Financial Accounting

Robert Libby
Cornell University

Patricia A. Libby
Ithaca College

Daniel G. Short
Miami University

McGraw Hill Irwin

Boston   Burr Ridge, IL   Dubuque, IA   Madison, WI   New York   San Francisco   St. Louis
Bangkok   Bogotá   Caracas   Kuala Lumpur   Lisbon   London   Madrid   Mexico City
Milan   Montreal   New Delhi   Santiago   Seoul   Singapore   Sydney   Taipei   Toronto

To:

Jenni, John, and Emma Rose Drago

Herman and Doris Hargenrater

Laura Libby, Oscar and Selma Libby

Bob and Mary Ann Short, Heather Short, *and* Maryrose Short

 Irwin

FINANCIAL ACCOUNTING

Published by McGraw-Hill/Irwin, a business unit of The McGraw-Hill Companies, Inc., 1221 Avenue of the Americas, New York, NY, 10020. Copyright © 2004, 2001, 1998, 1996, by The McGraw-Hill Companies, Inc. All rights reserved. No part of this publication may be reproduced or distributed in any form or by any means, or stored in a database or retrieval system, without the prior written consent of The McGraw-Hill Companies, Inc., including, but not limited to, in any network or other electronic storage or transmission, or broadcast for distance learning.

Some ancillaries, including electronic and print components, may not be available to customers outside the United States.

This book is printed on acid-free paper.

4 5 6 7 8 9 0 QPD/QPD 0 9 8 7 6 5

ISBN 0-07-247350-9

Publisher: *Brent Gordon*
Sponsoring editor: *Steve DeLancey*
Senior developmental editors: *Tracey Douglas/Kristin Leahy*
Senior marketing manager: *Rich Kolasa*
Senior project manager: *Kimberly D. Hooker*
Senior production supervisor: *Michael McCormick*
Design team leader: *Mary Christianson*
Photo research coordinator: *Jeremy Cheshareck*
Senior supplement coordinator: *Carol Loreth*
Senior producer, new media: *David Barrick*
Interior freelance designer: *Amanda Kavanaugh*
Cover freelance design: *Asylum Studios*
Cover photographs: *©Getty Images*
Conceptual line art: *Leighton & Co., Inc.*
Compositor: *GAC Indianapolis*
Typeface: *10.5/12 Times Roman*
Printer: *Quebecor, Dubuque*

Library of Congress Cataloging-in-Publication Data
Libby, Robert.
    Financial accounting/Robert Libby, Patricia A. Libby, Danial G. Short—4th ed.
        p. cm.
    Includes index.
    ISBN 0-07-247350-9 (alk. paper)
    1. Accounting. 2. Corporations—Accounting. 3. Financial statements. I. Libby, Patricia
A. II. Short, Daniel G. III. Title
HF5635.L684 2004
657—dc21   2002034780

Robert Libby

Robert Libby is the David A. Thomas Professor of Management at the Johnson Graduate School of Management at Cornell University, where he teaches the introductory financial accounting course. He previously taught at the University of Illinois, Pennsylvania State University, the University of Texas at Austin, the University of Chicago, and the University of Michigan. He received his B.S. from Pennsylvania State University and his M.A.S. and Ph.D. from the University of Illinois; he is also a CPA.

Bob is a widely published author specializing in behavioral accounting. He was selected as the AAA Outstanding Educator in 2000. His prior text, *Accounting and Human Information Processing* (Prentice Hall, 1981), was awarded the AICPA/AAA Notable Contributions to the Accounting Literature Award. He received this award again in 1996 for a paper. He has published numerous articles in the *Journal of Accounting Research*; *Accounting, Organizations, and Society*; and other accounting journals. He is Vice President-Publications of the American Accounting Association and is a member of the American Institute of CPAs and the editorial boards of *The Accounting Review*; *Accounting, Organizations, and Society*; *Journal of Accounting Literature*; and *Journal of Behavioral Decision Making*.

Patricia A. Libby

Patricia Libby is Chair of the Department of Accounting and Associate Professor of Accounting at Ithaca College, where she teaches the undergraduate financial accounting course. She previously taught graduate and undergraduate financial accounting at Eastern Michigan University and the University of Texas at Austin. Before entering academe, she was an auditor with Price Waterhouse (now PricewaterhouseCoopers) and a financial administrator at the University of Chicago. She received her B.S. from Pennsylvania State University, her M.B.A. from DePaul University, and her Ph.D. from the University of Michigan; she is also a CPA.

Pat conducts research on using cases in the introductory course and other parts of the accounting curriculum. She has published articles in *The Accounting Review, Issues in Accounting Education,* and *The Michigan CPA*. She has also conducted seminars nation-wide on active learning strategies, including cooperative learning methods.

Daniel G. Short

Dan Short is Professor of Accountancy at the Richard T. Farmer School of Business at Miami University. Dan has served as dean at both the Farmer School and the College of Business at Kansas State University. Previously, he was associate dean at the University of Texas at Austin, where he taught the undergraduate and graduate financial accounting courses. He also taught at the University of Michigan and the University of Chicago. He received his undergraduate degree from Boston University and his M.B.A. and Ph.D. from the University of Michigan.

Dan has won numerous awards for his outstanding teaching abilities and has published articles in *The Wall Street Journal, The Accounting Review,* the *Journal of Accounting Research,* and other business journals. He has worked with a number of Fortune 500 companies, commercial banks, and investment banks to develop and teach executive education courses on the effective use of accounting information. Dan has also served on boards of directors in several industries, including manufacturing, commercial banking, and medical services.

About the Authors

FOURTH *edition*

Financial Accounting

L I B B Y

L I B B Y

S H O R T

FOCUS COMPANIES:

Finally, a textbook on which both students and instructors *can agree.*

McGRAW-HILL/IRWIN and the authors would like to thank all of the financial accounting faculty and students who helped make *Financial Accounting, 3/e,* by Libby/Libby/Short **the market-leading financial accounting textbook**. It is clear that this IS the financial accounting text that you both can agree on.

Over three editions, *Financial Accounting* has built a reputation as the most interesting, up-to-date textbook on the market. This author team has continually led the way in making financial accounting more relevant and interesting to students, introducing cutting edge technology supplements to help students with divergent learning styles, and striving to provide students with the most readable and accessible textbook on the market.

The Libby author team achieves these goals by focusing on three key concepts.

RELEVANCE.
Unlike other books Libby makes financial accounting come alive by using real world focus companies in each chapter to teach fundamental accounting concepts. Your students learn why accounting is important and how businesses use accounting information to make decisions. The real world flavor is integrated throughout each chapter and even the problem material uses real world data. In light of the recent turmoil in the accounting profession, the fictitious **Maxidrive focus company in Chapter 1—a realistic representation of an actual case of fraud**—provides a perfect setting for discussing Enron and WorldCom and an easy way to get your students interested in and excited about accounting!

CLARITY.
The success of *Financial Accounting* also comes from writing that is lively and fun to read—**students just love this textbook!** To continue to meet the changing needs of financial accounting faculty and students, the presentation of material has been streamlined while maintaining effective coverage of all important topics.

TECHNOLOGY AIDES.
Today's students have diverse learning styles and numerous time commitments, and they want technology supplements that help them study more efficiently and effectively. **Topic Tackler, NetTutor, Homework Manager, and ALEKS for Financial Accounting** provide your students with four powerful tools tied directly to *Financial Accounting, 4/e,* that will help them maximize their study time and make their learning experience more enjoyable.

The McGraw-Hill/Irwin Libby/Libby/Short team would like to invite you to take the Libby challenge and discover why this is the book on which both students and faculty agree.

Relevance | Clarity | Technology

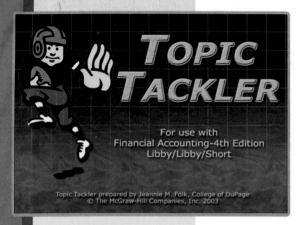

TOPIC TACKLER

For use with
Financial Accounting-4th Edition
Libby/Libby/Short

Topic Tackler prepared by Jeannie M. Folk, College of DuPage
© The McGraw-Hill Companies, Inc. 2003

TOPIC TACKLER

Topic Tackler 1–1

Concepts appearing
in the text that receive
additional treatment
in Topic Tackler are
marked with a
unique icon.

New and *Relevant:* *Additions* to Financial Accounting

FINANCIAL ACCOUNTING'S NEWEST FEATURES ARE EVEN MORE RELEVANT TO THE WAYS IN WHICH YOUR STUDENTS LEARN AND WORK.

STUDENT CD-ROM, *featuring Topic Tackler and Excel Templates for use with the Annual Report Cases*

For today's technologically savvy students, **TOPIC TACKLER** is a CD-ROM tutorial that offers a virtual helping hand in understanding the most troublesome topics of the financial accounting course. Through a step-by-step sequence of video clips, PowerPoint® slides, interactive practice exercises, and self-tests, Topic Tackler offers help on two key topics for every chapter, keeping your students engaged and learning every step of the way.

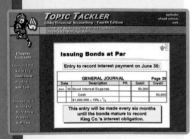

Video clips
provide real-world
perspectives from a
variety of accounting
experts.

VIDEO CLIPS

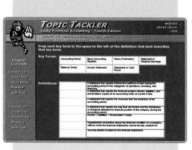

Fun, interactive
exercises help
students remember
key terminology.

EXERCISES

PowerPoint slide
shows offer step-by-
step coverage of
challenging topics
and make a great
resource for review.
Many also feature
animations.

POWERPOINT

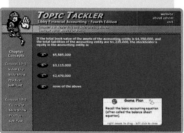

Self-grading quizzes
cover all of the main
topics, providing an
ideal way to brush up
before a test.

SELF-TESTS

EXCEL TEMPLATES FOR USE WITH THE ANNUAL REPORT CASES

If you're going to work in accounting (or business in general), you have to know Microsoft Excel. Students use the real financial statements of American Eagle Outfitters and Abercrombie & Fitch with accompanying Excel Templates to manipulate real-world data and solve problems. These assignments allow students to experience problem solving as it truly happens in real companies. (The financial statements are found in the textbook appendices and on this CD. The Excel Templates are found on the CD and on the book's Website.)

	A	B
1	CP9-3 Comparing Companies within an Industry	
2	Required:	
3	1.	Compute the current ratio for each company for each year.
4	2.	Compare the latest year current ratio for each company to the industry average from the Industry Ratio Report. Based solely on the current ratio, are these companies more or less liquid than the average company in their industry?
5	3.	Compute the payable turnover ratio for each company for each year. What is the amount of long-term liabilities for the current year?
6	4.	Compare the latest year payable turnover ratio for each company to the industry average from the Industry Ratio Report. Are these companies doing better or worse than the average company in their industry at paying trade creditors?
7	5.	Using this information and any other data from the annual report, write a brief assessment of the liquidity for the two companies.
8		
9	This spreadsheet is organized as follows:	
10	Sheet Name	Contents
11	CP9-3	CP9-3 and Spreadsheet Layout
12	Industry Ratio Report	Industry Ratio Report
13	AEOS B.S.	American Eagle Outfitters Consolidated Balance Sheets
14	AEOS I.S.	American Eagle Outfitters Consolidated Statements of Operations
15	AEOS S.S.E.	American Eagle Outfitters Consolidated Statements of Stockholders' Equity
16	AEOS S.C.F.	American Eagle Outfitters Consolidated Statements of Cash Flows
17	ANF B.S.	Abercrombie & Fitch Consolidated Balance Sheets
18	ANF I.S.	Abercrombie & Fitch Consolidated Statements of Income
19	ANF S.S.E.	Abercrombie & Fitch Consolidated Statements of Shareholders' Equity
20	ANF S.C.F.	Abercrombie & Fitch Consolidated Statements of Cash Flows
21		

MULTIPLE CHOICE QUESTIONS

As a result of reviewer feedback, ten multiple choice questions have been added to the end of each chapter. These questions allow students to check their grasp of basic concepts quickly prior to moving on to the rest of the end-of-chapter materials.

INFOGRAPHICS

Twenty-eight new infographics have been included throughout the text to help students visualize accounting concepts.

	A	B
1	CP14-3 Comparing Companies within an Industry	
2	Required:	
3	1.	From the list of ratios that were discussed in this chapter, select and compute the ratios that help you evaluate the companies' operations and compare the ratio for each company to the industry average ratios.
5	This spreadsheet is organized as follows:	
6	Sheet Name	Contents
7	CP14-3	CP14-3 and Spreadsheet Layout
8	Industry Ratio Report	Industry Ratio Report
9	AEOS B.S.	American Eagle Outfitters Consolidated Balance Sheets
10	AEOS I.S.	American Eagle Outfitters Consolidated Statements of Operations
11	AEOS S.S.E.	American Eagle Outfitters Consolidated Statements of Stockholders' Equity
12	AEOS S.C.F.	American Eagle Outfitters Consolidated Statements of Cash Flows
13	ANF B.S.	Abercrombie & Fitch Consolidated Balance Sheets
14	ANF I.S.	Abercrombie & Fitch Consolidated Statements of Income
15	ANF S.S.E.	Abercrombie & Fitch Consolidated Statements of Shareholders' Equity
16	ANF S.C.F.	Abercrombie & Fitch Consolidated Statements of Cash Flows
17		

EXCEL TEMPLATES

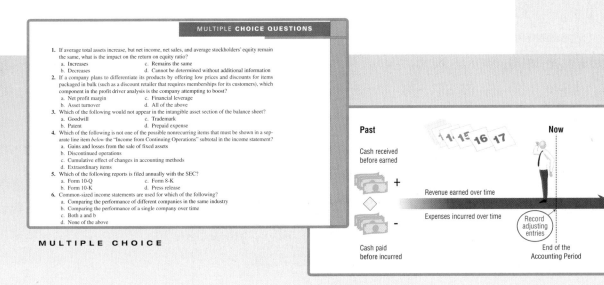

MULTIPLE CHOICE QUESTIONS

1. If average total assets increase, but net income, net sales, and average stockholders' equity remain the same, what is the impact on the return on equity ratio?
   a. Increases   c. Remains the same
   b. Decreases   d. Cannot be determined without additional information
2. If a company plans to differentiate its products by offering low prices and discounts for items packaged in bulk (such as a discount retailer that requires memberships for its customers), which component in the profit driver analysis is the company attempting to boost?
   a. Net profit margin   c. Financial leverage
   b. Asset turnover   d. All of the above
3. Which of the following would not appear in the intangible asset section of the balance sheet?
   a. Goodwill   c. Trademark
   b. Patent   d. Prepaid expense
4. Which of the following is not one of the possible nonrecurring items that must be shown in a separate line item *below* the "Income from Continuing Operations" subtotal in the income statement?
   a. Gains and losses from the sale of fixed assets
   b. Discontinued operations
   c. Cumulative effect of changes in accounting methods
   d. Extraordinary items
5. Which of the following reports is filed annually with the SEC?
   a. Form 10-Q   c. Form 8-K
   b. Form 10-K   d. Press release
6. Common-sized income statements are used for which of the following?
   a. Comparing the performance of different companies in the same industry
   b. Comparing the performance of a single company over time
   c. Both a and b
   d. None of the above

MULTIPLE CHOICE

INFOGRAPHICS

Additions to Financial Accounting

Relevant *Pedagogy*

Financial Accounting offers a host of pedagogical tools that complement the way you like to teach and the ways your students like to learn. Some call out special topics that help you in presenting a complex subject; others highlight issues relevant to what your students read in the papers or watch on TV. Either way, *Financial Accounting's* pedagogical support will make a real difference in your course and to your students.

INTERNATIONAL PERSPECTIVE

Highlights the emergence of global competition and resulting business issues in each chapter as well as the end-of-chapter material.

A QUESTION OF ETHICS

These boxes, located throughout the chapter, convey the importance of acting responsibly in business practice. The Libby author team has always stressed the importance of ethical conduct, and recent events in the accounting profession have made ethics more crucial than ever.

FINANCIAL ANALYSIS

Ties important chapter concepts to real-world decision-making examples. They also highlight alternative viewpoints and add to the critical thinking and decision-making focus of the text.

Hiding Billions in Expenses through Capitalization

FINANCIAL ANALYSIS

When expenditures that should be recorded as current period expenses are improperly capitalized as part of the cost of an asset, the effects on the financial statements can be enormous. In one of the largest accounting frauds in history, WorldCom inflated its income and cash flows from operations by billions of dollars in just such a scheme. Over five quarters in 2001 and 2002, the company initially announced that it had capitalized $3.8 billion that should have been recorded as operating expenses. By the time this chapter was written, it had raised its estimate to $7.2 billion in false profits reported in 1999 through 2002. This fraud turned WorldCom's actual losses into large profits. Accounting for expenses as capital expenditures increases current income because it spreads a single period's operating expenses over many future periods as depreciation expense. It increases cash flows from operations by moving

WorldCom

FINANCIAL ANALYSIS

Are Generally Accepted Accounting Principles Similar in Other Countries?

INTERNATIONAL PERSPECTIVE

While businesspeople compete in a single global economy, different sets of generally accepted accounting principles have developed within particular countries. Differences in political, cultural, and economic histories have produced a great number of cross-national differences in practice. These differences can have dramatic effects on the numbers presented in financial statements. The International Accounting Standards Board (IASB) and others are attempting to eliminate these differences. But for now, users of financial statements who cross national borders must be aware of the specific nature of these reporting differences to inter-...ates how firms such as Sum-...orts with foreign investors.

INTERNATIONAL PERSPECTIVE

A QUESTION OF ETHICS

Conflicting Interests of Managers, Stockholders, and Creditors

The economic interests of managers, stockholders, and creditors often differ. For example, paying dividends to stockholders benefits the stockholders but leaves less money available to pay creditors. Refurnishing managers' offices benefits managers but leaves less money to pay dividends. Ethical conduct and mutual trust play a major role in balancing these conflicting interests.

Accounting and financial statements also play a major role in enforcing these relationships of trust. Compliance with agreements (contracts) between managers and stockholders and between stockholders and creditors are monitored with financial statement data.* Enron, WorldCom, and other recent cases have made the wisdom of famed analyst Jack Ciesielski's warning for managers, shareholders, directors, creditors, and analysts more evident:

A QUESTION OF ETHICS

SELF-STUDY QUIZZES

This active learning feature engages the student, provides interactivity, and promotes efficient learning. Research shows that students learn best when they are actively engaged in the learning process. These quizzes ask students to pause at strategic points throughout each chapter to ensure they understand key points before moving ahead.

FOCUS ON CASH FLOWS

Each of the first twelve chapters includes a discussion and analysis of changes in the cash flow of the focus company and explores the decisions that caused those changes. The early and consistent coverage of cash flows encourages students to think more critically about the decisions they will face as managers and the impact those decisions will have on the company's cash flow.

KEY RATIO ANALYSIS

We believe that students will be better prepared to use financial information if they learn to evaluate different elements of financial performance as they learn how to measure and report them. As a result, we introduce relevant key ratios in each chapter in Key Ratio Analysis sections. Each Key Ratio Analysis box presents ratio analysis for the focus company in the chapter as well as for comparative companies. Cautions are also provided to help students understand the limitations of certain ratios.

REAL WORLD EXCERPTS

These excerpts include annual report information from the focus companies, as well as numerous other companies, articles from several different publications, analysts' reports, form 10-Ks, press releases, and First Call notes.

Pedagogy

SELF-STUDY QUIZ

1. Complete the following tabulation, indicating the direction (+ for increase, − for decrease, and NE for no effect) and amount of the effect of each transaction. Consider each item independently.

   a. Recorded and paid rent expense of $200.

   b. Recorded the sale of goods on account for $400 and cost of goods sold of $300.

TRANSACTION	CURRENT ASSETS	GROSS PROFIT	INCOME FROM OPERATIONS
a.			
b.			

2. Assume that Callaway executives received maximum bonuses if pretax earnings (before the cumulative effect of the accounting change) growth met or exceeded a target of 30 percent. Use Exhibit 5.5 to see whether Callaway executives would earn their maximum bonuses in the most recent year.

Computations _____

Discuss why companies might choose to pay executives based on the company's performance and why they use the accounting numbers in reports to shareholders to measure the executives' performance.

After you have completed your answers, check them with the solutions that follow:

1. a. −200, NE, −200; b. +100, +100, +100
2. Pretax earnings growth % = (129,322 − 85,497) ÷ 85,497 = 51.3% versus 30% target. They would earn their maximum bonuses. (In reality, their bonuses are now at the discretion of the board.) Many companies believe that higher pretax earnings growth will result in higher prices for the...

SELF-STUDY QUIZZES

FOCUS ON CASH FLOWS   **Investing and Financing Activities**

Cash Cash

Learning Objective 7
Identify investing and financing transactions and demonstrate how they are reported on the statement of cash flows.

Recall from Chapter 1 that companies report on cash inflows and outflows over a period in their statement of cash flows. This statement divides all transactions that affect cash into three categories: operating, investing, and financing activities. Operating activities are covered in Chapter 3. Investing activities include buying and selling noncurrent assets and investments; financing activities include borrowing and repaying debt, issuing and repurchasing stock, and paying dividends. When cash is involved, these activities are reported on the statement of cash flows. (When cash is not included in the transaction, such as when a building is acquired with a long-term mortgage note payable, there is no cash effect to include on the statement of cash flows.) In general, the effects of such activities are as follows:

FOCUS ON CASH FLOWS

Net Profit Margin   **KEY RATIO ANALYSIS**

In Chapter 2, we introduced the financial leverage ratio to examine managers' use of debt as a tool to increase resources that would generate more profit for the shareholders. In Chapter 3, we introduced the total asset turnover ratio to examine managers' effectiveness at utilizing assets efficiently to generate more profit for the shareholders. Now let's examine the third ratio, net profit margin, to examine managers' effectiveness at controlling revenues and ... shareholders. These three ratios are the primary ... holders to be discussed in Chapter 5.

... ng profit on every dollar of sales?

Learning Objective 4
Compute and interpret the net profit margin.

KEY RATIO ANALYSIS

For actively traded stocks such as Callaway Golf, most of the stock market reaction (stock price increases and decreases from investor trading) to the news in the press release usually occurs quickly. Recall that a number of analysts follow Callaway and regularly predict the company's earnings. When the actual earnings are published, the market reacts *not* to the amount of earnings but to the difference between expected earnings and actual earnings. This amount is called **unexpected earnings.** For example, *The San Diego Union-Tribune* recently reported the following:

Callaway Posts Strong Sales Profits

Bolstered by strong first-quarter earnings, Callaway Golf Co. shares jumped 15 percent yesterday, topping the $26 level for one of the few times in the past three years.

The Carlsad company reported earnings of 47 cents per share Wednesday, up from 17 cents for the same period last year. The company beat analysts' consensus estimate of 44 cents per share.

SOURCE: *The San Diego Union-Tribune*, April 27, 2001, p. C-1.

REAL WORLD EXCERPT
The San Diego Union-Tribune

REAL WORLD EXCERPTS

More Relevant *Pedagogy*

LEARNING OBJECTIVES

Outlined at the beginning of each chapter, these Learning Objectives are cross-referenced to the end-of-chapter material.

ORGANIZATION OF THE CHAPTER SCHEMATIC

This visual framework is a quick reference guide that helps students easily find a topic in the chapter.

INTEGRATION OF THE INTERNET

Throughout each chapter and its assignments, where appropriate, students are encouraged to explore actual Internet sites. At publication, all sites referenced were current and active. Because Internet sites are time and date sensitive, professors and students may need to use the Yahoo! database (www.yahoo.com) or a favorite search engine to locate the most current site.

ALL JOURNAL ENTRIES TIED TO THE ACCOUNTING EQUATION

Journal entries marked with (A), (L), (SE), (R), (E), or (X, if a contra-account) and plus and minus signs in early chapters assist students in transaction analysis. In addition, following each journal entry is a summary of the effects of the transaction on the fundamental accounting equation.

LEARNING OBJECTIVES

INTEGRATION OF THE INTERNET

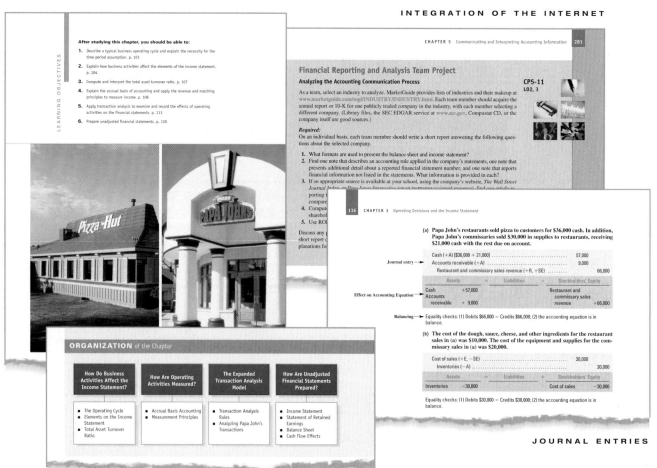

CHAPTER SCHEMATIC

JOURNAL ENTRIES

FLEXIBLE END-OF-CHAPTER CONTENT AND ORGANIZATION

Each chapter is followed by an extensive selection of end-of-chapter assignments that examine single concepts or integrate multiple concepts presented in the chapter, arranged by level of difficulty and in learning objective order. To maintain the real-world flavor of the chapter material, they are often based on other real domestic and international companies, and require analysis, conceptual thought, calculation, and written communication. Assignments suitable for individual or group written projects and oral presentations are included in strategic locations.

CHAPTER TAKE-AWAYS: Bulleted end-of-chapter summaries that compliment the learning objectives outlined at the beginning of the chapter.

KEY RATIOS: Summary of the key ratios presented in the chapter.

KEY TERMS: Page referenced to the chapter text.

FINDING FINANCIAL INFORMATION: highlights the chapter's key concepts, numbers, and totals in an easy-to-review graphic. The graphic includes Balance Sheet, Income Statement, Statement of Cash Flows, and Note Information.

MULTIPLE CHOICE: Questions that allow for a quick check of basic concepts (new—see page vii).

QUESTIONS: Allow students and faculty to ensure that chapter concepts have been grasped.

MINI-EXERCISES: Assignments that illustrate and apply a single learning objective from the chapter.

EXERCISES: Additional assignments that cover multiple learning objectives from each chapter.

PROBLEMS: Cross-referenced in blue to the Alternative Problems.

ALTERNATIVE PROBLEMS: Similar in level and content to the end of chapter problems.

CASES AND PROJECTS: This section includes Annual Report Cases, Financial Reporting and Analysis Cases, Critical Thinking Cases, and a Financial Reporting and Analysis Team Project.

Pedagogy

Contents

Detailed *Content* Changes

STREAMLINED TEXT

One of the major goals for this edition was to streamline the presentation of material while making it clearer to students what they should take away from each chapter. The authors were able to shorten chapters—some by 20%—without deleting any learning objectives or major topics.

CHAPTER 01

Chapter presentation streamlined, reducing word count by 20%

Overview of financial statements reorganized to focus on basic structure and elements of each statement

Financial analysis features shortened and consolidated

New Exhibit 1.6 illustrating relationships among the statements

New graphics to reinforce key concepts

New demonstration case based on Krispy Kreme Donuts focuses on the basic structure of the balance sheet and income statement

CHAPTER 02

Updated all information for Papa John's International

Simplified account titles and amounts in the balance sheet and in transactions for Papa John's and in the demonstration case

Included explanations of account titles on the balance sheet in Exhibit 2.2

Added more visual illustrations of key concepts

Shifted ratio analysis earlier to motivate the use of balance sheet information

Many new and revised end-of-chapter exercises and problems

CHAPTER 03

Updated all information for Papa John's International

Incorporated new SEC revenue recognition rules

Simplified account titles and amounts in the income statement and in transactions for Papa John's and in the demonstration case

Multiple-step income statement introduced

Added more visual illustrations of key concepts

Included explanations of account titles on the income statement in Exhibit 3.1

Shifted ratio analysis earlier to motivate the use of income statement information

CHAPTER 04

Updated all information for Papa John's International

Simplified account titles and amounts in the income statement and in transactions for Papa John's and in the demonstration case

Added more visual illustrations of key concepts

Created a new illustration of the Accounting Cycle (Exhibit 4.1)

Moved the computation of depreciation to Chapter 8

Modified the steps in the analysis of adjusting entries to add clarity

Illustrated the use of adjustments on the trial balance worksheet (Exhibit 4.3)

CHAPTER 05

Updated all information for Callaway Golf

New discussion of the effect of Enron and WorldCom on investors' faith in accounting numbers

Updated discussion of Web-based financial information sources

Multiple step income statement moved to Chapter 3

Short discussion of unusual items remains in this chapter and the longer discussion has been moved to chapter Supplement A, including a complete example with extraordinary items, cumulative effect, and discontinued operations

Updated demonstration case based on Microsoft

New end-of-chapter exercises and problems based on Lance, Inc; Cadbury Schweppes; GAP, Inc; and Tommy Hilfiger

CHAPTER 06

Updated all information on Timberland

New table and graphic summarizing the accounting process for bad debts

New t-account presentations for percent of sales and aging estimation methods

Simplified aging schedule

Advanced revenue recognition issues moved from chapter supplement to website

Added additional basic level exercises on bad debts to end-of-chapter material

CHAPTER 07

Updated all information on Harley-Davidson

New LIFO, FIFO, and weighted average inventory graphics

Simplified approach to the effects of LIFO and FIFO on financial statement analysis

Inventory errors and accounting systems combined in new section on control of inventory

Journal entries for periodic inventory system moved to chapter supplement

CHAPTER 08

Reorganized the chapter to improve the flow of topics

Updated all information for Delta Airlines

Added more visual illustrations of key concepts

Shifted ratio analysis earlier to reinforce the use of accounting information in analytic decisions

Deleted discussion and illustration of acquisition by a basket purchase to simplify the content

Moved discussion of changes in depreciation estimates to a chapter supplement to simplify the content

Shifted cash flow effects to later in the chapter

WorldCom scandal used to motivate importance of capitalization decisions

CHAPTER 09

Reorganized discussion of current liabilities

Revised discussion of accrued liabilities

Revised discussion of estimated liabilities

Improved discussion of working capital management

Expanded discussion of lease liabilities

Moved discussion of deferred taxes and retirement benefits to chapter supplement

Simplified presentation of present values and future values

Eliminated discussion of contra accounts and debt issued at a discount

Eliminated presentation of debt amortization schedule

Changed location of cash flow discussion to provide users with greater flexibility

CHAPTER 10

Simplified discussion of financial leverage

Improved graphics to enhance understanding

Simplified discussion of the process of issuing a bond

Improved focus of discussion of types of bonds

Simplified present value presentation

Eliminated discussion of bonds issued at a variable interest rate

Eliminated discussion of bond sinking fund

Simplified discussion of early retirement of debt

Discussion of bond investments moved to Chapter 12

Changed location of cash flow discussion to provide users with greater flexibility

CHAPTER 11

New focus company (Outback Steakhouse)

Improved presentation of issued and outstanding stock

Simplified discussion of par value and legal capital

Reorganized discussion of the sale of common stock

Simplified discussion of initial public offerings

Separated the discussion of common and preferred stock to achieve greater clarity

Changed location of cash flow discussion to provide users with greater flexibility

Improved and simplified discussion of dividends on preferred stock

Simplified discussion of retained earnings

Eliminated discussion of dividend payout ratio

Added discussion of earnings per share ratio

CHAPTER 12

Reorganized and simplified the chapter illustrations

Added more visual illustrations of key concepts

Integrated investments in debt securities previously presented in Chapter 10

New simplified illustration of accounting and reporting for mergers

Moved the discussion and illustration of consolidations to a chapter supplement to simplify the content

Many new and modified exercises and problems

CHAPTER 13

Dramatic revision allowing *either or both* the direct method or indirect method to be taught

Simplified step-by-step approach to statement construction

Simplified examples based on real companies

Extensive use of t-accounts and graphics to illustrate process for direct and indirect methods

New summary tables for reinforcement

New, well-known comparison companies Anheuser Busch and Coors

New mini-exercises and exercises focusing on the direct method

CHAPTER 14

Improved graphics to support discussions

Improved focus of discussion of individual ratios

Eliminated discussion of book value per share

Reorganized discussion of the interpretation of ratios

Eliminated some supplementary information based on user suggestions

01 RELEVANCE in the Classroom
Chapter 1's focus company, Maxidrive, deals with many of the same issues brought to light by the recent controversies involving Enron and WorldCom.

05 FLEXIBILITY in the Classroom
For those instructors who wish to emphasize ratio analysis, Chapter 5 can be used to summarize and integrate the ratios introduced in Chapters 2-4. This integration can also be saved for Chapter 14.

05 RELEVANCE in the Classroom
Chapter 5 covers the process of communicating accounting information to investors, another topic relevant to recent real-world events.

07 FLEXIBILITY in the Classroom
Chapter 7's supplements allow you to add more detail on the operation of alternative accounting systems and LIFO liquidations.

13 FLEXIBILITY in the Classroom
Chapter 13 makes it equally easy to cover either or both the direct and indirect methods, and can be covered at any point in the course following Chapter 5.

13 RELEVANCE in the Classroom
Chapter 13's contrast company illustrates the value of highlighting different approaches to common financial decision problems. The differences are readily apparent in class and provide valuable insight to your students.

Contents

Supplements for the Instructor

INSTRUCTOR CD-ROM

ISBN 0072473517

This integrated CD-ROM allows you to access most of the text's ancillary materials. You no longer need to worry about the various supplements that accompany your text. Instead, most everything is available on one convenient CD-ROM: PowerPoint slides, Solutions Manual, Instructor's Resource Manual, Test Bank and Computerized Test Bank, Annual Report Cases Templates, Excel Templates for the end-of-chapter material (along with a guide), text exhibits, video, and links to the Web.

WEBSITE

www.mhhe.com/libby4e
See page xvi for details.

INSTRUCTOR'S RESOURCE MANUAL

ISBN 0072473576

All supplements, including the Test Bank, Videos, Study Guide, and PowerPoint, are topically cross-referenced in the IRM to help instructors direct students to specific ancillaries to reinforce key concepts. Transparency masters of text exhibits are included. Electronic files are available on the Website.

SOLUTIONS MANUAL

ISBN 0072473703

Provides solutions for end-of-chapter questions, mini-exercises, exercises, problems, and cases. Electronic files are available on the Website.

POWERPOINT SLIDES

Completely customized PowerPoint presentations for use in your classroom. They are available on the Instructor CD-ROM and the Website.

SOLUTIONS ACETATES

ISBN 0072473592

These overhead transparencies provide both in-class visuals as well as solutions to most of the end-of-chapter material.

TEST BANK (PRINT VERSION)

ISBN 0072473711

This comprehensive Test Bank includes more than 3,000 true/false, multiple choice, essay, and matching questions.

COMPUTERIZED TESTBANK
(FROM BROWNSTONE)

ISBN 0072473533

Add and edit questions; create up to 99 versions of each test; attach graphic files to questions; import and export ASCII files; and select questions based on type, level of difficulty, or learning objective. This software provides password protection for saved tests and question databases, and is able to run on a network.

INSTRUCTOR EXCEL TEMPLATES

These Excel Templates allow students to develop important spreadsheet skills by using them to solve selected end of chapter assignments. They are available on the Instructor CD-ROM and on the Website.

INSTRUCTOR GENERAL LEDGER APPLICATION SOFTWARE (GLAS)

GLAS is tied to the end-of-chapter material and is available on the Instructor CD-ROM.

CHECK FIGURES

Provide answers to select problems and cases. These figures are available on the book's Website.

INSTRUCTOR'S MANUAL to accompany the MBA Supplement

ISBN 0072553898

The MBA Supplement includes expanded material on leases and deferred taxes.

INSTRUCTOR'S MANUAL to Accompany *Understanding Corporate Annual Reports,* William R. Pasewark

ISBN 0072387165

FINANCIAL ACCOUNTING VIDEO LIBRARY

ISBN 0072376163

Created to stimulate classroom discussion, illustrate key concepts, and review important material. Selected videos were produced by Dallas TeleLearning of the Dallas County Community College District © 1999. To acquire Accounting in Action as a Comprehensive Telecourse package, call Dallas TeleLearning at 972-669-6666, fax 972-669-6668 or visit their Website at *www.lecroy.dcccd.edu*.

Supplements

INSTRUCTOR PACKAGE for Interactive Financial Accounting Lab

ISBN 0072361344

Prepared by Ralph E. Smith and Rick Birney of Arizona State University, this package contains a network CD-ROM, an Installation/Setup Manual, and instructions for the Interactive Financial Accounting Lab's instructor grade book.

STUDENT SUPPLEMENTS

STUDENT CD-ROM

ISBN 0072473525

See page vi for details.

WEBSITE

www.mhhe.com/libby4e

See page xvi for details.

WORKING PAPERS

ISBN 0072473665

Selected by the authors, this booklet contains all the forms necessary for completing end-of-chapter materials.

STUDY GUIDE

ISBN 0072473673

An outstanding learning tool, this guide gives students a deeper understanding of the course material and reinforces, step by step, what they are learning in the main text.

POWERPOINT NOTES

ISBN 0072473657

Selected PowerPoint slides are reproduced for students in a handy booklet, allowing them to focus on the lecture and selectively annotate the slide rather than scramble to recreate the slide themselves.

STUDENT EXCEL TEMPLATES

These templates are tied to selected end-of-chapter material and are available on the Website.

STUDENT GENERAL LEDGER APPLICATION SOFTWARE (GLAS)

This software is tied to selected end-of-chapter material and is available on CD-ROM.

TELECOURSE GUIDE

ISBN 007247372X

This Telecourse Guide accompanies the instructional videos produced by Dallas County Community College.

MBA COMPANION

ISBN 007255388X

This supplement includes expanded material on leases and deferred taxes.

UNDERSTANDING CORPORATE ANNUAL REPORTS, William R. Pasewark

ISBN 007286821X

This financial analysis project emphasizes the interpretation and analysis of financial statements. It contains extensive instructions for obtaining an annual report from a publicly traded corporation. Students gain hands-on experience working with annual reports and are then better prepared to understand financial accounting concepts and their use in the business world.

INTERACTIVE FINANCIAL ACCOUNTING LAB

ISBN 0072361360

The Interactive Financial Accounting Lab (developed by Ralph E. Smith and Rick Birney of Arizona State University) is Windows-based software that uses a multimedia setting to help students learn the fundamentals of the accounting cycle and its various procedures.

COMPUTERIZED ACCOUNTING PRACTICE SETS

Business Simulations and practice sets using Windows by Leland Mansuetti and Keith Weidkamp of Sierra College include:

	3.5" Disks	CD-ROM
Granite Bay Jet Ski		
Level 1	0256221146	0072340886
Level 2	0256220980	007234105X
Wheels Exquisite, Inc.,		
Level 1	0075612437	0072341114
Thunder Mountain Snowmobile		
	025622112X	0072341149
Gold Run Snowmobile, Inc.		
	0073660981	0072341076

Supplements

Teaching With *Technology*

Technology brings a whole new level of flexibility and relevance to your financial accounting course. From teaching aids that make in-class presentation easy and stimulating to comprehensive study aids that work in the lab or the dorm as well as the classroom, our technology supplements give you more power than ever before to teach your class exactly the way you want it.

WEBSITE

www.mhhe.com/libby4e

For instructors, the book's Website contains the Instructor's Resource Manual, PowerPoint slides, Solutions Manual, GLAS (General Ledger Applications Software), Excel Templates tied to the end-of-chapter material, and the Annual Report Cases Templates, all organized by chapter. There are also links to professional resources.

In addition, for students and instructors, there are two appendices linked to the text material, check figures, articles tied to end-of-chapter material, Web links to the focus company financial statements, and Homework Manager (see below). Instructors can pull all of this material into their PageOut course syllabus or use it as part of another online course management system.

The student section of the site also includes (in addition to the elements mentioned above) self-quizzes, learning objectives, PowerPoint slides, chapter outlines, chapter take-aways, flashcards, and a link to NetTutor (see below).

POWERWEB

Keeping your course current can be a job in itself, and now McGraw-Hill does that job for you. PowerWeb extends the learning experience beyond the core textbook by offering all of the latest news and developments pertinent to financial accounting, without the clutter and dead links of a typical online search.

PowerWeb offers timely articles and links culled by a real-world expert in financial accounting. PowerWeb users can also take advantage of self-grading quizzes, interactive glossaries and exercises, and study tips.

Visit the PowerWeb site at *www.dushkin.com/powerweb* to see firsthand what PowerWeb can mean to your course.

PAGEOUT

PageOut is McGraw-Hill's unique point-and click course Website tool. With PageOut you can post your syllabus online, assign McGraw-Hill Online Learning Center or eBook content, add links to important off-site resources, and maintain student results in the online grade book. PageOut is free for every McGraw-Hill/Irwin user and, if you're short on time, we even have a team ready to build your site from scratch!

You can also use PageOut content with WebCT, eCollege.com, or Blackboard. To learn more about these digital solutions, visit *www.mhhe.com/solutions*.

KNOWLEDGE GATEWAY

Knowledge Gateway

Developed with the help of our partner Eduprise, the McGraw-Hill Knowledge Gateway is an all-purpose service and resource center for instructors teaching online. While training programs from WebCT and Blackboard will help teach you their software, only McGraw-Hill has services to help you actually *manage and teach* your online course, as well as run and maintain the software. To see how these platforms can assist your online course, visit *www.mhhe.com/solutions*.

ONLINE COURSE MANAGEMENT

No matter which online course solution you choose, you can count on the highest level of service. Our specialists offer free training and answer any question you have through the life of your adoption.

INSTRUCTOR ADVANTAGE AND INSTRUCTOR ADVANTAGE PLUS

Instructor Advantage is a special level of service McGraw-Hill offers in conjunction with WebCT and Blackboard. A team of platform specialists is always available, either by toll-free phone or e-mail, to ensure everything runs smoothly. Instructor Advantage is available free to all McGraw-Hill customers.

Instructor Advantage Plus guarantees you a full day of on-site training by a Blackboard or WebCT specialist, for yourself and up to nine colleagues. Thereafter, you will enjoy the benefits of unlimited telephone and e-mail support throughout the life of your adoption. IA Plus is available to qualifying McGraw-Hill adopters (see your representative for details).

NETTUTOR

NetTutor is a breakthrough program that allows one-on-one assistance completely online. Qualified accounting tutors equipped with a copy of *Financial Accounting 4/e* work online with your students on specific problems or concepts from their text.

The **Live Tutor Center** via NetTutor's WWWhiteboard enables a tutor to hold an interactive, on-line tutorial session with a student or several students. The **Q&A Center** allows students to submit questions at any time and retrieve answers within 24 hours. Finally, the **Archive Center** allows students to browse for answers to previously asked questions. They can also search for questions pertinent to a particular topic, and can ask a follow-up question if they encounter an answer they do not understand.

ALEKS® for Financial Accounting

 ALEKS (Assessment and Learning in Knowledge Spaces) delivers precise, qualitative diagnostic assessments of students' knowledge, guides them in the selection of appropriate new study material, and records their progress toward mastery of curricular goals in a robust classroom management system.

ALEKS interacts with the student much as a skilled human tutor would, moving between explanation and practice as needed, correcting and analyzing errors, defining terms and changing topics on request.

By sophisticated modeling of a student's knowledge state for a given subject, ALEKS can focus clearly on what the student is most ready to learn next. When students focus on exactly what they are ready to learn, they build confidence, and a learning momentum that fuels success.

ALEKS® Math Prep for Accounting

 Math Prep for Accounting provides coverage of the basic math skills needed to succeed in introductory financial accounting, including basic arithmetic, fractions, decimals, percents, and simple algebra concepts. Refreshing and improving these skills helps students perform better throughout the course.

For more information, visit the ALEKS website at *www.business.aleks.com*.

GRADESUMMIT

GradeSummit™ is a dynamic self-assessment and exam preparation service for students and instructors. Detailed diagnostic analysis of strengths and weaknesses enables efficient and effective study for students and effortless information for instructors. Find out more at *www.gradesummit.com*.

HOMEWORK MANAGER

 Homework Manager will help your students learn financial accounting by duplicating selected problem structures from each chapter of *Financial Accounting, 4/e* and presenting them with new data an infinite number of times. That way, students can work on fresh problems with the same problem structure until they master the topics covered. Each student also receives immediate scoring and feedback from the program to guide their studies.

Homework Manager may be used in practice, homework, or exam mode, as well as a variety of other standard assignment modes. In the homework and exam modes, Homework Manager records all the individual responses, grades the exams, and registers the grades in the online grade book. You not only know how your class performed on the exam, but also which topics or learning objectives your students struggled with.

Homework Manager is powered by Brownstone Learning.

Technology

Acknowledgments

Writing a successful text requires a team effort, and we have enjoyed working with excellent teammates. Throughout the process of writing this text, many people stepped forward with tremendous efforts that allowed us to accomplish our stated goals. We would like to recognize the sincere and devoted efforts of the many people who added their input to the process of developing this text. For this assistance, we thank the following colleagues:

FOURTH EDITION TEXT REVIEWERS

Matthew Anderson, *Michigan State University*
Richard Anderson, *Stonehill College*
Stephen Kwaku Asare, *University of Florida*
Wendy Bailey, *University of California—Riverside*
Eric Blazer, *Millersville University*
Charles Bokemeier, *Michigan State University*
Daniel Brickner, *Eastern Michigan University*
Virginia Clark, *University of Cincinnati*
Ann Clem, *Iowa State University*
Paul Clikeman, *University of Richmond*
Patricia Doherty, *Boston University*
Allan Drebin, *Northwestern University*
Tom English, *Boise State University*
Larry Farmer, *Middle Tennessee State University*
Kimberly Frank, *University of Nevada—Las Vegas*
Alan Glazer, *Franklin and Marshall College*
Norman Godwin, *Auburn University*
Bill Harden, *University of North Carolina—Greensboro*
John Hatcher, *Purdue University*
Richard Hulme, *California State University—Pomona*
Sharon Jackson, *Samford University*
Christopher Jones, *George Washington University*
Jefferson Jones, *Auburn University*
Sungsoo Kim, *Rutgers University*
Charles Klemstine, *University of Michigan*
Michael Knapp, *University of Oklahoma*
Donald Leonard, *Nichols College*
Seth Levine, *University of Miami—Keller*
Elliott Levy, *Bentley College*
Lawrence Logan, *University of Massachusetts—Dartmouth*
Gina Lord, *Santa Rosa Junior College*
George Machlan, *Susquehanna University*
David Marcinko, *University at Albany—SUNY*
Bharat Merchant, *Baruch College*
Alfred Michenzi, *Loyola College*
Paul Mihalek, *University of Hartford*

Ronald Milne, *University of Nevada—Las Vegas*
Muroki Mwaura, *William Patterson University*
Kanalis Ockree, *Washburn University*
Emeka Ofobike, *University of Akron*
Marge O'Reily-Allen, *Rider University*
Margaret Pollard, *American River College*
Glenn Rechtshaffen, *University of Auckland*
Anne Rich, *Quinnipiac University*
Iris Stuart, *California State University—Fullerton*
Pamela Stuerke, *Case Western Reserve University*
John Surdick, *Xavier University*
Diane Tanner, *University of North Florida*
Theodore Tully, *DeVry Institute—Fremont*
Marilyn Vito, *Richard Stockton College*
James Wallace, *University of California—Irvine*
Nancy Weatherholt, *University of Missouri—Kansas City*
Sterling Wetzel, *Oklahoma State University*
Gail Wright, *Bryant College*

FOURTH EDITION TECHNOLOGY REVIEWERS

Eric Blazer, *Millersville University*
Sue Cook, *Tulsa CC/SE Campus*
Charles Davis, *CSU–Sacramento*
Allan Drebin, *Northwestern University*
Bill Harden, *UNC/Greensboro*
Russell Hardin, *Pittsburg State University of Pittsburg, KS*
Roger Hehman, *University of Cincinnati*
Cindi Khanlarian, *UNC/Greensboro*
Linda Kropp, *Modesto Jr. College*
Elliott Levy, *Bentley College*
Meg Pollard, *American River College*
Jeffrey Quirin, *University of Wichita*
Thomas Robinson, *University of Alaska/Fairbanks*
Virginia Smith, *St. Mary's College*
Beverly Soriano, *Framingham State College*
Patricia Williams, *Friends University*

PREVIOUS EDITION REVIEWERS

Dawn Addington, *University of New Mexico*

Anwer Ahmed, *Syracuse University*

William Appleyard, *Salem State College*

Susan Armstrong, *Inver Hills Community College*

Holly Ashbaugh, *University of Northern Iowa*

Wendy Bailey, *University of Pittsburgh*

Roderick Barclay, *University of Texas—Dallas*

Cecil Battiste, *El Paso Community College*

Paul Bayes, *East Tennessee State University*

D'Arcy Becker, *University of New Mexico*

Linda Bell, *William Jewell College*

Martin Birr, *Indiana University at Indianapolis*

Robert Bloom, *John Carroll University*

Wayne Boutell, *University of California at Berkeley*

Ken Boze, *University of Alaska—Anchorage*

Russell Briner, *University of Texas—San Antonio*

Kevin Brown, *Drexel University*

David Byrd, *Southwest Missouri State University*

Matthew Calderisi, *Farleigh Dickinson University*

Thomas Calderon, *University of Akron*

Michael Capsuto, *Cypress College*

Barbara Cassidy, *St. Edward's University*

Nancy Cassidy, *Texas A&M University*

Ted Christensen, *Case Western University*

Anne Clem, *Iowa State University*

Mark Coffey, *Western New England College*

Michael Cornick, *University of North Carolina—Charlotte*

Rosalind Cranor, *Virginia Polytechnic Institute and State University*

Barbara Croteau, *Santa Rosa Junior College*

Gary Cunningham, *University of Minnesota*

Bruce Dehning, *University of New Hampshire*

Carol Dicino, *University of Southern Colorado*

Manuel Dieguez, *Florida International University*

Patricia Doherty, *Boston University*

Patricia Douglas, *Loyola Marymount University*

Tim Doupnik, *University of South Carolina*

Allan Drebin, *Northwestern University*

Marie Dubke, *University of Memphis*

David Durkee, *Weber State University*

Robert Egenolf, *University of Texas—Austin*

Jim Emig, *Villanova University*

Taylor Ernst, *Lehigh University*

Jack Ethridge, *Stephen Austin State University*

Thomas Evans, *University of Central Florida*

Kel-Ann Eyler, *Brenau University*

Alan Falcon, *Loyola Marymount University*

Gary Fish, *Illinois State University*

Al Frakes, *Washington State University*

Joseph Galanate, *Millersville University*

Arthur Goldman, *University of Kentucky*

Tim Griffin, *University of Missouri—KC*

Flora Guidry, *University of New Hampshire*

Marcia Halvorsen, *University of Cincinnati*

Leon Hanouille, *Syracuse University*

Russell Hardin, *Pittsburg State University*

John Hatcher, *Purdue University*

Paul Healy, *Harvard University*

Robin Hegedus, *Franklin University*

Kurt Heisinger, *Sierra College*

Donna Hetzel, *Western Michigan University*

Ken Hiltebeitel, *Villanova University*

Peggy Hite, *Indiana University*

David Hoffman, *University of North Carolina at Chapel Hill*

Jim Hood, *Mt. Hood Community College*

Kathy Horton, *University of Illinois at Chicago*

Marge Hubbert, *Cornell University*

Afshad Irani, *University of New Hampshire*

Sharon Jackson, *Auburn University at Montgomery*

Chris Jones, *George Washington University*

Naida Kaen, *University of New Hampshire*

Susan Kattelus, *Eastern Michigan University*

Howard Keller, *Indiana University at Indianapolis*

Charles Klemstine, *University of Michigan*

John Koeplin, *University of San Francisco*

Frank Korman, *Mountain View College*

Jim Kurtenbach, *Iowa State University*

David Lavin, *Florida International University*

Cynthia Levick, *Austin Community College*

Larry Logan, *University of Massachusetts—Dartmouth*

Gina Lord, *Santa Rosa Junior College*

Joan Luft, *Michigan State University*

Ron Mannino, *University of Massachusetts—Amherst*

Bobbie Martindale, *Dallas Baptist College*

Dawn Massey, *Fairfield University*

Alan Mayer-Sommer, *Georgetown University*

Paul McGee, *Salem State College*

Noel McKeon, *Florida Community College*

Betty McMechen, *Mesa State College*

Greg Merrill, *California State University at Fullerton*

Paul Mikalek, *University of Hartford*

Richard Muchow, *Palomar College*

Dennis Murphy, *California State University—Los Angeles*

Brian Nagle, *Duquesne University*

Sarah Nutter, *George Mason University*

Kanalis Ockree, *Washburn University*

John Osborn, *California State University—Fresno*

John O'Shaughnessy, *San Francisco State University*

Ron Pawliczek, *Boston College*

Kathy Petroni, *Michigan State University*

Rosemarie Pilcher, *Richland College*

Elizabeth Plummer, *Southern Methodist University*

Peter Poznanski, *Cleveland State University*

Don Putnam, *California State University Polytechnic at Pomona*

Mawdudur Rahman, *Suffolk University*

Jane Reimers, *Florida State University*

Keith Richardson, *Indiana State University*

Shirley Rockel, *Iowa Wesleyan College*

Michael Ruble, *Western Washington University*

Clayton Sager, *University of Wisconsin—Whitewater*

Bruce Samuelson, *Pepperdine University*

Shahrokh Saudagaran, *Santa Clara University*

Gene Sauls, *California State University—Sacramento*

Kenneth Schwartz, *Boston College*

Richard Scott, *University of Virginia*

Wayne Shaw, *Southern Methodist University*

Franklin Shuman, *Utah State University*

Mike Slaubaugh, *Indiana University—Purdue University*

Ken Smith, *Idaho State University*

William Smith, *Xavier University*

Ralph Spanswick, *California State University at Los Angeles*

Kevin Stocks, *Brigham Young University*

Kathryn Sullivan, *George Washington University*

Bill Svihla, *Indiana State University*

Karen Taylor, *Butte Community College*

Martin Taylor, *University of Texas—Arlington*

Blair Terry, *Fresno City College*

Laverne Thompson, *St. Louis Community College at Meramec*

Ben Trotter, *Texas Tech University*

Joan VanHise, *Fairfield University*

Michael Welker, *Drexel University*

Paul Wertheim, *Pepperdine University*

T. Sterling Wetzel, *Oklahoma State University*

L.K. Williams, *Morehead State University*

Steven Wong, *San Jose City College*

Suzanne Wright, *Penn State University*

William Zorr, *University of Wisconsin—Oshkosh*

Linda Zucca, *Kent State University*

Acknowledgments

In addition, we are deeply indebted to the following individuals who helped develop, critique, and shape the extensive ancillary package: Jeanne Simon, University of Texas at Austin; Betty McMechen, Mesa State College; Jeannie Folk, College of DuPage; Bruce Dehning, Chapman University; Barbara Croteau, Santa Rosa College; Larry Logan, University of Massachusetts/Dartmouth; Kim Temme, Maryville University; Patricia Doherty, Boston University; Peggy Bishop, the Wharton School at the University of Pennsylvania; Cathy Schrand, the Wharton School at the University of Pennsylvania; Jon Booker, Tennessee Technological University; Charles Caldwell, Tennessee Technological University; Susan Galbreath, Tennessee Technological University; Richard Rand, Tennessee Technological University; Jack Terry, ComSource Associates, Inc.; Deborah Jackson-Jones, Boardwork, Inc.; and Beth Woods, Accuracy Counts.

We also received invaluable input and support through the years from present and former colleagues and students, in particular William Wright, Marge Hubbard, Kristina Szafara, Steve Gallucci, Carol Marquardt, Susan Krische, Steve Smith, Jennifer Bremner, Susan Dahl, Brian Shearer, and Derek Oler. Furthermore, we appreciate the additional comments, suggestions, and support of our students and our colleagues at Cornell University, Ithaca College, and Miami University.

Finally, the extraordinary efforts of a talented group of individuals at McGraw-Hill/Irwin made all of this come together. We would especially like to thank our sponsoring editor, Steve DeLancey; Rich Kolasa, our marketing manager; Mary Christianson, our designer; Kimberly Hooker, our tireless project manager; Dan Wiencek in Advertising; Carol Loreth, our supplements coordinator; and Tracey Douglas and Kristin Leahy, our development editors.

ROBERT LIBBY

PATRICIA A. LIBBY

DANIEL G. SHORT

Acknowledgments

Chapter Three

Operating Decisions and the Income Statement 100

Chapter Four

Adjustments, Financial Statements, and the Quality of Earnings 160

Chapter Five

Communicating and Interpreting Accounting Information   222

Chapter Six

Reporting and Interpreting Sales Revenue, Receivables, and Cash 282

Chapter Seven

Reporting and Interpreting Cost of Goods Sold and Inventory 336

Chapter Nine

Reporting and Interpreting Liabilities   456

Chapter Ten

Reporting and Interpreting Bonds   508

Chapter 11

Reporting and Interpreting Owners' Equity 548

OUTBACK STEAKHOUSE 549

Chapter 12

Reporting and Interpreting Investments in Other Corporations 594

DOW JONES & CO., INC. 595

Chapter Fourteen

Analyzing Financial Statements 698

Financial Accounting

After studying this chapter, you should be able to:

1. Recognize the information conveyed in each of the four basic financial statements and the way that it is used by different decision makers (investors, creditors, and managers). p. 5

2. Identify the role of generally accepted accounting principles (GAAP) in determining the content of financial statements. p. 19

3. Distinguish the roles of managers and auditors in the accounting communication process. p. 21

4. Appreciate the importance of ethics, reputation, and legal liability in accounting. p. 23

Financial Statements and Business Decisions

1

FOCUS COMPANY:

Maxidrive Corporation

VALUING AN ACQUISITION USING

FINANCIAL STATEMENT INFORMATION*

In January, Exeter Investors purchased Maxidrive Corp., a fast-growing manufacturer of personal computer disk drives, for $33 million. The price Exeter paid was determined by considering the value of Maxidrive's assets, its debts to others, its ability to sell goods for more than the cost to produce them, and its ability to generate the cash necessary to pay its current bills. Much of this assessment was based on financial information that Maxidrive provided to Exeter in the form of financial statements. By July, Exeter had discovered a variety of problems in the company's operations and its financial statements. Maxidrive appeared to be worth only about half of what Exeter had paid for the company. Furthermore, Maxidrive did not have enough cash to pay its debt to American Bank. Exeter Investors filed a lawsuit against the previous owners and others responsible for Maxidrive's financial statements to recover its losses.

UNDERSTANDING THE BUSINESS

The Players

Maxidrive was founded by two engineers who had formerly worked for General Data, then a manufacturer of large computers. Predicting the rise in demand for personal computers with a hard disk drive, they started a company to manufacture this component. The founders invested a major portion of their savings, becoming the sole owners of Maxidrive. As is common in new businesses, the founders also functioned as managers of the business (they were **owner-managers**).

The founders soon discovered that they needed additional money to develop the business. Based on the recommendation of a close friend, they asked American Bank for a loan. American Bank continued to lend to Maxidrive as the need arose, becoming its largest lender, or **creditor.** Early last year, one of the founders of the business became gravely ill. This event, plus the stresses of operating in their highly competitive industry, led the founders to search for a buyer for their company. In January of this year, they struck a deal

*The Maxidrive case is a realistic representation of an actual case of fraud. No names in the case are real. The actual fraud is discussed in the epilogue to the chapter.

for the sale of the company to Exeter Investors, a small group of wealthy private **investors.** Both founders retired and a new manager was hired to run Maxidrive for the new owners. The new **manager** worked on behalf of Exeter Investors, but was not an owner of the company.

Whether investors are groups such as Exeter who recently bought all of Maxidrive Corp. or individuals who buy small percentages of large corporations, they make their purchases hoping to gain in two ways. They hope to receive a portion of what the company earns in the form of cash payments called **dividends** and eventually sell their share of the company at a higher price than they paid. As the Maxidrive case suggests, not all companies increase in value or have sufficient cash to pay dividends. Creditors lend money to a company for a specific length of time. They hope to gain by charging interest on the money they lend. As American Bank, Maxidrive's major creditor, has learned, some borrowers cannot repay their debts.

The Business Operations

To understand any company's financial statements, you must first understand its operations. As noted, Maxidrive designs and manufactures hard disk drives for personal computers. The major parts that go into the drive include the disks on which information is stored, the motors that spin the disks, the heads that read and write to the disks, and the computer chips that control the operations of the drive. Maxidrive purchases the disks and motors from other companies, called **suppliers.** It designs and manufactures the heads and chips and then assembles the drives. Maxidrive does not sell disk drives directly to the public. Instead, its **customers** are computer manufacturers such as Compaq and Apple Computer, which install the drives in machines they sell to retailers such as CompUSA. Thus, Maxidrive is a supplier to Compaq and Apple.

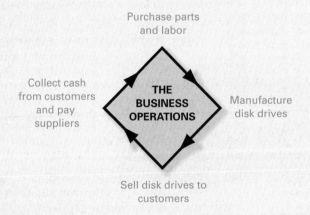

The Accounting System

ACCOUNTING is a system that collects and processes (analyzes, measures, and records) financial information about an organization and reports that information to decision makers.

Like all businesses, Maxidrive has an accounting system that collects and processes financial information about an organization and reports that information to decision makers. Maxidrive's managers (often called **internal decision makers**) and parties outside the firm such as Exeter Investors and American Bank (often called **external decision makers**) use the reports produced by this system. Exhibit 1.1 outlines the two parts of the accounting system. Internal managers typically require continuous, detailed information because they must plan and manage the day-to-day operations of the organization. Developing accounting information for internal decision makers, called **managerial** or **management accounting,** is the subject of a separate accounting course. The focus of this text is accounting for external decision makers, called **financial accounting,** and the four basic financial statements and related disclosures that are the output of that system.

EXHIBIT 1.1

The Accounting System
and Decision Makers

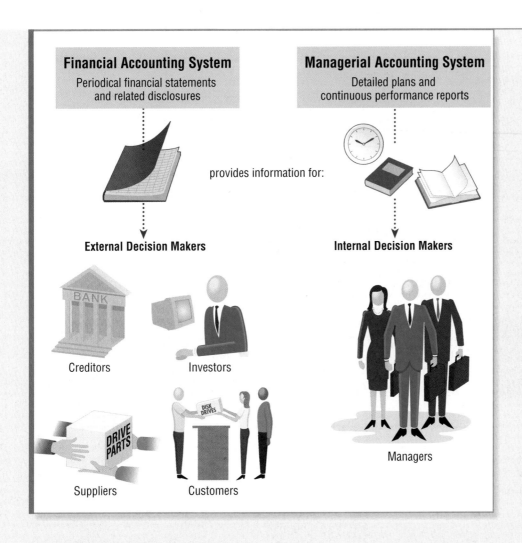

Financial Accounting System
Periodical financial statements
and related disclosures

Managerial Accounting System
Detailed plans and
continuous performance reports

provides information for:

External Decision Makers

Internal Decision Makers

BANK

Creditors

Investors

DISK DRIVES

DRIVE PARTS

Suppliers

Customers

Managers

We begin with a brief but comprehensive overview of the information reported in four basic financial statements and the people and organizations involved in their preparation and use. This overview provides you a context in which you can learn the more detailed material presented in the following chapters. In particular, we focus on how two primary users of the statements, investors (owners) and creditors (lenders), relied on each of Maxidrive's four basic financial statements in their ill-fated decisions to buy and lend money to Maxidrive. Then we test what you have learned by trying to correct the errors in the statements and discuss the implications of the errors for Maxidrive's value. Finally, we discuss the ethical and legal responsibilities of various parties for those errors.

To understand the way in which Exeter Investors used Maxidrive's financial statements in its decision and the way it was misled, we must first understand what specific information is presented in the four basic financial statements for a company such as Maxidrive. **Rather than trying to memorize the definitions of every term used in this chapter, try to focus your attention on learning the general structure and content of the statements. Specifically:**

1. What categories of items (often called **elements**) are reported on each of the four statements? (What type of information does a statement convey, and where can you find it.)

2. How are the elements within a statement related? (These **relationships** are usually described by an equation that tells you how the elements fit together.)

Learning Objective 1
Recognize the information conveyed in the four basic financial statements and the way that it is used by different decision makers (investors, creditors, and managers).

3. Why is each element important to owners' or creditors' decisions? (How **important** is the information to decision makers?)

The self-study quizzes will help you assess whether you have reached these goals. Remember that since this chapter is an overview, each concept discussed here will be discussed again in Chapters 2 through 5.

ORGANIZATION of the Chapter

Financial Statements and Business Decisions

The Four Basic Financial Statements

- Balance Sheet
- Income Statement
- Statement of Retained Earnings
- Statement of Cash Flows
- Relationships Among the Statements
- Notes

Using Financial Statements to Determine Maxidrive's Value

- Correcting Maxidrive's Income Statement
- Determining Maxidrive's Purchase Price

Responsibilities for the Accounting Process

- Generally Accepted Accounting Principles
- Management Responsibility and the Demand for Auditing
- Ethics, Reputation, and Legal Liability

THE FOUR BASIC FINANCIAL STATEMENTS: AN OVERVIEW

Both Exeter Investors (Maxidrive's new owner) and American Bank (Maxidrive's largest creditor) used Maxidrive's financial statements to learn more about the company before making their purchase and lending decisions. In doing so, Exeter and American Bank assumed that the statements accurately represented Maxidrive's financial condition. As they soon learned, and now have claimed in their lawsuits, the statements were in error.

Topic Tackler 1-1

1. On its **balance sheet,** Maxidrive overstated the economic resources it owned and understated its debts to others.

2. On its **income statement,** Maxidrive overstated its ability to sell goods for more than the cost to produce and sell them,

3. On its **statement of retained earnings,** Maxidrive overstated the amount of income it reinvested in the company for future growth, and

4. On its **statement of cash flows,** Maxidrive overstated its ability to generate from sales of disk drives the cash necessary to meet its current debts.

These four financial statements are the basic statements normally prepared by profit-making organizations for use by investors, creditors, and other external decision makers.

The four basic statements summarize the financial activities of the business. They can be prepared at any point in time (such as the end of the year, quarter, or month) and can apply to any time span (such as one year, one quarter, or one month). Like most companies, Maxidrive prepares financial statements for investors and creditors at the end of each quarter (known as **quarterly reports**) and at the end of the year (known as **annual reports**).

The Balance Sheet

The purpose of the **balance sheet** is to report the financial position (amount of assets, liabilities, and stockholders' equity) of an accounting entity at a particular point in time. We can learn a great deal about what the balance sheet reports just by reading the statement from the top. The balance sheet of Maxidrive Corp., presented by its former owners to Exeter Investors, is shown in Exhibit 1.2.

A **BALANCE SHEET** (Statement of Financial Position) reports the amount of assets, liabilities, and stockholders' equity of an accounting entity at a point in time.

Structure

Notice that the **heading** specifically identifies four significant items related to the statement:

1. **name of the entity,** Maxidrive Corp.
2. **title of the statement,** Balance Sheet.
3. **specific date of the statement,** At December 31, 2003.
4. **unit of measure** (in thousands of dollars).

The organization for which financial data are to be collected, called an **accounting entity,** must be precisely defined. On the balance sheet, the business entity itself, not

An **ACCOUNTING ENTITY** is the organization for which financial data are to be collected.

EXHIBIT 1.2

Balance Sheet

MAXIDRIVE CORP. Balance Sheet At December 31, 2003 (in thousands of dollars)		
		name of the entity
		title of the statement
		specific date of the statement
		unit of measure
Assets		
Cash	$ 4,895	*the amount of cash in the company's bank accounts*
Accounts receivable	5,714	*amounts owed by customers from prior sales*
Inventories	8,517	*parts and completed but unsold disk drives*
Plant and equipment	7,154	*factories and production machinery*
Land	981	*land on which the factories are built*
Total assets	$27,261	
Liabilities		
Accounts payable	$ 7,156	*amounts owed to suppliers for prior purchases*
Notes payable	9,000	*amounts owed on written debt contracts*
Total liabilities	16,156	
Stockholders' Equity		
Contributed capital	2,000	*amounts invested in the business by stockholders*
Retained earnings	9,105	*past earnings not distributed to stockholders*
Total stockholders' equity	11,105	
Total liabilities and stockholders' equity	$27,261	

The notes are an integral part of these financial statements.

the business owners, is viewed as owning the resources it uses and as owing its debts. The heading of each statement indicates the time dimension of the report. The balance sheet is like a financial snapshot indicating the entity's financial position at a specific point in time—in this case, December 31, 2003—which is stated clearly on the balance sheet. Financial reports are normally denominated in the currency of the country in which they are located. U.S. companies report in U.S. dollars, Canadian companies in Canadian dollars, and Mexican companies in Mexican pesos. Medium-sized companies such as Maxidrive often report in thousands of dollars; that is, they round the last three digits to the nearest thousand. The listing of Cash $4,895 on Maxidrive's balance sheet actually means $4,895,000.

Maxidrive's balance sheet first lists the company's assets. Assets are economic resources owned by the entity. It next lists its liabilities and stockholders' equity. They are the sources of financing or claims against the company's economic resources. Financing provided by creditors creates a liability. Financing provided by owners creates owners' equity. Since Maxidrive is a corporation, its owners' equity is designated as stockholders' equity.[1] Since each asset must have a source of financing, a company's assets must, by definition, equal its liabilities and stockholders' equity. This **basic accounting equation,** often called the balance sheet equation, is written:

BASIC ACCOUNTING EQUATION (balance sheet equation): Assets = Liabilities + Stockholders' Equity.

Assets	=	**Liabilities + Stockholders' Equity**
Economic resources		Sources of financing for the economic resources
(e. g., cash, inventory)		Liabilities: From creditors
		Stockholders' Equity: From stockholders

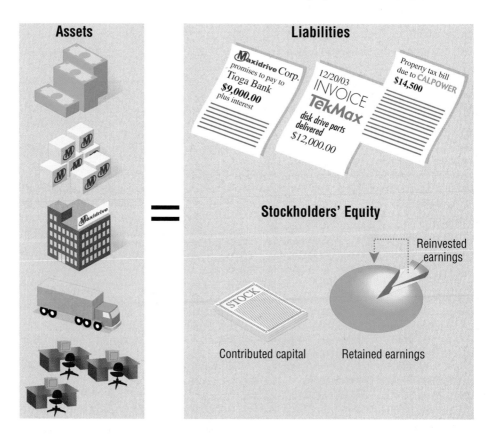

Assets

Liabilities

Stockholders' Equity

Maxidrive Corp. promises to pay to Tioga Bank $9,000.00 plus interest

12/20/03 INVOICE TekMax disk drive parts delivered $12,000.00

Property tax bill due to CALPOWER $14,500

Reinvested earnings

Contributed capital   Retained earnings

---

[1] A corporation is a business that is incorporated under the laws of a particular state. The owners are called **stockholders** or **shareholders.** Ownership is represented by shares of capital stock that usually can be bought and sold freely. The corporation operates as a separate legal entity, separate and apart from its owners. The stockholders enjoy limited liability; they are liable for the debts of the corporation only to the extent of their investments. Chapter Supplement A discusses forms of ownership in more detail.

Interpreting Assets, Liabilities, and Stockholders' Equity on the Balance Sheet

FINANCIAL
ANALYSIS

69,0	00	13,
67,000	137,00	
70,000	140,000	13,*
48,778	89,678	13,5

Assessment of Maxidrive's assets was important to its creditor, American Bank, and its prospective investor, Exeter, because assets provide a basis for judging whether the company has sufficient resources available to operate. Assets were also important because they could be sold for cash in the event that Maxidrive went out of business.

Exeter Investors was interested in Maxidrive's debts because of its concern whether the company has sufficient sources of cash to pay its debts. Maxidrive's debts were also relevant to American Bank's decision to lend money to the company because existing creditors share American Bank's claim against Maxidrive's assets. If a business does not pay its creditors, the creditors may force the sale of assets sufficient to meet their claims. The sale of assets often fails to cover all of a company's debts, and some creditors may take a loss.

Maxidrive's stockholders' equity or net worth is important to American Bank because creditors' claims legally come before those of owners. If Maxidrive goes out of business and its assets are sold, the proceeds of that sale must be used to pay back creditors such as American Bank before the owners receive any money. Thus, creditors consider stockholders' equity a protective "cushion."

The basic accounting equation shows what we mean when we refer to a company's **financial position:** the economic resources that the company owns and the sources of financing for those resources.

Elements

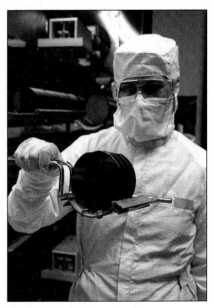

Assets are the economic resources owned by the company. Maxidrive lists five items under the category Assets. The exact items listed as assets on a company's balance sheet depend on the nature of its operations. But these are common names used by many companies. The five items listed by Maxidrive are the economic resources needed to manufacture and sell disk drives to companies such as Compaq. Each of these economic resources is expected to provide future benefits to the firm. To prepare to manufacture the drives, Maxidrive first needed cash to purchase land on which to build factories and install production machinery (buildings and equipment). Maxidrive then began purchasing parts and producing disk drives, which led to the balance assigned to inventories. When Maxidrive sells its disk drives to Compaq and others, it sells them on credit and receives promises to pay called accounts receivable, which are collected in cash later.

Every asset on the balance sheet is initially measured at the total cost incurred to acquire it. For example, the balance sheet for Maxidrive reports Land, $981; this is the amount paid (in thousands) for the land when it was acquired. Balance sheets do not generally show the amounts for which the assets could currently be sold.

Liabilities are the company's debts or obligations. Under the category Liabilities, Maxidrive lists two items. The accounts payable arise from the purchase of goods or services from suppliers on credit without a formal written contract (or a note). The notes payable result from cash borrowings based on a formal written debt contract with lending institutions such as banks.

Stockholders' equity indicates the amount of financing provided by owners of the business and earnings. It comes from two sources: (1) contributed capital, or the investment of cash and other assets in the business by the owners, and (2) retained earnings, or the amount of earnings (profits) reinvested in the business (and thus not distributed to stockholders in the form of dividends).

In Exhibit 1.2, the Stockholders' Equity section reports two items. The two founding stockholders' investment of $2,000,000 is reported as contributed capital. Maxidrives' total earnings (or losses incurred) less all dividends paid to the stockholders since formation of the corporation equaled $9,105,000 and is reported as retained earnings. Total stockholders' equity is the sum of the contributed capital plus the retained earnings.

SELF-STUDY QUIZ

1. Maxidrive's **assets** are listed in one section and **liabilities and stockholders' equity** in another. Notice that the two sections balance in conformity with the basic accounting equation. In the following chapters, you will learn that the basic accounting equation is the basic building block for the entire accounting process. Your task here is to verify that the assets of $27,261,000 is correct using the numbers for liabilities and stockholders' equity presented in Exhibit 1.2. Recall the basic accounting equation:

$$\text{Assets} = \text{Liabilities} + \text{Stockholders' Equity}$$

2. Learning which items belong in each of the balance sheet categories is an important first step in understanding their meaning. Without referring to Exhibit 1.2, mark each balance sheet item in the following list as an asset (A), liability (L), or stockholders' equity (SE).

_____ Accounts payable	_____ Inventories
_____ Accounts receivable	_____ Land
_____ Cash	_____ Notes payable
_____ Contributed capital	_____ Retained earnings
_____ Buildings and equipment	

After you have completed your answers, check them with the solutions that follow:

1. Assets ($27,261,000) = Liabilities ($16,156,000) + Stockholders' Equity ($11,105,000).
2. L, A, A, SE, A, A, A, L, SE (reading down the columns).

The Income Statement

Structure

The **income statement** (statement of income, statement of earnings, or statement of operations) reports the accountant's primary measure of performance of a business, revenues less expenses during the accounting period. While the term profit is used widely for this measure of performance, accountants prefer to use the technical terms **net income** or net earnings. Maxidrive's net income measures its success in selling disk drives for more than the cost to generate those sales.

A quick reading of Maxidrive's income statement (Exhibit 1.3) indicates a great deal about its purpose and content. The heading identifies the name of the entity, the title of the report, and the unit of measure used in the statement. Unlike the balance sheet, however, which reports as of a certain date, the income statement reports for a specified period of time (for the year ended December 31, 2003). The time period covered by the financial statements (one year in this case) is called an **accounting period.** Notice that Maxidrive's income statement has three major captions, revenues, expenses, and net income. The income statement equation that describes their relationship is

$$\text{Revenues} - \text{Expenses} = \text{Net Income}$$

The **INCOME STATEMENT** (Statement of Income, Statement of Earnings, Statement of Operations) reports the revenues less the expenses of the accounting period.

Income Statement

Revenues
– Expenses
Net Income

The **ACCOUNTING PERIOD** is the time period covered by the financial statements.

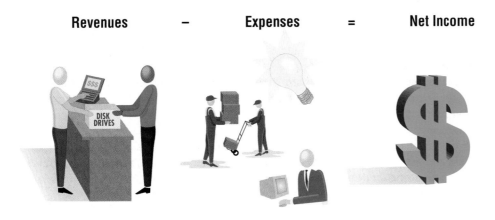

Revenues   −   **Expenses**   =   **Net Income**

Elements

Companies earn **revenues** from the sale of goods or services to customers (in Maxidrive's case, from the sale of disk drives). Revenues normally are reported for goods or services that have been sold to a customer **whether or not they have been paid for.** Retail stores such as Wal-Mart or McDonald's often receive cash at the time of sale. However, when Maxidrive sells its disk drives to Compaq and Apple Computer, it receives a promise of future payment called an account receivable, which later is collected in cash. In either case, the business recognizes total sales (cash and credit) as revenue for the period. Various terms are used in income statements to describe different sources of revenue (e.g., provision of services, sale of goods, rental of property). Maxidrive lists only one, sales revenue, in its income statement.

Expenses represent the dollar amount of resources the entity used to earn revenues during the period. Expenses reported in one accounting period may actually be paid for in another accounting period. Some expenses require the payment of cash immediately while some require payment at a later date. Some may also require the use of another

MAXIDRIVE CORP. Income Statement For the Year Ended December 31, 2003 (in thousands of dollars)		
name of the entity		
title of the statement		
accounting period		
unit of measure		
Revenues		
Sales revenue	$37,436	*revenue earned from sale of disk drives*
Total revenues	$37,436	
Expenses		
Cost of goods sold expense	26,980	*cost to produce disk drives sold*
Selling, general, and administrative expense	3,624	*operating expenses not directly related to production*
Research and development expense	1,982	*expenses incurred to develop new products*
Interest expense	450	*cost of using borrowed funds*
Total expenses	33,036	
Pretax income	4,400	
Income tax expense	1,100	*income taxes on period's pretax income ($4,400 × 25%)*
Net income	$ 3,300	

EXHIBIT 1.3

Income Statement

The notes are an integral part of these financial statements.

resource, such as an inventory item, which may have been paid for in a prior period. Maxidrive lists five types of expenses on its income statement, which are described in Exhibit 1.3. These expenses include income tax expense, which, as a corporation, Maxidrive must pay on pretax income.[2]

Net income or net earnings (often "the bottom line") is the excess of total revenues over total expenses. If total expenses exceed total revenues, a net loss is reported.[3] When revenues and expenses are equal for the period, the business has operated at breakeven.

We noted earlier that revenues are not necessarily the same as collections from customers and expenses are not necessarily the same as payments to suppliers. As a result, net income normally **does not equal** the net cash generated by operations. This latter amount is reported on the cash flow statement discussed later in this chapter.

FINANCIAL ANALYSIS

69,0	00	13,
67,000	137,00	
70,000	140,000	13,
48,778	89,678	13,5

Analyzing the Income Statement: Beyond the Bottom Line

Investors such as Exeter and creditors such as American Bank closely monitor a firm's net income because it indicates the firm's ability to sell goods and services for more than they cost to produce and deliver. Investors buy stock when they believe that future earnings will improve and lead to a higher stock price. Lenders also rely on future earnings to provide the resources to repay loans. The details of the statement also are important. For example, Maxidrive had to sell more than $37 million worth of disk drives to make just over $3 million. If a competitor were to lower prices just 10 percent, forcing Maxidrive to do the same, or if Maxidrive had to triple research and development expense to catch up to a competitor, its net income could easily turn into a net loss. These factors and others help investors and creditors estimate the company's future earnings.

SELF-STUDY **QUIZ**

1. Learning which items belong in each of the income statement categories is an important first step in understanding their meaning. Without referring to Exhibit 1.3, mark each income statement item in the following list as a revenue (R) or an expense (E).

    _____ Cost of goods sold   _____ Sales

    _____ Research and development   _____ Selling, general, and administrative

2. During the period 2003, Maxidrive delivered disk drives for which customers paid or promised to pay amounts totaling $37,436,000. During the same period, it collected $33,563,000 in cash from its customers. Without referring to Exhibit 1.3, indicate which of these two amounts will be shown on Maxidrive's income statement as **sales revenue** for 2003. Why did you select your answer?

3. During the period 2003, Maxidrive **produced** disk drives with a total cost of production of $27,130,000. During the same period, it **delivered** to customers disk drives that had cost a total of $26,980,000 to produce. Without referring to Exhibit 1.3, indicate which of the two numbers will be shown on Maxidrive's income statement as **cost of goods sold expense** for 2003. Why did you select your answer?

After you have completed your answers, check them with the solutions that follow:

---

[2]This example uses a 25 percent rate. Federal tax rates for corporations actually ranged from 15 percent to 35 percent at the time this book was written. State and local governments may levy additional taxes on corporate income, resulting in a higher total income tax rate.
[3]Net losses are normally noted by parentheses around the income figure.

1. E, E, R, E (reading down the columns).

2. Sales revenue in the amount of $37,436,000 is recognized. Sales revenue is normally reported on the income statement when goods or services have been delivered to customers who have either paid or promised to pay for them in the future.

3. Cost of goods sold expense is $26,980,000. Expenses are the dollar amount of resources used up to earn revenues during the period. Only those disk drives that have been delivered to customers have been used up. Those disk drives that are still on hand are part of the asset inventory.

Statement of Retained Earnings

Structure

Maxidrive prepares a separate **statement of retained earnings,** shown in Exhibit 1.4. The heading identifies the name of the entity, the title of the report, and the unit of measure used in the statement. Like the income statement, the statement of retained earnings covers a specified period of time (the accounting period), which in this case is one year. The statement reports the way that net income and the distribution of dividends affected the company's financial position during the accounting period.[4] Net income earned during the year increases the balance of retained earnings, showing the relationship of the income statement to the balance sheet. The declaration of dividends to the stockholders decreases retained earnings.[5]

The retained earnings equation that describes these relationships is

Beginning Retained Earnings + Net Income − Dividends = Ending Retained Earnings

The **STATEMENT OF RETAINED EARNINGS** reports the way that net income and the distribution of dividends affected the financial position of the company during the accounting period.

Elements

The statement begins with Maxidrive's **beginning-of-the-year retained earnings.** The current year's **net income** reported on the income statement is added and the current year's **dividends** are subtracted from this amount. During 2003, Maxidrive earned $3,300,000, as shown on the income statement (Exhibit 1.3). This amount was added to the beginning-of-the-year retained earnings. Also, during 2003, Maxidrive declared and paid a total of $1,000,000 in dividends to its two original stockholders. This amount was subtracted in computing **end-of-the-year retained earnings** on the balance sheet. Note that retained earnings increased by the portion of income reinvested in the business ($3,300,000 − 1,000,000 = $2,300,000). The ending retained earnings

MAXIDRIVE CORP. Statement of Retained Earnings For the Year Ended December 31, 2003 (in thousands of dollars)		
Retained earnings, January 1, 2003	$6,805	*last period's ending retained earnings*
Net income for 2003	3,300	*net income reported on the income statement*
Dividends for 2003	(1,000)	*dividends declared during the period*
Retained earnings, December 31, 2003	$9,105	*ending retained earnings on the balance sheet*

name of the entity
title of the statement
accounting period
unit of measure

EXHIBIT 1.4

Statement of Retained Earnings

The notes are an integral part of these financial statements.

[4]Other corporations report these changes at the end of the income statement or in a more general statement of stockholders' equity, which we discuss in Chapter 4.
[5]Net losses are subtracted.

amount of $9,105,000 is the same as that reported in Exhibit 1.2 on Maxidrive's balance sheet. Thus, the retained earnings statement indicates the relationship of the income statement to the balance sheet.

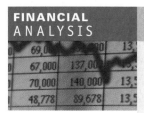

FINANCIAL ANALYSIS

Interpreting Retained Earnings

Reinvestment of earnings, or retained earnings, is an important source of financing for Maxidrive, representing more than one-third of its financing. Creditors such as American Bank closely monitor a firm's retained earnings statement because the firm's policy on dividend payments to the stockholders affects its ability to repay its debts. Every dollar Maxidrive pays to stockholders as a dividend is not available for use in paying back its debt to American Bank. Investors examine retained earnings to determine whether the company is reinvesting a sufficient portion of earnings to support future growth.

Statement of Cash Flows

Structure

The **STATEMENT OF CASH FLOWS** reports inflows and outflows of cash during the accounting period in the categories of operating, investing, and financing.

Maxidrive's statement of cash flows is presented in Exhibit 1.5. The **statement of cash flows** divides Maxidrive's cash inflows and outflows (receipts and payments) into the three primary categories of cash flows in a typical business: cash flows from operating, investing, and financing activities. The heading identifies the name of the entity, the title of the report, and the unit of measure used in the statement. Like the income

---

EXHIBIT 1.5

Statement of Cash Flows

name of the entity	**MAXIDRIVE CORP.**
title of the statement	**Statement of Cash Flows**
accounting period	**For the Year Ended December 31, 2003**
unit of measure	**(in thousands of dollars)**

directly related to earning income	**Cash flows from operating activities**
	Cash collected from customers	$33,563
	Cash paid to suppliers and employees	(30,854)
	Cash paid for interest	(450)
	Cash paid for taxes	(1,190)
	Net cash flow from operating activities	$ 1,069
purchase/sale of productive assets	**Cash flows from investing activities**
	Cash paid to purchase manufacturing equipment	(1,625)
	Net cash flow from investing activities	(1,625)
from investors and creditors	**Cash flows from financing activities**
	Cash received from bank loan	1,400
	Cash paid for dividends	(1,000)
	Net cash flow from financing activities	400
change in cash during the period ($1,069 − 1,625 + 400)	**Net decrease in cash during the year**	(156)
last period's ending cash balance	**Cash at beginning of year**	5,051
ending cash on the balance sheet	**Cash at end of year**	$ 4,895

The notes are an integral part of these financial statements.

statement, the cash flow statement covers a specified period of time (the accounting period), which in this case is one year.

As discussed earlier in this chapter, reported revenues do not always equal cash collected from customers because some sales may be on credit. Also, expenses reported on the income statement may not be equal to the cash paid out during the period because expenses may be incurred in one period and paid for in another. Because the income statement does not provide information concerning cash flows, accountants prepare the statement of cash flows to report inflows and outflows of cash. The cash flow statement equation describes the causes of the change in cash reported on the balance sheet from the end of last period to the end of the current period:

+/− Cash Flows from Operating Activities (CFO)

+/− Cash Flows from Investing Activities (CFI)

+/− Cash Flows from Financing Activities (CFF)

Change in Cash

Note that each of the three cash flow sources can be positive or negative.

Elements

Cash flows from operating activities are cash flows that are directly related to earning income. For example, when Compaq, Apple Computer, and other customers pay Maxidrive for the disk drives it has delivered to them, it lists the amounts collected as cash collected from customers. When Maxidrive pays salaries to its employees in research and development or pays bills received from its parts suppliers, it includes the amounts in cash paid to suppliers and employees.[6]

Cash flows from investing activities include cash flows related to the acquisition or sale of the company's productive assets. This year, Maxidrive had only one cash outflow from investing activities, the purchase of additional manufacturing equipment to meet growing demand for its products. **Cash flows from financing activities** are directly related to the financing of the enterprise itself. They involve receipt or payment of money to investors and creditors (except for suppliers). This year, Maxidrive borrowed an additional $1,400,000 from the bank to purchase most of the new manufacturing equipment. It also paid out $1,000,000 in dividends to the founding stockholders.

Interpreting the Cash Flow Statement

FINANCIAL ANALYSIS

Many analysts believe that the statement of cash flows is particularly useful in predicting future cash flows that may be available for payment of debt to creditors and dividends to investors. Bankers often consider the Operating Activities section to be most important because it indicates the company's ability to generate cash from sales to meet its current cash needs. Any amount left over can be used to pay back the bank debt or expand the company.

Stockholders will invest in a company only if they believe that it will eventually generate more cash from operations than it uses so that cash will become available to pay dividends and expand. The Investing Activities section shows that Maxidrive is making heavy investments in new manufacturing capacity, a good sign if demand continues to increase. But, as the Financing Activities section indicates, if Maxidrive is not able to sell more drives, it may have trouble meeting the payments on the new bank debt.

---

[6]Alternative ways to present cash flows from operations are discussed in Chapter 5.

1. During the period 2003, Maxidrive delivered disk drives to customers who paid or promised to pay a total of $37,436,000. During the same period, it collected $33,563,000 in cash from customers. Without referring to Exhibit 1.5, indicate which of the two amounts will be shown on Maxidrive's cash flow statement for 2003.

2. Learning which items belong in each cash flow statement category is an important first step in understanding their meaning. Without referring to Exhibit 1.5, mark each item in the following list as a cash flow from operating activities (O), investing activities (I), or financing activities (F). Place **parentheses** around the letter only if it is a cash **outflow.**

   _____ Cash paid for dividends

   _____ Cash received from bank loan

   _____ Cash paid for taxes

   _____ Cash paid to purchase manufacturing equipment

   _____ Cash paid to suppliers and employees

   _____ Cash collected from customers

After you have completed your answers, check them with the solutions that follow:

---

1. The firm recognizes $33,563,000 on the cash flow statement because this number represents the actual cash collected from customers related to current and prior years' sales.
2. (F), F, (O), (I), (O), O.

Relationships among the Statements

Our discussion of the four basic financial statements focused on what elements are reported in each statement, how the elements are related by the equation for each statement, and how the elements are important to the decisions of investors, creditors, and others. We have also discovered how the statements, all of which are outputs from the same system, are related to one another. In particular, we learned:

1. Net income from the income statement results in an increase in ending retained earnings on the statement of retained earnings.

2. Ending retained earnings from the statement of retained earnings is one of the two components of stockholders' equity on the balance sheet.

3. The change in cash on the cash flow statement added to the beginning-of-the-year balance in cash equals the end-of-year balance in cash on the balance sheet.

Thus, we can think of the income statement as explaining, through the statement of retained earnings, how the operations of the company improved or harmed the financial position of the company during the year. The cash flow statement explains how the operating, investing, and financing activities of the company affected the cash balance on the balance sheet during the year. These relationships are illustrated in Exhibit 1.6 for Maxidrive's financial statements.

Notes

At the bottom of each of Maxidrive's four basic financial statements is this statement: **"The notes are an integral part of these financial statements."** This is the accounting equivalent of the Surgeon General's warning on a package of cigarettes. It warns users that failure to read the **notes** (or footnotes) to the financial statements will result in an incomplete picture of the company's financial health. Notes provide supplemental information about the financial condition of a company, without which the financial statements cannot be fully understood.

NOTES (footnotes) provide supplemental information about the financial condition of a company without which the financial statements cannot be fully understood.

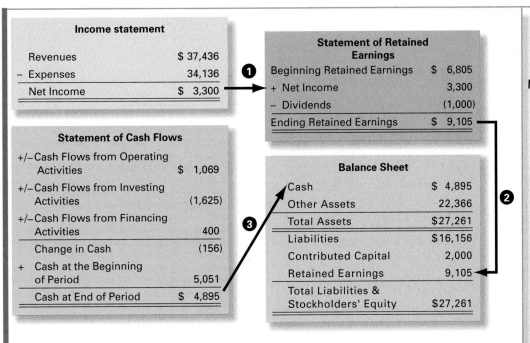

EXHIBIT 1.6

Relationships among Maxidrive's Statements

There are three basic types of notes. The first type provides descriptions of the accounting rules applied in the company's statements. The second presents additional detail about a line on the financial statements. For example, Maxidrive's inventory note indicates the amount of parts, drives under construction, and finished disk drives included in the total inventory amount listed on the balance sheet. The third type of note provides additional financial disclosures about items not listed on the statements themselves. For example, Maxidrive leases one of its production facilities; terms of the lease are disclosed in a note. Throughout this book, we will discuss many note disclosures because understanding their content is critical to understanding the company.

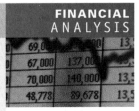

A few additional formatting conventions are worth noting here. Assets are listed on the balance sheet by ease of conversion to cash. Liabilities are listed by their maturity (due date). Most financial statements include the monetary unit sign (in the United States, the $) beside the first dollar amount in a group of items (e.g., the cash amount in the assets). Also, it is common to place a single underline below the last item in a group before a total or subtotal (e.g., land). A dollar sign is also placed beside group totals (e.g., total assets) and a double underline below. The same conventions are followed in all four basic financial statements.

Management Uses of Financial Statements

FINANCIAL ANALYSIS

In our discussion of financial analysis thus far, we have focused on the perspectives of investors and creditors. Managers within the firm also make direct use of financial statements. For example, Maxidrive's **marketing managers** and **credit managers** use customers' financial statements to decide whether to extend credit for purchases of disk drives. Maxidrive's **purchasing managers** analyze parts suppliers' financial statements to see whether the suppliers have the resources to meet Maxidrive's demand and invest in the development of new parts. Both the **employees' union** and Maxidrive's **human resource managers** use Maxidrive's financial statements as a basis for contract negotiations over pay rates. The net income figure even serves as a basis for calculating **employee bonuses.**

Regardless of the functional area of management in which you are employed, you will use financial statement data. You also will be evaluated based on the impact of your decisions on your company's financial statement data.

USING FINANCIAL STATEMENTS TO DETERMINE MAXIDRIVE'S VALUE

Correcting Maxidrive's Income Statement

Let's look at the errors Exeter Investors later found in Maxidrive's statements to see whether we have learned enough to make the necessary corrections.

Among Exeter's claims are that

1. Disk drives inventory included $1,000,000 of obsolete drives that could not be sold and must be scrapped.

2. Reported sales to customers and accounts receivable for last year included $1,200,000 of overstatements. Maxidrive had cut the price of a certain type of disk drive by 40 percent, but employees had created fake customer bills (called invoices) at the old higher prices to inflate reported sales.

Together, these two items significantly overstated Maxidrive's assets and its net income.

For purposes of our discussion, we focus on the effects on the income statement because they were most relevant to Exeter Investors' evaluation of Maxidrive. The simplest way to determine the effects of these two errors on the income statement is to use the income statement equation as we have in Exhibit 1.7. Correcting the two errors reduces pretax income to $2,200,000. After we subtract 25 percent for income tax expense, we are left with a corrected net income equal to $1,650,000, just *half* of the $3,300,000 amount Maxidrive initially reported.

Determining the Purchase Price for Maxidrive

Even at this early stage in your study of accounting, we can illustrate part of the process Exeter Investors went through in determining the price it was willing to pay for Maxidrive Corp. The price Exeter paid was decided by considering a variety of factors

EXHIBIT 1.7		Computations	Corrected Income Statement
Correction of the Income Statement Amounts (in thousands of dollars)	**Revenues** (as reported)	$37,436	
	Error 1: Employees created fake invoices for $1,200,000 in sales revenue. Accordingly revenues should decrease by $1,200,000.	(1,200)	
	Revenues (corrected)		$36,236
	Expenses (as reported)	33,036	
	Error 2: The cost of obsolete inventory items should be added to this year's expenses. Accordingly, expenses should increase by $1,000,000.	1,000	
	Expenses (corrected)		34,036
	Pretax income (corrected)		2,200
	Income tax expense (corrected) 25% × $2,200		550
	Net Income (corrected)		$ 1,650

including the value of Maxidrive's assets, its debts to others, its ability to sell goods for more than their production cost, and its ability to generate the cash necessary to pay its current bills. These factors are the subject matter of the balance sheet, income statement, and cash flow statement.

Maxidrive's current and prior years' income statements played a particularly important part in Exeter's evaluation. Prior years' income statements (which were not presented here) indicated that the company had earned income every year since its founding except for the first year. Many new companies do not become profitable this quickly. Further, both sales revenue and net income had risen every year.

One method for estimating the value of a company is with a **price/earnings ratio** (P/E ratio, or P/E multiple).The P/E ratio measures how many times current year's earnings that investors are willing to pay for a company's stock. All other things equal, a high P/E ratio means that investors have confidence in the company's ability to produce higher profits in future years. As in Maxidrive's case, competitors' P/E ratios often serve as a starting point in analyzing the price that should be paid for a company or its stock.

A key to Exeter's decision to buy Maxidrive was the fact that other companies in the same industry with similar performance and past growth were selling for 12 times their current earnings. Accordingly, the opportunity to buy Maxidrive for 10 times its current earnings seemed to be an excellent one, particularly since economic forecasts suggested that the next five years would see continuing growth and profitability for disk drive manufacturers. The key calculation that determined the price Exeter paid was based on the following manipulation of the P/E ratio:

$$\text{Price/Earnings Ratio} = \frac{\text{Market Price}}{\text{Net Income}}$$

$$\text{Market (Purchase)Price} = \text{P/E Ratio} \times \text{Net Income}$$

$$\text{Market (Purchase) Price} = 10 \times \text{Net Income}$$

$$\$33{,}000{,}000 = 10 \times \$3{,}300{,}000$$

Using the same formula, the corrected net income figure suggests a much lower price for Maxidrive:

$$\$16{,}500{,}000 = 10 \times \$1{,}650{,}000$$

The P/E ratio provides a good approximation of Exeter's loss—a $16.5 million overpayment ($33 million minus $16.5 million estimated value based on corrected earnings). This is the amount that Exeter hopes to recover from those responsible for the fraudulent financial statements it relied on in its analysis. (The role of net income in determining the value of a company will be discussed in more detail in your corporate finance course and more advanced courses in financial statement analysis.[7])

RESPONSIBILITIES FOR THE ACCOUNTING COMMUNICATION PROCESS

For the decision makers at Exeter to use the information in Maxidrive's financial statements effectively, they had to understand what information each of the statements conveyed. Yet the fraud perpetrated by Maxidrive employees suggests that this understanding is not sufficient. Exeter clearly needed to know that the numbers in the statements represented what they claimed. Numbers that do not represent what they claim to are meaningless. For example, if the balance sheet lists $2,000,000 for a factory that does not exist, that part of the statement does not convey useful information.

Topic Tackler 1–2

Learning Objective 2
Identify the role of generally accepted accounting principles (GAAP) in determining the content of financial statements.

[7]See, for example, K.R. Palepu, P.M. Healy, and V.B. Bernard, *Business Analysis and Valuation* (Cincinnati, OH: South-Western, 2000), chapter 11.

Decision makers also need to understand the **measurement rules** applied in computing the numbers on the statements. A swim coach would never try to evaluate a swimmer's time in the 100 freestyle without first asking if the time was for a race in meters or in yards. Likewise, a decision maker should never attempt to use accounting information without first understanding the measurement rules that were used to develop the information. These measurement rules are called **generally accepted accounting principles,** or GAAP.

Generally Accepted Accounting Principles

How Are Generally Accepted Accounting Principles Determined?

The accounting system in use today has a long history. Its foundations are normally traced back to the works of an Italian monk and mathematician, Fr. Luca Pacioli, published in 1494. However, prior to 1933, each company's management largely determined its financial reporting practices. Thus, little uniformity in practice existed among companies.

Following the dramatic stock market decline of 1929, the Securities Act of 1933 and The Securities Exchange Act of 1934 were passed into law by the U.S. Congress. These acts created the **Securities and Exchange Commission** (SEC) and gave it broad powers to determine the measurement rules for financial statements that companies must provide to stockholders.[8] The SEC has worked with organizations of professional accountants to establish groups that are given the primary responsibilities to work out the detailed rules that become generally accepted accounting principles. Today, the **Financial Accounting Standards Board** (FASB) has this responsibility. The Board has seven full-time voting members and a permanent staff who consider the appropriate financial reporting responses to ever-changing business practices. As of the date of publication of this book, the official pronouncements of the FASB (**Financial Accounting Standards**) and its predecessors totaled more than 4,700 pages of very fine print. Such detail is made necessary by the enormous diversity and complexity of current business practices.

Most managers do not need to learn all the details included in these standards. Our approach is to focus on those details that have the greatest impact on the numbers presented in financial statements and are appropriate for an introductory course.

Why is GAAP Important to Managers and External Users?

Generally accepted accounting principles (GAAP) are of great interest to the companies that must prepare financial statements, their auditors, and the readers of the statements. Companies and their managers and owners are most directly affected by the information presented in financial statements. Companies incur the cost of preparing the statements and bear the major economic consequences of their publication, which include, among others,

1. Effects on the selling price of a company's stock.

2. Effects on the amount of bonuses received by management and employees.

3. Loss of competitive information to other companies.

Recall that the amount that Exeter was willing to pay to purchase Maxidrive was determined in part by net income computed under GAAP. This presents the possibility that changes in GAAP can affect the price buyers are willing to pay for companies. Employees who receive part of their pay based on reaching stated targets for net income are directly concerned with any changes in how net income is computed under GAAP. Managers and owners also often are concerned that publishing certain information in financial statements will give away trade secrets to other companies that

---

[8]Contrary to popular belief, these rules are different from those that companies follow when filing their income tax returns. We discuss these differences further in later chapters.

compete with them. As a consequence of these and other concerns, changes in GAAP are actively debated, political lobbying often takes place, and final rules are often a compromise among the wishes of interested parties.

Are Generally Accepted Accounting Principles Similar in Other Countries?

INTERNATIONAL PERSPECTIVE

While businesspeople compete in a single global economy, different sets of generally accepted accounting principles have developed within particular countries. Differences in political, cultural, and economic histories have produced a great number of cross-national differences in practice. These differences can have dramatic effects on the numbers presented in financial statements. The International Accounting Standards Board (IASB) and others are attempting to eliminate these differences. But for now, users of financial statements who cross national borders must be aware of the specific nature of these reporting differences to interpret financial statements successfully. The following article indicates how firms such as Sumitomo Electric of Japan have increased the credibility of their reports with foreign investors.

SUMITOMO ELECTRIC GETS US AUDIT TO UP INTERNATIONAL CREDIBILITY

OSAKA (Nikkei)—Sumitomo Electric Industries Ltd. has undergone an audit by a U.S. accounting firm so that its English-language annual report will be more credible among overseas investors . . . and disclosed the differences created by Japan and U.S. accounting differences in the company's group net profit and group net assets. . . . Other Japanese firms are expected to follow suit.

06/27/2001
Dow Jones International News

(Copyright (c) 2001, Dow Jones & Company, Inc.)

REAL WORLD EXCERPT

Dow Jones
International News

Management Responsibility and the Demand for Auditing

Exeter's owners and managers were well aware of the details of U.S. GAAP, but they were still misled. Although the measurement rules that Maxidrive had used to produce its financial statements were consistent with GAAP, the underlying figures were fictitious. Who was responsible for the accuracy of the numbers in Maxidrive's financial statements?

Primary responsibility for the information in the financial statements lies with management, as represented by the highest officer of the company and the highest financial officer. Companies take three important steps to ensure the accuracy of the company's records: (1) they maintain a system of controls over both the records and the assets of the company, (2) they hire outside independent auditors to verify the fairness of the financial statements, and (3) they form a committee of the board of directors to review these other two safeguards. These three safeguards failed in Maxidrive's case. Some companies reiterate these responsibilities in a formal **report of management** in the annual report.

Learning Objective 3
Distinguish the roles of managers and auditors in the accounting communication process.

Three steps to ensure the accuracy of records:

System of controls   External Auditors   Board of Directors

The role of the independent auditor is described in more detail in the **audit report,** or report of independent accountants (Exhibit 1.8). The audit report describes the auditor's opinion of the fairness of the financial statements and the evidence gathered to support that opinion. An accountant may be licensed as a **certified public accountant,** or **CPA,** only on completion of requirements specified by each state. Only a licensed CPA can issue an audit report. In this role, accountants are known as independent CPAs (or independent accountants) because they have certain responsibilities that extend to the general public as well as to the specific business that pays for this service.

EXHIBIT 1.8

Report of Independent Accountants

Report of Independent Accountants To the Stockholders and Board of Directors of Maxidrive Corp.

We have audited the accompanying balance sheet of Maxidrive Corp. as of December 31, 2003, and the related statements of income, retained earnings and cash flows for the period ended December 31, 2003. These financial statements are the responsibility of the Company's management. Our responsibility is to express an opinion on these financial statements based on our audits.

We conducted our audits in accordance with generally accepted auditing standards. Those standards require that we plan and perform the audit to obtain reasonable assurance about whether the financial statements are free of material misstatement. An audit includes examining, on a test basis, evidence supporting the amounts and disclosures in the financial statements. An audit also includes assessing the accounting principles used and significant estimates made by management, as well as evaluating the overall financial statement presentation. We believe that our audits provide a reasonable basis for our opinion.

In our opinion, the financial statements referred to above present fairly, in all material respects, the financial position of Maxidrive Corp. at December 31, 2003, and the results of its operations and its cash flows for the period ended December 31, 2003, in conformity with generally accepted accounting principles.

Smith and Walker, CPAs
Smith and Walker, CPAs

An **audit** involves the examination of the financial reports (prepared by the management of the entity) to ensure that they represent what they claim to and conform with generally accepted accounting principles (GAAP). In performing an audit, the independent CPA examines the underlying transactions and the accounting methods used to account for these transactions. Because of the enormous number of transactions involving a major enterprise such as General Motors, the CPA does not examine each of these transactions. Rather, professional approaches are used to ascertain beyond reasonable doubt that transactions were measured and reported properly.

Many unintentional and intentional opportunities exist to prepare misleading financial reports. An audit performed by an independent CPA is the best protection available to the public. When that protection fails, however, the independent CPA is often found liable for losses incurred by those who rely on the statements. You can learn more about auditing and other information **assurance services** offered by CPAs in an auditing and assurance course.[9]

An **AUDIT** is an examination of the financial reports to ensure that they represent what they claim and conform with GAAP.

ASSURANCE SERVICES are independent professional services that improve the quality of information for decision makers.

Ethics, Reputation, and Legal Liability

If financial statements are to be of any value to decision makers, users must have confidence in the fairness of the information they present. Users will have greater confidence in the information if they know that the people who audited the statements were required to meet professional standards of ethics and competence.

The American Institute of Certified Public Accountants (AICPA) requires all of its members to adhere to a professional code of ethics and professional auditing standards. Failure to comply with the rules of conduct can result in serious professional penalties. CPAs' reputations for honesty and competence are their most important assets. The potential economic effects of damage to reputation and malpractice liability provide even stronger incentives to abide by professional standards.

In case of malpractice, the independent CPA may be held liable for losses suffered by those who relied on the statements the CPA examined. As a result of the fraud, Maxidrive filed for bankruptcy and will likely be sold in an attempt to pay off creditors. In a civil lawsuit, Exeter Investors and American Bank claimed losses of $16.5 million and $9 million, respectively, charging that the officers of Maxidrive had "perpetrated a massive fraud" and the auditors had "overlooked the errors" in the audit. Exeter and American Bank also have asked for punitive damages for gross negligence. In addition, the president and the chief financial officer of Maxidrive were convicted by a federal jury on three counts of criminal securities fraud for which they were fined and imprisoned.

Learning Objective 4
Appreciate the importance of ethics, reputation, and legal liability in accounting.

EPILOGUE

Although financial statement fraud is a fairly rare event, the misrepresentations in Maxidrive's statements aptly illustrate the importance of fairly presented financial statements to investors and creditors. They also indicate the crucial importance of the public accounting profession in ensuring the integrity of the financial reporting system. The recent Enron and WorldCom debacles have brought the importance of these issues to the attention of the general public.

As noted at the beginning of this chapter, Maxidrive is not a real company but is based on a real company that perpetrated a similar fraud. (The focus companies and contrasting examples in the remaining chapters are **real** companies.) Maxidrive is loosely based on the infamous fraud at MiniScribe, a real disk drive manufacturer. The size of the real fraud, however, was more than 10 times as great as that in the fictional case, as were the losses incurred and the damages claimed in the lawsuits that followed. (Many of the numbers in Maxidrive's financial statements are simply one-tenth the amounts presented in MiniScribe's fraudulent statements.) The nature of the fraud also was quite similar. At MiniScribe, sales revenue was overstated by transferring

---

[9]See, for example, William R. Kinney, *Information Quality Assurance and Internal Control for Management Decision Making* (New York: McGraw-Hill/Irwin, 2000).

nonexistent inventory between two facilities and creating phony documents to make it look as though the inventory were transferred to customers. MiniScribe even packaged bricks as finished products, shipped them to distributors, and counted them as sold. Cost of goods sold was understated by activities such as counting scrap parts and damaged drives as usable inventory. MiniScribe managers even broke into the auditors' locked trunks to change numbers on their audit papers.

As a consequence, MiniScribe reported net income of $31 million, which was subsequently shown to be $9 million. MiniScribe's investors and creditors filed lawsuits claiming more than $1 billion in damages. Actual damages in the hundreds of millions were paid. Both the chairman and the chief financial officer of MiniScribe were convicted of federal securities and wire fraud charges and sentenced to jail. Although most managers and owners act in an honest and responsible fashion, this incident, and the much larger frauds at Enron and WorldCom, are stark reminders of the economic consequences of lack of fair presentation in financial reports.

DEMONSTRATION **CASE**

At the end of most chapters, one or more demonstration cases are presented. These cases provide an overview of the primary issues discussed in the chapter. Each demonstration case is followed by a recommended solution. You should read the case carefully and then prepare your own solution before you study the recommended solution. This self-evaluation is highly recommended. The introductory case presented here reviews the elements reported on the income statement and balance sheet and how the elements within the statements are related.

Krispy Kreme Donuts

The stores owned and franchised by Krispy Kreme Donuts can each make between 4,000 and 10,000 donuts per day. This capacity and the fanatical loyalty of its customers have made this expanding company a great success. Following is a list of the financial statement items and amounts adapted from a recent Krispy Kreme Donuts Inc. income statement and balance sheet. The numbers are presented in thousands of dollars for the year ended January 28, 2001.

Accounts payable	$ 14,697
Accounts receivable	24,733
Cash	7,026
Contributed capital	85,060
General and administrative expenses	20,061
Income tax expense	9,058
Inventories	12,031
Net income	14,725
Notes payable	3,526
Operating expenses	250,690
Other assets	31,260
Other expenses	6,181
Other liabilities	26,474
Pretax income	23,783
Property and equipment	78,340
Retained earnings	41,736
Sales revenues	300,715
Short-term investments	18,103
Total assets	171,493
Total expenses	276,932
Total liabilities	44,697
Total liabilities and stockholders' equity	171,493
Total revenues	300,715
Total stockholders' equity	126,796

Required:

1. Prepare a balance sheet and an income statement for the year following the formats in Exhibits 1.2 and 1.3.

2. Specify what information these two statements provide.

3. Indicate the other two statements that would be included in its annual report.

4. Suggest why Krispy Kreme would voluntarily subject its statements to an independent audit.

SUGGESTED SOLUTION

1.

KRISPY KREME DONUTS INC. Balance Sheet At January, 28, 2001 (in thousands of dollars)	
Assets	
Cash	$ 7,026
Short-term investments	18,103
Accounts receivable	24,733
Inventories	12,031
Property and equipment	78,340
Other assets	31,260
Total assets	$171,493
Liabilities	
Accounts payable	$ 14,697
Notes payable	3,526
Other liabilities	26,474
Total liabilities	44,697
Stockholders' Equity	
Contributed capital	85,060
Retained earnings	41,736
Total stockholders' equity	126,796
Total liabilities and stockholders' equity	$171,493

KRISPY KREME DONUTS INC. Income Statement For the Year Ended January, 28, 2001 (in thousands of dollars)	
Revenues	
Sales revenues	$300,715
Total revenues	300,715
Expenses	
Operating expenses	250,690
General and administrative expenses	20,061
Other expenses	6,181
Total expenses	276,932
Pretax income	23,783
Income tax expense	9,058
Net income	$ 14,725

2. The balance sheet reports the amount of assets, liabilities, and stockholders' equity of an accounting entity at a point in time. The income statement reports the accountant's primary measure of performance of a business, revenues less expenses during the accounting period.

3. Krispy Kreme would also present a statement of retained earnings and a statement of cash flows.

4. Users will have greater confidence in the accuracy of financial statement information if they know that the people who audited the statements were required to meet professional standards of ethics and competence.

1. **Recognize the information conveyed in each of the four basic financial statements and the way that it is used by different decision makers (investors, creditors, and managers).** p. 5

   The **balance sheet** is a statement of financial position that reports dollar amounts for the assets, liabilities, and stockholders' equity at a specific point in time.

   The **income statement** is a statement of operations that reports revenues, expenses, and net income for a stated period of time.

   The **statement of retained earnings** explains changes to the retained earnings balance that occurred during the reporting period.

   The **statement of cash flows** reports inflows and outflows of cash for a specific period of time.

   The statements are used by investors and creditors to evaluate different aspects of the firm's financial position and performance.

2. **Identify the role of generally accepted accounting principles (GAAP) in determining the content of financial statements.** p. 19

   GAAP are the measurement rules used to develop the information in financial statements. Knowledge of GAAP is necessary for accurate interpretation of the numbers in financial statements.

3. **Distinguish the roles of managers and auditors in the accounting communication process.** p. 21

   Management has primary responsibility for the accuracy of a company's financial information. Auditors are responsible for expressing an opinion on the fairness of the financial statement presentations based on their examination of the reports and records of the company.

4. **Appreciate the importance of ethics, reputation, and legal liability in accounting.** p. 23

   Users will have confidence in the accuracy of financial statement numbers only if the people associated with their preparation and audit have reputations for ethical behavior and competence. Management and auditors can also be held legally liable for fraudulent financial statements and malpractice.

In this chapter, we studied the basic financial statements that communicate financial information to external users. Chapters 2, 3, and 4 provide a more detailed look at financial statements and examine how to translate data about business transactions into these statements. Learning how to translate back and forth between business transactions and financial statements is the key to using financial statements in planning and decision making. Chapter 2 begins our discussion of the way that the accounting function collects data about business transactions and processes the data to provide periodic financial statements, with emphasis on the balance sheet. To accomplish this purpose, Chapter 2 discusses key accounting concepts, the accounting model, transaction analysis, and analytical tools. We examine typical business activities of an actual service-oriented company to demonstrate the concepts in Chapters 2, 3, and 4.

Chapter Supplement A

Types of Business Entities

This textbook emphasizes **accounting for profit-making business entities.** The three main types of business entities are sole proprietorship, partnership, and corporation. A **sole proprietorship** is an unincorporated business owned by one person; it usually is small in size and is common in the service, retailing, and farming industries. Often the owner is the manager. Legally, the business and the owner are not separate entities. Accounting views the business as a separate entity, however, that must be accounted for separately from its owner.

A **partnership** is an unincorporated business owned by two or more persons known as **partners.** Some partnerships are large in size (e.g., international public accounting firms and law firms). The agreements between the owners are specified in a partnership contract. This contract deals with matters such as division of income each reporting period and distribution of resources of the business on termination of its operations. A partnership is not legally separate from its owners. Legally, each partner in a general partnership is responsible for the debts of the business (each general partner has

unlimited liability). The partnership, however, is a separate business entity to be accounted for separately from its several owners.

A **corporation** is a business incorporated under the laws of a particular state. The owners are called **stockholders** or **shareholders.** Ownership is represented by shares of capital stock that usually can be bought and sold freely. When an approved application for incorporation is filed by the organizers, the state issues a charter. This charter gives the corporation the right to operate as a separate legal entity, separate and apart from its owners. The stockholders enjoy **limited liability.** Stockholders are liable for the corporation's debts only to the extent of their investments. The corporate charter specifies the types and amounts of capital stock that can be issued. Most states require a minimum of two or three stockholders and a minimum amount of resources to be contributed at the time of organization. The stockholders elect a governing board of directors, which in turn employs managers and exercises general supervision of the corporation. Accounting also views the corporation as a separate business entity that must be accounted for separately from its owners.

In terms of economic importance, the corporation is the dominant form of business organization in the United States. This dominance is caused by the many advantages of the corporate form: (1) limited liability for the stockholders, (2) continuity of life, (3) ease in transferring ownership (stock), and (4) opportunities to raise large amounts of money by selling shares to a large number of people. The primary disadvantage of a corporation is that its income may be subject to double taxation (it is taxed when it is earned and again when it is distributed to stockholders as dividends). In this textbook, we emphasize the corporate form of business. Nevertheless, the accounting concepts and procedures that we discuss also apply to other types of businesses.

Chapter Supplement B

Employment in the Accounting Profession Today

Since 1900, accounting has attained the stature of professions such as law, medicine, engineering, and architecture. As with all recognized professions, accounting is subject to professional competence requirements, is dedicated to service to the public, requires a high level of academic study, and rests on a common body of knowledge. An accountant may be licensed as a certified public accountant, or CPA. This designation is granted only on completion of requirements specified by the state that issues the license. Although CPA requirements vary among states, they include a college degree with a specified number of accounting courses, good character, one to five years of professional experience, and successful completion of a professional examination. The CPA examination is prepared by the American Institute of Certified Public Accountants.

Accountants (including CPAs) commonly are engaged in professional practice or are employed by businesses, government entities, nonprofit organizations, and so on. Accountants employed in these activities may take and pass a professional examination to become a certified management accountant or CMA (the CMA examination is administered by the Institute of Management Accountants) or a certified internal auditor or CIA (the CIA examination is administered by the Institute of Internal Auditors).

Practice of Public Accounting

Although an individual may practice public accounting, usually two or more individuals organize an accounting firm in the form of a partnership (in many cases, a limited liability partnership, or LLP). Accounting firms vary in size from a one-person office, to regional firms, to the Big Four firms (Deloitte & Touche, Ernst & Young, KPMG, and PricewaterhouseCoopers), which have hundreds of offices located worldwide. Accounting firms usually render three types of services: assurance services, management consulting services, and tax services.

Assurance Services

Assurance services are independent professional services that improve the quality of information, or its context, for decision makers. The most important assurance service performed by the CPA in public practice is financial statement auditing. The purpose of an audit is to lend credibility to the financial reports, that is, to ensure that they fairly represent what they claim. An audit involves an examination of the financial reports (prepared by the management of the entity) to ensure that they conform with GAAP. Other areas of assurance services include electronic commerce integrity and security and information systems reliability.

Management Consulting Services

Many independent CPA firms offer **management consulting services.** These services usually are accounting based and encompass activities such as the design and installation of accounting, data processing, and profit-planning and control (budget) systems; financial advice; forecasting; inventory controls; cost-effectiveness studies; and operational analysis. This facet of public CPA practice is growing rapidly.

Tax Services

CPAs in public practice usually provide income tax services to their clients. These services include both tax planning as a part of the decision-making process and the determination of the income tax liability (reported on the annual income tax return). Because of the increasing complexity of state and federal tax laws, a high level of competence is required, which CPAs specializing in taxation can provide. The CPA's involvement in tax planning often is quite significant. Most major business decisions have significant tax impacts; in fact, tax-planning considerations often govern certain business decisions.

Employment by Organizations

Many accountants, including CPAs, CMAs, and CIAs, are employed by profit-making and nonprofit organizations. An organization, depending on its size and complexity, may employ from a few to hundreds of accountants. In a business enterprise, the chief financial officer (usually a vice president or controller) is a member of the management team. This responsibility usually entails a wide range of management, financial, and accounting duties.

In a business entity, accountants typically are engaged in a wide variety of activities, such as general management, general accounting, cost accounting, profit planning and control (budgeting), internal auditing, and computerized data processing. A primary function of the accountants in organizations is to provide data that are useful for internal managerial decision making and for controlling operations. The functions of external reporting, tax planning, control of assets, and a host of related responsibilities normally are also performed by accountants in industry.

Employment in the Public and Not-for-Profit Sector

The vast and complex operations of governmental units, from the local to the international level, create a need for accountants. The same holds true for other not-for-profit organizations such as hospitals and universities. Accountants employed in the public and not-for-profit sector perform functions similar to those performed by their counterparts in private organizations. The General Accounting Office (GAO) and the regulatory agencies, such as the SEC and Federal Communications Commission (FCC), also use the services of accountants in carrying out their regulatory duties.

FINDING **FINANCIAL INFORMATION**

Balance Sheet

Assets = Liabilities + Stockholders' Equity

Income Statement

Revenues
− Expenses

Net Income

Statement of Retained Earnings

Retained Earnings, beginning of the period
+ Net Income
− Dividends

Retained Earnings, end of the period

Statement of Cash Flows

+/− Cash Flow from Operating Activities
+/− Cash Flow from Investing Activities
+/− Cash Flow from Financing Activities

Net Change in Cash

KEY TERMS

Accounting p. 4
Accounting Entity p. 7
Accounting Period p. 10
Assurance Services p. 23
Audit p. 23
Balance Sheet (Statement of Financial Position) p. 7
Basic Accounting Equation (Balance Sheet Equation) p. 8

Financial Accounting Standards Board (FASB) p. 20
Generally Accepted Accounting Principles (GAAP) p. 20
Income Statement (Statement of Income, Statement of Earnings, or Statement of Operations) p. 10
Notes (Footnotes) p. 16

Securities and Exchange Commission (SEC) p. 20
Statement of Cash Flows p. 14
Statement of Retained Earnings p. 13

QUESTIONS

1. Define *accounting*.
2. Briefly distinguish financial accounting from managerial accounting.
3. The accounting process generates financial reports for both internal and external users. Identify some of the groups of users.
4. Briefly distinguish investors from creditors.
5. What is an accounting entity? Why is a business treated as a separate entity for accounting purposes?
6. Complete the following:

Name of Statement	Alternative Title
a. Income statement	*a.* _____
b. Balance sheet	*b.* _____
c. Audit report	*c.* _____

7. What information should be included in the heading of each of the four primary financial statements?
8. What are the purposes of (*a*) the income statement, (*b*) the balance sheet, (*c*) the statement of cash flows, and (*d*) the statement of retained earnings?
9. Explain why the income statement and the statement of cash flows are dated "For the Year Ended December 31, 2005," whereas the balance sheet is dated "At December 31, 2005."
10. Briefly explain the importance of assets and liabilities to the decisions of investors and creditors.
11. Briefly define the following: *net income, net loss,* and *breakeven.*
12. Explain the accounting equation for the income statement. What are the three major items reported on the income statement?
13. Explain the accounting equation for the balance sheet. Define the three major components reported on the balance sheet.
14. Explain the accounting equation for the statement of cash flows. Explain the three major components reported on the statement.
15. Explain the accounting equation for the statement of retained earnings. Explain the four major items reported on the statement of retained earnings.
16. Financial statements discussed in this chapter are aimed at *external users.* Briefly explain how a company's *internal* managers in different functional areas (e.g., marketing, purchasing, human resources) might use financial statement information.
17. Briefly describe the way that accounting measurement rules (generally accepted accounting principles) are determined in the United States.
18. Briefly explain the responsibility of company management and the independent auditors in the accounting communication process.
19. (Supplement A) Briefly differentiate between a sole proprietorship, a partnership, and a corporation.
20. (Supplement B) List and briefly explain the three primary services that CPAs in public practice provide.

MULTIPLE **CHOICE QUESTIONS**

1. Which of the following is *not* one of the four basic financial statements?
   a. balance sheet
   b. audit report
   c. income statement
   d. statement of cash flows

2. As stated in the audit report, or *Report of Independent Accountants,* the primary responsibility for a company's financial statements lies with
   a. the owners of the company
   b. independent financial analysts
   c. the auditors
   d. the company's management

3. Which of the following is true?
   a. FASB creates SEC
   b. GAAP creates FASB
   c. SEC creates AICPA
   d. FASB creates GAAP

4. Which of the following regarding retained earnings is false?
   a. Retained earnings is increased by net income and decreased by a net loss.
   b. Retained earnings is a component of stockholders' equity on the balance sheet.
   c. Retained earnings is an asset on the balance sheet.
   d. Retained earnings represents earnings not distributed to stockholders in the form of dividends.

5. Which of the following is *not* one of the four items required to be shown in the heading of a financial statement?
   a. the financial statement preparer's name
   b. the title of the financial statement
   c. the unit of measure in the financial statement
   d. the name of the business entity

6. How many of the following statements regarding the statement of cash flows is/are true?
   • The statement of cash flows separates cash inflows and outflows into three major categories: operations, investing and financing.
   • The ending cash balance shown on the statement of cash flows must agree with the amount shown on the balance sheet for the same fiscal period.
   • The total increase or decrease in cash shown on the statement of cash flow must agree with the "bottom line" (net income or net loss) reported on the income statement.
   a. none
   b. one
   c. two
   d. three

7. Which of the following is *not* a typical footnote included in an annual report?
   a. A note describing the auditor's opinion of the management's past and future financial planning for the business
   b. A note providing more detail about a specific item shown in the financial statements
   c. A note describing the accounting rules applied in the financial statements
   d. A note describing financial disclosures about items not appearing in the financial statements

8. Which of the following is true regarding the income statement?
   a. The income statement is sometimes called the statement of operations.
   b. The income statement reports revenues, expenses, and liabilities.
   c. The income statement reports only revenue for which cash was received at the point of sale.
   d. The income statement reports the financial position of a business at a particular point in time.

9. Which of the following is false regarding the balance sheet?
   a. The accounts shown on a balance sheet represent the basic accounting equation for a particular business entity.
   b. The retained earnings balance shown on the balance sheet must agree to the ending retained earnings balance shown on the statement of retained earnings.
   c. The balance sheet reports the changes in specific account balances over a period of time.
   d. The balance sheet reports the amount of assets, liabilities, and stockholders' equity of an accounting entity at a point in time.

10. Which of the following regarding GAAP is true?
    a. U.S. GAAP is the body of accounting knowledge followed by all countries in the world.
    b. Changes in GAAP can affect the interests of managers and stockholders.
    c. GAAP is the abbreviation for generally accepted auditing procedures.
    d. Changes to GAAP must be approved by the Senate Finance Committee.

For more practice with multiple choice questions, go to our website at www.mhhe.com/libby4e, click on "Student Center" in the upper left menu, click on this chapter's name and number from the list of contents, and then click on "Multiple Choice Quiz" from the menu on the left.

MINI-**EXERCISES**

Matching Elements with Financial Statements

M1-1
L01

Match each element with its financial statement by entering the appropriate letter in the space provided.

Element	Financial Statement
___ (1) Expenses	A. Balance sheet
___ (2) Cash flow from investing activities	B. Income statement
___ (3) Assets	C. Statement of retained earnings
___ (4) Dividends	D. Statement of cash flows
___ (5) Revenues	
___ (6) Cash flow from operating activities	
___ (7) Liabilities	
___ (8) Cash flow from financing activities	

Matching Financial Statement Items to Financial Statement Categories

M1-2
L01

Mark each item in the following list as an asset (A), liability (L), or stockholders' equity (SE) that would appear on the balance sheet or a revenue (R) or expense (E) that would appear on the income statement.

_____ (1) Retained earnings	_____ (6) Inventories	
_____ (2) Accounts receivable	_____ (7) Interest expense	
_____ (3) Sales revenue	_____ (8) Accounts payable	
_____ (4) Property, plant, and equipment	_____ (9) Land	
_____ (5) Cost of goods sold expense		

Identifying Important Accounting Abbreviations

M1-3
L02

The following is a list of important abbreviations used in the chapter. These abbreviations also are used widely in business. For each abbreviation, give the full designation. The first one is an example.

Abbreviation	Full Designation
(1) CPA	Certified Public Accountant
(2) GAAP	_____
(3) CMA	_____
(4) AICPA	_____
(5) SEC	_____
(6) FASB	_____

EXERCISES

Matching Definitions with Terms or Abbreviations

E1-1
L01, 2

Match each definition with its related term or abbreviation by entering the appropriate letter in the space provided.

Term or Abbreviation	Definition
___ (1) SEC	A. A system that collects and processes financial information about an organization and reports that information to decision makers.
___ (2) Audit	
___ (3) Sole proprietorship	
___ (4) Corporation	B. Measurement of information about an entity in the monetary unit—dollars or other national currency.
___ (5) Accounting	

____ (6) Separate entity	C. An unincorporated business owned by two or more persons.
____ (7) Audit report	D. The organization for which financial data are to be collected (separate and distinct from its owners).
____ (8) Cost principle	
____ (9) Partnership	E. An incorporated entity that issues shares of stock as evidence of ownership.
____ (10) AICPA	
____ (11) FASB	F. Initial recording of financial statement elements at acquisition cost.
____ (12) CPA	
____ (13) Unit of measure	G. An examination of the financial reports to ensure that they represent what they claim and conform with generally accepted accounting principles.
____ (14) GAAP	
____ (15) Publicly traded	

H. Certified Public Accountant.

I. An unincorporated business owned by one person.

J. A report that describes the auditors' opinion of the fairness of the financial statement presentations and the evidence gathered to support that opinion.

K. Securities and Exchange Commission.

L. Financial Accounting Standards Board.

M. A company that can be bought and sold by investors on established stock exchanges.

N. Generally accepted accounting principles.

O. American Institute of Certified Public Accountants.

E1-2 Matching Financial Statement Items to Financial Statement Categories

L01

Procter & Gamble

According to its annual report, "Procter & Gamble markets a broad range of laundry, cleaning, paper, beauty care, health care, food and beverage products in more than 140 countries around the world. P&G's more than 250 brands include Pampers, Tide, Ariel, Always, Whisper, Pantene, Bounty, Pringles, Folgers, Charmin, Downy, Lenor, Iams, Olay, Crest, Vicks and Actonel." The following are items taken from its recent balance sheet and income statement. Note that different companies use slightly different titles for the same item. Mark each item in the following list as an asset (A), liability (L), or stockholders' equity (SE) that would appear on the balance sheet or a revenue (R) or expense (E) that would appear on the income statement.

____ (1) Accounts payable		____ (9) Land
____ (2) Accounts receivable		____ (10) Marketing, administrative, and other operating expenses
____ (3) Cash and cash equivalents		
____ (4) Cost of products sold		____ (11) Long-term debt
____ (5) Property, plant, and equipment		____ (12) Net sales
____ (6) Income taxes		____ (13) Notes payable
____ (7) Interest expense		____ (14) Retained earnings
____ (8) Inventories		____ (15) Taxes payable

E1-3 Matching Financial Statement Items to Financial Statement Categories

L01

Tootsie Roll

Tootsie Roll Industries is engaged in the manufacture and sale of candy. Major products include Tootsie Roll, Tootsie Roll Pops, Tootsie Pop Drops, Tootsie Flavor Rolls, Charms, and Blow-Pop lollipops. The following items were listed on Tootsie Roll's recent income statement and balance sheet. Mark each item from the balance sheet as an asset (A), liability (L), or shareholders' equity (SE) and each item from the income statement as a revenue (R) or expense (E).

____ (1) Accounts payable		____ (10) Buildings
____ (2) Accounts receivable		____ (11) Cash and cash equivalents
____ (3) Cost of goods sold		____ (12) Land
____ (4) Distribution and warehousing		____ (13) Machinery and equipment
____ (5) Dividends payable		____ (14) Marketing, selling, and advertising
____ (6) General and administrative		____ (15) Net sales
____ (7) Income taxes payable		____ (16) Notes payable to banks
____ (8) Inventories		____ (17) Provision for income taxes*
____ (9) Investments		____ (18) Retained earnings

*In the United States, "provision for income taxes" is most often used as a synonym for "income tax expense."

Preparing a Balance Sheet

E1-4
L01
Honda
Motor Co.

Established less than 50 years ago, Honda Motor Co., Ltd. of Japan is a leading international manufacturer of automobiles and the largest manufacturer of motorcycles in the world. As a Japanese company, it follows Japanese GAAP and reports its financial statements in millions of yen (the sign for yen is ¥). Its recent balance sheet contained the following items (in millions). Prepare a balance sheet as of March 31, 2003, solving for the missing amount.

Cash and cash equivalents	¥ 150,554
Contributed capital	281,208
Accounts payable and other current liabilities	1,308,748
Inventories	606,689
Investments	212,294
Long-term debt	569,479
Net property, plant, and equipment	1,008,196
Other assets	213,845
Other liabilities	94,485
Retained earnings	755,419
Total assets	3,009,339
Total liabilities and stockholders' equity	?
Trade accounts, notes, and other receivables	817,761

Completing a Balance Sheet and Inferring Net Income

E1-5
L01

Terry Lloyd and Joan Lopez organized Read More Store as a corporation; each contributed $50,000 cash to start the business and received 4,000 shares of common stock. The store completed its first year of operations on December 31, 2003. On that date, the following financial items for the year were determined: December 31, 2003, cash on hand and in the bank, $48,900; December 31, 2003, amounts due from customers from sales of books, $26,000; unused portion of store and office equipment, $48,000; December 31, 2003, amounts owed to publishers for books purchased, $8,000; one-year note payable to a local bank for $2,000. No dividends were declared or paid to the stockholders during the year.

Required:
1. Complete the following balance sheet as of the end of 2003.
2. What was the amount of net income for the year?

_____
_____
_____

Assets		Liabilities	
Cash	$ _____	Accounts payable	$ _____
Accounts receivable	_____	Note payable	_____
Store and office equipment	_____	Interest payable	120
		Total liabilities	$ _____
		Stockholders' Equity	
		Contributed capital	$ _____
		Retained earnings	12,780
		Total stockholders' equity	_____
Total assets	$ _____	Total liabilities and stockholders' equity	$ _____

Analyzing Revenues and Expenses and Preparing an Income Statement

E1-6
L01

Assume that you are the owner of The Collegiate Shop, which specializes in items that interest students. At the end of January 2003, you find (for January only) this information:

a. Sales, per the cash register tapes, of $120,000, plus one sale on credit (a special situation) of $1,000.

b. With the help of a friend (who majored in accounting), you determined that all of the goods sold during January had cost $40,000 to purchase.

c. During the month, according to the checkbook, you paid $38,000 for salaries, rent, supplies, advertising, and other expenses; however, you have not yet paid the $600 monthly utilities for January on the store and fixtures.

Required:

On the basis of the data given, what was the amount of income for January (disregard income taxes)? Show computations. (*Hint:* A convenient form to use has the following major side captions: Revenue from Sales, Expenses, and the difference—Net Income.)

E1-7   Preparing an Income Statement and Inferring Missing Values

LO1

Wal-Mart

Wal-Mart Stores, Inc., is the largest retail chain in the United States, operating more than 2,000 stores. Its recent quarterly income statement contained the following items (in thousands). Solve for the missing amounts and prepare a condensed income statement for the quarter ended October 31, 2003. (*Hint:* First order the items as they would appear on the income statement and then solve for the missing values.)

Cost of sales	$16,200,873
Interest costs	184,190
Net income	?
Net sales	20,417,717
Operating, selling, and general and administrative expenses	3,340,263
Provision for income taxes*	339,422
Rental and other income	235,116
Total costs and expenses	?
Total revenues	?
Pretax income	?

E1-8   Analyzing Revenues and Expenses and Completing an Income Statement

LO1

Home Realty, Incorporated, has been operating for three years and is owned by three investors. J. Doe owns 60 percent of the total outstanding stock of 9,000 shares and is the managing executive in charge. On December 31, 2005, the following financial items for the entire year were determined: commissions earned and collected in cash, $150,000, plus $16,000 uncollected; rental service fees earned and collected, $20,000; salaries expense paid, $62,000; commissions expense paid, $35,000; payroll taxes paid, $2,500; rent paid, $2,200 (not including December rent yet to be paid); utilities expense paid, $1,600; promotion and advertising paid, $8,000; income taxes paid, $18,500; and miscellaneous expenses paid, $500. There were no other unpaid expenses at December 31. Also during the year, the company paid the owners "out-of-profit" cash dividends amounting to $12,000. Complete the following income statement:

Revenues		
Commissions earned	$ _____	
Rental service fees	_____	
Total revenues		$ _____
Expenses		
Salaries expense	$ _____	
Commission expense	_____	
Payroll tax expense	_____	
Rent expense	_____	
Utilities expense	_____	
Promotion and advertising expense	_____	
Miscellaneous expenses	_____	
Total expenses (excluding income taxes)		_____
Pretax income		$ _____
Income tax expense		_____
Net income		$55,500

*In the United States, "provision for income taxes" is a common synonym for "income tax expense."

Inferring Values Using the Income Statement and Balance Sheet Equations

E1-9
L01

Review the chapter explanations of the income statement and the balance sheet equations. Apply these equations in each independent case following to compute the two missing amounts for each case. Assume that it is the end of 2003, the first full year of operations for the company. (*Hint:* Organize the listed items as they are presented in the balance sheet and income statement equations and then compute the missing amounts.)

Independent Cases	Total Revenues	Total Expenses	Net Income (Loss)	Total Assets	Total Liabilities	Stockholders' Equity
A	$100,000	$82,000	$	$150,000	$70,000	$
B		80,000	12,000	112,000		60,000
C	80,000	86,000		104,000	26,000	
D	50,000		13,000		22,000	77,000
E		81,000	(6,000)		73,000	28,000

Preparing an Income Statement and Balance Sheet

E1-10
L01

Clay Corporation was organized by five individuals on January 1, 2003. At the end of January 2003, the following monthly financial data are available:

Total revenues	$130,000
Total expenses (excluding income taxes)	80,000
Income tax expense (all unpaid as of January 31)	15,000
Cash balance, January 31, 2003	30,000
Receivables from customers (all considered collectible)	15,000
Merchandise inventory (by inventory count at cost)	42,000
Payables to suppliers for merchandise purchased from them (will be paid during February 2003)	11,000
Contributed capital (2,600 shares)	26,000

No dividends were declared or paid during 2003.

Required:
Complete the following two statements:

CLAY CORPORATION
Income Statement
For the Month of January 2003

Total revenues	$ _____
Less: Total expenses (excluding income tax)	_____
Pretax income	_____
Less: Income tax expense	_____
Net income	$ _____

CLAY CORPORATION
Balance Sheet
At January 31, 2003

Assets	
Cash	$ _____
Receivables from customers	_____
Merchandise inventory	_____
Total assets	$ _____
Liabilities	
Payables to suppliers	$ _____

Income taxes payable	_____
Total liabilities	_____
Stockholders' equity	
Contributed capital	_____
Retained earnings	_____
Total stockholders' equity	_____
Total liabilities and stockholders' equity	$ _____

E1-11
L01

Analyzing and Interpreting an Income Statement and Price/Earnings Ratio

Pest Away Corporation was organized by three individuals on January 1, 2003, to provide insect extermination services. At the end of 2003, the following income statement was prepared:

PEST AWAY CORPORATION
Income Statement
For the Year Ended December 31, 2003

Revenues		
Service revenue (cash)	$192,000	
Service revenue (credit)	24,000	
Total revenues		$216,000
Expenses		
Salaries expense	$ 76,000	
Rent expense	21,000	
Utilities expense	12,000	
Advertising expense	14,000	
Supplies expense	25,000	
Interest expense	8,000	
Total expenses		156,000
Pretax income		$ 60,000
Income tax expense		21,000
Net income		$ 39,000

Required:
1. What was the average monthly revenue amount?
2. What was the monthly rent amount?
3. Explain why supplies are reported as an expense.
4. Explain why interest is reported as an expense.
5. Can you determine how much cash the company had on December 31, 2003? Explain.
6. If the company had a market value of $468,000, what is its price/earnings ratio?

E1-12
L01

Compaq
Computer

Focus on Cash Flows: Matching Cash Flow Statement Items to Categories

Compaq Computer is a leading designer and manufacturer of personal computers. The following items were taken from its recent cash flow statement. Note that different companies use slightly different titles for the same item. Without referring to Exhibit 1.5, mark each item in the list as a cash flow from operating activities (O), investing activities (I), or financing activities (F). Also place parentheses around the letter only if it is a cash outflow.

_____ (1) Cash paid to suppliers and employees
_____ (2) Cash received from customers
_____ (3) Income taxes paid
_____ (4) Interest and dividends received
_____ (5) Interest paid
_____ (6) Proceeds from sale of investment in Conner Peripherals, Inc.
_____ (7) Purchases of property, plant, and equipment
_____ (8) Repayment of borrowings

Preparing a Statement of Cash Flows

E1-13
LO1

NITSU Manufacturing Corporation is preparing the annual financial statements for the stockholders. A statement of cash flows must be prepared. The following data on cash flows were developed for the entire year ended December 31, 2006: cash inflow from operating revenues, $270,000; cash expended for operating expenses, $180,000; sale of unissued NITSU stock for cash, $30,000; cash dividends declared and paid to stockholders during the year, $22,000; and payments on long-term notes payable, $80,000. During the year, a tract of land was sold for $15,000 cash (which was the same price that NITSU had paid for the land in 2005), and $38,000 cash was expended for two new machines. The machines were used in the factory. The beginning-of-the-year cash balance was $63,000.

Required:
Prepare the statement of cash flows for 2006. Follow the format illustrated in the chapter.

Analyzing Cash Flows from Operations

E1-14
LO1

Paul's Painters, a service organization, prepared the following special report for the month of January 2003:

Service Revenue, Expenses, and Income		
Service revenue		
Cash services (per cash register tape)	$105,000	
Credit services (per charge bills; not yet collected by end of January)	30,500	
		$135,500
Expenses		
Salaries and wages expense (paid by check)	$ 50,000	
Salary for January not yet paid	3,000	
Supplies used (taken from stock, purchased for cash during December)	2,000	
Estimated cost of using company-owned truck for the month (called "depreciation")	500	
Other expenses (paid by check)	26,000	81,500
Pretax income		$ 54,000
Income tax expense (not yet paid)		13,500
Income for January		$ 40,500

Required:
1. The owner (who knows little about the financial part of the business) asked you to compute the amount by which cash had increased in January 2003 from the operations of the company. You decided to prepare a detailed report for the owner with the following major side captions: Cash Inflows (collections), Cash Outflows (payments), and the difference—Net Increase (or decrease) in Cash.
2. See if you can reconcile the difference—net increase (or decrease) in cash—you computed in requirement (1) with the income for January 2003.

PROBLEMS

Preparing an Income Statement and Balance Sheet (AP1-1)

P1-1
LO1

Assume that you are the president of Nuclear Company. At the end of the first year (December 31, 2003) of operations, the following financial data for the company are available:

Cash	$ 25,000
Receivables from customers (all considered collectible)	12,000
Inventory of merchandise (based on physical count and priced at cost)	90,000

Equipment owned, at cost less used portion	45,000
Accounts payable owed to suppliers	47,370
Salary payable for 2003 (on December 31, 2003, this was owed to an employee who was away because of an emergency; will return around January 10, 2004, at which time the payment will be made)	2,000
Total sales revenue	140,000
Expenses, including the cost of the merchandise sold (excluding income taxes)	89,100
Income taxes expense at 30% × pretax income; all paid during 2003	?
Contributed capital, 7,000 shares outstanding	87,000

No dividends were declared or paid during 2003.

Required (show computations):

1. Prepare a summarized income statement for the year 2003.
2. Prepare a balance sheet at December 31, 2003.

P1-2   **Analyzing a Student's Business and Preparing an Income Statement** (AP1-2)

LO1

During the summer between her junior and senior years, Susan Irwin needed to earn sufficient money for the coming academic year. Unable to obtain a job with a reasonable salary, she decided to try the lawn care business for three months. After a survey of the market potential, Susan bought a used pickup truck on June 1 for $1,500. On each door she painted "Susan's Lawn Service, Phone 471-4487." She also spent $900 for mowers, trimmers, and tools. To acquire these items, she borrowed $2,500 cash by signing a note payable promising to pay the $2,500 plus interest of $75 at the end of the three months (ending August 31).

At the end of the summer, Susan realized that she had done a lot of work, and her bank account looked good. This fact prompted her to become concerned about how much profit the business had earned.

A review of the check stubs showed the following: Bank deposits of collections from customers totaled $12,600. The following checks had been written: gas, oil, and lubrication, $920; pickup repairs, $210; mower repair, $75; miscellaneous supplies used, $80; helpers, $4,500; payroll taxes, $175; payment for assistance in preparing payroll tax forms, $25; insurance, $125; telephone, $110; and $2,575 to pay off the note including interest (on August 31). A notebook kept in the pickup, plus some unpaid bills, reflected that customers still owed her $800 for lawn services rendered and that she owed $200 for gas and oil (credit card charges). She estimated that the cost for use of the truck and the other equipment (called *depreciation*) for three months amounted to $500.

Required:

1. Prepare a quarterly income statement for Susan's Lawn Service for the months June, July, and August 2003. Use the following main captions: Revenues from Services, Expenses, and Net Income. Because this is a sole proprietorship, the company will not be subject to income tax.
2. Do you see a need for one or more additional financial reports for this company for 2003 and thereafter? Explain.

P1-3   **Comparing Income with Cash Flow (A Challenging Problem)**

LO1

New Delivery Company was organized on January 1, 2003. At the end of the first quarter (three months) of operations, the owner prepared a summary of its operations as shown in the first row of the following tabulation:

	COMPUTATION OF	
Summary of Transactions	**Income**	**Cash**
a. Services performed for customers, $66,000, of which one-sixth remained uncollected at the end of the quarter.	+$66,000	+$55,000
b. Cash borrowed from the local bank, $30,000 (one-year note).		

c. Small service truck purchased for use in the business: cost, $9,000; paid 30% down, balance on credit.		
d. Expenses, $36,000, of which one-sixth remained unpaid at the end of the quarter.		
e. Service supplies purchased for use in the business, $3,000, of which one-fourth remained unpaid (on credit) at the end of the quarter. Also, one-fifth of these supplies were unused (still on hand) at the end of the quarter.		
f. Wages earned by employees, $21,000, of which one-half remained unpaid at the end of the quarter.		
Based only on these transactions, compute the following for the quarter: Income (or loss) Cash inflow (or outflow)	═══	═══

Required:
1. For each of the six transactions given in this tabulation, enter what you consider the correct amounts. Enter a zero when appropriate. The first transaction is illustrated.
2. For each transaction, explain the basis for your dollar responses.

Evaluating Data to Support a Loan Application (A Challenging Problem)

P1-4
L01

On January 1, 2003, three individuals organized West Company as a corporation. Each individual invested $10,000 cash in the business. On December 31, 2003, they prepared a list of resources owned (assets) and a list of the debts (liabilities) to support a company request for $70,000 submitted to a local bank. None of the three investors had studied accounting. The two lists prepared were as follows:

Company resources	
Cash	$ 12,000
Service supplies inventory (on hand)	7,000
Service trucks (four practically new)	68,000
Personal residences of organizers (three houses)	190,000
Service equipment used in the business (practically new)	30,000
Bills due from customers (for services already completed)	15,000
Total	$322,000

Company obligations	
Unpaid wages to employees	$ 19,000
Unpaid taxes	8,000
Owed to suppliers	10,000
Owed on service trucks and equipment (to a finance company)	50,000
Loan from organizer	10,000
Total	$ 97,000

Required:
Prepare a short memo indicating:

1. Which of these items do not belong on the balance sheet (bear in mind that the company is considered to be separate from the owners)?
2. What additional questions would you raise about measurement of items on the list? Explain the basis for each question.
3. If you were advising the local bank on its loan decision, which amounts on the list would create special concerns? Explain the basis for each concern and include any recommendations that you have.
4. In view of your response to (1) and (2), what do you think the amount of stockholders' equity (i.e., assets minus liabilities) of the company would be? Show your computations.

ALTERNATE **PROBLEMS**

AP1-1
LO1

Preparing an Income Statement and Balance Sheet (P1-1)

Assume that you are the president of McClaren Corporation. At the end of the first year (June 30, 2005) of operations, the following financial data for the company are available:

Cash	$13,150
Receivables from customers (all considered collectible)	9,500
Inventory of merchandise (based on physical count and priced at cost)	57,000
Equipment owned, at cost less used portion	36,000
Accounts payable owed to suppliers	31,500
Salary payable for 2005 (on June 30, 2005, this was owed to an employee who was away because of an emergency; will return around July 7, 2005, at which time the payment will be made)	1,500
Total sales revenue	90,000
Expenses, including the cost of the merchandise sold (excluding income taxes)	60,500
Income taxes expense at 30% × pretax income; all paid during 2005	?
Contributed capital, 5,000 shares outstanding	62,000
No dividends were declared or paid during 2005.	

Required (show computations):
1. Prepare a summarized income statement for the year 2005.
2. Prepare a balance sheet at June 30, 2005.

AP1-2
LO1

Analyzing a Student's Business and Preparing an Income Statement (P1-2)

Upon graduation from high school, John Abel immediately accepted a job as an electrician's assistant for a large local electrical repair company. After three years of hard work, John received an electrician's license and decided to start his own business. He had saved $12,000, which he invested in the business. First, he transferred this amount from his savings account to a business bank account for Abel Electric Repair Company, Incorporated. His lawyer had advised him to start as a corporation. He then purchased a used panel truck for $9,000 cash and secondhand tools for $1,500; rented space in a small building; inserted an ad in the local paper; and opened the doors on October 1, 2003. Immediately, John was very busy; after one month, he employed an assistant.

Although John knew practically nothing about the financial side of the business, he realized that a number of reports were required and that costs and collections had to be controlled carefully. At the end of the year, prompted in part by concern about his income tax situation (previously he had to report only salary), John recognized the need for financial statements. His wife Jane developed some financial statements for the business. On December 31, 2003, with the help of a friend, she gathered the following data for the three months just ended. Bank account deposits of collections for electric repair services totaled $32,000. The following checks had been written: electrician's assistant, $8,500; payroll taxes, $175; supplies purchased and used on jobs, $9,500; oil, gas, and maintenance on truck, $1,200; insurance, $700; rent, $500; utilities and telephone, $825; and miscellaneous expenses (including advertising), $600. Also, uncollected bills to customers for electric repair services amounted to $3,000. The $200 rent for December had not been paid. John estimated that the cost of using the truck and tools (depreciation) during the three months to be $1,200. Income taxes for the three-month period were $3,480.

Required:
1. Prepare a quarterly income statement for Abel Electric Repair for the three months October through December 2003. Use the following main captions: Revenue from Services, Expenses, Pretax Income, and Net Income.
2. Do you think that John may need one or more additional financial reports for 2003 and thereafter? Explain.

Annual Report Cases

Finding Financial Information

CP1-1
LO1, 3

AMERICAN EAGLE OUTFITTERS

Refer to the financial statements of American Eagle Outfitters in Appendix B at the end of this book, or open file AEOS.pdf in the Annual Report Cases directory on the student CD-ROM.

Required:
1. What is the amount of net income for the current year?
2. What amount of revenue was earned in the current year?
3. How much inventory does the company have at the end of the current year?
4. By what amount did cash and cash equivalents* change during the year?
5. Who is auditor for the company?

Finding Financial Information

CP1-2
LO1, 3

ABERCROMBIE & FITCH

Refer to the financial statements of Abercrombie & Fitch in Appendix C at the end of this book, or open file ANF.pdf in the Annual Report Cases directory on the student CD-ROM.

Required:
Read the annual report. Look at the income statement, balance sheet, and cash flow statement closely and attempt to infer what kinds of information they report. Then answer the following questions based on the report.

1. What types of products does it sell?
2. Did the chief executive officer (CEO) believe that the company had a good year?
3. On what day of the year does its fiscal year end?
4. For how many years does it present complete
   a. Balance sheets?
   b. Income statements?
   c. Cash flow statements?
5. Are its financial statements audited by independent CPAs? How do you know?
6. Did its total assets increase or decrease over the last year?
7. What was the ending balance of inventories?
8. Write out its basic accounting (balance sheet) equation in dollars at year-end.

Comparing Companies Within an Industry

CP1-3
LO1

AMERICAN EAGLE OUTFITTERS

ABERCROMBIE & FITCH

Refer to the financial statements of American Eagle Outfitters given in Appendix B and Abercrombie & Fitch given in Appendix C and the Industry Ratio Report given in Appendix D at the end of this book, or open file CP1-3.xls in the Annual Report Cases directory on the student CD-ROM.

Required:
1. Both companies report "basic" earnings per share on their income statements and the market price per share of their stock in a note near the end of the annual report. Using current year's earnings per share and the highest stock price per share reported for the last quarter of the most recent year, compute the price/earnings ratio. Which company provided the highest price/earnings ratio for the current year?
2. Which company do investors believe will have the higher growth in earnings in the future?
3. Examine the Industry Ratio Report. Compare the price/earnings ratio for each company to the industry average. Did you expect these two companies, which are relative newcomers to the industry, to have price/earnings ratios above or below the industry average? Why?

Cash equivalents are short-term investments readily convertible to cash whose value is unlikely to change.

Financial Reporting and Analysis Cases

CP1-4
LO1

Using Financial Reports: Identifying and Correcting Deficiencies in an Income Statement and Balance Sheet

Performance Corporation was organized on January 1, 2003. At the end of 2003, the company had not yet employed an accountant; however, an employee who was "good with numbers" prepared the following statements at that date:

PERFORMANCE CORPORATION
December 31, 2003

Income from sales of merchandise	$175,000
Total amount paid for goods sold during 2003	(90,000)
Selling costs	(25,000)
Depreciation (on service vehicles used)	(10,000)
Income from services rendered	52,000
Salaries and wages paid	(62,000)

PERFORMANCE CORPORATION
December 31, 2003

Resources		
Cash		$ 32,000
Merchandise inventory (held for resale)		42,000
Service vehicles		50,000
Retained earnings (profit earned in 2003)		30,000
Grand total		$154,000
Debts		
Payables to suppliers		$ 22,000
Note owed to bank		25,000
Due from customers		13,000
Total		$ 60,000
Supplies on hand (to be used in rendering services)	$15,000	
Accumulated depreciation* (on service vehicles)	10,000	
Contributed capital, 6,500 shares	65,000	
Total		90,000
Grand total		$150,000

Required:

1. List all the deficiencies that you can identify in these statements. Give a brief explanation of each one.
2. Prepare a proper income statement (correct net income is $30,000) and balance sheet (correct total assets are $142,000).

CP1-5
LO1

Using Financial Reports: Applying the Balance Sheet Equation to Liquidate a Company

On June 1, 2008, Bland Corporation prepared a balance sheet just prior to going out of business. The balance sheet totals showed the following:

Assets (no cash)	$90,000
Liabilities	50,000
Stockholders' equity	40,000

Accumulated depreciation represents the used portion of the asset and should be subtracted from the asset balance.

Shortly thereafter, all of the assets were sold for cash.

Required:

1. How would the balance sheet appear immediately after the sale of the assets for cash for each of the following cases? Use the format given here.

		BALANCES IMMEDIATELY AFTER SALE			
	Cash Received for the Assets	Assets	− Liabilities	=	Stockholders' Equity
Case A	$ 90,000	$_____	$_____		$_____
Case B	80,000	$_____	$_____		$_____
Case C	100,000	$_____	$_____		$_____

2. How should the cash be distributed in each separate case? (*Hint:* Creditors must be paid in full before owners receive any payment.) Use the format given here:

	To Creditors	To Stockholders	Total
Case A	$_____	$_____	$_____
Case B	$_____	$_____	$_____
Case C	$_____	$_____	$_____

Critical Thinking Cases

Making Decisions as a Manager: Reporting the Assets and Liabilities of a Business

CP1-6
LO1, 3

Elizabeth Watkins owns and operates Liz's Boutique (a sole proprietorship). An employee prepares a financial report for the business at each year-end. This report lists all of the resources (assets) owned by Watkins, including such personal items as the home she owns and occupies. It also lists all of the debts of the business, but not her personal debts.

Required:

1. From the accounting point of view, in what ways do you disagree with what is being included in and excluded from the report of business assets and liabilities?
2. Upon questioning, Watkins responded, "Don't worry about it; we use it only to support a loan from the bank." How would you respond to this comment?

Making Decisions as an Owner: Deciding about a Proposed Audit

CP1-7
LO3

You are one of three partners who own and operate Mary's Maid Service. The company has been operating for seven years. One of the other partners has always prepared the company's annual financial statements. Recently you proposed that the statements be audited each year because it would benefit the partners and preclude possible disagreements about the division of profits. The partner who prepares the statements proposed that his Uncle Ray, who has a lot of financial experience, can do the job and at little cost. Your other partner remained silent.

Required:

1. What position would you take on the proposal? Justify your response.
2. What would you strongly recommend? Give the basis for your recommendation.

Evaluating an Ethical Dilemma: Ethics and Auditor Responsibilities

CP1-8
LO3, 4

A key factor that an auditor provides is independence. The *AICPA Code of Professional Conduct* states that "a member in public practice should be independent in fact and appearance when providing auditing and other attestation service."

Required:

Do you consider the following circumstances to suggest a lack of independence? Justify your position. (Use your imagination. Specific answers are not provided in the chapter.)

1. Jack Jones is a partner with a large audit firm and is assigned to the Ford audit. Jack owns 10 shares of Ford.
2. Jane Winkler has invested in a mutual fund company that owns 500,000 shares of Sears stock. She is the auditor of Sears.
3. Bob Franklin is a clerk/typist who works on the audit of AT&T. He has just inherited 50,000 shares of AT&T stock. (Bob enjoys his work and plans to continue despite his new wealth.)
4. Nancy Sodoma worked on weekends as the controller for a small business that a friend started. Nancy quit the job in midyear and now has no association with the company. She works full-time for a large CPA firm and has been assigned to do the audit of her friend's business.
5. Mark Jacobs borrowed $100,000 for a home mortgage from First City National Bank. The mortgage was granted on normal credit terms. Mark is the partner in charge of the First City audit.

Financial Reporting and Analysis Team Project

CP1-9
LO1, 3

Team Project: Examining an Annual Report

As a team, select an industry to analyze. MarketGuide provides lists of industries and their makeup at www.marketguide.com/mgi/INDUSTRY/INDUSTRY.html. Each group member should acquire the annual report or 10-K for one publicly traded company in the industry, with each member selecting a different company. (Library files, the SEC EDGAR service at www.sec.gov, Compustat CD, or the company's website are good sources. The Annual Report Gallery at www.reportgallery.com provides links to the websites of well-known companies.) On an individual basis, each group member should write a short report answering the following questions about the selected company.

1. What types of products or services does it sell?
2. On what day of the year does its fiscal year end?
3. For how many years does it present complete
   a. Balance sheets?
   b. Income statements?
   c. Cash flow statements?
4. Are its financial statements audited by independent CPAs? If so, by whom?
5. Did its total assets increase or decrease over the last year?
6. Did its net income increase or decrease over the last year?

Discuss any patterns that you as a team observe. Then, as a team, write a short report comparing and contrasting your companies using the preceding list of six attributes.

After studying this chapter, you should be able to:

1. Define the objective of financial reporting, the elements of the balance sheet, and the related key accounting assumptions and principles. p. 49

2. Compute and interpret the financial leverage ratio. p. 53

3. Identify what constitutes a business transaction and recognize common balance sheet account titles used in business. p. 56

4. Apply transaction analysis to simple business transactions in terms of the accounting model: Assets = Liabilities + Stockholders' Equity. p. 57

5. Determine the impact of business transactions on the balance sheet using two basic tools, journal entries and T-accounts. p. 62

6. Prepare and analyze a simple balance sheet. p. 69

7. Identify investing and financing transactions and demonstrate how they are reported on the statement of cash flows. p. 70

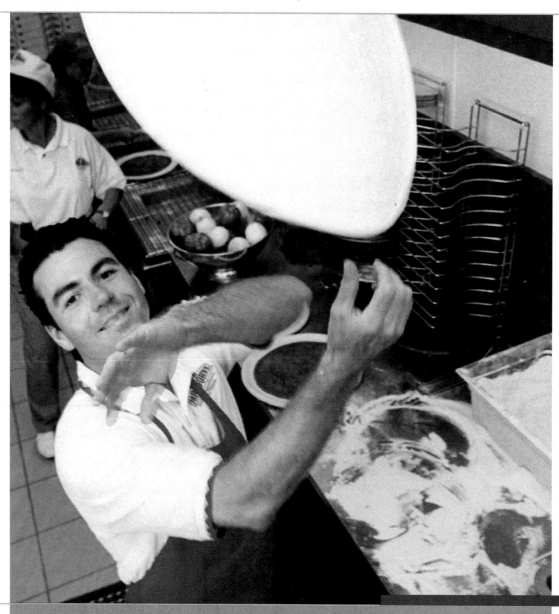

Investing and Financing Decisions and the Balance Sheet

2

I n the pizza segment of the highly competitive restaurant business, Papa John's shows it knows how to fight the battle "to become the No. 1 pizza brand in the world," taking on industry leader Pizza Hut as its primary target. *Time* magazine reports: "Papa John's scares Pizza Hut. That's because, since 1993, for every point Pizza Hut has lost in market share, Papa John's has gained one. . . . So far, nothing Pizza Hut has tried has slowed Papa John's."*

In 2000, Papa John's moved ahead of Little Caesar's to a ranking of third in sales behind giants Pizza Hut and Domino's. With more than 2,800 restaurants in the United States and abroad, the company has grown tremendously since its beginnings in 1983 when John Schnatter, founder and chief executive officer, knocked down closet walls at a bar he was tending to install a pizza oven. Ten years later, Papa John's became a public company with stock trading on the NASDAQ exchange (under the symbol PZZA). The company's balance sheets for the end of 2000 compared to the end of 1994 (in thousands of dollars†) highlight its growth:

FOCUS COMPANY:

Papa John's International

EXPANSION STRATEGY IN THE "PIZZA WARS"

www.papajohns.com

	Assets	=	Liabilities	+	Stockholders' Equity
End of 2000	$395,658		$229,337		$166,321
End of 1994	76,173		13,564		62,609
Change	+$319,485		+$215,773		+$103,712

The company's plans were to add 259 new restaurants to the chain in 2001. The Pizza Wars continue.

*John Greenwald, "Slice, Dice and Devour," Time *magazine, October 26, 1998. © 1998 Time Inc. Reprinted by permission.
†These totals are rounded amounts from the actual financial statements for the respective years. Amounts used in illustrations throughout Chapters 2, 3, and 4 are realistic estimates of actual monthly amounts.

UNDERSTANDING THE BUSINESS

Pizza is a global commodity, generating more than $29 billion in sales annually. While the business depends heavily on human capital, companies can compete through high-technology marketing. Papa John's strategy is to offer "Better Ingredients. Better Pizza." To do so requires an almost fanatical focus on testing ingredients and checking product quality, right down to the size of the black olives and the fat content of the mozzarella and meat. The company keeps operations simple, sticking to a focused menu of pizza, breadsticks, cheesesticks, and soft drinks for pick-up or delivery. To control quality and increase efficiency, the company builds regional commissaries (called quality control centers) that make the dough and sell it to the stores. The commissaries plus the opening of new company-owned stores and the sale of franchises‡ explain most of the growth in Papa John's assets and liabilities from year to year.

To understand how the results of Papa John's growth strategy are communicated in the financial statements, we must answer the following questions:

- What business activities cause changes in the balance sheet amounts from one period to the next?
- How do specific business activities affect each of the balance sheet amounts?
- How do companies keep track of the balance sheet amounts?

Once we have answered these questions, we will be able to perform two key analytical tasks:

1. Analyze and predict the effects of business decisions on a company's financial statements.
2. Use the financial statements of other companies to identify and evaluate the activities managers engaged in during a past period. This is a key task in **financial statement analysis.**

In this chapter, we focus on some typical asset acquisition activities (often called **investing activities**), along with related **financing activities,** such as borrowing funds from creditors or selling stock to investors to acquire the assets. We examine only those activities that affect balance sheet amounts; operating activities that affect both the income statement and the balance sheet are covered in Chapters 3 and 4. To begin, let's return to the basic concepts introduced in Chapter 1.

---

‡*Franchises are contracts in which a franchisor (such as Papa John's International) provides rights to franchisees (in this case, local restaurant operators) to sell or distribute a specific line of products or provide a particular service. In return, franchisees usually pay an initial fee to obtain the franchise, along with annual payments for ongoing services such as accounting, advertising, and training. Approximately 77 percent of Papa John's restaurants worldwide are franchises.*

ORGANIZATION of the Chapter

Overview of the Conceptual Framework	What Business Activities Cause Changes in Financial Statement Amounts?	How Do Transactions Affect Accounts?	How Do Companies Keep Track of Account Balances?	How Is the Balance Sheet Prepared?

■ Elements of the Balance Sheet
■ Financial Leverage Ratio
	■ Nature of Business Transactions
	■ Accounts
		■ Principles of Transaction Analysis
		■ Analyzing Papa John's Transactions
			■ The Direction of Transaction Effects
			■ Analytical Tools:
			    The Journal Entry
			    The T-account
			■ Transaction Analysis Illustrated	

OVERVIEW OF THE CONCEPTUAL FRAMEWORK

The key accounting terms and concepts defined in Chapter 1 are part of a theoretical framework developed over many years and synthesized by the Financial Accounting Standards Board (FASB). This conceptual framework is presented in Exhibit 2.1 as an overview with key concepts discussed in each of the next four chapters. An understanding of these accounting concepts will be helpful as you study because learning and remembering **how** the accounting process works is much easier if you know **why** it works a certain way. A clear understanding of these concepts will also help you in future chapters as we examine more complex business activities.

> **Learning Objective 1**
> Define the objective of financial reporting, the elements of the balance sheet, and the related key accounting assumptions and principles.

Concepts Emphasized in Chapter 2

Objective of Financial Reporting

The top of the pyramid in Exhibit 2.1 indicates the **primary objective of external financial reporting,** which guides the remaining sections of the conceptual framework. The primary objective of financial accounting is to provide useful economic information about a business to help external parties, primarily investors and creditors, make sound financial decisions. The users of accounting information are identified as **decision makers.** These decision makers include average investors, creditors, and experts who provide financial advice. They are all expected to have a reasonable understanding of accounting concepts and procedures (this may be one of the reasons you are studying accounting). Of course, as we discussed in Chapter 1, many other groups, such as suppliers and customers, also use external financial statements.

Users usually are interested in information to assist them in projecting a business's future cash inflows and outflows. For example, creditors and potential creditors need to assess an entity's ability to pay interest over time and pay back the principal on the loan. Investors and potential investors want to assess the entity's ability to pay dividends in the future. They also want to judge how successful the company might be so that the stock price rises and investors can then sell the stock for more than was paid.

> The **PRIMARY OBJECTIVE OF EXTERNAL FINANCIAL REPORTING** is to provide useful economic information about a business to help external parties make sound financial decisions.

EXHIBIT 2.1

Financial Accounting and
Reporting Conceptual
Framework

PRIMARY OBJECTIVE OF EXTERNAL FINANCIAL REPORTING [Ch. 2]

To provide useful economic information to external users for decision making (for assessing future cash flows)

QUALITATIVE CHARACTERISTICS OF FINANCIAL INFORMATION [Ch. 5]

To be useful, information should possess:

Relevancy—be capable of making a difference in decisions
- Predictive value (extrapolate into the future)
- Feedback value (assess prior expectations)
- Timeliness (available to help with decisions)

Reliability—can be relied upon
- Verifiability (can be verified independently)
- Representational faithfulness (represents reality)
- Neutrality (unbiased)

Information should also be
    Comparable across companies
    Consistent over time

ELEMENTS OF FINANCIAL STATEMENTS

Asset—economic resource with probable future benefits. [Ch. 2]

Liability—probable future sacrifices of economic resources. [Ch. 2]

Stockholders' Equity—financing provided by owners and operations (residual interest to owners). [Ch. 2]

Revenue—increase in assets or settlement of liabilities from ongoing operations. [Ch. 3]

Expense—decrease in assets or increase in liabilities from ongoing operations. [Ch. 3]

Gain—increase in assets or settlement of liabilities from peripheral activities. [Ch. 3]

Loss—decrease in assets or increase in liabilities from peripheral activities. [Ch. 3]

ASSUMPTIONS

- **Separate entity**—activities of the business are separate from activities of the owners. [Ch. 2]
- **Unit of measure**—accounting measurements will be in the national monetary unit. [Ch. 2]
- **Continuity** (going concern)—entity will not go out of business in the near future. [Ch. 2]
- **Time period**—the long life of a company can be reported over a series of shorter time periods. [Ch. 3]

PRINCIPLES

- **Historical cost**—cash equivalent price on the transaction date is used initially to measure elements. [Ch. 2]
- **Revenue recognition**—record when *measurable, realizable* and *earned* (i.e. company performs, evidence of customer payment arrangement exists, price is determinable, and collection is reasonably assured). [Ch. 3]
- **Matching**—record when expenses are incurred to generate revenues. [Ch. 3]
- **Full disclosure**—provide information sufficiently important to influence a decision (e.g., notes). [Ch. 5]

CONSTRAINTS [Ch. 5]

- **Cost benefit**—benefits to users should outweigh costs of providing information.
- **Materiality**—relatively small amounts not likely to influence decisions are to be recorded in the most cost-beneficial way.
- **Industry practices**—industry-specific measurements and reporting deviations may be acceptable.
- **Conservatism**—exercise care not to overstate assets and revenues or understate liabilities and expenses.

SEPARATE-ENTITY ASSUMPTION states that business transactions are separate from the transactions of the owners.

UNIT-OF-MEASURE ASSUMPTION states that accounting information should be measured and reported in the national monetary unit.

CONTINUITY (GOING-CONCERN) ASSUMPTION states that businesses are assumed to continue to operate into the foreseeable future.

Underlying Assumptions of Accounting

Three of the four basic assumptions that underlie accounting measurement and reporting were discussed briefly in Chapter 1. Under the **separate-entity assumption,** each business must be accounted for as an individual organization, separate and apart from its owners, all other persons, and other entities. Under the **unit-of-measure assumption,** each business entity accounts for and reports its financial results in terms primarily of the national monetary unit (dollars in the United States, yen in Japan, Euro in Germany). Under the **continuity assumption** (sometimes called the **going-concern assumption**), a business normally is assumed to continue operating long enough to meet its contractual commitments and plans. If a company was not expected to continue, for example, due to the likelihood of bankruptcy, then the assets and liabilities should be valued and reported on the balance sheet as if the company were to be liquidated (that is, discontinued, with all its assets sold and all debts paid). In future chapters, unless otherwise indicated, we assume that businesses meet the continuity assumption.

Assets, liabilities, and shareholders' equity are the key elements of a corporation's balance sheet, as we learned in Chapter 1. Let's review the definitions.

Elements of the Balance Sheet

Assets are probable future economic benefits owned or controlled by an entity as a result of past transactions. In other words, they are the resources the entity can use to operate in the future. So as not to mislead users when reporting information to them, managers use judgment (and past experience) to determine an asset's most likely future benefit. For example, a company may have a list of customers who owe $10,000. History suggests, however, that only $9,800 is likely to be collected. The lower, more probable and more conservative figure is reported to users for purposes of projecting future cash flows.

ASSETS are probable future economic benefits owned by the entity as a result of past transactions.

As shown in Papa John's balance sheet presented in Exhibit 2.2, most companies list assets **in order of liquidity,** or how soon an asset is expected to be turned into cash or used. Notice that several of Papa John's assets are categorized as **current assets.** Current assets are those resources that Papa John's will use or turn into cash within one year. Note that inventory is always considered a current asset, regardless of how long it takes to produce and sell the inventory. As indicated in Exhibit 2.2, Papa John's current assets include Cash, Short-term Investments, Accounts Receivable, Inventories, Prepaid Expenses, and Other Current Assets.

CURRENT ASSETS are assets that will be used or turned into cash within one year. Inventory is always considered a current asset regardless of the time needed to produce and sell it.

All other assets are considered long term, to be used or turned into cash beyond the coming year. For Papa John's, that includes Property and Equipment (net of amounts used in the past), Notes Receivable, Intangibles, and Other Assets. The Papa John's balance sheet includes assets of its company-owned restaurants, about 23 percent of all Papa John's restaurants. The assets of the remaining 77 percent belong to franchisees and are appropriately reported in their own financial statements.

Liabilities are probable debts or obligations that result from an entity's past transactions and will be paid for with assets or services. Those entities that a company owes money to are called **creditors.** Creditors usually receive payment of the amounts owed and sometimes interest on those amounts. Papa John's balance sheet includes six liabilities: Accounts Payable, Accrued Expenses Payable, Other Current Liabilities, Unearned Franchise Fees, Long-term Notes Payable, and Other Long-term Liabilities. These and other liabilities will be discussed in subsequent chapters.

LIABILITIES are probable debts or obligations of the entity that result from past transactions, which will be paid with assets or services.

Just as assets are reported in order of liquidity, liabilities are usually listed on the balance sheet **in order of maturity** (how soon an obligation is to be paid). Those liabilities that Papa John's will need to pay within the coming year (in cash, services, or other current assets) are classified as **current liabilities.** Distinguishing current assets and current liabilities assists external users of the financial statements in assessing the amounts and timing of future cash flows. Most corporations report current assets and liabilities separately, even though classifying them as such is not required.

CURRENT LIABILITIES are obligations that will be paid in cash (or other current assets) or satisfied by providing service within the coming year.

Environmental Liabilities

A QUESTION OF ETHICS

Due to changing legal requirements and concerns about social responsibility, companies are facing significant pressure to estimate and disclose environmental liabilities, such as the cleanup of hazardous waste sites. Determining the amounts and the likelihood of obligations, though, can be very difficult. Past estimates of the total cost to clean up air emissions, water quality, and remove asbestos have exceeded $250 billion per year, or approximately 2 to 5 percent of the gross domestic product.

Recent studies suggest that many companies face environmental liabilities, yet most fail to disclose the financial risk involved in complying with environmental regulations. In a study of 13 pulp and paper companies, at least half could have negative financial impacts between 5 percent and 10 percent of the market value of the shareholders' stock; however, few had adequately disclosed the financial risk in their financial reports.* Likewise, financial reports by semiconductor manufacturers facing potential liabilities from the environmental impact of using chemicals in the manufacturing process were also reviewed. The study found "no reporting at all on environmental performance." These studies now call for the Securities and Exchange Commission "to vigorously enforce its disclosure rules to ensure that investors are aware of the financial risk involved in corporate environmental compliance."

*Bryan Lee, "SEC Urged to Up Compliance," Dow Jones Newswires, January 31, 2001, Article 6.

EXHIBIT 2.2

Papa John's Balance Sheet

PAPA JOHN'S INTERNATIONAL, INC. AND SUBSIDIARIES	
Consolidated Balance Sheet	
December 31, 2000	
(dollars in thousands)	
Assets	
Current assets	
Cash	$ 6,000
Short-term investments	6,000
Accounts receivable	23,000
Inventories	18,000
Prepaid expenses	7,000
Other current assets	6,000
Total current assets	66,000
Property and equipment (net of accumulated depreciation of $83,000)	246,000
Notes receivable	17,000
Intangibles	49,000
Other assets	18,000
Total assets	$396,000
Liabilities and stockholders' equity	
Current liabilities	
Accounts payable	$ 24,000
Accrued expenses payable	45,000
Other current liabilities	1,000
Total current liabilities	70,000
Unearned franchise fees	6,000
Long-term notes payable	146,000
Other long-term liabilities	8,000
Stockholders' equity	
Contributed capital	1,000
Retained earnings	165,000
Total stockholders' equity	166,000
Total liabilities and stockholders' equity	$396,000

Annotations at left of exhibit:

- stocks and bonds purchased with excess cash
- payments due from franchisees and others on account
- food, beverages, and paper supplies
- rent and insurance paid in advance
- a summary of accounts with smaller balances

- the remaining cost of long-lived assets to be used in future operations (original cost minus the estimated portion of cost already used in the past)
- from franchisees
- patents, trademarks, and goodwill
- a summary of several long-term assets with smaller balances

- payments due to suppliers
- a summary of payroll, rent, and other obligations

- amounts paid by franchisees for services they will receive
- loans from creditors

STOCKHOLDERS' EQUITY (OWNERS' OR SHAREHOLDERS' EQUITY) is the financing provided by the owners and the operations of business.

Stockholders' equity (also called **owners' equity** or **shareholders' equity**) is the financing provided by the owners and by business operations. Owner-provided cash (and sometimes other assets) is referred to as **contributed capital**. Owners invest in the business and receive shares of stock as evidence of ownership. The major investor in Papa John's International, Inc., is John Schnatter, founder and CEO, who owns approximately 30 percent of the stock. FMR Corporation of Boston owns another 15 percent of the stock; corporate employees, directors, and the general public own the rest.

Owners invest (or buy stock) in a company in the hope of receiving two types of cash flows: **dividends,** which are a distribution of a company's earnings (a return on the shareholders' investment), and gains from selling the stock for more than they paid (known as **capital gains**). Earnings that are not distributed to the owners but instead are reinvested in the business by management are called **retained earnings**.[1] A look at Papa John's balance sheet (Exhibit 2.2) indicates that its growth has been financed by substantial reinvestment of retained earnings. Ninety-nine percent of Papa John's stockholders' equity is retained earnings ($165 million Retained Earnings ÷ $166 million total stockholders' equity).

> **CONTRIBUTED CAPITAL** results from owners providing cash (and sometimes other assets) to the business.

> **RETAINED EARNINGS** refers to the cumulative earnings of a company that are not distributed to the owners and are reinvested in the business.

A Note on Ratio Analysis

Users of financial information compute a number of ratios in analyzing a company's past performance and financial condition as input in predicting its future potential. For example, using the elements and classifications on the balance sheet, creditors can assess a company's ability to pay off its debt obligations or what the company's trend is in taking on more debt. One of the most common ratios is the current ratio that measures the company's ability to pay off its current liabilities when they come due. It is computed as follows:

$$\text{Current Ratio} = \frac{\text{Current Assets}}{\text{Current Liabilities}}$$

How ratios change over time and how they compare to the ratios of the company's competitors provide valuable information for users' decisions. This ratio and many others will be presented throughout the rest of this textbook with a final summary of ratio analysis in Chapter 14.

We begin our look at ratio analysis by presenting a different general ratio in Chapters 2, 3, and 4. In Chapter 5, we discuss the powerful effects of combining these three general ratios. The remaining chapters discuss the specific ratios affecting each of the general ratios for a more precise assessment of a company's strategies, strengths, and areas for concern.

The Financial Leverage Ratio	**KEY RATIO** ANALYSIS

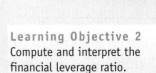

❓ ANALYTICAL QUESTION

How is management using debt to increase the amount of assets the company employs to earn income for stockholders?

% RATIO AND COMPARISONS

$$\text{Financial Leverage Ratio} = \frac{\text{Average Total Assets}}{\text{Average Stockholders' Equity}}$$

The 2000 ratio for Papa John's is:

$$\frac{(\$395,658 + \$372,051)/2}{(\$166,312 + \$292,133)/2} = 1.67$$

> **Learning Objective 2**
> Compute and interpret the financial leverage ratio.

---

[1]Retained earnings can increase only from profitable operations. Retained earnings decrease when a firm has a loss. In addition, as we discuss in Chapter 3, a company's annual income from operations is usually not equal to the net cash flows for the year.

COMPARISONS OVER TIME			COMPARISONS WITH COMPETITORS*	
Papa John's International, Inc.			Uno Restaurant Corp. (& Chicago Bar & Grill)	Chuck E. Cheese (CEC, Inc.)
1998	1999	2000	2000	2000
1.24	1.27	1.67	1.96	1.42

You cannot always compare the closest competitors. Pizza Hut and Domino's, noted as primary competitors for Papa John's, were not used in this analysis because both were involved in a change in ownership in previous years, causing them to reflect negative amounts in stockholders' equity. The results would be unusual and, therefore, not useful as a basis for comparison.

Selected Focus Companies' Financial Leverage Ratios

Delta Air Lines	4.08
Callaway Golf	1.23
Timberland	1.65

💡 INTERPRETATIONS

In General   The financial leverage ratio measures the relationship between total assets and the stockholders' equity that finances the assets. As noted, companies finance their assets with stockholders' equity and debt. The higher the proportion of assets financed by debt, the higher the financial leverage ratio. Conversely, the higher the proportion of assets financed with stockholders' equity, the lower the ratio. Increasing debt (and the leverage ratio) increases the amount of assets the company employs to earn income for stockholders, which increases the chances of earning higher income. However, it also increases **risk.** Debt financing is riskier than financing with stockholders' equity because the interest payments on debt must be made every period (they are legal obligations), whereas dividends on stock can be postponed. An increasing ratio over time signals more reliance on debt financing and more risk.

Creditors and security analysts use this ratio to assess a company's risk level, while managers use the ratio in deciding whether to expand by adding debt. As long as the interest on borrowing is less than the additional earnings generated, utilizing debt will enhance the stockholders' earnings.

Focus Company Analysis   Papa John's financial leverage increased dramatically in 2000, although the ratio over the prior three years remained fairly constant. Since December 1999, Papa John's has undertaken a major repurchase of its stock financed primarily by borrowing. This results in decreasing stockholders' equity and increasing liabilities, and thus, an increase in the financial leverage ratio. Papa John's has assumed more risk.

When compared against two other pizza restaurants, Papa John's 2000 financial leverage ratio falls in the middle. The two competitors listed are eat-in restaurants that must invest more in facilities than Papa John's, which primarily rents space instead of constructing buildings. Dun & Bradstreet reports that the average restaurant chain has a leverage ratio of 3.25 (nearly twice as much debt as equity financing). This suggests that Papa John's at 1.67 is following a less risky (more conservative) financing strategy than are other companies in the restaurant industry.

A Few Cautions   A financial leverage ratio near 1:1 indicates a company that is choosing not to utilize debt to expand. This suggests the company has lower risk but is not enhancing the return to stockholders. When comparing competitors, the ratio may be influenced by differences in business strategies, such as whether the company rents or buys facilities.

SELF-STUDY QUIZ

Wendy's International

Wendy's International, Inc., had the following balances on its recent balance sheets (in thousands):

Beginning of year: Assets—$1,941,680; Liabilities—$757,446; Stockholders' equity—$1,184,234

End of year: Assets—$1,837,947; Liabilities—$769,880; Stockholders' equity—$1,068,067

Compute Wendy's financial leverage ratio. What does this ratio tell you about Wendy's financing strategy?

After you have completed your answers, check them with the solutions that follow:

_____

($1,837,947 + $1,941,680)/2 ÷ ($1,068,067 + $1,184,234)/2 = 1.68, so Wendy's is following a slightly less risky financing strategy than other companies in the industry. This ratio is lower than the industry average, and is similar to Papa John's.

Basic Accounting Principle

The **historical cost principle** states that the cash-equivalent cost needed to acquire the asset on the date of the acquisition (the historical cost) should be used for recording all financial statement elements when acquired. Under the cost principle, cost is measured on the date of the transaction as the cash paid plus the current dollar value of all non-cash considerations (any assets, privileges, or rights) also given in the exchange. For example, if you trade your computer plus cash for a new car, the cost of the new car is equal to the cash paid plus the market value of the computer. Thus, in most cases, cost is relatively easy to determine and can be verified. A disadvantage of this approach is that, subsequent to the date of acquisition, the continued reporting of historical cost on the balance sheet does not reflect any changes in market value, usually because market value is a less verifiable and objective measure.

The **HISTORICAL COST PRINCIPLE** requires assets to be recorded at the historical cash-equivalent cost, which on the date of the transaction is cash paid plus the current dollar value of all noncash considerations also given in the exchange.

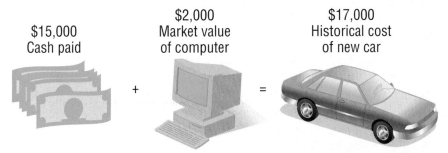

| $15,000 Cash paid | + | $2,000 Market value of computer | = | $17,000 Historical cost of new car |

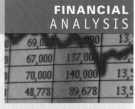

Unrecorded but Valuable Assets

FINANCIAL ANALYSIS

Managers use the balance sheet as a basis for managing the company's assets; analysts use it for valuing the firm. Both groups recognize that often a company's most valuable assets are *not* listed on the balance sheet (they have no "book value").* One such asset is a firm's trademark or brand name. General Electric's balance sheet reveals no listing for the GE trademark. Its book value is zero because it was developed internally over time, created through research, development, and advertising (it was not purchased). Many valuable intangible assets, such as trademarks, patents, and copyrights developed inside a company, have no book value.

This asset recognition rule (that assets are recorded at cost based on an exchange with an external party) suggests the circumstances in which trademarks and brand names *are* reported on the balance sheet. Several years ago, GE sold its television business to a French company, Thomson SA, the world's largest producer of televisions. Since the Thomson brand name has no value in the United States, Thomson also purchased the right to use GE's trademark for 10 years, at a cost of 250 million French francs (approximately $50 million). Thomson's balance sheet lists GE's trademark recorded at its acquisition cost of 250 million francs less the amount used over time.

*Book value *is the unused cost reported on the balance sheet, usually an asset's original acquisition cost minus the estimated portion reflecting the use of the asset in past operations.*

Now that we have reviewed the basic elements of the balance sheet, let's see what economic activities cause changes in the amounts reported on this financial statement.

WHAT BUSINESS ACTIVITIES CAUSE CHANGES IN FINANCIAL STATEMENT AMOUNTS?

Nature of Business Transactions

Learning Objective 3
Identify what constitutes a business transaction and recognize common balance sheet account titles used in business.

A **TRANSACTION** is (1) an exchange between a business and one or more external parties to a business or (2) a measurable internal event such as the use of assets in operations.

Topic Tackler 2–1

Accounting focuses on certain events that have an economic impact on the entity. Those events that are recorded as part of the accounting process are called **transactions.** The first step in translating the results of business events to financial statement numbers is determining which events to include. As the definitions of assets and liabilities indicate, only economic resources and debts **resulting from past transactions** are recorded on the balance sheet. Transactions include two types of events:

1. **External events:** These are **exchanges** of assets and liabilities between the business and one or more other parties. Examples include the purchase of a machine, the sale of merchandise, the borrowing of cash, and investment in the business by the owners.

2. **Internal events:** These include certain events that are not exchanges between the business and other parties but nevertheless have a direct and measurable effect on the entity. Examples include losses due to fire or other natural disasters and the use of property, plant, and equipment.

Throughout this textbook, the word *transaction* is used in the broad sense to include both types of events.

Some important events that have a future economic impact on a company are *not* reflected in the financial statements. In most cases, signing a contract is not considered to be a transaction because it involves only the exchange of promises, not of assets such as cash, goods, services, or property. For example, if Papa John's signs an employment contract with a new regional manager, from an accounting perspective, no transaction has occurred because no exchange of assets or liabilities has been made. Each party to the contract has exchanged promises (the manager agrees to work; Papa John's agrees to pay the manager for work rendered). For each day the new manager works, however, the exchange of services for pay results in a transaction that Papa John's must record. Because of their importance, long-term employment contracts, leases, and other commitments may need to be disclosed in notes to the financial statements.

Accounts

An **ACCOUNT** is a standardized format that organizations use to accumulate the dollar effect of transactions on each financial statement item.

To accumulate the dollar effect of transactions on each financial statement item, organizations use a standardized format called an **account**. The resulting balances are kept separate for financial statement purposes. To facilitate the recording of transactions, each company establishes a **chart of accounts,** a list of all the account titles and their unique numbers. The accounts are usually organized by financial statement element, with asset accounts listed first, followed by liability, stockholders' equity, revenue, and expense accounts in that order. The following account titles are quite common and are used by most companies.

Assets	Liabilities	Stockholders' Equity	Revenues	Expenses
Cash	Accounts Payable	Contributed Capital	Sales Revenue	Cost of Goods Sold
Accounts Receivable	Accrued Expenses Payable	Retained Earnings	Fee Revenue	Wages Expense
Notes Receivable	Notes Payable		Interest Revenue	Rent Expense
Inventory	Taxes Payable		Rent Revenue	Interest Expense
Supplies	Unearned Revenue			Depreciation Expense
Prepaid Expenses	Bonds Payable			Advertising Expense
Investments				Income Tax Expense
Equipment				
Buildings				
Land				
Intangibles				

Notice that

1. Accounts with "receivable" in the title are always assets; they represent amounts owed by customers and others to the business.
2. Accounts with "payable" in the title are always liabilities and represent amounts owed by the company to be paid to others in the future.
3. The account Prepaid Expenses is an asset since it represents amounts paid to others for future benefits, such as future insurance coverage or rental of property.
4. Accounts with "unearned" in the title are always liabilities representing amounts paid to the company from others expecting future goods or services from the company.

Every company has a different chart of accounts, depending on the nature of its business activities. For example, a small lawn care service may have an asset account Lawn Mowing Equipment, but a large corporation such as General Motors is unlikely to need such an account. These differences in accounts will become more apparent as we examine the balance sheets of various companies. Because each company has a different chart of accounts, you should *not* try to memorize a typical chart of accounts. In homework problems, you will either be given the account names or be expected to select appropriate names. Once you select a name for an account, you must use the exact name in all transactions affecting that account.

The accounts you see in the financial statements of most large corporations are actually summations (or aggregations) of a number of specific accounts. For example, Papa John's keeps separate inventory accounts for paper supplies, food, and beverages but combines them under Inventories on the balance sheet. Equipment, buildings, and land are also combined into an account called Property and Equipment. Since our aim is to understand financial statements of actual entities, we will focus on aggregated accounts.

SELF-STUDY **QUIZ**

Wendy's International

The following is a list of accounts from a recent Wendy's International, Inc., balance sheet. Indicate on the line provided whether each of the following is an asset (A), liability (L), or stockholders' equity account (SE).

_____ Accrued Expenses   _____ Long-Term Obligations   _____ Notes Receivable

_____ Property and Equipment   _____ Retained Earnings

_____ Accounts Payable   _____ Inventories

After you have completed your answers, check them with the solutions that follow:

_____

Column 1: L; A; L. Column 2: L; SE; A. Column 3: A.

How Do Transactions Affect Accounts?

Managers' business decisions often result in transactions that affect the financial statements. For example, the decisions to expand the number of stores, advertise a new product, change an employee benefit package, and invest excess cash would all affect the financial statements. Sometimes these decisions have unintended consequences as well. The decision to purchase additional inventory for cash in anticipation of a major sales initiative, for example, will increase inventory and decrease cash. But if there is

Learning Objective 4
Apply transaction analysis to simple business transactions in terms of the accounting model: Assets = Liabilities + Stockholders' Equity.

The News Corporation Limited

Understanding the Meaning of Account Titles in Foreign Financial Statements

We learned in Chapter 1 that differences in the political, cultural, and economic environments of other countries have produced significant variations in accounting and reporting rules. Foreign companies often use different account titles from U.S. companies. Some use additional accounts for financial statement items not normally reported under U.S. accounting rules. The Australian company, The News Corporation Limited, headed by K. Rupert Murdoch, is one example. The principal activities of The News Corporation Limited include printing and publishing books, newspapers, and magazines, television broadcasting, and film production and distribution. The News Corporation Limited includes some U.S. companies such as Fox Broadcasting Company and Twentieth Century Fox Film Corporation. A glance at a recent financial report shows that this entity's account titles are similar to those used by U.S. companies, except for liabilities and stockholders' equity:

Australian Accounts	U.S. Equivalents
Liabilities	
Borrowings	Similar to Notes and Bonds Payable
Creditors	Similar to Accounts Payable; relates to what is owed to suppliers and others
Provisions	A summary of payables for income tax, dividends, payroll, and other liabilities
Shareholders' Equity	
Share Capital	Similar to Contributed Capital
Retained Profits	Similar to Retained Earnings

no demand for the additional inventory, the lower cash balance will also reduce the company's ability to pay its other obligations.

Because business decisions often involve an element of risk, managers should understand exactly how transactions impact the financial statements. The process for determining the effects of transactions is called **transaction analysis.**

Principles of Transaction Analysis

TRANSACTION ANALYSIS is the process of studying a transaction to determine its economic effect on the business in terms of the accounting equation.

Transaction analysis is the process of studying a transaction to determine its economic effect on the entity in terms of the accounting equation (also known as the **accounting model**). We outline the process in this section of the chapter and create a visual tool representing the process (the transaction analysis model). The basic accounting equation and two principles are the foundation for this model. Recall from Chapter 1 that the basic accounting equation for a business that is organized as a corporation is as follows:

Assets (A) = Liabilities (L) + Stockholders' Equity (SE)

The two principles underlying the transaction analysis process follow:

1. Every transaction affects at least two accounts; correctly identifying those accounts and the direction of the effect (whether an increase or a decrease) is critical.

2. The accounting equation must remain in balance after each transaction.

Success in performing transaction analysis depends on a clear understanding of these principles. Study the following material well.

The Duality of Effects

The idea that every transaction has **at least two effects** on the basic accounting equation is known as the **duality of effects**.[2] Most transactions with external parties involve an exchange by which the business entity both gives up something and receives something in return. For example, suppose that Papa John's purchased some paper napkins for cash. In this exchange, Papa John's would receive supplies (an increase in an asset) and in return would give up cash (a decrease in an asset).

Transaction	Papa John's Received	Papa John's Gave
Purchased paper napkins for cash	Supplies (increased)	Cash (decreased)

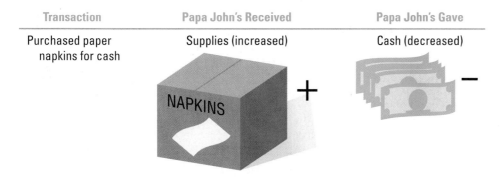

In analyzing this transaction, we determined that the accounts affected were Supplies and Cash. As we discussed in Chapter 1, however, most supplies are purchased on credit (that is, money is owed to suppliers). In that case, Papa John's would engage in **two** transactions: (1) the purchase of an asset on credit and (2) the eventual payment. In the first transaction, Papa John's would receive supplies (an increase in an asset) and would give in return a promise to pay later called *accounts payable* (an increase in a liability). In the second transaction, Papa John's would eliminate or receive back its promise to pay (a decrease in the accounts payable liability) and would give up cash (a decrease in an asset).

Transaction	Papa John's Received	Papa John's Gave
(1) Purchased paper napkins on credit	Supplies (increased)	Accounts Payable (increased) [a promise to pay]
(2) Paid on its accounts payable	Accounts Payable (decreased) [a promise was eliminated]	Cash (decreased)

As noted earlier, not all important business activities result in a transaction that affects the financial statements. Most important, signing a contract involving the exchange of two promises to perform does not result in an accounting transaction that is recorded. For example, if Papa John's sent an order for more napkins to its paper

---

[2]From the duality concept, accountants have developed what is known as the *double-entry system* of recordkeeping.

supplier and the supplier accepted the order but did not fill it immediately, no transaction took place. As soon as the goods are shipped to Papa John's, however, the supplier has given up its inventory in exchange for a promise from Papa John's to pay for the items in the near future, and Papa John's has exchanged its promise to pay for the supplies it receives. Because a promise has been exchanged for goods, a transaction has taken place; both Papa John's and the supplier's statements will be affected.

Maintaining the Accounting Equation Balance

The accounting equation must remain in balance after each transaction. That is, total assets must equal total liabilities and stockholders' equity. If all the correct accounts have been identified and the appropriate direction of the effect on each account has been determined, the equation should remain in balance. A systematic transaction analysis includes the following steps, in this order:

1. *Accounts and effects*
   a. **Identify the accounts (by title) affected and classify them by type of account**, making sure that at least two accounts change. Ask yourself what is given and what is received. Classifications are an asset (A), a liability (L), or a stockholders' equity account (SE).
   b. **Determine the direction of the effect** (an increase [+] or decrease [−] on each account).
2. *Balancing*
   c. **Verify that the accounting equation (A = L + SE) remains in balance.**

Analyzing Papa John's Transactions

To illustrate the use of the transaction analysis process, let's consider some typical transactions of Papa John's that are also common to most businesses. Remember that this chapter presents transactions that affect only the balance sheet accounts. Assume that Papa John's engages in the following events during January 2001, the month following the balance sheet in Exhibit 2.2. Account titles are from that balance sheet, and remember that **all amounts are in thousands of dollars:**

(a) **Papa John's issues $2,000 of additional common stock, receiving cash from investors.**

> 1. *Identify and classify accounts and effects:*
>   Cash (A) is received + $2,000. Additional stock certificates are given, Contributed Capital (SE) + $2,000.
> 2. *Is the accounting equation in balance?*
>   Yes. There is a $2,000 increase on the left side and a $2,000 increase on the right side of the equation.

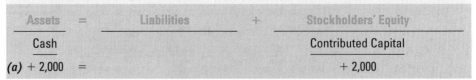

Assets	=	Liabilities	+	Stockholders' Equity
Cash				Contributed Capital
(a) + 2,000	=			+ 2,000

(b) **Papa John's borrows $6,000 from its local bank, signing a note to be paid in three years.**

> 1. *Identify and classify accounts and effects:*
>   Cash (A) is received + $6,000. A written promise to pay is given to the bank, Notes Payable (L) + $6,000.
> 2. *Is the accounting equation in balance?*
>   Yes. There is a $6,000 increase on the left side and a $6,000 increase on the right side of the equation.

Assets	=	Liabilities	+	Stockholders' Equity
Cash		Long-Term Notes Payable		Contributed Capital
(a) + 2,000 =				+ 2,000
(b) + 6,000 =		+ 6,000		

Events (a) and (b) are *financing* transactions. Companies that need cash for *investing* purposes (to buy or build additional facilities) often seek funds by selling stock to investors as in Event (a) or by borrowing from creditors as in Event (b).

(c) Papa John's purchases $10,000 of new ovens, counters, refrigerators, and other equipment, paying $2,000 in cash and signing a two-year note payable to the equipment manufacturer for the rest.

1. *Identify and classify accounts and effects:*

   Property and Equipment (A) is received + $10,000. Cash (A) −$2,000 is given and a written promise to pay is given to the manufacturer, Notes Payable (L) +$8,000.

2. *Is the accounting equation in balance?*

   Yes. There is an $8,000 increase on the left side and an $8,000 increase on the right side of the equation.

	Assets	=	Liabilities	+	Stockholders' Equity
Cash	Property and Equipment		Long-Term Notes Payable		Contributed Capital
(a) + 2,000		=			+ 2,000
(b) + 6,000		=	+ 6,000		
(c) − 2,000	+ 10,000	=	+ 8,000		

Notice that more than two accounts were affected by this transaction.

The effects of Events (a), (b), and (c) are listed in the chart at the end of the Self-Study Quiz. Space is left on the chart for your analysis of Events (d), (e), and (f).

SELF-STUDY **QUIZ**

Practice is the most effective way to develop your transaction analysis skills. Review the analysis in Events (a) through (c) and complete the analysis of Events (d) through (f) in the following chart. Repeat the steps until they become a natural part of your thought process. After you have completed the chart, check your answers with the solutions at the end of quiz.

(d) Papa John's lends $3,000 to new franchisees who sign notes agreeing to repay the loans in five years.

1. *Identify and classify accounts and effects:*

   Written promises from the franchisees are received, Notes Receivable (A) +$3,000. What and how much is given? _____

2. *Is the accounting equation in balance?*

   Yes. The equation remains the same because assets increase and decrease by the same amount.

(e) Papa John's purchases the stock of other companies as a short-term investment, paying $1,000 in cash.

1. *Identify and classify accounts and effects:*

   Cash (A) is given −$1,000. Stock certificates from the other companies are received, Short-term Investments (A) +$1,000.

2. *Is the accounting equation in balance?*

   _____ Why? _____

(f) Papa John's board of directors declares and pays $3,000 in dividends to shareholders.[†]

1. *Identify and classify accounts and effects:*

   In this transaction, earnings retained in the business are distributed to investors, Retained Earnings (SE) − $3,000. What and how much is given? _____

2. *Is the accounting equation in balance?*

   _____ Why? _____

		Assets			**=**	**Liabilities +**	**Stockholders' Equity**
	Cash	**Notes Receivable**	**Property and Equipment**	**Short-Term Investments**		**Long-Term Notes Payable**	**Contributed Capital**	**Retained Earnings**
(a)	+ 2,000				=		+ 2,000	
(b)	+ 6,000				=	+ 6,000		
(c)	− 2,000		+ 10,000		=	+ 8,000		
(d)	_____	+ 3,000			=			
(e)	− 1,000			+ 1,000	=			
(f)	_____				=			− 3,000

_____

(*d*) Cash (A) is given −$3,000.

(*e*) Yes. The equation remains the same because assets increase and decrease by the same amount.

(*f*) Cash (A) is given −$3,000. Yes, there is a $3,000 decrease on the left side of the equation and a $3,000 decrease on the right side.

If your answers did not agree with ours, we recommend that you go back to each event to make sure that you have completed each of the steps of transaction analysis.

HOW DO COMPANIES KEEP TRACK OF ACCOUNT BALANCES?

Learning Objective 5
Determine the impact of transaction analysis using two basic tools, journal entries and T-accounts.

Topic Tackler 2–2

For most organizations, recording transaction effects and keeping track of account balances in the manner just presented is impractical. To handle the multitude of daily transactions that business generates, accountants rely on two very important tools: journal entries and T-accounts. From the standpoint of accounting systems design, these analytical tools are a more efficient way to reflect the effects of transactions, determine account balances, and prepare financial statements. As future business managers, you should develop your understanding and use of these tools in financial analysis. For those studying accounting, this knowledge is the foundation for an understanding of the accounting system and future accounting coursework. After we explain how to perform transaction analysis using these tools, we illustrate their use in financial analysis.

_____

[†]*At the time this chapter is being written, Papa John's has not declared dividends; this transaction is included for purposes of illustration only.*

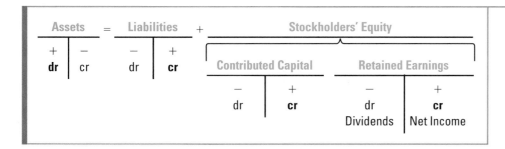

EXHIBIT 2.3

Transaction Analysis Model

The Direction of Transaction Effects

As we saw earlier, transactions increase and decrease assets, liabilities, and stockholders' equity. To reflect these effects efficiently, we need to structure the transaction analysis model in a manner that shows the **direction** of the effects. In Exhibit 2.3, notice that:

- The increase symbol + is located on the left side of the T for accounts on the left side of the accounting equation and on the right side of the T for accounts on the right side of the equation.
- The symbol **dr** for **debit** and **cr** for **credit** are always written on the left and the right of each account, respectively. **Debit** means the left side of an account, and **credit** means the right.

From this transaction analysis model, we can observe the following:

- Asset accounts increase on the left (debit) side; they have debit balances. It would be highly unusual for an asset account, such as Inventory, to have a negative (credit) balance.
- Liability and stockholders' equity accounts increase on the right (credit) side, creating credit balances.

As you are learning to perform transaction analysis, you should refer to this model often until you can construct it on your own without assistance.

Many students have trouble with accounting because they forget that the meaning of *debit* is simply the left side of an account and the meaning of *credit* is simply the right side of an account. Perhaps someone once told you that you were a credit to your school or your family. As a result, you may think that credits are good and debits are bad. Such is not the case. Just remember that **debit means left** and **credit means right.**

To remember which accounts debits increase and which accounts credits increase, recall that a debit (left) increases asset accounts because assets are on the left side of the accounting equation (A = L + SE). Similarly, a credit (right) increases liability and stockholders' equity accounts because they are on the right side of the accounting equation.

If you have identified the correct accounts and effects through transaction analysis, the accounting equation will remain in balance. Moreover, **the total dollar value of all debits will equal the total dollar value of all credits** in a transaction. For an extra measure of assurance, add this equality check (Debits = Credits) to the transaction analysis process.

Analytical Tool: The Journal Entry

In a bookkeeping system, transactions are recorded in chronological order in a **journal.** (See www.mhhe.com/libby4e [Appendix E] for an illustration of formal record-keeping procedures.) After analyzing the business documents that describe a transaction, the bookkeeper enters the effects on the accounts in the journal using debits and credits. The **journal entry**, then, is an accounting method for expression of the effects of a transaction on accounts and it is written in a debits-equal-credits format.

DEBIT means the left side of an account.

CREDIT means the right side of an account.

A **JOURNAL ENTRY** is an accounting method for expressing the effects of a transaction on accounts in a debits-equal-credits format.

The journal entry for Event (*c*) in the Papa John's illustration is as follows:

(date or reference)	Property and equipment (+A)	10,000	
	Cash (−A)		2,000
	Notes payable (+L)		8,000

Notice the following:

- It is useful to include a date or some form of reference for each transaction.
- The debits are written first (on top); the credits are written below the debits and are indented to the right (both the words and the amounts). The order of the debited accounts or credited accounts does not matter, as long as the debits are on top and the credits are on the bottom and indented.
- Total debits ($10,000) equal total credits ($2,000 + $8,000).
- Three accounts are affected by this transaction. Any journal entry that affects more than two accounts is called a **compound entry.** Although this is the only transaction in the Papa John's illustration that affects more than two accounts, many transactions in subsequent chapters require a compound journal entry.

While you are learning to perform transaction analysis, use the symbols A, L, and SE next to each account title, as in the preceding journal entry. Specifically identifying accounts as assets (A), liabilities (L), or stockholders' equity (SE) clarifies the transaction analysis and makes journal entries easier to write. In the next few chapters, we include the direction of the effect along with the symbol. For example, if Cash is to be increased, we write Cash (+A).

Many students try to memorize journal entries without understanding or using the transaction analysis model. As more detailed transactions are presented in subsequent chapters, the task becomes increasingly more difficult. In the long run, **memorizing, understanding, and using the transaction analysis model** presented here will save you time and prevent confusion.

Analytical Tool: The T-Account

By themselves, journal entries do not provide the balances in accounts. After the journal entries have been recorded, the bookkeeper posts (transfers) the dollar amounts to each account affected by the transaction to determine the new account balances. (In most computerized accounting systems, this happens automatically.)

As a group, the accounts are called a **ledger.** In the manual accounting system used by some small organizations, the ledger is often a three-ring binder with a separate

---

EXHIBIT 2.4	Illustration of a Journal Page and a Ledger Account in Columnar Format

GENERAL JOURNAL

Page 1

Date	Account Titles and Explanations	Posted Ref.	Debit	Credit
4/1/2003	Cash	101	9,000	
	Contributed capital	301		9,000
	Issued 1,500 shares of stock to investors (names).			
4/3/2003	Equipment	110	600	
	Cash	101		200
	Notes payable	201		400
	Purchased hand tools (supplier and invoice data			
	indicated), paying part in cash (check number			
	indicated) and part on account.			

GENERAL LEDGER

Account Title _Cash_   Account Number _101_

Date	Explanation	Posted Ref.	Debit	Credit	Balance
4/1/2003	Investments by owners	1	9,000		9,000
4/3/2003	Hand tools purchased	1		200	8,800
4/4/2003	Land purchased	1		5,000	3,800
4/5/2003	Fuel purchased	1		90	3,710
4/6/2003	Revenue in advance	2	1,600		5,310
4/8/2003	Insurance purchased	2		300	5,010
4/10/2003	Collection from customers	2	3,500		8,510
4/14/2003	Wages paid	3		3,900	4,610
4/18/2003	Note and interest paid	3		740	3,870
4/21/2003	Suppliers paid	3		100	3,770
4/29/2003	Collection from city	4	1,262		5,032

page for each account. In a computerized system, accounts are stored on a disk. See Exhibit 2.4 for an illustration of a journal page and the related Cash ledger page. Note that the cash effects from the journal entries have been posted to the Cash ledger page.

One very useful tool for summarizing the transaction effects and determining the balances for individual accounts is a **T-account,** a simplified representation of a ledger account. Exhibit 2.5 shows the T-accounts for Papa John's Cash and Notes Payable accounts based on Events (*a*) through (*f*). Notice that for Cash, which is classified as an asset, increases are shown on the left and decreases on the right side of the T-account. For Notes Payable, however, increases are shown on the right and decreases on the left since notes payable is a liability. Many small businesses still use handwritten or manually maintained accounts in this T-account format. Computerized systems retain the concept but not the format of the T-account.

The **T-ACCOUNT** is a tool for summarizing transaction effects for each account, determining balances, and drawing inferences about a company's activities.

+ Cash (A) −				− Long-Term Notes Payable (L) +		
Beg. balance	6,000				Beg. balance	146,000
(a)	2,000	(c)	2,000		(b)	6,000
(b)	6,000	(d)	3,000		(c)	8,000
		(e)	1,000		End. balance	160,000
		(f)	3,000			
End. balance	5,000					

EXHIBIT 2.5

T-Accounts Illustrated

In Exhibit 2.5, notice that the ending balance is indicated on the positive side with a double underline. To find the account balances, we can express the T-accounts as equations:

	Cash	Long-Term Notes Payable
Beginning balance	$ 6,000	$146,000
+ "+" side	+ 8,000	+ 14,000
− "−" side	− 9,000	− 0
Ending balance	$ 5,000	$160,000

A word on terminology: The words *debit* and *credit* may be used as verbs, nouns, and adjectives. For example, we can say that Papa John's Cash account was debited (verb) when stock was issued to investors, meaning that the amount was entered on the left side of the T-account. Or we can say that a credit (noun) was entered on the right side of an account. Notes Payable may be described as a credit account (adjective). These terms will be used instead of *left* and *right* throughout the rest of this textbook. The next section illustrates the steps to follow in analyzing the effects of transactions, recording the effects in journal entries, and determining account balances using T-accounts.

Transaction Analysis Illustrated

In this section, we use the monthly transactions for Papa John's that were presented earlier to demonstrate transaction analysis and the use of journal entries and T-accounts. We analyze each transaction, checking to make sure that the accounting equation remains in balance and that debits equal credits. In the T-accounts, located together at the end of the illustration, the amounts from Papa John's December 31, 2000, balance sheet have been inserted as the beginning balances. After reviewing or preparing each journal entry, trace the effects to the appropriate T-accounts using the transaction letters (*a*) to (*f*) as a reference. The first transaction has been highlighted for you.

Study this illustration carefully, including the explanations of transaction analysis. Careful study is **essential** to an understanding of (1) the accounting model, (2) transaction analysis, (3) the dual effects of each transaction, and (4) the dual-balancing system. The most effective way to learn these critical concepts, which are basic to material throughout the rest of the text, is to practice, practice, practice.

(a) **Papa John's issues $2,000 of additional common stock, receiving cash from investors.**

Cash (+A) 2,000
  Contributed capital (+SE) 2,000

Assets	=	Liabilities	+	Stockholders' Equity	
Cash +2,000				Contributed capital +2,000	

Equality checks: (1) Debits $2,000 = Credits $2,000; (2) the accounting equation is in balance.

These effects have been posted to the appropriate T-accounts at the end of the illustration (see the shaded amounts). To post the amounts, transfer or copy the debit or credit amount on each line to the appropriate T-account. For example, the $2,000 debit is listed in the debit (increase) column of the Cash T-account.

(b) **Papa John's borrows $6,000 from its local bank, signing a note to be paid in three years.**

Cash (+A) 6,000
  Long-term notes payable (+L) 6,000

Assets	=	Liabilities	+	Stockholders' Equity
Cash +6,000		Long-term notes payable +6,000		

Equality checks: (1) Debits $6,000 = Credits $6,000; (2) the accounting equation is in balance.

(c) **Papa John's purchases new ovens, counters, refrigerators, and other equipment, paying $2,000 in cash and signing a two-year note payable to the equipment manufacturer for $8,000.**

Property and equipment (+A) 10,000
  Cash (−A) 2,000
  Long-term notes payable (+L) 8,000

Assets	=	Liabilities	+	Stockholders' Equity
Property and equipment +10,000		Long-term notes payable +8,000		
Cash − 2,000				

Equality checks: (1) Debits $10,000 = Credits $10,000; (2) the accounting equation is in balance.

SELF-STUDY **QUIZ**

For Events *(d)*, *(e)*, and *(f)*, fill in the missing information indicated; then post the entries to the T-accounts. After you have completed your answers, check them with the solutions at the end of quiz.

(d) **Papa John's lends $3,000 to new franchisees who sign notes agreeing to repay the loans in five years.** Write the journal entry, post it to the T-accounts, and complete the equality checks.

_____ ( ) .... _____
_____ ( ) .... _____

Assets	=	Liabilities	+	Stockholders' Equity

Cash   −3,000
Notes receivable   +3,000

Equality checks: (1) Debits $_____ = Credits $_____; (2) the accounting equation is in balance.

(e) **Papa John's purchases the stock of other companies as a short-term investment, paying $1,000 in cash.** Complete the effects on the accounting equation by indicating the accounts, amounts, and direction of the effect.

Short-term investments (+A)   1,000
    Cash (−A)   1,000

Assets	=	Liabilities	+	Stockholders' Equity

_____ _____
_____ _____

Equality checks: (1) Debits $1,000 = Credits $1,000; (2) Is the accounting equation in balance? _____

(f) **Papa John's board of directors declares and pays $3,000 in dividends to shareholders.*** Write the journal entry, post it to the T-accounts, and complete the effects on the accounting equation.

_____ (   )   3,000
    _____ (   )   3,000

Assets	=	Liabilities	+	Stockholders' Equity
_____ −3,000				_____ −3,000

Equality checks: (1) Debits $3,000 = Credits $3,000; (2) the accounting equation is in balance.

_____

(d) *Journal entry:*
    Notes receivable (+A).   3,000
        Cash (−A).   3,000
    Debits $3,000 = Credits $3,000

(e) *Effect on the Accounting Equation:*

Assets	=	Liabilities	+	Stockholders' Equity
Cash − 1,000				
Short-term investments +1,000				

The accounting equation is in balance.

(f) *Journal entry:*
    Retained earnings (−SE)   3,000
        Cash (−A).   3,000

Effect on the Accounting Equation:

Assets	=	Liabilities	+	Stockholders' Equity
Cash − 3,000				Retained earnings − 3,000

_____

*At the time this chapter was being written, Papa John's has not declared dividends; this transaction is included for purposes of illustration only.

Following are the T-accounts that *changed* during the period because of these transactions. The beginning balances are the amounts from the December 31, 2000, Papa John's balance sheet. The balances of all other accounts remained the same.

+ Cash (A) −			
12/31/00 bal. 6,000			
(a) 2,000	2,000		(c)
(b) 6,000	____		(d)
	____		(e)
	____		(f)
1/31/01 bal. 5,000			

+ Short-Term Investments (A) −	
12/31/00 bal. 6,000	
(e) ____	
1/31/01 bal. 7,000	

+ Notes Receivable (A) −	
12/31/00 bal. 17,000	
(d) ____	
1/31/01 bal. 20,000	

− Contributed Capital (SE) +	
	1,000 12/31/00 bal.
	2,000 (a)
	3,000 1/31/01 bal.

+ Property and Equipment, net (A) −	
12/31/00 bal. 246,000	
(c) 10,000	
1/31/01 bal. 256,000	

− Long-Term Notes Payable (L) +	
	146,000 12/31/00 bal.
	6,000 (b)
	8,000 (c)
	160,000 1/31/01 bal.

− Retained Earnings (SE) +	
	165,000 12/31/00 bal.
(f) ____	
	162,000 1/31/01 bal.

You can verify that you posted the entries properly by adding the increase side and subtracting the decrease side of each T-account and comparing your answer with the ending balance for each T-account.

FINANCIAL ANALYSIS

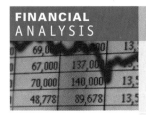

Inferring Business Activities from T-Accounts

T-accounts are useful primarily for instructional and analytical purposes. In many cases, we will use T-accounts to determine what transactions a company engaged in during a period. For example, the primary transactions affecting Accounts Payable for a period are purchases of assets on account and cash payments to suppliers. If we know the beginning and ending balances of Accounts Payable and all the amounts that were purchased on credit during a period, we can determine the amount of cash paid. A T-account analysis would include the following:

− Accounts Payable (L) +			
		600	Beg. bal.
Cash payments to suppliers	?	1,500	Purchase on account
		300	End. bal.

Solution:

Beginning Balance	+	Purchases on Account	−	Cash Payments to Suppliers	=	Ending Balance
$600	+	$1,500	−	?	=	$ 300
		$2,100	−	?	=	$ 300
				?	=	$1,800

EXHIBIT 2.6

Papa John's Balance Sheet

PAPA JOHN'S INTERNATIONAL, INC. AND SUBSIDIARIES Consolidated Balance Sheets (dollars in thousands)	January 31, 2001	December 31, 2000
Assets		
Current assets		
Cash	$ 5,000	$ 6,000
Short-term investments	7,000	6,000
Accounts receivable	23,000	23,000
Inventories	18,000	18,000
Prepaid expenses	7,000	7,000
Other current assets	6,000	6,000
Total current assets	66,000	66,000
Property and equipment		
(net of accumulated depreciation of $83,000)	256,000	246,000
Notes receivable	20,000	17,000
Intangibles	49,000	49,000
Other assets	18,000	18,000
Total assets	$409,000	$396,000
Liabilities and stockholders' equity		
Current liabilities		
Accounts payable	$ 24,000	$ 24,000
Accrued expenses payable	45,000	45,000
Other current liabilities	1,000	1,000
Total current liabilities	70,000	70,000
Unearned franchise fees	6,000	6,000
Long-term notes payable	160,000	146,000
Other long-term liabilities	8,000	8,000
Stockholders' equity		
Contributed capital	3,000	1,000
Retained earnings	162,000	165,000
Total stockholders' equity	165,000	166,000
Total liabilities and stockholders' equity	$409,000	$396,000

How Is the Balance Sheet Prepared?

It is possible to prepare a balance sheet at any point in time using the balances in the accounts. The balance sheet in Exhibit 2.6 was prepared using the new balances shown in the T-accounts in the preceding Papa John's illustration (shaded lines in the exhibit) plus the original balances in the accounts that did not change. It compares the account balances at January 31, 2001, with those at December 31, 2000. Note that when multiple periods are presented, the most recent balance sheet amounts are usually listed on the left.

Learning Objective 6
Prepare and analyze a simple balance sheet.

At the beginning of the chapter, we presented the changes in Papa John's balance sheets from the years 1994 to 2000. We questioned what made the accounts change and what the process was for reflecting the changes. Now we can see that the accounts have changed again in one month due to the transactions illustrated in this chapter:

	Assets	=	Liabilities	+	Stockholders' Equity
End of January 2001	$409,000		$244,000		$165,000
End of 2000	396,000		230,000		166,000
Change	+$ 13,000		+$ 14,000		–$ 1,000

FOCUS ON CASH FLOWS

Investing and Financing Activities

Learning Objective 7
Identify investing and financing transactions and demonstrate how they are reported on the statement of cash flows.

Recall from Chapter 1 that companies report on cash inflows and outflows over a period in their statement of cash flows. This statement divides all transactions that affect cash into three categories: operating, investing, and financing activities. Operating activities are covered in Chapter 3. Investing activities include buying and selling noncurrent assets and investments; financing activities include borrowing and repaying debt, issuing and repurchasing stock, and paying dividends. When cash is involved, these activities are reported on the statement of cash flows. (When cash is not included in the transaction, such as when a building is acquired with a long-term mortgage note payable, there is no cash effect to include on the statement of cash flows.) In general, the effects of such activities are as follows:

	Effect on Cash Flows
Operating activities	
(No transactions in this chapter were operating activities.)	
Investing activities	
Purchasing long-term assets for cash	–
Selling long-term assets for cash	+
Lending cash to others	–
Receiving principal payments on loans made to others	+
Financing activities	
Borrowing cash from banks	+
Repaying the principal on borrowings from banks	–
Issuing stock for cash	+
Repurchasing stock with cash	–
Paying cash dividends	–

Focus Company Analysis   Exhibit 2.7 shows a statement of cash flows for Papa John's based on the activities listed in this chapter. It reports the sources and uses of cash that created the $1,000 decrease in cash (from $6,000 to $5,000) in January 2001. Remember that only transactions that affect cash are reported on the cash flow statement.

The pattern of cash flows shown in Exhibit 2.7 (net cash outflows for investing activities and net cash inflows from financing activities) is typical of Papa John's past several annual statements of cash flows. Companies seeking to expand usually report cash outflows for investing activities.

PAPA JOHN'S INTERNATIONAL, INC.

PAPA JOHN'S INTERNATIONAL, INC.
Consolidated Statement of Cash Flows
For the month ended January 31, 2001
(in thousands)

Operating Activities	
(None in this chapter.)	
Investing Activities	
Purchased property and equipment (*c*)	$(2,000)
Purchased investments (*e*)	(1,000)
Lent funds to franchisees (*d*)	(3,000)
Net cash used in investing activities	**(6,000)**
Financing Activities	
Issued common stock (*a*)	2,000
Borrowed from banks (*b*)	6,000
Paid dividends (*f*)	(3,000)
Net cash provided by financing activities	**5,000**
Net decrease in cash	**(1,000)**
Cash at beginning of month	6,000
Cash at end of month	**$ 5,000**

EXHIBIT 2.7

Papa John's Statement of Cash Flows

Items are referenced to Events (a) through (f) illustrated in this chapter.

←*Agrees with the amount on the balance sheet.*

SELF-STUDY QUIZ

Lance, Inc.

Lance, Inc., manufactures and sells snack products. Indicate whether these transactions from a recent annual statement of cash flows were investing (I) or financing (F) activities and the direction of their effects on cash (+ = increases cash; − = decreases cash):

TRANSACTIONS	TYPE OF ACTIVITY (I OR F)	EFFECT ON CASH FLOWS (+ OR −)
1. Paid dividends.	_____	_____
2. Sold property.	_____	_____
3. Sold marketable securities (investments).	_____	_____
4. Purchased vending machines.	_____	_____
5. Repurchased its own common stock.	_____	_____

After you have completed the schedule, check it with the solutions that follow:

_____

1. F −   2. I +   3. I +   4. I −   5. F −

DEMONSTRATION CASE

On April 1, 2003, three ambitious college students started Terrific Lawn Maintenance Corporation. A summary of transactions completed through April 30, 2003, for Terrific Lawn Maintenance Corporation follows:

(*a*)	Issued 500 shares of stock (1,500 shares in total) to each of the three investors in exchange for $9,000 cash.
(*b*)	Acquired rakes and other hand tools (equipment) with a list price of $690 for $600; paid the hardware store $200 cash and signed a note for the balance.
(*c*)	Ordered three lawn mowers and two edgers from XYZ Lawn Supply, Inc., for $4,000.
(*d*)	Purchased 4 acres of land for the future site of a storage garage. Paid cash, $5,000.
(*e*)	Received the mowers and edgers that had been ordered, signing a note to pay XYZ Lawn Supply in full in 30 days.
(*f*)	Sold for $1,250 one acre of land to the city for a park. Accepted a note from the city for payment by the end of the month.
(*g*)	One of the owners borrowed $3,000 from a local bank for personal use.

Required:

1. Set up T-accounts for Cash, Notes Receivable (from the city), Equipment (hand tools and mowing equipment), Land, Notes Payable (to equipment supply companies), and Contributed Capital. Beginning balances are $0; indicate these beginning balances in the T-accounts. Analyze each transaction using the process outlined in the chapter. Prepare journal entries in chronological order. Enter the effects of the transactions in the appropriate T-accounts; identify each amount with its letter in the preceding list.

2. Use the amounts in the T-accounts developed in requirement (1) to prepare a classified balance sheet for Terrific Lawn Maintenance Corporation at April 30, 2003. Show the account balances for all assets, liabilities, and stockholders' equity. Use the following transaction analysis model.

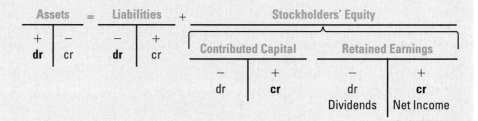

3. Prepare the investing and financing sections of the statement of cash flows. Check your answers with the solution in the following section.

SUGGESTED SOLUTION

1. Transaction analysis, journal entries, and T-accounts:

(*a*) Cash (+A)	9,000	
Contributed capital (+SE)		9,000

Assets	=	Liabilities	+	Stockholders' Equity
Cash +9,000				Contributed capital +9,000

Equality checks: (1) Debits $9,000 = Credits $9,000; (2) the accounting equation is in balance.

(*b*) Equipment (+A)	600	
Cash (−A)		200
Notes payable (+L)		400

Assets	=	Liabilities	+	Stockholders' Equity
Equipment +600		Notes payable +400		
Cash −200				

Equality checks: (1) Debits $600 = Credits $600; (2) the accounting equation is in balance.

The **historical cost principle** states that assets should be recorded at the amount paid on the date of the transaction, or $600, rather than at the $690 list price.

(c) This is not an accounting transaction; no exchange has taken place. No accounts are affected.

(d) Land (+A) 5,000
    Cash (−A) 5,000

Assets	=	Liabilities	+	Stockholders' Equity
Land +5,000				
Cash −5,000				

Equality checks: (1) Debits $5,000 = Credits $5,000; (2) the accounting equation is in balance.

(e) Equipment (+A) 4,000
    Notes payable (+L) 4,000

Assets	=	Liabilities	+	Stockholders' Equity
Equipment +4,000		Notes payable +4,000		

Equality checks: (1) Debits $4,000 = Credits $4,000; (2) the accounting equation is in balance.

(f) Notes receivable (+A) 1,250
    Land (−A) 1,250

Assets	=	Liabilities	+	Stockholders' Equity
Notes receivable + 1,250				
Land − 1,250				

Equality checks: (1) Debits $1,250 = Credits $1,250; (2) the accounting equation is in balance.

(g) There is no transaction for the company. The separate-entity assumption states that transactions of the owners are separate from transactions of the business.

Cash (A)			
+ (dr)		**− (cr)**	
Beg. bal.	0		
(a)	9,000	(b)	200
		(d)	5,000
End. bal.	3,800		

Notes Receivable (A)			
+ (dr)		**− (cr)**	
Beg. bal.	0		
(f)	1,250		
End. bal.	1,250		

Equipment (A)			
+ (dr)		**− (cr)**	
Beg. bal.	0		
(b)	600		
(e)	4,000		
End. bal.	4,600		

Land (A)				Notes Payable (L)			Contributed Capital (SE)		
+ (dr)		− (cr)		− (dr)	+ (cr)		− (dr)	+ (cr)	
Beg. bal.	0				Beg. bal.	0		Beg. bal.	0
(d)	5,000	(f)	1,250		(b)	400		(a)	9,000
End. bal.	3,750				(e)	4,000		End. bal.	9,000
					End. bal.	4,400			

2. Balance sheet:

TERRIFIC LAWN MAINTENANCE CORPORATION
Balance Sheet
At April 30, 2003

Assets			**Liabilities**	
Current Assets			*Current Liability*	
Cash	$ 3,800		Notes payable	$ 4,400
Notes receivable	1,250			
Total current assets	5,050		**Stockholders' Equity**	
Equipment	4,600		Contributed capital	9,000
Land	3,750		Total liabilities and	
Total assets	$13,400		stockholders' equity	$13,400

Notice that the balance sheets presented earlier in the text listed assets on the top and liabilities and stockholders' equity on the bottom. It is also acceptable practice to prepare a balance sheet with assets on the left side and liabilities and stockholders' equity on the right side, such as shown above.

3. Investing and financing effects of the statement of cash flows:

TERRIFIC LAWN MAINTENANCE CORPORATION
Statement of Cash Flows
For the Month Ended April 30, 2003

Operating Activities	
(none in this case)	
Investing Activities	
Purchased land (d)	$(5,000)
Purchased equipment (b)	(200)
Net cash used in investing activities	**(5,200)**
Financing Activities	
Issued common stock (a)	9,000
Net cash provided by financing activities	**9,000**
Change in cash	3,800
Beginning cash balance	0
Ending cash balance	**$ 3,800**

1. **Define the objective of financial reporting, the elements of the balance sheet, and the related key accounting assumptions and principles.   p. 49**
   - The primary objective of external financial reporting is to provide useful economic information about a business to help external parties, primarily investors and creditors, make sound financial decisions.
   - Elements of the balance sheet:
     - *a.* Assets—probable future economic benefits owned by the entity as a result of past transactions.
     - *b.* Liabilities—probable debts or obligations acquired by the entity as a result of past transactions, to be paid with assets or services.
     - *c.* Stockholders' equity—the financing provided by the owners and by business operations.
   - Key accounting assumptions and principles:
     - *a.* Separate-entity assumption—transactions of the business are accounted for separately from transactions of the owner.
     - *b.* Unit-of-measure assumption—financial information is reported in the national monetary unit.
     - *c.* Continuity (going-concern) assumption—a business is expected to continue to operate into the foreseeable future.
     - *d.* Historical cost principle—financial statement elements should be recorded at the cash-equivalent cost on the date of the transaction.
2. **Compute and interpret the financial leverage ratio.   p. 53**
   The financial leverage ratio (Average Total Assets ÷ Average Stockholders' Equity) measures the relationship between total assets and the stockholders' capital that finances the assets. The higher the ratio, the more debt is used to finance the assets. As the ratio (and thus debt) increases, risk increases.
3. **Identify what constitutes a business transaction and common balance sheet account titles used in business.   p. 56**
   A transaction includes:
   - An exchange between a business and one or more external parties to a business.
   or
   - A measurable internal event, such as adjustments for the use of assets in operations.
   An account is a standardized format that organizations use to accumulate the dollar effects of transactions related to each financial statement item. Typical balance sheet account titles include the following:
   - Assets: Cash, Accounts Receivable, Inventory, Prepaid Expenses, and Buildings and Equipment.
   - Liabilities: Accounts Payable, Notes Payable, Accrued Expenses Payable, and Taxes Payable.
   - Stockholders' equity: Contributed Capital and Retained Earnings.
4. **Apply transaction analysis to simple business transactions in terms of the accounting model: Assets = Liabilities + Stockholders' Equity.   p. 57**
   To determine the economic effect of a transaction on an entity in terms of the accounting equation, each transaction must be analyzed to determine the accounts (at least two) that are affected. In an exchange, the company receives something and gives up something. If the accounts, direction of the effects, and amounts are correctly analyzed, the accounting equation must stay in balance. The transaction analysis model is

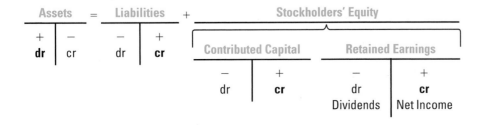

5. **Determine the impact of business transactions on the balance sheet using two basic tools, journal entries and T-accounts.   p. 62**
   - Journal entries express the effects of a transaction on accounts in a debits-equal-credits format. The accounts and amounts to be debited are listed first. Then the accounts and amounts to be credited are listed below the debits and indented, resulting in debits on the left and credits on the right.

(date or reference)	Account	xxx	
	Account		xxx

   - T-accounts summarize the transaction effects for each account. These tools can be used to determine balances and draw inferences about a company's activities.

+ Assets −		− Liabilities and Stockholders' Equity +	
Beginning balance Increases	Decreases	Decreases	Beginning balance Increases
Ending balance			Ending balance

6. **Prepare and analyze a simple balance sheet.   p. 69**
   Classified balance sheets are structured with
   - Assets categorized as "current assets" (those to be used or turned into cash within the year, with inventory always considered a current asset) and noncurrent assets, such as long-term investments, property and equipment, and intangible assets.
   - Liabilities categorized as "current liabilities" (those that will be paid with current assets) and long-term liabilities.
   - Stockholders' equity accounts are listed as Contributed Capital first followed by Retained Earnings.
7. **Identify investing and financing transactions and demonstrate how they are reported on the statement of cash flows.   p. 70**

   A statement of cash flows reports the sources and uses of cash for the period by the type of activity that generated the cash flow: operating, investing, and financing. Investing activities are purchasing and selling long-term assets and making loans and receiving principal repayments from others. Financing activities are borrowing and repaying to banks the principal on loans, issuing and repurchasing stock, and paying dividends.

   In this chapter, we discussed the fundamental accounting model and transaction analysis. Journal entries and T-accounts were used to record the results of transaction analysis for investing and financing decisions that affect balance sheet accounts. In Chapter 3, we continue our detailed look at the financial statements, in particular the income statement. The purpose of Chapter 3 is to build on your knowledge by discussing the measurement of revenues and expenses and illustrating the transaction analysis of operating decisions.

KEY **RATIO**

Financial leverage ratio measures the relationship between total assets and the stockholders' capital that finances them. The higher the ratio, the more debt is assumed by the company to finance assets. It is computed as follows (p. 53):

$$\text{Financial Leverage Ratio} = \frac{\text{Average Total Assets}}{\text{Average Stockholders' Equity}}$$

"Average" is (Last Year's Amount + This Year's Amount) ÷ 2

FINDING FINANCIAL INFORMATION

Balance Sheet

Current Assets
Cash
Accounts and notes
    receivable
Inventory
Prepaid expenses

Noncurrent Assets
Long-term investments
Property and equipment
Intangibles

Current Liabilities
Accounts payable
Notes payable
Accrued expenses payable
Unearned revenue

Noncurrent Liabilities
Long-term debt

Stockholders' Equity
Contributed capital
Retained earnings

Income Statement
To be presented in Chapter 3

Statement of Cash Flows

Under Investing Activities
+ Sales of noncurrent assets for cash
− Purchases of noncurrent assets for cash
− Loans to others
+ Receipt of loan principal payments from others

Under Financing Activities
+ Borrowing from banks
− Repayment of loan principal to banks
+ Issuance of stock
− Repurchasing stock
− Payment of dividends

Notes
To be discussed in future
    chapters

KEY TERMS

Account p. 56
Assets p. 51
Continuity (Going-Concern)
    Assumption p. 50
Contributed Capital p. 53
Credits p. 63
Current Assets p. 51
Current Liabilities p. 51

Debits p. 63
Historical Cost Principle p. 55
Journal Entry p. 63
Liabilities p. 51
Primary Objective of External
    Financial Reporting p. 49
Retained Earnings p. 53
Separate-Entity Assumption p. 50

Stockholders' Equity (Owners' or
    Shareholders' Equity) p. 52
T-account p. 65
Transaction p. 56
Transaction Analysis p. 58
Unit-of-Measure Assumption p. 50

QUESTIONS

1. What is the primary objective of financial reporting for external users?
2. Define the following:
    a. Asset.
    b. Current asset.
    c. Liability.
    d. Current liability.
    e. Contributed capital.
    f. Retained earnings.
3. Explain what the following accounting terms mean:
    a. Separate-entity assumption.
    b. Unit-of-measure assumption.
    c. Continuity assumption.
    d. Historical cost principle.
4. Why are accounting assumptions necessary?

5. How is the financial leverage ratio computed and interpreted?
6. For accounting purposes, what is an account? Explain why accounts are used in an accounting system.
7. What is the fundamental accounting model?
8. Define a business transaction in the broad sense, and give an example of two different kinds of transactions.
9. Explain what *debit* and *credit* mean.
10. Briefly explain what is meant by *transaction analysis*. What are the two steps in transaction analysis?
11. What two accounting equalities must be maintained in transaction analysis?
12. What is a *journal entry?*
13. What is a *T-account?* What is its purpose?
14. What transactions are classified as investing activities in a statement of cash flows? What transactions are classified as financing activities?
15. What is the difference between a bookkeeper and an accountant?

MULTIPLE **CHOICE QUESTIONS**

1. If a publicly traded company is trying to maximize its perceived value to decision makers external to the corporation, the company is most likely to *understate* which of the following on its balance sheet?
   a. assets
   b. liabilities
   c. retained earnings
   d. contributed capital
2. Which of the following is not an asset?
   a. short-term investments in stock
   b. land
   c. prepaid expense
   d. contributed capital
3. Which of the following is false if a company's financial leverage ratio is increasing over time?
   a. The amount of average stockholders' equity is decreasing relative to average total assets.
   b. The amount of average total liabilities is increasing relative to average total assets.
   c. The company is decreasing its risk related to required interest payments associated with debt.
   d. The company is increasing its risk related to required interest payments associated with debt.
4. Total assets on a balance sheet prepared on any date must agree with which of the following?
   a. the sum of total liabilities and net income as shown on the income statement
   b. the sum of total liabilities and contributed capital
   c. the sum of total liabilities and retained earnings
   d. the sum of total liabilities and contributed capital and retained earnings
5. The "duality of effects" can best be described as follows:
   a. When one records a transaction in the accounting system, at least two effects on the basic accounting equation will result.
   b. When an exchange takes place between two parties, both parties must record the transaction.
   c. When a transaction is recorded, both the balance sheet and the income statement must be impacted.
   d. When a transaction is recorded, one account will always increase and one account will always decrease.
6. The T-account is a tool commonly used for analyzing which of the following?
   a. increases and decreases to a single account in the accounting system
   b. debits and credits to a single account in the accounting system
   c. changes in specific account balances over a time period
   d. all of the above describe how T-accounts are used by accountants
7. Which of the following describes how assets are listed on the balance sheet?
   a. in alphabetical order
   b. in order of magnitude, lowest value to highest value

c. from most liquid to least liquid
d. from least liquid to most liquid

8. Which of the following is not a financing activity on the statement of cash flows?
   a. when the company lends money
   b. when the company borrows money
   c. when the company pays dividends
   d. when the company issues stock to shareholders

9. How many of the following are true regarding *debits* and *credits?*
   ■ In any given transaction, the total amount of the debits and the total amount of the credits must be equal.
   ■ Debits decrease certain accounts and credits decrease certain accounts.
   ■ Liabilities and Stockholders' Equity accounts usually end in credit balances, while assets usually end in debit balances.
   a. none   b. one   c. two   d. three

10. How many of the following statements are true regarding the balance sheet?
   ■ One cannot determine the true "fair market value" of a company by reviewing its balance sheet.
   ■ Certain internally generated assets, such as a trademark, are not reported on a company's balance sheet.
   ■ A balance sheet shows only the ending balances, in a summarized format, of all "balance sheet accounts" in the accounting system as of a particular date.
   a. none   b. one   c. two   d. three

For more practice with multiple choice questions, go to our website at www.mhhe.com/libby4e, click on "Student Center" in the upper left menu, click on this chapter's name and number from the list of contents, and then click on "Multiple Choice Quiz" from the menu on the left.

MINI-EXERCISES

Matching Definitions with Terms

M2-1
LO1

Match each definition with its related term by entering the appropriate letter in the space provided. There should be only one definition per term (that is, there are more definitions than terms).

Term	Definition
___ (1) Separate-entity assumption	A. = Liabilities + Stockholders' Equity.
___ (2) Historical cost principle	B. Reports assets, liabilities, and stockholders' equity.
___ (3) Credits	C. Accounts for a business separate from its owners.
___ (4) Assets	D. Increase assets; decrease liabilities and stockholders' equity.
___ (5) T-account	E. An exchange between an entity and other parties.
	F. The concept that businesses will operate into the foreseeable future.
	G. Decrease assets; increase liabilities and stockholders' equity.
	H. The concept that assets should be recorded at cash-equivalent cost.
	I. A standardized format used to accumulate data about each item reported on financial statements.

Matching Definitions with Terms

M2-2
LO1

Match each definition with its related term by entering the appropriate letter in the space provided. There should be only one definition per term (that is, there are more definitions than terms).

Term	Definition
___ (1) Journal entry	A. Accounting model.
___ (2) A = L + SE, and Debits = Credits	B. Four periodic financial statements.

___ (3) Assets = Liabilities + Stockholders' Equity

___ (4) Liabilities

___ (5) Income statement, balance sheet, statement of retained earnings, and statement of cash flows

C. The two equalities in accounting that aid in providing accuracy.

D. The results of transaction analysis in accounting format.

E. The account that is debited when money is borrowed from a bank.

F. Probable future economic benefits owned by an entity.

G. Cumulative earnings of a company that are not distributed to the owners.

H. Every transaction has at least two effects.

I. Probable debts or obligations to be paid with assets or services.

M2-3
LO2

Computing and Interpreting the Financial Leverage Ratio

Calculate the financial leverage ratio for Fullem Company based on the following data:

	Assets	Liabilities	Stockholders' Equity
End of 2002	$245,600	$ 90,300	$155,300
End of 2003	278,100	110,200	167,900

What does the result suggest about the company? What can you say about Fullem's ratio when compared to Papa John's 2000 ratio?

M2-4
LO3

Identifying Events as Accounting Transactions

For each of the following events, which events result in an exchange transaction for O'Brien Company (Y for yes and N for no)?

_____ (1) O'Brien purchased a machine that it paid for by signing a note payable.

_____ (2) Six investors in O'Brien Company sold their stock to another investor.

_____ (3) The company lent $150,000 to a member of the board of directors.

_____ (4) O'Brien Company ordered supplies from Office Max to be delivered next week.

_____ (5) The founding owner, Meaghan O'Brien, purchased additional stock in another company.

_____ (6) The company borrowed $1,000,000 from a local bank.

M2-5
LO3

Classifying Accounts on a Balance Sheet

The following are several of the accounts of Gomez-Sanchez Company:

___ (1) Accounts Payable

___ (2) Accounts Receivable

___ (3) Buildings

___ (4) Cash

___ (5) Contributed Capital

___ (6) Land

___ (7) Merchandise Inventory

___ (8) Income Taxes Payable

___ (9) Long-Term Investments

___ (10) Notes Payable (due in three years)

___ (11) Notes Receivable (due in six months)

___ (12) Prepaid Rent

___ (13) Retained Earnings

___ (14) Supplies

___ (15) Utilities Payable

___ (16) Wages Payable

In the space provided, classify each as it would be reported on a balance sheet. Use CA for current asset, NCA for noncurrent asset, CL for current liability, NCL for noncurrent liability, and SE for stockholders' equity.

M2-6
LO4

Determining Financial Statement Effects of Several Transactions

For each of the following transactions of Nardozzi Inc. for the month of January 2003, indicate the accounts, amounts, and direction of the effects on the accounting equation. A sample is provided.

a. *(Sample)* Borrowed $1,000 from a local bank.

b. Sold $3,000 additional stock to investors.

c. Purchased $500 in equipment, paying $100 cash and the rest on a note due in one year.

d. Declared and paid $100 in dividends to stockholders.

e. Lent $200 to an affiliate; accepted a note due in one year.

	Assets	=	Liabilities	+	Stockholders' Equity
a. Sample:	Cash	+1,000	Notes Payable	+1,000	

Identifying Increase and Decrease Effects on Balance Sheet Elements

M2-7
L05

Complete the following table by entering either the word *increases* or *decreases* in each column.

	Debit	Credit
Assets	_____	_____
Liabilities	_____	_____
Stockholders' equity	_____	_____

Identifying Debit and Credit Effects on Balance Sheet Elements

M2-8
L05

Complete the following table by entering either the word *debit* or *credit* in each column.

	Increase	Decrease
Assets	_____	_____
Liabilities	_____	_____
Stockholders' equity	_____	_____

Recording Simple Transactions

M2-9
L05

For each transaction in M2-6 (including the sample), write the journal entry in good form.

Completing T-Accounts

M2-10
L05

For each transaction in M2-6 (including the sample), post the effects to the appropriate T-accounts and determine ending account balances. Beginning balances are provided.

Cash	
Beg. bal. 1,000	
=====	

Notes Receivable	
Beg. bal. 1,000	
=====	

Equipment	
Beg. bal. 16,300	
=====	

Notes Payable	
	Beg. bal. 3,000
	=====

Contributed Capital	
	Beg. bal. 5,500
	=====

Retained Earnings	
	Beg. bal. 9,800
	=====

Reporting a Simple Balance Sheet

M2-11
L06

Given the transactions in M2-6 (including the sample), prepare a balance sheet for Nardozzi Inc. as of January 31, 2003, classified into current and noncurrent assets and liabilities.

Identifying Transactions as Investing or Financing Activities on the Statement of Cash Flows

M2-12
L07

For the transactions in M2-6, identify each as an investing (I) activity or financing (F) activity on the statement of cash flows.

EXERCISES

Matching Definitions with Terms

E2-1
L01

Match each definition with its related term by entering the appropriate letter in the space provided. There should be only one definition per term (that is, there are more definitions than terms).

Term	Definition
___ (1) Transaction	A. Economic resources to be used or turned into cash within one year.
___ (2) Continuity assumption	
___ (3) Balance sheet	B. Reports assets, liabilities, and stockholders' equity.
___ (4) Liabilities	C. Accounts for a business separate from its owners.
___ (5) Assets = Liabilities + Stockholders' Equity	D. Increase assets; decrease liabilities and stockholders' equity.
	E. An exchange between an entity and other parties.
___ (6) Current assets	F. The concept that businesses will operate into the foreseeable future.
___ (7) Note payable	
___ (8) Duality	G. Decrease assets; increase liabilities and stockholders' equity.
___ (9) Retained earnings	
___ (10) Debits	H. The concept that assets should be recorded at cash-equivalent cost.
	I. A standardized format used to accumulate data about each item reported on financial statements.
	J. The accounting model.
	K. The two equalities in accounting that aid in providing accuracy.
	L. The account that is credited when money is borrowed from a bank.
	M. Cumulative earnings of a company that are not distributed to the owners.
	N. Every transaction has at least two effects.
	O. Probable debts or obligations to be paid with assets or services.

E2-2   Identifying Account Titles

L03

The following are independent situations.

a. A company orders and receives 10 personal computers for office use for which it signs a note promising to pay $25,000 within three months.

b. A company purchases for $21,000 cash a new delivery truck that has a list, or sticker, price of $24,000.

c. A women's clothing retailer orders 30 new display stands for $300 each for future delivery.

d. A new company is formed and sells 100 shares of stock for $12 per share to investors.

e. A manufacturing company signs a contract for the construction of a new warehouse for $500,000. At the signing, the company writes a check for $50,000 to the construction company as the initial payment for the construction (receiving construction in progress).

f. A publishing firm purchases for $40,000 cash the copyright (an intangible asset) to a manuscript for an introductory accounting text.

g. A manufacturing firm pays stockholders a $100,000 cash dividend.

h. A company purchases 100 shares of Apple Computer common stock for $5,000 cash.

i. A company purchases a piece of land for $50,000 cash. An appraiser for the buyer valued the land at $52,500.

j. A manufacturing company acquires the patent (an intangible asset) on a new digital satellite system for television reception, paying $500,000 cash and signing a $400,000 note payable due in one year.

k. A local company is a sole proprietorship (one owner); its owner buys a car for $10,000 for personal use. Answer from the company's point of view.

l. A company borrows $1,000 from a local bank and signs a six-month note for the loan.

m. A company pays $1,500 principal on its note payable (ignore interest).

Required:

1. Indicate the appropriate account titles, if any, affected in each of the preceding events. Consider what is given and what is received.

2. At what amount would you record the truck in (b)? The land in (i)? What measurement principle are you applying?

3. For (c), what accounting concept did you apply? For (k), what accounting concept did you apply?

Classifying Accounts and Their Usual Balances

As described in a recent annual report, Polaroid Corporation designs, manufactures, and markets world-wide a variety of products primarily in instant image-recording fields, including instant photographic cameras and films, electronic imaging recording devices, conventional films, and light-polarizing filters and lenses. The following are accounts from a recent balance sheet for Polaroid.

E2-3
LO3, 5
Polaroid
Corporation

(1) Land	(6) Contributed Capital
(2) Retained Earnings	(7) Machinery and Equipment
(3) Notes Payable (due in 3 years)	(8) Accounts Payable
(4) Prepaid Expenses	(9) Short-Term Investments
(5) Long-Term Investments	(10) Taxes Payable

Required:

For each account, indicate whether the account is classified as a current asset (CA), noncurrent asset (NCA), current liability (CL), noncurrent liability (NCL), or stockholders' equity (SE), and whether the account usually has a debit or credit balance.

Determining Financial Statement Effects of Several Transactions

The following events occurred for Favata Company:

E2-4
LO4

a. Received investment of $20,000 cash by organizers and distributed stock to them.
b. Borrowed $6,000 cash from a bank.
c. Purchased $12,000 in land; paid $1,000 in cash and signed a mortgage note for the balance.
d. Loaned $300 to an employee who signed a note.
e. Purchased $8,000 of equipment, paying $1,000 in cash and signing a note for the rest.

Required:

For each of the events (*a*) through (*e*), perform transaction analysis and indicate the account, amount, and direction of the effect (+ for increase and − for decrease) on the accounting equation. Check that the accounting equation remains in balance after each transaction. Use the following headings:

Event	Assets	=	Liabilities	+	Stockholders' Equity

Determining Financial Statement Effects of Several Transactions

Nike, Inc., with headquarters in Beaverton, Oregon, is one of the world's leading manufacturers of athletic shoes and sports apparel. The following activities occurred during a recent year. The amounts are rounded to millions of dollars.

E2-5
LO4
Nike, Inc.

a. Purchased $216.3 in property, plant, and equipment; paid by signing a $5 long-term note and the rest in cash.
b. Issued $21.1 in additional stock for cash.
c. Declared $100 in dividends; paid $78.8 during the year and owed the rest to be paid in the following year.
d. Several Nike investors sold their own stock to other investors on the stock exchange for $21.
e. Sold $1.4 in investments in other companies for $1.4 cash.

Required:

1. For each of these events, perform transaction analysis and indicate the account, amount, and direction of the effect on the accounting equation. Check that the accounting equation remains in balance after each transaction. Use the following headings:

Event	Assets	=	Liabilities	+	Stockholders' Equity

2. Explain your response to Event (*d*).

Recording Investing and Financing Activities

Refer to E2-4.

E2-6
LO5

Required:

For each of the events in E2-4, prepare journal entries, checking that debits equal credits.

E2-7
LO5
Nike, Inc.

Recording Investing and Financing Activities

Refer to E2-5.

Required:
1. For each of the events in E2-5, prepare journal entries, checking that debits equal credits.
2. Explain your response to Event (*d*).

E2-8
LO5

Analyzing the Effects of Transactions in T-Accounts

Mulkeen Service Company, Inc., was organized by Conor Mulkeen and five other investors. The following activities occurred during the year:

a. Received $60,000 cash from the investors; each was issued 1,000 shares of capital stock.
b. Purchased equipment for use in the business at a cost of $12,000; one-fourth was paid in cash and the company signed a note for the balance (due in six months).
c. Signed an agreement with a cleaning service to pay it $120 per week for cleaning the corporate offices.
d. Lent $2,000 to one of the investors who signed a note due in six months.
e. Received an additional contribution from investors who provided $4,000 in cash and land valued at $10,000 in exchange for stock in the company.
f. Conor Mulkeen borrowed $10,000 for personal use from a local bank, signing a one-year note.

Required:
1. Create T-accounts for the following accounts: Cash, Note Receivable, Equipment, Land, Note Payable, and Contributed Capital. Beginning balances are zero. For each of the preceding transactions, record the effects of the transaction in the appropriate T-accounts. Include good referencing and totals for each T-account.
2. Using the balances in the T-accounts, fill in the following amounts for the accounting equation:
   Assets $_____ = Liabilities $_____ + Stockholders' Equity $_____
3. Explain your response to Events (*c*) and (*f*).

E2-9
LO4, 6

Inferring Investing and Financing Transactions and Preparing a Balance Sheet

During its first week of operations, January 1–7, 2003, Faith's Fine Furniture Company completed six transactions with the dollar effects indicated in the following schedule:

Accounts	Dollar Effect of Each of the Six Transactions						Ending Balance
	1	2	3	4	5	6	
Cash	$12,000	$50,000	$(4,000)	$(3,000)	$(7,000)		
Short-term note receivable				3,000			
Store fixtures					7,000		
Land			12,000			$3,000	
Short-term note payable		50,000	8,000			3,000	
Contributed capital	12,000						

Required:
1. Write a brief explanation of each transaction. Explain any assumptions that you made.
2. Compute the ending balance in each account and prepare a classified balance sheet for Faith's Fine Furniture Company on January 7, 2003.

E2-10
LO4, 6

Inferring Investing and Financing Transactions and Preparing a Balance Sheet

During its first month of operations, March 2004, Faye's Fashions, Inc., completed six transactions with the dollar effects indicated in the following schedule:

Accounts	Dollar Effect of Each of the Six Transactions						Ending Balance
	1	2	3	4	5	6	
Cash	$50,000	$(4,000)	$(4,000)	$(6,000)	$2,000		
Short-term investments				6,000	(2,000)		
Short-term note receivable			4,000				
Computer equipment						$4,000	
Delivery truck		25,000					
Long-term note payable		21,000					
Contributed capital	50,000					4,000	

Required:

1. Write a brief explanation of Transactions 1 through 6. Explain any assumptions that you made.
2. Compute the ending balance in each account and prepare a classified balance sheet for Faye's Fashions, Inc., at the end of March 2004.

Recording Journal Entries

E2-11
L05

Boyce Corporation was organized on May 1, 2003. The following events occurred during the first month.

a. Received $60,000 cash from the three investors who organized Boyce Corporation.
b. Borrowed $20,000 cash and signed a note due in two years.
c. Purchased $10,000 in equipment, paying $1,000 in cash and signing a six-month note for the balance.
d. Ordered store fixtures costing $16,000.
e. Lent $1,000 to an employee who signed a note to repay the loan in three months.
f. Received and paid for the store fixtures ordered in (*d*).

Required:
Prepare journal entries for each transaction. (Remember that debits go on top and credits go on the bottom, indented.) Be sure to use good referencing and categorize each account as an asset (A), liability (L), or stockholders' equity (SE). If a transaction does not require a journal entry, explain the reason.

Recording Journal Entries

E2-12
L05
Daimler-
Chrysler AG

DaimlerChrysler, headquartered in Stuttgart, Germany, manufactures several automotive brands including Mercedes-Benz, Chrysler, Jeep, and Dodge and has alliances with Mitsubishi Motors and Hyundai. Financial information is reported in the Euro (€) monetary unit. The following transactions were adapted from the annual report; amounts are in millions of Euros.

a. Declared €2,358 in dividends to be paid next month.
b. Ordered €22,100 in equipment.
c. Paid €2,379 in dividends previously declared.
d. Issued additional stock for €112 in cash.
e. Sold equipment at its cost of €809 for cash.
f. Received the equipment ordered in Event (*b*), paying €19,117 in cash and signing a note for the balance.
g. Purchased short-term investments for €4,883 cash.

Required:
Prepare journal entries for each transaction. (Remember that debits go on top and credits go on the bottom, indented.) Be sure to use good referencing and categorize each account as an asset (A), liability (L), or stockholders' equity (SE). If a transaction does not require a journal entry, explain the reason.

E2-13
L02, 5
Analyzing the Effects of Transactions Using T-Accounts and Interpreting the Financial Leverage Ratio as a Manager of the Company

Doane Company has been operating for one year (2003). You are a member of the management team investigating expansion ideas that will require borrowing funds from banks. At the start of 2004, Doane's T-account balances were as follows:

Assets:

Cash		Short-Term Investments		Property and Equipment	
5,000		2,000		4,000	

Liabilities:

Short-Term Notes Payable		Long-Term Notes Payable	
	300		600

Stockholders' Equity:

Contributed Capital		Retained Earnings	
	8,100		2,000

Required:

1. Using the data from these T-accounts, determine the amounts for the following on January 1, 2004:

   Assets $_____ = Liabilities $_____ + Stockholders' Equity $_____

2. Enter the following 2004 transactions in the T-accounts:
   a. Sold $1,500 of the investments for $1,500 cash.
   b. Sold one-fourth of the property and equipment for $1,000 in cash.
   c. Borrowed $1,600 at 10 percent interest from a local bank, signing a note with principal and interest due in three years.
   d. Paid $600 cash dividends to stockholders.

3. Compute ending balances in the T-accounts to determine amounts for the following on December 31, 2004:

   Assets $_____ = Liabilities $_____ + Stockholders' Equity $_____

4. Calculate the financial leverage ratio at December 31, 2004. If the industry average for the financial leverage ratio is 2.00, what does your computation suggest to you about Doane Company? Would you support expansion by borrowing? Why or why not?

E2-14
L06
Preparing a Balance Sheet

Refer to E2-13.

Required:

From the ending balances in the T-accounts in E2-13, prepare a classified balance sheet at December 31, 2004, in good form.

E2-15
L02, 5, 6
Analyzing the Effects of Transactions Using T-Accounts, Preparing a Balance Sheet, and Evaluating the Financial Leverage Ratio over Time as a Bank Loan Officer

Lee Delivery Company, Inc., was organized in 2003. The following transactions occurred during year 2003:

a. Received $40,000 cash from organizers in exchange for stock in the new company.
b. Purchased land for $12,000, signing a one-year note (ignore interest).
c. Bought two used delivery trucks for operating purposes at the start of the year at a cost of $10,000 each; paid $2,000 cash and signed a note due in three years for the rest (ignore interest).

d. Sold one-fourth of the land for $3,000 to Birkins Moving, which signed a six-month note.

e. Paid $2,000 cash to a truck repair shop for a new motor for one of the trucks. (*Hint:* Increase the account you used to record the purchase of the trucks since the productive life of the truck has been improved.)

f. Traded the other truck and $6,000 cash for a new one.

g. Stockholder Jonah Lee paid $22,000 cash for a vacant lot (land) for his personal use.

Required:

1. Set up appropriate T-accounts with beginning balances of $0 for Cash, Short-Term Note Receivable, Land, Equipment, Short-Term Notes Payable, Long-Term Notes Payable, and Contributed Capital. Using the T-accounts, record the effects of these transactions by Lee Delivery Company.

2. Prepare a classified balance sheet for Lee Delivery Company at the end of 2003.

3. At the end of the next two years, Lee Delivery Company reported the following amounts on its balance sheets:

	End of 2004	End of 2005
Assets	$90,000	$120,000
Liabilities	40,000	70,000
Stockholders' Equity	50,000	50,000

Compute the company's financial leverage ratio for 2004 and 2005. What is the trend and what does this suggest about the company?

4. At the beginning of year 2006, Lee Delivery Company applied to your bank for a $100,000 loan to expand the business. The vice president of the bank asked you to review the information and make a recommendation on lending the funds. What recommendation would you make to the bank's vice president about lending the money to Lee Delivery Company?

Explaining the Effects of Transactions on Balance Sheet Accounts Using T-Accounts

E2-16
L05

Heavey and Lovas Furniture Repair Service, a company with two stockholders, began operations on June 1, 2003. The following T-accounts indicate the activities for the month of June.

Cash (A)			
a.	17,000	*b.*	10,000
d.	800	*c.*	1,500

Notes Receivable (A)	
c.	1,500

Tools and Equipment (A)			
a.	3,000	*d.*	800

Building (A)	
b.	50,000

Notes Payable (L)	
	b. 40,000

Contributed Capital (SE)	
	a. 20,000

Required:
Explain Events (*a*) through (*d*) that resulted in the entries in the T-accounts. That is, for each account, what transactions made it increase and/or decrease?

Inferring Typical Investing and Financing Activities in Accounts

E2-17
L05

The following T-accounts indicate the effects of normal business transactions:

Equipment			
1/1	300		
	250	?	
12/31	450		

Note Receivable			
1/1	75		
	?	290	
12/31	50		

Notes Payable			
		130	1/1
	?	170	
		180	12/31

Required:
1. Describe the typical investing and financing transactions that affect each T-account. That is, what economic events occur to make each of these accounts increase and decrease?

2. For each T-account, compute the missing amounts.

E2-18
L07
Venator Group

Identifying Investing and Financing Activities Affecting Cash Flows

Venator Group (formally Woolworth Corporation) is a large global retailer of athletic footwear and apparel, including the Foot Locker family of stores, Champs Sports, and EastBay. The following are several of Venator's investing and financing activities as reflected in a recent annual statement of cash flows.

- *a.* Reduction of long-term debt.
- *b.* Sale of land.
- *c.* Issuance of common stock.
- *d.* Capital expenditures (for property, plant, and equipment).
- *e.* Issuance of short-term debt.

Required:
For each of these, indicate whether the activity is investing (I) or financing (F) and the direction of the effect on cash flows (+ = increases cash; − = decreases cash).

E2-19
L07
Hilton Hotels

Preparing the Investing and Financing Section of the Statement of Cash Flows

Hilton Hotels Corporation constructs, operates, and franchises domestic and international hotel and hotel-casino properties. Information from the company's recent annual statement of cash flows indicates the following investing and financing activities during that year (simplified, in millions of dollars):

Additional borrowing from banks	$438.5
Purchase of investments	282.2
Sale of property (assume sold at cost)	5.4
Issuance of stock	2.9
Purchase and renovation of properties	274.5
Payment of debt principal	32.2
Receipt of principal payment on a note receivable	5.4

Required:
Prepare the investing and financing sections of the statement of cash flows for Hilton Hotels. Assume that year-end is December 31, 2003.

E2-20
L03, 6, 7

Finding Financial Information as a Potential Investor

You are considering investing the cash you inherited from your grandfather in various stocks. You have received the annual reports of several major companies.

Required:
For each of the following, indicate where you would locate the information in an annual report. (*Hint:* The information may be in more than one location.)

1. Total current assets.
2. Amount of debt principal repaid during the year.
3. Summary of significant accounting policies.
4. Cash received from sales of noncurrent assets.
5. Amount of dividends paid during the year.
6. Short-term obligations.
7. Date of the statement of financial position.

PROBLEMS

P2-1
L01, 3, 5
Chevron Corporation

Identifying Accounts on a Classified Balance Sheet and Their Normal Debit or Credit Balances (AP2-1)

Chevron Corporation explores, produces, refines, markets, and supplies crude oil, natural gas, and petroleum products in the United States and 24 other countries. The following are accounts from a recent balance sheet of Chevron Corporation:

(1) Cash and Cash Equivalents
(2) Accounts and Notes Receivable
(3) Contributed Capital
(4) Long-Term Debt
(5) Prepaid Expenses
(6) Patents (an intangible asset)
(7) Federal and Other Taxes Payable
(8) Material, Supplies, and Other Inventories

(9) Accounts Payable
(10) Marketable Securities
(11) Capital Lease Obligations
(12) Retained Earnings
(13) Crude Oil and Petroleum Products
(14) Long-Term Investments
(15) Property, Plant, and Equipment

Required:

For each account, indicate how it normally should be categorized on a classified balance sheet. Use CA for current asset, NCA for noncurrent asset, CL for current liability, NCL for noncurrent liability, and SE for stockholders' equity. Also indicate whether the account normally has a debit or credit balance.

Determining Financial Statement Effects of Various Transactions (AP2-2)

P2-2
L03, 4

Lester's Home Healthcare Services was organized on January 1, 2003, by four friends. Each organizer invested $10,000 in the company and, in turn, was issued 8,000 shares of stock. To date, they are the only stockholders. During the first month (January 2003), the company had the following six events:

a. Collected a total of $40,000 from the organizers and, in turn, issued the shares of stock.
b. Purchased a building for $65,000, equipment for $16,000, and three acres of land for $12,000; paid $13,000 in cash and signed a note for the balance (the mortgage is due in 15 years). (*Hint:* Five different accounts are affected.)
c. One stockholder reported to the company that 500 shares of his Lester stock had been sold and transferred to another stockholder for $5,000 cash.
d. Purchased short-term investments for $3,000 cash.
e. Sold one acre of land for $4,000 cash to another company.
f. Lent one of the shareholders $5,000 for moving costs, receiving a signed six-month note from the shareholder.

Required:

1. Was Lester's Home Healthcare Services organized as a sole proprietorship, a partnership, or a corporation? Explain the basis for your answer.
2. During the first month, the records of the company were inadequate. You were asked to prepare the summary of the preceding transactions. To develop a quick assessment of their economic effects on Lester's Home Healthcare Services, you have decided to complete the tabulation that follows and to use plus ($+$) for increases and minus ($-$) for decreases for each account. The first event is used as an example.

		ASSETS					=	LIABILITIES +	STOCKHOLDERS' EQUITY	
Cash	Short-Term Investments	Notes Receivable	Land	Building	Equipment			Notes Payable	Contributed Capital	Retained Earnings
(a) +40,000							=		+40,000	

3. Did you include the transaction between the two stockholders—Event (c)—in the tabulation? Why?
4. Based only on the completed tabulation, provide the following amounts (show computations):
    a. Total assets at the end of the month.
    b. Total liabilities at the end of the month.
    c. Total stockholders' equity at the end of the month.
    d. Cash balance at the end of the month.
    e. Total current assets at the end of the month.

Recording Transactions in T-Accounts, Preparing the Balance Sheet, and Evaluating the Financial Leverage Ratio (AP2-3)

P2-3
L02, 5, 6

Patrie Plastics Company has been operating for three years. At December 31, 2003, the accounting records reflected the following:

Cash	$ 35,000	Intangibles	$ 5,000
Short-term investments	3,000	Accounts payable	25,000
Accounts receivable	5,000	Accrued liabilities payable	3,000
Inventory	40,000	Short-term note payable	12,000
Long-term note receivable	2,000	Long-term note payable	80,000
Equipment	80,000	Contributed capital	150,000
Factory building	150,000	Retained earnings	50,000

During the year 2004, the company had the following summarized activities:

a. Purchased equipment that cost $30,000; paid $10,000 cash and signed a one-year note for the balance.

b. Issued an additional 2,000 shares of capital stock for $20,000 cash.

c. Lent $12,000 to a supplier who signed a two-year note.

d. Purchased investments for $15,000 cash.

e. Borrowed $20,000 cash from a local bank, payable June 30, 2005.

f. Purchased a patent (an intangible asset) for $6,000 cash.

g. Built an addition to the factory for $42,000; paid $15,000 in cash and signed a three-year note for the balance.

h. Hired a new president at the end of the year. The contract was for $85,000 per year plus options to purchase company stock at a set price based on company performance.

i. Returned defective equipment to the manufacturer, receiving a cash refund of $2,000.

Required:

1. Create T-accounts for each of the accounts on the balance sheet and enter the balances at the end of 2003 as beginning balances for 2004.
2. Record each of the events for 2004 in T-accounts (including referencing) and determine the ending balances.
3. Explain your response to Event (*h*).
4. Prepare a classified balance sheet at December 31, 2004.
5. Compute the financial leverage ratio for 2004. What does this suggest about Patrie Plastics?

P2-4

LO7

Identifying Effects of Transactions on the Statement of Cash Flows (AP2-4)

Refer to P2-3.

Required:

Using the events (*a*) through (*i*) in P2-3, indicate whether each is an investing (I) or financing (F) activity for the year and the direction of the effect on cash flows (+ for increase and − for decrease). If there is no effect on cash flows, write NE.

P2-5

LO2, 5, 6

Bayer AG

Recording Transactions, Preparing Journal Entries, Posting to T-Accounts, Preparing the Balance Sheet, and Evaluating the Financial Leverage Ratio

Bayer AG, with headquarters in Leverkusen, Germany, is an international research-based group of companies active in health care, agriculture, polymers, and chemicals. Popular products include Bayer aspirin, Alka-Seltzer, and One-A-Day vitamins. The following is Bayer's (simplified) balance sheet from a recent year.

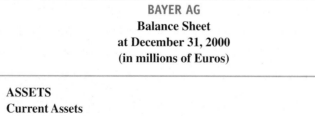

BAYER AG

Balance Sheet

at December 31, 2000

(in millions of Euros)

ASSETS	
Current Assets	
Cash	€ 704
Receivables and other assets	9,308
Inventories	6,095
	16,107

Noncurrent Assets	
Investments	2,156
Property, plant, and equipment	13,345
Intangible assets	4,843
	20,344
Total assets	**36,451**
LIABILITIES AND STOCKHOLDERS' EQUITY	
Current Liabilities	
Accounts payable	2,016
Other short-term obligations	9,597
	11,613
Long-term Liabilities	**8,461**
Stockholders' Equity	
Contributed capital	4,812
Retained earnings	11,565
Total stockholders' equity and liabilities	**36,451**

Assume that the following transactions occurred in 2001:

a. Issued additional shares of stock for €1,200 in cash.
b. Borrowed €3,952 from banks due in two years.
c. Declared and paid €953 in dividends to shareholders.
d. Purchased additional intangibles for €45 cash.
e. Purchased property, plant, and equipment; paid €2,647 in cash and €5,410 with additional long-term bank loans.
f. Acquired additional investments; paid €160 in cash.
g. Lent €250 to affiliates, who signed a six-month note.
h. Sold investments costing €115 for €115 cash.

Required:
1. Prepare a journal entry for each transaction.
2. Create T-accounts for each balance sheet account and include the December 31, 2000, balances. Post each journal entry to the appropriate T-accounts.
3. Prepare a balance sheet from the T-account ending balances for Bayer at December 31, 2001, based on these transactions.
4. Compute Bayer's financial leverage ratio for 2001. What does this suggest about the company?

Preparing the Investing and Financing Sections of a Statement of Cash Flows

Refer to P2-5.

P2-6
LO7
Bayer AG

Required:
Based on the activities for the year ended December 31, 2001, prepare the Investing and Financing sections of a statement of cash flows.

ALTERNATE PROBLEMS

Identifying Accounts on a Classified Balance Sheet and Their Normal Debit or Credit Balances (P2-1)

AP2-1
LO1, 3
Hasbro, Inc.

According to a recent Form 10-K report of Hasbro, Inc., "The Company is a worldwide leader in the design, manufacture and marketing of toys, games, interactive software, puzzles and infant products."

Hasbro produces products under several brands including Tonka, Milton Bradley, Playskool, and Parker Brothers. The following are several of the accounts from a recent balance sheet:

(1) Accounts Receivable   (8) Retained Earnings
(2) Short-term Borrowings   (9) Accounts Payable
(3) Contributed Capital   (10) Cash and Cash Equivalents
(4) Long-term Debt   (11) Accrued Liabilities Payable
(5) Prepaid Expenses   (12) Deferred Long-term Liabilities
(6) Intangibles   (13) Inventories
(7) Property, Plant, and Equipment   (14) Income Taxes Payable

Required:

Indicate how each account normally should be categorized on a classified balance sheet. Use CA for current asset, NCA for noncurrent asset, CL for current liability, NCL for noncurrent liability, and SE for stockholders' equity. Also indicate whether the account normally has a debit or credit balance.

AP2-2
LO2, 3, 4

Determining Financial Statement Effects of Various Transactions (P2-2)

Malamud Incorporated is a small manufacturing company that makes model trains to sell to toy stores. It has a small service department that repairs customers' trains for a fee. The company has been in business for five years. At the end of the most recent year, 2003, the accounting records reflected total assets of $500,000 and total liabilities of $200,000. During the current year, 2004, the following summarized events occurred:

a. Issued an additional 10,000 shares of capital stock for $100,000 cash.
b. Borrowed $120,000 cash from the bank and signed a 10-year note.
c. Built an addition on the factory for $200,000 and paid cash to the contractor.
d. Purchased equipment for the new addition for $30,000, paying $3,000 in cash and signing a note due in six months for the balance.
e. Purchased $85,000 in long-term investments.
f. Returned a $3,000 piece of equipment purchased in (d) because it proved to be defective; received a reduction of its short-term note payable.
g. Purchased a delivery truck (equipment) for $10,000; paid $5,000 cash and signed a short-term note payable for the remainder.
h. Lent $2,000 cash to the company president, Jennifer Malamud, who signed a note with terms showing the principal plus interest due in one year.
i. A stockholder sold $5,000 of his capital stock in Malamud Incorporated to his neighbor.

Required:

1. During 2004, the records of the company were inadequate. You were asked to prepare the summary of the preceding transactions. To develop a quick assessment of their economic effects on Malamud Incorporated, you have decided to complete the tabulation that follows and to use plus (+) for increases and minus (−) for decreases for each account. The first transaction is used as an example.

						ASSETS	=	LIABILITIES	+	STOCKHOLDERS' EQUITY	
Cash	Notes Receivable	Long-term Investments	Equipment	Building			Short-term Notes Payable	Long-term Notes Payable		Contributed Capital	Retained Earnings
(a)+100,000						=			+	100,000	

2. Did you include Event (i) in the tabulation? Why?
3. Based on beginning balances plus the completed tabulation, provide the following amounts (show computations):
   a. Total assets at the end of the month.
   b. Total liabilities at the end of the month.
   c. Total shareholders' equity at the end of the month.
4. Compute the financial leverage ratio for 2004. What does this suggest about the company?

Recording Transactions in T-Accounts, Preparing the Balance Sheet, and Evaluating the Financial Leverage Ratio (P2-3)

Ethan Allen Interiors, Inc., is a leading manufacturer and retailer of home furnishings in 310 retail stores in the United States and abroad. The following is adapted from Ethan Allen's June 30, 2000, annual financial report. Dollars are in thousands.

AP2-3
L02, 5, 6
Ethan Allen
Interiors, Inc.

Cash and cash equivalents	$ 14,024	Other assets	$ 5,276
Short-term investments	0	Accounts payable	65,879
Accounts receivable	34,336	Accrued expenses payable	33,969
Inventories	159,006	Long-term debt (includes the	
Prepaid expenses and other		current portion of $8,420)	17,907
current assets	28,421	Other long-term liabilities	35,307
Property, plant, and equipment	247,738	Contributed capital	144,668
Intangibles	54,770	Retained earnings	245,841

Assume that the following events occurred in the first quarter ended September 30, 2000:

a. Purchased $3,400 in additional intangibles for cash.
b. Sold equipment at its cost for $4,020 cash.
c. Purchased $2,980 in short-term investments for cash.
d. Issued additional shares of stock for $1,020 in cash.
e. Purchased property, plant, and equipment; paid $1,830 in cash and signed additional long-term notes for $9,400.
f. Sold at cost other assets for $310 cash.
g. Declared and paid $300 in dividends.

Required:
1. Create T-accounts for each of the accounts on the balance sheet; enter the balances at June 30, 2000.
2. Record each of the transactions for the first quarter ended September 30, 2000, in the T-accounts (including referencing) and determine the ending balances.
3. Prepare a classified balance sheet at September 30, 2000.
4. Compute the financial leverage ratio for the quarter ended September 30, 2000. What does this suggest about Ethan Allen Interiors, Inc.?

Identifying Effects of Transactions on the Statement of Cash Flows (P2-4)

Refer to AP2-3.

Required:
Using the events (*a*) through (*g*) in AP2-3, indicate whether each transaction is an investing (I) or financing (F) activity for the quarter and the direction of the effect on cash flows (+ for increase and − for decrease). If there is no effect on cash flows, write NE.

AP2-4
L07
Ethan Allen
Interiors, Inc.

CASES AND PROJECTS

Annual Report Cases

Finding Financial Information

Refer to the financial statements and accompanying notes of Abercrombie & Fitch given in Appendix C at the end of this book or open file ANF.pdf in the Annual Report Cases directory on the student CD-ROM.

CP2-1
L01, 2, 3, 4, 7

ABERCROMBIE
&
FITCH

Required:
1. Is the company a corporation, a partnership, or a proprietorship? How do you know?
2. Use the company's balance sheet to determine the amounts in the accounting equation (A = L + SE).
3. The company shows on the balance sheet that inventories are worth $120,997,000. Does this amount represent the expected selling price? Why or why not?
4. What is the company's fiscal year-end? Where did you find the exact date?

5. What are the company's obligations?
6. Compute the company's financial leverage ratio and explain its meaning.
7. How much cash did the company spend on purchasing property, plant, and equipment each year (capital expenditures)? Where did you find the information?

AMERICAN EAGLE OUTFITTERS

CP2-2 Finding Financial Information

LO1, 2, 3, 4, 7

Refer to the financial statements and accompanying notes of American Eagle Outfitters given in Appendix B at the end of this book or open file AEOS.pdf in the Annual Report Cases directory on the student CD-ROM.

Required:
1. Use the company's balance sheet to determine the amounts in the accounting equation (A = L + SE).
2. If the company was liquidated at the end of the current year, are the shareholders guaranteed to receive $367,695,000?
3. What are the company's noncurrent liabilities?
4. What is the company's financial leverage ratio?
5. Did the company have a cash inflow or outflow from financing activities? Of how much?

AMERICAN EAGLE OUTFITTERS

CP2-3 Comparing Companies within an Industry

LO2, 3, 7

Refer to the financial statements and accompanying notes of American Eagle Outfitters given in Appendix B, Abercrombie & Fitch given in Appendix C, and the Industry Ratio Report given in Appendix D at the end of this book or open file CP2-3.xls in the Annual Report Cases directory on the student CD-ROM.

Required:
1. Which company is larger in terms of total assets?
2. Compute the financial leverage ratio for both companies. Which company is assuming more risk? Why do you think that this is so?
3. Compare the financial leverage ratio for both companies to the industry average from the Industry Ratio Report. Are these two companies financing assets with debt more or less than the industry average? How is the financial leverage ratio influenced by these companies' choice to rent space instead of buying it?
4. In the most recent year, what were the net cash flows (that is, the increases in cash minus the decreases in cash) related to the buying, maturing, and selling of investments (marketable securities) for each company?
5. How much did each company pay in dividends for the most recent year?
6. What account title does each company use to report any land, buildings, and equipment it may have?

Financial Reporting and Analysis Cases

CP2-4 Broadening Financial Research Skills: Locating Financial Information on the EDGAR Database

LO2, 6, 7

The Securities and Exchange Commission (SEC) regulates companies that issue stock on the stock market. It receives financial reports from public companies electronically under a system called *EDGAR* (Electronic Data Gathering and Retrieval Service). Using the Internet, anyone may search the database for the reports that have been filed.

Using your Web browser, access the EDGAR database at www.freeedgar.com. To search the database, click on "Search Filings," type in "Papa Johns," and then click on "View Filings" when Papa John's International appears.*

---

*"A Crash Course for Online Investors: The SEC Can't Always Protect You," *Fortune,* May 24, 1999. ©1999 Time Inc. All rights reserved. Reprinted with permission.

Required:

To look at SEC filings,

1. Click on the 10-Q (quarterly) report dated 11/13/2001. Then skim down the Table of Contents to Item 1 (html.1) and click on "Balance Sheet."
   a. What was the amount of Papa John's total assets for the most recent quarter reported?
   b. Did long-term debt increase or decrease for the quarter?
   c. Compute the financial leverage ratio. How does it compare to the ratio indicated for Papa John's in the chapter? What does this suggest about the company?
2. Click on "Cash Flow Statement."
   a. What amount did Papa John's spend on property and equipment for the period?
   b. What was the total amount of cash flows from financing activities?

Interpreting the Financial Press

CP2-5
Fortune

The May 24, 1999, edition of *Fortune* magazine includes the article "A Crash Course for Online Investors: The SEC Can't Always Protect You."* You can access the article on the Libby/Libby/Short website at www.mhhe.com/libby4e.

Required:

Read the article and then answer the following questions:

1. What is a cyberinvestor according to the article?
2. What investment risk do cyberinvestors face?
3. List the rules suggested in the article to minimize risk from investing online.

Using Financial Reports: Evaluating the Reliability of a Balance Sheet

CP2-6
L01

Betsey Jordan asked a local bank for a $50,000 loan to expand her small company. The bank asked Betsey to submit a financial statement of the business to supplement the loan application. Betsey prepared the following balance sheet.

BALANCE SHEET June 30, 2004	
Assets	
Cash and CDs (investments)	$ 9,000
Inventory	30,000
Equipment	46,000
Personal residence (monthly payments, $2,800)	300,000
Remaining assets	20,000
Total assets	**$405,000**
Liabilities	
Short-term debt to suppliers	$ 62,000
Long-term debt on equipment	38,000
Total debt	100,000
Stockholders' equity	**305,000**
Total liabilities and stockholders' equity	**$405,000**

Required:

The balance sheet has several flaws. However, there is at least one major deficiency. Identify it and explain its significance.

*© 1999 Time Inc. All rights reserved.

CP2-7

LO2, 5, 6

Gateway, Inc.

Using Financial Reports: Analyzing the Balance Sheet

Recent balance sheets of Gateway, Inc. (producer and marketer of personal computers and PC-related products), are provided.

Required:

1. Is Gateway a corporation, sole proprietorship, or partnership? Explain the basis of your answer.
2. Use the company's balance sheet to determine the amounts in the accounting equation $(A = L + SE)$ for 2000.
3. Calculate the company's financial leverage ratio. Interpret the ratio that you calculated. What other information would make your interpretation more useful?
4. Give the journal entry the company will make when it pays its accrued liabilities.
5. Does the company appear to have been profitable over its years in business? On what account are you basing your answer? Assuming no dividends were paid, how much was net income in 2000? If impossible to determine without an income statement, state so.

GATEWAY INC.
Consolidated Balance Sheets
December 31, 2000 and 1999
(in millions)

	2000	1999
ASSETS		
Current assets		
Cash and cash equivalents	$ 484	$1,128
Marketable securities	130	209
Accounts receivable	545	646
Inventory	315	192
Other	793	522
Total current assets	2,267	2,697
Property, plant and equipment, net	897	746
Intangibles	166	52
Other assets	822	460
	$4,152	$3,955
Liabilities and Stockholders' Equity		
Current liabilities		
Accounts payable	$ 785	$ 899
Accrued liabilities	556	609
Accrued royalties	139	154
Other current liabilities	151	148
Total current liabilities	1,631	1,810
Other long-term obligations	141	128
Total liabilities	1,772	1,938
Stockholders' equity:		
Contributed capital	723	608
Retained earnings	1,657	1,409
Total stockholders' equity	2,380	2,017
	$4,152	$3,955

CP2-8

LO2, 6

McDonald's Corporation

Using Financial Reports: Preparing a Classified Balance Sheet and Analyzing the Financial Leverage Ratio

The following accounts, in alphabetical order, are adapted from a recent McDonald's Corporation's balance sheet (amounts are in millions of dollars):

	Current Year	Prior Year
Accounts and Notes Receivable	$ 609.4	$ 483.5
Accounts Payable	621.3	650.6
Accrued Liabilities	783.3	503.5
Cash and Equivalents	299.2	341.4
Contributed Capital	1,065.3	787.8
Current Maturities of Long-Term Debt	168.0	335.6
Intangible Assets	973.1	827.5
Inventories	77.3	70.5
Investments in and Advances to Affiliates (long-term)	854.1	634.8
Long-Term Debt	6,188.6	4,834.1
Notes Payable (short-term)	686.8	1,293.8
Notes Receivable due after One Year	67.9	67.0
Other Long-Term Liabilities	1,574.5	1,491.0
Other Noncurrent Assets	538.3	608.5
Prepaid Expenses and Other Current Assets	323.5	246.9
Property and Equipment, Net	16,041.6	14,961.4
Retained Earnings	8,458.9	8,144.1
Taxes Payable	237.7	201.0

Required:

1. Construct a classified balance sheet (with two years reported) for McDonald's Corporation in good form (assume that the current year ends on December 31, 2003).
2. Compute the company's financial leverage ratio for the current year.
3. In comparison to the ratio for the companies in the restaurant industry (as indicated in the chapter for Papa John's and others), how do you interpret this ratio for McDonald's?

Critical Thinking Cases

Making a Decision as a Financial Analyst: Preparing and Analyzing a Balance Sheet

CP2-9
LO2, 6

Your best friend from home writes you a letter about an investment opportunity that has come her way. A company is raising money by issuing shares of stock and wants her to invest $20,000 (her recent inheritance from her great-aunt's estate). Your friend has never invested in a company before and, knowing that you are a financial analyst, asks that you look over the balance sheet and send her some advice. An *unaudited* balance sheet, in only moderately good form, is enclosed with the letter:

DEWEY, CHEETUM, AND HOWE, INC.
Balance Sheet
For the Year Ending December 31, 2004

Accounts receivable	$ 8,000
Cash	1,000
Inventory	8,000
Furniture and fixtures	52,000
Delivery truck	12,000
Buildings (estimated market value)	98,000
Total assets	**$179,000**
Accounts payable	$ 16,000
Payroll taxes payable	13,000
Notes payable (due in three years)	15,000
Mortgage payable	50,000
Total liabilities	**$ 94,000**
Contributed capital	$ 80,000
Retained earnings	5,000
Total stockholder's equity	**$ 85,000**

There is only one footnote, and it states that the building was purchased for $65,000, has been depreciated by $5,000 on the books, and still carries a mortgage (shown in the liability section). The footnote further states that, in the opinion of the company president, the building is "easily worth $98,000."

Required:

1. Draft a new balance sheet for your friend, correcting any errors you note. (If any of the account balances need to be corrected, you may need to adjust the retained earnings balance correspondingly.) If no errors or omissions exist, state so.
2. Write a letter to your friend explaining the changes you made to the balance sheet, if any, and offer your comments on the company's apparent financial condition based only on this information. Suggest other information your friend might want to review before coming to a final decision on whether to invest.

CP2-10 Evaluating an Ethical Dilemma: Analyzing Management Incentives

L03

Leslie Fay

In 1993, Leslie Fay Companies, manufacturer of women's apparel, filed for Chapter 11 bankruptcy protection shortly after a scandal erupted over fraudulent accounting information. As reported in *The Wall Street Journal* (March 28, 1995, p. B1, B16), the company's audit committee report sharply criticized top management, suggesting that "it would have been difficult for senior management not to spot the extensive inventory and sales fraud."

There were numerous ways in which Leslie Fay committed the fraud, according to the report: To boost sales and lower costs, mid-level company officials forged inventory tags, ignored expected inventory shrinkage, multiplied the value of items in inventory, improperly inflated sales, and made up phantom inventory. These officials also constantly altered records to meet sales targets. In March 1995, Leslie Fay's independent auditors, BDO Seidman, filed charges against Leslie Fay management, suggesting a cause of the fraudulent activity was due to senior management's adoption of unrealistic budgets: "Senior management created an environment which encouraged and rewarded the cooking of Leslie Fay's books and records" (*The Wall Street Journal,* March 29, 1995).

Required:

1. Describe the parties who were harmed or helped by this fraud.
2. Explain how adopting unrealistic budgets may have contributed to the fraud.
3. Why do you think the independent auditor filed charges against its former client?

Financial Reporting and Analysis Team Project

CP2-11 Team Project: Analysis of Balance Sheets and Ratios

L02, 3, 7

As a team, select an industry to analyze. Using your web browser, each team member should acquire the annual report or 10-K for one publicly traded company in the industry, with each member selecting a different company.

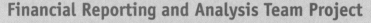

Required:

1. On an individual basis, each team member should write a short report that lists the following information.
   a. The date of the balance sheet.
   b. The asset accounts.
   c. The major investing and financing activities for the most recent period.
   d. The financial leverage ratio for the most recent period.
2. Then, as a team, write a short report comparing and contrasting your companies using the preceding attributes. Discuss any patterns across the companies that you as a team observe, and provide potential explanations for any differences discovered.

After studying this chapter, you should be able to:

1. Describe a typical business operating cycle and explain the necessity for the time period assumption. p. 103

2. Explain how business activities affect the elements of the income statement. p. 104

3. Compute and interpret the total asset turnover ratio. p. 107

4. Explain the accrual basis of accounting and apply the revenue and matching principles to measure income. p. 108

5. Apply transaction analysis to examine and record the effects of operating activities on the financial statements. p. 113

6. Prepare unadjusted financial statements. p. 120

Operating Decisions and the Income Statement

3

Papa John's and Pizza Hut follow different operating strategies:

- Number-one Pizza Hut regularly creates new pizza varieties (such as the Big New Yorker, the Twisted Crust, and the Stuffed Crust pizza you can eat backwards) to attract customers to its eat-in, take-out, and delivery services. The company releases a new variety, advertises like crazy, waits for the customers to rush in, and hopes they will return.

- Papa John's focuses on producing a limited variety of pizzas for pick up or delivery. The company hopes to build strong customer loyalty and repeat business by advertising the simple slogan "Better Ingredients. Better Pizza."

Despite these different strategies, Papa John's, ranked number three, has declared war on Pizza Hut, aiming to become the number-one pizza brand in the world. Until 1998, Papa John's took the battle directly to Pizza Hut, running commercials comparing what it believes is the superior quality of its dough and tomatoes with those used by Pizza Hut. But Pizza Hut fought back, first with commercials and newspaper ads suggesting that Papa John's ingredients are inferior and its "Better Ingredients. Better Pizza" slogan is false and misleading. Then the lawyers were brought into the scene. In 1998, Pizza Hut filed a lawsuit in a federal court accusing Papa John's of deceptive advertising and asked for $12.5 million in damages with an order to cease using its slogan. As *Fortune* recently noted, "This is a dough- (and mud-) slinging fight with no truce in sight."*

Taking the battle all the way, in March 2001 the Supreme Court rejected Pizza Hut's request to overturn a circuit court ruling that Papa John's could continue using the "Better Ingredients. Better Pizza" slogan.† Between 1998 and 2001, Papa John's added 586 stores

*Daniel Roth, "This Ain't No Pizza Party," Fortune *Magazine, November 9, 1998.* © *1998 Time Inc. All rights reserved.*
† *"High Court Rejects Review of Pizza Hut's Lawsuit Against Rival," The Wall Street Journal, March 29, 2001, section B2.*

while Pizza Hut's sales declined more than 11 percent. Other trends in the industry, such as the increase in independent pizza restaurant operators, a rise in consumer expectations for quality and consistency of product and service, and an increase in families dining out, will require the top pizza chains to reevaluate their operating strategies as the war continues.[‡]

UNDERSTANDING THE BUSINESS

To become the number-one pizza brand globally, Papa John's executives develop strategies, plans, and measurable indicators of progress toward their goals. For example, their growth plan in 2001 was to add 270 new restaurants and continue to tell customers about their fresh dough, tomato sauce, and high-quality cheese in three major national advertising campaigns. In developing their growth strategies, companies such as Papa John's plan their companywide operations in terms of the elements of the income statement (specific revenues and expenses).

Financial analysts develop their own set of expectations about Papa John's future performance. The published income statement provides the primary basis for comparing their projections to the actual results of operations. We will discuss these comparisons and the stock market's reactions to Papa John's results throughout this chapter as we learn about income recognition and measurement. To understand how business plans and the results of operations are reflected on the income statement, we need to answer the following questions:

1. How do business activities affect the income statement?
2. How are business activities measured?
3. How are business activities reported on the income statement?

In this chapter we focus on Papa John's operating activities that involve the sale of food to the public and the sale of ingredients, equipment, and services to franchisees. The results of these activities are reported on the income statement.

ORGANIZATION of the Chapter

How Do Business Activities Affect the Income Statement?	How Are Operating Activities Measured?	The Expanded Transaction Analysis Model	How Are Unadjusted Financial Statements Prepared?
■ The Operating Cycle ■ Elements on the Income Statement ■ Total Asset Turnover Ratio	■ Accrual Basis Accounting ■ Measurement Principles	■ Transaction Analysis Rules ■ Analyzing Papa John's Transactions	■ Income Statement ■ Statement of Retained Earnings ■ Balance Sheet ■ Cash Flow Effects

[‡]"Pizza Power 2001," Pizza Marketing Quarterly, August 9, 2001.

How Do Business Activities Affect the Income Statement?

Operating Cycle

The long-term objective for any business is to **turn cash into more cash.** If a company is to stay in business, this excess cash must be generated from operations (that is, from the activities for which the business was established), not from borrowing money or selling long-lived assets.

Companies (1) acquire inventory and the services of employees and (2) sell inventory or services to customers. The length of time between when inventory and employee services are paid for and when customers pay cash to the company (known as the **operating cycle**) depends on the nature of the business.

Learning Objective 1
Describe a typical business operating cycle and explain the necessity for the time period assumption.

The **OPERATING CYCLE (CASH-TO-CASH CYCLE)** is the time it takes for a company to pay cash to suppliers, sell goods and services to customers, and collect cash from customers.

Typical Operating Cycle

Purchase goods and services

Pay cash to suppliers

Sell goods and services to customers

Receive cash from customers

The operating cycle for Papa John's is relatively short. It spends cash to purchase ingredients, makes pizzas, and sells them to customers for cash. In some companies, inventory is paid for well before it is sold. Toys R Us, for example, builds its inventory for months preceding the year-end holiday season. It borrows funds from banks to pay for the inventory and repays the loans with interest when cash is received from customers. In other companies, cash is received from customers well after a sale takes place. For example, car dealerships often sell cars over time with monthly payments from customers due over several years. Shortening the operating cycle by creating incentives that encourage customers to buy sooner and/or pay faster improves a company's cash flows.

Managers know that reducing the time needed to turn cash into more cash (that is, shortening the operating cycle) means higher profit and faster growth. With the excess cash, managers may purchase additional inventory or other assets for growth, repay debt, or distribute it to owners as dividends.

Until a company ceases its activities, the operating cycle is repeated continuously. However, decision makers require information periodically about the company's financial condition and performance. To measure income for a specific period of time, accountants follow the **time period assumption**, which assumes that the long life of a company can be reported in shorter time periods, such as months, quarters, and years.[1] Two types of issues arise in reporting periodic income to users:

1. Recognition issues: *When* should the effects of operating activities be recognized (recorded)?

2. Measurement issues: *What amounts* should be recognized?

Before we examine the rules accountants follow in resolving these issues, however, let's review the elements of financial statements that are affected by operating activities.

> The **TIME PERIOD ASSUMPTION** indicates that the long life of a company can be reported in shorter time periods.

Elements of the Income Statement

> **Learning Objective 2**
> Explain how business activities affect the elements of the income statement.

Exhibit 3.1 shows a recent income statement for Papa John's, simplified for purposes of this chapter.[2] It has multiple subtotals, such as **operating income** and **income before income taxes.** This format is known as **multiple step** and is very common.[3] As we discuss the elements of the income statement, also refer to the conceptual framework outlined in Exhibit 2.1.

> **REVENUES** are increases in assets or settlements of liabilities from ongoing operations.

Revenues

Revenues are defined as increases in assets or settlements of liabilities from ongoing operations of the business (that is, an increase in net assets [A − L]). Operating revenues result from the sale of goods or services. When Papa John's sells pizza to consumers or equipment to franchisees, it has earned revenue. When revenue is earned, assets, usually cash or receivables, often increase. Sometimes if a customer pays for goods or services in advance, a liability account, usually deferred or unearned revenue, is created. At this point, no revenue has been earned. There is simply a receipt of cash in exchange for a promise to provide a good or service in the future. When the company provides the promised goods or services to the customer, the revenue is recognized and the liability settled.

Revenues earned

---

[1]In addition to the audited annual statements, most businesses prepare quarterly financial statements (also known as **interim reports** covering a three-month period) for external users. The Securities and Exchange Commission requires public companies to do so.

[2]For simplification, dollar amounts have been rounded and several accounts in the original statement have been combined with other accounts and/or shown in a different section of the statement in the exhibit. In addition, only one year's income statement is presented. Publicly traded companies such as Papa John's are actually required to present income information for three years to help users assess trends over time.

[3]Another common format, *single step,* reorganizes all accounts on the multiple-step format. All revenues and gains are listed together and all expenses and losses except taxes are listed together. The two subtotals are then subtracted to arrive at income before income taxes, the same subtotal as on the multiple-step statement.

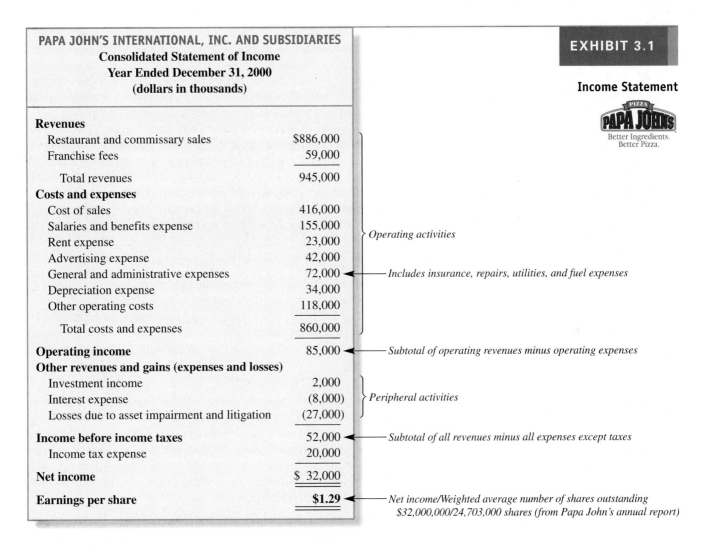

EXHIBIT 3.1

Income Statement

PAPA JOHN'S INTERNATIONAL, INC. AND SUBSIDIARIES
Consolidated Statement of Income
Year Ended December 31, 2000
(dollars in thousands)

Revenues	
Restaurant and commissary sales	$886,000
Franchise fees	59,000
Total revenues	945,000
Costs and expenses	
Cost of sales	416,000
Salaries and benefits expense	155,000
Rent expense	23,000
Advertising expense	42,000
General and administrative expenses	72,000
Depreciation expense	34,000
Other operating costs	118,000
Total costs and expenses	860,000
Operating income	85,000
Other revenues and gains (expenses and losses)	
Investment income	2,000
Interest expense	(8,000)
Losses due to asset impairment and litigation	(27,000)
Income before income taxes	52,000
Income tax expense	20,000
Net income	$ 32,000
Earnings per share	**$1.29**

> *Operating activities*

Includes insurance, repairs, utilities, and fuel expenses

Subtotal of operating revenues minus operating expenses

> *Peripheral activities*

Subtotal of all revenues minus all expenses except taxes

Net income/Weighted average number of shares outstanding
$32,000,000/24,703,000 shares (from Papa John's annual report)

Like most companies, Papa John's generates revenues from a variety of sources. Exhibit 3.1 shows revenues from two primary sources:

1. **Restaurant and Commissary Sales.** Approximately 25 percent of Papa John's stores are owned by the company, while 75 percent are franchises. In addition, to reduce costs and control quality and consistency, Papa John's builds regional commissaries (centralized kitchens and supply facilities) that provide all of the chain's pizza supplies and equipment. The largest revenue on Papa John's income statement, Restaurant and Commissary Sales, results from pizza sales in company-owned stores and sales by the commissaries. Pizza sales for the franchised restaurants are reported in the franchisees' financial statements.

2. **Franchise Fees.** Approximately 6 percent of all Papa John's revenues in 2000 came from selling franchises. Franchisees pay initial fees of $20,000 for the right to open and operate a specified number of restaurants in a specific geographic area. Papa John's records these fees as a liability (Unearned Franchise Fees) until it provides management training, site selection, restaurant design, and other promised services. As part of the franchise agreement, franchisees remit a fixed percentage of 4 to 5 percent of their store sales to Papa John's as franchise royalties. Both the initial development fees and royalties earned during the year are reported on Papa John's income statement as Franchise Fees.

Papa John's Primary Operating Revenues

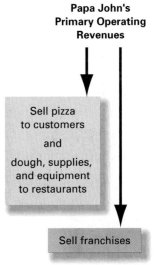

Sell pizza to customers
and
dough, supplies, and equipment to restaurants

Sell franchises

Costs and Expenses

Some students confuse the terms **expenditures** and **expenses.** An expenditure is any outflow of money for any purpose, whether to buy equipment or pay off a bank loan. An

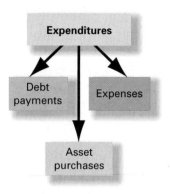

EXPENSES are decreases in assets or increases in liabilities from ongoing operations incurred to generate revenues during the period.

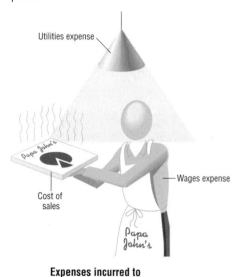

Expenses incurred to generate revenues

Papa John's Primary Operating Expenses

expense is more narrowly defined. When an asset is used to generate revenues during a period, all or a portion of the asset's cost is recorded as an **expense.** When an amount is **incurred to generate revenues during a period,** whether paid yet or to be paid in the future, an expense results. Therefore, not all expenditures are expenses, and expenses are necessary to generate revenues. Expenses are decreases in assets or increases in liabilities from ongoing operations incurred to generate revenues during the period.

Papa John's pays employees to make and serve food, uses electricity to operate equipment and light its facilities, advertises its pizza, and uses food and paper supplies. Without incurring these expenses, Papa John's could not generate revenues. Although some of the expenses may result from expenditures of cash at the time they are incurred, some may be incurred after cash has been paid in the past and others may be incurred before cash is paid in the future. When an expense occurs, assets such as supplies inventory and cash decrease or are used up **or** liabilities such as salaries or utilities payable increase.

The following are Papa John's primary expenses:

1. **Cost of sales.** In Papa John's restaurant operations, any ingredients or supplies that are part of inventory and are used to produce meals are expensed as they are used. In its commissary operations, any ingredients, supplies, and equipment that are part of inventory and sold to restaurants are expensed as they are used. In companies with a manufacturing or merchandising focus, cost of sales (also called cost of goods sold) is usually the most significant expense.

2. **Salaries and benefits expense.** In Papa John's restaurant operations, salaries and benefits expense to employees of $155,000,000 is more significant than its cost of sales by restaurants of $112,000,000 but less than cost of sales by commissaries of $304,000,000, totalling cost of sales of $416,000,000. In purely service-oriented companies in which no products are produced or sold, the cost of using employees to generate revenues is usually the largest expense.

3. **All other operating costs and expenses.** The remaining large expenses include Rent Expense, Advertising Expense, General and Administrative Expenses (for insurance, executive salaries, and rental of headquarters facilities), and Depreciation Expense reflecting the use of a part of long-lived assets such as buildings and equipment.

Other Revenues, Gains, Expenses, and Losses

Not all activities affecting an income statement are central to ongoing operations. Using excess cash to purchase stocks in other companies is an investing activity for Papa John's. However, any interest or dividends earned on the investment is called **investment income** or revenue. Likewise, borrowing money is a financing activity. However, the cost of then using that money is called **interest expense.** Except for financial institutions, incurring interest expense or earning investment income are not the central operations of most businesses including Papa John's. We say these are **peripheral** (normal but not central) **transactions.**

In similar fashion, companies sell property, plant, and equipment from time to time to maintain modern facilities. Selling land for more than the original purchase price does not result in a revenue because the transaction is not the central operating focus for the business. The **gain** results in an increase in assets or decrease in liabilities from a peripheral transaction. Papa John's did not report any gains in its 2000 income statement. However, it did report losses. **Losses** are decreases in assets or increases in liabilities from peripheral transactions. If land with a recorded cost of $2,800 were sold for $2,500, Papa John's would recognize a loss of $300 on the sale. "Losses due to asset impairment . . . " shown in Exhibit 3.1 will be discussed in Chapter 8. The losses due to "litigation" result primarily from the lawsuit brought by Pizza Hut.

Income Tax Expense

Income Tax Expense is the last expense listed on the income statement. All profit-making corporations are required to compute income taxes owed to federal, state, and foreign governments. Income tax expense is calculated as a percentage of the difference between revenues and expenses determined by applying the tax rates of the federal, state, local, and foreign taxing authorities. Papa John's effective tax rate in 2000 was 38.5 percent (income tax expense, $20,000,000, divided by income before income taxes, $52,000,000). This indicates that for every dollar of profit that Papa John's made in 2000, the company paid almost $.39 to taxing authorities.

GAINS are increases in assets or decreases in liabilities from peripheral transactions.

LOSSES are decreases in assets or increases in liabilities from peripheral transactions.

Earnings per Share

Corporations are required to disclose earnings per share on the income statement or in the notes to the financial statements. This ratio is widely used in evaluating the operating performance and profitability of a company. To compute earnings per share, net income is divided by the weighted average number of shares of stock outstanding. The calculation of the denominator is complex and is presented in other accounting courses. We used the actual number reported by Papa John's. For 2000, Papa John's reported $1.29 in earnings for each share of stock owned by investors.

As a final note, in Chapter 2, we discussed the financial leverage ratio, a tool to evaluate management's use of debt to improve earnings. We now introduce a ratio to assess managers' use of assets in total to improve earnings. As we will see in other chapters, similar analysis on the utilization of each specific type of asset provides additional information for decision makers.

The Total Asset Turnover Ratio	KEY RATIO ANALYSIS

? ANALYTICAL QUESTION

How effective is management in generating sales from assets (resources)?

% RATIO AND COMPARISONS

$$\text{Asset Turnover Ratio} = \frac{\text{Sales (or Operating) Revenues}}{\text{Average Total Assets}}$$

Learning Objective 3
Compute and interpret the total asset turnover ratio.

The 2000 ratio for Papa John's is:

$$\frac{\$945,000}{(\$396,000 + \$372,000)/2} = 2.46$$

COMPARISONS OVER TIME			COMPARISONS WITH COMPETITORS*	
Papa John's			Domino's Inc.	Tricon Global
1998	1999	2000	2000	2000
2.38	2.33	2.46	3.11	1.75

*Tricon Global is the parent company of Pizza Hut, KFC, and Taco Bell.

INTERPRETATIONS

In General   The total asset turnover ratio measures the sales generated per dollar of assets. A high asset turnover ratio signifies efficient management of assets; a low asset turnover ratio signifies inefficient management. A company's products and business strategy contribute significantly to its asset turnover ratio. However, when competitors are similar, manage-

Selected Focus Companies' Total Asset Turnover Ratios for 2000

Delta Air Lines 0.80

Harley-Davidson 1.28

Boston Beer 2.01

ment's ability to control the firm's assets is vital in determining its success. Stronger financial performance improves the asset turnover ratio.

Creditors and security analysts use this ratio to assess a company's effectiveness at controlling both current and noncurrent assets. In a well-run business, creditors expect the ratio to fluctuate due to seasonal upswings and downturns. For example, as inventory is built up prior to a heavy sales season, companies need to borrow funds. The asset turnover ratio declines with this increase in assets. Eventually, the season's high sales provide the cash needed to repay the loans. The asset turnover ratio then rises with the increased sales.

Focus Company Analysis Papa John's asset turnover ratio has increased slightly since 1998, suggesting an increase in management effectiveness in using assets to generate sales. In fact, Papa John's reported that, as the number of stores in a geographic area increased, regional commissaries showed higher sales, allowing management to use the commissary assets more efficiently.

Compared to its main competitors, Papa John's 2000 total asset turnover ratio falls in the middle. The difference in ratios is due in part to differences in operating strategy: Pizza Hut (and KFC and Taco Bell) operate primarily eat-in restaurants, so they must invest more in their facilities (that is, they are more asset intensive). Domino's, the leading pizza delivery company, operates primarily from rented facilities (that is, it is less asset intensive).

A Few Cautions While the total asset turnover ratio may decrease due to seasonal fluctuations, a declining ratio may also be caused by changes in corporate policies leading to a rising level of assets. Examples include relaxing credit policies for new customers or reducing collection efforts in accounts receivable. A detailed analysis of the changes in the key components of assets is needed to determine the causes of a change in the asset turnover ratio and thus management's decisions.

CASH BASIS ACCOUNTING records revenues when cash is received and expenses when cash is paid.

CASH BASIS
Income Measurement
Revenues (= cash receipts)
− Expenses (= cash payments)
Net Income (cash basis)

Learning Objective 4
Explain the accrual basis of accounting and apply the revenue and matching principles to measure income.

ACCRUAL BASIS ACCOUNTING records revenues when earned and expenses when incurred, regardless of the timing of cash receipts or payments.

ACCRUAL BASIS
Income Measurement
Revenues (= when earned)
− Expenses (= when incurred)
Net Income (accrual basis)

HOW ARE OPERATING ACTIVITIES RECOGNIZED AND MEASURED?

You probably determine your personal financial position by the cash balance in your bank account. Your financial performance is measured as the difference between your cash balance at the beginning of the period and the cash balance at the end of the period (that is, whether you end up with more or less cash). If you have a higher cash balance, cash receipts exceeded cash disbursements for the period. Many local retailers, medical offices, and other small businesses use the **cash basis of accounting** in which revenues are recorded when cash is received, and expenses are recorded when cash is paid, regardless of when the revenues were earned or the expenses incurred. This basis is often quite adequate for organizations that do not need to report to external users.

Accrual Accounting

Financial statements created under cash basis accounting normally postpone or accelerate recognition of revenues and expenses long before or after goods and services are produced and delivered (when cash is received or paid). They also do not necessarily reflect all assets or liabilities of a company on a particular date. For these reasons, cash basis financial statements are not very useful to external decision makers. Therefore, generally accepted accounting principles require **accrual basis accounting** for financial reporting purposes.

In accrual basis accounting, revenues and expenses are recognized when the transaction that causes them occurs, not necessarily when cash is received or paid. That is, **revenues are recognized when they are earned and expenses when they are incurred.** The two basic accounting principles that determine when revenues and expenses are recorded under accrual basis accounting are the **revenue principle** and the **matching principle.**

Revenue Principle

Under the **revenue principle,** four criteria or conditions must normally be met for revenue to be recognized.[4] If *any* of the following criteria is *not* met, revenue normally is *not* recognized and cannot be recorded.

1. **Delivery has occurred or services have been rendered.** The company has performed or substantially performed the acts promised to the customer by providing goods or services.

2. **There is persuasive evidence of an arrangement for customer payment.** In exchange for the company's performance, the customer has provided cash or a promise to pay cash (a receivable).

3. **The price is fixed or determinable.** There are no uncertainties as to the amount to be collected.

4. **Collection is reasonably assured.** For cash sales, collection is not an issue since it is received on the date of the exchange. For sales on credit, the company reviews the customer's ability to pay. If the customer is considered creditworthy, collecting cash from the customer is reasonably likely.

The **REVENUE PRINCIPLE** states that revenues are recognized when goods or services are delivered, there is evidence of an arrangement for customer payment, the price is fixed or determinable, and collection is reasonably assured.

Topic Tackler 3–1

These conditions normally occur when the title, risks, and rewards of ownership have transferred to the customers. For most businesses, these conditions are met at the point of delivery of goods or services. As is typical in the fast-food industry, Papa John's receives most of its revenues from restaurant sales at the time pizza is delivered to customers (criterion 1). Because a determinable amount of cash (criterion 3) is paid by customers in exchange for food service from Papa John's (criterion 2), there is no uncertainty as to the probability of collecting cash (criterion 4).

Papa John's also sells franchises from which the company receives cash from new franchisees **before** providing start-up services to them (criteria 2, 3, and 4 are met). Until the company provides the services it records no revenue. It records monies received from franchisees in the liability account Unearned Franchise Fees. This deferred or unearned revenue account represents the amount of goods or services owed to the franchisees. Later, when Papa John's provides the services (criterion 1), it earns and records the revenue by reducing the liability account.

Revenue is recorded according to the revenue principle when the four conditions are met, **regardless of when cash is received.** Cash may be received before or after revenue recognition, each resulting in two transactions—one on the date of the cash receipt and one on the date the revenue is earned.

---

[4]Thomas Phillips, Michael Leuhlfing, and Cynthia Daily, "The Right Way to Recognize Revenue," *Journal of Accountancy*, June 2001, pp. 39–46, providing a discussion of the SEC's Staff Accounting Bulletin 101 revenue recognition rules.

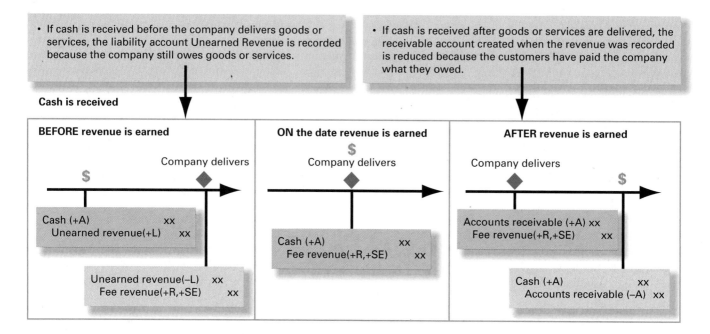

Companies usually disclose their revenue recognition practices in a note to the financial statements. The following excerpt from Papa John's note describes how it recognizes its two forms of franchise related income:

REAL WORLD EXCERPT

Better Ingredients.
Better Pizza.

ANNUAL REPORT

2. SIGNIFICANT ACCOUNTING POLICIES

Revenue Recognition

Franchise fees are recognized when a franchised restaurant begins operations, at which time we have performed our obligations related to such fees. Fees received pursuant to development agreements which grant the right to develop franchised restaurants in future periods in specific geographic areas are deferred and recognized on a pro rata basis as the franchised restaurants subject to the development agreements begin operations. Both franchise and development fees are nonrefundable. Franchise royalties, which are based on a percentage of franchised restaurants' sales, are recognized as earned.

SELF-STUDY QUIZ

This self-study quiz allows you to practice applying the revenue principle under accrual accounting. We recommend that you refer back to the four **revenue recognition criteria** presented earlier as you answer each question. Complete this quiz now to make sure you can apply the principle. The following transactions are samples of typical monthly operating activities of Papa John's (dollars in thousands). If revenue is to be recognized in **January,** indicate the title of the revenue account and the amount of revenue to be recognized.

ACTIVITY	REVENUE ACCOUNT TITLE	AMOUNT OF REVENUE RECOGNIZED IN JANUARY
(a) In January, Papa John's company-owned restaurants sold food to customers for $32,000 cash.		

(*b*) In January, Papa John's sold new franchises for $625 cash, providing $400 in services to these new franchisees during January; the remainder of services will be provided over the next three months.		
(*c*) In January, franchisees paid Papa John's $2,750 in cash for royalties based on the franchisees' weekly sales; $750 related to December sales and the rest to January sales.		
(*d*) In January, Papa John's commissaries sold sauce and dough to restaurants for $30,000 of which $20,000 was in cash and the rest was on account.		
(*e*) In January, franchisees paid $1,200 on account to Papa John's from December purchases of dough and sauce.		

After you have completed your answers, check them with the solutions that follow:

Revenue Account Title	Amount of Revenue Recognized in January
(a) Restaurant and Commissary Sales Revenue	$32,000
(b) Franchise Fees Revenue	$ 400
(c) Franchise Fees Revenue	$ 2,000
(d) Restaurant and Commissary Sales Revenue	$30,000
(e) No revenue earned in January.	—

Management's Incentives to Violate the Revenue Principle

A QUESTION OF ETHICS

Investors in the stock market base their decisions on their expectations of a company's future earnings. When companies announce quarterly and annual earnings information, investors evaluate how well the companies have met expectations and adjust their investing decisions accordingly. Companies that fail to meet expectations often experience a decline in stock price. Thus, managers are motivated to produce earnings results that meet or exceed investors' expectations. Sometimes they make unethical accounting and reporting decisions, as described in the August 2, 1999, issue of *Fortune*. Often such fraud involves falsifying revenues. As this text is being written, the collapse of Enron is being reported as a possible revenue recognition fraud among other types of potentially fraudulent activities.

Fraud is a criminal offense for which managers may be sentenced to jail. The following managers were convicted of revenue-related fraud in recent years.

The CEO	What He Did	Conviction/Plea	The Outcome
Donald Ferrarini, 71 Underwriters Financial Group	Reported nonexistent revenues; made losing company look like profit maker.	Convicted, 2/99.	Sentenced to 12 years, one month. He is appealing.
Richard Rubin, 57 Donnkenny	Concocted false invoices and revenues to meet earnings goals.	Pleaded guilty, 2/99.	Sentence pending; faces maximum of 5 years.

Chan Desaigoudar, 61, California Micro Devices	Led staff to record sales for products not shipped—or even manufactured.	Convicted, 7/98.	Served sentence of 36 months.
Paul Safronchik, 35 Home Theater Products Intl.	Invented customers and sales, showed profits when red ink was a reality.	Pleaded guilty, 12/96.	Served sentence of 37 months.

Besides the people who end up in jail, many others are affected by fraud. Stockholders lose stock value, employees may lose their jobs, and customers and suppliers may become wary of dealing with a company operating under the cloud of fraud. As a manager, you may face an ethical dilemma in the workplace. The ethical decision is the one you will be proud of 20 years later.

SOURCE: *Carol J. Loomis, "Lies, Damned Lies, and Managed Earnings: The Crackdown Is Here," Fortune, August 2, 1999, pp. 75–90.* © 1999 Time, Inc. All rights reserved.

The Matching Principle

The **MATCHING PRINCIPLE** requires that expenses be recorded when incurred in earning revenue.

The **matching principle** requires that costs incurred to generate revenues be recognized in the same period—a matching of costs with benefits. For example, when Papa John's restaurants provide food service to customers, revenue is earned. The costs of generating the revenue include expenses incurred such as these:

- Wages to employees who worked **during the period** (Wages Expense)
- Utilities for the electricity used **during the period** (Utilities Expense)
- Food and paper products used **during the period** (Cost of Sales)
- Facilities rental **during the period** (Rent Expense)
- The use of ovens and other equipment **during the period** (Depreciation Expense)

As with revenues and cash receipts, expenses are recorded as incurred, **regardless of when cash is paid.** Cash may be paid before or after expense recognition, resulting in two transactions: one on the date of the cash payment and one on the date the expense is incurred in generating revenue:

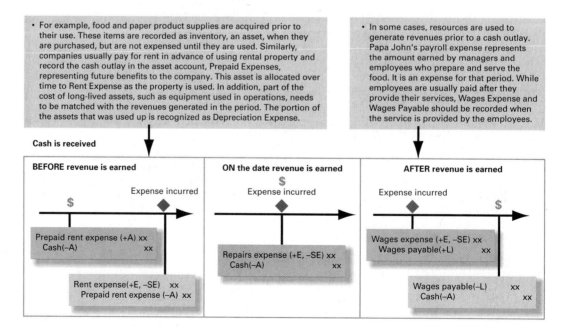

- For example, food and paper product supplies are acquired prior to their use. These items are recorded as inventory, an asset, when they are purchased, but are not expensed until they are used. Similarly, companies usually pay for rent in advance of using rental property and record the cash outlay in the asset account, Prepaid Expenses, representing future benefits to the company. This asset is allocated over time to Rent Expense as the property is used. In addition, part of the cost of long-lived assets, such as equipment used in operations, needs to be matched with the revenues generated in the period. The portion of the assets that was used up is recognized as Depreciation Expense.

- In some cases, resources are used to generate revenues prior to a cash outlay. Papa John's payroll expense represents the amount earned by managers and employees who prepare and serve the food. It is an expense for that period. While employees are usually paid after they provide their services, Wages Expense and Wages Payable should be recorded when the service is provided by the employees.

Cash is received

BEFORE revenue is earned	ON the date revenue is earned	AFTER revenue is earned
Expense incurred	Expense incurred	Expense incurred
Prepaid rent expense (+A) xx Cash(–A) xx	Repairs expense (+E, –SE) xx Cash(–A) xx	Wages expense (+E, –SE) xx Wages payable(+L) xx
Rent expense(+E, –SE) xx Prepaid rent expense (–A) xx		Wages payable(–L) xx Cash(–A) xx

This self-study quiz allows you to practice applying the **matching principle** under accrual accounting. Complete this quiz now to make sure you can apply this principle. The following transactions are samples of typical monthly operating activities of Papa John's (dollars in thousands). If expense is to be recognized in **January,** indicate the title of the expense account and the amount of the expense to be recognized. You should refer to the Papa John's income statement presented in Exhibit 3.1 for account titles.

ACTIVITY	EXPENSE ACCOUNT TITLE	AMOUNT OF EXPENSE RECOGNIZED IN JANUARY
(a) At the beginning of January, Papa John's restaurants paid $3,000 in rent for the months of January, February, and March.		
(b) In January, Papa John's paid suppliers $10,000 on account for supplies received in December.		
(c) In January, the food and paper products inventory used in selling pizza products to customers was $9,500.		
(d) In late January, Papa John's received a $500 utility bill for electricity used in January. The bill will be paid in February.		

After you have completed your answers, check them with the solutions that follow:

Expense Account Title	Amount of Expense Recognized in January
(a) Rent Expense	$1,000 ($3,000 ÷ 3 months)
(b) No expense in January	Supplies will be expensed when used.
(c) Cost of Sales	$9,500
(d) Utilities Expense (General and Administrative Expenses)	$ 500

THE EXPANDED TRANSACTION ANALYSIS MODEL

We have seen the variety of business activities affecting the income statement and how they are measured. Now we need to determine how these business activities are recorded in the accounting system and reflected in the financial statements. Chapter 2 covered investing and financing activities that affect assets, liabilities, and contributed capital. We now expand the transaction analysis model presented in that chapter to include operating activities.

Learning Objective 5
Apply transaction analysis to examine and record the effects of operating activities on the financial statements.

Transaction Analysis Rules

The complete transaction model presented in Exhibit 3.2 includes all five elements: Assets, Liabilities, Stockholders' Equity, Revenues, and Expenses. Recall that the Retained Earnings account is the accumulation of all past revenues and expenses minus

Topic Tackler 3–2

EXHIBIT 3.2

Transaction Analysis Model

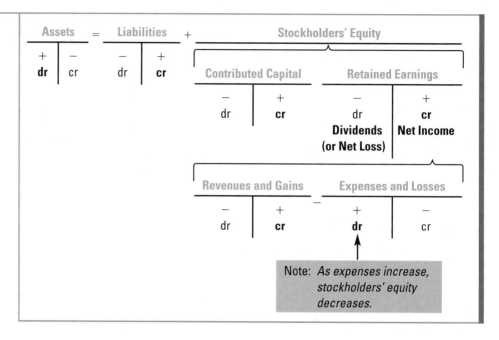

Assets = Liabilities + Stockholders' Equity

| + | − | | − | + |
| dr | cr | | dr | **cr** |

Contributed Capital

| − | + |
| dr | **cr** |

Retained Earnings

−	+
dr	**cr**
Dividends (or Net Loss)	**Net Income**

Revenues and Gains

| − | + |
| dr | **cr** |

Expenses and Losses

| + | − |
| **dr** | cr |

Note: *As expenses increase, stockholders' equity decreases.*

any income distributed to stockholders as dividends[5] (that is, earnings not retained in the business). When net income is positive, Retained Earnings increases; a net loss decreases Retained Earnings.

Before illustrating the use of the expanded transaction analysis model, we want to emphasize the following:

■ Revenues increase stockholders' equity through Retained Earnings and therefore have **credit** balances.

■ Expenses decrease stockholders' equity through Retained Earnings and therefore have **debit** balances. That is, to increase an expense, you debit it, which decreases Retained Earnings. Students often have difficulty with this concept. As expenses increase, Retained Earnings, and thus total stockholders' equity, decreases.

■ When revenues exceed expenses, the company reports net income, increasing Retained Earnings and stockholders' equity. However, when expenses exceed revenues, a net loss results, decreasing Retained Earnings and stockholders' equity.

When constructing and using the transactions analysis model, as we saw in Chapter 2:

■ All accounts can increase or decrease, although revenues and expenses tend to increase throughout a period. For accounts on the left side of the accounting equation, the increase symbol + is written on the left side of the T-account. For accounts on the right side of the accounting equation, the increase symbol + is written on the right side of the T-account.

■ Debits (dr) are written on the left side of each T-account and credits (cr) are written on the right.

■ Every transaction affects at least two accounts. In analyzing transactions:

    a. **Identify the accounts affected by title and classify them by type of account**, making sure that at least two accounts change. Ask yourself what is given and what is received. Classifications are an asset (A), a liability (L), a stockholders' equity (SE), a revenue (R), and an expense account (E).

    b. **Determine the direction of the effect** (an increase [+] or decrease [−] on each account).

    c. **Verify that the accounting equation (A = L + SE) remains in balance.**

Assets

| DR + | |

Liabilities

| | CR + |

Stockholders' Equity Accounts

| | CR + |

Revenue and Gains

| | CR + |

Expenses and Losses

| DR + | |

---

[5]Instead of reducing Retained Earnings directly when dividends are declared, companies may use the account Dividends Declared, which has a debit balance.

d. The total dollar value of the **debits** in the transaction **should equal** the total dollar value of the **credits**.

Since revenues are defined as inflows of net assets, then by definition recording a revenue results in either increasing an asset or decreasing a liability. In like manner, when recording an expense, an asset is decreased or a liability is increased. Revenues and expenses normally are not recorded in the same journal entry.

You should refer to the expanded transaction analysis model until you can construct it on your own without assistance. Study the following illustration carefully to make sure you understand the impact of operating activities on both the balance sheet and income statement.

Feedback Value Of Accounting Information and Stock Market Reaction

FINANCIAL ANALYSIS

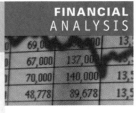

Stock market analysts and investors use accounting information to make their investment decisions. Thus the stock market, which is based on investors' expectations about a company's future performance, often reacts negatively when a company does not meet previously specified operating targets.

A net loss does not have to occur for a company to recognize that it is experiencing difficulty. Any unexpected variance in actual performance from the operating plan, such as lower than expected quarterly earnings, needs to be explained. On December 12, 2000, Papa John's announced that it anticipated it would report lower than expected earnings due to lower than expected franchisee sales, "fewer and later than expected restaurant openings," and "higher than expected labor and energy related costs."* On the day of the announcement, its stock had been selling at $26.81 per share. On the day following the announcement, the price dropped by $4.93 to $21.88 per share, an 18.4 percent decrease in one day.†

This is a clear example of how corporate decisions affect financial data and how internal and external users use the information. Accounting information has a pervasive effect on all forms of corporate decision making, as well as on the economic decisions that investors and creditors make.

*"Papa John's Announces November Comparable Sales and Revised Earnings Estimates and Restaurant Openings for 4Q, Full-Year 2000 and 2001," Business Wire, December 12, 2000.

†Bigcharts.com.

Analyzing Papa John's Transactions

We will begin with Papa John's January 31, 2001, balance sheet, presented at the end of Chapter 2 to include the effects of the operating activities in this chapter. All amounts are in thousands of dollars and the effects are posted to the appropriate T-accounts at the end of the illustration.

(a) **Papa John's restaurants sold pizza to customers for $36,000 cash. In addition, Papa John's commissaries sold $30,000 in supplies to restaurants, receiving $21,000 cash with the rest due on account.**

Journal entry →

Cash (+A) [$36,000 + 21,000]	57,000	
Accounts receivable (+A)	9,000	
Restaurant and commissary sales revenue (+R, +SE)		66,000

Effect on Accounting Equation →

Assets		=	Liabilities	+	Stockholders' Equity	
Cash	+57,000				Restaurant and	
Accounts					commissary sales	
receivable	+ 9,000				revenue	+66,000

Balancing → Equality checks: (1) Debits $66,000 = Credits $66,000; (2) the accounting equation is in balance.

(b) **The cost of the dough, sauce, cheese, and other ingredients for the restaurant sales in (a) was $10,000. The cost of the equipment and supplies for the commissary sales in (a) was $20,000.**

Cost of sales (+E, −SE)	30,000	
Inventories (−A)		30,000

Assets		=	Liabilities	+	Stockholders' Equity	
Inventories	−30,000				Cost of sales	−30,000

Equality checks: (1) Debits $30,000 = Credits $30,000; (2) the accounting equation is in balance.

(c) **Papa John's sold new franchises for $400 cash. The company earned $100 immediately by performing services for franchisees; the rest will be earned over the next several months.**

Cash (+A)	400	
Franchise fees revenue (+R, +SE)		100
Unearned franchise fees (+L)		300

Assets		=	Liabilities		+	Stockholders' Equity	
Cash	+400		Unearned			Franchise fees	
			franchise fees	+300		revenue	+100

Equality checks: (1) Debits $400 = Credits $400; (2) the accounting equation is in balance.

(d) **In January, Papa John's paid $7,000 for utilities, repairs, and fuel for delivery vehicles, all considered general and administrative expenses.**

General and administrative expenses (+E, −SE)	7,000	
Cash (−A)		7,000

Assets		=	Liabilities	+	Stockholders' Equity	
Cash	−7,000				General and	
					administrative	
					expenses	− 7,000

Equality checks: (1) Debits $7,000 = Credits $7,000; (2) the accounting equation is in balance.

(e) Papa John's commissaries ordered and received $29,000 in supplies inventories, paying $9,000 in cash and owing the rest on account to suppliers.

Inventories (+A)	29,000	
Cash (−A)		9,000
Accounts payable (+L)		20,000

Assets		=	Liabilities	+	Stockholders' Equity
Cash	−9,000		Accounts		
Inventories	+ 29,000		payable	+ 20,000	

Equality checks: (1) Debits $29,000 = Credits $29,000; (2) the accounting equation is in balance.

(f) Papa John's paid $14,000 cash to employees for their work in January.

| Salaries and benefits expense (+E, −SE) .... | 14,000 | |
| Cash (−A)... | | 14,000 |

Assets		=	Liabilities	+	Stockholders' Equity	
Cash	− 14,000				Salaries and	
					benefits expense	− 14,000

Equality checks: (1) Debits $14,000 = Credits $14,000; (2) the accounting equation is in balance.

(g) At the beginning of January, Papa John's paid the following: $2,000 for insurance covering the next four months beginning January 1, $6,000 for renting space in shopping centers over the next three months beginning January 1, and $1,000 for advertising to be run in February, all considered prepaid expenses when paid.

| Prepaid expenses (+A) .... | 9,000 | |
| Cash (−A) .... | | 9,000 |

Assets		=	Liabilities	+	Stockholders' Equity
Cash	− 9,000				
Prepaid expenses	+ 9,000				

Equality checks: (1) Debits $9,000 = Credits $9,000; (2) the accounting equation is in balance.

(h) Papa John's sold land with an historical cost of $1,000 for $4,000 cash.

Cash (+A)	4,000	
Property and equipment (−A)		1,000
Gain on sale of land (+Gain, +SE)		3,000

Assets		=	Liabilities	+	Stockholders' Equity	
Property and					Gain on sale of land	+3,000
equipment	− 1,000					
Cash	+ 4,000					

Equality checks: (1) Debits $4,000 = Credits $4,000; (2) the accounting equation is in balance.

SELF-STUDY **QUIZ**

For transactions (*i*) through (*k*), fill in the missing information. Be sure to transfer (post) the effects of the journal entries to the T-accounts at the end of the illustration. After you have completed your answers, check them with the solution at the end of the quiz.

(i) Papa John's received $3,500 in franchisee fees based on their weekly sales; $800 of the amount was due from franchisees' sales recorded as accounts receivable in December and the rest from January sales.

Write the journal entry; post the effects to the T-accounts.

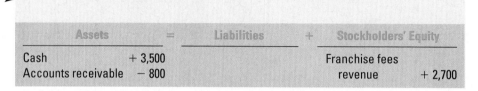

Assets	=	Liabilities	+	Stockholders' Equity
Cash	+ 3,500			Franchise fees
Accounts receivable	− 800			revenue + 2,700

Equality checks: (1) Debits $3,500 = Credits $3,500; (2) the accounting equation is in balance.

(j) Papa John's paid $10,000 on accounts owed to suppliers.

Write the journal entry; post the effects to the T-accounts.

Show the effects on the accounting equation.

Assets	=	Liabilities	+	Stockholders' Equity

Equality checks: (1) Debits $10,000 = Credits $10,000; (2) the accounting equation is in balance.

(k) Papa John's received $13,000 in cash: $1,000 in interest earned on investments and $12,000 in payments made by franchisees on their accounts.

Cash (+A) 13,000
    Investment income (+R, +SE) 1,000
    Accounts receivable (−A) 12,000

Show the effects on the accounting equation.

Assets	=	Liabilities	+	Stockholders' Equity

Equality checks: (1) Debits $_____ = Credits $_____ (2) Is the accounting equation is in balance?_____

(*i*) Cash (+A) 3,500
    Accounts receivable (−A)................................... 800
    Franchise fees revenue (+R, +SE) 2,700
(*j*) Accounts Payable (−L)....................................... 10,000
    Cash (−A)... 10,000

Assets	=	Liabilities	+	Stockholders' Equity
Cash	− 10,000	Accounts payable − 10,000		
(*k*) Assets	=	Liabilities	+	Stockholders' Equity
Cash	+ 13,000			Investment income + 1,000
Accounts receivable	− 12,000			

Debits $13,000 = Credits $13,000; the equation is in balance.

Balance Sheet Accounts (beginning balances are taken from Exhibit 2.6)

EXHIBIT 3.3

T-Accounts

Cash

Beg.	5,000			
(a)	57,000	7,000	(d)	
(c)	400	9,000	(e)	
(h)	4,000	14,000	(f)	
(i)	____	9,000	(g)	
(k)	13,000	____	(j)	
Bal.	33,900			

Accounts Receivable

Beg.	23,000	____	(i)	
(a)	9,000	12,000	(k)	
Bal.	19,200			

Property and Equipment

Beg.	339,000	1,000	(h)
Bal.	338,000		

Inventories

Beg.	18,000	30,000	(b)	
(e)	29,000			
Bal.	17,000			

Prepaid Expenses

Beg.	7,000	
(g)	9,000	
Bal.	16,000	

Accounts Payable

(j)	____	24,000	Beg.
		20,000	(e)
		34,000	Bal.

Unearned Franchise Fees

	6,000	Beg.
	300	(c)
	6,300	Bal.

Income Statement Accounts

Restaurant and Commissary Sales Revenue

	66,000	(a)
	66,000	Bal.

Franchise Fees Revenue

	100	(c)
	____	(i)
	2,800	Bal.

Cost of Sales

(b)	30,000	
Bal.	30,000	

Gain on Sale of Land

	3,000	(h)
	3,000	Bal.

Salaries and Benefits Expense

(f)	14,000	
Bal.	14,000	

Investment Income

	1,000	(k)
	1,000	Bal.

General and Administrative Expense

(d)	7,000	
Bal.	7,000	

Exhibit 3.3 shows the T-accounts that changed during the period because of transactions (a) through (k). The balances of all other accounts remained the same. Note that the amounts from Papa John's balance sheet at the end of Chapter 2 have been included as the beginning balances in Exhibit 3.3. At the beginning of every period, income

statement accounts have a zero beginning balance; therefore, there is no balance in the revenue and expense accounts at the beginning of the month.

You can verify that you posted the entries for transactions (*i*) through (*k*) properly by adding the increase side and subtracting the decrease side and then comparing your answer to the ending balance in each of the T-accounts.

HOW ARE UNADJUSTED FINANCIAL STATEMENTS PREPARED?

Learning Objective 6
Prepare unadjusted financial statements.

Based on the January transactions that have just been posted in the T-accounts, we can now prepare financial statements reflecting the operating activities for January. These statements are called **unadjusted** because, as is necessary under the accrual basis of accounting, not all revenues earned or expenses incurred in January have been recorded at this point. For example, the account Prepaid Expenses includes rent and insurance used in January, but the expenses are not yet recorded. This is true of the equipment used during the month as well.

Also notice that we have not calculated income taxes. Because the income statement is unadjusted, the amount of tax expense is not yet determinable. These statements do not at this point reflect generally accepted accounting principles based on accrual accounting until we adjust the accounts and financial statements in Chapter 4.

Unadjusted Income Statement

PAPA JOHN'S INTERNATIONAL, INC. AND SUBSIDIARIES Consolidated Statement of Income (unadjusted) Month Ended January 31, 2001 (dollars in thousands)	
Revenues	
Restaurant and commissary sales	$66,000
Franchise fees	2,800
Total revenues	68,800
Costs and expenses	
Cost of sales	30,000
Salaries and benefits expense	14,000
Rent expense	0
Advertising expense	0
General and administrative expenses	7,000
Depreciation expense	0
Other operating costs	0
Total costs and expenses	51,000
Operating income	17,800
Other revenues and gains (expenses and losses)	
Investment income	1,000
Interest expense	(0)
Gain on sale of land	3,000
Income before income taxes	21,800
Income tax expense	0
Net income	$21,800
Earnings per share (for the month)	$.88

$21,800,000 net income divided by average number → of shares outstanding (approximately 24,803,000)

Reporting Financial Information by Geographic and Operating Segments

Many companies, especially very large ones, operate in more than one geographic area. These companies are often called **multinationals.** A consolidated income statement that is based on aggregated data may not prove useful to investors seeking to assess possible risks and returns from companies operating in foreign markets. The same may be true if a company operates more than a single business. Therefore, many companies provide additional information about geographic and business segments in notes to the financial statements. An excerpt from Papa John's 2000 annual report provides information on segments:

REAL WORLD EXCERPT

ANNUAL REPORT

NOTES TO CONSOLIDATED FINANCIAL STATEMENTS

19. Segment Information

We have defined four reportable segments: domestic restaurants, domestic commissaries, domestic franchising and international operations. . . .
Segment information is as follows:

(*in thousands*)	2000	1999	1998
Revenues from external customers:			
Domestic restaurants	$456,637	$394,636	$344,089
Domestic commissaries	351,255	306,909	255,083
Domestic franchising	52,704	47,078	37,445
International	30,848	3,624	131
All others	53,233	53,078	45,404
Total revenues from external customers	$944,677	$805,325	$682,152

Unadjusted Statement of Retained Earnings

We also can prepare a statement of retained earnings that ties the information on Papa John's income statement to the balance sheet. Any transactions affecting Retained Earnings, such as generating net income and declaring dividends, are summarized in this statement.

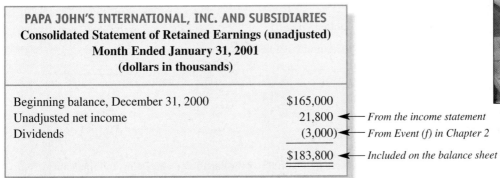

PAPA JOHN'S INTERNATIONAL, INC. AND SUBSIDIARIES
Consolidated Statement of Retained Earnings (unadjusted)
Month Ended January 31, 2001
(dollars in thousands)

Beginning balance, December 31, 2000	$165,000	
Unadjusted net income	21,800	◄— *From the income statement*
Dividends	(3,000)	◄— *From Event (f) in Chapter 2*
	$183,800	◄— *Included on the balance sheet*

Unadjusted Balance Sheet

Finally, we can revise the balance sheet from Chapter 2 to reflect the effects of the operating activities discussed in this chapter. Notice that the ending balance in the statement of retained earnings flows into the Stockholders' Equity section of the balance sheet. Revenues, expenses, and dividends are not listed separately on the balance sheet but are summarized in Retained Earnings. We explore the relationships among the financial statements further in the next chapter.

PAPA JOHN'S INTERNATIONAL, INC. AND SUBSIDIARIES	
Consolidated Balance Sheet (unadjusted)	
January 31, 2001	
(dollars in thousands)	
Assets	
Current assets:	
Cash	$ 33,900
Short-term investments	7,000
Accounts receivable	19,200
Inventories	17,000
Prepaid expenses	16,000
Other current assets	6,000
Total current assets	99,100
Property and equipment (net of accumulated depreciation of $83)	255,000
Notes receivable	20,000
Intangibles	49,000
Other assets	18,000
Total assets	$441,100
Liabilities and stockholders' equity	
Current liabilities:	
Accounts payable	$ 34,000
Accrued expenses payable	45,000
Other current liabilities	1,000
Total current liabilities	80,000
Unearned franchise fees	6,300
Long-term notes payable	160,000
Other long-term liabilities	8,000
Total liabilities	254,300
Stockholders' equity:	
Contributed capital	3,000
From the Statement of Retained Earnings → Retained earnings	183,800
Total stockholders' equity	186,800
Total liabilities and stockholders' equity	$441,100

FOCUS ON CASH FLOWS   **Operating Activities**

Chapter 2 presented a statement of cash flows for Papa John's investing and financing activities. Recall that investing activities relate primarily to transactions affecting long-term assets; financing activities are those from bank borrowings, stock issuances, and dividend payments to stockholders.

In this chapter, we focus on cash flows from operating activities. This section of the statement of cash flows reports **cash from** operating sources and **cash to** suppliers and others involved in operations.* The accounts most often associated with operating activities are current assets, such as Accounts Receivable, Inventories, and Prepaid Expenses, and current liabilities, such as Accounts Payable, Wages Payable, and Unearned Revenue.

When a transaction affects cash, it is included on the statement of cash flows. When a transaction does not affect cash, such as acquiring a building with a long-term mortgage note payable or selling goods on account to customers, there is no cash effect to include on the statement.

	Effect on Cash Flows
Operating activities	
Cash received: Customers	+
Interest and dividends on investments	+
Cash paid: Suppliers	−
Employees	−
Interest on debt obligations	−
Income taxes	−
Investing activities (see Chapter 2)	
Financing activities (see Chapter 2)	

Focus Company Analysis   The operating activities section of the following statement of cash flows for Papa John's is based on the transactions illustrated in this chapter, while the investing and financing activities relate primarily to transactions from Chapter 2. The statement reports the sources and uses of cash that created the overall $27,900 cash increase (from $6,000 to $33,900) in our Papa John's example. Remember that only the transactions that affect cash are reported.

In the long run, to remain in business, companies must generate positive cash flows from operations. Cash is needed to pay suppliers and employees. If the cash flow from operations is negative for a sustained period of time, the only other ways to obtain the necessary funds are to (1) sell long-lived assets (which reduces future productivity), (2) borrow from creditors (at increasing rates of interest as the risk of default rises), or (3) issue additional shares of stock (at a time when investors' expectations of poor future performance tends to drive the stock price down). Clearly, there are limits on how many of these activities companies can undertake.

Papa John's not only has realized positive cash flows from operations over the years but also has reported growth in the cash generated from operations in comparison to net income earned, from 2.01 times more cash than reported net income in 1998 to 2.41 times in 2000. This represents a conservative approach to reporting revenues and expenses that builds analysts' confidence about the reliability of the income information reported.

PAPA JOHN'S INTERNATIONAL, INC. AND SUBSIDIARIES
Consolidated Statement of Cash Flows
For the month ended January 31, 2001
(in thousands)

Each operating activity is referenced to the event illustrated in the chapter.

Operating Activities		
Cash from: Customers ($a + k$)	$69,000	*[$57,000 + 12,000]*
Franchisees ($c + i$)	3,900	*[$400 + 3,500]*
Interest on investments (k)	1,000	
Cash to: Suppliers ($d + e + g + j$)	(35,000)	*[$7,000 + 9,000 + 9,000 +*
Employees (f)	(14,000)	*10,000]*
Net cash provided by operating activities	**24,900**	

*When operating cash inflows and outflows are presented, the company is using the **direct method** of reporting cash flows from operations. However, most companies report cash from operations using the **indirect method** that will be discussed in later chapters.

Investing Activities		
Sold land (*h*)		4,000
Purchased property and equipment		(2,000)
Purchased investments		(1,000)
Lent funds to franchisees		(3,000)
Net cash used in investing activities		**(2,000)**
Financing Activities		
Issued common stock		2,000
Borrowed from banks		6,000
Paid dividends		(3,000)
Net cash provided by financing activities		**5,000**
Net increase in cash		**27,900**
Cash at beginning of month		6,000
Cash at end of month		**$33,900**

Except for the sale of land, investing and financing activities are illustrated in Chapter 2.

Agrees with the amount on the balance sheet.

Note that Papa John's had unadjusted net income of $21,800 in January, yet the balance in the Cash account increased by $27,900. This is a very clear example of the difference between the accrual basis of accounting and the cash basis. **On an accrual basis, net income is not equivalent to the change in cash for the period.**

SELF-STUDY QUIZ

PETCO Animal Supplies, Inc.

PETCO Animal Supplies, Inc., is a leading specialty retailer of premium pet food and supplies, with nearly 500 stores across the United States. Indicate whether the following transactions from a recent statement of cash flows affected cash flow as an operating (O), investing (I), or financing (F) activity, and show the direction of the effect (+ = an increase in cash; − = a decrease in cash):

TRANSACTIONS	TYPE OF ACTIVITY (O, I, OR F)	EFFECT ON CASH FLOWS (+ OR −)
1. Distribution to shareholders		
2. Receipt of cash from customers		
3. Additions to property		
4. Payment of income taxes		
5. Payment of cash to suppliers		
6. Repayment of long-term debt principal		
7. Receipt of interest on investments		
8. Borrowings of long-term debt		
9. Issuance of common stock		
10. Payment of interest on debt		
11. Payment of cash to employees		
12. Sale of property		

After you have completed your answers, check them with the solutions that follow:

1. F − 2. O + 3. I − 4. O − 5. O − 6. F − 7. O + 8. F + 9. F + 10. O − 11. O − 12. I +

DEMONSTRATION **CASE**

This case is a continuation of the Terrific Lawn Maintenance Corporation case introduced in Chapter 2. The company was established and supplies, property, and equipment were purchased. Terrific Lawn is ready for business. The balance sheet at April 30, 2003, based on investing and financing activities (from Chapter 2) is as follows:

TERRIFIC LAWN MAINTENANCE CORPORATION			
Balance Sheet			
At April 30, 2003			
Assets		**Liabilities**	
Current Assets		*Current Liability*	
Cash	$ 3,800	Notes payable	$ 4,400
Notes receivable	1,250		
Total current assets	5,050	**Stockholders' Equity**	
Equipment	4,600	Contributed capital	9,000
Land	3,750	Total liabilities and	
Total assets	$13,400	stockholders' equity	$13,400

The following completed activities occurred during April 2003:

a. Purchased and used gasoline for mowers and edgers, paying $90 in cash at a local gas station.

b. In early April, received from the city $1,600 cash in advance for lawn maintenance service for April through July ($400 each month). The entire amount was recorded as Unearned Revenue.

c. In early April, purchased $300 of insurance covering six months, April through September. The entire payment was recorded as Prepaid Expenses.

d. Mowed lawns for residential customers who are billed every two weeks. A total of $5,200 of service was billed in April.

e. Residential customers paid $3,500 on their accounts.

f. Paid wages every two weeks. Total cash paid in April was $3,900.

g. Received a bill for $320 from the local gas station for additional gasoline purchased on account and used in April.

h. Paid $700 principal and $40 interest on notes owed to XYZ Lawn Supply and the hardware store.

i. Paid $100 on accounts payable.

j. Collected $1,250 principal and $12 interest on the note owed by the city to Terrific Lawn Maintenance Corporation.

Required:

1. *a.* On a separate sheet of paper, set up T-accounts for Cash, Accounts Receivable, Notes Receivable, Prepaid Expenses, Equipment, Land, Accounts Payable, Unearned Revenue (same as deferred revenue), Notes Payable, Contributed Capital, Retained Earnings, Mowing Revenue, Interest Revenue, Wages Expense, Fuel Expense, and Interest Expense. Beginning balances for the balance sheet accounts should be taken from the

preceding balance sheet. Beginning balances for the operating accounts are $0. Indicate these balances on the T-accounts.

b. Analyze each transaction referring to the expanded transaction analysis model presented in this chapter.

c. On a separate sheet of paper, prepare journal entries in chronological order and indicate their effects on the accounting model (Assets = Liabilities + Stockholders' Equity). Include the equality checks: (1) Debits = Credits and (2) the accounting equation is in balance.

d. Enter the effects of each transaction in the appropriate T-accounts. Identify each amount with its letter in the list of preceding activities.

e. Compute balances in each of the T-accounts.

2. Use the amounts in the T-accounts to prepare a full set of unadjusted financial statements—income statement, statement of retained earnings, balance sheet, and statement of cash flows—for Terrific Lawn Maintenance Corporation at April 30, 2003. Refer to the statement presented in Chapter 2 for the investing and financing activities. (Adjustments to accounts will be presented in Chapter 4.)

Now check your answers with the following suggested solution.

SUGGESTED SOLUTION

1. Transaction analysis, journal entries, and T-accounts:

| (a) Fuel expense (+E, −SE) .... | 90 | |
| Cash (−A) .... | | 90 |

Assets	=	**Liabilities**	+	**Stockholders' Equity**
Cash − 90				Fuel expense − 90

Equality checks: (1) Debits $90 = Credits $90; (2) the accounting equation is in balance.

| (b) Cash (+A) .... | 1,600 | |
| Unearned revenue (+L) .... | | 1,600 |

Assets	=	**Liabilities**	+	**Stockholders' Equity**
Cash + 1,600		Unearned revenue +1,600		

Equality checks: (1) Debits $1,600 = Credits $1,600; (2) the accounting equation is in balance.

| (c) Prepaid expenses (+A) .... | 300 | |
| Cash (−A) .... | | 300 |

Assets	=	**Liabilities**	+	**Stockholders' Equity**
Prepaid expenses + 300				
Cash − 300				

Equality checks: (1) Debits $300 = Credits $300; (2) the accounting equation is in balance.

| (d) Accounts receivable (+A) .... | 5,200 | |
| Mowing revenue (+R, +SE) .... | | 5,200 |

Assets	=	**Liabilities**	+	**Stockholders' Equity**
Accounts receivable + 5,200				Mowing revenue + 5,200

Equality checks: (1) Debits $5,200 = Credits $5,200; (2) the accounting equation is in balance.

(e) Cash (+A) 3,500
    Accounts receivable (−A) 3,500

Assets	=	Liabilities	+	Stockholders' Equity
Cash + 3,500				
Accounts receivable − 3,500				

Equality checks: (1) Debits $3,500 = Credits $3,500; (2) the accounting equation is in balance.

(f) Wages expense (+E, −SE) 3,900
    Cash (−A) 3,900

Assets	=	Liabilities	+	Stockholders' Equity
Cash − 3,900				Wages expense − 3,900

Equality checks: (1) Debits $3,900 = Credits $3,900; (2) the accounting equation is in balance.

(g) Fuel expense (+E, −SE) 320
    Accounts payable (+L) 320

Assets	=	Liabilities	+	Stockholders' Equity
		Accounts payable +320		Fuel expense − 320

Equality checks: (1) Debits $320 = Credits $320; (2) the accounting equation is in balance.

(h) Interest expense (+E, −SE) 40
    Notes payable (−L) 700
    Cash (−A) 740

Assets	=	Liabilities	+	Stockholders' Equity
Cash − 740		Notes payable − 700		Interest expense − 40

Equality checks: (1) Debits $740 = Credits $740; (2) the accounting equation is in balance.

(i) Accounts payable (−L) 100
    Cash (−A) 100

Assets	=	Liabilities	+	Stockholders' Equity
Cash − 100		Accounts payable − 100		

Equality checks: (1) Debits $100 = Credits $100; (2) the accounting equation is in balance.

(j) Cash (+A) 1,262
    Notes receivable (−A) 1,250
    Interest revenue (+R,+SE) 12

Assets	=	Liabilities	+	Stockholders' Equity
Cash + 1,262				Interest revenue +12
Notes receivable − 1,250				

Equality checks: (1) Debits $1,262 = Credits $1,262; (2) the accounting equation is in balance.

T-Accounts:

Cash			
Beg.	3,800		
(b)	1,600	90	(a)
(e)	3,500	300	(c)
(j)	1,262	3,900	(f)
		740	(h)
		100	(i)
Bal.	5,032		

Accounts Receivable			
Beg.	0		
(d)	5,200	3,500	(e)
Bal.	1,700		

Notes Receivable			
Beg.	1,250	1,250	(j)
Bal.	0		

Prepaid Expenses		
Beg.	0	
(c)	300	
Bal.	300	

Equipment		
Beg.	4,600	
Bal.	4,600	

Land		
Beg.	3,750	
Bal.	3,750	

Accounts Payable			
		0	Beg.
(i)	100	320	(g)
		220	Bal.

Notes Payable			
		4,400	Beg.
(h)	700		
		3,700	Bal.

Unearned Revenue			
		0	Beg.
		1,600	(b)
		1,600	Bal.

Contributed Capital		
	9,000	Beg.
	9,000	Bal.

Retained Earnings		
	0	Beg.
	0	Bal.

Mowing Revenue		
	0	Beg.
	5,200	(d)
	5,200	Bal.

Interest Revenue		
	0	Beg.
	12	(j)
	12	Bal.

Wages Expense		
Beg.	0	
(f)	3,900	
Bal.	3,900	

Fuel Expense		
Beg.	0	
(a)	90	
(g)	320	
Bal.	410	

Interest Expense		
Beg.	0	
(h)	40	
Bal.	40	

2. Unadjusted financial statements:

TERRIFIC LAWN MAINTENANCE CORPORATION
Income Statement (unadjusted)
For the Month Ended April 30, 2003

Operating Revenues	
Mowing revenue	$5,200
Operating Expenses	
Fuel expense	410
Wages expense	3,900
	4,310
Operating Income	890
Other items	
Interest revenue	12
Interest expense	(40)
Pretax income	862
Income tax expense	0
Net Income	**$862**
Earnings per share for the month	**$.57**

← ($862 net income divided by 1,500 shares outstanding)

TERRIFIC LAWN MAINTENANCE CORPORATION
Statement of Retained Earnings (unadjusted)
For the Month Ended April 30, 2003

Balance, April 1, 2003	$ 0
Unadjusted net income	862
Dividends	0
Balance, April 30, 2003	$862

TERRIFIC LAWN MAINTENANCE CORPORATION
Statement of Cash Flows (unadjusted)
For the Month Ended April 30, 2003

Cash Flows from Operating Activities		
Cash received:	Customers (b, e)	$5,100
	Interest on notes receivable (j)	12
Cash paid:	Suppliers (a, c, i)	(490)
	Employees (f)	(3,900)
	Interest on notes payable (h)	(40)
Cash flows provided by operations		**682**
Cash Flows from Investing Activities		
Purchased land		(5,000)
Purchased equipment		(200)
Received principal payment on note receivable (j)		1,250
Cash flows used in investing activities		**(3,950)**
Cash Flows from Financing Activities		
Issued common stock		9,000
Payments on principal of notes payable (h)		(700)
Cash flows provided by financing activities		**8,300**
Change in cash		5,032
Beginning cash balance		0
Ending cash balance		**$5,032**

TERRIFIC LAWN MAINTENANCE CORPORATION
Balance Sheet (unadjusted)
April 30, 2003

Assets		Liabilities	
Current Assets		**Current Liabilities**	
Cash	$ 5,032	Accounts payable	$ 220
Accounts receivable	1,700	Notes payable	3,700
Prepaid expenses	300	Unearned revenue	1,600
Total current assets	7,032	Total current liabilities	5,520
Equipment	4,600	**Stockholders' Equity**	
Land	3,750	Contributed capital	9,000
		Retained earnings	862
Total assets	**$15,382**	**Total liabilities and stockholders' equity**	**$15,382**

CHAPTER **TAKE-AWAYS**

1. **Describe a typical business operating cycle and explain the necessity for the time period assumption. p. 103**
   - The operating cycle, or cash-to-cash cycle, is the time needed to purchase goods or services from suppliers, sell the goods or services to customers, and collect cash from customers.
   - Time period assumption—to measure and report financial information periodically, we assume the long life of a company can be cut into shorter periods.

2. **Explain how business activities affect the elements of the income statement. p. 104**
   - Elements on the income statement:
     - *a.* Revenues—increases in assets or settlements of liabilities from ongoing operations.
     - *b.* Expenses—decreases in assets or increases in liabilities from ongoing operations.
     - *c.* Gains—increases in assets or settlements of liabilities from peripheral activities.
     - *d.* Losses—decreases in assets or increases in liabilities from peripheral activities.

3. **Compute and interpret the total asset turnover ratio. p. 107**
   The total asset turnover ratio (Sales ÷ Average Total Assets) measures the sales generated per dollar of assets. The higher the ratio, the more efficient the company is at managing assets.

4. **Explain the accrual basis of accounting and apply the revenue and matching principles to measure income. p. 108**
   In accrual basis accounting, revenues are recognized when earned and expenses are recognized when incurred.
   - Revenue principle—recognize revenues when (1) delivery has occurred, (2) there is persuasive evidence of an arrangement for customer payment, (3) the price is fixed or determinable, and (4) collection is reasonably assured.
   - Matching principle—recognize expenses when they are incurred in generating revenue.

5. **Apply transaction analysis to examine and record the effects of operating activities on the financial statements. p. 113**
   The expanded transaction analysis model includes revenues and expenses:

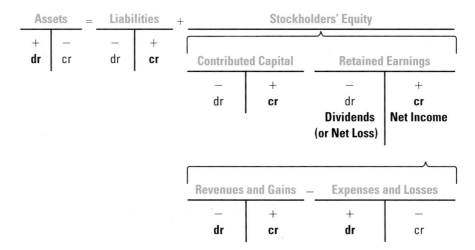

6. **Prepare unadjusted financial statements. p. 120**
   Until the accounts have been updated to include all revenues earned and expenses incurred in the period (due to a difference in the time when cash is received or paid), the financial statements are titled "unadjusted":
   - Unadjusted income statement.
   - Unadjusted statement of retained earnings.
   - Unadjusted balance sheet.
   - Unadjusted statement of cash flows.

   In this chapter, we discussed the operating cycle and accounting concepts relevant to income determination: the time period assumption, definitions of the income statement elements (revenues, expenses, gains, and losses), the revenue principle, and the matching principle. The accounting principles are defined in accordance with the accrual basis of accounting, which requires revenues to be recorded when earned and expenses to be recorded when incurred in the process of generating revenues. We expanded the transaction analysis model introduced in Chapter 2 by adding revenues and expenses and prepared unadjusted financial statements. In Chapter 4, we discuss the activities that occur at the end of the accounting period: the adjustment process, the preparation of adjusted financial statements, and the closing process.

KEY RATIO

Total asset turnover measures the sales generated per dollar of assets. A high ratio suggests that a company is managing its assets (the resources used to generate revenues) efficiently. The ratio is computed as follows (p. 107):

$$\text{Total Asset Turnover} = \frac{\text{Sales (or Operating) Revenues}}{\text{Average Total Assets}}$$

"Average" is (Last Year's Value + This Year's Value) ÷ 2.

FINDING FINANCIAL INFORMATION

BALANCE SHEET

Current Assets
Cash
Accounts and notes receivable
Inventory
Prepaid expense

Noncurrent Assets
Long-term investments
Property and equipment
Intangibles

Current Liabilities
Accounts payable
Notes payable
Accrued liabilities payable

Noncurrent Liabilities
Long-term debt

Stockholders' Equity
Contributed capital
Retained earnings

INCOME STATEMENT

Revenues
    Sales (from various operating activities)

Expenses
    Cost of sales (used inventory)
    Rent, wages, depreciation, insurance, etc.

Operating Income

Other items:
    Interest expense
    Investment income
    Gains on sale of assets
    Losses on sale of assets

Pretax Income
    Income tax expense

Net Income

Earnings per share

STATEMENT OF CASH FLOWS

Under Operating Activities
+ Cash from customers
+ Cash from interest and dividends
− Cash to suppliers
− Cash to employees
− Interest paid
− Income taxes paid

NOTES

Under Summary of Significant Accounting Policies
Description of the company's revenue recognition policy.

KEY TERMS

Accrual Basis Accounting p. 108
Cash Basis Accounting p. 108
Expenses p. 106
Gains p. 107

Losses p. 107
Matching Principle p. 112
Operating Cycle (Cash-to-Cash Cycle) p. 103

Revenues p. 104
Revenue Principle p. 109
Time Period Assumption p. 104

QUESTIONS

1. Describe a typical business operating cycle.
2. Explain what the time period assumption means.
3. Write the income statement equation and define each element.
4. Explain the difference between
   a. Revenues and gains.
   b. Expenses and losses.
5. Define *accrual accounting* and contrast it with cash basis accounting.
6. What four conditions must normally be met for revenue to be recognized under accrual basis accounting?
7. Explain the matching principle.
8. Explain why stockholders' equity is increased by revenues and decreased by expenses.
9. Explain why revenues are recorded as credits and expenses as debits.
10. Complete the following matrix by entering either *debit* or *credit* in each cell:

Item	Increase	Decrease
Revenues		
Losses		
Gains		
Expenses		

11. Complete the following matrix by entering either *increase* or *decrease* in each cell:

Item	Debit	Credit
Revenues		
Losses		
Gains		
Expenses		

12. Identify whether the following transactions affect cash flow from operating, investing, or financing activities, and indicate the effect of each on cash (+ for increase and − for decrease). If there is no cash flow effect, write "None":

Transaction	Operating, Investing, or Financing Effect on Cash	Direction of the Effect on Cash
Cash paid to suppliers		
Sale of goods on account		
Cash received from customers		
Purchase of investments		
Cash paid for interest		
Issuance of stock for cash		

13. State the equation for the asset turnover ratio and explain how it is interpreted.

1. Which of the following is *not* a specific account in a company's chart of accounts?
   a. Gains
   b. Net income
   c. Revenue
   d. Unearned Revenue

2. Which of the following is *not* one of the four conditions that normally must be met for revenue to be recognized according to the revenue principle for accrual basis accounting?
   a. The price is determinable.
   b. Services have been performed.
   c. Cash has been collected.
   d. Evidence of an arrangement exists.

3. The matching principle controls
   a. where on the income statement expenses should be presented.
   b. how costs are allocated between Cost of Sales (sometimes called Cost of Goods Sold) and general and administrative expenses.
   c. the ordering of current assets and current liabilities on the balance sheet.
   d. when costs are recognized as expenses on the income statement.

4. You have observed that the asset turnover ratio for a retail chain has increased steadily over the last three years. The *most* likely explanation is which of the following?
   a. A successful advertising campaign increased sales companywide, but no new store locations were added over the last three years.
   b. Salaries for upper management as a percentage of total expenses have decreased over the last three years.
   c. New stores were added throughout the last three years, and sales increased as a result of the additional new locations.
   d. The company began construction of a new, larger main office location three years ago that was put into use at the end of the second year.

5. Cash payments for salaries are reported in what section of the Statement of Cash Flows?
   a. Financing
   b. Operating
   c. Investing
   d. None of the above

6. A company collects $100 cash on an account receivable from a customer for a sale last period. How would the receipt of cash impact the following two financial statements this period?

	Income Statement	Statement of Cash Flows
a.	Revenue + $100	Inflow from investing
b.	No impact	Inflow from financing
c.	Revenue − $100	Inflow from operations
d.	No impact	Inflow from operations

7. When expenses exceed revenues in a given period,
   a. retained earnings is not impacted.
   b. retained earnings is increased.
   c. retained earnings is decreased.
   d. one cannot determine the impact on retained earnings without additional information.

8. Which account is *least* likely to be debited when revenue is recorded?
   a. Accounts Payable
   b. Accounts Receivable
   c. Cash
   d. Unearned Revenue

9. Which is the most likely goal of a business with regard to its operating cycle?
   a. To sustain its current operating cycle
   b. To expand its current operating cycle
   c. To shorten its current operating cycle
   d. To ignore its current operating cycle

10. Which of the following is the entry to be recorded by a law firm when it receives a retainer from a new client at the initial client meeting?
    a. *debit* to Accounts Receivable; *credit* to Sales Revenue
    b. *debit* to Unearned Revenue; *credit* to Sales Revenue
    c. *debit* to Cash; *credit* to Unearned Revenue
    d. *debit* to Unearned Revenue; *credit* to Cash

For more practice with multiple choice questions, go to our website at www.mhhe.com/libby4e, click on "Student Center" in the upper left menu, click on this chapter's name and number from the list of contents, and then click on "Multiple Choice Quiz" from the menu on the left.

MINI-EXERCISES

M3-1
LO1, 2, 4

Matching Definitions with Terms

Match each definition with its related term by entering the appropriate letter in the space provided. There should be only one definition per term (that is, there are more definitions than terms).

Term	Definition
___ (1) Losses	A. Decreases in assets or increases in liabilities from ongoing operations.
___ (2) Matching principle	B. Record revenues when earned and measurable (delivery of goods or services has been performed, there is persuasive evidence of an arrangement, the price is fixed or determinable, and collection is reasonably assured).
___ (3) Revenues	
___ (4) Time period assumption	
___ (5) Operating cycle	C. Report the long life of a company in shorter time periods.
	D. Record expenses when incurred in earning revenue.
	E. The time it takes to purchase goods or services from suppliers, sell goods or services to customers, and collect cash from customers.
	F. Decreases in assets or increases in liabilities from peripheral transactions.
	G. Increases in assets or decreases in liabilities from ongoing operations.

M3-2
LO3

Computing and Explaining the Total Asset Turnover Ratio

The following data are from annual reports of Justin's Jewelry Company

	2005	2004	2003
Total assets	$ 60,000	$ 50,000	$ 40,000
Total liabilities	12,000	10,000	5,000
Total stockholders' equity	48,000	40,000	35,000
Sales	154,000	144,000	130,000
Net income	50,000	38,000	25,000

Compute Justin's total asset turnover ratio for 2004 and 2005. What do these results suggest to you about Justin's Jewelry Company?

M3-3
LO2, 4

Reporting Cash Basis versus Accrual Basis Income

Mostert Music Company had the following transactions in March:

a. Sold instruments to customers for $10,000; received $6,000 in cash and the rest on account. The cost of the instruments was $7,000.

b. Purchased $4,000 of new instruments inventory; paid $1,000 in cash and owed the rest on account.

c. Paid $600 in wages for the month.

d. Received a $200 bill for utilities that will be paid in April.

e. Received $1,000 from customers as deposits on orders of new instruments to be sold to the customers in April.

Complete the following statements:

Cash Basis Income Statement		Accrual Basis Income Statement	
Revenues		Revenues	
Cash sales		Sales to customers	
Customer deposits			
Expenses		Expenses	
Inventory purchases		Cost of sales	
Wages paid		Wages expense	
	_____	Utilities expense	_____
Net income	=======	Net income	=======

Identifying Revenues

M3-4
LO2, 4

The following transactions are July 2004 activities of Bob's Bowling, Inc., which operates several bowling centers (for games and equipment sales). If revenue is to be recognized in July, indicate the revenue account title and amount. If revenue is not to be recognized in July, explain why.

Activity	Revenue Account Title and Amount
a. Bob's collected $10,000 from customers for games played in July.	
b. Bob's sold bowling equipment inventory for $5,000; received $3,000 in cash and the rest on account. [Ignore inventory cost.]	
c. Bob's received $1,000 from customers on account who purchased merchandise in June.	
d. The men's and ladies' bowling leagues gave Bob's a deposit of $1,500 for the upcoming fall season.	

Identifying Expenses

M3-5
LO2, 4

The following transactions are July 2004 activities of Bob's Bowling, Inc., which operates several bowling centers (for games and equipment sales). If expense is to be recognized in July, indicate the expense account title and amount. If expense is not to be recognized in July, explain why.

Activity	Expense Account Title and Amount
e. Bob's sold bowling merchandise costing $2,000.	
f. Bob's paid $2,000 for the June electricity bill and received the July bill for $2,200, which will be paid in August.	
g. Bob's paid $4,000 to employees for work in July.	
h. Bob's purchased $1,200 in insurance for coverage from July 1 to October 1.	
i. Bob's paid $1,000 to plumbers for repairing a broken pipe in the restrooms.	

Recording Revenues

M3-6
LO5

For each of the transactions in M3-4, write the journal entry in good form.

Recording Expenses

M3-7
LO5

For each of the transactions in M3-5, write the journal entry in good form.

M3-8 **Determining the Financial Statement Effects of Operating Activities Involving Revenues**

L05

The following transactions are July 2004 activities of Bob's Bowling, Inc., which operates several bowling centers (for games and equipment sales). For each of the following transactions, complete the tabulation, indicating the amount and effect (+ for increase and − for decrease) of each transaction. (Remember that A = L + SE, R − E = NI, and NI affects SE through Retained Earnings.) Write NE if there is no effect. The first transaction is provided as an example.

	BALANCE SHEET			INCOME STATEMENT		
Transaction	**Assets**	**Liabil-ities**	**Stock-holders' Equity**	**Revenues**	**Expenses**	**Net Income**
a. Bob's collected $10,000 from customers for games played in July.	+10,000	NE	+10,000	+10,000	NE	+10,000
b. Bob's sold $5,000 in bowling equipment inventory; received $3,000 in cash and the rest on account. [Ignore inventory cost.]						
c. Bob's received $1,000 from customers on account who purchased merchandise in June.						
d. The men's and ladies' bowling leagues gave Bob's a deposit of $1,500 for the upcoming fall season.						

M3-9 **Determining the Financial Statement Effects of Operating Activities Involving Expenses**

L05

The following transactions are July 2004 activities of Bob's Bowling, Inc., which operates several bowling centers (for games and equipment sales). For each of the following transactions, complete the tabulation, indicating the amount and effect (+ for increase and − for decrease) of each transaction. (Remember that A = L + SE, R − E = NI, and NI affects SE through retained earnings.) Write NE if there is no effect. The first transaction is provided as an example.

	BALANCE SHEET			INCOME STATEMENT		
Transaction	**Assets**	**Liabil-ities**	**Stock-holders' Equity**	**Revenues**	**Expenses**	**Net Income**
e. Bob's sold bowling merchandise costing $2,000.	−2,000	NE	−2,000	NE	+2,000	−2,000
f. Bob's paid $2,000 for the June electricity bill and received the July bill for $2,200 to be paid in August.						
g. Bob's paid $4,000 to employees for work in July.						
h. Bob's purchased $1,200 in insurance for coverage from July 1 to October 1.						
i. Bob's paid $1,000 to plumbers for repairing a broken pipe in the restrooms.						

Preparing a Simple Income Statement

Given the transactions in M3-8 and M3-9 (including the examples), prepare an income statement for Bob's Bowling, Inc., for the month of July 2004.

M3-10
LO6

Preparing the Operating Activities Section of a Statement of Cash Flows

Given the transactions in M3-8 and M3-9 (including the examples), prepare the operating activities section of the statement of cash flows for Bob's Bowling, Inc., for the month of July 2004.

M3-11
LO6

EXERCISES

Matching Definitions with Terms

Match each definition with its related term by entering the appropriate letter in the space provided. There should be only one definition per term (that is, there are more definitions than terms).

E3-1
LO1, 2, 4

Term	Definition
___ (1) Expenses	A. Report the long life of a company in shorter periods.
___ (2) Gains	B. Record expenses when incurred in earning revenue.
___ (3) Revenue principle	C. The time it takes to purchase goods or services from suppliers, sell goods or services to customers, and collect cash from customers.
___ (4) Cash basis accounting	
___ (5) Unearned revenue	
___ (6) Operating cycle	D. A liability account used to record cash received before revenues have been earned
___ (7) Accrual basis accounting	E. Increases in assets or decreases in liabilities from peripheral transactions.
___ (8) Prepaid expenses	
___ (9) Revenues − Expenses = Net Income	F. Decreases in assets or increases in liabilities from ongoing operations.
___ (10) Ending Retained Earnings = Beginning Retained Earnings + Net Income − Dividends	G. Record revenues when earned and measurable (delivery of goods or services has occurred, there is persuasive evidence of an arrangement for customer payment, the price is fixed or determinable, and collection is reasonably assured.)
	H. Decreases in assets or increases in liabilities from peripheral transactions.
	I. Record revenues when received and expenses when paid.
	J. The income statement equation.
	K. An asset account used to record cash paid before expenses have been incurred.
	L. The retained earnings equation.
	M. Record revenues when earned and expenses when incurred.

Identifying Revenues

Revenues are normally recognized when the delivery of goods or services has occurred, there is persuasive evidence of an arrangement, the price is fixed or determinable, and collection is reasonably assured. The amount recorded is the cash-equivalent sales price. The following transactions occurred in September 2003:

E3-2
LO2, 4

a. A customer orders and receives 10 personal computers from Gateway 2000; the customer promises to pay $25,000 within three months. Answer from Gateway's standpoint.

b. Sam Shell Dodge sells a truck with a list, or "sticker," price of $24,000 for $21,000 cash.

c. Hudson's Department Store orders 1,000 men's shirts from Arrow Shirt Company for $18 each for future delivery. The terms require payment in full within 30 days of delivery. Answer from Arrow's standpoint.

d. Arrow Shirt Company completes production of the shirts described in (c) and delivers the order. Answer from Arrow's standpoint.

e. Arrow receives payment from Hudson's for the order described in (c). Answer from Arrow's standpoint.

f. A customer purchases a ticket from American Airlines for $500 cash to travel the following January. Answer from American Airlines' standpoint.

g. General Motors issues $26 million in new common stock.

h. Penn State University receives $20,000,000 cash for 80,000 five-game season football tickets.

i. Penn State plays the first football game referred to in (h).

j. Hall Construction Company signs a contract with a customer for the construction of a new $500,000 warehouse. At the signing, Hall receives a check for $50,000 as a deposit on the future construction. Answer from Hall's standpoint.

k. On September 1, 2003, a bank lends $1,000 to a company; the note principal and 12 percent annual interest are due in one year. Answer from the bank's standpoint.

l. A popular ski magazine company receives a total of $1,800 today from subscribers. The subscriptions begin in the next fiscal year. Answer from the magazine company's standpoint.

m. Sears, a retail store, sells a $100 lamp to a customer who charges the sale on his store credit card. Answer from the standpoint of Sears.

Required:

For each of the transactions, if revenue is to be recognized in September, indicate the revenue account title and amount. If revenue is not to be recognized in September, explain why.

E3-3   Identifying Expenses
L02, 4

Revenues are normally recognized when goods or services have been provided and payment or promise of payment has been received. Expense recognition is guided by an attempt to match the costs associated with the generation of those revenues to the same time period. The following transactions occurred in January 2003:

a. Gateway 2000 pays its computer service technicians $90,000 in salaries for the two weeks ended January 7. Answer from Gateway's standpoint.

b. At the beginning of January, Turner Construction Company pays $4,500 in worker's compensation insurance for the first three months of the year.

c. McGraw-Hill Publishing Company uses $1,000 worth of electricity and natural gas in its headquarters building for which it has not yet been billed.

d. Arrow Shirt Company completes production of 500 men's shirts ordered by Bon Ton's Department Store at a cost of $9 each and delivers the order. Answer from Arrow's standpoint.

e. The campus bookstore receives 500 accounting texts at a cost of $50 each. The terms indicate that payment is due within 30 days of delivery.

f. During the last week of January, the campus bookstore sold 450 accounting texts received in (e) at a sales price of $80 each.

g. Sam Shell Dodge pays its salespersons $3,500 in commissions related to December automobile sales. Answer from Sam Shell Dodge's standpoint.

h. On January 31, Sam Shell Dodge determines that it will pay its salespersons $4,200 in commissions related to January sales. The payment will be made in early February. Answer from Sam Shell Dodge's standpoint.

i. A new grill is purchased and installed at a McDonald's restaurant at the end of the day on January 31; a $12,000 cash payment is made on that day.

j. The University of Florida orders 60,000 season football tickets from its printer and pays $6,000 in advance for the custom printing. The first game will be played in September. Answer from the university's standpoint.

k. Carousel Mall had janitorial supplies costing $1,000 in storage. An additional $600 worth of supplies was purchased during January. At the end of January, $900 worth of janitorial supplies remained in storage.

l. An Iowa State University employee works eight hours, at $15 per hour, on January 31; however, payday is not until February 3. Answer from the university's point of view.

m. Wang Company paid $3,600 for a fire insurance policy on January 1. The policy covers 12 months beginning on January 1. Answer from Wang's point of view.

n. Amber Incorporated has its delivery van repaired in January for $280 and charges the amount on account.

o. Ziegler Company, a farm equipment company, receives its phone bill at the end of January for $230 for January calls. The bill has not been paid to date.

p. Spina Company receives and pays in January a $1,500 invoice from a consulting firm for services received in January.

q. Felicetti's Taxi Company pays a $600 invoice from a consulting firm for services received and recorded in December.

Required:
For each of the transactions, if an expense is to be recognized in January, indicate the expense account title and the amount. If an expense is not to be recognized in January, indicate why.

Determining Financial Statement Effects of Various Transactions

E3-4
LO5

The following transactions occurred during a recent year:

a. Issued stock to organizers for cash (example).
b. Borrowed cash from local bank.
c. Purchased equipment on credit.
d. Earned revenue, collected cash.
e. Incurred expenses, on credit.
f. Earned revenue, on credit.
g. Paid cash on account.
h. Incurred expenses, paid cash.
i. Earned revenue, collected three-fourths in cash, balance on credit.
j. Experienced theft of $100 cash.
k. Declared and paid cash dividends.
l. Collected cash from customers on account.
m. Incurred expenses, paid four-fifths in cash, balance on credit.
n. Paid income tax expense for the period.

Required:
For each of the transactions, complete the tabulation, indicating the effect (+ for increase and − for decrease) of each transaction. (Remember that A = L + SE, R − E = NI, and NI affects SE through Retained Earnings.) Write NE if there is no effect. The first transaction is provided as an example.

	BALANCE SHEET			INCOME STATEMENT		
Transaction	**Assets**	**Liabilities**	**Stockholders' Equity**	**Revenues**	**Expenses**	**Net Income**
(a) (example)	+	NE	+	NE	NE	NE

Determining Financial Statement Effects of Various Transactions

E3-5
LO5
Wolverine World Wide, Inc.

Wolverine World Wide, Inc., manufactures military, work, sport, and casual footwear and leather accessories under a variety of brand names, such as Hush Puppies, Wolverine, and Bates, to a global market. The following transactions occurred during a recent year. Dollars are in thousands.

a. Issued common stock to investors for $48,869 cash (example).
b. Purchased $299,794 of additional raw materials inventory on account.
c. Borrowed $58,181 on long-term notes.
d. Sold $413,957 of products to customers on account; cost of the products sold was $290,469.
e. Paid cash dividends of $2,347.
f. Purchased $18,645 in additional property, plant, and equipment.
g. Incurred $85,993 in selling expenses, paying two-thirds in cash and owing the rest on account.
h. Earned $1,039 interest on investments, receiving 90 percent in cash.
i. Incurred $4,717 in interest expense to be paid at the beginning of next year.

Required:

For each of the transactions, complete the tabulation, indicating the effect (+ for increase and − for decrease) of each transaction. (Remember that A = L + SE, R − E = NI, and NI affects SE through Retained Earnings.) Write NE if there is no effect. The first transaction is provided as an example.

	BALANCE SHEET			INCOME STATEMENT		
Transaction	**Assets**	**Liabil-ities**	**Stock-holders' Equity**	**Revenues**	**Expenses**	**Net Income**
(*a*) (example)	+48,869	NE	+48,869	NE	NE	NE

E3-6 Recording Journal Entries

LO5

Sysco

Sysco, formed in 1969, is America's largest marketer and distributor of food service products, serving nearly 250,000 restaurants, hotels, schools, hospitals, and other institutions. The following summarized transactions are typical of those that occurred in a recent year.

a. Borrowed $80 million from a bank, signing a short-term note.
b. Provided $10.02 billion in service to customers during the year, with $9.5 billion on account and the rest received in cash.
c. Purchased plant and equipment for $127.9 million in cash.
d. Purchased $8.268 billion inventory on account.
e. Paid payroll, $1.02 billion during the year.
f. Received $410 million on account paid by customers.
g. Purchased and used fuel of $400 million in delivery vehicles during the year (paid for in cash).
h. Declared and paid $48.8 million in dividends for the year.
i. Paid $8.2 billion cash on accounts payable.
j. Incurred $20 million in utility usage during the year; paid $15 million in cash and owed the rest on account.

Required:

For each of the transactions, prepare journal entries. Determine whether the accounting equation remains in balance and debits equal credits after each entry.

E3-7 Recording Journal Entries

LO5

Greek Peak

Greek Peak Incorporated is a ski resort in upstate New York. The company sells lift tickets, ski lessons, and ski equipment. It operates several restaurants and rents townhouses to vacationing skiers. The following hypothetical December transactions are typical of those that occur at the resort.

a. Borrowed $500,000 from the bank on December 1, signing a note payable due in six months.
b. Purchased a new snow plow for $20,000 cash on December 31.
c. Purchased ski equipment inventory for $10,000 on account to sell in the ski shop.
d. Incurred $22,000 in routine maintenance expenses for the chair lifts; paid cash.
e. Sold $72,000 of season passes and received cash.
f. Sold daily lift passes for a total of $76,000 in cash.
g. Sold a pair of skis from the ski shop to a customer for $350 on account. (The cost of the skis was $250.)
h. Received a $320 deposit on a townhouse to be rented for five days in January.
i. Paid half the charges incurred on account in (*c*).
j. Received $200 on account from the customer in (*g*).
k. Paid $108,000 in wages to employees for the month of December.

Required:

1. Prepare journal entries for each transaction. (Remember to check that debits equal credits and that the accounting equation is in balance after each transaction.)
2. Assume that Greek Peak had a $1,200 balance in Accounts Receivable at the beginning of December. Determine the ending balance in the Accounts Receivable account at the end of December based on transactions (*a*) through (*k*). Show your work in T-account format.

Recording Journal Entries

Rowland & Sons Air Transport Service, Inc., has been in operation for three years. The following transactions occurred in February:

February 1	Paid $200 for rent of hangar space in February.
February 2	Purchased fuel costing $450 on account for the next flight to Dallas.
February 4	Received customer payment of $800 to ship several items to Philadelphia next month.
February 7	Flew cargo from Denver to Dallas; the customer paid $900 for the air transport.
February 10	Paid pilot $1,200 in wages for flying in January.
February 14	Paid $60 for an advertisement in the local paper to run on February 19.
February 18	Flew cargo for two customers from Dallas to Albuquerque for $1,700; one customer paid $500 cash and the other asked to be billed.
February 25	Purchased on account $1,350 in spare parts for the planes.
February 27	Declared a $200 cash dividend to be paid in March.

Required:
Prepare journal entries for each transaction. Be sure to categorize each account as an asset (A), liability (L), stockholders' equity (SE), revenue (R), or expense (E).

Analyzing the Effects of Transactions in T-Accounts and Computing Cash Basis versus Accrual Basis Net Income

Kline's Piano Rebuilding Company has been operating for one year (2003). At the start of 2004, its income statement accounts had zero balances and its balance sheet account balances were as follows:

Cash	$ 6,000	Accounts payable	8,000
Accounts receivable	25,000	Unearned fee revenue (deposits)	3,200
Supplies	1,200	Note payable	40,000
Equipment	8,000	Contributed capital	8,000
Land	6,000	Retained earnings	9,000
Building	22,000		

Required:
1. Create T-accounts for the balance sheet accounts and for these additional accounts: Rebuilding Fees Revenue, Rent Revenue, Wages Expense, and Utilities Expense. Enter the beginning balances.
2. Enter the following January 2004 transactions in the T-accounts, using the letter of each transaction as the reference:
   a. Received a $500 deposit from a customer who wanted her piano rebuilt.
   b. Rented a part of the building to a bicycle repair shop; received $300 for rent in January.
   c. Delivered five rebuilt pianos to customers who paid $14,500 in cash.
   d. Received $6,000 from customers as payment on their accounts.
   e. Received an electric and gas utility bill for $350 to be paid in February.
   f. Ordered $800 in supplies.
   g. Paid $1,700 on account in January.
   h. Received from the home of Ms. Kline, the major shareholder, a $600 tool (equipment) to use in the business.
   i. Paid $10,000 in wages to employees in January.
   j. Declared and paid a $3,000 dividend.
   k. Received and paid cash for the supplies in (f).
3. Using the data from the T-accounts, amounts for the following on January 31, 2004, were

   Revenues, $_____ − Expenses, $_____ = Net Income, $_____
   Assets, $_____ = Liabilities, $_____ + Stockholders' Equity, $_____
4. What is net income if Kline used the cash basis of accounting? Why does this differ from accrual basis net income (in requirement 3)?

Preparing an Income Statement, Statement of Retained Earnings, and Classified Balance Sheet

Refer to E3-9.

Required:

Use the ending balances in the T-accounts in E3-9 to prepare the following:

1. An unadjusted income statement for January 2004 in good form.
2. An unadjusted statement of retained earnings for January 2004.
3. An unadjusted classified balance sheet as of January 31, 2004, in good form.

E3-11
LO6

Preparing a Statement of Cash Flows

Refer to E3-9.

Required:

Use the transactions in E3-9 to prepare a statement of cash flows in good form.

E3-12
LO5

Analyzing the Effects of Transactions in T-Accounts

Karen Gorewit and Pat Nally had been operating a catering business, Traveling Gourmet, for several years. In March 2005, the partners were planning to expand by opening a retail sales shop and decided to form the business as a corporation called Traveling Gourmet, Inc. The following transactions occurred in March 2005:

a. Received $10,000 cash from each of the two shareholders to form the corporation, in addition to $2,000 in accounts receivable, $5,300 in equipment, a van (equipment) appraised at a fair market value of $13,000, and $1,200 in supplies.
b. Purchased a vacant store for sale in a good location for $60,000 with a $9,000 cash down payment and a mortgage from a local bank for the rest.
c. Borrowed $25,000 from the local bank on a 10 percent, one-year note.
d. Purchased and used food and paper supplies costing $8,830 in March; paid cash.
e. Made and sold food at the retail store for $10,900 cash.
f. Catered four parties in March for $3,200; $1,500 was billed, and the rest was received in cash.
g. Received a $320 telephone bill for March to be paid in April.
h. Paid $63 in gas for the van in March.
i. Paid $5,080 in wages to employees who worked in March.
j. Paid a $300 dividend from the corporation to each owner.
k. Purchased $15,000 of equipment (refrigerated display cases, cabinets, tables, and chairs) and renovated and decorated the new store for $10,000 (added to the cost of the building).

Required:

1. Set up appropriate T-accounts for Cash, Accounts Receivable, Supplies, Equipment, Building, Accounts Payable, Note Payable, Mortgage Payable, Contributed Capital, Retained Earnings, Food Sales Revenue, Catering Sales Revenue, Cost of Food and Paper Products, Utilities Expense, Wages Expense, and Fuel Expense.
2. Record in the T-accounts the effects of each transaction for Traveling Gourmet, Inc., in March. Identify the amounts with the letters starting with (a). Compute ending balances.

E3-13
LO6

Preparing an Income Statement, Statement of Retained Earnings, and Classified Balance Sheet

Refer to E3-12.

Required:

Use the balances in the completed T-accounts in E3-12 to respond to the following:

1. Prepare an unadjusted income statement in good form for the month of March 2005.
2. Prepare an unadjusted statement of retained earnings for the month of March 2005.
3. Prepare an unadjusted classified balance sheet in good form as of March 2005.
4. What do you think about the success of this company based on the results of the first month of operation?

E3-14
LO6

Preparing a Statement of Cash Flows

Refer to E3-12.

Required:
Use the transactions in E3-12 to prepare a statement of cash flows in good form.

Inferring Operating Transactions and Preparing an Income Statement and Balance Sheet

E3-15
LO2, 4, 5, 6

Kim's Kite Company (a corporation) sells and repairs kites from manufacturers around the world. Its stores are located in rented space in malls and shopping centers. During its first month of operations ended April 30, 2004, Kim's Kite Company completed eight transactions with the dollar effects indicated in the following schedule:

Accounts	(a)	(b)	(c)	(d)	(e)	(f)	(g)	(h)	Ending Balance
Cash	$50,000	$(10,000)	$(5,000)	$ 7,000	$(2,000)	$(1,000)		$3,000	
Accounts receivable				3,000					
Inventory			20,000	(3,000)					
Prepaid expenses					1,500				
Store fixtures		10,000							
Accounts payable			15,000				$1,200		
Unearned revenue								2,000	
Contributed capital	50,000								
Sales revenue				10,000				1,000	
Cost of sales				3,000					
Wages expense						1,000			
Rent expense					500				
Utilities expense							1,200		

Required:
1. Write a brief explanation of Transactions (*a*) through (*h*). Include any assumptions that you made.
2. Compute the ending balance in each account and prepare an income statement and a classified balance sheet for Kim's Kite Company on April 30, 2004.

Analyzing the Effects of Transactions Using T-Accounts and Interpreting the Total Asset Turnover Ratio as a Financial Analyst

E3-16
LO3, 5

DeVita Company, which has been operating for three years, provides marketing consulting services worldwide for dot.com companies. You are a financial analyst assigned to report on the DeVita management team's effectiveness at managing its assets efficiently. At the start of 2003 (its fourth year), DeVita's T-account balances were as follows. Dollars are in thousands.

Assets

Cash		Accounts Receivable		Long-Term Investments	
4,000		10,000		8,000	

Liabilities

Accounts Payable		Unearned Revenue		Long-Term Notes Payable	
	3,000		7,000		2,000

Stockholders' Equity

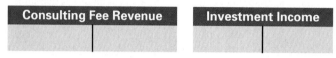

Contributed Capital		Retained Earnings	
	6,000		4,000

Revenues

Consulting Fee Revenue		Investment Income	

Expenses

Wages Expense		Travel Expense		Utilities Expense		Rent Expense	

Required:

1. Using the data from these T-accounts, amounts for the following on January 1, 2003, were

   Assets $_____ = Liabilities $_____ + Stockholders' Equity $_____.

2. Enter the following 2003 transactions in the T-accounts:

   a. Received $7,000 cash from clients on account.

   b. Provided $70,000 in services to clients who paid $60,000 in cash and owed the rest on account.

   c. Received $500 in cash as income on investments.

   d. Paid $20,000 in wages, $20,000 in travel, $12,000 rent, and $2,000 on accounts payable.

   e. Received a utility bill for $1,000.

   f. Paid $600 in dividends to stockholders.

   g. Received $2,000 in cash from clients in advance of services DeVita will provide next year.

3. Compute ending balances in the T-accounts to determine amounts for the following on December 31, 2003:

   Revenues $_____ − Expenses $_____ = Net Income $_____.
   Assets $_____ = Liabilities $_____ + Stockholders' Equity $_____.

4. Calculate the total asset turnover ratio for 2003. If the company had an asset turnover ratio in 2002 of 2.00 and in 2001 of 1.80, what does your computation suggest to you about DeVita Company? What would you say in your report?

E3-17

LO5

Dow Jones & Company

Inferring Transactions and Computing Effects Using T-Accounts

A recent annual report of Dow Jones & Company, the world leader in business and financial news and information (and publisher of *The Wall Street Journal*), included the following accounts. Dollars are in millions:

Accounts Receivable				Prepaid Expenses				Unearned Revenue			
1/1	313			1/1	25					240	1/1
	2,573	?			43	?			?	328	
12/31	295			12/31	26					253	12/31

Required:

1. For each T-account, describe the typical transactions that affect each account (that is, the economic events that occur to make these accounts increase and decrease).

2. For each T-account, compute the missing amounts.

E3-18

Finding Financial Information as an Investor

You are evaluating your current portfolio of investments to determine those that are not performing to your expectations. You have all of the companies' most recent annual reports.

Required:

For each of the following, indicate where you would locate the information in an annual report. (*Hint:* The information may be in more than one location.)

1. Description of a company's primary business(es).
2. Income taxes paid.
3. Accounts receivable.
4. Cash flow from operating activities.
5. Description of a company's revenue recognition policy.
6. The inventory sold during the year.
7. The data needed to compute the total asset turnover ratio.

PROBLEMS

Recording Nonquantitative Journal Entries (AP3-1)

P3-1
LO5

The following list includes a series of accounts for Norton Corporation that has been operating for three years. These accounts are listed and numbered for identification. Following the accounts is a series of transactions. For each transaction, indicate the account(s) that should be debited and credited by entering the appropriate account number(s) to the right of each transaction. If no journal entry is needed, use number 16. The first transaction is used as an example.

Account No.	Account Title	Account No.	Account Title
1	Cash	9	Wages payable
2	Accounts receivable	10	Income taxes payable
3	Supplies on hand	11	Contributed capital
4	Prepaid expense	12	Retained earnings
5	Equipment	13	Service revenue
6	Patents	14	Operating expenses (wages, supplies, interest)
7	Accounts payable	15	Income tax expense
8	Note payable	16	None of the above

Transactions	Debit	Credit
a. Example: Purchased equipment for use in the business; paid one-third cash and signed a note payable for the balance.	5	1, 8
b. Issued stock to new investors.		
c. Paid cash for salaries and wages.		
d. Collected cash for services performed this period.		
e. Collected cash on accounts receivable for services performed last period.		
f. Performed services this period on credit.		
g. Paid operating expenses incurred this period.		
h. Paid cash on accounts payable for expenses incurred last period.		
i. Incurred operating expenses this period to be paid next period.		
j. Purchased supplies to be used later; paid cash.		
k. Used some of the supplies inventory for operations.		
l. Purchased a patent (an intangible asset); paid cash.		
m. Made a payment on the equipment note in (a); the payment was part principal and part interest expense.		
n. Paid three-fourths of the income tax expense for the year; the balance will be paid next year.		
o. On the last day of the current period, paid cash for an insurance policy covering the next two years.		

Recording Journal Entries (AP3-2)

P3-2
LO5

Charles Badurski organized a new company, CollegeCaps, Inc. The company operates a small store in an area mall and specializes in baseball-type caps with logos printed on them. Charles, who is never without a cap, believes that his target market is college and high school students. You have been hired to record the transactions occurring in the first two weeks of operations.

May 1	Issued 1,000 shares of stock to investors for $30 per share.
May 1	Borrowed $50,000 from the bank to provide additional funding to begin operations; the note is due in two years.
May 1	Paid $1,200 for the current month's rent and another $1,200 for next month's rent.
May 1	Paid $2,400 for a one-year fire insurance policy (recorded as a prepaid expense).
May 3	Purchased furniture and fixtures for the store for $15,000 on account. The amount is due within 30 days.
May 4	Purchased a supply of The University of Texas, Southern Methodist University, and Michigan State University baseball caps for the store for $1,800 cash.
May 5	Placed advertisements in local college newspapers for a total of $250 cash.
May 9	Sold caps totaling $400, half of which was charged on account. The cost of the caps sold was $150.
May 10	Made full payment for the furniture and fixtures purchased on account on May 3.
May 14	Received $50 from a customer on account.

Required:

For each of the transactions, prepare journal entries. Be sure to categorize each account as an asset (A), liability (L), stockholders' equity (SE), revenue (R), or expense (E).

P3-3
LO5, 6

Wendy's
International, Inc.

Determining Financial Statement Effects of Various Transactions and Identifying Cash Flow Effects (AP3-3)

According to its annual report, Wendy's serves "the best hamburgers in the business" and other fresh food including salads, chicken sandwiches, and baked potatoes in more than 4,000 restaurants worldwide. The following activities were inferred from a recent annual report.

a. Purchased additional investments.
b. Served food to customers for cash.
c. Used food and paper products.
d. Paid cash dividends.
e. Incurred restaurant operating costs in company-owned facilities; paid part in cash and the rest on account.
f. Sold franchises, receiving part in cash and the rest in notes due from franchisees.
g. Paid interest on debt.
h. Purchased food and paper products; paid part in cash and the rest on account.

Required:

1. For each of the transactions, complete the tabulation, indicating the effect (+ for increase and − for decrease) of each transaction. (Remember that A = L + SE, R − E = NI, and NI affects SE through Retained Earnings.) Write NE if there is no effect. The first transaction is provided as an example.

	BALANCE SHEET			INCOME STATEMENT		
Transaction	**Assets**	**Liabil-ities**	**Stock-holders' Equity**	**Revenues**	**Expenses**	**Net Income**
(*a*) (example)	+/−	NE	NE	NE	NE	NE

2. Where, if at all, would each transaction be reported on the statement of cash flows? Use O for operating activities, I for investing activities, F for financing activities, and NE if the transaction would not be included on the statement.

P3-4
LO3, 5, 6

Analyzing the Effects of Transactions Using T-Accounts, Preparing Unadjusted Financial Statements, and Evaluating the Total Asset Turnover Ratio as a Manager (AP3-4)

Jenna Wohlwend, a connoisseur of fine chocolate, opened Jenna's Sweets in Collegetown on February 1, 2003. The shop specializes in a selection of gourmet chocolate candies and a line of gourmet ice cream. You have been hired as manager. Your duties include maintaining the store's financial records. The following transactions occurred in February 2003, the first month of operations.

a. Received four shareholders' contributions totaling $16,000 cash to form the corporation; issued stock.
b. Paid three months' rent for the store at $800 per month (recorded as prepaid expenses).
c. Purchased supplies for $300 cash.
d. Purchased and received candy for $5,000 on account, due in 60 days.
e. Negotiated a two-year $10,000 loan at the bank.
f. Used the money from (e) to purchase a computer for $2,500 (for recordkeeping and inventory tracking) and the balance for furniture and fixtures for the store.
g. Placed a grand opening advertisement in the local paper for $425 cash.
h. Made sales on Valentine's Day totaling $1,800; $1,525 was in cash and the rest on accounts receivable. The cost of the candy sold was $1,000.
i. Made a $500 payment on accounts payable.
j. Incurred and paid employee wages of $420.
k. Collected accounts receivable of $50 from customers.
l. Made a repair to one of the display cases for $118 cash.
m. Made cash sales of $2,000 during the rest of the month. The cost of the goods sold was $1,100.

Required:
1. Set up appropriate T-accounts for Cash, Accounts Receivable, Supplies, Merchandise Inventory, Prepaid Expenses, Equipment, Furniture and Fixtures, Accounts Payable, Notes Payable, Contributed Capital, Sales Revenue, Cost of Goods Sold (Expense), Advertising Expense, Wage Expense, and Repair Expense. All accounts begin with zero balances.
2. Record in the T-accounts the effects of each transaction for Jenna's Sweets in February, referencing each transaction in the accounts with the transaction letter. Show the unadjusted ending balances in the T-accounts.
3. Prepare unadjusted financial statements at the end of February (income statement, statement of retained earnings, and balance sheet).
4. Write a short memo to Jenna offering your opinion on the results of operations during the first month of business.
5. After three years in business, you are being evaluated for a promotion. One measure is how efficiently you managed the assets of the business. The following data are available:

	2005*	2004	2003
Total assets	$80,000	$45,000	$35,000
Total liabilities	45,000	20,000	15,000
Total stockholders' equity	35,000	25,000	20,000
Total sales	85,000	75,000	50,000
Net income	20,000	10,000	4,000

*At the end of 2005, Jenna decided to open a second store, requiring loans and inventory purchases prior to the opening in early 2006.

Compute the total asset turnover ratio for 2004 and 2005 and evaluate the results. Do you think you should be promoted? Why?

Preparing a Statement of Cash Flows (AP3-5)

Refer to P3-4.

Required:
For the transactions listed in P3-4, prepare a statement of cash flows for the month.

Analyzing the Effects of Transactions Using T-Accounts, Preparing Unadjusted Financial Statements, and Evaluating the Total Asset Turnover Ratio (AP3-6)

The following are several account balances (in millions of dollars) from a recent annual report of Federal Express Corporation, followed by several typical transactions. The business is described in the annual report as follows:

P3-5
L06

P3-6
L03, 5, 6
Federal Express

Federal Express Corporation offers a wide range of express services for the time-definite transportation of goods and documents throughout the world using an extensive fleet of aircraft and vehicles and leading-edge information technologies.

Assume that the following account balances are on June 30, 2003:

Account	Balance	Account	Balance
Flight and ground equipment	$3,476	Contributed capital	$ 702
Retained earnings	970	Receivables	923
Accounts payable	554	Other assets	1,011
Prepaid expenses	64	Cash	155
Accrued expenses payable	761	Spare parts, supplies, and fuel	164
Long-term notes payable	2,016	Other noncurrent liabilities	790

These accounts are not necessarily in good order and have normal debit or credit balances. The following transactions (in millions of dollars) occurred the next year ending June 30, 2004:

a. Provided delivery service to customers, receiving $7,200 in accounts receivable and $600 in cash.
b. Purchased new equipment costing $816; signed a long-term note.
c. Paid $744 cash to rent equipment and aircraft, with $648 for rental this month and the rest for rent next month.
d. Spent $396 cash to maintain and repair facilities and equipment during the month.
e. Collected $6,524 from customers on account.
f. Borrowed $900 by signing a long-term note.
g. Issued additional stock for $240.
h. Paid employees $3,804 during the month.
i. Purchased for cash and used $492 in fuel for the aircraft and equipment.
j. Paid $384 on accounts payable.
k. Ordered $72 in spare parts and supplies.

Required:
1. Prepare T-accounts for June 30, 2003, from the preceding list; enter the respective balances. You will need additional T-accounts for income statement accounts; enter $0 balances.
2. For each transaction, record the effects in the T-accounts. Label each using the letter of the transaction. Compute ending balances.
3. Prepare an unadjusted income statement, unadjusted statement of retained earnings, unadjusted balance sheet, and statement of cash flows in good form.
4. Based on the unadjusted amounts, compute the company's total asset turnover ratio. What does it suggest to you about Federal Express?

P3-7

L05

Cedar Fair

Recording Journal Entries and Identifying Cash Flow Effects

Cedar Fair, L. P. (Limited Partnership), owns and operates four seasonal amusement parks: Cedar Point in Ohio, Valleyfair near Minneapolis/St. Paul, Dorney Park and Wildwater Kingdom near Allentown, Pennsylvania, and Worlds of Fun/Oceans of Fun in Kansas City. The following are summarized transactions similar to those that occurred in a recent year (assume 2003):

a. Guests at the parks paid $89,664,000 cash in admissions.
b. The primary operating expenses (such as employee wages, utilities, and repairs and maintenance) for the year were $66,347,000 with $60,200,000 paid in cash and the rest on account.
c. Interest paid on long-term debt was $6,601,000.
d. The parks sell food and merchandise and operate games. The cash received during the year for these combined activities was $77,934,000.
e. The cost of products sold for cash during the year was $19,525,000.
f. Cedar Fair purchased and built additional buildings, rides, and equipment during the year, paying $23,813,000 in cash.

g. The most significant assets for the company are land, buildings, rides, and equipment. Therefore, a large expense for Cedar Fair is depreciation expense (related to using these assets to generate revenues during the year). For the year, the amount was $14,473,000 (credit Accumulated Depreciation).

h. Guests may stay in the parks at accommodations owned by the company. During the year, Accommodations Revenue was $11,345,000; $11,010,000 was paid by the guests in cash and the rest was owed on account.

i. Cedar Fair paid $2,900,000 principal on notes payable.

j. The company purchased $19,100,000 in food and merchandise inventory for the year, paying $18,000,000 in cash and owing the rest on account.

k. The selling, general, and administrative expenses such as the president's salary and advertising for the parks, classified as operating expenses, for the year were $21,118,000; $19,500,000 was paid in cash and the rest was owed on account.

l. Cedar Fair paid $8,600,000 on accounts payable during the year.

Required:

1. For each of these transactions, record journal entries. Use the letter of each transaction as its reference.

2. Use the following chart to identify whether each transaction results in a cash flow effect from operating (O), investing (I), or financing (F) activities, and indicate the direction and amount of the effect on cash (+ for increase and − for decrease). If there is no cash flow effect, write *none*. The first transaction is provided as an example.

Transaction	Operating, Investing, or Financing Effect	Direction and Amount of the Effect
(a)	O	+89,664,000

ALTERNATE PROBLEMS

Recording Nonquantitative Journal Entries (P3-1)

AP3-1
LO5

The following is a series of accounts for Murray & Morgan, Incorporated, that has been operating for two years. The accounts are listed and numbered for identification. Following the accounts is a series of transactions. For each transaction, indicate the account(s) that should be debited and credited by entering the appropriate account number(s) to the right of each transaction. If no journal entry is needed, write *none* after the transaction. The first transaction is given as an example.

Account No.	Account Title	Account No.	Account Title
1	Cash	9	Wages payable
2	Accounts receivable	10	Income taxes payable
3	Supplies	11	Contributed capital
4	Prepaid expense	12	Retained earnings
5	Buildings	13	Service revenue
6	Land	14	Operating expenses (wages,
7	Accounts payable		supplies, interest)
8	Mortgage payable	15	Income tax expense

Transactions	Debit	Credit
a. Example: Issued stock to new investors.	1	11
b. Performed services for customers this period on credit.	___	___
c. Purchased on credit but did not use supplies this period.	___	___
d. Prepaid a fire insurance policy this period to cover the next 12 months.	___	___
e. Purchased a building this period by making a 20 percent cash down payment and signing a mortgage loan for the balance.	___	___
f. Collected cash this year for services rendered and recorded in the prior year.	___	___

g. Paid cash this period for wages earned and recorded last period. ____ ____
h. Paid cash for operating expenses charged on accounts payable in the prior period. ____ ____
i. Paid cash for operating expenses incurred in the current period. ____ ____
j. Incurred and recorded operating expenses on credit to be paid next period. ____ ____
k. Collected cash for services rendered this period. ____ ____
l. Used supplies on hand to clean the offices. ____ ____
m. Recorded income taxes for this period to be paid at the beginning of the next period. ____ ____
n. Declared and paid a cash dividend this period. ____ ____
o. Made a payment on the building, which was part principal repayment and part interest. ____ ____
p. This period a shareholder sold some shares of her stock to another person for an amount above the original issuance price. ____ ____

AP3-2 **Recording Journal Entries** (P3-2)
L05

Julie Kellogg is the president of ServicePro, Inc., a company that provides temporary employees for not-for-profit companies. ServicePro has been operating for five years; its revenues are increasing with each passing year. You have been hired to help Julie analyze the following transactions for the first two weeks of April:

April 2	Purchased office supplies for $500 on account.
April 5	Billed the local United Way office $1,950 for temporary services provided.
April 8	Paid $250 for supplies purchased and recorded on account last period.
April 8	Placed an advertisement in the local paper for $400 cash.
April 9	Purchased a new computer for the office costing $2,300 cash.
April 10	Paid employee wages of $1,200. Of this amount, $200 had been earned and recorded in the Wages Payable account in the prior period.
April 11	Received $1,000 on account from the local United Way office billed on April 5.
April 12	Purchased land as the site of a future office for $10,000. Paid $2,000 down and signed a note payable for the balance.
April 13	Issued 2,000 additional shares of capital stock for $40 per share in anticipation of building a new office.
April 14	Billed Family & Children's Service $2,000 for services rendered.
April 15	Received the April telephone bill for $245 to be paid next month.

Required:
For each of the transactions, prepare journal entries. Be sure to categorize each account as an asset (A), liability (L), stockholders' equity (SE), revenue (R), or expense (E).

AP3-3 **Determining Financial Statement Effects of Various Transactions and Identifying Cash**
L05, 6 **Flow Effects** (P3-3)

Abercrombie & Fitch Co. is a specialty retailer of quality casual apparel for men and women. The company was established in 1892, purchased by The Limited in 1988, and in 1996 a newly incorporated Abercrombie & Fitch Co. exchanged stock with The Limited, which now owns 84.2 percent of the stock of the company. The following activities were inferred from a recent annual report.

a. Example: Incurred expenses, paid part cash and part on credit.
b. Sold merchandise to customers on account. (*Hint*: Indicate the effects for the sale; then reduce inventory for the amount sold—two transactions.)
c. Declared and paid cash dividends.
d. Collected cash on account.
e. Used supplies.
f. Repaid long-term debt principal and interest.

g. Purchased equipment; paid part cash and part on credit.
h. Paid cash on account.
i. Issued additional stock.
j. Paid rent to mall owners.
k. Received dividends and interest on investments.

Required:

1. For each of the transactions, complete the tabulation, indicating the effect (+ for increase and − for decrease) of each transaction. (Remember that A = L + SE, R − E = NI, and NI affects SE through Retained Earnings.) Write NE if there is no effect. The first transaction is provided as a sample.

	BALANCE SHEET			INCOME STATEMENT		
Transaction	**Assets**	**Liabilities**	**Stockholders' Equity**	**Revenues**	**Expenses**	**Net Income**
(a) (example)	−	+	−	NE	+	−

2. For each transaction, indicate where, if at all, it would be reported on the statement of cash flows. Use O for operating activities, I for investing activities, F for financing activities, and NE if the transaction would not be included on the statement.

Analyzing the Effects of Transactions Using T-Accounts, Preparing Unadjusted Financial Statements, and Evaluating the Total Asset Turnover Ratio as a Manager (P3-4)

AP3-4
LO3, 5, 6

Spicewood Stables, Inc., was established in Austin, Texas, on April 1, 2003. The company provides stables, care for animals, and grounds for riding and showing horses. You have been hired as the new Assistant Controller. The following transactions for April 2003 are provided for your review.

a. Received contributions from five investors of $50,000 in cash ($10,000 each), a barn valued at $100,000, land valued at $60,000, and supplies valued at $2,000. Each investor received 3,000 shares of stock.
b. Built a small barn for $42,000. The company paid half the amount in cash on April 1, 2003, and signed a three-year note payable for the balance.
c. Provided $15,260 in animal care services for customers, all on credit.
d. Rented stables to customers who cared for their own animals; received cash of $13,200.
e. Received from a customer $1,500 to board her horse in May, June, and July (record as unearned revenue).
f. Purchased hay and feed supplies on account for $3,210 to be used in the summer.
g. Paid $840 in cash for water utilities incurred in the month.
h. Paid $1,700 on accounts payable for previous purchases.
i. Received $1,000 from customers on accounts receivable.
j. Paid $4,000 in wages to employees who worked during the month.
k. At the end of the month, purchased a two-year insurance policy for $3,600.
l. Received an electric utility bill for $1,200 for usage in April; the bill will be paid next month.
m. Paid $100 cash dividend to each of the investors at the end of the month.

Required:

1. Set up appropriate T-accounts. All accounts begin with zero balances.
2. Record in the T-accounts the effects of each transaction for Spicewood Stables in April, referencing each transaction in the accounts with the transaction letter. Show the unadjusted ending balances in the T-accounts.
3. Prepare unadjusted financial statements at the end of April (income statement, statement of retained earnings, and balance sheet).
4. Write a short memo to the five owners offering your opinion on the results of operations during the first month of business.
5. After three years in business, you are being evaluated for a promotion to chief financial officer. One measure is how efficiently you managed the assets of the business. The following annual data are available:

	2005*	2004	2003
Total assets	$480,000	$320,000	$300,000
Total liabilities	125,000	28,000	30,000
Total stockholders' equity	355,000	292,000	270,000
Total sales	450,000	400,000	360,000
Net income	50,000	30,000	(10,000)

*At the end of 2005, Spicewood Stables decided to build an indoor riding arena for giving lessons year-round. The company borrowed construction funds from a local bank and the arena was opened in early 2006.

Compute the total asset turnover ratio for 2004 and 2005 and evaluate the results. Do you think you should be promoted? Why?

AP3-5
L06

Preparing a Statement of Cash Flows (P3-5)

Refer to AP3-4.

Required:

For the transactions listed in AP3-4, prepare a statement of cash flows for the month.

AP3-6
L05, 6
ExxonMobil Corporation

Analyzing the Effects of Transactions Using T-Accounts, Preparing Unadjusted Financial Statements, and Evaluating the Total Asset Turnover Ratio (P3-6)

The following are the summary account balances from a recent balance sheet of ExxonMobil Corporation. The accounts have normal debit or credit balances, but they are not necessarily listed in good order. The amounts are shown in millions of dollars. Assume the year-end is December 31, 2004.

Cash	$ 1,157	Marketable securities	$ 618
Notes payable	3,858	Accounts payable	13,391
Accounts receivable	8,073	Income tax payable	2,244
Inventories	5,541	Prepaid expenses	1,071
Other debt	30,954	Investments	5,394
Property & equipment, net	63,425	Intangibles, net	2,583
Shareholders' equity*	37,415		

*This account is a combination of Contributed Capital and Retained Earnings.

The following is a list of hypothetical transactions for January 2005.

a. Purchased on account $150 million of new equipment.
b. Received $500 million on accounts receivable.
c. Received and paid $1 million for utility bills.
d. Earned $5 million in sales on account with customers; cost of sales was $1 million.
e. Paid employees $1 million for wages earned during the month.
f. Paid half of the income taxes payable.
g. Purchased $23 million in supplies on account (include in Inventories).
h. Prepaid $12 million to rent a warehouse next month.
i. Paid $10 million of other debt and $1 million in interest on the debt.
j. Purchased a patent (an intangible asset) for $8 million cash.

Required:

1. Prepare T-accounts for December 31, 2004, from the preceding list; enter the beginning balances. You will need additional T-accounts for income statement accounts; enter $0 balances.
2. For each transaction, record the effects in the T-accounts. Label each using the letter of the transaction. Compute ending balances.
3. Prepare an unadjusted income statement, unadjusted statement of stockholders' equity (since contributed capital and retained earnings are not separately reported), unadjusted balance sheet, and unadjusted statement of cash flows in good form.
4. Based on the unadjusted amounts, compute the company's total asset turnover ratio. What does it suggest to you about ExxonMobil?

CASES AND **PROJECTS**

Annual Report Cases

Finding Financial Information

Refer to the financial statements and accompanying notes of Abercrombie & Fitch given in Appendix C at the end of the book, or open file ANF.pdf in the Annual Report Cases directory on the student CD-ROM.

Required:
1. State the amount of the largest expense on the 2000 income statement and describe the transaction represented by the expense.
2. Give the journal entry for interest income for the year ended February 3, 2001 (for this question, assume that the amount has not yet been received).
3. Assuming that all net sales are on credit, how much cash did Abercrombie & Fitch collect from customers? (*Hint:* Use a T-account of accounts receivable to infer collection.)
4. A shareholder has complained that "more dividends should be paid because the company had net earnings of $158.1 million. Since this amount is all cash, more of it should go to the owners." Explain why the shareholder's assumption that earnings equal net cash inflow is valid. If you believe that the assumption is not valid, state so and support your position concisely.
5. Describe and contrast the purpose of an income statement versus a balance sheet.
6. Compute the company's total asset turnover for 2000. Explain its meaning.

CP3-1
LO2, 3, 5

Finding Financial Information

Refer to the financial statements and accompanying notes of American Eagle Outfitters given in Appendix B at the end of the book, or open file AEOS.pdf in the Annual Report Cases directory on the student CD-ROM.

Required:
1. What is the company's revenue recognition policy?
2. Assuming that $30 million of cost of sales was due to noninventory purchase expenses (occupancy and warehousing costs), how much inventory did the company buy during the year? (*Hint:* Use a T-account of inventory to infer how much was purchased.)
3. Measuring general, administrative, and selling expenses as a percent of sales for 2000 and 1999, how much did it increase from 1999 to 2000? What explanation does management offer for this change?
4. Compute the company's total asset turnover for 2000, and explain its meaning.

CP3-2
LO2, 3, 5

Comparing Companies within an Industry

Refer to the financial statements of American Eagle Outfitters given in Appendix B, Abercrombie & Fitch given in Appendix C, and the Industry Ratio Report given in Appendix D at the end of this book, or open file CP3-3.xls in the Annual Report Cases directory on the student CD-ROM.

Required:
1. What title does each company call its income statement? Explain what "Consolidated" means.
2. Which company had higher net income at February 3, 2001?
3. What does each company report were the primary causes of the change in sales from 1999 to 2000? (*Hint:* Look in the Management's Discussion and Analysis section of the annual report.)
4. Compute the total asset turnover ratio for both companies for 2000. Which company is utilizing assets more effectively to generate sales? Why do you think that?
5. Compare the total asset turnover ratio for both companies to the industry average. On average, are these two companies utilizing assets to generate sales better or worse than their competitors?
6. How much cash was provided by operating activities for 2000 by each company? What was the percentage change in operating cash flows (1) from 1999 to 2000 and (2) from 1998 to 1999 for each company? (*Hint:* [Current Year Amount − Prior Year Amount] / Prior Year.)
7. How much did each company show as federal taxes currently payable at February 3, 2001? Where did you find this information?

CP3-3
LO2, 3, 5

Financial Reporting and Analysis Cases

CP3-4
L03

AMERICAN EAGLE
OUTFITTERS

Comparing a Company over Time

Refer to the annual report for American Eagle Outfitters in Appendix B, or open file AEOS.pdf in the Annual Report Cases directory on the student CD-ROM.

Required:
1. The annual report or 10-K report for American Eagle Outfitters provides selected financial data for the last five years. Compute the total asset turnover ratio for the most recent four years.
2. In Chapter 2, we discussed the financial leverage ratio. Compute this ratio for the most recent four years.
3. What do your results from the trends in the two ratios suggest to you about American Eagle Outfitters?

CP3-5
L04

Interpreting the Financial Press

The August 2, 1999, edition of *Fortune* presented numerous articles on accounting irregularities and fraud. One article entitled "Lies, Damned Lies, and Managed Earnings: The Crackdown Is Here" discusses the implications of unethical managerial decisions. You can access a portion of the article on the Libby/Libby/Short website at www.mhhe.com/libby4e.*

Required:
Read the article and then answer the following questions:

1. What is the SEC and what is its role? (Refer to Chapter 1.)
2. What are the four criteria for recording revenue under the revenue realization principle?
3. What fraudulent activities were committed by the three companies mentioned in the article? What accounting concepts were violated in each case?

CP3-6
L05, 6

Using Financial Reports: Analyzing Changes in Accounts and Preparing Financial Statements

Tastle Painting Service Company was organized on January 20, 2004, by three individuals, each receiving 5,000 shares of stock from the new company. The following is a schedule of the cumulative account balances immediately after each of the first 10 transactions ending on January 31, 2004.

Accounts	CUMULATIVE BALANCES									
	(a)	*(b)*	*(c)*	*(d)*	*(e)*	*(f)*	*(g)*	*(h)*	*(i)*	*(j)*
Cash	$75,000	$70,000	$85,000	$71,000	$61,000	$61,000	$57,000	$46,000	$41,000	$57,000
Accounts receivable			12,000	12,000	12,000	26,000	26,000	26,000	26,000	10,000
Office fixtures		20,000	20,000	20,000	20,000	20,000	20,000	20,000	20,000	20,000
Land				18,000	18,000	18,000	18,000	18,000	18,000	18,000
Accounts payable					3,000	3,000	3,000	10,000	5,000	5,000
Note payable		15,000	15,000	19,000	19,000	19,000	19,000	19,000	19,000	19,000
Contributed capital	75,000	75,000	75,000	75,000	75,000	75,000	75,000	75,000	75,000	75,000
Retained earnings							(4,000)	(4,000)	(4,000)	(4,000)
Paint revenue			27,000	27,000	27,000	41,000	41,000	41,000	41,000	41,000
Supplies expense					5,000	5,000	5,000	8,000	8,000	8,000
Wages expense					8,000	8,000	8,000	23,000	23,000	23,000

*"Lies, Damned Lies, and Managed Earnings: The Crackdown Is Here," *Fortune*, August 2, 1999. ©1999 Time Inc. All rights reserved. Reprinted with permission.

Required:

1. Analyze the changes in this schedule for each transaction; then explain the transaction. Transactions (*a*) and (*b*) are examples:

   a. Cash increased $75,000, and Contributed Capital (stockholders' equity) increased $75,000. Therefore, transaction (*a*) was an issuance of the capital stock of the corporation for $75,000 cash.

   b. Cash decreased $5,000, office fixtures (an asset) increased $20,000, and note payable (a liability) increased $15,000. Therefore, transaction (*b*) was a purchase of office fixtures that cost $20,000. Payment was made as follows: cash, $5,000; note payable, $15,000.

2. Based only on the preceding schedule after transaction (*j*), prepare an unadjusted income statement, a statement of retained earnings, and a balance sheet.

3. For each of the transactions, indicate the type of effect on cash flows (O for operating, I for investing, F for financing) and the direction (+ for increase and − for decrease) and amount of the effect. If there is no effect, write **none**. The first transaction is provided as an example.

Transaction	Operating, Investing, or Financing Effect	Direction and Amount of the Effect
(*a*)	F	+75,000

Using Financial Reports: Interpreting Challenging International Financial Statements

CP3-7
L05, 6
Volkswagen

Your cousin, an engineering major, has inherited some money and wants to invest in an auto company. She has never taken an accounting course and has asked you to help her compare a U.S. automaker's financial statements to those of a German automaker. Your cousin has given you the income statement, asset section of the balance sheet, and audit opinion for Volkswagen for a recent year.

AUDIT CERTIFICATE

The consolidated financial statements, which we have audited in accordance with professional standards, comply with the German legal provisions. With due regard to the generally accepted accounting principles, the consolidated financial statements give a true and fair view of the Group's assets, liabilities, financial position and profit or loss. The Group management report is consistent with the consolidated financial statements.

Hanover, February 24, 2002
C&L TREUARBEIT
DEUTSCHE REVISION
Aktiengesellschaft

STATEMENT OF EARNINGS OF THE VOLKSWAGEN GROUP FOR THE FISCAL YEAR
Ended December 31, 2002—DM million—

	2002	2001
Sales	85,403	76,315
Cost of sales	79,155	69,472
Gross profit	+ 6,248	+ 6,843
Selling and distribution expenses	5,661	5,414
General administration expenses	2,316	2,185
Other operating income	4,246	4,406
Other operating expenses	2,634	3,104
Results from participations	+ 55	+ 97
Interest results	+ 739	+ 1,228
Write-down of financial assets and securities classified as current assets	75	86
Results from ordinary business activities	+ 602	+ 1,785
Taxes on income	455	671
Net earnings	**147**	**1,114**

BALANCE SHEET OF THE VOLKSWAGEN GROUP
December 31, 2002—DM million—

Asset section only

Assets	Dec. 31, 2002	Dec. 31, 2001
Fixed assets		
Intangible assets	631	372
Tangible assets	24,050	21,126
Financial assets	2,747	2,655
Leasing and rental assets	7,393	6,293
	34,821	**30,446**
Current assets		
Inventories	9,736	9,049
Receivables and other assets	21,065	18,675
Securities	1,497	2,329
Cash on hand, deposits at German Federal		
Bank and postal giro balances, cash in banks	7,836	9,255
	40,134	**39,308**
Prepaid and deferred charges	**329**	**336**
BALANCE SHEET TOTAL	**75,284**	**70,090**

Required:

Review the excerpts of Volkswagen's financial statements. Write a letter to your cousin explaining the similarities and the dissimilarities you would expect to find if you compared Volkswagen's statements to those of a company in the United States. Offer your opinion on whether you would expect the underlying accounting principles of the two countries to be similar or dissimilar. On what are you basing your opinion?

Critical Thinking Cases

CP3-8
LO4, 5, 6

Making a Decision as a Bank Loan Officer: Analyzing and Restating Financial Statements That Have Major Deficiencies: A Challenging Case

Raul Tello started and operated a small boat repair service company during 2004. He is interested in obtaining a $100,000 loan from your bank to build a dry dock to store boats for customers in the winter months. At the end of the year, he prepared the following statements based on information stored in a large filing cabinet:

TELLO COMPANY
Profit for 2004

Service fees collected during 2004		$ 55,000
Cash dividends received		10,000
Total		65,000
Expense for operations paid during 2004	$22,000	
Cash stolen	500	
New tools purchased during 2004 (cash paid)	1,000	
Supplies purchased for use on service jobs (cash paid)	3,200	
Total		26,700
Profit		$ 38,300

Assets Owned at the End of 2004

Cash in checking account	$ 29,300
Building (at current market value)	32,000
Tools and equipment	18,000
Land (at current market value)	30,000
Stock in ABC Industrial	130,000
Total	$239,300

The following is a summary of completed transactions:

a. Received the following contributions (at fair market value) to the business from the owner when it was started in exchange for 1,000 shares of stock in the new company:

Building	$21,000	Land	$20,000
Tools and equipment	17,000	Cash	1,000

b. Earned service fees during 2004 of $87,000; of the cash collected, $20,000 was for deposits from customers on work to be done by Tello in the next year.

c. Received the cash dividends on shares of ABC Industrial stock purchased by Raul Tello six years earlier (not owned by the company).

d. Incurred expenses during 2004, $61,000.

e. Determined amount of supplies on hand (unused) at the end of 2004, $700.

Required:

1. Did Tello prepare the income statement on a cash basis or an accrual basis? Explain how you can tell. Which basis should be used? Explain why.
2. Reconstruct the correct entries under accrual accounting principles and post the effects to T-accounts.
3. Prepare an accrual-based income statement, balance sheet, and statement of cash flows. Explain (using footnotes) the reason for each change that you make to the income statement.
4. What additional information would assist you in formulating your decision regarding the loan to Mr. Tello?
5. Based on the revised statements and additional information needed, write a letter to Mr. Tello explaining your decision at this time regarding the loan.

Evaluating an Ethical Dilemma

CP3-9
LO4

Mike Lynch is the manager of an upstate New York regional office for an insurance company. As the regional manager, his compensation package comprises a base salary, commissions, and a bonus when the region sells new policies in excess of its quota. Mike has been under enormous pressure lately, stemming largely from two factors. First, he is experiencing a mounting personal debt due to a family member's illness. Second, compounding his worries, the region's sales of new policies have dipped below the normal quota for the first time in years.

You have been working for Mike for two years, and like everyone else in the office, you consider yourself lucky to work for such a supportive boss. You also feel great sympathy for his personal problems over the last few months. In your position as accountant for the regional office, you are only too aware of the drop in new policy sales and the impact this will have on the manager's bonus. While you are working late at year-end, Mike stops by your office.

Mike asks you to change the manner in which you have accounted for a new property insurance policy for a large local business. A check for the premium, substantial in amount, came in the mail on December 31, the last day of the reporting year. The premium covers a period beginning on January 5. You deposited the check and correctly debited cash and credited an **unearned revenue** account. Mike says, "Hey, we have the money this year, so why not count the revenue this year? I never did understand why you accountants are so picky about these things anyway. I'd like you to change the way you have recorded the transaction. I want you to credit a **revenue** account. And anyway, I've done favors for you in the past, and I am asking for such a small thing in return." With that, he leaves for the day.

Required:

How should you handle this situation? What are the ethical implications of Mike's request? Who are the parties who would be helped or harmed if you complied with the request? If you fail to comply with his request, how will you explain your position to him in the morning?

Financial Reporting and Analysis Team Project

CP3-10

LO2, 3, 4

Team Project: Analysis of Income Statements and Ratios

As a team, select an industry to analyze. Using your web browser, each team member should acquire the annual report or 10-K for one publicly traded company in the industry, with each member selecting a different company.

Required:

1. On an individual basis, each team member should write a short report that lists the following information:
    a. The major revenue and expense accounts on the most recent income statement.
    b. Computation of the total asset turnover ratio.
    c. Description of the company's revenue recognition policy, if reported.
    d. The percentage of cash from operating activities to net income for each year presented. This measures how liberal (that is, speeding up revenue recognition or delaying expense recognition) or conservative (that is, taking care not to record revenues too early or expenses too late) a company's management is in choosing among various revenue and expense recognition policies. A ratio above 1.0 suggests more conservative policies and below 1.0, more liberal policies.
2. Then, as a team, write a short report comparing and contrasting your companies using these attributes. Discuss any patterns across the companies that you as a team observe. Provide potential explanations for any differences discovered.

After studying this chapter, you should be able to:

1. Explain the purpose of a trial balance. p. 163

2. Analyze the adjustments necessary at the end of the period to update balance sheet and income statement accounts. p. 165

3. Present an income statement with earnings per share, statement of stockholders' equity, balance sheet, and supplemental cash flow information. p. 172

4. Compute and interpret the net profit margin. p. 177

5. Explain the closing process. p. 179

Adjustments, Financial Statements, and the Quality of Earnings

4

lthough Papa John's International, Inc., won the first big battle in the "Pizza Wars," it was left with scars. The litigation process is usually quite expensive, not only in terms of the actual costs for legal fees, but also in the time management spends fighting lawsuits instead of focusing on corporate growth strategies, the potential wavering of customer (and franchisee) confidence in the company that might result in lower sales, and potential damages to be paid should the lawsuit be lost. Papa John's faced the possibility of having to cease using its popular slogan "Better Ingredients. Better Pizza." This included deleting the phrase from broadcast advertising, pizza boxes, paper products, related promotional materials, and restaurant signage.

The years 1999 and 2000 were difficult for Papa John's due to the lawsuit. At the end of each fiscal year, Papa John's recorded Advertising Litigation Expense based on the costs it had incurred and those costs it expected to incur. As stated in the notes in its 2000 annual report, Papa John's disclosed that it recorded $7.1 million in litigation expenses, about half of the initial estimates:

FOCUS COMPANY:

Papa John's International

ESTIMATING THE COSTS OF THE PIZZA BATTLE

www.papajohns.com

REAL WORLD EXCERPT

ANNUAL REPORT

---

14. ADVERTISING LITIGATION

. . . We initially estimated that the pre-tax costs of complying with the court's order and certain related costs could have approximated $12.0 to $15.0 million, of which $6.1 million was recorded as pre-tax charges against 1999 earnings. . . . For the 2000 fiscal year, we incurred an additional $1.0 million of pre-tax charges related to this issue.

Applying sound judgment to estimate and record revenues when earned and expenses when incurred in the proper period is important for providing investors, creditors, and other users with reliable income measurement.

UNDERSTANDING THE BUSINESS

Managers are responsible for preparing financial statements that are useful to investors, creditors, and others. Financial information is most useful for analyzing the past and predicting the future when it is considered by users to be of **high quality.** High-quality information should be relevant (that is, important in the analysis and available in a timely manner) and reliable (that is, verifiable and unbiased in portraying economic reality).

Users expect revenues and expenses to be reported in the proper period based on the revenue and matching principles discussed in Chapter 3. Revenues are to be recorded when earned, and expenses are to be recorded when incurred regardless of when cash receipts or payments occur. Because many operating activities take place over a period of time, **adjustments** must be made at the end of the reporting period to record related revenues and expenses in the correct period. These entries update the records and are the focus of this chapter. Often, measuring revenues and expenses requires managers to make estimates and judgments, such as Papa John's did in estimating losses from the lawsuit.

Analysts assess the quality of financial information by determining how **conservative** the managers' estimates and judgments are. Choices that managers make that do not overstate assets and revenues or understate liabilities and expenses are considered more conservative. By applying conservative estimates and judgments, the resulting financial information is of higher quality for use by analysts. The information should not mislead the users in expecting the company to have a stronger financial position or higher earnings potential than exists. The effects of management's choices among alternative accounting methods and the use of estimates are presented throughout the rest of the text.

In this chapter, we emphasize the use of the same analytical tools illustrated in Chapters 2 and 3 (T-accounts and journal entries) to understand how the necessary adjustments are analyzed and recorded at the end of the accounting period. Then we prepare financial statements using adjusted accounts. Finally, we illustrate how to prepare the accounting records for the next period by "closing the books."

ORGANIZATION of the Chapter

Adjusting Revenues and Expenses	Preparing Financial Statements	Closing the Books
■ Accounting Cycle ■ Unadjusted Trial Balance ■ Analysis of Adjusting Entries ■ Papa John's Illustration ■ Adjusted Trial Balance	■ Income Statement ■ Statement of Stockholders' Equity ■ Balance Sheet ■ Supplemental Cash Flows Information ■ Net Profit Margin Ratio	■ End of the Accounting Cycle ■ Post-closing Trial Balance

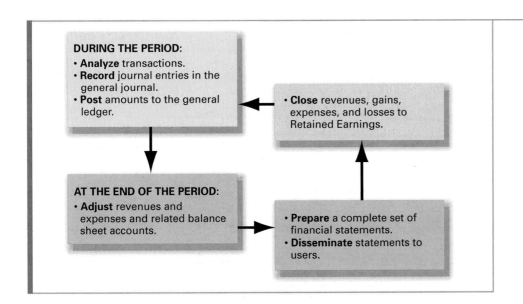

EXHIBIT 4.1

The Accounting Cycle

ADJUSTING REVENUES AND EXPENSES

Accounting Cycle

Exhibit 4.1 presents the fundamental steps in the **accounting cycle.** The accounting cycle is the process used by entities to analyze and record transactions, adjust the records at the end of the period, prepare financial statements, and prepare the records for the next cycle. **During the accounting period,** transactions that result in exchanges between the company and other external parties are analyzed and recorded (in the general journal in chronological order), and the related accounts are updated (in the general ledger), similar to our Papa John's illustrations in Chapters 2 and 3. In this chapter, we examine the **end-of-period** steps that focus primarily on adjustments to record revenues and expenses in the proper period and to update the balance sheet accounts for reporting purposes.

The **ACCOUNTING CYCLE** is the process used by entities to analyze and record transactions, adjust the records at the end of the period, prepare financial statements, and prepare the records for the next cycle.

Unadjusted Trial Balance

Before adjusting the accounting records, managers normally review an unadjusted trial balance produced either manually or, more often, generated by computerized software. A **trial balance** is a list of individual accounts in one column, usually in financial statement order, with their ending debit or credit balances in the next two columns. Debit balances are indicated in the left column and credit balances are indicated in the right column. Then the two columns are totaled to provide a check on the equality of the debits and credits. In fact, that is all that the trial balance reflects. Errors in a computer-generated trail balance may still exist even though debits equal credits when wrong accounts and/or amounts are used in the journal entries.[1]

Based on the T-accounts from the Papa John's illustration in Chapter 3, an unadjusted trial balance is presented in Exhibit 4.2. Notice that the Property and Equipment account is stated at original cost of $338,000 in the trial balance but was stated at $255,000 (original cost minus the portion allocated to past operations) in previous chapters.

Learning Objective 1
Explain the purpose of a trial balance.

A **TRIAL BALANCE** is a list of all accounts with their balances to provide a check on the equality of the debits and credits.

---

[1]Errors in a manually created trial balance also may occur in a manual recordkeeping system when wrong accounts and/or amounts are posted from correct journal entries. If the two columns are not equal, errors have occurred in one or more of the following:

- In preparing journal entries when debits do not equal credits.
- In posting the correct dollar effects of transactions from the journal entry to the ledger.
- In computing ending balances in accounts.
- In copying ending balances in the ledger to the trial balance.

These errors can be traced and should be corrected before adjusting the records.

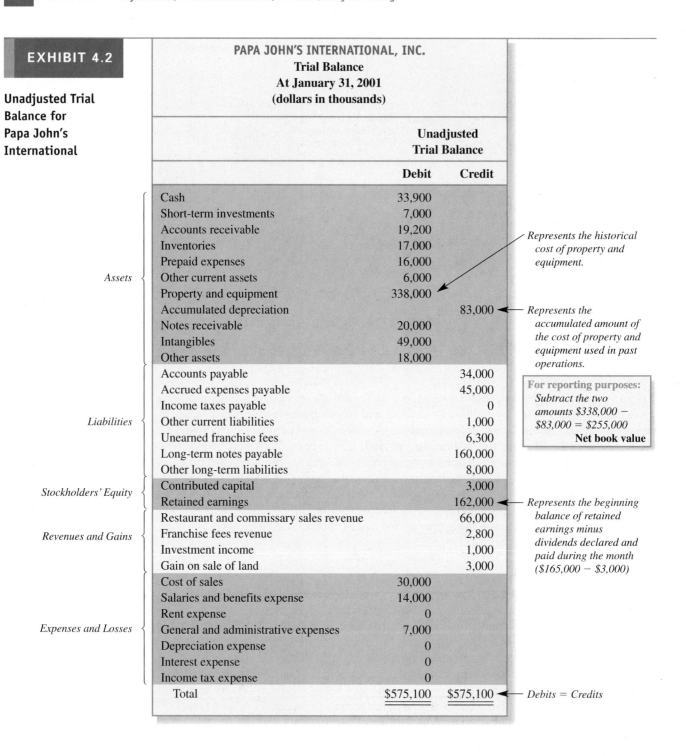

EXHIBIT 4.2

Unadjusted Trial
Balance for
Papa John's
International

PAPA JOHN'S INTERNATIONAL, INC.
Trial Balance
At January 31, 2001
(dollars in thousands)

| | Unadjusted Trial Balance | |
	Debit	Credit
Assets		
Cash	33,900	
Short-term investments	7,000	
Accounts receivable	19,200	
Inventories	17,000	
Prepaid expenses	16,000	
Other current assets	6,000	
Property and equipment	338,000	
Accumulated depreciation		83,000
Notes receivable	20,000	
Intangibles	49,000	
Other assets	18,000	
Liabilities		
Accounts payable		34,000
Accrued expenses payable		45,000
Income taxes payable		0
Other current liabilities		1,000
Unearned franchise fees		6,300
Long-term notes payable		160,000
Other long-term liabilities		8,000
Stockholders' Equity		
Contributed capital		3,000
Retained earnings		162,000
Revenues and Gains		
Restaurant and commissary sales revenue		66,000
Franchise fees revenue		2,800
Investment income		1,000
Gain on sale of land		3,000
Expenses and Losses		
Cost of sales	30,000	
Salaries and benefits expense	14,000	
Rent expense	0	
General and administrative expenses	7,000	
Depreciation expense	0	
Interest expense	0	
Income tax expense	0	
Total	$575,100	$575,100

Represents the historical cost of property and equipment.

Represents the accumulated amount of the cost of property and equipment used in past operations.

> **For reporting purposes:**
> *Subtract the two amounts $338,000 − $83,000 = $255,000*
> **Net book value**

Represents the beginning balance of retained earnings minus dividends declared and paid during the month ($165,000 − $3,000)

Debits = Credits

A **CONTRA-ACCOUNT** is an account that is an offset to, or reduction of, the primary account.

NET BOOK VALUE (BOOK VALUE, CARRYING VALUE) of an asset is the difference between its acquisition cost and accumulated depreciation, its related contra-account.

Long-lived asset accounts such as Property and Equipment increase when assets are purchased and decrease when assets are sold. These assets are also used in operations. To reflect the used-up portion of the long-lived assets' cost, a **contra-account** is created. **Any contra-account is directly related to another account but has the opposite balance.**

As a contra-account increases, the **net book value** (also called **book value** or **carrying value**) reported on the balance sheet decreases. Net book value is the historical cost balance less the contra-account balance. For property and equipment, the contra-account is called Accumulated Depreciation. For Papa John's, Accumulated Depreciation has a credit balance of $83,000. We will discuss many contra-accounts in other chapters and will designate contra-accounts with an X in front of the type of account to which it is related (e.g., Accumulated Depreciation [XA]).

Topic Tackler 4–1

Property and Equipment (A)		Accumulated Depreciation (XA)	
+	−	−	+
Beginning bal. *Purchases*	*Sales*		Beginning bal. *Use of assets*
Ending balance			Ending balance

= **Net book value**

Analysis of Adjusting Entries

Recall that, under accrual accounting concepts, revenues are recorded when earned (the revenue principle) and expenses are recorded when incurred to generate revenues during the same period (the matching principle). Operating income, therefore, is determined by measuring **all** revenues and expenses for a period regardless of when cash is received or paid. This difference in the timing of recording cash receipts and payments versus revenues and expenses requires adjustments at the end of the accounting period. **Adjusting entries** are necessary to update the accounts, reflecting appropriate amounts of revenues, expenses, assets, liabilities, and stockholders' equity for financial statement preparation. A good tool to help you visualize the impact of the timing difference is a timeline.

Deferred Revenues and Deferred Expenses

When cash is received prior to revenue recognition, the company records a journal entry to debit Cash and credit the liability account Unearned Revenue. The company promises to perform services or deliver goods in the future. Revenue recognition is deferred until the company meets its obligation. Unearned Revenue is considered a **deferred revenue** account. At the end of the accounting period, Unearned Revenue needs to be reduced and a revenue account needs to be increased by the amount of the revenue earned over time during the period.

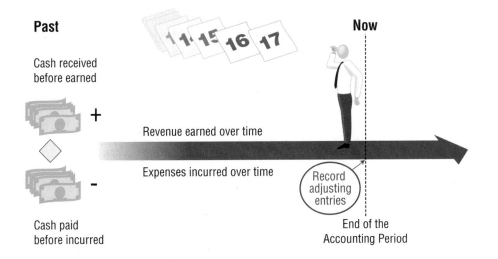

Past

Cash received before earned

Revenue earned over time

Expenses incurred over time

Record adjusting entries

Cash paid before incurred

Now

End of the Accounting Period

When cash is paid prior to incurring an expense, the company records a journal entry to debit an asset account and credit Cash. The company purchases a resource with probable future benefits that are expected to be received over time to generate revenues. Common examples of **deferred expenses** include Supplies, Prepaid Expenses such as rent, advertising, and insurance, Buildings, Equipment and Intangible Assets such as patents and copyrights. Expense recognition is deferred until the asset is used.

Learning Objective 2
Analyze the adjustments necessary at the end of the period to update balance sheet and income statement accounts.

ADJUSTING ENTRIES are entries necessary at the end of the accounting period to measure all revenues and expenses of that period.

DEFERRED REVENUES are previously recorded liabilities that need to be adjusted at the end of the accounting period to reflect the amount of revenue earned.

Examples:
• Unearned Ticket Revenue
• Deferred Subscription Revenue

Adjusting Entry:
↓ Liability and ↑ Revenue

DEFERRED EXPENSES are previously acquired assets that need to be adjusted at the end of the accounting period to reflect the amount of expense incurred in using the asset to generate revenue.

Examples:
• Supplies
• Prepaid Expenses (e.g., rent, advertising, insurance)
• Buildings and Equipment

Adjusting Entry:
↑ Expense and ↓ Asset

Accrued Revenues and Accrued Expenses

ACCRUED REVENUES are previously unrecorded revenues that need to be adjusted at the end of the accounting period to reflect the amount earned and its related receivable account.

Examples:
- Interest Receivable
- Rent Receivable

Adjusting Entry:
↑ Asset and ↑ Revenue

Unlike deferred revenues that were recorded because cash was received in the past, **accrued revenues** have not yet been recorded at the end of the accounting period even though revenue has been earned over time. No account exists to be adjusted. Since another entity owes the company money for services (or goods) that the company performed (or delivered) in the past, a Receivable account needs to be created along with the related revenue account in an adjusting entry. When the cash is received in the future, the receivable account is reduced.

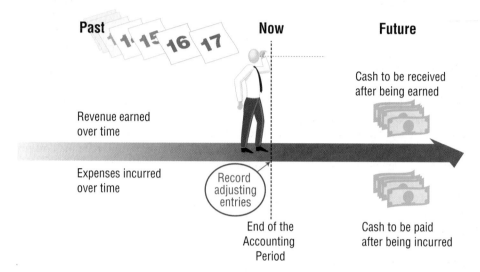

Likewise, numerous expenses are often incurred in the current period that companies pay for in the next period. These unrecorded **accrued expenses** require an adjusting entry to create a payable account along with the related expense account. Common examples of accrued expense accounts are Interest Expense incurred on debt, Wages Expense owed to employees, and Utilities Expense for bills received from utility suppliers. When the cash amounts are paid in the future, the payable accounts are reduced.

ACCRUED EXPENSES are previously unrecorded expenses that need to be adjusted at the end of the accounting period to reflect the amount incurred and its related payable account.

Examples:
- Interest Payable
- Wages Payable
- Property Taxes Payable

Adjusting Entry:
↑ Expense and ↑ Liability

Adjustment Process

To assist you in identifying and calculating adjusting entries, follow three steps:

Step 1: Determine whether the adjustment is to an existing deferred revenue or expense or an unrecorded accrued revenue or expense (ask, "Where's cash?"). If a deferred account is to be adjusted, create a T-account for the deferred revenue or expense account and its balance.

Step 2: Compute the revenue earned or expense incurred up to the end of the accounting period.

Step 3: Record the adjusting journal entry. (Students often have difficulty determining the accounts to use. The title of the revenue or expense account should be related to the asset or liability account. For example, Interest Expense is related to Interest Payable.)

We will now illustrate the use of these steps in our continuing Papa John's illustration.

Papa John's Illustration

As we review Papa John's trial balance in Exhibit 4.2, we can identify several deferred accounts resulting from the company's receiving or paying cash prior to earning revenue or incurring expenses. Since that time, revenues and expenses may have been earned or incurred during January, requiring adjustments to the deferred accounts:

Inventories (including supplies)	A portion of food and paper products has been used during the month.
Prepaid Expenses	All or a portion of the prepaid rent and insurance may have been used by month-end.

Property and Equipment The long-lived assets have been used during the month to generate revenues. A portion of their historical cost is recorded as an expense.

Unearned Franchise Fees All or a portion may have been earned by month-end.

In addition, the unadjusted trial balance contains a number of receivables and payables that suggest there may be earned revenues and incurred expenses that have not yet been recorded. Adjusting entries are needed to accrue the revenues and expenses for January:

Accounts Receivable Franchisees may owe additional royalties to Papa John's for the last week of January's sales.

Accrued Expenses Payable Any wages due to employees for work during the last week of January and amounts due for utilities used during the month but not yet billed to Papa John's need to be recorded as expenses for the month.

Long-Term Notes Payable Papa John's owes interest on any borrowed funds.

Income Taxes Payable Income tax expense needs to be recorded for the period.

Inventories

a. Inventories include food, paper products, and equipment for sale to franchisees by the commissaries. At the end of the month, Papa John's counted $13,000 in inventories on hand, but the Inventories account indicated a balance of $17,000 (from Exhibit 4.2). The difference is the inventory used or sold to franchisees during the month.

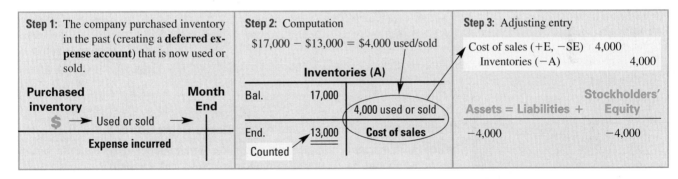

Prepaid Expenses

b. Prepaid Expenses includes $2,000 for insurance coverage over four months. One month has expired and there remains three months of future insurance benefits. Used insurance is called Insurance Expense and is categorized on the income statement as a general and administrative expense.

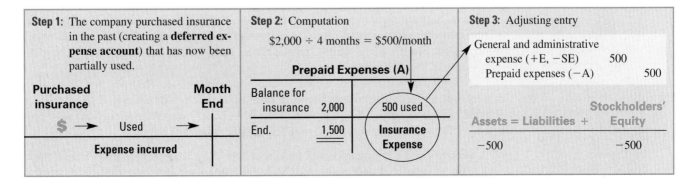

SELF-STUDY **QUIZ**

For (*c*), fill in the missing information. After you have completed your answers, check them with the solutions at the end of the quiz.

c. Prepaid Expenses also includes $6,000 for rental of space at shopping centers over the next three months. One month has expired and two months of future rental benefits remain.

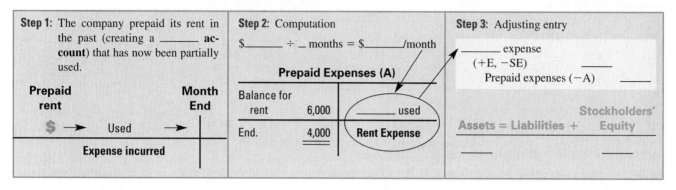

Step 1: The company prepaid its rent in the past (creating a _____ account) that has now been partially used.

Prepaid rent   **Month End**

$ → Used →

Expense incurred

Step 2: Computation

$_____ ÷ _ months = $_____/month

Prepaid Expenses (A)

| Balance for rent | 6,000 | _____ used |
| End. | 4,000 | **Rent Expense** |

Step 3: Adjusting entry

_____ expense (+E, −SE) _____
Prepaid expenses (−A) _____

Assets = Liabilities + Stockholders' Equity

_____   _____

(c) Step 1: A deferred expense

Step 2: Computation
$6,000 ÷ 3 months =
$2,000 used

Step 3: Adjusting entry
Rent expense
(+E, −SE) 2,000

Prepaid
expenses (−A)   2,000

Assets	= Liabilities +	Stockholders' Equity
− 2,000		− 2,000

Property and Equipment (and Accumulated Depreciation)

When buildings and equipment are used over time to generate revenues, a part of their cost should be expensed in the same period (the matching principle). Accountants say that buildings and equipment are **depreciated** over time as used. Depreciation expense is computed as an allocation of an asset's cost over its useful life to the company.

A common misconception held by students and others unfamiliar with accounting terminology is that depreciation reflects the asset's decline in market value. You may have heard the statement that a new car "depreciates" when it is driven off the dealer's lot. The car's market value has declined; it is now a "used" car. However, until the car is actually used to generate revenues, it has not depreciated from an accounting standpoint. **In accounting, depreciation is simply a cost allocation concept, not a way of reporting a reduction in market value.** Depreciation describes the portion of the asset's historical cost estimated to have been used during the period.

As previously discussed, a contra-account, Accumulated Depreciation, is used to accumulate the amount of the historical cost allocated to prior periods. It is directly related to the Property and Equipment account but has the opposite balance (a credit balance). Depreciation is discussed in much greater detail in Chapter 8.

d. Property and equipment has an historical cost of $338,000 at the end of the month. The accumulated depreciation of $83,000 is the used-up portion of the historical cost prior to this month. The depreciation is estimated to be $30,000 per year or $2,500 per month.

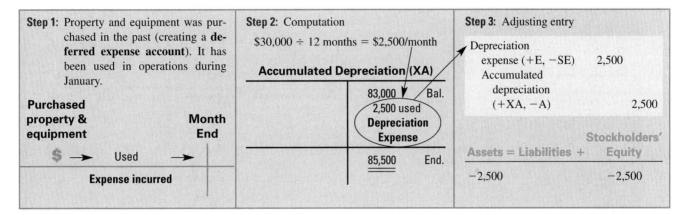

Unearned Revenues

e. Papa John's performed $100 in additional services in January for new franchisees who had previously paid Papa John's.

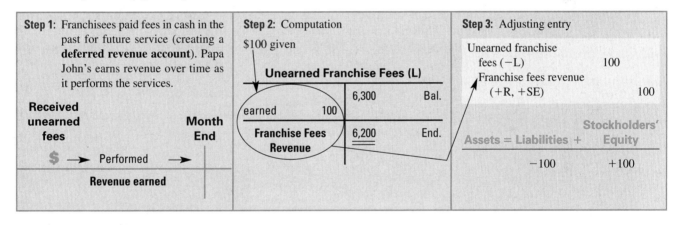

Receivables

f. Papa John's franchisees reported that they will pay Papa John's in February $900 in royalties for sales the franchisees made in the last week of January.

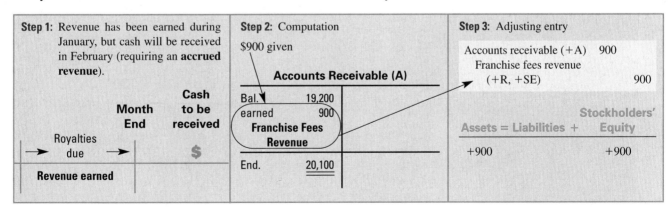

Accrued Expenses Payable (such as Salaries, Utilities, and Interest)

g. Papa John's owed its employees salaries and benefits for working four days at the end of January at $500 per day. The employees will be paid during the first week in February.

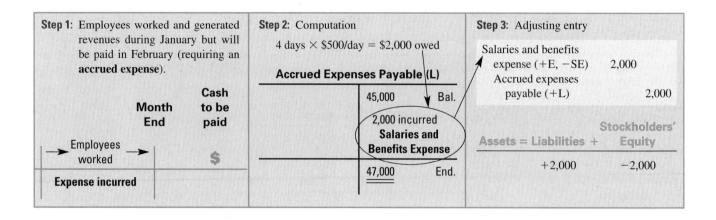

Step 1: Employees worked and generated revenues during January but will be paid in February (requiring an **accrued expense**).

Step 2: Computation

4 days × $500/day = $2,000 owed

Accrued Expenses Payable (L)

45,000 Bal.

2,000 incurred **Salaries and Benefits Expense**

47,000 End.

Step 3: Adjusting entry

Salaries and benefits expense (+E, −SE)   2,000
Accrued expenses payable (+L)   2,000

Assets = Liabilities + Stockholders' Equity

+2,000   −2,000

SELF-STUDY QUIZ

For (*h*), fill in the missing information. After you have completed your answers, check them with the solution that follows.

h. Papa John's received a $600 utility bill at the end of January for gas and electricity used in January. The company categorizes Utilities Expense as general and administrative expenses on the income statement. The bill will be paid during the first week in February.

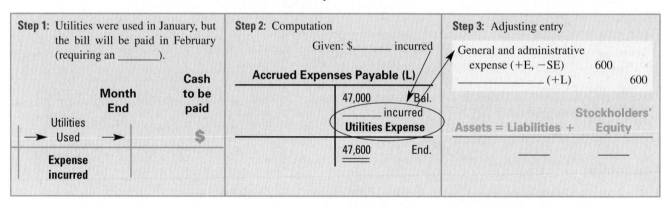

Step 1: Utilities were used in January, but the bill will be paid in February (requiring an _____).

Step 2: Computation

Given: $_____ incurred

Accrued Expenses Payable (L)

47,000 Bal.

_____ incurred **Utilities Expense**

47,600 End.

Step 3: Adjusting entry

General and administrative expense (+E, −SE)   600
_____ (+L)   600

Assets = Liabilities + Stockholders' Equity

_____   _____

(h) Step 1: An accrued expense Step 2: Computation $600 incurred amount was given Step 3: Adjusting entry General and administrative expense (+E, −SE)   600
Accrued expenses payable (+L)   600

Assets = Liabilities + Stockholders' Equity
+ 600   − 600

i. Papa John's borrowed $6,000 at the beginning of January, signing a note payable due in three years at 12 percent interest per year with interest to be paid at the end of each year. There are two components when borrowing money: **principal** and **interest**.

Note that principal was recorded properly in the past. However, interest expense is incurred over time as the bank's money is used. It is important to note that the interest rate is always given as an annual percentage. To compute interest expense for less than a full year, the number of months needed in the calculation is divided by 12.

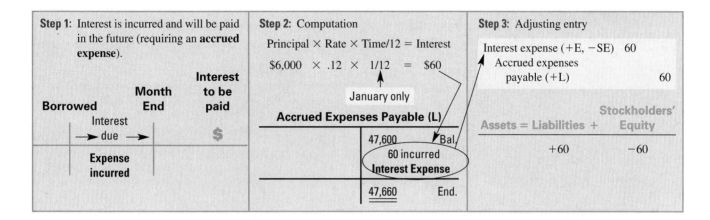

Income Taxes Payable

The final adjusting journal entry is to record the accrual of income taxes that will be paid in the next quarter. This requires computing adjusted pretax income:

	Revenues and Gains	Expenses and Losses	
Unadjusted totals	$72,800	$51,000	From Exhibit 4.2
Adjustments: (a)		4,000	
(b)		500	
(c)		2,000	
(d)		2,500	
(e)	100		
(f)	900		
(g)		2,000	
(h)		600	
(i)		60	
	$73,800	− $62,660	= **$11,140** Adjusted pretax income

j. Papa John's average income tax rate is 35 percent.

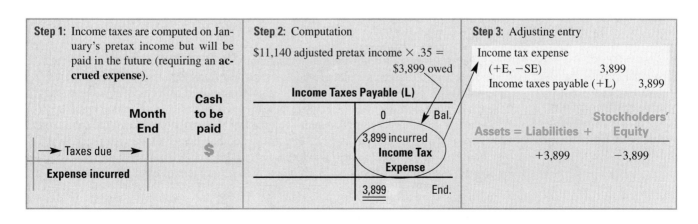

FINANCIAL ANALYSIS

Adjustments and Audits

Since end-of-period adjustments are the most complex portion of the annual recordkeeping process, they are prone to error. External auditors (independent CPAs) examine the company's records on a test, or sample, basis. To maximize the chance of detecting any errors significant enough to affect users' decisions, CPAs allocate more of their testing to transactions most likely to be in error.

Several accounting research studies have documented the most error-prone transactions for medium-sized manufacturing companies.* End-of-period adjustment errors such as failure to provide adequate product warranty liability, failure to include items that should be accrued, and end-of-period transactions recorded in the wrong period (called **cut-off errors**) are in the top category and thus receive a great deal of attention from the auditors.

For example, see J. R. Coakley and J. K. Loebbecke, "The Expectation of Accounting Errors in Medium-Sized Manufacturing Firms," Advances in Accounting, 2 (1985), pp. 199–245.

A QUESTION OF ETHICS

Adjustments and Incentives

Owners and managers of companies are most directly affected by the information presented in financial statements. If the financial performance and condition of the company appear strong, the company's stock price rises. Shareholders usually receive dividends and increase their investment value. Managers often receive bonuses based on the strength of a company's financial performance, and many in top management are compensated with options to buy their company's stock at prices below market.* The higher the market value, the more compensation they earn. When actual performance lags behind expectations, managers and owners may be tempted to manipulate accruals and deferrals to make up part of the difference. For example, managers may record cash received in advance of being earned as revenue in the current period or may fail to accrue certain expenses at year-end.

Evidence from studies of large samples of companies indicates that some managers do engage in such behavior. This research is borne out by enforcement actions of the Securities and Exchange Commission against companies and sometimes against their auditors. These SEC enforcement actions most often relate to accrual of revenue and receivables that should be deferred to future periods. In many of these cases, the firms involved, their managers, and their auditors are penalized for such actions. Furthermore, owners suffer because news of an SEC investigation negatively affects the company's stock price.

P. Healy, and J. Whalen, "A Review of the Earnings Management Literature and Its Implications for Standard Setting," Accounting Horizons, December 1999.

PREPARING FINANCIAL STATEMENTS

Learning Objective 3
Present an income statement with earnings per share, statement of stockholders' equity, balance sheet, and supplemental cash flow information.

Before we prepare a complete set of financial statements, let's update the trial balance to reflect the adjustments and provide us with adjusted balances for the statements.[2] In Exhibit 4.3, four new columns are added. Two are used to reflect the adjustments to each of the accounts. The other two are the updated balances, determined by adding (or subtracting) across each row. Again, we note that the total debits equal the total credits in each of the columns. It is from these adjusted balances that we will prepare an income statement, statement of stockholders' equity, and a balance sheet, with supplemental cash flow information to accompany the statement of cash flows.

---

[2]For a discussion and illustration of the use of a worksheet for end-of-period adjustments, refer to Appendix E located on the website at www.mhhe.com/libby4e.

EXHIBIT 4.3

Adjusted Trial Balance for Papa John's International

PAPA JOHN'S INTERNATIONAL, INC.
Trial Balance
At January 31, 2001
(dollars in thousands)

	Unadjusted Trial Balance		Adjustments		Adjusted Trial Balance		
	Debit	Credit	Debit	Credit	Debit	Credit	
Cash	33,900				33,900		
Short-term investments	7,000				7,000		
Accounts receivable	19,200		(f) 900		20,100		
Inventories	17,000			(a) 4,000	13,000		
Prepaid expenses	16,000			(b) 500	13,500		
				(c) 2,000			
Other current assets	6,000				6,000		
Property and equipment	338,000				338,000		Assets
Accumulated depreciation		83,000		(d) 2,500		85,500	
Notes receivable	20,000				20,000		
Intangibles	49,000				49,000		
Other assets	18,000				18,000		
Accounts payable		34,000				34,000	
Accrued expenses payable		45,000		(g) 2,000		47,660	
				(h) 600			
				(i) 60			
Income taxes payable		0		(j) 3,899		3,899	Liabilities
Other current liabilities		1,000				1,000	
Unearned franchise fees		6,300	(e) 100			6,200	
Long-term notes payable		160,000				160,000	
Other long-term liabilities		8,000				8,000	
Contributed capital		3,000				3,000	Stockholders' Equity
Retained earnings		162,000				162,000	
Restaurant and commissary sales revenue		66,000				66,000	
Franchise fees revenue		2,800		(e) 100		3,800	Revenues and Gains
				(f) 900			
Investment income		1,000				1,000	
Gain on sale of land		3,000				3,000	
Cost of sales	30,000		(a) 4,000		34,000		
Salaries and benefits expense	14,000		(g) 2,000		16,000		
Rent expense	0		(c) 2,000		2,000		
General and administrative expenses	7,000		(b) 500		8,100		Expenses and Losses
			(h) 600				
Depreciation expense	0		(d) 2,500		2,500		
Interest expense	0		(i) 60		60		
Income tax expense	0		(j) 3,899		3,899		
Total	$575,100	$575,100	$16,559	$16,559	$585,059	$585,059	

Income Statement

The financial statements are interrelated. That is, the numbers in one statement flow into the next statement. Exhibit 4.4 presents the transaction analysis model from Chapter 3 simplified for illustrating the connections between the statements. Starting on the right, we see that net income is a component of Retained Earnings, Retained Earnings is a component of Stockholders' Equity, and Stockholders' Equity is a component on the balance sheet.

EXHIBIT 4.4	
Relationships of the Financial Statements Using the Transaction Analysis Model	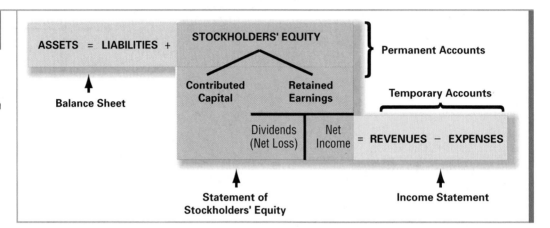

Another way of presenting the relationships among the statements follows. If a number on the income statement changes, it will impact the other statements.

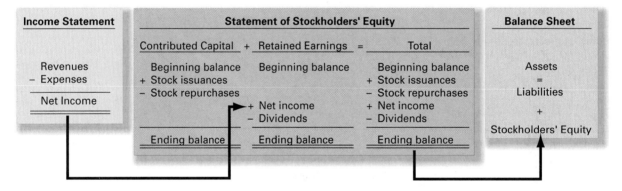

The income statement is prepared first because net income is a component of Retained Earnings. The January income statement for Papa John's based on transactions in Chapters 2 and 3 and adjustments in Chapter 4 follows. You will note that the earnings per share (EPS) ratio is reported on the income statement. It is widely used in evaluating the operating performance and profitability of a company, and it is the only ratio required to be disclosed on the statement or in the notes to the statements. Earnings per share is computed as:

$$\frac{\text{Earnings}}{\text{per Share}} = \frac{\text{Net Income Available to the Common Stockholders}}{\text{Average Number of Shares of Common Stock Outstanding during the Period}}$$

Based on Papa John's actual annual report for 2000, the average number of shares of stock outstanding was approximately 24,703,000. For simplicity, we use this same denominator in the computations of the earnings per share shown on the income statement.

$$\frac{\$7{,}241{,}000 \text{ Net Income}}{24{,}703{,}000 \text{ Shares}} = \$.29 \text{ earnings per share}$$

PAPA JOHN'S INTERNATIONAL, INC. AND SUBSIDIARIES
Consolidated Statement of Income
For the Month Ended January 31, 2001
(dollars in thousands)

Revenues:	
Restaurant and commissary sales	$66,000
Franchise fees	3,800
Total revenues	69,800
Costs and expenses:	
Cost of sales	34,000
Salaries and benefits expense	16,000
Rent expense	2,000
General and administrative expenses	8,100
Depreciation expense	2,500
Total costs and expenses	62,600
Operating income	7,200
Other revenues and gains (expenses and losses):	
Investment income	1,000
Interest expense	(60)
Gain on sale of land	3,000
Income before income taxes	11,140
Income tax expense	3,899
Net income	$7,241
Earnings per share	$.29 ←—— *For the month*

Statement of Stockholders' Equity

The final total from the income statement, net income, is carried forward to the Retained Earnings column of the statement of stockholders' equity. To this, the additional elements of the statement are added. Dividends declared and an additional stock issuance from prior chapters are also included in the statement:

PAPA JOHN'S INTERNATIONAL, INC. AND SUBSIDIARIES
Consolidated Statement of Stockholders' Equity
For the Month Ended January 31, 2001
(dollars in thousands)

	Contributed Capital	Retained Earnings	Stockholders' Equity	
Ending balance 12/31/00	$1,000	$165,000	$166,000	
Stock issuance	2,000		2,000	
Net income		7,241	7,241	←—— *From the income statement*
Dividends		(3,000)	(3,000)	
Ending balance 1/31/01	$3,000	$169,241	$172,241	

Balance Sheet

The ending balances for contributed capital and retained earnings from the statement of stockholders' equity are included on the balance sheet. You will notice that the contra-asset account, Accumulated Depreciation, has been subtracted from the Property and Equipment account to reflect net book value (or carrying value) at month-end for balance sheet purposes. Also recall that assets are listed in order of liquidity, and liabilities are listed in order of due dates. Current assets are those used or turned into cash within one year (as well as inventory). Current liabilities are obligations to be paid with current assets within one year.

PAPA JOHN'S INTERNATIONAL, INC. AND SUBSIDIARIES Consolidated Balance Sheet January 31, 2001 (dollars in thousands)	
Assets	
Current assets:	
Cash	$ 33,900
Short-term investments	7,000
Accounts receivable	20,100
Inventories	13,000
Prepaid expenses	13,500
Other current assets	6,000
Total current assets	93,500
Property and equipment (net of accumulated depreciation of $85,500)	252,500
Notes receivable	20,000
Intangibles	49,000
Other assets	18,000
Total assets	$433,000
Liabilities and stockholders' equity	
Current liabilities:	
Accounts payable	$ 34,000
Accrued expenses payable	47,660
Income taxes payable	3,899
Other current liabilities	1,000
Total current liabilities	86,559
Unearned franchise fees	6,200
Long-term notes payable	160,000
Other long-term liabilities	8,000
Total liabilities	260,759
Stockholders' equity:	
Contributed capital	3,000
From the Statement of→ Retained earnings	169,241
Stockholders' Equity	
Total stockholders' equity	172,241
Total liabilities and stockholders' equity	$433,000

FOCUS ON
CASH FLOWS

Disclosure

As presented in the previous chapters, the statement of cash flows explains the difference between the ending and beginning balances in the Cash account on the balance sheet during the accounting period. Put simply, the cash flow statement is a categorized list of all transactions of the period that affected the Cash account. The three categories are operating, investing, and financing activities. Since no adjustments made in this chapter affected cash, the statement of cash flows presented for Papa John's at the end of Chapter 3 has not changed.

For complete disclosure, however, companies are required to provide additional information on the statement itself or in the notes to the statements.

In General   Supplemental Disclosure (on the statement or in the notes): (1) Interest paid, (2) Income taxes paid, and (3) A list of the nature and amounts of significant noncash transactions (e.g., land exchanged for stock, acquisition of a building by signing a long-term mortgage payable).

Focus Company Analysis   For supplemental disclosure, no significant noncash transactions and no income taxes or interest were paid during January. In the notes to its 2000 annual report, Papa John's disclosed $6.9 million in interest paid and $23.8 million in income taxes paid. No significant noncash transactions were disclosed.

FINANCIAL
ANALYSIS

Cash Flows from Operations, Net Income, and the Quality of Earnings

Many standard financial analysis texts warn analysts to look for unusual deferrals and accruals when they attempt to predict future periods' earnings. They often suggest that wide disparities between net income and cash flow from operations is a useful warning sign. For example, Bernstein and Wild suggest that

> Cash flows are often less subject to distortion than is net income. Accounting accruals determining net income rely on estimates, deferrals, allocations, and valuations. These considerations typically admit more subjectivity than factors determining cash flows. For this reason we often relate cash flows from operations to net income in assessing its quality. **Certain users consider earnings of higher quality when the ratio of cash flows from operations divided by net income is greater.** This derives from a concern with revenue recognition or expense accrual criteria yielding high net income but low cash flows. (emphasis added)*

*L. Bernstein and J. Wild, Financial Statement Analysis (New York: McGraw-Hill/Irwin, 1998), p. 366.

KEY RATIO
ANALYSIS

Net Profit Margin

In Chapter 2, we introduced the financial leverage ratio to examine managers' use of debt as a tool to increase resources that would generate more profit for the shareholders. In Chapter 3, we introduced the total asset turnover ratio to examine managers' effectiveness at utilizing assets efficiently to generate more profit for the shareholders. Now let's examine the third ratio, net profit margin, to examine managers' effectiveness at controlling revenues and expenses to generate more profit for the shareholders. These three ratios are the primary components of Return on Equity to shareholders to be discussed in Chapter 5.

Learning Objective 4
Compute and interpret the net profit margin.

❓ ANALYTICAL QUESTION:

How effective is management in generating profit on every dollar of sales?

% RATIO AND COMPARISONS:

$$\text{Net Profit Margin} = \frac{\text{Net Income}}{\text{Net Sales (or Operating Revenues)}^*}$$

The 2000 ratio for Papa John's:

$$\frac{\$32,000,000}{\$945,000,000} = .0339 \ (3.39\%)$$

Net sales is sales revenue less any returns from customers and other reductions. For companies in the service industry, total operating revenues is equivalent to net sales.

COMPARISONS OVER TIME		
Papa John's		
1998	**1999**	**2000**
4.74%	5.87%	3.39%

COMPARISONS WITH COMPETITORS	
Domino's Inc.	**Tricon Global†**
2000	**2000**
2.2%	5.8%

†*Tricon Global is the parent company of Pizza Hut, KFC, and Taco Bell.*

💡 INTERPRETATIONS:

In General   Net profit margin measures how much of every sales dollar generated during the period is profit. A rising net profit margin signals more efficient management of sales and expenses. Differences among industries result from the nature of the products or services provided and the intensity of competition. Differences among competitors in the same industry reflect how each company responds to changes in competition (and demand for the product or service) and changes in managing sales volume, sales price, and costs. Financial analysts expect well-run businesses to maintain or improve their net profit margin over time.

Focus Company Analysis   Papa John's net profit margin increased in 1999, suggesting an improvement in the control of sales and costs. As the regional commissaries serve an increasing number of restaurants and operate closer to anticipated capacity, they become more efficient, so costs per sale decrease. However, the net profit margin dropped in 2000. In the Management's Discussion and Analysis section of the annual report, Papa John's noted increases in the costs of salaries, rent, and advertising in 2000, offset slightly by a decrease in the cost of cheese, which is 35 percent of food costs. In addition, Papa John's recorded $25 million in litigation expense and special charges due to assets determined to be less productive.

Domino's is Papa John's main competitor in the delivery segment of the pizza business. Domino's has a 1.19 percent lower net profit margin. This may suggest reduced efficiency in commissary activities by Domino's. On the other hand, Tricon Global has a 5.8 percent net profit margin. This ratio is similar to Papa John's in 1999, but higher than Papa John's in 2000, even though Tricon operates dine-in, take-out, and delivery restaurants that rely more heavily on facilities (a higher cost structure). Differences in business strategies explain some of the variation in the ratio analysis.

A Few Cautions   The decisions that management makes to maintain the company's net profit margin in the current period may have negative long-run implications. Analysts should perform additional analysis of the ratio to identify trends in each component of revenues and expenses. This involves dividing each line on the income statement by net sales. Statements presented with these percentages are called **common-sized income statements.** Changes in the percentages of the individual components of net income provide information on shifts in management's strategies.

Selected Focus Companies' Net Profit Margin Ratios for 2000

Callaway Golf   9.7%

Harley-Davidson   12.0%

Wal-Mart Stores   3.3%

CLOSING THE BOOKS
End of the Accounting Cycle

The ending balance in each of the asset, liability, and stockholders' equity accounts becomes the beginning account balance for the next period. These accounts, called **permanent** or **real accounts** (highlighted in Exhibit 4.4), are not reduced to a zero balance at the end of the accounting period. For example, the ending Cash balance of the prior accounting period is the beginning Cash balance of the next accounting period. The only time a permanent account has a zero balance is when the item it represents is no longer owned or owed.

On the other hand, revenue, expense, gain, and loss accounts are used to accumulate data for the **current accounting period only;** they are called **temporary** or **nominal accounts** (see Exhibit 4.4). The final step in the accounting cycle, closing the books, is done to prepare income statement accounts for the next accounting cycle. Therefore, at the end of each period, the balances in the temporary accounts are transferred, or **closed,** to the Retained Earnings account by recording a closing entry.

The **closing entry** has two purposes:

1. To transfer net income or loss to Retained Earnings.[3]

2. To establish a zero balance in each of the temporary accounts to start the accumulation in the next accounting period.

In this way, the income statement accounts are again ready for their temporary accumulation function for the next period. The closing entry is dated the last day of the accounting period, entered in the usual debits-equal-credits format (in the journal), and immediately posted to the ledger (or T-accounts). Temporary accounts with debit balances are credited and accounts with credit balances are debited. The net amount, equal to net income, affects Retained Earnings.

To illustrate the process, we create an example using just a few accounts. The closing amounts are taken from the ending balances in the T-accounts:

Sales revenue (−R)	100
Gain on sale of assets (−Gain)	30
Wages expense (−E)	40
Loss on sale of assets (−Loss)	10
Retained earnings (+SE)	80

Learning Objective 5
Explain the closing process.

PERMANENT (REAL) ACCOUNTS are the balance sheet accounts that carry their ending balances into the next accounting period.

TEMPORARY (NOMINAL) ACCOUNTS are income statement accounts that are closed to Retained Earnings at the end of the accounting period.

CLOSING ENTRY transfers balances in temporary accounts to Retained Earnings and establishes zero balances in temporary accounts.

Topic Tackler 4–2

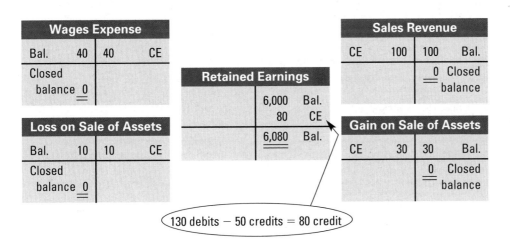

---

[3]Companies may close income statement accounts to a special temporary summary account, called **Income Summary,** that is then closed to Retained Earnings.

We now illustrate closing the books by preparing the closing entry for Papa John's at January 31, 2001, although companies close their records only at the end of the fiscal year.

Restaurant and commissary sales revenue (−R)	66,000	
Franchise fees revenue (−R)	3,800	
Investment income (−R)	1,000	
Gain on sale of land (−R)	3,000	
Cost of sales (−E)		34,000
Salaries and benefits expense (−E)		16,000
Rent expense (−E)		2,000
General and administrative expenses (−E)		8,100
Depreciation expense (−E)		2,500
Interest expense (−E)		60
Income tax expense (−E)		3,899
Retained earnings (+SE)		7,241

Post-Closing Trial Balance

A **POST-CLOSING TRIAL BALANCE** should be prepared as the last step of the accounting cycle to check that debits equal credits and all temporary accounts have been closed.

After the closing process is complete, all income accounts have a zero balance. These accounts are then ready for recording revenues and expenses in the new accounting period. The ending balance in Retained Earnings now is up-to-date (matches the amount on the balance sheet) and is carried forward as the beginning balance for the next period. As the last step of the accounting information processing cycle, a **post-closing trial balance** (Exhibit 4.5) should be prepared as a check that debits still equal credits and that all temporary accounts have been closed.

FINANCIAL ANALYSIS

Accruals and Deferrals: Judging Earnings Quality

Most of the adjustments discussed in this chapter, such as the allocation of prepaid insurance or the determination of accrued interest expense, involve direct calculations and require little judgment on the part of the company's management. In later chapters, we discuss many other adjustments that involve difficult and complex estimates about the future. These include, for example, estimates of customers' ability to make payments to the company for purchases on account, the useful lives of new machines, and future amounts that a company may owe on warranties of products sold in the past. Each of these estimates and many others can have significant effects on the stream of net earnings that companies report over time.

When attempting to value firms based on their balance sheet and income statement data, analysts also evaluate the estimates that form the basis for the adjustments. Those firms that make relatively pessimistic estimates that reduce current income are judged to follow **conservative** financial reporting strategies, and experienced analysts give these reports more credence. The earnings numbers reported by these companies are often said to be of "higher quality" because they are less influenced by management's natural optimism. Firms that consistently make optimistic estimates that result in reporting higher net income, however, are judged to be **aggressive.** Analysts judge these companies' operating performance to be of lower quality.

EXHIBIT 4.5

Post-Closing Trial Balance for Papa John's International

PAPA JOHN'S INTERNATIONAL, INC.
Trial Balance
At January 31, 2001
(dollars in thousands)

	Adjusted Trial Balance		Post-Closing Trial Balance		
	Debit	**Credit**	**Debit**	**Credit**	
Cash	33,900		33,900		Assets
Short-term investments	7,000		7,000		
Accounts receivable	20,100		20,100		
Inventories	13,000		13,000		
Prepaid expenses	13,500		13,500		
Other current assets	6,000		6,000		
Property and equipment	338,000		338,000		
Accumulated depreciation		85,500		85,500	
Notes receivable	20,000		20,000		
Intangibles	49,000		49,000		
Other assets	18,000		18,000		
Accounts payable		34,000		34,000	Liabilities
Accrued expenses payable		47,660		47,660	
Income taxes payable		3,899		3,899	
Other current liabilities		1,000		1,000	
Unearned franchise fees		6,200		6,200	
Long-term notes payable		160,000		160,000	
Other long-term liabilities		8,000		8,000	
Contributed capital		3,000		3,000	Stock-holders' Equity
Retained earnings		162,000		169,241	
Restaurant and commissary sales revenue		66,000		0	Revenues and Gains
Franchise fees revenue		3,800		0	
Investment income		1,000		0	
Gain on sale of land		3,000		0	
Cost of sales	34,000		0		Expenses and Losses
Salaries and benefits expense	16,000		0		
Rent expense	2,000		0		
General and administrative expenses	8,100		0		
Depreciation expense	2,500		0		
Interest expense	60		0		
Income tax expense	3,899		0		
Total	$585,059	$585,059	$518,500	$518,500	

DEMONSTRATION CASE

We take our final look at the accounting activities of Terrific Lawn Maintenance Corporation by illustrating the activities at the end of the accounting cycle: the adjustment process, financial statement preparation, and the closing process. No adjustments had been made to the accounts to reflect all revenues earned and expenses incurred in April. The trial balance for Terrific on April 30, 2003, based on the unadjusted balances in Chapter 3 is as follows:

TERRIFIC LAWN MAINTENANCE CORPORATION
Unadjusted Trial Balance
At April 30, 2003

	Unadjusted Trial Balance	
	Debit	Credit
Cash	5,032	
Accounts receivable	1,700	
Notes receivable	0	
Prepaid expenses	300	
Land	3,750	
Equipment	4,600	
Accumulated depreciation		0
Accounts payable		220
Accrued expenses payable		0
Notes payable		3,700
Income taxes payable		0
Unearned revenues		1,600
Contributed capital		9,000
Retained earnings		0
Mowing revenue		5,200
Interest revenue		12
Wages expense	3,900	
Fuel expense	410	
Insurance expense	0	
Utilities expense	0	
Depreciation expense	0	
Interest expense	40	
Income tax expense	0	
Total	$19,732	$19,732

In reviewing the trial balance, three deferred accounts (Prepaid Expenses, Equipment, and Unearned Revenues) may need to be adjusted and additional accruals may be necessary related to the interest on Notes Payable and Notes Receivable, Wages Expense, Income Tax Expense, and others. The following information is determined at the end of the accounting cycle:

Deferred Accounts

a. One-fourth of the $1,600 cash received from the city at the beginning of April for future mowing service has been earned in April. The $1,600 in Unearned Revenues represents four months of service (April through July).

b. Insurance costing $300 providing coverage for six months (April through September) paid by Terrific Lawn at the beginning of April has been partially used in April.

c. Mowers, edgers, rakes, and hand tools (equipment) have been used in April to generate revenues. The company estimates $300 in depreciation each year.

Accrued Accounts

d. Wages have been paid through April 28. Employees worked the last two days of April and will be paid in May. Wages accrue at $200 per day.

e. An extra telephone line was installed in April. The telephone bill for $52 including hookup and usage charges was received on April 30 and will be paid in May.

f. Interest accrues on the outstanding notes payable at an annual rate of 12 percent. The $3,700 in principal has been outstanding all month.

g. The estimated income tax rate for Terrific Lawn is 35 percent.

Required:

1. Using the process outlined in this chapter, analyze and record adjusting journal entries for April.

2. Prepare an adjusted trial balance.

3. Prepare an income statement, statement of stockholders' equity, and balance sheet from the amounts in the adjusted trial balance. Include earnings per share on the income statement. (The company issued 1500 shares.) Also prepare a schedule of supplemental disclosure for the statement of cash flows. If none is necessary, so indicate.

4. Prepare the closing entry for April 30, 2003.

5. Compute the company's net profit margin for the month.

Now you can check your answers with the following solution to these requirements.

SUGGESTED SOLUTION

1. Analysis of deferrals and accruals and related adjusting entries:

Unearned Revenue

a. One-fourth of the $1,600 cash received from the city at the beginning of April for future mowing service has been earned in April. The $1,600 in Unearned Revenues represents four months of service (April through July).

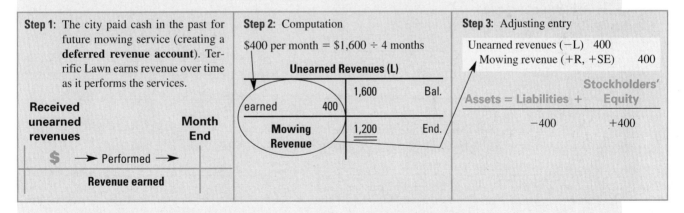

Prepaid Expenses

b. Insurance costing $300 providing coverage for six months (April through September) paid by Terrific Lawn at the beginning of April has been partially used in April.

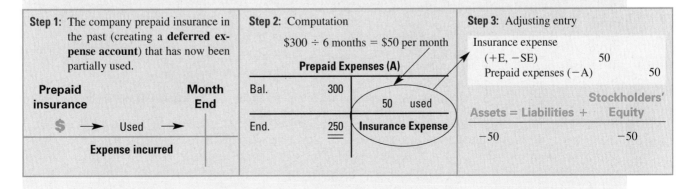

Equipment (and Accumulated Depreciation)

c. Mowers, edgers, rakes, and hand tools (equipment) have been used in April to generate revenues. The company estimates $300 in depreciation each year.

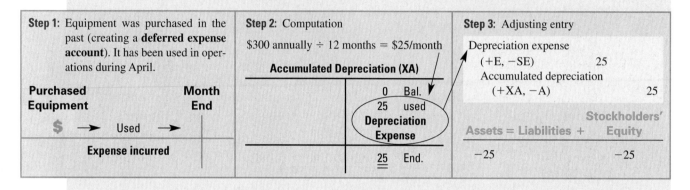

Accrued Expenses Payable (such as Wages, Utilities, and Interest)

d. Wages have been paid through April 28. Employees worked the last two days of April and will be paid in May. Wages accrue at $200 per day.

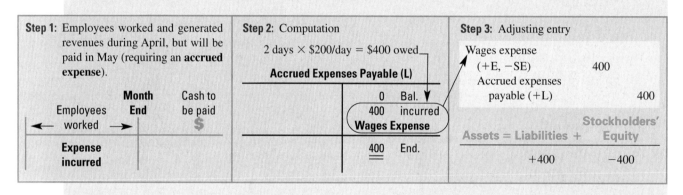

e. An extra telephone line was installed in April. The telephone bill for $52 including hookup and usage charges was received on April 30 and will be paid in May.

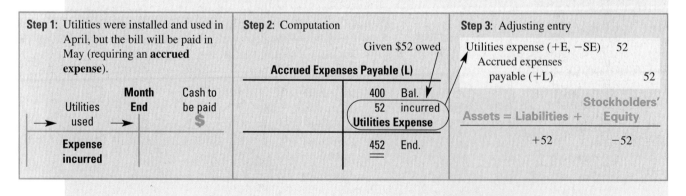

f. Interest accrues on the outstanding notes payable at an annual rate of 12 percent. The $3,700 in principal has been outstanding all month.

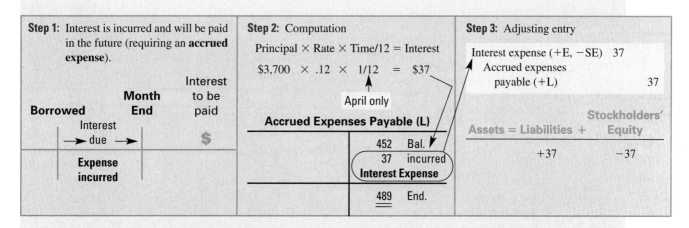

Income Taxes Payable

Computation of adjusted pretax income:

	Revenues and Gains	Expenses and Losses	
Unadjusted totals	$5,212	$4,350	From Chapter 3
Adjustments: (a)	400		
(b)		50	
(c)		25	
(d)		400	
(e)		52	
(f)		37	
	$5,612	— $4,914	= **$698** Adjusted pretax income

g. The estimated income tax rate for Terrific Lawn is 35 percent.

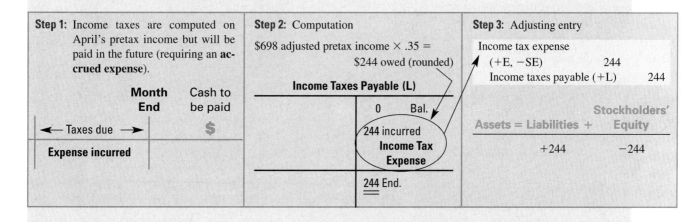

2. Adjusted trial balance:

TERRIFIC LAWN MAINTENANCE CORPORATION
Adjusted Trial Balance
At April 30, 2003

	Unadjusted Trial Balance		Adjustments		Adjusted Trial Balance	
	Debit	Credit	Debit	Credit	Debit	Credit
Cash	5,032				5,032	
Accounts receivable	1,700				1,700	
Notes receivable	0				0	
Prepaid expenses	300			(b) 50	250	
Land	3,750				3,750	
Equipment	4,600				4,600	
Accumulated depreciation		0		(c) 25		25
Accounts payable		220				220
Accrued expenses payable		0		(d) 400		489
				(e) 52		
				(f) 37		
Notes payable		3,700				3,700
Income taxes payable		0		(g) 244		244
Unearned revenues		1,600	(a) 400			1,200
Contributed capital		9,000				9,000
Retained earnings		0				0
Mowing revenue		5,200		(a) 400		5,600
Interest revenue		12				12
Wages expense	3,900		(d) 400		4,300	
Fuel expense	410				410	
Insurance expense	0		(b) 50		50	
Utilities expense	0		(e) 52		52	
Depreciation expense	0		(c) 25		25	
Interest expense	40		(f) 37		77	
Income tax expense	0		(g) 244		244	
Total	$19,732	$19,732	$1,208	$1,208	$20,490	$20,490

3. Financial statements

TERRIFIC LAWN MAINTENANCE CORPORATION
Income Statement
For the Month Ended April 30, 2003

Operating Revenues:	
Mowing revenue	$5,600
Operating Expenses:	
Wages expense	4,300
Fuel expense	410
Insurance expense	50
Utilities expense	52
Depreciation expense	25
	4,837
Operating income	763
Other items:	
Interest revenue	12
Interest expense	(77)
Pretax income	698
Income tax expense	244
Net Income	**$ 454**
Earnings per share	
($454 ÷ 1,500 shares)	$.30

TERRIFIC LAWN MAINTENANCE CORPORATION
Statement of Stockholders' Equity
For the Month Ended April 30, 2003

	Contributed Capital	Retained Earnings	Total
Balance, April 1, 2003	$ 0	$ 0	$ 0
Stock issuance	9,000		9,000
Net income		454	454
Dividends		0	0
Balance, April 30, 2003	**$9,000**	**$454**	**$9,454**

TERRIFIC LAWN MAINTENANCE CORPORATION
Balance Sheet
April 30, 2003

ASSETS		LIABILITIES	
Current Assets:		Current Liabilities:	
Cash	$ 5,032	Accounts payable	$ 220
Accounts receivable	1,700	Accrued expenses payable	489
Prepaid expenses	250	Notes payable	3,700
Total current assets	6,982	Income taxes payable	244
		Unearned revenues	1,200
		Total current liabilities	5,853
Land	3,750	**STOCKHOLDERS' EQUITY**	
Equipment (net of $25		Contributed capital	9,000
accumulated depreciation)	4,575	Retained earnings	454
		Total liabilities and	
Total assets	**$15,307**	**stockholders' equity**	**$15,307**

Statement of Cash Flows—Supplemental Disclosure

Interest paid: $40.
No income taxes were paid.
There were no significant noncash transactions.

4. Closing entry:

Mowing revenue (−R) 5,600	
Interest revenue (−R) 12	
Wages expense (−E)	4,300
Fuel expense (−E)	410
Insurance expense (−E).....................................	50
Utilities expense (−E)	52
Depreciation expense (−E)	25
Interest expense (−E)	77
Income tax expense (−E)	244
Retained earnings (+SE)	454

5. Net Profit Margin for April:

$$\frac{\text{Net Income}}{\text{Net Sales}} = \$454 \div \$5,600 = 8.1\% \text{ for the month of April}$$

CHAPTER **TAKE-AWAYS**

1. **Explain the purpose of a trial balance. p. 163**
   A trial balance is a list of all accounts with their debit or credit balances indicated in the appropriate column to provide a check on the equality of the debits and credits. The trial balance may be
   • Unadjusted—before adjustments are made.
   • Adjusted—after adjustments are made.
   • Post-closing—after revenues and expenses are closed to Retained Earnings.

2. **Analyze the adjustments necessary at the end of the period to update balance sheet and income statements accounts. p. 165**
   • Adjusting entries are necessary at the end of the accounting period to measure income properly, correct errors, and provide for adequate valuation of balance sheet accounts. The analysis involves
     a. Identifying deferred accounts (created in the past when cash was received or paid before being earned or incurred) and accrued accounts (revenues earned and expenses incurred before cash is to be received or paid in the future).
     b. Drawing a timeline and setting up T-accounts along with any computations.
     c. Recording the adjusting entry needed to obtain the appropriate ending balances in the accounts.
   • Recording adjusting entries has no effect on the Cash account.

3. **Present an income statement with earnings per share, statement of stockholders' equity, balance sheet, and supplemental cash flow information. p. 172**
   Adjusted account balances are used in preparing the following financial statements:
   • Income Statement: Revenues − Expenses = Net Income (including earnings per share computed as net income available to the common stockholders divided by the weighted-average number of shares of common stock outstanding during the period).
   • Statement of Stockholders' Equity: (Beginning Contributed Capital + Stock Issuances − Stock Repurchases) + (Beginning Retained Earnings + Net Income − Dividends) = Ending Total Stockholders' Equity.
   • Balance Sheet: Assets = Liabilities + Stockholders' Equity.
   • Supplemental cash flow information: Interest paid, income taxes paid, and significant noncash transactions.

4. **Compute and interpret the net profit margin. p. 177**
   Net profit margin (Net Income ÷ Net Sales) measures how much of every dollar of sales generated during the period is profit. A rising net profit margin signals more efficient management of sales and expenses.

FOR DEFERRED ACCOUNTS— Adjusting Entry:

↓ Liability and ↑ Revenue

or

↑ Expense and ↓ Asset

FOR ACCRUED ACCOUNTS— Adjusting Entry:

↑ Expense and ↑ Liability

or

↑ Asset and ↑ Revenue

5. Explain the closing process. p. 179

Temporary accounts (revenues, expenses, gains, and losses) are closed to a zero balance at the end of the accounting period to allow for the accumulation of income items in the following period. To close these accounts, debit each revenue and gain account, credit each expense and loss account, and record the difference (equal to net income) to Retained Earnings.

This chapter discussed the important steps in the accounting process that take place at year-end. These include the adjustment process, the preparation of the basic financial statements, and the closing process that prepares the records for the next accounting period. This end to the internal portions of the accounting process, however, is just the beginning of the process of communicating accounting information to external users.

In the next chapter we take a closer look at more sophisticated financial statements and related disclosures. We also examine the process by which financial information is disseminated to professional analysts, investors, the Securities and Exchange Commission, and the public, and the role each plays in analyzing and interpreting the information. These discussions will help you consolidate much of what you have learned about the financial reporting process from previous chapters. It will also preview many of the important issues we address later in the book.

Closing Entry:		
Each revenue	xx	
Each gain	xx	
Each expense		xx
Each loss		xx
Retained earnings		xx
(assumes net income is positive)		

KEY **RATIO**

Net profit margin measures how much of every sales dollar generated during the period is profit. A high or rising ratio suggests that the company is managing its sales and expenses efficiently. It is computed as follows (p. 177):

$$\text{Net Profit Margin} = \frac{\text{Net Income}}{\text{Net Sales}}$$

FINDING **FINANCIAL INFORMATION**

Balance Sheet

Current Assets

Accruals include:
  Interest receivable
  Rent receivable
Deferrals include:
  Inventory
  Prepaid expenses

Noncurrent Assets

Deferrals include:
 Property and equipment
 Intangibles

Current Liabilities

Accruals include:
  Interest payable
  Wages payable
  Utilities payable
  Income tax payable
Deferrals include:
  Unearned revenue

Income Statement

Revenues
  Increased by adjusting entries

Expenses
  Increased by adjusting entries

Pretax Income
  Income tax expense

Net Income

Notes

In Various Notes If Not on the Balance Sheet

Details of accrued expenses payable
Interest paid, income taxes paid, significant noncash transactions (if not reported on the statement of cash flows)

Statement of Cash Flows

Adjusting Entries Do Not Affect Cash
  Interest paid
  Income taxes paid
  Significant noncash transactions

KEY **TERMS**

Accounting Cycle p. 163
Accrued Expenses p. 166
Accrued Revenues p. 166
Adjusting Entries p. 165
Closing Entries p. 179

Contra-Account p. 164
Deferred Expenses p. 165
Deferred Revenues p. 165
Net Book Value (Book Value, Carrying Value) p. 164

Permanent (Real) Accounts p. 179
Post-Closing Trial Balance p. 180
Temporary (Nominal) Accounts p. 179
Trial Balance p. 163

QUESTIONS

1. What is a trial balance? What is its purpose?
2. Briefly explain adjusting entries. List the four types of adjusting entries, and give an example of each type.
3. What is a contra-asset? Give an example of one.
4. Explain how the financial statements relate to each other.
5. What is the equation for each of the following statements: (a) income statement, (b) balance sheet, (c) statement of cash flows, and (d) statement of stockholders' equity?
6. Explain the effect of adjusting entries on cash.
7. How is earnings per share computed and interpreted?
8. How is net profit margin computed and interpreted?
9. Contrast an unadjusted trial balance with an adjusted trial balance. What is the purpose of each?
10. What is the purpose of closing entries?
11. Differentiate among (a) permanent, (b) temporary, (c) real, and (d) nominal accounts.
12. Why are the income statement accounts closed but the balance sheet accounts are not?
13. What is a post-closing trial balance? Is it a useful part of the accounting information processing cycle? Explain.

MULTIPLE **CHOICE QUESTIONS**

1. Which of the following accounts would not appear in a closing entry?
    a. Interest Income
    b. Accumulated Depreciation
    c. Retained Earnings
    d. Salary Expense
2. Which account is least likely to appear in an adjusting journal entry?
    a. Cash
    b. Interest Receivable
    c. Property Tax Expense
    d. Salaries Payable
3. When a concert promoting company collects cash for tickets sales two months in advance of the show date, which of the following accounts is recorded?
    a. Accrued Expense
    b. Accrued Revenue
    c. Deferred Expense
    d. Deferred Revenue
4. On December 31 (fiscal year-end), an adjustment is made to reclassify a portion of unearned revenue as earned revenue. How many accounts will be affected on the year-end balance sheet by this entry?
    a. None
    b. One
    c. Two
    d. Three
5. Failure to make an adjusting entry to recognize accrued salaries payable would cause which of the following?
    a. an overstatement of assets and stockholders' equity
    b. an overstatement of assets and liabilities
    c. an understatement of expenses, liabilities, and stockholders' equity
    d. an understatement of expenses and liabilities and an overstatement of stockholders' equity
6. An adjusted trial balance
    a. shows the ending balances in a "debit" and "credit" format before posting the adjusting journal entries.

    b. is prepared after closing entries have been posted.

    c. is a tool used by financial analysts to review the performance of publicly traded companies.

    d. shows the ending balances resulting from the adjusting journal entries in a "debit" and "credit" format.

7. Company A owns a building. Which of the following statements regarding depreciation as used by accountants is false?

    a. As the value of the building decreases over time, it "depreciates."

    b. Depreciation is an estimated expense to be recorded over the building's estimated useful life.

    c. As depreciation is recorded, stockholders' equity is reduced.

    d. As depreciation is recorded, assets are reduced.

8. Which of the following columns in a trial balance are used as a source for preparing the income statement?

    a. Unadjusted Trial Balance   c. Adjusted Trial Balance

    b. Adjustments   d. Post-Closing Trial Balance

9. What ratio is required by GAAP to be reported on the financial statements or in the notes to the statements?

    a. Return on equity ratio   c. Current ratio

    b. Net profit margin ratio   d. Earnings per share ratio

10. If a company is successful in reducing selling and administrative costs while maintaining sales volume and the sales price of its product, what is the effect on the net profit margin ratio?

    a. The ratio will not change.   c. The ratio will decrease.

    b. The ratio will increase.   d. Either (a) or (c).

For more practice with multiple choice questions, go to our website at www.mhhe.com/libby4e, click on "Student Center" in the upper left menu, click on this chapter's name and number from the list of contents, and then click on "Multiple Choice Quiz" from the menu on the left.

MINI-**EXERCISES**

Preparing a Trial Balance

M4-1
LO1

DeVita Company has the following adjusted accounts and balances at year-end (June 30, 2003):

Accounts payable	200	Contributed capital	300	Long-term debt	1,300
Accounts receivable	350	Cost of sales	820	Prepaid expenses	40
Accrued expenses		Depreciation expense	110	Salaries expense	660
payable	150	Income taxes expense	110	Sales revenue	2,400
Accumulated		Income taxes payable	30	Rent expense	400
depreciation	250	Interest expense	80	Retained earnings	120
Buildings and		Interest income	50	Unearned fees	100
equipment	1,400	Inventories	610		
Cash	120	Land	200		

Required:
Prepare an adjusted trial balance in good form for the DeVita Company at June 30, 2003.

Matching Definitions with Terms

M4-2
LO2

Match each definition with its related term by entering the appropriate letter in the space provided.

Definition	Term
____ 1. A revenue not yet earned; collected in advance.	A. Accrued expense
____ 2. Office supplies on hand to be used next accounting period.	B. Deferred expense
____ 3. Rent revenue collected; not yet earned.	C. Accrued revenue
____ 4. Rent not yet collected; already earned.	D. Deferred revenue
____ 5. An expense incurred; not yet paid or recorded.	
____ 6. A revenue earned; not yet collected.	
____ 7. An expense not yet incurred; paid in advance.	
____ 8. Property taxes incurred; not yet paid.	

M4-3
L02

Matching Definitions with Terms

Match each definition with its related term by entering the appropriate letter in the space provided.

Definition	Term
___ 1. At year-end, wages payable of $3,600 had not been recorded or paid.	A. Accrued expense
___ 2. Office supplies were purchased during the year for $500, and $100 of them remained on hand (unused) at year-end.	B. Deferred expense
___ 3. Interest of $250 on a note receivable was earned at year-end, although collection of the interest is not due until the following year.	C. Accrued revenue
___ 4. At year-end, service revenue of $2,000 was collected in cash but was not yet earned.	D. Deferred revenue

M4-4
L02

Recording Adjusting Entries (Deferred Accounts)

For each of the following transactions for Hosey Company, give the adjusting entry required for the year ended December 31, 2003, using the process illustrated in the chapter:

a. Collected $900 rent for the period December 1, 2003, to March 1, 2004, which was credited to Unearned Rent Revenue on December 1, 2003.

b. Paid $2,400 for a two-year insurance premium on July 1, 2003; debited Prepaid Insurance for that amount.

c. Purchased a machine for $12,000 cash on January 1, 2000. The company estimates annual depreciation of $2,000.

M4-5
L02

Determining Financial Statement Effects of Adjusting Entries (Deferred Accounts)

For each of the transactions in M4-4, indicate the amounts and direction of effects of the adjusting entry on the elements of the balance sheet and income statement. Using the following format, indicate + for increase, − for decrease, and NE for no effect.

	BALANCE SHEET			INCOME STATEMENT		
Transaction	Assets	Liabilities	Stockholders' Equity	Revenues	Expenses	Net Income
a.						
b.						
c.						

M4-6
L02

Recording Adjusting Entries (Accrued Accounts)

For each of the following transactions for Hosey Company, give the adjusting entry required for the year ended December 31, 2003, using the process illustrated in the chapter:

a. Received a $220 utility bill for electricity usage in December to be paid in January 2004.

b. Owed wages to 10 employees who worked three days at $120 each per day at the end of December. The company will pay employees at the end of the first week of January 2004.

c. On September 1, 2003, loaned $3,000 to an officer who will repay the loan in one year at an annual interest rate of 12 percent.

M4-7
L02

Determining Financial Statement Effects of Adjusting Entries (Accrued Accounts)

For each of the transactions in M4-6, indicate the amounts and direction of effects of the adjusting entry on the elements of the balance sheet and income statement. Using the following format, indicate + for increase, − for decrease, and NE for no effect.

	BALANCE SHEET			INCOME STATEMENT		
Transaction	**Assets**	**Liabilities**	**Stockholders' Equity**	**Revenues**	**Expenses**	**Net Income**
a.						
b.						
c.						

Reporting an Income Statement with Earnings per Share

M4-8
LO3

Hosey Company has the following adjusted trial balance at December 31, 2003. No dividends were declared. However, 400 additional shares were issued during the year for $2,000:

	Debit	Credit
Cash	$ 1,500	
Accounts receivable	2,000	
Interest receivable	120	
Prepaid insurance	1,800	
Notes receivable	3,000	
Equipment	12,000	
Accumulated depreciation		$ 2,000
Accounts payable		1,600
Accrued expenses payable		3,820
Income taxes payable		2,900
Unearned rent revenue		600
Contributed capital (500 shares)		2,400
Retained earnings		1,000
Sales revenue		42,000
Interest revenue		120
Rent revenue		300
Wages expense	21,600	
Depreciation expense	2,000	
Utilities expense	220	
Insurance expense	600	
Rent expense	9,000	
Income tax expense	2,900	
Total	$56,740	$56,740

Prepare an income statement in good form for 2003. Include earnings per share.

Reporting a Statement of Stockholders' Equity

M4-9
LO3

Refer to M4-8. Prepare a statement of stockholders' equity in good form for 2003.

Reporting a Balance Sheet and Explaining the Effects of Adjustments on the Statement of Cash Flows

M4-10
LO3

Refer to M4-8. Prepare a classified balance sheet in good form at December 31, 2003. Then explain how the adjustments in M4-4 and M4-6 affected the operating, investing, and financing activities on the statement of cash flows.

Analyzing Net Profit Margin

M4-11
LO4

Compute net income based on the trial balance in M4-8. Then compute Hosey Company's net profit margin for 2003.

M4-12   **Recording Closing Entries**

L05

Refer to the adjusted trial balance in M4-8. Prepare closing entries on December 31, 2003.

EXERCISES

E4-1   **Preparing a Trial Balance**

L01

Goodison Consultants, Inc., provides marketing research for clients in the retail industry. The company had the following unadjusted balances at September 30, 2004:

Accumulated Depreciation		Accrued Expenses Payable	
	18,100		25,650

Cash		General and Administrative Expenses		Supplies Inventory	
173,000		320,050		12,200	

Wages and Benefits Expense		Prepaid Expenses		Interest Expense	
1,590,000		10,200		17,200	

Accounts Receivable		Consulting Fees Earned		Retained Earnings	
225,400			2,564,200		?

Income Taxes Payable		Travel Expense		Building and Equipment	
	2,030	23,990		323,040	

Utilities Expense		Gain on Sale of Land		Unearned Consulting Fees	
25,230			5,000		32,500

Investment Income		Accounts Payable		Land	
	10,800		86,830	60,000	

Other Operating Expenses		Contributed Capital		Professional Development Expense	
188,000			233,370	18,600	

Notes Payable		Rent Expense (on leased computers)		Investments	
	160,000	152,080		145,000	

Required:

Prepare in good form an unadjusted trial balance for Goodison Consultants, Inc., at September 30, 2004.

Identifying Adjusting Entries from Unadjusted Trial Balance

As stated in its annual report, "Compaq Computer Corporation is a global information technology company, developing and marketing hardware, software, solutions, and services." Following is a trial balance listing accounts that Compaq uses. Assume that the balances are unadjusted at the end of a recent fiscal year ended December 31.

E4-2
LO1, 2
Compaq
Computer
Corporation

COMPAQ COMPUTER CORPORATION
Unadjusted Trial Balance
At December 31, 2003
(millions of dollars)

	Debit	Credit
Cash	$ 4,091	
Accounts receivable	6,998	
Inventories	2,005	
Prepaid expenses	624	
Property, plant, and equipment	5,223	
Accumulated depreciation		$ 2,321
Intangible assets	3,641	
Other assets	3,414	
Accounts payable		4,237
Accrued liabilities		1,110
Income taxes payable		282
Pension obligations		545
Other liabilities		5,104
Contributed capital		7,270
Retained earnings		8,633
Product revenue		27,372
Services revenue		3,797
Cost of products sold	21,383	
Cost of services sold	2,597	
Selling, general, and administrative expenses	4,978	
Research and development costs	1,353	
Other operating expenses	4,283	
Income tax expense	81	
	$60,671	$60,671

Required:
1. Based on the information in the unadjusted trial balance, list the balance sheet deferred accounts that may need to be adjusted at December 31 and the related account for each (no computations are necessary).
2. Based on the information in the unadjusted trial balance, list the balance sheet accrued accounts that may need to be recorded at December 31 and the related account for each (no computations are necessary).

Recording Adjusting Entries

E4-3
LO2

Yellin Company completed its first year of operations on December 31, 2003. All of the 2003 entries have been recorded except for the following:

a. At year-end, employees earned wages of $6,000, which will be paid on the next payroll date, January 6, 2004.
b. At year-end, the company had earned interest revenue of $3,000. The cash will be collected March 1, 2004.

Required:

1. What is the annual reporting period for this company?
2. Identify whether each transaction results in a deferred or an accrued account. Using the process illustrated in the chapter, give the required adjusting entry for transactions (*a*) and (*b*). Include appropriate dates and write a brief explanation of each entry.
3. Why are these adjustments made?

E4-4   Recording Adjusting Entries and Reporting Balances in Financial Statements

LO2

Thapa Company is making adjusting entries for the year ended December 31, 2004. In developing information for the adjusting entries, the accountant learned the following:

a. A two-year insurance premium of $7,200 was paid on September 1, 2004, for coverage beginning on that date.

b. At December 31, 2004, the following data relating to shipping supplies was obtained from the records and supporting documents.

Shipping supplies on hand, January 1, 2004	$15,000
Purchases of shipping supplies during 2004	72,000
Shipping supplies on hand, counted on December 31, 2004	11,000

Required:

1. What amount should be reported on the 2004 income statement for Insurance Expense? For Shipping Supplies Expense?
2. What amount should be reported on the December 31, 2004, balance sheet for Prepaid Insurance? For Shipping Supplies?
3. Using the process illustrated in the chapter, record the adjusting entry for insurance at December 31, 2004, assuming that the premium was paid on September 1, 2004, and the bookkeeper debited the full amount to Prepaid Insurance.
4. Using the process illustrated in the chapter, record the adjusting entry for supplies at December 31, 2004, assuming that the purchases of shipping supplies were debited in full to Shipping Supplies.

E4-5   Determining Financial Statement Effects of Adjusting Entries

LO2

Refer to E4-3 and E4-4.

Required:

For each of the transactions in E4-3 and E4-4, indicate the amount and direction of effects of the adjusting entry on the elements of the balance sheet and income statement. Using the following format, indicate + for increase, − for decrease, and NE for no effect.

	BALANCE SHEET			INCOME STATEMENT		
Transaction	**Assets**	**Liabilities**	**Stockholders' Equity**	**Revenues**	**Expenses**	**Net Income**
E4-3 a.						
E4-3 b.						
E4-4 a.						
E4-4 b.						

E4-6   Recording Seven Typical Adjusting Entries

LO2

Cutter's Variety Store is completing the accounting process for the year just ended, December 31, 2003. The transactions during 2003 have been journalized and posted. The following data with respect to adjusting entries are available:

a. Office supplies on hand at January 1, 2003, was $250. Office supplies purchased and debited to Office Supplies during the year amounted to $600. The year-end count showed $300 of supplies on hand.

b. Wages earned by employees during December 2003, unpaid and unrecorded at December 31, 2003, amounted to $2,700. The last payroll was December 28; the next payroll will be January 6, 2004.

c. Three-fourths of the basement of the store is rented for $1,100 per month to another merchant, M. Dittman. Dittman sells compatible, but not competitive, merchandise. On November 1, 2003, the store collected six months' rent in the amount of $6,600 in advance from Dittman; it was credited in full to Unearned Rent Revenue when collected.

d. The remaining basement space is rented to Kathy's Specialty Shop for $520 per month, payable monthly. On December 31, 2003, the rent for November and December 2003 had not been collected or recorded. Collection is expected January 10, 2004.

e. The store used delivery equipment that cost $30,000 and $6,000 was the estimated depreciation for 2003.

f. On July 1, 2003, a two-year insurance premium amounting to $3,000 was paid in cash and debited in full to Prepaid Insurance. Coverage began on July 1, 2003.

g. Cutter's operates a repair shop to meet its own needs. The shop also does repairs for M. Dittman. At the end of December 31, 2003, Dittman had not paid for $750 in completed alterations. This amount has not yet been recorded as Repair Shop Revenue. Collection is expected during January 2004.

Required:

1. Identify each transaction as a deferred revenue, deferred expense, accrued revenue, or accrued expense.

2. Using the process illustrated in the chapter, for each situation record the adjusting entry that should be recorded for Cutter's at December 31, 2003.

Determining Financial Statement Effects of Seven Typical Adjusting Entries

E4-7
LO2

Refer to E4-6.

Required:

For each transaction in E4-6, indicate the amount and direction of effects of the adjusting entry on the elements of the balance sheet and income statement. Using the following format, indicate + for increase, − for decrease, and NE for no effect.

	BALANCE SHEET			INCOME STATEMENT		
Transaction	**Assets**	**Liabilities**	**Stockholders' Equity**	**Revenues**	**Expenses**	**Net Income**
a.						
b.						
c.						
etc.						

Recording Transactions Including Adjusting and Closing Entries (Nonquantitative)

E4-8
LO2, 5

The following accounts are used by Britt's Knits, Inc.

Codes	Accounts	Codes	Accounts
A	Cash	J	Contributed capital
B	Office supplies	K	Retained earnings
C	Accounts receivable	L	Service revenue
D	Office equipment	M	Interest revenue
E	Accumulated depreciation	N	Wage expense
F	Note payable	O	Depreciation expense
G	Wages payable	P	Interest expense
H	Interest payable	Q	Supplies expense
I	Unearned service revenue	R	None of the above

Required:

For each of the following nine independent situations, give the journal entry by entering the appropriate code(s) and amount(s).

	DEBIT		CREDIT	
Independent Situations	**Code**	**Amount**	**Code**	**Amount**
a. Accrued wages, unrecorded and unpaid at year-end, $400 (example).	N	400	G	400
b. Service revenue collected in advance, $800.				
c. Dividends declared and paid during the year, $900.				
d. Depreciation expense for the year, $1,000.				
e. Service revenue earned but not yet collected at year-end, $600.				
f. Office Supplies on hand during the year, $400; supplies on hand at year-end, $150.				
g. At year-end, interest on note payable not yet recorded or paid, $220.				
h. Balance at year-end in Service Revenue account, $62,000. Give the closing entry at year-end.				
i. Balance at year-end in Interest Expense account, $420. Give the closing entry at year-end.				

E4-9   **Determining Financial Statement Effects of Three Adjusting Entries**

L02

Iowa Company started operations on January 1, 2004. It is now December 31, 2004, the end of the annual accounting period. The part-time bookkeeper needs your help to analyze the following three transactions:

a. On January 1, 2004, the company purchased a special machine for a cash cost of $12,000. The machine's cost is estimated to depreciate at $1,200 per year.

b. During 2004, the company purchased office supplies that cost $1,400. At the end of 2004, office supplies of $400 remained on hand.

c. On July 1, 2004, the company paid cash of $400 for a two-year premium on an insurance policy on the machine that begins coverage on July 1, 2004.

Required:

Complete the following schedule of the amounts that should be reported for 2004:

Selected Balance Sheet Amounts at December 31, 2004	**Amount to Be Reported**
Assets	
Equipment	$_____
Accumulated depreciation	_____
Carrying value of equipment	_____
Office supplies	_____
Prepaid insurance	_____

Selected Income Statement Amounts for the Year Ended December 31, 2004	
Expenses	
Depreciation expense	$_____
Office supplies expense	_____
Insurance expense	_____

Determining Financial Statement Effects of Adjustments for Interest on Two Notes

E4-10
L02

Note 1: On April 1, 2003, Seaquist Corporation received a $10,000, 10 percent note from a customer in settlement of a $10,000 open account receivable. According to the terms, the principal of the note and interest are payable at the end of 12 months. The annual accounting period for Seaquist ends on December 31, 2003.

Note 2: On August 1, 2003, to meet a cash shortage, Seaquist Corporation obtained a $20,000, 12 percent loan from a local bank. The principal of the note and interest expense are payable at the end of 12 months.

Required:

For the relevant transaction dates of each note, indicate the amounts and direction of effects on the elements of the balance sheet and income statement. Using the following format, indicate + for increase, − for decrease, and NE for no effect. (*Reminder:* Assets = Liabilities + Stockholders' Equity; Revenues − Expenses = Net Income; and Net Income accounts are closed to Retained Earnings, a part of Stockholders' Equity.)

		BALANCE SHEET			INCOME STATEMENT		
Date	**Transaction**	**Assets**	**Liabil-ities**	**Stock-holders' Equity**	**Revenues**	**Expenses**	**Net Income**
April 1, 2003	Receipt of Note 1						
December 31, 2003	Adjustment for Note 1						
March 31, 2004	Collection of Note 1						
August 1, 2003	Borrowing on Note 2						
December 31, 2003	Adjustment for Note 2						
July 31, 2004	Payment on Note 2						

Inferring Transactions

E4-11
L02
Deere & Company

Deere & Company is the world's leading producer of agricultural equipment; a leading supplier of a broad range of industrial equipment for construction, forestry, and public works; a producer and marketer of a broad line of lawn and grounds care equipment; and a provider of credit, managed health care plans, and insurance products for businesses and the general public. The following information was from a recent annual report (in millions of dollars):

Income Taxes Payable			
		Beg. bal.	71
(a)	?	(b)	332
		End. bal.	80

Interest Payable			
		Beg. bal.	45
(e)	297	(f)	?
		End. bal.	51

Dividends Payable			
		Beg. bal.	43
(c)	?	(d)	176
		End. bal.	48

Required:

1. Identify the nature of each of the transactions (*a*) through (*f*). Specifically, what activities cause the accounts to increase and decrease?
2. For transactions (*a*), (*c*), and (*f*), compute the amount.

E4-12 **Analyzing the Effects of Errors on Financial Statement Items**

LO2

Graham & Crumb, Inc., publishers of movie and song trivia books, made the following errors in adjusting the accounts at year-end (December 31):

  a. Did not record $10,000 depreciation on the equipment costing $130,000.

  b. Failed to adjust the Unearned Revenue account to reflect that $3,000 was earned by the end of the year.

  c. Recorded a full year of accrued interest expense on a $15,000, 12 percent note payable that has been outstanding only since November 1.

  d. Failed to adjust Prepaid Insurance to reflect that $400 of insurance coverage has been used.

  e. Did not accrue $750 owed to the company by another company renting part of the building as a storage facility.

Required:

  1. For each error, prepare the adjusting journal entry (a) that was made, if any, and (b) that should have been made at year-end.

  2. Using the following headings, indicate the effect of each error and the amount of the effect (that is, the difference between the entry that was or was not made and the entry that should have been made). Use O if the effect overstates the item, U if the effect understates the item, and NE if there is no effect. (*Reminder:* Assets = Liabilities + Stockholders' Equity; Revenues − Expenses = Net Income; and Net Income accounts are closed to Retained Earnings, a part of Stockholders' Equity.)

	BALANCE SHEET			INCOME STATEMENT		
Transaction	**Assets**	**Liabilities**	**Stockholders' Equity**	**Revenues**	**Expenses**	**Net Income**
a.						
b.						
c.						
etc.						

E4-13 **Analyzing the Effects of Adjusting Entries on the Income Statement and Balance Sheet**

LO2

On December 31, 2004, Alan and Company prepared an income statement and balance sheet and failed to take into account four adjusting entries. The income statement, prepared on this incorrect basis, reflected pretax income of $30,000. The balance sheet (before the effect of income taxes) reflected total assets, $90,000; total liabilities, $40,000; and stockholders' equity, $50,000. The data for the four adjusting entries follow:

  a. Depreciation of $8,000 for the year on equipment that cost $85,000 was not recorded.

  b. Wages amounting to $17,000 for the last three days of December 2004 were not paid and not recorded (the next payroll will be on January 10, 2005).

  c. Rent revenue of $4,800 was collected on December 1, 2004, for office space for the period December 1, 2004, to February 28, 2005. The $4,800 was credited in full to Unearned Rent Revenue when collected.

  d. Income taxes were not recorded. The income tax rate for the company is 30 percent.

Required:

Complete the following tabulation to correct the financial statements for the effects of the four errors (indicate deductions with parentheses):

Items	Net Income	Total Assets	Total Liabilities	Stockholders' Equity
Balances reported	$30,000	$90,000	$40,000	$50,000
Effect of depreciation	_____	_____	_____	_____
Effect of wages	_____	_____	_____	_____
Effect of rent revenue	_____	_____	_____	_____
Adjusted balances	_____	_____	_____	_____
Effect of income taxes	_____	_____	_____	_____
Correct balances	_____	_____	_____	_____

Recording the Effects of Adjusting Entries and Reporting a Corrected Income Statement and Balance Sheet

E4-14
LO2, 3

On December 31, 2003, the bookkeeper for Joseph Company prepared the following income statement and balance sheet summarized here but neglected to consider three adjusting entries.

	As Prepared	Effects of Adjusting Entries	Corrected Amounts
Income Statement			
Revenues	$98,000	_____	_____
Expenses	(72,000)	_____	_____
Income tax expense	_____	_____	_____
Net income	$26,000		_____
Balance Sheet			
Assets			
Cash	$20,000	_____	_____
Accounts receivable	22,000	_____	_____
Rent receivable		_____	_____
Equipment	50,000	_____	_____
Accumulated depreciation	(10,000)	_____	_____
	$82,000		_____
Liabilities			
Accounts payable	$10,000	_____	_____
Income taxes payable		_____	_____
Stockholders' Equity			
Contributed capital	40,000	_____	_____
Retained earnings	32,000	_____	_____
	$82,000		_____

Data on the three adjusting entries follow:

  a. Depreciation of $5,000 on the equipment for 2003 was not recorded.
  b. Rent revenue of $2,000 earned for December 2003 was neither collected nor recorded.
  c. Income tax expense of $6,900 for 2003 was neither paid nor recorded.

Required:
  1. Prepare the three adjusting entries that were omitted. Use the account titles shown in the income statement and balance sheet data.
  2. Complete the two columns to the right in the preceding tabulation to show the correct amounts on the income statement and balance sheet.

Reporting a Correct Income Statement with Earnings per Share to Include the Effects of Adjusting Entries and Evaluating the Net Profit Margin as an Auditor

E4-15
LO2, 3, 4

Derek, Inc., completed its first year of operations on December 31, 2004. Because this is the end of the annual accounting period, the company bookkeeper prepared the following tentative income statement:

Income Statement, 2004		
Rental revenue		$114,000
Expenses		
Salaries and wages expense	$28,500	
Maintenance expense	12,000	
Rent expense	9,000	
Utilities expense	4,000	
Gas and oil expense	3,000	
Miscellaneous expenses		
(items not listed elsewhere)	1,000	
Total expenses		57,500
Income		$ 56,500

You are an independent CPA hired by the company to audit the company's accounting systems and review the financial statements. In your audit, you developed additional data as follows:

a.   Wages for the last three days of December amounting to $310 were not recorded or paid.
b.   The $400 telephone bill for December 2004 has not been recorded or paid.
c.   Depreciation on rental autos, amounting to $23,000 for 2004, was not recorded.
d.   Interest on a $20,000, one-year, 10 percent note payable dated October 1, 2004, was not recorded. The 10 percent interest is payable on the maturity date of the note.
e.   The Unearned Rental Revenue account includes $4,000 revenue to be earned in January 2005.
f.   Maintenance expense excludes $1,000, which is the cost of maintenance supplies used during 2004.
g.   The income tax expense is $7,000. Payment of income tax will be made in 2005.

Required:
1.   What adjusting entry for each item (*a*) through (*g*) do you recommend Derek should record at December 31, 2004? If none is required, explain why.
2.   Prepare a corrected income statement for 2004 in good form including earnings per share, assuming that 7,000 shares of stock are outstanding. Show computations.
3.   Compute the net profit margin based on the corrected information. What does this ratio suggest? If the average net profit margin for the industry is 18 percent, what might you infer about Derek?

E4–16
LO2

Evaluating the Effect of Adjusting Unearned Subscriptions on Cash Flows and Performance as a Manager

You are the regional sales manager for Abruzzo News Company. Abruzzo is making adjusting entries for the year ended March 31, 2004. On September 1, 2003, customers in your region paid $18,000 cash for three-year magazine subscriptions beginning on that date. The magazines are published and mailed to customers monthly. These were the only subscription sales in your region during the year.

Required:
1.   What amount should be reported as cash from operations on the statement of cash flows?
2.   What amount should be reported on the income statement for subscriptions revenue for the year ended March 31, 2004?
3.   What amount should be reported on the March 31, 2004, balance sheet for unearned subscriptions revenue?
4.   Give the adjusting entry at March 31, 2004, assuming that the subscriptions received on September 1, 2003, were recorded for the full amount in Unearned Subscriptions Revenue.
5.   The company expects your region's annual revenue target to be $4,000.
   a.   Evaluate your region's performance, assuming that the revenue target is based on cash sales.
   b.   Evaluate your region's performance, assuming that the revenue target is based on accrual accounting.

E4–17
LO1, 2

Recording Four Adjusting Entries and Completing the Trial Balance Worksheet

Seneca Company prepared the following trial balance at the end of its first year of operations ending December 31, 2003. To simplify the case, the amounts given are in thousands of dollars.

Account Titles	UNADJUSTED		ADJUSTMENTS		ADJUSTED	
	Debit	Credit	Debit	Credit	Debit	Credit
Cash	38					
Accounts receivable	9					
Prepaid insurance	6					
Machinery	80					
Accumulated depreciation						
Accounts payable		9				
Wages payable						
Income taxes payable						
Contributed capital (4,000 shares)		76				
Retained earnings	4					
Revenues (not detailed)		84				
Expenses (not detailed)	32					
Totals	169	169				

Other data not yet recorded at December 31, 2003:

a. Insurance expired during 2003, $5.
b. Depreciation expense for 2003, $4.
c. Wages payable, $7.
d. Income tax expense, $9.

Required:
1. Prepare the adjusting entries for 2003.
2. Complete the trial balance Adjustments and Adjusted columns.

Reporting an Income Statement, Statement of Stockholders' Equity, and Balance Sheet

Refer to E4-17.

Required:
Using the adjusted balances in E4-17, prepare an income statement, statement of stockholders' equity, and balance sheet for 2003.

E4-18
LO3

Recording Closing Entries

Refer to E4-17.

Required:
Using the adjusted balances in E4-17, give the closing entries for 2003. What is the purpose of "closing the books" at the end of the accounting period?

E4-19
LO5

PROBLEMS

Preparing a Trial Balance (AP4-1)

Dell Computer Corporation is the world's largest computer systems company selling directly to customers. Products include desktop computer systems, notebook computers, workstations, network server and storage products, and peripheral hardware and software. The following is a list of accounts and amounts reported. The accounts have normal debit or credit balances and the dollars are rounded to the nearest million. Assume the year ended on January 29, 2003, in recent financial statements.

P4-1
LO1
Dell
Computer
Corporation

Accounts payable	$ 2,397	Other assets	$ 806
Accounts receivable	2,094	Other expenses	38
Accrued expenses payable	1,298	Other liabilities	349
Accumulated depreciation	252	Property, plant, and equipment	775
Cash	520	Research and	
Contributed capital	1,781	development expense	272
Cost of sales	14,137	Retained earnings	?
Income tax expense	624	Sales revenue	18,243
Inventories	273	Selling, general, and	
Long-term debt	512	administrative expenses	1,788
Marketable securities	2,661		

Required:

Prepare an adjusted trial balance at January 29, 2003. How did you determine the amount for retained earnings?

P4-2

L02

Recording Adjusting Entries (AP4-2)

McCall Company's annual accounting year ends on December 31. It is December 31, 2004, and all of the 2004 entries except the following adjusting entries have been made:

a. On September 1, 2004, McCall collected six months' rent of $4,800 on storage space. At that date, McCall debited Cash and credited Unearned Rent Revenue for $4,800.

b. The company earned service revenue of $3,000 on a special job that was completed December 29, 2004. Collection will be made during January 2005. No entry has been recorded.

c. On November 1, 2004, McCall paid a one-year premium for property insurance, $4,200, for coverage starting on that date. Cash was credited and Prepaid Insurance was debited for this amount.

d. At December 31, 2004, wages earned by employees totaled $1,100. The employees will be paid on the next payroll date, January 15, 2005.

e. Depreciation of $1,000 must be recognized on a service truck purchased on July 1, 2004, at a cost of $12,000.

f. Cash of $1,500 was collected on November 1, 2004, for services to be rendered evenly over the next year beginning on November 1. Unearned Service Revenue was credited when the cash was received.

g. On December 27, 2004, the company received a tax bill of $400 from the city for 2004 property taxes on land. The tax bill is payable during January 2005.

h. On October 1, 2004, the company borrowed $10,000 from a local bank and signed a 12 percent note for that amount. The principal and interest are payable on maturity date, September 30, 2005.

Required:

1. Indicate whether each transaction relates to a deferred revenue, deferred expense, accrued revenue, or accrued expense.

2. Give the adjusting entry required for each transaction at December 31, 2004.

P4-3

L02

Determining Financial Statement Effects of Adjusting Entries (AP4-3)

Refer to P4-2.

Required:

1. Indicate whether each transaction relates to a deferred revenue, deferred expense, accrued revenue, or accrued expense.

2. Using the following headings, indicate the effect of each adjusting entry and the amount of the effect. Use + for increase, − for decrease, and NE for no effect. (*Reminder:* Assets = Liabilities + Stockholders' Equity; Revenues − Expenses = Net Income; and Net Income accounts are closed to Retained Earnings, a part of Stockholders' Equity.)

	BALANCE SHEET			INCOME STATEMENT		
Transaction	Assets	Liabilities	Stockholders' Equity	Revenues	Expenses	Net Income
a.						
b.						
c.						
etc.						

Recording Adjusting Entries (AP4-4)

Totka Towing Company is at the end of its accounting year, December 31, 2003. The following data that must be considered were developed from the company's records and related documents:

P4-4
L02

a. On July 1, 2003, a three-year insurance premium on equipment in the amount of $1,200 was paid and debited in full to Prepaid Insurance on that date. Coverage began on July 1.

b. During 2003, office supplies amounting to $800 were purchased for cash and debited in full to Supplies. At the end of 2002, the count of supplies remaining on hand was $200. The inventory of supplies counted on hand at December 31, 2003, was $300.

c. On December 31, 2003, HH's Garage completed repairs on one of the company's trucks at a cost of $800; the amount is not yet recorded and by agreement will be paid during January 2004.

d. In December 2003, a tax bill for $1,600 on land owned during 2003 was received from the city. The taxes, which have not been recorded, are due and will be paid on February 15, 2004.

e. On December 31, 2003, the company completed a contract for an out-of-state company for $8,000 payable by the customer within 30 days. No cash has been collected, and no journal entry has been made for this transaction.

f. On July 1, 2003, the company purchased a new hauling van at a cash cost of $23,600. Depreciation estimated at $1,100 for the year has not been recorded for 2003.

g. On October 1, 2003, the company borrowed $10,000 from the local bank on a one-year, 12 percent note payable. The principal plus interest is payable at the end of 12 months.

h. The income before any of the adjustments or income taxes was $30,000. The company's federal income tax rate is 30 percent. Compute adjusted income based on (a) through (g) to determine income tax expense.

Required:
1. Indicate whether each transaction relates to a deferred revenue, deferred expense, accrued revenue, or accrued expense.
2. Give the adjusting entry required for each transaction at December 31, 2003.

Determining Financial Statement Effects of Adjusting Entries (AP4-5)

Refer to P4-4.

P4-5
L02

Required:
1. Indicate whether each transaction relates to a deferred revenue, deferred expense, accrued revenue, or accrued expense.
2. Using the following headings, indicate the effect of each adjusting entry and the amount of each. Use + for increase, − for decrease, and NE for no effect. (*Reminder:* Assets = Liabilities + Stockholders' Equity; Revenues − Expenses = Net Income; and Net Income accounts are closed to Retained Earnings, a part of Stockholders' Equity.)

	BALANCE SHEET			INCOME STATEMENT		
Transaction	**Assets**	**Liabilities**	**Stockholders' Equity**	**Revenues**	**Expenses**	**Net Income**
a.						
b.						
c.						
etc.						

P4-6
LO2

Computing Amounts on Financial Statements and Finding Financial Information (AP4-6)

The following information was provided by the records of Collegetown Apartments (a corporation) at the end of the annual fiscal period, December 31, 2003:

Cash Receipts
a.	Rent revenue collected in cash during 2003 for occupancy in 2003	$512,000
b.	Rent revenue earned for occupancy in December 2003; not collected until 2004	16,000
c.	In December 2003, collected rent revenue in advance for January 2004	12,000

Cash Disbursements for Salaries
d.	Cash payment in January 2003 for employee salaries earned in December 2002	4,000
e.	Salaries incurred and paid during 2003	62,000
f.	Salaries earned by employees during December 2003 that will be paid in January 2004	3,000
g.	Cash advance to employees in December 2003 for salaries that will be earned in January 2004	1,500

Cash Disbursements for Supplies
h.	Maintenance supplies on January 1, 2003 (balance on hand)	3,000
i.	Maintenance supplies purchased for cash during 2003	8,000
j.	Maintenance supplies counted on December 31, 2003	1,700

Required:
Using T-accounts, compute the amounts that should be reported in Collegetown Apartments' 2003 financial statements for the following items and indicate on which financial statement the item is located. For Cash, create one T-account and label each effect to determine the amounts from renters, to suppliers, and to employees:

1. Rent revenue
2. Salary expense
3. Maintenance supplies expense
4. Cash from renters
5. Rent receivable
6. Cash to suppliers
7. Receivables from employees
8. Maintenance supplies inventory
9. Unearned rent revenue
10. Salaries payable
11. Cash to employees

P4-7
LO1, 2, 4, 5

Inferring Year-End Adjustments, Computing Earnings per Share and Net Profit Margin, and Recording Closing Entries (AP4-7)

Wagonblatt Company is completing the information processing cycle at its fiscal year-end, December 31, 2003. Following are the correct balances at December 31, 2003, for the accounts both before and after the adjusting entries for 2003.

	TRIAL BALANCE, DECEMBER 31, 2003					
Items	**Before Adjusting Entries**		**Adjustments**		**After Adjusting Entries**	
	Debit	**Credit**	**Debit**	**Credit**	**Debit**	**Credit**
a. Cash	$ 9,000				$ 9,000	

b. Accounts receivable			400		
c. Prepaid insurance	600		400		
d. Equipment	120,200		120,200		
e. Accumulated depreciation, equipment		$ 31,500		$ 40,000	
f. Income taxes payable				4,700	
g. Contributed capital		80,000		80,000	
h. Retained earnings, January 1, 2003		14,000		14,000	
i. Service revenue		46,000		46,400	
j. Salary expense	41,700		41,700		
k. Depreciation expense			8,500		
l. Insurance expense			200		
m. Income tax expense			4,700		
	$171,500	$171,500	$185,100	$185,100	

Required:

1. Compare the amounts in the columns before and after the adjusting entries to reconstruct the adjusting entries made in 2003. Provide an explanation of each.
2. Compute the amount of income assuming that it is based on the amounts (a) before adjusting entries and (b) after adjusting entries. Which income amount is correct? Explain why.
3. Compute earnings per share, assuming that 3,000 shares of stock are outstanding.
4. Compute the net profit margin. What does this suggest to you about the company?
5. Record the closing entries at December 31, 2003.

Recording Adjusting and Closing Entries and Preparing a Balance Sheet and Income Statement Including Earnings per Share (AP4-8)

P4-8
LO1, 2, 3, 5

Dorn, Inc., a small service company, keeps its records without the help of an accountant. After much effort, an outside accountant prepared the following unadjusted trial balance as of the end of the annual accounting period, December 31, 2004:

Account Titles	Debit	Credit
Cash	60,000	
Accounts receivable	13,000	
Supplies	800	
Prepaid insurance	1,000	
Service trucks	20,000	
Accumulated depreciation, service trucks		12,000
Other assets	11,200	
Accounts payable		3,000
Wages payable		
Income taxes payable		
Note payable (3 years; 10% interest due each December 31)		20,000
Contributed capital (5,000 shares outstanding)		28,200
Retained earnings		7,500
Service revenue		77,000
Remaining expenses (not detailed; excludes income tax)	41,700	
Income tax expense		
Totals	147,700	147,700

Data not yet recorded at December 31, 2004:

a. The supplies counted on December 31, 2004, reflected $300 remaining on hand to be used in 2005.
b. Insurance expired during 2004, $500.
c. Depreciation expense for 2004, $4,000.
d. Wages earned by employees not yet paid on December 31, 2004, $900.
e. Income tax expense was $7,350.

Required:

1. Record the 2004 adjusting entries.
2. Prepare an income statement and a classified balance sheet that include the effects of the preceding five transactions.
3. Record the 2004 closing entries.

P4-9

LO1, 2, 3, 4, 5

Comprehensive Review Problem: From Recording Transactions (including Adjusting and Closing Entries) to Preparing a Complete Set of Financial Statements and Performing Ratio Analysis (see Chapters 2, 3, and 4) (AP4-9)

Brothers Steve and Herman Hargenrater began operations of their tool and die shop (H & H Tool, Inc.) on January 1, 2002. The annual reporting period ends December 31. The trial balance on January 1, 2003, follows (the amounts are rounded to thousands of dollars to simplify):

Account No.	Account Titles	Debit	Credit
01	Cash	3	
02	Accounts receivable	5	
03	Supplies	12	
04	Land		
05	Equipment	60	
06	Accumulated depreciation (on equipment)		6
07	Remaining assets (not detailed to simplify)	4	
11	Accounts payable		5
12	Notes payable		
13	Wages payable		
14	Interest payable		
15	Income taxes payable		
21	Contributed capital (65,000 shares)		65
31	Retained earnings		8
35	Service revenue		
40	Depreciation expense		
41	Income tax expense		
42	Interest expense		
43	Remaining expenses (not detailed to simplify)	—	—
	Totals	84	84

Transactions during 2003 (summarized in thousands of dollars) follow:

a. Borrowed $10 cash on a five year, 12 percent note payable, dated March 1, 2003.
b. Purchased land for a future building site; paid cash, $9.
c. Earned revenues for 2003, $160, including $40 on credit.
d. Sold 3,000 additional shares of capital stock for $1 cash per share (show dollars in thousands; number of shares and price per share are as presented).
e. Recognized $85 in remaining expenses for 2003, including $15 on credit.
f. Collected accounts receivable, $24.
g. Purchased additional assets, $10 cash (debit Remaining Assets).
h. Paid accounts payable, $13.
i. Purchased supplies on account for future use, $18.
j. Signed a $25 service contract to start February 1, 2004.
k. Declared and paid a cash dividend, $17.

Data for adjusting entries:

l. Supplies counted on December 31, 2003, $14 (debit Remaining Expenses).
m. Depreciation for the year on the equipment, $6.
n. Interest accrued on notes payable (to be computed).
o. Wages earned since the December 24 payroll not yet paid, $12.
p. Income tax expense was $8, payable in 2004.

Required:
1. Set up T-accounts for the accounts on the trial balance and enter beginning balances.
2. Record transactions (*a*) through (*k*) and post them to the T-accounts.
3. Record and post the adjusting entries (*l*) through (*p*).
4. Prepare an income statement (including earnings per share), statement of stockholders' equity, balance sheet, and statement of cash flows.
5. Record and post the closing entries.
6. Prepare a post-closing trial balance.
7. Compute the following ratios for 2003:
   a. Financial leverage
   b. Total asset turnover
   c. Net profit margin

ALTERNATE **PROBLEMS**

Preparing a Trial Balance (P4-1)

AP4-1
L01
Starbucks Corporation

Starbucks Corporation purchases and roasts high-quality whole bean coffees and sells them along with fresh-brewed coffees, Italian-style espresso beverages, a variety of pastries and confections, coffee-related accessories and equipment, and a line of premium teas. In addition to sales through its company-operated retail stores, Starbucks also sells coffee and tea products through other channels of distribution. The following is a simplified list of accounts and amounts reported in recent financial statements. The accounts have normal debit or credit balances and the dollars are rounded to the nearest million. Assume the year ended on September 30, 2003.

Accounts payable	$ 56	Inventories	$ 181
Accounts receivable	48	Long-term investments	68
Accrued liabilities	131	Long-term liabilities	40
Accumulated depreciation	321	Net revenues	1,680
Cash	66	Other current assets	21
Contributed capital	647	Other long-lived assets	38
Cost of sales	741	Other operating expenses	51
Depreciation	98	Prepaid expenses	19
General and administrative		Property, plant, and equipment	1,081
expenses	90	Retained earnings	?
Income tax expense	62	Short-term bank debt	64
Interest expense	1	Short-term investments	51
Interest income	9	Store operating expenses	544

Required:
Prepare an adjusted trial balance at September 30, 2003. How did you determine the amount for retained earnings?

Recording Adjusting Entries (P4-2)

AP4-2
L02

Brandon Company's annual accounting year ends on June 30. It is June 30, 2003, and all of the 2003 entries except the following adjusting entries have been made:

    a. On March 30, 2003, Brandon paid a six-month premium for property insurance, $3,200, for coverage starting on that date. Cash was credited and Prepaid Insurance was debited for this amount.

    b. At June 30, 2003, wages of $900 were earned by employees but not yet paid. The employees will be paid on the next payroll date, July 15, 2003.

    c. On June 1, 2003, Brandon collected two months' maintenance revenue of $450. At that date, Brandon debited Cash and credited Unearned Maintenance Revenue for $450.

    d. Depreciation of $3,000 must be recognized on a service truck that cost $15,000 on July 1, 2002.

    e. Cash of $4,200 was collected on May 1, 2003, for services to be rendered evenly over the next year beginning on May 1. Unearned Service Revenue was credited when the cash was received.

    f. On February 1, 2003, the company borrowed $16,000 from a local bank and signed a 9 percent note for that amount. The principal and interest are payable on maturity date, January 31, 2004.

    g. On June 15, 2003, the company received a $500 tax bill from the city for the first half of 2003 property taxes on land; the bill is payable during July 2003.

    h. The company earned service revenue of $2,000 on a special job that was completed June 29, 2003. Collection will be made during July 2003; no entry has been recorded.

Required:

  1. Indicate whether each transaction relates to a deferred revenue, deferred expense, accrued revenue, or accrued expense.

  2. Give the adjusting entry required for each transaction at June 30, 2003.

AP4-3
L02

Determining Financial Statement Effects of Adjusting Entries (P4-3)

Refer to AP4-2.

Required:

  1. Indicate whether each transaction relates to a deferred revenue, deferred expense, accrued revenue, or accrued expense.

  2. Using the following headings, indicate the effect of each adjusting entry and the amount of the effect. Use + for increase, − for decrease, and NE for no effect. (*Reminder:* Assets = Liabilities + Stockholders' Equity; Revenues − Expenses = Net Income; and Net Income accounts are closed to Retained Earnings, a part of Stockholders' Equity.)

	BALANCE SHEET			INCOME STATEMENT		
Transaction	**Assets**	**Liabilities**	**Stockholders' Equity**	**Revenues**	**Expenses**	**Net Income**
a.						
b.						
c.						
etc.						

AP4-4
L02

Recording Adjusting Entries (P4-4)

Wendy's Catering Company is at its accounting year-end, December 31, 2004. The following data that must be considered were developed from the company's records and related documents:

    a. During 2004, office supplies amounting to $1,200 were purchased for cash and debited in full to Supplies. At the beginning of 2004, the count of supplies on hand was $350 and, at December 31, 2004, was $400.

    b. On December 31, 2004, the company catered an evening gala for a local celebrity. The $7,500 bill was payable by the end of January 2005. No cash has been collected, and no journal entry has been made for this transaction.

    c. On December 15, 2004, repairs on one of the company's delivery vans were completed at a cost of $600; the amount is not yet recorded and by agreement will be paid at the beginning of January 2005.

    d. On October 1, 2004, a one-year insurance premium on equipment in the amount of $1,200 was paid and debited in full to Prepaid Insurance on that date. Coverage began on November 1.

e. In November 2004, Wendy's signed a lease for a new retail location, providing a down payment of $2,100 for the first three months rent. The lease began on December 1, 2004.

f. On July 1, 2004, the company purchased new refrigerated display counters at a cash cost of $18,000. Depreciation of $1,600 has not been recorded for 2004.

g. On November 1, 2004, the company loaned $4,000 to one of its employees on a one-year, 12 percent note payable. The principal plus interest is payable by the employee at the end of 12 months.

h. The income before any of the adjustments or income taxes was $22,400. The company's federal income tax rate is 30 percent. Compute adjusted income based on (a) through (g) to determine income tax expense.

Required:
1. Indicate whether each transaction relates to a deferred revenue, deferred expense, accrued revenue, or accrued expense.
2. Give the adjusting entry required for each transaction at December 31, 2004.

Determining Financial Statement Effects of Adjusting Entries (P4-5)

AP4-5
LO2

Refer to AP4-4.

Required:
1. Indicate whether each transaction relates to a deferred revenue, deferred expense, accrued revenue, or accrued expense.
2. Using the following headings, indicate the effect of each adjusting entry and the amount of each. Use + for increase, − for decrease, and NE for no effect. (*Reminder:* Assets = Liabilities + Stockholders' Equity; Revenues − Expenses = Net Income; and Net Income accounts are closed to Retained Earnings, a part of Stockholders' Equity.)

	BALANCE SHEET			INCOME STATEMENT		
Transaction	Assets	Liabilities	Stockholders' Equity	Revenues	Expenses	Net Income
a.						
b.						
c.						
etc.						

Computing Amounts on Financial Statements and Finding Financial Information (P4-6)

AP4-6
LO2

The following information was provided by the records of Clifford's Cleaning Company at the end of the annual fiscal period, December 31, 2003:

Cash Receipts

a.	Collected cash in January 2003 for the only cleaning contracts completed in past years that were not yet paid by customers.	$ 11,000
b.	Service revenue collected in cash during 2003 for cleaning contracts in 2003.	213,000
c.	Service revenue earned for contracts in December 2003; not collected until 2004.	14,000
d.	In December 2003, collected contract revenue in advance for January 2004.	19,000

Cash Disbursements for Salaries

e.	Cash payment made in January 2003 for employee salaries earned in 2002; no other amounts were due to employees for past periods.	1,500
f.	Salaries incurred and paid during 2003.	78,000
g.	Salaries earned by employees during December 2003 that will be paid in January 2004.	1,900

Cash Disbursements for Supplies

h.	Cleaning supplies on hand on January 1, 2003.	1,800
i.	Cleaning supplies purchased for cash during 2003.	14,500
j.	Cleaning supplies counted on December 31, 2003.	2,700

Required:

Using T-accounts, compute the amounts that should be reported in Clifford's 2003 financial statements for the following items and indicate on which financial statement the item is located. For cash, create one T-account and label each effect to determine the amounts from customers, to suppliers, and to employees:

1. Service revenue
2. Cash to employees
3. Cleaning supplies expense
4. Receivables from customers
5. Cash to suppliers

6. Cleaning supplies
7. Wages expense
8. Cash from customers
9. Unearned revenue
10. Wages payable

AP4-7
LO1, 2, 4, 5

Inferring Year-End Adjustments, Computing Earnings per Share and Net Profit Margin, and Recording Closing Entries (P4-7)

Hormoz Company is completing the information processing cycle at the end of its fiscal year, December 31, 2003. Following are the correct balances at December 31, 2003, for the accounts both before and after the adjusting entries for 2003.

TRIAL BALANCE, DECEMBER 31, 2003						
	Before Adjusting Entries		Adjustments		After Adjusting Entries	
Items	Debit	Credit	Debit	Credit	Debit	Credit
a. Cash	$ 18,000				$ 18,000	
b. Accounts receivable					1,500	
c. Prepaid rent	1,200				800	
d. Property, plant, and equipment	210,000				210,000	
e. Accumulated depreciation		$ 52,500				$ 70,000
f. Income taxes payable						6,500
g. Deferred revenue		16,000				8,000
h. Contributed capital		110,000				110,000
i. Retained earnings, January 1, 2003		21,700				21,700
j. Service revenue		83,000				92,500
k. Salary expense	54,000				54,000	
l. Depreciation expense					17,500	
m. Rent expense					400	
n. Income tax expense					6,500	
	$283,200	$283,200			$308,700	$308,700

Required:

1. Compare the amounts in the columns before and after the adjusting entries to reconstruct the adjusting entries made in 2003. Provide an explanation of each.
2. Compute the amount of income assuming that it is based on the amount (a) before adjusting entries and (b) after adjusting entries. Which income amount is correct? Explain why.
3. Compute earnings per share, assuming that 5,000 shares of stock are outstanding.
4. Compute the net profit margin. What does this suggest to you about the company?
5. Record the closing entries at December 31, 2003.

AP4-8
LO1, 2, 3, 5

Recording Adjusting and Closing Entries and Preparing a Balance Sheet and Income Statement Including Earnings per Share (P4-8)

Rhoades Co., a small service repair company, keeps its records without the help of an accountant. After much effort, an outside accountant prepared the following unadjusted trial balance as of the end of the annual accounting period, December 31, 2004:

Account Titles	Debit	Credit
Cash	19,600	
Accounts receivable	7,000	
Supplies inventory	1,300	
Prepaid insurance	900	
Equipment	27,000	
Accumulated depreciation, equipment		12,000
Other assets	5,100	
Accounts payable		2,500
Wages payable		
Income taxes payable		
Note payable (2 years; 12% interest due each December 31)		5,000
Contributed capital (4,000 shares outstanding)		16,000
Retained earnings		10,300
Service revenue		48,000
Remaining expenses (not detailed; excludes income tax)	32,900	
Income tax expense		
Totals	93,800	93,800

Data not yet recorded at December 31, 2004:

 a. Depreciation expense for 2004, $3,000.
 b. Insurance expired during 2004, $450.
 c. Wages earned by employees not yet paid on December 31, 2004, $1,100.
 d. The supplies count on December 31, 2004, reflected $600 remaining on hand to be used in 2005.
 e. Income tax expense was $2,950.

Required:
 1. Record the 2004 adjusting entries.
 2. Prepare an income statement and a classified balance sheet for 2004 to include the effects of the preceding five transactions.
 3. Record the 2004 closing entries.

Comprehensive Review Problem: From Recording Transactions (including Adjusting and Closing Entries) to Preparing a Complete Set of Financial Statements and Performing Ratio Analysis (see Chapters 2, 3, and 4) (P4-9)

AP4-9
LO1, 2, 3, 4, 5

Kim Torge and Ben Guiliano began operations of their furniture repair shop (New Again Furniture, Inc.) on January 1, 2002. The annual reporting period ends December 31. The trial balance on January 1, 2003, was as follows (the amounts are rounded to thousands of dollars to simplify):

Account No.	Account Titles	Debit	Credit
01	Cash	5	
02	Accounts receivable	4	
03	Supplies	2	
04	Small tools	6	
05	Equipment		
06	Accumulated depreciation (equipment)		
07	Remaining assets (not detailed to simplify)	9	
11	Accounts payable		7
12	Notes payable		
13	Wages payable		
14	Interest payable		
15	Income taxes payable		
16	Unearned revenue		
21	Contributed capital (15,000 shares)		15

Continued

Account No.	Account Titles	Debit	Credit
31	Retained earnings		4
35	Service revenue		
40	Depreciation expense		
41	Income tax expense		
42	Interest expense		
43	Remaining expenses (not detailed to simplify)		
	Totals	26	26

Transactions during 2003 (summarized in thousands of dollars) follow:

a. Borrowed $20 cash on July 1, 2003, signing a 10 percent note payable.
b. Purchased equipment for $18 cash on July 1, 2003.
c. Sold 5,000 additional shares of capital stock for $1 cash per share (show dollars in thousands; numbers of shares and price per share are as presented).
d. Earned revenues for 2003, $65, including $9 on credit.
e. Recognized remaining expenses for 2003, $35, including $7 on credit.
f. Purchased additional small tools, $3 cash.
g. Collected accounts receivable, $8.
h. Paid accounts payable, $11.
i. Purchased on account supplies for future use, $10.
j. Received a $3 deposit on work to start January 15, 2004.
k. Declared and paid a cash dividend, $10.

Data for adjusting entries:

l. Supplies of $4 and small tools of $8 were counted on December 31, 2003 (debit Remaining Expenses).
m. Depreciation for 2003, $2.
n. Interest accrued on notes payable (to be computed).
o. Wages earned since the December 24 payroll not yet paid, $3.
p. Income tax expense was $4, payable in 2004.

Required:

1. Set up T-accounts for the accounts on the trial balance and enter beginning balances.
2. Record transactions (a) through (k) and post them to the T-accounts.
3. Record and post the adjusting entries (l) through (p).
4. Prepare an income statement (including earnings per share), statement of stockholders' equity, balance sheet, and the statement of cash flows.
5. Record and post the closing entries.
6. Prepare a post-closing trial balance.
7. Compute the following ratios for 2003:
   a. Financial leverage   c. Net profit margin
   b. Total asset turnover

CASES AND **PROJECTS**

Annual Report Cases

CP4-1   **Finding Financial Information**

L02, 3, 4, 5

Refer to the financial statements and accompanying notes of Abercrombie & Fitch given in Appendix C at the end of this book, or open file ANF.pdf in the Annual Report Cases directory on the student CD-ROM.

ABERCROMBIE
&
FITCH

Required:

1. How much is in the Store Supplies account at the end of the 2000 fiscal year?

2. What did the company report for unearned revenue at February 3, 2001? Where did you find this information?
3. What is included in the liability Accrued Rent? In Accrued Compensation?
4. How much did the company owe in currently payable state income taxes at the end of the 2000 fiscal year? Where did you find this information?
5. To what account is Interest Income related?
6. What company accounts would not appear on a post-closing trial balance?
7. Give the closing entry for Prepaid Expenses.
8. What is the company's earnings per share (basic only) for the three years reported?
9. Compute the company's net profit margin for the three years reported. What does the trend suggest to you about Abercrombie & Fitch?

Finding Financial Information

Refer to the financial statements and accompanying notes of American Eagle Outfitters given in Appendix B at the end of this book, or open file AEOS.pdf in the Annual Report Cases directory on the student CD-ROM.

CP4-2
LO2, 3, 4, 5

Required:
1. How much cash did the company pay for income taxes in its 2000 fiscal year?
2. What was the company's best quarter in terms of sales in its 2000 fiscal year? Where did you find this information?
3. Give the closing entry for the Other Income and Expense accounts.
4. What does Accounts and Notes Receivable consist of? Where did you find this information?
5. Compute the company's net profit margin for the three years reported. What does the trend suggest to you about American Eagle Outfitters?

AMERICAN EAGLE OUTFITTERS

Comparing Companies Within an Industry and over Time

Refer to the financial statements of American Eagle Outfitters in Appendix B, Abercrombie & Fitch given in Appendix C, and the Industry Ratio Report given in Appendix D at the end of this book or open file CP4-3.xls in the Annual Report Cases directory on the student CD-ROM.

CP4-3
LO2, 4

Required:
1. What was Advertising Expense for each company for 2000? Where did you find the information?
2. Compute the percentage of Advertising Expense to Net Sales for 2000 for both companies. Which company incurred the higher percentage? Show computations. Are you able to perform the same comparison for 1999 and 1998? If so, show the computations. If not, explain why not.
3. Compare the Advertising Expense to Net Sales ratio computed in requirement 2 to the industry average found in the Industry Ratio Report. Were these two companies spending more or less than their average competitor on advertising (on a relative basis)? What does this ratio tell you about the general effectiveness of each company's advertising strategy?
4. Both companies have a note to the financial statements explaining the accounting policy for advertising. How do the policies differ, if at all?
5. Compute each company's net profit margin for the three years reported. What do your results suggest to you about each company over time and in comparison to each other?
6. Compare each company's net profit margin for 2000 to the industry average net profit margin in the Industry Ratio Report. Were these two companies performing better or worse than the average company in the industry?

AMERICAN EAGLE OUTFITTERS

ABERCROMBIE & FITCH

Financial Report and Analysis Cases

Interpreting the Financial Press

A January 18, 2000, article in *Motley Fool* discusses the results of the initial court case between Papa John's and Tricon Global (Pizza Hut's parent company).* You can access the article on the Libby/Libby/Short website at www.mhhe.com/libby4e.

CP4-4

*Dave Mairo-Nachison, "Papa John's Q4 to Take a Slice," Fool Plate Special: An Investment Opinion, *Motley Fool*, January 18, 2000. © Copyright 2000. *The Motley Fool*. All rights reserved.

Required:

Read the brief article and answer the following questions:

1. What was the court's decision about Papa John's using the "Better Ingredients. Better Pizza." logo?
2. What did Papa John's estimate as the real cost of the lawsuit to the company?
3. What does the article suggest about the impact of the lawsuit on Papa John's stock price?

CP4-5   **Using Financial Reports: Inferring Adjusting Entries and Information Used in**
LO1, 2, 5   **Computations and Recording Closing Entries**

The pre-closing balances in the T-accounts of Hook M Horns Company at the end of the third year of operations, December 31, 2003, follow. The 2003 adjusting entries are identified by letters.

Cash	
Bal. 20,000	

Notes Payable 8%	
	Bal. 10,000

Contributed Capital (8,000 shares)	
	Bal. 56,000

Maintenance Supplies	
Bal. 500	(a) 300

Interest Payable	
	(b) 800

Retained Earnings	
	Bal. 9,000

Service Equipment	
Bal. 90,000	

Income Taxes Payable	
	(f) 13,020

Service Revenue	
(c) 6,000	Bal. 220,000

Accumulated Depreciation, Service Equipment	
	Bal. 18,000
	(d) 9,000

Wages Payable	
	(e) 500

Expenses	
Bal. 160,000	
(a) 300	
(b) 800	
(d) 9,000	
(e) 500	
(f) 13,020	

Remaining Assets	
Bal. 42,500	

Unearned Revenue	
	(c) 6,000

Required:

1. Develop three 2003 trial balances for Hook M Horns Company using the following format:

	UNADJUSTED TRIAL BALANCE		ADJUSTED TRIAL BALANCE		POST-CLOSING TRIAL BALANCE	
Account	Debit	Credit	Debit	Credit	Debit	Credit

2. Write an explanation for each adjusting entry for 2003.
3. Record the closing journal entries.
4. What was the average income tax rate for 2003?
5. What was the average issue (sale) price per share of the capital stock?

CP4-6   **Using Financial Reports: Analyzing the Effects of Adjustments**
LO2

Kreiser Land Company, a closely held corporation, invests in commercial rental properties. Kreiser's annual accounting period ends on December 31. At the end of each year, numerous adjusting entries

CRYSTAL'S DAY SPA, INC.		
Statement of Profits		
2003		
Spa fees collected		$115,000
Expenses paid:		
Rent for office space	$13,000	
Utilities expense	360	
Telephone expense	2,200	
Office salaries expense	22,000	
Office supplies expense	900	
Miscellaneous expenses	2,400	
Total expenses		40,860
Profit for the year		$ 74,140

Upon agreement of the parties, you have been asked to examine the financial figures for 2003. The other company's representative said, "I question the figures because, among other things, they appear to be on a 100 percent cash basis." Your investigations revealed the following additional data at December 31, 2003:

a. Of the $115,000 in spa fees collected in 2003, $32,000 was for services performed prior to 2003.
b. At the end of 2003, spa fees of $9,000 for services performed during the year were uncollected.
c. Office equipment owned and used by Crystal cost $5,000. Depreciation was estimated at $500 annually.
d. A count of office supplies at December 31, 2003, reflected $200 worth of items purchased during the year that were still on hand. Also, the records for 2002 indicate that the supplies on hand at the end of that year were about $125.
e. At the end of 2003, the secretary whose salary is $18,000 per year had not been paid for December because of a long trip that extended to January 15, 2004.
f. A $1,400 phone bill received for December 2003 was not paid until January 11, 2004.
g. The $13,000 office rent paid was for 13 months (it included the rent for January 2004).

Required:
1. On the basis of this information, prepare a corrected income statement for 2003 (ignore income taxes). Show your computations for any amounts changed from those in the statement prepared by Crystal's secretary. (Suggested solution format with four-column headings: Items; Cash Basis per Crystal's Statement, $; Explanation of Changes; and Corrected Basis, $.)
2. Write a memo to support your schedule prepared in requirement (1). The purpose should be to explain the reasons for your changes and to suggest other important items that should be considered in the pricing decision.

Critical Thinking Cases

Using Financial Reports: Evaluating Financial Information as a Bank Loan Officer

CP4-9
LO2, 3, 4

Monroeville Moving Corporation has been in operation since January 1, 2003. It is now December 31, 2003, the end of the annual accounting period. The company has not done well financially during the first year, although revenue has been fairly good. The three stockholders manage the company, but they have not given much attention to recordkeeping. In view of a serious cash shortage, they have applied to your bank for a $20,000 loan. You requested a complete set of financial statements. The following 2003 annual financial statements were prepared by a clerk and then were given to the bank.

MONROEVILLE MOVING CORPORATION

Income Statement For the Period Ended December 31, 2003		Balance Sheet At December 31, 2003	
Transportation revenue	$85,000	**Assets**	
Expenses:		Cash	$ 2,000
Salaries expense	17,000	Receivables	3,000
Supplies expense	12,000	Supplies	6,000
Other expenses	18,000	Equipment	40,000
Total expenses	47,000	Prepaid insurance	4,000
Net income	$38,000	Remaining assets	27,000
		Total assets	$82,000
		Liabilities	
		Accounts payable	$ 9,000
		Stockholders' Equity	
		Contributed capital	
		(10,000 shares outstanding)	35,000
		Retained earnings	38,000
		Total liabilities and	
		stockholders' equity	$82,000

After briefly reviewing the statements and "looking into the situation," you requested that the statements be redone (with some expert help) to "incorporate depreciation, accruals, inventory counts, income taxes, and so on." As a result of a review of the records and supporting documents, the following additional information was developed:

a. The supplies of $6,000 shown on the balance sheet has not been adjusted for supplies used during 2003. A count of the supplies on hand on December 31, 2003, showed $1,800.

b. The insurance premium paid in 2003 was for years 2003 and 2004. The total insurance premium was debited in full to Prepaid Insurance when paid in 2003 and no adjustment has been made.

c. The equipment cost $40,000 when purchased January 1, 2003. It had an estimated annual depreciation of $8,000. No depreciation has been recorded for 2003.

d. Unpaid (and unrecorded) salaries at December 31, 2003, amounted to $2,200.

e. At December 31, 2003, transportation revenue collected in advance amounted to $7,000. This amount was credited in full to Transportation Revenue when the cash was collected earlier during 2003.

f. Income tax expense was $3,650 (the tax rate is 25 percent).

Required:

1. Record the six adjusting entries required on December 31, 2003, based on the preceding additional information.

2. Recast the preceding statements after taking into account the adjusting entries. You do not need to use classifications on the statements. Suggested form for the solution:

		CHANGES		
Items	**Amounts Reported**	**Plus**	**Minus**	**Corrected Amounts**
(List here each item from the two statements)				

3. Omission of the adjusting entries caused:
    a. Net income to be overstated or understated (select one) by $_____.
    b. Total assets on the balance sheet to be overstated or understated (select one) by $_____.

4. For both of the unadjusted and adjusted balances, calculate these ratios for the company: (a) earnings per share and (b) net profit margin. Explain the causes of the differences and the impact of the changes on financial analysis.
5. Write a letter to the company explaining the results of the adjustments, your analysis, and your decision regarding the loan.

Financial Reporting and Analysis Team Project

Team Project: Analysis of Accruals, Earnings per Share, and Net Profit Margin

CP4-10
LO2, 3, 4

Using your web browser, as a team select an industry to analyze. Each team member should then use the Internet to obtain the annual report or 10-K for one publicly traded company in the industry, with each member selecting a different company.

Required:

1. On an individual basis, each team member should write a short report listing the following:
   a. The company's earnings per share for each year.
   b. The company's net profit margin for each year.
   c. The amount of accrued expenses (a liability) on the balance sheet and the ratio of accrued expenses to total liabilities.
   d. Summaries of any notes to the financial statements that describe accrued expenses in detail.
2. Discuss any patterns that you as a team observe. Then, as a team, write a short report comparing and contrasting your companies according to the preceding attributes. Provide potential explanations for any differences discovered.

After studying this chapter, you should be able to:

1. Recognize the people involved in the accounting communication process (managers, auditors, information intermediaries, government regulators, and users), their roles in the process, and the guidance they receive from legal and professional standards. p. 225

2. Identify the steps in the accounting communication process, including the issuance of press releases, annual reports, quarterly reports, and SEC filings as well as the role of electronic information services in this process. p. 232

3. Recognize and apply the different financial statement and disclosure formats used by companies in practice. p. 236

4. Analyze a company's performance based on return on equity and its components. p. 247

Communicating and Interpreting Accounting Information

5

I n just 19 years, Ely [pronounced EE-lee] Callaway took a small manufacturer of specialty golf clubs with $500,000 in annual sales and built it into the industry leader with sales of more than $830 million. Callaway attributes this success to the innovative Big Bertha oversized clubs, created by a team of aerospace and metallurgical engineers, which make the game easier to learn and play. Both touring pros and average golfers, including former presidents Bill Clinton and George Bush, carry a Big Bertha driver in their golf bags. But industry insiders attribute an equal portion of Ely Callaway's success to his marketing skills. Up until just before his death in July of 2001 at the age of 82, he spent hours each day talking to the pros who use his clubs at televised events and the dealers who sell them. He even wrote much of the company's ad copy.

FOCUS COMPANY

Callaway Golf

COMMUNICATING FINANCIAL INFORMATION

AND CORPORATE STRATEGY

www.callawaygolf.com

In 1989, Callaway and then chief financial officer (CFO) Carol Kerley applied that same personal marketing touch to the financial side of the business when they persuaded managers of the General Electric Pension Fund to invest $10 million in the company. The same enthusiasm and communication skill were apparent in the company's initial public offering (first stock issuance to the public, or IPO) in 1992. The CFO and her accounting staff worked tirelessly with the company's outside auditor, PricewaterhouseCoopers, and its investment bankers, Merrill Lynch, to prepare the detailed financial information necessary for the IPO. As a publicly traded company, Callaway is now required to provide detailed information in regular filings with the Securities and Exchange Commission.

Clear communication with the company's four customer groups—professional endorsers, dealers, golfing consumers, and investors and other users of financial statements—continues to be a hallmark of Callaway's business strategy. Callaway drivers are now the most popular on the PGA tours, and Callaway is the largest golf club company in the world.

UNDERSTANDING THE BUSINESS

Callaway Golf Company designs, manufactures, and markets high-quality innovative golf clubs that sell at premium prices. Its Big Bertha oversized stainless steel and titanium woods and irons account for most of its sales. Many golfers consider these clubs to be the "friendliest" in the game because they are less sensitive to off-center hits. The company manufactures its metal woods and irons in its new Carlsbad, California, factories using clubheads, shafts, and grips supplied by independent vendors such as Coastcast Corporation, Aldila, and True Temper. The clubs are sold primarily at high-end pro shops. Callaway invests considerable sums in research and development and is known for introducing new innovative products long before the end of existing products' life cycles.

Successful companies such as Callaway learn to match their financial reporting strategies to their business strategies. Marketing and communication are fundamental to both. Callaway executives value integrity in the communication of financial results as much as they do in relationships with suppliers, customers, and employees. They deal honestly and candidly with the financial press, financial analysts, and the investing public. The financial statements and related disclosures provided in its annual report are also a model of clarity. Callaway's management believes that this approach eases the company's access to capital, lowering both the costs of borrowing (interest rates) and the perceived riskiness of Callaway's stock.

Callaway knows that when investors lose faith in the truthfulness of a firm's accounting numbers, they also normally punish the company's stock. The accounting scandal at Enron and WorldCom are the best recent examples. They have even caused investors to question the accounting practices at other companies as suggested by this front-page story in *The Wall Street Journal.*

REAL WORLD EXCERPT

Wall Street Journal

BURDEN OF DOUBT: STOCKS TAKE A BEATING
AS ACCOUNTING WORRIES SPREAD BEYOND ENRON

It's not the economy anymore, stupid. It's the accounting.

Yesterday was the day that the smoldering corporate accounting scandal, which started with Enron Corp. . . . reached a wide group of U.S. companies and seriously singed their stock prices. Accounting problems surfaced in sectors ranging from banking to oil, prompting fears of new mini-Enrons and spurring a sell-off of shares at the slightest whiff of such trouble.

As a result, . . . the stock market took a tumble, with shares falling to their lowest levels in three months.

SOURCE: *The Wall Street Journal,* January 30, 2002.

Chapters 2 through 4 focused on the mechanics of preparing the income statement, balance sheet, statement of stockholders' equity, and cash flow statement. In this chapter, we will focus on the people involved and the process that conveys accounting information to statement users. We will also discuss the exact statement formats and additional disclosures provided in financial reports to help you learn how to find relevant information. Finally, we will examine a general framework for assessing a company's performance based on these reports.

ORGANIZATION of the Chapter

Players in the Accounting Communication Process	The Disclosure Process	A Closer Look at Financial Statement Formats and Notes	ROE Analysis: A Framework for Evaluating Company Performance
■ Managers (CEO, CFO, and Accounting Staff) ■ Auditors ■ Information Intermediaries: Analysts and Information Services ■ Government Regulators ■ Users: Institutional and Private Investors, Creditors, and Others ■ Guiding Principles for Communicating Useful Information	■ Press Releases ■ Annual Reports ■ Quarterly Reports ■ SEC Reports—10-K, 10-Q, 8-K	■ Classified Balance Sheet ■ Classified Income Statement ■ Statement of Stockholders' Equity ■ Statement of Cash Flows ■ Notes to Financial Statements ■ Voluntary Disclosures ■ Constraints of Accounting Measurement	• ROE Profit Driver Analysis • Profit Drivers and Business Strategy

PLAYERS IN THE ACCOUNTING COMMUNICATION PROCESS

Exhibit 5.1 summarizes the accounting communication process in terms of the people involved, their roles in the process, and the guidance they receive from legal and professional standards.

Managers (CEO, CFO, and Accounting Staff)

As noted in Chapter 1, the primary responsibility for the information in Callaway's financial statements and related disclosures lies with management, specifically the highest officer in the company, often called the *chairman and chief executive officer* (CEO), and the highest officer associated with the financial and accounting side of the business, often called the *chief financial officer* (CFO). The CEO and CFO of the very largest must personally certify their completeness and accuracy. At the time of Callaway's initial public offering (IPO), Ely Callaway, chairman and CEO, and Carol Kerley, CFO, were responsible for the reports filed with the Securities and Exchange Commission (SEC) and their conformance with GAAP. The members of the *accounting staff,* who actually prepare the details of the reports, also bear professional responsibility for the accuracy of this information, although their legal responsibility is smaller. Indeed, their future professional success depends heavily on their reputation for honesty and competence.

Auditors

As we saw in Chapter 1, the SEC requires publicly traded companies to have their statements audited by CPAs following generally accepted auditing standards. Many privately owned companies also have their statements audited. By signing an

Learning Objective 1
Recognize the people involved in the accounting communication process (managers, auditors, information intermediaries, government regulators, and users), their roles in the process, and the guidance they receive from legal and professional standards.

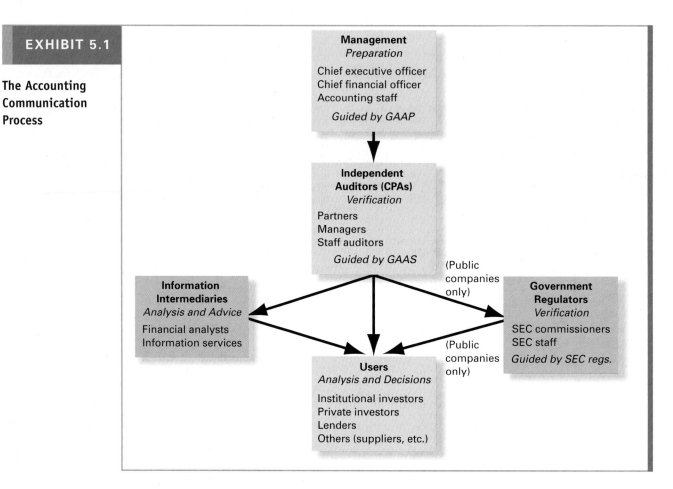

EXHIBIT 5.1

The Accounting Communication Process

Management
Preparation
Chief executive officer
Chief financial officer
Accounting staff
Guided by GAAP

Independent Auditors (CPAs)
Verification
Partners
Managers
Staff auditors
Guided by GAAS

Information Intermediaries
Analysis and Advice
Financial analysts
Information services

(Public companies only)

Government Regulators
Verification
SEC commissioners
SEC staff
Guided by SEC regs.

(Public companies only)

Users
Analysis and Decisions
Institutional investors
Private investors
Lenders
Others (suppliers, etc.)

UNQUALIFIED (clean) AUDIT OPINION. Auditors' statement that the financial statements are fair presentations in all material respects in conformity with GAAP.

unqualified, or clean, **audit opinion,** a CPA firm assumes financial responsibility for the fairness of the financial statements and related presentations. This opinion, which adds credibility to the statements, is often required by agreements with lenders and private investors. By voluntarily subjecting the company's statements to independent verification, private companies reduce the risk that the company's financial condition is not accurately represented in the statements. As a result, rational investors and lenders should lower the rate of return (interest) they charge for providing capital.

PricewaterhouseCoopers is currently Callaway Golf's auditor. This firm, along with KPMG, Deloitte & Touche, and Ernst & Young, make up what are referred to as the "Big 4" CPA firms. Each of these firms employs thousands of CPAs in offices scattered throughout the world. They audit the great majority of publicly traded companies, and many that are privately held. Some public companies and most private companies are audited by smaller CPA firms. A list of well-known companies and their auditors at the time this chapter was written follows.

Company	Industry	Auditor
The Boeing Company	Aircraft	Deloitte & Touche
Honda Motor Co. Ltd. (Japan)	Automobiles	KPMG
Singapore Airlines (Singapore)	Airline	Ernst & Young
Wendy's	Fast food	PricewaterhouseCoopers

Information Intermediaries: Analysts and Information Services

Students often view the communication process between companies and financial statement users as a simple process of mailing the report to individual shareholders who read the report and then make investment decisions based on what they have learned.

This simple picture is far from today's reality. Now most investors rely on sophisticated financial analysts and information services to gather and analyze information.

Financial Analysts

Financial analysts receive accounting reports and other information about the company from electronic information services. They also gather information through conversations with company executives and visits to company facilities and competitors. The results of their analyses are combined into analysts' reports. Analysts' reports normally include forecasts of future quarterly and annual earnings per share and share price; a buy, hold, or sell recommendation for the company's shares; and explanations for these judgments. In making their **earnings forecasts,** the analysts rely heavily on their knowledge of the way the accounting system translates business events into the numbers on a company's financial statements, which is the subject matter of this text. Individual analysts often specialize in particular industries (such as sporting goods or energy companies). Analysts are regularly evaluated based on the accuracy of their forecasts, as well as the profitability of their stock picks.[1] Recently, Beth Burnson of ABN Amro topped *The Wall Street Journal*'s list of all-star forecasters in the leisure and recreation industry. At the time this chapter was written, three major firms provided the following forecasts and recommendations for Callaway:

EARNINGS FORECASTS are predictions of earnings for future accounting periods.

REAL WORLD EXCERPT

First Call Notes

Firm	Stock Recommendation	Earnings Forecast for 2001	Earnings Forecast for 2002
Merrill Lynch	Neutral	1.59	1.80
Barrington Research	Buy	1.53	1.75
Hibernia Southcoast Capital	Buy	1.57	1.67

Analysts often work in the research departments of brokerage and investment banking houses such as Merrill Lynch, mutual fund companies such as Fidelity Investments, and investment advisory services such as Value Line, that sell their advice to others. Through their reports and recommendations, analysts are transferring their knowledge of accounting, the company, and the industry to their customers who lack this expertise. Many believe that decisions made based on analysts' advice cause stock market prices to react quickly to information in financial statements. A quick, unbiased reaction to information is called *market efficiency* in finance. It is highly unlikely that unsophisticated investors can glean more information from financial statements than the sophisticated analysts have already learned. The information services discussed in the next section allow investors to gather their own information about the company and monitor the recommendations of a variety of analysts.

Information Services

Companies actually file their SEC forms electronically through EDGAR (Electronic Data Gathering and Retrieval Service), which is sponsored by the SEC. Users can retrieve information from EDGAR within 24 hours of its submission, long before it is available through the mail. EDGAR is a free service available on the web at

www.sec.gov

---

[1]See M. B. Mikhail, B. R. Walther, and R. H. Willis, "Does Forecast Accuracy Matter to Security Analysts?" *The Accounting Review*, April 1999, pp. 185–200; and R. A. McEwen and J. E. Hunton, "Is Analyst Forecast Accuracy Associated With Accounting Information Use?" *Accounting Horizons*, March 1999, pp. 1–16.

Many companies also provide direct access to their financial statements and other information over the web. You can contact Callaway at

www.callawaygolf.com/corporate/investorrelations.asp

Financial analysts obtain much of the information they use from the wide variety of commercial on-line information services. Services such as Compustat and Global Access provide broad access to financial statements and news information. They also allow users to search the database by key words, including various financial statement terms. Their websites describe their services in more detail:

www.compustat.com

ga.primark.com/ga/

Readers should be aware that the definitions used to compute key ratios often differ across these sources.

More general information services include Dow Jones Interactive and Bloomberg. Dow Jones provides access to news stories about companies, current and historical stock prices, and company press releases, including the initial announcements of annual and quarterly financial results. The Bloomberg service also provides the ability to combine these sources of information in sophisticated analyses. The graph presented in Exhibit 5.2 plots Callaway's quarterly price per share and earnings per share over nine years. Their websites describe their services in more detail:

www.djnr.com

www.bloomberg.com

Some of the services provide specialized information. For example, First Call provides consensus (average) and analyst-by-analyst earnings forecasts for more than 18,000 domestic and foreign companies. More than 800 research analysts contribute earnings forecasts to the service. Their website describes their services:

www.firstcall.com

A growing number of other resources offer a mixture of free and fee-based information exist on the web. These include

www.multexinvestor.com/home.asp

www.hoovers.com

finance.yahoo.com

EXHIBIT 5.2

Price and Earnings per Share Graph from the Bloomberg Terminal

REAL WORLD EXCERPT

Bloomberg

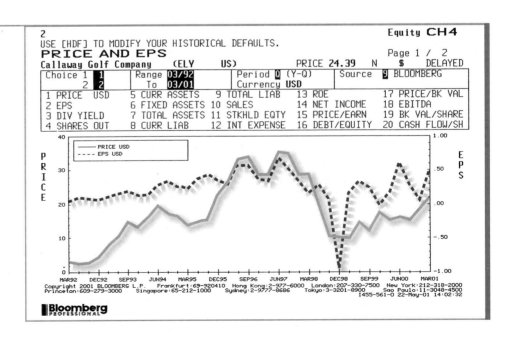

Information Services: Uses in Marketing, Classwork, and Job Searches

Information services have become the primary tool, not only of professional analysts but also of marketing strategists who use them to analyze competing firms. Sales representatives also use these services to analyze potential customers' needs for their products and creditworthiness. Growing, creditworthy companies are the most profitable targets for the sales representatives' efforts.

Information services are also an important source of information for student term papers and job searches. Potential employers expect job applicants to demonstrate knowledge of their companies during an interview, and electronic information services are an excellent source of company information. To learn more about electronic information services, contact the business or reference librarian at your college or university or explore some of the preceding websites.

Government Regulators

The *Securities and Exchange Commission* sets additional reporting standards for firms whose debt or equity securities are publicly traded. The SEC staff reviews these reports for compliance with these standards, investigates irregularities, and punishes violators. The SEC has increased efforts in this area as indicated by the cover story from *Fortune* magazine.

REAL WORLD EXCERPT

Fortune

The Crackdown Is Here

The nation's top earnings cop has put corporate America on notice: *Quit cooking the books.* Cross the line, you may do time.

SOURCE: *Fortune,* August 2, 1999, p. 75.

Research indicates that during a recent 11-year period, the SEC brought enforcement actions against nearly 300 firms for accounting-related violations.[2] In 72 percent of the cases, the CEO was implicated. In 29 percent, the company's auditors were also implicated. The *Fortune* article cited listed nine CEOs who had been sentenced to jail for accounting fraud during the prior five years. Consequences to the company included bankruptcy as in the cases of Enron and WorldCom, as well as financial penalties. In the wake of these accounting meltdowns, Congress has increased penalties for financial statement fraud. Funding for greater SEC scrutiny of company numbers has also been provided.

Users: Institutional and Private Investors, Creditors, and Others

Institutional investors include pension funds (associated with unions and employees of specific companies or government agencies); mutual funds; and endowment, charitable foundation, and trust funds (such as the endowment of your college or university). These institutional stockholders usually employ their own analysts who also rely on the information intermediaries just discussed. Institutional shareholders control the majority of publicly traded shares of U.S. companies. For example, at the end of the current fiscal year, institutional investors owned 63 percent of Callaway stock. Callaway's three largest institutional investors follow:

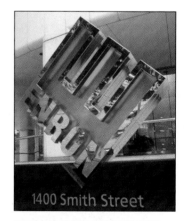

INSTITUTIONAL INVESTORS are managers of pension, mutual, endowment, and other funds that invest on the behalf of others.

[2]These statistics are reported in M. S. Beasley, J. V. Carcello, and D. R. Hermanson, "Fraudulent Financial Reporting: 1987–1997: An Analysis of U.S. Public Companies," *The Auditor's Report,* Summer 1999, pp. 15–17.

Institution	Approximate Ownership
Fidelity Management & Research	5.1 million shares
Barclays Bank	4.4 million shares
Wellington Management	1.6 million shares

Most small investors own stock in companies such as Callaway Golf indirectly through mutual and pension funds.

PRIVATE INVESTORS include individuals who purchase shares in companies.

Private investors include large individual investors such as Ely Callaway and his friends who originally invested directly in Callaway Golf, as well as small retail investors who buy shares of publicly traded companies through brokers such as Merrill Lynch. Retail investors normally lack the expertise to understand financial statements and the resources to gather data efficiently. They often rely on the advice of information intermediaries or turn their money over to the management of mutual and pension funds (institutional investors).

LENDERS (creditors) include suppliers and financial institutions that lend money to companies.

Lenders, or **creditors,** include suppliers, banks, commercial credit companies, and other financial institutions that lend money to companies. Lending officers and financial analysts in these organizations use the same public sources of information. They also use additional financial information (e.g., monthly statements) that companies often agree to provide as part of the lending contract. Lenders are the primary external user group for financial statements of private companies. Institutional and private investors also become creditors when they buy a company's publicly traded bonds.

A QUESTION OF ETHICS

Conflicting Interests of Managers, Stockholders, and Creditors

The economic interests of managers, stockholders, and creditors often differ. For example, paying dividends to stockholders benefits the stockholders but leaves less money available to pay creditors. Refurnishing managers' offices benefits managers but leaves less money to pay dividends. Ethical conduct and mutual trust play a major role in balancing these conflicting interests.

Accounting and financial statements also play a major role in enforcing these relationships of trust. Compliance with agreements (contracts) between managers and stockholders and between stockholders and creditors are monitored with financial statement data.* Enron, WorldCom, and other recent cases have made the wisdom of famed analyst Jack Ciesielski's warning for managers, shareholders, directors, creditors, and analysts more evident:

REAL WORLD EXCERPT

Analyst's Accounting Observer

One usual answer to the question "why does accounting matter?" is that it helps to avoid "blow-ups:" the unpleasant outcome when a stock crashes because the firm's management engaged in accounting chicanery that subsequently becomes visible. Actually, common sense and a good working knowledge of basic finance ("rising receivables and inventory are not a good thing") can help avoid blow-ups; but understanding accounting can help an analyst assess management candor with shareholders. And it can help an analyst understand more about the drivers of earnings and their sustainability; the analyst who understands accounting matters will know precisely where the "soft spots" are in financial reporting, the ones that can be manipulated in order to meet an expected earnings target or avoid breaking a loan covenant.

SOURCE: Analyst's Accounting Observer, www.aaopub.com, August 2000.

*Research that examines the use of accounting in contracting is called agency theory.

Financial statements also play an important role in the relationships between suppliers and customers. Customers evaluate the financial health of suppliers to determine whether they will be reliable, up-to-date sources of supply. Suppliers evaluate their customers to estimate their future needs and ability to pay debts. Competitors also attempt to learn useful information about a company from its statements. The potential loss of competitive advantage is one of the costs of public financial disclosures. Accounting regulators consider these costs as well as the direct costs of preparation when they consider requiring new disclosures. They apply what is called the **cost-benefit constraint,** which suggests that the benefits of accounting for and reporting information should outweigh the costs.

Guiding Principles for Communicating Useful Information

For accounting information to be useful, it must be relevant and reliable. **Relevant information** is capable of influencing decisions by allowing users to assess past activities and/or predict future activities. **Reliable information** is accurate, unbiased, and verifiable (independent parties can agree on the nature of the transaction and amount). Our discussions of ratio analysis have emphasized the importance of comparing ratios for the same company over time, as well as with those of competitors. Such comparisons are valid only if the information is prepared on a consistent and comparable basis. **Consistent information** means that within a company, similar accounting methods have been applied over time. **Comparable information** means that similar accounting methods have been applied across companies. These characteristics of useful information, along with the full-disclosure principle, guide the FASB in deciding what financial information should be reported.

> **THE COST-BENEFIT CONSTRAINT** suggests that the benefits of accounting for and reporting information should outweigh the costs.
>
> **RELEVANT INFORMATION** can influence a decision; it is timely and has predictive and/or feedback value.
>
> **RELIABLE INFORMATION** is accurate, unbiased, and verifiable.
>
> **CONSISTENT INFORMATION** can be compared over time because similar accounting methods have been applied.
>
> **COMPARABLE INFORMATION** allows comparisons across businesses because similar accounting methods have been applied.

SELF-STUDY QUIZ

Match the key terms in the left column with their definitions in the right column.

1. Relevant information   *a.* Management primarily responsible for accounting information.

2. CEO and CFO   *b.* An independent party who verifies financial statements.

3. Financial analyst   *c.* Information that influences users' decisions.

4. Auditor   *d.* Only information that provides benefits in excess of costs should be reported.

5. Cost-benefit constraint   *e.* An individual who analyzes financial information and provides advice.

After you have completed your answers, check them with the solutions that follow:

1c, 2a, 3e, 4b, 5d.

THE DISCLOSURE PROCESS

As noted in our discussion of information services and information intermediaries, the accounting communication process includes more steps and participants than one would envision in a world in which annual and quarterly reports are simply mailed to shareholders. SEC regulation FD, for "Fair Disclosure," requires that companies provide all investors with equal access to all important company news.

Learning Objective 2
Identify the steps in the accounting communication process, including the issuance of press releases, annual reports, quarterly reports, and SEC filings as well as the role of electronic information services in this process.

A **PRESS RELEASE** is a written public news announcement normally distributed to major news services.

Press Releases

To provide timely information to external users and to limit the possibility of selective leakage of information, Callaway and most public companies announce quarterly and annual earnings through a **press release** as soon as the verified figures (audited for annual and reviewed for quarterly earnings) are available. Callaway normally issues its earnings press releases within four weeks of the end of the accounting period. The announcements are sent electronically to the major print and electronic news services including *Dow Jones*, the *PR Newswire*, and *Bloomberg Business News,* which make them immediately available to subscribers. Exhibit 5.3 shows an excerpt from a typical quarterly press release for Callaway. It includes key financial figures and management's discussion of the results. Attached to the release are condensed income statements and balance sheets (unaudited) that will be included in the formal quarterly report to shareholders, distributed after the press release.

Many companies, including Callaway, follow these press releases with a conference call at which senior managers answer questions about the quarterly results from analysts. These calls are open to the investing public. Listening to these recordings is a good way to learn about a company's business strategy and its expectations for the future, as well as key factors that analysts consider when they evaluate a company. Callaway's most recent quarterly conference call can be accessed at

---

EXHIBIT 5.3

Earnings Press Release Excerpt for Callaway Golf Company

REAL WORLD EXCERPT

GOLF
PRESS RELEASE

GOLF

CALLAWAY GOLF REPORTS RECORD FIRST QUARTER SALES OF $261 MILLION; NET INCOME AND EARNINGS PER SHARE MORE THAN DOUBLE PREVIOUS LEVELS

CARLSBAD, Calif./April 25, 2001/Callaway Golf Company (NYSE:ELY) today reported record sales for the first quarter ended March 31, 2001. Reported net sales increased 32% to $261.4 million from $197.4 million during the first quarter of 2000. Net income increased 181% to $34.1 million in the first quarter of 2001 from $12.1 million in the first quarter of 2000. First quarter 2001 diluted earnings per share increased 181% to $0.47 from $0.17 in the same period last year.

Excluding the impact of recently adopted accounting pronouncements (SAB 101 on Revenue Recognition and Emerging Issues Task Force 00-10 on Accounting for Shipping and Handling Revenues and Costs), first quarter net sales increased 25% to $258.9 million from $206.6 million last year. Net income and diluted earnings per share increased 109% during the first quarter to $33.8 million and $0.47 per diluted share, respectively, as compared to $16.2 million and $0.22 per diluted share in the prior year. Implementing SAB 101 effectively shifts revenue from one period into a subsequent period, while adopting EITF 00-10 does not change earnings for any period.

"We are pleased with our overall first quarter results," stated Ely Callaway, Founder, Chairman, and CEO. "Good momentum has continued from last year into the first quarter of 2001 due to the success of several of our new product introductions and key sales programs. With the worldwide launch of the new Big Bertha ERC II Drivers, Hawk Eye VFT Drivers and Fairway Woods, and our Steelhead X-14 Pro Series Irons, we have continued to outpace the market and our brand is as strong as it's ever been."

Source: For more information about Callaway Golf Company, please visit our website on the Internet at www.callawaygolf.com.

2285 Rutherford Road • Carlsbad, CA 92008-8815
Telephone: (619) 931-1771 • Outside California (800) 228-2767
FAX: (619) 931-9539

www.callawaygolf.com/index.asp

For actively traded stocks such as Callaway Golf, most of the stock market reaction (stock price increases and decreases from investor trading) to the news in the press release usually occurs quickly. Recall that a number of analysts follow Callaway and regularly predict the company's earnings. When the actual earnings are published, the market reacts *not* to the amount of earnings but to the difference between expected earnings and actual earnings. This amount is called **unexpected earnings.** For example, *The San Diego Union-Tribune* recently reported the following:

Callaway Posts Strong Sales Profits

Bolstered by strong first-quarter earnings, Callaway Golf Co. shares jumped 15 percent yesterday, topping the $26 level for one of the few times in the past three years.

The Carlsad company reported earnings of 47 cents per share Wednesday, up from 17 cents for the same period last year. The company beat analysts' consensus estimate of 44 cents per share.

SOURCE: *The San Diego Union-Tribune*, April 27, 2001, p. C-1.

Unexpected earnings were +3 cents per share, and, as a result, the share price jumped over $3. The following excerpt from a recent article in *Harvard Business Review* points out the growing importance of meeting or beating the average or consensus analysts' estimate:

The Earnings Game: Everyone Plays, Nobody Wins

Quarterly earnings numbers dominate the decisions of executives, analysts, investors, and auditors . . . meeting analysts' expectations that earnings will rise in a smooth, steady, unbroken line has become, at many corporations, a game whose imperatives override even the imperative to deliver the highest possible return to shareholders.

SOURCE: *Harvard Business Review*, June 2001, p. 65.

Companies such as Callaway also issue press releases concerning other important events including new product announcements and new endorsement contracts with professional golfers. The stock market often appears to react to some of these important announcements. For example, a few years ago, Bloomberg reported the following:

Callaway Shares Rise after Spokesman Wins Pro-Am

New York, Feb. 7 (Bloomberg)—The shares of golf-club maker Callaway Golf Co. rose 6.6% today after Callaway's celebrity spokesman Johnny Miller won a California golf tournament yesterday . . . marking the 46-year-old golfer's first win in seven years.

SOURCE: *Bloomberg Business News,* New York, February 7, 1999.

Presumably, the stock market inferred that this would provide an impetus for future sales of the new product.

Press releases related to annual earnings and quarterly earnings often precede the issuance of the quarterly or annual report by 15 to 45 days. This time is necessary to prepare the additional detail and to print and distribute those reports.

Annual Reports

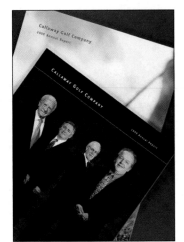

For privately held companies, **annual reports** are relatively simple documents photocopied on white bond paper. They normally include only the following:

1. Four basic financial statements: income statement, balance sheet, stockholders' equity or retained earnings statement, and cash flows statement.
2. Related notes (footnotes) as described earlier.
3. Report of Independent Accountants (Auditor's Opinion).

The annual reports of public companies are significantly more elaborate, both because of additional SEC reporting requirements and because many companies use their annual reports as public relations tools.

The annual reports of public companies are normally split into two sections. The first, "nonfinancial," section usually includes a letter to stockholders from the chairman and CEO; descriptions of the company's management philosophy, products, its successes (and occasionally its failures); and exciting prospects and challenges for the future. Beautiful photographs of products, facilities, and personnel often are included. The second, "financial," section includes the core of the report. The SEC sets minimum disclosure standards for the financial section of the annual reports of public companies. The principal components of the financial section include these:

1. Summarized financial data for a 5- or 10-year period.
2. Management's Discussion and Analysis of Financial Condition and Results of Operations.
3. The four basic financial statements.
4. Notes (footnotes).
5. Report of Independent Accountants (Auditor's Opinion) and sometimes the Report of Management Responsibility.
6. Recent stock price information.
7. Summaries of the unaudited quarterly financial data (described later).
8. Lists of directors and officers of the company and relevant addresses.

The order of these components varies.

Except for the Management's Discussion and Analysis, most of these elements have been covered in earlier chapters. This element includes an explanation of key figures on the financial statements and the risks the company faces in the future. Annual report information from American Eagle Outfitters and Abercrombie & Fitch is reprinted in Appendices B and C at the end of this book. As noted earlier, many companies make their annual reports available on the web.

Quarterly Reports

Quarterly reports normally begin with a short letter to shareholders. This is followed by a condensed income statement for the quarter, which often shows less detail than the annual income statement, and a condensed balance sheet dated at the end of the quarter (e.g., March 31 for the first quarter). These condensed financial statements are not audited and so are marked **unaudited.** Often the cash flow statement, statement of stockholders' equity (or retained earnings statement), and some notes to the financial statements are omitted. Private companies also normally prepare quarterly reports for their lenders. Callaway issues its quarterly reports about five weeks after the end of each quarter.

SEC Reports—10-K, 10-Q, 8-K

Public companies must file periodic reports with the SEC. They include the annual report on **Form 10-K**, quarterly reports on **Form 10-Q**, and current event reports on **Form 8-K**. These reports are normally referred to by number (for example, the "10-K"). The SEC requires that the 10-K be filed within 90 days of the fiscal year-end and the 10-Q within 45 days of the end of quarter. In general, the 10-K and 10-Q present all the information in the annual and quarterly reports, respectively, along with additional management discussion and several required schedules.

For example, the Form 10-K provides a more detailed description of the business including its products, product development, sales and marketing, manufacturing, and competitors. It also lists properties owned or leased, any legal proceedings it is involved in, and significant contracts it has signed. The 10-K also provides more detailed schedules concerning various figures on the income statement and balance sheet including bad debts, warranties, inventories, and advertising.

The **FORM 10-K** is the annual report that publicly traded companies must file with the SEC.

FORM 10-Q is the quarterly report that publicly traded companies must file with the SEC.

FORM 8-K is used by publicly traded companies to disclose any material event not previously reported that is important to investors.

| Judging International Sales Strategy from the Form 10-K | INTERNATIONAL PERSPECTIVE |

As part of the discussion of marketing and distribution strategy in its Form 10-K, Callaway disclosed a change in its international sales strategy:

REAL WORLD EXCERPT

Callaway GOLF

Form 10-K

Sales Outside of the United States

Approximately 46%, 42%, and 37% of the Company's net sales were derived from sales for distribution outside the United States in 2000, 1999 and 1998, respectively. The majority of the Company's international sales were made through its foreign subsidiaries and the rest through third party distributors. The Company does business (either directly or through its subsidiaries and distributors) in more than 70 countries throughout the world. The Company's management believes that controlling the distribution of its products in certain major markets in the world has been and will be an element in the future growth and success of the Company. The Company has been actively pursuing a reorganization of its international operations, including the acquisition of distribution rights in certain key countries in Europe, Asia and elsewhere around the world. The Company continued this strategy in the beginning of 2001 with the acquisition of distribution rights in Australia, New Zealand, Italy, Portugal and Spain.

While Callaway management believes that this change in strategy will be a source of future gains, it clearly will increase certain risks as well.

A CLOSER LOOK AT FINANCIAL STATEMENT FORMATS AND NOTES

To make financial statements more useful to investors, creditors, and analysts, specific **classifications** of information are included on the statements. Various classifications are used in practice. You should not be confused when you notice different formats used by different companies. You will find that each format is consistent with the principles discussed in this text.

Classified Balance Sheet

Topic Tackler 5–1

Exhibit 5.4 shows the December 31, 2000, balance sheet for Callaway Golf. Notice the title of the statement, Consolidated Balance Sheet. **Consolidated** means that the accounts of Callaway and those of its majority-owned subsidiaries (e.g., Callaway Golf [U.K.] Limited) have been added together and reported as a single number for each item. Note also that assets and liabilities are listed in a particular order on the balance sheet and are separated into current and noncurrent classifications.

Typically a balance sheet is classified as follows:

A. Assets (by order of liquidity)
1. Current assets (short term)
    a. Cash and cash equivalents
    b. Short-term investments (marketable securities)
    c. Accounts receivable
    d. Inventory
    e. Prepaid expenses
    f. Other current assets
2. Noncurrent assets
    a. Long-term investments
    b. Property, plant, and equipment—at cost less accumulated depreciation
    c. Intangible assets—at cost less accumulated amortization
    d. Other (miscellaneous) assets
        Total assets
B. Liabilities (by order of time to maturity)
1. Current liabilities (short-term)
    a. Accounts payable
    b. Accrued expenses payable
    c. Other short-term liabilities
2. Long-term liabilities
    a. Notes and mortgages payable
    b. Bonds payable
    c. Other long-term liabilities
        Total liabilities
C. Stockholders' equity (by source)
1. Contributed capital (by owners)
2. Retained earnings (accumulated earnings minus accumulated dividends declared)
3. Accumulated other comprehensive income
        Total stockholders' equity
        Total liabilities and stockholders' equity

A few of the items on Callaway's balance sheet are worthy of additional discussion. Callaway reports **Property, Plant, and Equipment, net** as one of its three noncurrent assets. This group includes tangible (physical) assets that were acquired for use in operating the business rather than for resale as inventory items or for investment. Examples include buildings; land on which the buildings sit; and equipment, tools, and furniture; fixtures used in operating the business. With the exception of land, property,

EXHIBIT 5.4

Balance Sheet of
Callaway Golf

REAL WORLD EXCERPT

Callaway
GOLF
ANNUAL REPORT

CALLAWAY GOLF COMPANY
Consolidated Balance Sheet
At December 31, 1999 and 2000

(in thousands, except share and per share data)	December 31, 2000	December 31, 1999
ASSETS		
Current assets:		
Cash and cash equivalents	$102,596	$112,602
Accounts receivable, net	58,836	54,252
Inventories, net	133,962	97,938
Deferred taxes	29,354	32,558
Other current assets	17,721	13,122
Total current assets	342,469	310,472
Property, plant, and equipment, net	134,712	142,214
Intangible assets	112,824	120,143
Other assets	40,929	43,954
	$630,934	$616,783
LIABILITIES AND SHAREHOLDERS' EQUITY		
Current liabilities:		
Accounts payable and accrued expenses	$44,173	$46,664
Accrued employee compensation and benefits	22,574	21,126
Accrued warranty expense	39,363	36,105
Accrued restructuring costs	—	1,379
Income taxes payable	3,196	—
Total current liabilities	109,306	105,274
Long-term liabilities:		
Deferred compensation	9,884	11,575
Commitment and contingencies (Note 13)		
Shareholders' equity:		
Common Stock, $.01 par value, 240,000,000 shares authorized, 78,958,963 and 76,302,196 issued December 31, 2000 and 1999	790	763
Paid-in capital	247,838	210,801
Accumulated other comprehensive income	(6,096)	280
Retained earnings	349,681	288,090
	592,213	499,934
Less: Common stock held in treasury, at cost, 4,815,241 shares at December 31, 2000 and none at December 31, 1999	(80,469)	—
Total shareholders' equity	511,744	499,934
	$630,934	$616,783

The accompanying notes are an integral part of these financial statements.

plant, and equipment is depreciated as it is used. The amount of depreciation computed for each period is reported on that period's income statement as depreciation expense. The accumulated amount of depreciation expense for all past periods is deducted from the initial cost of the asset to derive the **book value** or **net book value** reported on the balance sheet (Cost − Accumulated Depreciation).

To illustrate, assume that Callaway purchased a new computer system for $23,000. It had an estimated useful life of five years and a residual value of $1,000. Depreciation expense would be computed as $22,000 ÷ 5 years = $4,400 per year. If this were the company's only fixed asset, the balance sheets developed during the five-year period would report the following, probably in a note to the financial statements:

Computer System

	2003	2004	2005	2006	2007
Computer system (at cost)	$23,000	$23,000	$23,000	$23,000	$23,000
Less: Accumulated depreciation	4,400	8,800	13,200	17,600	22,000
Net book value	$18,600	$14,200	$ 9,800	$ 5,400	$ 1,000

Intangible Assets have no physical existence and a long life. Examples are patents, trademarks, copyrights, franchises, and goodwill from purchasing other companies. Most intangibles except goodwill are amortized as they are used, in a manner similar to the depreciation of tangible assets. They are reported net of accumulated amortization on the balance sheet. Callaway's intangible assets mostly relate to trademarks and goodwill resulting from the purchase of Odyssey Sports, Inc. Callaway's internally developed intangible assets are not shown on the balance sheet because they do not relate to an identifiable transaction.

The **Deferred Taxes** account represents the amount of income taxes that will most likely be paid or saved in the future based on differences in the application of tax laws and GAAP for recognizing revenues and expenses. If the amount is an asset (either current or noncurrent), future tax benefits (reductions) are expected. If the amount is a current or noncurrent liability, future tax payments are expected.

Until this chapter, we have identified the financing by investors as **Contributed Capital.** In practice, however, this account often is shown as two accounts: Common Stock and Paid-in Capital.[3] Each share of common stock usually has a nominal (low) **par value** printed on the face of the certificate. Par value is a legal amount per share established by the board of directors; it has no relationship to the market price of the stock. Its significance is that it establishes the minimum amount that a stockholder must contribute. Callaway's common stock has a par value of $.01 per share, but the 1,039,000 shares were sold in its 1992 initial public offering at a market price of $15.84 per share.[4] When a corporation issues capital stock, the amount received is recorded in part as Common Stock (Number of Shares × Par Value per Share) and the excess above par as **Paid-in Capital** (also called *Additional Paid-in Capital* or *Contributed Capital in Excess of Par*). The journal entry to record Callaway's 1992 initial public offering follows:

PAR VALUE is a legal amount per share established by the board of directors; it establishes the minimum amount a stockholder must contribute and has no relationship to the market price of the stock.

PAID-IN CAPITAL (Additional Paid-in Capital, Contributed Capital in Excess of Par) is the amount of contributed capital less the par value of the stock.

Cash (+A) ($15.84 × 1,039,000 shares)	16,457,760	
Common stock (+SE) ($.01 per share × 1,039,000 shares)		10,390
Paid-in capital (+SE) ($16,457,760 − 10,390)		16,447,370

Assets	=	Liabilities	+	Stockholders' Equity	
Cash +16,457,760				Common Stock +10,390	
				Paid-in Capital +16,447,370	

ACCUMULATED OTHER COMPREHENSIVE INCOME includes the net unrealized gains or losses on securities, net minimum pension liability adjustment, and net foreign currency translation adjustment, which are directly credited or debited to the stockholders' equity account.

The account **Accumulated Other Comprehensive Income** includes accumulated amounts of three additional types of gains or losses not included in the computation of net income. These are unrealized gain or loss on securities, minimum pension liability

[3]The face of Callaway's balance sheet (as is common for most companies) discloses information on the number of shares that the company is authorized to issue (240 million) and the number of shares issued (78,958,963). The amount listed as treasury stock is the number of previously issued shares that have been repurchased by the company from shareholders (4,815,241 shares). Chapter 11 discusses these terms in more detail.

[4]These numbers are rounded.

adjustment, and foreign currency translation adjustment. The first item, unrealized gain or loss on securities, will be discussed in Chapter 12. The latter two items are discussed in intermediate accounting and advanced accounting courses, respectively. Each period, the total amount of these gains and losses is directly credited or debited to this stockholders' equity account.

| **Balance Sheet Ratios and Debt Contracts** | **FINANCIAL ANALYSIS** |

When firms borrow money, they agree to make specific future payments of interest and principal. To provide protection for the creditors, they also often agree to other restrictions on their activities. For example, Callaway has a $120 million line of credit with its bank. As part of the agreement with the bank, Callaway agreed to maintain certain minimum financial ratios. Ratios typically used as part of these agreements are the current ratio and debt-to-equity ratio, which are defined as follows:

$$\text{Current Ratio} = \frac{\text{Current Assets}}{\text{Current Liabilities}} \qquad \text{Debt-to-Equity Ratio} = \frac{\text{Total Liabilities}}{\text{Stockholders' Equity}}$$

Maintaining a specified level of the current ratio assures the bank that the company has sufficient liquidity (liquid assets, after the payment of current liabilities) to pay its current debts. (The current ratio is discussed in more detail in Chapter 9.) The debt-to-equity ratio measures the portion of the company that is financed with debt as opposed to equity. By accepting the limit set by the debt-to-equity ratio, a company agrees to limit the amount of its additional borrowing, which limits the demands of new creditors on the company's cash. (The debt-to-equity ratio is discussed in more detail in Chapter 10.)

Classified Income Statement

Callaway Golf's 2000 consolidated income statement is reprinted for you in Exhibit 5.5. Other common titles include **statement of earnings** and **statement of operations.** This form of the income statement is called a *multiple-step income statement.* Income statements have two major sections. The first presents the income statement as we have in prior chapters. The second presents net income on a per share basis, or earnings per share. Notice that Callaway also reports income statement line items as a percentage of net sales, which are often called *common-size income statements.* Many analysts compute these common-size statements as a first step in analysis because they ease year-to-year comparisons.

Topic Tackler 5–2

Continuing Operations

Like most manufacturing and merchandising companies,[5] Callaway's income statements are prepared using the following basic structure.

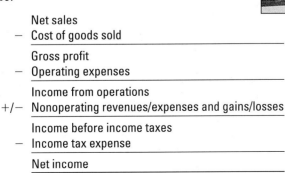

Net sales
− Cost of goods sold
_____
Gross profit
− Operating expenses
_____
Income from operations
+/− Nonoperating revenues/expenses and gains/losses
_____
Income before income taxes
− Income tax expense
_____
Net income

---

[5]A merchandiser buys products from manufacturers for resale, and a manufacturer produces goods for sale to wholesalers or retail merchandisers.

EXHIBIT 5.5	CALLAWAY GOLF COMPANY Consolidated Statement of Operations For the Years Ended December 31, 1998–2000					
Income Statement of Callaway Golf	**(in thousands, except per share data)**		**Year ended December 31,**			
		2000		**1999**		**1998**	

(in thousands, except per share data)	2000		1999		1998	
REAL WORLD EXCERPT	Net sales	$837,627	100%	$719,038	100%	$703,060	100%
	Cost of goods sold	440,119	53%	384,265	53%	410,341	58%
Callaway GOLF	Gross profit	397,508	47%	334,773	47%	292,719	42%
ANNUAL REPORT	Selling expenses	170,541	20%	128,565	18%	143,727	20%
	General and administrative expenses	70,333	8%	92,478	13%	98,048	14%
	Research and development costs	34,579	4%	34,002	5%	36,848	5%
	Restructuring costs			(5,894)	(1%)	54,235	8%
	Sumitomo transition costs			5,713	1%		
	Income (loss) from operations	122,055	15%	79,909	11%	(40,139)	(6%)
	Interest and other income, net	8,791		9,182		3,911	
	Interest expense	(1,524)		(3,594)		(2,671)	
	Income (loss) before income taxes and cumulative effect of accounting change	129,322	16%	85,497	12%	(38,899)	(6%)
	Income tax provision (benefit)	47,366		30,175		(12,335)	
	Income before cumulative effect of accounting change	81,956		55,322		(26,564)	
	Cumulative effect of accounting change	(957)					
	Net income (loss)	$ 80,999	10%	$ 55,322	8%	$ (26,564)	(4%)
	Earnings (loss) per common share: Basic						
	Income before cumulative effect of accounting change	$ 1.17		$ 0.79		$ (0.38)	
	Cumulative effect of accounting change	(0.01)					
		$ 1.16		$ 0.79		$ (0.38)	
	Diluted						
	Income before cumulative effect of accounting change	$1.14		$0.78		$ (0.38)	
	Cumulative effect of accounting change	(0.01)					
		$ 1.13		$ 0.78		$ (0.38)	
	Common equivalent shares: Basic	69,946		70,397		69,463	
	Diluted	71,412		71,214		69,463	
	The accompanying notes are an integral part of these financial statements.						

Net Sales refers to gross sales minus any discounts, returns, and allowances during the period. These latter items are discussed in Chapter 6. **Cost of Goods Sold** is the cost of inventory sold. **Gross Profit** (Gross Margin) is a subtotal, not an account. It is the difference between Net Sales and Cost of Goods Sold.

Operating expenses are the usual expenses incurred in operating a business. The specific expenses reported differ depending on the nature of the company and industry. Significant unusual items are reported separately. Callaway reports two such items in

GROSS PROFIT (Gross Margin) is net sales less cost of goods sold.

1999, the Restructuring Costs and Sumitomo Transition Costs. These two unusual items relate to the restructuring of Callaway's manufacturing and distribution systems. These items are included in operating expenses, even though they are unusual, because they relate to normal operations of the business. Another subtotal—**Income from Operations** (also called Operating Income)—is computed by subtracting operating expenses from gross profit.

INCOME FROM OPERATIONS (Operating Income) equals net sales less cost of goods sold and other operating expenses.

Nonoperating (other) Items are income, expenses, gains, and losses that do not relate to the company's primary operations. Examples include interest income, interest expense, and gains and losses on the sale of fixed assets and investment securities. Interest expense on debt is sometimes combined with interest revenue and listed as a single amount. These nonoperating items are added to or subtracted from income from operations to obtain **Income before Income Taxes,** also called Pretax Earnings. At this point, Income Tax Provision (Income Tax Expense) is normally subtracted to obtain Net Income. Income tax expense is incurred by a corporation but not by a sole proprietorship or partnership. Income taxes are payable each year (part in advance in quarterly installments).

INCOME BEFORE INCOME TAXES (Pretax Earnings) is revenues minus all expenses except income tax expense.

Some companies show fewer subtotals on their income statements. No difference exists in the revenue, expense, gain, and loss items reported using the different formats. Only the categories and subtotals differ.

Nonrecurring Items

Companies may also report one or more of three nonrecurring items on their income statements:

1. Discontinued operations.

2. Extraordinary items.

3. Cumulative effect of changes in accounting methods.

If any one of these three items exists, an additional subtotal is presented for Income from Continuing Operations (or Income before Nonrecurring Items), after which the nonrecurring items are presented. These three items are presented separately because they are not useful in predicting the future income of the company given their nonrecurring nature.

When a major component of a business is sold or abandoned, income or loss from that component, as well as any gain or loss on disposal, are included as discontinued operations. Extraordinary items are gains or losses incurred that are both unusual and infrequent in occurrence. The cumulative effect of changes in accounting methods presents the effects on the balance sheet of changing from one acceptable accounting method to another. For 2000, Callaway changed its method for recognizing revenues in response to new guidance provided by the SEC. The cumulative effect of that change on assets and liabilities on the balance sheet is reflected on the income statement, which flows through to retained earnings on the balance sheet. The Chapter Supplement explains these three nonrecurring items in more detail.

Earnings per Share

As we discussed in Chapter 4, simple computations for earnings per share (EPS) are as follows:

$$\text{EPS} = \frac{\text{Net Income Available to Common Shareholders}}{\substack{\text{Weighted Average Number of Shares Outstanding} \\ \text{During the Reporting Period}}}$$

Callaway discloses this amount as illustrated in Exhibit 5.5 (called **Basic EPS**). Any company that has a complex capital structure (that is, stock options or debt or equity securities convertible into common stock) must also compute the effect of these items as if they had been converted at the beginning of the period or when initially issued if during the current reporting period (called **Diluted EPS**). The computation of these amounts is beyond the scope of this text and is usually presented in advanced course-work for accounting majors. Any company that discloses discontinued operations, extraordinary items, or the cumulative effect of changes in accounting methods also must display these effects on a per share basis.

FINANCIAL ANALYSIS

Accounting-Based Executive Bonuses

Callaway Golf believes in tying executives' compensation to the company's performance as measured by pretax earnings. In prior years, Callaway paid its five executive officers bonuses of up to 75 percent of their base salary if pretax earnings growth (computed here) met target amounts. Smaller growth statistics result in smaller bonuses. The 1998 target for maximum bonus was as follows:

$$\text{Pretax Earnings Growth \%} = \frac{\substack{\text{Current Year} \\ \text{Pretax Earnings}} - \substack{\text{Last Year} \\ \text{Pretax Earnings}}}{\text{Last Year Pretax Earnings}} = 30\%$$

As a result of the large loss in 1998, no performance-based bonuses were paid.

SELF-STUDY QUIZ

1. Complete the following tabulation, indicating the direction (+ for increase, − for decrease, and NE for no effect) and amount of the effect of each transaction. Consider each item independently.

   a. Recorded and paid rent expense of $200.

   b. Recorded the sale of goods on account for $400 and cost of goods sold of $300.

TRANSACTION	CURRENT ASSETS	GROSS PROFIT	INCOME FROM OPERATIONS
a.			
b.			

2. Assume that Callaway executives received maximum bonuses if pretax earnings (before the cumulative effect of the accounting change) growth met or exceeded a target of 30 percent. Use Exhibit 5.5 to see whether Callaway executives would earn their maximum bonuses in the most recent year.

   Computations _____

   _____

   Discuss why companies might choose to pay executives based on the company's performance and why they use the accounting numbers in reports to shareholders to measure the executives' performance.

After you have completed your answers, check them with the solutions that follow:

_____
1. a. −200, NE, −200; b. +100, +100, +100
2. Pretax earnings growth % = (129,322 − 85,497) ÷ 85,497 = 51.3% versus 30% target.
They would earn their maximum bonuses. (In reality, their bonuses are now at the discretion of the board.) Many companies believe that higher pretax earnings growth will result in higher prices for the company's stock. Paying executives a bonus for increasing earnings growth thus

helps align the interests of the executives with those of the shareholders. In addition, companies often pay executive bonuses based on the numbers in the annual report because the auditors have independently verified those numbers.

Statement of Stockholders' Equity

The statement of stockholders' (shareholders') equity reports the changes in each of the company's stockholders' equity accounts during the accounting period. We will discuss this statement in Chapter 11.

Statement of Cash Flows

We introduced the three cash flow statement classifications in prior chapters:

Cash Flows from Operating Activities. This section reports cash flows associated with earning income.

Cash Flows from Investing Activities. Cash flows in this section are associated with purchase and sale of (1) productive assets (other than inventory) and (2) investments in other companies.

Cash Flows from Financing Activities. These cash flows are related to financing the business through debt issuances and repayments, stock (equity) issuances and repurchases, and dividend payments.

Exhibit 5.6 presents Callaway's 2000 consolidated statement of cash flows. The first section (Cash Flows from Operating Activities) can be reported using either the **direct** or **indirect** method. For Callaway, this first section is reported using the indirect method, which presents a reconciliation of net income on an accrual basis to cash flows from operations. This more common format differs from the format in the statement prepared for Papa John's at the end of Chapter 4, which was constructed using the direct method.

| Operating Activities (Indirect Method) | FOCUS ON CASH FLOWS |

The Operating Activities section prepared using the indirect method helps the analyst understand the causes of differences between a company's net income and its cash flows. Net income and cash flows from operating activities can be quite different. Remember that the income statement is prepared under the accrual concept. Revenues are recorded when earned without regard to when the related cash flows occur. Likewise, expenses are matched with revenues and recorded in the same period without regard to when the related cash flows occur.

In the indirect method, the Operating Activities section starts with net income computed under the accrual concept and converts it to cash flow from operating activities. The items listed between these two amounts explain the reasons they differ. For example, since no cash is paid during the current period for Callaway's depreciation expense reported on the income statement, this amount is added back in the conversion process. Similarly, increases and decreases in current assets and liabilities also account for some of the difference between net income and cash flow from operations. Note in Exhibit 5.6 that the buildup of inventories accounted for a major portion of the difference between Callaway's net income and cash flow from operations during 2000. As we cover different portions of the income statement and balance sheet in more detail in Chapters 6 through 12, we will also discuss the relevant sections of the cash flow statement. Then the complete cash flow statement will be discussed in detail in Chapter 13.

EXHIBIT 5.6

Cash Flows Statement
of Callaway Golf

REAL WORLD
EXCERPT

Callaway
GOLF

ANNUAL REPORT

CALLAWAY GOLF COMPANY
Consolidated Statement of Cash Flows
For the Years Ended December 31

(in thousands)	Year ended December 31,		
	2000	**1999**	**1998**
Cash flows from operating activities:			
Net Income (loss)	$ 80,999	$ 55,322	$(26,564)
Adjustments to reconcile net income to cash provided by operating activities			
Depreciation and amortization	40,249	39,877	35,885
Non-cash compensation	2,157	1,390	2,887
Tax benefit from exercise of stock options	6,806	2,377	3,068
Net non-cash foreign currency and hedging gains	(1,410)		
Deferred taxes	4,906	9,971	(36,235)
Non-cash restructuring costs		(8,609)	25,497
Loss on disposal of assets	342	315	1,298
Changes in assets and liabilities, net of effects from acquisitions:			
Accounts receivable, net	(9,047)	19,690	51,575
Inventories, net	(39,402)	51,092	(42,665)
Other assets	(3,074)	(12,966)	(12,149)
Accounts payable and accrued expenses	2,638	12,225	(4,357)
Accrued employee compensation and benefits	1,623	9,875	(3,411)
Accrued warranty expense	3,258	286	7,760
Income taxes payable	4,088	(10,001)	9,652
Accrued restructuring costs	(1,379)	(3,476)	7,389
Deferred compensation	(1,691)	3,969	(299)
Accrued restructuring costs—long term		(5,041)	11,117
Net cash provided by operating activities	91,063	166,296	30,448
Cash flows from investing activities:			
Capital expenditures	(28,386)	(56,244)	(67,859)
Acquisitions, net of cash acquired	(444)	(2,389)	(10,672)
Proceeds from sale of assets	244	5,095	3,417
Net cash used in investing activities	(28,586)	(53,538)	(75,114)
Cash flows from financing activities:			
Net proceeds from line of credit		(70,919)	70,919
Proceeds from note payable		35,761	12,971
Short-term debt retirement			(10,373)
Issuance of common stock	28,233	9,009	10,343
Acquisition of treasury stock	(80,469)		
Retirement of common stock			(917)
Proceeds from sale-leaseback of equipment	1,268		
Dividends paid, net	(19,538)	(19,760)	(19,485)
Net cash (used in) provided by financing activities	(70,506)	(45,909)	63,458
Effect of exchange rate changes on cash	(1,977)	135	622
Net (decrease) increase in cash and cash equivalents	(10,006)	66,984	19,414
Cash and cash equivalents at beginning of year	112,602	45,618	26,204
Cash and cash equivalents at end of year	$102,596	$112,602	$ 45,618
Supplemental disclosures:			
Non-cash financing		$ 48,732	
Cash paid for interest and fees	$ 805	$ 3,637	$ 2,162
Cash paid for income taxes	$ 29,245	$ 30,670	$ 8,165

The accompanying notes are an integral part of these financial statements.

Notes to Financial Statements

While the numbers reported on the various financial statements provide important information, users require additional details to facilitate their analysis. All financial reports include additional information in notes that follow the statements. Callaway's 2000 notes include three types of information:

1. Descriptions of the key accounting rules applied to the company's statements.

2. Additional detail supporting reported numbers.

3. Relevant financial information not disclosed on the statements.

Accounting Rules Applied in the Company's Statements

One of the first notes is typically a summary of significant accounting policies. As you will see in your study of subsequent chapters, generally accepted accounting principles (GAAP) permit companies to select from alternative methods for measuring the effects of transactions. The summary of significant accounting policies tells the user which accounting methods the company has adopted. Callaway's accounting policy for property, plant, and equipment is as follows:

REAL WORLD EXCERPT

Callaway
GOLF
ANNUAL REPORT

Note 2

SIGNIFICANT ACCOUNTING POLICIES

Property, Plant, and Equipment

Property, plant and equipment are stated at cost less accumulated depreciation. Depreciation is computed using the straight-line method over estimated useful lives of two to 30 years. The Company's property, plant and equipment generally are depreciated over the following periods:

Buildings and improvements	10–30 years
Machinery and equipment	5–15 years
Furniture, computers and equipment	3–5 years
Production molds	2 years

Without an understanding of the various accounting methods used, it is impossible to analyze a company's financial results effectively.

Alternative Accounting Methods and GAAP

FINANCIAL ANALYSIS

Many people mistakenly believe that GAAP permit only one accounting method to be used to compute each value on the financial statements (e.g., inventory). Actually, GAAP often allow a selection of an accounting method from a menu of acceptable methods. This permits a company to choose the methods that most closely reflect its particular economic circumstances. This flexibility complicates the financial statement users' task, however. Users must understand how the company's choice of accounting methods affects its financial statement presentations. As Gabrielle Napolitano and Abby Joseph Cohen of the investment banking firm of Goldman, Sachs & Co. note in their recent research report,

There are numerous legitimate ways in which company accounts can be made obscure. Further, investors must be wary of the means by which reported earnings can be manipulated or smoothed. Users of financial statements (e.g., shareholders, creditors, and others) are often forced to wrestle with dramatic differences in reporting practices between firms.*

*Gabrielle Napolitano and Abby Joseph Cohen, "The Quality of Reported Earnings Has Improved, But . . . Pointers on What to Look for in Company Reports," *U.S. Research* (New York: Goldman, Sachs & Co., January 2, 1997).

For example, before analyzing two companies' statements prepared using different accounting methods, one company's statements must be converted to the other's methods to make them comparable. Otherwise, the reader is in a situation analogous to comparing distances in kilometers and miles without converting to a common scale. In later chapters, we will focus on developing the ability to make these conversions.

Additional Detail Supporting Reported Numbers

The second category of notes provides supplemental information concerning the data shown on the financial statements. Among other information, these notes may show revenues broken out by geographic region or business segment, describe unusual transactions, and or offer expanded detail on a specific classification. For example, in Note 3, Callaway indicates the makeup of accounts receivable; inventory; property, plant, and equipment; intangible assets; and other items presented on the balance sheet. Note 16, which follows, shows sales reported on the income statement and long-lived assets from the balance sheet divided by geographic region:

Note 16

Segment Information

(in thousands)	Sales	Long-Lived Assets
2000		
United States	$451,264	$228,920
Europe	125,511	11,229
Japan	122,003	3,229
Rest of Asia	82,371	994
Other foreign countries	56,478	3,164
Total	$837,627	$247,536

Relevant Financial Information Not Disclosed on the Statements

The final category includes information that impacts the company financially but is not shown on the statements. Examples include information on stock option plans, legal matters, and any material event that occurred subsequent to year-end but before the financial statements are published. In Note 4, Callaway disclosed the details of its line of credit:

Note 4

Bank Line of Credit and Note Payable

In February 1999, the Company consummated the amendment of its credit facility to increase the facility to up to $120,000,000 (the "Amended Credit Agreement"). The Amended Credit Agreement expires on February 2004 and is secured by substantially all of the assets of the Company. The Amended Credit Agreement bears interest at the Company's election at the London Interbank Offering Rate ("LIBOR") plus a margin of the higher of the base rate on corporate loans at large U.S. money center commercial banks (prime rate), or the Federal Funds Rate plus 50 basis points. The line of credit requires the Company to maintain certain minimum financial ratios, including a fixed charge coverage ratio, as well as other restrictive covenants.

REAL WORLD EXCERPT

Callaway GOLF

ANNUAL REPORT

Voluntary Disclosures

GAAP and SEC regulations set only the minimum level of required financial disclosures. Many companies, including Callaway, provide important disclosures beyond those required. For example, in its annual report, 10-K, and recent earnings press release, Callaway discloses sales by major product category, which helps investors to track the success of new products.

Constraints of Accounting Measurement

Accurate interpretation of financial statements requires that the statement reader be aware of three important constraints of accounting measurement. First, small amounts do not have to be reported separately or accounted for precisely according to GAAP if they would not influence users' decisions. Accountants usually designate such items and amounts as **immaterial.** Determining material amounts is often very subjective.

Second, **conservatism** requires that special care be taken to avoid (1) overstating assets and revenues and (2) understating liabilities and expenses. This guideline attempts to offset managers' natural optimism about their operations, which sometimes creeps into the financial reports they prepare. This constraint produces more conservative income statement and balance sheet amounts.

Finally, the educated financial statement reader must be aware of special industry practices. For example, public utilities (an industry regulated by government) often present balance sheet information in what appears to be upside-down order. That is, property, plant, and equipment are listed first, followed by the more liquid assets (cash, accounts receivable, and supplies). The reason for this order of presentation is that regulatory commissions in many states require it.

MATERIAL AMOUNTS are amounts that are large enough to influence a user's decision.

CONSERVATISM suggests that care should be taken not to overstate assets and revenues or understate liabilities and expenses.

RETURN ON EQUITY ANALYSIS: A FRAMEWORK FOR EVALUATING COMPANY PERFORMANCE

Evaluating company performance is the primary goal of financial statement analysis. Company managers, as well as competitors, use financial statements to better understand and evaluate a company's business strategy. Analysts, investors, and creditors use these same statements to judge company performance when they estimate the value of the company's stock and its creditworthiness. Our discussion of the financial data contained in accounting reports has now reached the point where we can develop an overall framework for using that data to evaluate company performance. The most comprehensive framework of this type is called **return on equity** or **ROE analysis** (also called return on stockholders' equity or return on investment).

Learning Objective 4
Analyze a company's performance based on return on equity and its components.

Return on Equity

? ANALYTICAL QUESTION

How well has management used the stockholders' investment during the period?

% RATIO AND COMPARISONS

$$\text{Return on Equity} = \frac{\text{Net Income}}{\text{Average Stockholders' Equity*}}$$

The 2000 ratio for Callaway:

$$\frac{\$80,999}{(\$511,744 + 499,934) \div 2} = 0.160 \ (16.0\%)$$

COMPARISONS OVER TIME		
Callaway Golf		
1998	**1999**	**2000**
−5.7%	11.6%	16.0%

COMPARISONS WITH COMPETITORS	
S2 Golf	**Recreational Products Industry**
2000	**1996–2000**
4.0%	17.7%

💡 INTERPRETATIONS:

In General ROE measures how much the firm earned for each dollar of stockholders' investment. In the long run, firms with higher ROE are expected to have higher stock prices than firms with lower ROE, all other things equal. Managers, analysts, and creditors use this ratio to assess the effectiveness of the company's overall business strategy (its operating, investing, and financing strategies).

Focus Company Analysis ROE for large companies in the recreational products industry has averaged 17.7 percent over the last five years.† Callaway's ROEs from 1995 to 1997 were 47.5 percent, 41.7 percent, and 31.5 percent, which were significantly higher than that figure. Such high levels of ROE tend to be driven down over time by additional competition from new and existing competitors. Financial analysts sometimes call this *economic gravity.* Callaway is facing just such a situation as large companies such as American Brands—owned Cobra Golf—and Adidas-owned Taylor-Made invest millions in marketing to unseat Callaway from the top of its market. Callaway's performance dropped dramatically in 1998, which coincided with a decline in its share price from $28 per share in January 1998 to $10 by September 1998. Callaway's stock price returned to the $28 level when its improved 2000 results were announced. The relationship between ROE and share price is well established in the stock valuation literature.‡

A Few Cautions An increasing ROE can also indicate that a company is failing to invest in research and development or modernization of plant and equipment. While such a strategy will decrease expenses and thus increase ROE in the short run, it normally results in future declines in ROE as the company's products or plant and equipment reach the end of their life cycles. As a consequence, experienced decision makers evaluate ROE in the context of a company's business strategy.

Average Stockholders' Equity = (Beginning Stockholders' Equity + Ending Stockholders' Equity) ÷ 2

†Multex Investor, November 2001.

‡See Robert F. Halsey, "Using the Residual-Income Stock Price Valuation Model to Teach and Learn Ratio Analysis," Issues in Accounting Education, May 2001.

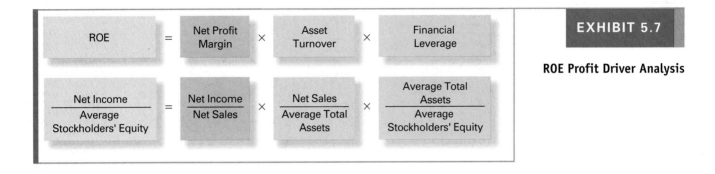

ROE Profit Driver Analysis

Effective analysis of Callaway's performance also requires an understanding of **why** its ROE differs both from prior levels and from those of its competitors. ROE profit driver analysis (also called ROE decomposition or DuPont analysis) breaks down ROE into the three factors shown in Exhibit 5.7. These factors are often called **profit drivers** or **profit levers** because they describe the three ways that management can improve ROE. They are measured by the key ratios we learned in Chapters 2 through 4.

A. Net profit margin. Net profit margin is Net Income/Net Sales. It measures how much of every sales dollar is profit. It can be increased by
  1. Increasing sales volume.
  2. Increasing sales price.
  3. Decreasing expenses.
B. Asset turnover (efficiency). Asset turnover is Net Sales/Average Total Assets. It measures how many sales dollars the company generates with each dollar of assets. It can be increased by
  1. Increasing sales volume.
  2. Disposing of (decreasing) less productive assets.
C. Financial leverage. Financial leverage is Average Total Assets/Average Stockholders' Equity. It measures how many dollars of assets are employed for each dollar of stockholder investment. It can be increased by
  1. Increased borrowing.
  2. Repurchasing (decreasing) outstanding stock.

Profit Drivers and Business Strategy

Successful manufacturers often follow one of two business strategies. The first is a high-value or product-differentiation strategy. Companies following this strategy rely on research and development and product promotion to convince customers of the superiority or distinctiveness of their products. This allows the company to charge higher prices and earn a higher net profit margin. The second is a low-cost strategy, which relies on efficient management of accounts receivable, inventory, and productive assets to produce high asset turnover.

Callaway Golf follows a classic high-value strategy. The ROE profit driver analysis presented in Exhibit 5.8 indicates the sources of Callaway's high ROE, as well as reasons for its increase over the last three years. After a particularly bad year in 1998, Callaway has shown steady improvement in ROE. The analysis indicates an increase in asset turnover as well as net profit margin from 1999 to 2000. This indicates that Callaway was able to generate more sales for each dollar of assets and higher profits on each dollar of sales. Callaway also decreased its financial leverage from 1999 to 2000 by financing its increase in assets more out of equity than from increased borrowing. Callaway's low financial leverage means less risk to shareholders if Callaway should face another bad year in the future.

EXHIBIT 5.8	Fiscal Year Ending	12/31/2000	12/31/1999	12/31/1998
	Net Income/Net Sales	0.10	0.08	(0.04)
Callaway Golf ROE Profit Driver Analysis	× Net Sales/Avg. Total Assets	1.34	1.13	1.15
	× Avg. Total Assets/Avg. Stockholders' Equity	1.23	1.34	1.30
	= Net Income/Avg. Stockholders' Equity	0.16	0.12	(0.06)

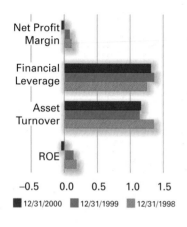

Companies often consider a variety of changes to increase ROE. These include

- Reducing promotional activities and fees paid to distributors to increase profit margin.

- Collecting accounts receivable more quickly, centralizing distribution to reduce inventory kept on hand, and consolidating production facilities in fewer factories to reduce the amount of assets necessary to generate each dollar of sales.

- Using more borrowed funds (financial leverage) so that more assets can be employed per dollar of stockholder investment.

Companies that follow a low-cost strategy, such as Gateway and Dell Computer, usually produce high ROE with higher asset turnover and higher leverage to make up for their lower net profit margin. This strategy is illustrated in the self-study quiz that follows this section.

As the preceding discussion indicates, companies can take many different actions to try to affect its profit drivers. To understand the impact of these actions, financial analysts disaggregate each of the profit drivers into more detailed ratios. For example, the asset turnover ratio is further disaggregated into turnover ratios for specific assets such as accounts receivable, inventory, and fixed assets. We will develop our understanding of these more specific ratios in the next eight chapters of the book. Then, in Chapter 14, we will combine the ratios in a comprehensive review.

SELF-STUDY QUIZ

Dell Computer
Gateway

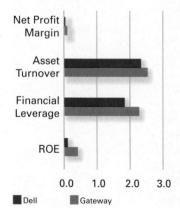

We used ROE analysis in Exhibit 5.8 to understand how Callaway's ROE had steadily improved over the last three years. This type of analysis is often called **time-series analysis.** ROE analysis can also be used to explain why a company has an ROE different from its competitors at a single point in time. This type of analysis is called **cross-sectional analysis.**

The following is the current year's ROE analysis for Dell Computer and Gateway, the largest computer manufacturers employing phone/Internet distribution. Both of these companies have followed a low-cost strategy, developing reputations for good products and service at low prices. Dell has produced a higher ROE than Gateway over the last two years, and its stock price has held up much better in the face of the general decline in technology stock prices. Using ROE analysis, explain how Dell has produced its higher ROE.

ROE PROFIT DRIVERS	DELL	GATEWAY
Net Income/Net Sales	.068	.025
× Net Sales/Average Total Assets	2.56	2.37
× Avg. Total Assets/Average Stockholders' Equity	2.28	1.84
= Net Income / Average Stockholders' Equity	0.40	0.11

After you have completed your answers, check them with the solutions that follow:

Both Dell and Gateway are well known for the efficiency of their operations, which is reflected in their high asset turnover ratios. Dell has the edge in asset efficiency, but the edge is small. Dell's major strength is its 170 percent higher net profit margin. This reflects Dell's success with its primary market segment, business customers. Dell purchases in higher quantity, which decreases order-processing and production costs. Its customers also often purchase higher-end, higher-net profit margin machines than customers in Gateway's primary market segment, individuals. The effect of this edge in net profit margin is multiplied further by Dell's greater reliance on leverage (debt financing). However, this greater leverage could come back to haunt Dell if there is a further downturn in the personal computer market.

EPILOGUE

The looming recession had begun to hurt golf club sales by the second quarter of 2001. In June, the company warned that earnings for the second quarter would be only about half of the amount forecasted by analysts. In response to that earnings warning, investors drove Callaway's stock price down to $14 per share. In July 2001, we were all saddened by the news of Ely Callaway's death. The world of golf, and Callaway Golf Company, must now face an uncertain future without Ely Callaway's passion to make golf more enjoyable for the average golfer. You can evaluate Callaway Golf's responses to these challenges by going to the web at www.callawaygolf.com to check its latest annual and quarterly reports.

DEMONSTRATION **CASE**

MICROSOFT CORPORATION

Complete the following requirements before proceeding to the suggested solution. Microsoft Corporation, developer of a broad line of computer software including the Windows operating systems, Word (word processing), and Excel (spreadsheet) programs is now the largest computer-related company in the world. Following is a list of the financial statement items and amounts adapted from a recent Microsoft income statement and balance sheet. These items have normal debit and credit balances and are reported in millions of dollars. For that year, 5,341 million (weighted average) shares of stock were outstanding. The company closes its books on June 30, 2001.

Microsoft

Accounts payable	$ 1,188	Other current liabilities	$ 2,120
Accounts receivable	3,671	Other investments	14,141
Accrued compensation	742	Other revenues and	
Cash and short-term		expenses (debit balance)	(534)
investments	31,600	Other noncurrent assets	3,170
Common stock and		Property, plant, and	
paid-in capital	28,390	equipment (net)	2,309
Cost of goods sold	3,455	Provision for income taxes	3,804
General and administrative	857	Research and development	4,379
Income taxes payable	1,468	Retained earnings	18,899
Investment income (loss)	(36)	Sales and marketing	4,885
Net revenues	25,296	Unearned revenue	5,614
Other current assets	3,530		

Required:

1. Prepare in good form a multiple-step income statement (showing both gross profit and operating income) and a classified balance sheet for the year.

2. Prepare an ROE profit driver analysis. Briefly explain its meaning and compare the result with that of Dell Computer as shown in the Self-Study Quiz. (Microsoft's total assets and total shareholders' equity at the beginning of the year were $52,150 million and $41,368 million, respectively.)

SUGGESTED SOLUTION

1.

MICROSOFT CORPORATION
Income Statement
For the Period Ended June 30, 2001
(in millions)

Net revenues	$25,296
Cost of goods sold	3,455
Gross profit	21,841
Operating expenses:	
Research and development	4,379
Sales and marketing	4,885
General and administrative	857
Total operating expenses	10,121
Operating income	**11,720**
Nonoperating income and expenses:	
Investment income (loss)	(36)
Other revenues and expenses	(534)
Income before income taxes	11,150
Provision for income taxes	3,804
Net income	$ 7,346
Earnings per share	**$1.38**

MICROSOFT CORPORATION
Balance Sheet
June 30, 2001
(in millions)

Assets	
Current assets	
Cash and short-term investments	$31,600
Accounts receivable	3,671
Other current assets	3,530
Total current assets	38,801
Noncurrent assets	
Property, plant, and equipment (net)	2,309
Other investments	14,141
Other noncurrent assets	3,170
Total assets	$58,421

Liabilities

Current liabilities

Accounts payable	$ 1,188
Accrued compensation	742
Income taxes payable	1,468
Unearned revenue	5,614
Other current liabilities	2,120
Total current liabilities	11,132

Noncurrent liabilities

Stockholders' equity

Common stock and paid-in-capital	28,390
Retained earnings	18,899
Total stockholders' equity	47,289
Total liabilities and stockholders' equity	$58,421

2.

Fiscal Year Ending	June 30, 2001
Net Income/Net Sales	0.29
× Net Sales/Average Total Assets	0.46
× Avg. Total Assets/Average Stockholders' Equity	1.25
= Net Income/Average Stockholders' Equity	0.17

For the year ended June 30, Microsoft's shareholders earned an ROE of 17 percent. This is much lower than Dell's recent results presented in the Self-Study Quiz, as the detailed analysis shows. In contrast to Dell's results (see the Self-Study Quiz), Microsoft maintains high profit margins, earning 29¢ of net income for every $1 of net sales but a lower asset efficiency with only $0.46 in sales generated for each $1 of assets. The analysis also indicates Microsoft's dominance of the computer software business, which allows the company to charge premium prices for its products. However, the financial leverage ratio indicates that Microsoft's capital is primarily equity (not debt) based. With $1.25 in assets for each $1.00 of shareholders' equity, Microsoft has chosen not to leverage (or borrow) as much, for example, as Dell Computer, which faces stiff competition in the computer hardware industry.

Chapter Supplement

Nonrecurring Items

As noted in the chapter, companies may report any of three nonrecurring items: discontinued operations, extraordinary items, and cumulative effects of accounting methods changes. The income statement of Tenneco Automotive Inc., a global manufacturer of automotive parts, contains all three items, and is presented in Exhibit 5.9

Discontinued Operations

Discontinued operations result from abandoning or selling a major business component. Operating income generated by the discontinued component and any gain or loss on the disposal (the difference between the book value of the net assets being disposed of and the sale price or the abandonment costs) are included. These amounts may be separately disclosed in a note or on the face of the income statement. Each amount is reported net of the income tax effects. Separate reporting of discontinued operations informs users that these results are not predictive of the company's future.

DISCONTINUED OPERATIONS
result from the disposal of a major component of the business and are reported net of income tax effects.

EXHIBIT 5.9

Income Statements for
Tenneco Inc.

REAL WORLD EXCERPT

Tenneco Automotive Inc.

ANNUAL REPORT

TENNECO AUTOMOTIVE INC. AND CONSOLIDATED SUBSIDIARIES
STATEMENTS OF INCOME (LOSS)
For the Years Ended
December 31, 1998–2000

	2000	1999	1998
	Millions Except Per Share Amounts		
Revenues			
Net sales and operating revenues	3,549	3,279	3,237
Costs and expenses			
Cost of sales (exclusive of depreciation shown below)	2,766	2,427	2,332
Engineering, research, and development	58	52	31
Selling, general, and administrative	459	521	472
Depreciation and amortization	151	144	150
	$3,434	$3,144	$2,985
Other income (expense)	5	13	(25)
Income before interest expense, income taxes, and minority interest	$120	$148	$227
Interest expense (net of interest capitalized)	186	106	69
Income tax expense (benefit)	(27)	82	13
Minority interest	2	23	29
Income (loss) from continuing operations	$(41)	$(63)	$116
Income (loss) from discontinued operations, net of income tax	—	(208)	139
Income (loss) before extraordinary loss	$(41)	$(271)	$255
Extraordinary loss, net of income tax	(1)	(18)	—
Income (loss) before cumulative effect of changes in accounting principles	$(42)	$(289)	$255
Cumulative effect of changes in accounting principles, net of income tax	—	(134)	—
Net income (loss)	$(42)	$(423)	$255

The accompanying notes to financial statements are an integral part of these statements of income (loss).

During 1999, Tenneco sold its paperboard manufacturing business. The results of the paperboard manufacturing operations and the loss on sale of the business are listed as discontinued operations, net of tax, on the income statement shown in Exhibit 5.9. The notes accompanying Tenneco's income statement reported the separate amounts of the operating loss and loss on sale.

Extraordinary Items

EXTRAORDINARY ITEMS are gains and losses that are both unusual in nature and infrequent in occurrence; they are reported net of tax on the income statement.

Extraordinary items are gains or losses that are considered both unusual in nature and infrequent in occurrence. Most extraordinary gains and losses relate to early retirement of long-term debt. Other examples include losses suffered from natural disasters such as floods and hurricanes in geographic areas where such disasters are rare. These items must be reported separately on the income statement net of income tax effects. Separate reporting again informs decision makers that these items are not likely to recur, and so are not predictive of the company's future. Note disclosure is needed to explain the nature of the extraordinary item. In 2000 and 1999, Tenneco reported extraordinary losses due to the early retirement of long-term debt (Exhibit 5.9). Accounting for early retirement of debt is discussed in Chapter 10.

Cumulative Effects of Changes in Accounting Methods

The final nonrecurring item reflects the income statement effects of any adjustment made to balance sheet accounts because of a change to a different acceptable accounting method. These amounts are called **cumulative effects of changes in accounting methods**. The goal is to determine what the balance sheet amount would be if the new accounting method had always been applied, net of any tax effects. Often these changes are required by new FASB pronouncements. At other times, corporate management determines that a change to an alternative accounting method is necessary because of changes in business activities. Note disclosure to explain the nature and effects of the change also is necessary. In 1999, Tenneco made two accounting method changes, one related to implementation of a new accounting standard and one voluntary change to improve the comparability of results with other automotive parts manufacturers. Again, the effects of accounting method changes are separated because they are normally not relevant to predicting the company's future.

CUMULATIVE EFFECTS OF CHANGES IN ACCOUNTING METHODS are the amounts reflected on the income statement for adjustments made to balance sheet accounts when applying different accounting principles.

CHAPTER TAKE-AWAYS

1. **Recognize the people involved in the accounting communication process (managers, auditors, information intermediaries, government regulators, and users), their roles in the process, and the guidance they receive from legal and professional standards.   p. 225**
   Management of the reporting company must decide on the appropriate format (categories) and level of detail to present in its financial reports. Independent audits increase the credibility of the information. Financial statement announcements from public companies usually are first transmitted to users through electronic information services. The SEC staff reviews public financial reports for compliance with legal and professional standards, investigates irregularities, and punishes violators. Analysts play a major role in making financial statement and other information available to average investors through their stock recommendations and earnings forecasts.

2. **Identify the steps in the accounting communication process, including the issuance of press releases, annual reports, quarterly reports, and SEC filings as well as the role of electronic information services in this process.   p. 232**
   Earnings are first made public in press releases. Companies follow these announcements with annual and quarterly reports containing statements, notes, and additional information. Public companies must file additional reports with the SEC, including the 10-K, 10-Q, and 8-K, which contain more details about the company. Electronic information services are the key source of dissemination of this information to sophisticated users.

3. **Recognize and apply the different financial statement and disclosure formats used by companies in practice.   p. 236**
   Most statements are classified and include subtotals that are relevant to analysis. On the balance sheet, the most important distinctions are between current and noncurrent assets and liabilities. On the income and cash flow statements, the distinction between operating and nonoperating items are most important. The notes to the statements provide descriptions of the accounting rules applied, add more information about items disclosed on the statements, and present information about economic events not included in the statements.

4. **Analyze a company's performance based on return on equity and its components.   p. 247**
   ROE measures how well management used the stockholders' investment during the period. Its three determinants, net profit margin, asset turnover, and financial leverage, indicate why ROE differs from prior levels or the ROEs of competitors. They also suggest strategies to improve ROE in future periods.

In Chapter 6, we will begin our in-depth discussion of financial statements. We will start with two of the most liquid assets, cash and accounts receivable, and transactions that involve revenues and certain selling expenses. Accuracy in revenue recognition and the related recognition of cost of goods sold (discussed in Chapter 7) are the most important determinants of the accuracy—and, thus, the usefulness—of financial statements. We will also introduce concepts related to the management and control of cash and receivables, a critical business function. A detailed understanding of these topics is crucial to future managers, accountants, and financial analysts.

KEY **RATIO**

Return on equity (ROE) measures how much the firm earned for each dollar of stockholders' investment. It is computed as follows (p. 248):

$$\text{Return on Equity} = \frac{\text{Net Income}}{\text{Average Stockholders' Equity}}$$

FINDING **FINANCIAL INFORMATION**

Balance Sheet

Key Classifications:
Current and non-current assets and liabilities
Contributed capital and retained earnings

Income Statement

Key Subtotals:
Gross profit
Income from operations
Net income
Earnings per share

Statement of Cash Flows

Under Operating Activities
  (indirect method):
Net income
$\pm$ differences between net income and cash
  provided by operating activities

Cash provided by operating activities

Notes

Key Classifications:
Descriptions of accounting rules applied in the
  statements
Additional detail supporting reported numbers
Relevant financial information not disclosed
  on the statements

KEY **TERMS**

Accumulated Other Comprehensive Income   p. 238
Comparable Information   p. 231
Conservatism   p. 247
Consistent Information   p. 231
Cost-Benefit Constraint   p. 231
Cumulative Effects of Changes in Accounting Methods   p. 255
Discontinued Operations   p. 253
Earnings Forecasts   p. 227

Extraordinary Items   p. 254
Form 8-K   p. 235
Form 10-K   p. 235
Form 10-Q   p. 235
Gross Profit (Gross Margin)   p. 240
Income before Income Taxes (Pretax Earnings)   p. 241
Income from Operations (Operating Income)   p. 241
Institutional Investors   p. 229

Lenders (Creditors)   p. 230
Material Amounts   p. 247
Paid-in Capital   p. 238
Par Value   p. 238
Press Release   p. 232
Private Investors   p. 230
Relevant Information   p. 231
Reliable Information   p. 231
Unqualified (Clean) Audit Opinion   p. 226

QUESTIONS

1. Describe the roles and responsibilities of management and independent auditors in the financial reporting process.
2. Define the following three users of financial accounting disclosures and the relationships among them: *financial analysts, private investors,* and *institutional investors.*
3. Briefly describe the role of information services in the communication of financial information.
4. Explain why information must be relevant and reliable to be useful.

5. What basis of accounting do GAAP require on the (a) income statement, (b) balance sheet, and (c) statement of cash flows?
6. Briefly explain the normal sequence and form of financial reports produced by private companies in a typical year.
7. Briefly explain the normal sequence and form of financial reports produced by public companies in a typical year.
8. What are the five major classifications on the income statement?
9. Define *extraordinary items.* Why should they be reported separately on the income statement?
10. List the six major classifications reported on a balance sheet.
11. For property, plant, and equipment, as reported on the balance sheet, explain (a) cost, (b) accumulated depreciation, and (c) net book value.
12. Briefly explain the major classifications of stockholders' equity for a corporation.
13. What are the three major classifications on a statement of cash flows?
14. What are the three major categories of notes or footnotes presented in annual reports? Cite an example of each.
15. Briefly define *return on equity* and what it measures.

MULTIPLE **CHOICE QUESTIONS**

1. If average total assets increase, but net income, net sales, and average stockholders' equity remain the same, what is the impact on the return on equity ratio?
   a. Increases
   b. Decreases
   c. Remains the same
   d. Cannot be determined without additional information
2. If a company plans to differentiate its products by offering low prices and discounts for items packaged in bulk (such as a discount retailer that requires memberships for its customers), which component in the profit driver analysis is the company attempting to boost?
   a. Net profit margin
   b. Asset turnover
   c. Financial leverage
   d. All of the above
3. Which of the following would not appear in the intangible asset section of the balance sheet?
   a. Goodwill
   b. Patent
   c. Trademark
   d. Prepaid expense
4. Which of the following is not one of the possible nonrecurring items that must be shown in a separate line item *below* the "Income from Continuing Operations" subtotal in the income statement?
   a. Gains and losses from the sale of fixed assets
   b. Discontinued operations
   c. Cumulative effect of changes in accounting methods
   d. Extraordinary items
5. Which of the following reports is filed annually with the SEC?
   a. Form 10-Q
   b. Form 10-K
   c. Form 8-K
   d. Press release
6. Common-sized income statements are used for which of the following?
   a. Comparing the performance of different companies in the same industry
   b. Comparing the performance of a single company over time
   c. Both a and b
   d. None of the above
7. Which of the following is *not* a normal function of a financial analyst?
   a. Issue earnings forecasts
   b. Examine the records underlying the financial statements to certify their conformance with GAAP
   c. Make buy, hold, and sell recommendations on companies' stock
   d. Advise institutional investors on their securities holdings
8. The classified balance sheet format allows one to ascertain quickly which of the following?
   a. The most valuable asset of the company
   b. The specific due date for all liabilities of the company
   c. What liabilities must be paid within the upcoming year
   d. None of the above

9. When companies issue par value stock for cash, which accounts are normally affected?
   a. Common Stock, Paid-in Capital, and Property, Plant, and Equipment, Net
   b. Cash and Property, Plant, and Equipment, Net
   c. Common Stock, Paid-in Capital, and Retained Earnings
   d. Common Stock, Paid-in Capital, and Cash
10. What type of audit report does a client hope to include with its annual report?
   a. Conservative   c. Comparable
   b. Qualified   d. Unqualified

For more practice with multiple choice questions, go to our website at www.mhhe.com/libby4e, click on "Student Center" in the upper left menu, click on this chapter's name and number from the list of contents, and then click on "Multiple Choice Quiz" from the menu on the left.

MINI-**EXERCISES**

M5-1   **Matching Players in the Accounting Communication Process with Their Definitions**
LO1
Match each player with the related definition by entering the appropriate letter in the space provided.

Players	Definitions
___ (1) CEO and CFO	A. Adviser who analyzes financial and other economic information to form forecasts and stock recommendations.
___ (2) Independent auditor	
___ (3) Users	B. Institutional and private investors and creditors (among others).
___ (4) Financial analyst	
	C. Chief executive officer and chief financial officer who have primary responsibility for the information presented in financial statements.
	D. Independent CPA who examines financial statements and attests to their fairness.

M5-2   **Identifying the Disclosure Sequence**
LO2
Indicate the order in which the following disclosures or reports are normally issued by public companies.

No.	Title
___	Annual report
___	Form 10-K
___	Earnings press release

M5-3   **Finding Financial Information: Matching Financial Statements with the Elements of Finan-**
LO3   **cial Statements**

Match each financial statement with the items presented on it by entering the appropriate letter in the space provided.

Elements of Financial Statements	Financial Statements
___ (1) Liabilities	A. Income statement
___ (2) Cash from operating activities	B. Balance sheet
___ (3) Losses	C. Cash flows statement
___ (4) Assets	D. None of the above
___ (5) Revenues	
___ (6) Cash from financing activities	
___ (7) Gains	
___ (8) Owners' equity	
___ (9) Expenses	
___ (10) Assets owned by a stockholder	

Determining the Effects of Transactions on Balance Sheet and Income Statement Categories

M5-4
LO3

Complete the following tabulation, indicating the sign of the effect (+ for increase, − for decrease, and NE for no effect) of each transaction. Consider each item independently.

a. Recorded sales on account of $100 and related cost of goods sold of $60.
b. Recorded advertising expense of $10 incurred but not paid for.

Transaction	Current Assets	Gross Profit	Current Liabilities
a.			
b.			

Determining Financial Statement Effects of Sales and Cost of Goods Sold and Issuance of Par Value Stock

M5-5
LO3

Using the following categories, indicate the effects of the following transactions. Use + for increase and − for decrease and indicate the accounts affected and the amounts.

a. Sales on account were $500 and related cost of goods sold was $360.
b. Issued 10,000 shares of $1 par value stock for $90,000 cash.

Event	Assets	=	Liabilities	+	Stockholders' Equity

Recording Sales and Cost of Goods Sold and Issuance of Par Value Stock

M5-6
LO3

Prepare journal entries for each transaction listed in M5-5.

Computing Net Book Value of Property, Plant, and Equipment

M5-7
LO3

May's Diner purchases new tables for $5,000 on January 1, 2003. The tables are expected to have a 10-year useful life and a $500 salvage value. What would be the net book value of the tables on December 31, 2005?

Computing and Interpreting Return on Equity

M5-8
LO4

Chen, Inc., recently reported the following December 31 amounts in its financial statements (in thousands):

	Current Year	Prior Year
Gross profit	$ 170	$140
Net income	85	70
Total assets	1,000	900
Total shareholders' equity	800	750

Compute return on equity for the current year. What does this ratio measure?

EXERCISES

Matching Players in the Accounting Communication Process with Their Definitions

E5-1
LO1

Match each player with the related definition by entering the appropriate letter in the space provided.

Players	Definitions
_____ (1) SEC	A. Adviser who analyzes financial and other economic
_____ (2) Independent auditor	information to form forecasts and stock recommendations.
_____ (3) Institutional investor	B. Financial institution or supplier that lends money to the
_____ (4) CEO and CFO	company.

_____ (5) Creditor

_____ (6) Financial analyst

_____ (7) Private investor

_____ (8) Information service

C. Chief executive officer and chief financial officer who have primary responsibility for the information presented in financial statements.

D. Independent CPA who examines financial statements and attests to their fairness.

E. Securities and Exchange Commission, which regulates financial disclosure requirements.

F. A company that gathers, combines, and transmits (paper and electronic) financial and related information from various sources.

G. Individual who purchases shares in companies.

H. Manager of pension, mutual, and endowment funds that invests on the behalf of others.

E5–2
LO2

Matching Definitions with Information Releases Made by Public Companies

Following are the titles of various information releases. Match each definition with the related release by entering the appropriate letter in the space provided.

Information Release	Definitions
_____ (1) Annual report	A. Written public news announcement that is normally distributed to major news services.
_____ (2) Form 8-K	B. Report containing the four basic statements for the year, related notes, and often statements by management and auditors.
_____ (3) Press release	
_____ (4) Form 10-Q	C. Brief unaudited report for quarter normally containing summary income statement and balance sheet (unaudited).
_____ (5) Quarterly report	
_____ (6) Form 10-K	D. Annual report filed by public companies with the SEC that contains additional detailed financial information.
	E. Quarterly report filed by public companies with the SEC that contains additional unaudited financial information.
	F. Report of special events (e.g., auditor changes, mergers) filed by public companies with the SEC.

E5–3
LO2

Finding Financial Information: Matching Information Items to Financial Reports

Following are information items included in various financial reports. Match each information item with the report(s) where it would most likely be found by entering the appropriate letter(s) in the space provided.

Information Item	Report
_____ (1) Summarized financial data for 5- or 10-year period.	A. Annual report
_____ (2) Initial announcement of quarterly earnings.	B. Form 8-K
_____ (3) Announcement of a change in auditors.	C. Press release
_____ (4) Complete quarterly income statement, balance sheet, and cash flows statement.	D. Form 10-Q
_____ (5) The four basic financial statements for the year.	E. Quarterly report
_____ (6) Summarized income statement information for the quarter.	F. Form 10-K
_____ (7) Detailed discussion of the company's competition.	G. None of the above
_____ (8) Notes to financial statements.	
_____ (9) Description of those responsible for the financial statements.	
_____ (10) Initial announcement of hiring of new vice president for sales.	

E5–4
LO3

Ordering the Classifications on a Typical Balance Sheet

Following is a list of classifications on the balance sheet. Number them in the order in which they normally appear on a balance sheet.

No.	Title
_____	Current liabilities
_____	Long-term liabilities

_____	Long-term investments
_____	Intangible assets
_____	Property, plant, and equipment
_____	Current assets
_____	Retained earnings
_____	Contributed capital
_____	Other noncurrent assets

Preparing a Classified Balance Sheet

Compaq Computer Corporation began as the first manufacturer of portable computers compatible with the MS-DOS operating system. These sewing machine–size computers found their most important market niche with independent CPAs for whom portability was a must. Today, Compaq is one of the leading manufacturers of computers compatible with the Windows operating systems. Compaq sells a wide variety of desktop, portable, and home computers, as well as powerful servers that run business networks. Presented here are the items listed on its recent balance sheet (in millions) presented in alphabetical order:

Accounts payable	$ 637
Accounts receivable, net	1,377
Cash and cash equivalents	627
Common stock and capital in excess of par value	586
Deferred income taxes (noncurrent)	186 credit
Income taxes payable	69
Inventories	1,123
Other current liabilities	538
Other noncurrent assets	14
Prepaid expenses	164
Property, plant, and equipment, less accumulated depreciation	779
Retained earnings	2,068

E5-5
LO3
Compaq Computer

Required:

Prepare a classified consolidated balance sheet for Compaq for the current year (ended December 31) using the categories presented in the chapter.

Preparing and Interpreting a Classified Balance Sheet with Discussion of Terminology (Challenging)

Lance, Inc., manufactures, markets, and distributes a variety of snack foods. Product categories include sandwich crackers, cookies, restaurant crackers and bread basket items, candy, chips, meat snacks, nuts, and cake items. These items are sold under tradenames including Lance, Toastchee, Toasty, Choc-O-Lunch, Captain's Wafers, and Cape Cod. Presented here are the items listed on its recent balance sheet (in millions) presented in alphabetical order:

Accounts payable	$ 14,718	
Accounts receivable, net	47,188	
Accrued compensation	8,844	
Accrued postretirement health care costs	11,317	
Accumulated other comprehensive income (loss)	(116)	
Additional paid-in capital	1,229	
Cash and cash equivalents	1,224	
Common stock, 28,947,222 shares outstanding	24,123	
Current portion of long-term debt	395	
Deferred income taxes (current)	4,161	debit
Deferred income taxes (noncurrent)	21,548	credit
Goodwill, net	42,069	
Inventories	23,205	
Long-term debt	63,536	
Other assets (noncurrent)	3,216	
Other intangible assets, net	10,177	
Other payables and accrued liabilities	15,439	

E5-6
LO3
Lance, Inc.

Prepaid expenses and other	6,550	
Property, plant, and equipment, net	179,283	
Retained earnings	149,357	
Other long-term liabilities	6,683	

Required:

1. Prepare a classified consolidated balance sheet for Lance, Inc., for the current year (ended December 31) using the categories presented in the chapter.
2. Four of the items end in the term *net*. Explain what this term means in each case.

E5-7

LO3

Reporting Property, Plant, and Equipment on the Balance Sheet

On January 1, 2004, Laura Anne's Bakery purchased a new oven for $6,800. The oven was expected to be used for four years and then to be sold for $2,000 on January 1, 2008. Prepare a schedule showing the amounts that would be reported on the balance sheets prepared at the end of 2004, 2005, 2006, and 2007 for the oven (at cost), accumulated depreciation, and net book value.

E5-8

LO3

Cadbury
Schweppes

Determining Financial Statement Effects of Stock Issuances with Par Value

Cadbury Schweppes plc, a company in the United Kingdom, is one of the largest beverage and candy companies in the world. In the United States, it is best known as the owner of the Snapple brand. Its financial statements are denominated in British pounds (symbol £). As part of its employee stock option plan, it recently issued 18 million shares of £0.125 par value shares for £51 million (these numbers are rounded). Using the following categories, indicate the effects of this transaction. Use + for increase and − for decrease and indicate the accounts affected and the amounts.

Assets	=	Liabilities	+	Stockholders' Equity

E5-9

LO3

Gap, Inc.

Recording Stock Issuances with Par Value

In a recent year, GAP, Inc., owner of GAP, Banana Republic, and OLD Navy stores, issued 13,000,000 shares of its $0.05 par value stock for $111,000,000 (these numbers are rounded). These additional shares were issued under an employee stock option plan. Prepare the journal entry required to record the stock issuance.

E5-10

LO3

Callaway GOLF

Inferring Stock Issuances and Cash Dividends from Changes in Stockholders' Equity

Callaway Golf recently reported the following December 31 balances in its stockholders' equity accounts (in thousands):

	Current Year	Prior Year
Common stock	$ 169	$ 140
Paid-in capital	57,807	31,948
Retained earnings	58,601	17,662
Total shareholders' equity	$116,577	$49,750

During the current year, Callaway reported net income of $42,862. Assume that the only other transactions that affected stockholders' equity during the current year were a single stock issuance and a single cash dividend that was declared and paid during the current year.

Required:

Recreate the two journal entries reflecting the stock issuance and dividend.

E5-11

LO3

Matching Definitions with Income Statement–Related Terms

Following are terms related to the income statement. Match each definition with its related term by entering the appropriate letter in the space provided.

Terms	Definitions
＿＿ (1) Cost of goods sold	A. Sales Revenue − Cost of Goods Sold.
＿＿ (2) Interest expense	B. Item that is both unusual and infrequent.
＿＿ (3) Extraordinary item	C. Sales of services for cash or on credit.
＿＿ (4) Service revenue	D. Revenues + Gains − Expenses − Losses
＿＿ (5) Income tax expense on operations	including effects of discontinued operations, extraordinary items, and cumulative effects of accounting changes (if any).
＿＿ (6) Income before extraordinary items	E. Amount of resources used to purchase or produce the goods that were sold during the reporting period.
＿＿ (7) Net income	F. Income Tax on Revenues − Operating Expenses.
＿＿ (8) Gross margin on sales	G. Cost of money (borrowing) over time.
＿＿ (9) EPS	H. Net income divided by average shares outstanding.
＿＿ (10) Operating expenses	I. Income before unusual and infrequent items and the related income tax.
＿＿ (11) Pretax income from operations	J. Total expenses directly related to operations.
	K. Income before all income tax and before discontinued operations, extraordinary items, and cumulative effects of accounting changes (if any).
	L. None of the above.

Inferring Income Statement Values

E5-12
LO3

Supply the missing dollar amounts for the 2004 income statement of Ultimate Style Company for each of the following independent cases:

	Case A	Case B	Case C	Case D	Case E
Sales revenue	$900	$700	$410	$?	$?
Selling expense	?	150	80	400	250
Cost of goods sold	?	380	?	500	310
Income tax expense	?	30	20	40	30
Gross margin	400	?	?	?	440
Pretax income	200	90	?	190	?
Administrative expense	150	?	60	100	80
Net income	170	?	50	?	80

Preparing a Multiple-Step Income Statement

E5-13
LO3

The following data were taken from the records of Village Corporation at December 31, 2004:

Sales revenue	$70,000
Gross profit	24,500
Selling (distribution) expense	8,000
Administrative expense	?
Pretax income	12,000
Income tax rate	30%
Shares of stock outstanding	3,000

Required:
Prepare a complete multiple-step income statement for the company (showing both gross profit and income from operations). Show all computations. (*Hint:* Set up the side captions starting with sales revenue and ending with earnings per share; rely on the amounts and percentages given to infer missing values.)

Preparing a Multiple-Step Income Statement

E5-14
LO3

The following data were taken from the records of Kimberly Appliances, Incorporated, at December 31, 2006:

Sales revenue	$120,000
Administrative expense	10,000
Selling (distribution) expense	18,000
Income tax rate	25%
Gross profit	48,000
Shares of stock outstanding	2,000

Required:

Prepare a complete multiple-step income statement for the company (showing both gross profit and income from operations). Show all computations. (*Hint:* Set up the side captions or rows starting with sales revenue and ending with earnings per share; rely on the amounts and percentages given to infer missing values.)

E5-15

L03

Fruit of the Loom

Determining the Effects of Transactions on Balance Sheet and Income Statement Categories

Fruit of the Loom, Inc., is one of the largest domestic producers of underwear and activewear, selling products under the FRUIT OF THE LOOM®, BVD®, MUNSINGWEAR®, WILSON®, and other brand names. Listed here are selected aggregate transactions from the first quarter of a recent year (in millions). Complete the following tabulation, indicating the sign (+ for increase, − for decrease, and NE for no effect) and amount of the effect of each transaction. Consider each item independently.

a.   Recorded sales on account of $501.1 and related cost of goods sold of $360.4.
b.   Borrowed $306.5 on line of credit with a bank with principal payable within one year.
c.   Incurred research and development expense of $10, which was paid in cash.

Transaction	Current Assets	Gross Profit	Current Liabilities
a.			
b.			
c.			

E5-16

L03

Rowe Furniture

Determining the Effects of Transactions on Balance Sheet, Income Statement, and Statement of Cash Flows Categories

Rowe Furniture Corporation is a Virginia-based manufacturer of furniture. Listed here are selected aggregate transactions from the first quarter of a recent year (in millions). Complete the following tabulation, indicating the sign (+ for increase, − for decrease, and NE for no effect) and amount of the effect of each additional transaction. Consider each item independently.

a.   Recorded collections of cash from customers owed on open account of $32.2.
b.   Repaid $2.1 in principal on line of credit with a bank with principal payable within one year.

Transaction	Current Assets	Gross Profit	Current Liabilities	Cash Flow from Operating Activities
a.				
b.				

E5-17

L03

Preparing a Simple Statement of Cash Flows Using the Indirect Method

Blackwell Corporation is preparing its annual financial statements at December 31, 2003. Listed here are the items on its statement of cash flows presented in alphabetical order. Parentheses indicate that a listed amount should be subtracted on the cash flow statement. The beginning balance in cash was $36,000 and the ending balance was $41,000.

Cash borrowed on three-year note	$25,000
Decrease in inventory	2,000
Decrease in accounts payable	(4,000)

Increase in accounts receivable	(10,000)
Net income	18,000
Stock issued for cash	22,000
New delivery truck purchased	(12,000)
Land purchased	(36,000)

Required:

Prepare the 2003 statement of cash flows for Blackwell Corporation. The section reporting cash flows from operating activities should be prepared using the indirect method discussed in the chapter.

Analyzing and Interpreting Return on Equity

E5-18
LO4
Lands' End

Lands' End Inc. is a mail-order and Internet-based direct merchant of traditionally styled casual clothing accessories, domestics, shoes, and soft luggage. Presented here are selected income statement and balance sheet amounts (in thousands).

	Current Year	Prior Year
Net sales	$1,371,375	$1,263,629
Net income	31,185	64,150
Average shareholders' equity	349,211	338,092
Average total assets	913,647	848,551

Required:

1. Compute ROE for the current and prior years and explain the meaning of the change.
2. Explain the major cause(s) of the decline in Lands' End's ROE using ROE profit driver analysis.

Analyzing and Evaluating Return on Equity from a Security Analyst's Perspective

E5-19
LO4

Papa John's is one of the fastest-growing pizza delivery and carry-out restaurant chains in the country. Presented here are selected income statement and balance sheet amounts (in thousands).

	Current Year	Prior Year
Net sales	$508,784	$360,052
Net income	26,853	18,614
Average shareholders' equity	232,988	196,352
Average total assets	381,014	286,057

Required:

1. Compute ROE for the current and prior years and explain the meaning of the change.
2. Explain the major cause(s) of the improvement in Papa John's ROE using ROE profit driver analysis.
3. Would security analysts more likely increase or decrease their estimates of share value on the basis of this change? Explain.

PROBLEMS

Matching Transactions with Concepts

P5-1
LO1, 2

Following are the concepts of accounting covered in Chapters 2 through 5. Match each transaction with its related concept by entering the appropriate letter in the space provided. Use one letter for each blank.

Concepts	Transactions
_____ (1) Users of financial statements	A. Recorded a $1,000 sale of merchandise on credit.
_____ (2) Objective of financial statements	B. Counted (inventoried) the unsold items at the end of the period and valued them in dollars.
	C. Acquired a vehicle for use in operating the business.
Qualitative Characteristics	D. Reported the amount of depreciation expense because it likely will affect important decisions of statement users.
_____ (3) Relevance	E. Identified as the investors, creditors, and others interested in the business.
_____ (4) Reliability	F. Used special accounting approaches because of the uniqueness of the industry.
Assumptions	G. Sold and issued bonds payable of $1 million.
_____ (5) Separate entity	H. Paid a contractor for an addition to the building with $10,000 cash and $20,000 market value of the stock of the company ($30,000 was deemed to be the cash equivalent price).
_____ (6) Continuity	
_____ (7) Unit of measure	
_____ (8) Time period	I. Engaged an outside independent CPA to audit the financial statements.
Elements of Financial Statements	J. Sold merchandise and services for cash and on credit during the year; then determined the cost of those goods sold and the cost of rendering those services.
_____ (9) Revenues	
_____ (10) Expenses	
_____ (11) Gains	K. Established an accounting policy that sales revenue shall be recognized only when ownership to the goods sold passes to the customer.
_____ (12) Losses	
_____ (13) Assets	
_____ (14) Liabilities	L. To design and prepare the financial statements to assist the users in making decisions.
_____ (15) Stockholders' equity	M. Established a policy not to include in the financial statements the personal financial affairs of the owners of the business.
Principles	
_____ (16) Cost	N. Sold an asset at a loss that was a peripheral or incidental transaction.
_____ (17) Revenue	
_____ (18) Matching	O. The user value of a special financial report exceeds the cost of preparing it.
_____ (19) Full disclosure	
Constraints of Accounting	P. Valued an asset, such as inventory, at less than its purchase cost because the replacement cost is less.
_____ (20) Materiality threshold	Q. Dated the income statement "For the Year Ended December 31, 2004."
_____ (21) Cost-benefit constraint	R. Used services from outsiders—paid cash for some and put the remainder on credit.
_____ (22) Conservatism constraint	S. Acquired an asset (a pencil sharpener that will have a useful life of five years) and recorded it as an expense when purchased for $1.99.
_____ (23) Industry peculiarities	
	T. Disclosed in the financial statements all relevant financial information about the business; necessitated the use of notes to the financial statements.
	U. Sold an asset at a gain that was a peripheral or incidental transaction.
	V. Assets of $500,000 − Liabilities of $300,000 = Stockholders' Equity of $200,000.
	W. Accounting and reporting assume a "going concern."

P5-2

L03

Matching Definitions with Balance Sheet–Related Terms

Following are terms related to the balance sheet, which were discussed in Chapters 2 through 5. Match each definition with its related term by entering the appropriate letter in the space provided.

Terms	Definitions
_____ (1) Retained earnings	A. A miscellaneous category of assets.
_____ (2) Current liabilities	B. Amount of contributed capital less the par value of
_____ (3) Liquidity	the stock.
_____ (4) Contra-asset account	C. Total assets minus total liabilities.
_____ (5) Accumulated depreciation	D. Nearness of assets to cash (in time).
_____ (6) Intangible assets	E. Assets expected to be collected in cash within one
_____ (7) Other assets	year or operating cycle, if longer.
_____ (8) Shares outstanding	F. Same as carrying value; cost less accumulated
_____ (9) Normal operating cycle	depreciation to date.
_____ (10) Book value	G. Accumulated earnings minus accumulated dividends.
_____ (11) Capital in excess of par	H. Asset offset account (subtracted from asset).
_____ (12) Liabilities	I. Balance of the Common Stock account divided by
_____ (13) Fixed assets	the par value per share.
_____ (14) Shareholders' equity	J. Assets that do not have physical substance.
_____ (15) Current assets	K. Probable future economic benefits owned by the
_____ (16) Assets	entity from past transactions.
_____ (17) Long-term liabilities	L. Liabilities expected to be paid out of current assets
	normally within the next year.
	M. The average cash-to-cash time involved in the
	operations of the business.
	N. Sum of the annual depreciation expense on an asset
	from its acquisition to the current date.
	O. All liabilities not classified as current liabilities.
	P. Property, plant, and equipment.
	Q. Debts or obligations from past transactions to be paid
	with assets or services.
	R. None of the above.

Preparing a Balance Sheet and Analyzing Some of Its Parts (AP5-1)

P5-3
LO3

King Jewelers is developing its annual financial statements for 2005. The following amounts were correct at December 31, 2005: cash, $42,000; accounts receivable, $51,300; merchandise inventory, $110,000; prepaid insurance, $800; investment in stock of Z corporation (long-term), $26,000; store equipment, $48,000; used store equipment held for disposal, $7,000; accumulated depreciation, store equipment, $9,600; accounts payable, $42,000; long-term note payable, $30,000; income taxes payable, $7,000; retained earnings, $86,500; and common stock, 100,000 shares outstanding, par $1.00 per share (originally sold and issued at $1.10 per share).

Required:
1. Based on these data, prepare a 2005 balance sheet. Use the following major captions (list the individual items under these captions):
   a. Assets: Current Assets, Long-Term Investments, Fixed Assets, and Other Assets.
   b. Liabilities: Current Liabilities and Long-Term Liabilities.
   c. Stockholders' Equity: Contributed Capital and Retained Earnings.
2. What is the net book value of the
   a. Inventory?
   b. Accounts receivable?
   c. Store equipment?
   d. Note payable (long term)?

Explain what these values mean.

Reporting Building, Land, and Depreciation Expense (AP5-2)

P5-4
LO3

Stewart Company is preparing its balance sheet at December 31, 2005. The following assets are to be reported:

a. Building, purchased 15 years ago (counting 2005): original cost, $450,000; estimated useful life, 25 years from date of purchase; and no residual value.

b. Land, purchased 15 years ago (counting 2005): original cost, $70,000.

Required:

1. Show how the two assets should be reported on the balance sheet. What is the total book value of the property, plant, and equipment?

2. What amount of depreciation expense should be reported on the 2005 income statement? Show computations.

P5-5 **Reporting Stockholders' Equity on a Balance Sheet and Recording the Issuance of Stock**
L03 (AP5-3)

At the end of the 2003 annual reporting period, Mesa Corporation's balance sheet showed the following:

MESA CORPORATION	
Balance Sheet	
At December 31, 2003	
Stockholders' Equity	
Contributed capital	
Common stock (par $10; 7,000 shares)	$ 70,000
Contributed capital in excess of par	10,000
Total contributed capital	80,000
Retained earnings	
Ending balance	50,000
Total stockholders' equity	$130,000

During 2004, the following selected transactions (summarized) were completed:

a. Sold and issued 1,000 shares of common stock at $15 cash per share (at year-end).

b. Determined net income, $40,000.

c. Declared and paid a cash dividend of $3 per share on the beginning shares outstanding.

Required:

1. Prepare the stockholders' equity section of the balance sheet at December 31, 2004.

2. Give the journal entry to record the sale and issuance of the 1,000 shares of common stock.

P5-6 **Preparing a Multiple-Step Income Statement**
L03

Tommy Hilfiger

Tommy Hilfiger Corporation designs, sources, and markets men's and women's sportswear, jeanswear, and childrenswear under the Tommy Hilfiger trademarks. The company prides itself in producing distinctive designs that recognize tradition while adding a fresh, youthful perspective. The items reported on its income statement for a recent year (ended March 31) are presented here (in thousands) in alphabetical order:

Cost of goods sold	1,116,321
Depreciation and amortization	106,640
Interest expense	41,412
Interest income	17,450
Net revenue	1,880,935
Other selling, general, and administrative expenses	460,554
Provision for income taxes	42,497
Weighted average shares outstanding	91,239

Required:

Prepare a multiple-step consolidated income statement (showing gross profit, operating income, and income before income taxes). Include presentation of basic earnings per share.

Preparing Both an Income Statement and Balance Sheet from a Trial Balance (AP5-4)

P5-7
LO3

Thomas Real Estate Company (organized as a corporation on April 1, 2003) has completed the accounting cycle for the second year, ended March 31, 2005. Thomas also has completed a correct trial balance as follows:

THOMAS REAL ESTATE COMPANY		
Trial Balance		
At March 31, 2005		
Account Titles	**Debit**	**Credit**
Cash	53,000	
Accounts receivable	44,800	
Office supplies inventory	300	
Automobiles (company cars)	30,000	
Accumulated depreciation, automobiles		10,000
Office equipment	3,000	
Accumulated depreciation, office equipment		1,000
Accounts payable		20,250
Income taxes payable		0
Salaries and commissions payable		1,500
Note payable, long term		30,000
Capital stock (par $1; 30,000 shares)		30,000
Contributed capital in excess of par		5,000
Retained earnings (on April 1, 2004)		7,350
Dividends declared and paid during the current year	8,000	
Sales commissions earned		77,000
Management fees earned		13,000
Operating expenses (detail omitted to conserve your time)	48,000	
Depreciation expense (on autos and including $500 on office equipment)	5,500	
Interest expense	2,500	
Income tax expense (not yet computed)		
Totals	195,100	195,100

Required:

1. Complete the financial statements, as follows:

   a. Income statement for the reporting year ended March 31, 2005. Include income tax expense, assuming a 30 percent tax rate. Use the following major captions: Revenues, Expenses, Pretax Income, Income Tax, Net Income, and EPS (list each item under these captions).

   b. Balance sheet at the end of the reporting year, March 31, 2005. Include (1) income taxes for the current year in Income Taxes Payable and (2) dividends in Retained Earnings. Use the following captions (list each item under these captions).

   Assets

   Current Assets
   Noncurrent Assets

   Liabilities

   Current Liabilities
   Long-Term Liabilities

   Stockholders' Equity

   Contributed Capital
   Retained Earnings

2. Give the journal entry to record income taxes for the year (not yet paid).

P5-8 Preparing a Simple Statement of Cash Flows Using the Indirect Method
LO3

Following are the items on Srinivasan Company's 2004 statement of cash flows presented in alphabetical order. Parentheses indicate that a listed amount should be subtracted on the cash flow statement. The beginning balance in cash was $40,000 and the ending balance was $27,000.

Borrowing on long-term note	$20,000
Increase in accounts payable	6,000
Increase in accounts receivable	(5,000)
Increase in inventories	(10,000)
Net income	55,000
Paid cash dividend	(15,000)
Paid long-term note	(12,000)
Purchased equipment	(80,000)
Purchased land	(8,000)
Sale of capital stock (3,000 shares × $12)	36,000

Required:

Prepare the 2004 statement of cash flows for Srinivasan Company using the indirect method presented in the chapter.

P5-9 Determining and Interpreting the Effects of Transactions on Income Statement
LO3, 4 **Categories and Return on Equity** (AP5-5)

Apple Computer

Apple Computer popularized both the personal computer and the easy-to-use graphic interface. Today it is fighting for its life, however, against a bevy of companies that rely on Intel microprocessors and the Windows operating system. Presented here is a recent income statement (in millions).

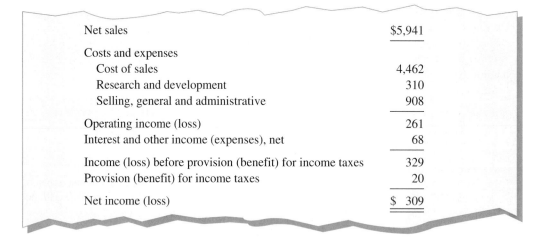

Net sales	$5,941
Costs and expenses	
Cost of sales	4,462
Research and development	310
Selling, general and administrative	908
Operating income (loss)	261
Interest and other income (expenses), net	68
Income (loss) before provision (benefit) for income taxes	329
Provision (benefit) for income taxes	20
Net income (loss)	$ 309

Its beginning and ending stockholders' equity was $1,200 and $1,642, respectively.

Required:

1. Listed here are hypothetical *additional* transactions. Assuming that they had *also* occurred during the fiscal year, complete the following tabulation, indicating the sign of the effect of each *additional* transaction (+ for increase, − for decrease, and NE for no effect). Consider each item independently and ignore taxes.
   a. Recorded sales on account of $500 and related cost of goods sold of $475.
   b. Incurred additional research and development expense of $100, which was paid in cash.
   c. Issued additional shares of common stock for $200 cash.
   d. Declared and paid dividends of $90.

Transaction	Gross Profit	Operating Income (Loss)	Return on Equity
a.			
b.			
c.			
d.			

2. Assume that next period, Apple does not pay any dividends, does not issue or retire stock, and earns the same income as during the current period. Will Apple's ROE next period be higher, lower, or the same as the current period? Why?

(Supplement A) Preparing a Multiple-Step Income Statement with Discontinued Operations and Cumulative Effects of Accounting Changes

P5-10

LO3

Adolph Coors Company

Adolph Coors Company, established in 1873, is the third-largest brewer of beer in the United States. Its products include Coors, Coors Light, ZIMA, and many other malt beverages. Recently, Coors discontinued its ceramics, aluminum, packaging, and technology-based developmental businesses. In the same year, it reported two changes in accounting methods mandated by the FASB. The items reported on its income statement for that year (ended December 26) are presented here (in thousands) in alphabetical order:

Cost of goods sold	$1,035,544
Cumulative effect of change in accounting for income taxes	30,500
Cumulative effect of change in accounting for post-retirement benefits (net of tax)	(38,800)
Income tax expense	22,900
Interest expense	16,014
Interest income	255
Marketing, general and administrative	429,573
Miscellaneous income—net	1,087
Net loss from discontinued operations	29,415
Net sales	1,550,788
Research and project development	12,370

Required:

Using appropriate headings and subtotals, prepare a multiple-step consolidated income statement (showing gross profit, operating income, and any other subheadings you deem appropriate).

(Supplement A) Inferring the Amounts on an Income Statement (Challenging)

P5-11

LO3

Following is a partially completed income statement of Reginold Corporation for the year ended December 31, 2004.

Items	Other Data		Amounts
Net sales revenue			$260,000
Cost of goods sold			
Gross margin on sales	Gross margin as percent of sales, 35%		
Expenses			

Selling expense			
General and administrative expense		28,000	
Interest expense		4,000	
Total expenses			
Pretax income			
Income tax on operations			
Income before extraordinary items			
Extraordinary gain		12,000	
Income tax effect			
Net extraordinary gain			
Net income			
EPS (on common stock)			
Income before extraordinary gain			1.20
Extraordinary gain			
Net income			

Required:

Based on these data and assuming (1) a 20 percent income tax rate on all items and (2) 25,000 common shares outstanding, complete the income statement. Show all computations.

ALTERNATE **PROBLEMS**

AP5-1   **Preparing a Balance Sheet and Analyzing Some of Its Parts** (P5-3)

L03

Carpet Bazaar is developing its annual financial statements for 2005. The following amounts were correct at December 31, 2005: cash, $35,000; investment in stock of ABC corporation (long term), $32,000; store equipment, $51,000; accounts receivable, $47,500; carpet inventory, $118,000; prepaid insurance, $1,300; used store equipment held for disposal, $3,500; accumulated depreciation, store equipment, $10,200; income taxes payable, $6,000; long-term note payable, $26,000; accounts payable, $45,000; retained earnings, $76,100; and common stock, 100,000 shares outstanding, par $1 per share (originally sold and issued at $1.25 per share).

Required:

1. Based on these data, prepare a 2005 balance sheet. Use the following major captions (list the individual items under these captions):
    a. Assets: Current Assets, Long-Term Investments, Fixed Assets, and Other Assets.
    b. Liabilities: Current Liabilities and Long-Term Liabilities.
    c. Stockholders' Equity: Contributed Capital and Retained Earnings.
2. What is the net book value of the
    a. Inventory?
    b. Accounts receivable?
    c. Store equipment?
    d. Note payable (long term)?

Explain what these values mean.

AP5-2   **Reporting Building, Land, and Depreciation Expense** (P5-4)

L03

Richmond Inc. is preparing its balance sheet at December 31, 2005. The following assets are to be reported:

a. Building, purchased 12 years ago (counting 2005): original cost, $630,000; estimated useful life, 20 years from date of purchase; and no residual value.

b. Land, purchased 12 years ago (counting 2005): original cost, $112,000.

Required:

1. Show how the two assets should be reported on the balance sheet. What is the total book value of the property, plant, and equipment?
2. What amount of depreciation expense should be reported on the 2005 income statement? Show computations.

Reporting Stockholders' Equity on a Balance Sheet and Recording the Issuance of Stock (P5-5)

AP5-3
LO3

At the end of the 2003 annual reporting period, Potamia Corporation's balance sheet showed the following:

POTAMIA CORPORATION	
Balance Sheet	
At December 31, 2003	
Stockholders' Equity	
Common stock (par $10; 9,500 shares)	$ 95,000
Additional paid-in capital	28,500
Retained earnings—Ending balance	70,000
Total stockholders' equity	$193,500

During 2004, the following selected transactions (summarized) were completed:

a. Sold and issued 1,500 shares of common stock at $17 cash per share (at year-end).
b. Determined net income, $50,000.
c. Declared and paid a cash dividend of $2 per share on the beginning shares outstanding.

Required:

1. Prepare the stockholders' equity section of the balance sheet at December 31, 2004.
2. Give the journal entry to record the sale and issuance of the 1,500 shares of common stock.

Preparing Both an Income Statement and Balance Sheet from a Trial Balance (P5-7)

AP5-4
LO3

ACME Pest Control Services (organized as a corporation on September 1, 2003) has completed the accounting cycle for the second year, ended August 31, 2005. ACME Pest Control also has completed a correct trial balance as follows:

ACME PEST CONTROL SERVICES		
Trial Balance		
At August 31, 2005		
Account Titles	**Debit**	**Credit**
Cash	26,000	
Accounts receivable	30,800	
Supplies inventory	1,300	
Service vehicles (company vans)	60,000	
Accumulated depreciation, automobiles		20,000
Equipment	14,000	
Accumulated depreciation, equipment		4,000
Accounts payable		16,700
Income taxes payable		0
Salaries payable		1,100
Note payable, long term		34,000

Capital stock (par $1; 10,000 shares)		10,000
Contributed capital in excess of par		30,000
Retained earnings (on September 1, 2004)		4,300
Dividends declared and paid during the current year	2,000	
Sales revenue		38,000
Maintenance contract revenue		17,000
Operating expenses (detail omitted to conserve your time)	27,000	
Depreciation expense (on vehicles and including $2,000 on equipment)	12,000	
Interest expense	2,000	
Income tax expense (not yet computed)		
Totals	175,100	175,100

Required:

1. Complete the financial statements, as follows:

   a. Income statement for the reporting year ended August 31, 2005. Include income tax expense, assuming a 30 percent tax rate. Use the following major captions: Revenues, Expenses, Pretax Income, Income Tax, Net Income, and EPS (list each item under these captions).

   b. Balance sheet at the end of the reporting year, August 31, 2005. Include (1) income taxes for the current year in Income Taxes Payable and (2) dividends in Retained Earnings. Use the following captions (list each item under these captions).

Assets

Current Assets
Noncurrent Assets

Liabilities

Current Liabilities
Long-Term Liabilities

Stockholders' Equity

Contributed Capital
Retained Earnings

2. Give the journal entry to record income taxes for the year (not yet paid).

AP5-5
LO3, 4
Barnes & Noble

Determining and Interpreting the Effects of Transactions on Income Statement Categories and Return on Equity (P5-9)

Barnes & Noble, Inc., revolutionized bookselling by making its stores public spaces and community institutions where customers may browse, find a book, relax over a cup of coffee, talk with authors, and join discussion groups. Today it is fighting increasing competition not only from traditional sources but also from on-line booksellers. Presented here is a recent income statement (in millions).

Net sales	$2,448
Costs and expenses	
Cost of sales	1,785
Selling, general and administrative	466
Depreciation and amortization	60
Preopening expenses	18
Operating income (loss)	119
Interest and other income (expenses), net	(38)
Income (loss) before provision (benefit) for income taxes	81
Provision (benefit) for income taxes	30
Net income (loss)	$ 51

Its beginning and ending stockholders' equity was $400 and $446, respectively.

Required:

1. Listed here are hypothetical *additional* transactions. Assuming that they had *also* occurred during the fiscal year, complete the following tabulation, indicating the sign of the effect of each *additional* transaction (+ for increase, − for decrease, and NE for no effect). Consider each item independently and ignore taxes.
    a. Recorded and received additional interest income of $4.
    b. Purchased $25 of additional inventory on open account.
    c. Recorded and paid additional advertising expense of $9.
    d. Additional shares of common stock are issued for $50 cash.

Transaction	Operating Income (Loss)	Net Income	Return on Equity
a.			
b.			
c.			
d.			

2. Assume that next period, Barnes & Noble does not pay any dividends, does not issue or retire stock, and earns 20 percent more than during the current period. Will Barnes & Noble's ROE next period be higher, lower, or the same as in the current period? Why?

CASES AND **PROJECTS**

Annual Report Cases

Finding Financial Information

Refer to the financial statements of American Eagle Outfitters given in Appendix B at the end of this book, or open file AEOS.pdf in the Annual Report Cases directory on the student CD-ROM. At the bottom of each statement, the company warns readers to "See notes to consolidated financial statements." The following questions illustrate the types of information that you can find in the financial statements and accompanying notes. (*Hint:* Use the notes.)

CP5-1
LO2, 3

AMERICAN EAGLE OUTFITTERS

Required:

1. What subtotals does it report on its income statement?
2. The company spent $87,825,000 on capital expenditures (property, plant, and equipment) this year. Were operating activities or financing activities the major source of cash for these expenditures?
3. What was the company's largest asset (net) at the end of the year?
4. Was women's apparel an increasing or decreasing percentage of its sales over the last three years?
5. Over what useful lives are buildings depreciated?
6. What portion of "Accounts and notes receivable" are composed of "Notes receivable"?

Finding Financial Information

Refer to the financial statements of Abercrombie & Fitch given in Appendix C at the end of this book, or open file ANF.pdf in the Annual Report Cases directory on the student CD-ROM. At the bottom of each statement, the company warns readers to "see accompanying notes." The following questions illustrate the types of information that you can find in the financial statements and accompanying notes. (*Hint:* Use the notes.)

CP5-2
LO2, 3, 4

ABERCROMBIE & FITCH

Required:

1. What items were included as noncurrent assets on the balance sheet?
2. How much land did the company own at the end of the current year?
3. What portion of accrued expenses were "Rent and landlord charges" during the current year?
4. At what point were catalogue and e-commerce sales recognized as revenue?

5. The company reported cash flows from operating activities of $151,189,000. However, its cash and cash equivalents decreased for the year. Explain how that happened.
6. What was the highest stock price for the company during the current year?
7. Did the company's ROE increase or decrease in the current year? How would you expect this to be reflected in the company's share price? Abercrombie & Fitch's shareholders' equity balance was $186,105 at the end of the 1998 fiscal year.

CP5-3
LO4

Comparing Companies within an Industry

Refer to the financial statements of American Eagle Outfitters given in Appendix B, Abercrombie & Fitch given in Appendix C, and the Industry Ratio Report given in Appendix D at the end of this book or open file CP5-3.xls in the Annual Report Cases directory on the student CD-ROM.

Required:
1. Compute return on equity for the current year. Which company provided the highest return to shareholders during the current year?
2. Use ROE profit driver analysis to determine the cause(s) of any differences. How might the ownership versus the rental of property, plant, and equipment affect the total asset turnover ratio?
3. Compare the ROE profit driver analysis for American Eagle Outfitters and Abercrombie & Fitch to the ROE profit driver analysis for their industry. Where does American Eagle Outfitters outperform or underperform the industry? Where does Abercrombie & Fitch outperform or underperform the industry?

Financial Reporting and Analysis Cases

CP5-4
LO1
The Auditor's
Report

Interpreting the Financial Press

The Committee of Sponsoring Organizations (COSO) recently published a research study that examined financial statement fraud occurrences between 1987 and 1997. A summary of the findings by M. S. Beasley, J. V. Carcello, and D. R. Hermanson, "Fraudulent Financial Reporting: 1987–1997: An Analysis of U.S. Public Companies," *The Auditor's Report*, Summer 1999, pp. 15–17 is available on the Libby/Libby/Short website at www.mhhe.com/libby4e.* You should read the article and then write a short memo outlining the following:

1. The size of the companies involved.
2. The extent of top management involvement.
3. The specific accounting fraud techniques involved.
4. What might lead managers to introduce misstatements into the income statement near the end of the accounting period.

CP5-5
LO2, 3

Using Financial Reports: Financial Statement Inferences

The following amounts were selected from the annual financial statements for Genesis Corporation at December 31, 2005 (end of the third year of operations):

From the 2005 income statement:	
Sales revenue	$275,000
Cost of goods sold	(170,000)
All other expenses (including income tax)	(95,000)
Net income	$10,000
From the December 31, 2005, balance sheet:	
Current assets	90,000
All other assets	212,000
Total assets	302,000
Current liabilities	40,000
Long-term liabilities	66,000
Capital stock (par $10)	100,000

*Copyright © 1999 by American Institute of Certified Public Accountants, Inc. Reprinted with permission.

Contributed capital in excess of par	16,000
Retained earnings	80,000
Total liabilities and stockholders' equity	$302,000

Required:

Analyze the data on the 2005 financial statements of Genesis by answering the questions that follow. Show computations.

1. What was the gross margin on sales?
2. What was the amount of EPS?
3. If the income tax rate was 25 percent, what was the amount of pretax income?
4. What was the average sales price per share of the capital stock?
5. Assuming that no dividends were declared or paid during 2005, what was the beginning balance (January 1, 2005) of retained earnings?

Using Financial Reports: Interpreting International Financial Statement Classifications (Challenging)

CP5-6
LO3
Diageo

As the economy becomes more international in scope, users of financial statements may be expected to analyze companies that are not incorporated in the United States. Diageo is a major world corporation located in London. It owns many familiar U.S. businesses such as the Pillsbury Company, Burger King, and Häagen-Dazs ice cream.

Required:

Based on the concepts presented in this book, explain the meaning of the various account classifications shown on the portion of the Diageo annual report presented here. (*Note:* There are five reserve accounts. The middle three relate to topics that are discussed in advanced accounting courses.)

DIAGEO
Consolidated Balance Sheet
At 30th September

	Notes	Current Year £m	Current Year £m	Prior Year £m	Prior Year £m
Fixed assets					
Intangible assets	11		2,652		588
Tangible assets	12		3,839		3,280
Investments	13		144		206
			6,635		4,074
Current assets					
Stocks	14	1,269		761	
Debtors	15	1,451		873	
Cash at bank and in hand		215		138	
		2,935		1,772	
Creditors—due within one year					
Borrowings	17	(362)		(187)	
Other creditors	19	(2,316)		(1,301)	
		(2,678)		(1,488)	
Net current assets	15		257		284
Total assets less current liabilities			6,892		4,358
Creditors—due after more than one year					
Borrowings	17	(3,494)		(702)	
Other creditors	20	(231)		(163)	
			(3,725)		(865)

Provisions for liabilities and charges	21		(325)		(55)
			2,842		3,438
Capital and reserves					
Called-up share capital	22		506		443
Reserves	23				
Share premium account		436		7	
Revaluation reserve		(944)		649	
Special reserve		—		282	
Related companies' reserves		10		16	
Profit and loss account		2,802		2,010	
			2,304		2,964
			2,810		3,407
Minority interests			32		31
			2,842		3,438

CP5-7
L01, 2

Callaway GOLF

Using Financial Reports: Analyzing Income Statement–Based Executive Bonuses

As noted in the chapter, Callaway Golf believes in tying executives' compensation to the company's performance as measured by accounting numbers. In a recent year, Callaway had agreed to pay its five executive officers bonuses of up to 200 percent of base salary if sales growth and pretax earnings as a percentage of sales (computed here) met or exceeded target amounts. Callaway's income statements for the relevant years are presented here.

(in thousands, except per share data)	Year Ended December 31,			
	Current Year		**Prior Year**	
Net sales	$254,645	100%	$132,058	100%
Cost of goods sold	115,458	45%	62,970	48%
Gross profit	139,187	55%	69,088	52%
Selling expenses	38,485	15%	19,810	15%
General and administrative expenses	28,633	11%	14,990	11%
Research and development costs	3,653	1%	1,585	1%
Income from operations	68,416	27%	32,703	25%
Other income (expense)				
Interest income (expense), net	1,024		403	
Other income, net	160		69	
Income before income taxes and cumulative effect of accounting change	69,600	27%	33,175	25%
Provision for income taxes	28,396		13,895	
Income before cumulative effect of accounting change	41,204	16%	19,280	15%
Cumulative effect of accounting change	1,658			
Net income	$ 42,862	17%	$ 19,280	15%

Callaway executives will receive bonuses if *sales growth* and *pretax earnings as a percent of sales* meet or exceed target amounts (35.1 percent and 21.1 percent, respectively). Meeting these goals in the current year would result in bonuses ranging from $400,000 to $700,000 for each of the five executive officers.

Required:

1. Use the preceding information to determine whether Callaway executives earned their bonuses in the most recent year presented.
2. Sales increased three years later by 22.6 percent to $678,512. What might explain the slower growth rate in this later year compared to the current year presented here?

Critical Thinking Cases

Making Decisions as a Manager: Evaluating the Effects of Business Strategy on Return on Equity

CP5-8
LO4
Sony

Sony is a world leader in the manufacture of consumer and commercial electronics as well as the entertainment and insurance industries. Its ROE has increased from 9 percent to 14 percent over the last three years.

Required:

1. Indicate the most likely effect of each of the changes in business strategy on Sony's ROE for the next period and future periods (+ for increase, − for decrease, and NE for no effect), assuming all other things are unchanged.
2. Explain your answer for each. Treat each item independently.
   a. Sony decreases its investment in research and development aimed at products to be brought to market in more than one year.
   b. Sony begins a new advertising campaign for a movie to be released during the next year.
   c. Sony issues additional stock for cash, the proceeds to be used to acquire other high-technology companies in future periods.

Strategy Change	Current Period ROE	Future Periods' ROE
a.		
b.		
c.		

Making a Decision as an Auditor: Effects of Errors on Income, Assets, and Liabilities

CP5-9
LO1

Megan Company (not a corporation) was careless about its financial records during its first year of operations, 2003. It is December 31, 2003, the end of the annual accounting period. An outside CPA examined the records and discovered numerous errors, all of which are described here. Assume that each error is independent of the others.

Required:

Analyze each error and indicate its effect on 2003 and 2004 income, assets, and liabilities if not corrected. Do not assume any other errors. Use these codes to indicate the effect of each dollar amount: O = overstated, U = understated, and NE = no effect. Write an explanation of your analysis of each transaction to support your response.

		EFFECT ON				
	NET INCOME		ASSETS		LIABILITIES	
Independent Errors	**2003**	**2004**	**2003**	**2004**	**2003**	**2004**
1. Depreciation expense for 2003, not recorded in 2003, $950.	O $950	NE	O $950	O $950	NE	NE
2. Wages earned by employees during 2003 not recorded or paid in 2003 but will be paid in 2004, $500.						
3. Revenue earned during 2003 but not collected or recorded until 2004, $600.						

4. Amount paid in 2003 and recorded as expense in 2003 but not an expense until 2004, $200.						
5. Revenue collected in 2003 and recorded as revenue in 2003 but not earned until 2004, $900.						
6. Sale of services and cash collected in 2003. Recorded as a debit to Cash and as a credit to Accounts Receivable, $300.						
7. On December 31, 2003, bought land on credit for $8,000, not recorded until payment was made on February 1, 2004.						

Following is a sample explanation of analysis of errors if not corrected, using the first error as an example:

1. Failure to record depreciation in 2003 caused depreciation expense to be too low; therefore, income was overstated by $950. Accumulated depreciation also is too low by $950, which causes assets to be overstated by $950 until the error is corrected.

CP5-10
L03

Mercury
Finance

Evaluating an Ethical Dilemma: Management Incentives and Fraudulent Financial Statements

Mercury Finance Co. was a fast-growing auto-finance and insurance company. In January 1997, however, the auditors discovered that recently announced 1996 earnings had been grossly overstated and prior years' earnings had been overstated to a lesser extent. The estimated size of the earnings overstatement for 1996 is described in the following excerpt:

BUSINESS BRIEF—MERCURY FINANCE CO.

Estimates for 1996 Revised Again, Now to a Big Loss
  04/24/97 p. A8
The Wall Street Journal

Mercury Finance Co., which previously warned that it had grossly overstated earlier years' earnings, said it now expects to report up to a $55 million loss for 1996. In January, the Lake Forest, Ill., auto-finance company initially reported earnings of $120.7 million for 1996. Soon afterward, however, Mercury disclosed the accounting "irregularities" and estimated that last year's earnings probably would be about $56.7 million. Yesterday, Mercury said in an "update" that 1996 results will include an additional $125 million in loss provisions, as well as a $25 million reserve to cover the planned sale of its Lyndon insurance unit. As a result, the company anticipates a 1996 net loss of between $48 million and $55 million. In New York Stock Exchange composite trading, Mercury closed down 25 cents, or 13%, at $1.75.

Required:
Using more recent new reports (*The Wall Street Journal Index, Dow Jones Interactive,* and *Bloomberg Business News* are good sources), answer the following questions.

1. Whom did the courts and regulatory authorities hold responsible for the misstated financial statements?
2. What were Mercury's closing stock prices on the day before (January 28, 1997) and the day after (January 30, 1997) the announcement of the misstatement?
3. How might executive compensation plans that tied bonuses to accounting earnings motivate unethical conduct in this case?

Financial Reporting and Analysis Team Project

Analyzing the Accounting Communication Process

CP5-11
LO2, 3

As a team, select an industry to analyze. MarketGuide provides lists of industries and their makeup at www.marketguide.com/mgi/INDUSTRY/INDUSTRY.html. Each team member should acquire the annual report or 10-K for one publicly traded company in the industry, with each member selecting a different company. (Library files, the SEC EDGAR service at www.sec.gov, Compustat CD, or the company itself are good sources.)

Required:
On an individual basis, each team member should write a short report answering the following questions about the selected company.

1. What formats are used to present the balance sheet and income statement?
2. Find one note that describes an accounting rule applied in the company's statements, one note that presents additional detail about a reported financial statement number, and one note that reports financial information not listed in the statements. What information is provided in each?
3. If an appropriate source is available at your school, using the company's website, *The Wall Street Journal Index*, or *Dow Jones Interactive* (or an instructor-assigned resource), find one article reporting the company's annual earnings announcement. How does the date of the announcement compare with the date on the annual report or 10-K?
4. Compute return on equity for the current year. Which company provided the highest return to shareholders during the current year?
5. Use ROE profit driver analysis to determine the cause(s) of any differences.

Discuss any patterns across the three companies that you as a team observe. Then, as a team, write a short report comparing and contrasting your companies using these attributes. Provide potential explanations for any differences discovered.

LEARNING OBJECTIVES

Reporting and Interpreting Sales Revenue, Receivables, and Cash

6

I nitially known among hunters and hikers for its trademark yellow waterproof boots, Timberland is well on its way to becoming the most powerful brand of rugged, outdoor-inspired products on the planet. Its premium footwear, apparel, and accessories are now sold through quality department, retail, and specialty stores in more than 90 countries and through company-owned specialty and outlet stores in the United States and abroad. Timberland achieved an important benchmark in 2000: Its revenues went past the $1 billion dollar mark, achieving double-digit revenue growth in both the footwear and apparel product lines. This amazing rate of growth requires that Timberland continually refresh its product lines by introducing new technologies, new styles, and new product categories, as well as broadening its brand image.

However, as Timberland learned in 1995, when it reported the first net loss in its history, higher revenues do not always produce higher profits. Profits are also determined by the relationship between sales prices and costs. Effective marketing and an emphasis on comfort, style, high-quality construction, and protection from the elements have convinced customers of the superiority of Timberland's products. This allows Timberland to charge higher prices for their quality products. When combined with careful management of production costs, inventory, and collections of accounts receivable, this allowed Timberland also to report that 2000 gross profit on sales and net income were the highest in its history.

FOCUS COMPANY

The Timberland Company

PRODUCT DEVELOPMENT, PRODUCTION, AND WORKING CAPITAL MANAGEMENT: KEYS TO GROSS PROFIT

www.timberland.com

UNDERSTANDING THE BUSINESS

Planning Timberland's growth strategy requires careful coordination of marketing and production activities. The success of each element of Timberland's strategy can be seen in the information presented in the comparative statements of income presented in Exhibit 6.1. Revenue (Net Sales Revenue) is reported first, and Cost of Goods Sold (an expense) is set out separately from the remaining expenses. (Other titles for this account are Cost of Sales and Cost of Products Sold.) Next, the income statement shows **gross profit (gross**

THE TIMBERLAND COMPANY
Consolidated Statements of Income
For the Years Ended December 31, 2000, 1999, and 1998
(amounts in thousands, except per share data)

	2000	1999	1998
Revenue	$1,091,478	$917,216	$862,168
Cost of goods sold	582,966	524,114	519,329
Gross profit	508,512	393,102	342,839
Operating Expense			
Selling	258,081	219,545	195,688
General and administrative	65,129	55,321	50,876
Amortization of goodwill	1,130	1,685	1,685
Total operating expense	324,340	276,551	248,249
Operating income	184,172	116,551	94,590
Other expense (income)			
Interest expense	5,648	9,342	9,538
Other, net	(8,128)	(3,449)	(1,942)
Total other expense (income)	(2,480)	5,893	7,596
Income before income taxes	186,652	110,658	86,994
Provision for income taxes	62,528	35,411	27,838
Net income before extraordinary item	124,124	75,247	59,156
Extraordinary item—loss on debt extinguishment net of tax benefit of $1,071 (see Note 3)	2,126	—	—
Net income	$ 121,998	$ 75,247	$ 59,156
Earnings per share before extraordinary item			
Basic	$ 3.09	$ 1.75	$ 1.29
Diluted	$ 2.91	$ 1.70	$ 1.26
Earnings per share after extraordinary item			
Basic	$ 3.04	$ 1.75	$ 1.29
Diluted	$ 2.86	$ 1.70	$ 1.26
Weighted-average shares outstanding			
Basic	40,119	42,895	45,698
Diluted	42,647	44,355	47,035

The accompanying notes are an integral part of these consolidated financial statements.

margin, gross profit margin), which is net sales revenue minus cost of goods sold. Revenue, gross profit, and net income for 2000 are at an all-time high.

To assess the effectiveness of Timberland's strategy, we need to know how net sales and cost of goods sold are determined. In this chapter, we will focus on the transactions that affect **net sales revenue** on the income statement and **cash** and **accounts receivable** on the balance sheet. We will also introduce the gross profit percentage ratio as a basis for evaluating changes in gross profit, as well as the receivables turnover ratio as a measure of the efficiency of credit-granting and collection activities. Finally, since the cash collected from customers is also a tempting target for fraud and embezzlement, we will discuss how accounting systems commonly include controls to prevent and detect such misdeeds.

ORGANIZATION of the Chapter

Accounting for Sales Revenue	Measuring and Reporting Receivables	Reporting and Safeguarding Cash
■ Credit Card Sales to Consumers ■ Sales Discounts to Businesses ■ Sales Returns and Allowances ■ Reporting Net Sales	■ Classifying Receivables ■ Accounting for Bad Debts ■ Reporting Accounts Receivable and Bad Debts ■ Estimating Bad Debts ■ Receivables Turnover Ratio ■ Control over Accounts Receivable	■ Cash and Cash Equivalents Defined ■ Cash Management ■ Internal Control of Cash ■ Reconciliation of Cash Accounts and the Bank Statements

ACCOUNTING FOR SALES REVENUE

As indicated in Chapter 3, the **revenue principle** requires that revenues be recorded when they are earned (delivery has occurred or services have been rendered, there is persuasive evidence of an arrangement for customer payment, the price is fixed or determinable, and collection is reasonably assured). For sellers of goods, these criteria are most often met and sales revenue is recorded when goods pass from the seller to the buyer. This is the point where title and risks of ownership transfer to the buyer.[1] Service companies most often record sales revenue when they have provided services to the buyer. Companies disclose the revenue recognition rule they follow in the footnote to the financial statements entitled Summary of Significant Accounting Policies. In that note, Timberland reports the following:

Learning Objective 1
Apply the revenue principle to determine the accepted time to record sales revenue for typical retailers, wholesalers, manufacturers, and service companies.

NOTES TO CONSOLIDATED FINANCIAL STATEMENTS

1. Summary of Significant Accounting Policies

Recognition of Revenue

. . . Sales are recognized upon shipment of product to customers.

REAL WORLD EXCERPT

THE
TIMBERLAND
COMPANY

ANNUAL REPORT

Like Timberland, many manufacturers, wholesalers, and retailers recognize revenue at shipment. This is when title and risks of ownership pass for Timberland's sales.

---

[1]The point at which title (ownership) changes hands is determined by the shipping terms in the sales contract. When goods are shipped **FOB (free on board) shipping point,** title changes hands at shipment, and the buyer normally pays for shipping. When they are shipped **FOB destination,** title changes hands on delivery, and the seller normally pays for shipping. Revenues from goods shipped FOB shipping point are normally recognized at shipment. Revenues from goods shipped FOB delivery are normally recognized at delivery (SEC Staff Accounting Bulletin 101, *Revenue Recognition in Financial Statements,* 2000). Auditors expend a great deal of effort ensuring that revenues are recognized in the proper period.

The appropriate **amount** of revenue to record is the **cash equivalent sales price**. Some sales practices differ depending on whether sales are made to businesses or consumers. Timberland sells footwear and apparel to other **businesses** (retailers) including Athletes Foot and The Shoe Dept., which then sell the goods to consumers. It also operates its own factory outlet stores and specialty stores that sell footwear and apparel directly to **consumers.**

Timberland uses a variety of methods to motivate both groups of customers to buy its products and make payment for their purchases. The principal methods include (1) allowing consumers to use credit cards to pay for purchases, (2) providing business customers direct credit and discounts for early payment, and (3) allowing returns from all customers under certain circumstances. These methods, in turn, affect the way we compute **net sales revenue**.

Credit Card Sales to Consumers

Learning Objective 2
Analyze the impact of credit card sales, sales discounts, and sales returns on the amounts reported as net sales.

Timberland accepts cash or credit card payment at its company-owned stores. Timberland managers decided to accept credit cards (mainly Visa, Mastercard, and American Express) for a variety of reasons:

1. Increasing customer traffic at its stores.

2. Avoiding the costs of providing credit directly to customers, including recordkeeping and bad debts (discussed later).

3. Lowering losses due to bad checks.

4. Avoiding losses from fraudulent credit card sales. (As long as Timberland follows the credit card company's verification procedure, the credit card company [e.g., Visa] absorbs any losses.)

5. Faster receipt of its money. (Since credit card receipts can be directly deposited in its bank account, Timberland receives its money faster than it would if it provided credit directly to consumers.)

A **CREDIT CARD DISCOUNT** is the fee charged by the credit card company for services.

The credit card company charges a fee for the service it provides. When Timberland deposits its credit card receipts in the bank, it might receive credit for only 97 percent of the sales price. The credit card company is charging a 3 percent fee (the **credit card discount**) for its service. If daily credit card sales at a factory store were $3,000, Timberland would report the following:

Sales revenue	$3,000
Less: Credit card discounts (0.03 × 3,000)	90
Net sales (reported on the income statement)	$2,910

Sales Discounts to Businesses

Most of Timberland's sales to businesses are credit sales on open account; that is, there is no formal written promissory note or credit card. When Timberland sells footwear to retailers on credit, credit terms are printed on the sales document and invoice (bill) sent to the customer. Often credit terms are abbreviated using symbols. For example, if the full price is due within 30 days of the invoice date, the credit terms would be noted as *n*/30. Here, the *n* means the sales amount **net** of, or less, any sales returns.

A **SALES DISCOUNT** (cash discount) is a cash discount offered to encourage prompt payment of an account receivable.

In some cases, a **sales discount** (often called a cash discount) is granted to the purchaser to encourage early payment.[2] For example, Timberland may offer standard

---

[2]It is important not to confuse a **cash discount** with a **trade discount.** Vendors sometimes use a **trade discount** for quoting sales prices; the sales price is the list or printed catalog price **less** the trade discount. For example, an item may be quoted at $10 per unit subject to a 20 percent trade discount on orders of 100 units or more; thus, the price for the large order is $8 per unit. Sales revenue should always be recorded net of trade discounts.

credit terms of 2/10, n/30, which means that the customer may deduct 2 percent from the invoice price if cash payment is made within 10 days from the date of sale. If cash payment is not made within the 10-day discount period, the full sales price (less any returns) is due within a maximum of 30 days.

Early Payment Incentive

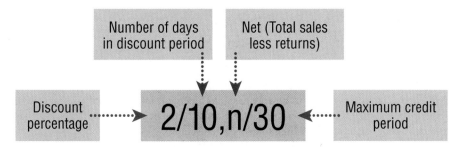

Timberland offers this sales discount to encourage customers to pay more quickly. This provides two benefits to Timberland.

1. Prompt receipt of cash from customers reduces the necessity to borrow money to meet operating needs.

2. Since customers tend to pay bills providing discounts first, a sales discount also decreases the chances that the customer will run out of funds before Timberland's bill is paid.

Companies commonly record sales discounts taken by subtracting the discount from sales if payment is made **within** the discount period (the usual case).[3] For example, if credit sales of $1,000 are recorded with terms 2/10, n/30 and payment of $980 ($1,000 $\times$ 0.98 = $980) is made within the discount period, net sales of the following amount would be reported:

Sales revenue	$1,000
Less: Sales discounts (0.02 $\times$ $1,000)	20
Net sales (reported on the income statement)	$ 980

If payment is made after the discount period, the full $1,000 would be reported as net sales.

Note that both the purpose and accounting for sales discounts are very similar to the purpose of and the accounting for credit card discounts. Both sales discounts and credit card discounts provide an attractive service to customers while promoting faster receipt of cash, reducing recordkeeping costs, and minimizing bad debts. Accounting for sales discounts is discussed in more detail in Supplement A.

To Take or Not to Take the Discount, That Is the Question

FINANCIAL ANALYSIS

Customers usually pay within the discount period because the savings are substantial. With terms 2/10, n/30, customers save 2 percent by paying 20 days early (on the 10th day instead of the 30th). This translates into a 37 percent annual interest rate. To calculate the annual interest rate, first compute the interest rate for the discount period. When the 2 percent discount is taken, the customer pays only 98 percent of the gross sales price. For example, on a $100 sale with terms 2/10, n/30, $2 would be saved and $98 would be paid 20 days early.

---

[3]We use the gross method in all examples in this text. Some companies use the alternative net method, which records sales revenue after deducting the amount of the cash discount. Since the choice of method has little effect on the financial statements, discussion of this method is left for an advanced course.

The interest rate for the 20-day discount period is computed as follows:

$$\frac{\text{Amount Saved}}{\text{Amount Paid}} = \text{Interest Rate for 20 Days}$$

$$\frac{\$2}{\$98} = 2.04\% \text{ for 20 Days}$$

The annual interest rate is:

$$\text{Interest Rate for 20 Days} \times \frac{365 \text{ Days}}{20 \text{ Days}} = \text{Annual Interest Rate}$$

$$2.04\% \times \frac{365 \text{ Days}}{20 \text{ Days}} = 37.23\% \text{ Annual Interest Rate}$$

Even if credit customers had to borrow cash at 15 percent interest to take advantage of this cash discount, they would save a great deal. Normally, the bank's interest rate is less than the interest rate associated with failing to take cash discounts.

Sales Returns and Allowances

SALES RETURNS AND ALLOWANCES is a reduction of sales revenues for return of or allowances for unsatisfactory goods.

Retailers and consumers have a right to return unsatisfactory or damaged merchandise and receive a refund or an adjustment to their bill. Such returns are often accumulated in a separate account called **Sales Returns and Allowances** and must be deducted from gross sales revenue in determining net sales. This account informs Timberland's managers of the volume of returns and allowances providing an important measure of the quality of customer service. Assume that Fontana shoes of Ithaca, New York, buys 40 pairs of hiking boots from Timberland for $2,000 on account. Before paying for the boots, Fontana discovers that 10 pairs of boots are not the color ordered and returns them to Timberland.[4] Timberland computes net sales as follows:

Sales revenue	$2,000
Less: Sales returns and allowances (0.25 × $2,000)	500
Net sales (reported on the income statement)	$1,500

Cost of goods sold related to the 10 pairs of boots would also be reduced.

Reporting Net Sales

On the company's books, credit card discounts, sales discounts,[5] and sales returns and allowances are accounted for separately to allow managers to monitor the costs of credit card use, sales discounts, and returns. Using the numbers in the preceding examples, the amount of net sales reported on the income statement is computed in the following manner:

Sales revenue	$6,000
Less: Credit card discounts (a contra-revenue)	90
Sales discounts (a contra-revenue)	20
Sales returns and allowances (a contra-revenue)	500
Net sales (reported on the income statement)	$5,390

Most companies, including Timberland, do not disclose the contra-revenue amounts. Timberland competitor, Deckers Outdoor Corp., indicates in its revenue recognition footnote that the appropriate subtractions are made, but does not disclose their amounts.

---

[4]Alternatively, Timberland might offer Fontana a $200 allowance to keep the wrong-color boots. If Fontana accepts the offer, Timberland reports $200 as sales returns and allowances.

[5]Sales and credit card discounts may also be reported as expenses on the income statement.

NOTES TO CONSOLIDATED FINANCIAL STATEMENTS

1. The Company and Summary of Significant Accounting Policies

Revenue Recognition

. . . Allowances for estimated returns and discounts are provided for when related revenue is recorded.

REAL WORLD EXCERPT

Deckers Outdoor Corp.

ANNUAL REPORT

So determining the effects of these items is usually impossible, even for well-educated external users.

As we noted earlier, net sales less cost of goods sold equals the subtotal **gross profit** or **gross margin.** Analysts often examine gross profit as a percentage of sales (the gross profit or gross margin percentage).

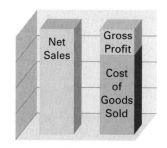

Gross Profit Percentage

KEY RATIO
ANALYSIS

❓ ANALYTICAL QUESTION:

By what amount (percentage) did sales prices exceed the costs to purchase or produce the goods or services sold?

％ RATIO AND COMPARISONS:

The gross profit percentage ratio is computed as follows:

$$\text{Gross Profit Percentage} = \frac{\text{Gross Profit}}{\text{Net Sales}}$$

The 2000 ratio for Timberland (see Exhibit 6.1):

$$\frac{\$508,512}{\$1,091,478} = 0.466 \ (46.6\%)$$

Learning Objective 3
Analyze and interpret the gross profit percentage.

Selected Focus Company Comparisons

Papa John's	59.7%
Harley-Davidson	34.1%
General Mills	75.6%

COMPARISONS OVER TIME		
Timberland		
1998	1999	2000
39.8%	42.9%	46.6%

COMPARISONS WITH COMPETITORS	
Skechers U.S.A.	Wolverine World Wide
2000	2000
42.1%	31.9%

💡 INTERPRETATIONS:

In General The gross profit percentage measures a company's ability to charge premium prices and produce goods and services at low cost. All other things equal, a higher gross profit results in higher net income.

Business strategy, as well as competition, affects the gross profit percentage. Companies pursuing a product-differentiation strategy use research and development and product promotion activities to convince customers of the superiority or distinctiveness of the company's products. This allows them to charge premium prices, producing a higher gross profit percentage. Companies following a low-cost strategy rely on more efficient management of production to reduce costs and increase the gross profit percentage. Managers, analysts, and creditors use this ratio to assess the effectiveness of the company's product development, marketing, and production strategy.

Focus Company Analysis Timberland's gross profit percentage has risen from a 1995 low of 31 percent to nearly 47 percent in 2000 and is well above the industry average of 40 percent.* At the beginning of the chapter, we discussed key elements of Timberland's business strategy that focused on introducing new technologies, product lines, and styles, as well as managing production and inventory costs. According to Timberland's annual report, the increases in gross profit percentage were "primarily due to improved design and development of footwear and apparel, a reduction in third party sourcing costs and internal manufacturing efficiencies . . . " indicating that the company's strategy was successful.

A Few Cautions: To assess the company's ability to sustain its new gross margins, you must understand the sources of any change in the gross profit percentage. For example, an increase in margin resulting from increased sales of high-margin boots during a hard winter would be less sustainable than an increase resulting from introducing new products. Also, higher prices must often be sustained with higher R&D and advertising costs, which can eat up any increase in gross margin. Finally, be aware that a small change in the gross profit percentage can lead to a large change in net income.

www.MARKET GUIDE.com

SELF-STUDY QUIZ

1. Assume that Timberland sold $30,000 worth of footwear to various retailers with terms 1/10, n/30 and half of that amount was paid within the discount period. Gross sales at company-owned stores were $5,000 for the same period, 80 percent being paid with credit cards with a 3 percent discount, the rest in cash. Compute net sales for the period.

2. During the first quarter of 2001, Timberland's net sales totaled $245,429, and cost of goods sold was $136,841. Verify that its gross profit percentage was 44.2 percent.

After you have completed your answers, check them with the solutions that follow:

1.	Gross Sales		$35,000
	Less: Sales discounts (0.01 × 1/2 × $30,000)		150
	Credit card discounts (0.03 × 0.80 × $5,000)		120
	Net Sales		$34,730

2.	Net Sales	$245,429
	Cost of goods sold	136,841
	Gross Profit	$108,588

$108,588 / 245,429 = 44.2% Gross profit percentage

MEASURING AND REPORTING RECEIVABLES

Classifying Receivables

ACCOUNTS RECEIVABLE (trade receivables, receivables) are open accounts owed to the business by trade customers.

Receivables may be classified in three common ways. First, they may be classified as either an account receivable or a note receivable. An **account receivable** is created by a credit sale on an open account. For example, an account receivable is created when Timberland sells shoes on open account to Fontana Shoes in Ithaca, New York.

A **note receivable** is a promise in writing (a formal document) to pay (1) a specified amount of money, called the **principal,** at a definite future date known as the **maturity date** and (2) a specified amount of **interest** at one or more future dates. The interest is the specified amount charged for use of the principal. We discuss the computation of interest when we discuss notes payable in a later chapter.

Second, receivables may be classified as trade or nontrade receivables. A **trade receivable** is created in the normal course of business when a sale of merchandise or services on credit occurs. A **nontrade receivable** arises from transactions other than the normal sale of merchandise or services. For example, if Timberland loaned money to a new vice president for international operations to help finance a home at the new job location, the loan would be classified as a nontrade receivable. Third, in a classified balance sheet, receivables also are classified as either **current** or **noncurrent** (short term or long term), depending on when the cash is expected to be collected. Like many companies, Timberland reports only one type of receivable account, Accounts Receivable, from customers (trade receivables) and classifies the asset as a current asset (short term) because the accounts receivable are all due to be paid within one year.

Timberland allows its business customers (the retail stores that buy and then resell its footwear) to purchase goods on open account because it believes that providing this service will result in more sales to this type of customer. Providing this service to business customers also has a cost. Timberland must pay to maintain a credit-granting and collections system, and it must realize that not all customers will pay their debts.

NOTES RECEIVABLE are written promises that require another party to pay the business under specified conditions (amount, time, interest).

Topic Tackler 6–1

Accounting for Bad Debts

When Timberland extends credit to the retail stores that resell its footwear and apparel, it knows that some of these customers will not pay their debts. The matching principle requires recording of bad debt expense in the **same** accounting period in which the related sales are made. However, Timberland may not learn that any particular customers will not pay until the **next** accounting period.

Timberland resolves this problem and satisfies the matching principle by using the **allowance method** to measure bad debt expense. The allowance method is based on **estimates** of the expected amount of bad debts. Two primary steps in employing the allowance method are:

1. Making the end-of-period adjusting entry to record estimated bad debt expense.

2. Writing off specific accounts determined to be uncollectible during the period.

Learning Objective 4
Estimate, report, and evaluate the effects of uncollectible accounts receivable (bad debts) on financial statements.

The **ALLOWANCE METHOD** bases bad debt expense on an estimate of uncollectible accounts.

Recording Bad Debt Expense Estimates

BAD DEBT EXPENSE (doubtful accounts expense, uncollectible accounts expense, provision for uncollectible accounts) is the expense associated with estimated uncollectible accounts receivable.

Bad debt expense (also called doubtful accounts expense, uncollectible accounts expense, provision for uncollectible accounts) is the expense associated with estimated uncollectible accounts receivable. An **adjusting journal entry** at the **end of the accounting period** records the bad debt estimate. For the year ended December 31, 2000, Timberland estimated bad debt expense to be $2,395 (all numbers in thousands of dollars) and made the following adjusting entry:

Bad debt expense (+E, −SE)	2,395	
Allowance for doubtful accounts (+XA, −A)		2,395

Assets	= Liabilities +	Stockholders' Equity
Allowance for doubtful accounts −2,395		Bad debt expense −2,395

The Bad Debt Expense is included in the category "Selling" expenses on the income statement (see Exhibit 6.1). It decreases net income and stockholder's equity. Accounts Receivable could not be credited in the journal entry because there is no way to know which customers' accounts receivable are involved. So the credit is made, instead, to a contra-asset account called **Allowance for Doubtful Accounts** (Allowance for Bad Debts or Allowance for Uncollectible Accounts). As a contra-asset, the balance in Allowance for Doubtful Accounts is always subtracted from the balance of the asset Accounts Receivable. Thus, the entry decreases the net book value of Accounts Receivable and total assets.

ALLOWANCE FOR DOUBTFUL ACCOUNTS (allowance for bad debts, allowance for uncollectible accounts) is a contra-asset account containing the estimated uncollectible accounts receivable.

Writing Off Specific Uncollectible Accounts

Throughout the year, when it is determined that a customer will not pay its debts (e.g., due to bankruptcy), the write-off of that individual bad debt is recorded through a journal entry. Now that the specific uncollectible customer account receivable has been identified, it can be removed with a credit. At the same time, we no longer need the related estimate in the contra-asset Allowance for Doubtful Accounts, which is removed by a debit. The journal entry summarizing Timberland's total write-offs of $1,480 during 2000 follows:

Allowance for doubtful accounts (−XA, +A)	1,480	
Accounts Receivable (−A)		1,480

Assets	= Liabilities +	Stockholders' Equity
Allowance for doubtful accounts +1,480		
Accounts receivable −1,480		

Notice that this journal entry did **not affect any income statement accounts.** It did not record a bad debt expense because the estimated expense was recorded with an adjusting entry in the period of sale. Also, the entry did **not change the net book value of accounts receivable,** since the decrease in the asset account (Accounts Receivable) was offset by the decrease in the contra-asset account (Allowance for Doubtful Accounts). Thus, it also did not affect total assets.

When a customer makes a payment on an account that has already been written off, the journal entry to write off the account is reversed to put the receivable back on the books, and the collection of cash recorded.

Summary of the Accounting Process

It is important to remember that accounting for bad debts is a two-step process:

Step	Timing	Accounts Affected		Financial Statement Effects	
1. Record estimated bad debts adjustment	End of period in which sales are made	Bad Debt Expense (E)	↑	Net Income	↓
		Allowance for Doubtful Accounts (XA)	↑	Assets (Accounts Receivable, Net)	↓
2. Identify and write off actual bad debts	Throughout period as bad debts become known	Accounts Receivable (A)	↓	Net Income	No Effect
		Allowance for Doubtful Accounts (XA)	↓	Assets (Accounts Receivable, Net)	No Effect

Timberland's complete 2000 accounting process for bad debts can now be summarized in terms of the changes in Accounts Receivable (Gross) and the Allowance for Doubtful Accounts:[6]

Accounts Receivable (Gross) (A)			
Beginning balance	83,606	Collections on account	1,062,052
Sales on account	1,091,478	Write-offs	1,480
Ending balance	111,552		

Accounts Receivable

Accounts Receivable (gross) (A)
− Allowance for Doubtful Accounts (XA)

Accounts Receivable (net) (A)

Allowance for Doubtful Accounts (XA)			
		Beginning balance	4,910
Write-offs	1,480	Bad debt expense adjustment	2,395
		Ending balance	5,825

Accounts Receivable (Gross) includes the total accounts receivable, both collectible and uncollectible. The balance in the Allowance for Doubtful Accounts is the portion of the accounts receivable balance the company estimates to be uncollectible. Accounts Receivable (Net) reported on the balance sheet is the portion of the accounts the company expects to collect (or its estimated net realizable value).

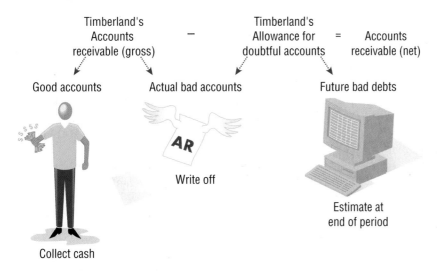

Timberland's Accounts receivable (gross)	−	Timberland's Allowance for doubtful accounts	=	Accounts receivable (net)
Good accounts		Actual bad accounts		Future bad debts
Collect cash		Write off		Estimate at end of period

---

[6]This assumes that all sales to businesses (wholesale sales) are on account.

| EXHIBIT 6.2 | THE TIMBERLAND COMPANY
Consolidated Balance Sheets
As of December 31, 2000 and 1999
(amounts in thousands, except share and per share data) | | |

Accounts Receivable on the Balance Sheet

REAL WORLD EXCERPT

THE
TIMBERLAND
COMPANY

ANNUAL REPORT

	2000	1999
Assets		
Current Assets		
Cash and equivalents	$114,852	$196,085
Accounts receivable, net of allowance for doubtful accounts of $5,825 in 2000 and $4,910 in 1999	105,727	78,696
Inventory	131,917	114,673
Prepaid expense	13,717	9,890
Prepaid income taxes	15,547	15,297
Total current assets	381,760	414,641

Reporting Accounts Receivable and Bad Debts

Analysts who want information on Timberland's receivables will find Accounts Receivable, Net of Allowance for Doubtful Accounts (the **net book value**), of $105,727 and $78,696 for 2000 and 1999 reported on the balance sheet (Exhibit 6.2). The balance in the Allowance for Doubtful Accounts ($5,825 in 2000 and $4,910 in 1999) is also reported. Accounts Receivable (Gross), the total accounts receivable, can be computed by adding the two amounts together.

The amounts of bad debt expense and accounts receivable written off for the period normally are not disclosed in the annual report. If they are material, these amounts are reported on a schedule that publicly traded companies include in their Annual Report Form 10-K filed with the SEC. Exhibit 6.3 presents this schedule from Timberland's 2000 filing.[7]

Estimating Bad Debts

The bad debt expense amount recorded in the end-of-period adjusting entry often is estimated based on either (1) total credit sales for the period or (2) an aging of accounts receivable. Both methods are acceptable under GAAP and are widely used in practice.[8]

Percentage of Credit Sales Method

PERCENTAGE OF CREDIT SALES METHOD bases bad debt expense on the historical percentage of credit sales that result in bad debts.

Many companies make their estimates using the **percentage of credit sales method,** which bases bad debt expense on the historical percentage of credit sales that result in bad debts. The average percentage of credit sales that result in bad debts can be computed by dividing total bad debt losses by total **credit** sales. A company that has been operating for some years has sufficient experience to project probable future bad debt losses. For example, if Timberland had experienced bad debt losses of 0.2395 percent of credit sales in similar years, and its credit sales were $1,000,000, it could estimate current year's bad debts as:

Credit sales	$1,000,000
× **Bad debt loss rate** (.2395%)	× .002395
Bad debt expense	$ 2,395

---

[7] Write-offs are reported on Timberland's 10-K net of (less) recoveries of previously written-off accounts.

[8] In our example, both methods produce the same estimate, which rarely occurs in practice. The percentage of credit sales method is simpler to apply, while the aging method is generally more accurate.

EXHIBIT 6.3

**Accounts Receivable
Valuation Schedule
(Form 10-K)**

REAL WORLD EXCERPT

THE
TIMBERLAND
COMPANY

FORM 10-K

THE TIMBERLAND COMPANY
Valuation and Qualifying Amounts
(dollars in thousands)

Description	Balance at Beginning of Period	Additions Charged to Costs and Expenses	Additions Charged to Other Accounts	Deductions Write-Offs, Net of Recoveries	Balance at End of Period
Allowance for doubtful accounts:					
Year ended					
December 31, 2000	$4,910	$2,395	—	$1,480	$5,825
December 31, 1999	4,769	3,618	—	3,477	4,910
December 31, 1998	3,742	2,383	—	1,356	4,769

This amount would be directly recorded as Bad Debt Expense (and an increase in Allowance for Doubtful Accounts) in the current year and the ending balance in the Allowance for Doubtful Accounts is computed as follows:

Allowance for Doubtful Accounts (XA)			
		Beginning balance	4,910
Write-offs	1,480	Bad debt expense adjustment	2,395
		Ending balance	?

percent of credit sales estimate
= $5,825

Aging of Accounts Receivable

As an alternative to the percentage of credit sales method, many companies use the **aging of accounts receivable method.** This method relies on the fact that, as accounts receivable become older and more overdue, it is less likely that they will prove to be collectible. For example, a receivable that was due in 30 days but has not been paid after 45 days is more likely to be collected, on average, than a similar receivable that remains unpaid after 120 days. Based on prior experience, the company can estimate what portion of receivables of different ages will not be paid.

Suppose that Timberland split its receivables into three age categories, as presented in Exhibit 6.4. Management would first examine the individual customer accounts receivable and sort them into the three age categories. Management would then **estimate** the probable bad debt loss rates for each category: for example, not yet due, 2 percent; 1 to 90 days past due, 17.4 percent; over 90 days, 35.12 percent. The total of the amounts estimated to be uncollectible under the aging method is the balance that

AGING OF ACCOUNTS RECEIVABLE METHOD estimates uncollectible accounts based on the age of each account receivable.

Age	Estimated % Uncollectible		Total Accounts Receivable		Estimated Uncollectible Accounts
Not yet due	2.00%	×	$ 90,000	=	$1,800
0–90 days past due	17.40%	×	20,000	=	3,480
Over 90 days past due	35.12%	×	1,552	=	545
Total			$111,552		$5,825

EXHIBIT 6.4

Aging Schedule

should be in the Allowance for Doubtful Accounts at the end of the period. This is called the **estimated balance.**

The approach to recording bad debt expense using the aging method is different from that for the percentage of credit sales method. Recall that using the percentage of credit sales, we directly computed the amount to be recorded as Bad Debt Expense on the income statement for the period in the adjusting journal entry. Alternatively, when using the aging method, we are computing the **final ending balance** we would like to have in the Allowance for Doubtful Accounts on the balance sheet after we make the necessary entry. As indicated in the following T-account, the **difference** between the actual balance in the account and the estimated balance is recorded as the adjusting entry for Bad Debt Expense for the period:

Allowance for Doubtful Accounts (XA)			
Write-offs	1,480	Beginning balance	4,910
		Bad debt expense adjustment	? = $2,395
		Ending balance	$5,825 uncollectible accounts estimate

Actual Write-Offs Compared with Estimates

The amount of uncollectible accounts actually written off seldom equals the estimated amount previously recorded. This situation is resolved when the next adjusting entry is made at the end of the accounting period: A higher or lower amount is recorded to make up for the previous period's error in estimate. **When estimates are found to be incorrect, financial statement values for prior annual accounting periods are not corrected.**

Control over Accounts Receivable

Many managers forget that extending credit will increase your sales volume, but unless the related receivables are collected, they do not add to the bottom line. These companies that emphasize sales without monitoring the collection of credit sales will soon find much of their current assets tied up in accounts receivable. The following practices can help minimize bad debts:

1. Require approval of customers' credit history by a person independent of the sales and collections functions.

2. Age accounts receivable periodically and contact customers with overdue payments.

3. Reward both sales and collections personnel for speedy collections so that they work as a team.

To assess the effectiveness of overall credit granting and collection activities, managers and analysts often compute the receivables turnover ratio.

KEY RATIO
ANALYSIS

Receivables Turnover

? ANALYTICAL QUESTION:
How effective are credit-granting and collection activities?

% RATIO AND COMPARISONS:
The receivables turnover ratio is computed as follows (see Exhibits 6.1 and 6.2):

$$\text{Receivables Turnover} = \frac{\text{Net Sales*}}{\text{Average Net Trade Accounts Receivable†}}$$

The 2000 receivables turnover ratio for Timberland:

$$\frac{\$1,091,478}{(\$105,727 + 78,696) \div 2} = 11.8$$

Learning Objective 5
Analyze and interpret the accounts receivable turnover ratio and the effects of accounts receivable on cash flows.

COMPARISONS OVER TIME		
Timberland		
1998	1999	2000
11.1	11.6	11.8

COMPARISONS WITH COMPETITORS	
Skechers U.S.A.	Wolverine World Wide
2000	2000
8.4	4.2

💡 INTERPRETATIONS:

In General   The receivables turnover ratio reflects how many times average trade receivables are recorded and collected during the period. The higher the ratio, the faster the collection of receivables. A higher ratio benefits the company because it can invest the money collected to earn interest income or reduce borrowings to reduce interest expense. Overly generous payment schedules and ineffective collection methods keep the receivables turnover ratio low. Analysts and creditors watch this ratio because a sudden decline may mean that a company is extending payment deadlines in an attempt to prop up lagging sales or is even recording sales that will later be returned by customers. Many managers and analysts compute the related number **average collection period** or **average days sales in receivables,** which is equal to 365 ÷ Receivables Turnover Ratio, or 30.9 days for Timberland. It indicates the average time it takes a customer to pay its accounts.

Focus Company Analysis   Timberland's receivables turnover rose slightly from a 1998 low of 11.1 to 11.8 in 2000, well above the industry average of 7.8,‡ and its competitors Skechers and Wolverine World Wide. This is also a considerable improvement over Timberland's 1996 ratio of only 7.0. This indicates the success of the element of Timberland's 1997 turnaround strategy focusing on better receivables management.

A Few Cautions: Since differences across industries in the manner in which customer purchases are financed can cause dramatic differences in the ratio, a particular firm's ratio should be compared only with its prior years' figures or with other firms in the same industry.

Since the amount of net credit sales is normally not reported separately, most analysts use net sales in this equation.
†*Average Net Trade Accounts Receivable = (Beginning Net Trade Accounts Receivable + Ending Net Trade Accounts Receivable) ÷ 2.*
‡*Dun and Bradstreet Industry Norms and Key Business Ratios (1999–2000).*

Selected Industry Comparisons: Receivables Turnover Ratio

Variety stores 98.6

Malt beverages 14.9

Lumber and building materials 12.7

Accounts Receivable

 FOCUS ON CASH FLOWS

The change in accounts receivable can be a major determinant of a company's cash flow from operations. While the income statement reflects the revenues of the period, the cash flow from operating activities reflects cash collections from customers. Since sales on account increase the balance in accounts receivable and cash collections from customers decrease the balance in accounts receivable, the change in accounts receivable from the beginning to the end of the period is the difference between sales and collections.

EFFECT ON STATEMENT OF CASH FLOWS

In General   When there is a net **decrease in accounts receivable** for the period, cash collected from customers is more than revenue; thus, the decrease must be **added** in computing cash flows from operations.

When a net **increase in accounts receivable** occurs, cash collected from customers is less than revenue; thus, the increase must be **subtracted** in computing cash flows from operations.*

Effect on Cash Flows	
Operating activities (indirect method)	
Net income	$xxx
Adjusted for	
Add accounts receivable decrease	+
or	
Subtract accounts receivable increase	−

Focus Company Analysis Exhibit 6.5 shows the Operating Activities section of Timberland's statement of cash flows. When sales rise quickly, as they have at Timberland over the past three years, receivables usually rise, decreasing cash flow from operations. The growth of accounts receivable produced a net decrease in cash flow from operating activities of $29,887 (24,419 + 2,687 + 2,781) during this period. Note that in 2000, growth in accounts receivables was 34.3 percent, while growth in sales was only 19.0 percent. If this trend continues, Timberland may need to take steps to again improve collections.

For companies with receivables in foreign currency or business acquisitions/dispositions, such as Timberland, the change reported on the cash flow statement will not equal the change in the accounts receivable reported on the balance sheet.

EXHIBIT 6.5

Accounts Receivable on the Cash Flow Statement

REAL WORLD EXCERPT

THE TIMBERLAND COMPANY

ANNUAL REPORT

THE TIMBERLAND COMPANY Consolidated Statements of Cash Flows For the Years Ended December 31, 2000, 1999 and 1998 (dollars in thousands)			
	2000	**1999**	**1998**
Cash flows from operating activities			
Net Income	$121,998	$75,247	$59,156
Adjustments to reconcile net income to net cash provided by operating activities			
Deferred income taxes	137	(714)	(35)
Depreciation and amortization	19,291	24,410	18,199
Loss (gain) on disposal of property, plant, and equipment	(131)	396	1,303
Extraordinary item	2,126	—	—
Tax benefit from stock option plans	12,600	2,500	2,300
Increase (decrease) in cash from changes in working capital:			
Accounts receivable	(24,419)	(2,687)	(2,781)
Inventory	(10,479)	15,817	11,637
Prepaid expense	(1,104)	1,679	1,112
Accounts payable	14,120	10,144	5,083
Accrued expense	7,681	15,290	(9,975)
Income taxes	(507)	(4,301)	459
Net cash provided by operating activities	$141,313	$137,781	$86,458

1. Assume that Timberland estimated that 0.5 percent of credit sales would prove uncollectible for the year, what adjusting journal entry would they make for bad debts at the end of a year in which credit sales were $700 million?

2. Indicate whether **granting later payment deadlines** (e.g., 60 days instead of 30 days) will most likely **increase** or **decrease** the accounts receivable turnover ratio. Explain.

3. In an earlier year, Timberland's Form 10-K reported beginning and ending balances in the Allowance for Doubtful Accounts of $723 and $904, respectively. It also reported that write-offs of bad debts amounted to $648 (all numbers in thousands). Assuming that no previously written-off accounts had been collected (there were no reinstatements), what amount did Timberland record as bad debt expense for the period? (**Solution approach:** Use the Allowance for Doubtful Accounts T-account to solve for the missing value.)

Allowance for Doubtful Accounts (XA)	

After you have completed your answer, check it with the solutions that follow.

1. Bad debt expense (+E , −SE)   3.5
       Allowance for doubtful accounts (+XA, −A)   3.5

2. Granting later payment deadlines will most likely **decrease** the accounts receivable turnover ratio, because later collections from customers will increase the average accounts receivable balance (the denominator of the ratio), decreasing the ratio.

3.

Allowance for Doubtful Accounts (XA)			
		Beginning balance	723
Write-offs	648	Bad debt expense (*solve*)	829
		Ending balance	904

Beginning + Bad Debt Expense − Write-Offs = Ending; $723 + X − 648 = $904; X = $829

REPORTING AND SAFEGUARDING CASH

Cash and Cash Equivalents Defined

Cash is defined as money or any instrument that banks will accept for deposit and immediate credit to a company's account, such as a check, money order, or bank draft. **Cash equivalents** are investments with original maturities of three months or less that are readily convertible to cash and whose value is unlikely to change (that is, are not sensitive to interest rate changes). Typical instruments included as cash equivalents are bank certificates of deposit and treasury bills that the U.S. government issues to finance its activities.

Even though a company may have several bank accounts and several types of cash equivalents, all cash accounts and cash equivalents are usually combined in one amount for financial reporting purposes. Timberland reports a single account, Cash and Equivalents. It also reports that the book values of cash equivalents on the balance

Learning Objective 6
Report, control, and safeguard cash.

CASH is money or any instrument that banks will accept for deposit and immediate credit to a company's account, such as a check, money order, or bank draft.

CASH EQUIVALENTS are short-term investments with original maturities of three months or less that are readily convertible to cash and whose value is unlikely to change.

sheet equal their fair market values—which we should expect given the nature of the instruments (investments whose value is unlikely to change).

Cash Management

Many businesses receive a large amount of cash, checks, and credit card receipts from their customers each day. Anyone can spend cash, so management must develop procedures to safeguard the cash it uses in the business. Effective cash management involves more than protecting cash from theft, fraud, or loss through carelessness. Other cash management responsibilities include:

1. Accurate accounting so that reports of cash flows and balances may be prepared.

2. Controls to ensure that enough cash is on hand to meet (a) current operating needs, (b) maturing liabilities, and (c) unexpected emergencies.

3. Prevention of the accumulation of excess amounts of idle cash. Idle cash earns no revenue. Therefore, it is often invested in securities to earn a return until it is needed for operations.

Internal Control of Cash

INTERNAL CONTROLS are the processes by which a company provides reasonable assurance regarding the reliability of the company's financial reporting, the effectiveness and efficiency of its operations, and its compliance with applicable laws and regulations.

The term **internal controls** refers to the process by which a company provides reasonable assurance regarding the reliability of the company's financial reporting, the effectiveness and efficiency of its operations, and its compliance with applicable laws and regulations. Internal control procedures should extend to all assets: cash, receivables, investments, plant and equipment, and so on. Controls that ensure the accuracy of the financial records are designed to prevent inadvertent errors and outright fraud such as occurred in the Maxidrive case discussed in Chapter 1. Because internal control increases the reliability of the financial statements, it is reviewed by the outside independent auditor.

Because cash is the asset most vulnerable to theft and fraud, a significant number of internal control procedures should focus on cash. You have already observed internal control procedures for cash, although you may not have known it at the time. At most movie theaters, one employee sells tickets and another employee collects them. Having one employee do both jobs would be less expensive, but that single employee could easily steal cash and admit a patron without issuing a ticket. If different employees perform the tasks, a successful theft requires participation of both.

Effective internal control of cash should include the following:

1. Separation of duties.
   a. Complete separation of the jobs of receiving cash and disbursing cash.
   b. Complete separation of the procedures of accounting for cash receipts and cash disbursements.
   c. Complete separation of the physical handling of cash and all phases of the accounting function.

2. Prescribed policies and procedures.
   a. Require that all cash receipts be deposited in a bank daily. Keep any cash on hand under strict control.
   b. Require separate approval of the purchases and the actual cash payments. Prenumbered checks should be used. Special care must be taken with payments by electronic funds transfers since they involve no controlled documents (checks).
   c. Assign the responsibilities for cash payment approval and check-signing or electronic funds transfer transmittal to different individuals.

d. Require monthly reconciliation of bank accounts with the cash accounts on the company's books (discussed in detail in the next section).

The separation of duties and the use of prescribed policies and procedures are important elements of the control of cash. Separation of duties deters theft because it requires the collusion of two or more persons to steal cash and then conceal the theft in the accounting records. Prescribed procedures are designed so that work done by one individual is checked against the results reported by other individuals. For example, the amount of cash collected at the cash register by the sales clerk can be compared with the amount of cash deposited at the bank by another employee. Reconciliation of the cash accounts to the bank statements provides a further control on deposits.

Ethics and the Need for Internal Control

A QUESTION OF ETHICS

Some people are bothered by the recommendation that all well-run companies should have strong internal control procedures. These people believe that control procedures suggest that management does not trust the company's employees. Although the vast majority of employees are trustworthy, employee theft does cost businesses billions of dollars each year. Interviews with convicted felons indicate that in many cases they stole from their employers because they thought that it was easy and that no one cared (there were no internal control procedures).

Many companies have a formal code of ethics that requires high standards of behavior in dealing with customers, suppliers, fellow employees, and the company's assets. Although each employee is ultimately responsible for his or her own ethical behavior, internal control procedures can be thought of as important value statements from management.

Reconciliation of the Cash Accounts and the Bank Statements

Content of a Bank Statement

Proper use of the bank accounts can be an important internal cash control procedure. Each month, the bank provides the company (the depositor) with a **bank statement** that lists (1) each deposit recorded by the bank during the period, (2) each check cleared by the bank during the period, and (3) the balance in the company's account. The bank statement also shows the bank charges or deductions (such as service charges) made directly to the company's account by the bank. A typical bank statement for ROW.COM, Inc., is shown in Exhibit 6.6.

Exhibit 6.6 lists three items that need explanation. Notice that listed under Checks and Debits, there is a deduction for $18 coded NSF.[9] This entry refers to a check for $18 received from a customer and deposited by ROW.COM with its bank. The bank processed the check through banking channels to the customer's bank, but the account did not have sufficient funds to cover the check. The customer's bank therefore returned it to ROW.COM's bank, which then charged it back to ROW.COM's account. This type of check often is called an **NSF check** (not sufficient funds). The NSF check is now a receivable; consequently, ROW.COM must make an entry to debit Receivables and credit Cash for the $18.

Notice the $6 listed on June 30 under Checks and Debits and coded **SC**. This is the code for bank service charges. The bank statement included a memo by the bank explaining this service charge (which was not documented by a check). ROW.COM must make an entry to reflect this $6 decrease in the bank balance as a debit to a relevant expense account, such as Bank Service Expense, and a credit to Cash.

A BANK STATEMENT is a monthly report from a bank that shows deposits recorded, checks cleared, other debits and credits, and a running bank balance.

---

[9]These codes vary among banks.

Example of a Bank Statement

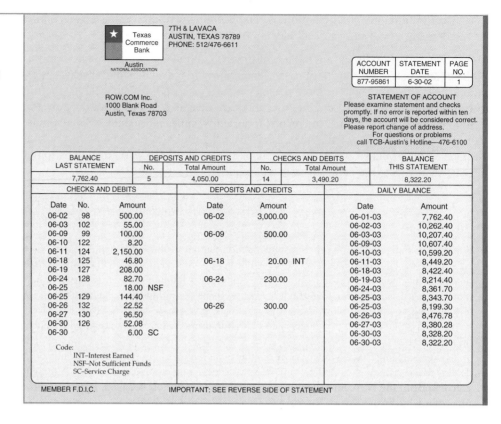

Notice the $20 listed on June 18 under Deposits and Credits and the code **INT** for interest earned. The bank pays interest on checking account balances, and increased ROW.COM's account for interest earned during the period. ROW.COM must record the interest by making an entry to debit Cash and credit Interest Income for the $20.

Need for Reconciliation

A **BANK RECONCILIATION** is the process of verifying the accuracy of both the bank statement and the cash accounts of a business.

A **bank reconciliation** is the process of comparing (reconciling) the ending cash balance in the company's records and the ending cash balance reported by the bank on the monthly bank statement. A bank reconciliation should be completed at the end of each month. Usually, the ending cash balance as shown on the bank statement does not agree with the ending cash balance shown by the related Cash ledger account on the books of the company. For example, the Cash ledger account of ROW.COM showed the following at the end of June (ROW.COM has only one checking account):

Topic Tackler 6–2

Cash (A)			
June 1 balance	7,090.00	June checks written	3,800.00
June deposits	5,750.00		
Ending balance	9,040.00		

The $8,322.20 ending cash balance shown on the bank statement (Exhibit 6.6) differs from the $9,040.00 ending balance of cash shown on the books of ROW.COM. Most of this difference exists because of timing differences in the recording of transactions:

1. Some transactions affecting cash were recorded in the books of ROW.COM but were not shown on the bank statement.

2. Some transactions were shown on the bank statement but had not been recorded in the books of ROW.COM.

Some of the difference may also be caused by errors in recording transactions.

The most common causes of differences between the ending bank balance and the ending book balance of cash are as follows:

1. **Outstanding checks.** These are checks written by the company and recorded in the company's ledger as credits to the Cash account that have not cleared the bank (they are not shown on the bank statement as a deduction from the bank balance). The outstanding checks are identified by comparing the list of canceled checks on the bank statement with the record of checks (such as check stubs or a journal) maintained by the company.

2. **Deposits in transit.** These are deposits sent to the bank by the company and recorded in the company's ledger as debits to the Cash account. The bank has not recorded these deposits (they are not shown on the bank statement as an increase in the bank balance). Deposits in transit usually happen when deposits are made one or two days before the close of the period covered by the bank statement. Deposits in transit are determined by comparing the deposits listed on the bank statement with the company deposit records.

3. **Bank service charges.** An expense for bank services that is listed on the bank statement but is not recorded on the company's books.

4. **NSF checks.** A "bad check" or "bounced check" that was deposited but must be deducted from the company's cash account and rerecorded as an account receivable.

5. **Interest.** The interest paid by the bank to the company on its bank balance.

6. **Errors.** Both the bank and the company may make errors, especially when the volume of cash transactions is large.

Bank Reconciliation Illustrated

The company should make a bank reconciliation immediately after receiving each bank statement. The general format for the bank reconciliation follows:

Ending cash balance per books	$xxx	Ending cash balance per bank statement	$xxx
+ Interest paid by bank	xx	+ Deposits in transit	xx
− NSF checks/Service charges	xx	− Outstanding checks	xx
± Company errors	xx	± Bank errors	xx
Ending correct cash balance	$xxx	Ending correct cash balance	$xxx

Exhibit 6.7 shows the bank reconciliation prepared by ROW.COM for the month of June to reconcile the ending bank balance ($8,322.20) with the ending book balance ($9,040.00). On the completed reconciliation, the correct cash balance is $9,045.00. This correct balance is the amount that should be shown in the Cash account after the reconciliation. Since ROW.COM has only one checking account and no cash on hand, it is also the correct amount of cash that should be reported on the balance sheet.

ROW.COM followed these steps in preparing the bank reconciliation:

1. **Identify the outstanding checks.** A comparison of the checks listed on the bank statement with the company's record of all checks drawn showed the following checks were still outstanding (had not cleared the bank) at the end of June:

Check No.	Amount
101	$ 145.00
123	815.00
131	117.20
Total	$1,077.20

EXHIBIT 6.7	ROW.COM INC.			
	Bank Reconciliation			
	For the Month Ending June 30, 2003			
Bank Reconciliation Illustrated	**Company's Books**		**Bank Statement**	
	Ending cash balance		Ending cash balance per bank	
	per books	$9,040.00	statement	$ 8,322.20
	Additions		Additions	
	Interest paid by the bank	20.00	Deposit in transit	1,800.00
	Error in recording check			
	No. 99	9.00		
		9,069.00		10,122.20
	Deductions		Deductions	
	NSF check of R. Smith	18.00	Outstanding checks	1,077.20
	Bank service charges	6.00		
	Ending correct cash balance	$9,045.00	Ending correct cash balance	$ 9,045.00

This total was entered on the reconciliation as a deduction from the bank account. These checks will be deducted by the bank when they clear the bank.

2. **Identify the deposits in transit.** A comparison of the deposit slips on hand with those listed on the bank statement revealed that a deposit of $1,800 made on June 30 was not listed on the bank statement. This amount was entered on the reconciliation as an addition to the bank account. It will be added by the bank when it records the deposit.

3. **Record bank charges and credits:**

   a. Interest received from the bank, $20—entered on the bank reconciliation as an addition to the book balance; it already has been included in the bank balance.

   b. NSF check of R. Smith, $18—entered on the bank reconciliation as a deduction from the book balance; it has been deducted from the bank statement balance.

   c. Bank service charges, $6—entered on the bank reconciliation as a deduction from the book balance; it has been deducted from the bank balance.

4. **Determine the impact of errors.** At this point, ROW.COM found that the reconciliation did not balance by $9. Upon checking the journal entries made during the month, check No. 99 written for $100 to pay an account payable was found. The check was recorded in the company's accounts as $109. Therefore, $9 (i.e., $109 − $100) must be added to the book cash balance on the reconciliation; the bank cleared the check for the correct amount, $100.

Note that in Exhibit 6.7 the two sections of the bank reconciliation now agree at a correct cash balance of $9,045.00.

A bank reconciliation as shown in Exhibit 6.7 accomplishes two major objectives:

1. Checks the accuracy of the bank balance and the company cash records, which involves developing the correct cash balance. The correct cash balance (plus cash on hand, if any) is the amount of cash that is reported on the balance sheet.

2. Identifies any previously unrecorded transactions or changes that are necessary to cause the company's Cash account(s) to show the correct cash balance. Any transactions or changes on the **Company's Books side** of the bank reconciliation need journal entries. Therefore, the following journal entries based on the Company's Books side of the bank reconciliation (Exhibit 6.7) must be entered into the company's records.

Accounts of ROW.COM

(a) Cash (+A)	20	
Interest income (+R, +SE)		20
To record interest by bank.		
(b) Accounts receivable (+A)	18	
Cash (−A)		18
To record NSF check.		
(c) Bank service expense (+E, −SE)	6	
Cash (−A)		6
To record service fees charged by bank.		
(d) Cash (+A)	9	
Accounts payable (+L)		9
To correct error made in recording a check payable to a creditor.		

Assets	=	Liabilities	+	Stockholders' Equity	
Cash (+20, −18, −6, +9) +5		Accounts payable +9		Interest income	+20
Accounts receivable +18				Bank service expense	−6

Notice again that all of the additions and deductions on the Company's Books side of the reconciliation need journal entries to update the Cash account. The additions and deductions on the Bank Statement side do not need journal entries because they will work out automatically when they clear the bank.

SELF-STUDY QUIZ

Indicate which of the following items discovered while preparing a company's bank reconciliation will result in adjustment of the cash balance on the balance sheet.

1. Outstanding checks.

2. Deposits in transit.

3. Bank service charges.

4. NSF checks that were deposited.

After you have completed your answer, check it with the solution that follows:

_____

3. Bank service charges are deducted from the company's account; thus, cash must be reduced and an expense must be recorded. 4. NSF checks that were deposited were recorded on the books as increases in the cash account; thus, cash must be decreased and the related accounts receivable increased if payment is still expected.

EPILOGUE

As we noted at the beginning of the chapter, Timberland recognized that to turn growth into profits, it had to (1) continually refresh its product lines by introducing new technologies, new styles, and new product categories, (2) become a leaner manufacturer, taking advantage of lower-cost production locations, and (3) focus more attention on inventory management and collections of accounts receivable since an uncollected account is of no value to the company. Each of these efforts is aimed at increasing net sales and/or decreasing cost of goods sold, thereby increasing gross profit. The first quarter of 2001 has sent mixed signals about the continued success of Timberland's strategy. While sales revenue was 17.7 percent higher than the first quarter of 2000, Timberland's gross profit percentage decreased from 45.7 percent to 44.2 percent. This indicates that competitive pressure and the looming recession may present new challenges for Timberland's management team. You can evaluate Timberland's responses to these challenges by going to the web at www.timberland.com to check Timberland's latest annual and quarterly reports.

DEMONSTRATION **CASE A**

(Complete the requirements before proceeding to the suggested solutions.) Wholesale Warehouse Stores sold $950,000 in merchandise during 2005, $400,000 of which was on credit with terms 2/10, n/30 (75 percent of these amounts were paid within the discount period), $500,000 was paid with credit cards (there was a 3 percent credit card discount), and the rest was paid in cash. On December 31, 2005, the Accounts Receivable balance was $80,000, and the Allowance for Doubtful Accounts was $3,000 (credit balance).

Required:

1. Compute net sales for 2005, assuming that sales and credit card discounts are treated as contra-revenues.

2. Assume that Wholesale uses the percentage of sales method for estimating bad debt expense and that it estimates that 2 percent of credit sales will produce bad debts. Record bad debt expense for 2005.

3. Assume instead that Wholesale uses the aging of accounts receivable method and that it estimates that $10,000 worth of current accounts are uncollectible. Record bad debt expense for 2005.

SUGGESTED SOLUTION

1. Both sales discounts and credit card discounts should be subtracted from sales revenues in the computation of net sales.

Sales Revenue	$950,000
Less: Sales Discounts (0.02 × 0.75 × $400,000)	6,000
Credit Card Discounts (0.03 × $500,000)	15,000
Net Sales	$929,000

2. The percentage estimate of bad debts should be applied to credit sales. Cash sales never produce bad debts.

Bad debt expense (+E, −SE) (0.02 × $400,000)	8,000	
Allowance for doubtful accounts (+XA, −A)		8,000

Assets	=	Liabilities	+	Stockholders' Equity
Allowance for doubtful accounts −8,000				Bad debt expense −8,000

3. The entry made when using the aging of accounts receivable method is the estimated balance minus the unadjusted balance.

Bad debt expense (+E, −SE) ($10,000 − $3,000)	7,000	
Allowance for doubtful accounts (+XA, −A)		7,000

Assets	=	Liabilities	+	Stockholders' Equity	
Allowance for				Bad debt expense	−7,000
doubtful accounts −7,000					

DEMONSTRATION **CASE B**

(Complete the requirements before proceeding to the suggested solution that follows.)
Heather Ann Long, a freshman at a large state university, has just received her first checking
account statement. This was her first chance to attempt a bank reconciliation. She had the
following information to work with:

Bank balance, September 1	$1,150
Deposits during September	650
Checks cleared during September	900
Bank service charge	25
Bank balance, October 1	875

Heather was surprised that the deposit of $50 she made on September 29 had not been posted
to her account and was pleased that her rent check of $200 had not cleared her account. Her
checkbook balance was $750.

Required:

1. Complete Heather's bank reconciliation.

2. Why is it important for individuals such as Heather and businesses to do a bank reconciliation each month?

SUGGESTED SOLUTION

1. Heather's bank reconciliation:

Heather's Books		Bank Statement	
October 1 cash balance	$750	October 1 cash balance	$875
Additions		Additions	
None		Deposit in transit	50
Deductions		Deductions	
Bank service charge	(25)	Outstanding check	(200)
Correct cash balance	$725	Correct cash balance	$725

2. Bank statements, whether personal or business, should be reconciled each month. This
   process helps ensure that a correct balance is reflected in the customer's books. Failure to
   reconcile a bank statement increases the chance that an error will not be discovered and
   may result in bad checks being written. Businesses must reconcile their bank statements
   for an additional reason: The correct balance that is calculated during reconciliation is
   recorded on the balance sheet.

Chapter Supplement A

Recording Discounts and Returns

In this chapter, both **credit card discounts** and **cash discounts** have been recorded as contra-revenues. For example, if the credit card company is charging a 3 percent fee for its service and credit card sales were $3,000 at a factory store for January 2, Timberland records the following:

Cash (+A)	2,910	
Credit card discount (+XR, −R, −SE)	90	
Sales revenue (+R, +SE)		3,000

Assets	=	Liabilities	+	Stockholders' Equity	
Cash	+2,910			Sales revenue	+3,000
				Credit card discount	−90

Similarly, if credit sales of $1,000 are recorded with terms 2/10, n/30 ($1,000 × 0.98 = $980), and payment is made within the discount period, Timberland would record the following:

| Accounts receivable (+A) | 1,000 | |
| Sales revenue (+R, +SE) | | 1,000 |

Assets	=	Liabilities	+	Stockholders' Equity	
Accounts receivable	+1,000			Sales revenue	+1,000

Cash (+A)	980	
Sales discount (+XR, −R, −SE)	20	
Accounts receivable (−A)		1,000

Assets	=	Liabilities	+	Stockholders' Equity	
Cash	+980			Sales discount	−20
Accounts receivable	−1,000				

Sales returns and allowances should always be treated as a contra-revenue. Assume that Fontana Shoes of Ithaca, New York, bought 40 pairs of hiking boots from Timberland for $2,000 on account. On the date of sale, Timberland makes the following journal entry:

| Accounts receivable (+A) | 2,000 | |
| Sales revenue (+R, +SE) | | 2,000 |

Assets	=	Liabilities	+	Stockholders' Equity	
Accounts receivable	+2,000			Sales revenue	+2,000

Before paying for the boots, Fontana discovered that 10 pairs of boots were not the color ordered and returned them to Timberland. On that date Timberland records:

| Sales returns and allowances (+XR, −R, −SE) | 500 | |
| Accounts receivable (−A) | | 500 |

	Assets	=	Liabilities	+	Stockholders' Equity	
Accounts receivable	−500				Sales returns and allowances	−500

In addition, the related cost of goods sold entry for the 10 pairs of boots would be reversed.

Chapter Supplement B

Applying the Revenue Principle in Special Circumstances
(This supplement can be found on our website www.mhhe.com/libby4e.)

CHAPTER **TAKE-AWAYS**

1. **Apply the revenue principle to determine the accepted time to record sales revenue for typical retailers, wholesalers, manufacturers, and service companies.   p. 285**
   Revenue recognition policies are widely recognized as one of the most important determinants of the fair presentation of financial statements. For most merchandisers and manufacturers, the required revenue recognition point is the time of shipment or delivery of goods. For service companies, it is the time that services are provided.

2. **Analyze the impact of credit card sales, sales discounts, and sales returns on the amounts reported as net sales.   p. 286**
   Both *credit card discounts* and *cash discounts* can be recorded either as contra-revenues or as expenses. When recorded as contra-revenues, they reduce net sales. *Sales returns and allowances,* which should always be treated as a contra-revenue, also reduce net sales.

3. **Analyze and interpret the gross profit percentage.   p. 289**
   Gross profit percentage measures the ability to charge premium prices and produce goods and services at lower cost. Managers, analysts, and creditors use this ratio to assess the effectiveness of the company's product development, marketing, and production strategy.

4. **Estimate, report, and evaluate the effects of uncollectible accounts receivable (bad debts) on financial statements.   p. 291**
   When receivables are material, companies must employ the allowance method to account for uncollectibles. These are the steps in the process:
   a. The end-of-period adjusting entry to record bad debt expense estimates.
   b. Writing off specific accounts determined to be uncollectible during the period.
   The adjusting entry reduces net income as well as net accounts receivable. The write-off affects neither.

5. **Analyze and interpret the accounts receivable turnover ratio and the effects of accounts receivable on cash flows.   p. 297**
   a. Accounts receivable turnover ratio—Measures the effectiveness of credit-granting and collection activities. It reflects how many times average trade receivables were recorded and collected during the period. Analysts and creditors watch this ratio because a sudden decline in it may mean that a company is extending payment deadlines in an attempt to prop up lagging sales or even is recording sales that later will be returned by customers.
   b. Effects on cash flows—When a net decrease in accounts receivable for the period occurs, cash collected from customers is always more than revenue, and cash flows from operations increases. When a net increase in accounts receivable occurs, cash collected from customers is always less than revenue. Thus, cash flows from operations declines.

6. **Report, control, and safeguard cash.   p. 299**
   Cash is the most liquid of all assets, flowing continually into and out of a business. As a result, a number of critical control procedures, including the reconciliation of bank accounts, should be applied. Also, management of cash may be critically important to decision makers who must have cash available to meet current needs yet must avoid excess amounts of idle cash that produce no revenue.

Closely related to recording revenue is recording the cost of what was sold. Chapter 7 will focus on transactions related to inventory and cost of goods sold. This topic is important because cost of goods sold has a major impact on a company's gross profit and net income, which are watched closely by investors, analysts, and other users of financial statements. Increasing emphasis on quality, productivity, and costs have further focused production managers' attention on cost of goods sold and inventory. Since inventory cost figures play a major role in product introduction and pricing decisions, they also are important to marketing and general managers. Finally, since inventory accounting has a major effect on many companies' tax liabilities, this is an important place to introduce the effect of taxation on management decision making and financial reporting.

KEY **RATIOS**

Gross profit percentage measures the excess of sales prices over the costs to purchase or produce the goods or services sold as a percentage. It is computed as follows (p. 289):

$$\text{Gross Profit Percentage} = \frac{\text{Gross Profit}}{\text{Net Sales}}$$

Receivables turnover ratio measures the effectiveness of credit-granting and collection activities. It is computed as follows (p. 296):

$$\text{Receivables Turnover} = \frac{\text{Net Sales}}{\text{Average Net Trade Accounts Receivable}}$$

FINDING **FINANCIAL INFORMATION**

Balance Sheet

Under Current Assets
Accounts receivable (net of allowance for
    doubtful accounts)

Income statement

Revenues
Net sales (sales revenue less discounts and
    sales returns and allowances)

Expenses
Selling expenses (including bad
    debt expense)

Statement of Cash Flows

Under Operating Activities (indirect method)
Net income
+ decreases in accounts receivable (net)
− increases in accounts receivable (net)

Notes

*Under Summary of Significant Accounting
    Policies*
Revenue recognition policy

Under a Separate Note on Form 10-K
Bad debt expense and write-offs of bad debts

KEY **TERMS**

Accounts Receivable (trade
    receivables or receivables) p. 290
**Aging of Accounts Receivable
    Method** p. 295
Allowance for Doubtful Accounts
    (allowance for bad debts or

    allowance for uncollectible
    accounts) p. 292
Allowance Method p. 291
Bad Debt Expense (doubtful
    accounts expense, uncollectible
    accounts expense, or provision

    for uncollectible accounts)
    p. 292
Bank Reconciliation p. 302
Bank Statement p. 301
Cash p. 299
Cash Equivalents p. 299

QUESTIONS

1. Explain the difference between sales revenue and net sales.
2. What is gross profit or gross margin on sales? How is the gross profit ratio computed? In your explanation, assume that net sales revenue was $100,000 and cost of goods sold was $60,000.
3. What is a credit card discount? How does it affect amounts reported on the income statement?
4. What is a sales discount? Use 1/10, n/30 in your explanation.
5. What is the distinction between *sales allowances* and *sales discounts?*
6. Differentiate accounts receivable from notes receivable.
7. Which basic accounting principle is the allowance method of accounting for bad debts designed to satisfy?
8. Using the allowance method, is bad debt expense recognized in (a) the period in which sales related to the uncollectible account were made or (b) the period in which the seller learns that the customer is unable to pay?
9. What is the effect of the write-off of bad debts (using the allowance method) on (a) net income and (b) accounts receivable, net?
10. Does an increase in the receivables turnover ratio generally indicate faster or slower collection of receivables? Explain.
11. Define *cash* and *cash equivalents* in the context of accounting. Indicate the types of items that should be included and excluded.
12. Summarize the primary characteristics of an effective internal control system for cash.
13. Why should cash-handling and cash-recording activities be separated? How is this separation accomplished?
14. What are the purposes of a bank reconciliation? What balances are reconciled?
15. Briefly explain how the total amount of cash reported on the balance sheet is computed.
16. (Chapter Supplement A) Under the gross method of recording sales discounts, is the amount of sales discount taken recorded (a) at the time the sale is recorded or (b) at the time the collection of the account is recorded?

MULTIPLE **CHOICE QUESTIONS**

1. What is the best description of a *credit card discount*?
   a. The discount offered by a seller to a consumer for using a national credit card such as VISA
   b. The fee charged by a seller to a consumer for the right to use a credit card, calculated as a percentage of total revenue for the sale
   c. The discount offered by a seller to a customer for early payment of an account receivable
   d. The percentage fee charged by a credit card company to a seller
2. Sales discounts with terms 2/10, n/30 mean:
   a. 10 percent discount for payment within 30 days
   b. 2 percent discount for payment within 10 days or the full amount (less returns) is due within 30 days
   c. Two-tenths of a percent discount for payment within 30 days
   d. None of the above
3. A company has been successful in reducing the costs of its manufacturing process by relocating the factory to another locale. What effect will this factor have on the company's gross profit percentage ratio, all other things equal?
   a. The ratio will not change.   c. The ratio will decrease.
   b. The ratio will increase.   d. Either (b) or (c).
4. When a company using the allowance method writes off a specific customer's account receivable from the accounting system, how many of the following are true?
   ■ Total stockholders' equity remains the same.
   ■ Total assets remain the same.

- Total expenses remain the same.
  - a. none
  - b. one
  - c. two
  - d. three

5. You have determined that Company X estimates bad debt expense with an aging of accounts receivable schedule. Company X's estimate of uncollectible receivables resulting from the aging analysis equals
   - a. bad debt expense for the current period.
   - b. the ending balance in the allowance for doubtful accounts for the period.
   - c. the change in the allowance for doubtful accounts for the period.
   - d. both (a) and (c).

6. Upon review of the most recent bank statement, you discover that you recently received an "insufficient funds check" from a customer. Which of the following describes the actions to be taken when preparing your next bank reconciliation?

	Balance per Books	Balance per Bank
a.	No change	Decrease
b.	Decrease	Increase
c.	Decrease	No change
d.	Increase	Decrease

7. Which of the following is *not* a step toward effective internal control over cash?
   - a. Require signatures from a manager and one financial officer on all checks
   - b. Require that cash be deposited daily at the bank
   - c. Require that the person responsible for removing the cash from the register have no access to the accounting records
   - d. All of the above are steps toward effective internal control

8. When using the allowance method, as bad debt expense is recorded,
   - a. total assets remain the same and stockholders' equity remains the same.
   - b. total assets decrease and stockholders' equity decreases.
   - c. total assets increase and stockholders' equity decreases.
   - d. total liabilities increase and stockholders' equity decreases.

9. Which of the following best describes the proper presentation of accounts receivable in the financial statements?
   - a. gross accounts receivable plus the allowance for doubtful accounts in the asset section of the balance sheet
   - b. gross accounts receivable in the asset section of the balance sheet and the allowance for doubtful accounts in the expense section of the income statement
   - c. gross accounts receivable less bad debt expense in the asset section of the balance sheet
   - d. gross accounts receivable less the allowance for doubtful accounts in the asset section of the balance sheet

10. Which of the following is not a component of net sales?
    - a. sales returns and allowances
    - b. sales discounts
    - c. cost of goods sold
    - d. credit card discounts

For more practice with multiple choice questions, go to our website at www.mhhe.com/libby4e, click on "Student Center" in the upper left menu, click on this chapter's name and number from the list of contents, and then click on "Multiple Choice Quiz" from the menu on the left.

MINI-EXERCISES

M6-1
L01

Interpreting the Revenue Principle

Indicate the *most likely* time you expect sales revenue to be recorded for each of the listed transactions.

Transaction	Point A	Point B
a. Airline tickets sold by an airline on a credit card	_____ Point of sale	_____ Completion of flight

b. Computer sold by mail order
company on a credit card   _____ Shipment   _____ Delivery
c. Sale of inventory to a business
customer on open account   _____ Shipment   _____ Collection of account

Reporting Net Sales with Sales Discounts

Merchandise invoiced at $2,000 is sold on terms 2/10, n/30. If the buyer pays within the discount pe-
riod, what amount will be reported on the income statement as net sales?

M6-2
LO2

Reporting Net Sales with Sales Discounts, Credit Card Discounts, and Sales Returns

Total gross sales for the period include the following:

Credit card sales (discount 3%)	$8,000
Sales on account (2/15, n/60)	$9,500

Sales returns related to sales on account were $500. All returns were made before payment. One-half of
the remaining sales on account was paid within the discount period. The company treats all discounts
and returns as contra-revenues. What amount will be reported on the income statement as net sales?

M6-3
LO2

Computing and Interpreting the Gross Profit Percentage

Net sales for the period was $56,000 and cost of sales was $48,000. Compute gross profit percentage
for the current year. What does this ratio measure?

M6-4
LO3

Recording Bad Debts

Prepare journal entries for each transaction listed.

a. During the period, bad debts are written off in the amount of $17,000.
b. At the end of the period, bad debt expense is estimated to be $14,000.

M6-5
LO4

Determining Financial Statement Effects of Bad Debts

Using the following categories, indicate the effects of the following transactions. Use + for increase
and − for decrease and indicate the accounts affected and the amounts.

a. At the end of the period, bad debt expense is estimated to be $10,000.
b. During the period, bad debts are written off in the amount of $8,000.

M6-6
LO4

Assets	=	Liabilities	+	Stockholders' Equity

Determining the Effects of Credit Policy Changes on Receivables Turnover Ratio

Indicate the most likely effect of the following changes in credit policy on the receivables turnover ratio (+ for increase, − for decrease, and NE for no effect).

_____ *a.* Granted credit with shorter payment deadlines.
_____ *b.* Increased effectiveness of collection methods.
_____ *c.* Granted credit to less creditworthy customers.

M6-7
LO5

Matching Reconciling Items to the Bank Reconciliation

Indicate whether the following items would be added (+) or subtracted (−) from the company's books
or the bank statement during the construction of a bank reconciliation.

M6-8
LO6

Reconciling Item	+	−	Company's Books	Bank Statement
a. Outstanding checks				
b. Bank service charge				
c. Deposit in transit				

M6-9   **(Chapter Supplement A) Recording Sales Discounts**

A sale is made for $700; terms are 2/10, n/30. At what amount should the sale be recorded under the gross method of recording sales discounts? Give the required entry. Also give the collection entry, assuming that it is during the discount period.

EXERCISES

E6-1   **Reporting Net Sales with Credit Sales and Sales Discounts**

LO2

During the months of January and February, Bronze Corporation sold goods to three customers. The sequence of events was as follows:

> Jan. 6 Sold goods for $1,000 to S. Green and billed that amount subject to terms 2/10, n/30.
>   6 Sold goods to M. Munoz for $800 and billed that amount subject to terms 2/10, n/30.
>   14 Collected cash due from S. Green.
> Feb. 2 Collected cash due from M. Munoz.
>   28 Sold goods for $500 to R. Reynolds and billed that amount subject to terms 2/10, n/45.

Required:
Assuming that Sales Discounts is treated as a contra-revenue, compute net sales for the two months ended February 28.

E6-2   **Reporting Net Sales with Credit Sales, Sales Discounts, and Credit Card Sales**

LO2

The following transactions were selected from the records of Evergreen Company:

> July 12 Sold merchandise to Customer R, who charged the $1,000 purchase on his Visa credit card. Visa charges Evergreen a 2 percent credit card fee.
> July 15 Sold merchandise to Customer S at an invoice price of $5,000; terms 3/10, n/30.
>   20 Sold merchandise to Customer T at an invoice price of $3,000; terms 3/10, n/30.
>   23 Collected payment from Customer S from July 15 sale.
> Aug. 25 Collected payment from Customer T from July 20 sale.

Required:
Assuming that Sales Discounts and Credit Card Discounts are treated as contra-revenues, compute net sales for the two months ended August 31.

E6-3   **Reporting Net Sales with Credit Sales, Sales Discounts, Sales Returns, and Credit Card Sales**

LO2

The following transactions were selected from among those completed by Hailey Retailers in 2004:

> Nov. 20 Sold two items of merchandise to Customer B, who charged the $400 sales price on her Visa credit card. Visa charges Hailey a 2 percent credit card fee.
>   25 Sold 20 items of merchandise to Customer C at an invoice price of $4,000 (total); terms 3/10, n/30
>   28 Sold 10 identical items of merchandise to Customer D at an invoice price of $6,000 (total); terms 3/10, n/30.
>   30 Customer D returned one of the items purchased on the 28th; the item was defective, and credit was given to the customer.
> Dec. 6 Customer D paid the account balance in full.
>   30 Customer C paid in full for the invoice of November 25, 2004.

Required:
Assume that Sales Discounts and Credit Card Discounts are treated as contra-revenues; compute net sales for the two months ended December 31, 2004.

Determining the Effects of Credit Sales, Sales Discounts, Credit Card Sales, and Sales Returns and Allowances on Income Statement Categories

E6-4
LO2

Rockland Shoe Company records sales returns and allowances as contra-revenues and sales discounts and credit card discounts as selling expenses. Complete the following tabulation, indicating the effect (+ for increase, − for decrease, and NE for no effect) of each transaction. Do not record related cost of goods sold.

July 12 Sold merchandise to customer at factory store who charged the $300 purchase on her American Express card. American Express charges a 1 percent credit card fee.

July 15 Sold merchandise to Customer T at an invoice price of $5,000; terms 3/10, n/30.

July 20 Collected cash due from Customer T.

July 21 Before paying for the order, a customer returned shoes with an invoice price of $1,000.

Transaction	Net Sales	Gross Profit	Income from Operations
July 12			
July 15			
July 20			
July 21			

Evaluating the Annual Interest Rate Implicit in a Sales Discount with Discussion of Management Choice of Financing Strategy

E6-5
LO2

Laura's Landscaping bills customers subject to terms 3/10, n/60.

Required:
1. Compute the annual interest rate implicit in the sales discount.
2. If his bank charges 15 percent interest, should the customer borrow from the bank so that he can take advantage of the discount? Explain your recommendation.

Analyzing Gross Profit Percentage on the Basis of a Multiple-Step Income Statement

E6-6
LO3

The following summarized data were provided by the records of Slate, Incorporated, for the year ended December 31, 2004:

Sales of merchandise for cash	$220,000
Sales of merchandise on credit	32,000
Cost of goods sold	147,000
Selling expense	40,200
Administrative expense	19,000
Sales returns and allowances	7,000
Items not included in above amounts:	
Estimated bad debt loss, 2.5% of credit sales	
Average income tax rate, 30%	
Number of shares of common stock outstanding, 5,000	

Required:
1. Based on these data, prepare a multiple-step income statement (showing both gross profit and income from operations). Include a Percentage Analysis column.
2. What was the amount of gross profit margin? What was the gross profit percentage ratio? Explain what these two amounts mean.

Analyzing Gross Profit Percentage on the Basis of a Multiple-Step Income Statement and Within-Industry Comparison

E6-7
LO3
Wolverine
World Wide

Wolverine World Wide Inc. prides itself as being the "world's leading marketer of U.S. branded non-athletic footwear." It competes in many markets with Timberland, often offering products at a lower price point. The following data were taken from its recent annual report (in thousands):

Sales of merchandise	$413,957
Income taxes	10,047
Cash dividends declared	2,347
Selling and administrative expense	85,993
Cost of products sold	290,469
Interest expense	3,678
Other income	297
Items not included in above amounts:	
Number of shares of common stock outstanding, 17,114	

Required:

1. Based on these data, prepare a multiple-step income statement (showing both gross profit and income from operations). There were no extraordinary items. Include a Percentage Analysis column.
2. How much was the gross profit margin? What was the gross profit percentage ratio? Explain what these two amounts mean. Compare the gross profit percentage with that of Timberland. What do you believe accounts for the difference?

E6-8

LO4

Recording Bad Debt Expense Estimates and Write-Offs Using the Percentage of Credit Sales Method

During 2003, Kim Productions, Inc., recorded credit sales of $650,000. Based on prior experience, it estimates a 1.5 percent bad debt rate on credit sales.

Required:
Prepare journal entries for each transaction:

a. The appropriate bad debt expense adjustment was recorded for the year 2003.
b. On December 31, 2003, an account receivable for $1,000 from March of the current year was determined to be uncollectible and was written off.

E6-9

LO4

Recording Bad Debt Expense Estimates and Write-Offs Using the Percentage of Credit Sales Method

During 2003, Gonzales Electronics, Incorporated, recorded credit sales of $720,000. Based on prior experience, it estimates a 0.5 percent bad debt rate on credit sales.

Required:
Prepare journal entries for each transaction:

a. The appropriate bad debt expense adjustment was recorded for the year 2003.
b. On December 31, 2003, an account receivable for $300 from a prior year was determined to be uncollectible and was written off.

E6-10

LO4

Determining Financial Statement Effects of Bad Debts

Using the following categories, indicate the effects of the transactions listed in E6-9. Use + for increase and − for decrease and indicate the accounts affected and the amounts.

Assets	=	Liabilities	+	Stockholders' Equity

E6-11

LO4

Recording and Determining the Effects of Bad Debt Transactions on Income Statement Categories

During 2003, Choi and Goldstein Furniture recorded credit sales of $650,000. Based on prior experience, it estimates a 2 percent bad debt rate on credit sales.

Required:

1. Prepare journal entries for each transaction below.
    a. The appropriate bad debt expense adjustment was recorded for the year 2003.
    b. On December 31, 2003, an account receivable for $1,600 from a prior year was determined to be uncollectible and was written off.

2. Complete the following tabulation, indicating the amount and effect (+ for increase, − for decrease, and NE for no effect) of each transaction.

Transaction	Net Sales	Gross Profit	Income from Operations
a.			
b.			

Interpreting Bad Debt Disclosures

E6-12
LO4
DaimlerChrysler
AG

DaimlerChrysler is the largest industrial group headquartered in Germany. Best known as the manufacturer of Mercedes-Benz and Chrysler cars and trucks, it also manufactures products in the fields of rail systems, aerospace, propulsion, defense, and information technology. In a recent filing pursuant to its listing on the New York Stock Exchange, it disclosed the following information concerning its allowance for doubtful accounts (in millions of German marks denoted DM):

Balance at Beginning of Period	Charged to Costs and Expenses	Amounts Written Off	Balance at End of Period
1,933	92	(52)	1,973

Required:
1. Record summary journal entries related to bad debts for the current year.
2. If DaimlerChrysler had written off an additional DM10 million of accounts receivable during the period, how would receivables, net, and net income have been affected? Explain why.

Inferring Bad Debt Write-Offs and Cash Collections from Customers

E6-13
LO4
Microsoft

Microsoft develops, produces, and markets a wide range of computer software including the Windows operating system. On a recent balance sheet, Microsoft reported the following information about net sales revenue and accounts receivable.

	Current Year	Prior Year
Accounts receivable, net of allowances of $76 and $57	$ 338	$ 270
Net revenues	3,753	2,759

According to its Form 10-K, Microsoft recorded bad debt expense of $47 and did not reinstate any previously written-off accounts during the current year.

Required:
1. What amount of bad debts was written off during the current year?
2. Assuming that all of Microsoft's sales during the period were on open account, solve for cash collected from customers for the current year.

Determining the Impact of Uncollectible Accounts on Income and Working Capital

E6-14
LO4
Sears

A recent annual report for Sears contained the following information at the end of its fiscal year:

	Year 1	Year 2
Accounts receivable	$7,022,075,000	$7,336,308,000
Allowance for doubtful accounts	(86,605,000)	(96,989,000)
	$6,935,470,000	$7,239,319,000

A footnote to the financial statements disclosed that uncollectible accounts amounting to $55,000,000 were written off as bad during year 1 and $69,000,000 during year 2. Assume that the tax rate for Sears was 30 percent.

Required:

1. Determine the bad debt expense for year 2 based on the preceding facts.
2. *Working capital* is defined as current assets minus current liabilities. How was Sears's working capital affected by the write-off of $69,000,000 in uncollectible accounts during year 2? What impact did the recording of bad debt expense have on working capital in year 2?
3. How was net income affected by the $69,000,000 write-off during year 2? What impact did recording bad debt expense have on net income for year 2?

E6-15   Computing Bad Debt Expense Using Aging Analysis

LO4

Brown Cow Dairy uses the aging approach to estimate bad debt expense. The balance of each account receivable is aged on the basis of three time periods as follows: (1) not yet due $12,000, (2) up to 120 days past due $5,000, and (3) more than 120 days past due $3,000. Experience has shown that for each age group, the average loss rate on the amount of the receivables at year-end due to uncollectability is (1) 2 percent, (2) 10 percent, and (3) 30 percent, respectively. At December 31, 2005 (end of the current year), the Allowance for Doubtful Accounts balance was $300 (credit) before the end-of-period adjusting entry is made.

Required:

What amount should be recorded as Bad Debt Expense for the current year?

E6-16   Recording and Reporting a Bad Debt Estimate Using Aging Analysis

LO4

Arias Company uses the aging approach to estimate bad debt expense. The balance of each account receivable is aged on the basis of three time periods as follows: (1) not yet due $65,000, (2) up to 180 days past due $10,000, and (3) more than 180 days past due $4,000. Experience has shown that for each age group, the average loss rate on the amount of the receivables at year-end due to uncollectability is (1) 1 percent, (2) 15 percent, and (3) 40 percent, respectively. At December 31, 2005 (end of the current year), the Allowance for Doubtful Accounts balance was $100 (credit) before the end-of-period adjusting entry is made.

Required:

1. Prepare the appropriate bad debt expense adjusting entry for the year 2005.
2. Show how the various accounts related to accounts receivable should be shown on the December 31, 2005 balance sheet.

E6-17   Recording, Reporting, and Evaluating a Bad Debt Estimate

LO4

During 2009, Martin's Camera Shop had sales revenue of $170,000, of which $85,000 was on credit. At the start of 2009, Accounts Receivable showed a $10,000 debit balance, and the Allowance for Doubtful Accounts showed an $800 credit balance. Collections of accounts receivable during 2009 amounted to $68,000.

Data during 2009 follows:

a. On December 31, 2009, an Account Receivable (J. Doe) of $1,500 from a prior year was determined to be uncollectible; therefore, it was written off immediately as a bad debt.
b. On December 31, 2009, on the basis of experience, a decision was made to continue the accounting policy of basing estimated bad debt losses on 2 percent of credit sales for the year.

Required:

1. Give the required journal entries for the two items on December 31, 2009 (end of the accounting period).
2. Show how the amounts related to Accounts Receivable and Bad Debt Expense would be reported on the income statement and balance sheet for 2009. Disregard income tax considerations.
3. On the basis of the data available, does the 2 percent rate appear to be reasonable? Explain.

E6-18   Analyzing and Interpreting the Receivables Turnover Ratio

LO5

A recent annual report for Federal Express contained the following data:

Federal Express

	(IN THOUSANDS)	
	Current Year	Previous Year
Accounts receivable	$1,034,608	$805,495
Less: Allowance for doubtful accounts	36,800	38,225
Net accounts receivable	$ 997,808	$767,270
Net sales (assume all on credit)	$7,015,069	

Required:

1. Determine the accounts receivable turnover ratio and average days sales in receivables for the current year.
2. Explain the meaning of each number.

Determining the Effects of Bad Debts on Receivables Turnover Ratio

E6-19
LO4, 5

During 2003, Leung Enterprises Corporation recorded credit sales of $650,000. Based on prior experience, it estimates a 1 percent bad debt rate on credit sales. At the beginning of the year, the balance in Net Trade Accounts Receivable was $50,000. At the end of the year, but *before* the bad debt expense adjustment was recorded and *before* any bad debts had been written off, the balance in Net Trade Accounts Receivable was $55,500.

Required:

1. Assume that on December 31, 2003, the appropriate bad debt expense adjustment was recorded for the year 2003 and accounts receivable totaling $6,000 for the year were determined to be uncollectible and written off. What was the receivables turnover ratio for 2003?
2. Assume instead that on December 31, 2003, the appropriate bad debt expense adjustment was recorded for the year 2003 and $7,000 of accounts receivable was determined to be uncollectible and written off. What was the receivables turnover ratio for 2003?
3. Explain why the answers to requirements (1) and (2) differ or do not differ.

Interpreting the Effects of Sales Declines and Changes in Receivables on Cash Flow from Operations

E6-20
LO5
Stride Rite

Stride Rite Corporation manufactures and markets shoes under the brand names Stride Rite®, Keds®, and Sperry Top-Sider®. Three recent years produced a combination of declining sales revenue and net income culminating in a net loss of $8,430,000. Each year, however, Stride Rite was able to report positive cash flows from operations. Contributing to that positive cash flow was the change in accounts receivable. The current and prior year balance sheets reported the following:

	(IN THOUSANDS)	
	Current Year	Previous Year
Accounts and notes receivable, less allowances	$48,066	$63,403

Required:

1. On the current year's cash flow statement (indirect method), how would the change in accounts receivable affect cash flow from operations? Explain why it would have this effect.
2. Explain how declining sales revenue often leads to (a) declining accounts receivable and (b) cash collections from customers being higher than sales revenue.

Interpreting the Effects of Sales Growth and Changes in Receivables on Cash Flow from Operations

E6-21
LO5
Nike

Nike, Inc., is the best known sports apparel and equipment company in the world. Three recent years produced a combination of dramatic increases in sales revenue and net income. Cash flows from operations declined during the period, however. Contributing to that declining cash flow was the change in accounts receivable. The current and prior year balance sheets reported the following:

	(IN THOUSANDS)	
	Current Year	Previous Year
Accounts receivable, less allowance for doubtful accounts	$1,346,125	$1,053,237

Required:

1. On the current year's cash flow statement (indirect method), how would the change in accounts receivable affect cash flow from operations? Explain why it would have this effect.
2. Explain how increasing sales revenue often leads to (a) increasing accounts receivable and thus (b) cash collections from customers being lower than sales revenue.

E6-22

LO6

Preparing Bank Reconciliation, Entries, and Reporting

Jones Company has the June 30, 2004, bank statement and the June ledger accounts for cash, which are summarized here:

	BANK STATEMENT		
	Checks	Deposits	Balance
Balance, June 1, 2004			$ 7,200
Deposits during June		$17,000	24,200
Checks cleared through June	$18,100		6,100
Bank service charges	50		6,050
Balance, June 30, 2004			6,050

Cash (A)				
June 1	Balance	6,800	June	Checks written 18,400
June	Deposits	19,000		

Cash on hand (A)		
June 30	Balance	300

Required:

1. Reconcile the bank account. A comparison of the checks written with the checks that have cleared the bank shows outstanding checks of $700. Some of the checks that cleared in June were written prior to June. No deposits in transit were carried over from May, but a deposit is in transit at the end of June.
2. Give any journal entries that should be made as a result of the bank reconciliation.
3. What is the balance in the Cash account after the reconciliation entries?
4. What is the total amount of cash that should be reported on the balance sheet at June 30?

E6-23

LO6

Preparing Bank Reconciliation, Entries, and Reporting

The September 30, 2006, bank statement for Russell Company and the September ledger accounts for cash are summarized here:

	BANK STATEMENT		
	Checks	Deposits	Balance
Balance, September 1, 2006			$ 6,300
Deposits recorded during September		$27,000	33,300
Checks cleared during September	$28,500		4,800
NSF checks—Betty Brown	150		4,650
Bank service charges	50		4,600
Balance, September 30, 2006			4,600

Cash (A)				
Sept 1	Balance	6,300	Sept.	Checks written 28,600
Sept.	Deposits	28,000		

Cash on hand (A)		
Sept 30	Balance	400

No outstanding checks and no deposits in transit were carried over from August; however, there are deposits in transit and checks outstanding at the end of September.

Required:
1. Reconcile the bank account.
2. Give any journal entries that should be made as the result of the bank reconciliation.
3. What should the balance in the Cash account be after the reconciliation entries?
4. What total amount of cash should the company report on the September 30 balance sheet?

(Chapter Supplement A) Recording Credit Sales, Sales Discounts, Sales Returns, and Credit Card Sales   E6-24

The following transactions were selected from among those completed by Hailey Retailers in 2004:

Nov. 20   Sold two items of merchandise to Customer B, who charged the $400 sales price on her Visa credit card. Visa charges Hailey a 2 percent credit card fee.

  25   Sold 20 items of merchandise to Customer C at an invoice price of $4,000 (total); terms 3/10, n/30.

  28   Sold 10 identical items of merchandise to Customer D at an invoice price of $6,000 (total); terms 3/10, n/30.

  30   Customer D returned one of the items purchased on the 28th; the item was defective, and credit was given to the customer.

Dec. 6   Customer D paid the account balance in full.

  30   Customer C paid in full for the invoice of November 25, 2004.

Required:
Give the appropriate journal entry for each of these transactions, assuming the company records sales revenue under the gross method. Do not record cost of goods sold.

PROBLEMS

Applying the Revenue Principle   P6-1
LO1

At what point should revenue be recognized in each of the following independent cases?

Case A. For Christmas presents, a McDonald's restaurant sells coupon books for $10. Each of the $1 coupons may be used in the restaurant any time during the following 12 months. The customer must pay cash when purchasing the coupon book.

Case B. Howard Land Development Corporation sold a lot to Quality Builders to construct a new home. The price of the lot was $50,000. Quality made a down payment of $100 and agreed to pay the balance in six months. After making the sale, Howard learned that Quality Builders often entered into these agreements but refused to pay the balance if it did not find a customer who wanted a house built on the lot.

Case C. Driscoll Corporation has always recorded revenue at the point of sale of its refrigerators. Recently, it has extended its warranties to cover all repairs for a period of seven years. One young accountant with the company now questions whether Driscoll has completed its earning process when it sells the refrigerators. She suggests that the warranty obligation for seven years means that a significant amount of additional work must be performed in the future.

P6-2
LO2, 4

Reporting Net Sales and Expenses with Discounts, Returns, and Bad Debts (AP6-1)

The following data were selected from the records of May Company for the year ended December 31, 2005.

Balances January 1, 2005	
Accounts receivable (various customers)	$120,000
Allowance for doubtful accounts	6,000

In the following order, except for cash sales, the company sold merchandise and made collections on credit terms 2/10, n/30 (assume a unit sales price of $500 in all transactions and use the gross method to record sales revenue).

Transactions during 2005

a. Sold merchandise for cash, $228,000.
b. Sold merchandise to R. Jones; invoice price, $12,000.
c. Sold merchandise to K. Black; invoice price, $26,000.
d. Two days after purchase date, R. Jones returned one of the units purchased in (b) and received account credit.
e. Sold merchandise to B. Sears; invoice price, $24,000.
f. R. Jones paid his account in full within the discount period.
g. Collected $98,000 cash from customer sales on credit in prior year, all within the discount periods.
h. K. Black paid the invoice in (c) within the discount period.
i. Sold merchandise to R. Roy; invoice price, $17,000.
j. Three days after paying the account in full, K. Black returned seven defective units and received a cash refund.
k. After the discount period, collected $7,000 cash on an account receivable on sales in a prior year.
l. Wrote off a 2003 account of $2,900 after deciding that the amount would never be collected.
m. The estimated bad debt rate used by the company was 1 percent of credit sales net of returns.

Required:

1. Using the following categories, indicate the effect of each listed transaction, including the write-off of the uncollectible account and the adjusting entry for estimated bad debts (ignore cost of goods sold).

Sales Revenue	Sales Discounts (taken)	Sales Returns and Allowances	Bad Debt Expense

2. Show how the accounts related to the preceding sale and collection activities should be reported on the 2005 income statement. (Treat sales discounts as a contra-revenue.)

P6-3
LO3

Understanding the Income Statement Based on the Gross Profit Percentage

The following data were taken from the year-end records of Nomura Export Company. You are to fill in all of the missing amounts. Show computations.

	INDEPENDENT CASES	
Income Statement Items	Case A	Case B
Gross sales revenue	$160,000	$232,000
Sales returns and allowances	?	18,000
Net sales revenue	?	?
Cost of goods sold	(68%)?	?
Gross profit	?	(30%)?
Operating expenses	18,500	?
Pretax income	?	20,000
Income tax expense (20%)	?	?
Income before extraordinary items	?	?
Extraordinary items	10,000 (gain)	2,000 (loss)
Less: Income tax (20%)	?	?
Net income	?	?
EPS (10,000 shares)	3.00	?

Interpreting Disclosure of Allowance for Doubtful Accounts (AP6-2)

P6-4
LO4
Kimberly-Clark

Kimberly-Clark manufactures and markets a variety of paper and synthetic fiber products, of which the best known is Kleenex tissues. It recently disclosed the following information concerning the allowance for doubtful accounts on its Form 10-K Annual Report submitted to the Securities and Exchange Commission.

SCHEDULE VIII Valuation and Qualifying Accounts (millions of dollars)					
Description: Allowances for Doubtful Accounts	Balance at Beginning of Period	Charged to Costs and Expenses	Charged to Other Accounts*	Write-Offs	Balance at End of Period
Year 3	$8.2	$4.5	$.2	$2.7	$10.2
Year 2	7.1	4.8	—	(?)	8.2
Year 1	6.4	(?)	.2	3.3	7.1

*These are primarily bad debt recoveries. (Hint: These require a reversal of the previous entry made when they were written off.)

Required:
1. Record summary journal entries related to bad debts for Year 3.
2. Supply the missing dollar amounts noted by (?) for Year 1 and Year 2.

Determining Bad Debt Expense Based on Aging Analysis (AP6-3)

P6-5
LO4

Green Pastures Equipment Company uses the aging approach to estimate bad debt expense at the end of each accounting year. Credit sales occur frequently on terms n/60. The balance of each account receivable is aged on the basis of three time periods as follows: (1) not yet due, (2) up to one year past due, and (3) more than one year past due. Experience has shown that for each age group, the average loss rate on the amount of the receivable at year-end due to uncollectability is (a) 1 percent, (b) 5 percent, and (c) 30 percent.

At December 31, 2008 (end of the current accounting year), the Accounts Receivable balance was $41,000, and the Allowance for Doubtful Accounts balance was $1,020 (credit). To simplify, only five customer accounts are used; the details of each on December 31, 2008, follow:

B. BROWN—ACCOUNT RECEIVABLE				
Date	Explanation	Debit	Credit	Balance
3/11/2007	Sale	14,000		14,000
6/30/2007	Collection		5,000	9,000

B. BROWN—ACCOUNT RECEIVABLE (CONTINUED)				
Date	Explanation	Debit	Credit	Balance
1/31/2008	Collection		4,000	5,000

D. DONALDS—ACCOUNT RECEIVABLE				
2/28/2008	Sale	22,000		22,000
4/15/2008	Collection		10,000	12,000
11/30/2008	Collection		8,000	4,000

N. NAPIER—ACCOUNT RECEIVABLE				
11/30/2008	Sale	9,000		9,000
12/15/2008	Collection		2,000	7,000

S. STROTHERS—ACCOUNT RECEIVABLE				
3/2/2006	Sale	5,000		5,000
4/15/2006	Collection		5,000	0
9/1/2007	Sale	10,000		10,000
10/15/2007	Collection		8,000	2,000
2/1/2008	Sale	19,000		21,000
3/1/2008	Collection		5,000	16,000
12/31/2008	Sale	3,000		19,000

T. THOMAS—ACCOUNT RECEIVABLE				
12/30/2008	Sale	6,000		6,000

Required:

1. Compute the total accounts receivable in each age category.
2. Compute the estimated uncollectible amount for each age category and in total.
3. Give the adjusting entry for bad debt expense at December 31, 2008.
4. Show how the amounts related to accounts receivable should be presented on the 2008 income statement and balance sheet.

P6-6
LO2, 3, 4
Preparing a Multiple-Step Income Statement and Computing the Gross Profit Percentage with Discounts, Returns, and Bad Debts (AP6-4)

Builders Company, Inc., sells heavy construction equipment. There are 10,000 shares of capital stock outstanding. The annual fiscal period ends on December 31. The following condensed trial balance was taken from the general ledger on December 31, 2006:

Account Titles	Debit	Credit
Cash	$ 42,000	
Accounts receivable	18,000	
Inventory, ending	65,000	
Operational assets	50,000	
Accumulated depreciation		$ 21,000
Liabilities		30,000
Capital stock		90,000
Retained earnings, January 1, 2006		11,600
Sales revenue		182,000
Sales returns and allowances	7,000	
Cost of goods sold	98,000	
Selling expense	17,000	
Administrative expense	18,000	
Bad debt expense	2,000	
Sales discounts	8,000	
Income tax expense	9,600	
Totals	$334,600	$334,600

Required:

1. Beginning with the amount for net sales, prepare a multiple-step income statement (showing both gross profit and income from operations). Treat sales discounts as a contra-revenue.
2. Compute the gross profit percentage and explain its meaning.

Evaluating the Effects of Credit Policy Changes on Receivables Turnover Ratio and Cash Flows from Operating Activities

P6-7
LO5

V. R. Rao and Company has been operating for five years as a software consulting firm specializing in the installation of industry standard products. During this period, it has experienced rapid growth in sales revenue and in accounts receivable. Ms. Rao and her associates all have computer science backgrounds. This year, the company hired you as its first corporate controller. You have put into place new credit-granting and collection procedures that are expected to reduce receivables by approximately one-third by year-end. You have gathered the following data related to the changes:

	(IN THOUSANDS)	
	Beginning of Year	End of Year (projected)
Accounts receivable	$1,000,608	$ 660,495
Less: Allowance for doubtful accounts	36,800	10,225
Net accounts receivable	$ 963,808	$ 650,270
		Current Year (projected)
Net sales (assume all on credit)		$7,015,069

Required:

1. Compute the accounts receivable turnover ratio based on two different assumptions:
   a. Those presented in the preceding table (a decrease in the balance in accounts receivable, net).
   b. No change from the beginning of the year in the accounts receivable balance.
2. Compute the effect of the projected change in the balance in accounts receivable on cash flow from operating activities for the year (the sign and amount of effect).
3. On the basis of your findings in requirements (1) and (2), write a brief memo explaining how an increase in accounts receivable turnover can result in an increase in cash flow from operating activities. Also explain how this increase can benefit the company.

Evaluating Internal Control

P6-8
LO6

Cripple Creek Company has one trusted employee who, as the owner said, "handles all of the book-keeping and paperwork for the company." This employee is responsible for counting, verifying, and recording cash receipts and payments, making the weekly bank deposit, preparing checks for major expenditures (signed by the owner), making small expenditures from the cash register for daily expenses, and collecting accounts receivable. The owners asked the local bank for a $20,000 loan. The bank asked that an audit be performed covering the year just ended. The independent auditor (a local CPA), in a private conference with the owner, presented some evidence of the following activities of the trusted employee during the past year:

a. Cash sales sometimes were not entered in the cash register, and the trusted employee pocketed approximately $50 per month.
b. Cash taken from the cash register (and pocketed by the trusted employee) was replaced with expense memos with fictitious signatures (approximately $12 per day).
c. A $300 collection on an account receivable of a valued out-of-town customer was pocketed by the trusted employee and was covered by making a $300 entry as a debit to Sales Returns and a credit to Accounts Receivable.
d. An $800 collection on an account receivable from a local customer was pocketed by the trusted employee and was covered by making an $800 entry as a debit to Allowance for Doubtful Accounts and a credit to Accounts Receivable.

Required:

1. What was the approximate amount stolen during the past year?
2. What would be your recommendations to the owner?

P6-9 Preparing a Bank Reconciliation and Related Journal Entries

L06

The bookkeeper at Hopkins Company has not reconciled the bank statement with the Cash account, saying, "I don't have time." You have been asked to prepare a reconciliation and review the procedures with the bookkeeper.

The April 30, 2006, bank statement and the April ledger accounts for cash showed the following (summarized):

	BANK STATEMENT		
	Checks	Deposits	Balance
Balance, April 1, 2006			$25,850
Deposits during April		$36,000	61,850
Interest collected		1,070	62,920
Checks cleared during April	$44,200		18,720
NSF check—A. B. Wright	140		18,580
Bank service charges	50		18,530
Balance, April 30, 2006			18,530

Cash (A)					
Apr. 1	Balance	23,250	Apr.	Checks written	43,800
Apr.	Deposits	42,000			

Cash on hand (A)		
Apr. 30	Balance	100

A comparison of checks written before and during April with the checks cleared through the bank showed outstanding checks at the end of April of $2,200. No deposits in transit were carried over from March, but a deposit was in transit at the end of April.

Required:
1. Prepare a detailed bank reconciliation for April.
2. Give any required journal entries as a result of the reconciliation. Why are they necessary?
3. What were the balances in the cash accounts in the ledger on May 1, 2006?
4. What total amount of cash should be reported on the balance sheet at the end of April?

P6-10 Computing Outstanding Checks and Deposits in Transit and Preparing a Bank

L06 Reconciliation and Journal Entries (AP6-5)

The August 2004 bank statement for Martha Company and the August 2004 ledger accounts for cash follow:

	BANK STATEMENT		
Date	Checks	Deposits	Balance
Aug. 1			$17,470
2	$ 300		17,170
3		$12,000	29,170
4	400		28,770
5	250		28,520
9	900		27,620
10	300		27,320
15		4,000	31,320
21	400		30,920
24	21,000		9,920
25		7,000	16,920
30	800		16,120
30		2,180*	18,300
31	100†		18,200

*$2,180 interest collected.
†Bank service charge.

Cash (A)			
Aug. 1 Balance	16,520	Checks written	
Deposits		Aug. 2	300
Aug. 2	12,000	4	900
12	4,000	15	290
24	7,000	17	550
31	5,000	18	800
		20	400
		23	21,000

Cash on hand (A)		
Aug. 31 Balance	200	

Outstanding checks at the end of July were for $250, $400, and $300. No deposits were in transit at the end of July.

Required:
1. Compute the deposits in transit at the end of August.
2. Compute the outstanding checks at the end of August.
3. Prepare a bank reconciliation for August.
4. Give any journal entries that the company should make as a result of the bank reconciliation. Why are they necessary?
5. After the reconciliation journal entries are posted, what balances would be reflected in the cash accounts in the ledger?
6. What total amount of cash should be reported on the August 31, 2004, balance sheet?

(Chapter Supplement A) Recording Sales, Returns, and Bad Debts   **P6-11**

Use the data presented in P6-2, which was selected from the records of May Company for the year ended December 31, 2005.

Required:
1. Give the journal entries for these transactions, including the write-off of the uncollectible account and the adjusting entry for estimated bad debts. Do not record cost of goods sold. Show computations for each entry.
2. Show how the accounts related to the preceding sale and collection activities should be reported on the 2005 income statement. (Treat sales discounts as a contra-revenue.)

ALTERNATE **PROBLEMS**

Reporting Net Sales and Expenses with Discounts, Returns, and Bad Debts (P6-2)   **AP6-1**
                                                                                        LO2, 4
The following data were selected from the records of Fluwars Company for the year ended December 31, 2004.

Balances January 1, 2004:	
Accounts receivable (various customers)	$97,000
Allowance for doubtful accounts	5,000

In the following order, except for cash sales, the company sold merchandise and made collections on credit terms 3/10, n/30 (assume a unit sales price of $400 in all transactions and use the gross method to record sales revenue).

Transactions during 2004

a. Sold merchandise for cash, $122,000.

b. Sold merchandise to Abbey Corp; invoice price, $6,800.

c. Sold merchandise to Brown Company; invoice price, $14,000.

d. Abbey paid the invoice in (*b*) within the discount period.

e. Sold merchandise to Cavendish Inc; invoice price, $12,400.

f. Two days after paying the account in full, Abbey returned four defective units and received a cash refund.

g. Collected $78,000 cash from customer sales on credit in prior year, all within the discount periods.

h. Three days after purchase date, Brown returned two of the units purchased in (*c*) and received account credit.

i. Brown paid its account in full within the discount period.

j. Sold merchandise to Decca Corporation; invoice price, $9,000.

k. Cavendish paid its account in full after the discount period.

l. Wrote off a 2003 account of $1,600 after deciding that the amount would never be collected.

m. The estimated bad debt rate used by the company was 2 percent of credit sales net of returns.

Required:

1. Using the following categories, indicate the effect of each listed transaction, including the write-off of the uncollectible account and the adjusting entry for estimated bad debts (ignore cost of goods sold).

Sales Revenue	Sales Discounts (taken)	Sales Returns and Allowances	Bad Debt Expense

2. Show how the accounts related to the preceding sale and collection activities should be reported on the 2004 income statement. (Treat sales discounts as a contra-revenue.)

AP6-2
LO4
Saucony, Inc.

Interpreting Disclosure of Allowance for Doubtful Accounts (P6-4)

Under various registered brand names, Saucony, Inc., and its subsidiaries develop, manufacture, and market bicycles and component parts, athletic apparel, and athletic shoes. It recently disclosed the following information concerning the allowance for doubtful accounts on its Form 10-K Annual Report submitted to the Securities and Exchange Commission.

SCHEDULE II
Valuation and Qualifying Accounts
(dollars in thousands)

Allowances for Doubtful Accounts and Discounts	Balance at Beginning of Year	Additions Charged to Costs and Expenses	Deductions from Reserve	Balance at End of Year
Year 3	$2,032	$4,908	$5,060	(?)
Year 2	1,234	(?)	4,677	$2,032
Year 1	940	5,269	(?)	1,234

Required:

1. Record summary journal entries related to bad debts for Year 3.
2. Supply the missing dollar amounts noted by (?) for Year 1, Year 2, and Year 3.

AP6-3
LO4

Determining Bad Debt Expense Based on Aging Analysis (P6-5)

Briggs & Stratton Engines Inc. uses the aging approach to estimate bad debt expense at the end of each accounting year. Credit sales occur frequently on terms n/45. The balance of each account receivable is aged on the basis of four time periods as follows: (1) not yet due, (2) up to 6 months past due, (3) 6 to 12 months past due, and (4) more than one year past due. Experience has shown that for each age group, the average loss rate on the amount of the receivable at year-end due to uncollectability is (a) 1 percent, (b) 5 percent, (c) 20 percent, and (d) 50 percent.

At December 31, 2006 (end of the current accounting year), the Accounts Receivable balance was $39,500, and the Allowance for Doubtful Accounts balance was $1,550 (credit). To simplify, only five customer accounts are used; the details of each on December 31, 2006, follow:

Date	Explanation	Debit	Credit	Balance
R. DEVENS—ACCOUNT RECEIVABLE				
3/13/2006	Sale	19,000		19,000
5/12/2006	Collection		10,000	9,000
9/30/2006	Collection		7,000	2,000
C. HOWARD—ACCOUNT RECEIVABLE				
11/01/2005	Sale	31,000		31,000
06/01/2005	Collection		20,000	11,000
12/01/2006	Collection		5,000	6,000
D. MCCLAIN—ACCOUNT RECEIVABLE				
10/31/2006	Sale	12,000		12,000
12/10/2006	Collection		8,000	4,000
T. SKIBINSKI—ACCOUNT RECEIVABLE				
05/02/2006	Sale	15,000		15,000
06/01/2006	Sale	10,000		25,000
06/15/2006	Collection		15,000	10,000
07/15/2006	Collection		10,000	0
10/01/2006	Sale	26,000		26,000
11/15/2006	Collection		16,000	10,000
12/15/2006	Sale	4,500		14,500
H. WU—ACCOUNT RECEIVABLE				
12/30/2006	Sale	13,000		13,000

Required:

1. Compute the total accounts receivable in each age category.
2. Compute the estimated uncollectible amount for each age category and in total.
3. Give the adjusting entry for bad debt expense at December 31, 2006.
4. Show how the amounts related to accounts receivable should be presented on the 2006 income statement and balance sheet.

Preparing a Multiple-Step Income Statement and Computing the Gross Profit Percentage with Discounts, Returns, and Bad Debts (P6-6)

AP6-4
LO2, 3, 4

Big Tommy Corporation is a local grocery store organized seven years ago as a corporation. At that time, 6,000 shares of common stock were issued to the three organizers. The store is in an excellent location, and sales have increased each year. At the end of 2009, the bookkeeper prepared the following statement (assume that all amounts are correct; note the incorrect terminology and format):

BIG TOMMY CORPORATION Profit and Loss December 31, 2009		
	Debit	Credit
Sales		$420,000
Cost of goods sold	$279,000	
Sales returns and allowances	10,000	
Selling expense	58,000	
Administrative and general expense	16,000	
Bad debt expense	1,000	
Sales discounts	6,000	
Income tax expense	15,000	
Net profit	35,000	
Totals	$420,000	$420,000

Required:

1. Beginning with the amount of net sales, prepare a multiple-step income statement (showing both gross profit and income from operations). Treat sales discounts as an expense.
2. Compute the gross profit percentage and explain its meaning.

AP6-5
LO6
Computing Outstanding Checks and Deposits in Transit and Preparing a Bank Reconciliation and Journal Entries (P6-10)

The December 31, 2004, bank statement for Packer Company and the December 2004 ledger accounts for cash follow.

BANK STATEMENT			
Date	Checks	Deposits	Balance
Dec. 1			$48,000
2	$400; 300	$17,000	64,300
4	7,000; 90		57,210
6	120; 180; 1,600		55,310
11	500; 1,200; 70	28,000	81,540
13	480; 700; 1,900		78,460
17	12,000; 8,000		58,460
23	60; 23,500	36,000	70,900
26	900; 2,650		67,350
28	2,200; 5,200		59,950
30	17,000; 1,890; 300*	19,000	59,760
31	1,650; 1,350; 150†	5,250‡	61,860

*NSF check, J. Left, a customer.
†Bank service charge.
‡Interest collected.

Cash (A)				
Dec. 1 Balance	64,100	Checks written during December:		
Deposits		60	5,000	2,650
Dec.11	28,000	17,000	5,200	1,650
23	36,000	700	1,890	2,200
30	19,000	3,300	1,600	7,000
31	13,000	1,350	120	300
		180	90	480
		12,000	23,500	8,000
		70	500	1,900
		900	1,200	

Cash on hand (A)	
Dec. 31 Balance	300

The November 2004 bank reconciliation showed the following: correct cash balance at November 30, $64,100; deposits in transit on November 30, $17,000; and outstanding checks on November 30, $400 + $500 = $900.

Required:

1. Compute the deposits in transit December 31, 2004.
2. Compute the outstanding checks at December 31, 2004.
3. Prepare a bank reconciliation at December 31, 2004.
4. Give any journal entries that should be made as a result of the bank reconciliation made by the company. Why are they necessary?
5. After the reconciliation journal entries, what balances would be reflected in the cash accounts in the ledger?
6. What total amount of cash should be reported on the December 31, 2004, balance sheet?

CASES AND PROJECTS

Annual Report Cases

Finding Financial Information

Refer to the financial statements of American Eagle Outfitters given in Appendix B at the end of this book, or open file AEOS.pdf in the Annual Report Cases directory on the student CD-ROM.

Required:

1. How much cash and cash equivalents does the company report at the end of the current year?
2. Does the company report an allowance for doubtful accounts on the balance sheet or in the notes? Explain why it does or does not. (*Hint:* Consider the makeup of its receivables.)
3. Compute the company's gross profit percentage for the most recent two years. Has it risen or fallen? Explain the meaning of the change.
4. Where does the company disclose its revenue recognition policy? When does the company record revenues for the "sale" of stored value cards and gift certificates?

CP6-1
LO1, 3, 4, 6

AMERICAN EAGLE OUTFITTERS

Finding Financial Information

Refer to the financial statements of Abercrombie & Fitch given in Appendix C at the end of this book, or open file ANF.pdf in the Annual Report Cases directory on the student CD-ROM.

Required:

1. What does the company include in its category of cash and cash equivalents? How close do you think the disclosed amount is to actual fair market value?
2. What expenses does Abercrombie & Fitch subtract from net sales in the computation of gross profit? How does this differ from Timberland's practice and how might it affect the manner in which you interpret the gross profit percentage?
3. Compute Abercrombie & Fitch's receivables turnover ratio for the year ended February 3, 2001. What characteristics of its business might cause it to be so high?
4. What was the change in accounts receivable and how did it affect net cash provided by operating activities for the current year?

CP6-2
LO2, 5, 6

ABERCROMBIE & FITCH

Comparing Companies within an Industry

Refer to the financial statements of American Eagle Outfitters given in Appendix B, Abercrombie & Fitch given in Appendix C, and the Industry Ratio Report given in Appendix D at the end of this book or open file CP6-3.xls in the Annual Report Cases directory on the student CD-ROM.

CP6-3
LO3, 5

AMERICAN EAGLE OUTFITTERS

ABERCROMBIE
&
FITCH

Required:

1. Compute gross profit percentage for both companies for the current and previous years. Does the respective Management's Discussion and Analysis suggest a reason that their gross profit percentage might be lower than the previous year?
2. Knowing that these two companies are specialty or niche retailers compared to some others in their industry (see the list of companies used in the Industry Ratio Report), do you expect their gross profit percentage to be higher or lower than the industry average? Why?
3. Compare the gross profit percentage for each company for the current year to the industry average. Are these two companies doing better or worse than the industry average? Does this match your expectations from requirement (2)?
4. On January 30, 1999, Abercrombie & Fitch's balance in Accounts Receivable (net) was $4,101,000. Compute its accounts receivable turnover ratio for the most current two years. What accounts for its change?

Financial Reporting and Analysis Cases

CP6-4

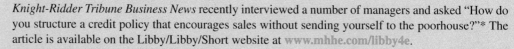

Knight-Ridder Tribune
Business News

Interpreting the Financial Press

Knight-Ridder Tribune Business News recently interviewed a number of managers and asked "How do you structure a credit policy that encourages sales without sending yourself to the poorhouse?"* The article is available on the Libby/Libby/Short website at www.mhhe.com/libby4e.

Required:

Read the article, organize the recommendations into categories, and write a short memo outlining the key recommended steps.

CP6-5
LO4, 5

Foster's Brewing

Using Financial Reports: International Bad Debt Disclosure

Foster's Brewing controls more than 50 percent of the beer market in Australia and owns 40 percent of Molson Breweries of Canada and 100 percent of Courage Limited of the United Kingdom. As an Australian company, it follows Australian GAAP and uses Australian accounting terminology. In the footnotes to its recent annual report, it discloses the information on receivables (all numbers are reported in thousands of Australian dollars).

Note 3: Receivables	Year 2	Year 1
Current		
Trade debtors	792,193	999,159
Provision for doubtful debts	(121,449)	(238,110)
Other debtors	192,330	130,288
Provision for doubtful debts	(384)	(2,464)
Non-current		
Trade debtors	164,808	200,893
Other debtors	15,094	16,068
Provision for doubtful debts	(7,920)	(7,400)
Note 15: Operation Profit	**Year 2**	**Year 1**
Amounts set aside to provisions for		
Doubtful debts—trade debtors	(21,143)	(53,492)
Doubtful debts—other debtors	(228)	(2,570)

*Barbara Pletcher, "Debt Service: If you don't collect the money, it's hard to pay the bills," *Knight-Ridder Tribune Business News*, 2001. Reprinted with permission of Tribune Media Services.

Required:

1. The account titles used by Foster's are different from those normally used by U.S. companies. What account titles does it use in place of Allowance for Doubtful Accounts and Bad Debt Expense?

2. Sales on account for Year 2 were $9,978,875. Compute the accounts receivable (trade debtors) turnover ratio for Year 1 (ignore uncollectible accounts).

3. Compute the provision for doubtful debts as a percentage of current receivables separately for receivables from trade debtors and receivables from others. Explain why these percentages might be different.

4. What was the total amount of receivables written off in Year 2?

Critical Thinking Cases

Making Decisions as an Independent CPA

CP6-6
LO6

Lane Manufacturing Company is a relatively small local business that specializes in the repair and renovation of antique furniture. The owner is an expert craftsperson. Although a number of skilled workers are employed, there is always a large backlog of work to be done. A long-time employee who serves as clerk-bookkeeper handles cash receipts, keeps the records, and writes checks for disbursements. The owner signs the checks. The clerk-bookkeeper pays small amounts in cash, subject to a month-end review by the owner. Approximately 80 regular customers are extended credit that typically amounts to less than $1,000. Although credit losses are small, in recent years the bookkeeper had established an allowance for doubtful accounts, and all write-offs were made at year-end. During January 2007 (the current year), the owner decided to start as soon as possible the construction of a building for the business that would provide many advantages over the presently rented space and would have space to expand facilities. As a part of the considerations in financing, the financing institution asked for 2006 audited financial statements. The company statements never had been audited. Early in the audit, the independent CPA found numerous errors and one combination of amounts, in particular, that caused concern.

There was some evidence that a $2,500 job completed by Lane had been recorded as a receivable (from a new customer) on July 15, 2006. The receivable was credited for a $2,500 cash collection a few days later. The new account never was active again. The auditor also observed that shortly thereafter, three write-offs of accounts receivable balances had been made to Allowance for Doubtful Accounts as follows: Jones, $800; Blake, $750; and Sellers, $950—all of whom were known as regular customers. These write-offs drew the attention of the auditor.

Required:

1. Explain what caused the CPA to be concerned. Should the CPA report the suspicions to the owner?

2. What recommendations would you make with respect to internal control procedures for this company?

Making a Decision as a Manager: Choosing among Alternative Recognition Points

CP6-7
LO1
UPS,
Federal Express,
and Airborne

UPS, Federal Express, and Airborne are three of the major players in the highly competitive package delivery industry. Comparability is a key qualitative characteristic of accounting numbers that allows analysts to compare similar companies. The revenue recognition footnotes of the three competitors reveal three different revenue recognition points for package delivery revenue: package delivery, percentage of service completed, and package pickup. These points correspond to the end, continuous recognition, and the beginning of the earnings process.

UNITED PARCEL SERVICE OF AMERICA, INC.

Revenue is recognized upon delivery of a package.

FEDERAL EXPRESS CORPORATION

Revenue is generally recognized upon delivery of shipments. For shipments in transit, revenue is recorded based on the percentage of service completed.

AIRBORNE FREIGHT CORP.

Domestic revenues and most domestic operating expenses are recognized when shipments are picked up from the customer. . . .

The Airborne footnote goes on to say, however: "The net revenue resulting from existing recognition policies does not materially differ from that which would be recognized on a delivery date basis."

Required:

1. Do you believe that the difference between Airborne's and UPS's revenue recognition policies materially affects their reported earnings? Why or why not?
2. Assume that all three companies pick up packages from customers and receive payment of $1 million for services each day of the year and that each package is delivered the next day. What would each company's service revenue for a year be given its stated revenue recognition policy?
3. Given your answers to requirement (2), under what conditions would that answer change?
4. Which revenue recognition rule would you prefer as a manager? Why?

CP6-8
LO1
Platinum
Software

Evaluating an Ethical Dilemma: Management Incentives, Revenue Recognition, and Sales with the Right of Return

Platinum Software was a fast-growing maker of accounting software. According to the federal charges, when business slowed and the company was unable to meet the stock market's expectation for continued growth, the former chairman and CEO (the company's founder), former CFO, and former controller responded by improperly recording revenue and allowances for returns resulting in overstatement of net income by $18 million. The three recently settled both federal charges brought by the SEC and a shareholder suit by paying nearly $2.8 million in restitution and fines and being suspended from practice for differing periods. The exact nature of the fraud is described in the following excerpt:

Three Ex-Officers of O.C. Software Firm Sanctioned; SEC:

Platinum founder Gerald Blackie agrees to 10-year ban as officer of public company to settle suit over falsifying books. Two other former executives are fined.

JOHN O'DELL TIMES STAFF WRITER
Los Angeles Times Orange County Edition 5/10/96

. . .

The SEC suit charged that Blackie, Tague and Erickson began falsifying sales records in 1993 and early 1994 in order to pump up Platinum's quarterly sales figures and make the company's financial situation appear stronger than it was.

For a period of at least nine months, ending early in 1994, the men backdated sales orders and reported as actual revenue fees that had not yet been received and were subject to secret cancellation agreements that the customers often exercised, the suit said.

In one case in 1993, the suit alleges, Blackie personally closed a $1.5-million software licensing deal with the Wackenhut Corp. on the day the fiscal year ended. He also executed a separate letter giving Wackenhut a 60-day right to cancel. Blackie then instructed Erickson to enter the $1.5 million as revenue in the just-completed fiscal year, even though the money had not been received.

Wackenhut later canceled the contract, the suit says, but Platinum did not disclose the cancellation or adjust for it when it later filed its annual report with the SEC.

In August 1993, with the company's stock price rising on the strength of the falsified financial reports, Blackie, Tague, and Erickson all sold large amounts of stock. Blackie profited again with a stock sale in November 1993, the SEC suit says. After the company revealed the accounting irregularities and announced Blackie's resignation in April 1994, the stock price plummeted 64 percent.

The suit also says Blackie received $128,125 in performance bonuses for the nine-month period in which he was falsifying financial reports; Erickson got $50,000 and Tague received $6,000. "If they had been any lower in the company they would never have gotten away with this for as long as they did," said SEC attorney Nathan.

John O'Dell. "Three Ex-Officers of O.C. Software Firm Sanctioned." *Los Angeles Times Orange County Edition,* May 10, 1996.

Required:
1. What facts, if any, presented in the article suggest that Platinum violated the revenue principle?
2. Assuming that Platinum did recognize revenue when contracts were signed, how could it have properly accounted for the fact that customers had a right to cancel the contracts (make an analogy with accounting for bad debts)?
3. What do you think may have motivated management to falsify the statements? Why was management concerned with reporting continued growth in net income?
4. Explain who was hurt by management's unethical conduct.
5. Assume that you are the auditor for other software licensing firms. After reading about the fraud, what types of transactions would you pay special attention to in the audit of your clients in this industry?

Financial Reporting and Analysis Team Project

Team Project: Analyzing Revenues and Receivables

CP6-9
LO1,4,5

As a team, select an industry to analyze (industry lists can be found at www.marketguide.com/mgi/INDUSTRY/INDUSTRY.html and www.hoovers.com; click on companies and industries). Each team member should acquire the annual report or 10-K for one publicly traded company in the industry, with each member selecting a different company. (Library files, the SEC EDGAR service at www.sec.gov, Compustat CD, or the company websites are good sources.) On an individual basis, each team member should then write a short report answering the following questions about the selected company.

1. What specific revenue recognition rule does the company follow?
2. What is the receivables turnover ratio?
3. If the 10-K is available, determine what additional disclosures are available concerning the allowance for doubtful accounts. If the necessary information is provided, what is bad debt expense as a percentage of sales?
4. What was the effect of the change in accounts receivable on cash flows from operations? Explain your answer.

Discuss any patterns across the companies that you as a team observe. Then, as a group, write a short report comparing and contrasting your companies using these attributes. Provide potential explanations for any differences discovered.

Reporting and Interpreting Cost of Goods Sold and Inventory

CHAPTER

7

The Harley-Davidson eagle trademark was once known best as a popular request in tattoo parlors. Now, as the company celebrates its one-hundredth anniversary, the stunning popularity of its products has created a problem that most other companies envy. Though the Milwaukee-based company has more than doubled motorcycle production in the last six years, meeting increases in customer demand is still difficult. Many of its motorcycle models sell out a year in advance. Harley has also dramatically expanded its riding and fashion apparel lines and programs to provide insurance and financing services to dealers and customers.

To close the gap between supply and demand for its products, Harley-Davidson continues to expand its production facilities in Wisconsin, Missouri, and Pennsylvania. However, increasing production numbers is only part of Harley's strategy. It is introducing new products to stay ahead of major competitors Honda, Yamaha, and BMW. It also focuses on controlling inventory quality and cost to maintain gross profit margin. Empowering, educating, and training both salaried and unionized employees; establishing long-term, mutually beneficial relationships with its suppliers; and developing accounting information systems that provide accurate and timely inventory information are keys to many of these efforts. Furthermore, selection of appropriate accounting methods for inventory can have a dramatic effect on the amount Harley-Davidson pays in income taxes. Continuous improvement in product development, manufacturing, inventory management, and information system design will be necessary for the Harley-Davidson eagle to continue its rise.

FOCUS COMPANY

Harley-Davidson, Inc.

FROM TURMOIL TO TRIUMPH AS A WORLD-CLASS MANUFACTURER

www.harley-davidson.com

UNDERSTANDING THE BUSINESS

Concerns about the cost and quality of inventory face all modern manufacturers and merchandisers and turn our attention to **cost of goods sold** (cost of sales, cost of products sold) on the income statement and **inventory** on the balance sheet. Exhibit 7.1

EXHIBIT 7.1

Income Statement and
Balance Sheet Excerpts

REAL WORLD EXCERPT

HARLEY-
DAVIDSON,
INC.

ANNUAL REPORT

HARLEY-DAVIDSON, INC.
Consolidated Statements of Income
(in thousands, except per share amounts)

Years Ended December 31,	2000	1999	1998
Net sales	$2,906,365	$2,452,939	$2,063,956
Cost of goods sold	1,915,547	1,617,253	1,373,286
Gross profit	990,818	835,686	690,670

HARLEY-DAVIDSON, INC.
Consolidated Balance Sheets
(in thousands, except share amounts)

December 31,	2000	1999
ASSETS		
Current Assets		
Cash and cash equivalents	$ 419,736	$183,415
Accounts receivable, net	98,311	101,708
Finance receivables, net	530,859	440,951
Inventories	191,931	168,616
Deferred income taxes	28,280	29,434
Prepaid expenses	28,147	24,870
Total current assets	1,297,264	948,994

presents the relevant excerpts from Harley-Davidson's financial statements that include these accounts. Note that Cost of Goods Sold is subtracted from Net Sales to produce gross profit on its income statement. On the balance sheet, Inventory is a current asset; it is reported below Cash and Accounts Receivable because it is less liquid than those assets.

The primary goals of inventory management are to have sufficient quantities of high-quality inventory available to serve customers' needs while minimizing the costs of carrying inventory (production, storage, obsolescence, and financing). Low quality leads to customer dissatisfaction, returns, and a decline in future sales. Also, purchasing or producing too few units of a hot-selling item causes stock-outs that mean lost sales revenue and decreases in customer satisfaction. Conversely, purchasing too many units of a slow-selling item increases storage costs as well as interest costs on short-term borrowings that finance the purchases. It may even lead to losses if the merchandise cannot be sold at normal prices.

The accounting system plays three roles in the inventory management process. First, the system must provide accurate information for preparation of periodic financial statements and tax returns. Second, it must provide up-to-date information on inventory

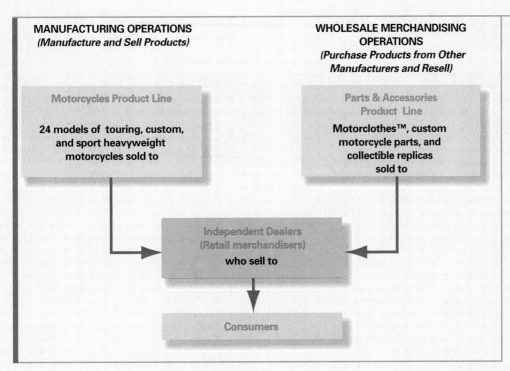

EXHIBIT 7.2

Harley-Davidson Motorcycle Division Product Lines

quantities and costs to facilitate ordering and manufacturing decisions. Third, since inventories are subject to theft and other forms of misuse, the system must also provide the information needed to help protect these important assets.

Harley's successful production and inventory management strategy and its mix of product lines (see Exhibit 7.2) make it a particularly good example for this chapter. Although best known as a **manufacturer** of motorcycles, Harley also purchases and resells completed products such as its popular line of Motorclothes™ apparel. In the second case, it acts as a **wholesaler.** Both the motorcycle and Motorclothes product lines are sold to their network of independent dealers. From an accounting standpoint, these independent dealers are Harley-Davidson's customers. The independent dealers are the **retailers** who sell the products to the public.

First we discuss the makeup of inventory, the important choices management must make in the financial and tax reporting process, and how these choices affect taxes paid. Then we will discuss how managers and analysts evaluate the efficiency of inventory management. Finally, we will briefly discuss how accounting systems are organized to keep track of inventory quantities and costs for decision making and control. This topic will be the principal subject matter of your managerial accounting course.

ORGANIZATION of the Chapter

Nature of Inventory and Cost of Goods Sold	Inventory Costing Methods	Valuation at Lower of Cost or Market	Evaluating Inventory Management	Control of Inventory

Nature of Inventory and Cost of Goods Sold
- Items Included in Inventory
- Flow of Inventory Costs
- Nature of Cost of Goods Sold

Inventory Costing Methods
- Specific Identification Method
- Cost Flow Assumptions (FIFO, LIFO, Weighted Average)
- Financial Statement Effects of Inventory Methods
- Managers' Choice of Inventory Methods
- Inventory Methods and Financial Statement Analysis

Evaluating Inventory Management
- Measuring Efficiency in Inventory Management
- Inventory Turnover Ratio
- Inventory and Cash Flows

Control of Inventory
- Errors in Measuring Ending Inventory
- Perpetual and Periodic Inventory Systems

NATURE OF INVENTORY AND COST OF GOODS SOLD

Items Included in Inventory

Learning Objective 1
Apply the cost principle to identify the amounts that should be included in inventory and the matching principle to determine cost of goods sold for typical retailers, wholesalers, and manufacturers.

Inventory is tangible property that is (1) held for sale in the normal course of business or (2) used to produce goods or services for sale. Inventory is reported on the balance sheet as a current asset because it normally is used or converted into cash within one year or the next operating cycle. Goods in inventory are initially recorded at cost, which is the price paid or consideration given to acquire the asset. Inventory cost includes the sum of the costs incurred in bringing an article to usable or salable condition and location. The types of inventory normally held depend on the characteristics of the business.

INVENTORY is tangible property held for sale in the normal course of business or used in producing goods or services for sale.

Merchandisers (wholesale or retail businesses) hold the following:

Merchandise inventory Goods (or merchandise) held for resale in the normal course of business. The goods usually are acquired in a finished condition and are ready for sale without further processing.

MERCHANDISE INVENTORY
includes goods held for resale in the ordinary course of business.

For Harley-Davidson, merchandise inventory includes the Motorclothes line and the parts and accessories it purchases for sale to its independent dealers.

Manufacturing businesses hold three types of inventory:

Raw materials inventory Items acquired for processing into finished goods. These items are included in raw materials inventory until they are used, at which point they become part of work in process inventory.

Work in process inventory Goods in the process of being manufactured but not yet complete. When completed, work in process inventory becomes finished goods inventory.

Finished goods inventory Manufactured goods that are complete and ready for sale.

Inventories related to Harley-Davidson's motorcycle manufacturing operations are recorded in these accounts.

Harley-Davidson's recent inventory note reports the following:

RAW MATERIALS INVENTORY includes items acquired for the purpose of processing into finished goods.

WORK IN PROCESS INVENTORY includes goods in the process of being manufactured.

FINISHED GOODS INVENTORY includes manufactured goods that are complete and ready for sale.

REAL WORLD EXCERPT

HARLEY-DAVIDSON, INC.

ANNUAL REPORT

HARLEY-DAVIDSON, INC.

NOTES TO CONSOLIDATED FINANCIAL STATEMENTS

2. ADDITIONAL BALANCE SHEET AND CASH FLOWS INFORMATION
(in thousands)

	December 31,	
	2000	**1999**
Inventories:		
Components at the lower of FIFO cost or market:		
Raw materials and work in process	$73,065	$61,893
Motorcycle finished goods	37,851	29,977
Parts and accessories	99,840	97,422

Note that Harley-Davidson combines the raw materials and work in process into one number. Other companies separate the two components. The parts and accessories category includes purchased parts and Motorclothes and other accessories that make up merchandise inventory.[1]

When Harley-Davidson purchases raw materials and merchandise inventory, the amount recorded should include the invoice price plus other expenditures related to the purchase, such as freight charges to deliver the items to its warehouses (freight-in) and inspection and preparation costs. In general, the company should cease accumulating purchase costs when the raw materials are **ready for use** or when the merchandise inventory is **ready for shipment**. Any additional costs related to selling the merchandise inventory to the dealers, such as marketing department salaries and dealer training sessions, are incurred after the inventory is ready for use. So, they should be included in selling, general, and administrative expenses in the period they are incurred.

Applying the Materiality Constraint in Practice

FINANCIAL ANALYSIS

Incidental costs such as inspection and preparation costs often are not material in amount (see the discussion of the materiality constraint in Chapter 5) and do not have to be assigned to the inventory cost. Thus, for practical reasons, many companies use the invoice price, less returns and discounts, to assign a unit cost to raw materials or merchandise and record other indirect expenditures as a separate cost that is reported as an expense.

---

[1]These do not add up to the balance reported in Exhibit 7.1 because they do not include the LIFO adjustment discussed later.

Flow of Inventory Costs

The flow of inventory costs for merchandisers (wholesalers and retailers) is relatively simple, as Exhibit 7.3A shows. When merchandise is purchased, the Merchandise Inventory account is increased. When the goods are sold, cost of goods sold is increased and merchandise inventory is decreased.

The flow of inventory costs in a manufacturing environment is more complex, as diagrammed in Exhibit 7.3B. First, **raw materials** (also called direct materials) must be purchased. For Harley-Davidson, these raw materials include steel and aluminum castings, forgings, sheet, and bars, as well as certain motorcycle component parts produced by its small network of suppliers, including carburetors, batteries, and tires. When they are used, the cost of these materials is removed from the raw materials inventory and added to the work in process inventory.

Two other components of manufacturing cost, direct labor and factory overhead, are also added to the work in process inventory when they are used. **Direct labor** cost represents the earnings of employees who work directly on the products being manufactured. **Factory overhead** costs include all other manufacturing costs. For example, the factory supervisor's salary and the cost of heat, light, and power to operate the factory are included in factory overhead. When the motorcycles are completed and ready for sale, the related amounts in work in process inventory are transferred to finished goods inventory. When the finished goods are sold, cost of goods sold increases, and finished goods inventory decreases.

As Exhibit 7.3 indicates, there are three stages to inventory cost flows for both merchandisers and manufacturers. The first involves purchasing and/or production activities. In the second, these activities result in additions to inventory accounts on the balance sheet. In the third stage, the inventory items are sold and the amounts become cost of goods sold expense on the income statement. Since the flow of inventory costs from merchandise inventory and finished goods to cost of goods sold are very similar, we will focus the rest of our discussion on merchandise inventory.

DIRECT LABOR refers to the earnings of employees who work directly on the products being manufactured.

FACTORY OVERHEAD are manufacturing costs that are not raw material or direct labor costs.

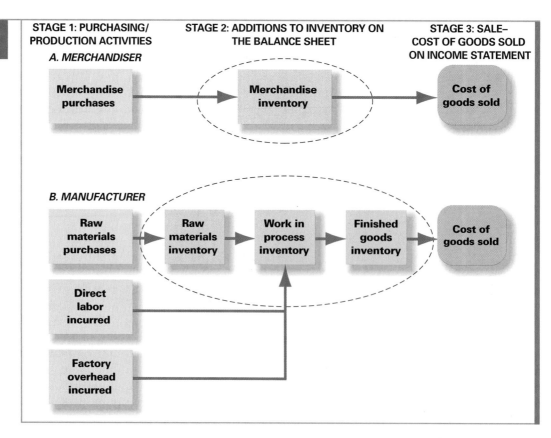

| EXHIBIT 7.3 | STAGE 1: PURCHASING/ PRODUCTION ACTIVITIES | STAGE 2: ADDITIONS TO INVENTORY ON THE BALANCE SHEET | STAGE 3: SALE– COST OF GOODS SOLD ON INCOME STATEMENT |

Flow of Inventory Costs

A. MERCHANDISER

Merchandise purchases → Merchandise inventory → Cost of goods sold

B. MANUFACTURER

Raw materials purchases → Raw materials inventory → Work in process inventory → Finished goods inventory → Cost of goods sold

Direct labor incurred → Work in process inventory

Factory overhead incurred → Work in process inventory

Modern Manufacturing Techniques and Inventory Costs	FINANCIAL ANALYSIS

69,0	0	13
67,000	137,00	
70,000	140,000	13,
48,778	89,678	13,

The flows of inventory costs diagrammed in Exhibit 7.3 represent the keys to manufacturing cost and quality control. Since the company must pay to finance and store raw materials and purchased parts, minimizing the size of these inventories in keeping with projected manufacturing demand is the first key to the process. To do so, Harley-Davidson must work closely with suppliers in design, production, and delivery of manufactured parts and the delivery of raw materials. (This approach to inventory management is called *just in time*.) Review and redesign of manufacturing operations and worker training and involvement programs are the keys to minimizing direct labor and factory overhead costs. New products are often designed to be simpler to manufacture, which improves product quality and reduces scrap and rework costs.

Harley-Davidson's management accounting system is designed to monitor the success of these changes and promote continuous improvements in manufacturing. The design of such systems is the subject matter of management accounting and cost accounting courses.

Nature of Cost of Goods Sold

Cost of goods sold (CGS) expense is directly related to sales revenue. Sales revenue during an accounting period is the number of units sold multiplied by the sales price. Cost of goods sold is the same number of units multiplied by their unit costs.

Let's examine the relationship between cost of goods sold on the income statement and inventory on the balance sheet. Harley-Davidson starts each accounting period with a stock of inventory called **beginning inventory** (BI). During the accounting period, new **purchases** (P) are added to inventory. The sum of the two amounts is the goods available for sale during that period. What remains unsold at the end of the period becomes **ending inventory** (EI) on the balance sheet. The portion of goods available for sale that is sold becomes **cost of goods sold** on the income statement. The ending inventory for one accounting period then becomes the beginning inventory for the next period. The relationships between these various inventory amounts are brought together in the **cost of goods sold equation.**

To illustrate, assume that Harley-Davidson began the period with $40,000 worth of Motorclothes in beginning inventory, purchased additional merchandise during the period for $55,000, and had $35,000 left in inventory at the end of the period. These amounts are combined as follows to compute cost of goods sold of $60,000:

GOODS AVAILABLE FOR SALE refers to the sum of beginning inventory and purchases (or transfers to finished goods) for the period.

COST OF GOODS SOLD EQUATION: $BI + P - EI = CGS$

Beginning inventory	$40,000
+ Purchases of merchandise during the year	55,000
Goods available for sale	95,000
− Ending inventory	35,000
Cost of goods sold	$60,000

These same relationships are illustrated in Exhibit 7.4 and can be represented in the merchandise inventory T-account as follows:

Merchandise Inventory (A)			
Beginning inventory	40,000		
Add: Purchases of inventory	55,000	Deduct: Cost of goods sold	60,000
Ending inventory	35,000		

If three of these four values are known, either the cost of goods sold equation or the inventory T-account can be used to solve for the fourth value.

EXHIBIT 7.4

Cost of Goods Sold for Merchandise Inventory

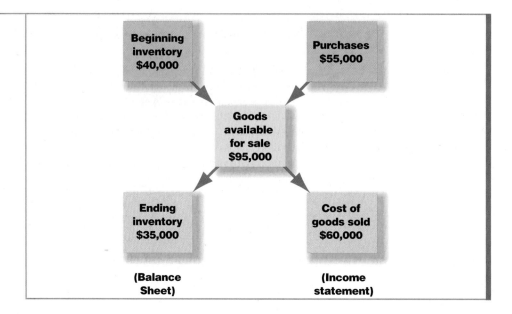

SELF-STUDY QUIZ

Assume the following facts for Harley-Davidson's Motorclothes leather baseball jacket product line for the year 2008:

> Beginning inventory 500 units at unit cost of $75.
> Ending inventory 600 units at unit cost of $75.
> Sales 1,100 units at a sales price of $100 (cost per unit $75).

1. Using the cost of goods sold equation, compute the dollar amount of purchases of leather baseball jackets for the period.

> Beginning inventory
> + Purchases of merchandise during the year
> − Ending inventory
> ————————————————————————
> Cost of goods sold

2. Prepare the first three lines of the income statement (showing computation of gross profit) for the leather baseball jacket line for the year 2008.

After you have completed your answers, check them with the solutions that follow:

1. BI = 500 × $75 = $37,500   BI + P − EI = CGS
   EI = 600 × $75 = $45,000   37,500 + P − 45,000 = 82,500
   CGS = 1,100 × $75 = $82,500   P = 90,000

2. Net sales $110,000
   Cost of goods sold   82,500
   Gross profit $ 27,500

Learning Objective 2
Report inventory and cost of goods sold using the four inventory costing methods.

INVENTORY COSTING METHODS

In the Motorclothes example presented in the Self-Study Quiz, the cost of all units of the leather baseball jackets was the same—$75. If inventory costs normally did not change, this would be the end of our discussion. As we are all aware, the prices of most goods do change. In recent years, the costs of many manufactured items such as automobiles and motorcycles have risen moderately. In some industries such as computers, costs of production have dropped dramatically along with retail prices.

When inventory costs have changed, which inventory items are treated as sold or remaining in inventory can turn profits into losses and cause companies to pay or save hundreds of millions of dollars in taxes. A simple example will illustrate these dramatic effects. Do not let the simplicity of our example mislead you. It applies broadly to actual company practices.

Assume that a Harley-Davidson shop made the following purchases:

Jan. 1 Had beginning inventory of 2 units of a Model A leather jacket at $70 each.

March 12 Purchased 4 units of Model A leather jacket at $80 each.

June 9 Purchased 1 unit of Model A leather jacket at $100 each.

Nov. 5 Sold 4 units for $120 each.

Note that **cost of the leather jackets rose** rapidly between January and June! On November 5, four units are sold for $120 each and revenues of $480 are recorded. What amount is recorded as cost of goods sold? The answer depends on which specific goods we assume are sold. Four generally accepted inventory costing methods are available for doing so:

1. Specific identification.

2. First-in, first-out (FIFO).

3. Last-in, first-out (LIFO).

4. Weighted average.

The four inventory costing methods are alternative ways to assign the total dollar amount of goods available for sale between (1) ending inventory and (2) cost of goods sold. The first method identifies individual items that remain in inventory or are sold. The remaining three methods assume that the inventory follow a certain physical flow.

Specific Identification Method

When the **specific identification method** is used, the cost of each item sold is individually identified and recorded as cost of goods sold. This method requires keeping track of the purchase cost of each item. This is done by either (1) coding the purchase cost on each unit before placing it in stock or (2) keeping a separate record of the unit and identifying it with a serial number. In the leather jacket example, any four of the items could have been sold. If we assume that one of the $70 items, two of the $80 items, and the one $100 item have been sold, the cost of those items ($70 + $80 + $80 + $100) would become cost of goods sold ($330). The cost of the remaining items would be ending inventory.

The specific identification method is impractical when large quantities of similar items are stocked. On the other hand, when dealing with expensive unique items such as houses or fine jewelry, this method is appropriate. This method may also be manipulated when the units are identical because one can affect the cost of goods sold and the ending inventory accounts by picking and choosing from among the several available unit costs. As a consequence, most inventory items are accounted for using one of three cost flow assumptions.

The **SPECIFIC IDENTIFICATION METHOD** identifies the cost of the specific item that was sold.

Cost Flow Assumptions

The **choice of an inventory costing method is not based on the physical flow of goods** on and off the shelves. That is why they are called **cost flow assumptions.** A useful tool for representing inventory cost flow assumptions is a bin, or container. Try

Topic Tackler 7–1

visualizing these inventory costing methods as flows of inventory in and out of the bin. Following practice, we will apply the methods **as if** all purchases during the period take place before any sales and cost of goods sold are recorded.

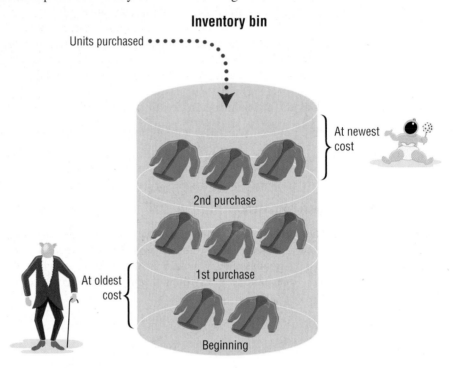

Inventory bin

First-In, First-Out Method

The **FIRST-IN, FIRST-OUT (FIFO) METHOD** assumes that the first goods purchased (the first in) are the first goods sold.

First-In, First-Out Method

The **first-in, first-out method,** frequently called **FIFO,** assumes that the earliest goods purchased (the first ones in) are the first goods sold, and the last goods purchased are left in ending inventory. Under FIFO, cost of goods sold and ending inventory are computed as if the flows in and out of the FIFO inventory bin in Exhibit 7.5 had taken place. First, each purchase is treated as if it were deposited in the bin from the top in sequence (two units at $70 followed by four units at $80, and one unit at $100) producing goods available for sale of $560. Each good sold is then removed from the **bottom** in sequence (two units at $70 and two at $80); **first in is first out.** These goods totaling $300 become cost of goods sold (CGS). The remaining units (two units at $80 and one at $100 = $260) become ending inventory. FIFO allocates the **oldest** unit costs **to cost of goods sold** and the **newest** unit costs **to ending inventory.**

The **LAST-IN, FIRST-OUT (LIFO) METHOD** assumes that the most recently purchased units (the last in) are sold first.

Last-In, First-Out Method

The **last-in, first-out method,** often called **LIFO,** assumes that the most recently purchased goods (the last ones in) are sold first and the oldest units are left in ending inventory. It is illustrated by the LIFO inventory bin in Exhibit 7.5. As in FIFO, each purchase is treated as if it were deposited in the bin from the top (two units at $70 followed by four units at $80, and one unit at $100) resulting in the goods available for sale of $560. Unlike FIFO, however, each good sold is treated as if it were removed from the top in sequence (one unit at $100 followed by three units at $80). These goods totaling $340 become cost of goods sold (CGS). The remaining units (one at $80 and two at $70) become ending inventory. LIFO allocates the **newest** unit costs **to cost of goods sold** and the **oldest** unit costs **to ending inventory.** The LIFO flow assumption is the exact opposite of the FIFO flow assumption:

	FIFO	LIFO
Cost of goods sold on income statement	Oldest unit costs	Newest unit costs
Inventory on balance sheet	Newest unit costs	Oldest unit costs

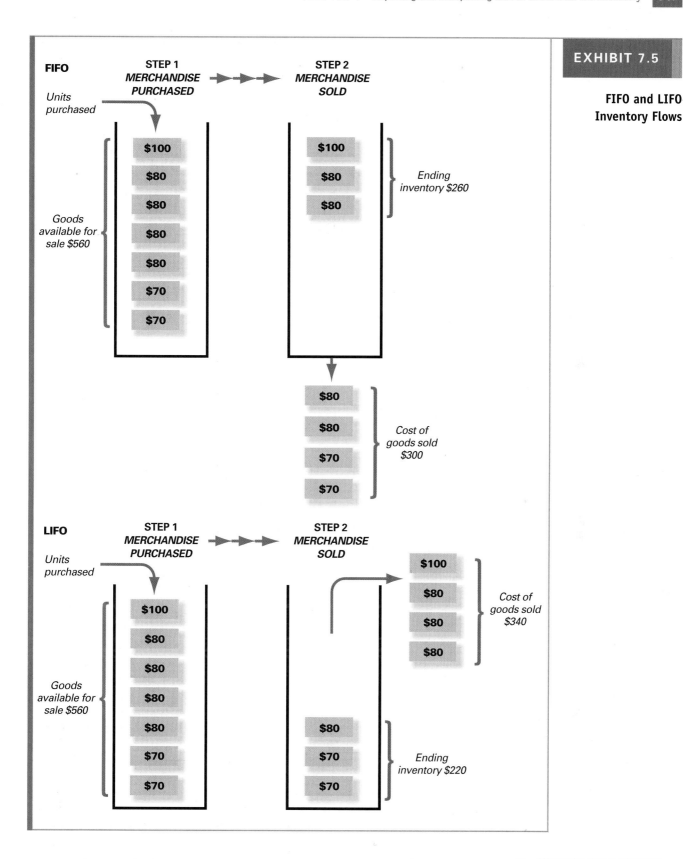

EXHIBIT 7.5

FIFO and LIFO Inventory Flows

Average Cost Method

The **average cost method** uses the weighted average unit cost of the goods available for sale for both cost of goods sold and ending inventory. The weighted average unit cost of the goods available for sale is computed as follows.

The **AVERAGE COST METHOD** uses the weighted average unit cost of the goods available for sale for both cost of goods sold and ending inventory.

EXHIBIT 7.6

Average Cost Inventory Flows

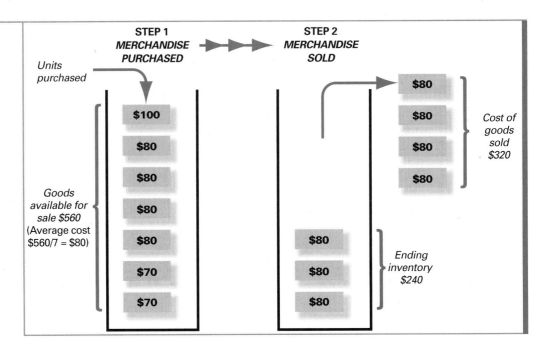

$$\text{Number of Units} \times \text{Unit Cost} = \text{Total Cost}$$

Number of Units		Unit Cost		Total Cost
2	×	$70	=	$140
4	×	$80	=	320
1	×	$100	=	100
7				$560

$$\text{Average Cost} = \frac{\text{Cost of Goods Available for Sale}}{\text{Number of Units Available for Sale}}$$

$$\text{Average Cost} = \frac{\$560}{7 \text{ Units}} = \$80 \text{ per Unit}$$

Cost of goods sold and ending inventory are assigned the same weighted average cost per unit of $80.

$$\text{Cost of Goods Sold} = 4 \text{ units} \times \$80 = \$320$$

$$\text{Ending Inventory} = 3 \text{ units} \times \$80 = \$240$$

These flows are illustrated in Exhibit 7.6.

Financial Statement Effects of Inventory Methods

Each of the four alternative inventory costing methods is in conformity with GAAP and the tax law. To understand why managers choose different methods in different circumstances, we must first understand their effects on the income statement and balance sheet. Exhibit 7.7 summarizes the financial statement effects of FIFO, LIFO, and weighted average methods in our example. Remember that the methods differ only in the portion of goods available for sale allocated to cost of goods sold versus ending inventory. For that reason, the method that gives the highest ending inventory amount also gives the lowest cost of goods sold and the highest gross profit, income tax expense, and income amounts, and vice versa. The weighted average cost method gives income and inventory amounts that are between the FIFO and LIFO extremes.

In the comparison in Exhibit 7.7, unit costs were increasing. **When unit costs are rising, LIFO produces lower income and a lower inventory valuation than FIFO.** Even in inflationary times, some companies' costs decline. **When unit costs are**

	FIFO	LIFO	Weighted Average
Cost of Goods Sold Calculation			
Beginning inventory	$140	$140	$140
Add: Purchases	420	420	420
Goods available for sale	560	560	560
Subtract: Ending inventory (to balance sheet)	260	220	240
Cost of goods sold (to income statement)	$300	$340	$320
Effect on the Income Statement			
Sales	$480	$480	$480
Cost of goods sold	300	340	320
Gross profit	180	140	160
Other expenses	80	80	80
Income before income taxes	100	60	80
Income tax expense (25%)	25	15	20
Net income	$ 75	$ 45	$ 60
Effect on the Balance Sheet			
Inventory	$260	$220	$240

EXHIBIT 7.7

Financial Statement Effects of Inventory Costing Methods

declining, **LIFO produces higher income and higher inventory valuation than FIFO.** These effects, which hold as long as inventory quantities are constant or rising,[2] are summarized in the following table:

Normal Financial Statement Effects of Increasing Costs

	FIFO	LIFO
Cost of goods sold on income statement	Lower	Higher
Net income	Higher	Lower
Income taxes	Higher	Lower
Inventory on balance sheet	Higher	Lower

Normal Financial Statement Effects of Decreasing Costs

	FIFO	LIFO
Cost of goods sold on income statement	Higher	Lower
Net income	Lower	Higher
Income taxes	Lower	Higher
Inventory on balance sheet	Lower	Higher

These effects occur because LIFO causes the newer unit costs to be reflected in cost of goods sold on the income statement. FIFO causes the older unit costs to be reflected in cost of goods sold on the income statement. In contrast, on the balance sheet, the ending inventory amount under LIFO is based on the oldest unit costs, whereas FIFO ending inventory is based on the newest costs.

Managers' Choice of Inventory Methods

What motivates companies to choose different inventory costing methods? Most managers choose accounting methods based on two factors:

---

[2]The impact of a decline in inventory *quantity* on LIFO amounts is discussed in Supplement A to this chapter.

Learning Objective 3
Decide when the use of different inventory costing methods is beneficial to a company.

1. Net income effects (managers prefer to report higher earnings for their companies).

2. Income tax effects (managers prefer to pay the least amount of taxes allowed by law as late as possible—the "**least-latest rule**").

Any conflict between the two motives is normally resolved by choosing one accounting method for external financial statements and a different method for preparing its tax return. The choice of inventory costing methods is a special case, however, because of what is called the **LIFO conformity rule:** If LIFO is used on the income tax return, it must also be used to calculate inventory and cost of goods sold for the financial statements.

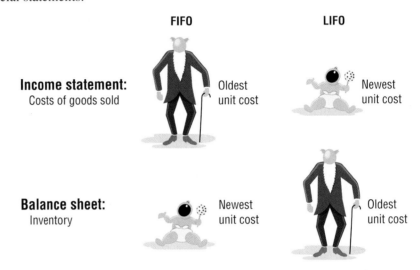

Increasing Cost Inventories

For inventory with increasing costs, LIFO is used on the tax return because it normally results in lower income taxes. This is illustrated in Exhibit 7.7, where income before income taxes was lowered from $100 under FIFO to $60 under LIFO. On the income tax expense line, this lowers income taxes from $25 under FIFO to $15 under LIFO, generating cash tax savings of $10 under LIFO.[3] The LIFO conformity rule leads companies to adopt LIFO for **both** tax and financial reporting purposes for increasing cost inventories located in the United States. Harley-Davidson is a fairly typical company facing increasing costs. It has saved approximately $7.0 million in taxes from the date it adopted the LIFO method through 2000.

Decreasing Cost Inventories

For inventory with decreasing costs, FIFO is most often used for both the tax return and financial statements. Using this method (along with lower of cost or market valuation, discussed later) produces the highest tax payments for companies with decreasing cost inventories. Many high-technology companies are facing declining costs. In such circumstances, the FIFO method, in which the oldest, most expensive goods become cost of goods sold, produces the highest cost of goods sold, the lowest pretax earnings, and thus the lowest income tax liability. For example, Apple Computer and Dell Computer account for inventories at FIFO.

For inventory located in countries that do not allow LIFO for tax purposes or that do not have a LIFO conformity rule, companies with increasing costs most often use FIFO or weighted average to report higher income on the income statement. Since most companies in the same industry face similar cost structures, clusters of companies in the same industries often choose the same accounting method.

---

[3]In theory, LIFO cannot provide permanent tax savings because (1) when inventory levels drop or (2) costs drop, the income effect reverses and the income taxes deferred must be paid. The economic advantage of deferring income taxes in such situations is due to the fact that interest can be earned on the money that otherwise would be paid as taxes for the current year.

Consistency in Use of Inventory Methods

It is important to remember that regardless of the physical flow of goods, a company can use any of the inventory costing methods. Also, a company is not required to use the same inventory costing method for all inventory items, and no particular justification is needed for the selection of one or more of the acceptable methods. Harley-Davidson, and most large companies, use different inventory methods for different inventory items.[4] However, accounting rules require companies to apply their accounting methods on a consistent basis over time. A company is not permitted to use LIFO one period, FIFO the next, and then go back to LIFO. A change in method is allowed only if the change will improve the measurement of financial results and financial position.

LIFO and Conflicts between Managers' and Owners' Interests

A QUESTION OF ETHICS

We have seen that the selection of an inventory method can have significant effects on the financial statements. Unfortunately, company managers may have an incentive to select a method that is not consistent with the owners' objectives. For example, during a period of rising prices, using LIFO may be in the best interests of the owners because LIFO often reduces a company's tax liability. If managers' compensation is tied to reported profits, they may prefer FIFO, which typically results in higher profits.

While a well-designed compensation plan should reward managers for acting in the best interests of the owners, that is not always the case. Clearly, a manager who selects an accounting method that is not optimal for the company solely to increase his or her compensation is engaging in questionable ethical behavior.

SELF-STUDY QUIZ

Assume that a company began operations this year. Its purchases for the year included:

Purchases January	10 units @ $6 each
Purchases May	5 units @ $10 each
Purchases November	5 units @ $12 each

During the year, 15 units were sold for $20 each, and other operating expenses totaled $100.

1. Compute cost of goods sold and pretax income for the year under the FIFO and LIFO accounting methods.
2. Which method would you recommend that the company adopt? Why?

After you have completed your answers, check them with the solutions that follow:

1.	FIFO	LIFO
Sales revenue (15 × $20)	$300	$300
Cost of goods sold	110	140
Gross Profit	190	160
Other expenses	100	100
Pretax income	$ 90	$ 60

FIFO cost of goods sold = (10 × $6) + (5 × $10) = $110
LIFO cost of goods sold = (5 × $12) + (5 × $10) + (5 × $6) = $140

2. LIFO would be recommended because it produces lower pretax income and lower taxes.

---

[4]*Accounting Trends & Techniques* (New York: AICPA, 2000) reported that although 301 (50 percent) of the 600 companies surveyed reported using LIFO for some portion of inventories, only 24 (4 percent) use LIFO for all inventories.

Inventory Methods and Financial Statement Analysis

Learning Objective 4
Compare companies that use different inventory costing methods.

What would analysts do if they wanted to compare two companies that prepared their statements using different inventory accounting methods? Before meaningful comparisons could be made, one company's statements would have to be converted to a comparable basis. Making such a conversion is eased by the requirement that U.S. public companies using LIFO also report beginning and ending inventory on a FIFO basis in the notes if the FIFO values are materially different. We can use this information along with the cost of goods sold equation to convert the balance sheet and income statement to the FIFO basis.

Converting the Income Statement to FIFO

Recall that the choice of a cost flow assumption affects how goods available for sale are allocated to ending inventory and cost of goods sold. It does not affect the recording of purchases. Ending inventory will be different under the alternative methods, and, since last year's ending inventory is this year's beginning inventory, beginning inventory will also be different:

Beginning inventory	*Different*
+ Purchases of merchandise during the year	*Same*
− Ending inventory	*Different*
Cost of goods sold	*Different*

This equation suggests that if we know the differences between a company's inventory valued at LIFO and FIFO for both beginning and ending inventory, we can compute the difference in cost of goods sold. Exhibit 7.8 shows Harley-Davidson's 1997 disclosure of the differences between LIFO and FIFO values for beginning and ending inventory. These amounts, referred to as the **LIFO reserve** or "Excess of FIFO over LIFO inventory," are disclosed by LIFO users in their inventory footnotes.

LIFO RESERVE is a contra-asset for the excess of FIFO over LIFO inventory.

Using Harley-Davidson's LIFO reserve values reported in the footnote in Exhibit 7.8, we see that, cost of goods sold would have been $1,891 **lower** had it used FIFO.

Beginning LIFO Reserve (Excess of FIFO over LIFO)	$20,722
− Less: Ending LIFO Reserve (Excess of FIFO over LIFO)	− 22,613
Difference in Cost of Goods Sold under FIFO	($1,891)

EXHIBIT 7.8

Financial Statement Effects of Inventory Costing Methods

REAL WORLD EXCERPT

HARLEY-
DAVIDSON,
INC.

ANNUAL REPORT

HARLEY-DAVIDSON, INC.

NOTES TO CONSOLIDATED FINANCIAL STATEMENTS

2. ADDITIONAL BALANCE SHEET AND CASH FLOW INFORMATION
(in thousands)

	December 31,	
	1997	1996
Inventories:		
Components at FIFO:	140,088	122,108
Excess of FIFO over LIFO inventories	22,613	20,722	◄— LIFO Reserve
Components at LIFO:	$117,475	$101,386

Since FIFO cost of goods sold expense is **lower,** income before income taxes would have been $1,891 **higher.** As a result, income taxes would be that amount times its tax rate of 37 percent **higher** had it used FIFO.

Difference in pretax income under FIFO	$1,891
Tax rate	× .37
Difference in taxes under FIFO	$ 700

Combining the two effects, net income would be increased by the change in cost of goods sold of $1,891 and decreased by the change in income tax expense of $700, resulting in an overall increase in net income of $1,191.

Decrease in Cost of Goods Sold Expense (**Income increases**)	$1,891
Increase in Income Tax Expense (**Income decreases**)	(700)
Increase in Net Income	$1,191

These Harley-Davidson computations are for 1997. It is important to note that even companies that usually face increasing costs occasionally face decreasing costs. For example, during 2000, Harley-Davidson's costs of new inventory declined due to manufacturing efficiencies. Consequently, when we convert from LIFO to FIFO, cost of goods sold for 2000 actually increase by $1,851, and the conversion's effect on pretax income is the opposite—a decrease of $1,851. As a result, even though LIFO usually saves it taxes, Harley paid $685 extra in taxes in 2000 (0.37 × $1,851).

Converting Inventory on the Balance Sheet to FIFO

You can adjust the inventory amounts on the balance sheet to FIFO by substituting the FIFO values in the note ($140,088 and $122,108 for 1997 and 1996, respectively) for the LIFO values (see Exhibit 7.8). Alternatively, you can add the LIFO reserve to the FIFO value on the balance sheet to arrive at the same numbers.

LIFO and International Comparisons
INTERNATIONAL PERSPECTIVE

The methods of accounting for inventories discussed in this chapter are used in most major industrialized countries. In several countries, however, the LIFO method is not generally used. In England and Canada, for example, LIFO is not acceptable for tax purposes, nor is it widely used in financial reporting. LIFO is not used in Australia and Singapore, but it may be used in China for both financial reporting and tax purposes. These differences can create comparability problems when one attempts to compare companies across international borders. For example, General Motors and Ford use LIFO to value U.S. inventories and average cost or FIFO for non-U.S. inventories, while Honda (of Japan) uses FIFO for all inventories.

SELF-STUDY QUIZ

Caterpillar Inc.

1. In a recent year, Caterpillar Inc., a major manufacturer of farm and construction equipment, reported pretax earnings of $1,615 million. Its inventory note indicated "if the FIFO (first-in, first-out) method had been in use, inventories would have been $2,103 and $2,035 higher than reported at the end of the current and prior year, respectively." (The amounts noted are for the LIFO reserve.) Convert pretax earnings for the current year from a LIFO to a FIFO basis.

Beginning LIFO Reserve (Excess of FIFO over LIFO) _____

Less: Ending LIFO Reserve (Excess of FIFO over LIFO) _____

Difference in cost of goods sold under FIFO _____

Pretax income (LIFO) _____

Difference in pretax income under FIFO _____

Pretax income (FIFO) _____

After you have completed your answers, check them with the solutions that follow:

_____

1.

Beginning LIFO Reserve	$2,035		Pretax income (LIFO)	$1,615
Less: Ending LIFO Reserve	2,103		Difference in pretax income	68
Difference in cost of goods sold	($68)		Pretax income (FIFO)	$1,683

VALUATION AT LOWER OF COST OR MARKET

Learning Objective 5
Report inventory at the lower of cost or market (LCM).

Inventories should be measured at their purchase cost in conformity with the cost principle. When the goods remaining in ending inventory can be replaced with identical goods at a lower cost, however, the lower cost should be used as the inventory valuation. Damaged, obsolete, and deteriorated items in inventory should also be assigned a unit cost that represents their current estimated net realizable value (sales price less costs to sell) if that is below cost. This rule is known as measuring inventories at the **lower of cost or market** (LCM).

LOWER OF COST OR MARKET (LCM) is a valuation method departing from the cost principle; it serves to recognize a loss when replacement cost or net realizable value drops below cost.

This departure from the cost principle is based on the conservatism constraint, which requires special care to avoid overstating assets and income. It is particularly important for two types of companies: (1) high-technology companies such as Dell Computer that manufacture goods for which the cost of production and the selling price are declining and (2) companies such as American Eagle Outfitters that sell seasonal goods such as clothing, the value of which drops dramatically at the end of each selling season (fall or spring).

REPLACEMENT COST is the current purchase price for identical goods.

Under LCM, companies recognize a "holding" loss in the period in which the **replacement cost** of an item drops rather than the period in which the item is sold. The holding loss is the difference between the purchase cost and the lower replacement cost. It is added to the cost of goods sold of the period. To illustrate, assume that Dell Computer had the following in the current period ending inventory:

Item	Quantity	Cost per Item	Replacement Cost (Market) per Item	Lower of Cost or Market per Item	Total Lower of Cost or Market
Pentium chips	1,000	$250	$200	$200	1,000 × $200 = $200,000
Disk drives	400	100	110	100	400 × $100 = 40,000

The 1,000 Pentium chips should be recorded in the ending inventory at the current market value ($200) because it is **lower** than the cost ($250). Dell makes the following journal entry to record the write-down:

Cost of goods sold (+E, −SE) (1,000 × $50)	50,000	
Inventory (−A)		50,000

Assets	=	Liabilities	+	Stockholders' Equity	
Inventory −50,000				Cost of Goods Sold	−50,000

Since the market price of the disk drives ($110) is higher than the original cost ($100), no write-down is necessary. The drives remain on the books at their cost of $100 per unit ($40,000 in total). Recognition of holding gains on inventory is not permitted by GAAP.

The write-down of the Pentium chips to market produces the following effects on the income statement and balance sheet:

Effects of LCM Write-Down	Current Period	Next Period (if sold)
Cost of goods sold	Increase $50,000	Decrease $50,000
Pretax income	Decrease $50,000	Increase $50,000
Ending inventory on balance sheet	Decrease $50,000	Unaffected

Note that the effects in the period of sale are the opposite of those in the period of the write-down. Lower of cost or market changes only the timing of cost of goods sold. It transfers cost of goods sold from the period of sale to the period of write-down.

In the case of seasonal goods such as clothing, obsolete goods, or damaged goods, if the sales price less selling costs (or **net realizable value**) drops below cost, this difference is subtracted from ending inventory and added to cost of goods sold of the period. This has the same effect on current and future periods' financial statements as the write-down to replacement cost.

NET REALIZABLE VALUE is the expected sales price less selling costs (e.g., repair and disposal costs).

Note that in the two examples that follow, both Harley-Davidson, which is a mixed LIFO company, and Dell Computer, which is a FIFO company, report the use of lower of cost or market for financial statement purposes.[5]

HARLEY-DAVIDSON, INC.

NOTES TO CONSOLIDATED FINANCIAL STATEMENTS

1. SUMMARY OF SIGNIFICANT ACCOUNTING POLICIES

INVENTORIES—Inventories are valued at the lower of cost or market. Substantially all inventories located in the United States are valued using the last-in, first-out (LIFO) method. Other inventories totaling $43.7 million in 1998 and $33.3 million in 1997, are valued at the lower of cost or market using the first-in, first-out (FIFO) method.

DELL COMPUTER

NOTES TO CONSOLIDATED FINANCIAL STATEMENTS

NOTE 1—Description of Business and Summary of Significant Accounting Policies

Inventories—Inventories are stated at the lower of cost or market with cost being determined on a first-in, first-out basis.

[5]For tax purposes, lower of cost or market may be applied with all inventory costing methods except LIFO.

EVALUATING INVENTORY MANAGEMENT

Measuring Efficiency in Inventory Management

Learning Objective 6
Evaluate inventory management using the inventory turnover ratio and the effects of inventories on cash flows.

As noted at the beginning of the chapter, the primary goals of inventory management are to have sufficient quantities of high-quality inventory available to serve customers' needs while minimizing the costs of carrying inventory (production, storage, obsolescence, and financing). The inventory turnover ratio is an important measure of the company's success in balancing these conflicting goals:

KEY RATIO
ANALYSIS

Inventory Turnover

? ANALYTICAL QUESTION:
How efficient are inventory management activities?

% RATIO AND COMPARISONS:

$$\text{Inventory Turnover} = \frac{\text{Cost of Goods Sold}}{\text{Average Inventory}}$$

The 2000 ratio for Harley-Davidson:

$$\frac{\$1,915,547}{(\$191,931 + 168,616)/2} = 10.6$$

COMPARISONS OVER TIME			COMPARISONS WITH COMPETITORS	
Harley-Davidson			**Titan Motorcycle**	**Honda Motor**
1998	**1999**	**2000**	**2000**	**2000**
10.1	10.0	10.6	1.9	7.2

💡 INTERPRETATIONS:

In General   The inventory turnover ratio reflects how many times average inventory was produced and sold during the period. A higher ratio indicates that inventory moves more quickly through the production process to the ultimate customer, reducing storage and obsolescence costs. Because less money is tied up in inventory, the excess can be invested to earn interest income or reduce borrowing, which reduces interest expense. More efficient purchasing and production techniques such as just-in-time inventory, as well as high product demand cause this ratio to be high. Analysts and creditors also watch the inventory turnover ratio because a sudden decline may mean that a company is facing an unexpected drop in demand for its products or is becoming sloppy in its production management. Many managers and analysts compute the related number of average days to sell inventory, which is equal to 365 ÷ inventory turnover ratio, or 34.4 days for Harley-Davidson. It indicates the average time it takes the company to produce and deliver inventory to customers.

Selected Focus Company Inventory Turnover	
Outback Steakhouse	26.51
General Mills	5.76
Boston Beer	5.35
Home Depot	5.53

Focus Company Analysis   Harley-Davidson's inventory turnover has increased from 10.1 in 1998 to 10.6 in 2000. This increase in inventory turnover resulted from increases in production volume at each of Harley's plants as well as use of just-in-time inventory principles. Harley's ratio is much higher than its smaller U.S. rival (Titan) whose operations are much less efficient. Harley-Davidson benefits from what economists call "economies of scale." Harley's turnover is even higher than the ratio for the giant Japanese auto and motorcycle manufacturer Honda.

A Few Cautions: Differences across industries in purchasing, production, and sales processes cause dramatic differences in this ratio. For example, restaurants such as Outback Steakhouse, which must turn over their perishable inventory very quickly, tend to have much higher inventory turnover. A particular firm's ratio should be compared only with its figures from prior years' or with figures for other firms in the same industry.

LIFO and Inventory Turnover Ratio

For many LIFO companies, the inventory turnover ratio can be deceptive. Remember that, for these companies, the beginning and ending inventory numbers that make up the denominator of the ratio will be artificially small because they reflect old lower costs. Consider Deere & Co., manufacturer of John Deere farm, lawn, and construction equipment. Its inventory note lists the following values:

REAL WORLD EXCERPT

Deere & Company
ANNUAL REPORT

DEERE & COMPANY
NOTES TO CONSOLIDATED FINANCIAL STATEMENTS
INVENTORIES
(in millions)

	2000	1999
Total FIFO value	$2,531	$2,349
Adjustment to LIFO basis	978	1,054
Inventories	$1,553	$1,295

John Deere's cost of goods sold for 2000 was $8,936.1 million. If the ratio is computed using the reported LIFO inventory values for the ratio, it would be

$$\text{Inventory Turnover Ratio} = \frac{\$8,936.10}{(\$1,553 + \$1,295)/2} = 6.3$$

Converting cost of goods sold (the numerator) to a FIFO basis and using the more current FIFO inventory values in the denominator, it would be

$$\text{Inventory Turnover Ratio} = \frac{\$8,936.10 + 76}{(\$2,531 + \$2,349)/2} = 3.7$$

Note that the major difference between the two ratios is in the denominator. FIFO inventory values are nearly two times the LIFO values. So the FIFO ratio is just over half the LIFO amount. The LIFO beginning and ending inventory numbers are artificially small because they reflect older lower costs. Thus, the numerator in the first calculation does not relate in a meaningful way to the denominator.[6]

Inventory and Cash Flows

When companies expand production to meet increases in demand, this increases the amount of inventory reported on the balance sheet. However, when companies overestimate demand for a product, they usually produce too many units of the slow-selling item. This increases storage costs as well as the interest costs on short-term borrowings that finance the inventory. It may even lead to losses if the excess inventory cannot be sold at normal prices. The cash flow statement often provides the first sign of such problems.

---

[6]Since the LIFO values for cost of goods sold on the income statement and the FIFO inventory numbers on the balance sheet are closer to current prices, they are often thought to be the most appropriate numerator and denominator, respectively, for use in this ratio.

FOCUS ON
CASH FLOWS   **Inventory**

As with a change in accounts receivable, a change in inventories can have a major effect on a company's cash flow from operations. Cost of goods sold on the income statement may be more or less than the amount of cash paid to suppliers during the period. Since most inventory is purchased on open credit (borrowing from suppliers is normally called accounts payable), reconciling cost of goods sold with cash paid to suppliers requires consideration of the changes in both the Inventory and Accounts Payable accounts.

The simplest way to think about the effects of changes in inventory is that buying (increasing) inventory eventually decreases cash, while selling (decreasing) inventory eventually increases cash. Similarly, borrowing from suppliers, which increases accounts payable, increases cash. Paying suppliers, which decreases accounts payable, decreases cash.

EFFECT ON STATEMENT OF CASH FLOWS

In General   When a net **decrease in inventory** for the period occurs, sales are greater than purchases; thus, the decrease must be **added** in computing cash flows from operations.

When a net **increase in inventory** for the period occurs, sales are less than purchases; thus, the increase must be **subtracted** in computing cash flows from operations.

When a net **decrease in accounts payable** for the period occurs, payments to suppliers are greater than new purchases; thus, the decrease must be **subtracted** in computing cash flows from operations.

When a net **increase in accounts payable** for the period occurs, payments to suppliers are less than new purchases; thus, the increase must be **added** in computing cash flows from operations.

Selected Focus Company Comparisons: 3-Year Change in Cash Flows Related to Inventory Changes (in millions)	
Timberland	+17
Wal-Mart	−4,262
Callaway Golf	−31

Effect on Cash Flows

Operating activities (indirect method)	
Net income	$xxx
Adjusted for	
Add inventory **decrease**	+
or	
Subtract inventory **increase**	−
Add accounts payable **increase**	+
or	
Subtract accounts payable **decrease**	−

Focus Company Analysis   Exhibit 7.9 is the Operating Activities section of Harley-Davidson's statement of cash flows. When the inventory balance increases during the period, as was the case at Harley-Davidson in 1999 and 2000, the company has purchased or produced more inventory than it sold. Thus, the increase is subtracted in the computation of cash flow from operations. When the accounts payable balance increases during the period, the company has borrowed more from suppliers than it has paid them. Thus, the increase is added in the computation of cash flow from operations.*

When sales rise quickly, as they did at Harley-Davidson, inventories usually rise, decreasing cash flow from operations. However, as the highlighted section of Exhibit 7.9 indicates, increases in borrowing from suppliers offset the rise in inventories.

For companies with foreign currency or business acquisitions/dispositions, the amount of the change reported on the cash flow statement will not equal the change in the accounts reported on the balance sheet.

	2000	1999

HARLEY-DAVIDSON, INC.
Consolidated Statements of Cash Flows
Years Ended December 31, 2000 and 1999
(in thousands)

	2000	1999
Cash flows from operating activities:		
Net Income	$347,713	$267,201
Adjustments to reconcile net income to net cash provided by operating activities:		
Depreciation and amortization	133,348	113,822
Gain on sale of credit card business	(18,915)	—
Tax benefit of stock options	35,876	15,504
Provision for credit losses	9,919	17,919
Deferred income taxes	1,363	11,393
Long-term employee benefits	4,631	(8,480)
Other	1,945	1,781
Net changes in current assets and current liabilities:		
Accounts receivable	3,397	11,709
Inventories	(23,315)	(13,000)
Prepaid expenses	(3,277)	(3,527)
Accounts payable and accrued liabilities	72,804	17,320
Total adjustments	217,776	164,441
Net cash provided by operating activities	565,489	431,642

EXHIBIT 7.9

Inventories on the Cash Flow Statement

REAL WORLD EXCERPT

HARLEY-DAVIDSON, INC.

ANNUAL REPORT

SELF-STUDY QUIZ

1. Refer to the Key Ratio Analysis for Harley-Davidson's inventory turnover. Based on the computations for 2000, answer the following question. If Harley-Davidson had been able to manage its inventory more efficiently and decrease purchases and ending inventory by $10,000, would its inventory turnover ratio have increased or decreased? Explain.

2. Based on the Focus on Cash Flows section, answer the following question. If Harley-Davidson had been able to manage its inventory more efficiently and *decrease* ending inventory, would its cash flow from operations have increased or decreased?

After you have completed your answers, check them with the solutions that follow:

1. Inventory turnover would have increased because the denominator of the ratio would have decreased by $5,000.

$$\frac{\$1,915,547}{(181,931 + 168,616) \div 2} = 10.9$$

2. A decrease in inventory would have increased cash flow from operations. (See the Focus on Cash Flows section.)

CONTROL OF INVENTORY

Errors in Measuring Ending Inventory

As the cost of goods sold equation indicates, a direct relationship exists between ending inventory and cost of goods sold because items not in the ending inventory are assumed to have been sold. Thus, the measurement of ending inventory quantities and

Learning Objective 7
Analyze the effects of inventory errors on financial statements and methods for keeping track of inventory.

costs affects both the balance sheet (assets) and the income statement (cost of goods sold, gross profit, and net income). The measurement of ending inventory affects not only the net income for that period but also the net income for the next accounting period. This two-period effect occurs because the ending inventory for one period is the beginning inventory for the next accounting period.

Greeting card maker Gibson Greetings had overstated its net income by 20 percent because one division had overstated ending inventory for the year. You can compute the effects of the error on both the current year's and the next year's income before taxes using the cost of goods sold equation. Assume that ending inventory was overstated by $10,000 due to a clerical error that was not discovered until the next year. This would have the following effects in the current year:

Current Year

Beginning inventory	
+ Purchases of merchandise during the year	
− Ending inventory	Overstated $10,000
Cost of goods sold	Understated $10,000

Topic Tackler 7–2

Because cost of goods sold was understated, **income before taxes would be overstated** by $10,000 in the **current year.**

And, since the current year's ending inventory becomes next year's beginning inventory, it would have the following effects next year:

Next Year

Beginning inventory	Overstated $10,000
+ Purchases of merchandise during the year	
− Ending inventory	
Cost of goods sold	Overstated $10,000

Because cost of goods sold was overstated, **income before taxes would be understated** by the same amount in the **next year.**

Each of these errors would flow into retained earnings so that at the end of the current year, retained earnings would be overstated by $10,000 (less the related income tax expense). This error would be offset in the next year, and retained earnings and inventory at the end of next year would be correct.

In this example, we assumed that the overstatement of ending inventory was inadvertent, the result of a clerical error. As we noted in Chapter 6, however, inventory fraud is one of the two most common forms of financial statement fraud. It occurred in the Maxidrive case discussed in Chapter 1 as well as in the real MiniScribe fraud. A similar fraud has been alleged at Nesmont, the Canadian gold refining and processing company as reported in the following article:

REAL WORLD EXCERPT

Dow Jones News Service

SEC Sues Ex-Intl Nesmont Officers, Claiming Asset Inflation

WASHINGTON (Dow Jones)—The Securities and Exchange Commission filed a civil complaint Thursday against three former officers of International Nesmont Industrial Corp. (NESFE), accusing them of falsifying the company's financial results. . . . The suit alleges . . . a deliberate scheme to overstate income and inflate assets of the Canadian gold refining and processing company. Among their more creative schemes was a practice of passing off brass bars as gold in order to pump up inventory, the SEC said. They are also accused of creating phony documents and lying about earnings.

SOURCE: Matthew Benjamin, "SEC Sues Ex-Intl. Nesmont Officers, Claiming Asset Inflation," *Dow Jones News Service,* July 24, 1997. Copyright 1997 by Dow Jones & Co. Inc. Reproduced with permission of Dow Jones & Co. Inc. in the format textbook via copyright clearance center.

Perpetual and Periodic Inventory Systems

The amount of purchases for the period is always accumulated in the accounting system. The amount of cost of goods sold and ending inventory can be determined by using one of two different inventory systems: perpetual or periodic. To simplify the discussion of how accounting systems keep track of these amounts, we will focus this discussion on the Motorclothes™ line for which Harley-Davidson is a wholesaler.

Perpetual Inventory System

In a **perpetual inventory system,** a detailed record is maintained for each type of merchandise stocked, showing (1) units and cost of the beginning inventory, (2) units and cost of each purchase, (3) units and cost of the goods for each sale, and (4) units and cost of the goods on hand at any point in time. This up-to-date record is maintained on a transaction-by-transaction basis. In a complete perpetual inventory system, the inventory record gives the amount of both ending inventory and cost of goods sold at any point in time. Under this system, a physical count should also be performed from time to time to ensure that records are accurate in case of errors or theft.

> In a **PERPETUAL INVENTORY SYSTEM,** a detailed inventory record is maintained, recording each purchase and sale during the accounting period.

To this point in the text, all journal entries for purchase and sale transactions have been recorded using a perpetual inventory system. In a perpetual inventory system, purchase transactions are recorded directly in an inventory account. When each sale is recorded, a companion cost of goods sold entry is made, decreasing inventory and recording cost of goods sold. As a result, information on cost of goods sold and ending inventory is available on a continuous (perpetual) basis.

Periodic Inventory System

Under the **periodic inventory system,** no up-to-date record of inventory is maintained during the year. An actual physical count of the goods remaining on hand is required at the **end of each period.** The number of units of each type of merchandise on hand is multiplied by their unit cost to compute the dollar amount of the ending inventory. Cost of goods sold is calculated using the cost of goods sold equation.

> In a **PERIODIC INVENTORY SYSTEM,** ending inventory and cost of goods sold are determined at the end of the accounting period based on a physical count.

Because the amount of inventory is not known until the end of the period when the inventory count is taken, the amount of cost of goods sold cannot be reliably determined until the inventory count is complete. Inventory purchases are debited to an account called Purchases, which is part of the asset inventory. Revenues are recorded at the time of each sale. However, cost of goods sold is not recorded until after the inventory count is completed. At other times, companies using a periodic system must estimate the amount of inventory on hand. Estimation methods are discussed in intermediate accounting courses.

Before affordable computers and bar code readers were available, the primary reason for using a periodic inventory system was its low cost. The primary disadvantage of a periodic inventory system is the lack of inventory information. Managers are not informed about low stock or overstocked situations. Most modern companies could not survive without this information. As noted at the beginning of the chapter, cost and quality pressures brought on by increasing competition, combined with dramatic declines in the cost of computers, have made sophisticated perpetual inventory systems a requirement at all but the smallest companies. The entries made when using both systems are compared in Supplement C at the end of this chapter.

SELF-STUDY QUIZ

Assume that it is now the end of 2005, and for the first time, the company will undergo an audit by an independent CPA. The annual income statement prepared by the company is presented below. Assume further that the independent CPA discovered that the ending inventory for 2005 was understated by $15,000. Correct and reconstruct the income statement in the space provided.

	FOR THE YEAR ENDED DECEMBER 31	
	2005 UNCORRECTED	2005 CORRECTED
Sales revenue	$750,000	
Cost of goods sold		
Beginning inventory	$ 45,000	
Add purchases	460,000	
Goods available for sale	505,000	
Less ending inventory	40,000	
Cost of goods sold	465,000	
Gross margin on sales	285,000	
Operating expenses	275,000	
Pretax income	10,000	
Income tax expense (20%)	2,000	
Net income	$ 8,000	

After you have completed your answers, check them with the solutions that follow:

_____

Sales revenue		$750,000
Cost of goods sold		
Beginning inventory	45,000	
Add purchases	460,000	
Goods available for sale	505,000	
Less ending inventory	55,000	
Cost of goods sold		450,000
Gross margin on sales		300,000
Operating expenses		275,000
Pretax income		25,000
Income tax expense (20%)		5,000
Net income		$ 20,000

Note: An ending inventory error in one year affects pretax income by the amount of the error and in the next year affects pretax income again by the same amount, but in the opposite direction.

DEMONSTRATION CASE

(Complete the requirements before proceeding to the suggested solution that follows.) This case reviews the application of the FIFO and LIFO inventory costing methods and the inventory turnover ratio.

Balent Appliances distributes a number of household appliances. One product, microwave ovens, has been selected for case purposes. Assume that the following summarized transactions were completed during the year ended December 31, 2005 in the order given (assume that all transactions are cash):

	Units	Unit Cost
a. Beginning inventory	11	$200
b. New inventory purchases	9	220
c. Sales (selling price, $420)	8	?

Required:

1. Compute the following amounts, assuming the application of the FIFO and LIFO inventory costing methods:

	ENDING INVENTORY		COST OF GOODS SOLD	
	Units	**Dollars**	**Units**	**Dollars**
FIFO				
LIFO				

2. Assuming that inventory cost was expected to follow current trends, which method would you suggest that Balent select to account for these inventory items? Explain your answer.

3. Assuming that other operating expenses were $500 and the income tax rate is 25 percent, prepare the income statement for the period using your selected method.

4. Compute the inventory turnover ratio for the current period using your selected method. What does it indicate?

SUGGESTED SOLUTION

1.

	ENDING INVENTORY		COST OF GOODS SOLD	
	Units	**Dollars**	**Units**	**Dollars**
FIFO	12	$2,580	8	$1,600
LIFO	12	$2,420	8	$1,760

Computations

Goods Available for Sale = Beginning Inventory + Purchases

$$= (11 \text{ units} \times \$200 = \$2,200) + (9 \text{ units} \times \$220 = \$1,980)$$

$$= \$4,180$$

FIFO inventory (costed at end of period)

Ending inventory: (9 units × $220 = $1,980) + (3 units × $200 = $600) = $2,580.
Cost of goods sold: 8 units × $200 = $1,600.

LIFO inventory (costed at end of period)

Ending inventory: (11 units × $200 = $2,200) + (1 unit × $220 = $220) = $2,420.
Cost of goods sold: 8 units × $220 = $1,760.

2. LIFO should be selected. Because costs are rising, LIFO produces higher cost of goods sold, lower pretax income, and lower income tax payments. It is used on the tax return and income statement because of the LIFO conformity rule.

3.

BALENT APPLIANCES
Statement of Income
Year Ended December 31, 2005

Sales	$3,360
Cost of goods sold	1,760
Gross profit	1,600
Other expenses	500
Income before income taxes	1,100
Income tax expense (25%)	275
Net income	$ 825

Computations

$$\text{Sales} = 8 \times \$420 = \$3{,}360.$$

4.

Inventory turnover ratio	=	Cost of Goods Sold	÷	Average Inventory
	=	$1,760	÷	[($2,200 + $2,420) ÷ 2 = $2,310]
	=	0.76		

The inventory turnover ratio reflects how many times average inventory was produced and sold during the period. Thus, Balent Appliances produced and sold its average inventory less than one time during the year.

Chapter Supplement A

LIFO Liquidations

A **LIFO LIQUIDATION** is a sale of a lower-cost inventory item from beginning LIFO inventory.

When a LIFO company sells more inventory than it purchases or manufactures, items from beginning inventory become part of cost of goods sold. This is called a **LIFO liquidation.** When inventory costs are rising, these lower cost items in beginning inventory produce a higher gross profit, higher taxable income, and higher taxes when they are sold. We illustrate this process by continuing our Harley-Davidson store Model A leather jacket example into its second year.

Financial Statement Effects of LIFO Liquidations

Recall that, in its first year of operation, the store purchased units for $70, $80, and $100 in sequence. Then the $100 unit and three of the $80 units were sold under LIFO, leaving one $80 unit and two $70 units in ending inventory. These events were represented using the LIFO inventory bin in Exhibit 7.5. Exhibit 7.10 continues this illustration into a second year. The ending inventory from year 1 becomes the beginning inventory for year 2. In part (a) of Exhibit 7.10, we assume that in year 2, the Harley-Davidson store purchased a total of three inventory units at the current $120 price, the sales price has been raised to $140, and three units are sold. Using LIFO, the three recently purchased $120 inventory items become part of cost of goods sold of $360, and the old $80 and $70 items from beginning inventory become ending inventory. Given that revenue is $140 per unit, the gross profit on the three newly purchased units is 3 units × $20 = $60.

Now assume instead, as we do in part (b) of Exhibit 7.10, that the store purchased only **two** additional units at $120 each. Using LIFO, these two new $120 units and the old $80 unit would become cost of goods sold. Given that revenue is $140 per unit, the gross profit on the newly purchased units is 2 units × $20 = $40. Since the cost of the old unit is only $80, the gross profit on this one unit is $60 ($140 − $80) instead of $20, raising total gross profit to $100.

Compared to part (a), cost of goods sold has decreased by $40, and gross profit and income before taxes have increased by $40. This $40 change is the **pretax effect of the LIFO liquidation.** Given the assumed tax rate of 25 percent, taxes paid are $10 (0.25 × $40) higher than in part (a).

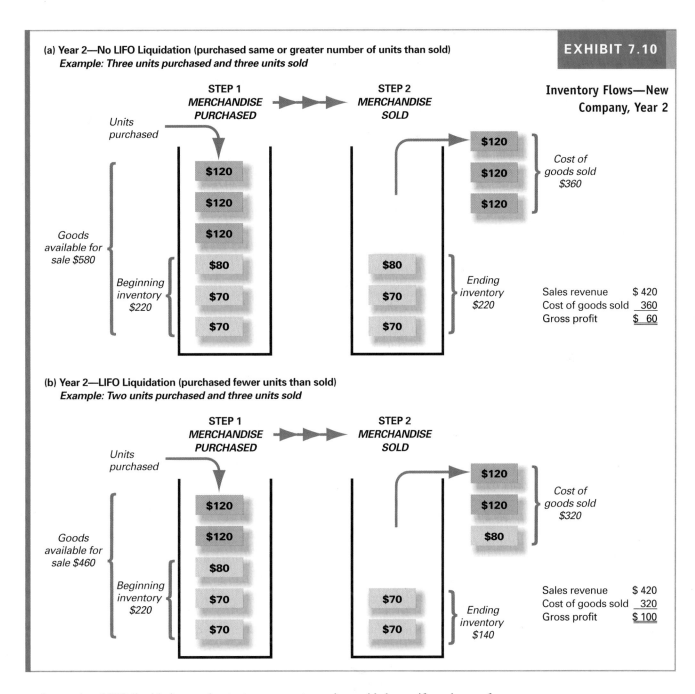

(a) Year 2—No LIFO Liquidation (purchased same or greater number of units than sold)
Example: Three units purchased and three units sold

EXHIBIT 7.10

Inventory Flows—New Company, Year 2

STEP 1 MERCHANDISE PURCHASED

STEP 2 MERCHANDISE SOLD

Units purchased

$120 / $120 / $120 / $80 / $70 / $70

Goods available for sale $580

Beginning inventory $220

Cost of goods sold $360: $120 / $120 / $120

Ending inventory $220: $80 / $70 / $70

Sales revenue	$ 420
Cost of goods sold	360
Gross profit	$ 60

(b) Year 2—LIFO Liquidation (purchased fewer units than sold)
Example: Two units purchased and three units sold

STEP 1 MERCHANDISE PURCHASED

STEP 2 MERCHANDISE SOLD

Units purchased

$120 / $120 / $80 / $70 / $70

Goods available for sale $460

Beginning inventory $220

Cost of goods sold $320: $120 / $120 / $80

Ending inventory $140: $70 / $70

Sales revenue	$ 420
Cost of goods sold	320
Gross profit	$ 100

In practice, LIFO liquidations and extra tax payments can be avoided even if purchases of additional inventory take place **after** the sale of the item it replaces. Tax law allows LIFO to be applied **as if** all purchases during an accounting period took place before any sales and cost of goods sold were recorded. Thus, temporary LIFO liquidations can be eliminated by purchasing additional inventory before year-end. Most companies apply LIFO in this manner.

LIFO Liquidations and Financial Statement Analysis

During the decade prior to 1993, Deere & Company and other companies in its industry faced declining demand and increasing competition in most major segments of their businesses. These economic changes reduced the inventory quantities necessary to meet customers' needs. Deere had also instituted modern manufacturing techniques that further decreased inventory levels. Deere, a long-time LIFO user, experienced continuing LIFO liquidations over this period. Companies must disclose the effects of LIFO liquidations in the notes when they are material, as Deere did in the note that follows. The second paragraph of the note explains the effect. The last sentence lists the pretax (after-tax) effects of the liquidations.

DEERE & COMPANY

NOTES TO CONSOLIDATED FINANCIAL STATEMENTS

Inventories

Substantially all inventories owned by Deere & Company and its United States equipment subsidiaries are valued at cost on the "last-in, first-out" (LIFO) method. . . .

Under the LIFO inventory method, cost of goods sold ordinarily reflects current production costs, thus providing a matching of current costs and current revenues in the income statement. However when LIFO–valued inventories decline, as they did in 1993 and 1992, lower costs that prevailed in prior years are matched against current year revenues, resulting in higher reported net income. Benefits from the reduction of LIFO inventories totaled $51 million ($33 million or $0.43 per share after income taxes) in 1993, $65 million ($43 million or $0.56 per share after income taxes) in 1992 and $128 million ($84 million or $1.11 per share after income taxes) in 1991.

According to this note, over the prior three years, LIFO liquidations increased Deere's reported income before taxes by a total of $244 million ($51 + $65 + $128). (These numbers are the equivalent of the $40 effect of the liquidation computed in the Harley-Davidson store example.) To compute pretax income as if the liquidations had not taken place (as if current year's production were large enough so that no items from beginning inventory were sold), simply subtract the LIFO liquidation effect from pretax income.

Pretax income on LIFO for 3 years (reported on the income statements)	$290
Less: Pretax effect of LIFO liquidations (from note)	244
Pretax income on LIFO for 3 years as if no liquidations	$ 46

Fully 84 percent ($244 ÷ $290) of Deere's reported pretax profit over the three years resulted from LIFO liquidations. Since the $46 million pretax profit figure reflected Deere's current costs of production, educated analysts used it when comparing Deere's performance to that of other LIFO companies. It is important to emphasize that these numbers still are on a **LIFO** basis but are computed **as if no liquidation had taken place.**

FINANCIAL
ANALYSIS

Inventory Management and LIFO Liquidations

Several research studies[7] have documented the year-end inventory purchasing decisions of firms that use LIFO. Many firms avoid LIFO liquidations and the accompanying increase in tax expense by purchasing sufficient quantities of inventory at year-end to ensure that ending inventory quantities are greater than or equal to beginning inventory quantities. While this practice increases the costs of carrying inventory (storage, financing, etc.), for these firms, the taxes saved exceed these amounts.

As noted earlier in the chapter, Harley-Davidson and many other firms have moved to more efficient just-in-time inventory techniques that greatly reduce the amount of inventory manufacturers keep on hand. When managers compare the savings in carrying costs against the costs of implementing the new system (new computers, training, etc.), they must also consider the added taxes they may pay if they account for the inventory using the LIFO method. When the company switches to the new just-in-time system, ending inventory quantity will normally decline below beginning inventory quantity, causing a LIFO liquidation and a one-time increase in taxes. This cost should be considered when deciding whether to adopt the new system. In this case, the tax law provides an incentive for U.S. companies not to become more efficient.

[7]See, for example, M. Frankel and R. Trezevant, "The Year-End LIFO Inventory Purchasing Decision: An Empirical Test," *The Accounting Review* (April 1994), pp. 382–98.

Chapter Supplement B

Additional Issues in Measuring Purchases
Purchase Returns and Allowances

Purchased goods may be returned to the vendor if they do not meet specifications, arrive in damaged condition, or are otherwise unsatisfactory. **Purchase returns and allowances** require a reduction in the cost of inventory purchases and the recording of a cash refund or a reduction in the liability to the vendor. For example, assume that Harley-Davidson returned to a supplier damaged harness boots that cost $1,000. The return would be recorded as follows:

> **PURCHASE RETURNS AND ALLOWANCES** are a reduction in the cost of purchases associated with unsatisfactory goods.

Accounts payable (−L) (or Cash)	1,000	
Inventory (−A)		1,000

Assets		=	Liabilities		+	Stockholders' Equity
Inventory	−1000		Accounts Payable	−1000		

Purchase Discounts

Cash discounts must be accounted for by both the seller and the buyer (accounting by the seller was discussed in Chapter 6). When merchandise is bought on credit, terms such as 2/10, n/30 are sometimes specified. That is, if payment is made within 10 days from the date of purchase, a 2 percent cash discount known as the **purchase discount** is granted. If payment is not made within the discount period, the full invoice cost is due 30 days after the purchase.

Assume that on January 17, Harley-Davidson bought goods that had a $1,000 invoice price with terms 2/10, n/30. The purchase should be recorded as follows (using what is called the gross method):

> A **PURCHASE DISCOUNT** is a cash discount received for prompt payment of an account.

Date of Purchase

Jan. 17	Inventory (+A)	1,000	
	Accounts payable (+L)		1,000

Assets		=	Liabilities		+	Stockholders' Equity
Inventory	+1000		Accounts Payable	+1000		

Date of Payment, within the Discount Period

Jan. 26	Accounts payable (−L)	1,000	
	Inventory (−A)		20
	Cash (−A)		980

Assets		=	Liabilities		+	Stockholders' Equity
Inventory	−20		Accounts Payable	−1000		
Cash	−980					

If for any reason Harley-Davidson did not pay within the 10-day discount period, the following entry would be needed:

Date of Payment, after the Discount Period

Feb. 1	Accounts payable (−L)	1,000	
	Cash (−A)		1,000

Assets		=	Liabilities		+	Stockholders' Equity
Cash	−1000		Accounts Payable	−1000		

Chapter Supplement C

Comparison of Perpetual and Periodic Inventory Systems

Assume, for this illustration only, that Harley-Davidson stocks and sells only one item, its Eagle Harness Boots, and that only the following events occurred in 2005:

Jan.   1   Had beginning inventory: 800 units, at unit cost of $50.

April   14   Purchased: 1,100 additional units, at unit cost of $50.

Nov.   30   Sold: 1,300 units, at unit sales price of $83.

In the two types of inventory systems, the following sequential steps would take place:

Perpetual Records	Periodic Records

1. Record all purchases in the Inventory account and in a detailed perpetual inventory record.
 	
April 14, 2005:
Inventory (+A) (1,100 units at $50)* 55,000
   Accounts payable (+L) (or Cash−A) .. 55,000
 	
*Also entered in the detailed perpetual inventory record as 1,100 harness boots at $50 each.
	1. Record all purchases in an account called Purchases.
	
	April 14, 2005:
	Purchases (+A) (1,100 units at $50) 55,000
	   Accounts payable (+L) (or Cash−A) .. 55,000

2. Record all sales in the Sales Revenue account and record the cost of goods sold.
 	
November 30, 2005:
Accounts receivable (+A) (or Cash+A) .. 107,900
   Sales revenue (+R, +SE) (1,300 units at $83) 107,900
Cost of goods sold (+E, −SE) 65,000
   Inventory (−A) (1,300 units at $50)* ... 65,000
 	
*Also entered in the perpetual inventory record as a reduction of 1,300 units at $50 each.
	2. Record all sales in a Sales Revenue account.
	
	November 30, 2005:
	Accounts receivable (+A) (or Cash+A) .. 107,900
	   Sales revenue (+R, +SE) (1,300 units at $83) 107,900

3. Use cost of goods sold and inventory amounts. At the end of the accounting period, the balance in the Cost of Goods Sold account is reported on the income statement. It is not necessary to compute cost of goods sold because the Cost of Goods Sold account is up-to-date. Also, the Inventory account shows the ending inventory amount reported on the balance sheet. A physical inventory count is still necessary to assess the accuracy of the perpetual records and identify theft and other forms of misuse (called shrinkage).
 	
No entry
	3. At end of period:
	  a. Count the number of units on hand.
	  b. Compute the dollar valuation of the ending inventory.
	  c. Compute and record the cost of goods sold.

Beginning inventory (last period's ending)	$40,000
Add purchases (balance in the Purchases account)	55,000
Goods available for sale	95,000
Deduct ending inventory (physical count—600 units at $50)	30,000
Cost of goods sold	$65,000

December 31, 2005:
Transfer beginning inventory and purchases to cost of goods sold:

Cost of goods sold (+E, −SE) 95,000
   Inventory (−A) (beginning) 40,000
   Purchases (−A) 55,000

Subtract the ending inventory amount from the cost of goods sold to complete its computation and establish the ending inventory balance:

Inventory (+A) (ending) 30,000
   Cost of goods sold (−E, +SE) 30,000

Perpetual Records				Periodic Records			
Assets	**= Liabilities**	**+**	**Stockholders' Equity**	**Assets**	**= Liabilities**	**+**	**Stockholders' Equity**
Inventory +55,000	Accounts Payable +55,000			Purchases +55,000	Accounts Payable +55,000		
Accts. Rec. +107,900			Sales Revenue +107,900	Accts. Rec. +107,900			Sales Revenue +107,900
Inventory −65,000			Cost of Goods Sold −65,000	Inventory −40,000			Cost of Goods Sold −95,000
				Purchases −55,000			
				Inventory +30,000			Cost of Goods Sold +30,000

Note that the effects of the entries on the accounting equation are the same under both systems. Only the timing of the recording of amounts changes.

Perpetual Inventory Records in Practice

Systems that do keep track of the costs of individual items or lots normally do so on a FIFO or estimated average (or standard) cost basis. For distinguishable high-value items, specific identification may be used. Perpetual records are rarely kept on a LIFO basis for two reasons: (1) doing so is more complex and costly and (2) it can increase tax payments. LIFO companies convert the outputs of their perpetual inventory system to LIFO with an adjusting entry.

CHAPTER **TAKE-AWAYS**

1. **Apply the cost principle to identify the amounts that should be included in inventory and the matching principle to determine cost of goods sold for typical retailers, wholesalers, and manufacturers. p. 340**
   Inventory should include all items owned that are held for resale. Costs flow into inventory when goods are purchased or manufactured. They flow out (as an expense) when they are sold or disposed of. In conformity with the matching principle, the total cost of the goods sold during the period must be matched with the sales revenue earned during the period.

2. **Report inventory and cost of goods sold using the four inventory costing methods. p. 344**
   The chapter discussed four different inventory costing methods used to allocate costs between the units remaining in inventory and to the units sold, and their applications in different economic circumstances. The methods discussed were FIFO, LIFO, weighted average cost, and specific identification. Each of the inventory costing methods conforms with GAAP. Public companies using LIFO must provide note disclosures that allow conversion of inventory and cost of goods sold to FIFO amounts. Remember that the cost flow assumption need not match the physical flow of inventory.

3. **Decide when the use of different inventory costing methods is beneficial to a company. p. 350**
   The selection of an inventory costing method is important because it will affect reported income, income tax expense (and hence cash flow), and the inventory valuation reported on the balance sheet. In a period of rising prices, FIFO normally results in a higher income and higher taxes than LIFO; in a period of falling prices, the opposite occurs. The choice of methods is normally made to minimize taxes.

4. **Compare companies using different inventory costing methods. p. 352**
   These comparisons can be made by converting the LIFO company's statements to FIFO. Public companies using LIFO must disclose the differences between LIFO and FIFO values for beginning and ending inventory. These amounts are often called the *LIFO reserve*. The beginning LIFO reserve minus the ending LIFO reserve equals the difference in cost of goods sold under FIFO. Pretax income is affected by the same amount in the opposite direction. This amount times the tax rate is the tax effect.

5. **Report inventory at the lower of cost or market (LCM). p. 354**
   Ending inventory should be measured based on the lower of actual cost or replacement cost (LCM basis). This practice can have a major effect on the statements of companies facing declining costs. Damaged, obsolete, and out-of-season inventory should also be written down to their current estimated net realizable value if below cost. The LCM adjustment increases cost of goods sold, decreases income, and decreases reported inventory in the year of the write-down.

6. **Evaluate inventory management using the inventory turnover ratio and the effects of inventory on cash flows. p. 356**

The inventory turnover ratio measures the efficiency of inventory management. It reflects how many times average inventory was produced and sold during the period. Analysts and creditors watch this ratio because a sudden decline may mean that a company is facing an unexpected drop in demand for its products or is becoming sloppy in its production management. When a net *decrease in inventory* for the period occurs, sales are more than purchases; thus, the decrease must be *added* in computing cash flows from operations. When a net *increase in inventory* for the period occurs, sales are less than purchases; thus, the increase must be *subtracted* in computing cash flows from operations.

7. **Analyze the effects of inventory errors on financial statements and methods for keeping track of inventory. p. 359**

An error in the measurement of ending inventory affects cost of goods sold on the current period's income statement and ending inventory on the balance sheet. Because this year's ending inventory becomes next year's beginning inventory, it also affects cost of goods sold in the following period, by the same amount, but in the opposite direction. These relationships can be seen through the cost of goods sold equation (BI + P − EI = CGS). A company can keep track of the ending inventory and cost of goods sold for the period using (1) the perpetual inventory system, which is based on the maintenance of detailed and continuous inventory records, and (2) the periodic inventory system, which is based on a physical count of ending inventory and use of the inventory equation to determine cost of goods sold.

In this and previous chapters, we discussed the current assets of a business. These assets are critical to operations, but many of them do not directly produce value. In Chapter 8, we will discuss the noncurrent assets property, plant, and equipment; natural resources; and intangibles that are the elements of productive capacity. Many of the noncurrent assets produce value, such as a factory that manufactures cars. These assets present some interesting accounting problems because they benefit a number of accounting periods.

KEY **RATIO**

Inventory turnover ratio measures the efficiency of inventory management. It reflects how many times average inventory was produced and sold during the period. (p. 356):

$$\text{Inventory Turnover} = \frac{\text{Cost of Goods Sold}}{\text{Average Inventory}}$$

FINDING **FINANCIAL INFORMATION**

Balance Sheet

Under Current Assets
Inventories

Income Statement

Expenses
Cost of goods sold

Statement of Cash Flows

Under Operating Activities (indirect method):
Net income
 − increases in inventory
 + decreases in inventory
 + increases in accounts payable
 − decreases in accounts payable

Notes

Under Summary of Significant Accounting Policies:
Description of management's choice of inventory accounting policy (FIFO, LIFO, LCM, etc.)

In Separate Note
If not listed on balance sheet, components of inventory (merchandise, raw materials, work in progress, finished goods)
If using LIFO, LIFO reserve (excess of FIFO over LIFO)

KEY TERMS

Average Cost Method p. 347
Cost of Goods Sold Equation p. 343
Direct Labor p. 342
Factory Overhead p. 342
Finished Goods Inventory p. 341
First-In, First-Out (FIFO) Method
  p. 346
Goods Available for Sale p. 343
Inventory p. 340

Last-In, First-Out (LIFO) Method
  p. 346
LIFO Liquidation p. 364
LIFO Reserve p. 352
Lower of Cost or Market (LCM)
  p. 354
Merchandise Inventory p. 340
Net Realizable Value p. 355
Periodic Inventory System p. 361

Perpetual Inventory System p. 361
Purchase Discount p. 367
Purchase Returns and Allowances
  p. 367
Raw Materials Inventory p. 341
Replacement Cost p. 354
Specific Identification Method
  p. 345
Work in Process Inventory p. 341

QUESTIONS

1. Why is inventory an important item to both internal (management) and external users of financial statements?
2. What are the general guidelines for deciding which items should be included in inventory?
3. Explain the application of the cost principle to an item in the ending inventory.
4. Define *goods available for sale*. How does it differ from cost of goods sold?
5. Define *beginning inventory* and *ending inventory*.
6. The chapter discussed four inventory costing methods. List the four methods and briefly explain each.
7. Explain how income can be manipulated when the specific identification inventory costing method is used.
8. Contrast the effects of LIFO versus FIFO on reported assets (i.e., the ending inventory) when (a) prices are rising and (b) prices are falling.
9. Contrast the income statement effect of LIFO versus FIFO (i.e., on pretax income) when (a) prices are rising and (b) prices are falling.
10. Contrast the effects of LIFO versus FIFO on cash outflow and inflow.
11. Explain briefly the application of the LCM concept to the ending inventory and its effect on the income statement and balance sheet when market is lower than cost.
12. When a perpetual inventory system is used, unit costs of the items sold are known at the date of each sale. In contrast, when a periodic inventory system is used, unit costs are known only at the end of the accounting period. Why are these statements correct?

MULTIPLE CHOICE QUESTIONS

1. How many of the following statements are true regarding *Cost of Goods Sold*?
   - ▩ Cost of goods sold represents the cost that a company incurred to purchase or produce inventory in the current period.
   - ▩ Cost of goods sold is an expense on the income statement.
   - ▩ Cost of goods sold is affected by the inventory method selected by a company (FIFO, LIFO, etc.).
   - a. none
   - b. one
   - c. two
   - d. three
2. The inventory costing method selected by a company will affect
   - a. the balance sheet.
   - b. the income statement.
   - c. the statement of retained earnings.
   - d. all of the above.
3. Which of the following is *not* a component of the cost of inventory?
   - a. administrative overhead
   - b. direct labor
   - c. raw materials
   - d. factory overhead

4. Each period, the cost of goods available for sale is allocated between
   a. assets and liabilities.
   b. assets and expenses.
   c. assets and revenues.
   d. expenses and liabilities.

5. A New York bridal dress designer who makes high-end custom wedding dresses most likely uses which inventory costing method?
   a. FIFO
   b. LIFO
   c. Weighted average
   d. Specific identification

6. An increasing inventory turnover ratio
   a. indicates a longer time span between the ordering and receiving of inventory.
   b. indicates a shorter time span between the ordering and receiving of inventory.
   c. indicates a shorter time span between the purchase and sale of inventory.
   d. indicates a longer time span between the purchase and sale of inventory.

7. If the ending balance in accounts payable decreases from one period to the next, which of the following is true?
   a. Cash payments to suppliers exceeded current period purchases.
   b. Cash payments to suppliers were less than current period purchases.
   c. Cash receipts from customers exceeded cash payments to suppliers.
   d. Cash receipts from customers exceeded current period purchases.

8. How many of the following regarding the *lower of cost or market* rule for inventory are true?

   ■ The lower of cost or market rule is an example of the historical cost principle.
   ■ When the replacement cost of inventory drops below the cost shown in the financial records, net income is reduced.
   ■ When the replacement cost of inventory drops below the cost shown in the financial records, total assets are reduced.

   a. none
   b. one
   c. two
   d. three

9. Which inventory method provides a better matching of current costs with sales revenue on the income statement and outdated values for inventory on the balance sheet?
   a. FIFO
   b. weighted average
   c. LIFO
   d. specific identification

10. Which of the following is false regarding a perpetual inventory system?
    a. Physical counts are not needed since records are maintained on a transaction-by-transaction basis.
    b. The balance in the inventory account is updated with each inventory purchase and sale transaction.
    c. Cost of goods sold is increased as sales are recorded
    d. The account Purchases is not used as inventory is acquired.

For more practice with multiple choice questions, go to our website at www.mhhe.com/libby4e, click on "Student Center" in the upper left menu, click on this chapter's name and number from the list of contents, and then click on "Multiple Choice Quiz" from the menu on the left.

MINI-EXERCISES

M7-1
LO1

Matching Inventory Items to Type of Business

Match the type of inventory with the type of business in the following matrix:

	TYPE OF BUSINESS	
Type of Inventory	**Merchandising**	**Manufacturing**
Merchandise		
Finished goods		
Work in process		
Raw materials		

Recording the Cost of Purchases for a Merchandiser

M7-2
LO1

Elite Apparel purchased 80 new shirts and recorded a total cost of $3,140 determined as follows:

Invoice cost	$2,600
Shipping charges	165
Import taxes and duties	115
Interest paid in advance (10%) on $2,600 borrowed to finance the purchase	260
	$3,140

Required:
Make the needed corrections in this calculation. Give the journal entry(ies) to record this purchase in the correct amount, assuming a perpetual inventory system. Show computations.

Identifying the Cost of Inventories for a Manufacturer

M7-3
LO1

Operating costs incurred by a manufacturing company become either (*a*) part of the cost of inventory to be expensed as cost of goods sold at the time the finished goods are sold or (*b*) expenses at the time they are incurred. Indicate whether each of the following costs belongs in category *a.* or *b.*

	a. Part of Inventory	*b.* Expense as Incurred
1. Wages of factory workers		
2. Sales salaries		
3. Costs of raw materials purchased		
4. Heat, light, and power for the factory building		
5. Heat, light, and power for the headquarters office building		

Inferring Purchases Using the Cost of Goods Sold Equation

M7-4
LO1
JCPenney

JCPenney Company, Inc., is a major retailer with department stores in all 50 states. The dominant portion of the company's business consists of providing merchandise and services to consumers through department stores that include catalog departments. In a recent annual report, JCPenney reported cost of goods sold of $10,969 million, ending inventory for the current year of $3,062 million, and ending inventory for the previous year of $2,969 million.

Required:
Is it possible to develop a reasonable estimate of the merchandise purchases for the year? If so, prepare the estimate; if not, explain why.

Matching Financial Statement Effects to Inventory Costing Methods

M7-5
LO2

Indicate whether the FIFO or LIFO inventory costing method normally produces each of the following effects under the listed circumstances.

a. Rising costs
       Highest net income _____
       Highest inventory _____
b. Declining costs
       Highest net income _____
       Highest inventory _____

Matching Inventory Costing Method Choices to Company Circumstances

M7-6
LO3

Indicate whether the FIFO or LIFO inventory costing method would normally be selected under each of the listed circumstances.

a. Rising costs _____
b. Declining costs _____

M7-7 Reporting Inventory Under Lower of Cost or Market

LO5

Kinney Company had the following inventory items on hand at the end of the year.

	Quantity	Cost per Item	Replacement Cost per Item
Item A	50	$75	$100
Item B	25	60	50

Computing the lower of cost or market on an item-by-item basis, determine what amount would be reported on the balance sheet for inventory.

M7-8 Determining the Effects of Inventory Management Changes on Inventory Turnover Ratio

LO6

Indicate the most likely effect of the following changes in inventory management on the inventory turnover ratio (1 for increase, 2 for decrease, and NE for no effect).

_____ *a.* Parts inventory delivered daily by suppliers instead of weekly.
_____ *b.* Shorten production process from 10 days to 8 days.
_____ *c.* Extend payments for inventory purchases from 15 days to 30 days.

M7-9 Determining the Financial Statement Effects of Inventory Errors

LO7

Assume the 2003 ending inventory was understated by $100,000. Explain how this error would affect the 2003 and 2004 pretax income amounts. What would be the effects if the 2003 ending inventory were overstated by $100,000 instead of understated?

EXERCISES

E7-1 Inferring Missing Amounts Based on Income Statement Relationships

LO1

Supply the missing dollar amounts for the 2004 income statement of Lewis Retailers for each of the following independent cases:

Cases	Sales Revenue	Beginning Inventory	Purchases	Total Available	Ending Inventory	Cost of Goods Sold	Gross Profit	Expenses	Pretax Income or (Loss)
A	$ 650	$100	$700	$?	$500	$?	$?	$200	$?
B	900	200	800	?	?	?	?	150	0
C	?	150	?	?	300	200	400	100	?
D	800	?	600	?	250	?	?	250	100
E	1,000	?	900	1,100	?	?	500	?	(50)

E7-2 Inferring Missing Amounts Based on Income Statement Relationships

LO1

Supply the missing dollar amounts for the 2006 income statement of Travis Company for each of the following independent cases:

	Case A	Case B	Case C
Sales revenue	$ 8,000	$ 6,000	$?
Sales returns and allowances	150	?	275
Net sales revenue	?	?	5,920
Beginning inventory	11,000	6,500	4,000
Purchases	5,000	?	9,420
Goods available for sale	?	15,270	13,420
Ending inventory	10,250	11,220	?
Cost of goods sold	?	?	5,400
Gross profit	?	1,450	?
Expenses	1,300	?	520
Pretax income	$ 800	$ (500)	$ 0

Inferring Merchandise Purchases

The Gap, Inc., is a specialty retailer that operates stores selling clothes under the trade names Gap, GapKids, BabyGap, and Banana Republic. Assume that you are employed as a stock analyst and your boss has just completed a review of the new Gap annual report. She provided you with her notes, but they are missing some information that you need. Her notes show that the ending inventory for Gap in the current year was $243,482,000 and in the previous year was $193,268,000. Net sales for the current year were $1,586,596,000. Gross profit was $540,360,000; net income was $97,628,000. For your analysis, you determine that you need to know the amount of purchases for the year and cost of goods sold.

Required:
Do you need to ask your boss for her copy of the annual report, or can you develop the information from her notes? Explain and show calculations.

E7-3
LO1
The Gap, Inc.

Analyzing and Interpreting the Financial Statement Effects of LIFO and FIFO

Lunar Company uses a periodic inventory system. At the end of the annual accounting period, December 31, 2004, the accounting records provided the following information for Product 2:

E7-4
LO2, 3

Transactions	Units	Unit Cost
a. Inventory, December 31, 2003	3,000	$12
For the year 2004:		
b. Purchase, April 11	9,000	10
c. Purchase, June 1	8,000	13
d. Sale, May 1 ($40 each)	5,000	
e. Sale, July 3 ($40 each)	6,000	
f. Operating expenses (excluding income tax expense), $195,000		

Required:
1. Prepare a separate income statement through pretax income that details cost of goods sold for Cases A and B. For each case, show the computation of the ending inventory. (*Hint:* Set up adjacent columns for each case.)
   a. Case A: FIFO.
   b. Case B: LIFO.
2. Compare the pretax income and the ending inventory amounts between the two cases. Explain the similarities and differences.
3. Which inventory costing method may be preferred for income tax purposes? Explain.

Analyzing and Interpreting the Financial Statement Effects of LIFO and FIFO

Scoresby Inc. uses a periodic inventory system. At the end of the annual accounting period, December 31, 2006, the accounting records provided the following information for Product 2:

E7-5
LO2, 3

Transactions	Units	Unit Cost
a. Inventory, December 31, 2005	6,000	$ 8
For the year 2006:		
b. Purchase, March 5	19,000	9
c. Purchase, September 19	10,000	11
d. Sale, April 15 ($29 each)	8,000	
e. Sale, October 31 ($31 each)	16,000	
f. Operating expenses (excluding income tax expense), $500,000		

Required:

1. Prepare a separate income statement through pretax income that details cost of goods sold for Cases A and B. For each case, show the computation of the ending inventory. (*Hint:* Set up adjacent columns for each case.)
   a. Case A: FIFO.
   b. Case B: LIFO.
2. Compare the pretax income and the ending inventory amounts between the two cases. Explain the similarities and differences.
3. Which inventory costing method may be preferred for income tax purposes? Explain.

E7-6

LO2, 3

Evaluating the Choice among Three Alternative Inventory Methods Based on Income and Cash Flow Effects

Courtney Company uses a periodic inventory system. Data for 2004: beginning merchandise inventory (December 31, 2003), 2,000 units at $35; purchases, 8,000 units at $38; expenses (excluding income taxes), $142,000; ending inventory per physical count at December 31, 2004, 1,800 units; sales price per unit, $70; and average income tax rate, 30 percent.

Required:

1. Prepare income statements under the FIFO, LIFO, and weighted average costing methods. Use a format similar to the following:

		INVENTORY COSTING METHOD		
Income Statement	Units	FIFO	LIFO	Weighted Average
Sales revenue	_____	$_____	$_____	$_____
Cost of goods sold	_____	_____	_____	_____
Beginning inventory	_____	_____	_____	_____
Purchases	_____	_____	_____	_____
Goods available for sale	_____	_____	_____	_____
Ending inventory	_____	_____	_____	_____
Cost of goods sold	_____	_____	_____	_____
Gross profit		_____	_____	_____
Expenses		_____	_____	_____
Pretax income		_____	_____	_____
Income tax expense		_____	_____	_____
Net income		_____	_____	_____

2. Between FIFO and LIFO, which method is preferable in terms of (a) net income and (b) cash flow? Explain.
3. What would your answer to requirement 2 be, assuming that prices were falling? Explain.

E7-7

LO2, 3

Evaluating the Choice among Three Alternative Inventory Methods Based on Cash Flow Effects

Following is partial information for the income statement of Timber Company under three different inventory costing methods, assuming the use of a periodic inventory system:

	FIFO	LIFO	Weighted Average
Unit sales price, $50			
Cost of goods sold			
Beginning inventory (330 units)	$11,220	$11,220	$11,220
Purchases (475 units)	17,100	17,100	17,100
Goods available for sale			
Ending inventory (510 units)			
Cost of goods sold			
Expenses, $1,600			

Required:

1. Compute cost of goods sold under the FIFO, LIFO, and weighted average inventory costing methods.
2. Prepare an income statement through pretax income for each method.
3. Rank the three methods in order of favorable cash flow and explain the basis for your ranking.

Analyzing Notes to Adjust Inventory from LIFO to FIFO

E7-8
L04
Ford Motor Company

The following note was contained in a recent Ford Motor Company annual report:

> **Inventory Valuation—Automotive.** Inventories are stated at the lower of cost or market. The cost of most US inventories is determined by the last-in, first-out ("LIFO") method. The cost of the remaining inventories is determined substantially by the first-in, first-out ("FIFO") method.
>
> If FIFO were the only method of inventory accounting used by the company, inventories would have been $1,235 million higher than reported this year and $1,246 million higher than reported last year.

The major classes of inventory for the company's automotive business segment at December 31 were as follows:

	INVENTORY (in $ millions)	
	Current Year	Previous Year
Finished products	$3,413.8	$3,226.7
Raw material and work in process	2,983.9	2,981.6
Supplies	419.1	429.9
Total	$6,816.8	$6,638.2

Required:

1. Determine the ending inventory that would have been reported in the current year if Ford had used only FIFO.
2. The cost of goods sold reported by Ford for the current year was $74,315 million. Determine the cost of goods sold that would have been reported if Ford had used only FIFO for both years.

Reporting Inventory at Lower of Cost or Market

E7-9
L05

Peterson Company is preparing the annual financial statements dated December 31, 2004. Ending inventory information about the five major items stocked for regular sale follows:

ENDING INVENTORY, 2004			
Item	Quantity on Hand	Unit Cost When Acquired (FIFO)	Replacement Cost (Market) at Year-End
A	50	$15	$13
B	75	40	40
C	10	50	52
D	30	30	30
E	400	8	6

Required:

Compute the valuation that should be used for the 2004 ending inventory using the LCM rule applied on an item-by-item basis. (*Hint:* Set up columns for Item, Quantity, Total Cost, Total Market, and LCM Valuation.)

E7-10
L05

Reporting Inventory at Lower of Cost or Market

Demski Company was formed on January 1, 2004, and is preparing the annual financial statements dated December 31, 2004. Ending inventory information about the four major items stocked for regular sale follows:

ENDING INVENTORY, 2004			
Item	Quantity on Hand	Unit Cost When Acquired (FIFO)	Replacement Cost (Market) at Year-End
A	20	$12	$13
B	75	40	38
C	35	55	52
D	10	30	35

Required:

1. Compute the valuation that should be used for the 2004 ending inventory using the LCM rule applied on an item-by-item basis. (*Hint:* Set up columns for Item, Quantity, Total Cost, Total Market, and LCM Valuation.)
2. What will be the effect of the write-down of inventory to lower of cost or market on cost of goods sold for the year ended December 31, 2004?

E7-11
L06
Dell Computer

Analyzing and Interpreting the Inventory Turnover Ratio

Dell Computer is the leading manufacturer of personal computers. In a recent year, it reported the following:

Net sales revenue	$12,327
Cost of sales	9,605
Beginning inventory	251
Ending inventory	233

Required:

1. Determine the inventory turnover ratio and average days to sell inventory for the current year.
2. Explain the meaning of each number.

E7-12
L04, 6

Analyzing and Interpreting the Effects of the LIFO/FIFO Choice on Inventory Turnover Ratio

The records at the end of January 2004 for All Star Company showed the following for a particular kind of merchandise:

Inventory, December 31, 2003 at FIFO 19 Units @ $14 = 266
Inventory, December 31, 2003 at LIFO 19 Units @ $10 = 190

Transactions	Units	Unit Cost	Total Cost
Purchase, January 9, 2004	25	15	$375
Purchase, January 20, 2004	50	16	800
Sale, January 11, 2004 (at $38 per unit)	40		
Sale, January 27, 2004 (at $39 per unit)	28		

Required:

Compute the inventory turnover ratio under the FIFO and LIFO inventory costing methods (show computations and round to the nearest dollar). Explain which you believe is the more accurate indicator of the liquidity of inventory.

Interpreting the Effect of Changes in Inventories and Accounts Payable on Cash Flow from Operations

E7-13
LO6
First Team
Sports, Inc.

First Team Sports, Inc., is engaged in the manufacture (through independent contractors) and distribution of in-line roller skates, ice skates, street hockey equipment, and related accessory products. Its recent annual report included the following on its balance sheet:

CONSOLIDATED BALANCE SHEETS
February 29, Current Year and February 28, Previous Year

	Current Year	Previous Year
. . . .		
Inventory (Note 3)	22,813,850	20,838,171
. . . .	. . .	. . .
Trade accounts payable	9,462,883	9,015,376

Required:

Explain the effects of the changes in inventory and trade accounts payable on cash flow from operating activities for the current year.

Analyzing the Effects of an Error in Recording Purchases

E7-14
LO7

Garraway Ski Company mistakenly recorded purchases of inventory on account received during the last week of December 2003 as purchases during January of 2004 (this is called a *purchases cutoff error*). Garraway uses a periodic inventory system, and ending inventory was correctly counted and reported each year. Assuming that no correction was made in 2003 or 2004, indicate whether each of the following financial statement amounts will be understated, overstated, or correct.

1. Net Income for 2003.
2. Net Income for 2004.
3. Retained Earnings for December 31, 2003.
4. Retained Earnings for December 31, 2004.

Analyzing the Effect of an Inventory Error Disclosed in an Actual Note to a Financial Statement

E7-15
LO7
Gibson
Greeting
Cards

Several years ago, the financial statements of Gibson Greeting Cards contained the following note:

On July 1, the Company announced that it had determined that the inventory . . . had been overstated. . . . The overstatement of inventory . . . was $8,806,000.

Gibson reported an incorrect net income amount of $25,852,000 for the year in which the error occurred and the income tax rate was 39.3 percent.

Required:

1. Compute the amount of net income that Gibson reported after correcting the inventory error. Show computations.
2. Assume that the inventory error was not discovered. Identify the financial statement accounts that would have been incorrect for the year the error occurred and for the subsequent year. State whether each account was understated or overstated.

E7-16

L07

Analyzing and Interpreting the Impact of an Inventory Error

Dallas Corporation prepared the following two income statements (simplified for illustrative purposes):

	First Quarter 2004		Second Quarter 2004	
Sales revenue		$15,000		$18,000
Cost of goods sold				
Beginning inventory	$ 3,000		$4,000	
Purchases	7,000		12,000	
Goods available for sale	10,000		16,000	
Ending inventory	4,000		9,000	
Cost of goods sold		6,000		7,000
Gross profit		9,000		11,000
Expenses		5,000		6,000
Pretax income		$ 4,000		$ 5,000

During the third quarter, it was discovered that the ending inventory for the first quarter should have been $4,400.

Required:

1. What effect did this error have on the combined pretax income of the two quarters? Explain.
2. Did this error affect the EPS amounts for each quarter? (See Chapter 5 discussion of EPS.) Explain.
3. Prepare corrected income statements for each quarter.
4. Set up a schedule with the following headings to reflect the comparative effects of the correct and incorrect amounts on the income statement:

	1st Quarter			2nd Quarter		
Income Statement Item	**Incorrect**	**Correct**	**Error**	**Incorrect**	**Correct**	**Error**

E7-17

Standard Oil

(Supplement A) Analyzing the Effects of a Reduction in the Amount of LIFO Inventory

An annual report of Standard Oil Company (Indiana) contained the following note:

> During this year and last year, the company reduced certain inventory quantities that were valued at lower LIFO costs prevailing in prior years. The effect of these reductions was to increase aftertax earnings this year by $71 million, or $0.24 per share, and $74 million, or $0.25 per share last year.

Required:

1. Explain why the reduction in inventory quantity increased after-tax earnings (net income) for Standard Oil.
2. If Standard Oil had used FIFO, would the reductions in inventory quantity during the two years have increased after tax earnings? Explain.

E7-18

(Supplement B) Recording Sales and Purchases with Cash Discounts

The Cycle Shop sells merchandise on credit terms of 2/10, n/30. A sale invoiced at $800 (cost of sales $500) was made to Missy Clemons on February 1, 2004. The company uses the gross method of recording sales discounts.

Required:

1. Give the journal entry to record the credit sale. Assume use of the perpetual inventory system.
2. Give the journal entry, assuming that the account was collected in full on February 9, 2004.
3. Give the journal entry, assuming, instead, that the account was collected in full on March 2, 2004.

On March 4, 2004, the company purchased bicycles and accessories from a supplier on credit, invoiced at $8,000; the terms were 1/15, n/30. The company uses the gross method to record purchases.

Required:

4. Give the journal entry to record the purchase on credit. Assume the use of the perpetual inventory system.
5. Give the journal entry, assuming that the account was paid in full on March 12, 2004.
6. Give the journal entry, assuming, instead, that the account was paid in full on March 28, 2004.

(Supplement C) Recording Purchases and Sales Using a Perpetual and Periodic Inventory System

E7-19

Demski Company reported beginning inventory of 100 units at a unit cost of $25. It engaged in the following purchase and sale transactions during 2003:

Jan. 14 Sold 25 units at unit sales price of $45 on open account.

April 9 Purchased 15 additional units at unit cost of $25 on open account.

Sep. 2 Sold 50 units at sales price of $50 on open account.

At the end of the 2003, a physical count showed that Demski Company had 40 units of inventory still on hand.

Required:

Record each transaction, assuming that Demski Company uses (a) a perpetual inventory system and (b) a periodic inventory system (including any necessary entries at the end of the accounting period on December 31).

PROBLEMS

Analyzing Items to Be Included in Inventory

P7-1
LO1

Reggie Company has just completed a physical inventory count at year-end, December 31, 2004. Only the items on the shelves, in storage, and in the receiving area were counted and costed on a FIFO basis. The inventory amounted to $70,000. During the audit, the independent CPA developed the following additional information:

a. Goods costing $500 were being used by a customer on a trial basis and were excluded from the inventory count at December 31, 2004.
b. Goods in transit on December 31, 2004, from a supplier, with terms FOB destination (explained in the "Required" section), cost $600. Because these goods had not arrived, they were excluded from the physical inventory count.
c. On December 31, 2004, goods in transit to customers, with terms FOB shipping point, amounted to $1,000 (expected delivery date January 10, 2005). Because the goods had been shipped, they were excluded from the physical inventory count.
d. On December 28, 2004, a customer purchased goods for cash amounting to $2,000 and left them "for pickup on January 3, 2005." Reggie Company had paid $1,200 for the goods and, because they were on hand, included the latter amount in the physical inventory count.
e. On the date of the inventory count, the company received notice from a supplier that goods ordered earlier at a cost of $2,200 had been delivered to the transportation company on December 27, 2004; the terms were FOB shipping point. Because the shipment had not arrived by December 31, 2004, it was excluded from the physical inventory.
f. On December 31, 2004, the company shipped $950 worth of goods to a customer, FOB destination. The goods are expected to arrive at their destination no earlier than January 8, 2005. Because the goods were not on hand, they were not included in the physical inventory count.

g. One of the items sold by the company has such a low volume that the management planned to drop it last year. To induce Reggie Company to continue carrying the item, the manufacturer-supplier provided the item on a "consignment basis." This means that the manufacturer-supplier retains ownership of the item, and Reggie Company (the consignee) has no responsibility to pay for the items until they are sold to a customer. Each month, Reggie Company sends a report to the manufacturer on the number sold and remits cash for the cost. At the end of December 2004, Reggie Company had five of these items on hand; therefore, they were included in the physical inventory count at $1,000 each.

Required:

Assume that Reggie's accounting policy requires including in inventory all goods for which it has title. Note that the point where title (ownership) changes hands is determined by the shipping terms in the sales contract. When goods are shipped "F.O.B. shipping point," title changes hands at shipment and the buyer normally pays for shipping. When they are shipped "F.O.B. destination," title changes hands on delivery, and the seller normally pays for shipping. Begin with the $70,000 inventory amount and compute the correct amount for the ending inventory. Explain the basis for your treatment of each of the preceding items. (*Hint:* Set up three columns: Item, Amount, and Explanation.)

P7-2
LO2

Analyzing the Effects of Four Alternative Inventory Methods (AP7-1)

Allsigns Company uses a periodic inventory system. At the end of the annual accounting period, December 31, 2007, the accounting records for the most popular item in inventory showed the following:

Transactions	Units	Unit Cost
Beginning inventory, January 1, 2007	400	$30
Transactions during 2007:		
a. Purchase, February 20	600	32
b. Sale, April 1 ($46 each)	(700)	
c. Purchase, June 30	500	36
d. Sale, August 1 ($46 each)	(100)	
e. Sales return, August 5 (related to transaction *d*)	20	

Required:

Compute the amount of (a) goods available for sale, (b) ending inventory, and (c) cost of goods sold at December 31, 2007, under each of the following inventory costing methods (show computations and round to the nearest dollar):

1. Weighted average cost.
2. First-in, first-out.
3. Last-in, first-out.
4. Specific identification, assuming that the April 1, 2007, sale was selected one-fifth from the beginning inventory and four-fifths from the purchase of February 20, 2007. Assume that the sale of August 1, 2007, was selected from the purchase of June 30, 2007.

P7-3
LO2, 3

Evaluating Four Alternative Inventory Methods Based on Income and Cash Flow

At the end of January 2004, the records of Atlanta Company showed the following for a particular item that sold at $18 per unit:

Transactions	Units	Amount
Inventory, January 1, 2004	500	$2,500
Sale, January 10	(400)	
Purchase, January 12	600	3,600
Sale, January 17	(300)	
Purchase, January 26	160	1,280
Purchase return, January 28	(10)	Out of Jan. 26 purchase

Required:

1. Assuming the use of a periodic inventory system, prepare a summarized income statement through gross profit on sales under each method of inventory: (a) weighted average cost, (b) FIFO, (c) LIFO, and (d) specific identification. For specific identification, assume that the first sale was out of the beginning inventory and the second sale was out of the January 12 purchase. Show the inventory computations in detail.
2. Of FIFO and LIFO, which method would result in the higher pretax income? Which would result in the higher EPS?
3. Of FIFO and LIFO, which method would result in the lower income tax expense? Explain, assuming a 30 percent average tax rate.
4. Of FIFO and LIFO, which method would produce the more favorable cash flow? Explain.

Analyzing and Interpreting Income Manipulation under the LIFO Inventory Method

P7-4
LO2, 3

Pacific Company sells electronic test equipment that it acquires from a foreign source. During the year 2008, the inventory records reflected the following:

	Units	Unit Cost	Total Cost
Beginning inventory	15	$12,000	$180,000
Purchases	40	10,000	400,000
Sales (45 units at $25,000 each)			

Inventory is valued at cost using the LIFO inventory method. On December 28, 2008, the unit cost of the test equipment was decreased to $8,000. The cost will be decreased again during the first quarter of the next year.

Required:

1. Complete the following income statement summary using the LIFO method and the periodic inventory system (show computations):

Sales revenue	$_____
Cost of goods sold	_____
Gross profit	_____
Expenses	300,000
Pretax income	$_____
Ending inventory	$_____

2. The management, for various reasons, is considering buying 20 additional units before December 31, 2008, at $8,000 each. Restate the income statement (and ending inventory), assuming that this purchase is made on December 31, 2008.
3. How much did pretax income change because of the decision on December 31, 2008? Is there any evidence of income manipulation? Explain.

Evaluating the LIFO and FIFO Choice When Costs Are Rising and Falling

P7-5
LO2, 3

Income is to be evaluated under four different situations as follows:

a. Prices are rising:
   1. Situation A: FIFO is used.
   2. Situation B: LIFO is used.
b. Prices are falling:
   1. Situation C: FIFO is used.
   2. Situation D: LIFO is used.

The basic data common to all four situations are sales, 500 units for $12,500; beginning inventory, 300 units; purchases, 400 units; ending inventory, 200 units; and operating expenses, $4,000. The following tabulated income statements for each situation have been set up for analytical purposes:

	PRICES RISING		PRICES FALLING	
	Situation A FIFO	Situation B LIFO	Situation C FIFO	Situation D LIFO
Sales revenue	$12,500	$12,500	$12,500	$12,500
Cost of goods sold				
Beginning inventory	3,600	?	?	?
Purchases	5,200	?	?	?
Goods available for sale	8,800	?	?	?
Ending inventory	2,600	?	?	?
Cost of goods sold	6,200	?	?	?
Gross profit	6,300	?	?	?
Expenses	4,000	4,000	4,000	4,000
Pretax income	2,300	?	?	?
Income tax expense (30%)	690	?	?	?
Net income	$ 1,610			

Required:

1. Complete the preceding tabulation for each situation. In Situations A and B (prices rising), assume the following: beginning inventory, 300 units at $12 = $3,600; purchases, 400 units at $13 = $5,200. In Situations C and D (prices falling), assume the opposite; that is, beginning inventory, 300 units at $13 = $3,900; purchases, 400 units at $12 = $4,800. Use periodic inventory procedures.
2. Analyze the relative effects on pretax income and on net income as demonstrated by requirement 1 when prices are rising and when prices are falling.
3. Analyze the relative effects on the cash position for each situation.
4. Would you recommend FIFO or LIFO? Explain.

P7-6
LO4
General
Motors

Evaluating the Choice between LIFO and FIFO Based on an Inventory Note (AP7-2)

An annual report for General Motors Corporation included the following note:

> Inventories are stated generally at cost, which is not in excess of market. The cost of substantially all domestic inventories was determined by the last-in, first-out (LIFO) method. If the first-in, first-out (FIFO) method of inventory valuation had been used by the Corporation for U.S. inventories, it is estimated that they would be $2,077.1 million higher at the end of this year, compared with $1,784.5 million higher at the end of last year.

For the year, GM reported net income (after taxes) of $320.5 million. At year-end, the balance of the GM retained earnings account was $15,340 million.

Required:

1. Determine the amount of net income that GM would have reported for the year if it had used the FIFO method (assume a 30 percent tax rate).
2. Determine the amount of retained earnings that GM would have reported at year-end if it always had used the FIFO method (assume a 30 percent tax rate).
3. Use of the LIFO method reduced the amount of taxes that GM had to pay for the year compared with the amount that would have been paid if it had used FIFO. Calculate the amount of this reduction (assume a 30 percent tax rate).

P7-7
LO5

Evaluating the Income Statement and Cash Flow Effects of Lower of Cost or Market

Smart Company prepared its annual financial statements dated December 31, 2004. The company applies the FIFO inventory costing method; however, the company neglected to apply LCM to the ending inventory. The preliminary 2004 income statement follows:

Sales revenue		$280,000
Cost of goods sold		
Beginning inventory	$ 30,000	
Purchases	182,000	
Goods available for sale	212,000	
Ending inventory (FIFO cost)	44,000	
Cost of goods sold		168,000
Gross profit		112,000
Operating expenses		61,000
Pretax income		51,000
Income tax expense (30%)		15,300
Net income		$ 35,700

Assume that you have been asked to restate the 2004 financial statements to incorporate LCM. You have developed the following data relating to the 2004 ending inventory:

		ACQUISITION COST		CURRENT REPLACEMENT UNIT COST
Item	Quantity	Unit	Total	(Market)
A	3,000	$3	$ 9,000	$4
B	1,500	4	6,000	2
C	7,000	2	14,000	4
D	3,000	5	15,000	3
			$44,000	

Required:
1. Restate this income statement to reflect LCM valuation of the 2004 ending inventory. Apply LCM on an item-by-item basis and show computations.
2. Compare and explain the LCM effect on each amount that was changed in requirement 1.
3. What is the conceptual basis for applying LCM to merchandise inventories?
4. Thought question: What effect did LCM have on the 2004 cash flow? What will be the long-term effect on cash flow?

Evaluating the Effects of Manufacturing Changes on Inventory Turnover Ratio and Cash Flows from Operating Activities (AP7-3)

P7-8
LO6

H.–T. Tan and Company has been operating for five years as an electronics component manufacturer specializing in cellular phone components. During this period, it has experienced rapid growth in sales revenue and in inventory. Mr. Tan and his associates have hired you as its first corporate controller. You have put into place new purchasing and manufacturing procedures that are expected to reduce inventories by approximately one-third by year-end. You have gathered the following data related to the changes:

	(IN THOUSANDS)	
	Beginning of Year	End of Year (projected)
Inventory	$463,808	$310,270
		Current Year (projected)
Cost of goods sold		$7,015,069

Required:

1. Compute the inventory turnover ratio based on two different assumptions:
   a. Those presented in the preceding table (a decrease in the balance in inventory).
   b. No change from the beginning of the year in the inventory balance.
2. Compute the effect of the projected change in the balance in inventory on cash flow from operating activities for the year (the sign and amount of effect).
3. On the basis of the preceding analysis, write a brief memo explaining how an increase in inventory turnover can result in an increase in cash flow from operating activities. Also explain how this increase can benefit the company.

P7-9
L07

Analyzing and Interpreting the Effects of Inventory Errors (AP7-4)

The income statements for four consecutive years for Clement Company reflected the following summarized amounts:

	2003	2004	2005	2006
Sales revenue	$50,000	$51,000	$62,000	$58,000
Cost of goods sold	32,500	35,000	43,000	37,000
Gross profit	17,500	16,000	19,000	21,000
Expenses	10,000	12,000	14,000	12,000
Pretax income	$ 7,500	$ 4,000	$ 5,000	$ 9,000

Subsequent to development of these amounts, it has been determined that the physical inventory taken on December 31, 2004, was understated by $3,000.

Required:

1. Recast the income statements to reflect the correct amounts, taking into consideration the inventory error.
2. Compute the gross profit percentage for each year (a) before the correction and (b) after the correction. Do the results lend confidence to your corrected amounts? Explain.
3. What effect would the error have had on the income tax expense assuming a 30 percent average rate?

P7-10
General
Electric

(Supplement A) Analyzing LIFO and FIFO When Inventory Quantities Decline Based on an Actual Note

In a recent annual report, General Electric reported the following in its inventory note:

December 31 (in millions)	Current Year	Prior Year
Raw materials and work in progress	$5,603	$5,515
Finished goods	2,863	2,546
Unbilled shipments	246	280
	8,712	8,341
Less revaluation to LIFO	(2,226)	(2,076)
LIFO value of inventories	$6,486	$6,265

It also reported a $23 million change in cost of goods sold due to "lower inventory levels."

Required:

1. Compute the increase or decrease in the pretax operating profit (loss) that would have been reported for the current year had GE employed FIFO accounting for all inventory for both years.
2. Compute the increase or decrease in pretax operating profit that would have been reported had GE employed LIFO but not reduced inventory quantities during the current year.

(Supplement B) Recording Sales and Purchases with Cash Discounts and Returns

P7-11

Campus Stop, Incorporated, is a student co-op. On January 1, 2009, the beginning inventory was $150,000, the Accounts Receivable balance was $4,000, and the Allowance for Doubtful Accounts had a credit balance of $800. Campus Stop uses a perpetual inventory system and records inventory purchases using the gross method.

The following transactions (summarized) have been selected from 2009 for case purposes:

a. Sold merchandise for cash (cost of sales $137,500)	$275,000
b. Received merchandise returned by customers as unsatisfactory, for cash refund (cost of sales $800)	1,600

Purchased merchandise from vendors on credit; terms 3/10, n/30 as follows:

c. August Supply Company invoice price before deduction of cash discount	5,000
d. Other vendors, invoice price before deduction of cash discount	120,000
e. Purchased equipment for use in store; paid cash	2,200
f. Purchased office supplies for future use in the store; paid cash	700
g. Freight on merchandise purchased; paid cash	400

Paid accounts payable in full during the period as follows:

h. Paid August Supply Company after the discount period	5,000
i. Paid other vendors within the 3% discount period	116,400

Required:
Prepare journal entries for each of the preceding transactions.

ALTERNATE PROBLEMS

Analyzing the Effects of Four Alternative Inventory Methods (P7-2)

AP7-1
LO2

Yalestone Company uses a periodic inventory system. At the end of the annual accounting period, December 31, 2005, the accounting records for the most popular item in inventory showed the following:

Transactions	Units	Unit Cost
Beginning inventory, January 1, 2005	1,800	$2.50
Transactions during 2005:		
a. Purchase, January 30	2,500	3.10
b. Sale, March 14 ($5 each)	(1,450)	
c. Purchase, May 1	1,200	4.00
d. Sale, August 31 ($5 each)	(1,900)	
e. Sales return, September 5 (related to transaction [d])	150	

Required:
Compute the amount of (a) goods available for sale, (b) ending inventory, and (c) cost of goods sold at December 31, 2005, under each of the following inventory costing methods (show computations and round to the nearest dollar):

1. Weighted average cost.
2. First-in, first-out.
3. Last-in, first-out.
4. Specific identification, assuming that the March 14, 2005, sale was selected two-fifths from the beginning inventory and three-fifths from the purchase of January 30, 2005. Assume that the sale of August 31, 2005, was selected from the remainder of the beginning inventory, with the balance from the purchase of May 1, 2005.

AP7-2

L04

DaimlerChrysler
Corporation

Evaluating the Choice between LIFO and FIFO Based on an Inventory Note (P7-6)

The following note was contained in a recent DaimlerChrysler Corporation annual report:

Inventories

Inventories are valued at the lower of cost or market. The cost of approximately 44 percent and 50 percent of inventories for the current and previous years, respectively, is determined on a Last-In, First-Out (LIFO) basis. The balance of inventory cost is determined on a First-In, First-Out (FIFO) basis.

Inventories and Cost of Sales

Inventories are summarized by major classification as follows (in $ millions):

	Current Year	Previous Year
Finished products, including service parts	$1,145	$ 972
Raw materials, finished production parts and supplies	985	1,165
Vehicles held for short-term lease	760	336
Total	$2,890	$2,473

Inventories valued on the LIFO basis would have been $160 million and $123 million higher than reported had they been valued on the FIFO basis at December 31 of the current year and previous year, respectively.

Total automotive manufacturing cost of sales aggregated $27.2 billion and $26.3 billion for the current year and previous year, respectively.

Required:

1. Determine the ending inventory that would have been reported in the current year if Daimler-Chrysler had used only FIFO.
2. Determine the cost of goods sold that would have been reported if DaimlerChrysler had used only FIFO for both years.
3. Explain why DaimlerChrysler management chose to use LIFO for certain of its inventories.

AP7-3

L06

Arctic
Enterprises

Evaluating the Effects of Failed Expansion Plans on Inventory Turnover Ratio and Cash Flows from Operating Activities (P7-8)

Arctic Enterprises, Inc., was the world's second-largest manufacturer of snowmobiles and had experienced exceptional growth in recent years. It planned for a major increase in sales in the following period by increasing production dramatically. Unfortunately, North America experienced less snow that year than in any of the preceding 20 years. As a consequence, sales remained flat, and Arctic reported a small profit of $1.9 million. However, its inventory balance increased by $24 million. Based on the following information, answer the questions that follow:

	(IN THOUSANDS)	
	Beginning of Year	End of Year (projected)
Inventory	$23,808	$47,270
		Current Year
Cost of goods sold		$161,069

Required:

1. Compute the inventory turnover ratio based on two different assumptions:
    a. Those presented in the preceding table.
    b. No change from the beginning of the year in the inventory balance.

2. Compute the effect of the change in the balance in inventory on cash flow from operating activities for the year (the sign and amount of effect).
3. On the basis of your analysis, write a brief memo explaining how a decrease in inventory turnover can result in a decrease in cash flow from operating activities.

Analyzing and Interpreting the Effects of Inventory Errors (P7-9)

AP7-4
LO7

The income statement for Sherwood Company summarized for a four-year period shows the following:

	2003	2004	2005	2006
Sales revenue	$2,000,000	$2,400,000	$2,500,000	$3,000,000
Cost of goods sold	1,400,000	1,630,000	1,780,000	2,100,000
Gross profit	600,000	770,000	720,000	900,000
Expenses	450,000	500,000	520,000	550,000
Pretax income	150,000	270,000	200,000	350,000
Income tax expense (30%)	45,000	81,000	60,000	105,000
Net income	$ 105,000	$ 189,000	$ 140,000	$ 245,000

An audit revealed that in determining these amounts, the ending inventory for 2004 was overstated by $20,000. The company uses a periodic inventory system.

Required:
1. Recast these income statements on a correct basis.
2. Did the error affect cumulative net income for the four-year period? Explain.
3. What effect would the error have had on the income tax expense assuming a 30 percent average rate?

CASES AND **PROJECTS**

Annual Report Cases

Finding Financial Information

CP7-1
LO1, 3, 6

Refer to the financial statements of American Eagle Outfitters given in Appendix B at the end of this book, or open file AEOS.pdf in the Annual Report Cases directory on the student CD-ROM.

AMERICAN EAGLE OUTFITTERS

1. How much inventory does the company hold at the end of the current year?
2. Estimate the amount of merchandise that the company purchased during the current year. (*Hint:* Use the cost of goods sold equation and ignore "certain buying, occupancy, and warehousing expenses.")
3. What method does the company use to determine the cost of its inventory?
4. What was the change in inventory? How did it affect net cash provided by operating activities for the current year?

Finding Financial Information

CP7-2
LO5, 6, 7

Refer to the financial statements of Abercrombie & Fitch given in Appendix C at the end of this book, or open file ANF.pdf in the Annual Report Cases directory on the student CD-ROM.

ABERCROMBIE & FITCH

Required:
1. The company uses lower of cost or market to account for its inventory. At the end of the year, do you expect the company to write its inventory down to replacement cost or net realizable value? Explain your answer.
2. If the company overstated ending inventory by $10 million for the year ended February 3, 2001, what would be the corrected value for Income before Income Taxes?
3. Compute Abercrombie & Fitch's inventory turnover ratio for the year ended February 3, 2001. What does it tell you?

CP7-3 **Comparing Companies within an Industry**

LO6

AMERICAN EAGLE
OUTFITTERS

ABERCROMBIE
&
FITCH

Refer to the financial statements of American Eagle Outfitters given in Appendix B and Abercrombie & Fitch given in Appendix C, and the Industry Ratio Report given in Appendix D at the end of this book or open file CP7-3.xls in the Annual Report Cases directory on the student CD-ROM.

Required:

1. Compute the inventory turnover ratio for both companies for the current year. What would you infer from the difference?
2. Compare the inventory turnover ratio for both companies to the industry average. Are these two companies doing better or worse than the industry average in turning over their inventory?

Financial Reporting and Analysis Cases

CP7-4 **Using Financial Reports: An International Perspective**

Diageo

As the economy becomes more international in scope, users of financial statements are often expected to analyze companies that are not incorporated in the United States. Diageo is a major world corporation located in London. It owns many U.S. businesses such as The Pillsbury Company, Burger King, and Hägen-Dazs ice cream.

Required:

Based on the concepts presented in this book, explain the meaning of the various account classifications shown on the portion of the Diageo annual report presented here. (*Note:* "Share of profits of related companies" and "Minority interests and preference dividends" pertain to topics introduced in subsequent chapters.)

DIAGEO
Consolidated Profit and Loss Account
For the Year Ended 30th September

	Notes	Current Year £m	Prior Year £m
Turnover	1	9,298	6,029
Operating costs	2	(8,349)	(5,387)
		949	642
Share of profits of related companies		18	12
Trading profit	3	967	654
Profit on sale of property		80	39
Reorganisation costs		(35)	(25)
Interest	4	(280)	(93)
Profit on ordinary activities before taxation		732	575
Taxation on profit on ordinary activities		(216)	(155)
Profit on ordinary activities after taxation		516	420
Minority interests and preference dividends	5	(8)	(8)
Profit attributable to ordinary shareholders	6	508	412
Extraordinary items		560	290
Profit for the financial year		1,068	702
Ordinary dividends		(167)	(129)
Transferred to reserves	7	901	573
Earnings per share		55.6p	46.9p

Using Financial Reports: Interpreting Effect of a Change in Accounting for Production-Related Costs

CP7-5
LO1
Dana
Corporation

Dana Corporation designs and manufactures component parts for the vehicular, industrial, and mobile off-highway original equipment markets. In a recent annual report, Dana's inventory note indicated the following:

> Dana changed its method of accounting for inventories effective January 1 . . . to include in inventory certain production-related costs previously charged to expense. This change in accounting principle resulted in a better matching of costs against related revenues. The effect of this change in accounting increased inventories by $23.0 and net income by $12.9.

Required:
1. Under Dana's previous accounting method, certain production costs were recognized as expenses on the income statement in the period they were incurred. When will they be recognized under the new accounting method?
2. Explain how including these costs in inventory increased both inventories and net income for the year.

Using Financial Reports: Interpreting Effects of the LIFO/FIFO Choice on Inventory Turnover

CP7-6
LO4, 6
Caterpillar

In a recent annual report, Caterpillar, Inc., a major manufacturer of farm and construction equipment, reported the following information concerning its inventories:

> The cost of inventories is determined principally by the LIFO (last-in, first-out) method of inventory valuation. This method was first adopted for the major portion of inventories in 1950. The value of inventories on the LIFO basis represented approximately 90% of total inventories at current cost value on December 31, 1995, 1994, and 1993. If the FIFO (first-in, first-out) method had been in use, inventories would have been $2,103, $2,035, and $1,818 higher than reported at December 31, 1995, 1994, and 1993, respectively.

On its balance sheet, it reported:

	1995	1994	1993
Inventories	$1,921	$1,835	$1,525

On its income statement, it reported:

	1995	1994	1993
Cost of goods sold	$12,000	$10,834	$9,075

Required:
As a recently hired financial analyst, you have been asked to analyze the efficiency with which Caterpillar has been managing its inventory and to write a short report. Specifically, you have been asked to compute inventory turnover for 1995 based on FIFO and on LIFO and compare the two ratios with two standards: (1) Caterpillar for the prior year 1994 and (2) its chief competitor, John Deere. For 1995, John Deere's inventory turnover was 4.2 based on FIFO and 9.8 based on LIFO. In your report, include

1. The appropriate ratios computed based on FIFO and LIFO.
2. An explanation for the differences in the ratios across the FIFO and LIFO methods.
3. An explanation of whether the FIFO or LIFO ratios provide a more accurate representation of the companies' efficiency in use of inventory.

CP7-7

General Motors

(Supplement A) Using Financial Reports: Analysis of the Effects of LIFO Liquidations

Several years ago, General Motors reported the following in its inventory note:

> The cost of substantially all domestic inventories was determined by the last-in, first-out (LIFO) method. If the first-in, first-out (FIFO) method of inventory valuation had been used by the Corporation for U.S. inventories, it is estimated they would be $1,886.0 million higher at December 31, [current year] compared with $2,077.1 million at December 31, [prior year]. As a result of decreases in unit sales and actions taken to reduce inventories, certain LIFO inventory quantities carried at lower costs prevailing in prior years, as compared with the costs of current purchases, were liquidated. . . . These inventory adjustments favorably affected income (loss) before income taxes by approximately $305.0 million [current year].

In the current year, GM recorded a small pretax operating profit of $22.8 million.

Required:
1. Compute the amount of pretax operating profit (loss) that GM would have reported had it not reduced inventory quantities during the current year.
2. Compute the amount of pretax operating profit (loss) for the current year that GM would have reported had it employed FIFO accounting in both years.
3. What is the normal relationship between pretax operating profit computed using LIFO and FIFO when costs are rising? Why is this relationship not in evidence in this case?

Critical Thinking Cases

CP7-8

L04

Quaker Oats

Making a Decision as a Financial Analyst: Analysis of the Effect of a Change to LIFO

A recent annual report for Quaker Oats included the following information:

> The company adopted the LIFO cost flow assumption for valuing the majority of remaining U.S. Grocery Products inventories. The Company believes that the use of the LIFO method better matches current costs with current revenues. The cumulative effect of this change on retained earnings at the beginning of the year is not determinable, nor are the pro forma effects of retroactive application of LIFO to prior years. The effect of this change on the current year was to decrease net income by $16.0 million, or $0.20 per share.

Required:
As a new financial analyst at a leading Wall Street investment banking firm, you are assigned to write a memo outlining the effects of the accounting change on Quaker's financial statements. Assume a 34 percent tax rate. In your report, be sure to include the following:
1. In addition to the reason that was cited, why did management adopt LIFO?
2. As an analyst, how would you react to the $0.20 per share decrease in income caused by the adoption of LIFO?

CP7-9

L07

Micro Warehouse

Evaluating an Ethical Dilemma: Earnings, Inventory Purchases, and Management Bonuses

Micro Warehouse is a computer software and hardware on-line and catalogue sales company. A recent *Wall Street Journal* article disclosed the following:

MICRO WAREHOUSE IS REORGANIZING TOP MANAGEMENT

Micro Warehouse Inc. announced a "significant reorganization" of its management, including the resignation of three senior executives.

The move comes just a few weeks after the Norwalk, Conn., computer catalogue sales company said it overstated earnings by $28 million since 1992 as a result of accounting irregularities. That previous disclosure prompted a flurry of shareholder lawsuits against the company. In addition, Micro Warehouse said it is cooperating with an "informal inquiry" by the Securities and Exchange Commission.

SOURCE: Stephan E. Frank, *The Wall Street Journal,* November 21, 1996, p. B2.

Its Form 10-Q quarterly report filed with the Securities and Exchange Commission two days before indicated that inaccuracies involving understatement of purchases and accounts payable in current and prior periods amounted to $47.3 million. It also indicated that, as a result, $2.2 million of executive bonuses for 1995 would be rescinded. Micro Warehouse's total tax rate is approximately 40.4 percent. Both cost of goods sold and executive bonuses are fully deductible for tax purposes.

Required:
As a new staff member at Micro Warehouse's auditing firm, you are assigned to write a memo outlining the effects of the understatement of purchases and the rescinding of the bonuses. In your report, be sure to include the following:

1. The total effect on pretax and after-tax earnings of the understatement of purchases.
2. The total effect on pretax and after-tax earnings of the rescinding of the bonuses.
3. An estimate of the percentage of after-tax earnings management is receiving in bonuses.
4. A discussion of why Micro Warehouse's board of directors may have decided to tie managers' compensation to reported earnings and the possible relation between this type of bonus scheme and the accounting errors.

Financial Reporting and Analysis Team Project

Team Project: Analyzing Inventories

As a team, select an industry to analyze (industry lists can be found at www.marketguide.com/mgi/INDUSTRY/INDUSTRY.html and www.hoovers.com, click on companies and industries). Each team member should acquire the annual report or 10-K for one publicly traded company in the industry, with each member selecting a different company. (Library files, the SEC EDGAR service at www.sec.gov, Compustat CD, or the company websites are good sources.) On an individual basis, each team member should then write a short report answering the following questions about the selected company.

CP7-10
LO3, 4, 6

1. What inventory costing method is applied to U.S. inventories? What do you think motivated this choice?
2. If the company used LIFO, how much higher or lower would net income before taxes be if it had used FIFO or a similar method instead?
3. What is the inventory turnover ratio?
4. What was the effect of the change in inventories on cash flow from operations? Explain your answer.

Discuss any patterns across the companies that you as a team observe. Then, as a team, write a short report comparing and contrasting your companies using these attributes. Provide potential explanations for any differences discovered.

Reporting and Interpreting Property, Plant, and Equipment; Natural Resources; and Intangibles

8

A s of December 2001, Delta Air Lines provided service to 179 domestic cities in 42 states and 45 international cities in 32 foreign countries. Delta is a capital-intensive company with more than $16.0 billion in property, plant, and equipment reported on its balance sheet. In fiscal year 2001, Delta spent $2.3 billion on aircraft and other flight equipment. Since the demand for air travel is seasonal, with peak demand occurring during the summer months, planning for optimal productive capacity in the airline industry is very difficult. Delta's managers must determine how many aircraft are needed in which cities at what points in time to fill all seats demanded. Otherwise, the company loses revenue (not enough seats) or has higher costs (too many seats).

FOCUS COMPANY:

Delta Air Lines

MANAGING PROFITS THROUGH CONTROL OF PRODUCTIVE CAPACITY

www.delta.com

Demand is also highly sensitive to general economic conditions and other events beyond the control of the company. Even the best corporate planners could not have predicted the September 11, 2001, terrorist attacks against the United States that rocked the airline industry. In response to the precipitous drop in the demand for air travel, Delta accelerated retirement of various aircraft, temporarily grounded aircraft, and considered delaying the purchase of new aircraft.

UNDERSTANDING THE BUSINESS

One of the major challenges managers of most businesses face is forecasting the company's long-term productive capacity (that is, the amount of plant and equipment) it will need. If managers underestimate the need, the company will not be able to produce enough goods or services to meet demand and will miss an opportunity to earn revenue. On the other hand, if they overestimate the need, the company will incur excessive costs that will reduce its profitability.

The airline industry provides an outstanding example of the difficulty of planning for and analyzing productive capacity. If an airplane takes off from Kansas City, Missouri, en route to New York City with empty seats, the economic value associated with those seats is lost for that flight. There is obviously no way to sell the seat to a customer after the airplane has left the gate. Unlike a manufacturer, an airline cannot "inventory" seats for the future.

Likewise, if an unexpectedly large number of people wants to board a flight, the airline must turn away some customers. You might be willing to buy a television set from Sears even if you had to wait one week for delivery, but you probably wouldn't book a flight home on Thanksgiving weekend on an airline that told you no seats were available. You would simply pick another airline or use a different mode of transportation.

Delta has a number of large competitors with familiar names such as U•S Airways, American, United, and Southwest. Delta's 10-K report mentions that "all domestic routes served by Delta are subject to competition from both new and existing carriers, and service over virtually all of Delta's domestic routes is highly competitive." Service over most of Delta's international routes is also highly competitive.

Much of the battle for passengers in the airline industry is fought in terms of property, plant, and equipment. Passengers want convenient schedules (that requires a large number of aircraft), and they want to fly on new, modern airplanes. Because airlines have such a large investment in equipment but no opportunity to inventory unused seats, they work very hard to fill their aircraft to capacity for each flight. The frequent fare wars you read about in newspaper advertisements occur when airlines try to build customer demand for their productive capacity. Delta's 10-K report for 2000 contains a note addressing this issue.

REAL WORLD EXCERPT

2000 10-K REPORT

> The airline industry is highly competitive and is characterized by substantial price competition. If price reductions are not offset by increases in traffic or changes in the mix of traffic that improve our passenger mile yield, our operating results will be adversely affected.
>
> SOURCE: Courtesy of Delta Air Lines, Inc.

As you can see from this discussion, issues surrounding property, plant, and equipment have a pervasive impact on a company in terms of strategy, pricing decisions, and profitability. Managers devote considerable time to planning optimal levels of productive capacity, and financial analysts closely review a company's statements to determine the impact of management's decisions.

This chapter is organized according to the life cycle of long-lived assets—acquisition, use, and disposal. First we will discuss the measuring and reporting issues related to land, buildings, and equipment. Then we will discuss the measurement and reporting issues for natural resources and intangible assets. Among the issues we will discuss are maintaining, using, and disposing of property and equipment over time and measuring and reporting assets considered impaired in their ability to generate future cash flows.

ORGANIZATION of the Chapter

Acquisition and Maintenance of Plant and Equipment	Use, Impairment, and Disposal of Plant and Equipment	Natural Resources and Intangible Assets
■ Classifying Long-Lived Assets ■ Fixed Asset Turnover Ratio ■ Measuring and Recording Acquisition Cost ■ Repairs, Maintenance, and Additions	■ Depreciation Concepts ■ Alternative Depreciation Methods ■ How Managers Choose ■ Measuring Asset Impairment ■ Disposal of Property, Plant, and Equipment	■ Acquisition and Depletion of Natural Resources ■ Acquisition and Amortization of Intangible Assets

ACQUISITION AND MAINTENANCE OF PLANT AND EQUIPMENT

Exhibit 8.1 shows the asset section of the balance sheet from Delta's annual report for the fiscal year ended December 31, 2000. Nearly 68 percent of Delta's total assets is flight and ground equipment. Delta also reports other assets with probable long-term benefits. Let's begin by classifying these assets.

Classifying Long-Lived Assets

The resources that determine a company's productive capacity are often called **long-lived assets**. These assets that are listed as noncurrent assets on the balance sheet may be either tangible or intangible, and have the following characteristics:

1. **Tangible assets** have physical substance; that is, they can be touched. This classification is called **property, plant, and equipment** or **fixed assets.** The three kinds of long-lived tangible assets are

   a. **Land** used in operations. As is the case with Delta, land often is not shown as a separate item on the balance sheet.

   b. **Buildings, fixtures, and equipment** used in operations. For Delta, this category includes aircraft, ground equipment to service the aircraft, and office space.

   c. **Natural resources** used in operations. Delta does not report any natural resources on its balance sheet. However, companies in other industries report natural resources such as timber tracts and silver mines.

2. **Intangible assets** are long-lived assets without physical substance that confer specific rights on their owner. Examples are patents, copyrights, franchises, licenses, and trademarks. Operating rights and other intangibles are shown on Delta's balance sheet.

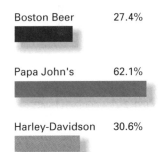

Plant and Equipment as a Percent of Total Assets for Selected Focus Companies

Boston Beer	27.4%
Papa John's	62.1%
Harley-Davidson	30.6%

Learning Objective 1
Define, classify, and explain the nature of long-lived productive assets and interpret the fixed asset turnover ratio.

LONG-LIVED ASSETS are tangible and intangible resources owned by a business and used in its operations over several years.

TANGIBLE ASSETS (or fixed assets) have physical substance.

INTANGIBLE ASSETS have special rights but not physical substance.

EXHIBIT 8.1

Delta Air Lines'
Asset Section of the
Balance Sheet

REAL WORLD EXCERPT

2000 ANNUAL REPORT

DELTA AIR LINES, INC.
Consolidated Balance Sheets
December 31, 2000 and 1999

Assets (in millions)	2000	1999
Current Assets: *(summarized)*	$ 3,205	$ 4,011
Property and Equipment:		
Flight equipment *(owned and leased)*	17,565	14,950
Less: Accumulated depreciation and amortization	5,173	4,859
	12,392	10,091
Ground property and equipment	4,371	4,008
Less: Accumulated depreciation	2,313	2,186
	2,058	1,822
Advance payments for equipment	390	537
Total property and equipment	14,840	12,450
Other Assets:		
Cost in excess of net assets acquired, net of accumulated amortization of $196 at December 31, 2000 and $137 at December 31, 1999	2,149	2,060
Operating rights and other intangibles, net of accumulated amortization of $236 at December 31, 2000 and $225 at December 31, 1999	102	108
Other noncurrent assets and investments *(summarized)*	1,635	1,313
Total other assets	3,886	3,481
Total assets	$21,931	$19,942

} Intangible assets

KEY RATIO ANALYSIS

Fixed Asset Turnover

? ANALYTICAL QUESTION:

How effectively is management utilizing fixed assets to generate revenues?

% RATIO AND COMPARISONS:

$$\text{Fixed Asset Turnover} = \frac{\text{Net Sales}}{\text{Average Net Fixed Assets*}}$$

[Beginning + Ending Fixed Asset Balance (net of accumulated depreciation)] ÷ 2

The 2000 ratio for Delta is:

$16,741 operating revenues ÷ [($14,840 + $12,450) ÷ 2] = 1.23 times

COMPARISONS OVER TIME			COMPARISONS WITH COMPETITORS	
Delta Air Lines			**Southwest**	**United**
1998	1999	2000	2000	2000
1.63	1.42	1.23	1.04	1.47

🔍 INTERPRETATIONS:

IN GENERAL   The fixed asset turnover ratio measures the sales dollars generated by each dollar of fixed asset used. A high rate normally suggests effective management. An increasing rate over time signals more efficient fixed asset use. Creditors and security analysts use this ratio to assess a company's effectiveness in generating sales from its long-lived assets.

FOCUS COMPANY ANALYSIS   Delta's fixed asset turnover ratio decreased considerably over the past few years (from a recent high of 1.83 in 1997). Although Delta continues to have a higher asset turnover than Southwest, United's asset turnover is higher, implying that United has maintained its efficiency while Delta's has decreased.

One reason for the reduced turnover ratio is the growth in Delta's fleet, from 569 aircraft in 1998 to 831 aircraft in 2000. Delta also reports commitments to buy another 74 aircraft in 2001. Future turnover rates will remain low unless Delta can either (1) dispose of older aircraft at a faster rate than it has in the past or (2) increase its revenues from flights, either by adding more flights or increasing the revenues it generates per passenger (which is unlikely given the level of competition in the industry at this time).

A FEW CAUTIONS: A lower or declining fixed asset turnover rate may indicate that a company is expanding (by acquiring additional productive assets) in anticipation of higher future sales. An increasing ratio could also signal that a firm has cut back on capital expenditures due to a downturn in business. As a consequence, appropriate interpretation of the fixed asset turnover ratio requires an investigation of related activities.

Selected Focus Companies' Fixed Asset Turnover Ratios for 2000

Company	Ratio
Papa John's	3.99
Timberland	16.92
Callaway Golf	6.05

Measuring and Recording Acquisition Cost

Under the **cost principle,** all reasonable and necessary expenditures made in acquiring and preparing an asset for use (or sale as in the case of inventory) should be recorded as the cost of the asset. We say that the expenditures are **capitalized** when they are recorded as part of the cost of an asset instead of as expenses in the current period. Any sales taxes, legal fees, transportation costs, and installation costs are then added to the purchase price of the asset. However, special discounts are subtracted and any interest charges associated with the purchase are expensed as incurred.

In addition to purchasing buildings and equipment, a company may acquire undeveloped land, typically with the intent to build a new factory or office building. When a company purchases land, all of the incidental costs of the purchase, such as title fees, sales commissions, legal fees, title insurance, delinquent taxes, and surveying fees, should be included in its cost.

Sometimes a company purchases an old building or used machinery for the business operations. Renovation and repair costs incurred by the company prior to the asset's use should be included as a part of its cost. Also, when purchasing land, building, and equipment as a group, the total cost is allocated to each asset in proportion to the market value of the assets as a whole.

For the sake of illustration, let's assume that Delta purchased a new 737 aircraft from Boeing on January 1, 2001 (the beginning of Delta's fiscal year) for a list price of $63 million. Let's also assume that Boeing offered Delta a discount of $4 million for signing the purchase agreement. That means the price of the new plane to Delta would actually be $59 million. In addition, Delta paid $200,000 to have the plane delivered and $800,000 to prepare the new plane for use. The amount recorded for the purchase, called the **acquisition cost,** is the net cash amount paid for the asset or, when noncash assets are used as payment, the fair market value of the asset given or asset received, whichever can be more clearly determined (called the **cash equivalent price**). Delta would calculate the acquisition cost of the new aircraft as follows:

Learning Objective 2
Apply the cost principle to measure the acquisition and maintenance of property, plant, and equipment.

Topic Tackler 8–1

The **ACQUISITION COST** is the net cash equivalent amount paid or to be paid for the asset.

Invoice price	$63,000,000
Less: Discount from Boeing	4,000,000
Net cash invoice price	59,000,000
Add: Transportation charges paid by Delta	200,000
Preparation costs paid by Delta	800,000
Cost of the aircraft (added to the asset account)	$60,000,000

For Cash

Assuming that Delta paid cash for the aircraft and related transportation and preparation costs, the transaction is recorded as follows:

Flight equipment (+A)	60,000,000	
Cash (−A)		60,000,000

Assets	=	Liabilities	+	Stockholders' Equity
Cash − 60,000,000				
Flight equipment + 60,000,000				

It might seem unusual for Delta to pay cash to purchase new assets that cost $60 million, but this is often the case. When it acquires productive assets, a company may pay with cash that was generated from operations or cash recently borrowed. It also is possible for the seller to finance the purchase on credit.

For Debt

Now let's assume that Delta signed a note payable for the new aircraft and paid cash for the transportation and preparation costs. In that case, Delta would record the following journal entry:

Flight equipment (+A)	60,000,000	
Cash (−A)		1,000,000
Note payable (+L)		59,000,000

Assets	=	Liabilities	+	Stockholders' Equity
Cash −1,000,000		Note payable +59,000,000		
Flight equipment + 60,000,000				

For Equity (or Other Noncash Considerations)

A noncash consideration, such as the company's common stock or a right given by the company to the seller to purchase the company's goods or services at a special price, might also be part of the transaction. When a noncash consideration is included in the purchase of an asset, the cash-equivalent cost (fair market value of the asset given or received) is determined.

Assume that Delta gave Boeing 400,000 shares of its $3 par value common stock with a market value of $85 per share and paid the balance in cash. The journal entry and transaction effects follow:

Flight equipment (+A)	60,000,000	
Common stock (+SE) ($3 par value × 400,000 shares)		1,200,000
Additional paid-in capital (+SE) ($82 × 400,000 shares)		32,800,000
Cash (−A)		26,000,000

Assets		= Liabilities +	Stockholders' Equity	
Cash	−26,000,000		Common stock	+1,200,000
Flight equipment	+60,000,000		Additional paid-in capital	+32,800,000

By Construction

In some cases, a company may construct an asset for its own use instead of buying it from a manufacturer. When a company does so, the cost of the asset includes all the necessary costs associated with construction, such as labor, materials, and, in most situations, a portion of the interest incurred during the construction period, called **capitalized interest.** The amount of interest expense that is capitalized is recorded by debiting the asset and crediting cash when the interest is paid. The amount of interest to be capitalized is a complex computation discussed in detail in other accounting courses.

CAPITALIZED INTEREST represents interest expenditures included in the cost of a self-constructed asset.

Capitalizing labor, materials, and a portion of interest expense has the effect of increasing assets, decreasing expenses, and increasing net income. Let's assume Delta constructed a new hangar, paying $600,000 in labor costs and $1,300,000 in supplies and materials. Delta also paid $400,000 in interest expense during the year with $100,000 of that amount related to the construction project:

Building (+A)	2,000,000	
Interest expense (+E, −SE)	300,000	
Cash (−A)		2,300,000

Capitalized Expenses:

Wages expense	600,000
Supplies expense	1,300,000
Interest expense	100,000

Delta Air Lines includes a note on capitalized interest in a recent annual report:

NOTES TO CONSOLIDATED FINANCIAL STATEMENTS

1. Summary of Significant Accounting Policies:

. . .

Interest Capitalized—We capitalize interest paid on advance payments used to acquire new aircraft and to construct ground facilities as an additional cost of the related assets. Interest is capitalized at our weighted average interest rate on long-term debt or, if applicable, the interest rate of specific borrowings. Interest capitalization ends when the property or equipment is ready for service or its intended use.

SOURCE: Courtesy of Delta Air Lines, Inc.

REAL WORLD EXCERPT

2000 ANNUAL REPORT

SELF-STUDY **QUIZ**

**McDonald's
Corporation**

In a recent year, McDonald's Corporation purchased property, plant, and equipment priced at $1.8 billion. Assume that the company also paid $70 million for sales tax; $8 million for transportation costs; $1.3 million for installation and preparation of the property, plant, and equipment before use; and $100,000 in maintenance contracts to cover repairs to the property, plant, and equipment during use.

1. Compute the acquisition cost for the property, plant, and equipment:

2. Under the following assumptions, indicate the effects of the acquisition on the accounting equation. Use + for increase and − for decrease and indicate the accounts and amounts:

	ASSETS	LIABILITIES	STOCKHOLDERS' EQUITY
a. Paid 30% in cash and the rest by signing a note payable.			
b. Issued 10 million shares of common stock ($.10 per share stated value) at a market price of $45 per share and paid the balance in cash.			

After you have completed your answers, check them with the solutions that follow:

1. Property, Plant, and Equipment (PPE)

Acquisition cost	$1,800,000,000
Sales tax	70,000,000
Transportation	8,000,000
Installation	1,300,000
Total	$1,879,300,000

Because the maintenance contracts are not necessary to readying the assets for use, they are not included in the acquisition cost.

2.

	ASSETS	LIABILITIES	STOCKHOLDERS' EQUITY
a.	PPE + 1,879,300,000 Cash −563,790,000	Note payable +1,315,510,000	
b.	PPE + 1,879,300,000 Cash −1,429,300,000		Common stock + 1,000,000 Additional paid-in capital +449,000,000

Repairs, Maintenance, and Additions

Most assets require substantial expenditures during their lives to maintain or enhance their productive capacity. These expenditures include cash outlays for ordinary repairs and maintenance, major repairs, replacements, and additions. Expenditures that are made after an asset has been acquired are classified as follows:

1. **Revenue expenditures**—expenditures that maintain the productive capacity of the asset during the current accounting period only. These cash outlays are recorded as **expenses** in the current period. **Ordinary repairs and maintenance** are expenditures for the normal maintenance and upkeep of long-lived assets. These expenditures are recurring in nature, involve relatively small amounts at each occurrence, and do not directly lengthen the useful life of the asset.

   In the case of Delta Air Lines, examples of ordinary repairs would include changing the oil in the aircraft engines, replacing the lights in the control panels, and fixing torn fabric on passenger seats. Although the cost of individual ordinary repairs is relatively small, in the aggregate these expenditures can be substantial. In a recent year, Delta paid $723 million for aircraft maintenance and repairs. This amount was reported as an expense on its income statement.

2. **Capital expenditures**—expenditures that increase the productive life, operating efficiency, or capacity of the asset. Capital expenditures are added to the appropriate **asset** accounts. **Extraordinary repairs** occur infrequently, involve large amounts of money, and increase an asset's economic usefulness in the future through either increased efficiency or longer life. Examples include additions, major overhauls, complete reconditioning, and major replacements and improvements, such as the complete replacement of an engine on an aircraft.

   In many cases, no clear line distinguishes capital expenditures (assets) from revenue expenditures (expenses). In these situations, managers must exercise professional judgment and make a subjective decision. Many managers prefer to capitalize expenditures for financial reporting purposes because net income for the period is higher if the total amount is not reported as an expense in the current period. Of course, for income tax purposes, most managers prefer to classify the expenditure as a deductible expense to pay lower taxes in the current period. Because these decisions are subjective, auditors review the items reported as capital and revenue expenditures closely.

   To avoid spending too much time classifying capital and revenue expenditures, some companies develop simple policies to govern the accounting for these expenditures. For example, one large computer company expenses all individual items that cost less than $1,000. Such policies are acceptable because of the **materiality constraint.**

REVENUE EXPENDITURES maintain the productive capacity of the asset during the current accounting period only and are recorded as expenses.

ORDINARY REPAIRS AND MAINTENANCE are expenditures for normal operating upkeep of long-lived assets.

CAPITAL EXPENDITURES increase the productive life, operating efficiency, or capacity of the asset and are recorded as increases in asset accounts, not as expenses.

EXTRAORDINARY REPAIRS are infrequent expenditures that increase an asset's economic usefulness in the future.

Hiding Billions in Expenses through Capitalization

FINANCIAL ANALYSIS

When expenditures that should be recorded as current period expenses are improperly capitalized as part of the cost of an asset, the effects on the financial statements can be enormous. In one of the largest accounting frauds in history, WorldCom inflated its income and cash flows from operations by billions of dollars in just such a scheme. Over five quarters in 2001 and 2002, the company initially announced that it had capitalized $3.8 billion that should have been recorded as operating expenses. By the time this chapter was written, it had raised its estimate to $7.2 billion in false profits reported in 1999 through 2002. This fraud turned WorldCom's actual losses into large profits. Accounting for expenses as capital expenditures increases current income because it spreads a single period's operating expenses over many future periods as depreciation expense. It increases cash flows from operations by moving cash outflows from the operating section to the investing section of the cash flows statement. Go to WorldCom's website at www.worldcom.com to read the latest press releases about this growing accounting scandal.

WorldCom

SELF-STUDY **QUIZ**

A building that originally cost $400,000 has been used over the past 10 years and needs continuous maintenance and repairs. For each of the following expenditures, indicate whether it should be expensed in the current period or capitalized as part of **the cost of the asset.**

	EXPENSE OR CAPITALIZE?
1. Replacing electrical wiring throughout the building.	_____
2. Repairs to the front door of the building.	_____
3. Annual cleaning of the filters on the building's air conditioning system.	_____
4. Significant repairs due to damage from an unusual and infrequent flood.	_____

After you have completed your answers, check them with the solutions that follow:

_____

1. Capitalize   2. Expense   3. Expense   4. Capitalize

USE, IMPAIRMENT, AND DISPOSAL OF PLANT AND EQUIPMENT

Depreciation Concepts

Learning Objective 3
Apply various cost allocation methods as assets are held and used over time.

Except for land that is considered to have an unlimited life, a long-lived asset with a limited useful life, such as an airplane, represents the prepaid cost of a bundle of future services or benefits. The **matching principle** requires that a portion of an asset's cost be allocated as an expense in the same period that revenues were generated by its use. Delta Air Lines earns revenue when it provides air travel service and incurs an expense when using its aircraft to generate the revenue.

Topic Tackler 8–2

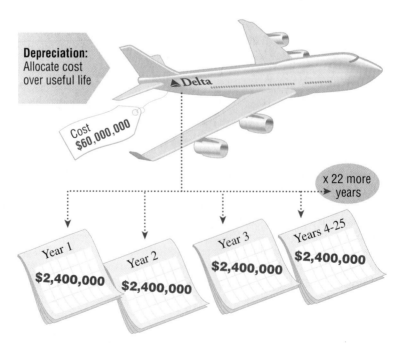

Depreciation:
Allocate cost over useful life

Cost $60,000,000

x 22 more years

Year 1
$2,400,000

Year 2
$2,400,000

Year 3
$2,400,000

Years 4-25
$2,400,000

Using the asset→depreciation expense each year

The term used to identify the matching of the cost of using buildings and equipment with the revenues they generated is **depreciation.** Thus, depreciation is **the process of allocating the cost of buildings and equipment over their productive lives using a systematic and rational method.**

Students often are confused by the concept of depreciation as accountants use it. In accounting, depreciation is a process of **cost allocation,** not a process of determining an asset's current market value or worth. When an asset is depreciated, the remaining balance sheet amount **probably does not represent its current market value.** On balance sheets subsequent to acquisition, the undepreciated cost is not measured on a market value basis.

An adjusting journal entry is needed at the end of each period to reflect the use of buildings and equipment for the period:

DEPRECIATION is the process of allocating the cost of buildings and equipment over their productive lives using a systematic and rational method.

Depreciation expense (+E, −SE)	xxxxx	
Accumulated depreciation (+XA, −A)		xxxxx

The amount of depreciation recorded during each period is reported on the income statement as **Depreciation Expense.** The amount of depreciation expense accumulated since the acquisition date is reported on the balance sheet as a contra-account, **Accumulated Depreciation,** and deducted from the related asset's cost. The net amounts on the balance sheet are called **net book values** or **carrying values.** The **net book (or carrying) value** of a long-lived asset is its acquisition cost less the accumulated depreciation from acquisition date to the balance sheet date. From Exhibit 8.1, we see that Delta's acquisition cost for flight equipment is $17,565,000,000 at the end of 2000. The accumulated depreciation on the equipment is $5,173,000,000. Thus, the book value is reported at $12,392,000,000. Delta also reported depreciation expense of $1,187,000,000 on its income statement for 2000. Failure to record depreciation for the period overstates income and overstates the asset's book value.

NET BOOK (OR CARRYING) VALUE is the acquisition cost of an asset less accumulated depreciation.

Book Value: Cost less accumulated depreciation

$60,000,000

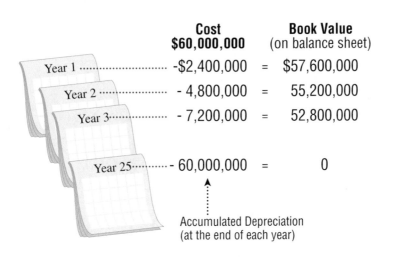

	Cost $60,000,000		Book Value (on balance sheet)
Year 1	-$2,400,000	=	$57,600,000
Year 2	- 4,800,000	=	55,200,000
Year 3	- 7,200,000	=	52,800,000
Year 25	- 60,000,000	=	0

Accumulated Depreciation (at the end of each year)

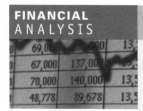

FINANCIAL ANALYSIS

Book Value as an Approximation of Remaining Life

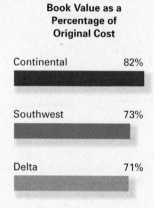

Book Value as a Percentage of Original Cost

Continental	82%
Southwest	73%
Delta	71%

Some analysts compare the book value of assets to their original cost as an approximation of their remaining life. If the book value of an asset is 100 percent of its cost, it is a new asset; if the book value is 25 percent of its cost, the asset has about 25 percent of its estimated life remaining. In Delta's case, the book value of its flight equipment is 71 percent of its original cost, compared to 82 percent for Continental Airlines and 73 percent for Southwest Airlines. This comparison suggests that Delta's flight equipment may have less estimated life remaining than that of Continental. This comparison is only a rough approximation and is influenced by some of the accounting issues discussed in the next section.

To calculate depreciation expense, three amounts are required for each asset:

1. Acquisition cost.
2. **Estimated** useful life to the company.
3. **Estimated** residual (or salvage) value at end of the asset's useful life to the company.

Of these three amounts, two, the asset's useful life and residual value, are estimates. Therefore, **depreciation expense is an estimate.**

ESTIMATED USEFUL LIFE is the expected service life of an asset to the present owner.

Useful life represents management's estimate of the asset's useful **economic life** to the company rather than its total economic life to all potential users. The asset's expected physical life is often longer than the company intends to use the asset. Economic life may be expressed in terms of years or units of capacity, such as the number of hours a machine is expected to operate or units it can produce. Delta's aircraft fleet is expected to fly for more than 25 years, but Delta wants to offer its customers a high level of service by replacing its older aircraft with modern equipment. For accounting purposes, Delta uses a 25-year estimated useful life. The subsequent owner of the aircraft (a regional airline) would use an estimated useful life based on its own policies.

RESIDUAL (OR SALVAGE) VALUE is the estimated amount to be recovered at the end of the company's estimated useful life of an asset.

Residual (or salvage) value represents management's estimate of the amount the company expects to recover upon disposal of the asset at the end of its estimated useful life. The residual value may be its estimated value of the asset as salvage or scrap or its expected value if sold to another user. In the case of Delta's aircraft, residual value may be the amount it expects to receive when it sells the asset to a small regional airline that operates older equipment. The notes to Delta's financial statements indicate that the company estimates residual value to be between 5 and 40 percent of the cost of the asset, depending on the asset.

FINANCIAL ANALYSIS

Differences in Estimated Lives within a Single Industry

Notes to recent actual financial statements of various companies in the airline industry reveal the following estimates for the useful lives of flight equipment:

Company	Estimated Life (in years)
Delta	20 to 25
Continental	20 to 25
U•S Airways	11 to 30
Singapore Airlines	5 to 15
Southwest	20 to 25

The differences in the estimated lives may be attributed to a number of factors such as the type of aircraft used by each company, equipment replacement plans, operational differences, and the degree of management's conservatism. In addition, given the same type of aircraft, companies that plan to use the equipment over fewer years may estimate higher residual values than companies that plan to use the equipment longer. For example, Singapore Airlines uses a residual value of 20 percent over a relatively short useful life, compared to 5 percent for Delta Air Lines over a 25-year useful life.

Differences in estimated lives and residual values of assets can have a significant impact on a comparison of the profitability of the competing companies. Analysts must be certain to identify the causes of differences in depreciable lives.

Alternative Depreciation Methods

Because of significant differences among companies and the assets they own, accountants have not been able to agree on a single best method of depreciation. As a result, managers may choose from several different acceptable depreciation methods, basing their decision on how they believe the asset will generate revenues over time. Once selected, the method should be applied consistently over time to enhance comparability of financial information to users. We will discuss the three most common depreciation methods:

- Straight-line (the most common, used by more than 95 percent of companies surveyed).
- Units-of-production.
- Declining-balance.

To illustrate each method, let's assume that Delta Air Lines acquired a new service vehicle (ground equipment) on January 1, 2003. The relevant information is shown in Exhibit 8.2.

Number of Companies Using Alternative Depreciation Methods*

Straight-line	577
Units-of-production	31
Declining-balance	27
Other	66

* Methods reported by 600 companies sampled in *Accounting Trends & Techniques* (AICPA), 2000.

Straight-Line Method

More companies, including Delta, use **straight-line depreciation** in their financial statements than all other methods combined. Under the straight-line method, an equal portion of an asset's depreciable cost is allocated to each accounting period over its estimated useful life. The formula to estimate annual depreciation expense follows:

STRAIGHT-LINE DEPRECIATION is the method that allocates the cost of an asset in equal periodic amounts over its useful life.

Straight-Line Formula:

$$(\text{Cost} - \text{Residual Value}) \times \frac{1}{\text{Useful Life}} = \text{Depreciation Expense}$$

$$(\$62,500 - \$2,500) \times \frac{1}{3 \text{ years}} = \$20,000$$

DELTA AIR LINES		EXHIBIT 8.2
Acquisition of a New Service Vehicle		

Cost, purchased on January 1, 2003	$62,500	
Estimated residual value	$ 2,500	
Estimated useful life	3 years **OR** 100,000 miles	
Actual miles driven in: Year 2003	30,000 miles	
Year 2004	50,000 miles	
Year 2005	20,000 miles	

Data for Illustrating the Computation of Depreciation Under Alternative Methods

In this formula, "Cost minus Residual Value" is the total amount to be depreciated, also called the **depreciable cost.** "1 ÷ Useful Life" is the **straight-line rate.** Using the data provided in Exhibit 8.2, the depreciation expense for Delta's new truck would be $20,000 per year. A **depreciation schedule** for the entire useful life of the machine follows:

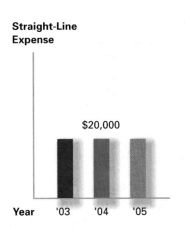

Straight-Line Expense

$20,000

Year '03 '04 '05

Amount for the Adjusting Entry: Reported on the Income Statement

Cost less Accumulated Depreciation: Reported on the Balance Sheet

Year	Computation	Depreciation Expense	Accumulated Depreciation	Net Book Value
At acquisition				$62,500
2003	($62,500 − $2,500) × 1/3	$20,000	$20,000	42,500
2004	($62,500 − $2,500) × 1/3	20,000	40,000	22,500
2005	($62,500 − $2,500) × 1/3	20,000	60,000	2,500
	Total	$60,000		

Notice that

1. Depreciation expense is a constant amount each year.

2. Accumulated depreciation increases by an equal amount each year.

3. Net book value decreases by the same amount each year.

This is the reason for the name **straight-line method.** Notice, too, that the adjusting entry can be prepared from this schedule, and the effect on the income statement and balance sheet are known. Delta Air Lines uses the straight-line method for all its assets. The company reported depreciation expense in the amount of $1,187,000,000 for 2000 equal to 7.1 percent of the airline's revenues for the year. Most companies in the airline industry use the straight-line method.

Units-of-Production Method

UNITS-OF-PRODUCTION DEPRECIATION is a method to allocate the cost of an asset over its useful life based on the relation of its periodic output to its total estimated output.

The **units-of-production depreciation** method relates depreciable cost to total estimated productive output. The formula to estimate annual depreciation expense under this method is as follows:

Units-of-Production Formula:

$$\frac{(\text{Cost} - \text{Residual Value})}{\text{Estimated Total Production}} \times \text{Actual Production} = \text{Depreciation Expense}$$

$$\frac{(\$62,500 - \$2,500)}{100,000 \text{ miles}} \times 30,000 \text{ miles in 2003} = \$18,000$$

Depreciation Rate per unit = $0.60 per mile

Dividing the depreciable cost by the estimated total production yields the depreciation rate per unit of production, which is then multiplied by the actual production for the period to determine depreciation expense. In our illustration, for every mile that the new vehicle is driven, Delta would record depreciation expense of $0.60. The depreciation schedule for the truck under the units-of-production method would appear as follows:

Year	Computation	Depreciation Expense	Accumulated Depreciation	Net Book Value
At acquisition				$62,500
2003	$.60 rate × 30,000 miles	$18,000	$18,000	44,500
2004	$.60 rate × 50,000 miles	30,000	48,000	14,500
2005	$.60 rate × 20,000 miles	12,000	60,000	2,500
	Total	$60,000		

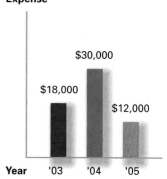

Units-of-Production Expense

$30,000

$18,000

$12,000

Year '03 '04 '05

Notice that, from period to period, depreciation expense, accumulated depreciation, and book value vary directly with the units produced. In the units-of-production method, depreciation expense is a **variable expense** because it varies directly with production or use. Although Delta does not use this method, the ExxonMobil Corporation, a major energy company that explores, produces, transports, and sells crude oil and natural gas worldwide, does as a note to its company's annual report explains.

1. Summary of Accounting Policies

Property, Plant and Equipment. Depreciation, depletion, and amortization, based on cost less estimated salvage value of the asset, are primarily determined under either the unit of production method or the straight-line method. Unit of production rates are based on oil, gas and other mineral reserves estimated to be recoverable from existing facilities. The straight-line method of depreciation is based on estimated asset service life taking obsolescence into consideration.

REAL WORLD EXCERPT

ExxonMobil Corporation
2000 ANNUAL REPORT

The units-of-production method is based on an estimate of an asset's total future productive capacity or output that is difficult to estimate. This is another example of the degree of subjectivity inherent in accounting.

Declining-Balance Method

Under the declining-balance depreciation method, depreciation expense amounts are higher in the early years of an asset's life and lower in the later years. We say, then, that this is an **accelerated depreciation** method. Although accelerated methods are seldom used for financial reporting purposes, the method that is used more frequently than others is the declining-balance method.

Declining-balance depreciation is based on applying a rate exceeding the straight-line rate to the asset's net book value over time. The rate is often double (two times) the straight-line rate and is termed the **double-declining-balance rate.** For example, if the straight-line rate is 10 percent (1 ÷ 10 years) for a 10-year estimated useful life, then the declining-balance rate is 20 percent (2 × the straight-line rate). Other typical acceleration rates are 1.5 times and 1.75 times. The double-declining-balance rate is adopted most frequently by companies employing an accelerated method, so we will use it in our illustration.

DECLINING-BALANCE DEPRECIATION is the method that allocates the cost of an asset over its useful life based on a multiple of the straight-line rate (often two times).

Double-Declining-Balance Formula:

$$(\text{Cost} - \text{Accumulated Depreciation}) \times \frac{2}{\text{Useful Life}} = \text{Depreciation Expense}$$

$$(\$62{,}500 - \$0 \text{ in } 2003) \times \frac{2}{3 \text{ years}} = \$41{,}667$$

Accumulated
Depreciation
increases over time

Note that **residual value is not included in computing depreciation expense** at this stage. It is not subtracted from cost as in the other methods presented. However, an asset's book value cannot be depreciated below residual value. Therefore, if the annual computation reduces net book value below residual value, a lower amount of depreciation expense must be recorded so that net book value equals residual value. No additional depreciation expense is computed in subsequent years. Computation of declining-balance depreciation expense is illustrated in the depreciation schedule:

Double-Declining-Balance Expense

Year	Computation	Depreciation Expense	Accumulated Depreciation	Net Book Value
At acquisition				$62,500
2003	($62,500 − $0) × 2/3	$41,667	$41,667	20,833
2004	($62,500 − $41,667) × 2/3	13,889	55,556	6,944
2005	($62,500 − $55,556) × 2/3	~~4,629~~	~~60,185~~	~~2,315~~
		4,444	60,000	2,500
	Total	$60,000		

Computed amount
is too large.

The calculated depreciation expense for 2005 ($4,629) is not the same as the amount actually reported on the income statement ($4,444). An asset should never be depreciated below the point at which net book value equals its residual value. The asset owned by Delta has an estimated residual value of $2,500. If depreciation expense were recorded in the amount of $4,629, the book value of the asset would be less than $2,500. The correct depreciation expense for year 2005 is therefore $4,444, the amount that will reduce the book value to exactly $2,500.

Companies in industries that expect fairly rapid obsolescence of their equipment use the declining-balance method. Sony is one of the companies that uses this method, as a note to its annual report shows.

2. Summary of significant accounting policies:

Property, plant and equipment and depreciation

Property, plant and equipment is stated at cost. Depreciation of property, plant and equipment is principally computed on the declining-balance method for Sony Corporation and Japanese subsidiaries and on the straight-line method for foreign subsidiary companies at rates based on estimated useful lives of the assets, principally, ranging from 15 up to 50 years for buildings and from 2 years up to 10 years for machinery and equipment.

As this note indicates, companies may use different depreciation methods for different classes of assets. Under the consistency principle, they are expected to apply the same methods to those assets over time.

In Summary

The following table summarizes the three depreciation methods and computations. The graph reflects the differences in depreciation expense over time for each method.

Depreciation Expense Summary

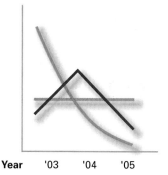

Method	Computation
Straight line	(Cost − Residual Value) × 1/Useful Life
Units of production	(Cost − Residual Value)/Estimated Total Production × Annual Production
Double declining balance	(Cost − Accumulated Depreciation) × 2/Useful Life

Year   '03   '04   '05

Impact of Alternative Depreciation Methods

FINANCIAL ANALYSIS

Assume that you are comparing two companies that are exactly the same, except for the fact that one uses accelerated depreciation and the other uses the straight-line method. Which company would you expect to report a higher net income? Actually, this question is a bit tricky. The answer is that you cannot say for certain which company's income would be higher.

The accelerated methods report higher depreciation and therefore lower net income during the early years of an asset's life. As the age of the asset increases, this effect reverses. Therefore, companies that use accelerated depreciation report lower depreciation expense and higher net income during the later years of an asset's life. The graph in the margin shows the pattern of depreciation over the life of an asset for the methods discussed in this chapter. When the curve for the accelerated method falls below the curve for the straight-line method, the accelerated method produces a higher net income than the straight-line method. The units-of-production method varies with activity.

Users of financial statements must understand the impact of alternative depreciation methods used over time. Differences in depreciation methods rather than real economic differences can cause significant variation in reported net incomes.

SELF-STUDY QUIZ

Assume that Delta has acquired new computer equipment at a cost of $240,000. The equipment has an estimated life of six years, an estimated operating life of 50,000 hours, and an estimated residual value of $30,000. Determine depreciation expense for the first full year under each of the following methods:

1. Straight-line depreciation

2. Double-declining-balance method

3. Units-of-production method (assume the equipment ran for 8,000 hours in the first year)

After you have completed your answers, check them with the solutions that follow:

---

1.   ($240,000 − $30,000) × 1/6 = $35,000
2.   ($240,000 − $0) × 2/6 = $80,000
3.   [($240,000 − $30,000) ÷ 50,000] × 8,000 = $33,600

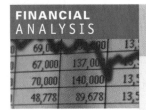

FINANCIAL ANALYSIS

Increased Profitability Due to an Accounting Adjustment? Reading the Notes

Financial analysts are particularly interested in changes in accounting estimates because they can have a large impact on a company's before-tax operating income. In Delta's case, the changes made in 1999 added $92 million in pretax income because of reduced depreciation expense, and would add a similar amount each year over the remaining life of the aircraft. Analysts pay close attention to this number because it represents increased profitability due merely to an accounting adjustment.

To give another example, in its news release, TransAlta Power, a power transmission limited partnership headquartered in Calgary, Alberta, Canada, announced first quarter earnings of $4.9 million for 2001, up from $3.6 million in the first quarter of 2000. Naturally, the president and director of TransAlta is "very pleased with the first quarter results . . . " and notes that "our operating performance continues at industry leading levels . . ."

However, in examining the information presented in the notes to the financial statements, the following disclosure is found: "Effective January 1, 2001, the estimated useful life of the power plant has increased to 27 years from 17 years." This change in estimate—a 59 percent increase in the estimated useful life of the plant—had the effect of increasing TransAlta's net income by $1.35 million.

Therefore, if the change in estimate had not been made, TransAlta's results for the first quarter of 2001 would be $3.55 million, a slight decrease from the first quarter of 2000. TransAlta may still be operating at industry leading levels, but without a convenient change in estimates, its bottom line would not have improved from the prior year.

SOURCE: *"TransAlta Power, L.P. announces first quarter results," CNN Newswire, April 19, 2001.*

How Managers Choose

Financial Reporting

Depreciation and Repair Expense over Time

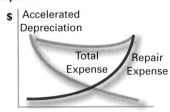

For financial reporting purposes, corporate managers must determine which depreciation method provides the best matching of revenues and expenses for any given asset. If the asset is expected to provide benefits evenly over time, then the straight-line method is preferred. Managers also find this method to be easy to use and to explain. If no other method is more systematic or rational, then the straight-line method is selected. Also, during the early years of an asset's life, the straight-line method reports higher income than the accelerated methods do. For these reasons, the straight-line method is, by far and away, the most common.

On the other hand, certain assets produce more revenue in their early lives because they are more efficient then than in later years. In this case, managers select an accelerated method to allocate cost. In addition, as the asset ages, repair costs are likely to increase. Thus, the total of the depreciation expense and repair expense for any given period is likely to provide a nearly constant amount charged to income each period.

Tax Reporting

Delta Air Lines, like most public companies, maintains two sets of accounting records. One set is prepared under GAAP for reporting to stockholders. The other set is prepared to determine the company's tax obligation under the Internal Revenue Code. When they first learn that companies maintain two sets of books, some people question the ethics or legality of the practice. In reality, **it is both legal and ethical to maintain separate records for tax and financial reporting purposes.**

The reason that it is legal to maintain two sets of books is simple: The objectives of GAAP and the Internal Revenue Code differ.

Financial Reporting (GAAP)	Tax Reporting (IRS)
The objective of financial reporting is to provide economic information about a business that is useful in projecting future cash flows of the business. Financial reporting rules follow generally accepted accounting principles.	The objective of the Internal Revenue Code is to raise sufficient revenues to pay for the expenditures of the federal government. Many of the Code's provisions are designed to encourage certain behaviors that are thought to benefit society (e.g., contributions to charities are made tax deductible to encourage people to support worthy programs).

While it is easy to understand why two sets of accounting records are permitted, perhaps the more interesting question is why managers elect to pay the extra cost of maintaining two sets of books. In some cases, differences between the Internal Revenue Code and GAAP leave the manager no choice but to maintain separate records. In other cases, the explanation is an economic one, called the **least and the latest rule.** All taxpayers want to pay the lowest amount of tax that is legally permitted and at the latest possible date. If you had the choice of paying $100,000 to the federal government at the end of this year or at the end of next year, you would choose the end of next year. By doing so, you could invest the money for an extra year and earn a significant return on the investment.

Similarly, by maintaining two sets of books, corporations can defer (delay) paying millions and sometimes billions of dollars in taxes. The following companies reported significant gross deferred tax obligations in a recent year. Much of these deferrals were due to differences in asset cost allocation methods:

Company	Deferred Tax Liabilities	Percentage Due to Applying Different Cost Allocation Methods
Delta Air Lines	$ 2,952 million	79%
PepsiCo	1,873 million	67
AT&T Corp.	41,236 million	93
Kmart Corp.	846 million	49

Most corporations use the IRS-approved Modified Accelerated Cost Recovery System (MACRS) to calculate depreciation expense for their tax returns. MACRS is similar to the declining-balance method and is applied over relatively short asset lives to yield high depreciation expense in the early years. The high depreciation expense reported under MACRS reduces a corporation's taxable income and therefore the amount it must pay in taxes. MACRS provides an incentive for corporations to invest in modern property, plant, and equipment in order to be competitive in world markets. **It is not acceptable for financial reporting purposes.**

Depreciation Methods in Other Countries

INTERNATIONAL
PERSPECTIVE

The various depreciation methods discussed in this chapter are used widely by corporations in most countries. Some methods used in other countries are not generally used in the United States. German companies may depreciate an asset's cost based on the number of hours it is used, and British companies may use the annuity method, which results in lower depreciation during the early years of an asset's life (contrasted with accelerated depreciation, which results in higher depreciation during the early years).

Many countries, including Australia, Brazil, England, Hong Kong, Mexico, and Singapore, also permit the revaluation of property, plant, and equipment to their current cost as of the balance sheet date. The primary argument in favor of revaluation is that the historical cost of an asset purchased 15 or 20 years ago is not meaningful because of the impact of inflation. For example, most people would not compare the original price of a 1973 Ford to the original price of a 2003 Ford because the purchasing power of the dollar changed dramatically between those years. However, revaluation to current cost is prohibited in the United States (under GAAP) and in Canada, Germany, and Japan. A primary argument against revaluation is the lack of objectivity involved in estimating an asset's current cost.

Measuring Asset Impairment

Learning Objective 4
Explain the effect of asset impairment on the financial statements.

Under a recent FASB pronouncement, corporations must review long-lived tangible and intangible assets for impairment. **Impairment** occurs when events or changed circumstances cause the estimated future cash flows (future benefits) of these assets to fall below their book value. If the estimated future cash flows are less than the asset's book value, an impairment loss should be recognized for the difference between the asset's book value and fair value. That is, the assets should be **written down.** Delta Air Lines reported the following write-down in its 2000 annual report:

REAL WORLD EXCERPT

1999 ANNUAL REPORT

> We accelerated the planned retirement of our 16 MD-90 aircraft and eight owned MD-11 aircraft over the next six to eight years as part of our fleet simplification strategy. As a result of this decision, we reviewed these fleet types for impairment, determining that the estimated future cash flows generated by these aircraft are less than their carrying values. The estimated future cash flows were based on projections of passenger yield, fuel costs, labor costs and other relevant factors in the markets in which these aircraft operate. These aircraft were written down to their fair values, as estimated by management, using published sources and bids received from third parties. Due to this impairment analysis, we recorded a pretax asset writedown of $320 million in the quarter ended December 31, 1999.
>
> SOURCE: Courtesy of Delta Air Lines, Inc.

Let's assume that the net book value of Delta's impaired aircraft was $8,320 million. If the future cash flows were estimated to be $8,000 million, then the asset was impaired because it was not expected to generate future benefits equal to its net book value. To compute the amount of the impairment loss, **fair value** is determined. For Delta, that process includes using published sources and third-party bids to obtain the value of the asset. If the assets' fair value was $8,000 million, then the loss is calculated as $320 million ($8,320 million net book value less $8,000 million fair value). The following journal entry would be recorded:

Loss due to impairment of assets (+Loss, − SE)	320,000,000	
Flight equipment (−A)		320,000,000

Assets	= Liabilities +	Stockholders' Equity
Flight equipment −320,000,000		Loss due to impairment −320,000,000

Fierce Pressure to Report Smooth, Ever-Higher Earnings

A QUESTION
OF ETHICS

Corporate executives have been under intense pressure over the past decade to keep earnings rising smoothly in order to meet analysts' expectations. As expectations have become more explicit, so too have the mechanisms executives use to manage earnings and hit their targets. Long-lived assets can play a significant role in a company's ability to meet or beat the estimated earnings, as indicated in the financial press:

"Learn to Play the Earnings Game (and Wall Street will love you)"

How the pros do it

Plan ahead: Time store openings or asset sales to keep earnings rising smoothly. In most cases, this is earnings management at its least controversial. The master of it is General Electric.

Capitalize it: Usually it's pretty clear which costs you capitalize and which you expense. But there are gray areas—software R&D is one—and you can get creative about the length of time an asset should be depreciated. America Online was, until it stopped in October, a noted aggressive capitalizer.

Write it off: Take a "big bath" and charge a few hundred million in restructuring costs, and meeting future earnings targets will be easier. Among the biggest restructurers in the 1990s: IBM.

SOURCE: *Fortune*, March 31, 1997, pp. 77–80. © 1997 Time, Inc. All rights reserved. Reprinted with permission.

REAL WORLD EXCERPT

Fortune

Disposal of Property, Plant, and Equipment

In some cases, a business may **voluntarily** decide not to hold a long-term asset for its entire life. The company may drop a product from its line and no longer need the equipment that was used to produce its product, or managers may want to replace a machine with a more efficient one. These disposals include sales, trade-ins, or retirements. When Delta disposes of an old aircraft, the company may sell it to a cargo airline or regional airline. A business may also dispose of an asset **involuntarily,** as the result of a casualty such as a storm, fire, or accident.

> **Learning Objective 5**
> Analyze the disposal of property, plant, and equipment.

Disposals of long-term assets seldom occur on the last day of the accounting period. Therefore, depreciation must be recorded to the date of disposal. The disposal of a depreciable asset usually requires two journal entries:

1. An adjusting entry to update the depreciation expense and accumulated depreciation accounts.

2. An entry to record the disposal. The cost of the asset and any accumulated depreciation at the date of disposal must be removed from the accounts. The difference between any resources received on disposal of an asset and its book value at the date of disposal is treated as a gain or loss on the disposal of the asset. This gain (or loss) is reported on the income statement. It is not a revenue (or expense), however, because it arises from peripheral or incidental activities rather than from central operations. Gains and losses from disposals are usually shown as a separate item on the income statement.

Assume that at the end of year 17, Delta sold an aircraft that was no longer needed because of the elimination of service to a small city. The aircraft was sold for $5 million cash. The original cost of the flight equipment of $20 million was depreciated using the straight-line method over 20 years with no residual value ($1 million depreciation expense per year). The last accounting for depreciation was at the end of year 16; thus, depreciation expense must be recorded for year 17. The computations are as follows:

Cash received		$5,000,000
Original cost of flight equipment	$20,000,000	
Less: Accumulated depreciation ($1,000,000 × 17 years)	17,000,000	
Book value at date of sale		3,000,000
Gain on sale of flight equipment		$2,000,000

The entries and effects of the transaction on the date of the sale are as follows:

(1) Update depreciation expense for year 17:
    Depreciation expense (+E, −SE) 1,000,000
        Accumulated depreciation (+XA, −A) 1,000,000
(2) Record the sale:
    Cash (+A) 5,000,000
    Accumulated depreciation (−XA, +A) 17,000,000
        Flight equipment (−A) 20,000,000
        Gain on sale of flight equipment (+Gain, +SE) 2,000,000

Assets	=	Liabilities	+	Stockholders' Equity	
(1) Accumulated				Depreciation	
depreciation −1,000,000				expense −1,000,000	
(2) Flight equipment −20,000,000				Gain on sale	
Accumulated				of asset +2,000,000	
depreciation +17,000,000					
Cash +5,000,000					

SELF-STUDY QUIZ

Now let's assume the same facts as above except that the asset was sold for $2,000,000 cash. Prepare the two entries on the date of the sale.

1. Update depreciation expense for year 17:

2. Record the sale:

ASSETS	=	LIABILITIES	+	STOCKHOLDERS' EQUITY

After you have completed your answers, check them with the solutions that follow:

(1) Depreciation expense (+E, −SE) 1,000,000
    Accumulated depreciation (+XA, −A) 1,000,000
(2) Cash (+A) 2,000,000
    Accumulated depreciation (−XA, +A) 17,000,000
    Loss on sale of flight equipment (+ Loss, −SE) 1,000,000
        Flight equipment (−A) 20,000,000

Assets		=	Liabilities	+	Stockholders' Equity	
(1) Accumulated					Depreciation	
depreciation	−1,000,000				expense	−1,000,000
(2) Flight					Loss on sale	
equipment	−20,000,000				of asset	−1,000,000
Accumulated						
depreciation	+17,000,000					
Cash	+2,000,000					

Taking a Different Strategy to Success

FINANCIAL ANALYSIS

Singapore Airlines, SIA, formed in 1972, has shown continued profitability as one of the world's largest operators of the most technologically advanced "jumbo jet," the Boeing 747-400. Unlike other airlines whose average fleet age is more than 12 years, Singapore Airlines uses its aircraft for an average of just under six years. This strategy has a dual effect. First, depreciation expense is significantly higher due to the aircraft's shorter estimated useful life and thus reduces net income. Singapore Airlines sells its used aircraft, however—an activity that has resulted in gains reported on the income statement. Both the depreciation computations through the use of estimates and asset sales through choosing the timing of the sales provide management with the flexibility to **manage earnings.**

For example, Singapore Airlines' 2001 annual report shows a gain on disposal of aircraft of $165.6 million representing 14.2 percent of pretax income. This is compared to only $85.8 million in 2000, or 7.8 percent of pretax income. Because the gains on disposals almost doubled, SIA enjoyed an increase in normal operating profit. Ignoring the effect of the gains, however, reveals that, in both 2000 and 2001, Singapore Airlines' normal operating profits would have **decreased** by 1.7 percent.

How can this lead to earnings management? SIA depreciates its aircraft faster than most other airlines. Therefore, when it sells its aircraft, the book value used to record the sale is quite low relative to the actual proceeds from the sale, resulting in a gain. Because management can decide to sell more or fewer aircraft in any given year, when ordinary earnings are low, management has the ability simply to retire more aircraft, recognize the gains, and increase net income.

In general, the practice of using conservative accounting policies (in this case, high depreciation from conservative useful life estimates) to increase subsequent net income is called creating a "cookie jar." These "cookies" (aircraft whose sale will result in a large gain) are available as needed to boost net income.

NATURAL RESOURCES AND INTANGIBLE ASSETS

Acquisition and Depletion of Natural Resources

You are probably most familiar with large companies that are involved in manufacturing (Ford, Black & Decker), distribution (Sears, Home Depot), or services (Federal Express, Holiday Inn). A number of large companies, some of which are less well known, develop raw materials and products from **natural resources,** including mineral deposits such as gold or iron ore, oil wells, and timber tracts. These resources are often called **wasting assets** because they are depleted (i.e., physically used up). Companies that develop natural resources are critical to the economy because they produce essential items such as lumber for construction, fuel for heating and transportation, and food for consumption. Because of the significant effect they can have on the environment, these companies attract considerable public attention. Concerned citizens often read the financial statements of companies involved in exploration for oil, coal, and various ores to determine the amount of money they spend to protect the environment.

Learning Objective 6
Apply measurement and reporting concepts for natural resources and intangible assets.

NATURAL RESOURCES are assets that occur in nature, such as mineral deposits, timber tracts, oil, and gas.

DEPLETION is the systematic and rational allocation of the cost of a natural resource over the period of exploitation.

When natural resources are acquired or developed, they are recorded in conformity with the **cost principle.** As a natural resource is used up, its acquisition cost must be apportioned among the periods in which revenues are earned in conformity with the **matching principle.** The term depletion describes the process of allocating a natural resource's cost over the period of its exploitation.[1] The units-of-production method is often applied to compute depletion.

When a natural resource such as an oil well is depleted, the company obtains inventory (oil). Since depleting the natural resource is necessary to obtain the inventory, the depletion computed during a period is added to the cost of the inventory, not expensed in the period. Consider the following illustration:

A timber tract costing $530,000 is depleted over its estimated cutting period based on a "cutting" rate of approximately 20 percent per year:

Timber inventory (+A) 106,000
    Timber tract (−A)   106,000
    (or Accumulated depletion XA)

> Note that the amount of the natural resource that is depleted is capitalized as inventory, not expensed. When the inventory is sold, the cost of goods sold will be included as an expense on the income statement.

Following is an excerpt from the asset section of International Paper's 2000 balance sheet along with the related footnote describing the accounting policies for the company's natural resource, forestland:

REAL WORLD EXCERPT

International Paper

2000 ANNUAL REPORT

CONSOLIDATED BALANCE SHEET (IN MILLIONS)

	2000	1999
Assets		
Cash	$1,198	$ 453
...		
Forestlands	5,966	2,921

Note:

Forestlands

At December 31, 2000, International Paper and its subsidiaries controlled about 12 million acres of forestlands in the U.S., 1.5 million acres in Brazil, 820,000 acres in New Zealand, and had, through licenses and forest management agreements, harvesting rights on government-owned timberlands in Canada. Forestlands include owned property as well as certain timber harvesting rights with terms of one or more years, and are stated at cost, less cost of timber harvested. Costs attributable to timber are charged against income as trees are cut. The depletion rate charged is determined annually based on the relationship of incurred costs to estimated current volume.

Acquisition and Amortization of Intangible Assets

Intangible assets are increasingly important resources for organizations. An intangible asset, like any other asset, has value because of certain rights and privileges often conferred by law on its owner. Unlike tangible assets such as land and buildings, however, an intangible asset has no material or physical substance. Examples of intangible assets include patents, trademarks, and licenses. Most intangible assets usually are evidenced by a legal document. Yet the growth in the importance of intangible assets has been the

---

[1]Consistent with the procedure for recording depreciation, an accumulated depletion account may be used. In practice, however, most companies credit the asset account directly for periodic depletion. This procedure is also typically used for intangible assets, which are discussed in the next section.

tremendous expansion in computer information systems and web technologies and the frenzy in companies purchasing other companies at high prices, with the expectation that these intangible resources will provide significant future benefits to the company.

Intangible assets are recorded **at historical cost only if they have been purchased.** If these assets are developed internally by the company, they are expensed when incurred. Upon acquisition of intangible assets, managers determine whether the separate intangibles have definite or indefinite lives:

Definite Life: The cost of an intangible with a definite life is allocated on a straight-line basis each period over its useful life in a process called **amortization** that is similar to depreciation and depletion. Most companies do not estimate a residual value for their intangible assets. Amortization expense is included on the income statement each period and the intangible assets are reported at cost less accumulated amortization on the balance sheet.

AMORTIZATION is the systematic and rational allocation of the acquisition cost of an intangible asset over its useful life.

Let's assume a company purchases a patent for $800,000 and intends to use it for 20 years. The adjusting entry to record $40,000 in patent amortization expense ($800,000 ÷ 20 years) is as follows:

Patent amortization expense (+E, −SE)	40,000	
Patents (−A) (or Accumulated amortization XA)		40,000

Indefinite Life: Intangible assets with indefinite lives are **not amortized.** Instead, these assets are to be tested at least annually for possible impairment, and the asset's book value is written down (decreased) to its fair value if impaired. The two-step process is similar to that used for other long-lived assets including intangibles with definite lives:

- **Test for Impairment:** The intangible asset is impaired if the book value exceeds possible future cash flows.

- **Amount of Impairment Loss:** The loss due to impairment is the difference between the book value and the fair value (that is, the current market value) of the asset.

An asset is impaired if: Book value > Future cash flows

Then the impairment loss is = Book value − Fair value

Let's assume a company purchases for $120,000 cash a copyright that is expected to have an indefinite life. At the end of the current year, management determines that the future cash flows will be $100,000. Because the book value exceeds future cash flows, the asset is impaired. Management also determines that the fair value of the copyright is $90,000. The $30,000 loss ($120,000 book value less $90,000 fair value) is recorded as follows:

Loss due to impairment (+Loss, − SE)	30,000	
Copyright (−A)		30,000

The AICPA's 2000 *Accounting Trends & Techniques* summarizes intangible assets most frequently disclosed by the 600 companies surveyed:

	Number of Companies	Percentage of 600
Goodwill recognized in a business combination	477	80%
Trademarks, brand names, copyrights	96	16
Patents, patent rights	79	13
Technology	40	7
Licenses, franchises, memberships	34	6
Noncompete covenants	25	4
Customer lists	19	3
Other—described in the annual report	63	11

Goodwill

For accounting purposes, **GOODWILL (COST IN EXCESS OF NET ASSETS ACQUIRED)** is the excess of the purchase price of a business over the fair market value of the business's assets and liabilities.

By far the most frequently reported intangible asset is **goodwill (cost in excess of net assets acquired).** The term *goodwill,* as used by most businesspeople, means the favorable reputation that a company has with its customers. Goodwill arises from factors such as customer confidence, reputation for good service or quality goods, location, outstanding management team, and financial standing. From its first day of operations, a successful business continually builds goodwill. In this context, the goodwill is said to be **internally generated** and is not reported as an asset (i.e., it was not purchased).

The only way to report goodwill as an asset is to purchase another business. Often the purchase price of the business exceeds the fair market value of all of its net assets (assets minus liabilities). Why would a company pay more for a business as a whole than it would pay if it bought the assets individually? The answer is to obtain its goodwill. You could easily buy modern bottling equipment to produce and sell a new cola drink, but you would not make as much money as you would if you acquired the goodwill associated with Coke or Pepsi brand names.

For accounting purposes, goodwill is defined as the difference between the purchase price of a company as a whole and the fair market value of its net assets:

> Purchase price
> − Fair market value of identifiable assets and liabilities
> —————————————————————————————
> Goodwill to be reported

Both parties to the sale estimate an acceptable amount for the goodwill of the business and add it to the appraised fair value of the business's assets and liabilities. Then the sale price of the business is negotiated. In conformity with the **cost principle,** the resulting amount of goodwill is recorded as an intangible asset only when it is actually purchased at a measurable cost.

Delta Air Lines recently acquired two companies: Comair Holdings for $1.8 billion and ASA Holdings for $700 million. Delta's balance sheet presented in Exhibit 8.1 includes the individual assets from these companies plus an item valued at $2.1 billion called *Cost in Excess of Net Assets Acquired.* The notes to the statements include the following:

Note 18.

BUSINESS ACQUISITIONS

. . .

The purchase price of the shares [of Comair and ASA] was allocated to the assets acquired and the liabilities assumed based on estimated fair values at the respective acquisition date . . . Based on the allocation, total costs of the acquisitions exceeded the estimated fair values of the underlying net assets by $1.45 billion and $534 million . . .

Source: Courtesy of Delta Air Lines, Inc.

Goodwill is considered to have an indefinite life and must be reviewed at least annually for possible impairment of value.

Trademarks

A **trademark** is a special name, image, or slogan identified with a product or a company; it is protected by law. Trademarks are among the most valuable assets a company can own. For example, most of us cannot imagine the Walt Disney Company without Mickey Mouse. Similarly, you probably enjoy your favorite soft drink more because of the image that has been built up around its name than because of its taste. Many people can identify the shape of a corporate logo as quickly as they can recognize the shape of a stop sign. Although trademarks are valuable assets, they are rarely seen on balance sheets. The reason is simple; intangible assets are not recorded unless they are purchased. Companies often spend millions of dollars developing trademarks, but most of those expenditures are recorded as expenses rather than capitalized as an intangible asset.

A **TRADEMARK** is an exclusive legal right to use a special name, image, or slogan.

Copyrights

A **copyright** gives the owner the exclusive right to publish, use, and sell a literary, musical, or artistic piece for a period not exceeding 70 years after the author's death.[2] The book you are reading has a copyright to protect the publisher and authors. It is against the law, for example, for an instructor to copy several chapters from this book and hand them out in class. A copyright that is purchased is recorded at cost.

A **COPYRIGHT** is the exclusive right to publish, use, and sell a literary, musical, or artistic work.

Patents

A **patent** is an exclusive right granted by the federal government for a period of 20 years, typically granted to a person who invents a new product or discovers a new process.[3] The patent enables the owner to use, manufacture, and sell both the subject of the patent and the patent itself. It prevents a competitor from simply copying a new invention or discovery until the inventor has had time to earn an economic return on the new product. Without the protection of a patent, inventors likely would be unwilling to search for new products. Patents are recorded at their purchase price or, if **developed internally,** at only their registration and legal costs because GAAP require the immediate expensing of research and development costs.

A **PATENT** is granted by the federal government for an invention; it is an exclusive right given to the owner to use, manufacture, and sell the subject of the patent.

Technology

The number of companies reporting a **technology** intangible asset jumped by nearly 75 percent between 1998 and 2000. Computer software and web development costs are becoming increasingly significant. In 2000, IBM Corporation reported $782 million in

TECHNOLOGY includes costs for computer software and web development.

---

[2] In general, the limit is 70 years beyond the death of an author. For anonymous authors, the limit is 95 years from the first publication date. For more detail, go to lcweb.loc.gov/copyright.

[3] For more details, go to www.uspto.gov.web/pac/general/#patent.

software on its balance sheet and disclosed the following in the notes to the financial statements:

REAL WORLD EXCERPT

International Business Machines Corporation

2000 ANNUAL REPORT

> The company capitalizes certain costs that are incurred to purchase or to create and implement internal use computer software, which include software coding, installation, testing and data conversion. Capitalized costs are amortized on a straight-line basis over two years.
>
> The company capitalizes costs incurred during certain phases of internal Web site development. Capitalized costs are amortized on a straight-line basis over two years.

Franchises

A **FRANCHISE** is a contractual right to sell certain products or services, use certain trademarks, or perform activities in a geographical region.

Franchises may be granted by the government or a business for a specified period and purpose. A city may grant one company a franchise to distribute gas to homes for heating purposes, or a company may sell franchises, such as the right to operate a KFC restaurant. Franchise agreements are contracts that can have a variety of provisions. They usually require an investment by the franchisee; therefore, they should be accounted for as intangible assets. The life of the franchise agreement depends on the contract. It may be a single year or an indefinite period. Blockbuster Video's franchise agreement covers a period of 20 years. Blockbuster has more than 900 stores under franchise agreements.

Licenses and Operating Rights

LICENSES and **OPERATING RIGHTS**, obtained through agreements with governmental units or agencies, permit owners to use public property in performing its services.

The Delta balance sheet presented in Exhibit 8.1 shows an asset **operating rights** and other intangibles for $102 million. The operating rights are authorized landing slots that are regulated by the government and are in limited supply at many airports. They are intangible assets that can be bought and sold by the airlines. Other types of **licenses** that grant permission to companies include using airwaves for radio and television broadcasts and land for cable and telephone lines.

Research and Development Expense—*Not an Intangible Asset*

If an intangible asset is developed internally, the cost of development normally is recorded as **research and development expense.** For example, Abbott Laboratories (a manufacturer of pharmaceutical and nutritional products) recently spent more than $1,351 million on research to discover new products. This amount was reported as an expense, not an asset, because research and development expenditures typically do not possess sufficient probability of resulting in measurable future cash flows. If Abbott Labs had spent an equivalent amount to purchase patents for new products from other drug companies, it would have recorded the expenditure as an asset.

FOCUS ON CASH FLOWS

Cash

Productive Assets and Depreciation

Depreciation expense is commonly called a **noncash expense** because it **does not directly affect cash flows.** The cash outflow associated with depreciation occurs when the related asset is acquired. When depreciation is recorded, no cash payment is made (i.e., there is no credit to Cash). Most other expenses cause an immediate or subsequent outflow of cash. The recording of salary expense, for example, is associated with either the immediate payment of cash or a subsequent payment when the Salaries Payable account is paid.

EFFECT ON STATEMENT OF CASH FLOWS

In General Acquiring, selling, and depreciating long-term assets affect a company's cash flows as indicated in the following table:

Learning Objective 7
Explain the impact on cash flows of acquiring, using, and disposing of long-lived assets.

	Effect on Cash Flows
Operating activities (indirect method)	
Net income	$xxx
Adjusted for: Depreciation and amortization expense	+
Gains on sale of long-term assets	−
Losses on sale of long-term assets	+
Losses due to asset impairment write-downs	+
Investing activities	
Purchase of long-term assets	−
Sale of long-term assets	+

Focus Company Analysis The following is a condensed version of Delta's statement of cash flows for 2000. Buying and selling long-term assets are investing activities. In 2000, Delta used $4,060 million in cash to purchase flight equipment and ground property and equipment. Delta also sold flight equipment for $384 million in cash. Since selling long-term assets is not an operating activity, any gains (losses) on sales of long-term assets that were included in net income must be deducted from (added to) net income in the operating activities section to eliminate the effect of the sale. Unless they are large, these gain and loss adjustments normally are not specifically highlighted on the statement of cash flows. Delta did not list any gains or losses in 2000.

Finally, in capital-intensive industries such as airlines, depreciation is a significant noncash expense. In Delta's case, depreciation and amortization expense was the single largest adjustment to net income in determining cash flows from operations. It averaged 41 percent of operating cash flows in 2000 and has steadily increased over the past three years. Other focus companies that are less capital intensive, such as Timberland and Harley-Davidson, have significantly lower depreciation adjustments as a percentage of cash flows from operations.

Selected Focus Companies: Percentage of Depreciation to Cash Flows from Operations

Timberland	14%
Harley-Davidson	24%
Delta Air Lines	41%

DELTA AIR LINES, INC.
Consolidated Statements of Cash Flows
For the Years Ended December 31, 2000, 1999, and 1998

(in millions)	2000	1999	1998
Cash flows from Operating Activities			
Net income	$828	$1,208	$1,078
Adjustment to reconcile net income to cash provided by operating activities:			
Asset write-downs (due to impairment)	108	469	—
Depreciation and amortization	1,187	1,057	902
Other (summarized)	775	(87)	746
Net cash provided by operating activities	2,898	2,647	2,726
Cash flows from Investing Activities			
Property and equipment additions:			
Flight equipment	(3,426)	(2,497)	(2,090)
Ground property and equipment	(634)	(558)	(633)
Proceeds from sale of flight equipment	384	215	17
Other (summarized)	(20)	(1,122)	365
Net cash used in investing activities	(3,396)	(3,962)	(2,341)

A Misinterpretation

Some analysts misinterpret the meaning of a noncash expense, saying that "cash is provided by depreciation." Although depreciation is added in the operating section of the statement of cash flows, **depreciation is not a source of cash.** Cash from operations can be provided only by selling goods and services. A company with a large amount of depreciation expense does not generate more cash compared with a company that reports a small amount of depreciation expense, assuming that they are exactly the same in every other respect. While depreciation expense reduces the amount of reported net income for a company, it does not reduce the amount of cash generated by the company, because it is a noncash expense. Remember that the effects of recording depreciation are a reduction in stockholders' equity and in fixed assets, not in cash. That is why, on the statement of cash flows, depreciation expense is added back to net income on an accrual basis to compute cash flows from operations (on a cash basis).

Although depreciation is a noncash expense, the **depreciation method used for tax purposes can affect a company's cash flows.** Depreciation is a deductible expense for income tax purposes. The higher the amount of depreciation recorded by a company for tax purposes, the lower the company's taxable income and the taxes it must pay. Because taxes must be paid in cash, a reduction in a company's results reduces the company's cash outflows (that is, lower net income leads to lower tax payments).

DEMONSTRATION **CASE**

(Resolve the requirements before proceeding to the suggested solution that follows.) Diversified Industries started as a residential construction company. In recent years, it has expanded into heavy construction, ready-mix concrete, sand and gravel, construction supplies, and earth-moving services. The company completed the following transactions during 2003. Amounts have been simplified.

2003

Jan. 1   The management decided to buy a 10-year-old building for $175,000 and the land on which it was situated for $130,000. It paid $100,000 in cash and signed a mortgage note payable for the rest.

Jan. 12   Paid $38,000 in renovation costs on the building prior to use.

June 19   Bought a third location for a gravel pit (designated Gravel Pit No. 3) for $50,000 cash. It was estimated that 100,000 cubic yards of gravel could be removed.

July 10   Paid $1,200 for ordinary repairs on the building.

Aug. 1   Paid $10,000 for costs of preparing the new gravel pit for exploitation.

Dec. 31   Year-end adjustments:

a. The building will be depreciated on a straight-line basis over an estimated useful life of 30 years. The estimated residual value is $33,000.

b. During 2003, 12,000 cubic yards of gravel were removed from Gravel Pit No. 3.

c. Diversified purchased another company several years ago at $100,000 over the fair values of the net assets acquired. The goodwill has an indefinite life.

d. At the beginning of the year, the company owned equipment with a cost of $650,000 and accumulated depreciation of $150,000. The equipment is being depreciated using the double-declining-balance method, with a useful life of 20 years and no residual value.

e. At year-end, the company tested its long-lived assets for possible impairment of their value. It identified a piece of old excavation equipment with a cost of $156,000 and remaining book value of $120,000. Due to its smaller size and lack of safety features, the old equipment has limited use. The future cash flows are expected to be $40,000 and the fair value is determined to be $35,000. Goodwill was found not to be impaired.

December 31, 2003, is the end of the annual accounting period.

Required:

1. Indicate the accounts affected and the amount and direction (+ for increase and − for decrease) of the effect of each of the preceding events on the financial statement categories at the end of the year. Use the following headings:

Date	Assets	=	Liabilities	+	Stockholders' Equity

2. Record the adjusting journal entries for December 31(*a*) and (*b*) only.
3. Show the December 31, 2003, balance sheet classification and amount for each of the following items:
   Fixed assets—land, building, equipment, and gravel pit
   Intangible asset—goodwill
4. Assuming that the company had sales of $1,000,000 for the year and a net book value of $500,000 for fixed assets at the beginning of the year, compute the fixed asset turnover ratio. Explain its meaning.

SUGGESTED SOLUTION

1. Effects of events (with computations):

Date	Assets		=	Liabilities		+	Stockholders' Equity	
Jan. 1	Cash	−100,000		Note payable +205,000				
	Land	+130,000						
	Building	+175,000						
Jan. 12 (1)	Cash	−38,000						
	Building	+38,000						
June 19 (2)	Cash	−50,000						
	Gravel Pit No. 3	+50,000						
July 10 (3)	Cash	−1,200					Repairs expense	−1,200
Aug. 1 (4)	Cash	−10,000						
	Gravel Pit No. 3	+10,000						
Dec. 31 *a* (5)	Accumulated depreciation	−6,000					Depreciation expense	−6,000
Dec. 31 *b* (6)	Gravel Pit No. 3	−7,200						
	Gravel inventory	+7,200						
Dec. 31 *c* (7)	No entry							
Dec. 31 *d* (8)	Accumulated depreciation	−50,000					Depreciation expense	−50,000
Dec. 31 *e* (9)	Equipment	−85,000					Loss due to asset impairment	−85,000

(1) Capitalize the $38,000 expenditure because it is necessary to prepare the asset for use.
(2) This is a natural resource.
(3) This is a revenue expenditure and should be expensed.
(4) Capitalize the $10,000 expenditure because it is necessary to prepare the asset for use.

(5)

Cost of building		Straight-line depreciation
Initial purchase price	$175,000	($213,000 cost − $33,000 residual value) ×
Repairs prior to use	38,000	1/30 years = **$6,000** annual depreciation
Acquisition cost	$213,000	

(6)

Cost of gravel pit		Units-of-production depletion
Initial payment	$ 50,000	($60,000 cost ÷ 100,000 estimated production) ×
Preparation costs	10,000	12,000 actual cubic yards = **$7,200** annual depletion
Acquisition cost	$ 60,000	Capitalize the depletion to gravel inventory.

(7) Goodwill has indefinite life and is therefore not amortized. We will test for impairment later.

(8) **Double-declining-balance depreciation**
($650,000 cost − $150,000 accumulated depreciation) × 2/20 years = $50,000 annual depreciation

(9) **Asset impairment**
Impairment Test: The book value of old equipment, $120,000, exceeds expected future cash flows, $40,000. The asset is impaired.

Impairment Loss	
Book value	$120,000
Less: Fair value	−35,000
Loss due to impairment	$ 85,000

2. Adjusting entries at December 31, 2003:

a.	Depreciation expense, building (+E, −SE)	6,000	
	Accumulated depreciation (+XA, −A)		6,000
b.	Gravel inventory (+A)	7,200	
	Gravel pit No. 3 (−A)		7,200

3. Partial balance sheet, December 31, 2003:

Assets		
Fixed assets		
Land		$130,000
Building	$213,000	
Less: Accumulated depreciation	6,000	207,000
Equipment ($650,000 − 85,000)	565,000	
Less: Accumulated depreciation ($150,000 + 50,000)	200,000	365,000
Gravel pit		52,800
Total fixed assets		$754,800
Intangible asset		
Goodwill		$100,000

4. Fixed asset turnover ratio:

$$\frac{\text{Sales}}{(\text{Beginning Net Fixed Asset Balance} + \text{Ending Net Fixed Asset Balance}) \div 2} = \frac{\$1,000,000}{(\$500,000 + \$754,800) \div 2} = 1.59$$

This construction company is capital intensive. The fixed asset turnover ratio measures the company's efficiency at using its investment in property, plant, and equipment to generate sales.

Chapter Supplement A

Changes in Depreciation Estimates

Depreciation is based on two estimates, useful life and residual value. These estimates are made at the time a depreciable asset is acquired. As experience with the asset accumulates, one or both of these initial estimates may need to be revised. In addition, extraordinary repairs and additions may be added to the original acquisition cost at some time during the asset's use. When it is clear that either estimate should be revised to a material degree or that the asset's cost has changed, the undepreciated asset balance (less any residual value at that date) should be apportioned over the remaining estimated life from the current year into the future. This is called a prospective **change in estimate.**

To compute the new depreciation expense due to a change in estimate for any of the depreciation methods described here, substitute the net book value for the original acquisition cost, the new residual value for the original amount, and the estimated remaining life in place of the original estimated life. As an illustration, the formula using the straight-line method follows.

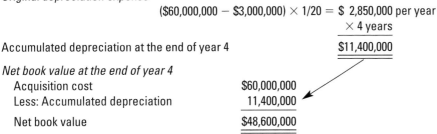

Original Straight-Line Formula Modified for a Change in Estimate:

$$(\text{Cost} - \text{Residual Value}) \times \frac{1}{\text{Useful Life}} = \text{Depreciation Expense}$$

$$(\text{Net Book Value} - \text{New Residual Value}) \times \frac{1}{\text{Remaining Life}} = \text{Depreciation Expense}$$

Assume Delta purchased an aircraft for $60,000,000 with an estimated useful life of 20 years and estimated residual value of $3,000,000. Shortly after the start of year 5, Delta changed the initial estimated life to 25 years and lowered the estimated residual value to $2,400,000. At the end of year 5, the computation of the new amount for depreciation expense is as follows:

Original depreciation expense

$$(\$60,000,000 - \$3,000,000) \times 1/20 = \$\ 2,850,000 \text{ per year}$$
$$\times 4 \text{ years}$$

Accumulated depreciation at the end of year 4 $11,400,000

Net book value at the end of year 4

Acquisition cost	$60,000,000
Less: Accumulated depreciation	11,400,000
Net book value	$48,600,000

Depreciation in years 5 through 25 based on changes in estimates:

$$(\text{Net book value} - \text{New residual value}) \times 1/\text{remaining years} = \text{New depreciation expense}$$

$$(\$48,600,000 - \$2,400,000) \times 1/21\ (25 - 4 \text{ years}) = \underline{\$2,200,000} \text{ per year}$$

Companies may also change depreciation methods (for example, from declining-balance to straight-line). Such a change requires significantly more disclosure since it violates the consistency principle that requires that accounting information reported in the financial statements be comparable across accounting periods. Under GAAP, changes in accounting estimates and depreciation methods should be made only when a new estimate or accounting method "better measures" the periodic income of the business.

Delta Air Lines changed depreciation estimates in the 1990s. The company's financial statements contained the following note:

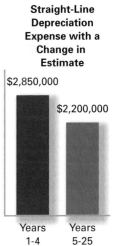

Straight-Line
Depreciation
Expense with a
Change in
Estimate

$2,850,000
$2,200,000

Years Years
1-4   5-25

As of July 1, 1998, we increased the depreciable lives of certain aircraft types from 20 to 25 years. The change in estimate reduced depreciation expense by $92 million ($.064 basic and $.060 diluted earnings per share) for fiscal 1999.

SOURCE: Courtesy of Delta Air Lines, Inc.

Notice that Delta changed the estimated life of its flight equipment. Why would Delta's management revise the estimates of useful life? The notes to the financial statements in 1999 indicate that Delta received delivery of several new aircraft from Boeing including the Boeing 777. This popular and efficient jet is a type of "new generation aircraft." Delta suggests by the increase in estimated useful life to 25 years that such aircraft will be flown longer than prior jet purchases.

SELF-STUDY **QUIZ**

Assume that Delta Air Lines owned a service truck that originally cost $100,000. When purchased, the truck had an estimated useful life of 10 years with no residual value. After operating the truck for 5 years, Delta determined that the remaining life was only two more years. Based on this change in estimate, what amount of depreciation should be recorded over the remaining life of the asset? Delta uses the straight-line method.

After you have completed your answer, compare it with the solution that follows:

_____
$50,000 (book value after 5 years) ÷ 2 years (remaining life) = $25,000 depreciation expense per year.

CHAPTER **TAKE-AWAYS**

1. **Define, classify, and explain the nature of long-lived productive assets and interpret the fixed asset turnover ratio. p. 397**
   a. Noncurrent assets are those that a business retains for long periods of time for use in the course of normal operations rather than for sale. They may be divided into tangible assets (land, buildings, equipment, natural resources) and intangible assets (including goodwill, patents, and franchises).
   b. The cost allocation method utilized affects the amount of net property, plant, and equipment that is used in the computation of the fixed asset turnover ratio. Accelerated methods reduce book value and increase the turnover ratio.
2. **Apply the cost principle to measure the acquisition and maintenance of property, plant, and equipment. p. 399**
   Acquisition cost of property, plant, and equipment is the cash-equivalent purchase price plus all reasonable and necessary expenditures made to acquire and prepare the asset for its intended use. These assets may be acquired using cash, debt, stock, or through self-construction. Expenditures made after the asset is in use are either capital expenditures or revenue expenditures:
   a. **Capital expenditures** provide benefits for one or more accounting periods beyond the current period. Amounts are debited to the appropriate asset accounts and depreciated, depleted, or amortized over their useful lives.
   b. **Revenue expenditures** provide benefits during the current accounting period only. Amounts are debited to appropriate current expense accounts when the expenses are incurred.
3. **Apply various cost allocation methods as assets are held and used over time. p. 404**
   Cost allocation methods: In conformity with the matching principle, cost (less any estimated residual value) is allocated to periodic expense over the periods benefited. Because of depreciation, the net book value of an asset declines over time and net income is reduced by the amount of the expense. Common depreciation methods include straight-line (a constant amount over time), units-of-production (a variable amount over time), and double-declining-balance (a decreasing amount over time).
   • Depreciation—buildings and equipment.

- Depletion—natural resources.
- Amortization—intangibles.

4. **Explain the effect of asset impairment on the financial statements. p. 414**

   When events or changes in circumstances reduce the estimated future cash flows of long-lived assets below their book value, the book values should be written down (by recording a loss) to the fair value of the assets.

5. **Analyze the disposal of property, plant, and equipment. p. 415**

   When assets are disposed of through sale or abandonment,
   - Record additional depreciation since the last adjustment was made.
   - Remove the cost of the old asset and its related accumulated depreciation, depletion, or amortization.
   - Recognize the cash proceeds.
   - Recognize any gains or losses when the asset's net book value is not equal to the cash received.

6. **Apply measurement and reporting concepts for natural resources and intangible assets. p. 417**

   The cost principle should be applied in recording the acquisition of natural resources and intangible assets. Natural resources should be depleted (usually by the units-of-production method) usually with the amount of the depletion expense capitalized to an inventory account. Intangibles with definite useful lives are amortized using the straight-line method. Intangibles with indefinite useful lives, including goodwill, are not amortized, but are reviewed at least annually for impairment. Report intangibles at net book value on the balance sheet.

7. **Explain the impact on cash flows of acquiring, using, and disposing of long-lived assets. p. 423**

   Depreciation expense is a noncash expense that has no effect on cash. It is added back to net income on the statement of cash flows to determine cash from operations. Acquiring and disposing of long-lived assets are investing activities.

In previous chapters, we discussed business and accounting issues related to the assets a company holds. In Chapters 9, 10, and 11, we shift our focus to the other side of the balance sheet to see how managers finance business operations and the acquisition of productive assets. We discuss various types of liabilities in Chapters 9 and 10 and examine stockholders' equity in Chapter 11.

KEY **RATIO**

The **fixed asset turnover ratio** measures how efficiently a company utilizes its investment in property, plant, and equipment over time. Its ratio can then be compared to competitors' ratios. The fixed asset turnover ratio is computed as follows (p. 398):

$$\text{Fixed Asset Turnover} = \frac{\text{Net Sales}}{(\text{Beginning Net Fixed Asset Balance} + \text{Ending Net Fixed Asset Balance}) \div 2}$$

FINDING **FINANCIAL INFORMATION**

Balance Sheet

Under Noncurrent Assets

Property, plant, and equipment (net of accumulated depreciation)

Natural resources (net of accumulated depletion)

Intangibles (net of accumulated amortization, if any)

Income Statement

Under Operating Expenses

Depreciation, depletion, and amortization expense or included in

Selling, general, and administrative expenses and

Cost of goods sold (with the amount for depreciation expense disclosed in a note)

Statement of Cash Flows

Under Operating Activities (indirect method)
Net income
+ Depreciation and amortization expense
− Gains on sales of assets
+ Losses on sales of assets

Under Investing Activities
+ Sales of assets for cash
− Purchases of assets for cash

Notes

Under Summary of Significant Accounting Policies
Description of management's choice for depreciation and amortization methods, including useful lives, and the amount of annual depreciation expense, if not listed on the income statement.

Under a Separate Footnote
If not specified on the balance sheet, a listing of the major classifications of long-lived assets at cost and the balance in accumulated depreciation, depletion, and amortization.

KEY TERMS

QUESTIONS

1. Define *long-lived assets*. Why are they considered to be a "bundle of future services"?
2. How is the fixed asset turnover ratio computed? Explain its meaning.
3. What are the classifications of long-lived assets? Explain each.
4. Relate the cost principle to the accounting for long-lived assets. Under the cost principle, what amounts should be included in the acquisition cost of a long-lived asset?
5. Describe the relationship between the matching principle and accounting for long-lived assets.
6. Distinguish between
   a. Capital expenditures and revenue expenditures. How is each accounted for?
   b. Ordinary repairs and extraordinary repairs. How is each accounted for?
7. Distinguish among depreciation, depletion, and amortization.
8. In computing depreciation, three values must be known or estimated; identify and explain the nature of each.
9. The estimated useful life and residual value of a long-lived asset relate to the current owner or user rather than all potential users. Explain this statement.
10. What type of depreciation expense pattern is used under each of the following methods and when is its use appropriate?
    a. The straight-line method.
    b. The units-of-production method.
    c. The double-declining-balance method.
11. Over what period should an addition to an existing long-lived asset be depreciated? Explain.

12. What is an *asset impairment?* How is it accounted for?
13. When equipment is sold for more than net book value, how is the transaction recorded? For less than net book value? What is net book value?
14. Define *intangible asset.* What period should be used to amortize an intangible asset with a definite life?
15. Define *goodwill.* When is it appropriate to record goodwill as an intangible asset?
16. Why is depreciation expense added to net income on the statement of cash flows?

MULTIPLE **CHOICE QUESTIONS**

1. Simon Company and Allen Company both bought a new delivery truck on January 1, 2001. Both companies paid exactly the same cost, $30,000 for their respective vehicle. As of December 31, 2004, the net book value of Simon's truck was less than the Allen Company's net book value for the same vehicle. Which of the following is an acceptable explanation for the difference in net book value?
   a. Both companies elected straight-line depreciation, but Simon Company used a longer estimated life.
   b. Simon Company estimated a lower residual value, but both estimated the same useful life and both elected straight-line depreciation.
   c. Because GAAP specifies rigid guidelines regarding the calculation of depreciation, this situation is not possible.
   d. Simon Company is using the straight-line method of depreciation, and Allen Company is using the double-declining-balance method of depreciation.

2. Barber, Inc., followed the practice of depreciating its building on a straight-line basis. A building was purchased in 2003 and had an estimated useful life of 20 years and a residual value of $20,000. The company's depreciation expense for 2003 was $20,000 on the building. What was the original cost of the building?
   a. $360,000   c. $400,000
   b. $380,000   d. $420,000

3. ACME, Inc., uses straight-line depreciation for all of its depreciable assets. ACME sold a used piece of machinery on December 31, 2003, that it purchased on January 1, 2002, for $10,000. The asset had a five-year life, zero residual value, and $2,000 accumulated depreciation as of December 31, 2002. If the sales price of the used machine was $7,500, the resulting gain or loss upon the sale was which of the following amounts?
   a. loss of $500   d. gain of $1,500
   b. gain of $500   e. No gain or loss upon the sale
   c. loss of $1,500

4. Under what method(s) of depreciation is an asset's *net book value* the depreciable base (the amount to be depreciated)?
   a. Straight-line method   c. Declining-balance method
   b. Units-of-production method   d. All of the above

5. What assets should be amortized using the straight-line method?
   a. Natural resources   c. Intangible assets with indefinite lives
   b. Intangible assets with definite lives   d. All of the above

6. A company wishes to report the highest earnings possible for financial reporting purposes. Therefore, when calculating depreciation,
   a. it will follow the MACRS depreciation tables prescribed by the IRS.
   b. it will select the shortest lives possible for its assets.
   c. it will select the longest lives possible for its assets.
   d. it will estimate higher residual values for its assets.

7. How many of the following statements regarding goodwill are true?

   ■ Goodwill is not reported unless purchased in an exchange.
   ■ Goodwill must be reviewed annually for possible impairment.
   ■ Impairment of goodwill results in a decrease in net income.

   a. none   c. two
   b. one   d. three

8. Company X is going to retire equipment that is fully depreciated. The equipment will simply be disposed of, not sold. Which of the following statements is false?
   a. Total assets will not change as a result of this transaction.
   b. Net income will not be impacted as a result of this transaction.
   c. This transaction will not impact cash flow.
   d. All of the above statements are true.

9. When recording depreciation, which of the following statements is true?
   a. Total assets increase and stockholders' equity increases.
   b. Total assets decrease and total liabilities increase.
   c. Total assets decrease and stockholders' equity increases.
   d. None of the above are true.

10. (Supplement) Thornton Industries purchased a machine for $45,000 and is depreciating it with the straight-line method over a life of 10 years, using a residual value of $3,000. At the beginning of the sixth year, a major overhaul was made costing $5,000, and the estimated useful life was extended to 13 years. Depreciation expense for Year 6 is:
    a. $1,885.
    b. $2,000.
    c. $3,250.
    d. $3,625.
    e. $4,200.

For more practice with multiple choice questions, go to our website at www.mhhe.com/libby4e, click on "Student Center" in the upper left menu, click on this chapter's name and number from the list of contents, and then click on "Multiple Choice Quiz" from the menu on the left.

MINI-EXERCISES

M8-1
LO1, 3, 6

Classifying Long-Lived Assets and Related Cost Allocation Concepts

For each of the following long-lived assets, indicate its nature and related cost allocation concept. Use the following symbols:

Nature			Cost Allocation Concept	
L	Land		DR	Depreciation
B	Building		DP	Depletion
E	Equipment		A	Amortization
NR	Natural resource		NO	No cost allocation
I	Intangible		O	Other
O	Other			

Asset	Nature	Cost Allocation	Asset	Nature	Cost Allocation
(1) Copyright	____	____	(6) Operating license	____	____
(2) Land held for use	____	____	(7) Land held for sale	____	____
(3) Warehouse	____	____	(8) Delivery vans	____	____
(4) Oil well	____	____	(9) Timber tract	____	____
(5) New engine for old machine	____	____	(10) Production plant	____	____

M8-2
LO1

Computing and Evaluating the Fixed Asset Turnover Ratio

The following information was reported by Cutter's Air Cargo Service for 2000:

Net fixed assets (beginning of year)	$1,450,000
Net fixed assets (end of year)	2,250,000
Net sales for the year	3,250,000
Net income for the year	1,700,000

Compute the company's fixed asset turnover ratio for the year. What can you say about Cutter's ratio when compared to Delta's 2000 ratio?

Identifying Capital and Revenue Expenditures

For each of the following items, enter the correct letter to the left to show the type of expenditure. Use the following:

Type of Expenditure		Transactions
C	Capital expenditure	_____ (1) Paid $400 for ordinary repairs.
R	Revenue expenditure	_____ (2) Paid $6,000 for extraordinary repairs.
N	Neither	_____ (3) Paid cash, $20,000, for addition to old building.
		_____ (4) Paid for routine maintenance, $200, on credit.
		_____ (5) Purchased a machine, $7,000; gave long-term note.
		_____ (6) Paid three-year insurance premium, $900.
		_____ (7) Purchased a patent, $4,300 cash.
		_____ (8) Paid $10,000 for monthly salaries.
		_____ (9) Paid cash dividends, $20,000.

M8-3
LO2

Computing Book Value (Straight-Line Depreciation)

Calculate the book value of a three-year-old machine that cost $21,500, has an estimated residual value of $1,500, and has an estimated useful life of four years. The company uses straight-line depreciation.

M8-4
LO3

Computing Book Value (Double-Declining-Balance Depreciation)

Calculate the book value of a three-year-old machine that cost $21,500, has an estimated residual value of $1,500, and has an estimated useful life of four years. The company uses double-declining-balance depreciation. Round to the nearest dollar.

M8-5
LO3

Computing Book Value (Units-of-Production Depreciation)

Calculate the book value of a three-year-old machine that cost $21,500, has an estimated residual value of $1,500, and has an estimated useful life of 20,000 machine hours. The company uses units-of-production depreciation and ran the machine 3,000 hours in year 1, 8,000 hours in year 2, 7,000 hours in year 3, and 2,000 hours in year 4.

M8-6
LO3

Identifying Asset Impairment

For each of the following scenarios, indicate whether an asset has been impaired (Y for yes and N for no) and, if so, the amount of loss that should be recorded.

M8-7
LO4

	Book Value	Estimated Future Cash Flows	Fair Value	Is Asset Impaired?	If so, Amount of Loss?
a. Machine	$16,000	$10,000	$9,000		
b. Copyright	40,000	41,000	39,000		
c. Factory building	50,000	35,000	30,000		
d. Building	230,000	230,000	210,000		

Recording the Disposal of a Long-Lived Asset (Straight-Line Depreciation)

As part of a major renovation at the beginning of the year, Mullins' Pharmacy, Inc., sold shelving units (store fixtures) that were 10 years old for $1,400 cash. The original cost of the shelves was $6,200 and had been depreciated on a straight-line basis over an estimated useful life of 12 years with an estimated residual value of $200. Record the sale of the shelving units.

M8-8
LO5

Computing Goodwill and Patents

Elizabeth Pie Company has been in business for 30 years and has developed a large group of loyal restaurant customers. Bonanza Foods made an offer to buy Elizabeth Pie Company for $5,000,000. The book value of Elizabeth Pie's recorded assets and liabilities on the date of the offer is $4,400,000 with a market value of $4,600,000. Elizabeth Pie also (1) holds a patent for a pie crust fluting machine that the company invented (the patent with a market value of $200,000 was never recorded by Eliza-

M8-9
LO6

beth Pie because it was developed internally) and (2) estimates goodwill from loyal customers to be $300,000 (also never recorded by the company). Should Elizabeth Pie Company management accept Bonanza Foods' offer of $5,000,000? If so, compute the amount of goodwill that Bonanza Foods should record on the date of the purchase.

M8-10
L07

Preparing the Statement of Cash Flows

Wagner Company had the following activities for the year ended December 31, 2004: Sold land for cash at its cost of $15,000. Purchased $80,000 of equipment, paying $75,000 in cash and the rest on a note payable. Recorded $3,000 in depreciation expense for the year. Net income for the year was $10,000. Prepare the operating and investing sections of a statement of cash flows for the year based on the data provided.

EXERCISES

E8-1
L01

Hasbro, Inc.

Preparing a Classified Balance Sheet

The following is a list of account titles and amounts (in millions) reported by Hasbro, Inc., a leading manufacturer of games, toys, and interactive entertainment software for children and families:

Buildings and improvements	$197	Cost in excess of net assets, net of	
Prepaid expenses and other		accumulated amortization	$ 704
current assets	319	Machinery and equipment	296
Allowance for doubtful accounts	64	Accumulated depreciation	227
Other noncurrent assets	131	Inventories	335
Accumulated amortization		Other intangibles	1,030
(other intangibles)	192	Land and improvements	15
Cash and cash equivalents	178	Accounts receivable	1,022
		Tools, dies, and molds	50

Required:

Prepare the asset section of the balance sheet for Hasbro, Inc., classifying the assets into Current Assets, Property, Plant, and Equipment (net), and Other Assets.

E8-2
L01, 2, 7

Evaluating the Impact of Capitalized Interest on Cash Flows and Fixed Asset Turnover from an Analyst's Perspective

You are a financial analyst charged with evaluating the asset efficiency of companies in the hotel industry. The financial statements for Hilton Hotels include the following note:

REAL WORLD EXCERPT

Hilton Hotels

> **Summary of Significant Accounting Policies**
>
> *Property, Equipment and Depreciation*
>
> Property and equipment are stated at cost. Interest incurred during construction of facilities is capitalized and amortized over the life of the asset.

Required:

1. Assume that Hilton followed this policy for a major construction project this year. How does Hilton's policy affect the following (+ for increase, − for decrease, and NE for no effect)?
   a. Cash flows.
   b. Fixed asset turnover ratio.
2. Normally, how would your answer to requirement (1*b*) affect your evaluation of Hilton's effectiveness in utilizing fixed assets?
3. If the fixed asset turnover ratio decreases due to interest capitalization, does this change indicate a real decrease in efficiency? Why or why not?

Computing and Interpreting the Fixed Asset Turnover Ratio from a Financial Analyst's Perspective

E8-3
LO1
Apple
Computer

The following data were included in a recent Apple Computer annual report:

In millions	2000	1999	1998	1997	1996	1995	1994	1993
Net sales	$7,983	$6,134	$5,941	$7,081	$9,833	$11,062	$9,180	$7,977
Net property, plant, and equipment	313	318	348	486	598	711	667	660

Required:
1. Compute Apple's fixed asset turnover ratio for 1994, 1996, 1998, and 2000 (the even years).
2. How might a financial analyst interpret the results?

Computing and Recording Cost and Depreciation of Assets (Straight-Line Depreciation)

E8-4
LO2, 3

Sweet Company bought a building for $71,200 cash and the land on which it is located for $106,800 cash. The company paid transfer costs of $2,000. Renovation costs on the building were $21,200.

Required:
1. Give the journal entry to record the purchase of the property, including all expenditures. Assume that all transactions were for cash and that all purchases occurred at the start of the year.
2. Compute straight-line depreciation at the end of one year, assuming an estimated 12-year useful life and a $14,000 estimated residual value.
3. What would be the net book value of the property at the end of year 2?

Determining Financial Statement Effects of an Asset Acquisition and Depreciation (Straight-Line Depreciation)

E8-5
LO2, 3

Conover Company ordered a machine on January 1, 2003, at an invoice price of $20,000. On date of delivery, January 2, 2003, the company paid $8,000 on the machine, and the balance was on credit at 12 percent interest. On January 3, 2003, it paid $250 for freight on the machine. On January 5, Conover paid installation costs relating to the machine amounting to $1,200. On July 1, 2003, the company paid the balance due on the machine plus the interest. On December 31, 2003 (the end of the accounting period), Conover recorded depreciation on the machine using the straight-line method with an estimated useful life of 10 years and an estimated residual value of $3,450.

Required (round all amounts to the nearest dollar):
1. Indicate the effects (accounts, amounts, and + or −) of each transaction (on January 1, 2, 3, 5, and July 1) on the accounting equation. Use the following schedule:

Date	Assets	=	Liabilities	+	Stockholders' Equity

2. Compute the acquisition cost of the machine.
3. Compute the depreciation expense to be reported for 2003.
4. What is the impact on the cost of the machine of the interest paid on the 12 percent note? Under what circumstances can interest expense be included in acquisition cost?
5. What would be the net book value of the machine at the end of 2004?

Recording Depreciation and Repairs (Straight-Line Depreciation)

E8-6
LO2, 3

Wiater Company operates a small manufacturing facility as a supplement to its regular service activities. At the beginning of 2004, an asset account for the company showed the following balances:

Manufacturing equipment	$80,000
Accumulated depreciation through 2003	55,000

During 2004, the following expenditures were incurred for repairs and maintenance:

| Routine maintenance and repairs on the equipment | $ 850 |
| Major overhaul of the equipment that improved efficiency | 10,500 |

The equipment is being depreciated on a straight-line basis over an estimated life of 15 years with a $5,000 estimated residual value. The annual accounting period ends on December 31.

Required:
1. Give the adjusting entry that was made at the end of 2003 for depreciation on the manufacturing equipment.
2. Starting at the beginning of 2004, what is the remaining estimated life?
3. Give the journal entries to record the two expenditures for repairs and maintenance during 2004.

E8-7 **Determining Financial Statement Effects of Depreciation and Repairs**
LO2, 3 **(Straight-Line Depreciation)**

Refer to the information in E8-6.

Required:
Indicate the effects (accounts, amounts, and + or −) of the following on the accounting equation:

Date	Assets	=	Liabilities	+	Stockholders' Equity

1. The adjustment for depreciation at the end of 2003.
2. The two expenditures for repairs and maintenance during 2004.

E8-8 **Computing Depreciation under Alternative Methods**
LO3

Dorn Corporation bought a machine at the beginning of the year at a cost of $6,400. The estimated useful life was four years, and the residual value was $800. Assume that the estimated productive life of the machine is 80,000 units. Yearly production was year 1, 28,000 units; year 2, 22,000 units; year 3, 18,000 units; and year 4, 12,000 units.

Required:
1. Complete a separate depreciation schedule for each of the alternative methods. You can round your answers to the nearest dollar.
   a. Straight-line.
   b. Units-of-production.
   c. Double-declining-balance.

| Method: _____ | | Depreciation | Accumulated | Net |
Year	Computation	Expense	Depreciation	Book Value
At acquisition				
1				
2				
3				
4				

2. Assuming that the machine was used directly in the production of one of the products that the company manufactures and sells, what factors might management consider in selecting a preferable depreciation method in conformity with the matching principle?

E8-9 **Explaining Depreciation Policy**
LO2, 3

The annual report for Eastman Kodak contained the following note:

Significant Accounting Policies

Depreciation

Depreciation expense is provided based on historical cost and the estimated useful lives of the assets. The Company generally uses the straight-line method for calculating the provision for depreciation. For assets in the United States acquired prior to January 1, 1992, the provision for depreciation is generally calculated using accelerated methods.

REAL WORLD EXCERPT

Eastman Kodak

Required:

1. Explain the term *historical cost*. What is the meaning of "provision for depreciation"?
2. Why do you think the company changed its depreciation method for assets acquired in 1992 and subsequent years? What impact did the change have on net income?

Interpreting Management's Choice of Different Depreciation Methods for Tax and Financial Reporting

E8-10
LO3

The annual report for Federal Express Corporation includes the following information:

REAL WORLD EXCERPT

Federal Express

For financial reporting purposes, depreciation and amortization of property and equipment is provided on a straight-line basis over the asset's service life. For income tax purposes, depreciation is generally computed using accelerated methods.

Required:

Explain why Federal Express uses different methods of depreciation for financial reporting and tax purposes.

Computing Depreciation and Book Value for Two Years Using Alternative Depreciation Methods and Interpreting the Impact on Cash Flows

E8-11
LO3, 7

Torge Company bought a machine for $65,000 cash. The estimated useful life was five years, and the estimated residual value was $5,000. Assume that the estimated useful life in productive units is 150,000. Units actually produced were 40,000 in year 1 and 45,000 in year 2.

Required:

1. Determine the appropriate amounts to complete the following schedule. Show computations, and round to the nearest dollar.

	Depreciation Expense for		Net Book Value at the End of	
Method of Depreciation	Year 1	Year 2	Year 1	Year 2
Straight-line				
Units-of-production				
Double-declining-balance				

2. Which method would result in the lowest EPS for year 1? For year 2?
3. Which method would result in the highest amount of cash outflows in year 1? Why?
4. Indicate the effects of (a) acquiring the machine and (b) recording annual depreciation on the operating and investing activities on the statement of cash flows (indirect method) for year 1 (assume the straight-line method).

E8-12
L04

Inferring Asset Impairment

REAL WORLD EXCERPT

Sunglass Hut
International

Sunglass Hut International is the world's largest specialty retailer of sunglasses with stores located in a wide variety of high-traffic shopping and tourist destinations. The following note and data were reported in a recent annual report:

NOTE 1—ORGANIZATION AND SUMMARY OF SIGNIFICANT ACCOUNTING POLICIES

Property and Equipment

The Company performed an analysis of the recoverability of the net book value of property and equipment for underperforming operations. As a result of the analysis, the Company reduced property and equipment by . . .

	In millions
Cost of property and equipment (beginning of year)	$192
Cost of property and equipment (end of year)	178
Capital expenditures during the year	29
Accumulated depreciation (beginning of year)	63
Accumulated depreciation (end of year)	77
Depreciation expense during the year	27
No property or equipment was sold	0

Required:

Based on the preceding information, compute the amount of property and equipment (both cost and accumulated depreciation) that Sunglass Hut wrote off as impaired during the year. (*Hint:* Set up T-accounts.)

E8-13
L05

Federal
Express

Recording the Disposal of an Asset at Three Different Sale Prices

Federal Express is the world's leading express-distribution company. In addition to the world's largest fleet of all-cargo aircraft, the company has more than 53,700 ground vehicles that pick up and deliver packages. Assume that Federal Express sold a small delivery truck that had been used in the business for three years. The records of the company reflected the following:

Delivery truck	$18,000
Accumulated depreciation	13,000

Required:
1. Give the journal entry for the disposal of the truck, assuming that
   a. The sales price was $5,000.
   b. The sales price was $5,600.
   c. The sales price was $4,600.
2. Based on the three preceding situations, explain the effects of the disposal of the asset.

E8-14
L05

Federal Express

Determining Financial Statement Effects of the Disposal of an Asset at Three Assumed Sale Prices

Refer to the information in E8-13.

Required:
1. Using the following structure, indicate the effects (accounts, amounts, and + or −) for the disposal of the truck assuming that
   a. The sales price was $5,000.
   b. The sales price was $5,600.
   c. The sales price was $4,600.

Assumption	Assets	=	Liabilities	+	Stockholders' Equity

2. For the three preceding situations, explain the effects of the disposal of the asset.

**Inferring Asset Age and Recording Accidental Loss on a Long-Lived Asset
(Straight-Line Depreciation)**

E8-15
LO5

On January 1, 2004, the records of Pastuf Corporation showed the following regarding a truck:

Equipment (estimated residual value, $2,000)	$12,000
Accumulated depreciation (straight line, three years)	6,000

On December 31, 2004, the delivery truck was a total loss as the result of an accident.

Required:
1. Based on the data given, compute the estimated useful life of the truck.
2. Give all journal entries with respect to the truck on December 31, 2004. Show computations.

Computing the Acquisition and Depletion of a Natural Resource

E8-16
LO6
Freeport-
McMoran

Freeport-McMoran is a natural resources company involved in the exploration, development, and ex-traction of natural resources. Annual revenues exceed $1 billion. Assume that in February 2003, Freeport-McMoran paid $700,000 for a mineral deposit in Wyoming. During March, it spent $65,000 in preparing the deposit for exploitation. It was estimated that 900,000 total cubic yards could be ex-tracted economically. During 2003, 60,000 cubic yards were extracted. During January 2004, the com-pany spent another $6,000 for additional developmental work. After conclusion of the latest work, the estimated remaining recovery was increased to 1,200,000 cubic yards over the remaining life. During 2004, 50,000 cubic yards were extracted.

Required:
1. Compute the acquisition cost of the deposit in 2003.
2. Compute depletion for 2003.
3. Compute the acquisition cost of the deposit after payment of the January 2004 developmental costs.

**Computing and Reporting the Acquisition and Amortization of
Three Different Intangible Assets**

E8-17
LO6

Kreiser Company had three intangible assets at the end of 2004 (end of the accounting year):
a. A patent purchased from J. Miller on January 1, 2004, for a cash cost of $5,640. Miller had regis-tered the patent with the U.S. Patent Office five years ago.
b. An internally developed trademark registered with the federal government for $10,000. Manage-ment decided the trademark has an indefinite life.
c. Computer software and web development technology purchased on January 1, 2003 for $60,000. The technology is expected to have a four-year useful life to the company.

Required:
1. Compute the acquisition cost of each intangible asset.
2. Compute the amortization of each intangible at December 31, 2004. The company does not use contra-accounts.
3. Show how these assets and any related expenses should be reported on the balance sheet and in-come statement for 2004.

Recording Leasehold Improvements and Related Amortization

E8-18
LO6
Starbucks Coffee
Company

Starbucks Coffee Company is a rapidly expanding retailer of specialty coffee with more than 2,600 company-operated stores in 35 states. Assume that Starbucks planned to open a new store on Com-monwealth Avenue near Boston University and obtained a 20-year lease starting January 1, 2004. The company had to renovate the facility by installing an elevator costing $175,000. Amounts spent to en-hance leased property are capitalized as intangible assets called Leasehold Improvements. The eleva-tor will be amortized over the useful life of the lease.

Required:
1. Give the journal entry to record the installation of the new elevator.
2. Give any adjusting entries required at the end of the annual accounting period on December 31, 2004, related to the new elevator. Show computations.

E8-19   Finding Financial Information as a Potential Investor

L01, 2, 3, 4, 5, 6, 7

You are considering investing the cash gifts you received for graduation in various stocks. You have received several annual reports of major companies.

Required:

For each of the following, indicate where you would locate the information in an annual report (*Hint:* The information may be in more than one location):

1. The detail on major classifications of long-lived assets.
2. The accounting method(s) used for financial reporting purposes.
3. Whether the company has had any capital expenditures for the year.
4. Net amount of property, plant, and equipment.
5. Policies on amortizing intangibles.
6. Depreciation expense.
7. Any significant gains or losses on disposals of fixed assets.
8. Prior year's accumulated depreciation.
9. The amount of assets written off as impaired during the year.

E8-20   (Supplement) Recording a Change in Estimate

Refer to E8-6.

Required:

Give the adjusting entry that should be made at the end of 2004 for depreciation of the manufacturing equipment, assuming no change in the original estimated life or residual value. Show computations.

E8-21   (Supplement) Determining Financial Statement Effects of a Change in Estimate

Refer to E8-6.

Required:

Using the following format, indicate the effects (accounts, amounts, and + or −) of the adjustment for depreciation of the manufacturing equipment, assuming no change in the estimated life or residual value. Show computations.

Date	Assets	=	Liabilities	+	Stockholders' Equity

E8-22   (Supplement) Recording and Explaining Depreciation, Extraordinary Repairs, and Changes in Estimated Useful Life and Residual Value (Straight-Line Depreciation)

L02, 3

At the end of the annual accounting period, December 31, 2003, Shafer Company's records reflected the following for Machine A:

Cost when acquired	$28,000
Accumulated depreciation	10,000

During January 2004, the machine was renovated at a cost of $11,000. As a result, the estimated life increased from five years to eight years, and the residual value increased from $3,000 to $5,000. The company uses straight-line depreciation.

Required:

1. Give the journal entry to record the renovation.
2. How old was the machine at the end of 2003?
3. Give the adjusting entry at the end of 2004 to record straight-line depreciation for the year.
4. Explain the rationale for your entries in requirements 1 and 3.

E8-23   (Supplement) Computing the Effect of a Change in Useful Life and Residual Value on Financial Statements and Cash Flows (Straight-Line Depreciation)

L03, 7

Todd Company owns the office building occupied by its administrative office. The office building was reflected in the accounts at the end of last year as follows:

Cost when acquired	$450,000
Accumulated depreciation (based on straight-line depreciation, an estimated life of 30 years, and a $30,000 residual value)	196,000

During January of this year, on the basis of a careful study, management decided that the total estimated useful life should be changed to 25 years (instead of 30) and the residual value reduced to $23,000 (from $30,000). The depreciation method will not change.

Required:
1. Compute the annual depreciation expense prior to the change in estimates.
2. Compute the annual depreciation expense after the change in estimates.
3. What will be the net effect of changing estimates on the balance sheet, net income, and cash flows for the year?

PROBLEMS

Explaining the Nature of a Long-Lived Asset and Determining the Financial Statement Effects of Its Purchase (AP8-1)

P8-1
LO1, 2

On January 2, 2003, Blumkin Company bought a machine for use in operations. The machine has an estimated useful life of eight years and an estimated residual value of $1,500. The company provided the following expenditures:

a. Invoice price of the machine, $70,000.
b. Freight paid by the vendor per sales agreement, $800.
c. Installation costs, $2,000.
d. Payment of the $70,000 was made as follows:

On January 2:

- Blumkin Company common stock, par $1; 2,000 shares (market value, $3 per share).
- Note payable, $40,000, 12 percent due April 16, 2003 (principal plus interest).
- Balance of the invoice price to be paid in cash. The invoice allows for a 2 percent discount for cash paid by January 12.

On January 15:

- Blumkin Company paid the balance due.

Required:
1. What are the classifications of long-lived assets? Explain their differences.
2. Indicate the accounts, amounts, and effects (+ for increase and − for decrease) of the purchase and subsequent cash payment on the accounting equation. Use the following structure:

Date	Assets	=	Liabilities	+	Stockholders' Equity

3. Explain the basis you used for any questionable items.

Explaining the Nature of a Long-Lived Asset and Recording Its Purchase (AP8-2)

P8-2
LO1, 2

Refer to the information in P8-1.

Required:
1. What are the classifications of long-lived assets? Explain their differences.
2. Record the purchase on January 2 and the subsequent payment on January 15. Show computations.
3. Explain the basis you used for any questionable items.

Analyzing the Effects of Repairs, an Addition, and Depreciation (AP8-3)

P8-3
LO2, 3
Federal
Express

A recent annual report for Federal Express included the following note:

Property and equipment

Expenditures for major additions, improvements, flight equipment modifications and overhaul costs are capitalized. Maintenance and repairs are charged to expense as incurred.

Assume that Federal Express made extensive repairs on an existing building and added a new wing. The building is a garage and repair facility for delivery trucks that serve the Denver area. The existing building originally cost $420,000, and by the end of 2003 (10 years), it was half depreciated on the basis of a 20-year estimated useful life and no residual value. Assume straight-line depreciation computed to the nearest month. During 2004, the following expenditures related to the building were made:

a. Ordinary repairs and maintenance expenditures for the year, $7,000 cash.
b. Extensive and major repairs to the roof of the building, $22,000 cash. These repairs were completed on December 31, 2004.
c. The new wing was completed on December 31, 2004, at a cash cost of $130,000.

Required:
1. Applying the policies of Federal Express, complete the following, indicating the effects for the preceding expenditures. If there is no effect on an account, write NE on the line:

	Building	Accumulated Depreciation	Depreciation Expense	Repairs Expense	Cash
Balance January 1, 2004	$420,000	$210,000			
Depreciation for 2004		_____	_____		_____
Balance prior to expenditures	420,000	_____	_____		
Expenditure *(a)*	_____	_____	_____	_____	_____
Expenditure *(b)*	_____	_____	_____	_____	_____
Expenditure *(c)*	_____	_____	_____	_____	_____
Balance December 31, 2004	_____	_____	_____	_____	

2. What was the book value of the building on December 31, 2004?
3. Explain the effect of depreciation on cash flows.

P8-4
LO2, 3

Computing the Acquisition Cost and Recording Depreciation under Three Alternative Methods (AP8-4)

At the beginning of the year, Montgomery Company bought three used machines from Hosey, Inc. The machines immediately were overhauled, installed, and started operating. The machines were different; therefore, each had to be recorded separately in the accounts.

	Machine A	Machine B	Machine C
Amount paid for asset	7,600	25,600	6,800
Installation costs	300	500	200
Renovation costs prior to use	2,000	400	600

By the end of the first year, each machine had been operating 8,000 hours.

Required:
1. Compute the cost of each machine.
2. Give the entry to record depreciation expense at the end of year 1, assuming the following:

| Machine | Estimates | | Depreciation Method |
	Life	Residual Value	
A	5	$1,500	Straight-line
B	40,000 hours	900	Units-of-production
C	4	2,000	Double-declining-balance

P8-5
LO1, 3
REX Stores
Corporation

Inferring Depreciation Amounts and Determining the Effects of a Depreciation Error on Key Ratios (AP8-5)

REX Stores Corporation, headquartered in Dayton, Ohio, is one of the nation's leading consumer electronics retailers operating more than 262 stores in 37 states. The following is a note from a recent annual report:

(1) SUMMARY OF SIGNIFICANT ACCOUNTING POLICIES—

(e) Property and Equipment—Property and equipment is recorded at cost. Depreciation is computed using the straight-line method. Estimated useful lives are 15 to 40 years for buildings and improvements, and 3 to 12 years for fixtures and equipment. Leasehold improvements are depreciated over 10 to 12 years. The components of cost at January 31, 2001 and 2000 are as follows:

	2001	2000
	(in thousands)	
Land	$ 36,866	$ 30,588
Buildings and improvements	93,582	77,645
Fixtures and equipment	19,716	17,213
Leasehold improvements	11,362	10,378
	161,526	135,824
Less: Accumulated depreciation	(25,883)	(22,023)
	$135,643	$113,801

Required:
1. Assuming that REX Stores did not sell any property, plant, and equipment in 2001, what was the amount of depreciation expense recorded in 2001?
2. Assume that REX Stores failed to record depreciation in 2001. Indicate the effect of the error (i.e., overstated or understated) on the following ratios:
   a. Earnings per share.
   b. Fixed asset turnover.
   c. Financial leverage.
   d. Return on equity.

Evaluating the Effect of Alternative Depreciation Methods on Key Ratios from an Analyst's Perspective

P8-6
LO1, 3

You are a financial analyst for General Motors Corporation and have been asked to determine the impact of alternative depreciation methods. For your analysis, you have been asked to compare methods based on a machine that cost $68,225. The estimated useful life is 10 years, and the estimated residual value is $2,225. The machine has an estimated useful life in productive output of 88,000 units. Actual output was 10,000 in year 1 and 8,000 in year 2.

Required:
1. For years 1 and 2 only, prepare separate depreciation schedules assuming:
   a. Straight-line method.
   b. Units-of-production method.
   c. Double-declining-balance method.

Method: _____		Depreciation	Accumulated	Net
Year	Computation	Expense	Depreciation	Book Value
At acquisition				
1				
2				

2. Evaluate each method in terms of its effect on cash flow, fixed asset turnover, and EPS. Assuming that General Motors is most interested in reducing taxes and maintaining a high EPS for year 1, what would you recommend to management? Would your recommendation change for year 2? Why or why not?

P8-7 Recording and Interpreting the Disposal of Three Long-Lived Assets (AP8-6)

L05

During 2003, Jensen Company disposed of three different assets. On January 1, 2003, prior to their disposal, the accounts reflected the following:

Asset	Original Cost	Residual Value	Estimated Life	Accumulated Depreciation (straight line)
Machine A	$20,000	$3,000	8 years	$12,750 (6 years)
Machine B	42,600	4,000	10 years	30,880 (8 years)
Machine C	76,200	4,200	15 years	57,600 (12 years)

The machines were disposed of in the following ways:

a. Machine A: Sold on January 1, 2003, for $8,200 cash.

b. Machine B: Sold on December 31, 2003, for $7,000; received cash, $3,000, and a $4,000 interest-bearing (12%) note receivable due at the end of 12 months.

c. Machine C: On January 1, 2003, this machine suffered irreparable damage from an accident. On January 10, 2003, a salvage company removed the machine at no cost.

Required:

1. Give all journal entries related to the disposal of each machine in 2003.
2. Explain the accounting rationale for the way that you recorded each disposal.

P8-8 Inferring Activities Affecting Fixed Assets from Notes to the Financial Statements and Analyzing the Impact of Depreciation on Cash Flows

L05, 7

Singapore Airlines

Singapore Airlines reported the following information in the notes to a recent annual report (in Singapore dollars):

SINGAPORE AIRLINES

Notes to the Accounts

13. Fixed Assets (in $ Million)

The Company

	Beginning of Year	Additions	Disposals/ Transfers	End of Year
Cost				
Aircraft	10,293.1	954.4	296.4	10,951.1
Other fixed assets (summarized)	3,580.9	1,499.1	1,156.7	3,923.3
	13,874.0	2,453.5	1,453.1	14,874.4
Accumulated depreciation				
Aircraft	4,024.8	683.7	290.1	4,418.4
Other fixed assets (summarized)	1,433.4	158.5	73.8	1,518.1
	5,458.2	842.2	363.9	5,936.5

Singapore Airlines also reported the following cash flow details:

Cash Flow from Operating Activities (in $ Million)		
	The Company	
	Current Year	Prior Year
Operating Profit	755.9	816.5
Adjustments for		
Depreciation of fixed assets	842.2	837.5
Loss/(surplus) on sale of fixed assets	(1.3)	(0.3)
Other adjustments (summarized)	82.3	39.4
Net Cash Provided by Operating Activities	1,679.1	1,693.1

Required:

1. Reconstruct the information in Note 13 into T-accounts for Fixed Assets and Accumulated Depreciation:

Fixed Assets		
Beg. balance		
Acquisitions	Disposals/transfers	
End. balance		

Accumulated Depreciation		
	Beg. balance	
Disposals/transfers	Depreciation expense	
	End. balance	

2. Compute the amount of cash the company received for disposals and transfers. Show computations.
3. Compute the percentage of depreciation expense to cash flows from operations. What do you interpret from the result?

Determining Financial Statement Effects of Activities Related to Various Long-Lived Assets (AP8-7)

P8-9
LO2, 3, 6

During the 2005 annual accounting period, Terwilliger Company completed the following transactions:

a. On January 1, 2005, purchased a patent for $19,600 cash (estimated useful life, seven years).
b. On January 1, 2005, purchased the assets (not detailed) of another business for cash $60,000, including $16,000 for goodwill. The company assumed no liabilities. Goodwill has an indefinite life.
c. On December 31, 2005, constructed a storage shed on land leased from S. Rhoades. The cost was $10,800. The company uses straight-line depreciation. The lease will expire in three years.
d. Total expenditures during 2005 for ordinary repairs and maintenance were $4,800.
e. On December 31, 2005, sold Machine A for $6,000 cash. Original cost on January 1, 2001, was $26,000; accumulated depreciation (straight line) to December 31, 2004, $18,400 ($3,000 residual value and five-year useful life).
f. On December 31, 2005, paid $7,000 for a complete reconditioning of Machine B acquired on January 1, 2001. Original cost, $32,000; accumulated depreciation (straight line) to December 31, 2004, $13,000 ($6,000 residual value and ten-year useful life).

Required:

1. For each of these transactions, indicate the accounts, amounts, and effects (+ for increase and − for decrease) on the accounting equation. Use the following structure:

Date	Assets	=	Liabilities	+	Stockholders' Equity

2. For each of these assets, compute depreciation and amortization to be recorded at the end of the year on December 31, 2005.

Computing Goodwill from the Purchase of a Business and Related Depreciation and Amortization

P8-10
LO6
Reebok International

Reebok International is a leading worldwide designer, marketer, and distributor of sport, fitness, and lifestyle products, including footwear and apparel. The notes to a recent annual report from Reebok included the following:

Business Acquisitions

During the current year, the Company acquired the assets of Perfection Sport Fashions, Inc., a designer and marketer of performance apparel and accessories marketed under the *Tinley* brand name.

Assume that Reebok acquired Perfection Sport Fashions on January 5, 2003. Reebok acquired the name of the company and all of its assets, except cash, for $400,000 cash. Reebok did not assume the liabilities. The transaction was closed on January 5, 2003, at which time the balance sheet of Perfection Sport Fashions reflected the following book values and an independent appraiser estimated the following market values for the assets:

PERFECTION SPORT FASHIONS
January 5, 2003

	Book Value	Market Value*
Accounts receivable (net)	$ 45,000	$ 45,000
Inventory	220,000	210,000
Fixed assets (net)	32,000	60,000
Other assets	3,000	10,000
Total assets	$300,000	
Liabilities	$ 60,000	
Stockholders' equity	240,000	
Total liabilities and stockholders' equity	$300,000	

These values for the purchased assets were provided to Reebok by an independent appraiser.

Required:

1. Compute the amount of goodwill resulting from the purchase. (*Hint:* Assets are purchased at market value in conformity with the cost principle.)
2. Compute the adjustments that Reebok would make at the end of the annual accounting period, December 31, 2003, for the following:
   a. Depreciation of the fixed assets (straight line), assuming an estimated remaining useful life of 15 years and no residual value.
   b. Goodwill (an intangible asset with an indefinite life).

P8-11 **Computing Amortization, Book Value, and Asset Impairment Related to Different**
L04, 6 **Intangible Assets** (AP8-8)

Fearn Company has five different intangible assets to be accounted for and reported on the financial statements. The management is concerned about the amortization of the cost of each of these intangibles. Facts about each intangible follow:

a. *Patent.* The company purchased a patent at a cash cost of $54,600 on January 1, 2003. The patent has an estimated useful life of 13 years.
b. *Copyright.* On January 1, 2003, the company purchased a copyright for $22,500 cash. It is estimated that the copyrighted item will have no value by the end of 25 years.
c. *Franchise.* The company obtained a franchise from McKenna Company to make and distribute a special item. It obtained the franchise on January 1, 2003, at a cash cost of $14,400 for a 12-year period.
d. *License.* On January 1, 2002, the company secured a license from the city to operate a special service for a period of five years. Total cash expended to obtain the license was $14,000.
e. *Goodwill.* The company started business in January 2001 by purchasing another business for a cash lump sum of $400,000. Included in the purchase price was "Goodwill, $60,000." Company executives stated that "the goodwill is an important long-term asset to us." It has an indefinite life.

Required:

1. Compute the amount of amortization that should be recorded for each intangible asset at the end of the annual accounting period, December 31, 2003.
2. Give the book value of each intangible asset on December 31, 2004.
3. Assume that on January 2, 2005, the copyrighted item was impaired in its ability to continue to produce strong revenues. The other intangible assets were not affected. Fearn estimated that the copyright will be able to produce future cash flows of $18,000. The fair value of the copyright is determined to be $16,000. Compute the amount, if any, of the impairment loss to be recorded.

P8-12 **(Supplement) Analyzing and Recording Entries Related to a Change in Estimated Life and Residual Value**

Reader's Digest is a global publisher of magazines, books, and music and video collections, and is one of the world's leading direct mail marketers. Many direct mail marketers use high-speed Didde press equipment to print their advertisements. These presses can cost more than $1 million. Assume that Reader's Digest owns a Didde press acquired at an original cost of $400,000. It is being depreciated on a straight-line basis over a 20-year estimated useful life and has a $50,000 estimated residual value. At the end of 2003, the press had been depreciated for a full eight years. In January 2004, a decision was made, on the basis of improved maintenance procedures, that a total estimated useful life of 25 years and a residual value of $73,000 would be more realistic. The accounting period ends December 31.

Required:
1. Compute (*a*) the amount of depreciation expense recorded in 2003 and (*b*) the book value of the printing press at the end of 2003.
2. Compute the amount of depreciation that should be recorded in 2004. Show computations.
3. Give the adjusting entry for depreciation at December 31, 2004.

ALTERNATE **PROBLEMS**

Explaining the Nature of a Long-Lived Asset and Determining the Financial Statement Effects of Its Purchase (P8-1)

AP8-1
LO1, 2

On June 1, 2002, the Wilbur Corp. bought a machine for use in operations. The machine has an estimated useful life of six years and an estimated residual value of $2,000. The company provided the following expenditures:

a. Invoice price of the machine, $60,000.
b. Freight paid by the vendor per sales agreement, $650.
c. Installation costs, $1,500.
d. Payment of the $60,000 was made as follows:
   On June 1:
   • Wilbur Corp. common stock, par $2; 2,000 shares (market value, $5 per share).
   • Balance of the invoice price on a note payable, 12 percent due September 2, 2002 (principal plus interest).
   On September 2:
   • Wilbur Corp. paid the balance and interest due on the note payable.

Required:
1. What are the classifications of long-lived assets? Explain their differences.
2. Indicate the accounts, amounts, and effects (+ for increase and − for decrease) of the purchase and subsequent cash payment on the accounting equation. Use the following structure:

Date	Assets	=	Liabilities	+	Stockholders' Equity

3. Explain the basis you used for any questionable items.

Explaining the Nature of a Long-Lived Asset and Recording Its Purchase (P8-2)

AP8-2
LO1, 2

Refer to the information in AP8-1.

Required:
1. What are the classifications of long-lived assets? Explain their differences.
2. Record the purchase on July 1 and the subsequent payment on September 2. Show computations.
3. Explain the basis you used for any questionable items.

Analyzing the Effects of Repairs, an Addition, and Depreciation (P8-3)

AP8-3
LO2, 3

A recent annual report for AMERCO, the holding company for U-Haul International, Inc., included the following note:

REAL WORLD EXCERPT

AMERCO

PROPERTY, PLANT AND EQUIPMENT

Property, plant and equipment are carried at cost and are depreciated on the straight-line and accelerated methods over the estimated useful lives of the assets. . . . Maintenance is charged to operating expenses as incurred, while renewals and betterments are capitalized. Major overhaul costs are amortized over the estimated period benefited.

AMERCO subsidiaries own property, plant, and equipment that are utilized in the manufacture, repair, and rental of U-Haul equipment and that provide offices for U-Haul. Assume that AMERCO made extensive repairs on an existing building and added a new wing. The building is a garage and repair facility for rental trucks that serve the Seattle area. The existing building originally cost $230,000, and by the end of 2004 (its fifth year), the building was one-quarter depreciated on the basis of a 20-year estimated useful life and no residual value. Assume straight-line depreciation computed to the nearest month. During 2005, the following expenditures related to the building were made:

a. Ordinary repairs and maintenance expenditures for the year, $5,000 cash.
b. Extensive and major repairs to the roof of the building, $17,000 cash. These repairs were completed on December 31, 2005.
c. The new wing was completed on December 31, 2005, at a cash cost of $70,000.

Required:
1. Applying the policies of AMERCO, complete the following, indicating the effects for the preceding expenditures. If there is no effect on an account, write NE on the line:

	Building	Accumulated Depreciation	Depreciation Expense	Repairs Expense	Cash
Balance January 1, 2005	$230,000	$57,500			
Depreciation for 2005		_____	_____		_____
Balance prior to expenditures	230,000	_____	_____		
Expenditure *(a)*	_____	_____	_____	_____	_____
Expenditure *(b)*	_____	_____	_____	_____	_____
Expenditure *(c)*	_____	_____	_____	_____	_____
Balance December 31, 2005	_____	_____	_____	_____	

2. What was the book value of the building on December 31, 2005?
3. Explain the effect of depreciation on cash flows.

AP8-4   **Computing the Acquisition Cost and Recording Depreciation under Three Alternative**
LO2, 3   **Methods** (P8-4)

At the beginning of the year, Morgan Inc. bought three used machines from Abruzzo Corporation. The machines immediately were overhauled, installed, and started operating. The machines were different; therefore, each had to be recorded separately in the accounts.

	Machine A	Machine B	Machine C
Cost of the asset	$10,800	$32,500	$21,700
Installation costs	800	1,100	1,100
Renovation costs prior to use	600	1,400	1,600

By the end of the first year, each machine had been operating 7,000 hours.

Required:
1. Compute the cost of each machine.
2. Give the entry to record depreciation expense at the end of year 1, assuming the following:

Machine	Estimates		Depreciation Method
	Life	Residual Value	
A	4	$1,000	Straight-line
B	33,000 hours	2,000	Units-of-production
C	5	1,400	Double-declining-balance

AP8-5   **Inferring Depreciation Amounts and Determining the Effects of a Depreciation Error**
LO1, 3   **on Key Ratios** (P8-5)

Lechters, Inc.

Lechters, Inc., and its subsidiaries is a specialty retailer of primarily brand-name basic and decorative housewares. As of January 30, 2001, the Company operated 325 stores in 36 states and the District of Columbia. The following is a note from a recent annual report:

(1) SUMMARY OF SIGNIFICANT ACCOUNTING POLICIES—

(e) Property and Equipment—Property and equipment are stated at cost. Depreciation and amortization are computed principally by the straight-line method by charges to earnings in amounts sufficient to write-off the cost of depreciable assets over their estimated lives, or where applicable, the terms of the respective leases, whichever is shorter.

The components of cost at the end of the current and prior years are as follows (in thousands):

	Current Year	Prior Year
Property and Equipment		
Fixtures and equipment	$ 57,678	$ 58,403
Leasehold improvements	96,452	94,994
	154,130	153,397
Less accumulated depreciation and amortization	88,401	79,891
Net property and equipment	$ 65,729	$ 73,506

Required:
1. Assuming that Lechters, Inc., did not have any asset impairment write-offs and did not sell any property, plant, and equipment in the current year, what was the amount of depreciation expense recorded in the current year?
2. Assume that Lechters, Inc., failed to record depreciation in the current year. Indicate the effect of the error (i.e., overstated or understated) on the following ratios:
   a. Earnings per share.
   b. Fixed asset turnover.
   c. Financial leverage.
   d. Return on equity.

Recording and Interpreting the Disposal of Three Long-Lived Assets (P8-7)

AP8-6
L05

During 2003, Kosik Company disposed of three different assets. On January 1, 2003, prior to their disposal, the accounts reflected the following:

Asset	Original Cost	Residual Value	Estimated Life	Accumulated Depreciation (straight line)
Machine A	$24,000	$2,000	5 years	$17,600 (4 years)
Machine B	16,500	5,000	10 years	8,050 (7 years)
Machine C	59,200	3,200	14 years	48,000 (12 years)

The machines were disposed of in the following ways:
a. Machine A: Sold on January 1, 2003, for $5,750 cash.
b. Machine B: Sold on December 31, 2003, for $9,000; received cash, $4,000, and a $5,000 interest-bearing (10%) note receivable due at the end of 12 months.
c. Machine C: On January 1, 2003, this machine suffered irreparable damage from an accident.

Required:
1. Give all journal entries related to the disposal of each machine.
2. Explain the accounting rationale for the way that you recorded each disposal.

Determining Financial Statement Effects of Activities Related to Various Long-Lived Assets (P8-9)

AP8-7
L02, 3, 6

During the 2004 annual accounting period, Chu Corporation completed the following transactions:

a. On January 1, 2004, purchased a license for $7,200 cash (estimated useful life, three years).
b. On January 1, 2004, repaved the parking lot of the building leased from I. Kumara. The cost was $7,800; the estimated useful life was five years with no residual value. The company uses straight-line depreciation. The lease will expire in 10 years.

c. On July 1, 2004, purchased another business for $120,000 cash. The transaction included $115,000 for assets and $24,000 for the liabilities assumed by Chu. The remainder was goodwill with an indefinite life.

d. On December 31, 2004, sold Machine A for $5,000 cash. Original cost, $21,500; accumulated depreciation (straight line) to December 31, 2003, $13,500 ($3,500 residual value and four-year life).

e. Total expenditures during 2004 for ordinary repairs and maintenance were $6,700.

f. On December 31, 2004, paid $8,000 for a complete reconditioning of Machine B acquired on January 1, 2001. Original cost, $18,000; accumulated depreciation (straight line) to December 31, 2003, $10,200 ($2,000 residual value and four-year life).

Required:

1. For each of these transactions, indicate the accounts, amounts, and effects (+ for increase and − for decrease) on the accounting equation. Use the following structure:

Date	Assets	=	Liabilities	+	Stockholders' Equity

2. For each of these assets, compute depreciation and amortization to the nearest month to be recorded at the end of the year on December 31, 2004.

AP8-8
LO4, 6

Computing Amortization, Book Value, and Asset Impairment Related to Different Intangible Assets (P8-11)

Norton Corporation has five different intangible assets to be accounted for and reported on the financial statements. The management is concerned about the amortization of the cost of each of these intangibles. Facts about each intangible follow:

a. *Patent.* The company purchased a patent at a cash cost of $18,600 on January 1, 2002. It is amortized over its expected useful life of 15 years.

b. *Copyright.* On January 1, 2002, the company purchased a copyright for $24,750 cash. It is estimated that the copyrighted item will have no value by the end of 30 years.

c. *Franchise.* The company obtained a franchise from Farrell Company to make and distribute a special item. It obtained the franchise on January 1, 2002, at a cash cost of $19,200 for a 12-year period.

d. *License.* On January 1, 2001, the company secured a license from the city to operate a special service for a period of seven years. Total cash expended to obtain the license was $21,000.

e. *Goodwill.* The company started business in January 2000 by purchasing another business for a cash lump sum of $650,000. Included in the purchase price was "Goodwill, $75,000." Company executives stated that "the goodwill is an important long-term asset to us." It has an indefinite life.

Required:

1. Compute the amount of amortization that should be recorded for each intangible asset at the end of the annual accounting period, December 31, 2002.

2. Give the book value of each intangible asset on January 1, 2005.

3. Assume that on January 2, 2005, the franchise was impaired in its ability to continue to produce strong revenues. The other intangible assets were not affected. Norton estimated that the franchise will be able to produce future cash flows of $14,500, and the fair value is $13,000. Compute the amount, if any, of the impairment loss to be recorded.

CASES AND **PROJECTS**

Annual Report Cases

CP8-1
LO1, 3, 4, 6

**AMERICAN EAGLE
OUTFITTERS**

Finding Financial Information

Refer to the financial statements and accompanying notes of American Eagle Outfitters given in Appendix B at the end of this book, or open file AEOS.pdf in the Annual Report Cases directory on the student CD-ROM.

Required:

1. What method of depreciation does the company use?
2. What is the amount of accumulated depreciation and amortization at the end of the current year?
3. For depreciation purposes, what is the estimated useful life of fixtures and equipment?

4. What was the original cost of leasehold improvements owned by the company at the end of the current year?
5. What amount of depreciation and amortization was reported as expense for the current year?
6. What is the company's fixed asset turnover ratio? What does it suggest?
7. For each of the preceding questions, where did you locate the information?

Finding Financial Information

Refer to the financial statements and accompanying notes of Abercrombie & Fitch given in Appendix C at the end of this book, or open file ANF.pdf in the Annual Report Cases directory on the student CD-ROM.

Required:
1. How much did the company spend on capital expenditures in 2000?
2. What were the primary purposes of these capital expenditures?
3. What is the estimated useful life of leasehold improvements for depreciation purposes?
4. What was the original cost of furniture, fixtures, and equipment held by the company at the end of the current year?
5. What was the amount of depreciation and amortization reported as an expense for the current year? Compare this amount to the change in accumulated amortization and depreciation from 1999 to 2000. Why would these numbers be different?
6. What is the company's fixed asset turnover ratio?
7. For each of the preceding questions, where did you locate the information?

CP8-2
L01, 3, 4, 6

ABERCROMBIE & FITCH

Comparing Companies within an Industry

Refer to the financial statements of American Eagle Outfitters given in Appendix B and Abercrombie & Fitch given in Appendix C, and the Industry Ratio Report given in Appendix D at the end of this book or open file CP8-3.xls in the Annual Report Cases directory on the student CD-ROM.

Required:
1. Compute the percentage of net fixed assets to total assets for both companies for the most recent year. Why do the companies differ?
2. Compute the percentage of the fixed assets that have been depreciated for both companies for the most recent year. Why do you think the percentages differ?
3. Compute the fixed asset turnover ratio for the most recent year presented for both companies. Which has higher asset efficiency? Why?
4. Compare the fixed asset turnover ratio for both companies to the industry average. Are these companies doing better or worse than the industry average in asset efficiency?

CP8-3
L01, 3

AMERICAN EAGLE OUTFITTERS

ABERCROMBIE & FITCH

Financial Reporting and Analysis Cases

Broadening Financial Research Skills: Identifying Competitors in an Industry

MarketGuide provides lists of industries and the competitors in each at www.marketguide.com/mgi/INDUSTRY/INDUSTRY.html.

Required:
Using your web browser, contact MarketGuide and identify three competitors for the following industries:
1. Airline.
2. Hotels and motels.
3. Footwear.
4. Computer hardware.

CP8-4

Interpreting the Financial Press

The October 5, 1998, edition of *Business Week* includes the article, "Earnings Hocus-Pocus."* You can access the article on the Libby/Libby/Short website at www.mhhe.com/libby4e.

CP8-5
L04

---

*Reprinted from October 5, 1998 issue of *Business Week* by special permission, copyright © 1998 by The McGraw-Hill Companies, Inc.

Required:

Read pages 1 through 9 of the article (stopping at the paragraph beginning with "Meanwhile, the SEC . . . ." Then answer the following questions:

1. What is meant by the concept that many companies take a "big bath"?
2. List several companies mentioned in the article that have taken a big bath by writing down fixed assets or intangibles. Indicate for each the nature of the earnings manipulation.

CP8-6

L03

Black & Decker

Using Financial Reports: Analyzing the Age of Assets

A note to a recent annual report for Black & Decker contained the following information (in thousands of dollars):

	Current Year
Land and improvements	$ 69,091
Buildings	298,450
Machinery and equipment	928,151
	1,295,692
Less accumulated depreciation	468,511
	$ 827,181

Depreciation expense (in thousands of dollars) charged to operations was $99,234 in the current year. Depreciation generally is computed using the straight-line method for financial reporting purposes.

Required:

1. What is your best estimate of the average expected life for Black & Decker's depreciable assets?
2. What is your best estimate of the average age of Black & Decker's depreciable assets?

CP8-7

L03

The Coca-Cola
Company

Using Financial Reports: Analyzing a Note Concerning Depreciation

A recent annual report for The Coca-Cola Company contained the following note:

> Property, plant, and equipment is stated at cost, less allowance for depreciation. Depreciation expense is determined principally by the straight-line method. The annual rates of depreciation are 2 percent to 10 percent for buildings and improvements and 7 percent to 34 percent for machinery, equipment, and containers.

Required:

1. What is the range of expected lives for buildings and improvements?
2. Explain why Coca-Cola depreciates the cost of its containers instead of including the total in cost of goods sold in the year the product is sold.

CP8-8

L01, 6, 7

The Seagram
Company Ltd.

Using Financial Reports: Analyzing Fixed Asset Turnover Ratio and Cash Flows

The Seagram Company Ltd., with headquarters in Montreal, Quebec, Canada, operates in both the beverage and entertainment industries. Seagram produces well-known spirits and wines. In June 1995, Seagram purchased an 80 percent interest in MCA, Inc., which produces and distributes motion picture, television, and home video products and recorded music; publishes books; and operates theme parks (Universal Studios) and retail stores. The purchase resulted in $2.7 billion in goodwill. Since 1995, Seagram has undertaken a number of business acquisitions and divestitures (sales of businesses) as the company expands into the entertainment industry. Selected data from a recent annual report are as follows (amounts are in millions of U.S. dollars):

PROPERTY, PLANT, EQUIPMENT, AND INTANGIBLES FROM THE CONSOLIDATED BALANCE SHEET		
	Current Year	Prior Year
Film costs, net of amortization	$1,272	$ 991
Artists' contracts, advances, and other entertainment assets	761	645
Property, plant, and equipment, net	2,733	2,559
Excess of cost over fair value of assets acquired	3,076	3,355
FROM THE CONSOLIDATED STATEMENT OF INCOME		
Total revenues	$9,714	$10,644
FROM THE CONSOLIDATED STATEMENT OF CASH FLOWS		
Income from continuing operations	$ 880	$ 445
Adjustments		
Depreciation	289	265
Amortization	208	190
Other adjustments (summarized)	(1,618)	(256)
Net cash provided by continuing operations	(241)	644
FROM THE NOTES TO THE FINANCIAL STATEMENTS		
Accumulated depreciation on property, plant, and equipment	$ 1,178	$ 1,023

Required:
1. Compute the cost of the property, plant, and equipment at the end of the current year. Explain your answer.
2. What was the approximate age of the property, plant, and equipment at the end of the current year?
3. Compute the fixed asset turnover ratio for the current year. Explain your results.
4. What is Excess of Cost Over Fair Value of Assets Acquired?
5. On the consolidated statement of cash flows, why are the depreciation and amortization amounts added to income from continuing operations?

Using Financial Reports: Inferring the Sale of Assets

CP8-9
LO1, 5, 7
Eastman Kodak

A recent annual report for Eastman Kodak reported that the balance of property, plant, and equipment at the end of the current year was $16,774 million. At the end of the previous year, it had been $15,667 million. During the current year, the company bought $2,118 million worth of new equipment. The balance of accumulated depreciation at the end of the current year was $8,146 million and at the end of the previous year was $7,654 million. Depreciation expense for the current year was $1,181 million. The annual report does not disclose any gain or loss on the disposition of property, plant, and equipment, so you may assume that the amount was zero.

Required:
What amount of proceeds did Eastman Kodak receive when it sold property, plant, and equipment during the current year? (*Hint:* Set up T-accounts.)

Using Financial Reports: Comparing Depreciation Methods in Different Countries

CP8-10
LO3
Diageo

Diageo is a major international company located in London. A recent annual report contained the following information concerning its accounting policies.

Fixed assets and depreciation

Fixed assets are stated at cost or at professional valuation. Cost includes interest, net of any tax relief, on capital employed in major developments.

No depreciation is provided on freehold land. Other leaseholds are depreciated over the unexpired period of the lease. All other buildings, plant, equipment, and vehicles are depreciated to residual values over their estimated useful lives within the following ranges:

Industrial buildings	25 to 100 years
Plant and machinery	3 to 25 years
Fixtures and fittings	3 to 17 years

Required:

Compare accounting for fixed assets and depreciation in England with procedures used in this country.

Critical Thinking Cases

CP8-11

LO2

Amerada Hess
Corporation

Making a Decision as a Financial Analyst: Interpreting the Impact of the Capitalization of Interest on an Accounting Ratio

The capitalization of interest associated with self-constructed assets was discussed in this chapter. A recent annual report for Amerada Hess Corporation disclosed the following information concerning capitalization of interest:

> Interest costs related to certain long-term construction projects are capitalized to comply with FAS No. 34, "Capitalization of Interest Cost." Capitalized interest in the current year amounted to $34,897,000.

The income statement for that year disclosed that interest expense was $224,200,000. A popular accounting ratio used by some analysts is the interest coverage ratio (Income ÷ Interest Expense).

Required:

1. Explain why an analyst would calculate this ratio.
2. Did Amerada Hess include the $34,897,000 in the reported interest expense of $224,200,000? If not, should an analyst include it when calculating the interest coverage ratio? Explain.

CP8-12

LO3, 7

Ford Motor
Corporation

Evaluating an Ethical Dilemma: Analyzing an Accounting Change

An annual report for Ford Motor Company included the following information:

> **Note 6. Net Property, Depreciation and Amortization—Automotive**
>
> Assets placed in service before January 1, 1993, are depreciated using an accelerated method. Assets placed in service beginning in 1993 will be depreciated using the straight-line method of depreciation. This change in accounting principle is being made to reflect improvements in the design and flexibility of manufacturing machinery and equipment and improvements in maintenance practices. These improvements have resulted in more uniform productive capacities and maintenance costs over the useful life of an asset. Straight-line is preferable in these circumstances. The change is expected to improve 1993 after-tax results by $80 to $100 million.

Required:

1. What was the stated reason for the change in method? What other factors do you think management considered when it decided to make this accounting change?
2. Do you think this is an ethical decision?
3. Who were affected by the change and how were they benefited or harmed?
4. What impact did this change have on cash flows for Ford?
5. As an investor, how would you react to the fact that Ford's net income will increase by $80 to $100 million as the result of this change?

Financial Reporting and Analysis Team Project

Team Project: Analysis of Long-Lived Assets

CP8-13

MarketGuide provides lists of industries and the competitors in each at www.marketguide.com/mgi/ INDUSTRY/INDUSTRY.html. Using your web browser, contact MarketGuide. As a group, select an industry to analyze. Each team member should then use the web browser to obtain the annual report or 10-K for one publicly traded company in the industry, with each member selecting a different company.

Required:

1. On an individual basis, each team member should write a short report listing the following:
   a. The accounts and amounts of the company's long-lived assets (property, plant, and equipment; intangible assets; and natural resources).
   b. The cost allocation method(s) and estimates used for each type of long-lived asset.
   c. The approximate average life of the assets.
   d. The fixed asset turnover ratio.
2. Discuss any patterns that you as a team observe. Then, as a team, write a short report comparing and contrasting your companies according to the preceding attributes.

LEARNING OBJECTIVES

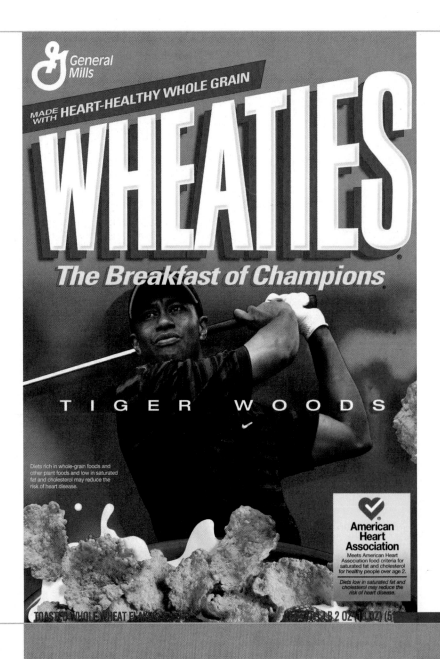

Reporting and Interpreting Liabilities

9

General Mills is a respected leader in the food industry. The company sells a full line of breakfast cereals, numerous snack foods, and the popular Betty Crocker products. While many consumers have grown up with Cheerios and Trix, more than a quarter of the company's recent growth has come from innovative new products, including Scooby Doo–shaped fruit snacks and changing-flavor Fruit by the Foot Flavor Wave.

To achieve its impressive financial results, General Mills executives establish aggressive goals for the company. While many of these goals focus on sales increases and improvements in operating efficiencies, some focus on financial results, such as growth in earnings per share and return on invested capital. One of the company's financial goals pertains to the liabilities, the focus of this chapter:

FOCUS COMPANY:

General Mills

MANAGING CAPITAL STRUCTURE

www.generalmills.com

General Mills' financial goal is to achieve performance that places us in the top 10 percent of major American companies, ranked by the combination of growth in earnings per share and return on capital over a five-year period. Our major financial targets for top-decile performance include: . . .

- Maintaining a balance sheet with a strong "A" bond rating that will allow access to financing at reasonable costs.

REAL WORLD EXCERPT

GENERAL
MILLS

ANNUAL REPORT*

*The financial information used for General Mills in this chapter is taken from their Form 10-K annual report submitted to the SEC for the fiscal year ended May 28, 2000.

Financial analysts consider a number of factors when they assess the strength of a company's balance sheet. One of the key factors they examine is how the company has financed its operations. Often, managing a company's liabilities is just as important as managing its assets.

UNDERSTANDING THE BUSINESS

Businesses finance the acquisition of their assets from two sources: funds supplied by creditors (debt) and funds provided by owners (equity). The mixture of debt and equity a business uses is called its *capital structure*. In addition to selecting a capital structure, management can select from a variety of sources from which to borrow money, as illustrated by the liability section of the balance sheet from General Mills shown in Exhibit 9.1.

What factors do managers consider when they borrow money? Two key factors are risk and cost. Debt capital is more risky than equity because payments associated with debt are a company's legal obligation. If a company cannot meet a required debt payment (either principal or interest) because of a temporary cash shortage, creditors may force the company into bankruptcy and require the sale of assets to satisfy the debt. As with any business transaction, borrowers and lenders attempt to negotiate the most favorable terms possible. Managers devote considerable effort to analyzing alternative borrowing arrangements.

Companies that include debt in their capital structure must also make strategic decisions concerning the balance between short-term and long-term debt. To evaluate a company's capital structure, financial analysts calculate a number of accounting ratios. In this chapter, we will discuss both short-term and long-term debt, as well as some important accounting ratios. We will also introduce you to present value concepts. In the next chapter, we discuss a special category of long-term debt, bonds payable.

EXHIBIT 9.1

Consolidated Balance Sheets

REAL WORLD EXCERPT

GENERAL MILLS

ANNUAL REPORT

GENERAL MILLS INC
Consolidated Balance Sheets
In Millions

	May 28, 2000	May 30, 1999
Liabilities and Equity		
Current Liabilities:		
Accounts payable	$ 641.5	$ 647.4
Current portion of long-term debt	413.5	90.5
Notes payable	1,085.8	524.4
Accrued taxes	104.9	135.0
Accrued payroll	142.4	138.6
Other current liabilities	141.0	164.4
Total Current Liabilities	2,529.1	1,700.3
Long-term Debt	1,760.3	1,702.4
Deferred Income Taxes	297.2	288.9
Deferred Income Taxes—Tax Leases	89.8	111.3
Other Liabilities	186.1	173.6
Total Liabilities	$4,862.5	$3,976.5

ORGANIZATION of the Chapter

Liabilities Defined and Classified	**Current Liabilities**	**Long-Term Liabilities**	**Present and Future Value Concepts**
■ Current Ratio	■ Accounts Payable ■ Accounts Payable Turnover Ratio ■ Accrued Liabilities ■ Notes Payable ■ Current Portion of Long-Term Debt ■ Deferred Revenues ■ Estimated Liabilities Reported on the Balance Sheet ■ Estimated Liabilities Reported in the Notes ■ Working Capital Management	■ Long-Term Notes Payable and Bonds ■ Lease Liabilities	■ Future and Present Values of a Single Amount ■ Future and Present Values of an Annuity ■ Accounting Applications of Future and Present Values

LIABILITIES DEFINED AND CLASSIFIED

Most people have a reasonable understanding of the definition of the word *liability.* Accountants formally define **liabilities** as probable debts or obligations of the entity that result from past transactions, which will be paid with assets or services. As Exhibit 9.1 shows, as of May 28, 2000, General Mills had borrowed long-term debt of $1,760.3 million. The company has a current obligation to pay cash to its creditors at some time in the future based on the borrowing agreements. Because of this obligation, General Mills must record long-term debt.

When a liability is first recorded, it is measured in terms of its current cash equivalent, which is the cash amount a creditor would accept to settle the liability immediately. Although General Mills borrowed $1,760.3 million, it will repay much more than that because the company must also pay interest on the debt. Interest that will be paid in the future is not included in the reported amount of the liability because it accrues and becomes a liability with the passage of time.

Like most businesses, General Mills has several kinds of liabilities as well as a wide range of creditors. The list of liabilities on the balance sheet differs from one company to the next because different operating activities result in different types of liabilities. The liability section of the General Mills report begins with the caption Current Liabilities. **Current liabilities** are defined as short-term obligations that will be paid within the current operating cycle of the business or within one year of the balance sheet date, whichever is longer. Because most companies have an operating cycle that is shorter than one year, current liabilities normally can be defined simply as liabilities that are due within one year. Noncurrent liabilities include all other liabilities.

Information about current liabilities is very important to managers and analysts because these obligations must be paid in the near future. Analysts say that a company has **liquidity** if it has the ability to meet its current obligations. A number of financial ratios are useful in evaluating liquidity, including the current ratio.

Learning Objective 1
Define, measure, and report current liabilities.

LIABILITIES Probable debts or obligations of the entity that result from past transactions, which will be paid with assets or services.

CURRENT LIABILITIES are short-term obligations that will be paid within the current operating cycle or one year, whichever is longer.

LIQUIDITY is the ability to pay current obligations.

Current Ratio

? ANALYTICAL QUESTION

Does a company currently have the resources to pay its short-term debt?

% RATIO AND COMPARISONS

The current ratio is computed as follows:

$$\text{Current Ratio} = \text{Current Assets} \div \text{Current Liabilities}$$

The 2000 current ratio for General Mills:

$$\$1,190.30 \div \$2,529.10 = 0.47$$

COMPARISONS OVER TIME			COMPARISONS WITH COMPETITORS	
General Mills			**Kellogg**	**Quaker Oats**
1998	**1999**	**2000**	**2000**	**2000**
0.72	0.65	0.47	0.66	1.06

💡 INTERPRETATIONS

Learning Objective 2
Use the current ratio.

In General While a high ratio normally suggests good liquidity, too high a ratio suggests inefficient use of resources. An old rule of thumb was that companies should have a current ratio between 1 and 2. Today, many strong companies use sophisticated management techniques to minimize funds invested in current assets and, as a result, have current ratios below 1.

Focus Company Analysis The current ratio for General Mills is very low and has been decreasing in recent years. While this trend might be a concern in many circumstances, it is not in the case of General Mills. The notes to the financial statements indicate that the company has "bank credit lines to ensure the availability of short-term funds on an as-needed basis." Instead of holding excess cash to enhance its liquidity, General Mills plans to borrow only when money is actually needed, avoiding significant interest expense. Most analysts would take this borrowing arrangement into consideration in assessing a company's liquidity.

A Few Cautions The current ratio may be a misleading measure of liquidity if significant funds are tied up in assets that cannot easily be converted into cash. A company with a high current ratio might still have liquidity problems if the majority of its current assets was made up of slow-moving inventory. Analysts recognize that managers can manipulate the current ratio by engaging in certain transactions just before the close of the fiscal year. In most cases, for example, the current ratio can be improved by paying creditors immediately prior to preparation of financial statements.

Liabilities are very important from an analytical perspective because they affect a company's future cash flows and risk characteristics. Most analysts devote a considerable amount of time to reviewing a company's liabilities. The simplest way to discuss liabilities is to review them in the same order that they are listed on most balance sheets.

CURRENT LIABILITIES

Accounts Payable

Most companies do not produce all the goods and services that they use in their basic operating activities. Instead, they purchase some goods and services from other businesses. Typically, these transactions are made on credit with cash payments made after the goods and services have been provided. As a result, these transactions create accounts payable, also called **trade accounts payable.** *Accounting Trends & Techniques* (published by the AICPA) examined the reporting practices of 600 companies and found that most companies use the term **accounts payable.**[1]

For many companies, trade credit is a relatively inexpensive way to finance the purchase of inventory because interest does not normally accrue on accounts payable. As an incentive to encourage more sales, some vendors offer very generous credit terms that may allow the buyer to resell merchandise and collect cash before payment must be made to the original vendor.

Some managers may be tempted to delay payment to suppliers as long as possible to conserve cash. This strategy normally is not advisable. Most successful companies develop positive working relationships with suppliers to ensure quality goods and services. A positive relationship can be destroyed by slow payment of debt. In addition, financial analysts become concerned if a business does not meet its obligations to trade creditors on a timely basis because such slowness often indicates that a company is experiencing financial difficulties. Both managers and analysts use the accounts payable turnover ratio to evaluate effectiveness in managing payables.

Accounts Payable Titles (sample of 600 companies)

	0	100	200	300	400	500
Combined with others						
Trade accounts payable						
Accounts payable						

Accounts Payable Turnover Ratio

KEY RATIO ANALYSIS

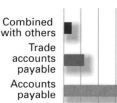

❓ ANALYTICAL QUESTION

How efficient is management in meeting obligations to suppliers?

% RATIO AND COMPARISONS

The accounts payable turnover ratio is computed as follows:

Accounts Payable Turnover = Cost of Goods Sold ÷ Average Accounts Payable

The 2000 accounts payable turnover ratio for General Mills:

$$\$2,697.6 \div \$644.4* = 4.19$$

($641.5 + $647.4) ÷ 2 = $644.4

Learning Objective 3
Analyze the accounts payable turnover ratio.

COMPARISONS OVER TIME		
General Mills		
1998	1999	2000
4.18	3.91	4.19

COMPARISONS WITH COMPETITORS	
Kellogg	Quaker Oats
2000	2000
9.59	11.19

💡 INTERPRETATIONS

In General   The accounts payable turnover ratio measures how quickly management is paying trade accounts. A high accounts payable ratio normally suggests that a company is paying its suppliers in a timely manner. The ratio can be stated more intuitively by dividing it into the number of days in a year:

Average Age of Payables = 365 Days ÷ Turnover Ratio

The 2000 average age of payables for General Mills:

365 Days ÷ 4.19 = 87 Days

Focus Company Analysis   The accounts payable turnover for General Mills is low compared to similar companies but has been fairly stable over time. Usually, a low ratio would raise questions concerning a company's liquidity. Most companies do not take 87 days on average to pay their creditors. While a low accounts payable turnover ratio might be a concern

---

[1]Reprinted with permission from *Accounting Trends & Techniques.* Copyright © 2000 by the American Institute of Certified Public Accounts, Inc.

in many circumstances, it is not in the case of General Mills because other indications of liquidity are good. The company is very aggressive in its cash management policy. By conserving cash with slow payment to suppliers, the company minimizes the amount of money it must borrow (and pay interest on).

A Few Cautions   The accounts payable turnover ratio is an average based on all accounts payable. The ratio might not reflect reality if a company pays some creditors on time but is late with others. The ratio is also subject to manipulation. Managers could be late in paying creditors during the entire year but catch up at year-end so that the ratio is at an acceptable level. As our focus company analysis indicates, a low ratio can indicate either liquidity problems or aggressive cash management. The first is a problem; the second is a strength. Analysts need to study other factors (such as the current ratio and the amount of cash generated from operating activities) to determine which is the case.

Accrued Liabilities

ACCRUED LIABILITIES are expenses that have been incurred but have not been paid at the end of the accounting period.

In many situations, a business incurs an expense in one accounting period and makes cash payment in another period. **Accrued liabilities** are expenses that have been incurred before the end of an accounting period but have not been paid. These expenses include items such as property taxes, electricity, and salaries. The balance sheet for General Mills lists both accrued taxes and accrued payroll. Accrued liabilities are recorded as adjusting entries at year-end.

Accrued Taxes Payable

Like individuals, corporations must pay taxes on the income they earn. Corporate tax rates are graduated with large corporations paying a top federal tax rate of 35 percent. Corporations may also pay state and local income taxes and, in some cases, foreign income taxes. The notes to the General Mills annual report include the following information pertaining to taxes:

REAL WORLD EXCERPT

GENERAL MILLS

ANNUAL REPORT

Note 17. Income Taxes

The components of earnings before income taxes and earnings (losses) of joint ventures and the income taxes thereon are as follows:

In Millions, Fiscal Year	2000	1999	1998
Earnings before income taxes:			
U.S.	$918.6	$825.4	$688.1
Foreign	28.4	21.3	(21.5)
Total earnings before income taxes	$947.0	$846.7	$666.6
Income taxes:			
Current:			
Federal	$280.1	$238.9	$242.8
State and local	14.1	21.5	31.0
Foreign	(1.8)	1.6	(2.6)
Total current	292.4	262.0	271.2

Notice that the 2000 federal income tax for General Mills ($280.1 million) was approximately 31 percent of its U.S. earnings ($918.6 million). For most corporations, federal income taxes represent a major cost.

Accrued Payroll

At the end of each accounting period, employees usually will have earned salaries that have not yet been paid. Unpaid salaries may be reported as part of accrued liabilities or as a separate item, as is the case with General Mills (the amount shown on the balance sheet is $142.4 million). In addition to reporting salaries that have been earned but not paid, companies must report the cost of unpaid benefits, including retirement programs, vacation time, and health insurance.

Let's look at vacation time as an example. Typically, a business grants employees paid vacation time based on the number of months they have worked. Under the matching concept, the cost of vacation time must be recorded in the year employees perform a service rather than the year they actually take vacation. If General Mills estimates the cost of accrued vacation time to be $125,000, accountants make the following adjusting entry at the end of the fiscal year:

| Compensation expense (+E, −SE) | 125,000 | |
| Accrued vacation liability (+L) | | 125,000 |

Assets	=	Liabilities	+	Stockholders' Equity
		Vacation liability +125,000		Compensation expense −125,000

When the vacations are taken (during the next summer), the accountants record the following:

| Accrued vacation liability (−L) | 125,000 | |
| Cash (−A) | | 125,000 |

Assets	=	Liabilities	+	Stockholders' Equity
Cash −125,000		Vacation liability −125,000		

General Mills does not separately disclose the amount of accrued vacation liability. Instead, the company reports this liability as part of accrued payroll. Apparently, the amount of accrued vacation liability is not material in management's opinion. Most analysts would probably agree.

Payroll Taxes

All payrolls are subject to a variety of taxes including federal, state, and local income taxes, Social Security taxes, and federal and state unemployment taxes. Employees pay some of these taxes and employers pay others. While we will look at only the two largest deductions for most people, reporting is similar for each type of payroll tax:

Employee Income Taxes   Employers are required to withhold income taxes for each employee. The amount of income tax withheld is recorded by the employer as a current liability between the date of the deduction and the date the amount is remitted to the government. Federal Income Tax Withheld is often referred to as **FITW.**

Employee FICA Taxes   The Social Security taxes paid by employees are called **FICA taxes** because they are required by the Federal Insurance Contributions Act. These taxes are imposed in equal amounts on both the employee and the employer. Effective January 1, 2003, the Social Security tax rate was 6.20 percent on the first $87,000 paid to each employee during the year. In addition, a separate 1.45 percent Medicare tax applies to all income. Therefore, the FICA tax rate is 7.65 percent on income up to $87,000 and 1.45 percent on all income above $87,000.

Employee compensation expense includes all funds earned by employees as well as funds paid to others on behalf of employees. To illustrate, let's assume General Mills accumulated the following information in its payroll records for the first two weeks of June 2003:

Salaries and wages earned	$1,800,000
Income taxes withheld	275,000
FICA taxes (employees' share)	105,000

Remember that both the employer and the employee must pay FICA taxes. As a result, the total liability associated with FICA taxes is $210,000 ($105,000 + $105,000). The entry to record the payroll follows:

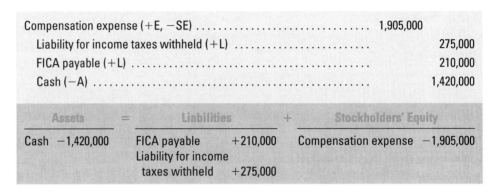

Compensation expense (+E, −SE)	1,905,000	
Liability for income taxes withheld (+L)		275,000
FICA payable (+L)		210,000
Cash (−A)		1,420,000

Assets	=	Liabilities	+	Stockholders' Equity
Cash −1,420,000		FICA payable +210,000		Compensation expense −1,905,000
		Liability for income		
		taxes withheld +275,000		

Types of Employee-Related Liabilities (sample of 600 companies)
0   100 200 300 400

Vacations
Benefits
Pensions
Compensation
Salaries and wages

Notice in the journal entry that compensation expense ($1,800,000 + $105,000) includes the employer's share of FICA taxes which is a fringe benefit earned by the employees. The cash paid to employees ($1,420,000) is not the total amount earned ($1,800,000) because the employer must withhold both income taxes ($275,000) and the employees' share of FICA taxes ($105,000).

Accounting Trends & Techniques found that most companies in its sample of 600 companies report employee-related liabilities.[2]

Notes Payable

Learning Objective 4
Report notes payable and explain the time value of money.

The **TIME VALUE OF MONEY** is interest that is associated with the use of money over time.

When a company borrows money, a formal written contract is usually prepared. Obligations supported by these contracts are called *notes payable*. A note payable specifies the amount borrowed, the date by which it must be repaid, and the interest rate associated with the borrowing.

Creditors are willing to lend cash because they will earn interest in return for giving up the use of their money for a period. This simple concept is called the **time value of money.** The longer borrowed money is held, the larger is the total dollar amount of interest expense. Interest at a given interest rate on a two-year loan is more than interest on a one-year loan. To the borrower, interest is an expense; to the creditor, it is a revenue.

To calculate interest, three variables must be considered: (1) the principal (i.e., the cash that was borrowed), (2) the annual interest rate, and (3) the time period for the loan. The interest formula is

$$\text{Interest} = \text{Principal} \times \text{Interest Rate} \times \text{Time}$$

To illustrate, assume that on November 1, 2003, General Mills borrows $100,000 cash on a one-year, 12 percent note payable. The interest is payable on March 31, 2004, and October 31, 2004. The principal is payable at the maturity date, October 31, 2004. The note is recorded in the accounts as follows:

[2]Reprinted with permission from *Accounting Trends & Techniques.* Copyright © 2000 by the American Institute of Certified Public Accounts, Inc.

```
Cash (+A) ................................................  100,000
    Note payable, short-term (+L) ................................      100,000
```

Assets	=	Liabilities	+	Stockholders' Equity
Cash +100,000		Notes payable +100,000		

Interest is an expense of the period in which the money is used. Under the matching concept, interest expense is recorded when it is incurred rather than when the cash actually is paid. Because General Mills uses the money for two months during 2003, it records interest expense in 2003 for two months, even though cash is not paid until March 31.

The computation of interest expense for 2003 is as follows:

$$\text{Interest} = \text{Principal} \times \text{Interest Rate} \times \text{Time}$$
$$\$2{,}000 = \$100{,}000 \times 12\% \times \tfrac{2}{12}$$

The entry to record interest expense on December 31, 2003 is

```
Interest expense (+E, −SE) ......................................  2,000
    Interest payable (+L) ........................................      2,000
```

Assets	=	Liabilities	+	Stockholders' Equity
		Interest payable +2,000		Interest expense −2,000

On March 31, 2004, General Mills would pay $5,000 in interest, which includes the $2,000 accrued and reported in 2003 plus the $3,000 interest accrued in the first three months of 2004. The following journal entry would be made:

```
Interest expense (+E, −SE) ......................................  3,000
Interest payable (−L) ...........................................  2,000
    Cash (−A) ................................................      5,000
```

Assets	=	Liabilities	+	Stockholders' Equity
Cash −5,000		Interest payable −2,000		Interest expense −3,000

Current Portion of Long-Term Debt

The distinction between current and long-term debt is important for both managers and analysts. Because current debt must be paid within the next year, companies must have sufficient cash to repay it. To provide accurate information on its current liabilities, a company must reclassify its long-term debt as a current liability within a year of its maturity date. Assume that General Mills signed a note payable of $5 million on January 1, 2003. Repayment is required on December 1, 2006. The December 31, 2004 and 2005, balance sheets would report the following:

December 31, 2004

Long-term liabilities:	
Note payable	$5,000,000

December 31, 2005

Current liabilities:
    Current portion of long-term note $5,000,000

An example of this type of disclosure can be seen in Exhibit 9.1. Notice that in 2000, General Mills reported $413.5 million as the current portion of long-term debt to be paid in full during the following accounting period. In some cases, companies will refinance debt when it comes due rather than pay out cash currently on hand.

FINANCIAL ANALYSIS

Refinanced Debt: Current or Noncurrent?

Instead of repaying a debt from current cash, a company may refinance it either by negotiating a new loan agreement with a new maturity date or by borrowing money from a new creditor and repaying the original creditor. If a company intends to refinance a currently maturing debt and has the ability to do so, should the debt be classified as a current or a long-term liability? Remember that analysts are interested in a company's current liabilities because those liabilities will generate cash outflows in the next accounting period. If a liability will not generate a cash outflow in the next accounting period, GAAP require that it not be classified as current. This rule is illustrated by a note from the General Mills annual report.

REAL WORLD EXCERPT

GENERAL MILLS

ANNUAL REPORT

We have a revolving credit agreement expiring in January 2002 that provides us with the ability to refinance short-term borrowing on a long-term basis. Therefore we have reclassified a portion of our notes payable to long-term debt.

Deferred Revenues

In most business transactions, cash is paid after the product or service has been delivered. In some cases, cash is paid before delivery. You have probably paid for magazines that you will receive at some time in the future. The publisher collects money for your subscription in advance, before the magazine is published. When a company collects cash before the related revenue has been earned, the cash is called **deferred revenues**.

Under the revenue principle, revenue cannot be recorded until it has been earned. Deferred revenues are reported as a liability because cash has been collected, but the related revenue has not been earned by the end of the accounting period. The obligation to provide services or goods in the future still exists. These obligations are classified as current or long-term, depending on when they must be satisfied.

DEFERRED REVENUES are revenues that have been collected but not earned; they are liabilities until the goods or services are provided.

Estimated Liabilities Reported on the Balance Sheet

Some recorded liabilities are based on estimates because the exact amount will not be known until a future date. For example, an estimated liability is created when a company offers a warranty with the products it sells. The cost of providing future repair work must be estimated and recorded as a liability (and expense) in the period in which the product is sold. General Mills, like most companies, quickly refunds money for any defective products it sells. The company does not report a liability for this type of obligation because it estimates the amount to be immaterial.

QUALITY GUARANTEE

We're committed to quality. In fact we unconditionally guarantee it. If you are not satisfied with the quality of this product, a prompt refund or adjustment of equal value will be made. Your comments and questions are welcome.
Save or send your box top and...
CALL: 1-800-328-1144 (7:30 AM – 5:30 PM, CST, Weekdays)
WRITE: General Mills, Box 200, Mpls., MN 55440
www.generalmills.com

A future service obligation that has generated considerable public interest is the adverse impact that some business activities have on the environment. In some cases, this adverse impact creates a financial obligation that must be reported. Freeport-McMoRan is a leading company in the production and sale of phosphate fertilizers that are used to grow grains. The process of extracting phosphates from the land has a major impact on the environment. Under state and federal laws, Freeport-McMoRan is obligated to restore the land once it has finished its operations. The balance sheet for the company reports a $129 million liability for land reclamation, and the notes included the following statement:

REAL WORLD EXCERPT

Freeport-McMoRan

ANNUAL REPORT

> **Environmental Remediation and Compliance.** Estimated future expenditures to restore properties and related facilities to a state required to comply with environmental and other regulations are accrued over the life of the properties. The future expenditures are estimated based on current costs, laws and regulations.

Liabilities associated with future service obligations are often based on estimates that are very difficult to develop accurately. The future cost of cleaning up pollution depends on a number of factors, including changing technology and legal standards. Many companies have faced bankruptcy because they underestimated the cost of complying with environmental regulations. Managers and analysts must be very cautious in evaluating the potential costs associated with activities that impact the environment.

Learning Objective 5
Report contingent liabilities.

Topic Tackler 9–1

Estimated Liabilities Reported in the Notes

Each of the liabilities that we have discussed is reported on the balance sheet at a specific dollar amount because each involves the probable future sacrifice of economic benefits. Some transactions or events create only a reasonably possible (but not probable) future sacrifice of economic benefits. These situations create **contingent liabilities,** which are potential liabilities that are created as a result of a past event. A contingent liability may or may not become a recorded liability depending on future events. A situation that produces a contingent liability also causes a contingent loss.

A **CONTINGENT LIABILITY** is a potential liability that has arisen as the result of a past event; it is not an effective liability until some future event occurs.

Contingent Liability Examples

Lawsuits   Environmental   Product
                  problems   warranties

Whether a situation produces a recorded or a contingent liability depends on two factors: the probability of a future economic sacrifice and the ability of management to estimate the amount of the liability. The following table illustrates the possibilities:

	Probable	Reasonably Possible	Remote
Subject to estimate	Record as liability	Disclose in note	Disclosure not required
Not subject to estimate	Disclose in note	Disclose in note	Disclosure not required

The probabilities of occurrence are defined in the following manner:

1. Probable—the chance that the future event or events will occur is high.
2. Reasonably possible—the chance that the future event or events will occur is more than remote but less than likely.
3. Remote—the chance that the future event or events will occur is slight.

In summary, (1) a liability that is both probable and capable of being reasonably estimated must be recorded and reported on the balance sheet, (2) a liability that is reasonably possible must be disclosed in a note in the financial statements whether it can be estimated or not, and (3) remote contingencies are not disclosed.

The notes to General Mills' annual report include the following:

> We are contingently liable under guarantees and comfort letters for $48.3 million. The guarantees and comfort letters are issued to support borrowing arrangements primarily for our joint ventures.

General Mills did not need to record a liability on the balance sheet because a loss was not probable. Harley-Davidson disclosed a common contingency in its notes:

> **Note 7**
> **Commitments and Contingencies**
>
> A state court jury in California found the Company liable for compensatory and punitive damages of $7.2 million, including interest, in a lawsuit brought by a supplier of aftermarket exhaust systems. The Company immediately appealed the verdict.

In this case, the existence of a liability was a reasonable possibility. As a result, GAAP required Harley-Davidson to disclose the lawsuit in its notes. The company subsequently reached an out-of-court settlement for $5 million. At that point, the loss was probable, which required recording the loss and the related liability on the balance sheet.

Accounting Trends & Techniques studied the financial statements of 600 companies and found that litigation was the most common type of contingent liability.[3]

Working Capital Management

Working capital is defined as the dollar difference between current assets and current liabilities. Working capital is important to both managers and financial analysts because it has a significant impact on the health and profitability of a company.

The working capital accounts are actively managed to achieve a balance between costs and benefits. If a business has too little working capital, it runs the risk of not being able to meet its obligations to creditors. On the other hand, too much working capital may tie up resources in unproductive assets and incur additional costs. Excess inventory, for example, ties up dollars that could be invested more profitably elsewhere in the business and incurs additional costs associated with storage and deterioration.

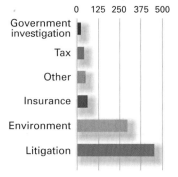

**Contingent Liabilities
(sample of 600 companies)**

WORKING CAPITAL is the dollar difference between total current assets and total current liabilities.

Learning Objective 6
Explain the importance of working capital and its impact on cash flows.

---

[3]Reprinted with permission from *Accounting Trends & Techniques*. Copyright © 2000 by the American Institute of Certified Public Accounts, Inc.

The annual report for General Mills states a number of financial goals, including "we have a goal of reducing working capital in fiscal year 2001."

Changes in working capital accounts are also important to managers and analysts because they have a direct impact on cash flows from operating activities reported on the statement of cash flows.

| **Working Capital and Cash Flows** | **FOCUS ON** CASH FLOWS |

Many working capital accounts have a direct relationship to income-producing activities. Accounts receivable, for example, are related to sales revenue: Accounts receivable increase when sales are made on credit. Cash is collected when the customer pays the bill. Similarly, accounts payable increase when an expense is incurred without a cash payment. A cash outflow occurs when the account is paid. Changes in working capital accounts that are related to income-producing activities must be considered when computing cash flows from operating activities.

EFFECT ON STATEMENT OF CASH FLOWS

In General Changes in working capital accounts will affect a company's cash flows as indicated in the following table:

Effect on Cash Flows

Operating activities (indirect method)	
Net income	$xxx
Adjusted for: Decreases in current assets* or increases in current liabilities	+
Adjusted for: Increases in current assets* or decrease in current liabilities	−

Other than cash

Focus Company Analysis A segment of the General Mills Consolidated Statements of Cash Flows, prepared using the indirect method, follows. Notice that between 1999 and 2000, cash flows from operations were essentially unchanged despite a significant increase in income. The annual report provides additional explanation: There was no change in cash flows from operations because of "increased use of working capital. The major factor was higher inventories related to additions for acquired businesses and our decision to buy extra inventory in anticipation of higher prices." This explanation demonstrates the impact that changes in working capital can have on cash flows from operating activities.

Selected Focus Company Comparisons: Change in Cash Flow Related to Working Capital (in millions)

Home Depot	$131
Wal-Mart	$1,840
Harrah's	$45

REAL WORLD EXCERPT

GENERAL MILLS

ANNUAL REPORT

GENERAL MILLS INC
Consolidated Statements of Cash Flows

In Millions, Fiscal Year Ended	May 28, 2000	May 30, 1999	May 31, 1998
Cash Flows—Operating Activities:			
Net earnings	$614.4	$534.5	$421.8
Adjustments to reconcile net earnings to cash flow:			
Depreciation and amortization	208.8	194.2	194.9
Deferred income taxes	43.5	42.0	(29.3)
Changes in current assets and liabilities, net of effects from businesses acquired	(125.6)	(93.3)	54.5
Unusual items	—	51.6	166.4
Other, net	(50.6)	(38.9)	(33.0)
Cash provided by continuing operations	690.5	690.1	775.3

Cash Flow from Changes in Current Assets and Liabilities:			
Receivables	$ 11.2	$(82.7)	$ 23.7
Inventories	(51.4)	(28.7)	(26.4)
Prepaid expenses and other current assets	(4.9)	9.2	1.6
Accounts payable	(49.4)	44.7	4.0
Other current liabilities	(31.1)	(35.8)	51.6
Changes in Current Assets and Liabilities	$(125.6)	$(93.3)	$ 54.5

SELF-STUDY QUIZ

Assume that the current ratio for General Mills is 2.0. For each of the following events, state whether the current ratio and working capital will increase or decrease:

1. General Mills incurs an account payable of $250,000 with no change in current assets.

2. The company borrows $1,000,000 in long-term debt.

3. The company pays taxes payable in the amount of $750,000.

4. The company finances a new building with long-term debt.

After you have completed your answers, check them with the solutions that follow:

_____

Current ratio	Working capital
1. Decrease	Decrease
2. Increase	Increase
3. Increase	No change
4. No change	No change

LONG-TERM LIABILITIES

Learning Objective 7
Report long-term liabilities.

LONG-TERM LIABILITIES are all of the entity's obligations not classified as current liabilities.

Long-term liabilities include all obligations that are not classified as current liabilities, such as long-term notes payable and bonds payable. Typically, a long-term liability will require payment more than one year in the future. These obligations may be created by borrowing money, or they may result from other activities.

Most companies borrow money on a long-term basis in order to purchase operational assets. To reduce risk for creditors, some companies agree to use specific assets as security. If the liability is not satisfied, the creditor may take ownership of the asset. A liability supported by this type of agreement is called a **secured debt.** An unsecured debt is one for which the creditor relies primarily on the borrower's integrity and general earning power.

Long-Term Notes Payable and Bonds

Companies can raise long-term debt capital directly from a number of financial service organizations including banks, insurance companies, and pension plans. Raising debt from one of these organizations is known as **private placement.** This type of debt is often called a **note payable,** which is a written promise to pay a stated sum at one or more specified future dates called the **maturity date(s).**

In many cases, a company's need for debt capital exceeds the financial ability of any single creditor. In these situations, the company may issue publicly traded debt called **bonds.** The opportunity to sell a bond in established markets provides bond-holders with an important benefit. They can sell their bonds to other investors prior to maturity if they have an immediate need for cash. Because bonds provide liquidity to investors, they are more likely to lend money to a company.

Both notes and bonds are written promises to pay a debt. Bonds will be discussed in detail in the next chapter.

Accounting for long-term debt is based on the same concepts used in accounting for short-term notes payable. A liability is recorded when the debt is incurred and interest expense is recorded with the passage of time.

Over the past years, business operations have become more global. Successful corporations market their products in many countries and locate manufacturing facilities around the world based on cost and productivity. The financing of corporations also has become international, even for companies that do not have international operations. Borrowing money in a foreign currency raises some interesting accounting and management issues.

Borrowing in Foreign Currencies

INTERNATIONAL PERSPECTIVE

Many corporations with foreign operations elect to finance those operations with foreign debt to lessen exchange rate risk. This type of risk exists because the relative value of each nation's currency varies on virtually a daily basis. As this book was being written, the British pound was worth approximately $1.45; a year earlier it was worth $1.65.

A U.S. corporation that conducts business operations in England might decide to borrow pounds to finance its operations there. The profits from the business, which will be in pounds, can be used to pay off the debt, which is in pounds. If this business earned profits in pounds but paid off debt in dollars, it would be exposed to exchange rate risk because the relative value of the dollar and the pound fluctuates.

Foreign corporations face this same problem. A note to a recent annual report from Toyota, a Japanese company that does significant business in the United States, stated:

> Earnings declined in the current year ended, as the appreciation of the yen aggravated the adverse effects of sluggish demand. . . . The movement in exchange rates reduced operating income of the company. Losses on currency exchange thus offset most of the cost savings we achieved.

REAL WORLD EXCERPT

Toyota
ANNUAL REPORT

Toyota has borrowed a large amount of money in the United States to lessen the exchange rate risk it faces. The company also owns and operates many factories in the United States.

Even if a company does not have international operations, it may elect to borrow in foreign markets. Interest rates often are low in countries experiencing a recession. These situations give corporations the opportunity to borrow at a lower cost.

For reporting purposes, accountants must convert, or translate, foreign debt into U.S. dollars. Conversion rates for all major currencies are published in most newspapers and can be found on the Internet. To illustrate foreign currency translation, assume that General Mills borrowed 1 million pounds (£). For the General Mills annual report, the accountant must use the conversion rate as of the balance sheet date, which we assume was £1.00 to $1.45. The dollar equivalent of the debt is $1,450,000 (£1,000,000 × 1.45). The dollar equivalent of foreign debt may change if the conversion rate changes even without any additional borrowings or repayments.

The notes to the balance sheet for General Mills indicate that the company has borrowed money primarily in the United States and Canada. In contrast, consider the following note from Toys "R" Us (amounts in millions):

	2000	**1999**
7% British pound sterling loan payable	$ 19	$ 33
Japanese yen loans payable in varying amounts through 2012	242	198
Swiss franc note payable, due 2004	342	342
8¼% sinking fund debentures, due 2017	12	24
Mortgage notes payable at annual interest rates from 10% to 11%	10	11

Toys "R" Us is an international company with more than 40 percent of its sales and assets located outside the United States. The company borrows heavily in international markets to minimize the risk associated with variations in exchange rates. This arrangement is typical for most large corporations and is further justification for business students to develop an understanding of international markets.

Lease Liabilities

An **OPERATING LEASE** does not meet any of the four criteria established by GAAP and does not cause the recording of an asset and liability.

Companies often lease assets rather than purchasing them. For example, renting extra delivery trucks during a busy period is more economical than owning them if they are not needed during the rest of the year. When a company leases an asset on a short-term basis, the agreement is called an **operating lease**. No liability is recorded when an operating lease is created. Instead, a company records rent expense as it uses the asset. Assume that on December 15, 2003, General Mills signed an operating lease contract to rent five large trucks during January 2004. No liability is recorded in 2003. Rent expense is recorded during January 2004 as the trucks are actually used.

A **CAPITAL LEASE** meets at least one of the four criteria established by GAAP and results in the recording of an asset and liability.

For a number of reasons, a company may prefer to lease an asset on a long-term basis rather than purchase it. This type of lease is called a **capital lease**. In essence, a capital lease contract represents the purchase and financing of an asset even though it is legally a lease agreement. Unlike an operating lease, capital leases are accounted for as if an asset has been purchased by recording an asset and a liability. Because of the significant differences between operating and capital leases, GAAP have specified criteria to distinguish between them. If a lease meets any of the following criteria, it is considered a capital lease:

- The lease term is 75 percent or more of the asset's expected economic life.
- Ownership of the asset is transferred to the lessee at the end of the lease term.
- The lease contract permits the lessee to purchase the asset at a price that is lower than its fair market value.
- The present value of the lease payments is 90 percent or more of the fair market value of the asset when the lease is signed.

The notes to the General Mills annual report indicate that the balance sheet includes $242 million in long-term debt associated with capital leases. The recorded value of debt associated with a capital lease is the present value of the required lease payments. The next section, on present value concepts, shows how this amount is actually computed.

PRESENT AND FUTURE VALUE CONCEPTS

Learning Objective 8
Apply the concepts of future and present values.

Our discussion of capital leases raised an interesting question about liabilities: Is the recorded amount of the liability the actual amount of cash that will be paid in the future? For example, if I agree to pay you $10,000 five years from now, should I report a liability of $10,000 on my personal balance sheet? To answer such questions, we will now introduce some relatively simple mathematics called **present** and **future value concepts.** These concepts will provide a foundation for our discussion of bond liabilities in the next chapter.

The concepts of **present value** (PV) and **future value** (FV) are based on the time value of money. Quite simply, money received today is worth more than money to be received one year from today (or at any other future date) because it can be used to earn interest. If you invest $1,000 today at 10 percent, you will have $1,100 in one year. In contrast, if you receive $1,000 one year from today, you will lose the opportunity to earn the $100 in interest revenue. The difference between the $1,000 and the $1,100 is the interest that can be earned during the year.

In some business situations, you will know the dollar amount of a cash flow that occurs in the future and will need to determine its value now. This type of question is known as a present value problem. The opposite situation occurs when you know the dollar amount of a cash flow that occurs today and need to determine its value at some point in the future. These questions are called future value problems. The value of money changes over time because money can earn interest. The following table illustrates the basic difference between present value and future value problems:

	Now	Future
Present value	?	$1,000
Future value	$1,000	?

Present and future value problems may involve two types of cash flow: a single payment or an annuity (a series of cash payments). Thus, four different situations are related to the time value of money:

1. Future value of a single payment.

2. Present value of a single payment.

3. Future value of an annuity.

4. Present value of an annuity.

Many inexpensive hand-held calculators can perform the detailed arithmetic computations required to solve future value and present value problems. In subsequent courses and in all business situations, you will probably use a calculator to solve these problems. At this stage, we encourage you to solve problems using Tables A-1 through A-4 in Appendix A at the end of this book. They give the value of a $1 cash flow (single payment or annuity) for different periods (*n*) and at different interest rates (*i*). If a problem involves payments other than $1, it is necessary to multiply the value from the table by the amount of the payment.[4] We believe that using the tables will give you a better understanding of how and why present and future value concepts apply to business problems.

Future and Present Values of a Single Amount

Future Value of a Single Amount

In future value of a single amount problems, you will be asked to calculate how much money you will have in the future as the result of investing a certain amount in the present. If you were to receive a gift of $10,000, for instance, you might decide to put it in a savings account and use the money as a down payment on a house after you graduate. The future value computation would tell you how much money will be available when you graduate.

To solve a future value problem, you need to know three items:

1. Amount to be invested.

2. Interest rate (*i*) the amount will earn.

3. Number of periods (*n*) in which the amount will earn interest.

PRESENT VALUE is the current value of an amount to be received in the future; a future amount discounted for compound interest rate.

FUTURE VALUE The sum to which an amount will increase as the result of compound interest.

Topic Tackler 9–2

---

[4]Present value and future value problems involve cash flows. The basic concepts are the same for cash inflows (receipts) and cash outflows (payments). No fundamental differences exist between present value and future value calculations for cash payments versus cash receipts.

Since the future value concept is based on compound interest, the amount of interest for each period is calculated by multiplying the principal plus any interest not paid out in prior periods. Graphically, the calculation of the future value of $1 for three periods and an interest rate of 10 percent may be represented as follows:

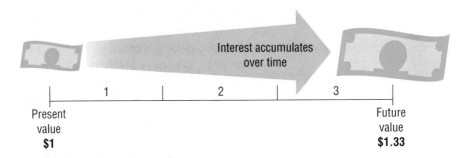

| | | Interest accumulates over time | |

Present value **$1**

Future value **$1.33**

Assume that on January 1, 2003, you deposit $1,000 in a savings account at 10 percent annual interest, compounded annually. At the end of three years, the $1,000 will have increased to $1,331 as follows:

Year	Amount at Start of Year	+	Interest During the Year	=	Amount at End of Year
1	$1,000	+	$1,000 × 10% = $100	=	$1,100
2	1,100	+	1,100 × 10% = $110	=	1,210
3	1,210	+	1,210 × 10% = $121	=	1,331

We can avoid the detailed arithmetic by referring to Table A-1, Future Value of $1. For $i = 10\%$, $n = 3$, we find the value 1.331. We then compute the balance at the end of year 3 as follows:

$$\$1{,}000 \times 1.3310 = \$1{,}331$$

From Table A-1,
Interest rate = 10%
N = 3

Note that the increase of $331 is due to the time value of money. It is interest revenue to the owner of the savings account and interest expense to the savings institution.

Present Value of a Single Amount

The present value of a single amount is the worth to you today of receiving that amount some time in the future. For instance, you might be offered an opportunity to invest in a debt instrument that would pay you $10,000 in 10 years. Before you decided whether to invest, you would want to determine the present value of the instrument.

To compute the present value of an amount to be received in the future, we must discount (a procedure that is the opposite of compounding) at i interest rate for n periods. In discounting, the interest is subtracted rather than added, as it is in compounding. Graphically, the present value of $1 due at the end of the third period with an interest rate of 10 percent can be represented as follows:

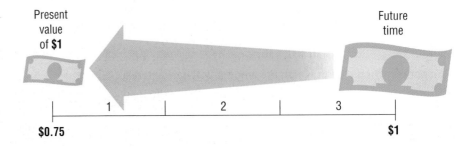

Present value of **$1**

Future time

$0.75

$1

Assume that today is January 1, 2003, and you have the opportunity to receive $1,000 cash on December 31, 2005. At an interest rate of 10 percent per year, how much is the $1,000 payment worth to you on January 1, 2003? You could discount the amount year by year,[5] but it is easier to use Table A-2, Appendix A, Present Value of $1. For $i = 10\%$, $n = 3$, we find that the present value of $1 is 0.7513. The present value of $1,000 to be received at the end of three years can be computed as follows:

$$\$1,000 \times 0.7513 = \$751.30$$

> From Table A-2,
> Interest rate = 10%
> N = 3

Learning how to compute a present value amount is not difficult, but it is more important that you understand what it means. The $751.30 is the amount you would pay now to have the right to receive $1,000 at the end of three years, assuming an interest rate of 10 percent. Conceptually, you should be indifferent between having $751.30 today and receiving $1,000 in three years, because you can use financial institutions to convert dollars from the present to the future and vice versa. If you had $751.30 today but preferred $1,000 in three years, you could simply deposit the money in a savings account and it would grow to $1,000 in three years. Alternatively, if you had a contract that promised you $1,000 in three years, you could sell it to an investor for $751.30 in cash today because it would permit the investor to earn the difference in interest.

SELF-STUDY QUIZ

1. If the interest rate in a present value problem increases from 8 percent to 10 percent, will the present value increase or decrease?

2. What is the present value of $10,000 to be received 10 years from now if the interest rate is 5 percent, compounded annually?

After you have completed your answers, check them with the solutions that follow:

————————

1. The present value will be less.
2. $10,000 \times 0.6139 = \$6,139$

Future and Present Values of an Annuity

Instead of a single payment, many business problems involve multiple cash payments over a number of periods. An **annuity** is a series of consecutive payments characterized by

> An **ANNUITY** is a series of periodic cash receipts or payments that are equal in amount each interest period.

1. An equal dollar amount each interest period.

2. Interest periods of equal length (year, half a year, quarter, or month).

3. An equal interest rate each interest period.

Examples of annuities include monthly payments on an automobile or home loan, yearly contributions to a savings account, and monthly pension benefits.

————————

[5]The detailed discounting is as follows:

Periods	Interest for the Year	Present Value*
1	$1,000 − ($1,000 × 1/1.10) = $90.91	$1,000 − $90.91 = $909.09
2	$909.09 − ($909.09 × 1/1.10) = $82.65	$909.09 − $82.65 = $826.44
3	$826.44 − ($826.44 × 1/1.10) = $75.14[†]	$826.44 − $75.14 = $751.30

*Verifiable in Table A-2.
[†]Adjusted for rounding.

Future Value of an Annuity

If you are saving money for some purpose, such as a new car or a trip to Europe, you might decide to deposit a fixed amount of money in a savings account each month. The future value of an annuity computation will tell you how much money will be in your savings account at some point in the future.

The future value of an annuity includes compound interest on each payment from the date of payment to the end of the term of the annuity. Each new payment accumulates less interest than prior payments only because the number of periods remaining in which to accumulate interest decreases. The future value of an annuity of $1 for three periods at 10 percent may be represented graphically as:

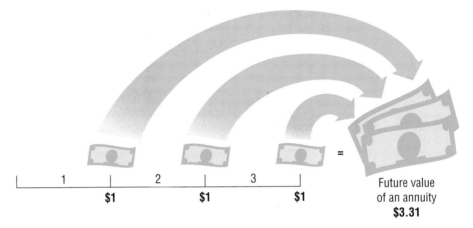

| 1 | 2 | 3 | Future value of an annuity $3.31 |
| $1 | $1 | $1 | |

Assume that each year for three years, you deposit $1,000 cash in a savings account at 10 percent interest per year. You make the first $1,000 deposit on December 31, 2003, the second one on December 31, 2004, and the third and last one on December 31, 2005. The first $1,000 deposit earns compound interest for two years (for a total principal and interest of $1,210); the second deposit earns interest for one year (for a total principal and interest of $1,100). The third deposit earns no interest because it was made on the day that the balance is computed. Thus, the total amount in the savings account at the end of three years is $3,310 ($1,210 + $1,100 + $1,000).

To derive the future value of this annuity, we could compute the interest on each deposit. However, we can refer to Table A-3, Appendix A, Future Value of an Annuity of $1 for $i = 10\%$, $n = 3$ to find the value 3.3100. The future value of your three deposits of $1,000 each can be computed as follows:

From Table A-3, Interest rate = 10% N = 3

$$\$1,000 \times 3.3100 = \$3,310.$$

The Power of Compounding

Compound interest is a remarkably powerful economic force. Indeed, the ability to earn interest on interest is the key to building economic wealth. If you save $1,000 per year for the first 10 years of your career, you will have more money when you retire than you would if you had saved $15,000 per year for the last 10 years of your career. This surprising outcome occurs because the money you save early in your career will earn more interest than the money you save at the end of your career. If you start saving money now, the majority of your wealth will not be the money you saved but the interest your money was able to earn.

The chart in the margin illustrates the power of compounding over a brief 10-year period. If you deposit $1 each year in an account earning 10 percent interest, at the end of just 10 years, only 64 percent of your balance will be made up of money you have saved; the rest will be interest you have earned. After 20 years, only 35 percent of your

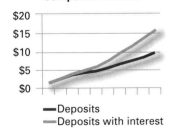

Effects of Compound Interest

| $20 |
| $15 |
| $10 |
| $5 |
| $0 |

Deposits
Deposits with interest

balance will be from saved money. The lesson associated with compound interest is clear: Even though saving money is difficult, you should start now.

Present Value of an Annuity

The present value of an annuity is the value now of a series of equal amounts to be received (or paid out) for some specified number of periods in the future. It is computed by discounting each of the equal periodic amounts. A good example of this type of problem is a retirement program that offers employees a monthly income after retirement. The present value of an annuity of $1 for three periods at 10 percent may be represented graphically as follows:

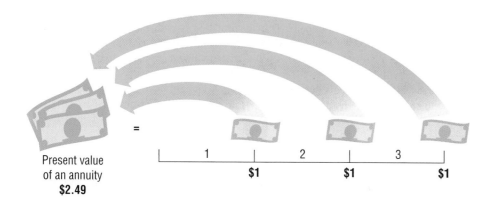

Present value
of an annuity
$2.49

Assume you are to receive $1,000 cash on each December 31, 2003, 2004, and 2005. How much would the sum of these three $1,000 future amounts be worth on January 1, 2003, assuming an interest rate of 10 percent per year? We could use Table A-2, Appendix A to calculate the present value as follows:

Year	Amount		Factor from Table A-2, Appendix A, $i = 10\%$		Present Value
1	$1,000	×	0.9091 ($n = 1$)	=	$ 909.10
2	$1,000	×	0.8264 ($n = 2$)	=	826.40
3	$1,000	×	0.7513 ($n = 3$)	=	751.30
			Total present value	=	$2,486.80

We can compute the present value of this annuity more easily however, by using Table A-4, Appendix A as follows:

$$\$1,000 \times 2.4869 = \$2,487 \text{ (rounded)}$$

From Table A-4,
Interest rate = 10%
N = 3

Interest Rates and Interest Periods

The preceding illustrations assumed annual periods for compounding and discounting. Although interest rates are almost always quoted on an annual basis, most compounding periods encountered in business are less than one year. When interest periods are less than a year, the values of n and i must be restated to be consistent with the length of the interest period.

To illustrate, 12 percent interest compounded annually for five years requires the use of $n = 5$ and $i = 12\%$. If compounding is quarterly, however, the interest period is one-quarter of a year (i.e., four periods per year), and the quarterly interest rate is one-quarter of the annual rate (i.e., 3 percent per quarter). Therefore, 12 percent interest compounded quarterly for five years requires use of $n = 20$ and $i = 3\%$.

Newspaper, magazine, and television advertisements are easy to misinterpret if the consumer does not understand present value concepts. For example, most car companies offer seasonal promotions with special financing incentives. A car dealer may advertise 4 percent interest on car loans when banks are charging 10 percent. Typically, the lower interest rate is not really an incentive because the dealer simply charges a higher price for cars the dealership finances. Borrowing from the bank and paying cash at the dealership may help the buyer to negotiate a lower price. Customers should use the present value concepts illustrated in this chapter to compare financing alternatives.

Another misleading advertisement, seen every January, promises magazine subscribers a chance to become an instant millionaire. The fine print discloses that the winner will receive $25,000 for 40 years, which amounts to $1,000,000 (40 × $25,000), but the present value of this annuity at 8 percent is only $298,000. While most winners are happy to get the money, they are not really millionaires.

Some consumer advocates argue that consumers should not have to study present value concepts to understand such advertisements. While some of these criticisms may be valid, the quality of information contained in advertisements that include interest rates has improved over the past few years.

Accounting Applications of Future and Present Values

Learning Objective 9
Apply present value concepts to liabilities.

Many business transactions require the use of future and present value concepts. So that you can test your understanding of these concepts, we illustrate two cases.

CASE A On January 1, 2003, General Mills bought some new delivery trucks. The company signed a note and agreed to pay $200,000 on December 31, 2004, an amount representing the cash equivalent price of the trucks plus interest for two years. The market interest rate for this note was 12 percent.

1. How should the accountant record the purchase?
Answer: This case requires the computation of the present value of a single amount. In conformity with the cost principle, the cost of the trucks is their current cash equivalent price, which is the present value of the future payment. The problem can be shown graphically as follows:

January 1, 2003	December 31, 2003	December 31, 2004

? $200,000

The present value of the $200,000 is computed as follows:

$$\$200,000 \times 0.7972 = \$159,440$$

From Table A-2,
Interest rate = 12%
N = 2

Therefore, the journal entry is as follows:

Delivery trucks (+A)	159,440	
Note payable (+L)		159,440

Assets	=	Liabilities	+	Stockholders' Equity
Delivery trucks +159,440		Note payable +159,440		

2. What journal entry should be made at the end of the first and second years to record interest expense?

Answer: Each year's interest expense is recorded in an adjusting entry as follows:

December 31, 2003 Interest expense (+E, −SE) 19,132*
                Note payable (+L)   19,132
*$159,440 × 12% = $19,132.

Assets	=	Liabilities	+	Stockholders' Equity	
		Note Payable +19,132		Interest Expense	−19,132

December 31, 2004 Interest expense (+E, −SE) 21,428*
                Note payable (+L)   21,428
*($159,440 + $19,132) × 12% = 21,428.

Assets	=	Liabilities	+	Stockholders' Equity	
		Note payable +21,428		Interest expense	−21,428

3. What journal entry should be made on December 31, 2004, to record payment of the debt?

Answer: At this date the amount to be paid is the balance of Note Payable, which is the same as the maturity amount on the due date. The journal entry to record full payment of the debt follows:

Note payable (−L) 200,000
    Cash (−A)   200,000

Assets	=	Liabilities	+	Stockholders' Equity
Cash −200,000		Note payable −200,000		

CASE B On January 1, 2003, General Mills bought new printing equipment. The company elected to finance the purchase with a note payable to be paid off in three years in annual installments of $163,686. Each installment includes principal plus interest on the unpaid balance at 11 percent per year. The annual installments are due on December 31, 2003, 2004, and 2005. This problem can be shown graphically as follows:

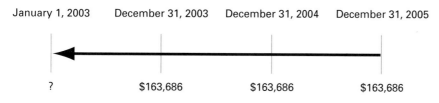

1. What is the amount of the note?

Answer: The note is the present value of each installment payment, $i = 11\%$ and $n = 3$. This is an annuity because payment is made in three equal installments. The amount of the note is computed as follows:

$$\$163,686 \times 2.4437 = \$400,000$$

From Table A-4,
Interest rate = 11%
N = 3

The acquisition on January 1, 2003 is recorded as follows:

| Printing equipment (+A) .... | 400,000 | |
| Note payable (+L) .... | | 400,000 |

Assets	=	Liabilities	+	Stockholders' Equity
Printing equipment	+400,000	Note Payable +400,000		

2. What journal entries should be made at the end of each year to record the payments on this note?

Answer:

December 31, 2003 Note payable (−L)	119,686	
Interest expense (+E, −SE) ($400,000 × 11%)	44,000	
Cash (−A)		163,686

Assets	=	Liabilities	+	Stockholders' Equity
Cash	−163,686	Note payable	−119,686	Interest Expense	−44,000

December 31, 2004 Note payable (−L)	132,851	
Interest expense (+E, −SE)		
[($400,000 − $119,686) × 11%]	30,835	
Cash (−A)		163,686

Assets	=	Liabilities	+	Stockholders' Equity
Cash	−163,686	Note payable	−132,851	Interest expense	−30,835

December 31, 2005 Note payable (−L)	147,463	
Interest expense (+E, −SE)	16,223*	
Cash (−A)		163,686

*Interest: ($400,000 − $119,686 − $132,851) × 11% = $16,223 (rounded to accommodate rounding errors).

Assets	=	Liabilities	+	Stockholders' Equity
Cash	−163,686	Note payable	−147,463	Interest expense	−16,223

In the next chapter, we will use the present value techniques you have just learned to understand how to account for bonds.

Chapter Supplement A

Income Taxes and Retirement Benefits

Two aspects of business operations, income taxes and employee retirement benefits, may result in the creation of either an asset or a liability. On most financial statements, you will see these items as liabilities, so we will discuss them along with other liabilities.

Deferred Taxes

Because separate rules govern the preparation of financial statements (GAAP) and tax returns (Internal Revenue Code), income tax expense and current taxes payable often differ in amount. To reflect this difference, companies establish a separate account called *Deferred Taxes*. In practice, deferred taxes can be either assets (such as taxes related to cash collected from a customer, which is taxable before it is reported as a revenue on the income statement) or liabilities (such as taxes related to depreciation, which is reported on the tax return before it is reported on the income statement). General Mills has deferred tax amounts reported as both assets and liabilities.

Deferred tax items exist because of timing differences in the reporting of revenues and expenses on the income statement and tax return. These **temporary differences** are caused by differences between GAAP, which govern financial statement preparation, and the Internal Revenue Code, which governs the preparation of tax returns.

Deferred tax amounts always reverse themselves. For example, at some point in the future the accelerated depreciation recorded on the tax return will be less than the straight-line depreciation reported on the income statement (recall from Chapter 8 that accelerated depreciation causes higher depreciation expense compared to straight line in the early years of an asset's life and lower depreciation in the later years). When a deferred tax liability reverses, the deferred tax amount is reduced, and the company pays more taxes to the IRS than the amount of income tax expense reported on the income statement.

The computation of deferred taxes involves some complexities that are discussed in advanced accounting courses. At this point, you need to understand only that deferred tax assets and liabilities are caused by temporary differences between the income statement and tax return. Each temporary difference has an impact on the income statement in one accounting period and on the tax return in another.

Accrued Retirement Benefits

Most employers provide retirement programs for their employees. In a defined contribution program, the employer makes cash payments to an investment fund. When employees retire, they are entitled to a portion of the fund. If the investment strategy of the fund is successful, the retirement income for the employees will be larger. If the strategy is not successful, it will be lower. The employer's only obligation is to make the required annual payments to the fund that are recorded as pension expense.

Other employers offer defined benefit programs. Under these programs, employees' retirement benefits are based on a percentage of their pay at retirement or a certain number of dollars for each year of employment. In these cases, the pension expense that must be accrued each year is the change in the current cash value of employees' retirement packages. The current cash value changes each year for a variety of reasons. For example, it will change (1) as employees draw closer to receiving benefits, (2) as employees' retirement benefits increase as a result of higher pay or longer service, and (3) if the employees' life expectancies change. The company must report a pension liability based on any portion of the current cash value of the retirement program that has not actually been funded. For example, if the company were to transfer $8 million to the pension fund while the current cash value of the pension obligation was $10 million, the company would report a $2 million pension liability on its balance sheet.

For many corporations, especially those with unionized work forces, the financial obligation associated with defined benefit retirement programs can be huge. A recent financial statement for Ford Motor Company disclosed the following information:

REAL WORLD EXCERPT

Ford Motor Company
ANNUAL REPORT

Note 2

Employee Retirement Benefits
(in millions)

Accumulated Postretirement Benefit Obligation	
Retirees	$ 7,035.0
Active employees eligible to retire	2,269.6
Other active employees	5,090.6
Total accumulated obligation	$14,395.2

To put the size of this obligation in perspective, it represents an amount nearly equal to Ford's total stockholders' equity. The retirement benefit expense for the year was $1.3 billion, which exceeded the income Ford earned for the previous three years.

DEFERRED TAX ITEMS exist because of timing differences caused by reporting revenues and expenses according to GAAP on a company's income statement and according to the Internal Revenue Code on the tax return.

TEMPORARY DIFFERENCES are timing differences that cause deferred income taxes and will reverse, or turn around, in the future.

General Mills does not have a pension liability on its balance sheet because cash payments to the retirement fund have been larger than the current value of pension benefits. The notes report the following:

Note 5

Balance Sheet Information

(in millions)	2000	1999
Other assets:		
Prepaid pension	$593.1	$528.3

This type of information is important to analysts who are interested in forecasting a company's future cash flows. Ford has a much larger obligation to transfer cash to its retirement fund than does General Mills.

In recent years, employer-provided health care benefits have been the subject of a great deal of discussion. Many large companies pay for a portion of their employees' health insurance costs. These payments are recorded as an expense in the current accounting period. In addition, some employers continue to pay for health care costs after their employees retire. The cost of these future benefits must be estimated and recorded as an expense for the periods in which the employees perform services. The recording of future health care costs for retired employees is an excellent example of the use of estimates in accounting. Imagine the difficulty of estimating future health care costs when you do not know how long employees will live, how healthy they will be during their retirements, and how much money doctors and hospitals will charge for their services in the future.

Accounting for retirement benefits is a complex topic that is discussed in detail in subsequent accounting courses. We introduce the topic at this point as another example of the application of the matching concept, which requires that expenses be recorded in the year in which benefits are received. This accounting procedure also avoids creating improper incentives for managers. If the future cost of retirement benefits were not included in the period in which work is performed, managers might have the incentive to offer employees increases in their retirement benefits instead of increases in their salaries. In this manner, managers could understate the true cost of employees' services and make their companies appear more profitable.

Chapter Supplement B

Federal Income Tax Concepts

Unlike sole proprietorships and partnerships, corporations are separate legal entities, so they are required to pay income taxes. Corporations must prepare a U.S. Corporate Tax Return (Form 1120), which lists their revenue and expenses for the year. The amount of the tax payable is based on the taxable income reported on their tax return. As was mentioned earlier, taxable income usually differs from the income reported on the income statement because the income statement is prepared in conformity with GAAP, but the tax return is prepared in conformity with the Internal Revenue Code.

Calculation of Taxes Payable

In most cases, a large corporation's tax obligation is determined by multiplying its taxable income by 35 percent. Rates are graduated, however, so that very small corporations pay lower rates than large corporations do.

Exhibit 9.2 illustrates the calculation of taxes payable at various income levels. Notice in Cases B and C that a portion of the income is taxed at a rate that is higher than the maximum of 35 percent. The purpose of the 39 percent rate is to phase out the benefits of the lower rates that were intended to benefit only smaller corporations. The $136,000 total taxes payable on taxable income of $400,000 is an effective tax rate of exactly 34 percent.

EXHIBIT 9.2

Calculation of Taxes Payable

Case A: Taxable Income	$ 90,000
Computation	
0.15 of first $50,000	$ 7,500
0.25 of next $25,000	6,250
0.34 of $15,000	5,100
Taxes payable	$ 18,850
Case B: Taxable Income	**$150,000**
Computation	
0.15 of first $50,000	$ 7,500
0.25 of next $25,000	6,250
0.34 of next $25,000	8,500
0.39 of $50,000 ($150,000 − $100,000)	19,500
Taxes payable	$ 41,750
Case C: Taxable Income	**$400,000**
Computation	
0.15 of first $50,000	$ 7,500
0.25 of next $25,000	6,250
0.34 of next $25,000	8,500
0.39 of next $235,000	91,650
0.34 of $65,000 ($400,000 − $335,000)	22,100
Taxes payable	$136,000

A 35 percent tax rate applies to taxable incomes higher than $10 million. A provision phases out the 34 percent tax rate for very large corporations. The tax rate from $15,000,000 to $18,333,333 is 38 percent. At higher incomes, the rate reverts to 35 percent. This provision results in an effective tax rate of 35 percent once a corporation earns more than $18,333,333.

Revenue and Expense Recognition for Income Tax Purposes

Several differences exist between GAAP and the rules that govern preparation of the federal income tax return. The following are common examples:

1. Interest revenue on state and municipal bonds is generally excluded from taxable income, although it is included in accounting income.

2. Revenue collected in advance (e.g., rent revenue) is included in taxable income when it is collected and in accounting income when it is earned.

3. Proceeds from life insurance policies (e.g., key executive insurance) is excluded from taxable income but included in accounting income.

4. Corporations that own less than 20 percent of another corporation's stock may exclude 70 percent of the dividends received from taxable income although all the dividends are included in accounting income. The exclusion is 80 percent if the corporation owns more than 20 percent of the other corporation's stock. A 100 percent exclusion is permitted if 80 percent or more of the stock is owned.

5. For tax purposes, depreciation expense is generally based on the Accelerated Cost Recovery System (ACRS) for assets placed in service after 1980 but before 1987, or on the Modified Accelerated Cost Recovery System (MACRS) for assets placed in service after 1986. These methods were discussed in Chapter 8.

Tax Minimization Versus Tax Evasion

Most large corporations spend considerable time and money developing strategies that *minimize* the amount of federal income taxes they must pay. Nothing is wrong with this approach because courts have stated there is no legal obligation to pay more taxes than the law demands. Even if you do not major in accounting, you will probably want to take a course in federal income taxation because knowledge of the Internal Revenue Code is important for most executives. This knowledge offers opportunities to save significant amounts of money.

In contrast, tax evasion involves the use of illegal means to avoid paying taxes. Use of accelerated depreciation is an example of *tax minimization;* failure to report revenue that was collected in cash is an example of *tax evasion.* While efforts at tax minimization represent good business practice, tax evasion is morally and legally wrong. Individuals who evade taxes run the risk of severe financial penalties as well as the possibility of being sent to jail.

CHAPTER **TAKE-AWAYS**

1. **Define, measure, and report liabilities. p. 459**
Strictly speaking, accountants define liabilities as probable future sacrifices of economic benefits that arise from past transactions. They are classified on the balance sheet as either current or long term. Current liabilities are short-term obligations that will be paid within the current operating cycle of the business or within one year of the balance sheet date, whichever is longer. Long-term liabilities are all obligations not classified as current.

2. **Use the current ratio. p. 460**
The current ratio is a comparison of current assets and current liabilities. Analysts use this ratio to assess the liquidity of a company.

3. **Analyze the accounts payable turnover ratio. p. 461**
This ratio is computed by dividing cost of goods sold by accounts payable. It shows how quickly management is paying its trade creditors and is considered to be a measure of liquidity.

4. **Report notes payable and explain the time value of money. p. 464**
A note payable specifies the amount borrowed, when it must be repaid, and the interest rate associated with the debt. Accountants must report the debt and the interest as it accrues. The time value of money refers to the fact that interest accrues on borrowed money with the passage of time.

5. **Report contingent liabilities. p. 467**
A contingent liability is a potential liability that has arisen as the result of a past event. Such liabilities are disclosed in a note if the obligation is reasonably possible.

6. **Explain the importance of working capital and its impact on cash flows. p. 468**
Working capital is used to fund the operating activities of a business. Changes in working capital accounts affect the statement of cash flows. Cash flows from operating activities are increased by decreases in current assets (other than cash) or increases in current liabilities. Cash flows from operating activities are decreased by increases in current assets (other than cash) or decreases in current liabilities.

7. **Report long-term liabilities. p. 470**
Usually, long-term liabilities will be paid more than one year in the future. Accounting for long-term debt is based on the same concepts used in accounting for short-term debt.

8. **Apply the concepts of present and future values. p. 472**
These concepts are based on the time value of money. Simply stated, a dollar to be received in the future is worth less than a dollar available today (present value). Alternatively, a dollar invested today will grow to a larger amount in the future (future value). These concepts are applied either to a single payment or multiple payments called *annuities.* Either tables or calculators can be used to determine present and future values.

9. **Apply present value concepts to liabilities. p. 478**
Accountants use present value concepts to determine the reported amounts of liabilities. A liability involves the payment of some amount at a future date. The reported liability is not the amount of the future payment. Instead, the liability is reported at the amount of the present value of the future payment.

In this chapter, we focused on current liabilities and introduced you to present value concepts. In the next chapter, we will use present value concepts to measure long-term liabilities. We will also discuss long-term liabilities in the context of the capital structure of the company.

KEY **RATIOS**

Current ratio measures the ability of a company to pay its current obligations. It is computed as follows (p. 460):

$$\text{Current Ratio} = \frac{\text{Current Assets}}{\text{Current Liabilities}}$$

Accounts payable turnover is a measure of how quickly a company pays its creditors. It is computed as follows (p. 461):

$$\text{Accounts Payable Turnover} = \frac{\text{Cost of Goods Sold}}{\text{Average Accounts Payable}}$$

FINDING **FINANCIAL INFORMATION**

Balance Sheet

Under Current Liabilities
Liabilities listed by account title, such as
Accounts payable
Accrued liabilities
Notes payable
Current portion of long-term debt

Under Noncurrent Liabilities
Liabilities listed by account title, such as
Long-term debt
Deferred taxes
Bonds

Income statement

Liabilities are shown only on the balance sheet, never on the income statement. Transactions affecting liabilities often affect an income statement account. For example, accrued salary compensation affects an income statement account (compensation expense) and a balance sheet account (salaries payable).

Statement of Cash Flows

Under Operating Activities (indirect method)
Net income
+ Increases in most current liabilities
− Decreases in most current liabilities

Under Financing Activities
+ Increase in long-term liabilities
− Decreases in long-term liabilities

Notes

Under Summary of Significant Accounting Policies
Description of pertinent information concerning accounting treatment of liabilities. Normally, there is minimal information.

Under a Separate Note
If not listed on the balance sheet, a listing of the major classifications of liabilities with information about maturities and interest rates. Information about contingent liabilities is reported in the notes.

KEY **TERMS**

Accrued Liabilities p. 462
Annuity p. 475
Capital Lease p. 472
Contingent Liability p. 467
Current Liabilities p. 459
Deferred Revenues p. 466

Deferred Tax Items p. 481
Future Value p. 473
Liabilities p. 459
Liquidity p. 459
Long-Term Liabilities p. 470

Operating Lease p. 472
Present Value p. 473
Temporary Differences p. 481
Time Value of Money p. 464
Working Capital p. 468

QUESTIONS

1. Define *liability*. Differentiate between a current liability and a long-term liability.
2. How can external parties be informed about the liabilities of a business?
3. Liabilities are measured and reported at their current cash equivalent amount. Explain.
4. A *liability* is a known obligation of either a definite or an estimated amount. Explain.
5. Define *working capital*. How is it computed?
6. What is the current ratio? How is it related to the classification of liabilities?
7. Define *accrued liability*. What type of entry usually reflects an accrued liability?
8. Define *deferred revenue*. Why is it a liability?
9. Define *note payable*. Differentiate between a secured and an unsecured note.
10. What is a contingent liability? How is a contingent liability reported?
11. Compute 2003 interest expense for the following note: face, $4,000; 12 percent interest; date of note, April 1, 2003.
12. Explain the concept of the time value of money.
13. Explain the basic difference between future value and present value.
14. If you deposited $10,000 in a savings account that earns 10 percent, how much would you have at the end of 10 years? Use a convenient format to display your computations.
15. If you hold a valid contract that will pay you $8,000 cash 10 years hence and the going rate of interest is 10 percent, what is its present value? Use a convenient format to display your computations.
16. What is an annuity?
17. Complete the following schedule:

	Table Values
Concept	$i = 5\%, n = 4; i = 10\%, n = 7; i = 14\%, n = 10$
FV of $1	
PV of $1	
FV of annuity of $1	
PV of annuity of $1	

18. If you deposit $1,000 for each of 10 interest periods (ordinary annuity) that earns 8 percent interest, how much would you have at the end of period 10? Use a convenient format to display your computations.
19. You purchased an XIT auto for $18,000 by making a $3,000 cash payment and six semiannual installment payments for the balance at 12 percent interest. Use a convenient format to display computation of the amount of each payment.

MULTIPLE **CHOICE QUESTIONS**

1. You and your spouse are planning your retirement. In addition to other savings, you have opened an account with Edward Jones. Your goal is to deposit $15,000 at the end of each year, starting in 12 months and continuing for 10 years. You expect to earn 5 percent each year. How much will be in the account at the end of 10 years?
   a. $24,433
   b. 150,000
   c. 188,668
   d. 495,990
2. The university spirit organization needs to buy a new trailer in which to haul the team mascot to the football games. A dealership in Lockhart has agreed to the following terms: $2,000 down plus monthly payments of $365 for 4 years, which includes interest at 6 percent. A dealership in Leander will agree to a $1,000 down payment, plus payments of $380 per month for four years, which includes interest at 12 percent. Which is the better deal, *and why*?
   a. The Leander offer is better because the total payments of $19,240 are less than the total payments of $19,520 to be made to the Lockhart dealership.
   b. The Lockhart offer is better because the cost in terms of present value is less than the present value cost of the Leander offer.
   c. The Lockhart offer is better because the financing rate is less.

d. The Leander offer is better because the cash down payment is less.

e. The Leander offer is better because the cost in terms of present value is less than the present value cost of the Lockhart offer.

3. Which of the following best describes *accrued liabilities?*

a. Long-term liabilities.

b. Current amounts owed to suppliers of inventory.

c. Current liabilities to be recognized as revenue in a future period.

d. Current amounts owed to various parties excluding suppliers of inventory.

4. Company X has borrowed $100,000 from the bank to be repaid over the next five years with payments beginning next month. Which of the following best describes the presentation of this debt in the balance sheet as of today (the date of borrowing)?

a. $100,000 in the Long-Term Liability section.

b. $100,000 plus the interest to be paid over the five-year period in the Long-Term Liability section.

c. A portion of the $100,000 in the Current Liability section and the remainder of the principal in the Long-Term Liability section.

d. A portion of the $100,000 plus interest in the Current Liability section and the remainder of the principal plus interest in the Long-Term Liability section.

5. A company is facing a class-action lawsuit in the upcoming year. It is possible, but not probable, that the company will have to pay a settlement of approximately $2,000,000. How would this fact be reported in the financial statements to be issued at the end of the current month?

a. $2,000,000 in the Current Liability section.

b. $2,000,000 in the Long-Term Liability section.

c. In a descriptive narrative in the footnote section.

d. Disclosure in this case is not required.

6. Which of the following transactions would usually cause accounts payable turnover to increase?

a. Collection of cash from a customer.   c. Purchase of merchandise on credit.

b. Payment of cash to a supplier.   d. None of the above.

7. How is working capital calculated?

a. Current assets multiplied by current liabilities.

b. Current assets plus current liabilities.

c. Current assets minus current liabilities.

d. Current assets divided by current liabilities.

8. Which of the following is least likely to be an annuity?

a. Monthly payments to a savings account.   c. Monthly payments on a home mortgage.

b. Monthly receipts from a pension plan.   d. Monthly utility bill payments.

9. Liabilities are presented in the financial statements at what value?

a. Net book value.   c. Future value.

b. Present value.   d. Cash flow value.

10. Fred wants to save enough money each year so that he can purchase a sports car in January 2008. Fred receives a large bonus from his employer every December 31. He anticipates that the car will cost $54,000 on January 1, 2008. In order for Fred to calculate how much he needs to save each December 31, he will need to have which of the following?

a. The anticipated interest rate and the present value of $1 table.

b. The anticipated interest rate and the future value of $1 table.

c. The anticipated interest rate and the present value table for annuities,

d. The anticipated interest rate and the future value table for annuities.

For more practice with multiple choice questions, go to our website at www.mhhe.com/libby4e, click on "Student Center" in the upper left menu, click on this chapter's name and number from the list of contents, and then click on "Multiple Choice Quiz" from the menu on the left.

MINI-EXERCISES

Computing Interest Expense

M9-1
LO4

Jacobs Company borrowed $500,000 on a 90-day note at 9 percent interest. The money was borrowed for 30 days in 2003 and 60 days in 2004; the note and interest were to be paid upon maturity in 2004. How much interest expense, if any, would be reported in 2003 and in 2004?

M9-2   Recording a Note Payable

L04

Farmer Corporation borrowed $100,000 on November 1, 2003. The note carried a 12 percent interest rate with the principal and interest payable on June 1, 2004. Prepare the journal entry to record the note on November 1. Prepare the adjusting entry to record accrued interest on December 31.

M9-3   Finding Financial Information

L01, 3, 6

For each of the following items, specify whether the information would be found in the balance sheet, the income statement, the statement of cash flows, the notes to the statements, or not at all.

1. The amount of working capital.
2. The total amount of current liabilities.
3. Information concerning company pension plans.
4. The accounts payable turnover ratio.
5. Information concerning the impact of changes in working capital on cash flows for the period.

M9-4   Computing Measures of Liquidity

L02

The balance sheet for Shaver Corporation reported the following: total assets, $250,000; noncurrent assets, $150,000; current liabilities, $40,000; total stockholders' equity, $90,000. Compute Shaver's current ratio and working capital.

M9-5   Analyzing the Impact of Transactions on Liquidity

L02

BSO, Inc., has a current ratio of 2.0 and working capital in the amount of $1,240,000. For each of the following transactions, determine whether the current ratio and working capital will increase, decrease, or remain the same.

a. Paid accounts payable in the amount of $50,000.
b. Recorded accrued salaries in the amount of $100,000.
c. Borrowed $250,000 from a local bank to be repaid in 90 days.
d. Purchased $20,000 of new inventory on credit.

M9-6   Reporting Contingent Liabilities

L05

Buzz Coffee Shops is famous for its large servings of hot coffee. After a case involving McDonald's, the lawyer for Buzz warned management (during 2003) that it could be sued if someone were to spill hot coffee and be burned: "With the temperature of your coffee, I can guarantee it's just a matter of time before you're sued for $1,000,000." Unfortunately, in 2005 the prediction came true when a customer filed suit. The case went to trial in 2006, and the jury awarded the customer $400,000 in damages, which the company immediately appealed. During 2007, the customer and the company settled their dispute for $150,000. What is the proper reporting of this liability each year?

M9-7   Computing the Present Value of a Single Payment

L08

What is the present value of $500,000 to be paid in 10 years, with an interest rate of 8 percent?

M9-8   Computing the Present Value of an Annuity

L08

What is the present value of 10 equal payments of $15,000, with an interest rate of 10 percent?

M9-9   Computing the Present Value of a Complex Contract

L08

As a result of a slowdown in operations, Mercantile Stores is offering to employees who have been terminated a severance package of $100,000 cash; another $100,000 to be paid in one year; and an annuity of $30,000 to be paid each year for 20 years. What is the present value of the package, assuming an interest rate of 8 percent?

M9-10   Computing the Future Value of an Annuity

L08

You plan to retire in 20 years. Is it better for you to save $25,000 a year for the last 10 years before retirement or $15,000 for each of the 20 years? You are able to earn 10 percent interest on your investments.

Making a Complex Computation of a Future Value

M9-11
LO8

You want a retirement fund of $500,000 when you retire in 20 years. You are able to earn 10 percent on your investments. How much should you deposit each year to build the retirement fund that you want?

EXERCISES

Computing Working Capital; Explaining the Current Ratio and Working Capital

E9-1
LO2, 4, 6

Flair Corporation is preparing its 2004 balance sheet. The company records show the following related amounts at the end of the accounting period, December 31, 2004:

Total current assets	$170,100
Total all remaining assets	525,000
Liabilities:	
Notes payable (8%, due in 5 years)	18,000
Accounts payable	60,000
Income taxes payable	12,000
Liability for withholding taxes	3,000
Rent revenue collected in advance	4,000
Bonds payable (due in 15 years)	100,000
Wages payable	7,800
Property taxes payable	2,000
Note payable (10%; due in 6 months)	10,000
Interest payable	400

Required:

1. Compute (a) working capital and (b) the current ratio (show computations). Why is working capital important to management? How do financial analysts use the current ratio?
2. Compute the amount of interest expense for 2004 on the long-term note. Assume that it was dated October 1, 2004.

Recording a Note Payable through Its Time to Maturity with Discussion of Management Strategy

E9-2
LO1, 4
Dayton
Hudson

Many businesses borrow money during periods of increased business activity to finance inventory and accounts receivable. Dayton Hudson is one of America's largest general merchandise retailers. Each Christmas, Dayton Hudson builds up its inventory to meet the needs of Christmas shoppers. A large portion of Christmas sales are on credit. As a result, Dayton Hudson often collects cash from the sales several months after Christmas. Assume that on November 1, 2003, Dayton Hudson borrowed $4.5 million cash from Metropolitan Bank for working capital purposes and signed an interest-bearing note due in six months. The interest rate was 10 percent per annum payable at maturity. The accounting period ends December 31.

Required:

1. Give the journal entry to record the note on November 1.
2. Give any adjusting entry required at the end of the annual accounting period.
3. Give the journal entry to record payment of the note and interest on the maturity date, April 30, 2004.
4. If Dayton Hudson needs extra cash during every Christmas season, should management borrow money on a long-term basis to avoid the necessity of negotiating a new short-term loan each year?

Determining Financial Statement Effects of Transactions Involving Notes Payable

E9-3
LO4
Dayton
Hudson

Using the data from the previous exercise, complete the following requirements.

Required:

1. Determine the financial statement effects for each of the following: (a) issuance of the note on November 1, (b) impact of the adjusting entry at the end of the accounting period, and (c) the payment of the note and interest on April 30, 2004. Indicate the effects (e.g., cash + or −), using the following schedule:

Date	Assets	Liabilities	Stockholders' Equity

2. If Dayton Hudson needs extra cash every Christmas season, should management borrow money on a long-term basis to avoid negotiating a new short-term loan each year?

E9-4   Recording Payroll Costs with Discussion

L01

McLoyd Company completed the salary and wage payroll for March 2003. The payroll provided the following details:

Salaries and wages earned	$230,000
Employee income taxes withheld	46,000
Union dues withheld	3,000
Insurance premiums withheld	1,200
FICA taxes*	16,445

*$16,445 each for employer and employees.

Required:
1. Give the journal entry to record the payroll for March including employee deductions.
2. Give the journal entry to record the employer's payroll taxes.
3. Give a combined journal entry to show the payment of amounts owed to governmental agencies and other organizations.
4. What was the total labor cost for the company? Explain. What percentage of the payroll was take-home pay? From the employers' perspective, does an economic difference between the cost of salaries and the cost of fringe benefits exist? From the employees' perspective, does a difference exist?

E9-5   Computing Payroll Costs; Discussion of Labor Costs

L01

Town Lake Company has completed the payroll for January 2004, reflecting the following data:

Salaries and wages earned	$82,000
Employee income taxes withheld	9,500
Union dues withheld	1,200
FICA payroll taxes*	6,013

*Assessed on both employer and employee (i.e., $6,013 each).

Required:
1. What amount of additional labor expense to the company was due to tax laws? What was the amount of the employees' take-home pay?
2. List the liabilities and their amounts that are reported on the company's January 31, 2004, balance sheet.
3. Would employers react differently to a 10 percent increase in the employer's share of FICA than to a 10 percent increase in the basic level of salaries? Would financial analysts react differently?

E9-6   Determining the Impact of Transaction, Including Analysis of Cash Flows

L01, 2, 4

Bryant Company sells a wide range of goods through two retail stores operated in adjoining cities. Most purchases of goods for resale are on invoices. Occasionally, a short-term note payable is used to obtain cash for current use. The following transactions were selected from those occurring during 2004:

a. Purchased merchandise on credit, $18,000 on January 10, 2004; the company uses a periodic inventory system.
b. Borrowed $40,000 cash on March 1, 2004 from City Bank and gave an interest-bearing note payable: face amount, $40,000, due at the end of six months, with an annual interest rate of 8 percent payable at maturity.

Required:
1. Describe the impact of each transaction on the balance sheet equation. Indicate the effects (e.g., cash + or −), using the following schedule:

Date	Assets	Liabilities	Stockholders' Equity

2. What amount of cash is paid on the maturity date of the note?
3. Discuss the impact of each transaction on Bryant's cash flows.
4. Discuss the impact of each transaction on the current ratio.

Evaluating Lease Alternatives

As the new vice president for consumer products at Acme Manufacturing, you are attending a meeting to discuss a serious problem associated with delivering merchandise to customers. Bob Smith, director of logistics, summarized the problem: "It's easy to understand, we just don't have enough delivery trucks given our recent growth." Barb Bader from the accounting department responded: "Maybe it's easy to understand but it's impossible to do anything. Because of Wall Street's concern about the amount of debt on our balance sheet, we're under a freeze and can't borrow money to acquire new assets. There's nothing we can do."

On the way back to your office after the meeting, your assistant offers a suggestion: "Why don't we just lease the trucks we need? That way we can get the assets we want without having to record a liability on the balance sheet."

How would you respond to this suggestion?

E9-7
LO7

(Supplement A) Reporting a Liability, with Discussion

The annual report for Ford Motor Company contained the following information:

E9-8
LO1, 7
Ford Motor
Company

Postretirement Health Care and Life Insurance Benefits

The company and certain of its subsidiaries sponsor unfunded plans to provide selected health care and life insurance benefits for retired employees. The company's employees may become eligible for those benefits if they retire while working for the company. However, benefits and eligibility rules may be modified from time to time.

Required:
Should Ford report a liability for these benefits on its balance sheet? Explain.

(Supplements A and B) Computing Deferred Income Tax: One Temporary Difference, with Discussion

E9-9
LO8, 9

The comparative income statements of Martin Corporation at December 31, 2004, showed the following summarized pretax data:

	Year 2003	Year 2004
Sales revenue	$65,000	$72,000
Expenses (excluding income tax)	50,000	54,000
Pretax income	$15,000	$18,000

Included in the 2004 data is a $2,800 expense that was deductible only in the 2003 income tax return (rather than in 2004). The average income tax rate was 30 percent. Taxable income from the income tax returns was 2003, $14,000, and 2004, $17,400.

Required:
1. For each year, compute (a) income taxes payable and (b) deferred income tax. Is the deferred income tax a liability or an asset? Explain.
2. Show what amounts related to income taxes should be reported each year on the income statement and balance sheet. Assume that income tax is paid on April 15 of the next year.
3. Explain why tax expense is not simply the amount of cash paid during the year.

(Supplements A and B) Recording Deferred Income Tax: One Temporary Difference; Discussion of Management Strategy

E9-10
LO7

The comparative income statement for Chung Corporation at the end of December 31, 2004, provided the following summarized pretax data:

	Year 2003	Year 2004
Revenue	$80,000	$88,000
Expenses (excluding income tax)	65,000	69,000
Pretax income	$15,000	$19,000

Included in the 2004 data is a $5,000 revenue that was taxable only in the 2003 income tax return. The average income tax rate was 32 percent. Taxable income shown in the tax returns was 2003, $13,000, and 2004, $18,500.

Required:
1. For each year, compute (a) income taxes payable and (b) deferred income tax. Is the deferred income tax a liability or an asset? Explain.
2. Give the journal entry for each year to record income taxes payable, deferred income tax, and income tax expense.
3. Show what amounts related to income taxes should be reported each year on the income statement and balance sheet. Assume that income tax is paid on April 15 of the next year.
4. Why would management want to incur the cost of maintaining separate tax and financial accounting records to defer the payment of taxes?

E9-11
L07
Colgate-Palmolive

(Supplements A and B) Reporting Deferred Taxes

The annual report for Colgate-Palmolive contains the following information (in millions):

Income Taxes
Differences between accounting for financial statement purposes and accounting for tax purposes result in taxes currently payable (lower) higher than the total provision for income taxes as follows:

	1999	1998	1997
Excess tax over book depreciation	$(18.0)	$(19.8)	$(18.9)
Other	(31.4)	76.6	(25.5)
Total	$(49.4)	$ 56.8	$(44.4)

Required:
1. Determine whether tax expense is higher or lower than taxes payable for each year.
2. Explain the most likely reason for tax depreciation to be higher than book depreciation.
3. Is the deferred tax liability reported on the 1999 balance sheet $49.4 million? Explain.

E9-12
L07
Carnival Cruise Lines

Reporting a Liability

Carnival Cruise Lines provides exotic vacations on board luxurious passenger ships. In 1998, the company moved its offices and included the following note in its current annual report:

Leases

On March 27, 1998, the Company entered into a ten-year lease for 230,000 square feet of office space located in Miami, Florida. The Company moved its operation to this location in October 1998. The total rent payable over the ten-year term of the lease is approximately $24 million.

Required:
Based on these facts, do you think the company should report this obligation on its balance sheet? Explain. If the obligation should be reported as a liability, how should the amount be measured?

E9-13
L08

Computing Four Types of Present and Future Values

On January 1, 2003, Wesley Company completed the following transactions (assume an 11 percent annual interest rate):

a. Deposited $12,000 in Fund A.
b. Established Fund B by agreeing to make six annual deposits of $2,000 each. Deposits are made each December 31.

c. Established Fund C by depositing a single amount that will increase to $40,000 by the end of year 7.

d. Decided to deposit a single sum in Fund D that will provide 10 equal annual year-end payments of $15,000 to a retired employee (payments starting December 31, 2003).

Required (show computations and round to the nearest dollar):
1. What will be the balance of Fund A at the end of year 9?
2. What will be the balance of Fund B at the end of year 6?
3. What single amount must be deposited in Fund C on January 1, 2003?
4. What single sum must be deposited in Fund D on January 1, 2003?

Computing Growth in a Savings Account: A Single Amount

E9-14
LO8

On January 1, 2003, you deposited $6,000 in a savings account. The account will earn 10 percent annual compound interest, which will be added to the fund balance at the end of each year.

Required (round to the nearest dollar):
1. What will be the balance in the savings account at the end of 10 years?
2. What is the interest for the 10 years?
3. How much interest revenue did the fund earn in 2003? 2004?

Computing Deposit Required and Accounting for a Single-Sum Savings Account

E9-15
LO8

On January 1, 2003, Alan King decided to deposit an amount in a savings account that will provide $80,000 four years later to send his son to college. The savings account will earn 8 percent, which will be added to the fund each year-end.

Required (show computations and round to the nearest dollar):
1. How much must Alan deposit on January 1, 2003?
2. Give the journal entry that Alan should make on January 1, 2003.
3. What is the interest for the four years?
4. Give the journal entry that Alan should make on (a) December 31, 2003, and (b) December 31, 2004.

Recording Growth in a Savings Account with Equal Periodic Payments

E9-16
LO8

On each December 31, you plan to deposit $2,000 in a savings account. The account will earn 9 percent annual interest, which will be added to the fund balance at year-end. The first deposit will be made December 31, 2003 (end of period).

Required (show computations and round to the nearest dollar):
1. Give the required journal entry on December 31, 2003.
2. What will be the balance in the savings account at the end of the 10th year (i.e., after 10 deposits)?
3. What is the interest earned on the 10 deposits?
4. How much interest revenue did the fund earn in 2004? 2005?
5. Give all required journal entries at the end of 2004 and 2005.

Computing Growth for a Savings Fund with Periodic Deposits

E9-17
LO8

On January 1, 2003, you plan to take a trip around the world upon graduation four years from now. Your grandmother wants to deposit sufficient funds for this trip in a savings account for you. On the basis of a budget, you estimate that the trip currently would cost $15,000. To be generous, your grandmother decided to deposit $3,500 in the fund at the end of each of the next four years, starting on December 31, 2003. The savings account will earn 6 percent annual interest, which will be added to the savings account at each year-end.

Required (show computations and round to the nearest dollar):
1. How much money will you have for the trip at the end of year 4 (i.e., after four deposits)?
2. What is the interest for the four years?
3. How much interest revenue did the fund earn in 2003, 2004, 2005, and 2006?

Computing Value of an Asset Based on Present Value

E9-18
LO9

You have the chance to purchase the royalty interest in an oil well. Your best estimate is that the net royalty income will average $25,000 per year for five years. There will be no residual value at that time. Assume that the cash inflow occurs at each year-end and that considering the uncertainty in your estimates, you expect to earn 15 percent per year on the investment. What should you be willing to pay for this investment on January 1, 2003?

PROBLEMS

P9-1
LO1, 2, 6

Recording and Reporting Current Liabilities with Discussion of Cash Flow Effects (AP9-1)

Curb Company completed the following transactions during 2004. The annual accounting period ends December 31, 2004.

Jan.	8	Purchased merchandise for resale at an invoice cost of $13,580; assume a periodic inventory system.
	17	Paid January 8 invoice.
Apr.	1	Borrowed $40,000 from National Bank for general use; executed a 12-month, 12 percent interest-bearing note payable.
June	3	Purchased merchandise for resale at an invoice cost of $17,820.
July	5	Paid June 3 invoice.
Aug.	1	Rented a small office in a building owned by the company and collected six months' rent in advance amounting to $5,100. (Record the collection in a way that will not require an adjusting entry at year-end.)
Dec.	20	Received a $100 deposit from a customer as a guarantee to return a large trailer "borrowed" for 30 days.
	31	Determined wages of $6,500 earned but not yet paid on December 31 (disregard payroll taxes).

Required:
1. Prepare journal entries for each of these transactions.
2. Prepare all adjusting entries required on December 31, 2004.
3. Show how all of the liabilities arising from these transactions are reported on the balance sheet at December 31, 2004.
4. For each transaction, state whether the current ratio is increased, decreased, or remains the same.
5. For each transaction, state whether cash flow from operating activities is increased, decreased, or there is no effect.

P9-2
LO1, 2, 6

Determining Financial Effects of Transactions Affecting Current Liabilities with Discussion of Cash Flow Effects (AP9-2)

Using data from the previous problem, complete the following requirements.

Required:
1. For each transaction (including adjusting entries) listed in the previous problem, indicate the effects (e.g., cash + or −), using the following schedule:

Date	Assets	Liabilities	Stockholders' Equity

2. For each transaction, state whether cash flow from operating activities is increased, decreased, or there is no effect.
3. For each transaction, state whether the current ratio is increased, decreased, or there is no change.

P9-3
LO1

Recording and Reporting Accrued Liabilities and Deferred Revenue with Discussion

During 2004, Riverside Company completed the following two transactions. The annual accounting period ends December 31.

a. Paid and recorded wages of $130,000 during 2004; however, at the end of December 2004, three days' wages are unpaid and unrecorded because the weekly payroll will not be paid until January 6, 2005. Wages for the three days are $3,600.

b. Collected rent revenue on December 10, 2004, of $2,400 for office space that Riverside rented to another party. The rent collected was for 30 days from December 10, 2004, to January 10, 2005, and was credited in full to Rent Revenue.

Required:
1. Give (a) the adjusting entry required on December 31, 2004, and (b) the January 6, 2005, journal entry for payment of any unpaid wages from December 2004.
2. Give (a) the journal entry for the collection of rent on December 10, 2004, and (b) the adjusting entry on December 31, 2004.
3. Show how any liabilities related to these transactions should be reported on the company's balance sheet at December 31, 2004.
4. Explain why the accrual method of accounting provides more relevant information to financial analysts than the cash method.

Determining Financial Statement Effects of Transactions Involving Accrued Liabilities and Deferred Revenue

P9-4
LO1

Using the data from the previous exercise, complete the following requirements.

Required:
1. Determine the financial statement effects for each of the following: (a) the adjusting entry required on December 31, 2004, (b) the January 6, 2005, journal entry for payment of any unpaid wages from December 2004, (c) the journal entry for the collection of rent on December 10, 2004, and (d) the adjusting entry on December 31, 2004. Indicate the effects (e.g., cash + or −), using the following schedule:

Date	Assets	Liabilities	Stockholders' Equity

2. Explain why the accrual method of accounting provides more relevant information to financial analysts than the cash method.

Determining Financial Statement Effects of Various Liabilities (AP9-3)

P9-5
LO1, 5
Polaroid

Polaroid designs, manufactures, and markets products primarily in instant image recording. Its annual report contained the following note:

> **Product Warranty**
>
> Estimated product warranty costs are accrued at the time products are sold.

1. Assume that estimated warranty costs for 2003 were $2 million and that the warranty work was performed during 2004. Describe the financial statement effects for each year.

Reader's Digest Association is a publisher of magazines, books, and music collections. The following note is from its annual report:

> **Revenues**
>
> Sales of subscriptions to magazines are recorded as unearned revenue at the time the order is received. Proportional shares of the subscription price are recognized as revenues when the subscription is fulfilled.

Reader's Digest
Association

2. Assume that Reader's Digest collected $10 million in 2003 for magazines that will be delivered in future years. During 2004, the company delivered $8 million worth of magazines on those subscriptions. Describe the financial statement effects for each year.

Brunswick Corporation is a multinational company that manufactures and sells marine and recreational products. Its annual report contained the following information:

Brunswick
Corporation

Litigation

A jury awarded $44.4 million in damages in a suit brought by Independent Boat Builders, Inc., a buying group of boat manufacturers and its 22 members. Under the antitrust laws, the damage award has been trebled, and the plaintiffs will be entitled to their attorney's fees and interest.

The Company has filed an appeal contending the verdict was erroneous as a matter of law, both as to liability and damages.

3. How should Brunswick account for this litigation?

The Coca-Cola
Company

4. A recent annual report for The Coca-Cola Company reported current assets of $4,247,677 and current liabilities of $5,303,222. Based on the current ratio, do you think that Coca-Cola is experiencing financial difficulty?

Alcoa

Alcoa is involved in the mining and manufacturing of aluminum. Its products can become an advanced alloy for the wing of a Boeing 777 or a common recyclable Coca-Cola can. The annual report for Alcoa stated the following:

Environmental Expenditures

Liabilities are recorded when remedial efforts are probable and the costs can be reasonably estimated.

5. In your own words, explain Alcoa's accounting policy for environmental expenditures. What is the justification for this policy?

P9-6
LO6

Determining Cash Flow Effects (AP9-4)

For each of the following transactions, determine whether cash flows from operating activities will increase, decrease, or remain the same:

a. Purchased merchandise on credit.
b. Paid an account payable in cash.
c. Accrued payroll for the month but did not pay it.
d. Borrowed money from the bank. The term of the note is 90 days.
e. Reclassified a long-term note as a current liability.
f. Paid accrued interest expense.
g. Recorded a contingent liability based on a pending lawsuit.
h. Paid back the bank for money borrowed in *d*.
i. Collected cash from a customer for services that will be performed in the next accounting period (i.e., deferred revenues are recorded).

P9-7
LO2, 7
PepsiCo

Analyzing the Reclassification of Debt (AP9-5)

PepsiCo, Inc., is a $25 billion company in the beverage, snack food, and restaurant businesses. PepsiCo's annual report included the following note:

At year-end, $3.5 billion of short-term borrowings were reclassified as long-term, reflecting PepsiCo's intent and ability to refinance these borrowings on a long-term basis, through either long-term debt issuances or rollover of existing short-term borrowings.

As a result of this reclassification, PepsiCo's current ratio improved from 0.51 to 0.79. Do you think the reclassification was appropriate? Why do you think management made the reclassification? As a financial analyst, would you use the current ratio before the reclassification or after the reclassification to evaluate PepsiCo's liquidity?

(Supplements A and B) Recording and Reporting Deferred Income Tax: Depreciation (AP9-6)

P9-8
LO7

At December 31, 2003, the records of Pearson Corporation provided the following information:

Income statement	
Revenues	$160,000*
Depreciation expense (straight line)	(11,000)†
Remaining expenses (excluding income tax)	(90,000)
Pretax income	$ 59,000

*These revenues include $20,000 interest on tax-free municipal bonds.

†Equipment depreciated—acquired January 1, 2003, cost $44,000; estimated useful life, four years and no residual value. Accelerated depreciation is used on the tax return as follows: 2003, $17,600; 2004, $13,200; 2005, $8,800; and 2006, $4,400.

a. Income tax rate, 30 percent. Assume that 85 percent is paid in the year incurred.
b. Taxable income from the 2003 income tax return, $80,000.

Required:
1. Compute income taxes payable and deferred income tax for 2003. Is the deferred income tax a liability or an asset? Explain.
2. Show what amounts related to 2003 income taxes should be reported on the income statement and balance sheet.

Computing Present and Future Values (AP9-7)

P9-9
LO8, 9

On January 1, 2003, Plymouth Company completed the following transactions (use an 8 percent annual interest rate for all transactions):

a. Deposited $50,000 in a debt retirement fund. Interest will be computed at six-month intervals and added to the fund at those times (i.e., semiannual compounding). (*Hint:* Think carefully about *n* and *i*.)
b. Established a plant addition fund of $400,000 to be available at the end of year 5. A single sum that will grow to $400,000 will be deposited on January 1, 2003.
c. Established a pension retirement fund of $500,000 to be available by the end of year 6 by making six equal annual deposits each at year-end, starting on December 31, 2003.
d. Purchased a $180,000 machine on January 1, 2003, and paid cash, $60,000. A four-year note payable is signed for the balance. The note will be paid in four equal year-end payments starting on December 31, 2003.

Required (show computations and round to the nearest dollar):
1. In transaction *a*, what will be the balance in the fund at the end of year 4? What is the total amount of interest revenue that will be earned?
2. In transaction *b*, what single sum amount must the company deposit on January 1, 2003? What is the total amount of interest revenue that will be earned?
3. In transaction *c*, what is the required amount of each of the six equal annual deposits? What is the total amount of interest revenue that will be earned?
4. In transaction *d*, what is the amount of each of the equal annual payments that will be paid on the note? What is the total amount of interest expense that will be incurred?

Comparing Options Using Present Value Concepts (AP9-8)

P9-10
LO8

After hearing a knock at your front door, you are surprised to see the Prize Patrol from a large, well-known magazine subscription company. It has arrived with the good news that you are the big winner, having won $20 million. You discover that you have three options: (1) you can receive $1 million per year for the next 20 years, (2) you can have $8 million today, or (3) you can have $2 million today and receive $700,000 for each of the next 20 years. Your lawyer tells you that it is reasonable to expect to earn 10 percent on investments. Which option do you prefer? What factors influence your decision?

Computing Amounts for a Debt Fund with Journal Entries (AP9-9)

P9-11
LO8, 9

On December 31, 2003, Post Company deposited in a fund the cash to pay the principal amount of a $140,000 debt due on December 31, 2006. The company will make four equal annual deposits on each

December 31 in 2003, 2004, 2005, and 2006. The fund will earn 7 percent annual interest, which will be added to the balance at each year-end. The fund trustee will pay the loan principal (to the creditor) upon receipt of the last fund deposit. The company's accounting period ends December 31.

Required (show computations and round to the nearest dollar):

1. How much must be deposited each December 31?
2. What amount of interest will be earned?
3. How much interest revenue will the fund earn in 2003, 2004, 2005, and 2006?
4. Give journal entries for the company on the following dates:
   a. For the first deposit on December 31, 2003.
   b. For all amounts at the end of 2004 and 2005.
   c. For payment of the debt on December 31, 2006.
5. Show how the effect of the fund will be reported on the December 31, 2004, income statement and balance sheet.

ALTERNATE **PROBLEMS**

AP9-1 **Recording and Reporting Current Liabilities with Discussion of Cash Flow Effects** (P9-1)

L01, 6

Curb Company completed the following transactions during 2004. The annual accounting period ends December 31, 2004.

Jan.	15	Recorded tax expense for the year in the amount of $125,000. Current taxes payable were $93,000.
	31	Paid accrued interest expense in the amount of $52,000.
Apr.	30	Borrowed $550,000 from Commerce Bank; executed a 12-month, 12 percent interest-bearing note payable.
June	3	Purchased merchandise for resale at an invoice cost of $75,820.
July	5	Paid June 3 invoice.
Aug.	31	Signed contract to provide security service to a small apartment complex and collected six months' fees in advance amounting to $12,000. (Record the collection in a way that will not require an adjusting entry at year-end.)
Dec.	31	Reclassified a long-term liability in the amount of $100,000 to a current liability classification.
	31	Determined salary and wages of $85,000 earned but not yet paid December 31 (disregard payroll taxes).

Required:

1. Prepare journal entries for each of these transactions.
2. Prepare all adjusting entries required on December 31, 2004.
3. Show how all of the liabilities arising from these transactions are reported on the balance sheet at December 31, 2004.
4. For each transaction, state whether cash flow from operating activities is increased, decreased, or there is no effect.

AP9-2 **Determining Financial Effects of Transactions Affecting Current Liabilities with**

L01, 6 **Discussion of Cash Flow Effects** (P9-2)

Using data from Problem AP9-1, complete the following requirements.

Required:

1. For each transaction (including adjusting entries) listed in the previous problem, indicate the effects (e.g., cash + or −), using the following schedule:

Date	Assets	Liabilities	Stockholders' Equity

2. For each transaction, state whether cash flow from operating activities is increased, decreased, or there is no effect.

Determining Financial Statement Effects of Various Liabilities (P9-5)

AP9-3
L01, 5
Pulte

Pulte Corporation is a national builder of homes that does more than $2 billion in business each year. Its annual report contained the following note:

> ### Allowance for Warranties
>
> Home purchasers are provided with warranties against certain building defects. Estimated warranty cost is provided in the period in which the sale is recorded.

1. Assume that estimated warranty costs for 2006 were $8.5 million and that the warranty work was performed during 2007. Describe the financial statement effects for each year.

Carnival Cruise Lines operates cruise ships in Alaska, the Caribbean, the South Pacific, and the Mediterranean. Some cruises are brief; others can last for several weeks. The company does more than $1 billion in cruise business each year. The following note is from its annual report:

Carnival Cruise Lines

> ### Revenues
>
> Customer cruise deposits, which represent unearned revenue, are included in the balance sheet when received and are recognized as cruise revenue upon completion of voyages of duration of 10 days or less and on a pro rata basis computed using the number of days completed for voyages in excess of 10 days.

2. In your own words, explain how unearned revenue is reported in the balance sheet for Carnival. Assume that Carnival collected $19 million in 2003 for cruises that will be completed in the following year. Of that amount, $4 million was related to cruises of 10 or fewer days that were not complete; $8 million to cruises more than 10 days that, on average were 60 percent complete; and $7 million was related to cruises that had not yet begun. What is the amount of unearned revenue that should be reported on the 2003 balance sheet?

Sunbeam Corporation is a consumer products company that manufactures and markets a number of familiar brands including Mr. Coffee, Osterizer, First Alert, and Coleman. Annual revenues for the company exceed $2 billion. Its annual report contained the following information:

Sunbeam

> ### Litigation
>
> The Company and its subsidiaries are involved in various lawsuits arising from time to time that the Company considers to be ordinary routine litigation incidental to its business. In the opinion of the Company, the resolution of these routine matters will not have a material adverse effect upon the financial position, results of operations, or cash flows of the Company. At the end of the current year, the Company had established accruals for litigation matters of $31.2 million.
>   In 1996, the Company recorded a $12.0 million charge related to a case for which an adverse development arose. In the fourth quarter of this year, the case was favorably resolved and, as a result, $8.1 million of the charge was reversed into income.

3. Explain the meaning of this note in your own words. Describe how litigation has affected the financial statements for Sunbeam.
4. A recent annual report for Exxon reported a current ratio of 0.90. For the previous year, the ratio was 1.08. Based on this information, do you think that Exxon is experiencing financial difficulty? What other information would you want to consider in making this evaluation?

Exxon

Brunswick

Brunswick Corporation is a multinational company that manufactures and sells marine and recreational products. Its annual report contained the following information:

> **Legal and Environmental**
>
> The company is involved in numerous environmental remediation and clean-up projects with an aggregate estimated exposure of approximately $21 million to $42 million. The Company accrues for environmental remediation-related activities for which commitments or clean-up plans have been developed and for which costs can be reasonably estimated.

5. In your own words, explain Brunswick's accounting policy for environmental expenditures. What is the justification for this policy?

AP9-4 Determining Cash Flow Effects (P9-6)
L06

For each of the following transactions, determine whether cash flows from operating activities will increase, decrease, or remain the same:

a. Purchased merchandise for cash.
b. Paid salaries and wages for the last month of the previous accounting period.
c. Paid taxes to the federal government.
d. Borrowed money from the bank. The term of the note is two years.
e. Withheld FICA taxes from employees' paychecks and immediately paid them to the government.
f. Recorded accrued interest expense.
g. Paid cash as the result of losing a lawsuit. A contingent liability associated with the liability had been recorded.
h. Paid salaries and wages for the current month in cash.
i. Performed services for a customer who had paid for them in the previous accounting period (i.e., deferred revenue is earned).

AP9-5 Analyzing the Reclassification of Debt (P9-7)
L07
General Mills

General Mills is a multibillion-dollar company that makes and sells products used in the kitchens of most American homes. The Company's annual report included the following note:

> We have a revolving credit agreement expiring in two years that provides for a credit line (which permits us to borrow money when needed). This agreement provides us with the opportunity to refinance short-term borrowings on a long-term basis.

Should General Mills classify the short-term borrowing as current or noncurrent debt based on this ability to borrow money to refinance the debt if needed? If you were a member of the management team, explain what you would want to do and why. If you were a financial analyst, would your answer be different?

AP9-6 (Supplements A and B) Recording and Reporting Deferred Income Tax: Two Temporary
L07 Differences (P9-8)

The records of Calib Corporation provided the following summarized data for 2006 and 2007:

	Year-End December 31	
	2006	2007
Income statement		
Revenues	$210,000	$218,000
Expenses (excluding income tax)	130,000	133,000
Pretax income	$ 80,000	$ 85,000

a. Income tax rate, 32 percent. Assume that income taxes payable are paid 80 percent in the current year and 20 percent on April 15 of the next year.

b. Temporary differences:

   (1) The 2007 expenses include an $8,000 expense that must be deducted only in the 2006 tax return.

   (2) 2007 revenues include a $6,000 revenue that was taxable only in 2008.

c. Taxable income shown in the tax returns was 2006, $82,000, and 2007, $85,000.

Required:

  1. For each year compute (a) income taxes payable and (b) deferred income tax. Is each deferred income tax a liability or an asset? Explain.

  2. Give the journal entry for each year to record income taxes payable, deferred income tax, and income tax expense.

  3. Show what amounts related to income taxes should be reported each year on the income statement and balance sheet.

  4. As a financial analyst, would you evaluate a deferred tax liability and taxes currently payable differently?

Computing Present and Future Values (P9-9)

AP9-7
LO8

On January 1, 2003, Dodge Company completed the following transactions (use a 10 percent annual interest rate for all transactions):

a. Deposited $200,000 in a debt retirement fund. Interest will be computed at six-month intervals and added to the fund at those times (i.e., semiannual compounding). (*Hint:* Think carefully about *n* and *i*.)

b. Established a plant addition fund of $1,000,000 to be available at the end of year 10. A single sum that will grow to $1,000,000 will be deposited on January 1, 2003.

c. Established a pension retirement fund of $800,000 to be available by the end of year 10 by making 10 equal annual deposits each at year-end, starting on December 31, 2003.

d. Purchased a $750,000 machine on January 1, 2003, and paid cash, $400,000. A four-year note payable is signed for the balance. The note will be paid in four equal year-end payments starting on December 31, 2003.

Required (show computations and round to the nearest dollar):

  1. In transaction *a*, what will be the balance in the fund at the end of year 5? What is the total amount of interest revenue that will be earned?

  2. In transaction *b*, what single sum amount must the company deposit on January 1, 2003? What is the total amount of interest revenue that will be earned?

  3. In transaction *c*, what is the required amount of each of the 10 equal annual deposits? What is the total amount of interest revenue that will be earned?

  4. In transaction *d*, what is the amount of each of the equal annual payments that will be paid on the note? What is the total amount of interest expense that will be incurred?

Comparing Options Using Present Value Concepts (P9-10)

AP9-8
LO8

After completing a long and successful career as senior vice president for a large bank, you are preparing for retirement. After visiting the human resources office, you have found that you have several retirement options: (1) you can receive an immediate cash payment of $1 million, (2) you can receive $60,000 per year for life (you have a life expectancy of 20 years), or (3) you can receive $50,000 per year for 10 years and then $70,000 per year for life (this option is intended to give you some protection against inflation). You have determined that you can earn 8 percent on your investments. Which option do you prefer and why?

Computing Amounts for a Fund with Journal Entries (P9-11)

AP9-9
LO8, 9

On January 1, 2003, Jalopy Company decided to accumulate a fund to build an addition to its plant. The company will deposit $320,000 in the fund at each year-end, starting on December 31, 2003. The fund will earn 9 percent interest, which will be added to balance at each year-end. The accounting period ends December 31.

Required:

  1. What will be the balance in the fund immediately after the December 31, 2005, deposit?

  2. Complete the following fund accumulation schedule:

Date	Cash Payment	Interest Revenue	Fund Increase	Fund Balance
12/31/2003				
12/31/2004				
12/31/2005				
Total				

3. Give journal entries on December 31, 2003, 2004, and 2005.
4. The plant addition was completed on January 1, 2006 for a total cost of $1,060,000. Give the entry, assuming that this amount is paid in full to the contractor.

CASES AND **PROJECTS**

Annual Report Cases

CP9-1

L01, 4, 5, 7

AMERICAN EAGLE
OUTFITTERS

Finding Financial Information

Refer to the financial statements of American Eagle Outfitters given in Appendix B at the end of this book, or open file AEOS.pdf in the Annual Report Cases directory on the student CD-ROM.

Required:
1. What is the amount of accrued compensation and payroll taxes liability for the current year?
2. How did changes in accounts payable affect cash flows from operating activities in the current year?
3. What is the amount of long-term liabilities for the current year?
4. What amount of federal income taxes was deferred during the current year?
5. What is the amount of the future minimum lease obligations under operating leases in effect at February 3, 2001?

CP9-2

L01, 5, 7

ABERCROMBIE
&
FITCH

Finding Financial Information

Refer to the financial statements of Abercrombie & Fitch given in Appendix C at the end of this book, or open file ANF.pdf in the Annual Report Cases directory on the student CD-ROM.

Required:
1. What is the amount of accrued compensation for the current year?
2. How did changes in accounts payable and accrued expenses affect cash flows from operating activities in the current year?
3. What is the amount of long-term liabilities for the current year?
4. What amount of catalog and advertising expense remains unpaid at the end of the current year?
5. Does the company have any contingent liabilities?

CP9-3

L02, 3

AMERICAN EAGLE
OUTFITTERS

ABERCROMBIE
&
FITCH

Comparing Companies within an Industry

Refer to the financial statements of American Eagle Outfitters given in Appendix B, Abercrombie & Fitch given in Appendix C, and the Industry Ratio Report given in Appendix D at the end of this book, or open file CP9-3.xls in the Annual Report Cases directory on the student CD-ROM.

Required:
1. Compute the current ratio for each company for each year.
2. Compare the latest year current ratio for each company to the industry average from the Industry Ratio report. Based solely on the current ratio, are these companies more or less liquid than the average company in their industry?
3. Compute the payable turnover ratio for each company for the current year. What is the amount of long-term liabilities for the current year?
4. Compare the latest year payable turnover ratio for each company to the industry average from the Industry Ratio report. Are these companies doing better or worse than the average company in their industry at paying trade creditors?
5. Using this information and any other data from the annual report, write a brief assessment of the liquidity for the two companies.

Financial Reporting and Analysis Cases

Explaining a Note: Accrued Liability for a Frequent Flyer Program

Most major airlines have frequent flyer programs that permit passengers to earn free tickets based on the number of miles they have flown. A recent Southwest Airlines annual report contained the following note:

> Frequent flyer awards. The Company accrues the estimated incremental cost of providing free travel awards under its Rapid Rewards frequent flyer program.

The phrase *incremental cost* refers to additional expense associated with an extra passenger taking the flight (e.g., the cost of a soft drink and a snack).

Required:
1. What cost measures other than incremental cost could Southwest use?
2. What account should Southwest debit when it accrues this liability?

CP9-4
LO1, 5
Southwest
Airlines

Reporting Short-Term Borrowings

PepsiCo, Inc., manufactures a number of products that are part of our daily lives. Its businesses include Pepsi-Cola, Slice, Mountain Dew, and Fritos. The company's annual revenues exceed $22 billion. A recent PepsiCo annual report contained the following information:

> At the end of the current year, $3.6 billion of short-term borrowings were classified as long-term, reflecting PepsiCo's intent and ability to refinance these borrowings on a long-term basis, through either long-term debt issuances or rollover of existing short-term borrowings. The significant amount of short-term borrowings classified as long-term, as compared to the end of the previous year when no such amounts were reclassified, primarily reflects the large commercial paper issuances in the current year but also resulted from a refined analysis of amounts expected to be refinanced beyond one year.

Required:
As an analyst, comment on the company's classification of short-term borrowings as long-term liabilities. What conditions should exist to permit a company to make this type of classification?

CP9-5
LO1, 7
PepsiCo. Inc.

Interpreting the Financial Press

Increasingly, companies are becoming sensitive to environmental issues surrounding their business operations. They recognize that some of their actions can have detrimental impacts on the environment in ways that may not be fully understood for years or even decades. Environmental issues present complex problems for companies that must report contingent liabilities. A related article, Munter, Sacasas, and Garcia, "Accounting and Disclosure of Environmental Contingencies," January 1996, pp. 36–37, 50–52, from the *CPA Journal* (www.cpaj.com)* is available on the Libby/Libby/Short website at www.mhhe.com/libby4e. Read the article and prepare a brief memo concerning how companies should report environment issues in their financial statements.

CP9-6
LO7

Analyzing Hidden Interest in a Real Estate Deal: Present Value

Many advertisements contain offers that seem too good to be true. A few years ago, an actual newspaper ad offered "a $150,000 house with a zero interest rate mortgage" for sale. If the purchaser made

CP9-7
LO8

*Munter, Sacasas, and Garcia, "Accounting and Disclosure of Environmental Contingencies," *CPA Journal,* January 1996, pp. 36–37, 50–52. Reprinted with permission.

monthly payments of $3,125 for four years ($150,000 ÷ 48 months), no interest would be charged. When the offer was made, mortgage interest rates were 12 percent. Present value for $n = 48$, and $i = 1\%$ is 37.9740.

Required:
1. Did the builder actually provide a mortgage at zero interest?
2. Estimate the true price of the home that was advertised. Assume that the monthly payment was based on an implicit interest rate of 12 percent.

CP9-8
L09
Exxon Corporation

Computing the Present Value of Lease Obligations

A recent annual report for Exxon included the following note:

At December 31, 1998, the corporation and its subsidiaries held noncancelable leases covering drilling equipment, tankers, service stations and other properties with minimum lease commitments as indicated in the table.

Years	Minimum Commitment (in millions)
1999	$ 864
2000	713
2001	564
2002	488
2003	373
2004 and beyond	1,448

You are a lending officer for a large commercial bank and for comparative purposes want to compute the present values of these leases.

Required:
Determine the present value of the minimum lease payments shown as of December 31, 1998. You may assume an interest rate of 10 percent. Identify other assumptions that you must make.

Critical Thinking Cases

CP9-9
L01, 2

Making Decisions as a Manager: Liquidity

In some cases, a manager can engage in transactions that improve the appearance of financial reports without affecting the underlying economic reality. In this chapter, we discussed the importance of liquidity as measured by the current ratio and working capital. For each of the following transactions, (a) determine whether reported liquidity is improved and (b) state whether you believe that the fundamental liquidity of the company has been improved. Assume that the company has positive working capital and a current ratio of 2.

a. Borrowed $1 million from the bank, payable in 90 days.
b. Borrowed $10 million with a long-term note, payable in five years.
c. Reclassified current portion of long-term debt as long term as the result of a new agreement with the bank that guarantees the company's ability to refinance the debt when it matures.
d. Paid $100,000 of the company's accounts payable.
e. Entered a borrowing agreement that guarantees the ability to borrow up to $10 million when needed.
f. Required all employees to take accrued vacation to reduce its liability for vacation compensation.

Evaluating an Ethical Dilemma: Managing Reported Results

CP9-10
LO2

The president of a regional wholesale distribution company planned to borrow a significant amount of money from a local bank at the beginning of the next fiscal year. He knew that the bank placed a heavy emphasis on the liquidity of potential borrowers. To improve the company's current ratio, the president told his employees to stop shipping new merchandise to customers and to stop accepting merchandise from suppliers for the last three weeks of the fiscal year. Is this behavior ethical? Would your answer be different if the president had been concerned about reported profits and asked all of the employees to work overtime to ship out merchandise that had been ordered at the end of the year?

Making a Decision as a Financial Analyst: Cash Flows

CP9-11
LO2, 6

As a young analyst at a large mutual fund, you have found two companies that meet the basic investment criteria of the fund. One company has a very high current ratio but a relatively low amount of cash flow from operating activity reported on the statement of cash flows. The other company has a very low current ratio but very significant cash flows from operating activities. Which company would you tend to prefer?

Making a Decision as an Auditor: Contingent Liabilities

CP9-12
LO5

For each of the following situations, determine whether the company should (a) report a liability on the balance sheet, (b) disclose a contingent liability, or (c) not report the situation. Justify and explain your conclusions.

1. An automobile company introduces a new car. Past experience demonstrates that lawsuits will be filed as soon as the new model is involved in any accidents. The company can be certain that at least one jury will award damages to people injured in an accident.
2. A research scientist determines that the company's best-selling product may infringe on another company's patent. If the other company discovers the infringement and files suit, your company could lose millions.
3. As part of land development for a new housing project, your company has polluted a natural lake. Under state law, you must clean up the lake once you complete development. The development project will take five to eight years to complete. Current estimates indicate that it will cost $2 to $3 million to clean up the lake.
4. Your company has just been notified that it lost a product liability lawsuit for $1 million that it plans to appeal. Management is confident that the company will win on appeal, but the lawyers believe that it will lose.
5. A key customer is unhappy with the quality of a major construction project. The company believes that the customer is being unreasonable but, to maintain goodwill, has decided to do $250,000 in repairs next year.

Assessing Contingent Liabilities

CP9-13
LO5

If a liability is both probable and subject to estimate, it must be recorded on the balance sheet. The Financial Accounting Standards Board has defined *probable* as "the future event or events are likely to occur." Working in a small group, decide on a specific probability that is appropriate for this standard. (For example, is an 80 percent chance of occurrence probable?) Be prepared to justify your determination.

Evaluating an Ethical Dilemma: Fair Advertising

CP9-14
LO8

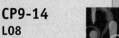

The New York State Lottery Commission ran the following advertisement in a number of New York newspapers:

> The Lotto jackpot for Wednesday, August 25, 1999, will be $3 million including interest earned over a 20-year payment period. Constant payments will be made each year.

Explain the meaning of this advertisement in your own words. Evaluate the "fairness" of this advertisement. Could anyone be misled? Do you agree that the lottery winner has won $3 million? If not, what amount is more accurate? State any assumptions you make.

Financial Reporting and Analysis Team Project

CP9-15
LO1, 4, 5

Team Project: Examining an Annual Report

As a team, select an industry to analyze. Each team member should acquire the annual report or 10-K for one publicly traded company in the industry, with each member selecting a different company. (Library files, the SEC EDGAR service at www.sec.gov, Compustat CD, or the company itself are good sources.) On an individual basis, each team member should then write a short report answering the following questions about the selected company.

1. Review the liabilities for your company. What strategy has the company followed with respect to borrowed funds?
2. Compare the individual liability accounts over several years. How have they changed?
3. Does the company have any contingent liabilities? If so, evaluate the risk associated with the contingency.
4. Compare the company's liabilities to its assets, income, and cash flows. Do you have any concerns?

Discuss any patterns across the companies that you as a team observe. Then, as a team, write a short report comparing and contrasting your companies using these attributes. Provide potential explanations for any differences discovered.

LEARNING OBJECTIVES

Reporting and Interpreting Bonds

10

Gaming (gambling) has become big business in this country. Casinos are now just a short drive from most major cities. Many of the most popular ones are owned and operated by major corporations whose stock is traded on the New York Stock Exchange. One of the most successful gaming companies is Harrah's Entertainment, Inc., which operates casinos under the names Harrah's, Showboat, and Rio. Harrah's annual report states the following:

"Harrah's Entertainment's strategy is different from that of our competitors. More casinos in more locations means Harrah's Entertainment has more opportunities to develop valuable relationships with more customers than any other company. Harrah's Entertainment's distribution allows us to serve customers both in their home casino markets and as they travel."

FOCUS COMPANY:

Harrah's Entertainment, Inc.

FINANCING GROWTH WITH BONDS PAYABLE

www.harrahs.com

As the gaming industry has grown and become more competitive, companies such as Harrah's have had to invest large amounts of money to create unique gaming environments. As Harrah's annual report states, "Nothing else matters if customers aren't dazzled with every encounter at every property." To illustrate the magnitude of the investment that is needed, consider the Harrah's casino in Tunica, Mississippi, 30 miles south of Memphis. The facility includes 50,000 square feet of gaming space, 1,296 slot machines, and 22 table games. To support the casino, Harrah's built a hotel with 182 rooms and 18 suites, three restaurants and a snack bar, a 250-seat showroom, and retail shops, 13,464 square feet of convention space, a golf course, and parking for 2,708 cars.

Because of the company's strategy of investing in large and unique casinos, Harrah's has had to raise large amounts of new capital in addition to retaining much of its income. In this chapter, we will study Harrah's sale of $500 million in new bonds. Harrah's has disclosed information concerning its long-term debt shown in Exhibit 10.1.

EXHIBIT 10.1

**Note from Harrah's
Annual Report**

HARRAH'S ENTERTAINMENT, INC.

NOTE 5—DEBT

Long-term debt consisted of the following:

	2000	1999
Bank Facility		
7.1%–9.5%, maturities to 2004	$1,574,600	$1,110,000
Secured Debt		
7.1%, maturity 2028	97,273	98,278
9¼%, maturity 2008	—	58,137
13%, maturity 2009	2,358	2,377
6.0%–9.0%, maturities to 2029	1,903	—
Unsecured Senior Notes		
7½%, maturity 2009	498,285	498,072
Unsecured Senior Subordinated Notes		
7⅞%, maturity 2005	750,000	750,000
Other Unsecured Borrowings		
5.5%–15.2%, maturities to 2001	41,366	23,409
Capitalized Lease Obligations		
4.9%–8.9%, maturities to 2004	989	2,872
	2,966,774	2,543,145
Current portion of long-term debt	(130,928)	(2,877)
	$2,835,846	$2,540,268

As of December 31, 2000, aggregate annual principal maturities for the four years subsequent to 2001 were: 2002, $1.4 million; 2003, $1.3 million; 2004, $1.5 billion; and 2005, $751.5 million.

UNDERSTANDING THE BUSINESS

Learning Objective 1
Describe bond characteristics and use the debt-to-equity ratio.

Capital structure is the mixture of debt and equity a company uses to finance its operations. Almost all companies employ some debt in their capital structure. Indeed, large corporations need to borrow billions of dollars, which makes borrowing from individual creditors impractical. Instead, these corporations issue bonds to raise debt capital.

Bonds are securities that corporations and governmental units issue when they borrow large amounts of money. After bonds have been issued, they can be traded on established exchanges such as the New York Bond Exchange. The ability to sell a bond on the bond exchange is a significant advantage for creditors because it provides them with liquidity or the ability to convert their investments into cash. If you lend money directly to a corporation for 20 years, you must wait that long before your cash investment is repaid. If you lend money by purchasing a bond, you can always sell it to another creditor if you need cash before it matures.

The liquidity of publicly traded bonds offers an important advantage to corporations. Because most creditors are reluctant to lend money for long periods with no opportunity to receive cash prior to maturity, they demand a higher interest rate for long-term loans. By issuing more liquid debt, corporations can reduce the cost of long-term borrowing.

The use of bonds to raise long-term capital offers other significant advantages to corporations such as Harrah's:

1. **Stockholders maintain control.** Bondholders do not vote or share in the company's earnings.

2. **Interest expense is tax deductible.** The tax deductibility of interest expense reduces the net cost of borrowing.

3. **The impact on earnings is positive.** Money can often be borrowed at a low interest rate and invested at a higher rate. Assume that Home Video, Inc., owns a video rental store. The company has stockholders' equity of $100,000 invested in the store and earns net income of $20,000 per year. Management plans to open a new store that will also cost $100,000 and earn $20,000 per year. Should management issue new stock or borrow the money at an interest rate of 8 percent? The following analysis shows that the use of debt will increase the return to the owners:

	Option 1 Stock	Option 2 Debt
Income before interest and taxes	$40,000	$ 40,000
Interest (8% × $100,000)		8,000
Income before taxes	40,000	32,000
Income taxes (35%)	14,000	11,200
Net income	26,000	20,800
Stockholders' equity	200,000	100,000
Return on equity	13%	20.8%

Unfortunately, bonds carry higher risk than equity. The following are the major disadvantages:

1. **Risk of bankruptcy.** Interest payments to bondholders are fixed charges that must be paid each period whether the corporation earns income or incurs a loss.

2. **Negative impact on cash flows.** Debt must be repaid at a specified time in the future. Management must be able to generate sufficient cash to repay the debt or the ability to refinance it.

This chapter provides a basic understanding of the management, accounting, and financial issues associated with bonds. We begin with a description of bonds payable. Then we see how bond transactions are analyzed and recorded. The chapter closes with a discussion of the early retirement of debt.

ORGANIZATION of the Chapter

Characteristics of Bonds Payable
- Debt-to-Equity Ratio

Reporting Bond Transactions
- Bonds Issued at Par
- Times Interest Earned Ratio
- Bonds Issued at a Discount
- Bonds Issued at a Premium

Additional Topics
- Effective-Interest Amortization
- Early Retirement of Debt
- Financing Activities on the SCF

CHARACTERISTICS OF BONDS PAYABLE

The **BOND PRINCIPAL** is the amount (1) payable at the maturity of the bond and (2) on which the periodic cash interest payments are computed.

A bond usually requires the payment of interest over its life with repayment of principal on the maturity date. The **bond principal** is the amount (1) that is payable at the maturity date and (2) on which the periodic cash interest payments are computed. The principal is also called the **par value**, **face amount**, and maturity value. All bonds have a par value, which is the amount that will be paid when the bond matures. For most individual bonds, the par value is $1,000, but it can be any amount.

PAR VALUE is another name for bond principal, or the maturity amount of a bond.

A bond always specifies a **stated rate** of interest and the timing of periodic cash interest payments, usually annually or semiannually. Each periodic interest payment is computed as principal times the stated interest rate. The selling price of a bond does not affect the periodic cash payment of interest. For example, a $1,000, 8 percent bond always pays cash interest of (1) $80 on an annual basis or (2) $40 on a semiannual basis.

FACE AMOUNT is another name for principal, or the principal amount of the bond.

Different types of bonds have different characteristics for good economic reasons. Individual creditors have different risk and return preferences. A retired person may be willing to receive a lower interest rate in return for greater security. This type of creditor might want a mortgage bond that pledges a specific asset as security in case the company cannot repay the bond. Another type of creditor might be willing to accept a low interest rate and an unsecured status in return for the opportunity to convert the bond into common stock at some point in the future. Companies try to design bond features that are attractive to different groups of creditors just as automobile manufacturers try to design cars that appeal to different groups of consumers. Some key types of bonds are shown here:

The **STATED RATE** is the rate of cash interest per period specified in the bond contract.

A **DEBENTURE** is an unsecured bond; no assets are specifically pledged to guarantee repayment.

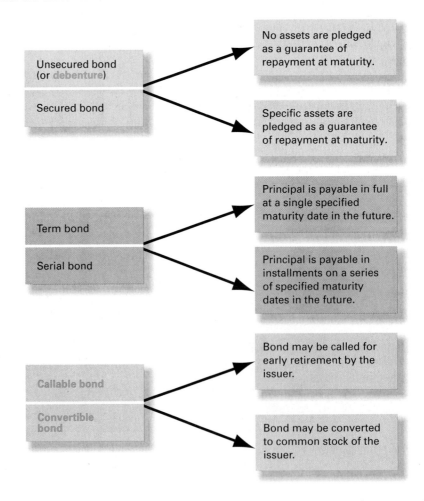

CALLABLE BONDS may be called for early retirement at the option of the issuer.

CONVERTIBLE BONDS may be converted to other securities of the issuer (usually common stock).

An **INDENTURE** is a bond contract that specifies the legal provisions of a bond issue.

When Harrah's decided to issue new bonds, it prepared a bond **indenture** (bond contract) that specified the legal provisions of the bonds. These provisions include the maturity date, rate of interest to be paid, date of each interest payment, and any conversion privileges. The indenture also contains covenants designed to protect the creditors. Harrah's indenture included limitations on new debt that the company might issue in the future. Other typical covenants include limitations on the payment of dividends and required minimums of certain accounting ratios, such as the current ratio. Because covenants may limit the company's future actions, management prefers those that are least restrictive. Creditors, however, prefer more restrictive covenants, which lessen the risk of the investment. As with any business transaction, the final result is achieved through negotiation.

Bond covenants are typically reported in the notes to the financial statements. *Accounting Trends & Techniques* (published by the AICPA) reviewed the reporting practices of 600 companies.[1] The graph in the margin shows the percentage of companies that disclosed debt covenants. Harrah's reported the following information about its debt covenants.

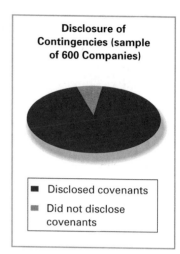

Disclosure of Contingencies (sample of 600 Companies)

■ Disclosed covenants
□ Did not disclose covenants

Long-Term Debt

Our debt agreements contain financial covenants requiring us to maintain a specific tangible net worth and to meet other financial ratios. Covenants limit our ability to pay dividends and to repurchase our outstanding shares.

REAL WORLD EXCERPT

Harrah's
ENTERTAINMENT, INC.
ANNUAL REPORT

The bond issuer also prepares a prospectus, which is a legal document that is given to potential bond investors. The prospectus describes the company, the bonds, and how the proceeds of the bonds will be used. In the prospectus for the Harrah's bonds, we learn that the company plans to use the proceeds to repay some of its outstanding debt. This debt reduction was required as part of an agreement to purchase another company (Showboat) a few months earlier.

When a bond is issued to an investor, the person receives a **bond certificate.** All bond certificates for a single bond issue are identical. The face of each certificate shows the same maturity date, interest rate, interest dates, and other provisions. An independent party, called the **trustee,** is usually appointed to represent the bondholders. A trustee's duties are to ascertain whether the issuing company fulfills all provisions of the bond indenture. Harrah's appointed IBJ Whitehall Bank & Trust Company to act as trustee.

A **BOND CERTIFICATE** is the bond document that each bondholder receives.

A **TRUSTEE** is an independent party appointed to represent the bondholders.

Because of the complexities associated with bonds, several agencies exist to evaluate the probability that a bond issuer will not be able to meet the requirements specified in the indenture. This risk is called *default risk.* Moody's and Standard and Poor's use letter ratings to specify the quality of a bond. Bonds with ratings above Baa/BBB are investment grade; bonds with ratings below that level are speculative and are often called *junk bonds.* Many banks, mutual funds, and trusts are permitted to invest only in investment-grade bonds. In addition to evaluating the risk of a specific bond, analysts also assess the overall risk of the issuer. One ratio that is important in this assessment is the debt-to-equity ratio.

---

[1]Reprinted with permission from *Accounting Trends & Techniques.* Copyright © 2000 by the American Institute of Certified Public Accounts, Inc.

? ANALYTICAL QUESTION

What is the relationship between the amount of capital provided by owners and the amount provided by creditors?

% RATIO AND COMPARISONS

The debt-to-equity ratio is computed as follows:

Debt-to-Equity = Total Liabilities ÷ Owners' Equity

The 2000 ratio for Harrah's is

$$\$3,877,653 \div \$1,269,718 = 3.05$$

COMPARISONS OVER TIME				COMPARISONS WITH COMPETITORS	
Harrah's				Mirage Resorts	Trump Casinos
1998	1999	2000		2000	2000
2.86	2.19	3.05		1.67	17.9

💡 INTERPRETATIONS

In General   A high ratio suggests that a company relies heavily on funds provided by creditors. Heavy reliance on creditors increases the risk that a company may not be able to meet its contractual financial obligations during a business downturn.

Focus Company Analysis   The debt-to-equity ratio for Harrah's has increased over the past few years and falls between the ratios for two major competitors. As discussed earlier, Harrah's has embarked on a strategy to create a national brand image in gaming. The company is investing heavily in the acquisition of other companies and the expansion of facilities. The debt-to-equity ratio has been significantly affected by this aggressive acquisition strategy. Given this context, most analysts would not be concerned about the increase in the company's debt-to-equity ratio over the past few years.

A Few Cautions   The debt-to-equity ratio tells only part of the story with respect to the risks associated with debt. It does not help the analyst understand whether the company's operations can support its debt. Remember that debt carries an obligation to make cash payments for interest and principal. As a result, most analysts would evaluate the debt-to-equity ratio within the context of the amount of cash the company can generate from operating activities.

REPORTING BOND TRANSACTIONS

Learning Objective 2
Report bonds payable and interest expense with bonds sold at par, at a discount, and at a premium.

When Harrah's issued its bonds, it specified two types of cash payment in the bond contract:

1. **Principal.** This amount is usually a single payment that is made when the bond matures. It is also called the **par,** or **face, value.**

2. **Cash interest payments.** These payments, which represent an annuity, are computed by multiplying the principal amount times the interest rate stated in the bond contract. This interest is called the **contract, stated,** or **coupon rate** of interest. The bond contract specifies whether the interest payments are made quarterly, semiannually, or annually.

The **COUPON RATE** is the stated rate of interest on bonds.

Topic Tackler 10–1

Neither the issuing company nor the underwriter determines the price at which the bonds sell. Instead, the market determines the price using the present value concepts introduced in the last chapter. To determine the present value of the bond, you compute the present value of the principal (a single payment) and the present value of the interest payments (an annuity) and add the two amounts.

Creditors demand a certain rate of interest to compensate them for the risks related to bonds, called the **market interest rate** (also known as the **yield** or **effective-interest rate**). Because the market rate is the interest rate on a debt when it is incurred, it is the rate that should be used in computing the present value of a bond.

The present value of a bond may be the same as par, above par (**bond premium**), or below par (**bond discount**). If the stated and the market interest rates are the same, a bond sells at par; if the market rate is higher than the stated rate, a bond sells at a discount; and if the market rate is lower than the stated rate, the bond sells at a premium. This relationship can be shown graphically as follows:

MARKET INTEREST RATE is the current rate of interest on a debt when incurred; also called the **YIELD** or **EFFECTIVE-INTEREST RATE.**

BOND PREMIUM is the difference between the selling price and par when the bond is sold for more than par.

BOND DISCOUNT is the difference between the selling price and par when the bond is sold for less than par.

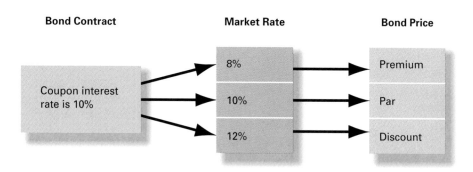

In commonsense terms, when a bond pays an interest rate that is less than the rate creditors demand, they will not buy it unless its price is reduced (i.e., a discount must be provided). When a bond pays more than creditors demand, they will be willing to pay a premium to buy it.

When a bond is issued at par, the issuer receives cash equal to its par value. When a bond is issued at a discount, the issuer receives less cash than the par value. When a bond is issued at a premium, the issuer receives more cash than the par value. Corporations and creditors do not care whether a bond is issued at par, at a discount, or at a premium because bonds are always priced to provide the market rate of interest. To illustrate, consider a corporation that issues three separate bonds on the same day. The bonds are the same except that one has a stated interest rate of 8 percent, another a rate of 10 percent, and a third a rate of 12 percent. If the market rate of interest were 10 percent, the first would be issued at a discount, the second at par, and the third at a premium. As a result, a creditor who bought any one of the bonds would earn the market interest rate of 10 percent.

During the life of the bond, its market price will change as market interest rates change. While this information is reported in the financial press, it does not affect the company's financial statements and the way its interest payments are accounted for from one period to the next.

In the next section of this chapter, we will see how to account for bonds issued at par, bonds issued at a discount, and bonds issued at a premium.

FINANCIAL ANALYSIS

Bond Information from the Business Press

Bond prices are reported each day in the business press based on transactions that occurred on the bond exchange. The following is typical of the information you will find:

Bond	Yield	Volume	Close	Change
Safeway 6.0 03	6.8	58	97.2	−1/4
Sears 7.0 07	6.77	25	101.4	−3/8
Harrah's 7.5 09	6.9	580	104.1	−7/8

This listing states that the Harrah's bond has a coupon interest rate of 7.5 percent and will mature in the year 2009. The bond currently provides a cash yield of 6.9 percent and has a selling price of 104.1 percent of par, or $1,040.10. On this date, 580 bonds were sold, and the price fell 7/8 point from the closing price on the previous trading day (a point is 1 percent).

It is important to remember that these changes do not affect the company's financial statements. For financial reporting purposes, the company uses the interest rates that existed when the bonds were first sold to the public.

SELF-STUDY QUIZ

Your study of bonds will be easier if you understand the new terminology that has been introduced in this chapter. Let's review some of those terms. Define the following:

1. Market interest rate.
2. Coupon interest rate.
3. Synonyms for coupon interest rate.
4. Bond discount.
5. Bond premium.
6. Synonyms for market interest rate.

After you have completed your answers, check them with the solutions that follow:

_____

1. The market rate is the interest rate demanded by creditors. It is the rate used in the present value computations to discount future cash flows.
2. Coupon interest rate is the stated rate on the bonds.
3. Coupon rate is also called stated rate and contract rate.
4. A bond that sells for less than par is sold at a discount. This occurs when the coupon rate is lower than the market rate.
5. A bond that sells for more than par is sold at a premium. This occurs when the coupon rate is higher than the market rate.
6. Market interest rate is also called *yield* or *effective-interest rate.*

Bonds Issued at Par

Bonds sell at their par value when buyers are willing to invest in them at the interest rate stated in the bond contract. To illustrate, let's assume that on January 1, 2003, Harrah's issued 10 percent bonds with a par value of $100,000 and received $100,000 in cash (which means that the bonds sold at par). The bonds were dated to start earning interest on January 1, 2003, and will pay interest each June 30 and December 31. The bonds mature in 10 years on December 31, 2012.

The amount of money a corporation receives when it sells bonds is the present value of the future cash flows associated with them. When Harrah's issued its bonds, it agreed to make two types of payments in the future: a single payment of $100,000 when the bond matures in 10 years and an annuity of $5,000 payable twice each year for 10 years. The bond payments can be shown graphically as follows:

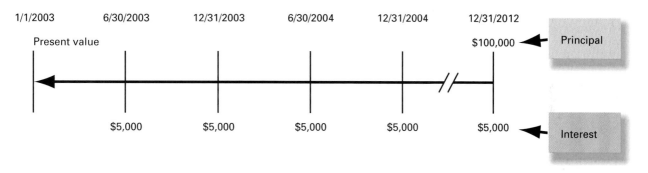

The present value of the bond payments can be computed with the tables contained in Appendix A using the factor for 20 periods and an interest rate of 5 percent (10 percent ÷ 2):

	Present Value
a. Single payment: $100,000 × 0.3769	$ 37,690
b. Annuity: $5,000 × 12.4622	62,310*
Issue price of Harrah's bonds	$100,000

Rounded.

If the effective rate of interest equals the stated rate of interest, the present value of the future cash flows associated with a bond always equals the bond's par amount. Remember that a bond's selling price is determined by the present value of its future cash flows, not the par value. On date of issue, bond liabilities are recorded at the present value of future cash flows on date of issue, not the par value, as follows:

Cash (+A) 100,000
  Bonds payable (+L) 100,000

Assets	=	Liabilities	+	Stockholders' Equity
Cash +100,000		Bonds payable +100,000		

Reporting Interest Expense on Bonds Issued at Par

The creditors who bought the bonds did so with the expectation that they would earn interest over the life of the bond. Harrah's will pay interest at 5 percent (i.e., 10 percent per year) on the par value of the bonds each June 30 and December 31 until the bond's maturity date. The amount of interest each period will be $5,000 (5% × $100,000). The entry to record the interest payments is as follows:

| Bond interest expense (+E, −SE) | 5,000 | |
| Cash (−A) | | 5,000 |

Assets	=	Liabilities	+	Stockholders' Equity	
Cash −5,000				Interest expense	−5,000

Bond interest payment dates rarely coincide with the last day of a company's fiscal year. Under the matching concept, interest expense that has been incurred but not paid must be accrued with an adjusting entry. If Harrah's fiscal year ended on May 31, the company would accrue interest for five months and record interest expense and interest payable.

Because interest payments are a legal obligation for the borrower, financial analysts want to be certain that a business is generating sufficient resources to meet its obligations. The times interest earned ratio is useful when making this assessment.

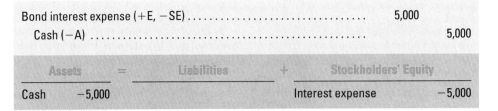

KEY RATIO
ANALYSIS

Times Interest Earned

Learning Objective 3
Analyze the times interest earned ratio.

❓ ANALYTICAL QUESTION

Is the company generating sufficient resources from its profit-making activities to meet its current interest obligations?

% RATIO AND COMPARISONS

The times interest earned ratio is computed as follows:

$$\text{Times Interest Earned} = \frac{\text{Net Income} + \text{Interest Expense} + \text{Income Tax Expense}}{\text{Interest Expense}}$$

The 2000 ratio for Harrah's is:

$$((\$12,060)^* + \$227,139 + \$15,417) \div \$227,139 = 1.01$$

Harrah's reported a loss in 2000.

COMPARISONS OVER TIME			COMPARISONS WITH COMPETITORS	
Harrah's			Mirage Resorts	Trump Casinos
1998	1999	2000	2000	2000
2.51	2.74	1.01	3.31	0.40

💡 INTERPRETATIONS

In General   A high times interest earned ratio is viewed more favorably than a low ratio. The ratio shows the amount of resources generated for each dollar of interest expense. A high ratio indicates an extra margin of protection in case profitability deteriorates. Analysts are particularly interested in a company's ability to meet its required interest payments because failure to do so could result in bankruptcy.

Focus Company Analysis   In 2000, profit-making activities for Harrah's generated only $1.01 for each dollar of interest, not a comfortable safety margin. The company's annual report provides an explanation: the financial impact of the bankruptcy of one of Harrah's affiliates. Despite the bankruptcy, Harrah's generated significant cash flows from operating activities. As a result, its required interest payments were never at risk.

A Few Cautions The times interest earned ratio is often misleading for new or rapidly growing companies that tend to invest considerable resources to build their capacity for future operations. In such cases, the times interest earned ratio will reflect significant amounts of interest expense associated with the new capacity but not the income that will be earned with the new capacity. Analysts should consider the company's long-term strategy when using this ratio. Some analysts prefer to compare interest expense to the amount of cash a company can generate, because creditors cannot be paid with "income" that is generated.

Bonds Issued at a Discount

Bonds sell at a discount when the market rate of interest is higher than the stated interest rate on them. Let's assume that the market rate of interest was 12 percent when Harrah's sold its bonds (which have a par value of $100,000). The bonds have a stated rate of 10 percent, payable semiannually, which is less than the market rate on the date of issue. Therefore, the bonds sold at a discount.

Topic Tackler 10–2

To compute the cash issue price of the bonds, we can use the tables in Appendix A. As in the previous example, the number of periods is 20, but we must use an interest rate of 6% (12% ÷ 2), which is the market rate of interest. The cash issue price of the Harrah's bonds is computed as follows:

	Present Value
a. Single payment: $100,000 × 0.3118	$31,180
b. Annuity: $5,000 × 11.4699	57,349
Issue (sale) price of Harrah's bonds	$88,529*

The amount of the discount: $100,000 − $88,529 = $11,471.

The cash price of the bonds issued by Harrah's is $88,529. Some people refer to this price as *88.5*, which means that the bonds were sold at 88.5 percent of their par value ($88,529 ÷ $100,000).

When a bond is sold at a discount, the Bonds Payable account is credited for the par amount, and the discount is recorded as a debit to Discount on Bonds Payable. The issuance of the Harrah's bonds at a discount is recorded as follows:

Cash (+A) 88,529
Discount on bonds payable (+XL, −L) 11,471
　　Bonds payable (+L) 100,000

Assets	=	Liabilities	+	Stockholders' Equity
Cash +88,529		Bonds payable +100,000		
		Discount on bonds −11,471		

Note that the discount is recorded in a separate contra-liability account (Discount on Bonds Payable) as a debit. The balance sheet reports the bonds payable at their book value, which is their maturity amount less any unamortized discount. Harrah's, like most companies, does not separately disclose the amount of unamortized discount or premium when the amount is small relative to other balance sheet amounts.

The annual report for ExxonMobil provides a good example of the reporting of a bond discount:

	2000	1999
	(in millions)	
ExxonMobil Corporation notes due 2004		
Face value ($1,146) net of unamortized discount	$749	$671

Notice that the book value of the ExxonMobil bonds increased from 1999 to 2000. This change was caused by the accounting procedure for discounts. In the next section we will see how and why the change occurs.

Reporting Interest Expense on Bonds Issued at a Discount

Based on our illustration, Harrah's must pay back $100,000 when the bond matures, but received only $88,529 when the bond was issued. The extra cash that must be paid is an adjustment of interest expense to ensure that creditors earn the market rate of interest. To adjust interest expense, the borrower apportions or amortizes the bond discount to each interest period as an increase in interest expense. Therefore, the amortization of bond discount results in an increase in bond interest expense.

The bond discount can be allocated using two amortization methods: (1) straight line and (2) effective interest. Because straight-line amortization is easy to compute, we will discuss it first. The effective-interest method is discussed later in this chapter.

STRAIGHT-LINE AMORTIZATION of a bond discount or premium is a simplified method that allocates an equal dollar amount to each interest period.

To amortize the $11,471 bond discount over the life of Harrah's bonds using **straight-line amortization**, we allocate an equal dollar amount to each interest period. Harrah's bonds have 20 six-month interest periods. The amortization of discount each period is $11,471 ÷ 20 periods = $574. We add this amount to the cash payment of interest ($5,000) to compute interest expense for the period ($5,574). The interest payments on Harrah's bonds each period are as follows:

Bond interest expense (+E, −SE)	5,574	
Discount on bonds payable (−XL,+L)		574
Cash (−A)		5,000

Assets	=	Liabilities	+	Stockholders' Equity	
Cash	−5,000	Discount on bonds	+574	Bond interest expense	−5,574

Bonds payable are reported on the balance sheet at their book value. On June 30, 2003, the book value of Harrah's bonds is $89,103 ($88,529 + $574). In each interest period, the book value of the bonds increases by $574 because the unamortized discount decreases by $574. At the maturity date of the bonds, the unamortized discount (i.e., the balance in the Discount on Bonds Payable account) is zero. At that time, the maturity amount of the bonds and the book value are the same (i.e., $100,000).

A note from the annual report for Ames Department Stores effectively summarizes our discussion to this point:

Debt

Debt obligations that carried face interest rates significantly less than market were discounted to their present values using estimated market rates. The discount amount will be amortized to interest expense over the term of the related obligation. The determination of appropriate interest rates was based upon evaluation of Ames' credit standing, the nature of the collateral, if any, and other terms pertaining to the debt, and the prevailing rates for similar instruments or issues with similar credit rating.

Accounting for Zero Coupon Bonds

Some bonds do not pay periodic cash interest because the coupon interest rate is zero. These bonds are often called *zero coupon bonds*. Why would an investor buy a bond that did not pay interest? Our discussion of bond discounts has probably given you a good idea of the answer. The coupon interest rate on a bond can be virtually any amount and the price of the bond will be adjusted so that investors earn the market rate of interest. A bond with a zero coupon interest rate is simply a deep discount bond that will sell for substantially less than its maturity value.

Let's use the $100,000 Harrah's bond to illustrate a zero coupon rate. Assume that market rate is 10 percent and the bond pays no cash interest. The selling price of the bond is the present value of the maturity amount because no other cash payments will be made over the life of the bond. We can compute the present value with the tables contained in Appendix A, using the factor for 10 periods and an interest rate of 10%:

	Present Value
Single payment: $100,000 × 0.3855	$38,550

Accounting for a zero coupon bond is no different from accounting for other bonds sold at a discount. The only difference is that the amount of the discount is much larger. The annual report for General Mills contained the following information concerning the company's zero coupon bonds:

Note 9. Long-Term Debt (in millions)	2000	1999
Zero Coupon notes, yield 11.1% $263 due 2013	$63.5	$59.4

Notice that while these bonds do not pay cash interest, they have been priced to provide the investor with an effective interest rate of 11.1 percent.

Bonds Issued at a Premium

Bonds sell at a premium when the market rate of interest is lower than their stated interest rate. Let's assume that the market rate of interest is 8 percent while the Harrah's bonds pay cash interest of 10 percent.

The present value of Harrah's 8 percent bonds can be computed from the tables contained in Appendix A using the factor for 20 periods and an interest rate of 4% (8% ÷ 2):

	Present Value
a. Single payment: $100,000 × 0.4564	$ 45,640
b. Annuity: $5,000 × 13.5903	67,952
Issue (sale) price of Harrah's bonds	$113,592

When a bond is sold at a premium, the Bonds Payable account is credited for the par amount, and the premium is recorded as a credit to Premium on Bonds Payable. The issuance of Harrah's bonds at a premium would be recorded as follows:

Cash (+A)	113,592	
Premium on bonds payable (+L)		13,592
Bonds payable (+L)		100,000

Assets	=	Liabilities	+	Stockholders' Equity
Cash +113,592		Premium on bonds +13,592		
		Bonds payable +100,000		

The book value of the bond is the sum of the two accounts, Premium on Bonds Payable and Bonds Payable, or $113,592.

Reporting Interest Expense on Bonds Issued at a Premium

As with a discount, the recorded premium of $13,592 must be apportioned to each interest period. Using the straight-line method, the amortization of premium each semi-annual interest period is $680 ($13,592 ÷ 20 periods). This amount is subtracted from the cash interest payment ($5,000) to calculate interest expense ($4,320). Thus, amortization of a bond premium decreases interest expense.

The payment of interest on the bonds is recorded as follows:

Bond interest expense (+E, −SE)	4,320	
Premium on bonds payable (−L)	680	
Cash (−A)		5,000

Assets	=	Liabilities	+	Stockholders' Equity
Cash −5,000		Premium on bonds −680		Bonds interest expense −4,320

Notice that the $5,000 cash paid each period includes $4,320 interest expense and $680 premium amortization. Thus, the cash payment to investors includes the current interest they have earned plus a return of part of the premium they paid when they bought the bonds.

The book value of the bonds is the amount in the Bonds Payable account plus any unamortized premium. On June 30, 2003, the book value of the bonds is $112,912 ($100,000 + $13,592 − $680).

At maturity, after the last interest payment, the bond premium is fully amortized, and the maturity amount equals the book value of the bonds. On December 31, 2012, the bonds are paid off in full, resulting in the same entry whether the bond was originally sold at par, at a discount, or at a premium. Exhibit 10.2 compares the effects of the amortization of bond discount and bond premium on a $1,000 bond.

SELF-STUDY QUIZ

Assume that Harrah's issued $100,000 bonds that will mature in 10 years. The bonds pay interest twice each year at an annual rate of 9 percent. They were sold when the market rate was 8 percent. Determine the bonds' selling price.

After you have completed your answers, check them with the solution that follows:

$4,500 × 13.5903 = $ 61,156
100,000 × 0.4564 = 45,640
$106,796

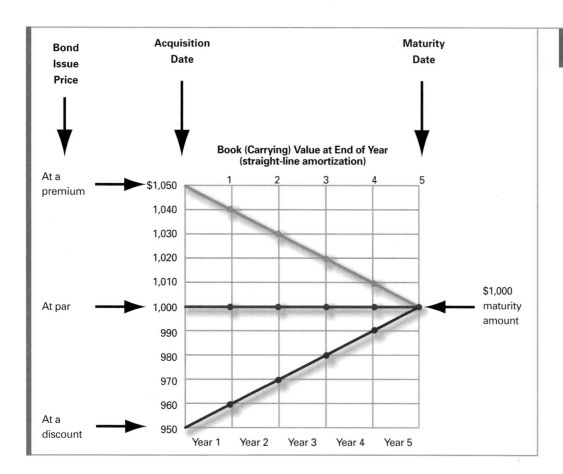

EXHIBIT 10.2

Amortization of Bond Discount and Premium Compared

ADDITIONAL TOPICS

In the following sections, we discuss three additional topics commonly encountered in accounting for bonds payable:

- Effective-interest amortization of bond discounts and premiums.
- Early retirement of debt.
- Report of financing activities on the statement of cash flows.

Effective-Interest Amortization

Earlier in this chapter, we introduced you to the straight-line method for amortizing a bond discount or premium. The only advantage of the straight-line method is the simplicity of its calculation. Under generally accepted accounting principles (GAAP), the straight-line method may be used only if the reported results are not materially different from those of the effective-interest method, a conceptually superior method of amortizing a bond discount or premium. We believe this method provides a better understanding of why the amortization of a bond discount or premium is an adjustment to interest expense.

Interest expense is the cost of borrowing money, which is correctly measured by multiplying the true interest rate times the amount of money actually borrowed. The true interest rate is the rate the market used to determine the present value of the bond when it was issued. The actual amount borrowed is the cash received when the bond was sold plus any accrued but unpaid interest.

Under the **effective-interest method**, interest expense for a bond is computed by multiplying the current unpaid balance (i.e., the amount actually borrowed) times the market rate of interest that existed on the date the bonds were sold. The periodic

Learning Objective 4
Use the effective-interest method of amortization.

The **EFFECTIVE-INTEREST METHOD** amortizes a bond discount or premium on the basis of the effective-interest rate; it is the theoretically preferred method.

amortization of a bond premium or discount is then calculated as the difference between interest expense and the amount of cash paid or accrued.

Effective-Interest Amortization of a Bond Discount

Earlier in this chapter we illustrated accounting for bonds issued at a discount. Let's expand that example to see how the discount is amortized under the effective-interest method. The example involved 10 percent Harrah's bonds with a par value of $100,000, issued when the market rate was 12 percent. The issue price of the bonds was $88,529, and the bond discount was $11,471.

The first interest payment on Harrah's bonds is made on June 30, 2003. The journal entry to record interest expense is similar to the one shown earlier, using the straight-line method. The only difference is the amount. Interest expense at the end of the first six months is calculated by multiplying the amount actually borrowed by the market rate of interest for six months ($88,529 $\times$ 12% $\times$ 6/12 = $5,312). The amount of cash paid is calculated by multiplying the principal by the stated rate of interest for six months ($100,000 $\times$ 10% $\times$ 6/12 = $5,000). The difference between the interest expense and the cash paid (or accrued) is the amount of discount that has been amortized ($5,312 − $5,000 = $312).

Effective-interest amortization causes these amounts to change each period.

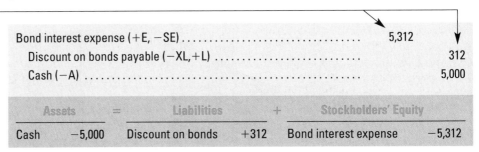

Bond interest expense (+E, −SE)		5,312	
Discount on bonds payable (−XL,+L)			312
Cash (−A)			5,000

Assets	=	Liabilities	+	Stockholders' Equity	
Cash	−5,000	Discount on bonds	+312	Bond interest expense	−5,312

The amortization of the bond discount reduces the balance of the Discount on Bonds Payable account. A reduction of a contra-liability account increases the book value of the liability, as shown:

	January 1, 2003	June 30, 2003
Bonds payable	$100,000	$100,000
Discount on bonds payable	(11,471)	(11,159)*
Book value	$ 88,529	$ 88,841

*$11,471 − $312 = $11,159.

Each period the amortization of the bond discount increases the bond's book value (or unpaid balance). The amortization of bond discount can be thought of as interest earned by the bondholders but not paid to them. During the first six months of 2003, the bondholders earned interest of $5,312 but received only $5,000 in cash. The additional $312 was added to the principal of the bond and will be paid to bondholders when the bond matures.

Interest expense for the second six months of 2003 must reflect the change in the unpaid balance of bonds payable that occurred with amortization of the bond discount. The interest expense for the second half of 2003 is calculated by multiplying the unpaid balance on June 30, 2003, by the market rate of interest for six months ($88,841 $\times$ 12% $\times$ 6/12 = $5,330). Thus amortization of the bond discount in the second period is $330.

Bond interest expense (+E, −SE)		5,330	
Discount on bonds payable (−XL, +L)			330
Cash (−A)			5,000

Assets	=	Liabilities	+	Stockholders' Equity	
Cash	−5,000	Discount on bonds	+330	Bond interest expense	−5,330

Notice that interest expense for the second half of 2003 is more than interest expense for the first six months of 2003. Harrah's effectively borrowed more money during the second half of the year because of the unpaid interest. Because of the amortization of the bond discount, interest expense increases each year during the life of the bond.

Some companies use a bond amortization schedule to assist them with the detailed computations required under the effective-interest amortization method. A typical schedule follows:

Amortization Schedule: Bond Discount

Date	(a) Interest Paid	(b) Interest Expense	(c) Amortization	(d) Book Value
1/1/2003				$88,529
6/30/2003	$5,000	$5,312	$312	88,841
12/31/2003	5,000	5,330	330	89,171

Interest expense (column b) is computed by multiplying the market rate of interest by book value of the bonds at the beginning of the period (column d). Amortization is computed by subtracting cash interest (column a) from interest expense (column b). The book value of the bonds (column d) is computed by adding amortization (column c) to the book value at the beginning of the period.

In summary, under the effective-interest method, interest expense changes each accounting period as the effective amount of the liability changes. Under the straight-line method, interest expense remains constant over the life of the bond. The chart in the margin illustrates these differences.

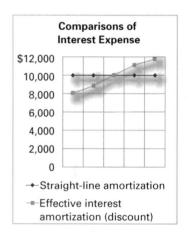

Comparisons of Interest Expense

◆ Straight-line amortization
■ Effective interest amortization (discount)

Effective-Interest Amortization of Bond Premium

The effective-interest method is basically the same for a discount or a premium. In either case, interest expense for a bond is computed by multiplying the current unpaid balance (i.e., the amount actually borrowed) times the market rate of interest on the date the bonds were sold. The periodic amortization of a bond premium or discount is then calculated as the difference between interest expense and the amount of cash paid or accrued. Let's use our earlier example of a bond premium to illustrate the similarity. The example involved 10 percent Harrah's bonds with a par value of $100,000 issued when the market rate was 8 percent. The issue price of the bonds was $113,592, and the bond premium was $13,592.

The first interest payment on Harrah's bonds is made on June 30, 2003. The interest expense at the end of the first six months is calculated by multiplying the amount actually borrowed by the market rate of interest for six months ($113,592 × 8% × 6/12 = $4,544). The amount of cash paid is calculated by multiplying the principal by the stated rate of interest for six months ($100,000 × 10% × 6/12 = $5,000). The difference between the interest expense and the cash paid (or accrued) is the amount of premium that has been amortized ($5,000 − $4,544 = $456).

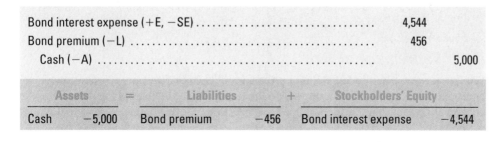

Bond interest expense (+E, −SE)	4,544	
Bond premium (−L)	456	
Cash (−A)		5,000

Assets	=	Liabilities	+	Stockholders' Equity	
Cash	−5,000	Bond premium	−456	Bond interest expense	−4,544

The basic difference between effective-interest amortization of a bond discount and a bond premium is that the amortization of a discount increases the book value of the liability and the amortization of a premium reduces it. An amortization schedule for the first year of this example follows. Compare it to the amortization schedule for a discount shown previously.

Amortization Schedule: Bond Premium

Date	(a) Interest Paid	(b) Interest Expense	(c) Amortization	(d) Book Value
1/1/2003				$113,592
6/30/2003	$5,000	$4,544	$456	113,136
12/31/2003	5,000	4,525	475	112,661

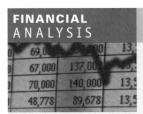

FINANCIAL
ANALYSIS

Understanding Alternative Amortization Methods

Although the effective-interest method is preferred conceptually, some companies use the straight-line method. Under the materiality constraint, accounting for various transactions should conform with GAAP unless the amounts involved are immaterial and will not affect decisions made by statement users. The straight-line method is permitted when the difference in periodic amortization between the two methods is not material in amount. Because differences are often immaterial, most financial statements do not disclose which method the company uses. Harrah's is an exception; it indicates the following in its notes:

REAL WORLD EXCERPT

ENTERTAINMENT, INC.®
ANNUAL REPORT

Summary of Significant Accounting Policies

Original issue discount is amortized over the life of the related indebtedness using the effective interest method.

Compare the note for Harrah's to one from Kansas City Southern Industries:

REAL WORLD EXCERPT

Kansas City Southern
Industries
ANNUAL REPORT

Note 5: Debt

Debt was issued at a discount of $1.6 million which will be amortized over the respective debt maturities on a straight line basis which is not materially different from the interest method.

Learning Objective 5
Report the early retirement of bonds.

Notice that both notes do not provide sufficient information to quantify the impact of using one method versus the other. As a result, most analysts are not concerned about which method a company chooses.

Early Retirement of Debt

Bonds are normally issued for long periods, such as 20 or 30 years. As mentioned earlier, bondholders who need cash prior to the maturity date can simply sell the bonds to another investor. This transaction does not affect the books of the company that issued the bonds.

In several situations, a corporation may decide to retire bonds before their maturity date. A bond with a call feature may be called in for early retirement at the issuer's option. Typically, the bond indenture includes a call premium for bonds retired before the maturity date, which often is stated as a percentage of par value. The prospectus for Harrah's bonds included the following:

REAL WORLD EXCERPT

The Notes are redeemable, in whole or in part, at any time, at our option, at a redemption price equal to the greater of (a) 100% of the principal amount of the Notes then outstanding or (b) the sum of the present values of the remaining scheduled payments of principal and interest thereon discounted at the Treasury Rate, plus .30% interest. . . .

ENTERTAINMENT, INC.

BOND PROSPECTUS

Assume that in 1994, Harrah's issued bonds in the amount of $1 million and that the bonds sold at par. If Harrah's called the bonds in 2003 at 102% of par, the company's accountants would make the following journal entry:

Bonds payable (−L)	1,000,000	
Loss on bond call (+Loss, −SE)	20,000	
Cash (−A)		1,020,000

Assets		=	Liabilities		+	Stockholders' Equity	
Cash	−1,020,000		Bonds payable	−1,000,000		Loss	−20,000

The loss on the bond call is the amount over par that must be paid according to the bond indenture. This loss on the bond call is reported on the income statement as an extraordinary item.

In some cases, a company may elect to retire debt early by purchasing it on the open market, just as an investor would. This approach is necessary when the bonds do not have a call feature. It might also be an attractive approach if the price of the bonds fell after the date of issue. What could cause the price of a bond to fall? The most common cause is a rise in interest rates. As you may have noticed during our discussion of present value concepts, bond prices move in the opposite direction of interest rates. If interest rates go up, bond prices fall, and vice versa. When interest rates have gone up, a company that wants to retire a bond before maturity may find buying the bond on the open market is less expensive than paying a call premium.

SELF-STUDY QUIZ

Which company has a higher level of risk, a company with a high debt-equity ratio and a high interest coverage ratio or a company with a low debt-equity ratio and a low interest coverage ratio?

After you have completed your answer, check it with the solution that follows:

———

A company can be forced into bankruptcy if it does not meet its interest obligations to creditors. Many successful companies borrow very large amounts of money without creating unreasonable risk because they generate sufficient funds from normal operations to meet their obligations. Even a small amount of debt can be a problem if a company does not generate funds to meet current interest obligations. Usually, the company with a high debt-to-equity ratio and a high interest coverage ratio is viewed as being less risky.

Learning Objective 6
Explain how financing activities are reported in the statement of cash flows.

The issuance of a bond payable is reported as a cash inflow from financing activities on the statement of cash flows. The repayment of principal is reported as a cash outflow from financing activities. Many students are surprised to learn that the payment of bond interest is not reported in the Financing Activities section of the statement of cash flows. Interest payments are related directly to the earning of income and are therefore reported in the Cash Flows from Operating Activities section of the statement. Companies are also required to report the amount of cash paid for interest expense each accounting period. *Accounting Trends & Techniques* reports that companies disclose this information in a variety of locations.

EFFECT ON STATEMENT OF CASH FLOWS

In General As we saw in the last chapter, transactions involving short-term creditors (e.g., accounts payable) affect working capital and are therefore reported in the operating activities section of the statement of cash flows. Cash received from long-term creditors is reported as an inflow from financing activities. Cash payments made to long-term creditors (with the exception of interest expense) are reported as outflows from financing activities. Examples are shown in the following table:

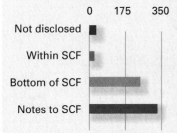

Disclosure of Cash Interest Payments (sample of 600 Companies)

	0	175	350
Not disclosed			
Within SCF			
Bottom of SCF			
Notes to SCF			

	Effect on Cash Flows
Financing activities	
Issuance of bonds	+
Debt retirement	−
Repayment of bond principal upon maturity	−

Focus Company Analysis A segment of Harrah's statement of cash flows follows. Several items pertain to issues discussed in this chapter. The remaining items will be discussed in other chapters. Notice that Harrah's reports both the early extinguishments (retirement) of debt and new borrowings. Although businesses normally borrow money to finance the acquisition of long-lived assets, they also borrow to rearrange their capital structure. In the case of Harrah's, the company had outstanding debt with an interest rate of 9.25 percent. The company was able to retire this debt by borrowing at an interest rate of 7.875 percent, saving the company nearly $8 million in annual interest cost.

Selected Focus Company Comparisons: Cash Flows from Financing Activities (in millions)

General Mills	($102.3)
Outback	(54.7)
Home Depot	737.0

Analysts are particularly interested in the Financing Activities section of the statement of cash flows because it provides important insights about the future capital structure for a company. Rapidly growing companies typically report significant amounts of funds in this section of the statement.

REAL WORLD EXCERPT

ANNUAL REPORT

HARRAH'S ENTERTAINMENT, INC.
Consolidated Statements of Cash Flows
(In Thousands)

	Year Ended December 31,		
	2000	**1999**	**1998**
Cash flows from financing activities			
Net borrowings under lending agreements, net of financing costs of $1,444 and $4,556	503,425	1,105,444	—
Net short-term borrowings	193,550	21,000	—
Proceeds from exercises of stock options	45,150	24,329	2,462
Purchases of treasury stock	(277,607)	(147,952)	—
Early extinguishments of debt	(213,063)	(620,493)	—

Scheduled debt retirements	(3,472)	(5,075)	(563,522)
Premiums paid on early			
extinguishments of debt	(1,104)	(9,278)	(24,569)
Minority interests' distributions,			
net of contributions	(14,003)	(7,122)	(6,200)
Net (repayments) borrowings under			
retired facility, net of financing			
costs of $9,332 in 1998	—	(1,086,000)	362,262
Proceeds from issuance of senior			
notes, net of discount and issue			
costs of $5,980	—	494,020	—
Proceeds from issuance of senior			
subordinated notes, net of issue			
costs of $12,552	—	—	737,448
Other	4,759	—	—
Cash flows provided by (used in)			
financing activities	237,635	(231,127)	507,881

DEMONSTRATION CASE

(Try to answer the questions before proceeding to the suggested solution that follows.) To raise funds to build a new plant, Reed Company's management issued bonds. The bond indenture specified the following:

Par value of the bonds: $100,000.

Date of issue: February 1, 2003; due in 10 years on January 31, 2013.

Interest rate: 12 percent per annum, payable 6 percent on each July 31 and January 31.

All the bonds were sold on February 1, 2003, at 106. The annual accounting period for Reed Company ends on December 31.

Required:

1. How much cash did Reed Company receive from the sale of the bonds payable? Show computations.

2. What was the amount of premium on the bonds payable? Over how many months should it be amortized?

3. Compute the amount of amortization of premium per month and for each six-month interest period, using straight-line amortization. Round your answer to the nearest dollar.

4. Give the journal entry on February 1, 2003, to record the sale and issuance of the bonds payable.

5. Give the journal entry for payment of interest and amortization of premium for the first interest payment on July 31, 2003.

SUGGESTED SOLUTION

1. Sale price of the bonds: $100,000 \times 106\% = \$106,000$.

2. Premium on the bonds payable: $\$106,000 - \$100,000 = \$6,000$.

> Months amortized: From date of sale,
> February 1, 2003, to maturity date, January 31, 2013 = 120 months.

3. Premium amortization: $\$6,000 \div 120$ months $= \$50$ per month, or $300 each six-month interest period (straight-line).

4. February 1, 2003 (issuance date):

Cash (+A)	106,000	
Premium on bonds payable (+L)		6,000
Bonds payable (+L)		100,000
To record sale of bonds payable at 106.		

5. July 31, 2003 (first interest payment date):

Bond interest expense (+E, −SE) ($6,000 − $300)	5,700	
Premium on bonds payable (−L)	300	
Cash (−A) ($100,000 × 6%)		6,000
To record payment of semiannual interest.		

CHAPTER TAKE-AWAYS

1. **Describe the characteristics of bonds and use the debt-to-equity ratio. p. 510**

   Bonds have a number of characteristics designed to meet the needs of both the issuing corporation and the creditor. A complete listing of bond characteristics is discussed in the chapter.

   Corporations use bonds to raise long-term capital. Bonds offer a number of advantages compared to stock, including the ability to earn a higher return for stockholders, the tax deductibility of interest, and the fact that control of the company is not diluted. Bonds do carry additional risk, however, because interest and principal payments are not discretionary.

   The debt-to-equity ratio compares the amount of capital supplied by creditors to the amount supplied by owners. It is a measure of a company's debt capacity. It is an important ratio because of the high risk associated with debt capital that requires obligatory interest and principal payments.

2. **Report bonds payable and interest expense for bonds sold at par, at a discount, and at a premium. p. 514**

   Three types of events must be recorded over the life of a typical bond: (1) the receipt of cash when the bond is first sold, (2) the periodic payment of cash interest, and (3) the repayment of principal upon the maturity of the bond.

   Bonds are sold at a discount whenever the coupon interest rate is less than the market rate of interest. A discount is the dollar amount of the difference between the par value of the bond and its selling price. The discount is recorded as a contra-liability when the bond is sold and is amortized over the life of the bond as an adjustment to interest expense.

   Bonds are sold at a premium whenever the coupon interest rate is more than the market rate of interest. A premium is the dollar amount of the difference between the selling price of the bond and its par value. The premium is recorded as a liability when the bond is sold and is amortized over the life of the bond as an adjustment to interest expense.

3. **Analyze the times interest earned ratio. p. 518**

   This ratio measures a company's ability to meet its interest obligations with resources from its profit-making activities. It is computed by comparing interest expense to earnings (including net income, interest expense, and income tax expense).

4. **Use the effective-interest method of amortization. p. 523**

There are two methods of amortizing bond discounts and premiums, the straight-line method and the effective-interest method. Under the effective-interest method, interest expense is computed by multiplying the current amount of the bond liability by the market rate of interest when the bonds were issued.

5. **Report the early retirement of bonds. p. 526**

A corporation may retire bonds before their maturity date. The difference between the book value and the amount paid to retire the bonds is reported as a gain or loss, depending on the circumstances.

6. **Explain how financing activities are reported on the statement of cash flows. p. 528**

Cash flows associated with transactions involving long-term creditors are reported in the Financing Activities section of the statement of cash flows. Interest expense is reported in the Operating Activities section.

KEY **RATIOS**

Debt-to-equity ratio measures the balance between debt and equity. Debt funds are viewed as being riskier than equity funds. The ratio is computed as follows (p. 514):

$$\text{Debt-to-Equity} = \frac{\text{Total Liabilities}}{\text{Owners' Equity}}$$

Times interest earned ratio measures a company's ability to generate resources from current operations to meet its interest obligations. The ratio is computed as follows (p. 518):

$$\text{Times Interest Earned} = \frac{\text{Net Income} + \text{Interest Expense} + \text{Income Tax Expense}}{\text{Interest Expense}}$$

FINDING **FINANCIAL INFORMATION**

Balance Sheet

Under Current Liabilities

Bonds are normally listed as long-term liabilities. An exception occurs when the bonds are within one year of maturity. Such bonds are reported as current liabilities with the following title:
Current Portion of Long-Term Debt

Under Noncurrent Liabilities

Bonds are listed under a variety of titles, depending on the characteristics of the bond. Titles include
Bonds Payable
Debentures
Convertible Bonds

Statement of Cash Flows

Under Financing Activities

+ Cash inflows from long-term creditors
− Cash outflows to long-term creditors

Under Operating Activities

The cash outflow associated with interest expense is reported as an operating activity.

Income Statement

Bonds are shown only on the balance sheet, never on the income statement. Interest expense associated with bonds is reported on the income statement. Most companies report interest expense in a separate category on the income statement.

Notes

Under Summary of Significant Accounting Policies

Description of pertinent information concerning accounting treatment of liabilities. Normally, there is minimal information. Some companies report the method used to amortize bond discounts and premiums.

Under a Separate Note

Most companies include a separate note called "Long-Term Debt" that reports information about each major debt issue, including amount and interest rate. The note also provides detail concerning debt covenants.

KEY **TERMS**

Bond Certificate p. 513
Bond Discount p. 515
Bond Premium p. 515
Bond Principal p. 512
Callable Bonds p. 512
Convertible Bonds p. 512

Coupon Rate p. 514
Debenture p. 512
Effective-Interest Method p. 523
Effective-Interest Rate p. 515
Face Amount p. 512
Indenture p. 512

Market Interest Rate p. 515
Par Value p. 512
Stated Rate p. 512
Straight-Line Amortization p. 520
Trustee p. 513
Yield p. 515

QUESTIONS

1. What are the primary characteristics of a bond? For what purposes are bonds usually issued?
2. What is the difference between a bond indenture and a bond certificate?
3. Differentiate secured bonds from unsecured bonds.
4. Differentiate between callable and convertible bonds.
5. From the perspective of the issuer, what are some advantages of issuing bonds instead of capital stock?
6. As the tax rate increases, the net cost of borrowing money decreases. Explain.
7. At the date of issuance, bonds are recorded at their current cash equivalent amount. Explain.
8. Explain the nature of the discount and premium on bonds payable.
9. What is the difference between the stated interest rate and the effective-interest rate on a bond?
10. Differentiate among the stated and effective rates of interest on a bond (a) sold at par, (b) sold at a discount, and (c) sold at a premium.
11. What is the book value of a bond payable?
12. Explain the basic difference between the straight-line and effective-interest methods of amortizing bond discount or premium. Explain when each method should or may be used.

MULTIPLE **CHOICE QUESTIONS**

1. Annual interest expense for a single bond issue continues to increase over the life of the bonds. Which of the following explains this?
   a. The market rate of interest has increased since the bonds were sold.
   b. The coupon rate of interest has increased since the bonds were sold.
   c. The bonds were sold at a discount.
   d. The bonds were sold at a premium.
2. Which of the following is not an advantage of issuing bonds when compared to issuing additional shares of stock in order to obtain additional capital?
   a. Stockholders maintain proportionate ownership percentages.
   b. Interest expense reduces taxable income.
   c. Timing flexibility associated with the payment of interest.
   d. All of the above are advantages associated with bonds.
3. Which of the following does not impact the calculation of the cash interest payments to be made to bondholders?
   a. par value of the bond   c. market rate of interest
   b. coupon rate of interest   d. the frequency of the payments
4. Which account would not be included in the debt-to-equity ratio calculation?
   a. Unearned Revenue   c. Income Taxes Payable
   b. Retained Earnings   d. All of the above are included
5. Which of the following is false when a bond is issued at a premium?
   a. The bond will issue for an amount above its par value.
   b. "Bonds payable" will be credited for the par value of the bond.
   c. Interest expense will exceed the cash interest payments.
   d. All of the above are false

6. When the issuing corporation has the right to terminate the relationship with the bondholder early and repay the amount borrowed ahead of schedule, we say that the bond is
   a. convertible
   b. secured
   c. amortizable
   d. callable

7. To determine whether a bond will be sold at a premium, discount, or at face value, one must know which of the following pairs of information?
   a. the par value and the coupon rate on the date the bonds were issued
   b. the par value and the market rate on the date the bonds were issued
   c. the coupon rate and the market rate on the date the bonds were issued
   d. the coupon rate and the stated rate on the date the bonds were issued

8. When using the effective-interest method of amortization, interest expense reported in the income statement is impacted by the
   a. par value of the bonds
   b. coupon rate of interest stated in the bond certificate
   c. market rate of interest on the date the bonds were issued
   d. both (a) and (b)

9. Which of the following would not appear in the Financing section of the statement of cash flows?
   a. cash interest payments to bondholders
   b. principal repayments to bondholders
   c. amounts borrowed from bondholders
   d. all of the above appear in the Financing section

10. When using the effective interest method of amortization, the book value of the bonds changes by what amount on each interest payment date?
    a. interest expense
    b. cash interest payment
    c. amortization
    d. none of the above

For more practice with multiple choice questions, go to our website at www.mhhe.com/libby4e, click on "Student Center" in the upper left menu, click on this chapter's name and number from the list of contents, and then click on "Multiple Choice Quiz" from the menu on the left.

MINI-**EXERCISES**

Finding Financial Information

For each of the following items, specify whether the information would be found in the balance sheet, the income statement, the statement of cash flows, the notes to the statements, or not at all.

1. The amount of a bond liability.
2. Interest expense for the period.
3. Cash interest paid for the period.
4. Interest rates for specific bond issues.
5. The names of major holders of bonds.
6. The maturity date of specific bond issues.

M10-1
LO1, 2

Computing Bond Issuance Price

Coopers Company plans to issue $500,000, 10-year, 10 percent bonds. Interest is payable semiannually each June 30 and December 31. All of the bonds will be sold on January 1, 2003. Determine the issuance price of the bonds, assuming a market yield of 8 percent.

M10-2
LO2

Computing Bond Issuance Price

Waterhouse Company plans to issue $300,000, 10-year, 10 percent bonds. Interest is payable semiannually each June 30 and December 31. All of the bonds will be sold on January 1, 2003. Determine the issuance price of the bonds assuming a market yield of 12 percent.

M10-3
LO2

M10-4
L02

Recording the Issuance of a New Bond and the Payment of Interest (Straight-Line Amortization)

Price Company issued $500,000, 10-year, 8 percent bonds on January 1, 2003. The bonds sold for $545,000. Interest is payable semiannually each June 30 and December 31. Record the sale of the bonds on January 1, 2003, and the payment of interest on June 30, 2003, using straight-line amortization.

M10-5
L02, 4

Recording the Issuance of a New Bond and the Payment of Interest (Effective-Interest Amortization)

IDS Company issued $1,000,000, 10-year, 8 percent bonds on January 1, 2003. The bonds sold for $1,070,000. Interest is payable semiannually each June 30 and December 31. Record the sale of the bonds on January 1, 2003, and the payment of interest on June 30, 2003, using the effective-interest method of amortization. The yield on the bonds is 7 percent.

M10-6
L02

Recording the Issuance of a New Bond and the Payment of Interest (Straight-Line Amortization)

Garland Company issued $600,000, 10-year, 10 percent bonds on January 1, 2003. The bonds sold for $580,000. Interest is payable semiannually each June 30 and December 31. Record the sale of the bonds on January 1, 2003, and the payment of interest on June 30, 2003, using straight-line amortization.

M10-7
L02, 4

Recording the Issuance of a New Bond and the Payment of Interest (Effective-Interest Amortization)

Hopkins Company issued $800,000, 10-year, 10 percent bonds on January 1, 2003. The bonds sold for $753,000. Interest is payable semiannually each June 30 and December 31. Record the sale of the bonds on January 1, 2003, and the payment of interest on June 30, 2003, using effective-interest amortization. The yield on the bonds is 11 percent.

M10-8
L02

Determining Cash Flow Effects

If a company issues a bond at a discount, will interest expense each period be more or less than the cash payment for interest? If another company issues a bond at a premium, will interest expense be more or less than the cash payment for interest? Is your answer to either question affected by the method used to amortize the discount or premium?

M10-9
L05

Determining Financial Statement Effects of an Early Retirement of Debt

If interest rates fell after the issuance of a bond and the company decided to retire the debt, would you expect the company to report a gain or loss on debt retirement? Describe the financial statement effects of a debt retirement under these circumstances.

EXERCISES

E10-1
L01, 2

Lennar Homes

Recording Bonds Based on an Annual Report

Lennar Homes is a nationwide builder of new homes that has constructed more than 140,000 single-family residences since its founding in 1954. The company is currently traded on the New York Stock Exchange. Lennar's annual report contained the following information (in thousands):

	2001	2000	1999
Interest expense	$ 119,503	$ 98,601	$ 48,859
Bonds payable	1,505,255	1,254,650	523,661

Required:

1. Record interest expense using a single journal entry for each year. Assume the bonds were sold at par.
2. Record the issuance of bonds payable, assuming that the full amount was sold during 2001.
3. Recognizing that Lennar is a home builder, why do you think that the amounts of bonds payable increased so much during this period?

Determining Financial Statement Effects for Bond Issue and First Interest Payment with Premium

E10-2
LO1, 2, 3

Grocery Corporation sold a $250,000, 11 percent bond issue on January 1, 2003, at a market rate of 8 percent. The bonds were dated January 1, 2003, with interest to be paid each December 31; they mature 10 years from January 1, 2003.

Required:

1. How are the financial statements affected by the issuance of the bonds? Describe the impact on the debt-to-equity and times interest earned ratios, if any.
2. How are the financial statements affected by the payment of interest on December 31? Describe the impact on the debt-to-equity and times interest earned ratios, if any.
3. Show how the bond interest expense and the bonds payable should be reported on the December 31, 2003, annual financial statements.

Explaining Why Debt Is Sold at a Discount

E10-3
LO2
Apple
Computer

The annual report of Apple Computer, Inc., contained the following note:

> ### Long-Term Debt
>
> On February 10, 1994, the Company issued $300 million aggregate principal amount of its 6.5% unsecured notes. The notes were sold at 99.925% of par, for an effective yield of 6.51%. The notes pay interest semiannually and mature on February 15, 2004.

After reading this note, one student asked why Apple didn't simply sell the notes for an effective yield of 6.5 percent and avoid having to account for a very small discount over the next 10 years. Prepare a written response to this question.

Explaining Bond Terminology

E10-4
LO1, 2
Carnival Cruise
Lines

The balance sheet for Carnival Cruise Lines includes "zero coupon convertible subordinated notes." In your own words, explain the features of this debt. The balance sheet does not report a premium or a discount associated with this debt. Do you think it is recorded at par?

Interpreting Information Reported in the Business Press

E10-5
LO1
AT&T

As this book was being written, the business press reported the following information concerning bonds issued by AT&T:

Bonds	Yield	Close
AT&T 6.5	7.3	89.5

Explain the meaning of the reported information. If you bought AT&T bonds with $10,000 face value, how much would you pay (based on the preceding information reported)? Assume that the bonds were originally sold at par. What impact would the decline in value have on the financial statements for AT&T?

Evaluating Bond Features

E10-6
LO1
PepsiCo, Inc.
The Walt
Disney Company

You are a personal financial planner working with a married couple in their early 40s who have decided to invest $100,000 in corporate bonds. You have found two bonds that you think will interest your clients. One is a zero coupon bond issued by PepsiCo with an effective interest rate of 9 percent and a maturity date of 2015. It is callable at par. The other is a Walt Disney bond that matures in 2093. It has an effective interest rate of 9.5 percent and is callable at 105 percent of par. Which bond would you recommend and why? Would your answer be different if you expected interest rates to fall significantly over the next few years? Would you prefer a different bond if the couple were in their late 60s and retired?

E10-7
L01, 2

Computing the Issue Price of a Bond, with Discussion

Charger Corporation issued a $150,000 bond that matures in five years. The bond has a stated interest rate of 8 percent and pays interest on February 1, May 1, August 1, and November 1. When the bond was issued, the market rate of interest was 12 percent. Record the issuance of the bond on February 1. Also record the payment of interest on May 1 and August 1. Use the straight-line method for amortization of any discount or premium. Explain why someone would buy a bond that did not pay the market rate of interest.

E10-8
L01, 2
The Walt
Disney Co.

Explaining an International Transaction

A recent Walt Disney annual report contained the following note:

> The Company issued Yen 100 billion (approximately $920 million) of Japanese yen bonds through a public offering in Japan. The bonds are senior, unsecured debt obligations of the Company. Interest on the bonds is payable semi-annually at a fixed interest rate of 5% per year through maturity. The bonds provide for principal payments in dollars and interest payments in Japanese yen.

Required:
1. Describe how this bond would be reported on the balance sheet.
2. Explain why management borrowed money in this manner.

E10-9
L01, 3

Analyzing Financial Ratios

You have just started you first job as a financial analyst for a large stock brokerage company. Your boss, a senior analyst, has finished a detailed report evaluating bonds issued by two different companies. She stopped by your desk and asked for help: "I have compared two ratios for the companies and found something interesting." She went on to explain that the debt-to-equity ratio for Applied Technologies, Inc., is much lower than the industry average and that the one for Innovative Solutions, Inc., is much higher. On the other hand, the times interest earned ratio for Applied Technologies is much higher than the industry average, and the ratio for Innovative Solutions is much lower. Your boss then asked you to think about what the ratios indicate about the two companies so that she could include the explanation in her report. How would you respond?

E10-10
L02

Computing the Issue Price of a Bond

Kaizen Corporation issued a $500,000 bond that matures in 10 years. The bond has a stated interest rate of 10 percent. When the bond was issued, the market rate was 10 percent. The bond pays interest twice per year. At what price was the bond issued?

E10-11
L02, 6

Computing the Issue Price of a Bond with Analysis of Income and Cash Flow Effects

Imai Company issued a $1 million bond that matures in five years. The bond has a 10 percent stated rate of interest. When the bond was issued, the market rate was 8 percent. The bond pays interest twice per year on June 30 and December 31. Record the issuance of the bond on June 30. Notice that the company received more than $1 million when it issued the bond. How will this premium affect future income and future cash flows?

E10-12
L02

Computing Issue Prices of Bonds for Three Cases

Thompson Corporation is planning to issue $100,000, five-year, 8 percent bonds. Interest is payable semiannually each June 30 and December 31. All of the bonds will be sold on January 1, 2003; they mature on December 31, 2007.

Required:

1. Compute the issue (sale) price on January 1, 2003, for each of the following independent cases (show computations):

   a. **Case A:** Market (yield) rate, 8 percent.

   b. **Case B:** Market (yield) rate, 6 percent.

   c. **Case C:** Market (yield) rate, 10 percent.

Recording Bond Issue and First Interest Payment with Discount

E10-13

LO2

On January 1, 2003, Seton Corporation sold a $200,000, 8 percent bond issue (9 percent market rate). The bonds were dated January 1, 2003, pay interest each December 31, and mature 10 years from January 1, 2003.

Required:

1. Give the journal entry to record the issuance of the bonds.
2. Give the journal entry to record the interest payment on December 31, 2003. Use straight-line amortization.
3. Show how the bond interest expense and the bonds payable should be reported on the December 31, 2003, annual financial statements.

Recording Bond Issue: Entries for Issuance and Interest

E10-14

LO2

Northland Corporation had $400,000, 10-year coupon bonds outstanding on December 31, 2003 (end of the accounting period). Interest is payable each December 31. The bonds were issued (sold) on January 1, 2003. The 2003 annual financial statements showed the following:

Income statement

Bond interest expense (straight-line amortization) $33,200

Balance sheet

Bonds payable (net liability)   389,200

Required (show computations):

1. What was the issue price of the bonds? Give the journal entry to record the issuance of the bonds.
2. What was the coupon rate on the bonds? Give the entry to record 2003 interest.

Analyzing a Bond Amortization Schedule: Reporting Bonds Payable

E10-15

LO2, 4

Stein Corporation issued a $1,000 bond on January 1, 2003. The bond specified an interest rate of 9 percent payable at the end of each year. The bond matures at the end of 2005. It was sold at a market rate of 11 percent per year. The following spreadsheet was completed:

	Cash Paid	Interest Expense	Amortization	Balance
January 1, 2003				$ 951
End of year 2003	$90	$105	$15	966
End of year 2004	90	106	16	982
End of year 2005	90	108	18	1,000

Required:

1. What was the bond's issue price?
2. Did the bond sell at a discount or a premium? How much was the premium or discount?
3. What amount of cash was paid each year for bond interest?
4. What amount of interest expense should be shown each year on the income statement?
5. What amount(s) should be shown on the balance sheet for bonds payable at each year-end? (For year 2005, show the balance just before retirement of the bond.)
6. What method of amortization was used?
7. Show how the following amounts were computed for year 2004: (a) $90, (b) $106, (c) $16, and (d) $982.
8. Is the method of amortization that was used preferable? Explain why.

E10-16
LO2, 4

Preparing a Debt Payment Schedule with Effective-Interest Method of Amortization and Determining Reported Amounts

Shuttle Company issued a $10,000, three-year, 10 percent bond on January 1, 2003. The bond interest is paid each December 31. The bond was sold to yield 9 percent.

Required:
1. Complete a bond payment schedule. Use the effective-interest method.
2. What amounts will be reported on the financial statements at the end of 2003, 2004, and 2005?

E10-17
LO6

Determining Effects on the Statement of Cash Flows

A number of events over the life of a bond have effects that are reported on the statement of cash flows. For each of the following events, determine whether the event affects the statement of cash flows. If so, describe the impact and specify where on the statement the effect is reported.

1. A $1,000,000 bond is issued at a discount. The reported amount of the bond on the balance sheet is $945,000.
2. At year-end, $50,000 accrued interest is reported and $1,000 of the bond discount is amortized using the straight-line method.
3. Early in the second year, accrued interest is paid. At the same time, $8,000 interest that accrued in the second year is paid.
4. The company elects to retire the debt in the fifth year. At that time, the reported carrying value of the bonds is $960,000 and the company reports a $25,000 gain on the early retirement of debt.

PROBLEMS

P10-1
LO1, 2

Comparing Bonds Issued at Par, Discount, and Premium

Sikes Corporation, whose annual accounting period ends on December 31, issued the following bonds:

Date of bonds: January 1, 2003
Maturity amount and date: $100,000 due in 10 years (December 31, 2012).
Interest: 10 percent per annum payable each December 31.
Date sold: January 1, 2003.
Straight-line amortization is used.

Required:
1. Provide the following amounts to be reported on the December 31, 2003, financial statements:

	Issued at Par Case A	at 96 Case B	at 102 Case C
a. Interest expense.	$	$	$
b. Bonds payable.			
c. Unamortized premium or discount.			
d. Net liability.			
e. Stated rate of interest.			
f. Cash interest paid.			

2. Explain why items *a* and *f* in requirement (1) are different.
3. Assume that you are an investment adviser and a retired person has written to you asking, "Why should I buy a bond at a premium when I can find one at a discount? Isn't that stupid? It's like paying list price for a car instead of negotiating a discount." Write a brief letter in response to the question.

P10-2
LO1, 5

Comparing Carrying Value and Market Value (AP10-1)

The name Hilton is well known in the hotel industry. The Hilton annual report contained the following information concerning long-term debt:

REAL WORLD EXCERPT

Hilton Hotels

ANNUAL REPORT

Long-Term Debt

The estimated current market value of long-term debt is based on the quoted market price for the same or similar issues. The current carrying value for long-term debt is $1,132.5 (million) and the current market value is $1,173.5 (million).

Required:

Explain why there is a difference between the carrying value and the current market value of the long-term debt for Hilton. Assume that Hilton decided to retire all of its long-term debt for cash (a very unlikely event). Prepare the journal entry to record the transaction.

Determining Reported Amounts with Discussion of Management Strategy (AP10-2)

Carter Corporation issued $400,000 in bonds that mature in 10 years. The bonds have a stated interest rate of 6 percent and pay interest on March 1 and September 1. When the bonds were sold, the market rate of interest was 8 percent. Carter uses the effective-interest method. By December 31, 2003, the market rate of interest had increased to 10 percent.

P10-3
LO2, 3, 4

Required:

1. What amount of bond liability is recorded on March 1, 2003?
2. What amount of interest is recorded on September 1, 2003?
3. As a manager of a company, would you prefer the straight-line or effective-interest method?
4. Determine the impact of these transactions at year-end on the debt-to-equity ratio and times interest earned ratio.

Completing Schedule Comparing Bonds Issued at Par, Discount, and Premium (AP10-3)

Quartz Corporation sold a $500,000, 7 percent bond issue on January 1, 2003. The bonds pay interest each December 31 and mature 10 years from January 1, 2003. For comparative study and analysis, assume three separate cases. Use straight-line amortization and disregard income tax unless specifically required. Assume three independent selling scenarios: Case A, bonds sold at par; Case B, bonds sold at 98; Case C, bonds sold at 102.

P10-4
LO2

Required:

1. Complete the following schedule as of December 31, 2003, to analyze the differences among the three cases.

	Case A (Par)	Case B (at 98)	Case C (at 102)
a. Cash received at issue.			
b. Bond interest expense, pretax for 2003.			
c. Bonds payable, 7 percent.			
d. Unamortized discount.			
e. Unamortized premium.			
f. Net liability.			
g. Stated interest rate.			

Recording Bond Issuance and Interest Payments (AP10-4)

West Company issued bonds with the following provisions:

P10-5
LO2

Maturity value: $600,000

Interest: 9 percent per annum payable semiannually each June 30 and December 31.

Terms: Bonds dated January 1, 2003, due five years from that date.

The annual accounting period ends December 31. The bonds were sold on January 1, 2003, at an 8 percent market rate.

Required:

1. Compute the issue (sale) price of the bonds (show computations).
2. Give the journal entry to record the issuance of the bonds.
3. Give the journal entries at the following dates (use straight-line amortization): June 30, 2003; December 31, 2003; and June 30, 2004.
4. How much interest expense would be reported on the income statement for 2003? Show how the liability related to the bonds should be reported on the December 31, 2003, balance sheet.

P10-6

LO2, 4

Completing an Amortization Schedule

Berkley Corporation issued bonds and received cash in full for the issue price. The bonds were dated and issued on January 1, 2003. The stated interest rate was payable at the end of each year. The bonds mature at the end of four years. The following schedule has been completed (amounts in thousands):

Date	Cash	Interest	Amortization	Balance
January 1, 2003				$6,101
End of year 2003	$450	$427	$23	6,078
End of year 2004	450	?	?	6,053
End of year 2005	450	?	?	?
End of year 2006	450	?	?	6,000

Required:

1. Complete the amortization schedule.
2. What was the maturity amount of the bonds?
3. How much cash was received at date of issuance (sale) of the bonds?
4. Was there a premium or a discount? If so, which and how much?
5. How much cash will be disbursed for interest each period and in total for the full life of the bond issue?
6. What method of amortization is being used? Explain.
7. What is the stated rate of interest?
8. What is the effective rate of interest?
9. What amount of interest expense should be reported on the income statement each year?
10. Show how the bonds should be reported on the balance sheet at the end of each year (show the last year immediately before retirement of the bonds).
11. Why is the method of amortization being used preferable to other methods? When must it be used?

P10-7

LO2, 4

Computing Amounts for Bond Issue and Comparing Amortization Methods (AP10-5)

Dektronik Corporation manufactures electrical test equipment. The company's board of directors authorized a bond issue on January 1, 2003, with the following terms:

Maturity (par) value: $800,000
Interest: 8 percent per annum payable each December 31.
Maturity date: December 31, 2007.
Effective-interest rate when sold: 12 percent.

Required:

1. Compute the bond issue price. Explain why both the stated and effective-interest rates are used in this computation.
2. Assume that the company used the straight-line method to amortize the discount on the bond issue. Compute the following amounts for each year (2003–2007):
   a. Cash payment for bond interest.
   b. Amortization of bond discount or premium.
   c. Bond interest expense.
   d. Interest rate indicated (Item *c* ÷ $800,000).
   e. The straight-line rate is theoretically deficient when interest expense, *d*, is related to the net liability (i.e., book value of the debt). Explain.

3. Assume instead that the company used the effective-interest method to amortize the discount. Prepare an effective-interest bond amortization schedule similar to the one in the text. The effective-interest method provides a constant interest rate when interest expense is related to the net liability. Explain by referring to the bond amortization schedule.
4. Which method should the company use to amortize the bond discount? As a financial analyst, would you prefer one method over the other? If so, why?

Explaining Note to a Financial Statement (AP10-6)

Federal Express is a name synonymous with overnight delivery of important packages. The annual report for FedEx contains the following note:

> An agreement was executed to issue $45,000,000 of City of Indianapolis Airport Facility Refunding Bonds. The refunding will be used to retire 11.25% Indianapolis Special Facilities Bonds, Series 1984, which were originally issued in November 1984 to finance the acquisition, construction and equipping of an express sorting hub at the Indianapolis International Airport. The refunding bonds have a maturity date of 2017 and a coupon rate of 6.85%.

P10-8
L05

REAL WORLD EXCERPT

Federal Express
ANNUAL REPORT

Required:
1. In your own words, explain the meaning of this note.
2. Why did management decide to make an early retirement of this debt?

ALTERNATE **PROBLEMS**

Understanding the Difference between Carrying Value and Market Value (P10-2)

Quaker Oats is a well-known name at most breakfast tables. The company does more than $6 billion in sales revenue each year. The Quaker annual report contained the following information concerning long-term debt:

> **Long-Term Debt**
>
> The fair value of long-term debt was $779.7 million at the end of the current fiscal year, which was based on market prices for the same or similar issues or on the current rates offered to the Company for similar debt of the same maturities. The carrying value of long-term debt as of the same date was $759.5 million.

AP10-1
L01, 5

REAL WORLD EXCERPT

Quaker Oats
ANNUAL REPORT

Required:
What is meant by "fair value"? Explain why there is a difference between the carrying value and the fair value of the long-term debt for Quaker Oats. Assume that Quaker Oats decided to retire all of its long-term debt for cash (a very unlikely event). Prepare the journal entry to record the transaction.

Using the Effective-Interest Method with Discussion of Management Strategy (P10-3)

Carter Corporation issued $2,000,000 in bonds that mature in 10 years. The bonds have a stated interest rate of 8 percent and pay interest on March 1 and September 1. When the bonds were sold on March 1, 2003, the market rate of interest was 6 percent. Carter uses the effective-interest method. By December 31, 2003, the market interest rate of interest had increased to 7 percent.

AP10-2
L01, 2, 3, 4

Required:
1. What amount of bond liability is recorded on March 1, 2003?
2. What amount of interest expense is recorded on September 1, 2003?
3. As a manager of a company, would you prefer the straight-line or effective-interest method?

4. Determine the impact of these transactions at year-end on the debt-to-equity ratio and times interest earned ratio.

AP10-3
LO2

Completing a Schedule That Involves a Comprehensive Review of the Issuance of Bonds at Par, Discount, and Premium (P10-4)

On January 1, 2003, Delaware Corporation sold and issued $100,000, five-year, 10 percent bonds. The bond interest is payable annually each December 31. Assume three separate and independent selling scenarios: Case A, at par; Case B, at 90; and Case C, at 110.

Required:

1. Complete a schedule similar to the following for each separate case assuming straight-line amortization of discount and premium. Disregard income tax. Give all dollar amounts in thousands.

	At End of 2003	At End of 2004	At End of 2005	At End of 2006
Case A: sold at par (100)	$	$	$	$
Interest expense on income statement				
Net liability on balance sheet				
Case B: sold at a discount (90)				
Interest expense on income statement				
Net liability on balance sheet				
Case C: sold at a premium (110)				
Interest expense on income statement				
Net liability on balance sheet				

AP10-4
LO2

Computing Issue Price of Bonds and Recording Issuance and Interest Payments (P10-5)

Jacobs Company issued bonds with the following provisions:

Maturity value: $1,000,000

Interest: 8 percent per annum payable semiannually each June 30 and December 31.

Terms: Bonds dated January 1, 2003, due 10 years from that date.

The annual accounting period ends December 31. The bonds were sold on January 1, 2003, at 10 percent market rate.

Required:

1. Compute the issue (sale) price of the bonds (show computations).
2. Give the journal entry to record the issuance of the bonds.
3. Give the journal entries at the following dates (use straight-line amortization): June 30, 2003; December 31, 2003; and June 30, 2004.
4. How much interest expense would be reported on the income statement for 2003? Show how the liability related to the bonds should be reported on the December 31, 2003, balance sheet.

AP10-5
LO2, 4

Straight-Line versus Effective-Interest Methods of Amortizing Bond Discount and Premium with Discussion (P10-7)

United Products Corporation manufactures office equipment and supplies. The company authorized a bond issue on January 1, 2003, with the following terms:

Maturity (par) value: $1,200,000

Interest: 10 percent per annum payable each December 31.

Maturity date: December 31, 2007.

Effective-interest rate when sold: 8 percent.

Required:

1. Compute the bond issue price. Explain why both the stated and effective-interest rates are used in this computation.
2. Assume that the company used the straight-line method to amortize the discount on the bond issue. Compute the following amounts for each year (2003–2007):

    a. Cash payment for bond interest.

    b. Amortization of bond discount or premium.

    c. Bond interest expense.

    d. Interest rate indicated.

    e. The straight-line rate is theoretically deficient when interest expense, *d*, is related to the net liability (i.e., book value of the debt). Explain.

3. Assume instead that the company used the effective-interest method to amortize the discount. Prepare an effective-interest bond amortization schedule similar to the one in the text. The effective-interest method provides a constant interest rate when interest expense is related to the net liability. Explain by referring to the bond amortization schedule.

4. Which method should the company use to amortize the bond discount? As a financial analyst, would you prefer one method over the other? If so, why?

Understanding the Early Retirement of Debt (P10-8)

AP10-6
LO5
AMC Entertainment, Inc.

AMC Entertainment, Inc., owns and operates 243 movie theaters with 1,617 screens in 22 states. On August 12, 1992, the company sold 11 7/8 percent bonds in the amount of $52,720,000 and used the cash proceeds to retire bonds with a coupon rate of 13.6 percent. At that time, the 13.6 percent bonds had a book value of $50,000,000.

Required:

1. Prepare the journal entry to record the early retirement of the 13.6 percent bonds.

2. How should AMC report any gain or loss on this transaction?

3. Why did the company issue new bonds in order to retire the old bonds?

CASES AND **PROJECTS**

Annual Reporting Cases

Finding Financial Information

CP10-1
LO1, 2, 6

AMERICAN EAGLE OUTFITTERS

Refer to the financial statements of American Eagle Outfitters given in Appendix B at the end of this book or open file AEOS.pdf in the Annual Report Cases directory on the student CD-ROM.

Required:

1. How much interest expense was paid in cash during the current fiscal year?

2. Explain why the company does not report bonds payable on its balance sheet.

3. Describe the company's established arrangements, if any, that permit it to borrow money if needed.

Finding Financial Information

CP10-2
LO1, 2, 6

ABERCROMBIE & FITCH

Refer to the financial statements of Abercrombie & Fitch given in Appendix C at the end of this book or open file ANF.pdf in the Annual Report Cases directory on the student CD-ROM.

Required:

1. How much interest expense was paid in cash during the current fiscal year?

2. Explain why the company does not report bonds payable on its balance sheet.

3. Describe the company's established arrangements, if any, that permit it to borrow money if needed.

Comparing Companies within an Industry

CP10-3
LO1, 3

AMERICAN EAGLE OUTFITTERS

Refer to the financial statements of American Eagle Outfitters given in Appendix B, Abercrombie & Fitch given in Appendix C, and the Industry Ratio Report given in Appendix D at the end of this book or open file CP10-3.xls in the Annual Report Cases directory on the student CD-ROM. Most companies report some amounts of bonds payable on their balance sheets. It is somewhat surprising, therefore, that neither American Eagle or Abercrombie & Fitch reports any bond liabilities.

Required:

1. Based on your analysis of the reports and your understanding of the industry, explain why both companies have built these rather unusual capital structures.

2. Two financial ratios (the debt-to-equity ratio and times interest earned) are discussed in this chapter. Are they relevant for these companies? Explain.

Financial Reporting and Analysis Cases

CP10-4

L01

Analyzing the Use of Debt

Cricket Corporation's financial statements for 2003 showed the following:

Income Statement	
Revenues	$300,000
Expenses	(198,000)
Interest expense	(2,000)
Pretax income	100,000
Income tax (30%)	(30,000)
Net income	$ 70,000

Balance Sheet	
Assets	$300,000
Liabilities (average interest rate, 10%)	$ 20,000
Common stock, par $10	200,000
Retained earnings	80,000
	$300,000

Notice in these data that the company had a debt of only $20,000 compared with common stock outstanding of $200,000. A consultant recommended the following: debt, $100,000 (at 10 percent) instead of $20,000 and common stock outstanding of $120,000 (12,000 shares) instead of $200,000 (20,000 shares). That is, the company should finance the business with more debt and less owner contribution.

Required (round to nearest percent):

1. You have been asked to develop a comparison between (a) the actual results and (b) the results had the consultant's recommendation been followed. To do this, you decided to develop the following schedule:

Item	Actual Results for 2003	Results with an $80,000 Increase in Debt
a. Total debt		
b. Total assets		
c. Total stockholders' equity		
d. Interest expense (total at 10 percent)		
e. Net income		
f. Return on total assets		
g. Earnings available to stockholders:		
(1) Amount		
(2) Per share		
(3) Return on stockholders' equity		

2. Based on the completed schedule in requirement (1), provide a comparative analysis and interpretation of the actual results and the recommendation.

CP10-5

L01

JCPenney
Company

Analyzing Zero Coupon Bonds from an Actual Company

JCPenney Company was one of the first companies to issue zero coupon bonds. It issued bonds with a face (maturity) value of $400 million due eight years after issuance. When the bonds were sold to the public, similar bonds paid 15 percent effective interest. An article in *Forbes* magazine discussed the JCPenney bonds and stated: "It's easy to see why corporations like to sell bonds that don't pay interest. But why would anybody want to buy that kind of paper [bond]?"

Required:

1. Explain why an investor would buy a JCPenney bond with a zero interest rate.
2. If investors could earn 15 percent on similar investments, how much did JCPenney receive when it issued the bonds with a face value of $400 million?

Explaining Bond Premiums and Effective-Interest Rate Amortization

CP10-6
LO4

Times Company issued a $100,000 bond with a stated interest rate of 8 percent. When the bond was issued, the market rate was 6 percent. The bond matures in 10 years and pays interest on December 31 each year. The bond was issued on January 1, 2003.

Required:

1. Compute the present value of the difference between the interest paid each year ($8,000) and the interest demanded by the market ($100,000 × 6% = $6,000). Use the market rate of interest and the 10-year life of the bond in your present value computation. Discuss what this demonstrates.
2. Why does interest expense change each year when the effective-interest method is used?
3. Compute the present value of the Times Company bonds, assuming that they had a 7-year life instead of 10-year life. Compare this amount to the book value of the bond at the end of year 2005. What does this comparison demonstrate?

Interpreting the Financial Press

CP10-7
LO1

In this chapter, we talked about bonds primarily from the perspective of the issuing corporation. To understand bonds, it is also necessary to develop an understanding of why investors buy bonds. An article on this topic is available on the Libby/Libby/Short website at www.mhhe.com/libby4e. You should read the article, "It's Time for Bonds to Get Some Respect,"* January 19, 1998, and then write a short memo summarizing the article in your own words. What type of investors are interested in buying bonds? Describe the impact of inflation on bonds.

Critical Thinking Cases

Making a Decision as a Financial Analyst

CP10-8
LO1

You are working for a large mutual fund company as a financial analyst. You have been asked to review two competitive companies in the same industry. Both have similar cash flows and net income, but one has no debt in its capital structure and the other has a debt-to-equity ratio of 3.2. Based on this limited information, which would you prefer? Justify your conclusion. Would your preference be influenced by the companies' industry?

Evaluating an Ethical Dilemma

CP10-9
LO1

You work for a small company considering investing in a new Internet business. Financial projections suggest that the company will be able to earn in excess of $40 million per year on an investment of $100 million. The company president suggests borrowing the money by issuing bonds that will carry a 7 percent interest rate. He says, "This is better than printing money! We won't have to invest a penny of our own money, and we get to keep $33 million per year after we pay interest to the bondholders." As you think about the proposed transaction, you feel a little uncomfortable about taking advantage of the creditors in this fashion. You feel that it must be wrong to earn such a high return by using money that belongs to other people. Is this an ethical business transaction?

Evaluating an Ethical Dilemma

CP10-10
LO1

Many retired people invest a significant portion of their money in bonds of corporations because of their relatively low level of risk. During the 1980s, significant inflation caused some interest rates to rise to as high as 15 percent. Retired people who bought bonds that paid only 6 percent continued to earn at the lower rate. During the 1990s, inflation subsided and interest rates declined. Many corporations took advantage of call options on bonds and refinanced high interest rate debt with low interest

---

*"It's Time for Bonds to Get Some Respect," Reprinted from January 19, 1998 issue of *Business Week* by special permission, copyright ©1998 by The McGraw-Hill Companies, Inc.

rate debt. In your judgment, is it ethical for corporations to continue paying low interest rates when rates increase but to call bonds when rates decrease?

CP10-11 Evaluating an Ethical Dilemma
LO1

Assume that you are a portfolio manager for a large insurance company. The majority of the money you manage is from retired school teachers who depend on the income you earn on their investments. You have invested a significant amount of money in the bonds of a large corporation and have just received a call from the company's president explaining that it is unable to meet its current interest obligations because of deteriorating business operations related to increased international competition. The president has a recovery plan that will take at least two years. During that time, the company will not be able to pay interest on the bonds and, she admits, if the plan does not work, bondholders will probably lose more than half of their money. As a creditor, you can force the company into immediate bankruptcy and probably get back at least 90 percent of the bondholders' money. You also know that your decision will cause at least 10,000 people to lose their jobs if the company ceases operations. Given only these two options, what should you do?

CP10-12 Analyzing Risk and Return
LO1

As explained in the chapter, the use of debt offers shareholders the opportunity to earn higher returns, but it also creates higher risk. Different individuals have different preferences for risk and return, so determining the optimal balance of risk and return is not an easy matter. To illustrate the problem, conduct the following exercise in a small group.

You are offered the opportunity to participate in one of the following lotteries that require an investment of $10,000:

1. There is a 100 percent probability that you will get back $10,500 at the end of one year.
2. There is a 50 percent probability that you will get back $10,000 at the end of one year and a 50 percent probability that you will get $12,000.
3. There is a 50 percent probability that you will get back $8,000 at the end of one year and a 50 percent probability that you will get $16,000.

Determine which of the three lotteries you prefer and then attempt to reach a group consensus as to which lottery the group will accept.

Financial Reporting and Analysis Team Project

CP10-13 Team Project: Examining an Annual Report
LO1, 2, 3, 6

As a team, select an industry to analyze. Each group member should acquire the annual report or 10-K for one publicly traded company in the industry, with each member selecting a different company. (Library files, the SEC EDGAR service at www.sec.gov, Compustat CD, and the company itself are good sources.) On an individual basis, each team member should then write a short report answering the following questions about his or her selected company.

1. Review the types of bonds issued by the company. Do you observe any unusual features?
2. Compute and analyze the debt-to-equity and times interest earned ratios.
3. Review the statement of cash flows. Has the company either issued or repaid money associated with a bond? If so, can you determine the reason?
4. Has the company issued bonds denominated in a foreign currency? Can you determine why?
5. Were bonds issued at either a premium or a discount? If so, does the company use the straight-line or effective-interest amortization method?

Discuss any patterns across the companies that you as a team observe. Then, as a team, write a short report comparing and contrasting your companies using these attributes. Provide potential explanations for any differences discovered.

After studying this chapter, you should be able to:

1. Explain the role of stock in the capital structure of a corporation. p. 552

2. Analyze the earnings per share ratio. p. 554

3. Describe the characteristics of common stock and analyze transactions affecting common stock. p. 555

4. Discuss dividends and analyze transactions. p. 559

5. Analyze the dividend yield ratio. p. 559

6. Discuss the purpose of stock dividends, stock splits, and report transactions. p. 562

7. Describe the characteristics of preferred stock and analyze transactions affecting preferred stock. p. 564

8. Discuss the impact of capital stock transactions on cash flows. p. 566

Reporting and Interpreting Owners' Equity

I n the early 1990s, Outback Steakhouse was a privately owned company with bold growth plans. To finance the company's growth, management recognized the need to raise large amounts of new capital. Outback would have to "go public," allowing the company's stock to be traded on a major stock exchange. In June 1991, Outback's stock was first sold to the public.

Outback's initial growth strategy has since become a reality. Today, there are more than 660 Outback restaurants as well as more than 100 others operated under different names. Company revenues have grown to exceed $2 billion in food and beverage sales. Still growing at a pace of 50 new restaurants a year, Outback plans to expand internationally in countries such as Japan, Portugal, China, Australia, Malaysia, Bahrain, and Korea.

Investors who bought Outback's stock when it first went public have benefited from its rapid growth. If you had invested $10,000 in the company in 1991, your stock would be worth $135,000 today. To achieve this level of success, Outback's management needed to develop and execute a sound business strategy. Equally important, however, was management's ability to develop a solid capital structure with which to finance the company's growth. In this chapter, we study the role that stockholders' equity plays in building a successful business.

FOCUS COMPANY:

Outback Steakhouse

FINANCING

CORPORATE

GROWTH WITH

CAPITAL SUPPLIED

BY OWNERS

www.outback.com

UNDERSTANDING THE BUSINESS

To some people, the words *corporation* and *business* are almost synonymous. You've probably heard friends refer to a career in business as "the corporate world." Equating business with corporations is understandable because corporations are the dominant form of business organization in terms of volume of operations. If you were to write the names of 50 familiar companies on a piece of paper, probably all of them would be corporations.

The popularity of the corporate form can be attributed to a critical advantage that corporations have over sole proprietorships and partnerships: They can raise large amounts of capital because both large and small investors can easily participate in their owner-ship. This ease of participation is related to several factors.

Percent of Americans Who Own Common Stock

- Shares of stock can be purchased in small amounts. You could buy a single share of Outback stock for less than $30 and become one of the owners of this successful company.
- Ownership interests can easily be transferred through the sale of shares on established markets such as the New York Stock Exchange.
- Stock ownership provides investors with limited liability.*

Many Americans own stock either directly or indirectly through a mutual fund or pension program. Stock ownership offers them the opportunity to earn higher returns than they could on deposits to bank accounts or investments in corporate bonds. Unfortunately, stock ownership also involves higher risk. The proper balance between risk and the expected return on an investment depends on individual preferences.

Exhibit 11.1 presents financial information from Outback's annual report. Notice that the stockholders' equity section of the balance sheet lists two primary sources of stockholders' equity:

1. **Contributed capital** from the sale of stock. This is the amount of money stockholders invested through the purchase of shares.
2. **Retained earnings** generated by the company's profit-making activities. This is the cumulative amount of net income the corporation has earned since its organization less the cumulative amount of dividends paid since organization.

Most companies generate a significant portion of their stockholders' equity from retained earnings. In the case of Outback, retained earnings represents nearly 80 percent of the company's total stockholders' equity.

ORGANIZATION of the Chapter

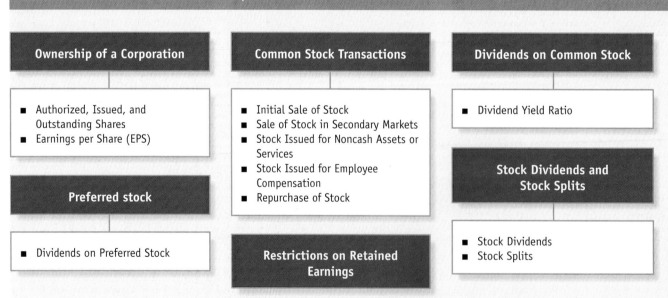

Ownership of a Corporation	Common Stock Transactions	Dividends on Common Stock
■ Authorized, Issued, and Outstanding Shares ■ Earnings per Share (EPS)	■ Initial Sale of Stock ■ Sale of Stock in Secondary Markets ■ Stock Issued for Noncash Assets or Services ■ Stock Issued for Employee Compensation ■ Repurchase of Stock	■ Dividend Yield Ratio

Preferred stock

- Dividends on Preferred Stock

Restrictions on Retained Earnings

Stock Dividends and Stock Splits

- Stock Dividends
- Stock Splits

*If a corporation becomes insolvent, creditors have recourse for their claims only to the corporation's assets. Thus, stockholders stand to lose only their equity in the corporation. In the case of a partnership or sole proprietorship, creditors have recourse to the owners' personal assets if the assets of the business are insufficient to meet its debts.

CONSOLIDATED BALANCE SHEETS
(in thousands)

	December 31, 2000	December 31, 1999
STOCKHOLDERS' EQUITY		
Common stock, $0.01 par value, 200,000 shares authorized; 78,514 and 77,519 shares issued; and 76,632 and 77,404 outstanding as of December 31, 2000 and 1999, respectively	785	775
Additional paid-in capital	214,541	194,251
Retained earnings	638,383	501,384
	853,709	696,410
Less treasury stock, 1,882 shares and 115 shares at December 31, 2000 and 1999, respectively, at cost	(46,119)	(3,445)
Total stockholders' equity	807,590	692,965

CONSOLIDATED STATEMENTS OF STOCKHOLDERS' EQUITY
(in thousands)

	Common Stock Shares	Common Stock Amount	Additional Paid-In Capital	Retained Earnings	Treasury Stock	Total
Balance, December 31, 1997	75,028	$762	$157,903	$292,617	$(13,900)	$437,382
Issuance of common stock	946	9	19,112			19,121
Distributions				(2,639)		(2,639)
Purchase of treasury stock	(300)				(6,345)	(6,345)
Reissuance of treasury stock	544		719	(5,266)	9,420	4,873
Net income				96,048		96,048
Balance, December 31, 1998	76,218	771	177,734	380,760	(10,825)	548,440
Issuance of common stock	442	4	16,230			16,234
Distributions				(2,522)		(2,522)
Purchase of treasury stock	(239)				(7,230)	(7,230)
Reissuance of treasury stock	983		287	(1,177)	14,610	13,720
Net income				124,323		124,323
Balance, December 31, 1999	77,404	775	194,251	501,384	(3,445)	692,965
Issuance of common stock	995	10	20,290			20,300
Purchase of treasury stock	(1,980)				(48,615)	(48,615)
Reissuance of treasury stock	213			(4,131)	5,941	1,810
Net income				141,130		141,130
Balance, December 31, 2000	76,632	$ 785	$214,541	$638,383	$(46,119)	$807,590

EXHIBIT 11.1

Excerpt from Consolidated Balance Sheets and Statements of Stockholders' Equity for Outback Steakhouse

REAL WORLD EXCERPT

NO RULES. JUST RIGHT.®

ANNUAL REPORT

OWNERSHIP OF A CORPORATION

The corporation is the only business form the law recognizes as a separate entity. As a distinct entity, the corporation enjoys a continuous existence separate and apart from its owners. It may own assets, incur liabilities, expand and contract in size, sue others, be sued, and enter into contracts independently of its stockholder owners.

To protect everyone's rights, the creation and governance of corporations are tightly regulated by law. Corporations are created by application to a state government (not the federal government). On approval of the application, the state issues a charter, sometimes called the *articles of incorporation.* Corporations are governed by a board of directors elected by the stockholders.

Each state has different laws governing the organization of corporations created within its boundaries. Although Outback has its headquarters in Florida, it elected to incorporate in the state of Delaware. You will find that an unusually large number of corporations were incorporated in Delaware. The reason is simple: That state has some of the most favorable laws for establishing corporations.

Benefits of Stock Ownership

Learning Objective 1
Explain the role of stock in the capital structure of a corporation.

When you invest in a corporation, you are known as a *stockholder* or *shareholder.* As a stockholder, you receive shares of stock that you subsequently can sell on established stock exchanges. Owners of common stock receive a number of benefits:

- **A voice in management.** You may vote in the stockholders' meeting on major issues concerning management of the corporation.
- **Dividends.** You receive a proportional share of the distribution of profits.
- **Residual claim.** You will receive a proportional share of the distribution of remaining assets upon the liquidation of the company.

Owners, unlike creditors, are able to vote at the annual stockholders' meeting, with a number of votes equal to the number of shares owned. The following Notice of Annual Meeting of Shareholders was recently sent to all owners of Outback stock:

REAL WORLD EXCERPT

NO RULES. JUST RIGHT.®

NOTICE OF
SHAREHOLDERS' MEETING

NOTICE OF ANNUAL MEETING OF STOCKHOLDERS

Notice is hereby given that the Annual Meeting of Stockholders of OUTBACK STEAKHOUSE, INC. (the "Company") will be held at the Tampa Bay Performing Arts Center Morsani Hall, 1010 MacInnes Place North, Tampa, Florida 33602, on Wednesday, April 25 at 10:00 A.M., Tampa time, for the following purposes:

1. To elect five directors, each to serve for a term of three years and until his or her successor is duly elected and qualified; and

2. To transact such other business as may properly come before the meeting.

Only stockholders of record at the close of business on March 1 are entitled to notice of and to vote at the meeting or any adjournment or postponement of the meeting.

This notice also contained several pages of information concerning the people who were nominated to be members of the board of directors as well as a variety of financial information. Since most owners do not actually attend the annual meeting, the notice included a proxy card, similar to an absentee ballot. Owners may complete the proxy and mail it to the company, which will include it in the votes at the annual meeting.

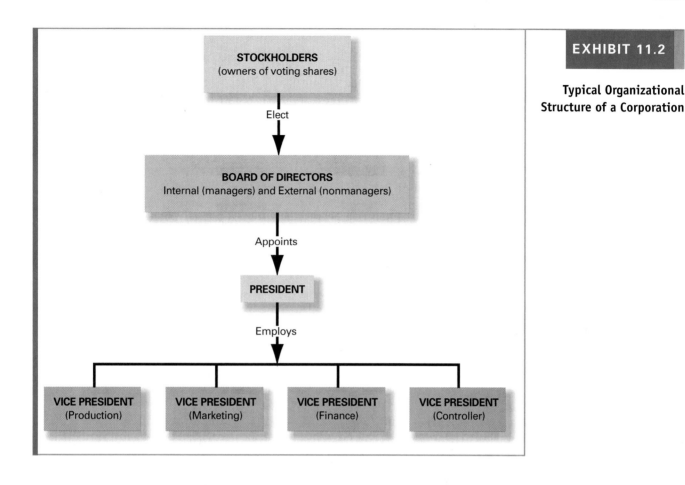

EXHIBIT 11.2

Typical Organizational Structure of a Corporation

As shown in Exhibit 11.2, stockholders have ultimate authority in a corporation. The board of directors and, indirectly, all the employees are accountable to the stockholders. The organizational structure shown is typical of most corporations, but the specific structure depends on the nature of the company's business.

Authorized, Issued, and Outstanding Shares

The corporate charter specifies the maximum number of shares that can be sold to the public. The financial statements must report information concerning the number of shares that have been sold to date. Let's look at the share information reported by Outback as of December 31, 2000, shown in Exhibit 11.1. For Outback, the maximum number of shares that can be sold, called the **authorized number of shares,** is 200,000 (thousand). As of December 31, 2000, the company had sold 78,514 (thousand) shares. Stock that has been sold to the public is called **issued shares.**

For a number of reasons, a company might want to buy back stock that has already been sold to the public. Stock that has been bought back is called *treasury stock.* When a company buys back its stock, a difference is created between the number of issued shares and the number of **outstanding shares**, or shares currently held by individual stockholders. We can compute outstanding shares for Outback using data from the December 31, 2000, balance sheet shown in Exhibit 11.1 (in thousands):

Issued Shares	78,514
Less: Treasury Stock	(1,882)
Outstanding Shares	76,632

The **AUTHORIZED NUMBER OF SHARES** is the maximum number of shares of a corporation's capital stock that can be issued as specified in the charter.

ISSUED SHARES represent the total number of shares of stock that have been sold.

OUTSTANDING SHARES refer to the total number of shares of stock that are owned by stockholders on any particular date.

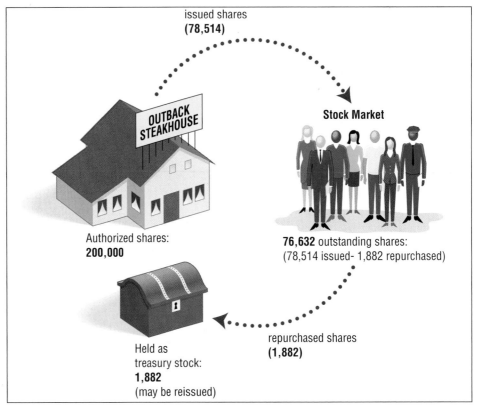

Notice that when treasury stock is held, the number of shares issued and the number of shares outstanding differ by the number of shares of treasury stock held (treasury stock is included in "issued" but not in "outstanding"). The number of shares outstanding is important to financial analysts who need to express certain dollar amounts on a per share basis. One example is the earnings per share ratio.

KEY RATIO ANALYSIS

Earnings per Share (EPS)

Learning Objective 2
Analyze the earnings per share ratio.

❓ ANALYTICAL QUESTION:

How profitable is a company?

% RATIO AND COMPARISONS

Earnings per share is computed as follows:

Earnings per Share = Income ÷ Average Number of Common Shares Outstanding

The 2000 ratio for Outback Steakhouse:

$$\$141 \text{ million} \div 77.5 \text{ million shares}^* = \$1.82$$

*As reported in the notes to the financial statements

COMPARISONS OVER TIME			COMPARISONS WITH COMPETITORS	
Outback			Ruby Tuesday	Wendy's
1998	1999	2000	2000	2000
$1.25	$1.59	$1.82	$1.44	$0.91

💡 INTERPRETATIONS

In General All analysts and investors are interested in a company's earnings. You have probably seen newspaper headlines announcing a company's earnings. Notice that those news stories normally report earnings on an earnings per share (EPS) basis. The reason is simple: numbers are much easier to compare on a per share basis. For example, in 2000, Outback earned income of $141,130,000 compared to $124,323,000 in the previous year. If we make that comparison on a per share basis, we can say that EPS increased from $1.59 to $1.82. EPS is also useful in comparing companies of different sizes. Ruby Tuesday, a smaller company than Outback, earned $59,200,000 in 2000. While net income for Ruby Tuesday is only 42 percent of the income earned by Outback, EPS for Ruby Tuesday is 79 percent of the EPS for Outback because Ruby Tuesday has fewer stockholders.

Focus Company Analysis   Outback has a strategy of rapid growth and reinvestment of earnings. Analysts are watching EPS to be sure the company will achieve its strategy. Outback's EPS increased by more than 45 percent between 1998 and 2000, a strong level of growth. In comparison, Ruby Tuesday's EPS increased by a greater percentage during the same period, and its stock price rose more rapidly than did Outback's.

A Few Cautions   While EPS is an effective and widely used measure of profitability, it can be misleading if there are significant differences in the market values of the shares being compared. Two companies earning $1.50 per share might appear to be comparable, but if shares in one company cost $10 while shares of the other cost $175, they are not comparable.

Common Stock Transactions

Most corporations issue two types of stock, common stock and preferred stock. All corporations must issue common stock while only some issue preferred stock. In this section, we discuss common stock and in a subsequent section, we discuss preferred stock.

Common stock is held by individuals who are often thought of as the "owners" of the corporation because they have the right to vote and share in the profitability of the business through dividends. The dividend rate for common stock is determined by the board of directors based on the company's profitability.

The fact that common stock dividends may increase with increases in the company's profitability helps to explain why investors can make money in the stock market. Basically, you can think of the price of a share of stock as the present value of all its future dividends. If a company's profitability improves so that it can pay higher dividends, the present value of its common stock will increase.

Common stock normally has a **par value,** a nominal value per share established in the corporate charter. Par value has no relationship to the market value of a stock. The notes to Outback's annual report state that their common stock has a par value of $0.01 while its market value is more than $25 per share.

Most states require stock to have a par value. The original purpose of this requirement was to protect creditors by specifying a permanent amount of capital that owners could not withdraw before a bankruptcy which would leave creditors with an empty corporate shell. This permanent amount of capital is called **legal capital**. Today, this requirement has little importance because of other contractual protections for creditors.

Some states require the issuance of **no-par value stock**, which does not have a specified amount per share. When a corporation issues no-par stock, legal capital is as defined by the state law.

Initial Sale of Stock

Two names are applied to transactions involving the initial sale of a company's stock to the public. An **initial public offering,** or IPO, involves the very first sale of a company's stock to the public (i.e., when the company first "goes public"). You have probably heard stories of Internet stocks that have increased dramatically in value the day of the IPO. While investors sometimes earn significant returns on IPOs, they also take significant risks. Once a company's stock has been traded on established markets, additional sales of new stock to the public are called **seasoned new issues.**

Learning Objective 3
Describe the characteristics of common stock and analyze transactions affecting common stock.

COMMON STOCK is the basic voting stock issued by a corporation.

PAR VALUE is the nominal value per share of capital stock specified in the charter; serves as the basis for legal capital.

LEGAL CAPITAL is the permanent amount of capital defined by state law that must remain invested in the business; serves as a cushion for creditors.

NO-PAR VALUE STOCK is capital stock that has no par value specified in the corporate charter.

Topic Tackler 11-1

Most sales of stock to the public are cash transactions. To illustrate the accounting for an initial sale of stock, assume that Outback sold 100,000 shares of its $0.01 par value stock for $22 per share. The company records the following journal entry:

Cash (+A) (100,000 × $22) 2,200,000
    Common stock (+SE) (100,000 × $0.01)   1,000
    Capital in excess of par value (+SE)   2,199,000

Assets	=	Liabilities	+	Stockholders' Equity	
Cash	+2,200,000			Common stock	+1,000
				Capital in excess of par	+2,199,000

Notice that the common stock account is credited for the number of shares sold times the par value per share, and the capital in excess of par value account is credited for the remainder. If the corporate charter does not specify a par value for the stock, the stated value is used in the same manner that par value is used. If there is no par or stated value, the amount of entire proceeds from the sale will be entered in the common stock account.

Sale of Stock in Secondary Markets

When a company sells stock to the public, the transaction is between the issuing corporation and the buyer. Subsequent to the initial sale, investors can sell shares to other investors without directly affecting the corporation. For example, if investor Jon Drago sold 1,000 shares of Outback stock to Jennifer Lea, Outback would not record a journal entry on its books. Mr. Drago received cash for the shares he sold, and Ms. Lea received stock for the cash she paid. Outback did not receive or pay anything.

Each business day, *The Wall Street Journal* reports the results of thousands of transactions between investors in secondary markets, such as the New York Stock Exchange (NYSE), the American Stock Exchange (AMEX), and the NASDAQ market. Managers of corporations closely follow the price movements of their company's stock. Stockholders expect to earn money on their investments through both dividends and increases in the stock price. In many instances, senior management has been replaced because of a stock's poor performance in the stock market. While managers watch the stock price on a daily basis, transactions between investors do not directly affect the company's financial statements.

Stock Issued for Noncash Assets or Services

Small companies are playing an increasingly important role in the U.S. economy. They created a large percentage of the new jobs in the United States in recent years. Indeed, many of today's corporate giants were small start-up companies just a few years ago. Companies such as Dell Computers, Microsoft, and Apple Computer began literally as basement operations in the homes of their founders.

One feature common to all start-up companies is a shortage of cash. Because these companies often cannot afford to pay cash for needed assets and services, they sometimes give stock in lieu of paying cash. Many executives, for instance, will join start-up companies at very low salaries because they will also earn shares of stock. An executive who received Microsoft or Amazon.com stock during its early days would be very wealthy today.

When a company issues stock to acquire noncash assets or services, the acquired items are recorded at the market value of the stock at the date of the transaction in accordance with the cost principle. If the market value of the stock cannot be determined, the market value of the assets or services received should be used. To illustrate, assume that during its early years, Outback was unable to pay cash for legal services. Instead, the company issued 10,000 shares of stock to the Rose law firm when the stock was selling for $15 per share. At that time, the company recorded the following journal entry:

Legal fees (+E, −SE)	150,000	
Common stock (+SE) (10,000 × $0.01)		100
Capital in excess of par value (+SE)		149,900

Assets	=	Liabilities	+	Stockholders' Equity	
				Legal fees	−150,000
				Common stock	+100
				Capital in excess of par	+149,900

Notice that the value of the legal services received is assumed to be the same as the market value of the stock. This assumption is reasonable because two independent parties usually keep negotiating until the value of what is given up equals the value of what is received.

Stock Issued for Employee Compensation

One of the advantages of the corporate form is the ability to separate the management of a business from its ownership. Separation can also be a disadvantage because some managers may not act in the owners' best interests. This problem can be overcome in a number of ways. Compensation packages can be developed to reward managers for meeting goals that are important to stockholders. Another strategy is to offer managers stock options, which permit them to buy stock at a fixed price.

The holder of a stock option has an interest in a company's performance just as an owner does. Stock option plans have become an increasingly common form of compensation over the past few years. Indeed, 98 percent of the companies surveyed by *Accounting Trends & Techniques* now offer stock option plans to their employees.

Outback's annual report contains the following note:

11. Stock Option and Other Benefit Plans

The purpose of the Stock Option Plan is to attract competent personnel, to provide long-term incentives to Directors and key employees, and to discourage employees from competing with the Company.

As of December 31, 2000, the Company had granted to employees of the Company a cumulative total of approximately 19,769,000 options to purchase the Company's Common Stock at prices ranging from $0.19 to $38.33 per share which was the estimated fair market value at the time of each grant.

REAL WORLD EXCERPT

ANNUAL REPORT

The options Outback issued specified that shares could be bought at the then current market price. Granting a stock option is a form of compensation, even if the grant price and the current stock price are the same. You can think of a stock option as a risk-free investment. If you hold a stock option and the stock price declines, you have lost nothing. If the stock price increases, you can exercise your option at the low grant price and sell the stock at the higher price for a profit.

REPURCHASE OF STOCK

A corporation may want to repurchase its stock from existing stockholders for a number of reasons. One common reason is the existence of an employee bonus plan that provides workers with shares of the company's stock as part of their compensation. Because of Securities and Exchange Commission regulations concerning newly issued shares, most companies find it less costly to give employees repurchased shares than to issue new ones. Stock that has been reacquired and held by the issuing corporation is called **treasury stock**. These shares have no voting, dividend, or other stockholder rights while held as treasury stock.

Most companies record the purchase of treasury stock based on the cost of the shares that were purchased. Assume that Outback bought 100,000 shares of its stock in the open market when it was selling for $20 per share. Using the cost method, the company would record the following journal entry:

Treasury stock (+XSE, −SE) (100,000 × $20)	2,000,000	
Cash (−A)		2,000,000

Assets	=	Liabilities	+	Stockholders' Equity	
Cash −2,000,000				Treasury stock −2,000,000	

TREASURY STOCK is a corporation's own stock that had been issued but was subsequently reacquired and is still being held by that corporation.

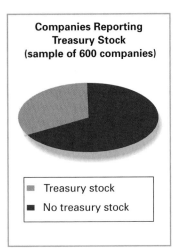

Companies Reporting Treasury Stock (sample of 600 companies)

■ Treasury stock
■ No treasury stock

Intuitively, many students expect the Treasury Stock account to be reported as an asset. Such is not the case because a company cannot create an asset by investing in itself. The Treasury Stock account is actually a contra-equity account, which means that it is subtracted from total stockholders' equity. This practice makes sense because treasury stock is stock that is no longer outstanding and therefore should not be included in stockholders' equity.

As the information in Exhibit 11.1 indicates, Outback reported treasury stock in the amount of $46,119 (thousand) on its balance sheet as of December 31, 2000. The statement of stockholders' equity reports the same amount plus additional information.

When a company sells its treasury stock, it does not report an accounting profit or loss on the transaction, even if it sells the stock for more or less than it paid. GAAP do not permit a corporation to report income or losses from investments in its own stock because transactions with the owners are not considered normal profit-making activities. Based on the previous example, assume that Outback resold 10,000 shares of treasury stock for $30 per share. Remember that the company had purchased the stock for $20 per share. Outback would record the following journal entry:

Cash (+A) (10,000 × $30)	300,000	
Treasury stock (−XSE, +SE) (10,000 × $20)		200,000
Capital in excess of par (+SE)		100,000

Assets	=	Liabilities	+	Stockholders' Equity	
Cash +300,000				Treasury stock +200,000	
				Capital in excess of par +100,000	

While most companies credit Capital in Excess of Par when recording treasury stock, some companies set up a separate account called Capital from Treasury Stock Transactions.

If treasury stock were sold at a price below its purchase price (i.e., at an economic loss), stockholders' equity would be reduced by the amount of the difference between purchase price and the sale price. Notice that this is the case in the Outback statement of stockholders' equity.

1. Assume that Applied Technology Corporation issued 10,000 shares of its common stock, par value $2, for $150,000 cash. Prepare the journal entry to record this transaction.

2. Assume that Applied Technology repurchased 5,000 shares of its stock in the open market when the stock was selling for $12 per share. Record this transaction using the cost method.

After you have completed your answers, check them with the solutions that follow:

1.	Cash	150,000	
	Common stock		20,000
	Capital in excess of par		130,000
2.	Treasury stock	60,000	
	Cash		60,000

DIVIDENDS ON COMMON STOCK

Investors buy common stock because they expect a return on their investment. This return can come in two forms: stock price appreciation and dividends. Some investors prefer to buy stocks that pay little or no dividends because companies that reinvest the majority of their earnings tend to increase their future earnings potential, along with their stock price. Wealthy investors in high tax brackets prefer to receive their return in the form of higher stock prices because capital gains may be taxed at a lower rate than dividend income. Other investors, such as retired people who need a steady income, prefer to receive their return in the form of dividends. These people often seek stocks that will pay very high dividends, such as utility stocks. Because of the importance of dividends to many investors, analysts often compute the dividend yield ratio to evaluate a corporation's dividend policy.

Learning Objective 4
Discuss dividends and analyze transactions.

Topic Tackler 11–2

Dividend Yield	**KEY RATIO** ANALYSIS

? ANALYTICAL QUESTION
What is return on investment based on dividends?

% RATIO AND COMPARISONS
The dividend yield ratio is computed as follows:

Dividend Yield = Dividends per Share ÷ Market Price per Share

The 2000 ratio for Outback Steakhouse:

$0.00 ÷ $27 = 0.0 percent

Learning Objective 5
Analyze the dividend yield ratio.

COMPARISONS OVER TIME		
Outback		
1998	1999	2000
0%	0%	0%

COMPARISONS WITH COMPETITORS	
Ruby Tuesday	**Wendy's**
2000	2000
0.2%	0.9%

⚲ INTERPRETATIONS

In General   Investors in common stock earn a return from both dividends and capital appreciation (increases in the market price of the stock). Growth-oriented companies often rely mainly on increases in their market price to provide a return to investors. Others pay large dividends but have more stable market prices. Each type of stock appeals to different types of investors with different risk and return preferences.

Focus Company Analysis   As a growth-oriented company, Outback has established a policy not to pay dividends, a policy that is reflected in its dividend yield ratio. Notice that while both the comparison companies are paying dividends, the yields are virtually immaterial in amount. None of these stocks would appeal to investors who need a steady income from dividends.

A Few Cautions   Remember that the dividend yield ratio tells only part of the return on investment story. Often potential capital appreciation is a much more important consideration. Outback is currently reinvesting all its earnings. As a result, the company is growing rapidly, and its stock price has increased significantly. Investors in Outback have bought the stock with the expectation of earning a return from increases in its market value, not from dividends.

A corporation does not have a legal obligation to pay dividends. The annual report for Outback discloses their policy of not paying dividends in order to finance growth.

REAL WORLD EXCERPT

NO RULES. JUST RIGHT.®

ANNUAL REPORT

> The Company has never paid a cash dividend on its Common Stock. The Board of Directors intends to retain earnings of the Company to support operations and to finance expansion and does not intend to pay cash dividends on Common Stock for the foreseeable future. The payment of cash dividends in the future will depend upon such factors as earnings levels, capital requirements, the Company's financial condition and other factors deemed relevant by the Board of Directors.

Once the board of directors formally declares a dividend, a liability is created. An actual press release announcing a dividend declaration for Wendy's contained the following information:

REAL WORLD EXCERPT

Wendy's
DIVIDEND DECLARATION

> **DATELINE: DUBLIN, OHIO, MAY 2, 2001**
>
> The Board of Directors of Wendy's today declared a quarterly cash dividend on common stock of six cents a share, payable May 25 to shareholders of record May 14.

The **DECLARATION DATE** is the date on which the board of directors officially approves a dividend.

The **RECORD DATE** is the date on which the corporation prepares the list of current stockholders as shown on its records; dividends can be paid only to the stockholders who own stock on that date.

The **PAYMENT DATE** is the date on which a cash dividend is paid to the stockholders of record.

Notice that this announcement contains three important dates:

1. **Declaration date—May 2, 2001.** The **declaration date** is the date on which the board of directors officially approves the dividend. As soon as it makes the declaration, it creates a dividend liability.

2. **Date of record—May 14, 2001.** The **record date** follows the declaration; it is the date on which the corporation prepares the list of current stockholders based on its records. The dividend is payable only to those names listed on the record date. No journal entry is made on this date.

3. **Date of payment—May 25, 2001.** The **payment date** is the date on which the cash is disbursed to pay the dividend liability. It follows the date of record, as specified in the dividend announcement.

Immediately on May 2, Wendy's records the following journal entry to reflect the declaration of the cash dividend. Assuming 1,000,000 shares are outstanding, the dividend amounts to $60,000 ($0.06 × 1,000,000):

Retained earnings (−SE) 60,000
    Dividends payable (+L) 60,000

Assets	=	Liabilities	+	Stockholders' Equity	
		Dividends payable	+60,000	Retained earnings	−60,000

The payment of the liability on May 25 is recorded as follows:

Dividends payable (−L) 60,000
    Cash (−A) 60,000

Assets		=	Liabilities		+	Stockholders' Equity
Cash	− 60,000		Dividends payable	−60,000		

Notice that the declaration and payment of a cash dividend reduce assets (cash) and stockholders' equity (retained earnings) by the same amount. This observation explains the two fundamental requirements for payment of a cash dividend:

1. **Sufficient retained earnings.** The corporation must have accumulated a sufficient amount of retained earnings to cover the amount of the dividend. State incorporation laws often limit cash dividends to the balance in the Retained Earnings account.

2. **Sufficient cash.** The corporation must have sufficient cash to pay the dividend and meet the operating needs of the business. The mere fact that the Retained Earnings account has a large credit balance does not mean that the board of directors can declare and pay a cash dividend. The cash generated in the past by earnings represented in the Retained Earnings account may have been expended to acquire inventory, buy operational assets, and pay liabilities. Consequently, no necessary relationship exists between the balance of retained earnings and the balance of cash on any particular date. Quite simply, retained earnings is not cash.

Impact of Dividends on Stock Price

FINANCIAL ANALYSIS

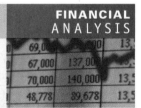

Another date that is important in understanding dividends has no accounting implications. The date two business days before the date of record is known as the *ex-dividend date.* This date is established by the stock exchanges to make certain that dividend checks are sent to the right people. If you buy stock before the ex-dividend date, you will receive the dividend. If you buy stock on the ex-dividend date or later, the previous owner will receive the dividend.

If you follow stock prices, you will notice that they often fall on the ex-dividend date. The reason is simple: On that date, the stock is worth less because it no longer includes the right to receive the next dividend.

SELF-STUDY **QUIZ**

Answer the following questions concerning dividends:

1. On which dividend date is a liability created?

2. A cash outflow occurs on which dividend date?

3. What are the two fundamental requirements for the payment of a dividend?

After you have completed your answers, check them with the solutions that follow:

1. Declaration date.
2. Date of payment.
3. Dividends can be paid only if sufficient retained earnings and sufficient cash are both available.

STOCK DIVIDENDS AND STOCK SPLITS

Stock Dividends

Learning Objective 6
Discuss the purpose of stock dividends, stock splits, and report transactions.

A **STOCK DIVIDEND** is a distribution of additional shares of a corporation's own stock.

Without a qualifier, the term *dividend* means a cash dividend, but dividends can also be paid with additional shares of stock. A **stock dividend** is a distribution of additional shares of a corporation's stock to its stockholders on a pro rata basis at no cost to the stockholder. The phrase *pro rata basis* means that each stockholder receives additional shares equal to the percentage of shares held. A stockholder with 10 percent of the outstanding shares would receive 10 percent of any additional shares issued as a stock dividend.

The term *stock dividend* is sometimes misused in annual reports and news articles. A recent *Wall Street Journal* headline announced that a particular company had just declared a "stock dividend." A close reading of the article revealed that the company had actually declared a cash dividend on the stock.

The value of a stock dividend is the subject of much debate. In reality, a stock dividend by itself has no economic value. All stockholders receive a pro rata distribution of shares, which means that each stockholder owns exactly the same portion of the company as before. The value of an investment is determined by the percentage of the company that is owned, not the number of shares held. If you get change for a dollar, you do not have more wealth because you hold four quarters instead of only one dollar. Similarly, if you own 10 percent of a company, you are not wealthier simply because the company declares a stock dividend and gives you (and all other stockholders) more shares of stock.

The stock market reacts immediately when a stock dividend is issued, and the stock price falls proportionally. Theoretically, if the stock price was $60 before a stock dividend and the number of shares is doubled, in the absence of events affecting the company, the price would fall to $30. Thus, an investor would own 100 shares worth $6,000 before the stock dividend (100 × $60) and 200 shares worth $6,000 after the stock dividend (200 × $30).

In reality, the fall in price is not exactly proportional to the number of new shares issued. In some cases, the stock dividend makes the stock more attractive to new investors. Many investors prefer to buy stock in round lots, which are multiples of 100 shares. An investor with $10,000 might not buy a stock selling for $150, for instance, because she cannot afford to buy 100 shares. She might buy the stock if the price were less than $100 as the result of a stock dividend. In other cases, stock dividends are associated with increases in cash dividends, which are attractive to some investors.

When a stock dividend occurs, the company must transfer an additional amount into the common stock account to reflect the additional shares issued. The amount transferred depends on whether the stock dividend is classified as large or small. A large stock dividend involves the distribution of additional shares that amount to more than 20–25 percent of currently outstanding shares. A small stock dividend involves the distribution of shares that amount to less than 20–25 percent of the outstanding shares. If the stock dividend is classified as large, the amount transferred to the Common Stock account is based on the par value of the additional shares issued. If the stock dividend is small (i.e., less than 20–25 percent), the amount transferred should be the total market value of the shares issued, with the par value of the stock transferred to the Common Stock account and the excess transferred to the Capital in Excess of Par Value account.

Outback Steakhouse issued its last stock dividend in 1999. If we assume that Outback issued 1,000,000 shares as a large stock dividend, the company would make the following journal entry:

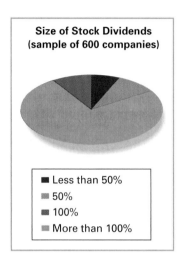

Size of Stock Dividends (sample of 600 companies)

■ Less than 50%
■ 50%
■ 100%
■ More than 100%

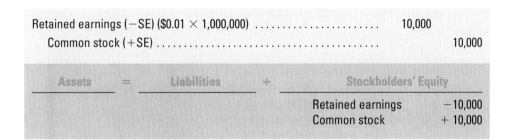

Retained earnings (−SE) ($0.01 × 1,000,000)	10,000	
Common stock (+SE)		10,000

Assets	=	Liabilities	+	Stockholders' Equity	
				Retained earnings	−10,000
				Common stock	+ 10,000

This journal entry moves an amount from Retained Earnings to the company's Common Stock account. Notice that the stock dividend did not change total stockholders' equity. It changed only the balances of some of the accounts that constitute stockholders' equity.

Stock Splits

Stock splits are not dividends. While they are similar to a stock dividend, they are quite different in terms of their impact on the stockholders' equity accounts. In a **stock split**, the total number of authorized shares is increased by a specified amount, such as 2 for 1. In this instance, each share held is called in and two new shares are issued in its place. Typically, a stock split is accomplished by reducing the par or stated value per share of all authorized shares, so that their total par value is unchanged. For instance, if Outback executes a 2-for-1 stock split, it reduces the par value of its stock from $0.01 to $0.005 and doubles the number of shares outstanding. In contrast to a stock dividend, a stock split does not result in the transfer of a dollar amount to the Common Stock account. The reduction in the par value per share compensates for the increase in the number of shares, so that no transfer is needed.

In both a stock dividend and a stock split, the stockholder receives more shares of stock without having to invest additional resources to acquire the shares. A stock dividend requires a journal entry; a stock split does not but is disclosed in the notes to the financial statements. The comparative effects of a large stock dividend versus a stock split may be summarized as follows:

A **STOCK SPLIT** is an increase in the total number of authorized shares by a specified ratio; does not decrease retained earnings.

STOCKHOLDERS' EQUITY

	Before	After a 100% Stock Dividend	After a Two-for-One Stock Split
Number of shares outstanding	30,000	60,000	60,000
Par value per share	$ 10	$ 10	$ 5
Total par value outstanding	300,000	600,000	300,000
Retained earnings	650,000	350,000	650,000
Total stockholders' equity	950,000	950,000	950,000

SELF-STUDY QUIZ

Barton Corporation issued 100,000 new shares of common stock (par value $10) in a stock dividend when the market value was $30 per share.

1. Record this transaction, assuming that it was a small stock dividend.

2. Record this transaction, assuming that it was a large stock dividend.

3. What journal entry would be required if the transaction were a stock split?

After you have completed your answers, check them with the solutions that follow:

——————

1. Retained earnings   3,000,000
    Common stock   1,000,000
    Capital in excess of par   2,000,000
2. Retained earnings   1,000,000
    Common stock   1,000,000
3. No journal entry is required in the case of a stock split.

Learning Objective 7
Describe the characteristics of preferred stock and analyze transactions affecting preferred stock.

PREFERRED STOCK is stock that has specified rights over common stock.

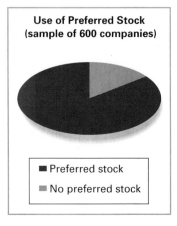

Use of Preferred Stock (sample of 600 companies)

■ Preferred stock
■ No preferred stock

PREFERRED STOCK

In addition to common stock, some corporations issue **preferred stock**. Preferred stock differs from common stock based on a number of rights granted to the stockholders. These are the most significant differences:

■ **Preferred stock does not grant voting rights.** As a result, preferred stock does not appeal to investors who want some control over the operations of a corporation. Indeed, this is one of the main reasons some corporations issue preferred stock to raise their equity capital: Preferred stock permits them to raise funds without diluting common stockholders' control. The chart in the margin shows the percentage of companies surveyed by *Accounting Trends & Techniques* that include preferred stock in their capital structure.

■ **Lower risk for preferred stock.** Generally, preferred stock is less risky than common stock because holders receive priority payment of dividends and distribution of assets if the corporation goes out of business. Usually a specified amount per share must be paid to preferred stockholders upon dissolution before any remaining assets can be distributed to the common stockholders.

■ **Preferred stock typically has a fixed dividend rate.** For example, "6 percent preferred stock, par value $10 per share" pays an annual dividend of 6 percent of par, or $0.60 per share. If preferred stock has no par value, the preferred dividend would be specified as $0.60 per share. The fixed dividend is attractive to certain investors who want a stable income from their investments.

Dividends on Preferred Stock

Because investors who purchase preferred stock give up certain advantages that are available to investors in common stock, preferred stock offers a dividend preference. The two most common dividend preferences are current and cumulative.

Current Dividend Preference

The **current dividend preference** requires the current preferred dividend must be paid before any dividends are paid on the common stock. This preference is always a feature of preferred stock. After the current dividend preference has been met and if no other preference is operative, dividends can be paid to the common stockholders.

   Declared dividends must be allocated between preferred stock and common stock. First, the preferred stock preference must be met; then the remainder of the total dividend can be allocated to the common stock. To illustrate, assume the Orban Company has the following stock outstanding:

Orban Company
Preferred stock outstanding, 6%, par $20; 2,000 shares = $40,000 par
Common stock outstanding, par $10; 5,000 shares = $50,000 par

Assuming a current dividend preference only, dividends would be allocated as follows:

Example	Total Dividends	6% Preferred Stock *	Common Stock
No. 1	$ 3,000	$2,400	$ 600
No. 2	18,000	2,400	15,600

Preferred dividend preference, $40,000 × 6% = $2,400.

Cumulative Dividend Preference

The **cumulative dividend preference** states that if all or a part of the current dividend is not paid in full, the cumulative unpaid amount, known as **dividends in arrears**, must be paid before any common dividends can be paid. Of course, if the preferred stock is noncumulative, dividends can never be in arrears; any preferred dividends that are not declared are permanently lost. Because preferred stockholders are unwilling to accept this unfavorable feature, preferred stock is usually cumulative.

   To illustrate the cumulative preference, assume that Orban Company has the same amount of stock outstanding as in the last example. In this case, dividends have been in arrears for two years.

Example	Total Dividends	6% Preferred Stock *	Common Stock
No. 1	$ 8,000	$ 7,200	$ 800
No. 2	30,000	7,200	22,800

Current dividend preference, $40,000 × 6% = $2,400; dividends in arrears preference, $2,400 × 2 years = $4,800; current dividend preference plus dividends in arrears = $7,200.

CURRENT DIVIDEND PREFERENCE is the feature of preferred stock that grants priority on preferred dividends over common dividends.

CUMULATIVE DIVIDEND PREFERENCE is the preferred stock feature that requires specified current dividends not paid in full to accumulate for every year in which they are not paid. These cumulative preferred dividends must be paid before any common dividends can be paid.

DIVIDENDS IN ARREARS are dividends on cumulative preferred stock that have not been declared in prior years.

	Impact of Dividends in Arrears	**FINANCIAL** ANALYSIS

The existence of dividends in arrears is important information because they limit a company's ability to pay dividends to common stockholders and can affect a company's future cash flows. Because dividends are never an actual liability until the board of directors declares them, dividends in arrears are not reported on the balance sheet. Instead, they are disclosed in the notes to the statements. The following note from Lone Star Industries is typical:

REAL WORLD EXCERPT

Lone Star Industries
ANNUAL REPORT

The total of dividends in arrears on the $13.50 preferred stock at the end of the year was $11,670,000. The aggregate amount of such dividend must be paid before any dividends are paid on common stock.

RESTRICTIONS ON RETAINED EARNINGS

Several types of business transactions may cause restrictions to be placed on retained earnings that limit a company's ability to pay dividends. The most typical example is borrowing money from a bank. For additional security, some banks include a loan covenant that limits the amount of dividends a corporation can pay. In addition, debt covenants often include a limit on borrowing and require a minimum balance of cash or working capital. If debt covenants are violated, the creditor can demand immediate repayment of the debt.

The full-disclosure principle requires restrictions on retained earnings be reported in the financial statements or in a separate note to the financial statements. Most companies report these restrictions in the notes, as illustrated in the following note from the annual report of May Department Store:

REAL WORLD EXCERPT

May Department Store
ANNUAL REPORT

Under the most restrictive covenants of long-term debt agreements, $1.2 billion of retained earnings was restricted as to the payment of dividends and/or common share repurchase.

Analysts are particularly interested in information concerning these restrictions because of the impact they have on the company's dividend policy.

**FOCUS ON
CASH FLOWS** **Financing Activities**

Transactions involving capital stock have a direct impact on the capital structure of a business. Because of the importance of these transactions, they are reported in the section of the statement of cash flows called Cash Flows from Financing Activities. Examples of cash flows associated with capital stock are included in the statement of cash flows for Outback Steakhouse, shown in Exhibit 11.3.

Learning Objective 8
Discuss the impact of capital stock transactions on cash flows.

EFFECT ON STATEMENT OF CASH FLOWS

In General   Cash received from owners is reported as an inflow; cash payments made to owners are reported as outflows. See the following example.

	Effect on Cash Flows
Financing activities	
Issuance of capital stock	+
Purchase of treasury stock	−
Sale of treasury stock	+
Payment of cash dividends	−

Focus Company Analysis Notice that for each of the last three years, Outback has repurchased its own capital stock (Exhibit 11.3). As discussed earlier, companies do so for a number of reasons. In Outback's case, notes to the annual report indicate that the company is buying treasury stock to support a stock option plan for restaurant managers.

Outback has an aggressive growth strategy; the company has invested more than $100 million dollars in new facilities in each of the last three years. Rather than raising additional capital from financing activities, the company has actually used funds each year in financing activities (e.g., the repurchase of stock and distributions to "partners," who individually have invested in some of Outback's operations). Outback has been able to use funds for both investing and financing activities because it generates significant cash flows from operating activities.

Selected Focus Company Comparisons: Proceeds from the Issuance of Common Stock (in millions)	
General Mills	$110.6
Outback	13.3
Home Depot	351.0

CONSOLIDATED STATEMENTS OF CASH FLOWS
(in thousands)

	Years Ended December 31,		
	2000	**1999**	**1998**
Cash flows from financing activities:			
Proceeds from issuance of common stock	$ 13,315	$ 13,292	$ 19,121
Proceeds from issuance of long-term debt	15,400		1,013
Proceeds from minority partners' contributions	4,450	1,250	5,525
Distributions to minority partners and stockholders	(39,198)	(38,755)	(24,952)
Repayments of long-term debt	(1,908)	(37,516)	(32,231)
Payments for purchase of treasury stock	(48,615)	(7,230)	(6,345)
Proceeds from reissuance of treasury stock	1,810	12,585	3,451
Net cash used in financing activities	$(54,746)	$(56,374)	$(34,418)

EXHIBIT 11.3

Excerpt from Statement of Cash Flows for Outback Steakhouse

REAL WORLD EXCERPT

NO RULES. JUST RIGHT.®

ANNUAL REPORT

DEMONSTRATION CASE

(Try to resolve the requirements before proceeding to the suggested solution that follows.) This case focuses on the organization and operations for the first year of Shelly Corporation, which was organized by 10 local entrepreneurs on January 1, 2003, for the purpose of operating a business to sell various supplies to hotels. The charter authorized the following capital stock:

Common stock, no-par value, 20,000 shares

Preferred stock, 5 percent, $100 par value, 5,000 shares

The laws of the state specify that the legal capital for no-par stock is the full sale amount.

The following summarized transactions, selected from 2003, were completed on the dates indicated:

a. Jan. Sold a total of 8,000 shares of common stock to the 10 entrepreneurs for cash at $50 per share. Credit the Common Stock account for the total issue amount.

b. Feb. Sold 2,000 shares of preferred stock at $102 per share; cash collected in full.

c. Mar. Purchased land for a store site and made full payment by issuing 100 shares of preferred stock. Early construction of the store is planned. Debit Land (store site). The preferred stock is selling at $102 per share.

d. July Purchased 100 shares of preferred stock that had been sold and issued earlier. Shelly Corporation paid the stockholder $104 per share.

e. Aug. Sold 20 shares of the preferred treasury stock at $105 per share.

Required:

1. Give the appropriate journal entries with a brief explanation for each transaction.

2. Prepare the Stockholders' Equity section of the balance sheet for Shelly Corporation at December 31, 2003. Assume retained earnings is $31,000.

SUGGESTED SOLUTION

1. Journal entries:

a. Jan. 2003
Cash (+A) 400,000
    Common stock (+SE) 400,000
Sale of no-par common stock ($50 × 8,000 shares = $400,000).

b. Feb. 2003
Cash (+A) 204,000
    Preferred stock (+SE) 200,000
    Capital in excess of par, preferred stock (+SE) .. 4,000
Sale of preferred stock ($102 × 2,000 shares = $204,000).

c. March 2003
Land (+A) 10,200
    Preferred stock (+SE) 10,000
    Capital in excess of par, preferred stock (+SE) .. 200
Purchased land for future store site; paid in full by issuance of 100 shares of preferred stock ($102 × 100 shares = $10,200).

d. July 2003
Treasury stock (+XSE, −SE) 10,400
    Cash (−A) 10,400
Purchased 100 shares of preferred treasury stock ($104 × 100 shares = $10,400).

e. Aug. 2003
Cash (+A) 2,100
    Treasury stock (−XSE, +SE) 2,080
    Capital in excess of par, preferred stock (+SE) .. 20
Sold 20 shares of the preferred treasury stock at $105.

2. Stockholders' equity section of the balance sheet:

<table>
<tr><td colspan="2" align="center">**SHELLY CORPORATION**
Balance Sheet
At December 31, 2003</td></tr>
<tr><td colspan="2">**Stockholders' Equity**</td></tr>
<tr><td colspan="2">Contributed capital</td></tr>
<tr><td> Preferred stock, 5% (par value $100; authorized 5,000 shares, issued 2,100 shares of which 80 shares are held as treasury stock)</td><td align="right">$210,000</td></tr>
<tr><td> Capital in excess of par, preferred stock</td><td align="right">4,220</td></tr>
<tr><td> Common stock (no-par value; authorized 20,000 shares, issued and outstanding 8,000 shares)</td><td align="right">400,000</td></tr>
<tr><td>   Total contributed capital</td><td align="right">$614,220</td></tr>
<tr><td>Retained earnings</td><td align="right">31,000</td></tr>
<tr><td>   Total contributed capital and retained earnings</td><td align="right">$645,220</td></tr>
<tr><td>Less cost of preferred treasury stock held (80 shares)</td><td align="right">(8,320)</td></tr>
<tr><td>   Total stockholders' equity</td><td align="right">$636,900</td></tr>
</table>

Chapter Supplement A

Accounting for Owners' Equity for Sole Proprietorships and Partnerships

Owner's Equity for a Sole Proprietorship

A *sole proprietorship* is an unincorporated business owned by one person. Only two owner's equity accounts are needed: (1) a capital account for the proprietor (J. Doe, Capital) and (2) a drawing (or withdrawal) account for the proprietor (J. Doe, Drawings).

The capital account of a sole proprietorship serves two purposes: to record investments by the owner and to accumulate periodic income or loss. The drawing account is used to record the owner's withdrawals of cash or other assets from the business. The drawing account is closed to the capital account at the end of each accounting period. Thus, the capital account reflects the cumulative total of all investments by the owner and all earnings of the entity less all withdrawals from the entity by the owner.

In most respects, the accounting for a sole proprietorship is the same as for a corporation. Exhibit 11.4 presents the recording of selected transactions of Doe Retail Store and the statement of owner's equity.

Because a sole proprietorship does not pay income taxes, its financial statements do not reflect income tax expense or income taxes payable. Instead, the net income of a sole proprietorship is taxed when it is included on the owner's personal income tax return. Likewise, the owner's salary is not recognized as an expense in a sole proprietorship because an employer/employee contractual relationship cannot exist with only one party involved. The owner's salary is therefore accounted for as a distribution of profits (i.e., a withdrawal).

Owners' Equity for a Partnership

The Uniform Partnership Act, which most states have adopted, defines partnership as "an association of two or more persons to carry on as co-owners of a business for profit." Small businesses and professionals such as accountants, doctors, and lawyers often use the partnership form of business.

A partnership is formed by two or more persons reaching mutual agreement about the terms of the relationship. The law does not require an application for a charter as in the case of a corporation. Instead, the agreement between the partners constitutes a partnership contract. This agreement should specify matters such as division of periodic income, management responsibilities, transfer or sale of partnership interests, disposition of assets upon liquidation, and procedures to be followed in case of the death of a partner. If the partnership agreement does not specify these matters, the laws of the resident state are binding.

The primary advantages of a partnership are (1) ease of formation, (2) complete control by the partners, and (3) lack of income taxes on the business itself. The primary disadvantage is the unlimited liability of each partner for the partnership's debts. If the partnership does not have sufficient assets to satisfy outstanding debt, creditors of the partnership can seize the partners' personal assets.

As with a sole proprietorship, accounting for a partnership follows the same underlying principles as any other form of business organization, except for those entries that directly affect owners' equity. Accounting for partners' equity follows the same pattern as for a sole proprietorship except that separate capital and drawings accounts must be established for each partner. Investments by each partner are credited to that partner's capital account; withdrawals are debited to the respective drawings account. The net income of a partnership is divided among the partners in accordance with the partnership agreement and credited to each account. The respective drawings accounts are closed to the partner capital accounts. After the closing process, each partner's capital account reflects the cumulative total of all that partner's investments plus that partner's share of the partnership earnings less all that partner's withdrawals.

Exhibit 11.5 presents selected journal entries and partial financial statements for AB Partnership to illustrate the accounting for the distribution of income and partners' equity.

The financial statements of a partnership follow the same format as those for a corporation except that (1) the income statement includes an additional section entitled Distribution of Net Income, (2) the partners' equity section of the balance sheet is detailed for each partner, (3) the partnership has no income tax expense because partnerships do not pay income tax (partners must report their share of the partnership profits on their individual tax returns), and (4) salaries paid to the partners are not recorded as expenses but are treated as distributions of earnings.

EXHIBIT 11.4

Accounting for Owner's Equity for a Sole Proprietorship

Selected Entries during 2003

January 1, 2003

J. Doe started a retail store by investing $150,000 of personal savings. The journal entry follows:

Cash (+A)   150,000
    J. Doe, capital (+OE)   150,000

Assets	=	Liabilities	+	Owner's Equity	
Cash +150,000				J. Doe, capital	+150,000

During 2003

Each month during the year, Doe withdrew $1,000 cash from the business for personal living costs. Accordingly, each month the following journal entry was made:

J. Doe, drawings (−OE)   1,000
    Cash (−A)   1,000

Assets	=	Liabilities	+	Owner's Equity	
Cash −1,000				J. Doe, drawings	−1,000

Note: At December 31, 2003, after the last withdrawal, the drawings account reflected a debit balance of $12,000.

December 31, 2003

The usual journal entries for the year, including adjusting and closing entries for the revenue and expense accounts, resulted in an $18,000 net income, which were closed to the capital account as follows:

Individual revenue and expense accounts (−R&E)   18,000
    J. Doe, capital (+OE)   18,000

Assets	=	Liabilities	+	Owner's Equity	
				Revenues and expenses	−18,000
				J. Doe, capital	+18,000

December 31, 2003

The drawings account was closed as follows:

J. Doe, capital (−OE)   12,000
    J. Doe, drawings (+OE)   12,000

Assets	=	Liabilities	+	Owner's Equity	
				J. Doe, capital	−12,000
				J. Doe, drawings	+12,000

Balance Sheet December 31, 2003 (partial)

Owner's equity	
J. Doe, capital, January 1, 2003	$150,000
Add: Net income for 2003	18,000
Total	168,000
Less: Withdrawals for 2003	(12,000)
J. Doe, capital, December 31, 2003	$156,000

Selected Entries during 2003

January 1, 2003

A. Able and B. Baker organized AB Partnership on this date. Able contributed $60,000 and Baker $40,000 cash to the partnership and agreed to divide net income (and net loss) 60% and 40%, respectively. The journal entry for the business to record the investment was as follows:

Cash (+A)	100,000	
A. Able, capital (+OE)		60,000
B. Baker, capital (+OE)		40,000

Assets	=	Liabilities	+	Owners' Equity	
Cash +100,000				A. Able, capital	+60,000
				B. Baker, capital	+40,000

During 2003

The partners agreed that Able would withdraw $1,000 and Baker $650 per month in cash. Accordingly, each month the following journal entry was made:

A. Able, drawings (−OE)	1,000	
B. Baker, drawings (−OE)	650	
Cash (−A)		1,650

Assets	=	Liabilities	+	Owners' Equity	
Cash −1,650				A. Able, drawings	−1,000
				B. Baker, drawings	− 650

December 31, 2003

Assume that the normal closing entries for the revenue and expense accounts resulted in a net income of $30,000. The partnership agreement specified Abel would receive 60% of earnings and Baker would get 40%. The closing entry was as follows:

Individual revenue and expense accounts (−R&E)	30,000	
A. Able, capital (+OE)		18,000
B. Baker, capital (+OE)		12,000

Assets	=	Liabilities	+	Owners' Equity	
				Revenues and expenses	−30,000
				A. Able, capital	+18,000
				B. Baker, capital	+12,000

December 31, 2003

The journal entry required to close the drawings accounts follows:

A. Able, capital (−OE)	12,000	
B. Baker, capital (−OE)	7,800	
A. Able, drawings (+OE)		12,000
B. Baker, drawings (+OE)		7,800

EXHIBIT 11.5

Accounting for Partners' Equity

STATEMENT OF STOCKHOLDERS' EQUITY

This statement reports detailed information concerning stockholders' equity, including
(1) amounts in each equity account,
(2) number of shares outstanding,
(3) impact of transactions such as earning income, payment of dividends, and purchase of treasury stock.

NOTES

Under Summary of Significant Accounting Policies

Usually, very little information concerning capital stock is provided in this summary.

Under a Separate Note

Most companies report information about their stock option plans and information about major transactions such as stock dividends or significant treasury stock transactions. A historical summary of dividends paid per share is typically provided.

KEY TERMS

Authorized Number of
  Shares p. 553
Common Stock p. 555
Cumulative Dividend
  Preference p. 565
Current Dividend Preference p. 565
Declaration Date p. 560

Dividends in Arrears p. 565
Issued Shares p. 553
Legal Capital p. 555
No-Par Value Stock p. 555
Outstanding Shares p. 553
Par Value p. 555

Payment Date p. 560
Preferred Stock p. 564
Record Date p. 560
Stock Dividend p. 562
Stock Split p. 563
Treasury Stock p. 558

QUESTIONS

1. Define the term *corporation* and identify the primary advantages of this form of business organization.
2. What is the charter of a corporation?
3. Explain each of the following terms: (a) authorized capital stock, (b) issued capital stock, and (c) outstanding capital stock.
4. Differentiate between common stock and preferred stock.
5. Explain the distinction between par value and no-par value capital stock.
6. What are the usual characteristics of preferred stock?
7. What are the two basic sources of stockholders' equity? Explain each.
8. Owners' equity is accounted for by source. What does *source* mean?
9. Define treasury stock. Why do corporations acquire treasury stock?
10. How is treasury stock reported on the balance sheet? How is the "gain or loss" on treasury stock that has been sold reported on the financial statements?
11. What are the two basic requirements to support the declaration of a cash dividend? What are the effects of a cash dividend on assets and stockholders' equity?
12. Differentiate between cumulative and noncumulative preferred stock.
13. Define *stock dividend*. How does a stock dividend differ from a cash dividend?
14. What are the primary reasons for issuing a stock dividend?
15. Identify and explain the three important dates with respect to dividends.
16. Define *retained earnings*. What are the primary components of retained earnings at the end of each period?
17. What does restrictions on retained earnings mean?

EXHIBIT 11.5

Accounting for Partners' Equity

Selected Entries during 2003

January 1, 2003

A. Able and B. Baker organized AB Partnership on this date. Able contributed $60,000 and Baker $40,000 cash to the partnership and agreed to divide net income (and net loss) 60% and 40%, respectively. The journal entry for the business to record the investment was as follows:

Cash (+A)	100,000	
A. Able, capital (+OE)		60,000
B. Baker, capital (+OE)		40,000

Assets	=	Liabilities	+	Owners' Equity	
Cash +100,000				A. Able, capital	+60,000
				B. Baker, capital	+40,000

During 2003

The partners agreed that Able would withdraw $1,000 and Baker $650 per month in cash. Accordingly, each month the following journal entry was made:

A. Able, drawings (−OE)	1,000	
B. Baker, drawings (−OE)	650	
Cash (−A)		1,650

Assets	=	Liabilities	+	Owners' Equity	
Cash −1,650				A. Able, drawings	−1,000
				B. Baker, drawings	− 650

December 31, 2003

Assume that the normal closing entries for the revenue and expense accounts resulted in a net income of $30,000. The partnership agreement specified Abel would receive 60% of earnings and Baker would get 40%. The closing entry was as follows:

Individual revenue and expense accounts (−R&E)	30,000	
A. Able, capital (+OE)		18,000
B. Baker, capital (+OE)		12,000

Assets	=	Liabilities	+	Owners' Equity	
				Revenues and expenses	−30,000
				A. Able, capital	+18,000
				B. Baker, capital	+12,000

December 31, 2003

The journal entry required to close the drawings accounts follows:

A. Able, capital (−OE)	12,000	
B. Baker, capital (−OE)	7,800	
A. Able, drawings (+OE)		12,000
B. Baker, drawings (+OE)		7,800

EXHIBIT 11.5

(continued)

Assets	=	Liabilities	+	Owners' Equity	
				A. Able, capital	−12,000
				B. Baker, capital	−7,800
				A. Able, drawings	+12,000
				B. Baker, drawings	+7,800

A separate statement of partners' capital, similar to the following, is customarily prepared to supplement the balance sheet:

AB PARTNERSHIP
Statement of Partners' Capital
For the Year Ended December 31, 2003

	A. Able	B. Baker	Total
Investment, January 1, 2003	$60,000	$40,000	$100,000
Add: Additional investments during the year	0	0	0
Net income for the year	18,000	12,000	30,000
Totals	78,000	52,000	130,000
Less: Drawings during the year	(12,000)	(7,800)	(19,800)
Partners' equity, December 31, 2003	$66,000	$44,200	$110,200

CHAPTER TAKE-AWAYS

1. **Explain the role of stock in the capital structure of a corporation. p. 552**
   The law recognizes corporations as separate legal entities. Owners invest in a corporation and receive capital stock that can be traded on established stock exchanges. Stock provides a number of rights, including the right to receive dividends.

2. **Analyze the earnings per share ratio. p. 554**
   The earnings per share ratio facilitates the comparison of a company's earnings over time or with other companies at a single point in time. By expressing earnings on a per share basis, differences in the size of companies becomes less important.

3. **Describe the characteristics of common stock and analyze transactions affecting common stock. p. 555**
   Common stock is the basic voting stock issued by a corporation. Usually it has a par value, but no-par stock can be issued. Common stock offers some special rights that appeal to certain investors.
   A number of key transactions involve capital stock: (1) initial sale of stock, (2) treasury stock transactions, (3) cash dividends, and (4) stock dividends and stock splits. Each is illustrated in this chapter.

4. **Discuss dividends and analyze transactions. p. 559**
   The return associated with an investment in capital stock comes from two sources: appreciation and dividends. Dividends are recorded as a liability when they are declared by the board of directors (i.e., on the date of declaration). The liability is satisfied when the dividends are paid (i.e., on the date of payment).

5. **Analyze the dividend yield ratio. p. 559**
   The dividend yield ratio measures the percentage of return on an investment from dividends. For most companies, the return associated with dividends is very small.

6. **Discuss the purpose of stock dividends, stock splits, and report transactions. p. 562**
   Stock dividends are pro rata distributions of a company's stock to existing owners. The transaction involves transferring an additional amount into the common stock account. A stock split also in-

volves the distribution of additional shares to owners but no additional amount is transferred into the common stock account. Instead, the par value of the stock is reduced.

7. **Describe the characteristics of preferred stock and analyze transactions affecting preferred stock. p. 564**
Preferred stock provides investors certain advantages including dividend preferences and a preference on asset distributions in the event the corporation is liquidated.

8. **Discuss the impact of capital stock transactions on cash flows. p. 566**
Both inflows (e.g., the issuance of capital stock) and outflows (e.g., the purchase of treasury stock) are reported in the Financing Activities section of the statement of cash flows. The payment of dividends is reported as an outflow in this section.

This chapter concludes a major section of the book. In the previous several chapters, we have discussed individual sections of the balance sheet. We now shift our focus to a common business transaction that affects many accounts on each of the financial statements. For a number of strategic reasons, businesses often invest in other businesses. In the next chapter, you will see why companies invest in other companies and how those investments affect their financial statements.

KEY **RATIOS**

The **earnings per share** ratio states the income of a corporation on a per share of common stock basis. The ratio is computed as follows (p. 554):

$$\text{Earnings per Share} = \frac{\text{Income}}{\text{Average Number of Shares of Common Stock Outstanding}}$$

The **dividend yield ratio** measures the dividend return on the current price of the stock. The ratio is computed as follows (p. 559):

$$\text{Dividend Yield Ratio} = \frac{\text{Dividend per Share}}{\text{Market Price per Share}}$$

FINDING **FINANCIAL INFORMATION**

BALANCE SHEET

Under Current Liabilities
Dividends, once declared by the board of directors, are reported as a liability (usually current).

Under Noncurrent Liabilities
Transactions involving capital stock do not generate noncurrent liabilities.

Under Stockholders' Equity
Typical accounts include
  Preferred stock
  Common stock
  Capital in excess of par
  Retained earnings
  Treasury stock

INCOME STATEMENT

Capital stock is never shown on the income statement. Dividends paid are not an expense. They are a distribution of income and are, therefore, not reported on the income statement.

STATEMENT OF CASH FLOWS

Under Financing Activities
+Cash inflows from initial sale of stock
+Cash inflows from sale of treasury stock
−Cash outflows for dividends
−Cash outflows for purchase of treasury stock

STATEMENT OF STOCKHOLDERS' EQUITY

This statement reports detailed information concerning stockholders' equity, including
(1) amounts in each equity account,
(2) number of shares outstanding,
(3) impact of transactions such as earning income, payment of dividends, and purchase of treasury stock.

NOTES

Under Summary of Significant Accounting Policies

Usually, very little information concerning capital stock is provided in this summary.

Under a Separate Note

Most companies report information about their stock option plans and information about major transactions such as stock dividends or significant treasury stock transactions. A historical summary of dividends paid per share is typically provided.

KEY TERMS

QUESTIONS

1. Define the term *corporation* and identify the primary advantages of this form of business organization.
2. What is the charter of a corporation?
3. Explain each of the following terms: (a) authorized capital stock, (b) issued capital stock, and (c) outstanding capital stock.
4. Differentiate between common stock and preferred stock.
5. Explain the distinction between par value and no-par value capital stock.
6. What are the usual characteristics of preferred stock?
7. What are the two basic sources of stockholders' equity? Explain each.
8. Owners' equity is accounted for by source. What does *source* mean?
9. Define treasury stock. Why do corporations acquire treasury stock?
10. How is treasury stock reported on the balance sheet? How is the "gain or loss" on treasury stock that has been sold reported on the financial statements?
11. What are the two basic requirements to support the declaration of a cash dividend? What are the effects of a cash dividend on assets and stockholders' equity?
12. Differentiate between cumulative and noncumulative preferred stock.
13. Define *stock dividend*. How does a stock dividend differ from a cash dividend?
14. What are the primary reasons for issuing a stock dividend?
15. Identify and explain the three important dates with respect to dividends.
16. Define *retained earnings*. What are the primary components of retained earnings at the end of each period?
17. What does restrictions on retained earnings mean?

1. Which feature is not applicable to common stock ownership?
   a. right to receive dividends before preferred stock shareholders
   b. right to participate in management through voting
   c. right to receive residual assets upon liquidation of the company
   d. All of the above are features of common stock ownership.

2. Which statement regarding treasury stock is false?
   a. Treasury stock is considered to be issued but not outstanding.
   b. Treasury stock has no voting, dividend, or liquidation rights.
   c. Treasury stock reduces total equity on the balance sheet.
   d. None of the above *are* false.

3. Which of the following statements about stock dividends is true?
   a. Stock dividends are reported on the statement of cash flow.
   b. Stock dividends are reported on the statement of retained earnings.
   c. Stock dividends increase total equity.
   d. Stock dividends decrease total equity.

4. Which order best describes the largest number of shares to the smallest number of shares?
   a. shares authorized, shares issued, shares outstanding
   b. shares issued, shares outstanding, shares authorized
   c. shares outstanding, shares issued, shares authorized
   d. shares in the treasury, shares outstanding, shares issued

5. Which combination would be the best for an investor when shopping for a new stock?
   a. high dividend yield ratio, high earnings per share
   b. low dividend yield ratio, high earnings per share
   c. high dividend yield ratio, low earnings per share
   d. low dividend yield ratio, low earnings per share

6. A journal entry is not recorded on what date?
   a. date of declaration
   b. date of record
   c. date of payment
   d. a journal entry is recorded on all of these dates.

7. Which section of the statement of cash flows would include cash payments for the purchase of treasury stock?
   a. Operating
   b. Investing
   c. Financing
   d. in the footnotes

8. Which statement regarding dividends is false?
   a. Dividends represent a sharing of corporate profits with owners.
   b. Both stock and cash dividends reduce retained earnings.
   c. Cash dividends paid to stockholders reduce net income.
   d. None of the above statements are false.

9. When treasury stock is purchased with cash, what is the impact on the balance sheet equation?
   a. No change: the reduction of the asset Cash is offset with the addition of the asset Treasury Stock.
   b. Assets decrease and Stockholders' Equity increases.
   c. Assets increase and Stockholders' Equity decreases.
   d. Assets decrease and Stockholders' Equity decreases.

10. In what situation does an investor's personal wealth increase immediately?
    a. when receiving a cash dividend
    b. when receiving a stock dividend
    c. when a stock split is announced
    d. in all of these situations

For more practice with multiple choice questions, go to our website at www.mhhe.com/libby4e, click on "Student Center" in the upper left menu, click on this chapter's name and number from the list of contents, and then click on "Multiple Choice Quiz" from the menu on the left.

MINI-EXERCISES

M11-1
LO1

Evaluating Stockholders' Rights

Name three rights of stockholders. Which of these is most important in your opinion? Why?

M11-2
LO3

Computing the Number of Unissued Shares

The balance sheet for Crutcher Corporation reported 147,000 shares outstanding, 200,000 shares authorized, and 10,000 shares in treasury stock. Compute the maximum number of new shares that Crutcher could issue.

M11-3
LO3

Recording the Sale of Common Stock

To expand operations, Aragon Consulting issued 100,000 shares of previously unissued stock with a par value of $1. The selling price for the stock was $75 per share. Record the sale of this stock. Would your answer be different if the par value was $2 per share? If so, record the sale of stock with a par value of $2.

M11-4
LO3, 7

Comparing Common Stock and Preferred Stock

Your parents have just retired and have asked you for some financial advice. They have decided to invest $100,000 in a company very similar to Outback Steakhouse. The company has issued both common and preferred stock. What factors would you consider in giving them advice? Which type of stock would you recommend?

M11-5
LO3

Determining the Effects of Treasury Stock Transactions

Trans Union Corporation purchased 20,000 shares of its own stock for $45 per share. The next year, the company sold 5,000 shares for $50 per share and the following year, it sold 10,000 shares for $37 per share. Determine the impact (increase, decrease, or no change) of each of these transactions on the following classifications:
1. Total assets.
2. Total liabilities.
3. Total stockholders' equity.
4. Net income.

M11-6
LO4

Determining the Amount of a Dividend

Jacobs Company has 300,000 shares of common stock authorized, 270,000 shares issued, and 50,000 shares of treasury stock. The company's board of directors declares a dividend of 50 cents per share. What is the total amount of the dividend that will be paid?

M11-7
LO4

Recording Dividends

On April 15, 2003, the board of directors for Auction.com declared a cash dividend of 20 cents per share payable to stockholders of record on May 20. The dividends will be paid on June 14. The company has 500,000 shares of stock outstanding. Prepare any necessary journal entries for each date.

M11-8
LO7

Determining the Amount of a Preferred Dividend

Colliers, Inc., has 200,000 shares of cumulative preferred stock outstanding. The preferred stock pays dividends in the amount of $2 per share but because of cash flow problems, the company did not pay any dividends last year. The board of directors plans to pay dividends in the amount of $1 million this year. What amount will go to preferred stockholders?

M11-9
LO6

Determining the Impact of Stock Dividends and Stock Splits

Armstrong Tools, Inc., announced a 100 percent stock dividend. Determine the impact (increase, decrease, no change) of this dividend on the following:
1. Total assets.
2. Total liabilities.
3. Common stock.

4. Total stockholders' equity.
5. Market value per share of common stock.
6. Now assume that the company announced a 2-for-1 stock split. Determine the impact of the stock split.

Recording a Stock Dividend

M11-10
LO6

Shriver Food Systems, Inc., has issued a 50 percent stock dividend. The company has 800,000 shares authorized and 200,000 shares outstanding. The par value of the stock is $5 per share, and the market value is $100 per share. Record the payment of this stock dividend.

EXERCISES

Reporting Stockholders' Equity and Determining Dividend Policy

E11-1
LO3, 4

Sampson Corporation was organized in 2003 to operate a financial consulting business. The charter authorized the following capital stock: common stock, par value $8 per share, 12,000 shares. During the first year, the following selected transactions were completed:

a. Sold and issued 6,000 shares of common stock for cash at $20 per share.
b. Issued 600 shares of common stock for a piece of land to be used for a facilities site; construction began immediately. Assume that the stock was selling at $22 per share at the date of issuance. Debit Land.
c. Sold and issued 2,000 shares of common stock for cash at $23 per share.
d. At year-end, the accounts reflected a $7,000 loss. Because a loss was incurred, no income tax expense was recorded.

Required:
1. Give the journal entry required for each of these transactions.
2. Prepare the stockholders' equity section as it should be reported on the year-end balance sheet.
3. Can Sampson pay dividends at this time? Explain.

Analyzing the Impact of Dividend Policy

E11-2
LO4

McDonald and Associates is a small manufacturer of electronic connections for local area networks. Consider three independent situations.

Case 1: McDonald increases its cash dividends by 50 percent, but no other changes occur in the company's operations.
Case 2: The company's income and cash flows increase by 50 percent, but this does not change its dividends.
Case 3: McDonald issues a 50 percent stock dividend, but no other changes occur.

Required:
1. How do you think each situation would affect the company's stock price?
2. If the company changed its accounting policies and reported higher net income, would the change have an impact on the stock price?

Determining the Effects of Transactions on Stockholders' Equity

E11-3
LO3, 7

Shelby Corporation was organized in January 2003 by 10 stockholders to operate an air conditioning sales and service business. The charter issued by the state authorized the following capital stock:

Common stock, $1 par value, 200,000 shares.
Preferred stock, $10 par value, 6 percent, 50,000 shares.

During January and February 2003, the following stock transactions were completed:

a. Collected $40,000 cash from each of the 10 organizers and issued 2,000 shares of common stock to each of them.
b. Sold 15,000 shares of preferred stock at $25 per share; collected the cash and immediately issued the stock.

Required:

Net income for 2003 was $40,000; cash dividends declared and paid at year-end were $10,000. Prepare the stockholders' equity section of the balance sheet at December 31, 2003.

E11-4   Determining the Effects of the Issuance of Common and Preferred Stock
L01, 3, 7

Kelly, Incorporated, was issued a charter on January 15, 2003, that authorized the following capital stock:

Common stock, no-par, 100,000 shares.

Preferred stock, 7 percent, par value $10 per share, 5,000 shares.

The board of directors established a stated value on the no-par common stock of $6 per share. During 2003, the following selected transactions were completed in the order given:

a. Sold and issued 20,000 shares of the no-par common stock at $18 cash per share.
b. Sold and issued 3,000 shares of preferred stock at $22 cash per share.
c. At the end of 2003, the accounts showed net income of $38,000.

Required:
1. Prepare the stockholders' equity section of the balance sheet at December 31, 2003.
2. Assume that you are a common stockholder. If Kelly needed additional capital, would you prefer to have it issue additional common stock or additional preferred stock? Explain.

E11-5   Recording Stockholders' Equity Transactions, Including Noncash Consideration:
L01, 3   Write a Brief Memo

Teacher Corporation obtained a charter at the start of 2003 that authorized 50,000 shares of no-par common stock and 20,000 shares of preferred stock, par value $10. The corporation was organized by four individuals who received 51 percent of the common stock. The remaining shares were to be sold to other individuals at $40 per share on a cash basis. During 2003, the following selected transactions occurred:

a. Collected $15 per share cash from three of the organizers and received two adjoining lots of land from the fourth organizer. Issued 4,000 shares of common stock to each of the four organizers and received title to the land.
b. Sold and issued 6,000 shares of common stock to an outsider at $40 cash per share.
c. Sold and issued 8,000 shares of preferred stock at $20 cash per share.

Required:
1. Give the journal entries indicated for each of these transactions.
2. Write a brief memo to explain the basis that you used to determine the cost of the land.

E11-6   Finding Amounts Missing from the Stockholders' Equity Section
L03, 7

The stockholders' equity section on the December 31, 2006, balance sheet of Chemfast Corporation follows:

Stockholders' Equity

Contributed capital	
Preferred stock (par $20; authorized 10,000 shares, ? issued, of which 500 shares are held as treasury stock)	$104,000
Common stock (no-par; authorized 20,000 shares, issued and outstanding 8,000 shares)	600,000
Capital in excess of par, preferred	14,300
Contributed capital, treasury stock transactions	1,500
Retained earnings	30,000
Cost of treasury stock, preferred	(9,500)

Required:
Complete the following statements and show your computations.
1. The number of shares of preferred stock issued was _____.
2. The number of shares of preferred stock outstanding was _____.
3. The average sale price of the preferred stock when issued was $_____ per share.

4. Have the treasury stock transactions (a) increased corporate resources or (b) decreased resources? _____ By how much? _____.
5. The treasury stock transactions increased (decreased) stockholders' equity by _____.
6. How much did the treasury stock held cost per share? $_____.
7. Total stockholders' equity is $_____.
8. The average issue price of the common stock was $_____.
9. Assuming that one-fourth of the treasury stock is sold at $35 per share, the remaining balance in the Treasury Stock account is $_____.

Finding Information Missing from an Annual Report

E11-7
LO3
Procter &
Gamble

Procter & Gamble is a $38 billion company that sells products that are part of most of our daily lives, including Mr. Clean, Cheer, Crest, Vicks, Scope, Pringles, Folgers, Vidal Sassoon, Zest, and Charmin. The annual report for P&G contained the following information:

a. Retained earnings at the end of 1998 totaled $11,144 million.
b. Treasury stock amounted to $1,929 million at the end of 1998 and $2,533 million at the end of 1999.
c. Net income for 1999 was $3,763 million.
d. Stated value of the stock is $1 per share.
e. Cash dividends declared in 1999 were $1.14 per share.
f. The Common Stock, Par Value account totaled $1,320 million at the end of both 1998 and 1999.

Required: (Assume that no other information concerning stockholders' equity is relevant.)
1. Estimate the number of shares outstanding during 1999.
2. Estimate the amount of retained earnings at the end of 1999.
3. Did the number of shares outstanding change during 1999?

Recording Treasury Stock Transactions and Analyzing Their Impact

E11-8
LO3, 8

During 2005, the following selected transactions affecting stockholders' equity occurred for Italy Corporation:

Feb. 1	Purchased in the open market 200 shares of the company's own common stock at $22 cash per share.
Jul. 15	Sold 100 of the shares purchased on February 1, 2005, for $24 cash per share.
Sept. 1	Sold 60 more of the shares purchased on February 1, 2005, for $20 cash per share.
Dec. 15	Sold an additional 20 of the treasury shares for $15 per share.

Required:
1. Give the indicated journal entries for each of the four transactions.
2. What impact does the purchase of treasury stock have on dividends paid?
3. What impact does the sale of treasury stock for an amount higher than the purchase price have on net income and the statement of cash flows?

Computing Shares Outstanding

E11-9
LO3
Philip Morris
Companies,
Inc.

The 1998 annual report for Philip Morris Companies, Inc., disclosed that 4 billion shares of common stock had been authorized. At the end of 1997, 2,805,961,317 shares had been issued and the number of shares in treasury stock was 380,474,028. During 1998, no additional shares were issued, but additional shares were purchased for treasury stock and shares were sold from treasury stock. The net change was a decrease of 5,047,286 shares. Determine the number of shares outstanding at the end of 1998.

Computing Dividends on Preferred Stock and Analyzing Differences

E11-10
LO4, 7

The records of Hoffman Company reflected the following balances in the stockholders' equity accounts at December 31, 2010:

Common stock, par $12 per share, 40,000 shares outstanding.
Preferred stock, 8 percent, par $10 per share, 6,000 shares outstanding.
Retained earnings, $220,000.

On September 1, 2010, the board of directors was considering the distribution of a $62,000 cash dividend. No dividends were paid during 2008 and 2009. You have been asked to determine dividend amounts under two independent assumptions (show computations):

a. The preferred stock is noncumulative.
b. The preferred stock is cumulative.

Required:

1. Determine the total and per share amounts that would be paid to the common stockholders and to the preferred stockholders under the two independent assumptions.
2. Write a brief memo to explain why the dividends per share of common stock were less for the second assumption.
3. What factor would cause a more favorable per share result to the common stockholders?

E11-11
LO7
Mission
Critical
Software, Inc.

Analyzing Dividends in Arrears

Mission Critical Software, Inc., is listed on the Nasdaq and is a leading provider of systems management software for Windows NT network and Internet infrastructure. Like many start-up companies, Mission Critical struggled with cash flows as it developed new business opportunities. A student found a financial statement for Mission Critical that included the following:

1998 increase in dividends in arrears on preferred stock was $264,000.

The student who read the note suggested that the Mission Critical preferred stock would be a good investment because of the large amount of dividend income that would be earned when the company started paying dividends again: "As the owner of the stock, I'll get dividends for the period I hold the stock plus some previous periods when I didn't even own the stock." Do you agree? Explain.

E11-12
LO4, 7

Determining the Impact of Dividends

Average Corporation has the following capital stock outstanding at the end of 2004:

Preferred stock, 6 percent, par $15, outstanding shares, 8,000.
Common stock, par $8, outstanding shares, 30,000.

On October 1, 2004, the board of directors declared dividends as follows:

Preferred stock: Full cash preference amount, payable December 20, 2004.
Common stock: 10 percent common stock dividend (i.e., one additional share for each 10 held), issuable December 20, 2004.

On December 20, 2004, the market prices were preferred stock, $40, and common stock, $32.

Required:
Explain the overall effect of each of the dividends on the assets, liabilities, and stockholders' equity of the company.

E11-13
LO4, 7
Sears,
Roebuck
and Company

Recording the Payment of Dividends

A recent annual report for Sears, Roebuck and Co. disclosed that the company paid preferred dividends in the amount of $119.9 million. It declared and paid dividends on common stock in the amount of $2 per share. During the year, Sears had 1,000,000,000 shares of common authorized; 387,514,300 shares had been issued; 41,670,000 shares were in treasury stock. Assume that the transaction occurred on July 15.

Required:
Prepare a journal entry to record the declaration and payment of dividends.

E11-14
LO6

Analyzing Stock Dividends

On December 31, 2007, the Stockholders' Equity section of the balance sheet of R & B Corporation reflected the following:

Common stock (par $10; authorized 60,000 shares,
outstanding 25,000 shares) $250,000
Capital in excess of par 12,000
Retained earnings 75,000

On February 1, 2008, the board of directors declared a 12 percent stock dividend to be issued April 30, 2008. The market value of the stock on February 1, 2008, was $18 per share.

Required:

1. For comparative purposes, prepare the Stockholders' Equity section of the balance sheet (a) immediately before the stock dividend and (b) immediately after the stock dividend. (*Hint:* Use two amount columns for this requirement.)
2. Explain the effects of this stock dividend on the assets, liabilities, and stockholders' equity.

Analyzing the Repurchase of Stock

E11-15
LO3, 4
Winnebago

Winnebago is a familiar name on vehicles traveling U.S. highways. The company manufactures and sells large motor homes for vacation travel. These motor homes can be quickly recognized because of the company's "flying W" trademark. A recent news article contained the following information:

> The Company's profits have been running double a year ago, revenues were up 27 percent in the May quarter and order backlog stands at 2,229 units. Those are the kind of growth statistics that build confidence in the boardroom. The Company has announced plans to spend $3.6 million to expand its manufacturing facilities and it recently authorized repurchase of $15 million worth of its own shares, the third buyback in two years. The Company's stock is now selling for $25 per share.

Required:

1. Determine the impact of the stock repurchase on the financial statements.
2. Why do you think the board decided to repurchase the stock?
3. What impact will this purchase have on Winnebago's future dividend obligations?

Preparing a Statement of Stockholders' Equity and Evaluating Dividend Policy

E11-16
LO3, 5

The following account balances were selected from the records of Blake Corporation at December 31, 2007, after all adjusting entries were completed:

Common stock (par $15; authorized 100,000 shares, issued 35,000 shares,
of which 1,000 shares are held as treasury stock) $525,000
Capital in excess of par 180,000
Dividends declared and paid in 2007 18,000
Retained earnings, January 1, 2007 76,000
Treasury stock at cost (1,000 shares) 20,000

Net income for the year was $28,000. Restriction on retained earnings equal to the cost of treasury stock held is required by law in this state. The stock price is currently $22.43 per share.

Required:

1. Prepare the stockholders' equity section of the balance sheet at December 31, 2007.
2. Compute and evaluate the dividend yield ratio. Determine the number of shares of stock that received dividends.

Recording Dividends

E11-17
LO4
Black &
Decker

Black & Decker is a leading global manufacturer and marketer of power tools, hardware, and home improvement products. A recent press release contained the following announcement:

> The Black & Decker Corporation announced today that its Board of Directors declared a quarterly cash dividend of 12 cents per share of the company's outstanding common stock payable December 31, 1999, to stockholders of record at the close of business on December 17, 1999.

At the time of this announcement, Black & Decker had 150,000,000 shares authorized and 87,498,000 issued and outstanding. The par value for the company's stock is $.01 per share.

Required:
Prepare journal entries as appropriate for each date mentioned in the note.

E11-18 Comparing Stock Dividends and Splits
LO6

On July 1, 2004, Jones Corporation had the following capital structure:

Common stock (par $1, authorized shares)	$200,000
Common stock (par $1, unissued shares)	50,000
Capital in excess of par	88,000
Retained earnings	72,000
Treasury stock, none	

Required:
Complete the following comparative tabulation based on two independent cases:

Case 1: The board of directors declared and issued a 10 percent stock dividend when the stock was selling at $4 per share.

Case 2: The board of directors voted a 6-to-5 stock split (i.e., a 20 percent increase in the number of shares). The market price prior to the split was $4 per share.

Items	Before Dividend and Split	After Stock Dividend	After Stock Split
Common stock account	$	$	$
Par per share	$ 1	$	$
Shares outstanding	#	#	#
Capital in excess of par	$88,000	$	$
Retained earnings	72,000		
Total stockholders' equity	$	$	$

E11-19 Evaluating Dividend Policy
LO4
H&R Block

H&R Block is a well-known name especially during income tax time each year. The company serves more than 18 million taxpayers in more than 10,000 offices in the United States, Canada, Australia, and England. A recent press release contained the following information:

> H&R Block today reported that revenues for the first quarter ended July 31, 1999, climbed 72 percent to $121 million. The company reported a first quarter net loss of $37 million, or 38 cents per share. The Board of Directors declared a quarterly dividend of 27 cents per share payable October 1, 1999, to shareholders of record on September 10, 1999.

Required:
1. Explain how H&R Block can pay dividends despite its loss.
2. What factors did the board of directors consider when it declared the dividends?

Evaluating the Dividend Yield Ratio

E11-20
L05
Cinergy
and
Starbucks

Cinergy is a utility company that provides gas and electric service in Ohio, Kentucky, and Indiana. The company's dividend yield is 6.6 percent. Starbucks, a well-known retailer of coffee products, does not pay dividends, resulting in a dividend yield of 0.0 percent. Both companies are approximately the same size with market values of $5 billion.

Required:
1. Based on this limited information, why do you think the dividend policies of the two companies are so different?
2. Will the two companies attract different types of investors? Explain.

PROBLEMS

Finding Missing Amounts (AP11–1)

P11-1
L03, 6

At December 31, 2007, the records of Nortech Corporation provided the following selected and incomplete data:

> Common stock (par $10; no changes during 2007)
> Shares authorized, 200,000.
> Shares issued, _____ ? _____ ; issue price $17 per share; cash collected in full, $2,125,000.
> Shares held as treasury stock, 3,000 shares, cost $20 per share.
> Net income for 2007, $118,000.
> Dividends declared and paid during 2007, $73,200.
> Retained earnings balance, January 1, 2007, $155,000.
> The treasury stock was acquired after the split was issued.

Required:
1. Complete the following tabulation:
   Shares authorized _____ .
   Shares issued _____ .
   Shares outstanding _____ .
2. The balance in the Capital in Excess of Par account appears to be $ _____ .
3. Earnings per Share is $ _____ .
4. Dividend paid per share of common stock is $ _____ .
5. Treasury stock should be reported on the balance sheet under the major caption _____ in the amount of $ _____ .
6. Assume that the board of directors voted a 100 percent stock split (the number of shares will double). After the stock split, the par value per share will be $ _____ , and the number of outstanding shares will be _____ .
7. Assuming the stock split mentioned above, give any journal entry that should be made. If none, explain why.
8. Disregard the stock split (assumed above). Assume instead that a 10 percent stock dividend was declared and issued when the market price of the common stock was $21. Give any journal entry that should be made.

Preparing the Stockholders' Equity Section of the Balance Sheet

P11-2
L03, 7

Skyhawk Corporation received its charter during January 2003. The charter authorized the following capital stock:

> Preferred stock: 8 percent, par $10, authorized 20,000 shares.
> Common stock: par $8, authorized 50,000 shares.

During 2003, the following transactions occurred in the order given:

a. Issued a total of 40,000 shares of the common stock to the four organizers at $11 per share.
b. Sold 5,000 shares of the preferred stock at $18 per share.

c. Sold 3,000 shares of the common stock at $14 per share and 1,000 shares of the preferred stock at $28.

d. Net income for the year was $48,000.

Required:

Prepare the stockholders' equity section of the balance sheet at December 31, 2003.

P11-3
L03, 7

Recording Transactions Affecting Stockholders' Equity (AP11–2)

Kerr Corporation began operations in January 2003. The charter authorized the following capital stock:

Preferred stock: 9 percent, $10 par, authorized 40,000 shares.

Common stock: No-par, authorized 80,000 shares, stated value per share is $5.

During 2003, the following transactions occurred in the order given:

a. Issued 20,000 shares of common stock to each of the three organizers. Collected $9 cash per share from two of the organizers and received a plot of land in full payment for the shares of the third organizer.

b. Sold 6,000 shares of the preferred stock at $18 per share.

c. Sold 500 shares of the preferred stock at $20 and 1,000 shares of common stock at $12 per share.

Required:

1. Give the journal entries indicated for each of these transactions.
2. Write a brief memo explaining what you used to determine the cost of the land.

P11-4
L01, 3

Recording Transactions and Comparing Par and No-Par Stock

McNally Company was issued a charter in January 2003, which authorized 100,000 shares of common stock with a par value of $25. During 2003, the following selected transactions occurred in the order given:

a. Sold 9,000 shares of the stock for cash at $60 per share. Collected the cash and issued the stock immediately.

b. Acquired land to be used as a future plant site; made payment in full by issuing 600 shares of stock. Assume a market value per share of $66.

Required:

1. Record the issuance of stock.
2. How would your previous answer change if (a) the stock was no-par, and (b) the stock had a stated value of $15 per share?
3. Does the type of stock issued (par, no-par, or stated value) affect the recorded value of the land? Explain.
4. Should a stockholder care whether a company issues par, no-par, or stated value stock? Explain.

P11-5
L03

Preparing the Stockholders' Equity Section after Selected Transactions (AP11–3)

Worldwide Company obtained a charter from the state in January 2003, which authorized 200,000 shares of common stock, $10 par value. The stockholders were 30 local citizens. During the first year, the company earned $38,200 and the following selected transactions occurred in the order given:

a. Sold 60,000 shares of the common stock to the 30 stockholders at $12 per share.

b. Purchased 2,000 shares at $15 cash per share from one of the 30 stockholders who needed cash and wanted to sell the stock back to the company.

c. Resold 1,000 of the shares of the treasury stock purchased in transaction *b* two months later to another individual at $18 cash per share.

Required:

Prepare the stockholders' equity section of the balance sheet at December 31, 2003.

P11-6
L03, 4, 6
Halliburton

Recording Stockholders' Equity Transactions (AP11–4)

Halliburton is a large multinational corporation with extensive operations in energy-related areas. The annual report for Halliburton reported the following transactions affecting stockholders' equity:

a. Purchased $3.5 million in treasury stock.
b. Declared and paid cash dividends in the amount of $254.2 million.
c. Issued 2-for-1 common stock dividend. 222.5 million additional shares were issued with a total par value of $556.3 million.

Required:
Prepare journal entries to record each of these transactions.

Analyzing Stockholders' Equity Transactions, Including Treasury Stock

P11-7
LO3, 4, 6

1. Compare a stock dividend with a cash dividend.
2. Compare a large stock dividend with a small stock dividend.
3. Describe the impact of the sale of treasury stock for more than cost on the income statement and the statement of cash flows.
4. Explain why a company might purchase treasury stock.

Comparing Stock and Cash Dividends (AP11–5)

P11-8
LO4, 6, 7

Water Tower Company had the following stock outstanding and retained earnings at December 31, 2007:

Common stock (par $8; outstanding, 30,000 shares)	$240,000
Preferred stock, 7% (par $10; outstanding, 6,000 shares)	60,000
Retained earnings	280,000

The board of directors is considering the distribution of a cash dividend to the two groups of stockholders. No dividends were declared during 2005 or 2006. Three independent cases are assumed:

Case A: The preferred stock is noncumulative; the total amount of dividends is $30,000.

Case B: The preferred stock is cumulative; the total amount of dividends is $12,600.

Case C: Same as Case B, except the amount is $66,000.

Required:
1. Compute the amount of dividends, in total and per share, that would be payable to each class of stockholders for each case. Show computations.
2. Assume the company issued a 10 percent common stock dividend on the outstanding shares when the market value per share was $24. Complete the following comparative schedule including explanation of the comparative differences.

	AMOUNT OF DOLLAR INCREASE (DECREASE)	
Item	Cash Dividend—Case C	Stock Dividend
Assets	$	$
Liabilities	$	$
Stockholders' equity	$	$

Analyzing Dividend Policy

P11-9
LO4, 8
Compaq

Dana and David, two young financial analysts, were reviewing financial statements for Compaq, one of the world's largest manufacturers of personal computers. Dana noted that the company did not report any dividends in the Financing Activity section of the statement of cash flows and said, "Just a few years ago, *Forbes* magazine named Compaq as one of the best performing companies. If it's so good, I wonder why it isn't paying any dividends." David wasn't convinced that Dana was looking in the right place for dividends but didn't say anything.

Dana continued the discussion by noting, "When *Forbes* selected it as a best performing company, Compaq's sales doubled over the previous two years just as they doubled over the prior two years. Its income was only $789 million that year compared with $867 million the previous year, but cash flow from operating activities was $943 million compared to an outflow of $101 million the prior year."

At that point, David noted that the statement of cash flows reported that Compaq had invested $703 million in new property this year compared with $408 million the prior year. He also was surprised to see that inventory and accounts receivable had increased by $1 billion and nearly $2 billion, respectively, the previous year. "No wonder it can't pay dividends; it generated less than $1 billion from operating activities and had to put it all back in accounts receivable and inventory."

Required:
1. Correct any misstatements that either Dana or David made. Explain.
2. Which of the factors presented in the case help you understand Compaq's dividend policy?

P11-10
LO4, 6, 7

Determining the Financial Statement Effects of Dividends

Lynn Company has outstanding 60,000 shares of $10 par value common stock and 25,000 shares of $20 par value preferred stock (8 percent). On December 1, 2004, the board of directors voted an 8 percent cash dividend on the preferred stock and a 10 percent common stock dividend on the common stock. At the date of declaration, the common stock was selling at $35 and the preferred at $20 per share. The dividends are to be paid, or issued, on February 15, 2005. The annual accounting period ends December 31.

Required:
Explain the comparative effects of the two dividends on the assets, liabilities, and stockholders' equity (a) through December 31, 2004, (b) on February 15, 2005, and (c) the overall effects from December 1, 2004, through February 15, 2005. A schedule similar to the following might be helpful:

COMPARATIVE EFFECTS EXPLAINED

Item	Cash Dividend on Preferred	Stock Dividend on Common

1. Through December 31, 2004:
   Assets, etc.

P11-11
LO4, 6
Adobe Systems

Recording Dividends

Adobe Systems develops and markets computer software including Adobe Acrobat that enables users to access information across all print and electronic media. A recent news article contained the following information:

September 16, 1999

Adobe Systems reported record revenue and operating profit for the third quarter of fiscal 1999. The Board of Directors announced a 100% stock dividend will occur on October 26, 1999 for stockholders of record on October 4, 1999. The Board also declared this quarter's cash dividend of $0.05 per share, payable on October 12, 1999 to stockholders of record as of September 28, 1999.

Required:
1. Prepare any journal entries that Adobe should make as the result of information in the preceding report. Assume that the company has 1 million shares outstanding, the par value is $0.50 per share, and the market value is $40 per share.
2. What do you think happened to the company's stock price after the September 16 announcement?
3. What factors did the board of directors consider in making this decision?

P11-12
LO1

(Chapter Supplement A) Comparing Stockholders' Equity Sections for Alternative Forms of Organization

Assume for each of the following independent cases that the annual accounting period ends on December 31, 2003, and that the Income Summary account at that date reflected a debit balance (loss) of $20,000.

Case A: Assume that the company is a *sole proprietorship* owned by Proprietor A. Prior to the closing entries, the capital account reflected a credit balance of $50,000 and the drawings account a balance of $8,000.

Case B: Assume that the company is a *partnership* owned by Partner A and Partner B. Prior to the closing entries, the owners' equity accounts reflected the following balances: A, Capital, $40,000; B, Capital, $38,000; A, Drawings, $5,000; and B, Drawings, $9,000. Profits and losses are divided equally.

Case C: Assume that the company is a *corporation.* Prior to the closing entries, the stockholders' equity accounts showed the following: Capital Stock, par $10, authorized 30,000 shares, outstanding 15,000 shares; Capital in excess of Par, $5,000; Retained Earnings, $65,000.

Required:
1. Give all the closing entries indicated at December 31, 2003, for each of the separate cases.
2. Show how the Owners' Equity section of the balance sheet would appear at December 31, 2003, for each case.

ALTERNATE **PROBLEMS**

Finding Missing Amounts (P11-1)

AP11-1
LO2, 3, 4, 6

At December 31, 2005, the records of Kozmetsky Corporation provided the following selected and incomplete data:

> Common stock (par $1; no changes during 2005)
> Shares authorized, 5,000,000.
> Shares issued, _____ ? _____ ; issue price $80 per share.
> Shares held as treasury stock, 100,000 shares, cost $60 per share.
> Net income for 2005, $4,800,000.
> Common stock account $1,500,000.
> Dividends declared and paid during 2005, $2 per share.
> Retained earnings balance, January 1, 2005, $82,900,000.
> The treasury stock was acquired after the split was issued.

Required:
1. Complete the following tabulation:
   Shares issued _____ .
   Shares outstanding _____ .
2. The balance in the Capital in excess of Par account appears to be $ _____ .
3. EPS on net income is $ _____ .
4. Total dividends paid on common stock during 2005 is $ _____ .
5. Treasury stock should be reported on the balance sheet under the major caption _____ in the amount of $ _____ .
6. Assume that the board of directors voted a 100 percent stock split (the number of shares will double). After the stock split, the par value per share will be $ _____ , and the number of outstanding shares will be _____ .
7. Disregard the stock split (assumed above). Assume instead that a 10 percent stock dividend was declared and issued when the market price of the common stock was $21. Explain how stockholders' equity will change.

Recording Transactions Affecting Stockholders' Equity (P11–3)

AP11-2
LO3, 7

Arnold Company was granted a charter that authorized the following capital stock:

Common stock: No-par, 100,000 shares. The no-par stock is not assigned a stated value per share.
Preferred stock: 8 percent, par $5, 20,000 shares.

During the first year, 2003, the following selected transactions occurred in the order given:

a. Sold 30,000 shares of the no-par common stock at $40 cash per share and 5,000 shares of the preferred stock at $26 cash per share.

b. Issued 2,000 shares of preferred stock as full payment for a plot of land. The stock was selling at $26.

c. Repurchased 3,000 shares of the no-par common stock sold earlier; paid cash, $38 per share.

Required:
1. Give the journal entries indicated for each of these transactions.
2. Explain the economic difference between acquiring an asset for cash compared with acquiring it by issuing stock. Is it "better" to acquire a new asset without having to give up another asset?

AP11-3
LO1, 3

Preparing the Stockholders' Equity Section After Selected Transactions (P11–5)

Global Marine obtained a charter from the state in January 2003, which authorized 1,000,000 shares of common stock, $5 par value. During the first year, the company earned $429,000, and the following selected transactions occurred in the order given:

a. Sold 700,000 shares of the common stock at $54 per share. Collected the cash and issued the stock.

b. Purchased 25,000 shares at $50 cash per share to use as stock incentives for senior management.

Required:
Prepare the stockholders' equity section of the balance sheet at December 31, 2003.

AP11-4
LO3, 4, 6, 7
Kmart

Recording Stockholders' Equity Transactions (P11–6)

The annual report for Kmart described the following transactions that affected stockholders' equity:

a. Declared cash dividends of $0.92 per share; total dividends were $374 million.

b. Sold series B preferred stock (no-par) in the amount of $157 million.

c. Sold treasury stock for $10 million; original cost was $8 million.

d. Issued a 100 percent stock dividend on common stock; its par value was $206 million, and the market value was $784 million.

Required:
Prepare journal entries to record each of these transactions.

AP11-5
LO4, 6, 7

Comparing Stock and Cash Dividends (P11–8)

Ritz Company had the following stock outstanding and retained earnings at December 31, 2006:

Common stock (par $1; outstanding, 500,000 shares)	$500,000
Preferred stock, 8% (par $10; outstanding, 21,000 shares)	210,000
Retained earnings	900,000

The board of directors is considering the distribution of a cash dividend to the two groups of stockholders. No dividends were declared during 2004 or 2005. Three independent cases are assumed:

Case A: The preferred stock is noncumulative; the total amount of dividends is $25,000.

Case B: The preferred stock is cumulative; the total amount of dividends is $25,000.

Case C: Same as Case B, except the amount is $75,000.

Required:
1. Compute the amount of dividends, in total and per share, payable to each class of stockholders for each case. Show computations.
2. Assume that the company issued a 15 percent common stock dividend on the outstanding shares when the market value per share was $50. Complete the following comparative schedule, including explanation of the comparative differences.

	AMOUNT OF DOLLAR INCREASE (DECREASE)	
	Cash Dividend—	
Item	Case C	Stock Dividend
Assets	$	$
Liabilities	$	$
Stockholders' equity	$	$

Annual Report Cases

Finding Financial Information

Refer to the financial statements of American Eagle Outfitters given in Appendix B at the end of this book, or open file AEOS.pdf in the Annual Report Cases directory on the student CD-ROM.

Required:

1. What is the approximate number of stockholders of record at the end of the current year?
2. Did the company pay dividends during the current year? If so, how much per share?
3. Does the company have any treasury stock? If so, how much?
4. Has the company ever issued a stock dividend or a stock split? If so, describe.
5. What is the par value of the common stock?
6. How many shares of common stock are authorized? How many shares are outstanding?

CP11-1
LO1, 2, 3, 4

AMERICAN EAGLE OUTFITTERS

Finding Financial Information

Refer to the financial statements of Abercrombie & Fitch given in Appendix C at the end of this book, or open file ANF.pdf in the Annual Report Cases directory on the student CD-ROM.

Required:

1. Does the company have any treasury stock? If so, how much?
2. What was the highest price for company stock during the fourth quarter of fiscal year 2000?
3. Did the company purchase any of its own stock during the period covered by the financial statements?
4. Describe the company's dividend policy.
5. Has the company ever issued a stock dividend or a stock split? If so, describe.
6. What is the par value of the common stock?

CP11-2
LO1, 2, 3, 4

ABERCROMBIE & FITCH

Comparing Companies within an Industry

Refer to the financial statements of American Eagle Outfitters given in Appendix B, Abercrombie & Fitch given in Appendix C, and the Industry Ratio Report given in Appendix D at the end of this book or open file CP11-3.xls in the Annual Report Cases directory on the student CD-ROM.

Required:

1. Notice that neither company has paid cash dividends since inception and neither plans to do so in the foreseeable future. As a result, the financial ratios discussed in this chapter are not useful for analyzing the companies. Why do you think both companies have similar dividend policies?
2. Examine the Industry Ratio Report for the family clothing stores industry. Does not paying dividends appear to be the norm for the industry?
3. Notice that both American Eagle Outfitters and Abercrombie & Fitch have split their stock. As an investor, would you buy the stock of a company that did not have plans to pay dividends in the foreseeable future?
4. Using the information from the following table, compare the dividend-related industry average ratios for the family clothing store industry to the variety store industry and the natural gas distribution industry. Why do public utilities distribute more of their profits as dividends than the other two industries? What type of investor would be interested in buying stock in a public utility instead of a retail store? Why?

CP11-3
LO3, 4

AMERICAN EAGLE OUTFITTERS

ABERCROMBIE & FITCH

DIVIDEND RATIOS FOR VARIOUS INDUSTRIES			
	Family Clothing Stores	Variety Stores	Natural Gas Distribution
Dividend/ Income	3.72%	7.48%	63.52%
Dividend yield	0.31	0.21	4.21
Example company	The GAP	Wal-Mart	Public Service of N.C.

Financial Reporting and Analysis Cases

CP11-4
LO4
Halliburton

Computing Dividends for an Actual Company

A recent annual report for Halliburton Company contained the following information (in millions of dollars):

Stockholders' Equity	Current Year	Previous Year
Common stock, par value $2.50, authorized 2,000 shares	$ 298.3	$ 298.4
Paid-in capital in excess of par	130.5	129.9
Retained earnings	2,080.8	2,052.3
Less 12.8 and 13.0 treasury stock, at cost	382.2	384.7

In the current year, Halliburton declared and paid cash dividends of $1 per share. What would be the total amount of dividends declared and paid if they had been based on the amount of stock outstanding at the end of the year?

CP11-5
LO4, 5
General Mills

Analyzing Dividend Policy

General Mills is a very successful company with substantial growth in revenues and earnings during the past 10 years. The following information was contained in a recent annual report:

	1999	1998	1997	1996	1995	1994	1993	1992	1991
Dividend/ Income	62%	80%	72%	63%	81%	64%	51%	49%	44%
Dividend yield ratio	2.7%	3.1%	3.2%	3.3%	3.1%	3.5%	2.5%	2.3%	2.2%
Dividends per share (dollars)	2.16	2.12	2.03	1.91	1.88	1.88	1.68	1.48	1.28

Based on this information, describe the dividend policy of General Mills. Assume that you are a financial analyst preparing a forecast of next year's operating results for General Mills. Net earnings for 1999 were $535 million, and the company paid out $331 million in dividends. Due to a number of factors, you believe that net income for next year will increase substantially and will be in the range of $900 to $950 million. To complete your financial forecast, you now need to estimate the total amount of dividends that General Mills will pay. What is your estimate?

CP11-6
LO4, 5, 6, 7
Dollar General

Inferring Financial Statement Amounts

Dollar General is a national retailer in direct competition with Wal-Mart. The annual report for Dollar General contained the following information:

Shareholders' Equity (amounts in thousands, except shares)	Preferred Stock	Common Stock	Paid-In Capital	Retained Earnings
Balance, January 30, 1998 (Common shares 167,052,000)	$858	$83,526	$379,954	$320,085
Net income				182,033
5-for-4 stock split		21,090		(21,090)
Issuance of common stock		1,488	27,523	

The company paid dividends in the amount of $3,497,000 to its preferred stockholders. It also paid dividends of $0.14 per share to its common stockholders. Assume that the common dividend was paid after the 5-for-4 stock split. Determine the total amount of dividends paid to common stockholders. When the annual report was issued, the common stock price was $25. Compute the dividend yield ratio.

Interpreting the Financial Press

As discussed in the chapter, companies buy back their own stock for a number of reasons. An article on this topic is available on the Libby/Libby/Short website at **www.mhhe.com/libby4e.** You should read the article, "Stock Market Time Bomb,"* November 15, 1999, and then write a short memo summarizing the article. In general, do you think large stock buybacks are good for investors?

CP11-7
LO2, 3

Critical Thinking Cases

Making a Decision as a Financial Analyst

Assume that you are a stockbroker with two clients. One is a recent college graduate and the other is a retired couple. You have recently reviewed the annual report for Philip Morris, which sells popular tobacco and beer products as well as Kraft brand foods. You were impressed with a 22 percent increase in net income for Philip Morris in 1998. You noticed that the company generated more than $8 billion in cash flows from operating activities and paid $1.68 per share in dividends. The dividend yield was 6.7 percent, one of the highest you have been able to find for large, well-known companies. Based on this information and your current knowledge of Philip Morris, would you recommend this stock for either of your clients?

CP11-8
LO4, 5
Philip Morris

Making a Decision as an Investor

You have retired after a long and successful career as a business executive and now spend a good portion of your time managing your retirement portfolio. You are considering three basic investment alternatives. You can invest in (1) corporate bonds currently paying 7 percent interest, (2) conservative stocks with average dividend yields of 5 percent and dividend payouts in excess of 80 percent of current earnings, and (3) growth-oriented technology stocks that pay no dividends. Analyze each of these alternatives and select one. Justify your selection.

CP11-9
LO4, 5

Evaluating an Ethical Dilemma

You are a member of the board of directors of a large company that has been in business for more than 100 years. The company is proud of the fact that it has paid dividends every year it has been in business. Because of this stability, many retired people have invested large portions of their savings in your common stock. Unfortunately, the company has struggled for the past few years as it tries to introduce new products and is considering not paying a dividend this year. The president wants to skip the dividend in order to have more cash to invest in product development: "If we don't invest this money now, we won't get these products to market in time to save the company. I don't want to risk thousands of jobs." One of the most senior board members speaks next: "If we don't pay the dividend, thousands of retirees will be thrown into financial distress. Even if you don't care about them, you have to recognize our stock price will crash when they all sell." The company treasurer proposes an alternative: "Let's skip the cash dividend and pay a stock dividend. We can still say we've had a dividend every year." The entire board now turns to you for your opinion. What should the company do?

CP11-10
LO4, 6

Evaluating an Ethical Dilemma

You are the president of a very successful Internet company that has had a remarkably profitable year. You have determined that the company has more than $10 million in cash generated by operating activities not needed in the business. You are thinking about paying it out to stockholders as a special dividend. You discuss the idea with your vice president, who reacts angrily to your suggestion:

CP11-11
LO4

*Reprinted from November 15, 1999 issue of *Business Week* by special permission, copyright ©1999 by the McGraw-Hill Companies, Inc.

"Our stock price has gone up by 200 percent in the last year alone. What more do we have to do for the owners? The people who really earned that money are the employees who have been working 12 hours a day, six or seven days a week to make the company successful. Most of them didn't even take vacations last year. I say we have to pay out bonuses and nothing extra for the stockholders." As president, you know that you are hired by the board of directors, which is elected by the stockholders. What is your responsibility to both groups? To which group would you give the $10 million?

Financial Reporting and Analysis Team Projects

CP11-12
LO1

Team Project: Evaluating Stock Compensation

Break into two teams. One team should play the role of labor union representatives and the other the role of senior management. The labor union wants all of its employees to receive an additional 10 percent of their compensation in the form of company stock. The union president argues that the stockholders will benefit from this proposal because the employees will work harder for the company if they are also owners. Management believes that this proposal is too expensive and that the board of directors would probably fire the management team if it ever approved the proposal. Outline the points to support your position and enter a negotiation to resolve the conflict. As a team, write a final recommendation to present to the board.

CP11-13
LO4

Team Project: Studying the Impact of Dividend Announcements

Each member of the team should find dividend announcements for different companies. Using a source such as *The Wall Street Journal,* determine the stock price for the company for each day one week before and one week after the announcement. Using spreadsheet software, prepare a chart of the stock price movement. Compare the charts for each company.

Required:

The team should summarize what a comparison of the charts indicates. Review the earnings announcements. Do they help explain any of the differences observed? Write a brief statement explaining how you think the stock market reacts to earnings announcements.

LEARNING OBJECTIVES

Reporting and Interpreting Investments in Other Corporations

12

Dow Jones & Co. is best known for its index of stock prices, the Dow Jones Industrial Average. However, the company does much more. It is the largest global provider of business news and information through print and electronic publishing.

Dow Jones's flagship publication, *The Wall Street Journal,* is the largest daily newspaper in the United States, with a circulation of more than 1.8 million. In print publishing, Dow Jones also produces *The Wall Street Journal Europe, The Asian Wall Street Journal, The Wall Street Journal Americas* (to Central and South America), *Barron's* (a business and financial weekly), *Far Eastern Economic Review,* and various financial magazines. The company also owns Ottaway Newspapers, Inc., which publishes 19 general-interest community newspapers.

Dow Jones recognizes that new technologies bring increased efficiency to its operations while expanding business opportunities. For example, *The Wall Street Journal* transmits page images to various printing plants via satellite, speeding delivery of material to the presses. Dow Jones also sells business news programming to CNBC and MSNBC. Moreover, the company is one of the leading providers of business and financial news over the World Wide Web. Its principal electronic products include Dow Jones Newswires, Dow Jones Interactive (a vast news library), and The Wall Street Journal Interactive Edition.

Dow Jones has achieved its diversity in part by investing in the stock of other companies. For example, Dow Jones owns half of CNBC Europe, CNBC Asia, and *SmartMoney* magazine. The announcement in early 2000 of the merger of two media giants, Time Warner and America Online, brought speculation of how other media companies might respond to the changing nature of the media industry and technology. To meet new challenges, will Dow Jones be seen "waltzing with Yahoo, AT&T, or Amazon.com"?*

*Felicity Barringer, "Media Megadeal: The Old Guard; Established Media Companies Are Nervous in Wake of Pact," *The New York Times,* January 12, 2000, p. 6, column 1.

UNDERSTANDING THE BUSINESS

Many strategic factors motivate managers to invest in securities. A company that has extra cash and simply wants to earn a return on the idle funds can invest those funds in the stocks and bonds of other companies, either long- or short-term. We say these investments are passive because the managers are not interested in influencing or controlling the other companies. Dow Jones's 2000 balance sheet, shown in Exhibit 12.1, does not reflect any short-term investments but does report a long-term Other Investments account.

EXHIBIT 12.1   Dow Jones & Company Balance Sheet

DOW JONES & COMPANY
Consolidated Balance Sheet
December 31, 2000 and 1999

(dollars in thousands)	2000	1999		2000	1999
Assets:			**Liabilities:**		
Current Assets:			Current Liabilities:		
Cash and cash equivalents	$ 49,347	$ 86,388	Accounts payable—trade	$ 66,699	$ 66,776
Accounts receivable—trade, net of allowance for doubtful accounts of $6,377 in 2000 and $5,919 in 1999	236,284	291,567	Accrued wages, salaries and commissions	73,119	62,659
			Retirement plan contributions payable	21,333	41,686
Accounts receivable—other	43,649	24,855	Other payables	185,138	124,470
Newsprint inventory	13,109	9,407	Income taxes	27,658	40,315
Prepaid expenses	18,105	16,041	Unearned revenue	213,277	225,157
Deferred income taxes	7,749	9,885	Total current liabilities	587,224	561,063
Total current assets	368,243	438,143	Long-term debt	150,865	149,945
Investments in associated companies, at equity	65,871	50,959	Deferred compensation, principally postretirement benefit obligation	227,948	217,612
Other investments	11,219	174,727	Other noncurrent liabilities	228,658	29,226
			Total liabilities	1,194,695	957,846
Plant and property, at cost			Minority Interests in Subsidiaries	8,593	1,377
Land	21,880	22,066	**Stockholders' Equity:**		
Buildings and improvements	415,297	313,138	Common stock	81,136	81,004
Equipment	969,365	902,230	Common stock, class B	21,045	21,177
Construction in progress	218,937	205,917	Additional paid-in capital	137,481	137,487
	1,625,479	1,443,351	Retained earnings	602,432	809,517
Less accumulated depreciation	864,616	766,939	Accumulated other comprehensive income:		
	760,863	676,412	Unrealized loss on investments	(4,960)	(941)
Goodwill, less accumulated amortization of $39,162 in 2000 and $38,660 in 1999	73,840	83,099	Foreign currency translation adjustment	405	(1,257)
Deferred income taxes	71,316	73,552		837,539	1,046,987
Other assets	10,704	15,821	Less, treasury stock (at cost)	678,771	493,497
Total assets	$1,362,056	$1,512,713	Total stockholders' equity	158,768	553,490
			Total liabilities and stockholders' equity	$1,362,056	$1,512,713

Sometimes a company decides to invest in another company with the purpose of influencing that company's policies and activities. Dow Jones's balance sheet reports these types of investments as Investments in Associated Companies. Finally, managers may determine that controlling another company, either by purchasing it directly or becoming the majority shareholder, is desirable. In this case, the two companies' financial reports are combined into consolidated financial statements, as Dow Jones has done (see the title to its "consolidated" balance sheet). In the notes to the annual report, we find that Dow Jones's significant past acquisitions include *Far Eastern Economic Review* and Ottaway Newspapers.

In this chapter, we discuss the accounting for four types of investments. First, we discuss using the amortized cost method to account for passive investments in bonds. Second, we examine the market value method of accounting for passive investments in stocks. Third, we present the equity method used to account for stock held to exert significant influence. The chapter closes with a discussion of accounting for mergers and consolidated statements.

ORGANIZATION of the Chapter

Types of Investments and Accounting Methods	Debt Held to Maturity: Amortized Cost Method	Passive Stock Investments: Market Value Method	Investments for Significant Influence: Equity Method	Controlling Interests: Mergers and Acquisitions
■ Passive Investments in Debt ■ Passive Investments in Stock ■ Investments in Stock for Significant Influence ■ Investments in Stock for Control	■ Bond Purchases ■ Interest Earned ■ Principal at Maturity	■ Classifying Passive Stock Investments ■ Securities Available for Sale ■ Comparing Trading and Available-for-Sale Securities	■ Recording Investments Under the Equity Method ■ Reporting Investments Under the Equity Method	■ What Are Consolidated Statements? ■ Recording a Merger ■ Reporting a Merger ■ Return on Assets

TYPES OF INVESTMENTS AND ACCOUNTING METHODS

The accounting methods used to record investments are directly related to the purpose of the investment.

Passive Investments in Debt

Passive investments are made to earn a high rate of return on funds that may be needed for future short-term or long-term purposes. This category includes both investments in debt (bonds and notes) and equity securities (stock). Debt securities are always considered passive investments. If the company intends to hold the securities until they reach maturity date, the investments are measured and reported at amortized cost. If they are to be sold before maturity, they are reported using the market value method.

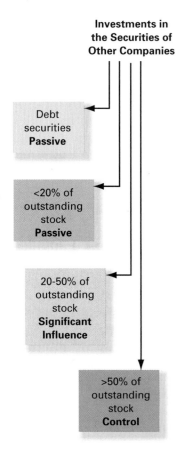

Investments in the Securities of Other Companies

Debt securities
Passive

<20% of outstanding stock
Passive

20-50% of outstanding stock
Significant Influence

>50% of outstanding stock
Control

Passive Investments in Stock

For investments in equity securities, the investment is presumed passive if the investing company owns less than 20 percent of the outstanding voting shares of the other company. The market value method is used to measure and report the investments.

Investments in Stock for Significant Influence

Significant influence is the ability to have an important impact on the operating and financing policies of another company in which it owns shares of voting stock. Significant influence is presumed if the investing company owns from 20 to 50 percent of the outstanding voting shares of the other company. However, other factors may also indicate that significant influence exists, such as membership on the board of directors of the other company, participation in the policy-making processes, evidence of material transactions between the two companies, an interchange of management personnel, or technological dependency. The equity method is used to measure and report this category of investments.

Investments in Stock for Control

Control is the ability to determine the operating and financing policies of another company through ownership of voting stock. For all practical purposes, control is presumed when the investing company owns more than 50 percent of the outstanding voting stock of the other company. Rules for consolidation are applied to combine the companies.

These categories and the appropriate measuring and reporting methods can be summarized as follows:

Investment Category	Level of Ownership (percentage of outstanding voting stock)	Measuring and Reporting Method
1. Passive: Debt held to maturity	—	Amortized cost
2. Passive: Stock	<20%	Market value method
3. Significant influence: Stock	Between 20 and 50%	Equity method
4. Control: Stock	>50%	Consolidated statement method

DEBT HELD TO MATURITY: AMORTIZED COST METHOD

Learning Objective 1
Analyze and report bond investments held to maturity.

HELD-TO-MATURITY INVESTMENTS are investments in bonds that management has the intent and ability to hold until maturity.

When management plans to hold a bond until its maturity date (when the principal is due), it is reported in an account appropriately called **Held-to-Maturity Investments.** Bonds should be classified as held-to-maturity investments if management has the intent and the ability to hold them until maturity. These bonds are listed at cost adjusted for the amortization of any bond discount or premium, not at their fair market value.

Bonds Purchases

On the date of purchase, a bond may be acquired at the maturity amount (at *par*), for less than the maturity amount (at a *discount*), or for more than the maturity amount (at a *premium*).[1] The total cost of the bond, including all incidental acquisition costs such as transfer fees and broker commissions, is debited to the Held-to-Maturity Investments account.

---

[1]The determination of the price of the bond is based on the present value techniques discussed in Chapter 9. Many analysts refer to a bond price as a percentage of par. For example, *The Wall Street Journal* might report that an ExxonMobil bond with a par value of $1,000 is selling at 82.97. This means it would cost $829.70 (82.97 percent of $1,000) to buy the bond.

To illustrate accounting for bond investments, assume that on July 1, 2008, Dow Jones paid the par value of $100,000[2] for 8 percent bonds that mature on June 30, 2013. The 8 percent interest is paid each June 30 and December 31. Management plans to hold the bonds for five years, until maturity.

The journal entry to record the purchase of the bond follows:

| Held-to-maturity investment (+A) .... | 100,000 | |
| Cash (−A) .... | | 100,000 |

Assets	=	Liabilities	+	Stockholders' Equity
Cash	−100,000			
Held-to-maturity investment	+100,000			

Interest Earned

The bonds in this illustration were purchased at par, or face value. Since no premium or discount needs to be amortized, the book value remains constant over the life of the investment. In this situation, revenue earned from the investment each period is measured as the amount of interest collected in cash or accrued at year-end. The following journal entry records the receipt of interest on December 31:

| Cash (+A) ($100,000 × 8% × 6/12) .... | 4,000 | |
| Interest revenue (+R, +SE) .... | | 4,000 |

Assets	=	Liabilities	+	Stockholders' Equity
Cash	+4,000			Interest revenue +4,000

The same entry is made on succeeding interest payment dates.

Principal at Maturity

When the bonds mature on June 30, 2013, the journal entry to record receipt of the principal payment would be:

| Cash (+A) .... | 100,000 | |
| Held-to-maturity investment (−A) .... | | 100,000 |

Assets	=	Liabilities	+	Stockholders' Equity
Cash	+100,000			
Held-to-maturity investment	−100,000			

If the bond investment must be sold before maturity, any difference between market value (the proceeds from the sale) and net book value would be reported as a gain or loss on sale. If management *intends* to sell the bonds before the maturity date, they are treated in the same manner as investments in stock classified as available-for-sale securities discussed in the next section.

---

[2]When bond investors accept a rate of interest on a bond investment that is the same as the stated rate of interest on the bonds, the bonds sell at par (i.e., at 100, or 100% of face value).

MARKET VALUE METHOD
reports securities at their current
market value.

**UNREALIZED HOLDING GAINS
AND LOSSES** are amounts
associated with price changes of
securities that are currently held.

PASSIVE STOCK INVESTMENTS:
THE MARKET VALUE METHOD

When the investing company owns less than 20 percent of the outstanding voting stock of another company, the investment is considered passive. Among the assets and liabilities on the balance sheet, only passive investments in marketable securities are reported using the **market value method** on the date of the balance sheet.[3] This violates the historical cost principle. Before we discuss the specific accounting for these investments, we should consider the implications of using market value:

1. **Why are passive investments reported at fair market value on the balance sheet?** Two primary factors determine the answer to this question:

   - **Relevance.** Analysts who study financial statements often attempt to forecast a company's future cash flows. They want to know how a company can generate cash for purposes such as expansion of the business, payment of dividends, or survival during a prolonged economic downturn. One source of cash is the sale of stock from its passive investments portfolio. The best estimate of the cash that could be generated by the sale of these securities is their current market value.

   - **Measurability.** Accountants record only items that can be measured in dollar terms with a high degree of reliability (an unbiased and verifiable measurement). Determining the fair market value of most assets is very difficult because they are not actively traded. For example, the John Hancock building is an important part of the Boston skyline. John Hancock's balance sheet reports the building in terms of its original cost in part because of the difficulty in determining an objective value for it. Contrast the difficulty of determining the value of a building with the ease of determining the value of securities that John Hancock may own. A quick look at *The Wall Street Journal* is all that is necessary to determine the current price of IBM or ExxonMobil stock because these securities are traded each day on established stock exchanges.

2. **When the investment account is adjusted to reflect changes in fair market value, what other account is affected when the asset account is increased or decreased?** Under the double-entry method of accounting, every journal entry affects at least two accounts. One account is a valuation allowance that is added to or subtracted from the investment account (maintained at cost) to report market value. The other account affected is for **unrealized holding gains or losses** that are recorded whenever the fair market value of investments changes. These are unrealized because no actual sale has taken place; simply by holding the security, the value has changed. If the value of the investments increased by $100,000 during the year, an adjusting journal entry records the increase in the asset account and an unrealized holding gain for $100,000. If the value of the investments decreased by $75,000 during the year, an adjusting journal entry records the decrease in the asset and an unrealized holding loss of $75,000. Recording an unrealized holding gain is a departure from the revenue principle that states that revenues and gains should be recorded when the company has completed the earnings process that generated them. The financial statement treatment of the unrealized holding gains or losses depends on the classification of the passive stock investments.

Classifying Passive Stock Investments

Depending on management's intent, passive investments may be classified as trading securities or securities available for sale.

Topic Tackler 12–1

---

[3]All **nonvoting** stock is accounted for under the market value method without regard to the level of ownership.

Trading Securities

Trading securities are actively traded with the objective of generating profits on short-term changes in the price of the securities. This approach is similar to the one taken by many mutual funds. The portfolio manager actively seeks opportunities to buy and sell securities. Trading securities are classified as **current assets** on the balance sheet.

Securities Available for Sale

Most companies do not actively trade the securities of other companies. Instead, they invest to earn a return on funds they may need for operating purposes in the near future. These investments are called **securities available for sale.** They are classified as current or noncurrent assets on the balance sheet depending on whether management intends to sell the securities during the next year.

Trading securities (TS for short) are most commonly reported by financial institutions that actively buy and sell short-term investments to maximize returns. Most corporations, however, invest in short- and long-term securities available for sale (SAS for short). We will focus on this category in the next section by analyzing Dow Jones's investing activities.

Securities Available for Sale

Dow Jones's Other Investments account is reported for the year 2000 at $11.2 million.[4] The notes to Dow Jones's annual report contain the following information concerning this investment portfolio:

TRADING SECURITIES are all investments in stocks or bonds held primarily for the purpose of active trading (buying and selling) in the near future (classified as short term).

SECURITIES AVAILABLE FOR SALE are all passive investments other than trading securities (classified as short or long term).

REAL WORLD EXCERPT

DOW JONES & CO.

ANNUAL REPORT

NOTES TO FINANCIAL STATEMENTS

Note 1. Summary of Significant Accounting Policies

INVESTMENTS in marketable equity securities, all of which are classified as available for sale, are carried at their market value in the consolidated balance sheets. The unrealized gains or losses of these investments are recorded directly to Stockholders' Equity. Any decline in market value below the investment's original cost that is determined to be other than temporary as well as any realized gains or losses would be recognized in income (see Note 15).

For simplification, let's assume that Dow Jones had no passive investments at the end of 2002. In the following illustration, we will apply the accounting policy used by Dow Jones.

Purchase of Stock

At the beginning of 2003, Dow Jones purchases 10,000 shares of Internet Financial News[5] (IFNews for short) common stock for $60 per share. There were 100,000 outstanding shares, so Dow Jones owns 10 percent of IFNews (10,000 ÷ 100,000), which is treated as a passive investment. Such investments are recorded initially at cost:

---

[4]This is down from $174.7 million in 1999 because of large write-offs of a number of investments whose market values had permanently fallen below book value. GAAP requires that investments in all categories whose market value has permanently and materially fallen below book value be written down to market.

[5]Internet Financial News is a fictitious company.

| Investment in SAS (+A) | .... | 600,000 | |
| Cash (−A) | .... | | 600,000 |

Assets		=	Liabilities	+	Stockholders' Equity
Investment in SAS	+600,000				
Cash	−600,000				

This entry and those that follow are illustrated in T-accounts in Exhibit 12.2.

Dividends Earned

Investments in equity securities earn a return from two sources: (1) price increases and (2) dividend income. Price increases (or decreases) are analyzed both at year-end and when a security is sold. Dividends earned are reported as investment income on the income statement and are included in the computation of net income for the period. Dow Jones received a $1 per share cash dividend from IFNews, which totals $10,000 ($1 × 10,000 shares).

EXHIBIT 12.2

T-Accounts for the Illustrated Transactions

Balance Sheet Accounts

Investment in SAS (at cost) (A)		
1/1/03	0	
Purchase	600,000	
12/31/03	600,000	
12/31/04	600,000	
		600,000 2005 Sale
12/31/05	0	

Allowance to Value at Market—SAS (A)		
		0 1/1/03
		20,000 2003 AJE
		20,000 12/31/03
2004 AJE	30,000	
12/31/04	10,000	
		10,000 2005 Sale
		0 12/31/05

Net Unrealized Gains and Losses—SAS (SE)		
1/1/03	0	
2003 AJE	20,000	
12/31/03	20,000	
		30,000 2004 AJE
		10,000 12/31/04
2005 Sale	10,000	
12/31/05	0	

Income Statement Accounts

Investment Income (R)		
		10,000 Earned
		10,000 12/31/03

Gain on Sale of Investments		
		0 1/1/05
		25,000 2005 Sale
		25,000 12/31/05

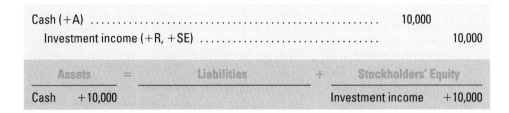

| Cash (+A) .... | 10,000 | |
| Investment income (+R, +SE) .... | | 10,000 |

Assets	=	Liabilities	+	Stockholders' Equity
Cash +10,000				Investment income +10,000

This entry is the same for both the trading securities and available-for-sale securities.

Year-End Valuation

At the end of the accounting period, passive investments are reported on the balance sheet at fair market value. Assume that IFNews had a $58 per share market value at the end of the year. That is, the investment had lost value ($60− $58 = $2 per share) for the year. However, since the investment has not been sold, there is only a holding loss, not a realized loss.

Reporting the SAS investment at market value requires adjusting it to market value at the end of each period using the account Allowance to Value at Market—SAS with an offset to Net Unrealized Gains and Losses in SAS. If the Allowance to Value at Market—SAS account has a **debit balance,** it is **added** to the Investment in SAS account. If it has a **credit balance,** it is **subtracted.** The Net Unrealized Gains and Losses in SAS account is reported in the stockholders' equity section of the balance sheet under Other Comprehensive Income. Thus, the balance sheet remains in balance. Since the SAS investment is expected to be held into the future, the unrealized holding gain or loss is not reported as part of net income. Only when the security is sold are any realized gains or losses included in net income.

The following chart is used to compute any unrealized gain or loss in the SAS portfolio:

Year	Market Value	−	Cost	=	Balance Needed in Valuation Allowance	−	Unadjusted Balance in Valuation Allowance	=	Amount for Adjusting Entry
2003	$580,000 ($58 × 10,000)	−	$600,000 ($60 × 10,000)	=	($20,000)	−	$0 (We assume there were no passive investments at the end of the prior year.)	=	($20,000) An unrealized loss for the period

The adjusting entry at the end of 2003 is recorded as follows:

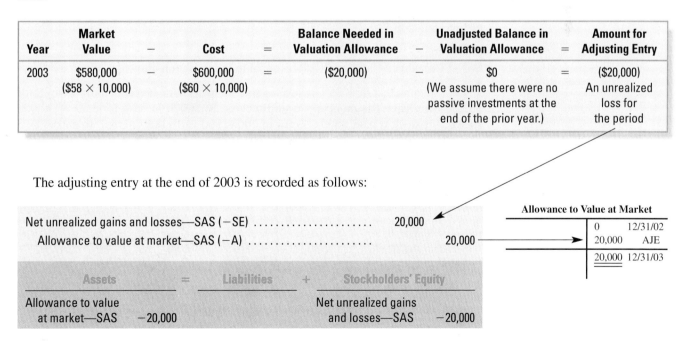

| Net unrealized gains and losses—SAS (−SE) .... | 20,000 | |
| Allowance to value at market—SAS (−A) .... | | 20,000 |

Allowance to Value at Market

0	12/31/02
20,000	AJE
20,000	12/31/03

Assets	=	Liabilities	+	Stockholders' Equity
Allowance to value at market—SAS −20,000				Net unrealized gains and losses—SAS −20,000

On the 2003 balance sheet under Other Investments, Dow Jones would report an investment in securities available for sale of $580,000 ($600,000 cost less the $20,000 credit balance in the valuation allowance). It would also report under Other Comprehensive Income its net unrealized loss on securities available for sale of $20,000. The only item reported on the income statement for 2003 would be investment income of $10,000 from the dividends earned, classified under other nonoperating items.

Now let's assume that the IFNews securities were held through the year 2004. At the end of 2004, the stock had a $61 per share market value. The adjustment for 2004 would be computed as follows:

Year	Market Value	−	Cost	=	Balance Needed in Valuation Allowance	−	Unadjusted Balance in Valuation Allowance	=	Amount for Adjusting Entry
2004	$610,000 ($61 × 10,000)	−	$600,000 ($60 × 10,000)	=	$10,000	−	($20,000)	=	$30,000 An unrealized gain for the period

The adjusting entry at the end of 2004 would be:

Allowance to Value at Market

		0	12/31/02
		20,000	AJE
		20,000	12/31/03
AJE	30,000		
12/31/04	10,000		

Allowance to value at market—SAS (+A) 30,000
   Net unrealized gains and losses—SAS (+SE)   30,000

Assets	=	Liabilities	+	Stockholders' Equity
Allowance to value at market—SAS +30,000				Net unrealized gains and losses—SAS +30,000

Sale of Stock

When securities available for sale are sold, **three** accounts on the balance sheet (in addition to Cash) are affected:

- Investment in SAS
- Allowance to Value at Market
- Net Unrealized Gains and Losses (equal to the valuation allowance).

Let's assume that in 2005 Dow Jones sold all of its SAS investment in IFNews for $62.50 per share. The company would receive $625,000 in cash ($62.50 × 10,000 shares) for stock it paid $600,000 for in 2003 ($60 × 10,000 shares). In entry (1), a gain on sale of $25,000 ($625,000− $600,000) would be recorded and the Investment in SAS would be eliminated. In entry (2), the valuation allowance and related net unrealized gains and losses account in stockholders' equity would be eliminated.

(1) Cash (+A) 625,000
   Investment in SAS (−A)   600,000
   Gain on sale of investments (+Gain, +SE)   25,000
(2) Net unrealized gains and losses—SAS (−SE) 10,000
   Allowance to value at market—SAS (−A)   10,000

Assets	=	Liabilities	+	Stockholders' Equity
(1) Cash +625,000				Gain on sale of investments +25,000
Investment in SAS −600,000				
(2) Allowance to value at market—SAS −10,000				Net unrealized gains and losses—SAS −10,000

Comparing Trading and Available-for-Sale Securities

The reporting impact of unrealized holding gains or losses depends on the classification of the investment:

Available-for-Sale Portfolio. As we learned in the previous section, the balance in net unrealized holding gains and losses is reported as a separate component of stockholders' equity (under **other comprehensive income**). It is not reported on the income statement and does not affect net income. At the time of sale, the difference between the proceeds from the sale and the original cost of the investment is recorded as a gain or loss on sale of available-for-sale securities. At the same time, the Net Unrealized Gains and Losses—SAS and Allowance to Value at Market—SAS are eliminated.

Trading Securities Portfolio. The amount of the adjustment to record net unrealized holding gains and losses is included in each period's income statement. Net holding gains increase and net holding losses decrease net income. This also means that the amount recorded as net unrealized gains and losses on trading securities is closed to Retained Earnings at the end of the period. Thus, when selling a trading security, Cash and only **two** other balance sheet accounts are affected: Investment in TS and the Allowance to Value at Market—TS for the trading securities portfolio. Also, only the difference between the cash proceeds from the sale and Investment in TS **net** of the Allowance to Value at Market is recorded as a gain or loss on sale of trading securities.

Exhibit 12.3 provides comparative journal entries and financial statement balances for the transactions illustrated for Dow Jones from 2003 to 2005. **Note that total income reported for the three years is the same for both trading securities and securities available for sale ($35,000). Only the allocation across the three periods differs.**

Equity Securities and Earnings Management

FINANCIAL ANALYSIS

Most managers prefer to treat their passive investments as securities available for sale. This treatment generally reduces variations in reported earnings by avoiding recognition of unrealized holding gains and losses resulting from quarter-to-quarter stock price changes. It also allows managers to smooth out earnings fluctuations by selling securities with unrealized gains when earnings decline and by selling those with unrealized losses when earnings increase. Diligent analysts can see through this strategy, however, by examining the required note on investments in the financial statements.

SELF-STUDY QUIZ

Dow Jones

Now let's reconstruct the activities that Dow Jones undertook in a recent year. Answer the following questions using the T-accounts to help you infer the amounts. The dollars are in thousands.

BALANCE SHEET ACCOUNTS

(In Other Investments)

Investment in SAS			
1/1	81,894		
Purchase	118,000	?	Sale
12/31	188,010		

Allowance to Value at Market—SAS			
1/1	3,396		
AJE	?	2,016	Sale
12/31	35,775		

EXHIBIT 12.3 Comparison of Accounting for Available-for-Sale and Trading Securities Portfolios

Part A: Entries	Trading Securities			Securities Available for Sale		
2003:						
• Purchase (for $600,000 cash)	Investment in TS (+A)	600,000		Investment in SAS (+A)	600,000	
	Cash(−A)		600,000	Cash (−A)		600,000
• Receipt of dividends ($10,000 cash)	Cash (+A)	10,000		Cash (+A)	10,000	
	Investment income (+R, +SE)		10,000	Investment income (+R, +SE)		10,000
• Year-end adjustment to market (market = $580,000)	Net unrealized gains/losses— TS (+Loss,−SE)	20,000		Net unrealized gains/ losses— SAS (−SE)	20,000	
	Allowance to value at market—TS (−A)		20,000	Allowance to value at market—SAS (−A)		20,000
2004:						
• Year-end adjustment to market (market = $610,000)	Allowance to value at market—TS (+A)	30,000		Allowance to value at market—SAS (+A)	30,000	
	Net unrealized gains/ losses—TS (+Gain, +SE)		30,000	Net unrealized gains/ losses—SAS (+SE)		30,000
2005:						
• Sale (for $625,000)	*Two balance sheet accounts are eliminated:*			*Three balance sheet accounts are eliminated:*		
	Cash (+A)	625,000		Cash (+A)	625,000	
	Allowance to value at market—TS (−A)		10,000	**Investment in SAS (−A)**		600,000
	Investment in TS (−A)		600,000	Gain on sale of investment (+Gain, +SE)		25,000
	Gain on sale of investment (+Gain, +SE)		15,000	**Net unrealized gains/ losses—SAS (−SE)**	10,000	
				Allowance to value at market—SAS (−A)		10,000

Part B: Financial Reporting	Trading Securities				Securities Available for Sale			
Balance Sheet reporting:	Assets	2005	2004	2003	Assets	2005	2004	2003
	Investment in TS	—	600,000	600,000	Investment in SAS	—	600,000	600,000
	Allow. to market—TS	—	10,000	(20,000)	Allow. to market—SAS	—	10,000	(20,000)
	Net Investment in TS	—	610,000	580,000	Net Investment in SAS	—	610,000	580,000
					Stockholders' Equity			
					Net unreal. gains/losses	—	10,000	(20,000)
Income Statement reporting:		2005	2004	2003		2005	2004	2003
	Investment income	—	—	10,000	Investment income	—	—	10,000
	Gain on sale	15,000	—	—	Gain on sale	25,000	—	—
	Net unreal. gains/losses	—	30,000	(20,000)				

(In Accumulated Other Comprehensive Income)

Net Unrealized Gains and Losses—SAS			
		3,396	1/1
Sale	?	?	AJE
		35,775	12/31

INCOME STATEMENT ACCOUNTS

Investment Income		
	?	Earned
	12,266	12/31

Loss on Sale of Investments		
Sale	2,384	
12/31	2,384	

a. Purchased securities available for sale for cash. Prepare the journal entry.	
b. Received cash dividends on the investments. Prepare the journal entry.	
c. Sold SAS investments at a loss. Prepare the journal entries.	
d. At year-end, the SAS portfolio had a market value of $223,785. Prepare the adjusting entry.	
e. What would be reported on the balance sheet related to the SAS investments on December 31? On the income statement for the year?	
f. How would year-end reporting change if the investments were categorized as trading securities instead of securities available for sale?	

After you have completed your answers, check them with the solutions that follow:

a. Investment in SAS (+A)	118,000	
Cash (−A)		118,000
b. Cash (+A)	12,266	
Investment income (+R, +SE)		12,266
c. (1) Cash (+A)	9,500	
Loss on sale of investment (+Loss, −SE)	2,384	
Investment in SAS (−A)		11,884
(2) Net unrealized gains/losses—SAS (−SE)	2,016	
Allowance to value at market—SAS (−A)		2,016
d. Allowance to value at market—SAS (+A)	34,395	
Net unrealized gains/losses—SAS (+SE)		34,395

e. Balance Sheet   Income Statement

Assets		*Nonoperating Items*

Balance Sheet

Assets
   Other investments $223,785

Stockholders' Equity
   Net unrealized gains/losses   35,775
     (in Accumulated Other Comprehensive Income)

Income Statement

Nonoperating Items
   Loss on sale of investments $ 2,384
   Investment income   12,266

f. If the securities were categorized as trading securities, no net unrealized gain would appear on the balance sheet. Therefore, when the securities were sold in c, no debit would be made to the Net Unrealized Gains/Losses account. Rather, there would be a loss on the sale of $4,400 (net of the valuation allowance) reported on the income statement. Then at year-end, the net unrealized gain of $34,395 would be reported on the income statement (not in stockholders' equity).

Market Value	−	Cost	=	Balance Needed in Valuation Allowance	−	Unadjusted Balance in Valuation Allowance	−	Adjustment to Valuation Allowance
$223,785	−	$188,010	=	35,775	−	$1,380 ($3,396 − $2,016)	=	$34,395

INVESTMENTS FOR SIGNIFICANT INFLUENCE: EQUITY METHOD

Learning Objective 3
Analyze and report investments involving significant influence using the equity method.

When Dow Jones invests cash in securities that are reported on its balance sheet as Other Investments, it is a passive investor. However, when the company reports Investments in Associated Companies on its balance sheet, it is taking a more active role as an investor. For a variety of reasons, an investor may want to exert influence (presumed by owning 20 to 50 percent of the outstanding voting stock) without becoming the controlling shareholder (presumed when owning over 50 percent of the voting stock). Examples follow:

EQUITY METHOD is used when an investor can exert significant influence over an investee; the method permits recording the investor's share of investee's income.

- A retailer may want to influence a manufacturer to be sure that it can obtain certain products designed to its specifications.

- A manufacturer may want to influence a computer consulting firm to ensure that it can incorporate the consulting firm's cutting-edge technology in its manufacturing processes.

- A manufacturer may recognize that a parts supplier lacks experienced management and could prosper with additional managerial support.

INVESTMENTS IN ASSOCIATED (OR AFFILIATED) COMPANIES are investments in stock held for the purpose of influencing the operating and financing strategies of the entity for the long term.

The **equity method** must be used when an investor can exert significant influence over an investee. On the balance sheet these long-term investments are classified as **investments in associated companies** (or affiliated companies). Dow Jones reported the following seven investments in associated companies in its 2000 annual report:

REAL WORLD EXCERPT

DOW JONES & CO.

ANNUAL REPORT

NOTES TO FINANCIAL STATEMENTS

Note 1. Summary of Significant Accounting Policies

. . . The equity method of accounting is used for companies and other investments in which the company has significant influence, generally this represents common stock ownership or partnership equity of at least 20% and not more than 50% . . . .

Note 4. Investments in Associated Companies, at Equity

At December 31, 2000, the principal components of investments in associated companies, at equity were the following:

Investment	Ownership	Description of Business
Business News (Asia) Private	50%	Business and financial news television company broadcasting as CNBC Asia, in partnership with NBC
Business News (Europe) L.P.	50	Business and financial news television company broadcasting as CNBC Europe, in partnership with NBC
Dow Jones Reuters Business Interactive LLC (Factiva)	50	Provides electronic-delivery of business news and on-line research, in partnership with Reuters Group Plc.
F.F. Soucy, Inc. & Partners, L.P.	40	Newsprint mill in Quebec, Canada
Handelsblattgruppe-Zeitung GmbH	22	Publisher of *Handelsblatt,* Germany's leading business newspaper.
HB-Dow Jones S.A.	42	A part-owner of a publishing company in the Czech Republic
SmartMoney	50	Publisher of *SmartMoney* magazine and SmartMoney.com serving the private-investor market throughout the U.S. and Canada, in partnership with Hearst Corp.

Recording Investments Under the Equity Method

Because the investing corporation can influence the operating and financing decisions of the investee, the investing company recognizes its share of the investee's net income in the period in which it is earned. Dividends are treated as distributions of already recognized earnings, specifically:

Topic Tackler 12–2

- **Net Income of Investee:** If the investee reports positive results of operations for the year, the investor then records investment income equal to its percentage share of the investee's net income and increases its asset account Investments in Associated Companies. If the investee reports a net loss, the investor records the opposite effect.

- **Dividends Paid by Investee:** If the investee declares and pays dividends during the year (a financing decision), the investor reduces its investment account and increases cash when it receives its share of the dividends.

Investments in Associated Companies (A)	

Beginning balance
Purchases
Company's % share of investee's
    net income (credit Equity in
    Investee's Net Earnings)
	Sales
	Company's % share of investee's
	    net loss (debit Equity in
	    Investee's Net Earnings)
	Company's % share of investee's dividends
	    declared for the period (debit Cash)

Ending balance	

Purchase of Stock

For simplification, let's assume that, at the beginning of 2003, Dow Jones had no long-term investments in companies over which it exerted significant influence. In 2003, Dow Jones purchased 40,000 shares of the outstanding voting common stock of Internet Financial News (IFNews) for $400,000 in cash. Since IFNews had 100,000 shares of common stock outstanding, Dow Jones acquired 40 percent and was presumed to have significant influence over the investee. Therefore, Dow Jones must use the equity method to account for this investment. The purchase of the asset would be recorded at cost.

Investments in associated companies (+A)	400,000	
Cash (−A)		400,000

Assets	=	Liabilities	+	Stockholders' Equity
Investments in associated				
companies	+400,000			
Cash	−400,000			

Investee Earnings

Because the investor can influence the process of earning income for the investee, the investor company bases its investment income on the investee's earnings rather than the dividends it pays. During 2003, IFNews reported a net income of $500,000 for the year. Dow Jones's percentage share of the IFNews's income was $200,000 (40% × $500,000) and is recorded as follows:

Investments in associated companies (+A)	200,000	
Equity in investee earnings (+R, +SE)		200,000

Assets	=	Liabilities	+	Stockholders' Equity	
Investments in associated				Equity in investee	
companies	+200,000			earnings	+200,000

If the investee reports a net loss for the period, the investor records its percentage share of the loss by decreasing the investment account and recording Equity in Investee Loss. The Equity in Investee Earnings (or Loss) is reported in the Other Items section of the income statement with interest revenue, interest expense, and gains and losses on sales of assets.

Dividends Received

Because Dow Jones can influence the dividend policies of its equity-method investments, any dividends it receives should **not** be recorded as investment income. Instead, dividends received reduce its investment account. During 2003, IFNews declared and paid a cash dividend of $2 per share to stockholders. Dow Jones received $80,000 in cash ($2 × 40,000 shares) from IFNews.

Cash (+A)	80,000	
Investments in associated companies (−A)		80,000

Assets	=	Liabilities	+	Stockholders' Equity
Cash	+80,000			
Investments in associated				
companies	−80,000			

In summary, the effects for 2003 are reflected in the following T-accounts:

Investments in Associated Companies			
1/1/03	0		
Purchase	400,000		
Share of investee net earnings	200,000	80,000	Share of investee dividends
12/31/03	520,000		

Equity in Investee Earnings			
		0	1/1/03
		200,000	Share of investee net earnings
		200,000	12/31/03

Reporting Investments Under the Equity Method

The Investments in Associated Companies account is reported on the balance sheet as a long-term asset. However, as these last two entries show, the investment account does not reflect either cost or market value. Instead, the following occurs:

- The investment account is increased by the cost of shares that were purchased and the proportional share of the investee company income.
- The account is reduced by the amount of dividends received from the investee company and the proportional share of any investee company losses.

At the end of the accounting period, accountants **do not adjust the investment account to reflect changes in the fair market value** of the securities that are held. When the securities are sold, the difference between the cash received and the book value of the investment is recorded as a gain or loss on the sale of the asset and is reported on the income statement in the Other Items section.

Improper Influence

A QUESTION OF ETHICS

A key assumption underlying accounting is that all transactions occur at "arm's length." That is, each party to the transaction is acting in his or her own self-interest. But when one corporation exerts significant influence over another (i.e., it owns 20 to 50 percent of the common stock), it is unreasonable to assume that transactions between the corporations are made at arm's length.

Consider what might happen if an investor corporation could affect the investee's dividend policy. If the investor reported dividends paid by the investee as dividend income, the investor could manipulate its income by influencing the other company's dividend policy. In a bad year, the investor might request large dividend payments to bolster its income. In a good year, it might try to cut dividend payments to build up the investee company's retained earnings to support large dividends in the future.

The equity method prevents this type of manipulation. Instead of recognizing dividends as income, income from the investment is based on a percentage of the affiliated company's reported net income.

SELF-STUDY **QUIZ**

Now let's reconstruct the activities that Dow Jones actually undertook in 2000 for its investments in associated companies with a few transactions being assumed. Answer the following questions, using the T-accounts to help you infer the amounts. The dollars are in thousands.

Investments in Associated Companies			
1/1/2000	50,959		
Purchase	44,255		
		12,161	Share of investee dividends
		?	Share of investee net losses
12/31/2000	65,871		

Equity in Net Earnings/Losses of Associated Companies		
1/1/2000	0	
Share of investee net losses	17,182	
12/31/2000	17,182	

a. Purchased additional investments in associated companies for cash. Prepare the journal entry.	
b. Received cash dividends on the investments. Prepare the journal entry.	
c. At year-end, the investments in associated companies had a market value of $62,000; the companies also reported $50,000 in net losses for the year. Prepare the adjusting entry.	
d. What would be reported on the December 31, 2000, balance sheet related to the investments in associated companies? What would be reported on the income statement for 2000?	

After you have completed your answers, check them with the solutions that follow:

_____

a. Investments in associated companies (+A)   44,255
        Cash (−A)   44,255
b. Cash (+A)   12,161
        Investments in associated companies (−A)   12,161
c. Equity in net losses of associated
        companies (+Loss, −SE)   17,182
        Investments in associated companies (−A)   17,182
d. **Balance Sheet**   **Income Statement**
      Assets   Other Items
        Investments in   Equity in net losses of
        associated companies $65,871   associated companies $17,182

Selecting Accounting Methods for Minority Investments

Managers can choose freely between LIFO and FIFO or accelerated depreciation and straight-line depreciation. In the case of minority (≤ 50% owned) investments, they may **not** simply choose between the market value and equity methods. Investments of less than 20 percent of a company's outstanding stock are usually accounted for under the market value method and investments of 20 percent to 50 percent under the equity method.

However, managers may be able to structure the acquisition of stock in a manner that permits them to use the accounting method that they prefer. For example, a company that wants to use the market value method could purchase only 19.9 percent of the outstanding stock of another company and achieve the same investment goals as they would with a 20 percent investment. Why might managers want to avoid using the equity method? Most managers prefer to minimize variations in reported earnings. If a company were planning to buy stock in a firm that reported large earnings in some years and large losses in others, it might want to use the market value method to avoid reporting its share of the investee's earnings and losses.

Analysts who compare several companies must understand management's reporting choices and the way in which differences between the market value and equity methods can affect earnings.

Investments | **FOCUS ON** CASH FLOWS

Many of the effects from applying the market value method to passive investments and the equity method to investments held for significant influence affect net income but not cash flow. These items require adjustments under the indirect method when converting net income to cash flows from operating activities.

In General   **Sales of securities** require a number of adjustments:

1. Any gain on the sale is subtracted from net income in the Operating Activities section.

2. Any loss on the sale is added back in the Operating Activities section.

The cash resulting from the sale or purchase is reflected in the Investing Activities section.

Income under the equity method also requires adjustments. Recall that cash dividends received from investees are not recorded as income. In addition, investors record as income their share of investees' earnings even though no cash is involved, resulting in the following:

1. Dividends received are added to net income in the Operating Activities section.

2. Any equity in investee earnings needs to be subtracted in the Operating Activities section.

3. Any equity in investee losses needs to be added in the Operating Activities section.

EFFECT ON STATEMENT OF CASH FLOWS

	EFFECT ON CASH FLOWS
Operating Activities	
Net income	$xxx
Adjusted for	
Gains/losses on sale of investments	−/+
Equity in net earnings/losses of associated companies	−/+
Dividends received from associated companies	+
Net unrealized holding gains/losses on trading securities	−/+
Investing Activities	
Purchase of investments	−
Sale of investments	+

Focus Company Analysis   A partial statement of cash flows for Dow Jones for 2000 follows. In both investment portfolios (SAS and associated companies), Dow Jones sold securities during the year; the gain is subtracted in the operating section. Dow Jones also added back the equity in losses of associated companies and dividends received from associated companies.

Dow Jones appropriately adjusted net income for these items. In both the Operating and Investing Activities sections, the effects related to accounting for investments have a significant impact on cash flows for Dow Jones.

DOW JONES & CO. INC.	
Consolidated Statement of Cash Flows (partial)	
For the year ended December 31, 2000	
(in thousands)	
Operating Activities	
Consolidated net loss	$(118,962)
Adjustments to reconcile net loss to net cash provided by operating activities:	
Gain on sale of business and investments	(24,053)
Equity in losses of associated companies, net of distributions	29,343
(other adjustments—not detailed here)	560,119
Net cash provided by operating activities	**446,447**
Investing Activities	
Businesses and investments acquired	(50,384)
Disposition of businesses and investments	28,760
(other investing activities—not detailed here)	(181,169)
Net cash used in investing activities	**(202,793)**

Equity in losses +17,182
Dividends +12,161
29,343

CONTROLLING INTERESTS: MERGERS AND ACQUISITIONS

Learning Objective 4
Analyze and report investments in controlling interests.

Before we discuss financial reporting issues for situations in which a company owns more than 50 percent of the outstanding common stock of another corporation, we should consider management's reasons for acquiring this level of ownership. The following are some of the reasons for acquiring control of another corporation:

1. **Vertical integration.** In this type of acquisition, a company acquires another at a different level in the channels of distribution. For example, Dow Jones owns a newsprint company that provides raw materials as well as a national delivery service.

2. **Horizontal growth.** These acquisitions involve companies at the same level in the channels of distribution. For example, Dow Jones has expanded internationally by creating or acquiring newspaper companies in major international markets in Asia and Europe.

3. **Synergy.** The operations of two companies together may be more profitable than the combined profitability of the companies as separate entities. Dow Jones has created or purchased a number of broadcast and internet news services. Merging these companies and sharing news content may create more profits than operating separate entities could.

Understanding why one company has acquired control over other companies is a key factor in understanding the company's overall business strategy.

The **PARENT COMPANY** is the entity that gains a control over another company.

The **SUBSIDIARY COMPANY** is the entity that is acquired by the parent.

CONSOLIDATED FINANCIAL STATEMENTS are the financial statements of two or more companies that have been combined into a single set of financial statements as if the companies were one.

What Are Consolidated Statements?

Any corporate acquisition involves two companies. The **parent** is the company that gains control over the other company. The **subsidiary** is the company that the parent acquires. When a company acquires another, **consolidated financial statements** must be presented. These statements combine the operations of two or more companies into a single set of statements. Basically, **consolidated statements can be thought of as the adding together of the separate financial statements for two or more companies to make it appear as if a single company exists.** Thus, the cash accounts for each company are added together as are the inventory accounts, land accounts, and others.

The notes to Dow Jones's 2000 annual report provide the following information:

REAL WORLD EXCERPT

DOW JONES
& CO.

ANNUAL REPORT

NOTES TO FINANCIAL STATEMENTS

Note 1. Summary of Significant Accounting Policies

THE CONSOLIDATED FINANCIAL STATEMENTS include the accounts of the company and its majority-owned subsidiaries. All significant intercompany transactions are eliminated in consolidation . . .

As the note indicates, eliminating any intercompany items is necessary when consolidated statements are prepared. **Remember that consolidated statements make it appear as though a single company exists when in fact there are two or more separate legal entities.** Intercompany items do not exist for a single corporation. For example, a debt owed by Dow Jones (the parent) to its newsprint subsidiary is not reported on a consolidated statement because a company cannot owe itself money. We discuss the preparation of consolidated statements in more detail in Supplement A at the end of this chapter.

Recording a Merger

We learned that consolidated statements are presented in such a way that two companies appear to have merged into one. In fact, the simplest way to understand the statements that result from the consolidation process is to consider the case of a simple merger where one company purchases all of the net assets of another and the target company goes out of existence. In such a situation, the purchasing company records the net assets of the target according to the cost principle, at the cash equivalent purchase price.

A **MERGER** occurs when one company purchases all of the net assets of another and the target company goes out of existence.

To illustrate, we will use simplified data for Dow Jones (the purchaser) and IFNews (the hypothetical target). Let's assume that, on January 1, 2001, Dow Jones paid $100 (all numbers in millions) in cash to buy all of IFNews's stock.[6] It then merges IFNews into its operations and IFNews goes out of existence as a separate legal entity. Exhibit 12.4 presents Dow Jones and IFNews's balance sheets, and market value data for IFNews's assets and liabilities, immediately **before** the merger.

(in millions)	Dow Jones	IFN Book Value	IFN Market Value
Assets			
Cash and other current assets	$ 368		
Plant and equipment (net)	761	$30	$35
Other assets	233	60	60
Total assets	$1,362	$90	
Liabilities and Stockholders' Equity			
Current liabilities	$ 587	$10	$10
Noncurrent liabilities	608		
Stockholders' equity	167	80	
Total liabilities and stockholders' equity	$1,362	$90	

EXHIBIT 12.4

Balance Sheets Immediately Before the Merger

---

[6]Purchasing 100 percent of the outstanding stock results in a wholly owned subsidiary. Purchasing less than 100 percent of the stock results in **minority interest** in the subsidiary, which represents the shares owned by other than the parent.

Note that Dow Jones paid $100 for 100 percent of IFNews even though the total book value of IFNews's net assets was only $80 ($90 assets − $10 liabilities). This is not surprising because **the book value of a company's net assets is not the same as the fair market value.** We will assume that an analysis of IFNews's assets and liabilities on the date of acquisition revealed the following facts:

- IFNews's Plant and Equipment had a current market value of $35 (net book value of $30).

- The book values of Other Assets ($60) and Current Liabilities ($10) on IFNews's balance sheet were equal to market values.

- IFNews had developed a good reputation with an important group of online investors, which increased IFNews's overall value. For these reasons, Dow Jones was willing to pay an additional $15 to acquire IFNews. The $15 difference between the purchase price of the company and the fair market value of its net assets (assets minus liabilities) is called **goodwill (or Cost in Excess of Net Assets Acquired)**. It may be computed as follows:

Purchase price for IFNews	$100
Less: Net assets purchased, at market ($35 + 60 − 10)	85
Goodwill purchased	$ 15

For accounting purposes, **GOODWILL (COST IN EXCESS OF NET ASSETS ACQUIRED)** is the excess of the purchase price of a business over the fair market value of the business's assets and liabilities.

The **PURCHASE METHOD** records assets and liabilities acquired in a merger or acquisition at their fair market value.

As noted, the cost principle requires that the assets and liabilities of IFNews be recorded by Dow Jones on its books at the purchase price (fair market value) on the date of the merger. This method of recording mergers and acquisitions, called the **purchase method,** is the only method allowed by U.S. GAAP. Dow Jones would record the merger as follows:

Plant and equipment (net) (+A)	35
Other assets (+A)	60
Goodwill (+A)	15
Current liabilities (+L)	10
Cash (−A)	100

Assets	=	Liabilities	+	Stockholders' Equity
Plant and equipment (net) +35		Current Liabilities +10		
Other assets +60				
Goodwill +15				
Cash −100				

It is important to remember that goodwill can be reported on the balance sheet **only if it is acquired in a purchase transaction.**

Reporting a Merger

Postmerger Balance Sheet

The postmerger balance sheet shown in Exhibit 12.5 was prepared by combining the above journal entry with Dow Jones's balance sheet shown in Exhibit 12.4.

(in millions)	Dow Jones
Assets	
Cash and other current assets ($368 − 100)	$ 268
Plant and equipment (net) ($761 + 35)	796
Other assets ($233 + 60)	293
Goodwill ($100 − 85)	15
Total assets	$1,372
Liabilities and Stockholders' Equity	
Current liabilities ($587 + 10)	$ 597
Noncurrent liabilities	608
Stockholders' equity	167
Total liabilities and stockholders' equity	$1,372

EXHIBIT 12.5

Dow Jones's Balance Sheet Immediately After the Merger

Remember the following:

1. IFNews's assets and liabilities are added at their fair market values, not their original book values.

2. Goodwill = Purchase Price − Net Assets Purchased (at their market prices).

3. The cash payment made for the acquisition is subtracted from cash on the balance sheet. If the company is purchased through issuance of additional stock, contributed capital is increased (credited) instead.

4. The balance sheet would be the same if Dow Jones and IFNews continued as separate legal entities after the purchase, and consolidated statements were prepared.

Postmerger Income Statements

After the merger, Dow Jones's accounting system will capture all of the revenues and expenses of the combined company. The resulting income statement is presented in Exhibit 12.6. The combined amounts include the following:

1. Revenues that would have been recorded in the separate accounting systems had the combination not taken place (Dow Jones $2,158 + IFNews's $120 = $2,278).

2. Expenses that would have been recorded in the separate accounting systems had the combination not taken place (Dow Jones $2,150 + IFNews's $106 = $2,256).

3. Additional expenses related to the recording of IFNews's assets and liabilities at market value; $1 additional depreciation assuming a 5-year useful life ($5 additional plant and equipment over book value ÷ 5 years = $1 per year).[7]

(in millions)	Dow Jones
Revenues ($2,158 + $120)	$2,278
Expenses ($2,150 + $106 + $1)	2,257
Net income	$ 21

EXHIBIT 12.6

Dow Jones's Income Statement for the Year Following the Acquisition

---

[7]Ignoring taxes.

Again, it is important to remember that the income statement would be the same if Dow Jones and IFNews continued as separate legal entities after the purchase and consolidated statements were prepared. These circumstances are illustrated in Chapter Supplement A.

As we noted in Chapter 8, goodwill is considered to have an indefinite life. As a consequence, it is not amortized, but, like all long-lived assets, goodwill is reviewed for possible impairment of value. Recording an impairment loss would increase expenses for the period and reduce the amount of goodwill on the balance sheet. Dow Jones described GAAP for goodwill in its recent SEC Form 10-Q.

REAL WORLD EXCERPT

DOW JONES & CO.

FORM 10-Q

[T]he FASB issued Statement of Financial Accounting Standards No. 142 (SFAS 142) "Goodwill and Other Intangible Assets." According to this Statement, goodwill shall not be amortized but be tested for impairment at least annually or between annual tests if an event occurs or circumstances change indicating that goodwill of a reporting unit might be impaired. The aggregate amount of goodwill impairment losses shall be presented as a separate line item in the operating section of the income statement.

FINANCIAL ANALYSIS

Accounting for Goodwill

Before 2001, GAAP required that goodwill be amortized over no more than 40 years. Beginning in 2002, companies were required to cease amortizing any previously recorded or newly recorded goodwill. For companies with large goodwill balances, this change caused a substantial increase in reported earnings. For example, Dow Jones Corporate Filings Alert recently reported the following effects for Wal-Mart:

REAL WORLD EXCERPT

DOW JONES & CO.

CORPORATE FILINGS ALERT

WAL-MART SAYS ACCTG CHANGE TO ADD $223M TO NET IN FY '03

WASHINGTON (Dow Jones)—Wal-Mart Stores Inc. (WMT) Tuesday projected an annual increase of $223 million in reported net income beginning in fiscal 2003 because of a new accounting pronouncement that requires that goodwill and intangible assets with indefinite lives no longer be amortized.

09/04/2001
Dow Jones Corporate Filings Alert
(Copyright (c) 2001, Dow Jones & Company, Inc.)

In evaluating Wal-Mart's post-2002 performance, analysts needed to adjust for the fact that this change in accounting rules artificially increased net income. Because the amortization of goodwill (like depreciation expense) is a noncash expense, ceasing the amortization had no impact on cash flows from operations.

KEY RATIO ANALYSIS

Return on Assets (ROA)

❓ ANALYTICAL QUESTION

During the period, how well has management used the company's total invested capital provided by both debt holders and stockholders?

% RATIO AND COMPARISONS:

$$\text{Return on Assets} = \frac{\text{Net Income*}}{\text{Average Total Assets**}}$$

Learning Objective 5
Analyze and interpret the return on assets ratio.

The 2000 ratio for Dow Jones:

$$\frac{\$(118,962)}{(\$1,362,056 + \$1,512,713) \div 2} = -0.083 \, (-8.3\%)$$

COMPARISONS OVER TIME		
Dow Jones		
1998	**1999**	**2000**
0.5%	18.1%	−8.3%

COMPARISONS WITH COMPETITORS	
New York Times	**Knight-Ridder**
2000	**2000**
11.2%	7.5%

Selected Focus Companies' Return on Assets Ratio for 2000

Papa John's	8.6%
Harley-Davidson	15.3%
Callaway Golf	13%

💡 INTERPRETATIONS:

In General ROA measures how much the firm earned for each dollar of investment. It is the broadest measure of profitability and management effectiveness, independent of financing strategy. ROA allows investors to compare management's investment performance against alternative investment options. Firms with higher ROA are doing a better job of selecting new investments, all other things equal. Company managers often compute the measure on a division-by-division basis and use it to evaluate division managers' relative performance.

Focus Company Analysis The average ROA for the printing and publishing industry is 5.7 percent.[†] Dow Jones's ROA is well below that amount. However, during the year, Dow Jones wrote down two of its major investments by $178.5 million and set up a reserve of $255 million on a contract guarantee related to a prior investment. Without these two nonrecurring losses, Dow Jones's ROA would have been in the ballpark of 19 percent. When analysts use ROA to predict the future, they often remove such nonrecurring items because they will not affect future periods' returns.

A Few Cautions: Like ROE, ROA can be decomposed into its components:

ROA	**=**	**Net Profit Margin**	**×**	**Asset Turnover**
$\dfrac{\text{Net Income}}{\text{Average Total Assets}}$	$=$	$\dfrac{\text{Net Income}}{\text{Net Sales}}$	$\times$	$\dfrac{\text{Net Sales}}{\text{Average Total Assets}}$

Like ROE, effective analysis of ROA requires understanding why ROA differs from prior levels and that of its competitors. The preceding decomposition, as well as more detailed analyses of components of net profit margin and asset turnover, provides that understanding.

*In more complex return on total asset analyses, interest expense (net of tax) and minority interest are added back to net income in the numerator of the ratio, since the measure assesses return on capital independent of its source.

**Average Total Assets = (Beginning Total Assets + Ending Total Assets) ÷ 2

[†]"Industry Norms & Key Business Ratios," *Dun & Bradstreet* (2000).

SELF-STUDY **QUIZ**

Lexis Corporation purchased 100 percent of Nexis Company for $10 million and merged Nexis into Lexis. On the date of merger, the market value of Nexis's Other Assets was $11 and the book value of Nexis's Liabilities was equal to market value. The two companies' summary balance sheets appeared as follows immediately **before** the merger:

	LEXIS (PARENT)	NEXIS (SUBSIDIARY)
Cash	$10	
Other Assets	90	$10
Liabilities	30	4
Stockholders' Equity	70	6

On the balance sheet after the merger was recorded, what would be the following balances?

1. Goodwill

2. Stockholders' Equity

3. Other Assets

After you have completed your answers, check them with the solutions that follow:

1. Purchase Price − Market Value of Net Assets = Goodwill $10 − (11 − 4) = $3.
2. Lexis's stockholders' equity is unchanged, leaving $70.
3. Lexis's other assets + Nexis's other assets (at market) = $90 + 11 = $101.

DEMONSTRATION CASE A

(Try to resolve the requirements before proceeding to the suggested solution that follows.) Howell Equipment Corporation sells and services a major line of farm equipment. Both sales and service operations have been profitable. The following transactions affected the company during 2004:

a. Jan. 1   Purchased 2,000 shares of common stock of Dear Company at $40 per share. This purchase represented 1 percent of the shares outstanding. Management intends to trade these shares actively.

b. Dec. 28   Received $4,000 cash dividend on the Dear Company stock.

c. Dec. 31   Determined that the current market price of the Dear stock was $39.

Required:

1. Prepare the journal entry for each of these transactions.

2. What accounts and amounts will be reported on the balance sheet at the end of 2004? On the income statement for 2004?

SUGGESTED SOLUTION FOR CASE A

1.   **a.** Jan. 1   Investment in TS (+A) 80,000

                  Cash (−A) (2,000 shares × $40)   80,000

     b. Dec. 28   Cash (+A) 4,000

                  Investment income (+R, +SE)   4,000

     c. Dec. 31   Net unrealized gains/losses—TS

                  (+Loss, −SE) 2,000

                  Allowance to value at market (−A)   2,000

Year	Market Value	−	Cost	=	Balance Needed in Valuation Allowance	−	Unadjusted Balance in Valuation Allowance	=	Adjustment to Valuation Allowance
2004	$78,000 ($39 × 2000 shares)	−	$80,000	=	($2,000)	−	$0	=	($2,000) an unrealized loss for the period

2. On the Balance Sheet:

Current Assets

Investment in TS $78,000
($80,000 cost −
$2,000 allowance)

On the Income Statement:

Other Nonoperating Items

Investment income $4,000
Net unrealized loss on
  trading securities 2,000

DEMONSTRATION CASE B

Assume the same facts as in Case A except that the securities were purchased as securities available for sale rather than as trading securities.

Required:

1. Prepare the journal entry for each of these transactions.
2. What accounts and amounts will be reported on the balance sheet at the end of 2004? On the income statement for 2004?

SUGGESTED SOLUTION FOR CASE B

1. **a.** Jan. 1 Investment in SAS (+A) 80,000
          Cash (−A) (2,000 shares × $40 per share) ...   80,000
    b. Dec. 28 Cash (+A) 4,000
          Investment income (+R, +SE)   4,000
    c. Dec. 31 Net unrealized gains/losses—SAS (−SE) 2,000
          Allowance to value at market (−A)   2,000

Year	Market Value	−	Cost	=	Balance Needed in Valuation Allowance	−	Unadjusted Balance in Valuation Allowance	=	Adjustment to Valuation Allowance
2004	$78,000 ($39 × 2000 shares)	−	$80,000	=	($2,000)	−	$0	=	($2,000) an unrealized loss for the period

2. On the Balance Sheet:

Current or Noncurrent Assets

Investment in SAS $78,000
($80,000 cost −
$2,000 allowance)

Stockholders' Equity

Accumulated other comprehensive income:

Net unrealized gains/losses on SAS (2,000)

On the Income Statement:

Other Items

Investment income $4,000

DEMONSTRATION **CASE C**

On January 1, 2003, Connaught Company purchased 40 percent of the outstanding voting shares of London Company on the open market for $85,000 cash. London declared $10,000 in cash dividends and reported net income of $60,000 for the year.

Required:

1. Prepare the journal entries for 2003.

2. What accounts and amounts were reported on Connaught's balance sheet at the end of 2003? On Connaught's income statement for 2003?

SUGGESTED SOLUTION FOR CASE C

1.	Jan. 1	Investments in associated companies (+A)	85,000	
		Cash (−A)		85,000
	Dividends	Cash (+A) (40% × $10,000)	4,000	
		Investments in associated companies (−A) ...		4,000
	Dec. 31	Investments in associated companies (+A) (40% × $60,000)	24,000	
		Equity in investee's net earnings (+R, +SE) ...		24,000

2. **On the Balance Sheet:**

Noncurrent Assets

Investments in associated companies ($85,000 − $4,000 + $24,000) $105,000

On the Income Statement:

Other Items

Equity in investee's net earnings $24,000

DEMONSTRATION **CASE D**

On January 1, 2005, Beaver Company purchased 100 percent of the outstanding voting shares of Paris Company in the open market for $85,000 cash and Paris was merged into Beaver. On the date of acquisition, the market value of Paris Company's Plant and Equipment was $79,000 (net book value, $70,000). Beaver had no liabilities or other assets.

Required:

1. Analyze the merger to determine the amount of goodwill purchased.

2. Give the journal entry that Beaver Company should make on the date of the acquisition. If none is required, explain why.

3. Should Paris Company's assets be included on Beaver's balance sheet at book value or market value? Explain.

SUGGESTED SOLUTION FOR CASE D

1. Purchase price for Paris Company	$85,000
Less: Market value of net assets purchased	79,000
Goodwill	$ 6,000

2.   Jan. 1, 2005 Plant and equipment (+A) 79,000

              Goodwill (+A) 6,000

                  Cash (−A) 85,000

3. Paris Company's assets should be included on the postmerger balance sheet at their market values as of the date of acquisition. The cost principle applies as it does with all asset acquisitions.

Chapter Supplement A

Preparing Consolidated Statements

As noted in the chapter, when a company acquires another and **both companies continue their separate legal existence, consolidated financial statements** must be presented. These statements combine the statements of two or more companies into a single set of statements prepared as if they were one company.

Recording Acquisition of a Controlling Interest

By offering cash or shares of its stock or a combination of the two to a target company's shareholders, one company can acquire control of another. When the target company's shareholders accept the offer and the exchange is made, the parent company records the investment in its accounts at the acquisition cost using the purchase method. When both companies maintain their separate legal identities after the acquisition, we say that a **parent-subsidiary relationship** exists. Since both companies continue to exist, both companies' accounting systems continue to record their respective transactions.

Using the same data we used when we discussed the merger of Dow Jones (the parent) and IFNews (the hypothetical subsidiary), let's assume that, on January 1, 2001, Dow Jones paid $100 (all numbers in millions) cash to buy all of IFNews's stock.[8] Dow Jones would record the acquisition as follows:

Investment in IFNews (+A) 100

   Cash (−A) 100

Assets	=	Liabilities	+	Stockholders' Equity
Investment in IFNews +100				
Cash −100				

Because the acquisition of IFNews is simply an exchange of shares among owners, no entry is made on IFNews's books. The spreadsheet in Exhibit 12.7 presents Dow Jones's and IFNews's balance sheets immediately **after** the acquisition is recorded by Dow Jones. The Investment in IFNews account is included in Dow Jones's balance sheet.

Preparing Consolidated Financial Statements After Acquisition

The Balance Sheet

In consolidation, the separate financial statements of the parent (Dow Jones) and the subsidiary (IFNews) are combined into a single consolidated statement. The investment account must be eliminated to avoid double counting the subsidiary's assets and liabilities and the parent company's investment in those assets. Dow Jones paid $100 for all of IFNews's stock even though the total **book value** of IFNews's stockholders' equity was only $80. Thus, the investment

---

[8]Purchasing 100 percent of the outstanding stock results in a wholly owned subsidiary. Purchasing less than 100 percent of the stock results in **minority interest** in the subsidiary.

EXHIBIT 12.7

Spreadsheet for Consolidated Balance Sheet on the Date of Acquisition

Immediately After Acquisition

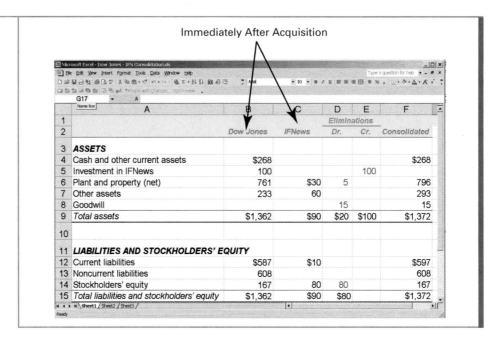

		Dow Jones	IFNews	Eliminations Dr.	Eliminations Cr.	Consolidated
3	**ASSETS**					
4	Cash and other current assets	$268				$268
5	Investment in IFNews	100			100	
6	Plant and property (net)	761	$30	5		796
7	Other assets	233	60			293
8	Goodwill			15		15
9	*Total assets*	$1,362	$90	$20	$100	$1,372
10						
11	**LIABILITIES AND STOCKHOLDERS' EQUITY**					
12	Current liabilities	$587	$10			$597
13	Noncurrent liabilities	608				608
14	Stockholders' equity	167	80	80		167
15	*Total liabilities and stockholders' equity*	$1,362	$90	$80		$1,372

account balance of $100 on Dow Jones's books represents the market value of IFNews's net assets (assets minus liabilities) on the date of acquisition. Dow Jones paid $20 in excess of book value for the following reasons:

■ IFNews's plant and equipment had a current market value of $35 and a net book value of $30. (The book values of all other assets and liabilities already on IFNews's balance sheet were equal to their market values.)

■ IFNews had developed a good reputation with an important group of online investors, which increased IFNews's overall value. For these reasons, Dow Jones was willing to pay $15 more than book value to acquire IFNews's stock. The $15 difference between the purchase price of the company and the fair market value of its net assets (assets minus liabilities) is called goodwill. It may be analyzed as follows:

Purchase price for 100% interest in IFNews	$100
Less: Net assets purchased, at market ($80 + $5)	85
Goodwill purchased	$ 15

To complete the process of consolidating Dow Jones and IFNews, we must **eliminate** Dow Jones's investment account and replace it with the assets and liabilities of IFNews along with the acquired goodwill. In this process, the goodwill is reported separately, and IFNews's assets and liabilities must be adjusted to market value for items where market value is different than book value, such as the plant and property in this illustration. We can accomplish this in the following five steps:

1. Subtracting the investment account balance of $100.

2. Adding the $15 goodwill purchased as an asset.

3. Adding $5 to plant and property to adjust the balance to market value.

4. Subtracting the IFNews stockholders' equity.

5. Adding together what remains of the Dow Jones and IFNews balance sheets.

When these procedures are accomplished, the balance sheet shown in Exhibit 12.8 is produced. Note that this is the same balance sheet presented in Exhibit 12.5 that resulted from the merger of Dow Jones and IFNews into one company. This should not be surprising because consolidated statements present a single set of statements as if the parent and subsidiary companies were one.

DOW JONES AND SUBSIDIARIES
Consolidated Balance Sheet
January 1, 2001

Assets	
Cash and other current assets	$ 268
Plant and property (net)	796
Other assets	293
Goodwill	15
Total assets	$1,372
Liabilities and Stockholders' Equity	
Current liabilities	$ 597
Noncurrent liabilities	608
Stockholders' equity	167
Total liabilities and stockholders' equity	$1,372

EXHIBIT 12.8

Consolidated Balance Sheet on the Date of Acquisition (in millions)

Income Statement

When we prepared the consolidated balance sheet, we combined the separate balance sheets to make it appear as if a single company exists. Consolidating the income statements requires a similar process. Prior to preparing consolidated statements for Dow Jones and its subsidiary IFNews, their separate income statements were as follows:

Simplified *Separate* Income Statements
Year ended December 31, 2001, One Year After Acquisition

(in millions)	Dow Jones	IFN
Revenues	$2,158	$120
Less: Expenses	2,150	106
Plus: Income from subsidiary	14	
Net income	$ 22	$ 14

The revenues and expenses generated by the parent company's own operations, excluding any investment income from the subsidiary, must now be combined with the subsidiary's revenues and expenses. The revaluation of assets to market value, if any, also has implications for the consolidated income statement. The increase in the assets must be depreciated or amortized in the consolidation process.

In this example, preparing the consolidated income statement requires three steps (ignoring taxes):

1. Add Dow Jones's revenues from its own operations of $2,158 and IFNews's revenues of $120.

2. Add Dow Jones's expenses related to its own operations of $2,150 and IFNews's expenses of $106.

3. Add to the expenses the $1 additional depreciation expense, assuming a 5-year useful life ($5 additional plant and equipment over book value ÷ 5 years = $1 per year).

Due to the simplicity of this example, you can directly prepare the simplified consolidated income statement in Exhibit 12.9. Complex adjustments and eliminations would normally be entered into a spreadsheet program.

EXHIBIT 12.9

Consolidated Income Statement

DOW JONES AND SUBSIDIARIES Consolidated Income Statement Year Ended December 31, 2001 (in millions)	
Revenues ($2,158 + $120)	$2,278
Expenses ($2,150 + $106 + $1)	2,257
Net income	$ 21

DEMONSTRATION **CASE E**

On January 1, 2004, Connaught Company purchased 100 percent of the outstanding voting shares of London Company on the open market for $85,000 cash. On the date of acquisition, the market value of London Company's operational assets was $79,000.

Required:

1. Give the journal entry that Connaught Company should make on the date of acquisition. If none is required, explain why.

2. Give the journal entry that London Company should make on the date of acquisition. If none is required, explain why.

3. Analyze the acquisition to determine the amount of goodwill that was purchased.

4. Should London Company's assets be included on the consolidated balance sheet at book value or market value? Explain.

SUGGESTED SOLUTION FOR CASE E

1. Jan. 1, 2004   Investment in subsidiary (+A)   85,000
                          Cash (−A)................................   85,000

2. London Company does not record a journal entry related to the purchase of its stock by Connaught Company. The transaction was between Connaught and the stockholders of London Company; it did not directly involve London Company.

3. Purchase price for London Company $85,000

   Market value of net assets purchased   79,000

   Goodwill $ 6,000

4. London Company's assets should be included on the consolidated balance sheet at their market values **as of the date of acquisition.** The cost principle applies as it does with all asset acquisitions.

CHAPTER **TAKE-AWAYS**

1. **Analyze and report bond investments held to maturity.**   p. 598
   When management intends to hold a bond investment until it matures, the held-to-maturity bond is recorded at cost when acquired and reported at amortized cost on the balance sheet. Any interest earned during the period is reported on the income statement.

2. **Analyze and report passive investments in stock using the market value method. p. 600**
   Acquiring less than 20 percent of the outstanding voting shares of an investee's common stock is presumed to be a passive stock investment. Passive investments may be classified as trading securities (actively traded to maximize return) or securities available for sale (earn a return but are not as actively traded), depending on management's intent. The investments are recorded at cost and adjusted to *market value* at year-end. A valuation allowance is increased or decreased to arrive at market value with the resulting unrealized holding gain or loss recorded. For trading securities, the net unrealized gains and losses are reported in net income; for securities available for sale, the net unrealized gains and losses are reported as a component of stockholders' equity in other comprehensive income. Any dividends earned are reported as revenue, and any gains or losses on sales of passive investments are reported on the income statement.

3. **Analyze and report investments involving significant influence using the equity method. p. 608**
   If between 20 and 50 percent of the outstanding voting shares are owned, significant influence over the investee firm's operating and financing policies is presumed, and the equity method is applied. Under the *equity method*, the investor records the investment at cost on the acquisition date. Each period thereafter, the investment amount is increased (or decreased) by the proportionate interest in the income (or loss) reported by the investee corporation and decreased by the proportionate share of the dividends declared by the investee corporation. Each period the investor recognizes as revenue its proportionate share of the income (or loss) reported by the investee company.

   The investing section of the statement of cash flows discloses purchases and sales of investments. In the operating section, net income is adjusted for any gains or losses on sales of investments and equity in the earnings of associated companies (net of dividends received).

4. **Analyze and report investments in controlling interests. p. 614**
   Mergers occur when one company purchases all of the net assets of another and the target company ceases to exist as a separate legal entity. Mergers and ownership of a controlling interest of another corporation (more than 50 percent of the outstanding voting shares) must be accounted for using the purchase method. The acquisition is accounted for in conformity with the cost principle, with the investee's assets and liabilities measured at their market values. Any amount paid above the market value of the net assets is reported as goodwill by the investor. The concept of consolidation is based on the view that a parent company and its subsidiaries constitute one economic entity. Therefore, the separate income statements, balance sheets, and statements of cash flows should be combined each period on an item-by-item basis as a single set of consolidated financial statements. Consolidated statements are the same as those that result from a merger when all of the assets and liabilities are acquired and the target company ceases to exist.

5. **Analyze and interpret the return on assets ratio. p. 619**
   The return on assets ratio measures how much the company earned for each dollar of assets. It provides information on profitability and management's effectiveness with an increasing ratio over time suggesting increased efficiency. ROA is computed as net income divided by average total assets.

Each year, many companies report healthy profits but file for bankruptcy. Some investors consider this situation to be a paradox, but sophisticated analysts understand how this situation can occur. These analysts recognize that the income statement is prepared under the accrual concept (revenue is reported when earned and the related expense is matched with the revenue). The income statement does not report cash collections and cash payments. Troubled companies usually file for bankruptcy because they cannot meet their cash obligations (for example, they cannot pay their suppliers or meet their required interest payments). The income statement does not help analysts assess the cash flows of a company. The statement of cash flows discussed in Chapter 13 is designed to help statement users evaluate a company's cash inflows and outflows.

KEY **RATIO**

Return on assets measures how much the company earned on every dollar of assets during the period. A high or rising ratio suggests that the company is managing its assets efficiently. It is computed as follows (p. 618):

$$\text{Return on Assets (ROA)} = \frac{\text{Net Income}}{\text{Average Total Assets*}}$$

(Beginning Total Assets + Ending Total Assets) ÷ 2

FINDING **FINANCIAL INFORMATION**

Balance Sheet

Current Assets

Investment in trading securities (net of valuation allowance)

Investment in securities available for sale (net of valuation allowance)

Noncurrent Assets

Investment in securities available for sale (net of valuation allowance)

Investment in associated companies

Investments held to maturity

Stockholders' Equity

Accumulated other comprehensive income:

Net unrealized gains and losses on securities available for sale

Statement of Cash Flows

Operating Activities

Net income adjusted for:

Gains/losses on sale of investments

Equity in earnings/losses of associated companies

Dividends received from associated companies

Net unrealized gains/losses on trading securities

Income Statement

Under "Other Items"

Investment income

Loss or gain on sale of investments

Net unrealized gains and losses on trading securities

Equity in investee earnings or losses

Notes

In Various Notes

Accounting policies for investments

Details on securities held as trading and available-for-sale securities and investments in associated companies

KEY **TERMS**

Consolidated Financial Statements p. 614

Equity Method p. 608

Goodwill (Cost in Excess of Net Assets Acquired) p. 616

Held-to-Maturity Investments p. 598

Investments in Associated (or Affiliated) Companies p. 608

Market Value Method p. 600

Merger p. 615

Parent Company p. 614

Purchase Method p. 616

Securities Available for Sale p. 601

Subsidiary Company p. 614

Trading Securities p. 601

Unrealized Holding Gains and Losses p. 600

QUESTIONS

1. Explain the difference between a short-term investment and a long-term investment.
2. Explain the difference in accounting methods used for passive investments, investments in which the investor can exert significant influence, and investments in which the investor has control over another entity.
3. Explain how bonds held to maturity are reported on the balance sheet.
4. Explain the application of the cost principle to the purchase of capital stock in another company.
5. Under the market value method, when and how does the investor company measure revenue?

6. Under the equity method, why does the investor company measure revenue on a proportionate basis when income is reported by the investee company rather than when dividends are declared?

7. Under the equity method, dividends received from the investee company are not recorded as revenue. To record dividends as revenue involves double counting. Explain.

8. What is a business combination by purchase?

9. What is goodwill?

10. What is a parent–subsidiary relationship?

11. Explain the basic concept underlying consolidated statements.

12. What is the basic element that must be present before consolidated statements are appropriate?

13. (Supplement A) What are intercompany eliminations?

MULTIPLE **CHOICE QUESTIONS**

1. Company A owns 40 percent of Company B and exercises significant influence over the management of Company B. Therefore, Company A uses what method of accounting for reporting its ownership of stock in Company B?
   a. the amortized cost method
   b. the market-value method
   c. the equity method
   d. consolidation of the financial statements of companies A and B

2. Company A purchases 10 percent of Company X and intends to hold the stock for at least five years. At the end of the current year, how would Company A's investment in Company X be reported on Company A's December 31 (year-end) balance sheet?
   a. at original cost in the Current Asset section
   b. at the December 31 market value in the Current Asset section
   c. at original cost in the Long-Term Asset section
   d. at the December 31 market value in the Long-Term Asset section

3. Dividends received from a stock that is reported as a *Security Available for Sale* in the long-term asset section of the balance sheet are reported as which of the following?
   a. an increase to cash and a decrease to the investment in stock account
   b. an increase to cash and an unrealized gain on the balance sheet
   c. an increase to cash and an increase to revenue
   d. an increase to cash and an unrealized gain on the income statement

4. Realized gains and losses are recorded on the income statement for which of the following transactions in *trading securities* and *available-for-sale securities?*
   a. when adjusting a *trading security* to its market value
   b. when adjusting an *available-for-sale* security to its market value
   c. only when recording the sale of a *trading security*
   d. when recording the sale of either a *trading security* or an *available-for-sale* security

5. When recording dividends received from a stock investment accounted for using the equity method, which of the following statements is true?
   a. Total assets are increased and net income is increased.
   b. Total assets are increased and total owners' equity is increased.
   c. Total assets are decreased and total owners' equity is decreased.
   d. Total assets and total owners' equity do not change.

6. When using the equity method of accounting, when is revenue recorded on the books of the investor company?
   a. when the market value of the investee stock increases
   b. when a dividend is received from the investee
   c. when the investee company reports net income
   d. both (b) and (c)

7. Which of the following items is reported in the Investing Section of the statement of cash flows when a stock investment is sold?
   a. the subtraction of a resulting gain on the sale   c. the addition of cash sales proceeds
   b. the addition of a resulting loss on the sale   d. all of the above

8. Which of the following statements regarding goodwill is false?
    a. Goodwill appears in the noncurrent asset section of the balance sheet.
    b. When the amortization of goodwill was halted in 2001, cash flows for those companies reporting goodwill increased accordingly.
    c. When companies develop goodwill internally rather than acquire the goodwill in an exchange, goodwill is not reported on the balance sheet.
    d. None of the above are false.
9. Which of the following is true regarding the return on assets ratio?
    a. This ratio is used to evaluate the efficiency of a company given the capital contributed by owners.
    b. This ratio is used to evaluate the financing strategy of a company.
    c. Return on assets can be separated into two components, net profit margin and inventory turnover.
    d. This ratio is used to evaluate how efficiently a company manages its total assets.
10. Consolidated financial statements are required in which of the following situations?
    a. only when a company can exert significant influence over another company
    b. only when a company acquires goodwill in the purchase of another company
    c. only when a parent company can exercise control over its subsidiary
    d. only when a company acquires another company for vertical integration

For more practice with multiple choice questions, go to our website at www.mhhe.com/libby4e, click on "Student Center" in the upper left menu, click on this chapter's name and number from the list of contents, and then click on "Multiple Choice Quiz" from the menu on the left.

MINI-EXERCISES

M12-1
LO1, 2, 3, 4

Matching Measurement and Reporting Methods

Match the following. Answers may be used more than once:

Measurement Method

A. Market value method	___ More than 50 percent ownership
B. Equity method	___ Bonds held to maturity
C. Consolidation	___ Less than 20 percent ownership
D. Unamortized cost	___ At least 20 percent but not more than 50 percent ownership
	___ Current market value
	___ Original cost less any amortization of premium or discount associated with the purchase
	___ Original cost plus proportionate part of the income of the investee less proportionate part of the dividends declared by investee.

M12-2
LO1

Recording a Bond Investment

Wall Company purchased $1,000,000, 8 percent bonds issued by Janice Company on January 1, 2003. The purchase price of the bonds was $1,070,000. Interest is payable semiannually each June 30 and December 31. Record the purchase of the bonds on January 1, 2003.

M12-3
LO2

Recording Trading Securities Transactions

During 2004, Princeton Company acquired some of the 50,000 outstanding shares of the common stock, par $10, of Cox Corporation as trading securities. The accounting period for both companies ends December 31. Give the journal entries for each of the following transactions that occurred during 2004:

July 2 Purchased 8,000 shares of Cox common stock at $28 per share.

Dec.15 Cox Corporation declared and paid a cash dividend of $2 per share.

     31 Determined the current market price of Cox stock to be $25 per share.

Recording Available-for-Sale Securities Transactions

M12-4
LO2

Using the data in M12-3, assume that Princeton Company purchased the voting stock of Cox Corporation for the available-for-sale portfolio instead of the trading securities portfolio. Give the journal entries for each of the transactions listed.

Determining Financial Statement Effects of Trading Securities Transactions

M12-5
LO2

Using the following categories, indicate the effects of the transactions listed in M12-3. Use + for increase and − for decrease and indicate the amounts.

	BALANCE SHEET			INCOME STATEMENT		
Transaction	Assets	Liabilities	Stockholders' Equity	Revenues	Expenses	Net Income

Determining Financial Statement Effects of Available-for-Sale Securities Transactions

M12-6
LO2

Using the following categories, indicate the effects of the transactions listed in M12-4. Use + for increase and − for decrease and indicate the amounts.

	BALANCE SHEET			INCOME STATEMENT		
Transaction	Assets	Liabilities	Stockholders' Equity	Revenues	Expenses	Net Income

Recording Equity Method Securities Transactions

M12-7
LO3

On January 1, 2003, Ubuy.com acquired 25 percent (10,000 shares) of the common stock of E-Net Corporation. The accounting period for both companies ends December 31. Give the journal entries for each of the following transactions that occurred during 2003:

July   2   E-Net declared and paid a cash dividend of $3 per share.

Dec. 31   E-Net reported net income of $200,000.

Determining Financial Statement Effects of Equity Method Securities

M12-8
LO3

Using the following categories, indicate the effects of the transactions listed in M12-7. Use + for increase and − for decrease and indicate the accounts affected and the amounts.

	BALANCE SHEET			INCOME STATEMENT		
Transaction	Assets	Liabilities	Stockholders' Equity	Revenues	Expenses	Net Income

Recording a Merger

M12-9
LO4

Philadelphia Textile Company acquired Boston Fabric Company for $600,000 cash when Boston's only assets, property and equipment, had a book value of $590,000 and a market value of $630,000. Philadelphia also assumed Boston's bonds payable of $100,000. After the acquisition, Boston would cease to exist as a separate legal entity after merging with Philadelphia. Record the acquisition.

Computing and Interpreting Return on Assets Ratio

M12-10
LO5

MAD Company reported the following information at the end of each year:

Year	Net Income	Total Assets
2003	$152,000	$ 52,000
2004	195,000	68,000
2005	201,000	134,000
2006	212,000	145,000

Compute return on assets for 2004, 2005, and 2006. What do the results suggest about MAD Company?

M12-11

The Walt Disney Company

(Supplement A) Interpreting Goodwill Disclosures

Disney owns theme parks, movie studios, television and radio stations, newspapers, and television networks, including ABC and ESPN. Its balance sheet recently reported goodwill in the amount of $16 billion, which is more than 30 percent of the company's total assets. This percentage is very large compared to that of most companies. Explain why you think Disney has such a large amount of goodwill reported on its balance sheet.

EXERCISES

E12-1

L01

Sears, Roebuck & Company

Recording Bonds Held to Maturity

Sears, Roebuck & Co. is perhaps best known for its mall-based retail stores that sell apparel, home, and automotive products. The company does more than $41 billion in sales each year.

Assume that as part of its cash management strategy, Sears purchased $10 million bonds at par for cash on July 1, 2004. The bonds pay 10 percent interest each June 30 and December 31 and mature in 10 years. Sears plans to hold the bonds until maturity.

Required:
1. Record the purchase of the bonds on July 1, 2004.
2. Record the receipt of interest on December 31, 2004.

E12-2

L02, 3

Comparing Market Value and Equity Methods

Company A purchased a certain number of Company B's outstanding voting shares at $18 per share as a long-term investment. Company B had outstanding 20,000 shares of $10 par value stock. Complete the following matrix relating to the measurement and reporting by Company A after acquisition of the shares of Company B stock.

Questions	Market Value Method	Equity Method
a. What is the applicable level of ownership by Company A of Company B to apply the method?	____%	____%
For *b, e, f,* and *g,* assume the following:		
Number of shares acquired of Company B stock	1,500	5,000
Net income reported by Company B in the first year	$60,000	$60,000
Dividends declared by Company B in the first year	$15,000	$15,000
Market price at end of first year, Company B stock	$ 15	$ 15
b. At acquisition, the investment account on the books of Company A should be debited at what amount?	$____	$____
c. When should Company A recognize revenue earned on the stock of Company B? Explanation required.	____	____
d. After acquisition date, how should Company A change the balance of the investment account with respect to the stock owned in Company B (other than for disposal of the investment)? Explanation required.	____	____
e. What is the net balance in the investment account on the balance sheet of Company A at the end of the first year?	$____	$____
f. What amount of revenue from the investment in Company B should Company A report at the end of the first year?	$____	$____
g. What amount of unrealized loss should Company A report at the end of the first year?	$____	$____

Recording Transactions in the Trading Securities Portfolio

On June 30, 2003, MetroMedia, Inc., purchased 10,000 shares of Mitek stock for $20 per share. Management purchased the stock for speculative purposes and recorded the stock in the trading securities portfolio. The following information pertains to the price per share of Mitek stock:

	Price
12/31/2003	$24
12/31/2004	31
12/31/2005	25

MetroMedia sold all of the Mitek stock on February 14, 2006, at a price of $23 per share. Prepare any journal entries that are required by the facts presented in this case.

E12-3
LO2

Recording Transactions in the Available-for-Sale Portfolio

Using the data in E12-3, assume that MetroMedia management purchased the Mitek stock for the available-for-sale portfolio instead of the trading securities portfolio. Prepare any journal entries that are required by the facts presented in the case.

E12-4
LO2

Reporting Gains and Losses in the Trading Securities Portfolio

On March 10, 2004, General Solutions, Inc., purchased 5,000 shares of MicroTech stock for $50 per share. Management purchased the stock for speculative purposes and recorded it in the trading securities portfolio. The following information pertains to the price per share of MicroTech stock:

	Price
12/31/2004	$55
12/31/2005	40
12/31/2006	42

General Solutions sold all of the MicroTech stock on September 12, 2007, at a price of $39 per share. Prepare any journal entries that are required by the facts presented in this case.

E12-5
LO2

Reporting Gains and Losses in the Available-for-Sale Portfolio

Using the data in E12-5, assume that General Solutions management purchased the MicroTech stock for the available-for-sale portfolio instead of the trading securities portfolio. Prepare any journal entries that are required by the facts presented in the case.

E12-6
LO2

Recording and Reporting an Equity Method Security

Felicia Company acquired some of the 60,000 shares of outstanding common stock (no-par) of Nueces Corporation during 2004 as a long-term investment. The annual accounting period for both companies ends December 31. The following transactions occurred during 2004:

Jan. 10 Purchased 21,000 shares of Nueces common stock at $12 per share.

Dec. 31 Received the 2004 financial statement of Nueces Corporation, which reported net income of $90,000.

Dec. 31 Nueces Corporation declared and paid a cash dividend of $0.60 per share.

Dec. 31 Determined the market price of Nueces stock to be $11 per share.

E12-7
LO3

Required:
1. What accounting method should the company use? Why?
2. Give the journal entries for each of these transactions. If no entry is required, explain why.
3. Show how the long-term investment and the related revenue should be reported on the 2004 financial statements of the company.

E12-8 Interpreting the Effects of Equity Method Investments on Cash Flow from Operations

LO3

Using the data in E12-7, answer the following questions.

Required:
1. On the current year cash flow statement, how would the investing section of the statement be affected by the preceding transactions?
2. On the current year cash flow statement (indirect method), how would the equity in the earnings of the associated company and the dividends from the associated company affect the operating section? Explain the reasons for the effects.

E12-9 Determining the Appropriate Accounting Treatment for an Acquisition

LO4

The Colgate-
Palmolive
Company

The notes to the financial statements of Colgate-Palmolive contained the following information:

> **2. Acquisitions**
>
> In March 1992, the Company acquired the Mennen Company for an aggregate price of $670 million paid with 11.6 million shares of the Company's common stock and $127 million in cash.

Assume that the fair value of the net assets of Mennen equaled $410 million and the par value of Colgate-Palmolive's common stock was $2 per share. Prepare the entry on the date of the acquisition assuming it is a merger.

E12-10 Analyzing and Interpreting the Return on Assets Ratio

LO5

Timberland is a leading designer of shoes and clothing. In a recent year, it reported the following:

	Current Year	Prior Year
Revenue	$862,168	$796,458
Net income	59,156	47,321
Total assets	469,467	420,003
Total stockholders' equity	266,193	214,895

TIMBERLAND

Required:
1. Determine the return on assets ratio for the current year.
2. Explain the meaning of the ratio.

E12-11 (Supplement A) Interpreting Consolidation Policy

DaimlerChrysler

The annual report for DaimlerChrysler includes the statement that "intercompany accounts and transactions have been eliminated in consolidation." In your own words, explain the meaning of this statement. Why is it necessary to eliminate all intercompany accounts and transactions in consolidation?

E12-12 (Supplement A) Analyzing Goodwill and Reporting the Consolidated Balance Sheet

On January 1, 2003, Company P purchased 100 percent of the outstanding voting shares of Company S in the open market for $80,000 cash. On that date, the separate balance sheets (summarized) of the two companies reported the following book values:

	IMMEDIATELY AFTER THE ACQUISITION JANUARY 1, 2003	
	Company P	Company S
Cash	$ 12,000	$18,000
Investment in Co. S (at cost)	80,000	
Property and Equipment (net)	48,000	42,000
Total assets	$140,000	$60,000

Liabilities	$ 40,000	$ 9,000
Common stock:		
Company P (no-par)	90,000	
Company S (par $10)		40,000
Retained earnings	10,000	11,000
Total liabilities and stockholders' equity	$140,000	$60,000

It was determined on the date of acquisition that the market value of the assets and liabilities of Company S were equal to their book values.

Required:
1. Give the journal entry that Company P made at date of acquisition to record the investment. If none is required, explain why.
2. Analyze the acquisition to determine the amount of goodwill purchased.
3. Prepare a consolidated balance sheet immediately after acquisition.

(Supplement A) Determining Consolidated Net Income

E12-13

Assume that P Company acquired S Company on January 1, 2005, for $100,000 cash. At the time, the net book value of S Company was $90,000. The market value was $96,000 with property and equipment having market value of $6,000 over book value. The property and equipment has a three-year remaining life and is depreciated straight-line with no residual value. During 2005, the companies reported the following operating results:

	P Company	S Company
Revenues related to their own operations	$500,000	$75,000
Expenses related to their own operations	350,000	50,000

Compute consolidated net income for the year ended December 31, 2005.

PROBLEMS

Determining Financial Statement Effects for Bonds Held to Maturity (AP12-1)

P12-1
LO1

Starbucks is a rapidly expanding company that provides high-quality coffee products. Assume that as part of its expansion strategy, Starbucks plans to open numerous new stores in Mexico in five years. The company has $5 million to support the expansion and has decided to invest the funds in corporate bonds until the money is needed. Assume that Starbucks purchased bonds with $5 million face value at par for cash on July 1, 2004. The bonds pay 8 percent interest each June 30 and December 31 and mature in five years. Starbucks plans to hold the bonds until maturity.

Required:
1. What accounts are affected when the bonds are purchased on July 2, 2004?
2. What accounts are affected when interest is received on December 31, 2004?
3. Should Starbucks prepare a journal entry if the market value of the bonds decreased to $4,000,000 on December 31, 2004? Explain.

Recording Passive Investments (AP12-2)

P12-2
LO2

On March 1, 2003, HiTech Industries purchased 10,000 shares of Integrated Services Company for $20 per share. The following information applies to the stock price of Integrated Services:

	Price
12/31/2003	$18
12/31/2004	24
12/31/2005	30

Required:

1. Prepare journal entries to record the facts in the case, assuming that HiTech purchased the shares for the trading portfolio.
2. Prepare journal entries to record the facts in the case, assuming that HiTech purchased the shares for the available-for-sale portfolio.

P12-3   **Reporting Passive Investments** (AP12-3)

L02

During January 2004, Crystal Company purchased the following shares as a long-term investment:

Stock	Number of Shares Outstanding	Purchase	Cost per Share
Q Corporation Common (no-par)	90,000	12,600	$ 5
R Corporation Preferred, nonvoting (par $10)	20,000	12,000	30

Subsequent to acquisition, the following data were available:

	2004	2005
Net income reported at December 31		
Q Corporation	$30,000	$36,000
R Corporation	40,000	48,000
Dividends declared and paid per share during the year		
Q Corporation common stock	$0.80	$0.85
R Corporation preferred stock	0.90	0.90
Market value per share at December 31		
Q Corporation common stock	$ 4.00	$ 4.00
R Corporation preferred stock	29.00	30.00

Required:

1. What accounting method should be used for the investment in Q common stock? R preferred stock? Why?
2. Give the journal entries for the company for each year in parallel columns (if none, explain why) for each of the following:
   a. Purchase of the investments.
   b. Income reported by Q and R Corporations.
   c. Dividends received from Q and R Corporations.
   d. Market value effects at year-end.
3. For each year, show how the following amounts should be reported on the financial statements:
   a. Long-term investment.
   b. Stockholders' equity—net unrealized gains and losses.
   c. Revenues.

P12-4   **Recording Passive Investments and Investments for Significant Influence**

L02, 3

On August 4, 2002, Coffman Corporation purchased 1,000 shares of Dittman Company for $45,000. The following information applies to the stock price of Dittman Company:

	Price
12/31/2002	$52
12/31/2003	47
12/31/2004	38

Dittman Company declares and pays cash dividends of $2 per share on June 1 of each year.

Required:

1. Prepare journal entries to record the facts in the case, assuming that Coffman purchased the shares for the trading portfolio.

2. Prepare journal entries to record the facts in the case, assuming that Coffman purchased the shares for the available-for-sale portfolio.

3. Prepare journal entries to record the facts in the case, assuming that Coffman used the equity method to account for the investment. Coffman owns 30 percent of Dittman and Dittman reported $50,000 in income each year.

Comparing Methods to Account for Various Levels of Ownership of Voting Stock

P12-5
LO2, 3

Company C had outstanding 30,000 shares of common stock, par value $10 per share. On January 1, 2003, Company D purchased some of these shares as a long-term investment at $25 per share. At the end of 2003, Company C reported the following: income, $50,000, and cash dividends declared and paid during the year, $25,500. The market value of Company C stock at the end of 2003 was $22 per share.

Required:

1. For each of the following cases (in the tabulation), identify the method of accounting that Company D should use. Explain why.
2. Give the journal entries for Company D at the dates indicated for each of the two independent cases, assuming that the investments will be held long term. If no entry is required, explain why. Use the following format:

Tabulation of Items	Case A: 3,600 Shares Purchased	Case B: 10,500 Shares Purchased
1. Accounting method?		
2. Journal entries:		
a. To record the acquisition at January 1, 2003.		
b. To recognize the income reported by Company C for 2003.		
c. To recognize the dividends declared and paid by Company C.		
d. Entry to recognize market value effect at end of 2003.		

3. Complete the following schedule to show the separate amounts that should be reported on the 2003 financial statements of Company D:

	Dollar Amounts	
	Case A	Case B
Balance sheet		
Investments		
Stockholders' equity		
Income statement		
Investment income		
Equity in earnings of investee		

4. Explain why assets, stockholders' equity, and revenues for the two cases are different.

Comparing the Market Value and Equity Methods (AP12-4)

P12-6
LO2, 3

Ship Corporation had outstanding 100,000 shares of no-par common stock. On January 10, 2004, Shore Company purchased a block of these shares in the open market at $20 per share for long-term investment purposes. At the end of 2004, Ship reported net income of $300,000 and cash dividends of $.60 per share. At December 31, 2004, Ship stock was selling at $18 per share. This problem involves two separate cases:

Case A Purchase of 10,000 shares of Ship common stock.

Case B Purchase of 40,000 shares of Ship common stock.

Required:

1. For each case, identify the accounting method that the company should use. Explain why.
2. For each case, in parallel columns, give the journal entries for each of the following (if no entry is required, explain why):

      a. Acquisition.

      b. Revenue recognition.

      c. Dividends received.

      d. Market value effects.

  3. For each case, show how the following should be reported on the 2004 financial statements:

      a. Long-term investments.

      b. Shareholders' equity.

      c. Revenues.

  4. Explain why the amounts reported in requirement (3) are different for the two cases.

P12-7
LO2, 3

Determining Cash Flow Statement Effects of Passive Investments and Investments for Significant Influence (AP12-5)

During 2005, Oscar Company purchased some of the 90,000 shares of common stock, par $8, of Selma, Inc., as a long-term investment. The annual accounting period for each company ends December 31. The following transactions occurred during 2005:

Jan.   7 Purchased 40,500 shares of Selma stock at $32 per share.

Dec. 31 Received the 2005 financial statement of Selma, which reported net income of $200,000.

      31 Selma declared and paid a cash dividend of $3 per share.

      31 Determined that the current market price of Selma stock was $40 per share.

Indicate how the Operating Activities and Investing Activities sections of the cash flow statement will be affected by each transaction.

P12-8
LO4

Analyzing Goodwill and Reporting a Merger (AP12-6)

On January 4, 2004, Pronti Company acquired all of the net assets of Scott Company for $120,000 cash. The two companies merged with Pronti Company surviving. The balance sheets for each company prior to the merger follow.

Balance Sheets at January 4, 2004	Pronti Company	Scott Company
Cash	$118,000	$23,000
Property and equipment (net)	132,000	65,000*
Total assets	$250,000	$88,000
Liabilities	$ 27,000	$12,000
Common stock (par $5)	120,000	40,000
Retained earnings	103,000	36,000
Total liabilities and stockholders' equity	$250,000	$88,000

Determined by Pronti Company to have a market value of $72,000 at date of acquisition.

Required:

  1. How much goodwill was involved in this merger? Show computations.

  2. Record the merger by Pronti Company on January 4, 2004.

  3. Prepare a consolidated balance sheet immediately after the acquisition.

P12-9
LO5
Verizon
Communications

Interpreting the Return on Assets Ratio (AP12-7)

Verizon Communications Inc. was formed by the merger of Bell Atlantic Corporation and GTE Corporation. It is the largest provider of wireline and wireless communication services in the United States with presence in over 40 other countries. The following information was reported in the company's 2000 annual report:

(in millions)	2000	1999	1998	1997
Net income	$ 11,797	$ 8,260	$ 4,980	$ 5,181
Total assets	164,735	112,830	98,164	95,742

Required:

1. Compute the return on assets ratio for 2000, 1999, and 1998.
2. What do the results in requirement (1) suggest about Verizon?

(Supplement A) Analyzing Goodwill and Reporting the Consolidated Balance Sheet

P12-10

On January 4, 2004, Penn Company acquired all 8,000 outstanding shares of Syracuse Company for $12 cash per share. Immediately after the acquisition, the balance sheets reflected the following:

Balance Sheets at January 4, 2004	Penn Company	Syracuse Company
Cash	$ 22,000	$23,000
Investment in Syracuse Company	96,000	
Property and equipment (net)	132,000	65,000*
Total assets	$250,000	$88,000
Liabilities	$ 27,000	$12,000
Common stock (par $5)	120,000	40,000
Retained earnings	103,000	36,000
Total liabilities and stockholders' equity	$250,000	$88,000

Determined by Penn Company to have a market value of $72,000 at date of acquisition.

Required:

1. Give the journal entry that Penn Company made to record the acquisition.
2. Analyze the acquisition to determine the amount of goodwill purchased.
3. Should Syracuse Company's assets be included on the consolidated balance sheet at book value or market value? Explain.
4. Prepare a consolidated balance sheet immediately after acquisition. (*Hint:* Consider your answer to requirement [3].)

ALTERNATE **PROBLEMS**

Determining Financial Statement Effects for Bonds Held to Maturity (P12-1)

AP12-1
L01
Blimpie
International

Blimpie International Inc. sells franchises for Blimpie Subs & Salads (offering a quick-service sub sandwich in approximately 2,000 franchise stores throughout the United States and 12 countries), Pasta Central, Maui Tacos, and Smoothie Island. Assume that Blimpie International has $10 million in cash to support future expansion and has decided to invest the funds in corporate bonds until the money is needed. Blimpie purchases bonds with $10 million face value for $10.3 million cash on January 1, 2004. The bonds pay 8 percent interest each June 30 and December 31 and mature in four years. Blimpie International plans to hold the bonds until maturity.

Required:

1. What accounts were affected when the bonds were purchased on January 1, 2004?
2. What accounts were affected when interest was received on June 30, 2004?
3. Should Blimpie prepare a journal entry if the market value of the bonds decreased to $9,700,000 on December 31, 2004? Explain.

Recording Passive Investments (P12-2)

AP12-2
L02

On September 15, 2004, James Media Corporation purchased 5,000 shares of Community Broadcasting Company for $30 per share. The following information applies to the stock price of Community Broadcasting:

	Price
12/31/2004	$32
12/31/2005	24
12/31/2006	20

Required:

1. Prepare journal entries to record the facts in the case, assuming that James Media purchased the shares for the trading portfolio.
2. Prepare journal entries to record the facts in the case, assuming that James Media purchased the shares for the available-for-sale portfolio.

AP12-3 **Reporting Passive Investments** (P12-3)

LO2

During January 2003, Hexagon Company purchased 12,000 shares of the 200,000 outstanding common shares (no-par value) of Seven Corporation at $30 per share. This block of stock was purchased as a long-term investment. Assume that the accounting period for each company ends December 31. Subsequent to acquisition, the following data were available:

	2003	2004
Income reported by Seven Corporation at December 31	$40,000	$60,000
Cash dividends declared and paid by Seven Corporation during the year	60,000	80,000
Market price per share of Seven common stock on December 31	28	29

Required:

1. What accounting method should the company use? Why?
2. Give the journal entries for the company for each year (use parallel columns) for the following (if none, explain why):
   a. Acquisition of Seven Corporation stock.
   b. Net income reported by Seven Corporation.
   c. Dividends received from Seven Corporation.
   d. Market value effects at year-end.
3. Show how the following amounts should be reported on the financial statements for each year:
   a. Long-term investment.
   b. Stockholders' equity—net unrealized gain/loss.
   c. Revenues.

AP12-4 **Comparing the Market Value and Equity Methods** (P12-6)

LO2, 3

Packer Company purchased, as a long-term investment, some of the 200,000 shares of the outstanding common stock of Boston Corporation. The annual accounting period for each company ends December 31. The following transactions occurred during 2005:

Jan. 10 Purchased shares of common stock of Boston at $15 per share as follows:
       Case A—30,000 shares.
       Case B—80,000 shares.

Dec. 31 Received the 2005 financial statements of Boston Corporation; the reported net income was $90,000.

    31 Received a cash dividend of $0.60 per share from Boston Corporation.

    31 Determined that the current market price of Boston stock was $9 per share.

Required:

1. For each case, identify the accounting method that the company should use. Explain why.
2. Give the journal entries for each case for these transactions. If no entry is required, explain why. (*Hint:* Use parallel columns for Case A and Case B.)
3. Give the amounts for each case that should be reported on the 2005 financial statements. Use the following format:

	Case A	Case B
Balance sheet (partial)		
Investments		
Investments in common stock, Boston Corporation		
Stockholders' equity		
Net unrealized gain or loss		
Income statement (partial)		
Investment income		
Equity in earnings of investee		

Determining Cash Flow Statement Effects of Passive Investments and Investments for Significant Influence (P12-7)

For each of the transactions in AP12-4, indicate how the operating activities and investing activities sections of the cash flow statement will be affected.

Analyzing Goodwill and Reporting a Merger (P12-8)

AP12-6
LO4

On June 1, 2003, Pi Company acquired all of the net assets of Sigma Company for $120,000 cash. The two companies merged with Pi Company surviving. The balance sheets for each company prior to the merger follow.

Balance Sheets at June 1, 2003	Pi Company	Sigma Company
Cash	$146,000	$ 13,000
Property and equipment (net)	352,000	165,000*
Total assets	$498,000	$178,000
Liabilities	$ 93,000	$ 82,000
Common stock (par $1)	220,000	65,000
Retained earnings	185,000	31,000
Total liabilities and stockholders' equity	$498,000	$178,000

Determined by Pi Company to have a market value of $180,000 at date of acquisition.

Required:
1. How much goodwill was involved in this merger? Show computations.
2. Record the merger by Pi Company on June 1, 2003.
3. Prepare a consolidated balance sheet immediately after the acquisition.

Interpreting the Return on Assets Ratio (P12-9)

Marriott International, Inc., is a global leader in the hospitality industry with more than 2,200 operating units in 60 countries. The following information was reported in the company's 2000 annual report:

(in millions)	2000	1999	1998	1997
Net income	$ 479	$ 400	$ 390	$ 324
Total assets	8,237	7,324	6,233	5,161

Required:
1. Compute the return on assets ratio for 2000, 1999, and 1998.
2. What do the results in requirement (1) suggest about Marriott?

CASES AND **PROJECTS**

Annual Report Cases

Finding Financial Information

Refer to the financial statements of American Eagle Outfitters given in Appendix B at the end of this book, or open file AEOS.pdf in the Annual Report Cases directory on the student CD-ROM.

AMERICAN EAGLE OUTFITTERS

Required:
1. What was the balance in short-term investments reported by the company on February 3, 2001? What types of securities were included in this account?
2. How much cash did the company realize from selling short-term securities during the year ended February 3, 2001? How large do you think the gain or loss was on these transactions?

3. What was the balance of goodwill reported by the company at February 3, 2001? What does the change in this balance from January 29, 2000, imply about corporate acquisition activities in the 2000 fiscal year?

4. What companies did American Eagle acquire in 2000? What accounting method did it use for each acquisition? If it did not disclose the accounting method, can you infer what it was?

5. Did the Schottenstein acquisition occur at arm's length? What could this imply about the amount of payment?

CP12-2
L01, 2, 3

Finding Financial Information

Refer to the financial statements of Abercrombie & Fitch given in Appendix C at the end of this book, or open file ANF.pdf in the Annual Report Cases directory on the student CD-ROM.

Required:

1. What types of securities were included in the marketable securities reported on the company's balance sheet as at January 29, 2000?

2. Was any gain or loss realized on their sale? How can you determine this?

3. Has the firm increased or decreased its performance as measured by return on assets from 1999 to 2000? Note that the company's 1998 balance for total assets was $319,278.

CP12-3
L04

Comparing Companies within an Industry

Refer to the financial statements of American Eagle Outfitters given in Appendix B, Abercrombie & Fitch given in Appendix C, and the Industry Ratio Report given in Appendix D at the end of this book, or open file CP12-3.xls in the Annual Report Cases directory on the student CD-ROM.

Required:

1. Compute the return on assets ratio for both companies for the current year. What would you infer from the difference? Which company provided the higher return on its total investments during the current year?

2. Was the difference in ROA due primarily to profitability or efficiency differences? How did you know?

3. Was the return on assets for American Eagle Outfitters higher or lower than the industry average? For Abercrombie & Fitch?

Financial Reporting and Analysis Cases

CP12-4
L02, 3

Using Financial Reports: Analyzing the Financial Effects of the Market Value and Equity Methods

On January 1, 2004, Woodrow Company purchased 30 percent of the outstanding common stock of Trevor Corporation at a total cost of $560,000. Management intends to hold the stock for the long term. On the December 31, 2004, balance sheet, the investment in Trevor Corporation was $720,000, but no additional Trevor stock was purchased. The company received $80,000 in cash dividends from Trevor. The dividends were declared and paid during 2004. The company used the equity method to account for its investment in Trevor. The market price of Trevor stock increased during 2004 to a total value of $600,000.

Required:

1. Explain why the investment account balance increased from $560,000 to $720,000 during 2004.

2. What amount of revenue from the investment was reported during 2004?

3. If Woodrow used the market value method, what amount of revenue from the investment should have been reported in 2004?

4. If the market value method were used, what amount should be reported as the investment in Trevor Corporation on the December 31, 2004, balance sheet?

CP12-5

Using Financial Reports: Interpreting International Goodwill Disclosures

L04

Diageo is a major international company located in London. A recent annual report contained the following information concerning its accounting policies.

Acquisitions On the acquisition of a business, including an interest in a related company, fair values are attributed to the group's share of net tangible assets and significant owned brands acquired. Where the cost of acquisition exceeds the values attributable to such net assets, the difference is treated as goodwill and is written off directly to reserves in the year of acquisition.

Intangible assets Significant owned brands, acquired after 1st January 1985, the value of which is not expected to diminish in the foreseeable future, are recorded in the balance sheet as fixed intangible assets. No amortisation is provided on these assets but their value is reviewed annually by the directors and the cost written down as an exceptional item where permanent diminution in value has occurred.

Diageo used the word *reserves* to mean *retained earnings*. Discuss how this accounting treatment compares with procedures used in this country.

Critical Thinking Cases

Evaluating an Ethical Dilemma: Using Inside Information

CP12-6

Assume that you are on the board of directors of a company that has decided to buy 80 percent of the outstanding stock of another company within the next three or four months. The discussions have convinced you that this company is an excellent investment opportunity, so you decide to buy $10,000 worth of the company's stock. Is there an ethical problem with your decision? Would your answer be different if you planned to invest $500,000? Are there different ethical considerations if you don't buy the stock but recommend that your brother do so?

Evaluating an Acquisition from the Standpoint of a Financial Analyst

CP12-7
LO5

Assume that you are a financial analyst for a large investment banking firm. You are responsible for analyzing companies in the retail sales industry. You have just learned that a large West Coast retailer has acquired a large East Coast retail chain for a price more than the net book value of the acquired company. You have reviewed the separate financial statements for the two companies before the announcement of the acquisition. You have been asked to write a brief report explaining what will happen when the financial results of the companies are consolidated under the purchase method, including the impact on the return on assets ratio.

Financial Reporting and Analysis Team Project

Team Project: Examining an Annual Report

CP12-8
LO2, 3, 4, 5

As a team, select an industry to analyze. Each team member should acquire the annual report or Form 10-K for one publicly traded company in the industry, with each member selecting a different company. (Library files, the SEC EDGAR service at www.sec.gov, Compustat CD, or the company itself are good sources.) On an individual basis, each group member should then write a short report answering the following questions about his or her selected company:

1. Determine whether the company prepared consolidated financial statements. If so, did it use the purchase method? How do you know?
2. Does the company use the equity method for any of its investments?
3. Does the company hold any investments in securities? If so, what is their market value? Does the company have any unrealized gains or losses?
4. Identify the company's lines of business. Why does management want to engage in these business activities?
5. Compute the return on assets ratio for the two most recent years reported. What do the results suggest about your company?

Discuss any patterns across the companies that you as a group observe. Then, as a group, write a short report comparing and contrasting your companies using these attributes. Provide potential explanations for any differences discovered.

Statement of Cash Flows

13

I̲t was no accident when Jim Koch, founder of Boston Beer Company, named his products for Samuel Adams, the American revolutionary who led the Boston Tea Party. When Koch delivered the first 25 cases of Samuel Adams Boston Lager to a Boston bar in 1985, he fired the first shot in a revolution that stunned the brewing industry. At that point, megabrewers such as Anheuser-Busch and Miller dominated beer brewing; annual sales by all small "craft" brewers totaled just over 100,000 barrels. By the year 2000, Boston Beer alone sold more than 1.2 million barrels and reported net income of $11.2 million.

Although it may seem puzzling, growing profitable operations do not always ensure positive cash flow. Also, seasonal fluctuations in sales, purchases of inventory, and advertising expenditures may bring **high profits and net cash outflows** in some quarters and **losses and net cash inflows** in others. As we have seen in earlier chapters, this results because the timing of revenues and expenses does not always match cash inflows and outflows. As a consequence, Boston Beer must carefully manage cash flows as well as profits. For the same reasons, financial analysts must consider the information provided in Boston Beer's cash flow statement in addition to its income statement and balance sheet.

FOCUS COMPANY:

Boston Beer Company

MANAGING PRODUCTION AND CASH FLOWS

IN A SEASONAL BUSINESS

www.bostonbeer.com

UNDERSTANDING THE BUSINESS

Clearly, net income is important, but cash flow is also critical to a company's success. Cash flow permits a company to expand operations, replace worn assets, take advantage of new investment opportunities, and pay dividends to its owners. Some Wall Street analysts go so far as to say "cash flow is king." Both managers and analysts need to understand the various sources and uses of cash that are associated with business activity.

The cash flow statement focuses attention on a firm's ability to generate cash internally, its management of current assets and current liabilities, and the details of its investments and its external financing. It is designed to help both managers and analysts answer important cash-related questions such as these:

■ Will the company have enough cash to pay its short-term debts to suppliers and other creditors without additional borrowing?

■ Is the company adequately managing its accounts receivable and inventory?

■ Has the company made necessary investments in new productive capacity?

■ Did the company generate enough cash flow internally to finance necessary investments, or did it rely on external financing?

■ Is the company changing the makeup of its external financing?

Boston Beer is a particularly good example to illustrate the importance of the cash flow statement for two reasons. First, like all companies in its industry, Boston Beer's inventory purchases and sales vary with the seasons. This seasonal variation has surprising effects on cash flows and net income. Second, an important element of Boston Beer's business strategy is the outsourcing of much of its product manufacturing. The decision to outsource dramatically affects investments in plant and equipment and the need for external financing.

We begin our discussion with an overview of the statement of cash flows. Then we examine the information reported in each section of the statement in depth. The chapter ends with a discussion of additional cash flow disclosures.

ORGANIZATION of the Chapter

Classifications of the Statement of Cash Flows	**Reporting and Interpreting Cash Flows from Operating Activities**	**Reporting and Interpreting Cash Flows from Investing Activities**	**Reporting and Interpreting Cash Flows from Financing Activities**	**Additional Cash Flow Disclosures**
■ Cash Flows from Operating Activities ■ Cash Flows from Investing Activities ■ Cash Flows from Financing Activities ■ Net Increase (Decrease) in Cash ■ Relationships to the Balance Sheet and Income Statement	■ **Part A:** Reporting Cash Flows from Operating Activities—Indirect Method **OR** ■ **Part B:** Reporting Cash Flows from Operating Activities—Direct Method ■ Interpreting Cash Flow from Operating Activities ■ Quality of Income Ratio	■ Reporting Cash Flows from Investing Activities ■ Interpreting Cash Flow from Investing Activities ■ Capital Acquisitions Ratio	■ Reporting Cash Flows from Financing Activities ■ Interpreting Cash Flow from Financing Activities	■ Noncash Investing and Financing Activities ■ Supplemental Cash Flow Information

CLASSIFICATIONS OF THE STATEMENT OF CASH FLOWS

Basically, the statement of cash flows explains how the amount of cash on the balance sheet at the beginning of the period became the amount of cash reported at the end of the period. For purposes of this statement, the definition of cash includes cash and cash equivalents. **Cash equivalents** are short-term, highly liquid investments that are both

1. Readily convertible to known amounts of cash.
2. So near to maturity there is little risk that their value will change if interest rates change.

Generally, only investments with original maturities of less than three months qualify as a cash equivalent under this definition.[1] Examples of cash equivalents are Treasury bills (a form of short-term U.S. government debt), money market funds, and commercial paper (short-term notes payable issued by large corporations).

As you can see in Exhibit 13.1, the statement of cash flows reports cash inflows and outflows in three broad categories: (1) operating activities, (2) investing activities, and (3) financing activities. Together, these three cash flow categories explain the change from the beginning balance to the ending balance in cash on the balance sheet.

Cash Flows from Operating Activities

Cash flows from operating activities (cash flows from operations) are the cash inflows and outflows that relate directly to revenues and expenses reported on the income statement. There are two alternative approaches for presenting the operating activities section of the statement:

1. The **direct method** reports the components of cash flows from operating activities as gross receipts and gross payments.

Inflows	Outflows
Cash received from	**Cash paid for**
Customers	Purchase of goods for resale and services
Dividends and interest on investments	(electricity, etc.)
	Salaries and wages
	Income taxes
	Interest on liabilities

The difference between the inflows and outflows is called the **net cash inflow (outflow) from operating activities.** Boston Beer experienced a net cash inflow of $2,922 (in thousands) from its operations for the first quarter of 2000. Though the FASB recommends the direct method, it is rarely used in the United States. The direct method is the required format in a number of countries. Many financial executives have reported that they do not use it because it is more expensive to implement than the indirect method.

2. The **indirect method** starts with net income from the income statement and then eliminates noncash items to arrive at net cash inflow (outflow) from operating activities.

> Net income
> +/− Adjustments for noncash items
> _____
> Net cash inflow (outflow) from operating activities

---

[1] **Original maturity** means original maturity to the entity holding the investment. For example, both a three-month Treasury bill and a three-year Treasury note purchased three months from maturity qualify as cash equivalents. A Treasury note purchased three years ago, however, does not become a cash equivalent when its remaining maturity is three months.

Learning Objective 1
Classify cash flow statement items as part of net cash flows from operating, investing, and financing activities.

A **CASH EQUIVALENT** is a short-term, highly liquid investment with an original maturity of less than three months.

Topic Tackler 13–1

CASH FLOWS FROM OPERATING ACTIVITIES (cash flows from operations) are cash inflows and outflows directly related to earnings from normal operations.

The **DIRECT METHOD** of presenting the Operating Activities section of the cash flow statement reports components of cash flows from operating activities as gross receipts and gross payments.

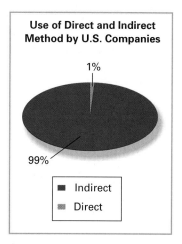

Use of Direct and Indirect Method by U.S. Companies

1%

99%

■ Indirect
▨ Direct

The **INDIRECT METHOD** of presenting the Operating Activities section of the cash flow statement adjusts net income to compute cash flows from operating activities.

EXHIBIT 13.1

Consolidated Statement
of Cash Flows

REAL WORLD EXCERPT

QUARTERLY REPORT

THE BOSTON BEER COMPANY, INC.	
Consolidated Statement of Cash Flows	
(in thousands*) (unaudited)	Three months ended March 25, 2000
Cash flows from operating activities:	
Net income	$3,573
Adjustments to reconcile net income to net cash provided by operating activities:	
Depreciation	1,408
Changes in assets and liabilities:	
Accounts receivable	(2,762)
Inventory	(220)
Prepaid expenses	1,549
Accounts payable	(1,892)
Accrued expenses	1,266
Net cash provided by operating activities	2,922
Cash flows from investing activities:	
Proceeds from sale of equipment	222
Purchases of equipment	(1,515)
Maturities (sale) of short-term investments	16,500
Purchase of short-term investments	(13,331)
Net cash provided by investing activities	1,876
Cash flows from financing activities:	
Purchase of treasury stock	(5,801)
Net proceeds from stock issuance	15
Net cash used in financing activities	(5,786)
Net decrease in cash and cash equivalents	(988)
Cash and cash equivalents at beginning of period	5,346
Cash and cash equivalents at end of period	$4,358

Certain amounts have been adjusted to simplify the presentation.

Almost 99 percent of large U.S. companies, including Boston Beer, use this method.[2] Notice in Exhibit 13.1 that in the first quarter of 2000, Boston Beer reported positive net income of $3,573 but generated positive cash flows from operating activities of only $2,922. Why should income and cash flows from operating activities differ? Remember that on the income statement, revenues are recorded when they are earned, without regard to when the related cash inflows occur. Similarly, expenses are matched with revenues and recorded without regard to when the related cash outflows occur.

For now, the most important thing to remember about the two methods is that they are simply alternative ways to arrive at the same number. The total amount of **cash flows from operating activities is always the same** (an inflow of $2,922 in Boston Beer's case), **regardless of whether it is computed using the direct or indirect method.**

[2]*Accounting Trends & Techniques* (New York: American Institute of CPAs, 2000).

Cash Flows from Investing Activities

Cash flows from investing activities are cash inflows and outflows related to the purchase and disposal of long-lived productive assets and investments in the securities of other companies. Typical cash flows from investing activities include:

Inflows	Outflows
Cash received from	**Cash paid for**
Sale or disposal of property, plant, and equipment	Purchase of property, plant, and equipment
Sale or maturity of investments in securities	Purchase of investments in securities

The difference between these cash inflows and outflows is called **net cash inflow (outflow) from investing activities.**

For Boston Beer, this amount was an inflow of $1,876 for the first quarter of 2000. Most of the activity related to the purchase and sale of short-term securities. Since sales exceeded purchases, there was a net cash inflow.

Cash Flows from Financing Activities

Cash flows from financing activities include exchanges of cash with creditors (debtholders) and owners (stockholders). Usual cash flows from financing activities include the following:

Inflows	Outflows
Cash received from	**Cash paid for**
Borrowing on notes, mortgages, bonds, etc. from creditors	Repayment of principal to creditors (excluding interest, which is an operating activity)
Issuing stock to owners	Repurchasing stock from owners
	Dividends to owners

The difference between these cash inflows and outflows is called **net cash inflow (outflow) from financing activities.**

Boston Beer experienced a net cash outflow from financing activities of $5,786 for the first quarter of 2000. The Financing Activities section of its statement shows that Boston Beer paid $5,801 in cash to repurchase its stock from owners and issued new shares for $15. No dividends were paid and no cash was borrowed or repaid.

Net Increase (Decrease) in Cash

The combination of **the net cash flows from operating activities, investing activities, and financing activities must equal the net increase (decrease) in cash** for the reporting period. For the first quarter of 2000, Boston Beer reported a net decrease in cash of $988, which explains the change in cash on the balance sheet from the beginning balance of $5,346 to the ending balance of $4,358.

Net cash provided by operating activities	$2,922
Net cash provided by investing activities	1,876
Net cash used in financing activities	(5,786)
Net decrease in cash and cash equivalents	(988)
Cash and cash equivalents at beginning of period	5,346
Cash and cash equivalents at end of period	$4,358

To give you a better understanding of the statement of cash flows, we now discuss Boston Beer's statement in more detail including the way that it relates to the balance sheet and income statement. Then we will examine the way each section of the statement describes a set of important decisions Boston Beer management made and the way financial analysts use each section to evaluate the company's performance.

CASH FLOWS FROM INVESTING ACTIVITIES are cash inflows and outflows related to the acquisition or sale of productive facilities and investments in the securities of other companies.

CASH FLOWS FROM FINANCING ACTIVITIES are cash inflows and outflows related to external sources of financing (owners and creditors) for the enterprise.

SELF-STUDY **QUIZ**

Big Rock Brewery

Big Rock Brewery Ltd. is one of the larger craft brewers in Canada. A listing of some of its cash flows follows. Indicate whether each item is disclosed in the Operating Activities (O), Investing Activities (I), or Financing Activities (F) section of the statement of cash flows.

_____ a. Shares repurchased from stockholders

_____ b. Collections from customers

_____ c. Payment of interest on debt

_____ d. Purchase of plant and equipment

_____ e. Acquisition of investment securities

After you have completed your answers, check them with the solutions that follow:

_____

a. F, b. O, c. O, d. I, e. I

Relationships to the Balance Sheet and Income Statement

Preparing and interpreting the cash flow statement requires an analysis of the balance sheet and income statement accounts that relate to the three sections of the cash flow statement. In previous chapters, we emphasized that companies record transactions as journal entries that are posted to T-accounts, which are used to prepare the income statement and the balance sheet. But companies cannot prepare the statement of cash flows using the amounts recorded in the T-accounts because those amounts are based on accrual accounting. Instead, they must analyze the numbers recorded under the accrual method and adjust them to a cash basis. To prepare the statement of cash flows, they need the following data:

1. **Comparative balance sheets** used in calculating the cash flows from all activities (operating, investing, and financing). To ease the preparation process, we recommend that you compute the change from the beginning to the end of the period for each balance sheet item.

2. A **complete income statement** used primarily in calculating cash flows from operating activities.

3. **Additional details** concerning selected accounts where the total change amount in an account balance during the year does not reveal the underlying nature of the cash flows.

Our approach to preparing and understanding the cash flow statement focuses on the changes in the balance sheet accounts. It relies on a simple manipulation of the balance sheet equation:

Assets = Liabilities + Stockholders' Equity

First, assets can be split into cash and noncash assets:

Cash + Noncash Assets = Liabilities + Stockholders' Equity

If we move the noncash assets to the right side of the equation, then

Cash = Liabilities + Stockholders' Equity − Noncash Assets

Given this relationship, the changes (Δ) in cash between the beginning and end of the period must equal the changes (Δ) in the amounts on the right side of the equation between the beginning and end of the period:

Δ Cash = Δ Liabilities + Δ Stockholders' Equity − Δ Noncash Assets

Category	Transaction	Cash Effect	Other Account Affected
Operating	Collect accounts receivable	+Cash	−Accounts Receivable (A)
	Pay accounts payable	−Cash	−Accounts Payable (L)
	Prepay rent	−Cash	+Prepaid Rent (A)
	Pay interest	−Cash	−Retained Earnings (SE)
	Sale for cash	+Cash	+Retained Earnings (SE)
Investing	Purchase equipment for cash	−Cash	+Equipment (A)
	Sell investment securities for cash	+Cash	−Investments
Financing	Pay back debt to bank	−Cash	−Notes Payable—Bank (L)
	Issue stock for cash	+Cash	+Common Stock and Paid-in Capital (SE)

EXHIBIT 13.2

Selected Cash Transactions and Their Effects on Other Balance Sheet Accounts

Thus, **any transaction that changes cash must be accompanied by a change in liabilities, stockholders' equity, or noncash assets.** Exhibit 13.2 illustrates this concept for selected cash transactions. In the next sections of the chapter, we will classify each balance sheet change as relating to operating (O), investing (I), or financing (F) activities.

REPORTING AND INTERPRETING CASH FLOWS FROM OPERATING ACTIVITIES

Since the operating section can be prepared in one of two formats, we discuss them separately. Part A describes the indirect method, and part B the direct method. Your instructor may choose to assign one, the other, or both. After you have completed the part(s) assigned, you should move on to the discussion of interpreting cash flow from operations.

Remember that

1. Cash flow from operating activities is always the same regardless of whether it is computed using the direct or indirect method.

2. The investing and financing sections are always presented in the same manner regardless of the format of the operating section.

Part A: Reporting Cash Flows from Operating Activities—Indirect Method

Exhibit 13.3 shows Boston Beer's comparative balance sheet and income statement. Remember that the indirect method starts with net income and converts it to cash flows from operating activities. To keep track of all the additions and subtractions made to convert net income to cash flows from operating activities, it is helpful to set up a schedule to record the computations. We will construct a schedule for Boston Beer in Exhibit 13.4.

Preparing the operating section using the indirect method involves the following three steps:

Learning Objective 2A
Report and interpret cash flows from operating activities using the indirect method.

Step 1: **Mark the changes in the balance sheet accounts related to earning income (operating items) with an O.** These accounts include the following:

- Current assets (other than cash and short-term investments which relate to investing activities).

- Current liabilities (other than amounts owed to investors and financial institutions,[3] all of which relate to financing activities).

---

[3]Examples of the accounts excluded are Dividends Payable, Short-Term Debt to Financial Institutions, and Current Maturities of Long-Term Debt. Current maturities of long-term debt are amounts of debt with an original term of more than one year that are due within one year of the statement date.

■ Retained earnings because it increases by the amount of net income, which is the starting point for the Operating section. (Retained earnings also decreases by dividends declared and paid, which is a financing outflow noted by an F.)

Equipment, net is relevant to the computation of Cash Flows from Operating Activities as well as Investing (noted by an I) because it is affected by depreciation expense.

In Exhibit 13.3, all of the relevant current assets and liabilities have been marked with an O. These items include

■ Accounts receivable

■ Inventories

■ Prepaid expenses

■ Accounts payable

■ Accrued expenses

As we have noted, retained earnings and equipment are also relevant to operations.

Step 2:   Begin the Operating Activities section with net income reported on the income statement. We begin our schedule presented in Exhibit 13.4 with net income of $3,573 taken from Boston Beer's income statement (Exhibit 13.3).

Step 3:   Adjust net income for the effects of items marked O that reflect differences in the timing of accrual basis net income and cash flows. The following adjustments are the ones most frequently encountered:

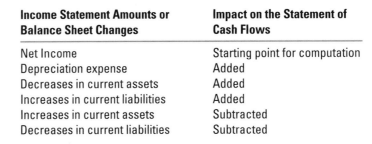

Income Statement Amounts or Balance Sheet Changes	Impact on the Statement of Cash Flows
Net Income	Starting point for computation
Depreciation expense	Added
Decreases in current assets	Added
Increases in current liabilities	Added
Increases in current assets	Subtracted
Decreases in current liabilities	Subtracted

This step is completed in two parts:

Step 3a: Adjust net income for depreciation and amortization expense. Recording depreciation and amortization expense does not affect the cash account (or any other current asset or liability). It affects a noncurrent asset (such as Equipment, net). **Since depreciation and amortization expense is subtracted in computing net income, but does not affect cash, we always add each back** to convert net income to cash flow from operating activities. In the case of Boston Beer, we need to remove the effect of depreciation expense by adding back $1,408 to net income (see Exhibit 13.4).[4]

Step 3b: Adjust net income for changes in current assets and current liabilities. Each change in current assets (other than cash and short-term investments) and current liabilities (other than amounts owed to owners and financial institutions) causes a difference between net income and cash flow from operating activities. When converting net income to cash flow from operating activities, apply the following general rules:

■ **Add the change when a current asset decreases or current liability increases.**

■ **Subtract the change when a current asset increases or current liability decreases.**

Understanding what makes these current assets and current liabilities increase and decrease is the key to understanding the logic of these additions and subtractions.

---

[4]Gains and losses on sales of equipment and investments are dealt with in a similar manner and are discussed in Chapter Supplement A. Other similar additions and subtractions are discussed in more advanced accounting courses.

EXHIBIT 13.3

The Boston Beer
Company:
Comparative Balance
Sheet and Current
Income Statement
(in thousands)

REAL WORLD
EXCERPT

QUARTERLY REPORT

Related Cash Flow Section Change in Cash	THE BOSTON BEER COMPANY, INC. Consolidated Balance Sheet			
	(unaudited) In Thousands	March 25, 2000	December 25, 1999*	Change
	Assets			
	Current Assets:			
I	Cash and cash equivalents	4,358	5,346	−988
O	Short-term investments	35,830	38,999	−3,169
O	Accounts receivable	19,052	16,290	+2,762
O	Inventories	15,876	15,656	+220
O	Prepaid expenses	4,532	6,081	−1,549
	Total current assets	79,648	82,372	
I†	Equipment, net	30,266	30,381	−115
	Total assets	$109,914	$112,753	
	Liabilities and Stockholders' Equity			
	Current Liabilities:			
O	Accounts payable	$14,414	$16,306	−1,892
O	Accrued expenses	14,108	12,842	+1,266
	Total current liabilities	28,522	29,148	
	Stockholders' Equity:			
F	Contributed capital	41,244	47,030	−5,786
O and F	Retained earnings	40,148	36,575	+3,573
	Total stockholders' equity	81,392	83,605	
	Total liabilities and stockholders' equity	$109,914	$112,753	

THE BOSTON BEER COMPANY, INC.
Consolidated Statements of Operations

(unaudited) In Thousands	Three Months Ended March 25, 2000
Net sales	$44,257
Cost of sales	19,615
Gross profit	24,642
Operating expenses:	
Selling, general and administrative expense	17,626
Depreciation	1,408
Total operating expenses	19,034
Operating income	5,608
Interest income	553
Income before provision for income taxes	6,161
Provision for income taxes	2,588
Net income	$ 3,573

*Certain balances have been adjusted to simplify the presentation.
†The Accumulated Depreciation account is also related to operations because it relates to depreciation.

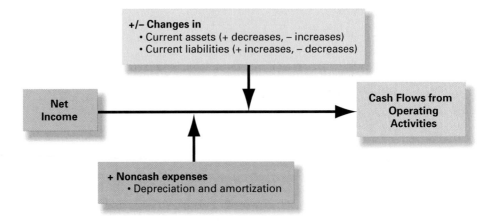

Change in Accounts Receivable

We illustrate this logic with the first operating item (O) listed on Boston Beer's Balance sheet (Exhibit 13.3), accounts receivable. Remember that the income statement reflects sales revenue, but the cash flow statement must reflect cash collections from customers. As the following accounts receivable T-account illustrates, when sales revenues are recorded, accounts receivable increases, and when cash is collected from customers, accounts receivable decreases.

Accounts Receivable (A)			
Beginning balance	16,290		
Sales revenue (on account)	44,257	Collections from customers	41,495
Ending balance	19,052		

Change +$2,762

In the Boston Beer example, sales revenue on account reported on the income statement is higher than cash collections from customers by $44,257 − $41,495 = $2,762. Since less money was collected from customers, this amount must be subtracted from net income to convert to cash flows from operating activities. Note that this amount is also the same as the **change** in the accounts receivable account:

Ending balance	$19,052
− Beginning balance	16,290
Change	$ 2,762

This same underlying logic is used to determine adjustments for the other current assets and liabilities.

To summarize, the income statement reflects revenues of the period, but cash flow from operating activities must reflect cash collections from customers. Sales on account increase the balance in accounts receivable, and collections from customers decrease the balance.

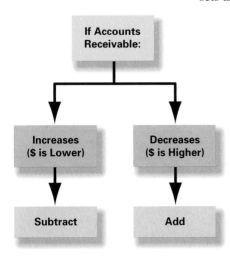

Accounts Receivable (A)		
Beg.	16,290	
Increase	2,762	
End.	19,052	

The balance sheet for Boston Beer Company (Exhibit 13.3) indicates an **increase** in accounts receivable of $2,762 for the period, which means cash collected from customers is lower than revenue. To convert to cash flows from operating activities, the amount of the increase (the extra revenues) must be **subtracted** in Exhibit 13.4. (A decrease is added.)

Conversion of Net Income to Net Cash Flow from Operating Activities		
Items	**Amount**	**Explanation**
Net income, accrual basis	$3,573	From income statement.
Add (subtract) to convert to cash basis:		
Depreciation	+1,408	Add back because depreciation expense does not affect cash.
Accounts receivable increase	−2,762	Subtract because accrual basis revenues are more than cash collected from customers.
Inventory increase	−220	Subtract because purchases are more than cost of goods sold expense.
Prepaid expense decrease	+1,549	Add back because accrual basis expenses are more than cash prepayments for expenses.
Accounts payable decrease	−1,892	Subtract because amounts purchased on account (borrowed from suppliers) are less than cash payments to suppliers.
Accrued expenses increase	+1,266	Add back because accrual basis expenses are more than the cash payments for expenses.
Net cash inflow from operating activities	$2,922	Reported on the statement of cash flows.

EXHIBIT 13.4

Boston Beer Company: Schedule for Net Cash Flow from Operating Activities, Indirect Method (in thousands)

Change in Inventory

The income statement reflects merchandise sold for the period, whereas cash flow from operating activities must reflect cash purchases. Purchases of goods increase the balance in inventory, and recording merchandise sold decreases the balance in inventory.

Inventories (A)	
Beg.	15,656
Increase	220
End.	15,876

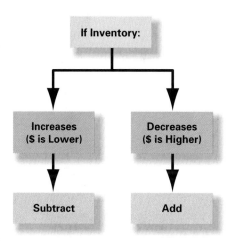

Boston Beer's balance sheet (Exhibit 13.3) indicates that inventory **increased** by $220, which means that the amount of purchases is more than the amount of merchandise sold. The increase (the extra purchases) must be **subtracted** from net income to convert to cash flow from operating activities in Exhibit 13.4. (A decrease is added.)

Change in Prepaid Expenses

The income statement reflects expenses of the period, but cash flow from operating activities must reflect the cash payments. Cash prepayments increase the balance in prepaid expenses, and expenses decrease the balance in prepaid expenses.

Prepaid Expenses (A)		
Beg.	6,081	
	Decrease	1,549
End.	4,532	

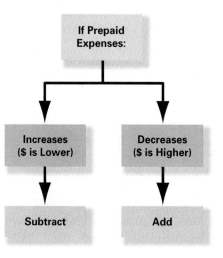

The Boston Beer balance sheet (Exhibit 13.3) indicates a $1,549 **decrease** in prepaid expenses, which means that the amount of expenses is more than new cash prepayments. The decrease (the extra expenses) must be **added** back to net income in Exhibit 13.4. (An increase is subtracted.)

Change in Accounts Payable

Cash flow from operations must reflect cash purchases, but not all purchases are for cash. Purchases on account increase accounts payable, and cash paid to suppliers decreases accounts payable.

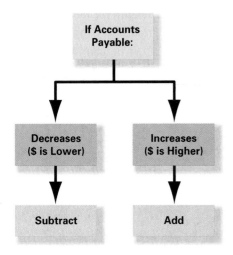

Accounts Payable (L)			
		Beg.	16,306
Decrease	1,892		
		End.	14,414

Boston Beer's accounts payable **decreased** by $1,892, which means that cash payments were more than purchases on account, and this decrease (the extra payments) must be **subtracted** in Exhibit 13.4. (An increase would be added.)

Change in Accrued Expenses

The income statement reflects all accrued expenses, but the cash flow statement must reflect actual payments for those expenses. Recording accrued expenses increases the balance in the liability Accrued Expenses and cash payments for the expenses decrease Accrued Expenses.

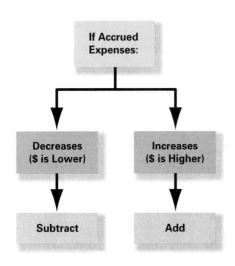

Accrued Expenses (L)		
	Beg.	12,842
	Increase	1,266
	End.	14,108

Boston Beer's accrued expenses (Exhibit 13.3) **increased** by $1,266, which indicates that accrual basis expenses are more than cash paid for the expenses. The increase (the extra expenses) must be **added** back in Exhibit 13.4. (A decrease is subtracted.)

Summary

We can summarize the typical additions and subtractions that are required to reconcile net income with cash flow from operating activities as follows:

	ADDITIONS AND SUBTRACTIONS TO RECONCILE NET INCOME TO CASH FLOW FROM OPERATING ACTIVITIES	
Item	When Item Increases	When Item Decreases
Depreciation and amortization	+	
Accounts receivable	−	+
Inventory	−	+
Prepaid expenses	−	+
Accounts payable	+	−
Accrued expense liabilities	+	−

Notice again in this table that to reconcile net income to cash flows from operating activities, you must:

- **Add the change when a current asset decreases or current liability increases.**
- **Subtract the change when a current asset increases or current liability decreases.**

The cash flow statement for Boston Beer (Exhibit 13.1) shows the same additions and subtractions to reconcile net income to cash flows from operating activities described in Exhibit 13.4.

INTERNATIONAL PERSPECTIVE

Foreign Currency and the Cash Flow Statement

Consolidated statements may include one or more subsidiaries located in other countries whose statements report in a currency other than the U.S. dollar (for example, the euro or Mexican peso). The process of translating those statements into dollars may cause the changes in the current assets and liabilities on the balance sheet not to match the changes reported on the cash flow statement. Acquisitions and sales of subsidiaries during the period can have a similar effect.*

*P. R. Bahnson, P. B. W. Miller, and B. P. Budge, "Nonarticulation in Cash Flow Statements and Implications for Education, Research and Practice," *Accounting Horizons,* December 1996, pp. 1–15.

SELF-STUDY QUIZ

Big Rock Brewery

Indicate which of the following items taken from Big Rock Brewery's cash flow statement would be added (+), subtracted (−), or not included (0) in the reconciliation of net income to cash flow from operations.

_____ *a.* Increase in inventories.
_____ *b.* Increase in bank indebtedness.
_____ *c.* Amortization expense.
_____ *d.* Decrease in accounts receivable.
_____ *e.* Increase in accounts payable.
_____ *f.* Increase in prepaid expenses.

After you have completed your answers, check them with the solutions that follow:

_____
a. −, b. 0, c. +, d. +, e. +, f. −.

If your instructor has assigned only the indirect method, you should skip the next section and go to the discussion of Interpreting Cash Flow from Operations (page 661).

Part B: Reporting Cash Flows from Operating Activities—Direct Method

The direct method presents a summary of all operating transactions that result in either a debit or a credit to cash. It is prepared by adjusting each item on the income statement from an accrual basis to a cash basis. We will complete this process for all of the revenues and expenses reported in Boston Beer's income statement in Exhibit 13.3 and accumulate them in a new schedule in Exhibit 13.5.

Learning Objective 2B
Report and interpret cash flows from operating activities using the direct method.

Cash Flows from Operating Activities

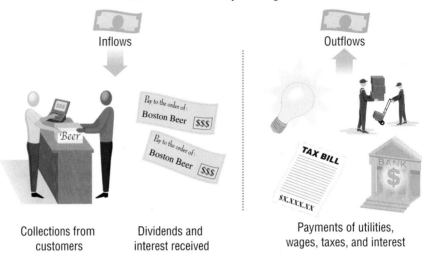

Inflows		Outflows
Collections from customers	Dividends and interest received	Payments of utilities, wages, taxes, and interest

Converting Revenues to Cash Inflows

When sales are recorded, accounts receivable increases, and when cash is collected, accounts receivable decreases. Thus, the following formula will convert sales revenue amounts from the accrual basis to the cash basis:

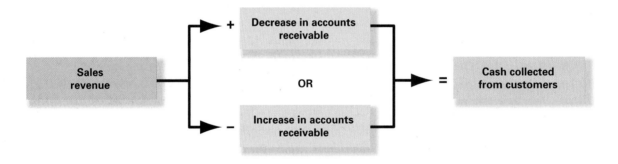

Accounts Receivable	
Beg.	16,290
Increase	2,762
End.	19,052

Using information from Boston Beer's income statement and balance sheet presented in Exhibit 13.3, we can compute cash collected from customers as follows:

Net Sales	$44,257
− Increase in accounts receivable	2,762
Cash collected from customers	$41,495

Boston Beer's second revenue is interest income. Since there is no interest receivable balance, using the same logic, we can see that interest income must be equal to cash collected for interest.

Interest income	$553
No change in interest receivable	0
Cash collected for interest	$553

Converting Cost of Goods Sold to Cash Paid to Suppliers

Cost of goods sold represents the cost of merchandise sold during the accounting period. It may be more or less than the amount of cash paid to suppliers during the period. In Boston Beer's case, inventory increased during the quarter because the company bought more merchandise from suppliers than it sold to customers. If the company paid cash to suppliers of inventory, it must have paid more cash to suppliers than the amount of cost of goods sold, so the increase in inventory must be added to compute cash paid to suppliers.

Typically, companies owe their suppliers money (an accounts payable balance will appear on the balance sheet). To convert cost of goods sold to cash paid to suppliers, the borrowing and repayments represented by the accounts payable must also be considered. Borrowing increases cash and accounts payable and repayment decreases cash and accounts payable, so Boston Beer's decrease in accounts payable must also be added in the computation. Cost of goods sold can therefore be converted to a cash basis in the following manner:

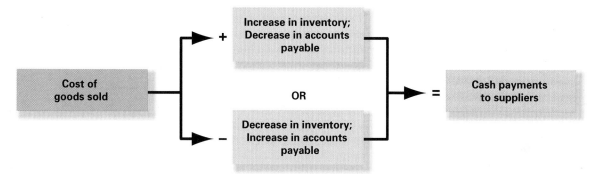

Using information from Exhibit 13.3, we can compute cash paid to suppliers as follows:

Cost of goods sold	$19,615
+ Increase in inventory	220
+ Decrease in accounts payable	1,892
Cash payments to suppliers	$21,727

Inventories		
Beg.	15,656	
Increase	220	
End.	15,876	

Accounts Payable		
		Beg. 16,306
Decrease 1,892		
		End. 14,414

Converting Operating Expenses to a Cash Outflow

The total amount of an expense on the income statement may differ from the cash outflow associated with that activity. Some expenses are paid before they are recognized as expenses (e.g., prepaid rent). When prepayments are made, the balance in the asset prepaid expenses increases; when expenses are recorded, prepaid expenses decreases. When Boston Beer's prepaid expenses decreased by $1,549 during the period, it paid less cash than it recorded as operating expenses. The decrease must be subtracted in computing cash paid for expenses.

Some other expenses are paid for after they are recognized (e.g., accrued expenses). In this case, when expenses are recorded, the balance in the liability accrued expenses increases; when payments are made, accrued expenses decreases. When Boston Beer's accrued expenses increased by $1,266, it paid less cash than it recorded as operating expenses. The increase must also be subtracted in computing cash paid for expenses.

Generally, other expenses can be converted from the accrual basis to the cash basis in the following manner:

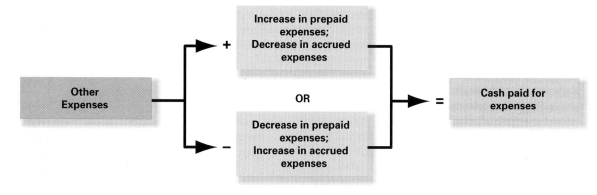

EXHIBIT 13.5

Boston Beer Company:
Schedule for Net Cash Flow
from Operating Activities,
Direct Method (in thousands)

Cash flows from operating activities	
Cash collected from customers	$41,495
Cash collected for interest	553
Cash payments to suppliers	(21,727)
Cash payments for expenses	(14,811)
Cash payments for income taxes	(2,588)
Net cash provided by operating activities	$ 2,922

Prepaid Expenses

Beg.	6,081		
		Decrease	1,549
End.	4,532		

Accrued Expenses

		Beg.	12,842
		Increase	1,266
		End.	14,108

Using information from Exhibit 13.3, we can compute cash paid for expenses as follows:

Selling, general and administrative expense	$17,626
− Decrease in prepaid expenses	1,549
− Increase in accrued expenses	1,266
Cash payments for expenses	$14,811

The same logic can be applied to income taxes. Boston Beer presents income tax expense of $2,588. Since there is no balance in Income Taxes Payable (or change in Deferred Taxes), income taxes paid must be the same as income tax expense.

Income tax expense	$2,588
No change in taxes payable	0
Cash payments for income taxes	$2,588

These amounts of the operating cash inflows and outflows are accumulated in Exhibit 13.5.

To summarize, the following adjustments must commonly be made to convert income statement items to the related operating cash flow amounts:

Income Statement Account	+/− Change in Balance Sheet Account(s)	= Operating Cash Flow
Sales revenue	+ Decrease in Accounts Receivable (A) − Increase in Accounts Receivable (A)	= Collections from customers
Interest/Dividend revenue	+ Decrease in Interest/Dividends Receivable (A) − Increase in Interest/Dividends Receivable (A)	= Collections of interest/dividends on investments
Cost of goods sold	+ Increase in Inventory (A) − Decrease in Inventory (A) − Increase in Accounts Payable (L) + Decrease in Accounts Payable (L)	= Payments to suppliers of inventory
Other expenses	+ Increase in Prepaid Expenses (A) − Decrease in Prepaid Expenses (A) − Increase in Accrued Expenses (L) + Decrease in Accrued Expenses (L)	= Payments to suppliers of services (e.g., rent, utilities, wages, interest)
Income tax expense	+ Increase in Prepaid Income Taxes (Deferred Taxes) (A) − Decrease in Prepaid Income Taxes (Deferred Taxes) (A) − Increase in Income Taxes Payable (Deferred Taxes) (L) + Decrease in Income Taxes Payable (Deferred Taxes) (L)	= Payments of income taxes

It is important to note again that the net cash inflow or outflow is the same regardless of whether the direct or indirect method of presentation is used (in this case, an inflow of $2,922). The two methods differ only in terms of the details reported on the statement.

Australian Practices

INTERNATIONAL PERSPECTIVE

Foster's Brewing is the first name in Australian beer and a major player in world beverage markets. Following Australian GAAP, which requires use of the direct method of presentation, Foster's cash flow from operations is presented as follows. Note that Foster's combines payments to suppliers, government, and employees, but other companies report these items separately. Like U.S. companies that choose the direct method, Foster's reports the indirect presentation in a note to the financial statements.

STATEMENT OF CASH FLOWS FOR THE YEAR ENDED 30 JUNE 2001 ($M)
Cash flows from operating activities

Receipts from customers	6,156.8
Payments to suppliers, governments and employees	(5,388.3)
Dividends received	0.2
Interest received	90.1
Borrowing costs [interest paid]	(269.6)
Income taxes paid	(306.0)
Net cash flows from operating activities	283.2

REAL WORLD EXCERPT

Foster's Brewing Int.

ANNUAL REPORT

SELF-STUDY QUIZ

Indicate which of the following line items taken from cash flow statement would be added (+), subtracted (−), or not included (0) in the cash flow from operations section when the direct method is used.

_____ *a.* Increase in inventories.

_____ *b.* Payment of dividends to stockholders.

_____ *c.* Cash collections from customers.

_____ *d.* Purchase of plant and equipment for cash.

_____ *e.* Payments of interest to debtholders.

_____ *f.* Payment of taxes to the government.

After you have completed your answers, check them with the solutions that follow:

_____

a. 0, b. 0, c. +, d. 0, e. −, f. −

Interpreting Cash Flow from Operations

The Operating Activities section of the cash flow statement focuses attention on the firm's ability to generate cash internally through operations and its management of current assets and current liabilities (also called **working capital**). Most analysts believe that this is the most important section of the statement because, in the long run,

operations are the only source of cash. That is, investors will not invest in a company if they do not believe that cash generated from operations will be available to pay them dividends or expand the company. Similarly, creditors will not lend money if they do not believe that cash generated from operations will be available to pay back the loan. For example, many dot.com companies crashed when investors lost faith in their ability to turn business ideas into cash flows from operations.

A common rule of thumb followed by financial and credit analysts is to avoid firms with rising net income but falling cash flow from operations. Rapidly rising inventories or receivables often predict a slump in profits and the need for external financing. In the first quarter of 2000, Boston Beer exhibited just such a pattern. Was it a sign of trouble for the leader of the craft beer industry? Why did net income also drop in the second quarter, even though cash flow from operations rose?

	Net Income		Cash Flows from Operations
1st quarter	$3,573	>	$2,922
2nd quarter	$3,542	<	$5,050

To answer these questions, we must carefully analyze how Boston Beer's operating activities are reported in its cash flow statement. To properly interpret this information, we also must learn more about the brewing industry.

Increases in receivables: A warning sign?

Managers sometimes attempt to boost declining sales by extending credit terms (for example, from 30 to 60 days) or by lowering credit standards (that is, lending to riskier customers). The resulting increase in accounts receivable can cause net income to outpace cash flow from operations. As a consequence, many analysts view this pattern as a warning sign.

Analysts who cover the beverage industry know that Boston Beer's increase in receivables results from normal seasonal fluctuations in beer sales to distributors. Beer sales to distributors are low in the last month of the fourth quarter (December) because of the onset of winter. As a result, the beginning balance in Accounts Receivable in January are low. However, sales are high at the end of the first quarter (March) in anticipation of spring. The higher March sales cause accounts receivable to grow, but the cash is not collected until April.

On the cash flow statement, this net increase in accounts receivable has a negative effect on cash flow from operations for the first quarter. This normal seasonal fluctuation in sales is clearly not a sign of problems for Boston Beer.

Analyzing Inventory Changes

An unexpected increase in inventory can also cause net income to outpace cash flow from operations. Such inventory growth can be a sign that planned sales growth did not materialize. A decline in inventory can be a sign that the company is anticipating lower sales in the next quarter. Many analysts compute the quality of income ratio as a general warning sign of these and similar problems.

KEY RATIO ANALYSIS   **Quality of Income Ratio**

Learning Objective 3
Analyze and interpret the quality of income ratio.

❓ ANALYTICAL QUESTION:
How much cash does each dollar of net income generate?

% RATIO AND COMPARISONS:

$$\text{Quality of Income Ratio} = \frac{\text{Cash Flow from Operating Activities}}{\text{Net Income}}$$

Boston Beer ratio for the *year** 2000 was:

$$\frac{\$17{,}336}{\$11{,}239} = \$1.54\ (154\%)$$

COMPARISONS OVER TIME			COMPARISONS WITH COMPETITORS	
Boston Beer (Annual)			**Anheuser Busch**	**Coors**
1998	**1999**	**2000**	**2000**	**2000**
2.82	1.25	1.54	1.44	2.60

Selected Focus Company Comparisons

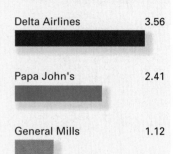

Delta Airlines	3.56
Papa John's	2.41
General Mills	1.12

💡 INTERPRETATIONS

In General   The quality of income ratio measures the portion of income that was generated in cash. All other things equal, a higher quality of income ratio indicates greater ability to finance operating and other cash needs from operating cash inflows.[†] A higher ratio also indicates that it is less likely that the company is using aggressive revenue recognition policies to increase net income. When this ratio does not equal 1.0, analysts must establish the sources of the difference to determine the significance of the findings. There are four potential causes of any difference:

1. **The corporate life cycle (growth or decline in sales).** When sales are increasing, receivables and inventory normally increase faster than accounts payable. This often reduces operating cash flows below income, which, in turn, reduces the ratio. When sales are declining, the opposite occurs, and the ratio increases.

2. **Seasonality.** As was the case for Boston Beer, seasonal variations in sales and purchases of inventory can cause the ratio to deviate from 1.0.

3. **Changes in revenue and expense recognition.** Aggressive revenue recognition or failure to accrue appropriate expenses will inflate net income and reduce the ratio.

4. **Changes in management of operating assets and liabilities.** Inefficient management will increase operating assets and decrease liabilities, reducing operating cash flows and the quality of income ratio. More efficient management will have the opposite effect.

Focus Company Analysis   During the past three years, Boston Beer's quality of income ratio has ranged from 1.25 to 2.82. As we noted earlier, the difference between net income and cash flow from operations in the case of Boston Beer for the first quarter of 2000 was not a cause for alarm. It was due to normal seasonal changes in sales and receivables. The annual results for 2000 support this conclusion, indicating a slight increase in quality of earnings from 1999. Its ratio is between those for Anheuser Busch and Coors. The wide variation in Boston Beer's ratio would prompt analysts to contact management to determine its causes.

A Few Cautions   The quality of income ratio can be interpreted only based on an understanding of the company's business operations and strategy. For example, a low ratio can be due simply to normal seasonal changes. However, it also can indicate obsolete inventory, slowing sales, or failed expansion plans. To test for these possibilities, analysts often analyze this ratio in tandem with the accounts receivable turnover and inventory turnover ratios.[‡]

---

*To eliminate the effects of seasonality, we look at the ratio for the annual period.

[†]When a net loss is reported, a more negative ratio indicates greater ability to finance the company from operations.

[‡]K. G. Palepu, P. M. Healy, and V. L. Bernard, *Business Analysis and Valuation Using Financial Statements,* 2e (Cincinnati, OH: South-Western, 2000).

Fraud and Cash Flows from Operations

REAL WORLD EXCERPT

Investors Chronicle

The cash flow statement often gives outsiders the first hint that financial statements may contain errors and irregularities. The importance of this indicator as a predictor is receiving more attention in the United States and internationally. *Investors Chronicle* recently reported on an accounting fraud at a commercial credit company, suggesting that

... a look at Versailles's cash flow statement—an invaluable tool in spotting creative accounting—should have triggered misgivings. In the company's last filed accounts in 1999 Versailles reported operating profits of GBP 15.37m [$25 million] but a cash outflow from operating activities of 15.12m [$24 million]. ... such figures should ... have served as a warning. After all, what use is a company to anyone if it reports only accounting profits which are never translated into cash?

As noted in earlier chapters, unethical managers sometimes attempt to reach earnings targets by manipulating accruals and deferrals of revenues and expenses to inflate income. Since these adjusting entries do not affect the cash account, they have no effect on the cash flow statement. A growing difference between net income and cash flow from operations can be a sign of such manipulations. This early warning sign has signaled some famous bankruptcies, such as that of W. T. Grant in 1975. The company had inflated income by failing to make adequate accruals of expenses for uncollectible accounts receivable and obsolete inventory. The more astute analysts noted the growing difference between net income and cash flow from operations and recommended selling the stock long before the bankruptcy.

SOURCE: James Chapman, "Creative Accounting: Exposed!" *Investors Chronicle*, February 3, 2001.

REPORTING AND INTERPRETING CASH FLOWS FROM INVESTING ACTIVITIES

Reporting Cash Flows from Investing Activities

Learning Objective 4
Report and interpret cash flows from investing activities.

Preparing this section of the cash flow statement requires an analysis of the accounts related to property, plant, and equipment; intangible assets; and investments in the securities of other companies. Normally, the relevant balance sheet accounts include short-term investments and long-term asset accounts such as Long-Term Investments and Property, Plant, and Equipment. The following relationships are the ones that you will encounter most frequently:

Related Balance Sheet Account(s)	Investing Activity	Cash Flow Effect
Property, plant, and equipment and intangible assets (patents, etc.)	Purchase of property, plant, and equipment or intangible assets for cash	Outflow
	Sale of property, plant, and equipment or intangible assets for cash	Inflow
Short- or long-term investments (stocks and bonds of other companies)	Purchase of investment securities for cash	Outflow
	Sale (maturity) of investment securities for cash	Inflow

Remember this:

- **Only purchases paid for with cash or cash equivalents are included.**
- **The amount of cash that is received from the sale of assets is included, regardless of whether the assets are sold at a gain or loss.**

In Boston Beer's case, the balance sheet (Exhibit 13.3) shows two investing assets (noted with an *I*) that have changed during the period: Equipment, net (fixed assets) and Short-Term Investments. To determine the causes of these changes, accountants need to search the related company records.

Cash Flows from Investing Activities

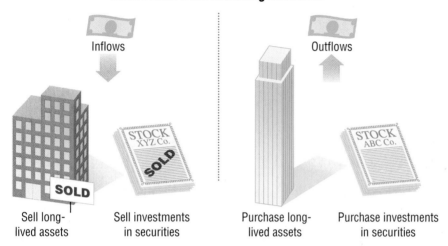

Inflows		Outflows	
Sell long-lived assets	Sell investments in securities	Purchase long-lived assets	Purchase investments in securities

Equipment, Net

They would discover that the company sold equipment for its net book value of $222 cash, which is a cash inflow. It also purchased new equipment for $1,515 cash, which is a cash outflow. Both of these investing items are listed in the schedule of investing activities in Exhibit 13.6. These two items, less the amount of depreciation expense added back in the Operations section ($1,408), explain the decrease in Equipment, net of $115.

Equipment, Net (A)			
Beg.	30,381	Sold	222
Purch.	1,515	Depr.	1,408
End.	30,266		

Investments

Boston Beer's records also indicate that it sold short-term investments and received $16,500 in cash, which is an investing cash inflow. The company also purchased an additional $13,331 in short-term investments during the quarter for cash, which is an investing cash outflow. Both of these investing items are listed in the schedule of investing activities in Exhibit 13.6. Together, they explain the $3,169 decrease ($13,331 − $16,500 = −$3,169) in short-term investments reported on the balance sheet.

Short-Term Investments (A)			
Beg.	38,999		
Purch.	13,331	Sold	16,500
End.	35,830		

The resulting net cash flow from investing activities is a $1,876 inflow (see Exhibit 13.6).

EXHIBIT 13.6

Boston Beer Company: Schedule for Net Cash Flow from Investing Activities (in thousands)

Items	Cash Inflow (Outflows)	Explanation
Proceeds from sale of equipment	$ 222	Receipt of cash from sale of equipment
Purchase of equipment	(1,515)	Payment in cash for equipment
Maturities (sale) of short-term investments	16,500	Receipt of cash from sale of short-term investments
Purchase of short-term investments	(13,331)	Payment in cash for new investments
Net cash inflow (outflow) from investing activities	$ 1,876	Reported on the statement of cash flows

Interpreting Cash Flows from Investing Activities

Two common ways to assess a company's ability to internally finance its expansion needs are the capital acquisitions ratio and free cash flow.

KEY RATIO ANALYSIS

Capital Acquisitions Ratio

Learning Objective 5
Analyze and interpret the capital acquisitions ratio.

❓ ANALYTICAL QUESTION:

To what degree was the company able to finance purchases of property, plant, and equipment with cash provided by operating activities?

% RATIO AND COMPARISONS:

$$\text{Capital Acquisitions Ratio} = \frac{\text{Cash Flow from Operating Activities}}{\text{Cash Paid for Property, Plant, and Equipment}}$$

Boston Beer's ratio for 1998 through 2000* was

$$\frac{\$53,511}{\$15,433} = 3.47$$

Examine the ratio using two techniques:

Selected Focus Company Comparisons

General Mills   2.53

Delta Airlines   0.84

Papa John's   1.08

COMPARISONS OVER TIME		COMPARISONS WITH COMPETITORS	
Boston Beer		**Minnesota Brewing**	**Redhook Ale**
1995–1997	**1998–2000**	**1998–2000**	**1998–2000**
0.71	3.47	0.44	3.82

Interpret the results carefully.

In General   The capital acquisitions ratio reflects the portion of purchases of property, plant, and equipment financed from operating activities (without the need for outside debt or equity financing or the sale of other investments or fixed assets). A high ratio indicates less need for outside financing for current and future expansion. It benefits the company because it provides the company opportunities for strategic acquisitions, avoids the cost of additional debt, and reduces the risk of bankruptcy that comes with additional leverage (see Chapter 10).

Focus Company Analysis   Boston Beer's capital acquisitions ratio has increased from 0.71 to 3.47 in recent years. However, the low ratio from the 1995–97 period was due primarily to the acquisition of a Cincinnati brewery in 1997. Since then, the firm's expenditures on capital assets have returned to more typical levels. When companies in an industry acquire

*Since capital expenditures for plant and equipment often vary greatly from year to year, this ratio is often computed over longer periods of time than one year, such as three years used here.

more productive capacity than is necessary to meet customer demand, the costs of maintaining and financing idle plant can drive a company to ruin. Boston Beer minimizes the risks of overcapacity by outsourcing a significant portion of its production to other brewers. This practice lowers Boston Beer's borrowing, depreciation, and transportation costs compared to companies with a single large brewery. Minnesota Brewing's ratio is low because it follows a strategy of building new plant and equipment. Redhook's high ratio for the 1998–2000 period indicates that it significantly decreased capital investments in recent years compared to 1996–1998 when its ratio was 0.30.

A Few Cautions   Since the needs for investment in plant and equipment differ dramatically across industries (for example, airlines versus pizza delivery restaurants), a particular firm's ratio should be compared only with its prior years figures or with other firms in the same industry. Also, a high ratio may indicate a failure to update plant and equipment, which can limit a company's ability to compete in the future.

Free Cash Flow

FINANCIAL ANALYSIS

Managers and analysts often calculate **free cash flow** as a measure of a firm's ability to pursue long-term investment opportunities. Free cash flow is normally calculated as follows:

$$\text{Free Cash Flow} = \text{Cash Flows from Operating Activities} - \text{Dividends} - \text{Capital Expenditures}$$

Any positive free cash flow is available for additional capital expenditures, investments in other companies, and mergers and acquisitions without the need for external financing. While free cash flow is considered a positive sign of financial flexibility, it also can represent a hidden cost to shareholders. Sometimes managers use free cash flow to pursue unprofitable investments just for the sake of growth or to obtain perquisites (such as fancy offices and corporate jets) that do not benefit the shareholders. In these cases, the shareholders would be better off if free cash flow were paid as additional dividends or used to repurchase the company's stock on the open market.

FREE CASH FLOW = Cash Flows from Operating Activities − Dividends − Capital Expenditures

---

REPORTING AND INTERPRETING CASH FLOWS FROM FINANCING ACTIVITIES

Reporting Cash Flows from Financing Activities

Financing activities are associated with generating capital from creditors and owners. This section of the cash flow statement reflects changes in two current liabilities, Notes Payable to Financial Institutions (often called *short-term debt*) and Current Maturities of Long-Term Debt, as well as changes in long-term liabilities and stockholders' equity accounts. These balance sheet accounts relate to the issuance and retirement of debt and stock and the payment of dividends. The following relationships are the ones that you will encounter most frequently:

Learning Objective 6
Report and interpret cash flows from financing activities.

Related Balance Sheet Account(s)	Financing Activity	Cash Flow Effect
Short-term debt (notes payable)	Borrowing cash from bank or other financial institution	Inflow
	Repayment of loan principal	Outflow
Long-term debt	Issuance of bonds for cash	Inflow
	Repayment of bond principal	Outflow
Common stock and additional paid-in capital	Issuance of stock for cash	Inflow
	Repurchase (retirement) of stock with cash	Outflow
Retained earnings	Payment of cash dividends	Outflow

Remember this:

- **If debt or stock is issued for other than cash, it is not included in this section.**
- **Cash repayments of principal are cash flows from financing activities.**
- **Interest payments are cash flows from operating activities.** Since interest expense is reported on the income statement, the related cash flow is shown in the operating section.
- **Dividend payments are cash flows from financing activities.** They are not reported on the income statement because they represent a distribution of income to owners, so they are shown in the financing section.

To compute cash flows from financing activities, you should review changes in debt and stockholders' equity accounts. In the case of Boston Beer Company, the analysis of changes in the balance sheet (Exhibit 13.3) finds that only contributed capital changed during the period (noted with an F).

Contributed Capital

The change in contributed capital resulted from two decisions. First, Boston Beer repurchased outstanding stock for $5,801 cash, which is a cash outflow. The company also issued common stock to employees for $15 in cash, which is a cash inflow. Together, these two amounts account for the $5,786 decrease in contributed capital. They are listed in the schedule of financing activities in Exhibit 13.7, which shows a net cash outflow of $5,786.

Contributed Capital (SE)			
		Beg.	47,030
Repurch.	5,801	Issue	15
		End.	41,244

Short- and Long-Term Debt

If Boston Beer had borrowed or repaid principal on short- or long-term debt during the period, these also would be listed in this section. The appropriate amounts would be determined by analyzing the short- and long-term debt accounts.

Retained Earnings

Finally, retained earnings should be analyzed. Retained earnings rises when income is earned and falls when dividends are declared and paid. Boston Beer's retained earnings rose by an amount equal to its net income, so no dividends were declared and paid. Should Boston Beer ever decide to pay dividends, it would also list them as financing cash outflows.

EXHIBIT 13.7			

Boston Beer Company: Schedule for Net Cash Flow from Financing Activities (in thousands)

Items	Cash Inflow (Outflows)	Explanation
Repurchase of stock (treasury stock)	($5,801)	Cash payments to repurchase outstanding stock
Net proceeds from stock issuance	15	Cash proceeds from issue of common stock
Net cash inflow (outflow) from financing activities	($5,786)	Reported on the statement of cash flows

Retained Earnings (SE)			
		Beg.	36,575
Dividends	0	Net Income	3,573
		End.	40,148

Cash Flows from Financing Activities

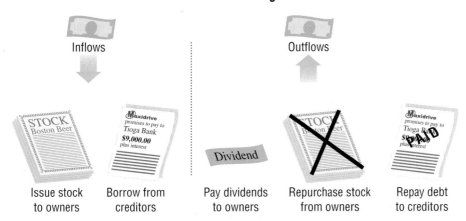

Inflows		Outflows		
Issue stock to owners	Borrow from creditors	Pay dividends to owners	Repurchase stock from owners	Repay debt to creditors

Interpreting Cash Flows from Financing Activities

The long-term growth of a company is normally financed from three sources: internally generated funds (cash from operating activities), the issuance of stock, and money borrowed on a long-term basis. As we discussed in Chapter 10, companies can adopt a number of different capital structures (the balance of debt and equity). The financing sources that management uses to fund growth will have an important impact on the firm's risk and return characteristics. The statement of cash flows shows how management has elected to fund its growth. This information is used by analysts who wish to evaluate the capital structure and growth potential of a business.

SELF-STUDY **QUIZ**

Pete's Brewing Co.

Indicate which of the following items taken from Pete's Brewing Company's cash flow statement would be reported in the Investing section (I) or Financing section (F) and whether the amount would be an inflow (+) or an outflow (−).

_____ *a.* Increase in bank indebtedness.

_____ *b.* Additions to capital assets (for cash).

_____ *c.* Acquisition of investments (for cash).

_____ *d.* Share repurchase (with cash).

After you have completed your answers, check them with the solutions that follow:

_____
a. F+, b. I−, c. I−, d. F−.

ADDITIONAL CASH FLOW DISCLOSURES

The formal statement of cash flows for Boston Beer Company is shown in Exhibit 13.1. As you can see, it is a simple matter to construct the statement after the detailed analysis of the accounts and transactions has been completed (shown in Exhibits 13.4,

Learning Objective 7
Explain the impact of additional cash flow disclosures.

13.5, 13.6, and 13.7). If the company uses the direct method for computing cash flow from operations, it must present the reconciliation of net income to cash flow from operations (the indirect method as presented in Exhibit 13.4) as a supplemental schedule. Companies also must provide two other disclosures related to the cash flow statement.

Noncash Investing and Financing Activities

Certain transactions are important investing and financing activities but have no cash flow effects. These are called **noncash investing and financing activities**. For example, the purchase of a $100,000 building with a $100,000 mortgage given by the former owner does not cause either an inflow or an outflow of cash. As a result, these noncash activities are not listed in the three main sections of the cash flow statement. However, supplemental disclosure of these transactions is required, in either narrative or schedule form. Boston Beer's statement of cash flows does not list any noncash investing and financing activities. The following schedule from the annual report of Pacific Aerospace & Electronics illustrates the significance and diversity of noncash transactions.

PACIFIC AEROSPACE & ELECTRONICS, INC.

Noncash investing and financing activities:

	Year Ended May 31,		
	1999	**2000**	**2001**
Seller financed acquisition of property, plant and equipment	$241,000	$—	$—
Conversion of notes and accrued interest to common stock	—	11,457,000	—
Short-term obligations refinanced with long-term debt	—	—	9,306,000
Reclassification of property, plant and equipment to other assets	1,217,000	—	—
Issuance of warrants in connection with debt	—	—	1,886,000

Supplemental Cash Flow Information

Companies that use the indirect method of presenting cash flows from operations also must provide two other figures: cash paid for interest and cash paid for income taxes. These are normally listed at the bottom of the statement or in the notes.

EPILOGUE

Our more detailed analysis of Boston Beer's first-quarter cash flow indicates that the difference between net income and cash flows in the first quarter was not a cause for alarm. In fact, it was a normal consequence of seasonal variations in sales, purchases of raw materials, and advertising expenditures. On the income statement, lower sales in the first quarter are usually more than offset by the decline in advertising in the same period, resulting in strong earnings. The upsurge in sales in March, however, causes receivables to rise, resulting in lower cash flow from operations. Collections of these receivables in the second quarter account for much of the upsurge in cash flows from operations in that quarter. Our further analysis of Boston Beer's investing and financing indicates that the cash needs to continue its investment strategy should be more than met by operations.

DEMONSTRATION **CASE**

(Try to resolve the requirements before proceeding to the suggested solution that follows.) During a recent year (ended December 31), Redhook Ale Brewery, a Seattle-based craft brewer, reported net income of $3,182 (all numbers in thousands) and cash and cash equivalents at the beginning of the year of $472. It also engaged in the following activities:

Redhook Ale Brewery

a. Paid $18,752 in principal on debt.

b. Received $46,202 in cash from initial public offering of common stock.

c. Incurred other noncurrent accrued operating expenses of $857.

d. Paid $18,193 in cash for purchase of fixed assets.

e. Accounts receivable increased by $881.

f. Borrowed $16,789 from various lenders.

g. Refundable deposits payable increased by $457.

h. Inventories increased by $574.

i. Made cash deposits on equipment of $5,830.

j. Income tax refund receivable decreased by $326.

k. Sold (issued) stock to employees for $13 in cash.

l. Accounts payable decreased by $391.

m. Received $4 from other investing activities.

n. Accrued expenses increased by $241.

o. Prepaid expenses increased by $565.

p. Recorded depreciation of $1,324.

q. Paid $5 cash in other financing activities.

Required:

Based on this information, prepare the cash flow statement using the indirect method.

SUGGESTED SOLUTION

REDHOOK ALE BREWERY
Statement of Cash Flows
For the Year Ended December 31
(in thousands)

Operating activities	
Net income	$ 3,182
Adjustments	
Depreciation	1,324
Other noncurrent accrued expenses	857
Change in accounts receivable	(881)
Change in inventories	(574)
Change in income taxes receivable	326
Change in prepaid expenses	(565)
Change in accounts payable	(391)
Change in accrued expenses	241
Change in refundable deposits payable	457
Net cash flow from operating activities	3,976

Investing activities	
Expenditures for fixed assets	(18,193)
Deposits on equipment	(5,830)
Other	4
Net cash flow from investing activities	(24,019)
Financing activities	
Proceeds from debt	16,789
Repayment of debt	(18,752)
Proceeds from sale of stock (IPO)	46,202
Proceeds from sale of stock (options)	13
Other	(5)
Net cash flow from financing activities	44,247
Increase in cash and cash equivalents	24,204
Cash and cash equivalents:	
Beginning of year	472
End of year	$24,676

Chapter Supplement A

Adjustment for Gains and Losses: Indirect Method

As noted earlier, the Operating Activities section of the statement may include an adjustment for gains and losses reported on the income statement. The transactions that cause gains and losses should be classified on the cash flow statement as operating, investing, or financing activities, depending on their dominant characteristics. For example, if the sale of a productive asset (e.g., a delivery truck) produced a gain, it would be classified as an investing activity.

An adjustment must be made in the Operating Activities section to avoid double counting the gain or loss. To illustrate, consider the following entry for Boston Beer to record the disposal of a delivery truck:

Cash (+A)	8,000	
Accumulated depreciation (−XA, +A)	4,000	
Property, plant, and equipment (−A)		10,000
Gain on disposal (+Gain, +SE)		2,000

Assets		=	Liabilities	+	Stockholders' Equity	
Cash	+8,000				Gain on disposal	+2,000
Accumulated depreciation	+4,000					
Property, plant, and equipment	− 10,000					

The inflow of cash was $8,000 is an investing cash inflow, but the reported gain of $2,000 was also shown on the income statement. Because the gain was included in the computation of income, it is necessary to remove (subtract) the $2,000 gain from the Operating Activities section of the statement to avoid double counting.

When a loss is reported on the income statement, it also must be removed from cash flows from operating activities. Consider the following entry to record the sale of assets:

Cash (+A)..	41,000	
Accumulated depreciation (−XA, +A).................	15,000	
Loss on disposal (−Loss, −SE)	12,000	
Property, plant, and equipment (−A)................		68,000

Assets		= Liabilities	+ Stockholders' Equity	
Cash	+41,000		Loss on disposal	− 12,000
Accumulated depreciation	+15,000			
Property, plant, and equipment	− 68,000			

On the cash flow statement, the loss of $12,000 must be removed (added back) in the computation of cash from operating activities, and the total cash collected of $41,000 must be shown in the Investing Activities section of the statement.

Chapter Supplement B

Spreadsheet Approach—Statement of Cash Flows: Indirect Method

As situations become more complex, the analytical approach that we used to prepare the statement of cash flows for Boston Beer Company becomes cumbersome and inefficient. In actual practice, many companies use a spreadsheet approach to prepare the statement of cash flows. The spreadsheet is based on the same logic that we used in our previous illustration. The spreadsheet's primary advantage is that it offers a more systematic way to keep track of data. You may find it useful even in simple situations.

Exhibit 13.8 shows Boston Beer Company's spreadsheet, which is organized as follows:

1. Four columns to record dollar amounts are established. The first column is for the beginning balances for items reported on the balance sheet; the next two columns reflect debit and credit changes to those balances; the final column contains the ending balances for the balance sheet accounts.

2. On the far left of the top half of the spreadsheet, each account name from the balance sheet is entered.

3. On the far left of the bottom half of the spreadsheet, the name of each item that will be reported on the statement of cash flows is entered.

Changes in the various balance sheet accounts are analyzed in terms of debits and credits in the top half of the spreadsheet with the offsetting debits and credits being recorded in the bottom half of the spreadsheet in terms of their impact on cash flows. Each change in the noncash balance sheet accounts explains part of the change in the Cash account. To illustrate, let's examine each of the entries on the spreadsheet for Boston Beer Company shown in Exhibit 13.8. You will note that they follow each of the items presented in the schedule to prepare the cash flow statement shown in Exhibits 13.4, 13.6, and 13.7.

a. This entry is used to start the reconciliation; net income of $3,573 is shown as an inflow in the Operating Activities section to be reconciled by the noncash reconciling entries. The credit to Retained Earnings reflects the effects of the original closing entry. This is the starting point for the reconciliation.

b. Depreciation expense of $1,408 is a noncurrent accrued expense. It is added back to net income because this type of expense does not cause a cash outflow when it is recorded. The credit to Accumulated Depreciation reflects the effects of the original entry to record depreciation.

c. When an asset that was classified as part of fixed assets is sold, the actual cash proceeds appear in the Investing Section of the statement of cash flows. In this case, $222 is shown as proceeds.

d. This entry reconciles the change in accounts receivable during the period with net income. It is subtracted from net income because cash collections from customers totaled less than sales revenue.

EXHIBIT 13.8 Spreadsheet to Prepare Statement of Cash Flows, Indirect Method

BOSTON BEER COMPANY
Quarter Ended March 25, 2000
(in thousands)

	Beginning Balances, 12/25/1999	Analysis of Change Debit		Analysis of Change Credit		Ending Balances, 3/25/2000
Items from Balance Sheet						
Cash and cash equivalents	5,346			(n)	988	4,358
Short-term investments	38,999	(k)	13,331	(j)	16,500	35,830
Accounts receivable	16,290	(d)	2,762			19,052
Inventories	15,656	(e)	220			15,876
Prepaid expenses	6,081			(f)	1,549	4,532
Equipment, net	30,381	(i)	1,515	(b)	1,408	30,266
				(c)	222	
Accounts payable	16,306	(g)	1,892			14,414
Accrued expenses	12,842			(h)	1,266	14,108
Contributed Capital	47,030	(l)	5,801	(m)	15	41,244
Retained earnings	36,575			(a)	3,573	40,148

		Inflows		Outflows		Subtotals
Statement of Cash Flows						
Cash flows from operating activities:						
Net income		(a)	3,573			
Adjustments to reconcile net income to cash provided by operating activities						
Depreciation and amortization		(b)	1,408			
Changes in assets and liabilities:						
Accounts receivable				(d)	2,762	
Inventories				(e)	220	
Prepaid expenses		(f)	1,549			
Accounts payable				(g)	1,892	
Accrued expenses		(h)	1,266			
						2,922
Cash flows from investing activities:						
Proceeds from sale of equipment		(c)	222			
Purchases of equipment				(i)	1,515	
Maturities (sale) of short-term investments		(j)	16,500			
Purchase of short-term investments				(k)	13,331	
						1,876
Cash flows from financing activities:						
Purchase of treasury stock				(l)	5,801	
Net proceeds from stock issuance		(m)	15			
						(5,786)
Net decrease in cash and cash equivalents		(n)	988			
			51,042		51,042	(988)

e. This entry reconciles the purchases of inventory with cost of goods sold. It is subtracted from net income because more inventory was purchased than was sold.

f. This entry reconciles the prepayment of expenses with their expiration. It is added to net income because cash payments for new prepayments are less than the amounts that expired and were recorded on the income statement during the period.

g. This entry reconciles cash paid to suppliers with purchases on account. It is subtracted because more cash was paid than was borrowed during the period.

h. This entry reconciles the accrual of expenses with payments for these expenses. It is added because cash payments for expenses are less than new accruals.

i. This entry records the purchases of new plant and equipment (fixed assets) for cash.

j. This entry records the receipt of cash on maturity of some short-term investments.

k. This entry records the purchases of short-term investments for cash.

l. This entry records cash paid to repurchase some of Boston Beer's own stock from shareholders.

m. This entry records the cash received from the issuance of stock.

n. This entry shows that the net increase or decrease reported on the statement of cash flows is the same as the change in the cash balance on the balance sheet during the period.

The preceding entries complete the spreadsheet analysis because all accounts are reconciled. The accuracy of the analysis can be checked by adding the two analysis columns to verify that Debits = Credits. You should also note that the debits and credits to the balance sheet accounts directly match those recorded in the T-accounts presented in the body of the chapter. The formal statement of cash flows can be prepared directly from the spreadsheet.

The analytical technique that you have learned for preparing the statement of cash flows will help you deal with other significant business problems. For example, this type of analysis is useful for developing cash budgets for a business. Many small businesses that experience rapid sales growth get into serious financial difficulties because they did not forecast the cash flow effects associated with credit sales and large increases in inventory.

CHAPTER **TAKE-AWAYS**

1. **Classify cash flow statement items as part of net cash flows from operating, investing, and financing activities. p. 647**
   The statement has three main sections: Cash Flows from Operating Activities, which are related to earning income from normal operations; Cash Flows from Investing Activities, which are related to the acquisition and sale of productive assets; and Cash Flows from Financing Activities, which are related to external financing of the enterprise. The net cash inflow or outflow for the year is the same amount as the increase or decrease in cash and cash equivalents for the year on the balance sheet. Cash equivalents are highly liquid investments with original maturities of less than three months.

2a. **Report and interpret cash flows from operating activities using the indirect method. p. 651**
   The indirect method for reporting cash flows from operating activities reports a conversion of net income to net cash flow from operating activities. The conversion involves additions and subtractions for (1) noncurrent accruals including expenses (such as depreciation expense) and revenues that do not affect current assets or current liabilities and (2) changes in each of the individual current assets (other than cash and short-term investments) and current liabilities (other than short-term debt to financial institutions and current maturities of long-term debt, which relate to financing), which reflect differences in the timing of accrual basis net income and cash flows.

2b. **Report and interpret cash flows from operating activities using the direct method. p. 657**
   The direct method for reporting cash flows from operating activities accumulates all of the operating transactions that result in either a debit or a credit to cash into categories. The most common inflows are cash received from customers and dividends and interest on investments. The most common outflows are cash paid for purchase of services and goods for resale, salaries and wages, income taxes, and interest on liabilities. It is prepared by adjusting each item on the income statement from an accrual basis to a cash basis.

3. **Analyze and interpret the quality of income ratio. p. 662**
   Quality of income ratio (Cash Flow from Operating Activities ÷ Net Income) measures the portion of income that was generated in cash. A higher quality of income ratio indicates greater ability to finance operating and other cash needs from operating cash inflows. A higher ratio also indicates that it is less likely that the company is using aggressive revenue recognition policies to increase net income.

4. **Report and interpret cash flows from investing activities. p. 664**
   Investing activities reported on the cash flow statement include cash payments to acquire fixed assets and short- and long-term investments and cash proceeds from the sale of fixed assets and short- and long-term investments.

5. **Analyze and interpret the capital acquisitions ratio. p. 666**
   The capital acquisitions ratio (Cash Flow from Operating Activities ÷ Cash Paid for Property, Plant, and Equipment) reflects the portion of purchases of property, plant, and equipment financed from operating activities without the need for outside debt or equity financing or the sale of other investments or fixed assets. A high ratio benefits the company because it provides the company with opportunities for strategic acquisitions.

6. **Report and interpret cash flows from financing activities. p. 667**
   Cash inflows from financing activities include cash proceeds from issuance of short- and long-term debt and common stock. Cash outflows include cash principal payments on short- and long-term debt, cash paid for the repurchase of the company's stock, and cash dividend payments. Cash payments associated with interest are a cash flow from operating activities.

7. **Explain the impact of additional cash flow disclosures. p. 669**
   Noncash investing and financing activities are investing and financing activities that do not involve cash. They include, for example, purchases of fixed assets with long-term debt or stock, exchanges of fixed assets, and exchanges of debt for stock. These transactions are disclosed only as supplemental disclosures to the cash flow statement along with cash paid for taxes and interest under the indirect method.

Throughout the preceding chapters, we emphasized the conceptual basis of accounting. An understanding of the rationale underlying accounting is important for both preparers and users of financial statements. In Chapter 14, we bring together our discussion of the major users of financial statements and how they analyze and use them. We discuss and illustrate many widely used analytical techniques discussed in earlier chapters, as well as additional techniques. As you study Chapter 14, you will see that an understanding of accounting rules and concepts is essential for effective analysis of financial statements.

KEY **RATIOS**

Quality of income ratio indicates what portion of income was generated in cash. It is computed as follows (p. 662):

$$\text{Quality of Income Ratio} = \frac{\text{Cash Flow from Operating Activities}}{\text{Net Income}}$$

Capital acquisitions ratio measures the ability to finance purchases of plant and equipment from operations. It is computed as follows (p. 666):

$$\text{Capital Acquisitions Ratio} = \frac{\text{Cash Flow from Operating Activities}}{\text{Cash Paid for Property, Plant, and Equipment}}$$

FINDING **FINANCIAL INFORMATION**

Balance Sheet	**Income Statement**
Changes in Assets, Liabilities, and Stockholders' Equity	*Net Income and Noncurrent Accruals*

Statement of Cash Flows

Cash Flows from Operating Activities

Cash Flows from Investing Activities

Cash Flows from Financing Activities

Separate Schedule (or note)
   Noncash investing and financing activities
   Interest and taxes paid

Notes

Under Summary of Significant Accounting Policies
   Definition of cash equivalents

Under Separate Note
   If not listed on cash flow statement:
   Noncash investing and financing activities
   Interest and taxes paid

KEY TERMS

Cash Equivalent p. 647
Cash Flows from Financing Activities p. 649
Cash Flows from Investing Activities p. 649

Cash Flows from Operating Activities (Cash Flows from Operations) p. 647
Direct Method p. 647

Free Cash Flow p. 667
Indirect Method p. 647
Noncash Investing and Financing Activities p. 670

QUESTIONS

1. Compare the purposes of the income statement, the balance sheet, and the statement of cash flows.
2. What information does the statement of cash flows report that is not reported on the other required financial statements? How do investors and creditors use that information?
3. What are cash equivalents? How are purchases and sales of cash equivalents reported on the statement of cash flows?
4. What are the major categories of business activities reported on the statement of cash flows? Define each of these activities.
5. What are the typical cash inflows from operating activities? What are the typical cash outflows from operating activities?
6. Under the indirect method, depreciation expense is added to net income to report cash flows from operating activities. Does depreciation cause an inflow of cash?
7. Explain why cash paid during the period for purchases and for salaries is not specifically reported on the statement of cash flows, indirect method, as cash outflows.
8. Explain why a $50,000 increase in inventory during the year must be included in developing cash flows for operating activities under both the direct and indirect methods.
9. Compare the two methods of reporting cash flows from operating activities in the statement of cash flows.
10. What are the typical cash inflows from investing activities? What are the typical cash outflows from investing activities?
11. What are the typical cash inflows from financing activities? What are the typical cash outflows from financing activities?
12. What are noncash investing and financing activities? Give two examples. How are they reported on the statement of cash flows?
13. How is the sale of equipment reported on the statement of cash flows using the indirect method?

MULTIPLE CHOICE QUESTIONS

1. Most companies use the indirect method of computing the change in cash from operating activities because of the following reason(s):
   a. The FASB prefers the indirect method.
   b. It is less costly to prepare than the direct method.

    c. The indirect method arrives at a higher cash inflow amount.

    d. Both (a) and (b) are correct.

2. In what order do the three sections of the statement of cash flows appear when reading from top to bottom?

    a. Financing, Investing, Operating   c. Operating, Financing, Investing

    b. Investing, Operating, Financing   d. Operating, Investing, Financing

3. Total cash inflow in the operating section of the statement of cash flows should include which of the following?

    a. cash received from customers at the point of sale

    b. cash collections from customer accounts receivable

    c. cash received in advance of revenue recognition (unearned revenue)

    d. All of the above

4. If the balance in prepaid expenses increased during the year, what action should be taken on the statement of cash flows when following the indirect method, *and why*?

    a. The change in the account balance should be subtracted from net income because the net increase in prepaid expenses did not impact net income but did reduce the cash balance.

    b. The change in the account balance should be added to net income because the net increase in prepaid expenses did not impact net income but did increase the cash balance.

    c. The net change in prepaid expenses should be subtracted from net income to reverse the income statement effect that had no impact on cash.

    d. The net change in prepaid expenses should be added to net income to reverse the income statement effect that had no impact on cash.

5. Which of the following would not appear in the investing section of the statement of cash flows?

    a. purchase of inventory

    b. sale of obsolete equipment used in the factory

    c. purchase of land for a new office building

    d. All of the above would appear

6. Which of the following items would not appear in the financing section of the statement of cash flows?

    a. the repurchase of the company's own stock

    b. the receipt of dividends

    c. the repayment of debt

    d. the payment of dividends

7. Which of the following is not added to net income when computing cash flows from operations under the indirect method?

    a. the net increase in accounts payable

    b. the net decrease in accounts receivable

    c. depreciation expense reported on the income statement

    d. all of the above are added

8. If a company engages in a noncash material transaction, which of the following is required?

    a. The company must include an explanatory narrative or schedule along with the statement of cash flows.

    b. No disclosure is necessary.

    c. The company must include an explanatory narrative or schedule along with the balance sheet.

    d. It must be reported in the investing and financing section of the statement of cash flow.

9. The change in cash shown *in the operating section* of the statement of cash flows should equal which of the following?

    a. net income on the income statement   c. the change in accounts payable

    b. the change in accounts receivable   d. none of the above

10. The *total* change in cash as shown near the bottom of the statement of cash flows for the year should agree to which of the following?

    a. the difference in retained earnings when reviewing the comparative balance sheet

    b. net income or net loss as found on the income statement

    c. the difference in cash when reviewing the comparative balance sheet

    d. none of the above

For more practice with multiple choice questions, go to our website at www.mhhe.com/libby4e, click on "Student Center" in the upper left menu, click on this chapter's name and number from the list of contents, and then click on "Multiple Choice Quiz" from the menu on the left.

Matching Items Reported to Cash Flow Statement Categories (Indirect Method)

Adolph Coors Company, founded in 1873, is the third largest U.S. brewer. Its tie to the magical appeal of the Rocky Mountains is one of its most powerful trademarks. Some of the items included in its recent annual consolidated statement of cash flows presented using the *indirect method* are listed here. Indicate whether each item is disclosed in the Operating Activities (O), Investing Activities (I), or Financing Activities (F) section of the statement or (NA) if the item does not appear on the statement. (*Note:* This is the exact wording used on the actual statement.)

M13-1
LO1, 2A
Adolph Coors

_____ 1. Proceeds from sale of properties.
_____ 2. Purchase of stock. [This involves repurchase of its own stock.]
_____ 3. Depreciation, depletion, and amortization.
_____ 4. Accounts payable (decrease).
_____ 5. Inventories (decrease).
_____ 6. Principal payment on long-term debt.

Determining the Effects of Account Changes on Cash Flow from Operating Activities (Indirect Method)

M13-2
LO2A

Indicate whether each item would be added ($+$) or subtracted ($-$) in the computation of cash flow from operating activities using the indirect method.

_____ 1. Depreciation, depletion, and amortization.
_____ 2. Inventories (increase).
_____ 3. Accounts payable (decrease).
_____ 4. Accounts receivable (decrease).
_____ 5. Accrued expenses (increase).

Matching Items Reported to Cash Flow Statement Categories (Direct Method)

M13-3
LO1, 2B
Lion Nathan

Lion Nathan, brewer of XXXX, Toohey's, and other well-known Australian brands, has net revenue of more than $1 billion Australian. Some of the items included in its recent annual consolidated statement of cash flows presented using the *direct method* are listed here. Indicate whether each item is disclosed in the Operating Activities (O), Investing Activities (I), or Financing Activities (F) section of the statement or (NA) if the item does not appear on the statement. (*Note:* This is the exact wording used on the actual statement.)

_____ 1. Repayments of borrowings (bank debt).
_____ 2. Dividends paid.
_____ 3. Proceeds from sale of property, plant and equipment.
_____ 4. Net interest paid.
_____ 5. Receipts from customers.
_____ 6. Payment for share buy-back.

Analyzing the Quality of Income Ratio

M13-4
LO3

Lisa K. Corporation reported net income of $80,000, depreciation expense of $3,000, and cash flow from operations of $60,000. Compute the quality of income ratio. What does the ratio tell you about the company's ability to finance operating and other cash needs from operating cash inflows?

Computing Cash Flows from Investing Activities

M13-5
LO4

Based on the following information, compute cash flows from investing activities.

Cash collections from customers	$800
Sale of used equipment	250
Depreciation expense	100
Purchase of short-term investments	300

M13-6 Computing Cash Flows from Financing Activities

LO6

Based on the following information, compute cash flows from financing activities.

Purchase of short-term investments	$ 250
Dividends paid	800
Interest paid	400
Additional short-term borrowing from bank	1,000

M13-7 Reporting Noncash Investing and Financing Activities

LO7

Which of the following transactions qualify as noncash investing and financing activities?

_____ Purchase of equipment with short-term investments
_____ Dividends paid in cash
_____ Purchase of building with mortgage payable
_____ Additional short-term borrowing from bank

EXERCISES

E13-1 Matching Items Reported to Cash Flow Statement Categories (Indirect Method)

LO1, 2A

Nike

Nike, Inc., is the best-known sports shoe, apparel, and equipment company in the world because of its association with sports legends such as Michael Jordan, teams such as the Michigan Wolverines, and events such as the Olympics. Some of the items included in its recent annual consolidated statement of cash flows presented using the *indirect method* are listed here.

Indicate whether each item is disclosed in the Operating Activities (O), Investing Activities (I), or Financing Activities (F) section of the statement or (NA) if the item does not appear on the statement. (*Note:* This is the exact wording used on the actual statement.)

_____ 1. Depreciation.
_____ 2. Additions to property, plant, and equipment.
_____ 3. Increase (decrease) in notes payable. (The amount is owed to financial institutions.)
_____ 4. (Increase) decrease in other current assets.
_____ 5. Disposal of property, plant, and equipment.
_____ 6. Reductions in long-term debt including current portion.
_____ 7. Repurchase of stock.
_____ 8. (Increase) decrease in inventory.
_____ 9. Net income.
_____ 10. Additions to long-term debt.

E13-2 Determining Cash Flow Statement Effects of Transactions

LO1

Stanley Furniture

Stanley Furniture Company is a Virginia-based furniture manufacturer. For each of the following first-quarter transactions, indicate whether *net cash inflows (outflows)* from operating activities (NCFO), investing activities (NCFI), or financing activities (NCFF) are affected and whether the effect is an inflow (+) or outflow (−), or (NE) if the transaction has no effect on cash. (*Hint:* Determine the journal entry recorded for the transaction. The transaction affects net cash flows if and only if the account Cash is affected.)

_____ 1. Paid cash to purchase new equipment.
_____ 2. Purchased raw materials inventory on account.
_____ 3. Collected payments on account from customers.
_____ 4. Recorded an adjusting entry to record accrued salaries expense.
_____ 5. Recorded and paid interest on debt to creditors.
_____ 6. Repaid principal on revolving credit loan from bank.
_____ 7. Prepaid rent for the following period.
_____ 8. Sold used equipment for cash at book value.

_____ 9. Made payment to suppliers on account.

_____ 10. Declared and paid cash dividends to shareholders.

Determining Cash Flow Statement Effects of Transactions

Compaq Computer Corporation is a leading manufacturer of personal computers and servers for the business and home markets. For each of the following recent transactions, indicate whether *net cash inflows (outflows)* from operating activities (NCFO), investing activities (NCFI), or financing activities (NCFF) are affected and whether the effect is an inflow (+) or outflow (−), or (NE) if the transaction has no effect on cash. (*Hint:* Determine the journal entry recorded for the transaction. The transaction affects net cash flows if and only if the account Cash is affected.)

_____ 1. Recorded and paid income taxes to the federal government.

_____ 2. Issued common stock for cash.

_____ 3. Prepaid rent for the following period.

_____ 4. Recorded an adjusting entry for expiration of a prepaid expense.

_____ 5. Paid cash to purchase new equipment.

_____ 6. Issued long-term debt for cash.

_____ 7. Collected payments on account from customers.

_____ 8. Purchased raw materials inventory on account.

_____ 9. Recorded and paid salaries to employees.

_____ 10. Purchased new equipment by signing a three-year note.

Interpreting Noncurrent Accruals from a Management Perspective

QuickServe, a chain of convenience stores, was experiencing some serious cash flow difficulties because of rapid growth. The company did not generate sufficient cash from operating activities to finance its new stores, and creditors were not willing to lend money because the company had not produced any income for the previous three years. The new controller for QuickServe proposed a reduction in the estimated life of store equipment to increase depreciation expense; thus, "we can improve cash flows from operating activities because depreciation expense is added back on the statement of cash flows." Other executives were not sure that this was a good idea because the increase in depreciation would make it more difficult to have positive earnings: "Without income, the bank will never lend us money."

Required:

What action would you recommend for QuickServe? Why?

Comparing the Direct and Indirect Methods

To compare statement of cash flows reporting under the direct and indirect methods, enter check marks to indicate which items are used with each method.

Cash Flows (and Related Changes)	Statement of Cash Flows Method	
	Direct	Indirect
1. Cash collections from customers		
2. Accounts receivable increase or decrease		
3. Payments to suppliers		
4. Inventory increase or decrease		
5. Accounts payable increase or decrease		
6. Payments to employees		
7. Wages payable, increase or decrease		
8. Depreciation expense		
9. Net income		
10. Cash flows from operating activities		
11. Cash flows from investing activities		
12. Cash flows from financing activities		
13. Net increase or decrease in cash during the period		

E13-6

LO2A

Reporting Cash Flows from Operating Activities (Indirect Method)

The following information pertains to Day Company:

Sales		$80,000
Expenses		
Cost of goods sold	$50,000	
Depreciation expense	6,000	
Salaries expense	12,000	68,000
Net income		$12,000
Accounts receivable increase	$ 5,000	
Merchandise inventory decrease	8,000	
Salaries payable increase	500	

Required:

Present the Operating Activities section of the statement of cash flows for Day Company using the indirect method.

E13-7

LO2A

Reporting and Interpreting Cash Flows from Operating Activities from an Analyst's Perspective (Indirect Method)

Kane Company completed its income statement and balance sheet for 2006 and provided the following information:

Service revenue		$50,000
Expenses		
Salaries	$42,000	
Depreciation	7,000	
Amortization of copyrights	300	
Utilities	7,000	
Other expenses	1,700	58,000
Net loss		($ 8,000)
Decrease in accounts receivable	$12,000	
Bought a small service machine	5,000	
Increase in salaries payable	9,000	
Decrease in other accrued liabilities	4,000	

Required:

1. Present the Operating Activities section of the statement of cash flows for Kane Company using the indirect method.
2. What were the major reasons that Kane was able to report a net loss but positive cash flow from operations? Why are the reasons for the difference between cash flow from operations and net income important to financial analysts?

E13-8

LO2A

Sizzler International, Inc.

Reporting and Interpreting Cash Flows from Operating Activities from an Analyst's Perspective (Indirect Method)

Sizzler International, Inc., operates 700 family restaurants around the world. The company's recent annual report contained the following information (in thousands):

Net loss	$(9,482)
Depreciation and amortization	33,305
Increase in receivables	170
Decrease in inventories	643
Increase in prepaid expenses	664
Decrease in accounts payable	2,282
Decrease in accrued liabilities	719
Increase in income taxes payable	1,861
Reduction of long-term debt	12,691
Additions to equipment	29,073

Required:

1. Based on this information, compute cash flow from operating activities using the indirect method.
2. What were the major reasons that Sizzler was able to report a net loss but positive cash flow from operations? Why are the reasons for the difference between cash flow from operations and net income important to financial analysts?

Inferring Balance Sheet Changes from the Cash Flow Statement

A recent statement of cash flows for Colgate-Palmolive reported the following information (in millions):

E13-9
LO2A
Colgate-
Palmolive

Operating Activities	
Net income	$477.0
Depreciation	192.5
Cash effect of changes in	
Receivables	(38.0)
Inventories	28.4
Other current assets	10.6
Payables	(10.0)
Other	(117.8)
Net cash provided by operations	$542.7

Required:

Based on the information reported on the statement of cash flows for Colgate-Palmolive, determine whether the following accounts increased or decreased during the period: Receivables, Inventories, Other Current Assets, and Payables.

Inferring Balance Sheet Changes from the Cash Flow Statement

A recent statement of cash flows for Apple Computer contained the following information (in thousands):

E13-10
LO2A
Apple
Computer,
Inc.

Operations	
Net income	$310,178
Depreciation	167,958
Changes in assets and liabilities	
Accounts receivable	(199,401)
Inventories	418,204
Other current assets	33,616
Accounts payable	139,095
Income taxes payable	50,045
Other current liabilities	39,991
Other adjustments	(222,691)
Cash generated by operations	$736,995

Required:

For each of the asset and liability accounts listed on the statement of cash flows, determine whether the account balances increased or decreased during the period.

Reporting and Interpreting Cash Flows from Operating Activities from an Analyst's Perspective (Direct Method)

Refer to the information for Kane Company in Exercise 13.7.

E13-11
LO2B

Required:

1. Present the Operating Activities section of the statement of cash flows for Kane Company using the direct method. Assume that other accrued liabilities relate to other expenses on the income statement.

2. What were the major reasons that Kane was able to report a net loss but positive cash flow from operations? Why are the reasons for the difference between cash flow from operations and net income important to financial analysts?

E13-12
LO2B
Sizzler
International,
Inc.

Reporting and Interpreting Cash Flows from Operating Activities from an Analyst's Perspective (Direct Method)

Refer back to the information given for Exercise 13.8 and the following summarized income statement for Sizzler International, Inc.:

Revenues	$136,500
Cost of sales	45,500
Gross margin	91,000
Salary expense	56,835
Depreciation and amortization	33,305
Other expense	7,781
Net loss before tax	(6,921)
Income tax expense	2,561
Net loss	$(9,482)

Required:

1. Based on this information, compute cash flow from operating activities using the direct method. Assume that prepaid expenses and accrued liabilities relate to other expenses.
2. What were the major reasons that Sizzler was able to report a net loss but positive cash flow from operations? Why are the reasons for the difference between cash flow from operations and net income important to financial analysts?

E13-13
LO2A, 3
PepsiCo

Analyzing Cash Flows from Operating Activities; Interpreting the Quality of Income Ratio

A recent annual report for PepsiCo contained the following information for the period (in millions):

Net income	$1,587.9
Depreciation and amortization	1,444.2
Increase in accounts receivable	161.0
Increase in inventory	89.5
Decrease in prepaid expense	3.3
Increase in accounts payable	143.2
Decrease in taxes payable	125.1
Decrease in other current liabilities	96.7
Cash dividends paid	461.6
Treasury stock purchased	463.5

Required:

1. Compute cash flows from operating activities for PepsiCo using the indirect method.
2. Compute the quality of income ratio.
3. What were the major reasons that Pepsi's quality of income ratio did not equal 1.0?

E13-14
LO4, 6
Rowe Furniture

Reporting Cash Flows from Investing and Financing Activities

Rowe Furniture Corporation is a Virginia-based manufacturer of furniture. In a recent quarter, it reported the following activities:

Net income	$ 4,135
Purchase of property, plant, and equipment	871

Continued

Continued

Borrowings under line of credit (bank)	1,417
Proceeds from issuance of stock	11
Cash received from customers	29,164
Payments to reduce long-term debt	46
Sale of marketable securities	134
Proceeds from sale of property and equipment	6,594
Dividends paid	277
Interest paid	90
Purchase of treasury stock (stock repurchase)	1,583

Required:

Based on this information, present the Cash Flow from Investing and Financing Activities sections of the cash flow statement.

Reporting and Interpreting Cash Flows from Investing and Financing Activities with Discussion of Management Strategy

E13-15
LO4, 6
Gibraltar
Steel

Gibraltar Steel Corporation is a Buffalo, New York–based manufacturer of high-value-added cold-rolled steel products. In a recent year, it reported the following activities:

Net income	$ 5,213
Purchase of property, plant, and equipment	10,468
Payments of notes payable (bank)	8,598
Net proceeds of initial public offering	26,061
Depreciation and amortization	3,399
Long-term debt reduction	17,832
Proceeds from sale of marketable securities	131
Proceeds from sale of property, plant, and equipment	1,817
Proceeds from long-term debt	10,242
Decrease in accounts receivable	1,137
Proceeds from notes payable (bank)	3,848

Required:

1. Based on this information, present the Cash Flow from Investing and Financing Activities sections of the cash flow statement.
2. What do you think was Gibraltar management's plan for the use of the cash generated by the initial public offering of stock?

Analyzing and Interpreting the Capital Acquisitions Ratio

E13-16
LO5
Pete's
Brewing

A recent annual report for Pete's Brewing Company contained the following data for the three most recent years:

	(in thousands)		
	Year 3	Year 2	Year 1
Cash flow from operating activities	$ 821	$1,460	$619
Cash flow from investing activities	(1,404)	(1,315)	(862)
Cash flow from financing activities	42,960	775	360

Assume that all investing activities involved acquisition of new plant and equipment.

Required:

1. Compute the capital acquisitions ratio for the three-year period in total.
2. What portion of Pete's investing activities was financed from external sources or preexisting cash balances during the three-year period?

3. What do you think is the likely explanation for the dramatic increase in cash flow from financing activities during the most recent year?

E13-17
LO5, 7

Reporting Noncash Transactions on the Statement of Cash Flows; Interpreting the Effect on the Capital Acquisitions Ratio

An analysis of Martin Corporation's operational asset accounts provided the following information:

a. Acquired a large machine that cost $26,000, paying for it by giving a $15,000, 12 percent interest-bearing note due at the end of two years and 500 shares of its common stock, with a par value of $10 per share and a market value of $22 per share.

b. Acquired a small machine that cost $8,700. Full payment was made by transferring a tract of land that had a book value of $8,700.

Required:
1. Show how this information should be reported on the statement of cash flows.
2. What would be the effect of these transactions on the capital acquisitions ratio? How might these transactions distort interpretation of the ratio?

E13-18
AMC Entertainment

(Supplement A) Determining Cash Flows from the Sale of Property

AMC Entertainment is the second-largest motion picture exhibitor in the United States. The following was abstracted from the company's statement of cash flows (in thousands):

	Year 3	Year 2	Year 1
Cash flows from operating activities			
Gain on sale of property	(9,638)	(7,314)	—
Cash flows from investing activities			
Proceeds from disposition of property	14,768	11,623	1,797

Required:
Determine the cash flow from the sale of property for each year for AMC.

E13-19

(Supplement A) Determining Cash Flows from the Sale of Equipment

During the period, English Company sold some excess equipment at a loss. The following information was collected from the company's accounting records:

From the Income Statement	
Depreciation expense	$ 700
Loss on sale of equipment	3,000
From the Balance Sheet	
Beginning equipment	12,500
Ending equipment	8,000
Beginning accumulated depreciation	2,000
Ending accumulated depreciation	2,400

No new equipment was bought during the period.

Required:
For the equipment that was sold, determine its original cost, its accumulated depreciation, and the cash received from the sale.

E13-20

(Supplement B) Preparing a Statement of Cash Flows, Indirect Method: Complete Spreadsheet

An analysis of accounts follows:

a. Purchased equipment, $20,000, and issued capital stock in full payment.
b. Purchased a long-term investment for cash, $15,000.
c. Paid cash dividend, $12,000.

d. Sold operational asset for $6,000 cash (cost, $21,000, accumulated depreciation, $19,000).

e. Sold capital stock, 500 shares at $12 per share cash.

Items from Financial Statements	Beginning Balances, 12/31/2003	Analysis of Changes		Ending Balances, 12/31/2004
		Debit	Credit	
Income statement items				
Sales			$140,000	
Cost of goods sold		$59,000		
Depreciation		3,000		
Wage expense		28,000		
Income tax expense		9,000		
Interest expense		5,000		
Remaining expenses		15,800		
Net income		20,200		
Balance sheet items				
Cash	$ 20,500			$ 19,200
Accounts receivable	22,000			22,000
Merchandise inventory	68,000			75,000
Investments, long-term				15,000
Equipment	114,500			113,500
Total debits	$225,000			$244,700
Accumulated depreciation	$ 32,000			$ 20,000
Accounts payable	17,000			14,000
Wages payable	2,500			1,500
Income taxes payable	3,000			4,500
Bonds payable	54,000			54,000
Common stock, no par	100,000			126,000
Retained earnings	16,500			24,700
Total credits	$225,000			$244,700
		Inflows	Outflows	
Statement of cash flows				
Cash flows from operating activities:				
Cash flows from investing activities:				
Cash flows from financing activities:				
Net increase (decrease) in cash				
Totals				

Required:

Complete the spreadsheet for the statement of cash flows, indirect method.

PROBLEMS

Using Schedule Approach to Prepare the Statement of Cash Flows (Indirect Method) (AP13-1)

P13-1
LO1, 2A, 4, 6, 7

The income statement of Frank Corporation follows on the next page.

Analysis of Selected 2004 Account Balances and Transactions:

a. Purchased investment securities for $5,000 cash.

b. Borrowed $15,000 on a two-year, 8 percent interest-bearing note.

c. During 2004, sold machinery for its net book value; received $11,000 in cash.

d. Purchased machinery for $50,000; paid $9,000 in cash and signed a four-year note payable to the dealer for $41,000.

e. At December 31, 2004, declared and paid a cash dividend of $10,000.

f. Cash balance on December 31, 2003 was $21,000.

FRANK CORPORATION
Income Statement
For the Year Ended December 31, 2004
Accrual Basis

Sales revenue (one-fourth on credit; accounts receivable at year's end 2003, $12,000; 2004, $17,000)		$400,000
Cost of goods sold (one-third on credit; accounts payable at year's end 2003, $10,000; 2004, $7,000; inventory at year's end—2003, $60,000; 2004, $52,000)		268,000
Expenses		
Salaries and wages (including accrued wages payable at year's end—2003, $1,000; 2004, $800)	$51,000	
Depreciation expense	9,200	
Rent expense (no accruals)	5,800	
Interest expense (no accruals)	12,200	
Income tax expense (income taxes payable at year's end— 2003, $3,000; 2004, $5,000)	11,800	
Total expenses		90,000
Net income		$42,000

Required:

Prepare a statement of cash flows, indirect method, using the schedule approach. Include any additional required note disclosures.

P13-2
L01, 2A, 4, 6
Rocky
Mountain
Chocolate
Factory

Using Schedule Approach to Prepare the Statement of Cash Flows (Indirect Method)

Rocky Mountain Chocolate Factory manufactures an extensive line of premium chocolate candies for sale at its franchised and company-owned stores in malls throughout the United States. Its balance sheet for the first quarter of 1996 is presented along with an analysis of selected accounts and transactions:

ROCKY MOUNTAIN CHOCOLATE FACTORY, INC.
Balance Sheets

Assets	May 31, 1996 (Unaudited)	February 29, 1996
CURRENT ASSETS		
Cash and cash equivalents	$ 921,505	$ 528,787
Accounts and notes receivable—trade, less allowance for doubtful accounts of $43,196 at May 31 and $28,196 at February 29	1,602,582	1,463,901
Inventories	2,748,788	2,504,908
Deferred tax asset	59,219	59,219
Other	581,508	224,001
Total current assets	5,913,602	4,780,816
PROPERTY AND EQUIPMENT—AT COST	14,010,796	12,929,675
Less accumulated depreciation and amortization	−2,744,388	−2,468,084
	11,266,408	10,461,591

Assets	May 31, 1996 (Unaudited)	February 29, 1996
OTHER ASSETS		
Notes and accounts receivable due after one year	100,206	111,588
Goodwill, net of accumulated amortization of $259,641 at May 31 and $253,740 at Feb. 29	330,359	336,260
Other	574,130	624,185
	1,004,695	1,072,033
	$18,184,705	$16,314,440
Liabilities and Equity		
CURRENT LIABILITIES		
Short-term debt	$ 0	$ 1,000,000
Current maturities of long-term debt	429,562	134,538
Accounts payable—trade	1,279,455	998,520
Accrued liabilities	714,473	550,386
Income taxes payable	11,198	54,229
Total current liabilities	2,434,688	2,737,673
LONG-TERM DEBT, less current maturities	4,193,290	2,183,877
DEFERRED INCOME TAXES	275,508	275,508
Stockholders' Equity		
Common stock—authorized 7,250,000 shares, $.03 par value; issued 3,034,302 shares at May 31 and at Feb. 29	91,029	91,029
Additional paid-in capital	9,703,985	9,703,985
Retained earnings	2,502,104	2,338,267
	12,297,118	12,133,281
Less common stock held in treasury, at cost— 129,153 shares at May 31 and at February 29	1,015,899	1,015,899
	11,281,219	11,117,382
	$18,184,705	$16,314,440

The accompanying notes are an integral part of these statements.

Analysis of Selected Accounts and Transactions

a. Net income was $163,837. Notes and accounts receivable due after one year relate to operations.

b. Depreciation and amortization totaled $282,205.

c. No "other" noncurrent assets (which relate to investing activities) were purchased this period.

d. No property, plant, and equipment were sold during the period. No goodwill was acquired or sold.

e. Proceeds from issuance of long-term debt were $4,659,466 and principal payments were $2,355,029. (Combine the current maturities with the long-term debt in your analysis.)

f. No dividends were declared or paid.

g. Ignore the "deferred tax asset" and "deferred income taxes" liability accounts.

Required:

Prepare a statement of cash flows, indirect method, using the schedule approach.

Using Schedule Approach to Prepare the Statement of Cash Flows (Direct Method)

P13-3

LO1, 2B, 4, 6, 7

Use the information concerning Frank Corporation provided in Problem 13-1 to fulfill the following requirement.

Required:

Prepare a statement of cash flows, direct method, using the schedule approach. Include any additional required note disclosures. (Do not prepare the reconciliation of net income to cash flow from operations.)

P13-4
LO2A, 2B

Comparing Cash Flows from Operating Activities (Direct and Indirect Methods)

Beta Company's accountants just completed the income statement and balance sheet for the year and have provided the following information (in thousands):

Income Statement		
Sales revenue		$20,600
Expenses		
Cost of goods sold	$9,000	
Depreciation expense	2,000	
Salaries expense	5,000	
Rent expense	2,500	
Insurance expense	800	
Utilities expense	700	
Interest expense on bonds	600	
Loss on sale of investments	400	21,000
Net loss		$ (400)

Selected Balance Sheet Accounts		
	2003	2004
Merchandise inventory	$ 60	$ 82
Accounts receivable	450	380
Accounts payable	210	240
Salaries payable	20	29
Rent payable	6	2
Prepaid rent	7	2
Prepaid insurance	5	14

Other Data:

The company issued $20,000, 8 percent bonds payable during the year.

Required:

1. Prepare the Cash Flows from Operating Activities section of the statement of cash flows using the direct method.
2. Prepare the Cash Flows from Operating Activities section of the statement of cash flows using the indirect method.

P13-5

(Supplement B) Preparing Statement of Cash Flows Spreadsheet, Statement of Cash Flows, and Schedules Using Indirect Method (AP13-2)

Hunter Company is developing its annual financial statements at December 31, 2004. The statements are complete except for the statement of cash flows. The completed comparative balance sheets and income statement are summarized:

	2003	2004
Balance sheet at December 31		
Cash	$ 18,000	$ 44,000
Accounts receivable	29,000	27,000
Merchandise inventory	36,000	30,000

Continued

Continued

Fixed assets (net)	72,000	75,000
	$155,000	$176,000
Accounts payable	$ 22,000	$ 25,000
Wages payable	1,000	800
Note payable, long-term	48,000	38,000
Common stock, no par	60,000	80,000
Retained earnings	24,000	32,200
	$155,000	$176,000

Income statement for 2004	
Sales	$100,000
Cost of goods sold	(61,000)
Expenses	(27,000)
Net income	$ 12,000

Additional Data:

a. Bought fixed assets for cash, $9,000.
b. Paid $10,000 on the long-term note payable.
c. Sold unissued common stock for $20,000 cash.
d. Declared and paid a $3,800 cash dividend.
e. Incurred expenses that included depreciation, $6,000; wages, $10,000; taxes, $3,000; other, $8,000.

Required:

1. Prepare a statement of cash flows spreadsheet using the indirect method to report cash flows from operating activities.
2. Prepare the statement of cash flows.
3. Prepare a schedule of noncash investing and financing activities if necessary.

ALTERNATE **PROBLEMS**

Using Schedule Approach to Prepare the Statement of Cash Flows (Indirect Method) (P13-1)

AP13-1
LO1, 2A, 4, 6, 7

Stonewall Company was organized on January 1, 2003. During the year ended December 31, 2003, the company provided the following data:

Income Statement	
Sales revenue	$ 80,000
Cost of goods sold	(35,000)
Depreciation expense	(4,000)
Remaining expenses	(32,000)
Net income	$ 9,000

Balance Sheet	
Cash	$48,000
Accounts receivable	18,000
Merchandise inventory	15,000
Machinery (net)	25,000
Total assets	$106,000

Continued

Continued

Accounts payable	$ 10,000
Accrued expenses payable	21,000
Dividends payable	2,000
Note payable, short-term	15,000
Common stock	54,000
Retained earnings	4,000
Total liabilities and stockholders' equity	$106,000

Analysis of Selected Accounts and Transactions:

a. Sold 3,000 shares of common stock, par $10, at $18 per share; collected cash.

b. Borrowed $15,000 on a one-year, 8 percent interest-bearing note; the note was dated June 1, 2003.

c. During 2003, purchased machinery; paid $29,000.

d. Purchased merchandise for resale at a cost of $50,000 (debited Inventory because the perpetual system is used); paid $40,000 cash, balance credited to Accounts Payable.

e. Exchanged plant machinery with a book value of $2,000 for office machines with a market value of $2,000.

f. At December 31, 2003, declared a cash dividend of $5,000; paid $3,000 in December 2003; the balance will be paid March 1, 2004.

g. Because this is the first year of operations, all account balances are zero at the beginning of the year; therefore, the changes in the account balances are equal to the ending balances.

Required:
Prepare a statement of cash flows, indirect method, using the schedule approach.

AP13-2
LO1, 2A, 4, 6, 7

(Supplement B) Preparing Statement of Cash Flows Spreadsheet and Statement of Cash Flows Using Indirect Method: Includes Noncash Investing and Financing Activity and Sale of an Asset at Book Value (P13-5)

Ellington Company is developing its 2004 annual report. The following information is provided:

	2003	2004
Cash	$21,000	$22,400
Accounts receivable	18,000	21,000
Inventory	35,000	32,000
Prepaid insurance	2,400	1,400
Investments, long-term	12,500	9,300
Fixed assets (net)	31,100	59,600
Patent	2,000	1,500
Accounts payable	27,000	15,000
Wages payable	4,000	1,000
Income taxes payable	2,000	2,200
Note payable, long-term	20,000	10,000
Common stock ($10 par)	50,000	80,000
Contributed capital in excess of par	3,000	6,000
Retained earnings	16,000	33,000

Other Information:

a. Sold long-term investment at book value, $3,200. Purchased fixed assets by issuing 3,000 shares of common stock; market value of common stock, $11 per share.

b. Revenues, $150,000.

c. Expenses: depreciation, $4,500; patent amortization, $500; insurance, $2,000; wages, $48,500; income taxes, $7,000; and cost of goods sold, $62,000.

Required:

1. Prepare a statement of cash flows spreadsheet using the indirect method to report cash flows from operating activities.
2. Prepare the statement of cash flows.
3. Prepare a schedule of noncash investing and financing activities.

CASES AND **PROJECTS**

Annual Report Cases

Finding Financial Information

Refer to the financial statements of American Eagle Outfitters given in Appendix B at the end of this book, or open file AEOS.pdf in the Annual Report Cases directory on the student CD-ROM.

Required:
1. Which of the two basic reporting approaches for the cash flows from operating activities did the company adopt?
2. What amount of tax payments did the company make during the current year?
3. Explain why the terms "stock compensation" and "loss on impairment and write-off of fixed assets" were added in the reconciliation of net income to net cash provided by operating activities.
4. What was free cash flow for the year ended February 3, 2001?
5. Has the company paid cash dividends during the last three years? How did you know?

CP13-1
LO2A, 4, 6

AMERICAN EAGLE OUTFITTERS

Finding Financial Information

Refer to the financial statements of Abercrombie & Fitch given in Appendix C at the end of this book, or open file ANF.pdf in the Annual Report Cases directory on the student CD-ROM.

Required:
1. What were the three largest "Adjustments to reconcile net income to net cash provided by operating activities"? Explain the direction of the effect of each in the reconciliation.
2. What have been Abercrombie & Fitch's major uses of cash over the past three years? What have been its major sources of cash for these activities? What are the company's plans for financing future expenditures? How did you know?
3. What was free cash flow for the year ended February 3, 2001? What does this imply about the company's financial flexibility?

CP13-2
LO2A, 4, 6

ABERCROMBIE & FITCH

Comparing Companies within an Industry

Refer to the financial statements of American Eagle Outfitters given in Appendix B, Abercrombie & Fitch given in Appendix C, and the Industry Ratio Report given in Appendix D at the end of this book, or open file CP13-3.xls in the Annual Report Cases directory on the student CD-ROM.

Required:
1. Compute the quality of income ratio for both companies for the current year. Why might they be different?
2. Compare the quality of income ratio for both companies to the industry average. Are these companies producing more or less cash from operating activities relative to net income than the average company in the industry? Does comparing the sales growth rate for these two companies to the industry average help explain why their quality of income ratio is above or below the industry average? Explain. Note that Sales Growth Rate = (Current Net Sales − Prior Net Sales)/Prior Net Sales.
3. Compute the capital acquisitions ratio for both companies for the current year. Compare their abilities to finance purchases of property, plant, and equipment with cash provided by operating activities.
4. Compare the capital acquisitions ratio for both companies to the industry average. How do these two companies' abilities to finance the purchase of property, plant, and equipment with cash provided by operating activities compare to those of the industry?

CP13-3
LO3, 5

AMERICAN EAGLE OUTFITTERS

ABERCROMBIE & FITCH

Financial Reporting and Analysis Cases

Using Financial Reports: Analyzing a U.K. Cash Flow Statement

Scottish & Newcastle serves up Courage by the pint. The U.K.'s largest brewer, it makes a number of popular beers, including Courage, John Smith's, Newcastle, and McEwan's. It also makes licensed brands such as Foster's, Kronenbourg, and Miller. As do all U.K. companies, the Edinburgh-based company follows U.K. generally accepted accounting principles. Its cash flow statement prepared according to those principles follows, along with one of the related notes.

CP13-4
LO1, 2A
Scottish & Newcastle

Required:

1. Which of the two basic reporting approaches for the statement of cash flows did the company adopt?

2. Compare Scottish & Newcastle's statement with that of Boston Beer presented in Exhibit 13.1. What differences do you see in the U.S. and U.K. versions of the statement?

SCOTTISH & NEWCASTLE PLC
Group Cash Flow Statement
Year ended 2 May 1999

	Notes	1999 (52 weeks)		1998 (53 weeks)	
		£m	£m	£m	£m
Net cash inflow from operating activities	32		542.7		565.0
Dividends from joint ventures			7.7		2.5
Returns on investments and servicing of finance					
Interest received		3.0		3.1	
Interest paid		(71.0)		(59.0)	
Preference dividends paid		(0.7)		(1.1)	
Net cash outflow for returns on investments and servicing of finance			(68.7)		(57.0)
Taxation			(88.2)		(82.5)
Capital expenditure and financial investment					
Purchase of tangible fixed assets		(374.0)		(314.2)	
Purchase of investments		(45.0)		(67.0)	
Sale of tangible fixed assets		108.5		43.0	
Realisation of investments		55.4		67.4	
Net cash outflow for capital expenditure and financial investment			(255.1)		(270.8)
Acquisition and disposals					
Purchase of businesses		—		(225.0)	
New Overdraft acquired with businesses		—		(1.0)	
Disposal of investment in joint venture		—		2.2	
Net cash outflow for acquisitions and disposals			—		(223.8)
Equity dividends paid			(148.8)		(135.8)
Net cash outflow before use of liquid resources and financing			(10.4)		(202.4)
Management of liquid resources					
Movement in short-term deposits with banks			14.4		(2.9)
Financing					
Issues of ordinary share capital		7.2		8.0	
Proceeds of loan capital		314.2		388.5	
Repayment of loan capital		(284.7)		(123.0)	
Net cash inflow from financing			36.7		273.5
Increase in cash in the period	33		40.7		68.2

Liquid resources comprise term deposits of less than one year.

Continued

NOTE 32: NET CASH INFLOW FROM OPERATING ACTIVITIES	1999 £m	1998 £m
Group operating profit	399.4	470.5
Exceptional charges against operating profit	63.5	—
Depreciation-normal	133.0	123.8
Provisions against investments	3.1	2.3
Decrease in stocks	14.0	4.6
Decrease in debtors	7.9	2.6
Decrease in creditors	(23.6)	(10.5)
Net cash inflow from ordinary operating activities	597.3	593.3
Reorganisation costs	(15.7)	(14.3)
Utilisation of acquisition and pensions provisions	(38.9)	(14.0)
Net cash inflow from operating activities	542.7	565.0

Critical Thinking Cases

Making a Decision as a Financial Analyst: Analyzing Cash Flow for a New Company

CP13-5
LO2A
Carlyle Golf, Inc.

Carlyle Golf, Inc., was formed in September of last year. The company designs, contracts for the manufacture of, and markets a line of men's golf apparel. A portion of the statement of cash flows for Carlyle follows:

	Current Year
Cash flows from operating activities	
Net income	$(460,089)
Depreciation	3,554
Noncash compensation (stock)	254,464
Deposits with suppliers	(404,934)
Increase in prepaid assets	(42,260)
Increase in accounts payable	81,765
Increase in accrued liabilities	24,495
Net cash flows	$(543,005)

Management expects a solid increase in sales in the near future. To support the increase in sales, it plans to add $2.2 million to inventory. The company did not disclose a sales forecast. At the end of the current year, Carlyle had less than $1,000 in cash. It is not unusual for a new company to experience a loss and negative cash flows during its start-up phase.

Required:
As a financial analyst recently hired by a major investment bank, you have been asked to write a short memo to your supervisor evaluating the problems facing Carlyle. Emphasize typical sources of financing that may or may not be available to support the expansion.

Financial Reporting and Analysis Team Project

Team Project: Analyzing Cash Flows

CP13-6
LO1, 2, 3, 4, 5, 6

As a team, select an industry to analyze (industry lists can be found at www.marketguide.com/mgi/ INDUSTRY/INDUSTRY.html and www.hoovers.com; click on companies and industries). Each team member should acquire the annual report or 10-K for one publicly traded company in the industry, with each member selecting a different company. (Library files, the SEC EDGAR service at www.sec.gov, Compustat CD, or the company itself are good sources.) On an individual basis, each team member should then write a short report answering the following questions about their selected company.

1. Which of the two basic reporting approaches for cash flows from operating activities did the company adopt?
2. What is the quality of earnings ratio for the most current year? What were the major causes of differences between net income and cash flow from operations?
3. What is the capital acquisitions ratio for the three-year period presented in total? How is the company financing its capital acquisitions?
4. What portion of the cash from operations in the current year is being paid to stockholders in the form of dividends?

Discuss any patterns across the three companies that your team observes. Then, as a team, write a short report comparing and contrasting your companies using these attributes. Provide potential explanations for any differences discovered.

LEARNING OBJECTIVES

Analyzing Financial Statements

14

The history of Home Depot is an unusual success story. Founded in 1978 in Atlanta, Home Depot has grown to be America's largest home improvement retailer, and according to *Fortune* magazine, one of the nation's 30 largest retailers. Financial statements for Home Depot are presented in Exhibit 14.1. As you can see, Home Depot's rapid growth has continued in recent years. Sales revenue for the year ended January 28, 2001, was 51 percent higher than in 1999, and the company's net earnings increased almost 60 percent.

With this rapid growth, would you want to invest in Home Depot? A number of professional analysts think you should, including those who work for Bear Stearns, a large investment firm. In a report in which they recommended investors buy stock in Home Depot, they wrote: "We continue to believe that the company's stock should be a core retail holding for investors, given the company's industry-leading position in a growing market, superb management, and focus on improving sales and gross margins."

Professional analysts consider a large number of factors in developing the type of recommendation contained in the Bear Stearns report, including information reported in a company's financial statements. In this chapter, we use accounting information and a variety of analytical tools to study Home Depot and its major competitor, Lowe's.

EXHIBIT 14.1

Home Depot Financial Statements

CONSOLIDATED BALANCE SHEETS
The Home Depot, Inc. and Subsidiaries

amounts in millions, except share data	January 28, 2001	January 30, 2000
Assets		
Current Assets:		
Cash and Cash Equivalents	$ 167	$ 168
Short-Term Investments, including current maturities of long-term investments	10	2
Receivables, net	835	587
Merchandise Inventories	6,556	5,489
Other Current Assets	209	144
Total Current Assets	7,777	6,390
Property and Equipment, at cost:		
Land	4,230	3,248
Buildings	6,167	4,834
Furniture, Fixtures and Equipment	2,877	2,279
Leasehold Improvements	665	493
Construction in Progress	1,032	791
Capital Leases	261	245
	15,232	11,890
Less Accumulated Depreciation and Amortization	2,164	1,663
Net Property and Equipment	13,068	10,227
Long-Term Investments	15	15
Notes Receivable	77	48
Cost in Excess of the Fair Value of Net Assets Acquired, net of accumulated amortization of $41 at January 28, 2001 and $33 at January 30, 2000	314	311
Other	134	90
	$21,385	$17,081
Liabilities and Stockholders' Equity		
Current Liabilities:		
Accounts Payable	$ 1,976	$ 1,993
Accrued Salaries and Related Expenses	627	541
Sales Taxes Payable	298	269
Other Accrued Expenses	1,402	763
Income Taxes Payable	78	61
Current Installments of Long-Term Debt	4	29
Total Current Liabilities	4,385	3,656
Long-Term Debt, excluding current installments	1,545	750
Other Long-Term Liabilities	245	237
Deferred Income Taxes	195	87
Minority Interest	11	10

EXHIBIT 14.1

continued

Stockholders' Equity

Common Stock, par value $0.05. Authorized: 10,000,000,000 shares; issued and outstanding— 2,323,747,000 shares at January 28, 2001 and 2,304,317,000 shares at January 30, 2000	116	115
Paid-In Capital	4,810	4,319
Retained Earnings	10,151	7,941
Accumulated Other Comprehensive Income	(67)	(27)
	15,010	12,348
Less Shares Purchased for Compensation Plans	6	7
Total Stockholders' Equity	15,004	12,341
	$21,385	$17,081

CONSOLIDATED STATEMENTS OF EARNINGS

amounts in millions, except per share data

	Fiscal Year Ended		
	January 28, 2001	January 30, 2000	January 31, 1999
Net Sales	**$45,738**	**$38,434**	**$30,219**
Cost of Merchandise Sold	32,057	27,023	21,614
Gross Profit	13,681	11,411	8,605
Operating Expenses:			
Selling and Store Operating	8,513	6,819	5,332
Pre-Opening	142	113	88
General and Administrative	835	671	515
Total Operating Expenses	9,490	7,603	5,935
Operating Income	4,191	3,808	2,670
Interest Income (Expense):			
Interest and Investment Income	47	37	30
Interest Expense	(21)	(41)	(46)
Interest, net	26	(4)	(16)
Earnings Before Income Taxes	4,217	3,804	2,654
Income Taxes	1,636	1,484	1,040
Net Earnings	$ 2,581	$ 2,320	$ 1,614
Basic Earnings Per Share	$ 1.11	$ 1.03	$ 0.73
Weighted Average Number of Common Shares Outstanding	2,315	2,244	2,206
Diluted Earnings Per Share	$ 1.10	$ 1.00	$ 0.71
Weighted Average Number of Common Shares Outstanding Assuming Dilution	2,352	2,342	2,320

EXHIBIT 14.1

continued

CONSOLIDATED STATEMENTS OF CASH FLOWS
The Home Depot, Inc. and Subsidiaries

amounts in millions,	Fiscal Year Ended		
	January 28, 2001	January 30, 2000	January 31, 1999
Cash Provided From Operations:			
Net Earnings	$ 2,581	$ 2,320	$ 1,614
Reconciliation of Net Earnings to Net Cash			
Provided by Operations:			
Depreciation and Amortization	601	463	373
(Increase) Decrease in Receivables, net	(246)	(85)	85
Increase in Merchandise Inventories	(1,075)	(1,142)	(698)
Increase in Accounts Payable			
and Accrued Expenses	754	820	423
Increase in Income Taxes Payable	151	93	59
Other	30	(23)	61
Net Cash Provided by Operations	2,796	2,446	1,917
Cash Flows From Investing Activities:			
Capital Expenditures, net of $16, $37 and $41			
of non-cash capital expenditures in fiscal			
2000, 1999 and 1998, respectively	(3,558)	(2,581)	(2,053)
Purchase of Remaining Interest in			
The Home Depot Canada	—	—	(261)
Payments for Businesses Acquired, net	(26)	(101)	(6)
Proceeds from Sales of Property and Equipment	95	87	45
Purchases of Investments	(39)	(32)	(2)
Proceeds from Maturities of Investments	30	30	4
Advances Secured by Real Estate, net	(32)	(25)	2
Net Cash Used in Investing Activities	(3,530)	(2,622)	(2,271)
Cash Flows From Financing Activities:			
Issuance (Repayments) of Commercial			
Paper Obligations, net	754	(246)	246
Proceeds from Long-Term Borrowings	32	522	—
Repayments of Long-Term Debt	(29)	(14)	(8)
Proceeds from Sale of Common Stock, net	351	267	167
Cash Dividends Paid to Stockholders	(371)	(255)	(168)
Minority Interest Contributions to Partnership	—	7	11
Net Cash Provided by Financing Activities	737	281	248
Effect of Exchange Rate Changes on Cash			
and Cash Equivalents	(4)	1	(4)
(Decrease) Increase in Cash and Cash Equivalents	(1)	106	(110)
Cash and Cash Equivalents at Beginning of Year	168	62	172
Cash and Cash Equivalents at End of Year	$ 167	$ 168	$ 62
Supplemental Disclosure of Cash			
Payments Made For:			
Interest, net of interest capitalized	$ 16	$ 26	$ 36
Income Taxes	$ 1,386	$ 1,396	$ 940

UNDERSTANDING THE BUSINESS

In the United States, companies spend billions of dollars each year preparing, auditing, and publishing their financial statements. These statements are then mailed to current and prospective investors. Most companies also make financial information available to investors on the Internet. Home Depot has a particularly interesting home page (http://www.homedepot.com) that contains current financial statements, recent news articles about the company, and a variety of relevant information.

The reason that Home Depot and other companies spend so much money to provide information to investors is simple: Financial statements help people to make better economic decisions. In fact, published financial statements are designed primarily to meet the needs of external decision makers, including present and potential owners, investment analysts, and creditors.

ORGANIZATION of the Chapter

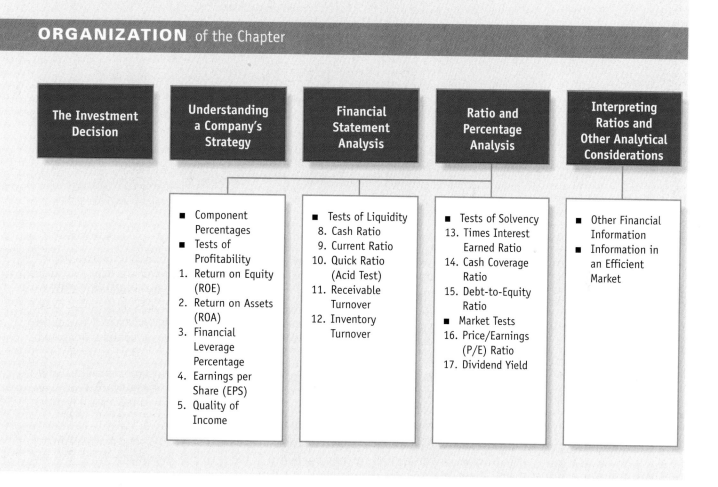

The Investment Decision	Understanding a Company's Strategy	Financial Statement Analysis	Ratio and Percentage Analysis	Interpreting Ratios and Other Analytical Considerations
	■ Component Percentages ■ Tests of Profitability 1. Return on Equity (ROE) 2. Return on Assets (ROA) 3. Financial Leverage Percentage 4. Earnings per Share (EPS) 5. Quality of Income	■ Tests of Liquidity 8. Cash Ratio 9. Current Ratio 10. Quick Ratio (Acid Test) 11. Receivable Turnover 12. Inventory Turnover	■ Tests of Solvency 13. Times Interest Earned Ratio 14. Cash Coverage Ratio 15. Debt-to-Equity Ratio ■ Market Tests 16. Price/Earnings (P/E) Ratio 17. Dividend Yield	■ Other Financial Information ■ Information in an Efficient Market

THE INVESTMENT DECISION

Of the people who use financial statements, investors are perhaps the single largest group. They often rely on the advice of professional analysts, who develop recommendations on widely held stocks such as Home Depot. Most individual investors use analysts' reports and track their recommendations. As this book was being written, professional analysts issued the following investment recommendations for Home Depot:

Analyst Ratings: Home Depot	Today	1 Month Ago	2 Months Ago	3 Months Ago
1—Strong Buy	**13**	12	10	9
2—Buy	**9**	9	7	9
3—Hold	**3**	4	5	5
4—Sell	**0**	0	0	0
5—Strong Sell	**0**	0	0	0
Average Rating	**1.56**	1.64	1.73	1.78

Source: Quicken.com/investments/

In considering an investment in stock, investors should evaluate the company's future income and growth potential on the basis of the following factors:

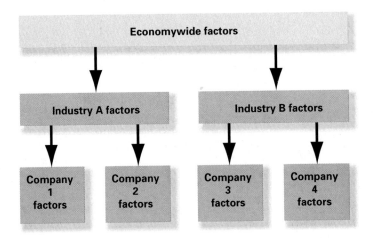

1. *Economywide factors.* Often the overall health of the economy has a direct impact on the performance of an individual business. Investors should consider data such as the unemployment rate, general inflation rate, and changes in interest rates. For example, in a research report issued by Lehman Brothers, a large investment bank, an analyst predicted increased sales revenue at Home Depot because of "the positive implications of the Fed's 275 basis points in interest rate reductions, along with tax rebates."

2. *Industry factors.* Certain events have a major impact on each company within an industry, but only a minor impact on other companies outside the industry. For example, The Lehman Brothers' report predicted increased sales at Home Depot because of "easing lumber prices and declining mortgage rates."

3. *Individual company factors.* To properly analyze a company, good analysts do not rely only on the information contained in the financial statements. They visit the company, buy its products, and read about it in the business press. If you evaluate McDonald's, it is equally important to assess the quality of its balance sheet and the quality of its Big Mac. An example of company-specific information is contained in the Lehman Brothers' report: "New Products Increase Profitability. Home Depot continues to add new product assortments to its stores. Its latest product addition is major appliances. Although well behind Sears, this year will be the first major step to potentially overtaking the No. 1 position."

Besides considering these factors, investors should understand a company's business strategy when evaluating its financial statements. Before discussing analytical techniques, we will show you how business strategy affects financial statement analysis.

UNDERSTANDING A COMPANY'S STRATEGY

Financial statement analysis involves more than just "crunching numbers." Before you start looking at numbers, you should know what you are looking for. While financial statements report on transactions, each of those transactions is the result of a company's operating decisions as it implements its business strategy.

Learning Objective 1
Explain how a company's business strategy affects financial analysis.

The DuPont model (introduced in Chapter 5) helps us understand that a number of business strategies affect the profitability of a business. The model follows:

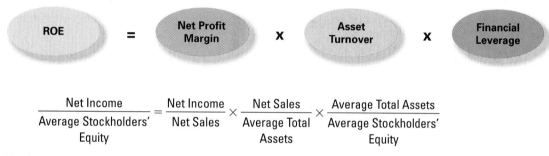

$$\frac{\text{Net Income}}{\text{Average Stockholders' Equity}} = \frac{\text{Net Income}}{\text{Net Sales}} \times \frac{\text{Net Sales}}{\text{Average Total Assets}} \times \frac{\text{Average Total Assets}}{\text{Average Stockholders' Equity}}$$

Businesses can earn a high rate of return by following different strategies. These are two fundamental strategies:

1. *Product differentiation.* Under this strategy, companies offer products with unique benefits, such as high quality or unusual style or features. These unique benefits allow a company to charge higher prices. In general, higher prices yield higher profit margins, which lead to higher returns on equity (as shown in the ROE model).

2. *Cost advantage.* Under this strategy, companies attempt to operate more efficiently than their competitors, which permits them to offer lower prices to attract customers. The efficient use of resources is captured in the asset turnover ratio, and as the ROE model illustrates, higher asset turnover ratio leads to higher return on investment.

You can probably think of a number of companies that have followed one of these two basic strategies. Here are some examples:

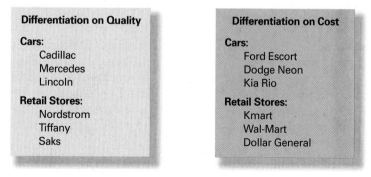

The best place to start financial analysis is with a solid understanding of a company's business strategy. To evaluate how well a company is doing, you must know what managers are trying to do. You can learn a great deal about a company's business strategy by reading its annual report, especially the letter from the president. It also is useful to read articles about the company in the business press.

Home Depot's business strategy is described in its 10-K report as follows:

REAL WORLD EXCERPT

10-K REPORT

OPERATING STRATEGY. The operating strategy for Home Depot stores is to offer a broad assortment of high-quality merchandise and services at competitive prices using highly knowledgeable, service-oriented personnel and aggressive advertising. We believe that our associates' knowledge of products and home improvement techniques and applications is very important in our marketing approach and our ability to maintain customer satisfaction. We regularly check our competitors' prices to ensure that our prices are competitive within each market.

Source: The Home Depot

This strategy has several implications for our analysis of Home Depot:

1. Cost control is critical. Home Depot must be able to purchase merchandise at low prices in order to beat competitors.

2. To cover the cost of operating large stores, Home Depot must be able to generate a high volume of business.

3. To offer a high level of service, Home Depot must incur employee compensation and training costs that are higher than competitors' costs. This puts pressure on Home Depot to control costs in other areas.

With these implications in mind, we can attach more meaning to the information contained in Home Depot's financial statements.

FINANCIAL STATEMENT ANALYSIS

Learning Objective 2
Discuss how analysts use financial statements.

Analyzing financial data without a basis for comparison is impossible. For example, would you be impressed with a company that earned $1 million last year? You are probably thinking, "It depends." A $1 million profit might be very good for a company that lost money the year before but not good for a company that made $500 million the preceding year. It might be good for a small company but not for a very large company. And it might be considered good if all the other companies in the industry lost money the same year but not good if they all earned much larger profits.

As you can see from this simple example, financial results cannot be evaluated in isolation. To properly analyze the information reported in financial statements, you must develop appropriate comparisons. The task of finding appropriate benchmarks requires judgment and is not always easy. Financial analysis is a sophisticated skill, not a mechanical process.

There are two methods for making financial comparisons, times series analysis and comparisons with similar companies.

1. Time series analysis. Information on a single company is compared over time. For example, a key measure of performance for a retail company is the change in sales volume each year for its existing stores. The following time series chart shows that in 2000, the percentage increase in sales volume for existing Home Depot stores was well below historical levels. Home Depot's managers plan to deal with this problem through a number of new advertising and promotional programs.

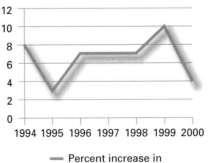

— Percent increase in
same store sales

2. **Comparison with similar companies.** We have seen that financial results are often affected by industry and economywide factors. By comparing a company with another one in the same line of business, an analyst can gain better insight into its performance. The comparison of various measures for Home Depot and Lowe's (in the following graph) indicates Home Depot's operating strength.

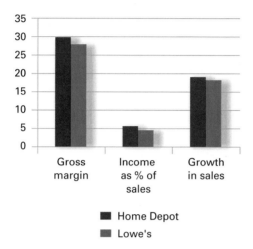

Finding comparable companies is often very difficult. American Brands, for example, is a well-known company that sells tobacco, distilled spirits, life insurance, home improvement products, office products, and golf equipment. No other company sells exactly that group of products. Care must be exercised in selecting comparable companies from the same basic industry. Days Inn, La Quinta, Hilton, Four Seasons, Marriott, and Mirage Resorts are all well-known companies in the hotel industry, but not all could be considered comparable companies for purposes of financial analysis. These hotels offer different levels of quality and appeal to different types of customers.

The federal government has developed the North American Industry Classification System for use in reporting economic data. The system assigns a specific industry code to each corporation based on its business operations. Analysts often use these six-digit codes to identify companies that have similar business operations. In addition, financial information services such as Robert Morris Associates provide averages for many common accounting ratios for various industries defined by the industrial classification codes. Because of the diversity of companies included in each industry classification, however, these data should be used with great care. For this reason, some analysts prefer to compare two companies that are very similar instead of using industrywide comparisons.

Topic Tackler 14–1

RATIO AND PERCENTAGE ANALYSIS

All financial analysts use **ratio analysis** or **percentage analysis** when they review companies. A ratio or percentage expresses the proportionate relationship between two different amounts, allowing for easy comparisons. Assessing a company's profitability is difficult if you know only that it earned a net income of $500,000. Comparing income to other numbers, such as stockholders' equity, provides additional insights. If stockholders' equity is $5 million, for example, then the relationship of earnings to investment is $500,000 ÷ $5,000,000 = 10 percent. This measure indicates a different level of performance than would be the case if stockholders' equity were $250 million. Ratio analysis helps decision makers to identify significant relationships and make meaningful comparisons between companies.

Ratios may be computed using amounts in one statement, such as the income statement, or in two different statements, such as the income statement and the balance sheet. In addition, amounts on a single statement may be expressed as a percentage of a base amount.

RATIO (PERCENTAGE) ANALYSIS is an analytical tool that measures the proportional relationship between two financial statement amounts

Learning Objective 3
Compute and interpret component percentages.

Component Percentages

COMPONENT PERCENTAGES express each item on a particular financial statement as a percentage of a single base amount.

Analysts often compute **component percentages,** which express each item on a financial statement as a percentage of a single base amount (the ratio's denominator). To compute component percentages for the income statement, the base amount is net sales revenue. Each expense is expressed as a percentage of net sales revenue. On the balance sheet, the base amount is total assets; each balance sheet account is divided by total assets.

Exhibit 14.2 shows a component percentage analysis for Home Depot's income statement (shown in Exhibit 14.1). If you simply reviewed the dollar amounts on the income statement, you might be concerned about several significant differences. For example, cost of merchandise sold increased more than $5 million between 2000 and 2001. But the component percentage provides an important insight: cost of merchandise sold actually decreased as a percentage of sales during that period. In other words, cost of merchandise sold increased primarily because of the increase in the company's sales revenue.

The component analysis (in Exhibit 14.2) helps to highlight several additional issues for Home Depot, such as these:

1. Income increased by $967 million between 1999 and 2001. A portion of the increase in income can be attributed to an increase in sales revenue, but a portion is attributable to improvement in the margin between cost and selling price for merchandise sold (gross profit increased from 28.5 percent to 29.9 percent). Unfortunately, this improvement was offset by an increase in selling and store operating expense as a percentage of sales (17.6 percent to 18.6 percent).

2. Some of the percentage changes may seem immaterial, but they involve significant amounts of money. The increase in the ratio of selling and store operating expense as a percentage of sales from 1999 to 2001 reduced earnings before taxes by $457 million.

3. Cost of merchandise sold as a percentage of sales declined consistently between 1999 and 2001. As we mentioned earlier, a key part of Home Depot's strategy is selling merchandise at low prices. The annual report indicates that the improvement in the ratio of cost of goods sold to sales revenue is a positive indication of the successful implementation of the company's strategy.

EXHIBIT 14.2	COMPONENT PERCENTAGES		
	Income Statement	**2001**	**2000**	**1999**
Component Percentages for Home Depot	Net sales	100.0%	100.0%	100.0%
	Cost of merchandise sold	70.1	70.3	71.5
	Gross profit	29.9	29.7	28.5
	Operating expenses			
	Selling and store operating	18.6	17.7	17.6
	Pre-opening	0.3	0.3	0.3
	General and administrative	1.8	1.7	1.7
	Total operating expenses	20.7	19.8	19.6
	Operating income	9.2	9.9	8.8
	Interest income	0.1	0.1	0.1
	Interest expense	0.0	(0.1)	(0.1)
	Interest, net	0.1	0.0	0.0
	Earnings, before taxes	9.2	9.9	8.8
	Income taxes	3.6	3.9	3.4
	Net earnings	5.6	6.0	5.3

4. Significant stability in all income statement relationships indicates a well-run company. Note that most of the individual income statement items changed less than one percentage point over the three-year period.

Many analysts use graphics software in their study of financial results. Graphic representation is especially useful when communicating findings during meetings or in printed form. The charts in the margin summarize key 2001 data from Exhibit 14.2 along with comparable data from Lowe's, a key competitor.

In addition to component percentages, analysts use ratios to compare related items from the financial statements. Of the many ratios that can be computed from a single set of financial statements, analysts use only those that can be helpful in a given situation. Comparing cost of goods sold to property, plant, and equipment is never useful because these items have no natural relationship. Instead, an analyst will often compute certain widely used ratios and then decide which additional ratios could be relevant to a particular decision. Research and development costs as a percentage of sales is not a commonly used ratio, for example, but it is useful when analyzing companies that depend on new products, such as drug or computer firms.

When you compute ratios, remember a basic fact about financial statements: Balance sheet amounts relate to an instant in time while income statement amounts relate to an entire period. In comparing an income statement amount to a balance sheet amount, you should express the balance sheet as an average of the beginning and ending balances. In practice, many analysts simply use the ending balance sheet amount, an approach that is appropriate only if no significant changes have occurred in the balance sheet amounts. For consistency, we always use average amounts.

Financial statement analysis is a judgmental process; not all ratios are helpful in a given situation. We will discuss several ratios that are appropriate to most situations. They can be grouped into the categories shown in Exhibit 14.3.

Component Percentages for Home Depot

- ■ Cost of merchandise
- ▨ Operating expense
- ■ Earnings

Component Percentages for Lowe's

- ■ Cost of merchandise
- ▨ Operating expense
- ■ Earnings

TESTS OF PROFITABILITY

Profitability is a primary measure of the overall success of a company. Indeed, it is necessary for a company's survival. Several **tests of profitability** focus on measuring the adequacy of income by comparing it to other items reported on the financial statements. Return on equity is a widely used measure of profitability.

Learning Objective 4
Compute and interpret profitability ratios.

TESTS OF PROFITABILITY compare income with one or more primary activities.

1. Return on Equity (ROE)

Return on equity relates income earned to the investment made by the owners. This ratio reflects the simple fact that investors expect to earn more money if they invest more money. Two investments that offer a return of $10,000 are not comparable if one requires a $100,000 investment and the other requires a $250,000 investment. The return on equity ratio is computed as follows:[1]

$$\text{Return on Equity} = \frac{\text{Income*}}{\text{Average Owners' Equity}}$$

$$\text{Home Depot 2001} = \frac{\$2,581}{\$13,672^\dagger} = 18.9\%$$

*Income before extraordinary items should be used.
†($15,004 + $12,341) ÷ 2 = $13,672.

Home Depot earned 18.9 percent on the owners' investment. Was that return good or bad? We can answer this question by comparing Home Depot's return on equity with the ratio for a similar company. Return on equity for Lowe's was 15.9 percent in 2001,

Topic Tackler 14–2

[1]The figures for Home Depot used throughout the following examples are taken from the financial statements in Exhibit 14.1.

	Ratio	Basic Computation

EXHIBIT 14.3

Widely Used Accounting Ratios

Tests of Profitability

1. Return on equity (ROE)

$$\frac{\text{Income}}{\text{Average Owners' Equity}}$$

2. Return on assets (ROA)

$$\frac{\text{Income} + \text{Interest Expense (net of tax)}}{\text{Average Total Assets}}$$

3. Financial leverage percentage

Return on Equity − Return on Assets

4. Earnings per share (EPS)

$$\frac{\text{Income}}{\text{Average Number of Shares of Common Stock Outstanding}}$$

5. Quality of income

$$\frac{\text{Cash Flows from Operating Activities}}{\text{Net Income}}$$

6. Profit margin

$$\frac{\text{Income (before extraordinary items)}}{\text{Net Sales Revenue}}$$

7. Fixed asset turnover

$$\frac{\text{Net Sales Revenue}}{\text{Average Net Fixed Assets}}$$

Tests of Liquidity

8. Cash ratio

$$\frac{\text{Cash} + \text{Cash Equivalents}}{\text{Current Liabilities}}$$

9. Current ratio

$$\frac{\text{Current Assets}}{\text{Current Liabilities}}$$

10. Quick ratio

$$\frac{\text{Quick Assets}}{\text{Current Liabilities}}$$

11. Receivable turnover

$$\frac{\text{Net Credit Sales}}{\text{Average Net Receivables}}$$

12. Inventory turnover

$$\frac{\text{Cost of Goods Sold}}{\text{Average Inventory}}$$

Tests of Solvency

13. Times interest earned

$$\frac{\text{Net Income} + \text{Interest} + \text{Income Tax Expense}}{\text{Interest Expense}}$$

14. Cash coverage

$$\frac{\text{Cash Flows from Operating Activities (before interest and tax expense)}}{\text{Interest Paid}}$$

15. Debt-to-equity

$$\frac{\text{Total Liabilities}}{\text{Owners' Equity}}$$

Market Tests

16. Price/earnings ratio

$$\frac{\text{Current Market Price per Share}}{\text{Earnings per Share}}$$

17. Dividend yield

$$\frac{\text{Dividends per Share}}{\text{Market Price per Share}}$$

much lower than that for Home Depot. Clearly, Home Depot produced a better return than its strongest competitor.

We can gain additional insight by examining Home Depot's ROE over time:

	2001	2000	1999
ROE	18.9%	22.0%	20.4%

This comparison shows that Home Depot's performance in 2001 as measured by its ROE was good but not as strong as in past years. In the annual report, management attributed the deterioration in the company's performance to slow growth in the economy.

2. Return on Assets (ROA)

Another test of profitability compares income to the total assets (i.e., total investment) used to earn the income. Many analysts consider the return on assets ratio to be a better measure (compared to ROE) of management's ability to utilize assets effectively because it is not affected by the way in which the assets were financed. For example, the return on equity could be very high for a company that has borrowed a large amount of debt compared to a company that earned the same return on the same amount of assets but borrowed less money. Return on assets is computed as follows:

$$\text{Return on Assets} = \frac{\text{Income* + Interest Expense (net of tax)}^\dagger}{\text{Average Total Assets}}$$

$$\text{Home Depot 2001} = \frac{\$2,581 + (\$21 \times 66\%)}{\$19,233^\ddagger} = 13.5\,\%$$

Income before extraordinary items should be used.

†*This illustration assumes a corporate tax rate of 34 percent.*

‡*($21,385 + $17,081) ÷ 2 = $19,233.*

Note that interest expense has been added to net income in the numerator of the ratio. Because the denominator of the ratio includes resources provided by both owners and creditors, the numerator must include the return that was available to each group. Interest expense is added back because it was previously deducted in the computation of net income. Note, too, that interest expense is measured net of income tax. This amount is used because it represents the net cost to the corporation for the funds provided by creditors.

The return on assets for Lowe's was 9.1 percent, much lower than Home Depot's. This comparison indicates that Home Depot utilizes its assets more effectively than Lowe's.

3. Financial Leverage Percentage

Financial leverage percentage measures the advantage or disadvantage that occurs when a company's return on equity differs from its return on assets (i.e., ROE − ROA). In the DuPont model discussed earlier in this chapter, **financial leverage** was defined as the proportion of assets acquired with funds supplied by owners. The ratio **financial leverage percentage** measures a related but different concept. This ratio describes the relationship between the return on equity and the return on assets. Leverage is positive when the rate of return on a company's assets exceeds the average after-tax interest rate on its borrowed funds. Basically, the company borrows at one rate and invests at a higher rate of return. Most companies have positive leverage.

Financial leverage percentage can be measured by comparing the two return ratios as follows:

$$\text{Financial Leverage Percentage} = \text{Return on Equity} - \text{Return on Assets}$$

$$\text{Home Depot 2001} = 18.9\% - 13.5\% = 5.4\% \text{ (positive leverage)}$$

When a company borrows funds at an after-tax interest rate and invests those funds to earn a higher after-tax rate of return, the difference accrues to the benefit of the owners. The notes to Home Depot's annual report indicate that the company borrowed money at rates ranging from 3.25 percent to 10.5 percent and invested it in assets earning 13.5 percent. The difference between the income earned on the money it borrows and the interest it paid to creditors is available for the owners of Home Depot. This benefit of financial leverage is the primary reason most companies obtain a significant amount of their resources from creditors rather than from the sale of capital stock. Note that financial leverage can be enhanced either by investing effectively (i.e., earning a high return on investment) or by borrowing effectively (i.e., paying a low rate of interest).

Lowe's financial leverage ratio (6.8 percent) is somewhat higher than Home Depot's. Lowe's has achieved its higher ratio by utilizing comparatively more debt in its capital structure.

4. Earnings per Share (EPS)

The earnings per share ratio is a measure of return on investment that is based on the number of shares outstanding instead of the dollar amounts reported on the balance sheet. In simple situations,[2] EPS is computed as follows:

$$\text{Earnings per Share} = \frac{\text{Income}}{\text{Average Number of Shares of Common Stock Outstanding}}$$

$$\text{Home Depot 2001} = \frac{\$2,581}{2,314^*} = \$1.11 \text{ per share}$$

$$^*(2,324 + 2,304) \div 2 = 2,314$$

Earnings per share is probably the single most widely watched ratio. Its importance is illustrated by a news story published in *USA Today* (October 13, 2000):

> Shares of blue chip retailer Home Depot were trashed yesterday. Shares fell by 28%, losing over $32 billion in market value. Home Depot's problem? The company announced that its earnings per share will grow this year 17% instead of the 25% that had been expected.
>
> Source: The Home Depot

5. Quality of Income

Most financial analysts are concerned about the quality of a company's earnings because some accounting procedures can be used to report higher income. For example, a company that uses LIFO and short estimated lives for depreciable assets will report lower earnings than a similar company that uses FIFO and longer estimated lives. One method of evaluating the quality of a company's earnings is to compare its reported earnings to its cash flows from operating activities, as follows:

$$\text{Quality of Income} = \frac{\text{Cash Flows from Operating Activities}}{\text{Net Income}}$$

$$\text{Home Depot 2001} = \frac{\$2,796}{\$2,581} = 1.08$$

---

[2]The computation of EPS is more complex if a company has issued different types of stock; these complexities are discussed in advanced accounting courses. Note, for example, that the average number of shares shown in Exhibit 14.1 differs from this simple calculation.

A quality of income ratio that is higher than 1 is considered to indicate high-quality earnings because each dollar of income is supported by one dollar or more of cash flow. A ratio that is below 1 represents lower-quality earnings.

6. Profit Margin

The profit margin measures the percentage of each sales dollar, on average, that represents profit. It is computed as follows:

$$\text{Profit Margin} = \frac{\text{Income (before Extraordinary Items)}}{\text{Net Sales Revenue}}$$

$$\text{Home Depot 2001} = \frac{\$2,581}{\$45,738} = 5.6\%$$

For 2001, each dollar of Home Depot's sales generated 5.6 cents of profit. In comparison, Lowe's earned only 4.3 cents for each dollar of sales. Although the difference might seem small, it represents a significant advantage for Home Depot.

Although profit margin is a good measure of operating efficiency, care must be used in analyzing it because it does not consider the resources (i.e., total investment) needed to earn income. It is very difficult to compare profit margins for companies in different industries. For example, profit margins are low in the food industry while profit margins in the jewelry business are high. Both types of business can be quite profitable, however, because a high sales volume can compensate for a low profit margin. Grocery stores have low profit margins, but they generate a high sales volume from their relatively inexpensive stores and inventory. Although jewelry stores earn comparatively more profit from each sales dollar, they require a large investment in luxury stores and very expensive inventory.

The trade-off between profit margin and sales volume can be stated in simple terms: Would you prefer to have 5 percent of $1,000,000 or 10 percent of $100,000? As you can see, a larger profit margin is not always better.

7. Fixed Asset Turnover

Another measure of operating efficiency is the fixed asset turnover ratio, which compares sales volume with a company's investment in fixed assets. The term *fixed assets* is synonymous with property, plant, and equipment. The ratio is computed as follows:

$$\text{Fixed Asset Turnover} = \frac{\text{Net Sales Revenue}}{\text{Average Net Fixed Assets}}$$

$$\text{Home Depot 2001} = \frac{\$45,738}{\$11,648^*} = 3.9$$

$$^*(\$13,068 + \$10,227) \div 2 = \$11,648.$$

In 2001, Home Depot's fixed asset turnover was better than Lowe's (3.1). In simple terms, this means that Home Depot had a competitive advantage over Lowe's in terms of its ability to effectively utilize its fixed assets to generate revenue. For each dollar Home Depot invested in property, plant, and equipment, the company was able to earn $3.90 in sales revenue while Lowe's could earn only $3.10. This comparison is extremely important because it indicates that management of Home Depot was able to operate more efficiently than its main competitor.

The fixed asset turnover ratio is used widely to analyze capital-intensive companies such as airlines and electric utilities. For companies that hold large amounts of inventory and accounts receivable, analysts often prefer to use the asset turnover ratio, which is based on total assets rather than fixed assets:

$$\text{Asset Turnover} = \frac{\text{Net Sales Revenue}}{\text{Average Total Assets}}$$

$$\text{Home Depot 2001} = \frac{\$45,738}{\$19,233^*} = 2.38$$

($21,385 + $17,081) ÷ 2 = $19,233.

In 2001, Home Depot was able to generate $2.38 in revenue for each dollar invested in assets. In comparison, Lowe's asset turnover ratio was 1.86. Both turnover ratios show that Home Depot was able to operate more efficiently than Lowe's. This comparison is important because operating efficiency has a significant impact on profitability as the DuPont model (presented earlier in this chapter) indicates.

SELF-STUDY **QUIZ**

Show how to compute the following ratios:

1. Return on equity =

2. Return on assets =

3. Profit margin =

After you have completed your answers, check them with the solutions that follow:

1. $\dfrac{\text{Income}}{\text{Average Owners' Equity}}$

2. $\dfrac{\text{Income} + \text{Interest Expense (net of tax)}}{\text{Average Total Assets}}$

3. $\dfrac{\text{Income (before extraordinary items)}}{\text{Net Sales Revenue}}$

TESTS OF LIQUIDITY

Learning Objective 5
Compute and interpret liquidity ratios.

TESTS OF LIQUIDITY are ratios that measure a company's ability to meet its currently maturing obligations.

Liquidity refers to a company's ability to meet its currently maturing debts. **Tests of liquidity** focus on the relationship between current assets and current liabilities. The ability to pay current liabilities is an important factor in evaluating a company's short-term financial strength. A company that does not have cash available to pay for purchases on a timely basis will lose its cash discounts and run the risk of having its credit discontinued by vendors. We discuss three ratios that are used to measure liquidity: the cash ratio, the current ratio, and the quick ratio.

8. Cash Ratio

Cash is the lifeblood of a business. Without cash, a company cannot pay its employees or meet its obligations to creditors. Even a profitable business will fail without sufficient cash. One measure of the adequacy of available cash, called the *cash ratio,* is computed as follows:

$$\text{Cash Ratio} = \frac{\text{Cash} + \text{Cash Equivalents}}{\text{Current Liabilities}}$$

$$\text{Home Depot 2001} = \frac{\$167}{\$4,385} = 0.04 \text{ to } 1$$

In 2001, Lowe's cash ratio was 0.15, indicating that its cash reserve was larger than Home Depot's. Would analysts be concerned about Home Depot's lower ratio? Probably not, because there were other factors to consider. For example, Home Depot's statement of cash flows showed that the company generated a large amount of cash from its operating activities. As a result, it did not need to keep a large amount of cash on hand to meet unexpected needs. Indeed, most analysts believe the cash ratio should not be too high because holding excess cash is usually uneconomical. It is far better to invest the cash in productive assets or reduce debt.

Home Depot's cash ratio has decreased in recent years. In most cases, deterioration of the cash ratio might be a cause for concern. For instance, it could be an early warning that the company was experiencing financial difficulty. Given Home Depot's strong performance, however, the deterioration of its cash ratio was more likely the result of aggressive efforts by managers to minimize the amount of cash used to operate the business.

Some analysts do not use the cash ratio because it is very sensitive to small events. The collection of a large account receivable, for example, could have a significant impact on a company's cash ratio. The current ratio and the quick ratio are much less sensitive to the timing of such transactions.

9. Current Ratio

The current ratio measures the relationship between total current assets and total current liabilities on a specific date. It is computed as follows:

$$\text{Current Ratio} = \frac{\text{Current Assets}}{\text{Current Liabilities}}$$

$$\text{Home Depot 2001} = \frac{\$7{,}777}{\$4{,}385} = 1.77 \text{ to } 1$$

The current ratio measures the cushion of working capital that companies maintain to allow for the inevitable unevenness in the flow of funds through the working capital accounts. At the end of 2001, Home Depot had $1.77 in current assets for each $1 in current liabilities. Most analysts would judge that ratio to be very strong, given Home Depot's ability to generate cash.

To properly use the current ratio, analysts must understand the nature of a company's business. Many manufacturing companies have developed sophisticated systems to minimize the amount of inventory they must hold. These systems, called *just-in-time inventory,* are designed to have an inventory item arrive just when it is needed. While these systems work well in manufacturing processes, they do not work as well in retailing. Customers expect to find merchandise in the store when they want it, and it has proven difficult to precisely forecast consumer behavior. As a result, most retailers have comparatively high current ratios because they must carry large inventories. Home Depot, for example, maintains an inventory of 45,000 different products in each store.

Analysts consider a current ratio of 2 to be financially conservative. Indeed, most companies have current ratios that are below 2. The optimal level of the current ratio depends on the business environment in which a company operates. If cash flows are predictable and stable (as they are for a utility company), the current ratio can be low, even less than 1. If cash flows are highly variable (as they are in the airline industry), a higher current ratio is desirable.

Analysts become concerned if a company's current ratio is high compared to that of other companies. A firm is operating inefficiently when it ties up too much money in inventory or accounts receivable. There is no reason, for instance, for a Home Depot store to hold 1,000 hammers in stock if it sells only 100 hammers a month.

10. Quick Ratio (Acid Test)

The quick ratio is a more stringent test of short-term liquidity than is the current ratio. The quick ratio compares quick assets, defined as *cash and near-cash assets,* to current liabilities. Quick assets include cash, short-term investments, and accounts receivable (net of the allowance for doubtful accounts). Inventory is omitted from quick assets because of the uncertainty of the timing of cash flows from its sale. Prepaid expenses are also excluded from quick assets. The quick ratio is computed as follows:

$$\text{Quick Ratio} = \frac{\text{Quick Assets}}{\text{Current Liabilities}}$$

$$\text{Home Depot 2001} = \frac{\$1,012}{\$4,385} = 0.23 \text{ to } 1$$

The quick ratio is a measure of the safety margin that is available to meet a company's current liabilities. Home Depot has 23 cents in cash and near-cash assets for every $1 in current liabilities. This margin of safety is typical of the retail industry and would be considered a good margin in light of the large amount of cash Home Depot generates from its operating activities. In comparison, the quick ratio for Lowe's is 0.21 to 1.

11. Receivable Turnover

Accounts receivable are closely related to both short-term liquidity and operating efficiency. A company that can quickly collect cash from its customers has good liquidity and does not needlessly tie up funds in unproductive assets. The receivable turnover ratio is computed as follows:

$$\text{Receivable Turnover} = \frac{\text{Net Credit Sales*}}{\text{Average Net Receivables}}$$

$$\text{Home Depot 2001} = \frac{\$45,738}{\$711^{\dagger}} = 64 \text{ Times}$$

When the amount of credit sales is not known, total sales may be used as a rough approximation.
$\dagger(\$835 + \$587) \div 2 = \$711$

A high receivable turnover ratio suggests that a company is effective in its credit-granting and collection activities. Granting credit to poor credit risks and making ineffective collection efforts will produce a low receivable turnover ratio. While a very low ratio is obviously a problem, a very high ratio also can be troublesome because it suggests an overly stringent credit policy that could cause lost sales and profits.

The receivable turnover ratio is often converted to a time basis known as the *average age of receivables.* The computation is as follows:

$$\text{Average Age of Receivables} = \frac{\text{Days in a Year}}{\text{Receivable Turnover}}$$

$$\text{Home Depot 2001} = \frac{365}{64} = 5.7 \text{ Average Days to Collect}$$

The effectiveness of credit and collection activities is sometimes judged by the rule of thumb that the average days to collect should not exceed 1.5 times the credit terms. For example, if the credit terms require payment in 30 days, the average days to collect should not exceed 45 days (i.e., not more than 15 days past due). Like all rules of thumb, this one has many exceptions.

Although the receivable turnover ratio normally provides useful insights, the one for Home Depot is not meaningful. It is highly unlikely that Home Depot collects cash from its credit customers in just 5.7 days, on average. Because we did not know the amount of Home Depot's credit sales, we used total sales as an approximation. In this case, the approximation is not reasonable. Think about the last time you watched a customer buying merchandise on credit in a retail store. Most customers use a bank credit card such as MasterCard or Visa. From the seller's perspective, a sales transaction involving a bank credit card is recorded in virtually the same manner as a cash sale. In other words, a sale involving a credit card does not create an account receivable on the seller's books; instead, the account receivable is recorded on the credit card company's books. In practice, the majority of Home Depot's credit sales involve bank credit cards. As a result, Home Depot's accounts receivable turnover ratio is not meaningful.

12. Inventory Turnover

Like receivable turnover, inventory turnover is a measure of both liquidity and operating efficiency. This ratio reflects the relationship of inventory to the volume of goods sold during the period. It is computed as follows:

$$\text{Inventory Turnover} = \frac{\text{Cost of Goods Sold}}{\text{Average Inventory}}$$

$$\text{Home Depot 2001} = \frac{\$32,057}{\$6,022^*} = 5.3 \text{ Times}$$

($6,556 + $5,489) ÷ 2 = $6,022.

Because a company normally realizes profit each time inventory is sold, an increase in this ratio is usually favorable. If the ratio is too high, however, it may be an indication that sales were lost because desired items were not in stock.

On average, Home Depot's inventory was acquired and sold to customers 5.3 times during the year. The inventory turnover ratio is critical for Home Depot because of its business strategy. They want to be able to offer customers the right product when they need it at a price that beats the competition. If Home Depot does not effectively manage its inventory levels, it will incur extra costs that must be passed on to the customer.

Inventory turnover for Lowe's was 4.4. Because of the magnitude of each company's investment in inventory, the relatively small difference between their inventory turnover ratios is still a significant competitive advantage for Home Depot.

During the early 1990s, Home Depot's inventory turnover was better than it is currently. The company recently spent $9 million to upgrade computer systems in all its stores and is now transmitting data via satellite. One of the announced goals of this investment is to increase inventory turnover. Both managers and analysts will be watching closely to see whether inventory turnover improves.

Turnover ratios vary significantly from one industry to the next. Companies in the food industry (grocery stores and restaurants) have high inventory turnover ratios because their inventory is subject to rapid deterioration in quality. Companies that sell expensive merchandise (automobiles and high-fashion clothes) have much lower ratios because although sales of those items are infrequent, customers want to have a selection to choose from when they do buy.

The turnover ratio is often converted to a time basis called the *average days' supply in inventory*. This is the computation:

$$\text{Average Days' Supply in Inventory} = \frac{\text{Days in Year}}{\text{Inventory Turnover}}$$

$$\text{Home Depot 2001} = \frac{365}{5.3} = 69 \text{ Average Days' Supply in Inventory}$$

SELF-STUDY QUIZ

Show how to compute the following ratios:

1. Quality of income =

2. Quick ratio =

3. Cash ratio =

After you have completed your answers, check them with the solutions that follow:

1. Cash Flows from Operating Activities/Net Income
2. Quick Assets/Current Liabilities
3. Cash + Cash Equivalents/Current Liabilities

TESTS OF SOLVENCY

Learning Objective 6
Compute and interpret solvency ratios.

TESTS OF SOLVENCY are ratios that measure a company's ability to meet its long-term obligations

Solvency refers to a company's ability to meet its long-term obligations. **Tests of solvency,** which are measures of a company's ability to meet these obligations, include the times interest earned, cash coverage, and debt-to-equity ratios.

13. Times Interest Earned Ratio

Interest payments are a fixed obligation. If a company fails to make required interest payments, creditors may force it into bankruptcy. Because of the importance of meeting interest payments, analysts often compute a ratio called *times interest earned:*

$$\text{Time Interest Earned} = \frac{\text{Net Income} + \text{Interest Expense} + \text{Income Tax Expense}}{\text{Interest Expense}}$$

$$\text{Home Depot 2001} = \frac{\$2,581 + \$21 + \$1,636}{\$21} = 202 \text{ Times}$$

The times interest earned ratio compares the income a company generated in a period to its interest obligation for the same period. It represents a margin of protection for creditors. In 2001, Home Depot generated more than $202 in income for each $1 of interest expense, a high ratio that indicates a secure position for creditors.

Some analysts prefer to calculate the times interest earned ratio based on all contractually required payments, including principal and rent payments. Others believe that the ratio is flawed because interest expense and other obligations are paid in cash, not with net income. These analysts prefer to use the cash coverage ratio.

14. Cash Coverage Ratio

Given the importance of cash flows and required interest payments, it is easy to understand why many analysts use the cash coverage ratio. It is computed as follows:

$$\text{Cash Coverage} = \frac{\text{Cash Flows from Operating Activities before Interest and Taxes}}{\text{Interest Paid (from statement of cash flows)}}$$

$$\text{Home Depot 2001} = \frac{\$2,796 + \$16 + \$1,386}{\$16} = 262$$

The cash coverage ratio compares the cash generated by a company to its cash obligations for the period. Remember that analysts are concerned about a company's ability to make required interest payments. Home Depot's cash coverage ratio shows that the company generated nearly $262 in cash for every $1 of interest expense, which is strong coverage. Note that the numerator and the denominator of the cash coverage ratio use **interest paid** from the statement of cash flows instead of **interest expense** from the income statement. Accrued interest and interest payments are normally similar in amount, but are not always the same.

15. Debt-to-Equity Ratio

The debt-to-equity ratio expresses a company's debt as a proportion of its owners' equity. It is computed as follows:

$$\text{Debt-to-Equity Ratio} = \frac{\text{Total Liabilities}}{\text{Owners' Equity}}$$

$$\text{Home Depot 2001} = \frac{\$6,381}{\$15,004} = 0.43$$

In 2001, for each $1 of owners' equity, Home Depot had 43 cents of liabilities. By comparison, Lowe's debt-to-equity ratio was 0.52.

Debt is risky for a company because specific interest payments must be made even if the company has not earned sufficient income to pay them. In contrast, dividends are always at the company's discretion and are not legally enforceable until they are declared by the board of directors. Thus, equity capital is usually considered much less risky than debt.

Despite the risk associated with debt, most companies obtain significant amounts of resources from creditors because of the advantages of financial leverage discussed earlier. In addition, interest expense is a deductible expense on the corporate income tax return. In selecting a capital structure, a company must balance the higher returns available through leverage against the higher risk associated with debt. Because of the importance of the risk-return relationship, most analysts consider the debt-to-equity ratio a key part of any company evaluation.

MARKET TESTS

Several ratios, often called **market tests,** relate the current price per share of stock to the return that accrues to investors. Many analysts prefer these ratios because they are based on the current value of an owner's investment in a company.

Learning Objective 7
Compute and interpret market test ratios.

16. Price/Earnings (P/E) Ratio

MARKET TESTS are ratios that tend to measure the market worth of a share of stock.

The price/earnings (P/E) ratio measures the relationship between the current market price of a stock and its earnings per share. Recently, when the price of Home Depot stock was $35 per share, EPS for Home Depot was $1.11. The P/E ratio for Home Depot is computed as follows:

$$\text{Price/Earnings Ratio} = \frac{\text{Current Market Price per Share}}{\text{Earnings per Share}}$$

$$\text{Home Depot 2001} = \frac{\$35}{\$1.11} = 31.5$$

This P/E ratio indicates that Home Depot's stock was selling at a price that was 31.5 times its earnings per share. The P/E ratio reflects the stock market's assessment of a company's future performance. A high ratio indicates that earnings are expected to grow rapidly. Home Depot's P/E ratio is high compared to those of most other companies, including Lowe's, which reported a P/E ratio of 14. In fact, it is currently more than twice the average for companies included in the S&P 500 stock index.

In economic terms, the value of a stock is related to the present value of the company's future earnings. Thus, a company that expects to increase its earnings in the future is worth more than one that cannot grow its earnings (assuming other factors are the same). But while a high P/E ratio and good growth prospects are considered favorable, there are risks. When a company with a high P/E ratio does not meet the level of earnings expected by the market, the negative impact on its stock can be dramatic. As mentioned earlier, Home Depot's stock price fell 28 percent on October 13, 2000, after the announcement that its rate of earnings growth had slowed. Clearly, the stock's value had been based on an assessment of significant growth in future earnings.

17. Dividend Yield

When investors buy stock, they expect two kinds of return: dividend income and price appreciation. The dividend yield ratio measures the relationship between the dividends per share paid to stockholders and the current market price of a stock. Home Depot paid dividends of 16 cents per share when the market price of its stock was $35 per share. Its dividend yield ratio is computed as follows:

$$\text{Dividend Yield Ratio} = \frac{\text{Dividend per Share}}{\text{Market Price per Share}}$$

$$\text{Home Depot 2001} = \frac{\$0.16}{\$35} = 0.45\%$$

You might be surprised that Home Depot's dividend yield was below 1 percent when an investor could earn more than 5 percent in a federally insured savings account. In fact, the dividend yield for most stocks is not high compared to alternative investments. Investors are willing to accept low dividend yields if they expect that the price of a stock will increase while they own it. Clearly, investors who bought Home Depot's stock did so with the expectation that its price would increase. In contrast, stocks with low growth potential tend to offer much higher dividend yields than do stocks with high growth potential. These stocks often appeal to retired investors who need current income rather than future growth potential.

Like Home Depot, the dividend yield for Lowe's was 0.45 percent in 2001. The chart in the margin shows dividend yields for some companies in other industries.

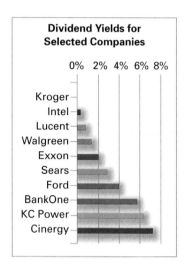

Dividend Yields for Selected Companies

0% 2% 4% 6% 8%

Kroger
Intel
Lucent
Walgreen
Exxon
Sears
Ford
BankOne
KC Power
Cinergy

SELF-STUDY **QUIZ**

Show how to compute the following ratios:

1. Current ratio =

2. Inventory turnover =

3. Price/earnings ratio =

After you have completed your answers, check them with the solutions that follow:

---

1. $\dfrac{\text{Current Assets}}{\text{Current Liabilities}}$

2. $\dfrac{\text{Cost of Goods Sold}}{\text{Average Inventory}}$

3. $\dfrac{\text{Current Market Price per Share}}{\text{Earnings per Share}}$

INTERPRETING RATIOS AND OTHER ANALYTICAL CONSIDERATIONS

Except for earnings per share, the computation of financial ratios has not been standardized by either the accounting profession or security analysts. Thus, users of financial statements should compute the various ratios in accordance with their decision objectives. Before using ratios computed by others, they should determine the computational approach that was used.

As we have seen, ratios can be interpreted only by comparing them to other ratios or to some optimal value. Some ratios, by their very nature, are unfavorable at either very high or very low values. For example, a very low current ratio may indicate an

	YEARS BEFORE BANKRUPTCY				
	5	4	3	2	1
Current ratio	1.8	1.7	1.7	1.2	1.2
Debt-to-equity ratio	1.6	1.8	2.0	5.0	5.6

EXHIBIT 14.4

Selected Financial Ratios for Hechinger

inability to meet maturing debts, and a very high current ratio may indicate an unprofitable use of funds. Furthermore, an optimal ratio for one company may not be optimal for another. Comparisons among the ratios for different companies are appropriate only if the companies are comparable in terms of their industry, operations, size, and accounting policies.

Because ratios are based on the aggregation of information, they may obscure underlying factors that are of interest to the analyst. For example, a current ratio that is considered optimal can obscure a short-term liquidity problem in a company with a large amount of inventory but a minimal amount of cash with which to pay debts as they mature. Careful analysis can uncover this type of problem.

In other cases, analysis cannot uncover obscured problems. For example, consolidated statements include financial information about a parent company and its subsidiaries. The parent company could have a high current ratio and the subsidiary a low one, but when their statements are consolidated, their current ratios are in effect averaged and can fall within an acceptable range. The fact that the subsidiary could have a serious liquidity problem is obscured.

Despite limitations, ratio analysis is a useful analytical tool. For instance, financial ratios are effective for predicting bankruptcy. Exhibit 14.4 presents the current and debt-to-equity ratios for Hechinger, a former competitor of Home Depot, for the five years before its bankruptcy in June 1999. Notice the progressive deterioration of these ratios. Analysts who studied these ratios probably were not surprised when Hechinger filed for bankruptcy.

Financial statements provide information to all investors, both sophisticated and unsophisticated. However, users who understand basic accounting principles and terminology are able to more effectively analyze the information contained in financial statements. For example, some unsophisticated users who do not understand the cost principle believe that assets are reported on the balance sheet at their fair market value. Interpreting accounting numbers correctly without an understanding of the concepts that were used to develop them is impossible.

In analyzing different companies, you will find that they rarely use exactly the same accounting policies. Comparisons among companies are appropriate only if the analyst who is making them understands the impact of different accounting alternatives. For example, one company may use conservative accounting alternatives such as accelerated depreciation and LIFO while another may use income-maximizing alternatives such as straight-line depreciation and FIFO. Analysts who do not understand the different effects of these accounting methods could misinterpret financial results. Perhaps the most important first step in analyzing financial statements is a review of the company's accounting policies, which are disclosed in a note to the statements.

Other Financial Information

The ratios we have discussed are useful for most analytical purposes. Because each company is different, however, you must exercise professional judgment when you conduct each financial analysis. To illustrate, let's look at some special factors that could affect our analysis of Home Depot.

1. Rapid growth. Growth in total sales volume does not always indicate that a company is successful. Sales volume from new stores may obscure the fact that existing stores are not meeting customer needs and are experiencing declines in sales. The family pizza chain Chuck-E-Cheese appeared to be a success when it reported rapid growth in total sales revenue by opening new restaurants. Unfortunately, the novelty of the new Chuck-E-Cheese restaurants proved to be short-lived fads, and their sales volume fell quickly. Because its older restaurants were unprofitable, Chuck-E-Cheese was forced to reorganize. In contrast, Home Depot's annual report shows that the company's stores posted sales increases ranging from 3 percent to 15 percent in each of the previous 10 years. Clearly, Home Depot can generate sales increases from both new and existing stores.

2. **Uneconomical expansion.** Some growth-oriented companies will open stores in less desirable locations if good locations cannot be found. These poor locations can cause a company's average productivity to decline. One measure of productivity in the retail industry is sales volume per square foot of selling space. For Home Depot, productivity results have been mixed:

Year	Sales per Square Foot
2001	$415
2000	423
1999	410
1998	406
1997	398

Sales per square foot have stabilized in recent years after rapid growth in the early 1990s when they increased by more than $100 per square foot. Management explains the slowdown in growth is the direct result of its strategy:

REAL WORLD EXCERPT

ANNUAL REPORT

We continue our cannibalization strategy, whereby we take the pressure off a busy store by opening another one nearby. While some challenge this approach because it tends to lower sales productivity, this strategy results in better service and greater customer satisfaction, which ultimately translates into higher sales and profits.

Source: The Home Depot

3. **Subjective factors.** Remember that vital information about a company is not contained in the annual report. The best way to evaluate Home Depot's strategy of being a price leader, for instance, is to visit its stores and those of competitors. An analyst who studied Home Depot for Salomon Smith Barney did exactly that:

REAL WORLD EXCERPT

SALOMON SMITH BARNEY
RESEARCH REPORT

On July 15, we surveyed the Boca Raton, Florida market. The Home Depot store is about two years old and was particularly impressive with respect to its in-stock position, customer service and total store presentation. We were able to compare Home Depot's pricing on 20 sample items. Our price analysis revealed that Home Depot is the price leader in the market by an average of 11 percent below the average total price of our 20-item market basket. Given the Home Depot's low cost structure, we believe that it will remain the price leader in this important market.

Source: The Home Depot

As these examples illustrate, no single approach can be used to analyze all companies. Furthermore, an effective analyst will look beyond the information contained in an annual report.

Financial statements are an important source of information for investors. Announcement of unexpected information can cause a substantial movement in the price of a company's stock.

A company's accountants often are aware of important financial information before it is made available to the public. This type of data is called *insider information*. Some people might be tempted to buy or sell stock based on insider information, but to do so is a serious criminal offense. The Securities and Exchange Commission has brought a number of cases against individuals who traded on insider information. Their convictions resulted in large fines and time served in jail.

In some cases, determining whether something is insider information is difficult. For example, an individual could overhear a comment made in the company elevator by two executives. A well-respected Wall Street investment banker gave good advice on dealing with such situations: "If you are not sure if something is right or wrong, apply the newspaper headline test. Ask yourself how you would feel to have your family and friends read about what you had done in the newspaper." Interestingly, many people who have spent time in jail and lost small fortunes in fines because of insider trading say that the most difficult part of the process was telling their families.

To uphold the highest ethical standard, many public accounting firms have adopted rules that prevent their staff from investing in companies that the firms audit. Such rules are designed to ensure that a company's auditors cannot be tempted to engage in insider trading.

Information in an Efficient Market

Considerable research has been performed on the way in which stock markets react to new information. Much of this evidence supports the view that the markets react very quickly to new information in an unbiased manner (that is, the market does not systematically overreact or underreact to new information). A market that reacts to information in this manner is called **efficient market.** In an efficient market, the price of a security fully reflects all available information.

It is not surprising that the stock markets react quickly to new information. Many professional investors manage stock portfolios valued in the hundreds of millions of dollars. These investors have a financial incentive to discover new information about a company and to trade quickly based on it.

The research on efficient markets has important implications for financial analysts. It probably is not beneficial to study old information (say an annual report that was released six months earlier) in an effort to identify an undervalued stock. In an efficient market, the price of a stock reflects all information contained in the annual report shortly after its release. In an efficient market, moreover, a company cannot manipulate the price of its stock by manipulating its accounting policy. The market should be able to differentiate between a company whose earnings are increasing due to improved productivity and one whose earnings have increased simply because of changes in accounting policies.

EFFICIENT MARKETS are securities markets in which prices fully reflect available information.

CHAPTER **TAKE-AWAYS**

1. **Explain how a company's business strategy affects financial analysis. p. 705**

   In simple terms, a business strategy establishes the objectives a business is trying to achieve. Performance is best evaluated by comparing the financial results to the objectives that the business was working to achieve. In other words, an understanding of a company's strategy provides the context for conducting financial statement analysis.

2. **Discuss how analysts use financial statements. p. 706**

   Analysts use financial statements to understand present conditions and past performance as well as to predict future performance. Financial statements provide important information to help users understand and evaluate corporate strategy. The data reported on statements can be used for either time-series analysis (evaluating a single company over time) or in comparison with similar companies at a single point in time. Most analysts compute component percentages and ratios when using statements.

3. **Compute and interpret component percentages. p. 707**

   To compute component percentages for the income statement, the base amount is net sales revenue. Each expense is expressed as a percentage of net sales revenue. On the balance sheet, the base amount is total assets; each balance sheet account is divided by total assets. Component percentages are evaluated by comparing them over time for a single company or by comparing them with percentages for similar companies.

4. **Compute and interpret profitability ratios. p. 709**

   Several tests of profitability focus on measuring the adequacy of income by comparing it to other items reported on the financial statements. Exhibit 14.3 lists these ratios and shows how to compute them. Profitability ratios are evaluated by comparing them over time for a single company or by comparing them with ratios for similar companies.

5. **Compute and interpret liquidity ratios. p. 714**

   Tests of liquidity measure a company's ability to meet its current maturing debt. Exhibit 14.3 lists these ratios and shows how to compute them. Liquidity ratios are evaluated by comparing them over time for a single company or by comparing them with ratios for similar companies.

6. **Compute and interpret solvency ratios. p. 718**

   Solvency ratios measure a company's ability to meet its long-term obligations. Exhibit 14.3 lists these ratios and shows how to compute them. Solvency ratios are evaluated by comparing them over time for a single company or by comparing them with ratios for similar companies.

7. **Compute and interpret market test ratios. p. 719**

   Market test ratios relate the current price of a stock to the return that accrues to investors. Exhibit 14.3 lists these ratios and shows how to compute them. Market test ratios are evaluated by comparing them over time for a single company or by comparing them with ratios for similar companies.

FINDING **FINANCIAL INFORMATION**

Balance Sheet

Ratios are not reported on the balance sheet, but analysts use balance sheet information to compute many ratios. Most analysts use an average of the beginning and ending amounts for balance sheet accounts when comparing the account to an income statement account.

Income Statement

Earnings per share is the only ratio that is required to be reported on the financial statements. It is usually reported at the bottom on the income statement

Statement of Cash Flows

Ratios are not reported on this statement, but some analysts use amounts from this statement to compute some ratios.

Statement of Stockholders' Equity

Ratios are not reported on this statement, but analysts use amounts from this statement to compute some ratios.

Notes

Under Summary of Significant Accounting Policies

This note has no information pertaining directly to ratios, but it is important to understand accounting differences if you are comparing two companies.

Under a Separate Note

Most companies include a 10-year financial summary as a separate note. These summaries include data for significant accounts, some accounting ratios, and nonaccounting information.

Component Percentages p. 708   Ratio (Percentage) Analysis p. 707   Tests of Profitability p. 709
Efficient Markets p. 723   Tests of Liquidity p. 714   Tests of Solvency p. 718
Market Tests p. 719

QUESTIONS

1. What are some of the primary items on financial statements about which creditors usually are concerned?
2. Why are the notes to the financial statements important to decision makers?
3. What is the primary purpose of comparative financial statements?
4. Why are statement users interested in financial summaries covering several years? What is the primary limitation of long-term summaries?
5. What is ratio analysis? Why is it useful?
6. What are component percentages? Why are they useful?
7. Explain the two concepts of return on investment.
8. What is financial leverage? How is it measured as a percentage?
9. Is profit margin a useful measure of profitability? Explain.
10. Compare and contrast the current ratio and the quick ratio.
11. What does the debt-to-equity ratio reflect?
12. What are market tests?
13. Identify two factors that limit the effectiveness of ratio analysis.

MULTIPLE **CHOICE QUESTIONS**

1. Which of the following ratios is *not* used to analyze profitability?
   a. quality of income ratio   c. quick ratio
   b. return on assets   d. return on equity
2. Which of the following would *not* change the receivables turnover ratio for a retail company?
   a. increases in the retail prices of inventory
   b. a change in credit policy
   c. increases in the cost incurred to purchase inventory
   d. none of the above would change the ratio
3. Which of the following ratios is used to analyze liquidity?
   a. earnings per share   c. current ratio
   b. debt-to-equity   d. both (a) and (c)
4. Positive financial leverage indicates
   a. positive cash flow from financing activities.
   b. a debt-to-equity ratio higher than 1.
   c. a rate of return on assets exceeding the interest rate on debt.
   d. a profit margin in one year exceeding the previous year's profit margin.
5. If a potential investor is analyzing three companies in the same industry and wishes to invest in only one, which ratio is least likely to affect the investor's decision?
   a. quick ratio   c. price to earnings ratio
   b. earnings per share   d. dividend yield ratio
6. Analysts use ratios to
   a. compare different companies in the same industry.
   b. track a company's performance over time.
   c. compare a company's performance to industry averages.
   d. All of the above describe ways that analysts use ratios.

7. Which of the following ratios incorporates cash flows from operations?
   a. inventory turnover
   b. earnings per share
   c. quality of income
   d. all of the above

8. Given the following ratios for four companies, which company is least likely to experience problems paying its current liabilities promptly?

	Quick ratio	Receivable turnover
a.	1.2	58
b.	1.2	45
c.	1.0	55
d.	.5	60

9. A decrease in selling and administrative expenses would impact what ratio?
   a. fixed asset turnover ratio
   b. times interest earned
   c. debt-to-equity ratio
   d. current ratio

10. A creditor is least likely to use what ratio when analyzing a company that has borrowed funds on a long-term basis?
    a. cash coverage ratio
    b. debt-to-equity ratio
    c. times interest earned ratio
    d. profit margin

For more practice with multiple choice questions, go to our website at www.mhhe.com/libby4e, click on "Student Center" in the upper left menu, click on this chapter's name and number from the list of contents, and then click on "Multiple Choice Quiz" from the menu on the left.

MINI-**EXERCISES**

M14-1
LO3

Inferring Financial Information Using Component Percentages

A large retailer reported revenue of $1,680,145,000. The company's gross profit percentage was 55.9 percent. What amount of cost of goods sold did the company report?

M14-2
LO3

Inferring Financial Information Using Component Percentages

A consumer products company reported a 6.8 percent increase in sales from 2003 to 2004. Sales in 2003 were $20,917. In 2004, the company reported cost of goods sold in the amount of $9,330. What was the gross profit percentage in 2004?

M14-3
LO4

Computing the Return on Owners' Investment Ratio

Compute the return on equity ratio for 2004 given the following data:

	2004	2003
Net income	$ 185,000	$ 160,000
Stockholders' equity	1,000,000	1,200,000
Total assets	2,400,000	2,600,000
Interest expense	40,000	30,000

M14-4
LO4

Inferring Financial Information Using Component Percentages

Compute the financial leverage percentage for 2004 given the following data:

	2004	2003
Return on equity	22%	24%
Return on assets	8	6
Profit margin	12	10

M14-5
LO5

Analyzing the Inventory Turnover Ratio

A manufacturer reported an inventory turnover ratio of 8.6 during 2003. During 2004, management introduced a new inventory control system that was expected to reduce average inventory levels by 25 percent without affecting sales volume. Given these circumstances, would you expect the inventory turnover ratio to increase or decrease during 2004? Explain.

Inferring Financial Information Using a Ratio

Scruggs Company reported total assets of $1,200,000 and noncurrent assets of $480,000. The company also reported a current ratio of 1.5. What amount of current liabilities did the company report?

M14-6
LO5

Analyzing Financial Relationships

Doritos Company has prepared draft financial results now being reviewed by the accountants. You notice that the financial leverage percentage is negative. You also note that the current ratio is 2.4 and the quick ratio is 3.7. You recognize that these financial relationships are unusual. Does either imply that a mistake has been made? Explain.

M14-7
LO4, 5

Inferring Financial Information Using a Ratio

In 2003, Drago Company reported earnings per share of $8.50 when its stock was selling for $212.50. In 2004, its earnings increased by 20 percent. If all other relationships remain constant, what is the price of the stock? Explain.

M14-8
LO7

Inferring Financial Information Using a Ratio

An Internet company earned $5 per share and paid dividends of $2 per share. The company reported a dividend yield of 5 percent. What was the price of the stock?

M14-9
LO7

Analyzing the Impact of Accounting Alternatives

Lexis Corporation is considering changing its inventory method from FIFO to LIFO and wants to determine the impact on selected accounting ratios. In general, what impact would you expect on the following ratios: profit margin, fixed asset turnover, current ratio, and quick ratio?

M14-10
LO3, 4, 5

EXERCISES

Matching Each Ratio with Its Computational Formula

Match each ratio or percentage with its computation by entering the appropriate letters in the blanks.

E14-1
LO3, 4, 5, 6, 7

Ratios or Percentages	Definitions
____ 1. Profit margin	A. Income (before extraordinary items) ÷ Net Sales.
____ 2. Inventory turnover ratio	B. Days in Year ÷ Receivable Turnover.
____ 3. Average collection period	C. Income ÷ Average Owners' Equity.
____ 4. Dividend yield ratio	D. Income ÷ Average number of Shares of Common
____ 5. Return on equity	Stock Outstanding.
____ 6. Current ratio	E. Return on Equity − Return on Assets.
____ 7. Debt-to-equity ratio	F. Quick Assets ÷ Current Liabilities.
____ 8. Price/earnings ratio	G. Current Assets ÷ Current Liabilities.
____ 9. Financial leverage percentage	H. Cost of Goods Sold ÷ Average Inventory.
____ 10. Receivable turnover ratio	I. Net Credit Sales ÷ Average Net Receivables
____ 11. Average days' supply	J. Days in Year ÷ Inventory Turnover.
of inventory	K. Total Liabilities ÷ Owners' Equity.
____ 12. Earnings per share	L. Dividends per Share ÷ Market Price per Share.
____ 13. Return on assets	M. Current Market Price per Share ÷ Earnings per Share.
____ 14. Quick ratio	N. Income + Interest Expense (net of tax) ÷ Average
____ 15. Times interest earned	Total Assets.
____ 16. Cash coverage ratio	O. Cash from Operating Activities (before interest and
____ 17. Fixed asset turnover	taxes) ÷ Interest Paid.
	P. Net Sales Revenue ÷ Net Fixed Assets.
	Q. (Net Income + Interest Expense + Income Tax
	Expense) ÷ Interest Expense.

E14-2
L03
Walgreens

Preparing a Schedule Using Component Percentages

Walgreens is one of the fastest-growing retailers in the United States. It claims to lead the chain drug-store industry in sales and profits. Complete component percentage analysis on the company's income statement that follows. Discuss any insights provided by this analysis.

WALGREENS
Income Statement
(Amounts in millions)

	2000	1999
Net sales	$21,206.9	$17,838.8
Cost sales	15,465.9	12,978.6
Selling, occupancy and administration	4,516.9	3,844.8
Interest expense	.4	.4
Interest income	6.1	12.3
Other income	33.5	
Income tax expense	486.4	403.2
Net earnings	776.9	624.1

E14-3
L05

Analyzing the Impact of Selected Transactions on the Current Ratio

Current assets totaled $54,000, and the current ratio was 1.8. Assume that the following transactions were completed: (1) purchased merchandise for $6,000 on short-term credit and (2) purchased a delivery truck for $10,000, paid $1,000 cash, and signed a two-year interest-bearing note for the balance.

Required:
Compute the cumulative current ratio after each transaction.

E14-4
L05
Sunbeam

Analyzing the Impact of Selected Transactions on the Current Ratio

Sunbeam is a leading designer, manufacturer, and marketer of branded consumer products, including Mr. Coffee, Osterizer, First Alert, and Coleman camping gear. Recently, the company has experienced significant financial difficulties and has been named in a number of lawsuits alleging material misstatements in its financial statements. The company's financial statements acknowledge that actions pending against the company "could have a material adverse impact on the Company's financial position." As a result, management must pay close attention to the impact that each operating decision has on the company's liquidity.

In the most recent statement, Sunbeam reported current assets of $1,090,068,000 and current liabilities of $602,246,000. Determine the impact of the following transactions on the current ratio for Sunbeam: (1) sold long-term assets that represented excess capacity, (2) accrued severance pay and fringes for employees who will be terminated, (3) wrote down the carrying value of certain inventory items that were deemed to be obsolete, and (4) acquired new inventory; supplier was not willing to provide normal credit terms, so an 18-month interest-bearing note was signed.

E14-5
L05
Procter & Gamble

Analyzing the Impact of Selected Transactions on Accounts Receivable and Inventory Turnover

Procter & Gamble is a multinational corporation that manufactures and markets many products that are probably in your home. Last year, sales for the company were $38,125 (all amounts in millions). The annual report did not disclose the amount of credit sales, so we will assume that 30 percent of sales was on credit. The average gross margin rate was 45 percent on sales. Account balances follow:

	Beginning	Ending
Accounts receivable (net)	$2,940	$2,781
Inventory	3,380	3,284

Required:
Compute the turnover for the accounts receivable and inventory, the average age of receivables, and the average days' supply of inventory.

Computing Financial Leverage

Motorola is a global leader in providing integrated communications and electronic solutions for businesses. Its financial statements reported the following at year-end (in millions):

Total assets	$28,728
Total debt (average 8% interest)	16,506
Net income (average tax rate 30%)	1,180

E14-6
LO4
Motorola

Required:
Compute the financial leverage percentage. Was it positive or negative?

Analyzing the Impact of Selected Transactions on the Current Ratio

Current assets totaled $100,000, and the current ratio was 1.5. Assume that the following transactions were completed: (1) paid $6,000 for merchandise purchased on short-term credit, (2) purchased a delivery truck for $10,000 cash, (3) wrote off a bad account receivable for $2,000, and (4) paid previously declared dividends in the amount of $25,000.

E14-7
LO5

Required:
Compute the cumulative current ratio after each transaction.

Inferring Financial Information

Dollar General Corporation operates general merchandise stores that feature quality merchandise at low prices to meet the needs of middle-, low-, and fixed-income families. All stores are located in the United States, predominantly in small towns in 24 midwestern and southeastern states. In a recent year, the company reported average inventories of $721,843,000 and an inventory turnover of 3. Average total fixed assets were $283,142,000, and the fixed asset turnover ratio was 11.4. Determine the gross margin for Dollar General.

E14-8
LO3
Dollar General Corporation

Computing Selected Ratios

Sales for the year were $600,000, of which one-half was on credit. The average gross margin rate was 40 percent on sales. Account balances follow:

E14-9
LO5

	Beginning	Ending
Accounts receivable (net)	$40,000	$60,000
Inventory	70,000	30,000

Required:
Compute the turnover for the accounts receivable and inventory, the average age of receivables, and the average days' supply of inventory.

Analyzing the Impact of Selected Transactions on the Current Ratio

Current assets totaled $500,000, the current ratio was 2.0, and the company uses the periodic inventory method. Assume that the following transactions were completed: (1) sold $12,000 in merchandise on short-term credit, (2) declared but did not pay dividends of $50,000, (3) paid prepaid rent in the amount of $12,000, (4) paid previously declared dividends in the amount of $50,000, (5) collected an account receivable in the amount of $12,000, and (6) reclassified $40,000 of long-term debt as a short-term liability.

E14-10
LO5

Required:
Compute the cumulative current ratio after each transaction.

Computing Liquidity Ratios

Cintas designs, manufactures, and implements corporate identity uniform programs that it rents or sells to customers throughout the United States and Canada. The company's stock is traded on the NASDAQ and has provided investors with significant returns over the past few years. Selected information from the company's balance sheet follows. For 2001, the company reported sales revenue of $2,160,700,000 and cost of goods sold of $1,264,433,000.

E14-11
LO5
Cintas

CINTAS
Balance Sheet
(Amounts in thousands)

Cintas	2001	2000
Cash	$ 73,724	$ 52,182
Marketable securities	35,140	57,640
Accounts receivable, less allowance of $8,765, $7,364	244,450	225,735
Inventories	214,349	164,906
Prepaid expense	8,470	7,237
Accounts payable	42,495	50,976
Accrued compensation	35,140	28,140
Accrued liabilities	78,308	66,218
Long-term debt due within one year	20,605	16,604

Required:

Compute the current ratio, quick ratio, inventory turnover, and accounts receivable turnover (assuming that 60 percent of sales was on credit).

E14-12 **Using Financial Information to Identify Mystery Companies**

LO3, 5, 6

The following selected financial data pertain to four unidentified companies:

	Companies			
	1	2	3	4
Balance Sheet Data				
(component percentage)				
Cash	3.5	4.7	8.2	11.7
Accounts receivable	16.9	28.9	16.8	51.9
Inventory	46.8	35.6	57.3	4.8
Property and equipment	18.3	21.7	7.6	18.7
Income Statement Data				
(component percentage)				
Gross profit	22.0	22.5	44.8	N/A*
Profit before taxes	2.1	0.7	1.2	3.2
Selected Ratios				
Current ratio	1.3	1.5	1.6	1.2
Inventory turnover	3.6	9.8	1.5	N/A
Debt-to-equity	2.6	2.6	3.2	3.2

*N/A = Not applicable

This financial information pertains to the following companies:

a. Retail fur store
b. Advertising agency
c. Wholesale candy company
d. Car manufacturer

Required:

Match each company with its financial information.

E14-13 **Using Financial Information to Identify Mystery Companies**

LO3, 5, 6

The following selected financial data pertain to four unidentified companies:

	Companies			
	1	2	3	4
Balance Sheet Data				
(component percentage)				
Cash	7.3	21.6	6.1	11.3
Accounts receivable	28.2	39.7	3.2	22.9
Inventory	21.6	0.6	1.8	27.5
Property and equipment	32.1	18.0	74.6	25.1
Income Statement Data				
(component percentage)				
Gross profit	15.3	N/A*	N/A	43.4
Profit before taxes	1.7	3.2	2.4	6.9
Selected Ratios				
Current ratio	1.5	1.2	0.6	1.9
Inventory turnover	27.4	N/A	N/A	3.3
Debt-to-equity	1.7	2.2	5.7	1.3

*N/A = Not applicable

This financial information pertains to the following companies:

a. Travel agency c. Meat packer
b. Hotel d. Drug company

Required:
Match each company with its financial information.

Using Financial Information to Identify Mystery Companies

E14-14
LO3, 5, 6

The following selected financial data pertain to four unidentified companies:

	Companies			
	1	2	3	4
Balance Sheet Data				
(component percentage)				
Cash	5.1	8.8	6.3	10.4
Accounts receivable	13.1	41.5	13.8	4.9
Inventory	4.6	3.6	65.1	35.8
Property and equipment	53.1	23.0	8.8	35.7
Income Statement Data				
(component percentage)				
Gross profit	N/A*	N/A	45.2	22.5
Profit before taxes	0.3	16.0	3.9	1.5
Selected Ratios				
Current ratio	0.7	2.2	1.9	1.4
Inventory turnover	N/A	N/A	1.4	15.5
Debt-to-equity	2.5	0.9	1.7	2.3

*N/A = Not applicable

This financial information pertains to the following companies:

a. Cable TV company c. Accounting firm
b. Grocery store d. Retail jewelry store

Required:
Match each company with its financial information.

Using Financial Information to Identify Mystery Companies

E14-15
LO3, 5, 6

The selected financial data shown below pertain to four unidentified companies.

	Companies			
	1	2	3	4
Balance Sheet Data				
(component percentage)				
Cash	11.6	6.6	5.4	7.1
Accounts receivable	4.6	18.9	8.8	35.6
Inventory	7.0	45.8	65.7	26.0
Property and equipment	56.0	20.3	10.1	21.9
Income Statement Data				
(component percentage)				
Gross profit	56.7	36.4	14.1	15.8
Profit before taxes	2.7	1.4	1.1	0.9
Selected Ratios				
Current ratio	0.7	2.1	1.2	1.3
Inventory turnover	30.0	3.5	5.6	16.7
Debt-to-equity	3.3	1.8	3.8	3.1

This financial information pertains to the following companies:

a. Full-line department store c. Automobile dealer (both new and used cars)
b. Wholesale fish company d. Restaurant

Required:
Match each company with its financial information.

PROBLEMS

P14-1 **Analyzing Comparative Financial Statement Using Percentages** (AP14-1)

LO3

The comparative financial statements prepared at December 31, 2004, for Goldfish Company showed the following summarized data:

	2004	2003
Income Statement		
Sales revenue	$180,000*	$165,000
Cost of goods sold	110,000	100,000
Gross margin	70,000	65,000
Operating expenses and interest expense	56,000	53,000
Pretax income	14,000	12,000
Income tax	4,000	3,000
Net income	$ 10,000	$ 9,000
Balance Sheet		
Cash	$ 4,000	$ 8,000
Accounts receivable (net)	14,000	18,000
Inventory	40,000	35,000
Operational assets (net)	45,000	38,000
	$103,000	$ 99,000
Current liabilities (no interest)	$ 16,000	$ 19,000
Long-term liabilities (10% interest)	45,000	45,000
Common stock (par $5)	30,000	30,000
Retained earnings†	12,000	5,000
	$103,000	$ 99,000

*One-third was credit sales.
†During 2004, cash dividends amounting to $3,000 were declared and paid.

Required:
1. Complete the following columns for each item in the preceding comparative financial statements:

Increase (Decrease)
2004 over 2003

Amount	Percent

2. By what amount did working capital change? What was the amount of cash inflow from revenues for 2004?

Analyzing Comparative Financial Statements Using Percentages and Selected Ratios (AP14-2)

P14-2
LO3, 4, 6

Use the data given in P14-1 for Goldfish Company.

Required:
1. Present component percentages for 2004 only.
2. Respond to the following for 2004:
   a. What was the average percentage markup on sales?
   b. What was the average income tax rate?
   c. Compute the gross profit margin. Was it a good or poor indicator of performance? Explain.
   d. What percentage of total resources was invested in operational assets?
   e. Compute the debt-to-equity ratio. Does it look good or bad? Explain.
   f. What was the return on equity?
   g. What was the return on assets?
   h. Compute the financial leverage percentage. Was it positive or negative? Explain.

Analyzing a Financial Statement Using Several Ratios

P14-3
LO3, 4, 5, 6, 7

Use the data in P14-1 for Goldfish Company. Assume a stock price of $28 per share. Compute appropriate ratios and explain the meaning of each.

Analyzing Ratios (AP14-3)

P14-4
LO3, 4, 5, 6, 7
Sears, Roebuck, and JCPenney

Sears, Roebuck and JCPenney are two giants of the retail industry. Both offer full lines of moderately priced merchandise. Annual sales for Sears total $41 billion. JCPenney is somewhat smaller with $30 billion in revenues. Compare the two companies as a potential investment based on the following ratios:

Ratio	Sears	JCPenney
P/E	8.1	9.7
Gross profit margin	33.5	23.1
Profit margin	3.6	1.7
Quick ratio	0.1	0.6
Current ratio	2.2	1.6
Debt-to-equity	2.8	1.4
Return on equity	23.5	7.5
Return on assets	4.1	3.2
Dividend yield	3.0%	5.9%
Dividend payout ratio	24.0%	118.0%

Analyzing a Financial Statement Using Several Ratios

P14-5
LO3, 4, 5, 6, 7

Summer Corporation has just completed its comparative statements for the year ended December 31, 2004. At this point, certain analytical and interpretive procedures are to be undertaken. The completed statements (summarized) are as follows:

	2004	2003
Income Statement		
Sales revenue	$450,000*	$420,000*
Cost of goods sold	250,000	230,000

Continued

	2004	2003
Gross margin	200,000	190,000
Operating expenses (including interest on bonds)	167,000	168,000
Pretax income	33,000	22,000
Income tax	10,000	6,000
Net income	$ 23,000	$ 16,000
Balance Sheet		
Cash	$ 6,800	$ 3,900
Accounts receivable (net)	42,000	28,000
Merchandise inventory	25,000	20,000
Prepaid expenses	200	100
Operational assets (net)	130,000	120,000
	$204,000	$172,000
Accounts payable	$ 17,000	$ 18,000
Income taxes payable	1,000	2,000
Bonds payable (10% interest rate)	70,000**	50,000
Common stock (par $5)	100,000†	100,000
Retained earnings	16,000‡	2,000
	$204,000	$172,000

*Credit sales totaled 40 percent.

**$20,000 of bonds were issued on 1/2/2004.

†The market price of the stock at the end of 2004 was $18 per share.

‡During 2004, the company declared and paid a cash dividend of $9,000.

Required:
1. Compute appropriate ratios for 2004 and explain the meaning of each.
2. Respond to the following for 2004:
    a. Evaluate the financial leverage. Explain its meaning using the computed amount(s).
    b. Evaluate the profit margin amount and explain how a stockholder might use it.
    c. Explain to a stockholder why the current ratio and the quick ratio are different. Do you observe any liquidity problems? Explain.
    d. Assuming that credit terms are 1/10, n/30, do you perceive an unfavorable situation for the company related to credit sales? Explain.

P14-6   **Identifying Companies Based on the Price/Earnings Ratio**

LO7

The price/earnings ratio provides important information concerning the stock market's assessment of the growth potential of a business. The following are price/earnings ratios for selected companies as of the date this book was written. Match the company with its ratio and explain how you made your selections. If you are not familiar with a company, you should contact its website.

Company	Price/Earnings Ratio
____ 1. Commerce Bank	A. 55
____ 2. Cinergy Gas and Electric	B. 12
____ 3. Compaq Computers	C. 26
____ 4. Home Depot	D. not applicable (no earnings)
____ 5. Motorola	E. 10
____ 6. Starbucks	F. 143
____ 7. America Online	G. 108
____ 8. Amazon.com	H. 65
____ 9. Pepsi	I. 82

P14-7   **Comparing Alternative Investment Opportunities** (AP14-4)

LO3, 4, 5, 6, 7

The 2004 financial statements for Armstrong and Blair companies are summarized here:

	Armstrong Company	Blair Company
Balance Sheet		
Cash	$ 35,000	$ 22,000
Accounts receivable (net)	40,000	30,000
Inventory	100,000	40,000
Operational assets (net)	140,000	400,000
Other assets	85,000	308,000
Total assets	$400,000	$800,000
Current liabilities	$100,000	$ 50,000
Long-term debt (10%)	60,000	70,000
Capital stock (par $10)	150,000	500,000
Contributed capital in excess of par	30,000	110,000
Retained earnings	60,000	70,000
Total liabilities and stockholders' equity	$400,000	$800,000
Income Statement		
Sales revenue (1/3 on credit)	$450,000	$810,000
Cost of goods sold	(245,000)	(405,000)
Expenses (including interest and income tax)	(160,000)	(315,000)
Net income	$ 45,000	$ 90,000
Selected data from the 2003 statements		
Accounts receivable (net)	$ 20,000	$ 38,000
Inventory	92,000	45,000
Long-term debt	60,000	70,000
Other data		
Per share price at end of 2004 (offering price)	$ 18	$ 15
Average income tax rate	30%	30%
Dividends declared and paid in 2004	$ 36,000	$150,000

The companies are in the same line of business and are direct competitors in a large metropolitan area. Both have been in business approximately 10 years, and each has had steady growth. The management of each has a different viewpoint in many respects. Blair is more conservative, and as its president said, "We avoid what we consider to be undue risk." Neither company is publicly held. Armstrong Company has an annual audit by a CPA but Blair Company does not.

Required:
1. Complete a schedule that reflects a ratio analysis of each company. Compute the ratios discussed in the chapter.
2. A client of yours has the opportunity to buy 10 percent of the shares in one or the other company at the per share prices given and has decided to invest in one of the companies. Based on the data given, prepare a comparative written evaluation of the ratio analyses (and any other available information) and give your recommended choice with the supporting explanation.

Analyzing the Impact of Alternative Inventory Methods on Selected Ratios

P14-8
LO4, 5

Company A uses the FIFO method to cost inventory, and Company B uses the LIFO method. The two companies are exactly alike except for the difference in inventory costing methods. Costs of inventory items for both companies have been rising steadily in recent years, and each company has increased its inventory each year. Each company has paid its tax liability in full for the current year (and all previous years), and each company uses the same accounting methods for both financial reporting and income tax reporting.

Required:
Identify which company will report the higher amount for each of the following ratios. If it is not possible, explain why.

1. Current ratio.
2. Quick ratio.
3. Debt-to-equity ratio.
4. Return on equity.
5. Earnings per share.

P14-9
LO3, 4, 5, 6, 7
Lands' End

Analyzing a Financial Statement Using Appropriate Ratios (AP14-5)

Lands' End is a direct merchant offering traditionally styled casual clothing and accessories through catalogs and the Internet. The following information was reported in a recent annual statement. For the year 2001, compute the ratios discussed in this chapter. If there is not sufficient information, describe what is missing and explain what you would do.

LANDS' END, INC. & SUBSIDIARIES
Consolidated Statement of Operations
(In thousands)

	FOR THE PERIOD ENDED		
	January 26, 2001	January 28, 2000	January 29, 1999
Revenue:			
Net merchandise sales	$1,354,974	$1,319,823	$1,371,375
Shipping and handling revenue	107,309	97,063	94,746
Total revenue	1,462,283	1,416,886	1,466,121
Cost of sales:			
Cost of merchandise sales	728,446	727,291	754,661
Shipping and handling costs	112,158	99,791	95,368
Total cost of sales	840,604	827,082	850,029
Gross profit	621,679	589,804	616,092
Selling, general and administrative expenses	560,019	512,647	543,824
Non-recurring charge (credit)	—	(1,774)	12,600
Income from operations	61,660	78,931	59,668
Other income (expense):			
Interest expense	(1,512)	(1,890)	(7,734)
Interest income	2,244	882	16
Other	(7,381)	(1,679)	(2,450)
Total other expense, net	(6,649)	(2,687)	(10,168)
Income before income taxes	55,011	76,244	49,500
Income tax provision	20,354	28,210	18,315
Net income	$ 34,657	$ 48,034	$ 31,185

LANDS' END, INC. & SUBSIDIARIES
Consolidated Balance Sheets

	January 26, 2001	January 28, 2000
(In thousands)		
Assets		
Current assets:		
Cash and cash equivalents	$ 75,351	$ 76,413
Receivables, net	19,808	17,753

Inventory	188,211	162,193
Prepaid advertising	17,627	16,572
Other prepaid expenses	9,715	5,816
Deferred income tax benefits	10,973	10,661
Total current assets	321,685	289,408
Property, plant and equipment, at cost:		
Land and buildings	104,815	102,776
Fixtures and equipment	103,866	102,886
Computer hardware and software	99,979	73,024
Leasehold improvements	4,630	4,453
Construction in progress	4,289	—
Total property, plant and equipment	317,579	283,139
Less-accumulated depreciation and amortization	132,286	117,317
Property, plant and equipment, net	185,293	165,822
Intangibles, net	651	966
Total assets	$507,629	$456,196

Liabilities and shareholders' investment

Current liabilities:

Lines of credit	$ 16,940	$ 11,724
Accounts payable	96,168	74,510
Reserve for returns	9,061	7,869
Accrued liabilities	41,135	43,754
Accrued profit sharing	2,357	2,760
Income taxes payable	13,213	10,255
Total current liabilities	178,874	150,872
Deferred income taxes	14,567	9,117
Shareholders' investment:		
Common stock, 40,221 shares issued	402	402
Donated capital	8,400	8,400
Additional paid-in capital	31,908	29,709
Deferred compensation	(121)	(236)
Accumulated other comprehensive income	5,974	2,675
Retained earnings	489,087	454,430
Treasury stock, 10,945 and 10,071		
shares at cost, respectively	(221,462)	(199,173)
Total shareholders' investment	314,188	296,207
Total liabilities and shareholders' investment	$507,629	$456,196

Analyzing an Investment by Comparing Selected Ratios (AP14-6)

P14-10
LO5, 6, 7

You have the opportunity to invest $10,000 in one of two companies from a single industry. The only information you have follows. The word *high* refers to the top third of the industry; *average* is the middle third; *low* is the bottom third. Which company would you select? Write a brief paper justifying your recommendation.

Ratio	Company A	Company B
Current	High	Average
Quick	Low	Average
Debt-to-equity	High	Average
Inventory turnover	Low	Average
Price/earnings	Low	Average
Dividend yield	High	Average

P14-11
LO5, 6, 7

Analyzing an Investment by Comparing Selected Ratios (AP14-7)

You have the opportunity to invest $10,000 in one of two companies from a single industry. The only information you have is shown here. The word *high* refers to the top third of the industry; *average* is the middle third; *low* is the bottom third. Which company would you select? Write a brief paper justifying your recommendation.

Ratio	Company A	Company B
Current	Low	Average
Quick	Average	Average
Debt-to-equity	Low	Average
Inventory turnover	High	Average
Price/earnings	High	Average
Dividend yield	Low	Average

ALTERNATE PROBLEMS

AP14-1
LO3, 4, 5, 6, 7

Analyzing a Financial Statement Using Ratios and Percentage Changes (P14-1)

Taber Company has just prepared the following comparative annual financial statements for 2004:

TABER COMPANY
Comparative Income Statement
For the Years Ended December 31, 2004, and 2003

		2004		2003
Sales revenue (one-half on credit)		$110,000		$99,000
Cost of goods sold		52,000		48,000
Gross margin		$ 58,000		$51,000
Expenses (including $4,000 interest expense each year)		40,000		37,000
Pretax income		$ 18,000		$14,000
Income tax on operations (30%)		5,400		4,200
Income before extraordinary items		$ 12,600		$ 9,800
Extraordinary loss	$2,000			
Less income tax saved	600	1,400		
Extraordinary gain			$3,000	
Applicable income tax			900	2,100
Net income		$ 11,200		$11,900

TABER COMPANY
Comparative Balance Sheet
At December 31, 2004, and 2003

	2004	2003
Assets		
Cash	$ 49,500	$ 18,000
Accounts receivable (net; terms 1/10, n/30)	37,000	32,000
Inventory	25,000	38,000
Operational assets (net)	95,000	105,000
Total assets	$206,500	$193,000

Liabilities

Accounts payable	$ 42,000	$ 35,000
Income taxes payable	1,000	500
Note payable, long-term	40,000	40,000
Stockholders' equity		
Capital stock (par $10)	90,000	90,000
Retained earnings	33,500	27,500
Total liabilities and stockholders' equity	$206,500	$193,000

Required (round percentage and ratios to two decimal places):

1. For 2004, compute the tests of (a) profitability, (b) liquidity, (c) solvency, and (d) market. Assume that the quoted price of the stock was $23 for 2004. Dividends declared and paid during 2004 were $6,750.
2. Respond to the following for 2004:
    a. Compute the percentage changes in sales, income before extraordinary items, net income, cash, inventory, and debt.
    b. What appears to be the pretax interest rate on the note payable?
3. Identify at least two problems facing the company that are suggested by your responses to requirements 1 and 2.

Using Ratios to Analyze Several Years of Financial Data (P14-2)

AP14-2
LO3, 4, 5

The following information was contained in the annual financial statements of Pine Company, which started business January 1, 2003 (assume account balances only in Cash and Capital Stock on this date; all amounts are in thousands of dollars).

	2003	2004	2005	2006
Accounts receivable (net; terms n/30)	$11	$12	$18	$ 24
Merchandise inventory	12	14	20	30
Net sales (3/4 on credit)	44	66	80	100
Cost of goods sold	28	40	55	62
Net income (loss)	(8)	5	12	11

Required (show computations):

1. Complete the following tabulation

Items	2003	2004	2005	2006

   a. Profit margin percentage
   b. Gross margin ratio
   c. Expenses as percentage of sales, excluding cost of goods sold
   d. Inventory turnover
   e. Days' supply in inventory
   f. Receivable turnover
   g. Average days to collect

2. Evaluate the results of the related ratios *a, b,* and *c* to identify the favorable or unfavorable factors. Give your recommendations to improve the company's operations.
3. Evaluate the results of the last four ratios (*d, e, f,* and *g*) and identify any favorable or unfavorable factors. Give your recommendations to improve the company's operations.

Analyzing Ratios (P14-4)

AP14-3
LO3, 4, 5, 6, 7
Coca-Cola
PepsiCo

Coke and Pepsi are well-known international brands. Coca-Cola sells more than $13 billion worth of beverages each year while annual sales of Pepsi products exceed $22 billion. Compare the two companies as a potential investment based on the following ratios:

Ratio	Coca-Cola	PepsiCo
P/E	65.0	26.5
Gross profit margin	69.3	58.4

Profit margin	12.2	8.8
Quick ratio	0.4	0.7
Current ratio	0.6	1.1
Debt-to-equity	0.7	0.4
Return on equity	27.4	29.1
Return on assets	28.0	16.6
Dividend yield	1.0%	1.6%
Dividend payout ratio	65.0%	41.0%

AP14-4 Comparing Loan Requests from Two Companies Using Several Ratios (P14-7)
LO3, 4, 5, 6, 7

The 2004 financial statements for Rand and Tand companies are summarized here:

	Rand Company	Tand Company
Balance Sheet		
Cash	$ 25,000	$ 45,000
Accounts receivable (net)	55,000	5,000
Inventory	110,000	25,000
Operational assets (net)	550,000	160,000
Other assets	140,000	57,000
Total assets	$880,000	$292,000
Current liabilities	$120,000	$15,000
Long-term debt (12%)	190,000	55,000
Capital stock (par $20)	480,000	210,000
Contributed capital in excess of par	50,000	4,000
Retained earnings	40,000	8,000
Total liabilities and stockholders' equity	$880,000	$292,000
Income Statement		
Sales revenue (on credit)	(1/2) $800,000	(1/4) $280,000
Cost of goods sold	(480,000)	(150,000)
Expenses (including interest and income tax)	(240,000)	(95,000)
Net income	$ 80,000	$ 35,000
Selected Data from the 2003 Statements		
Accounts receivable, net	$ 47,000	$ 11,000
Long-term debt (12%)	190,000	55,000
Inventory	95,000	38,000
Other Data		
Per share price at end of 2004	$ 14.00	$ 11.00
Average income tax rate	30%	30%
Dividends declared and paid in 2004	$ 20,000	$ 9,000

These two companies are in the same line of business and in the same state but in different cities. Each company has been in operation for about 10 years. Rand Company is audited by one of the national accounting firms; Tand Company is audited by a local accounting firm. Both companies received an unqualified opinion (i.e., the independent auditors found nothing wrong) on the financial statements. Rand Company wants to borrow $75,000 cash, and Tand Company needs $30,000. The loans will be for a two-year period and are needed for "working capital purposes."

Required:
1. Complete a schedule that reflects a ratio analysis of each company. Compute the ratios discussed in the chapter.
2. Assume that you work in the loan department of a local bank. You have been asked to analyze the situation and recommend which loan is preferable. Based on the data given, your analysis prepared in requirement 1, and any other information, give your choice and the supported explanation.

Analyzing a Financial Statement Using Appropriate Ratios (P14-9)

La-Z Boy manufactures and sells furniture including its popular reclining chair. Annual revenues exceed $2 billion. The following information was reported in a recent annual statement. Compute the ratios discussed in this chapter. If there is not sufficient information, describe what is missing and explain what you would do.

AP14-5
L04, 5, 6, 7
La-Z Boy

LA-Z BOY INCORPORATED
Consolidated Balance Sheet

(Amounts in thousands)	As of 4/28/01	4/29/00
Assets		
Current assets		
Cash and equivalents	$ 23,565	$ 14,353
Receivables, less allowance of $30,546		
in 2001 and $25,474 in 2000	380,867	394,453
Inventories		
Raw materials	90,381	91,018
Work-in-progress	62,465	63,635
Finished goods	115,425	98,623
FIFO inventories	268,271	253,276
Excess of FIFO over LIFO	(10,384)	(7,473)
Total inventories	257,887	245,803
Deferred income taxes	26,168	22,374
Other current assets	20,289	15,386
Total current assets	708,776	692,369
Property, plant and equipment		
Buildings and building fixtures	199,473	189,588
Machinery and equipment	177,851	162,485
Information systems	31,308	27,836
Land and land improvements	25,490	25,173
Transportation equipment	17,909	17,454
Network and production tracking systems	6,053	6,080
Other	24,284	22,755
	482,368	451,371
Less: accumulated depreciation	252,027	223,488
Property, plant and equipment, net	230,341	227,883
Goodwill, less accumulated amortization		
of $21,810 in 2001 and $17,360 in 2000	112,755	116,668
Trade names, less accumulated amortization		
of $5,792 in 2001 and $1,052 in 2000	134,667	135,340
Other long-term assets, less allowance		
of $6,404 in 2001 and $6,747 in 2000	35,964	46,037
Total assets	$1,222,503	$1,218,297
Liabilities and shareholders' equity		
Current liabilities		
Lines of credit	$ 10,380	$ 8,000
Current portion of long-term debt	5,304	5,119
Current portion of capital leases	541	457
Accounts payable	92,830	90,392
Payroll and other compensation	78,550	74,724
Income taxes	11,490	5,002
Other current liabilities	50,820	53,312
Total current liabilities	249,915	237,006

—continued

continued

Long-term debt	**196,923**	233,938
Capital leases	**2,496**	2,156
Deferred income taxes	**45,709**	50,280
Other long-term liabilities	**32,314**	31,825
Contingencies and commitments (Note 12)		
Shareholders' equity		
Preferred shares—5,000 authorized; none issued	—	—
Common shares, $1 par value-150,000		
authorized; 60,501 outstanding in 2001		
and 61,328 outstanding in 2000	**60,501**	61,328
Capital in excess of par value	**210,924**	211,450
Retained earnings	**427,616**	392,458
Accumulated other comprehensive loss	**(3,895)**	(2,144)
Total shareholders' equity	**695,146**	663,092
Total liabilities and shareholders' equity	**$1,222,503**	$1,218,297

Consolidated Statement of Income

(Amounts in thousands, except per share data) Fiscal year ended	4/28/01 (52 weeks)	4/29/00 (53 weeks)	4/24/99 (52 weeks)
Sales	**$2,256,197**	$1,782,916	$1,339,962
Cost of sales	**1,753,000**	1,350,561	997,975
Gross profit	**503,197**	432,355	341,987
Selling, general and administrative	**382,403**	289,507	235,228
Operating profit	**120,794**	142,848	106,759
Interest expense	**17,960**	9,655	4,440
Interest income	**1,779**	1,976	2,181
Other income, net	**7,431**	5,144	2,738
Pretax income	**112,044**	140,313	107,238
Income tax expense(benefit)			
Federal—current	**44,866**	49,491	41,286
—deferred	**(6,930)**	(3,288)	(4,727)
State—current	**6,576**	7,048	5,114
—deferred	**(804)**	(552)	(577)
Total income tax expense	**43,708**	52,699	41,096
Net income	**$ 68,336**	$ 87,614	$ 66,142

AP14-6 **Analyzing an Investment by Comparing Selected Ratios** (P14-10)

LO4, 5, 6, 7

You have the opportunity to invest $10,000 in one of two companies from a single industry. The only information you have is shown here. The word *high* refers to the top third of the industry; *average* is the middle third; *low* is the bottom third. Which company would you select? Write a brief paper justifying your recommendation.

Ratio	Company A	Company B
EPS	High	Low
ROA	Low	High
Debt to equity	High	Average
Current	Low	Average
Price/earnings	Low	High
Dividend yield	High	Average

Analyzing an Investment by Comparing Selected Ratios (P14-11)

You have the opportunity to invest $10,000 in one of two companies from a single industry. The only information you have is shown here. The word *high* refers to the top third of the industry; *average* is the middle third; *low* is the bottom third. Which company would you select? Write a brief paper justifying your recommendation.

Ratio	Company A	Company B
ROA	High	Average
Profit margin	High	Low
Financial leverage	High	Low
Current	Low	High
Price/earnings	High	Average
Debt-to-equity	High	Low

CASES AND **PROJECTS**

Annual Report Cases

Analyzing Financial Statements

Refer to the financial statements of American Eagle Outfitters given in Appendix B on page 749, or open file AEOS.pdf in the Annual Report Cases directory on the student CD-ROM. From the list of ratios discussed in this chapter, select and compute the ratios that help you evaluate the company's operations.

AMERICAN EAGLE OUTFITTERS

Analyzing Financial Statements

Refer to the financial statements of Abercrombie & Fitch given in Appendix C on page 788, or open file ANF.pdf in the Annual Report Cases directory on the student CD-ROM. From the list of ratios discussed in this chapter, select and compute the ratios that help you evaluate the company's operations.

ABERCROMBIE & FITCH

Comparing Companies within an Industry

Refer to the financial statements of American Eagle Outfitters given in Appendix B, Abercrombie & Fitch given in Appendix C, and the Industry Ratio Report given in Appendix D at the end of this book or open file CP14-3.xls in the Annual Report Cases directory on the student CD-ROM. From the list of ratios discussed in this chapter, select and compute the ratios that help you evaluate the companies' operations and compare the ratios for each company to the industry average ratios.

AMERICAN EAGLE OUTFITTERS

ABERCROMBIE & FITCH

Financial Reporting and Analysis Cases

Inferring Information from the ROE Model

In this chapter, we discussed the ROE profit driver (or DuPont model). Using that framework, find the missing amount in each case that follows:

Case 1: ROE is 10 percent, net income is $200,000; asset turnover is 5, and net sales are $1,000,000. What is the amount of average stockholders' equity?

Case 2: Net income is $1,500,000; net sales are $8,000,000; average stockholders' equity is $12,000,000; ROE is 22 percent and asset turnover is 8. What is the amount of average total assets?

Case 3: ROE is 15 percent; net profit margin is 10 percent; asset turnover is 5; and average total assets are $1,000,000. What is the amount of average stockholders' equity?

Case 4: Net income is $500,000; ROE is 15 percent; asset turnover is 5; net sales are $1,000,000; and financial leverage is 2. What is the amount of average total assets?

CP14-5

LO1

Interpreting Financial Results Based on Corporate Strategy

In this chapter, we discussed the importance of analyzing financial results based on an understanding of the company's business strategy. Using the ROE model, we illustrated how different strategies could earn high returns for investors. Assume that two companies in the same industry adopt fundamentally different strategies. One manufactures high-quality consumer electronics. Its products employ state-of-the-art technology, and the company offers a high level of customer service both before and after the sale. The other company emphasizes low cost with good performance. Its products utilize well-established technology but are never innovative. Customers buy these products at large, self-service warehouses and are expected to install the products using information contained in printed brochures. Which of the ratios discussed in this chapter would you expect to differ for these companies as a result of their different business strategies?

CP14-6

LO1, 4, 5, 6, 7

Nordstrom
and JCPenney

Interpreting Financial Results Based on Corporate Strategy

In this chapter, we discussed the importance of analyzing financial results based on an understanding of the company's business strategy. Using the ROE model, we illustrated how different strategies could earn high returns for investors. Both Nordstrom and JCPenney are in the retail industry. Nordstrom is a specialty apparel retailer operating in 23 states. Annual revenues exceed $5 billion. The store is well known for high-quality merchandise and a high level of customer service. JCPenney is a full-line retailer appealing to middle income shoppers. Its merchandise is moderately priced, and customers receive a lower level of service. The following are several ratios from each company. Identify which company is Nordstrom and which is JCPenney. Which of these ratios do you think are affected by the different strategies? Explain.

Ratio	Company A	Company B
Gross margin	34.4	23.1
Profit margin	4.0	1.7
Current ratio	1.8	1.6
Debt to equity	0.8	1.4
Return on equity	15.9	7.5
Return on assets	6.5	2.3
Dividend payout	22.1	117.0
Price/earnings	15.3	9.3

CP14-7

LO3, 4, 5, 6, 7

Interpreting Financial Publications

An important source of information for most investors is the analyst report published by all large investment firms. A professional analyst report* for Home Depot is available on the Libby/Libby/Short website at www.mhhe.com/libby4e. You should read this report and then write a short memo discussing the use of financial information in the report.

Critical Thinking Cases

CP14-8

LO4, 5, 6, 7

Analyzing the Impact of Alternative Depreciation Methods on Ratio Analysis

Speedy Company uses the sum-of-years'-digits method to depreciate its property, plant, and equipment, and Turtle Company uses the straight-line method. Both companies use 175 percent declining-balance depreciation for income tax purposes. The two companies are exactly alike except for the difference in depreciation methods.

Required:
1. Identify the financial ratios discussed in this chapter that are likely to be affected by the difference in depreciation methods.
2. Which company will report the higher amount for each ratio that you have identified? If you cannot be certain, explain why.

---

*Linda Bannister, "Home Depot's Analyst's Report," December 31, 1999. Reprinted with permission of Edward Jones.

Determining the Impact of Selected Transactions on Measures of Liquidity

CP14-9
L05

Three commonly used measures of liquidity are the current ratio, the quick ratio, and working capital. For each of the following transactions, determine whether the measure will increase, decrease, or not change. You should assume that both ratios are higher than 1 and that working capital is positive.

a. The company purchased $100,000 of inventory on credit.
b. Merchandise, which cost $35,000, was sold on credit for $50,000. The company uses the periodic inventory method.
c. Previously declared dividends are paid in cash.
d. Depreciation expense is recorded.
e. A customer pays money on his account receivable.

Evaluating an Ethical Dilemma

CP14-10
L05

Almost Short Company requested a sizable loan from First Federal Bank to acquire a large tract of land for future expansion. Almost Short reported current assets of $1,900,000 ($430,000 in cash) and current liabilities of $1,075,000. First Federal denied the loan request for a number of reasons, including the fact that the current ratio was below 2:1. When Almost Short was informed of the loan denial, the comptroller of the company immediately paid $420,000 that was owed to several trade creditors. The comptroller then asked First Federal to reconsider the loan application. Based on these abbreviated facts, would you recommend that First Federal approve the loan request? Why? Are the comptroller's actions ethical?

Financial Reporting and Analysis Team Project

Team Project: Examining an Annual Report

CP14-11
L03, 4, 5, 6, 7

As a team, select an industry to analyze. Each team member should acquire the annual report or 10-K for one publicly traded company in the industry, with each member selecting a different company. (Library files, the SEC EDGAR service at www.sec.gov, Compustat CD, or the company itself are good resources.) On an individual basis, each team member should write a brief report analyzing his or her company using the techniques discussed in this chapter.

Discuss any patterns across the companies that you as a team observe. Then, as a team, write a short report comparing and contrasting your companies. Provide potential explanations for any difference discovered.

TABLE A.1
Future Value of $1

Periods	2%	3%	3.75%	4%	4.25%	5%	6%	7%	8%
0	1.	1.	1.	1.	1.	1.	1.	1.	1.
1	1.02	1.03	1.0375	1.04	1.0425	1.05	1.06	1.07	1.08
2	1.0404	1.0609	1.0764	1.0816	1.0868	1.1025	1.1236	1.1449	1.1664
3	1.0612	1.0927	1.1168	1.1249	1.1330	1.1576	1.1910	1.2250	1.2597
4	1.0824	1.1255	1.1587	1.1699	1.1811	1.2155	1.2625	1.3108	1.3605
5	1.1041	1.1593	1.2021	1.2167	1.2313	1.2763	1.3382	1.4026	1.4693
6	1.1262	1.1941	1.2472	1.2653	1.2837	1.3401	1.4185	1.5007	1.5869
7	1.1487	1.2299	1.2939	1.3159	1.3382	1.4071	1.5036	1.6058	1.7138
8	1.1717	1.2668	1.3425	1.3686	1.3951	1.4775	1.5938	1.7182	1.8509
9	1.1951	1.3048	1.3928	1.4233	1.4544	1.5513	1.6895	1.8385	1.9990
10	1.2190	1.3439	1.4450	1.4802	1.5162	1.6289	1.7908	1.9672	2.1589
20	1.4859	1.8061	2.0882	2.1911	2.2989	2.6533	3.2071	3.8697	4.6610

Periods	9%	10%	11%	12%	13%	14%	15%	20%	25%
0	1.	1.	1.	1.	1.	1.	1.	1.	1.
1	1.09	1.10	1.11	1.12	1.13	1.14	1.15	1.20	1.25
2	1.1881	1.2100	1.2321	1.2544	1.2769	1.2996	1.3225	1.4400	1.5625
3	1.2950	1.3310	1.3676	1.4049	1.4429	1.4815	1.5209	1.7280	1.9531
4	1.4116	1.4641	1.5181	1.5735	1.6305	1.6890	1.7490	2.0736	2.4414
5	1.5386	1.6105	1.6851	1.7623	1.8424	1.9254	2.0114	2.4883	3.0518
6	1.6771	1.7716	1.8704	1.9738	2.0820	2.1950	2.3131	2.9860	3.8147
7	1.8280	1.9487	2.0762	2.2107	2.3526	2.5023	2.6600	3.5832	4.7684
8	1.9926	2.1436	2.3045	2.4760	2.6584	2.8526	3.0590	4.2998	5.9605
9	2.1719	2.3579	2.5580	2.7731	3.0040	3.2519	3.5179	5.1598	7.4506
10	2.3674	2.5937	2.8394	3.1058	3.3946	3.7072	4.0456	6.1917	9.3132
20	5.6044	6.7275	8.0623	9.6463	11.5231	13.7435	16.3665	38.3376	86.7362

TABLE A.2
Present Value of $1

Periods	2%	3%	3.75%	4%	4.25%	5%	6%	7%	8%
1	0.9804	0.9709	0.9639	0.9615	0.9592	0.9524	0.9434	0.9346	0.9259
2	0.9612	0.9426	0.9290	0.9246	0.9201	0.9070	0.8900	0.8734	0.8573
3	0.9423	0.9151	0.8954	0.8890	0.8826	0.8638	0.8396	0.8163	0.7938
4	0.9238	0.8885	0.8631	0.8548	0.8466	0.8227	0.7921	0.7629	0.7350
5	0.9057	0.8626	0.8319	0.8219	0.8121	0.7835	0.7473	0.7130	0.6806
6	0.8880	0.8375	0.8018	0.7903	0.7790	0.7462	0.7050	0.6663	0.6302
7	0.8706	0.8131	0.7728	0.7599	0.7473	0.7107	0.6651	0.6227	0.5835
8	0.8535	0.7894	0.7449	0.7307	0.7168	0.6768	0.6274	0.5820	0.5403
9	0.8368	0.7664	0.7180	0.7026	0.6876	0.6446	0.5919	0.5439	0.5002
10	0.8203	0.7441	0.6920	0.6756	0.6595	0.6139	0.5584	0.5083	0.4632
20	0.6730	0.5537	0.4789	0.4564	0.4350	0.3769	0.3118	0.2584	0.2145

TABLE **A.2** (*continued*)
Present Value of $1

Periods	9%	10%	11%	12%	13%	14%	15%	20%	25%
1	0.9174	0.9091	0.9009	0.8929	0.8850	0.8772	0.8696	0.8333	0.8000
2	0.8417	0.8264	0.8116	0.7972	0.7831	0.7695	0.7561	0.6944	0.6400
3	0.7722	0.7513	0.7312	0.7118	0.6931	0.6750	0.6575	0.5787	0.5120
4	0.7084	0.6830	0.6587	0.6355	0.6133	0.5921	0.5718	0.4823	0.4096
5	0.6499	0.6209	0.5935	0.5674	0.5428	0.5194	0.4972	0.4019	0.3277
6	0.5963	0.5645	0.5346	0.5066	0.4803	0.4556	0.4323	0.3349	0.2621
7	0.5470	0.5132	0.4817	0.4523	0.4251	0.3996	0.3759	0.2791	0.2097
8	0.5019	0.4665	0.4339	0.4039	0.3762	0.3506	0.3269	0.2326	0.1678
9	0.4604	0.4241	0.3909	0.3606	0.3329	0.3075	0.2843	0.1938	0.1342
10	0.4224	0.3855	0.3522	0.3220	0.2946	0.2697	0.2472	0.1615	0.1074
20	0.1784	0.1486	0.1240	0.1037	0.0868	0.0728	0.0611	0.0261	0.0115

TABLE **A.3**
Future Value of Annuity of $1

Periods*	2%	3%	3.75%	4%	4.25%	5%	6%	7%	8%
1	1.	1.	1.	1.	1.	1.	1.	1.	1.
2	2.02	2.03	2.0375	2.04	2.0425	2.05	2.06	2.07	2.08
3	3.0604	3.0909	3.1139	3.1216	3.1293	3.1525	3.1836	3.2149	3.2464
4	4.1216	4.1836	4.2307	4.2465	4.2623	4.3101	4.3746	4.4399	4.5061
5	5.2040	5.3091	5.3893	5.4163	5.4434	5.5256	5.6371	5.7507	5.8666
6	6.3081	6.4684	6.5914	6.6330	6.6748	6.8019	6.9753	7.1533	7.3359
7	7.4343	7.6625	7.8386	7.8983	7.9585	8.1420	8.3938	8.6540	8.9228
8	8.5830	8.8923	9.1326	9.2142	9.2967	9.5491	9.8975	10.2598	10.6366
9	9.7546	10.1591	10.4750	10.5828	10.6918	11.0266	11.4913	11.9780	12.4876
10	10.9497	11.4639	11.8678	12.0061	12.1462	12.5779	13.1808	13.8164	14.4866
20	24.2974	26.8704	29.0174	29.7781	30.5625	33.0660	36.7856	40.9955	45.7620

Periods*	9%	10%	11%	12%	13%	14%	15%	20%	25%
1	1.	1.	1.	1.	1.	1.	1.	1.	1.
2	2.09	2.10	2.11	2.12	2.13	2.14	2.15	2.20	2.25
3	3.2781	3.3100	3.3421	3.3744	3.4069	3.4396	3.4725	3.6400	3.8125
4	4.5731	4.6410	4.7097	4.7793	4.8498	4.9211	4.9934	5.3680	5.7656
5	5.9847	6.1051	6.2278	6.3528	6.4803	6.6101	6.7424	7.4416	8.2070
6	7.5233	7.7156	7.9129	8.1152	8.3227	8.5355	8.7537	9.9299	11.2588
7	9.2004	9.4872	9.7833	10.0890	10.4047	10.7305	11.0668	12.9159	15.0735
8	11.0285	11.4359	11.8594	12.2997	12.7573	13.2328	13.7268	16.4991	19.8419
9	13.0210	13.5975	14.1640	14.7757	15.4157	16.0853	16.7858	20.7989	25.8023
10	15.1929	15.9374	16.7220	17.5487	18.4197	19.3373	20.3037	25.9587	33.2529
20	51.1601	57.2750	64.2028	72.0524	80.9468	91.0249	102.4436	186.6880	342.9447

*There is one payment each period.

TABLE **A.4**
Present Value of Annuity of $1

Periods*	2%	3%	3.75%	4%	4.25%	5%	6%	7%	8%
1	0.9804	0.9709	0.9639	0.9615	0.9592	0.9524	0.9434	0.9346	0.9259
2	1.9416	1.9135	1.8929	1.8861	1.8794	1.8594	1.8334	1.8080	1.7833
3	2.8839	2.8286	2.7883	2.7751	2.7620	2.7232	2.6730	2.6243	2.5771
4	3.8077	3.7171	3.6514	3.6299	3.6086	3.5460	3.4651	3.3872	3.3121
5	4.7135	4.5797	4.4833	4.4518	4.4207	4.3295	4.2124	4.1002	3.9927
6	5.6014	5.4172	5.2851	5.2421	5.1997	5.0757	4.9173	4.7665	4.6229
7	6.4720	6.2303	6.0579	6.0021	5.9470	5.7864	5.5824	5.3893	5.2064
8	7.3255	7.0197	6.8028	6.7327	6.6638	6.4632	6.2098	5.9713	5.7466
9	8.1622	7.7861	7.5208	7.4353	7.3513	7.1078	6.8017	6.5152	6.2469
10	8.9826	8.5302	8.2128	8.1109	8.0109	7.7217	7.3601	7.0236	6.7101
20	16.3514	14.8775	13.8962	13.5903	13.2944	12.4622	11.4699	10.5940	9.8181

Periods*	9%	10%	11%	12%	13%	14%	15%	20%	25%
1	0.9174	0.9091	0.9009	0.8929	0.8550	0.8772	0.8696	0.8333	0.8000
2	1.7591	1.7355	1.7125	1.6901	1.6681	1.6467	1.6257	1.5278	1.4400
3	2.5313	2.4869	2.4437	2.4018	2.3612	2.3216	2.2832	2.1065	1.9520
4	3.2397	3.1699	3.1024	3.0373	2.9745	2.9137	2.8550	2.5887	2.3616
5	3.8897	3.7908	3.6959	3.6048	3.5172	3.4331	3.3522	2.9906	2.6893
6	4.4859	4.3553	4.2305	4.1114	3.9975	3.8887	3.7845	3.3255	2.9514
7	5.0330	4.8684	4.7122	4.5638	4.4226	4.2883	4.1604	3.6046	3.1611
8	5.5348	5.3349	5.1461	4.9676	4.7988	4.6389	4.4873	3.8372	3.3289
9	5.9952	5.7590	5.5370	5.3282	4.1317	4.9464	4.7716	4.0310	3.4631
10	6.4177	6.1446	5.8892	5.6502	5.4262	5.2161	5.0188	4.1925	3.5705
20	9.1285	8.5136	7.9633	7.4694	7.0248	6.6231	6.2593	4.8696	3.9539

*There is one payment each period.

ALIVE
AE Annual Report 2000

AMERICAN EAGLE
OUTFITTERS
www.ae.com

TABLE OF CONTENTS

AE Annual Report 2000

SELECTED CONSOLIDATED FINANCIAL DATA

For the years ended	Feb 3, 2001 (1)(2)	Jan 29, 2000	Jan 30, 1999	Jan 31, 1998	Feb 1, 1997

In thousands, except per share amounts and square foot data

Summary of Operations

Net sales	$1,093,477	$832,104	$587,600	$405,713	$326,404
Comparable store sales increase (decrease) (3)	5.8%	20.9%	32.1%	15.1%	(1.8%)
Gross profit	$436,225	$356,508	$234,511	$136,967	$98,756
Gross profit as a percentage of net sales	39.9%	42.8%	39.9%	33.8%	30.3%
Operating income	$146,551	$149,514	$87,053	$31,120	$8,859
Net income	$93,758	$90,660	$54,118	$19,537	$5,925
Net income as a percentage of net sales	8.6%	10.9%	9.2%	4.8%	1.8%

Per Share Results

Basic earnings per common share (4)	$1.35	$1.30	$0.80	$0.29	$0.09
Diluted earnings per common share (4)	$1.30	$1.24	$0.75	$0.29	$0.09
Weighted average common shares outstanding—basic (4)	69,652	69,555	67,921	66,272	65,849
Weighted average common shares outstanding—diluted (4)	72,132	73,113	71,928	68,449	68,082

(Financial data continued on next page)

(1) Represents the 53-week period ended February 3, 2001.
(2) Includes the results of operations, beginning October 29, 2000, for the divisions of Dylex Limited purchased by the Company as discussed in Note 3 of the Consolidated Financial Statements.
(3) The comparable store sales increase for the period ended February 3, 2001 is compared to the corresponding 53-week period last year.
(4) Earnings per common share and weighted average common shares outstanding amounts have been restated to reflect the February 2001 three-for-two stock split.
(5) Net sales per average square foot is calculated using retail sales for the year divided by the straight average of the beginning and ending square footage for the year.

AE Annual Report 2000

(Financial data continued from previous page)

For the years ended	Feb 3, 2001 (1)(2)	Jan 29, 2000	Jan 30, 1999	Jan 31, 1998	Feb 1, 1997

In thousands, except per share amounts and square foot data

Balance Sheet Information

	Feb 3, 2001 (1)(2)	Jan 29, 2000	Jan 30, 1999	Jan 31, 1998	Feb 1, 1997
Total assets	$543,046	$354,628	$210,948	$144,795	$110,438
Total cash and short-term investments	$161,373	$168,492	$85,300	$48,359	$34,326
Working capital	$169,514	$174,137	$94,753	$48,486	$34,378
Stockholders' equity	$367,695	$264,501	$151,197	$90,808	$71,056
Long-term debt	$24,889	-	-	-	-
Current ratio	2.14	2.97	2.59	1.90	1.87
Average return on stockholders' equity	29.7%	43.6%	44.7%	24.1%	8.8%

Other Financial Information

	Feb 3, 2001 (1)(2)	Jan 29, 2000	Jan 30, 1999	Jan 31, 1998	Feb 1, 1997
Total stores at year-end—United States	554	466	386	332	303
Total stores at year-end—Canada	109	-	-	-	-
Net sales per average selling square foot (5)	$549	$569	$497	$391	$340
Total selling square feet at end of period	2,354,245	1,625,731	1,276,889	1,080,657	990,980
Net sales per average gross square foot (5)	$441	$451	$388	$303	$261
Total gross square feet at end of period	2,919,556	2,039,380	1,624,933	1,393,361	1,285,598

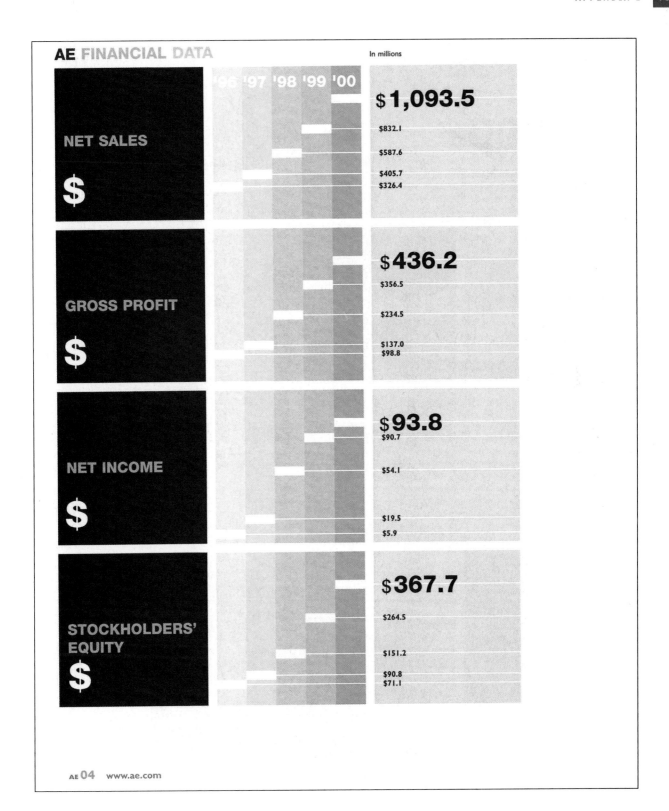

AE FINANCIAL DATA

In millions

NET SALES $

'96	'97	'98	'99	'00

$ **1,093.5**

$832.1

$587.6

$405.7
$326.4

GROSS PROFIT $

$ **436.2**

$356.5

$234.5

$137.0
$98.8

NET INCOME $

$ **93.8**
$90.7

$54.1

$19.5
$5.9

STOCKHOLDERS' EQUITY $

$ **367.7**

$264.5

$151.2

$90.8
$71.1

AE 04   www.ae.com

AE **2000** IN REVIEW

A clear focus on the AE brand strategy helped develop AE into a true 360° lifestyle brand.

Jason Biggs image provided by Dimension Films.

Sales exceeded one billion dollars for the first time in AE history.

$1 billion

Naturally, when you're living and breathing your customer's lifestyle, you watch what they watch. Because of this, we wardrobed Columbia Tristar's Dawson's Creek on the WB. We partnered with Dimension Films, a division of Miramax Films, to wardrobe four of their youth-oriented movies. In 2001, we began wardrobing MTV's Road Rules.

During back-to-school, we launched a unisex fragrance called **ALIVE**. Simply put the name **ALIVE** perfectly describes our brand and culture.

We estimate our combined advertising efforts consisting of national magazine advertising, direct mail, email, radio, and the AE Magazine made 142 million impressions on the AE target customer in 2000.

GROOVING IS ALIVE

AMERICAN EAGLE
OUTFITTERS

AE 06   www.ae.com

We opened our 500th store in Springfield, OH, on May 30, 2000, one of 90 stores opened in the U.S.

AMERICAN EAGLE
OUTFITTERS

Our strong back-to-school and holiday selling seasons resulted in an increase in EPS of 30% over the prior fall season. During the back-to-school season, we became the new destination store for denim. Holiday 2000 was all about sweaters and we had them in the right colors and styles and at the right price.

AE Cable Sweaters
$39.95 & up

GOING FAST IS ALIVE

AMERICAN EAGLE OUTFITTERS

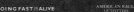

Canada

AE Magazine

Fiscal 2000 sales at ae.com increased 600% over 1999. A strong focus on the customer experience and integrating ae.com with our existing operation will set the stage for future success.

ae.com

In November 2000, we entered the Canadian market by acquiring the 109 store Thriftys/Bluenotes chain and prime mall real estate. We plan to expand AE into Canada with 46 locations by back-to-school 2001.

TO OUR STOCKHOLDERS

Fiscal 2000 was another record year for American Eagle Outfitters. We are especially pleased with our performance because of the challenges we faced in 2000. We met those challenges head on, increased our sales and profitability, invested wisely in talent and new opportunities, and continued the growth of the American Eagle Outfitters brand. Our net sales rose 31%, exceeding a billion dollars for the first time in our history. Same store sales grew 5.8% and net income reached a record $93.8 million or $1.30 per diluted share.

Our clear focus on the AE brand strategy is working. American Eagle Outfitters is a true 360° lifestyle brand. In 2000, customers shopped in our 554 stores, on our thriving website, ae.com, and from our magalog, the AE Magazine. At American Eagle Outfitters the customer experience is paramount. We listen to our customers 24/7/365, and give them what they want—value priced, fashion right, high quality, lifestyle merchandise. Our unwavering, disciplined process has served us well over the past few years, and it served us well again in 2000.

In 2000, we made a number of strategic investments in our future. We bought a second U.S. distribution center in Ottawa, Kansas to service our West Coast stores. We bought an import services company, Blue Star Imports, and we entered Canada with our first major acquisition. Enviably, after all of these strategic investments and stock repurchases of 1.8 million shares, our cash and investments totaled $161 million, and our debt to total capital ratio was just 8%. Working capital was strong, with current assets covering current liabilities 2.1 times at year-end. Our Fiscal 2000 average return on equity reached almost 30%.

We were challenged early in 2000. A rapid fashion shift made our spring and summer seasons difficult. We responded quickly, bringing our inventory position in-line with demand. Unfortunately, these markdowns hurt our bottom line in the second quarter.

Listening to our customers and living and breathing their lifestyle paid off again in the back-to-school season. They wanted denim in the coolest and newest washes and fits. We had it. American Eagle Outfitters became the new destination store for denim. We also launched a signature fragrance during back-to-school called Alive. Simply put, the name perfectly describes our brand and culture.

We followed back-to-school with an even more successful holiday season. We had the right sweaters in the right colors at the right price. As a result, 2000 was the strongest sales year we've ever had for sweaters. Our financial performance improved significantly during the fall and winter seasons. Comparable store sales rose an average of 9% during the second half of the year. Profits rose as well, increasing 28% over the second half of 1999.

Because we are a vertically-integrated retailer, controlling our product from the design stage all the way through to the store level, we can react rapidly and we did just that in 2000. Our process begins with a very talented team of merchants, designers, and marketers who constantly seek inspiration from our target customer. The center of our merchandising process is our New York City design office. When you enter our design office you can feel the energy. We are committed to continually seeking out, rewarding, and growing the best and brightest merchandising, design,

and marketing talent in the world. To be a world class brand you must have world class talent. Period. In 2001, we look forward to moving our design headquarters to a new location on Fifth Avenue in New York City. Our new facility is bigger, brighter, and there's room to grow our business.

Our core customers, men and women in the 16–34 age-range, are a powerful demographic group. They care a lot about how they look. They spend more on clothes than other age groups. And, they go to the mall and surf the net frequently. Importantly, this group is one of the fastest growing segments of the U.S. population. Over the next 10 years, 6 million people will be added to this group. We are ready for them.

Naturally, when you're living and breathing your customers' lifestyle, you watch what they watch. We continued to wardrobe the TV series, Dawson's Creek, one of the highest rated dramas among teens and twenty-somethings in both the U.S. and Canada. In 2000, we also partnered with Dimension Films, a division of Miramax Films, to wardrobe four of their youth-oriented movies. And, in March 2001, we began wardrobing the cast of MTV's Road Rules 10. Road Rules is a very popular MTV show with viewership averaging 4.5 million people per episode. Additionally, we continue to advertise in publications that are important to our customers, including: Maxim, In-Style, Seventeen, Teen People, Jane, and Rolling Stone.

In 2000, we opened 90 new U.S. stores and closed 2 stores, ending the year with 554 total locations. Additionally, we remodeled 47 stores, many of which were store expansions. We remain very pleased with our new store design. The stores are open and inviting. Our customers have found our new store design to be as much a hangout as a destination for fashion. New and expanded stores average 5,500 square feet, a little bigger than our overall store base, which averages 4,700 square feet. The slightly larger format will better accommodate new merchandise categories like underwear, dormwear, swimwear, gymwear, and personal care.

In 2001, we expect to open in new regions of the U.S., such as Southern California, and we will noticeably strengthen our presence in existing markets. In the U.S. alone, we have identified enough locations to sustain our growth over the next several years.

AE.com, our e-commerce business, strengthened in 2000 and far exceeded our expectations. Sales rose over 600% and traffic to the site increased dramatically. We invested in talent and have begun to build a business process that is integrated into our core stores business so that we can better serve our customers in 2001 and beyond.

The customer experience is also paramount at ae.com. In fact, we recently added new features like express checkout, outfit selling, and the ability to email friends and family a picture of a favorite item. We added these features because our customers asked for them.

In November 2000, we entered Canada with our first major acquisition. We acquired three businesses— the Thriftys/ Bluenotes chain, an established Canadian brand and a profitable retail business; 57 Braemar stores, with excellent real estate in prime mall locations, of which 46 will be converted to American Eagle stores

in 2001; and National Logistics Services, a 420,000 square foot distribution center near Toronto, which will handle all of the distribution needs for our Canadian operations.

Entering Canada makes strategic sense for American Eagle Outfitters. It's geographically close to our existing store base. It's predominately English speaking and the fashion is much like the U.S. We believe it is a market where the AE brand will translate well. Our brand offers tremendous value and fashionable, high-quality merchandise, all of which are important to Canadian customers. By back-to-school 2001, we plan to operate 46 American Eagle stores in Canada. By 2003, we could have as many as 90 American Eagle stores throughout Canada.

The Thriftys/Bluenotes chain is located throughout Canada. The brand targets a younger, slightly more urban inspired teen demographic than American Eagle Outfitters. The Bluenotes brand is well established, and ranks as the number one selling women's jean and the number three selling men's jean brand in Canada. In 2001, we will continue the process of converting Thriftys stores to the Bluenotes name. By year-end, nearly half of the stores will operate under the Bluenotes name. We are very excited about adding the Bluenotes brand to our Company and believe that it offers a number of future growth opportunities.

We are committed to increasing stockholder value. To that end, we announced our fourth stock split on January 22, 2001. This three-for-two stock split was distributed on February 23, 2001, to shareholders of record on February 2, 2001.

We entered 2001 energized with excitement for the year ahead. We've positioned ourselves well for future success. We are enthusiastic about the opening of 46 American Eagle stores in Canada. And to top it off, Thriftys/Bluenotes presents an awesome new prospect for growth. The American Eagle Outfitters brand continues to grow in momentum, scope, and reach, due in large part to the limitless energy of our associates, and our focus on our brand strategy and the customer experience. For all these reasons and more, we are looking forward to another successful year in 2001. We thank you for your continued support.

Jay L. Schottenstein

Jay L. Schottenstein
Chairman of the Board and Chief Executive Officer

James V. O'Donnell

James V. O'Donnell
Chief Operating Officer

Roger S. Markfield

Roger S. Markfield
President and Chief Merchandising Officer

AE Annual Report 2000

MANAGEMENT'S DISCUSSION AND ANALYSIS OF FINANCIAL CONDITION AND RESULTS OF OPERATIONS

Overview

For the fourth straight year, we achieved record sales and earnings. For the year ended February 3, 2001 ("Fiscal 2000"), we reached one billion dollars in sales for the first time in our history.

This performance was achieved primarily through the growth of our AE brand. We opened 90 new stores and closed 2 stores during the year, increasing our total store count in the United States to 554.

In November 2000, we expanded into the Canadian retail marketplace by acquiring the Thriftys/Bluenotes retail chain and 57 Braemar stores, of which 46 will be converted to American Eagle stores in 2001 (See Note 3 of the Consolidated Financial Statements). We continued to expand the non-store distribution of our merchandise through sales on our Internet web site, ae.com. In Fiscal 2000, sales from our site increased over 600%. We promoted our brand through print media by increasing magazine advertising circulation by 33% and increasing catalog and direct mail distribution by 29%.

As a result of this growth, our sales for Fiscal 2000 increased to $1,093.5 million from $832.1 million for the year ended January 29, 2000 (the "prior year" or "Fiscal 1999"), an increase of 31.4%. Comparable store sales increased 5.8% compared to the corresponding fifty-three week period last year. This was achieved on top of a 20.9% comparable store increase in Fiscal 1999. Our strong sales performance was driven primarily by a 35% increase in units sold. On an average store basis, units sold increased almost 9%.

Gross profit increased in Fiscal 2000 to $436.2 million from $356.5 million, but declined as a percent of sales to 39.9% from 42.8% of sales for the prior year.

Net income for Fiscal 2000 was $93.8 million, or $1.30 per diluted share, compared to $90.7 million, or $1.24 per diluted share, in the prior year.

Our balance sheet remained strong at the end of Fiscal 2000. As of February 3, 2001, working capital was $169.5 million. Inventory was $84.1 million compared to $60.4 million at the end of the prior year, and decreased approximately 1% on a per store basis for our U.S. stores. Stockholders' equity increased approximately 39% to $367.7 million, or $5.10 per diluted share, at the end of Fiscal 2000 compared to $264.5 million, or $3.62 per diluted share, at the end of the prior year. Average return on stockholders' equity was 29.7% for Fiscal 2000, compared to 43.6% for Fiscal 1999.

Results of Operations

This table shows, for the periods indicated, the percentage relationship to net sales of the listed items included in the Company's Consolidated Statements of Operations.

For the years ended	Feb 3, 2001	Jan 29, 2000	Jan 30, 1999
Net sales	100.0%	100.0%	100.0%
Cost of sales, including certain buying, occupancy and warehousing expenses	60.1	57.2	60.1
Gross profit	39.9	42.8	39.9
Selling, general and administrative expenses	24.4	23.4	23.6
Depreciation and amortization expense	2.1	1.4	1.5
Operating income	13.4	18.0	14.8
Other income (expense), net	0.6	–	0.4
Income before income taxes	14.0	18.0	15.2
Provision for income taxes	5.4	7.1	6.0
Net income	8.6%	10.9%	9.2%

AE Annual Report 2000

Comparison of Fiscal 2000 to Fiscal 1999

Net sales increased 31.4% to $1,093.5 million from $832.1 million. The increase includes:

- $52.3 million from comparable store sales,
- $174.1 million from new and noncomparable store sales and non-store sales, and
- $35.0 million from the Thriftys/ Bluenotes stores in Canada.

These amounts include $13.6 million in sales from the fifty-third week. Comparable store sales increased 5.8% compared to the corresponding fifty-three week period last year.

The sales increase resulted primarily from an increase of 35.1% in units sold. We operated 554 U.S. stores and 109 Thriftys/ Bluenotes stores at the end of the current year, compared to 466 total stores at the end of the prior year.

Gross profit increased 22.4% to $436.2 million from $356.5 million. Gross profit as a percent of net sales decreased to 39.9%

from 42.8%. The decrease in gross profit as a percent of net sales, was primarily attributable to a 2.8% decrease in merchandise margins. The decrease in merchandise margins resulted primarily from increased markdowns as a percent of sales during the second quarter.

Selling, general and administrative expenses increased to $266.5 million from $194.8 million. As a percent of net sales, these expenses increased to 24.4% from 23.4%. The $71.7 million increase includes:

- $40.3 million in operating expenses for our new stores in the United States and Canada,
- $13.2 million in compensation and benefit costs to support growth,
- $7.0 million in services purchased to support the non-store business, and additional outside service costs to support the growing business,
- $4.5 million related to equipment leases, primarily to improve in-store processing,
- $4.2 million in increased advertising costs, related to signage, direct mail, and catalog and non-store advertising costs, and
- $2.5 million for other selling, general and administrative expenses.

Depreciation and amortization expense increased to $23.2 million from $12.2 million. As a percent of net sales, these expenses increased to 2.1% from 1.4%. The increase includes $5.4 million related to new stores in the United States and Canada. The remaining increase is due primarily to depreciation expense related to technological improvements and investments in our distribution center infrastructure.

For Fiscal 2000, we had net other income of $6.2 million. This compared to net other expense of $0.2 million in the prior year. During the fourth quarter of Fiscal 1999, a valuation adjustment was recorded related to a marketable equity security. This investment was sold during Fiscal 2000. Investment income increased by $1.8 million as a result of higher cash reserves available for investment and higher average rates of return.

Income before income taxes increased to $152.8 million from $149.4 million. As a percent of net sales, income before income taxes decreased to 14.0% from 18.0%. The decrease in income before income taxes as a percent of sales was attributable to the factors noted above.

Comparison of Fiscal 1999 to Fiscal 1998

Net sales increased 41.6% to $832.1 million from $587.6 million. The increase includes:

- $118.8 million from comparable store sales, representing a 20.9% increase over the prior year, and
- $125.7 million from new and noncomparable store sales, and non-store sales.

The increase resulted primarily from an increase of 42.0% in units sold. We operated 466 stores at the end of Fiscal 1999, compared to 386 stores at the end of Fiscal 1998.

Gross profit increased 52.0% to $356.5 million from $234.5 million. Gross profit as a percent of net sales increased to 42.8% from 39.9%. The increase in gross profit as a percent of net sales was attributable to a 2.1% increase in merchandise margins as well as a 0.8% improvement in buying, occupancy, and warehousing costs. The increase in merchandise margins resulted from improved mark-ons and a decrease in

markdowns as a percent of sales. The improvement in buying, occupancy, and warehousing costs reflects improved leveraging achieved through comparable store sales growth.

Selling, general and administrative expenses increased to $194.8 million from $138.8 million. As a percent of net sales, these expenses decreased to 23.4% from 23.6%. The $56.0 million increase includes:

- $15.4 million in operating expenses for our new stores,
- $15.0 million in compensation and benefit costs related to additional personnel to support the increased sales volume and incentive programs that reward employees for the achievement of key performance indicators,
- $8.2 million for direct mail, signage, promotional advertising, and catalog and non-store advertising,
- $7.2 million in additional outside service costs to support the growing business, including the non-store business,
- $2.6 million related to equipment costs, primarily for leasing store registers and other hardware, and
- $7.6 million for other selling, general and administrative expenses.

Depreciation and amortization expense increased to $12.2 million from $8.6 million. As a percent of net sales, these expenses decreased to 1.4% from 1.5%.

For Fiscal 1999, we had interest income of $4.4 million, which was offset by investment expense of $4.6 million. Investment expense was a result of a valuation adjustment recorded during the fourth quarter of Fiscal 1999 related to a marketable equity security. Interest income increased from $2.4 million as a result of higher cash reserves available for investment.

Income before income taxes increased to $149.4 million from $89.5 million. As a percent of net sales, income before income taxes increased to 18.0% from 15.2%. The increase in income before income taxes as a percent of sales was attributable to the factors noted above.

AE Annual Report 2000

Liquidity and Capital Resources

The increase in cash and cash equivalents during Fiscal 2000 resulted primarily from an increase of $150.6 million in cash provided by operating activities, that was primarily derived from net income, adjusted for changes in working capital. Working capital at year-end was $169.5 million for Fiscal 2000, $174.1 million for Fiscal 1999, and $94.8 million for Fiscal 1998.

Sources of cash included $112.9 million resulting from the maturity of our short-term investments, $29.1 million in proceeds from debt used to partially finance the Canadian acquisition, and $10.2 million in proceeds from stock option exercises.

Our primary uses of cash included $87.8 million in capital expenditures, $78.2 million for the Canadian acquisition, $46.4 million to purchase short-term investments, $22.3 million to repurchase common stock, and $8.5 million to purchase an import services company, Blue Star Imports.

The remainder of the cash flow provided by operating activities is being retained for new store growth, store remodels, system enhancements, and other capital expenditures. We fund merchandise purchases through operating cash flow.

At February 3, 2001, the Company had an unsecured demand lending arrangement (the "facility") with a bank to provide a $125.0 million line of credit at either the lender's prime lending rate (8.50% at February 3, 2001) or a negotiated rate such as LIBOR. The facility has a limit of $40.0 million that can be used for direct borrowing. No borrowings were required

against the line for the current or prior year. At February 3, 2001, letters of credit in the amount of $66.8 million were outstanding leaving a remaining available balance on the line of $58.2 million.

The Company entered into a $29.1 million non-revolving term facility (the "term facility") and a $4.9 million revolving operating facility (the "operating facility") in November 2000 to finance the Canadian acquisition. The term facility matures in December 2007 and bears interest at the one-month Bankers' Acceptance Rate (5.50% at February 3, 2001) plus 140 basis points. The operating facility is due in November 2001, has six additional one year extensions, and bears interest at either the lender's prime lending rate (7.50% at February 3, 2001) or the Bankers' Acceptance Rate (5.50% at February 3, 2001) plus 120 basis points. There were no borrowings under the operating facility for the year ended February 3, 2001.

Capital expenditures, net of construction allowances, totaled $87.8 million for Fiscal 2000. These expenditures included:

- $32.2 million related to the addition of 90 new stores,
- $21.3 million for 47 remodeled locations,
- $13.3 million related to our second distribution facility,
- $5.0 million in fixtures and improvements to existing stores,
- $4.0 million in warehousing systems costs,
- $3.5 million in systems improvements,
- $3.1 million in improvements to our existing distribution center,
- $3.1 million in office renovations, and
- $2.3 million in other capital expenditures.

We expect capital expenditures for Fiscal 2001 to total approximately $153.0 million including the following:

- $35.0 million related to the addition of 86 new stores in the United States and Canada,
- $23.0 million for 53 remodeled locations in the United States and Canada,
- $25.0 million to convert certain Canadian store locations to American Eagle and Thriftys/Bluenotes stores,
- $21.0 million to complete construction on a second distribution facility,
- $19.0 million to install new systems, including hardware and software for our stores,
- $11.0 million to retrofit our stores, and
- $19.0 million in other capital expenditures.

Additionally, in Fiscal 2001, we plan to make $4.3 million in scheduled principal payments on the term facility. We plan to fund these capital expenditures and debt repayments primarily through available cash. These forward-looking statements will be influenced by our financial position, consumer spending, availability of financing, and the number of acceptable mall leases that may become available.

Our growth strategy includes the possibility of growth through acquisitions. We periodically consider and evaluate acquisitions and opportunities to support future growth, and may undertake acquisitions in 2001 and beyond. At this time, we have not committed to any material future acquisition. In the event we do pursue material future acquisitions, such actions could require additional equity or debt financing. There can be no assurance that we would be successful in closing any potential acquisition transaction, or that any acquisition we undertake would increase our profitability.

AE Annual Report 2000

Income Taxes

We had deferred tax assets of $35.0 million at February 3, 2001 which resulted primarily from financial and tax accounting differences. We have had taxable income during each of the past three tax years and anticipate that future taxable income will be able to recover the full amount of the deferred tax assets. A portion of the deferred tax assets has resulted from a capital loss. We anticipate that we will have sufficient capital gain income to recognize the benefit recorded from the loss. Assuming a 39% effective tax rate, we will need to recognize pretax net income of approximately $90.0 million in future periods to recover existing deferred tax amounts. See Note 10 of the Consolidated Financial Statements.

Impact of Inflation

We do not believe that the relatively modest levels of inflation experienced in the United States in recent years have had a significant effect on our net sales or our profitability. Substantial increases in cost, however, could have a significant impact on our business and the industry in the future.

Safe Harbor Statement, Business Risks, and Seasonality

This report contains various "forward-looking statements" within the meaning of Section 27A of the Securities Act of 1933, as amended, and Section 21E of the Securities Exchange Act of 1934, as amended, which represent our expectations or beliefs concerning future events, including the following:

- the planned opening of approximately 86 stores in the United States and Canada in Fiscal 2001,
- the selection of approximately 53 stores in the United States and Canada for remodeling,
- the plan to spend approximately $21.0 million to complete construction on our second distribution facility,
- the plan to convert certain Canadian store locations to American Eagle and Thriftys/Bluenotes stores,
- the sufficiency of existing cash and investment balances, cash flows and line of credit facilities to meet Fiscal 2001 cash requirements, and
- the possibility of growth through acquisitions.

We caution that these statements are further qualified by factors that could cause our actual results to differ materially from those in the forward-looking statements, including without limitation, the following:

- our ability to anticipate and respond to changing consumer preferences and fashion trends in a timely manner,
- decline in demand for our merchandise,
- the ability to obtain suitable sites for new stores at acceptable costs,
- the integration of new stores into existing operations,
- the acceptance of our AE brand in Canada,
- customer acceptance of our new store design,
- our ability to successfully acquire and integrate other businesses,
- the integration of our additional distribution facility into existing operations,
- the expansion of buying and inventory capabilities,
- the hiring and training of qualified personnel,
- the availability of capital,
- the effect of overall economic conditions and consumer spending patterns,
- the effect of changes in weather patterns,
- the change in currency and exchange rates, interest rates, duties, tariffs, or quotas, and
- the effect of competitive pressures from other retailers.

The impact of the aforementioned factors, some of which are beyond our control, may cause our actual results to differ materially from expected results in these statements and other forward-looking statements we may make from time-to-time.

Historically, our operations have been seasonal, with a significant amount of net sales and net income occurring in the fourth fiscal quarter, reflecting increased demand during the year-end holiday selling season and, to a lesser extent, the third quarter, reflecting increased demand during the back-to-school selling season. During Fiscal 2000, these periods accounted for approximately 65% of our sales. As a result of this seasonality, any factors negatively affecting us during the third and fourth fiscal quarters of any year, including adverse weather or unfavorable economic conditions, could have a material adverse effect on our financial condition and results of operations for the entire year. Our quarterly results of operations also may fluctuate based upon such factors as the timing of certain holiday seasons, the number and timing of new store openings, the amount of net sales contributed by new and existing stores, the timing and level of markdowns, store closings, refurbishments and relocations, competitive factors, weather and general economic conditions.

CONSOLIDATED FINANCIAL STATEMENTS

American Eagle Outfitters, Inc.
AE Annual Report 2000

FY 2000

American Eagle Outfitters, Inc.
Consolidated Balance Sheets

	Feb 3, 2001	Jan 29, 2000	Jan 30, 1999

In thousands

Assets

Current assets:

Cash and cash equivalents	$133,446	$76,581	$71,940
Short-term investments	27,927	91,911	13,360
Merchandise inventory	84,064	60,375	49,688
Accounts and note receivable, including related party	29,466	13,471	8,560
Prepaid expenses and other	18,864	6,640	2,757
Deferred income taxes	24,894	13,584	8,199
Total current assets	318,661	262,562	154,504
Property and equipment, at cost, net of accumulated depreciation and amortization	183,373	84,926	53,370
Goodwill, net of accumulated amortization	23,780	–	–
Deferred income taxes	10,129	4,029	2,200
Other assets, net of accumulated amortization	7,103	3,111	874
Total assets	$543,046	$354,628	$210,948

Liabilities and Stockholders' Equity

Current liabilities:

Accounts payable	$42,038	$30,700	$18,551
Current portion of note payable	4,300	–	–
Accrued compensation and payroll taxes	25,549	21,307	17,739
Accrued rent	22,577	17,755	13,042
Accrued income and other taxes	29,719	7,927	4,773
Unredeemed stored value cards and gift certificates	13,085	7,703	3,372
Other liabilities and accrued expenses	11,879	3,033	2,274
Total current liabilities	149,147	88,425	59,751
Non-current liabilities:			
Commitments and contingencies	–	–	–
Note payable	24,889	–	–
Other non-current liabilities	1,315	1,702	–
Total non-current liabilities	26,204	1,702	–
Stockholders' equity	367,695	264,501	151,197
Total liabilities and stockholders' equity	$543,046	$354,628	$210,948

See Notes to Consolidated Financial Statements

AE Annual Report 2000   Consolidated Financial Statements

American Eagle Outfitters, Inc.
Consolidated Statements of Operations

For the years ended	Feb 3, 2001	Jan 29, 2000	Jan 30, 1999
In thousands, except per share amounts			
Net sales	$1,093,477	$832,104	$587,600
Cost of sales, including certain buying, occupancy and warehousing expenses	657,252	475,596	353,089
Gross profit	436,225	356,508	234,511
Selling, general and administrative expenses	266,474	194,795	138,847
Depreciation and amortization expense	23,200	12,199	8,611
Operating income	146,551	149,514	87,053
Other income (expense), net	6,249	(160)	2,436
Income before income taxes	152,800	149,354	89,489
Provision for income taxes	59,042	58,694	35,371
Net income	$93,758	$90,660	$54,118
Basic earnings per common share	$1.35	$1.30	$0.80
Diluted earnings per common share	$1.30	$1.24	$0.75
Weighted average common shares outstanding—basic	69,652	69,555	67,921
Weighted average common shares outstanding—diluted	72,132	73,113	71,928

See Notes to Consolidated Financial Statements

American Eagle Outfitters, Inc.
Consolidated Statements of Stockholders' Equity

For the years ended February 3, 2001, January 29, 2000, and January 30, 1999

In thousands

	Shares (1)	Common Stock	Contributed Capital	Retained Earnings	Treasury Stock	Deferred Compensation Expense	Other Comprehensive Income/(Loss)	Stockholders' Equity
Balance at January 31, 1998	15,011	$150	$58,519	$35,756	($1,625)	($1,992)	$ –	$90,808
Net income and comprehensive income	–	–	–	54,118	–	–	–	54,118
Stock options and restricted stock	490	5	5,448	–	345	(427)	–	5,371
Merger costs incurred by Natco	–	–	900	–	–	–	–	900
Stock splits— May 8, 1998 and May 3, 1999	30,609	306	(306)	–	–	–	–	–
Balance at January 30, 1999	46,110	461	64,561	89,874	(1,280)	(2,419)	–	151,197
Stock options and restricted stock	630	6	25,909	–	–	(985)	–	24,930
Retirement of treasury stock	–	–	(1,280)	–	1,280	–	–	–
Comprehensive income:								
Net income	–	–	–	90,660	–	–	–	90,660
Unrealized loss on investments, net of tax	–	–	–	–	–	–	(2,286)	(2,286)
Total comprehensive income	–	–	–	–	–	–	–	88,374
Balance at January 29, 2000	46,740	467	89,190	180,534	–	(3,404)	(2,286)	264,501
Stock options and restricted stock	1,413	14	29,742	–	–	(621)	–	29,135
Repurchase of common stock	(1,207)	(12)	12	–	(22,339)	–	–	(22,339)
Three-for-two stock split—February 23, 2001	23,473	235	(235)	–	–	–	–	–
Comprehensive income:								
Net income	–	–	–	93,758	–	–	–	93,758
Other comprehensive income, net of tax:								
Unrealized gain on investments and reclassification adjustment	–	–	–	–	–	–	2,286	2,286
Foreign currency translation adjustment	–	–	–	–	–	–	354	354
Other comprehensive income	–	–	–	–	–	–	–	2,640
Total comprehensive income	–	–	–	–	–	–	–	96,398
Balance at February 3, 2001	70,419	$704	$118,709	$274,292	($22,339)	($4,025)	$354	$367,695

(1) 125 million authorized, 72 million issued and 70 million outstanding, $.01 par value common stock at February 3, 2001. Issued and outstanding were 70 million and 69 million (adjusted for stock splits) at January 29, 2000 and January 30, 1999, respectively. The Company has 5 million authorized, with none issued or outstanding, $.01 par value preferred stock at February 3, 2001.

See *Notes to Consolidated Financial Statements*

AE Annual Report 2000   Consolidated Financial Statements

American Eagle Outfitters, Inc.
Consolidated Statements of Cash Flows

For the years ended	Feb 3, 2001	Jan 29, 2000	Jan 30, 1999
In thousands			
Operating activities			
Net income	$93,758	$90,660	$54,118
Adjustments to reconcile net income to net cash provided by operating activities:			
Depreciation and amortization	23,200	12,199	8,611
Loss on impairment and write-off of fixed assets	2,902	1,907	1,467
Stock compensation	6,952	5,809	1,336
Deferred income taxes	(6,572)	(7,214)	(2,753)
Investment expense	–	4,554	–
Merger costs incurred by Natco	–	–	900
Changes in assets and liabilities:			
Merchandise inventory	(5,606)	(10,687)	(13,410)
Accounts and note receivable	(13,388)	(4,911)	(913)
Prepaid expenses and other	(12,185)	(6,205)	2,445
Accounts payable	12,175	12,121	(5,400)
Unredeemed stored value cards	5,373	4,331	1,669
Accrued liabilities	43,982	30,348	11,751
Total adjustments	56,833	42,252	5,703
Net cash provided by operating activities	150,591	132,912	59,821
Investing activities			
Capital expenditures	(87,825)	(45,556)	(24,913)
Purchase of an import services company, Blue Star Imports	(8,500)	–	–
Purchase of Dylex divisions, net of cash	(78,184)	–	–
Purchase of short-term investments	(46,421)	(124,166)	(54,559)
Sale of short-term investments	112,878	38,775	41,199
Other investing activities	(1,397)	–	–
Net cash used for investing activities	(109,449)	(130,947)	(38,273)
Financing activities			
Proceeds from issuance of note payable	29,101	–	–
Principal payments on note payable	(1,651)	–	–
Repurchase of common stock	(22,339)	–	–
Net proceeds from stock options exercised	10,191	2,676	2,033
Net cash provided by financing activities	15,302	2,676	2,033
Effect of exchange rates on cash	421	–	–
Net increase in cash and cash equivalents	56,865	4,641	23,581
Cash and cash equivalents—beginning of period	76,581	71,940	48,359
Cash and cash equivalents—end of period	$133,446	$76,581	$71,940

See Notes to Consolidated Financial Statements

American Eagle Outfitters, Inc.
Notes to Consolidated Financial Statements

For the year ended February 3, 2001

1. Business Operations

American Eagle Outfitters, Inc. (the "Company") designs, markets, and sells its AE brand of relaxed, clean, and versatile clothing for 16 to 34 year olds in its United States retail stores. We also operate via the Internet at *ae.com*. The AE brand provides high-quality merchandise at affordable prices. AE's lifestyle collection offers casual basics like cargos complemented by fashion looks in stretch, denim, and other modern fabrications.

The Thriftys/Bluenotes brand targets a slightly younger demographic, offering a more urban/suburban, denim-driven collection for 12 to 22 year olds.

The Company operates retail stores located primarily in regional enclosed shopping malls in the United States and Canada.

The following table sets forth the approximate consolidated percentage of net sales attributable to each merchandise group for each of the periods indicated:

For the years ended	Feb 3, 2001	Jan 29, 2000	Jan 30, 1999
Men's apparel	40%	39%	40%
Women's apparel	52%	53%	52%
Footwear and accessories— men's and women's	8%	8%	8%
Total	100%	100%	100%

AE Annual Report 2000   Consolidated Financial Statements

2. Summary of Significant Accounting Policies

Principles of Consolidation

The Consolidated Financial Statements include the accounts of the Company and its subsidiaries. The results of operations of the acquired Canadian businesses discussed in Note 3 are included in the Consolidated Financial Statements beginning October 29, 2000. All intercompany transactions and balances have been eliminated in consolidation.

Fiscal Year

The Company's financial year is a 52/53 week year that ends on the Saturday nearest to January 31. For tax purposes, the Company reports on a July year-end. As used herein, "Fiscal 2000" refers to the fifty-three week period ended February 3, 2001. "Fiscal 1999" and "Fiscal 1998" refer to the fifty-two week periods ended January 29, 2000 and January 30, 1999, respectively. "Fiscal 2001" refers to the fifty-two week period ending February 2, 2002.

Estimates

The preparation of financial statements in conformity with generally accepted accounting principles requires management to make estimates and assumptions that affect the reported amounts of assets and liabilities and disclosure of contingent assets and liabilities at the date of the financial statements and the reported amounts of revenues and expenses during the reporting period. Actual results could differ from those estimates. On an ongoing basis, management reviews its estimates based on currently available information. Changes in facts and circumstances may result in revised estimates.

Recent Financial Accounting Standards Board Pronouncements

FASB Interpretation No. 44, *Accounting for Certain Transactions Involving Stock Compensation*

In March 2000, the FASB issued FASB Interpretation No. 44, *Accounting for Certain Transactions Involving Stock Compensation* which interprets APB Opinion No. 25, *Accounting for Stock Issued to Employees*. The Company adopted the Interpretation on July 1, 2000, as required. Adoption of the Interpretation has resulted in no significant changes to the Company's accounting for stock option grants.

Staff Accounting Bulletin No. 101, *Revenue Recognition in Financial Statements*

The Securities and Exchange Commission (SEC) issued and subsequently amended guidance related to revenue recognition during December 1999 and in the first half of the calendar year 2000. These interpretations were implemented in Fiscal 2000. Adoption of this guidance has resulted in no material impact on the Company's financial statements.

SFAS 133, *Accounting for Derivative Instruments and Hedging Activities*

In 1998, the FASB issued Statement of Financial Accounting Standards No. 133, *Accounting for Derivative Instruments and Hedging Activities* as amended by SFAS 137 and 138 (collectively SFAS 133), which establishes standards for the recognition and measurement of derivative and hedging activities. This standard is effective for the Company's Fiscal 2001 financial statements. In November 2000, the Company entered into an effective interest rate swap in connection with the Canadian acquisition. The Company will adopt SFAS 133 in the first quarter of Fiscal 2001. The Company believes that the interest rate swap will be an effective hedge and any changes in the fair market value will be included in other comprehensive income, subsequent to the adoption of SFAS 133.

Foreign Currency Translation

The Canadian dollar is the functional currency for the Canadian businesses. In accordance with SFAS Statement No. 52, *Foreign Currency Translation*, assets and liabilities denominated in foreign currencies were translated into U.S. dollars at the exchange rate prevailing at February 3, 2001. Revenues and expenses denominated in foreign currencies were translated into U.S. dollars (the reporting currency) at the monthly average exchange rate for the period from acquisition through February 3, 2001. Gains or losses resulting from foreign currency transactions are included in the results of operations, whereas, related translation adjustments are reported as an element of other comprehensive income, net of income taxes, in accordance with SFAS Statement No. 130, *Reporting Comprehensive Income* (See Note 8 of the Consolidated Financial Statements).

Cash and Cash Equivalents

Cash includes cash equivalents. The Company considers all highly liquid investments purchased with a maturity of three months or less to be cash equivalents.

Short-term Investments

Cash in excess of operating requirements is invested in marketable equity or government debt obligations. As of February 3, 2001, short-term investments included investments with an original maturity of greater than three months (averaging approximately 8 months) and consisted primarily of tax-exempt municipal bonds, taxable federal agency notes, and commercial paper classified as available for sale.

Merchandise Inventory

Merchandise inventory is valued at the lower of average cost or market, utilizing the retail method. Average cost includes merchandise design and sourcing costs and related expenses.

The Company reviews its inventory levels in order to identify slow-moving merchandise and generally uses markdowns to clear merchandise. Markdowns may occur when inventory exceeds customer demand for reasons of style, seasonal adaptation, changes in customer preference, lack of consumer acceptance of fashion items, competition, or if it is determined that the inventory in stock will not sell at its currently ticketed price. Such markdowns may have an adverse impact on earnings, depending on the extent and amount of inventory affected.

Property and Equipment

Property and equipment is recorded on the basis of cost with depreciation computed utilizing the straight-line method over the estimated useful lives as follows:

Buildings—25 to 40 years
Leasehold improvements—5 to 10 years
Fixtures and equipment—3 to 8 years

In accordance with SFAS No. 121, *Accounting for the Impairment of Long-Lived Assets and for Long-Lived Assets to Be Disposed Of*, management evaluates the ongoing value of leasehold improvements and store fixtures associated with retail stores which have been open longer than one year. Impairment losses are recorded on long-lived assets used in operations when events and circumstances indicate that the assets might be impaired and the undiscounted cash flows estimated to be generated by those assets are less than the carrying amounts of those assets. When events such as these occur, the impaired assets are adjusted to estimated fair value. The impairment loss, included in selling, general and administrative expenses for Fiscal 2000 was $0.5 million. There were no impairment losses for Fiscal 1999. The impairment loss for Fiscal 1998 was $0.2 million.

Goodwill

Goodwill amounts of $16.3 million in connection with the Canadian acquisition and $8.5 million in connection with the purchase of importing operations from Schottenstein Stores Corporation are being amortized over 15 years using the straight-line method. The Company's policy is to periodically review the carrying value assigned to goodwill to determine if events have occurred which would require an adjustment to fair value. Management reviews the performance of the underlying operations including reviewing discounted cash flows from operations. There were no impairment losses relating to goodwill recognized for Fiscal 2000.

Other Assets

Other assets consist primarily of lease buyout costs, trademark costs, and organization costs. The lease buyout costs are amortized over the remaining life of the leases, generally for no greater than ten years. The trademark costs are amortized over five to fifteen years. Organization costs are amortized over five years. These assets, net of amortization, are presented as other assets (long-term) on the Consolidated Balance Sheets.

Interest Rate Swap

The Company's interest rate swap agreement is used to manage interest rate risk. Net settlement amounts under the interest rate swap agreement are recorded as adjustments to interest expense during the period incurred. The Company does not currently hold or issue derivative financial instruments for trading purposes.

Stock Split

On January 22, 2001, the Company's Board of Directors announced a three-for-two stock split which was distributed on February 23, 2001, to shareholders of record on February 2, 2001. Accordingly, all share amounts and per share data have been restated to reflect the stock split.

Stock Repurchases

On February 24, 2000, the Company's Board of Directors authorized the repurchase of up to 3,750,000 shares (adjusted for the February 2001 stock split) of its stock. For the year ended February 3, 2001, the Company purchased 1,809,750 shares (adjusted for the February 2001 stock split) of common stock on the open market for approximately $22.3 million. These repurchases have been recorded as treasury stock.

Stock Option Plan

In October 1995, the FASB issued SFAS No. 123, *Accounting for Stock-Based Compensation*, which establishes financial accounting and reporting standards for stock-based employee compensation plans. The Company continues to account for its stock-based employee compensation plan using the intrinsic value method under Accounting Principles Board Opinion No. 25. See pro forma disclosures required under SFAS 123 in Note 12 of the Consolidated Financial Statements.

Revenue Recognition

Revenue is recorded upon purchase of merchandise by customers. In connection with stored value cards and gift certificates, a deferred revenue amount is established upon purchase of the card by the customer and revenue is recognized upon redemption and purchase of the merchandise.

AE Annual Report 2000   Consolidated Financial Statements

Advertising Costs

Advertising costs are expensed as
incurred. Advertising expense is
summarized as follows:

For the years ended	Feb 3, 2001	Jan 29, 2000	Jan 30, 1999
In thousands			
Advertising expense	$36,262	$27,243	$16,431

**Supplemental Disclosures
of Cash Flow Information**

For the years ended	Feb 3, 2001	Jan 29, 2000	Jan 30, 1999
In thousands			
Cash paid during the periods for:			
Income taxes	$37,362	$45,741	$41,706
Interest	$ 607	$ –	$ –

Earnings Per Share

The following table shows the amounts
used in computing earnings per share and
the effect on income and the weighted
average number of shares of dilutive
potential common stock (stock options and
restricted stock).

For the years ended	Feb 3, 2001	Jan 29, 2000	Jan 30, 1999
In thousands			
Net income	$93,758	$90,660	$54,118
Weighted average common shares outstanding:			
Basic shares	69,652	69,555	67,921
Dilutive effect of stock options and non-vested restricted stock	2,480	3,558	4,007
Diluted shares	72,132	73,113	71,928

Reclassification

Certain reclassifications have been made to
the Consolidated Financial Statements for
prior periods in order to conform to the
Fiscal 2000 presentation.

3. Business Acquisitions

Effective October 29, 2000, the Company purchased certain assets associated with three Canadian businesses of Dylex Limited. The total purchase price, including fees and expenses, was $78.2 million. The results of operations of the acquired businesses are included in the Consolidated Financial Statements beginning October 29, 2000. The acquisition was accounted for using the purchase method and the resulting goodwill of approximately $16.3 million is being amortized over fifteen years.

In connection with the acquisition, the Company announced its intention to convert certain retail locations to American Eagle retail stores. Management has finalized and approved the plan related to this conversion. Accordingly, the Company accrued approximately $7.3 million in exit costs consisting primarily of operating losses of the discontinued businesses, lease costs, and severance costs. Substantially all of the costs accrued will be paid during Fiscal 2001. The conversion plan is expected to be completed by the end of July 2001.

The purchase price allocation is preliminary and may be adjusted as new facts become apparent. However, management does not believe that any potential change will be material.

The following unaudited pro forma consolidated results of operations of the Company assume that the purchase occurred on January 31, 1999.

These amounts are based upon certain assumptions and estimates, which the Company believes are reasonable. The pro forma results do not necessarily represent results which would have occurred if the business combination had taken place at the date and on the basis assumed above.

For the years ended	Feb 3, 2001	Jan 29, 2000
In thousands, except per share amounts		
Net sales	$1,209,878	$1,002,063
Net income	$82,596	$84,399
Basic earnings per common share	$1.19	$1.21
Diluted earnings per common share	$1.15	$1.15

Effective January 31, 2000, the Company acquired importing operations from Schottenstein Stores Corporation, a related party. The purpose of the acquisition was to integrate the expertise of the importing operation into the Company's supply chain process, and to streamline and improve the efficiency of the process.

The terms of the acquisition required a payment of $8.5 million to Schottenstein Stores Corporation, which was made on March 6, 2000. The majority of the acquisition price was recorded as goodwill which is being amortized over fifteen years.

AE Annual Report 2000   Consolidated Financial Statements

4. Related Party Transactions

The Company has various transactions with related parties. The nature of the relationship with each party is primarily through common ownership. In September 1999, our distribution center facility, which is owned by a related party, was expanded to add 120,000 square feet which increased our capacity to handle distribution needs for future growth. As a result, the Company entered into an amended operating lease for its corporate headquarters and distribution center with a related party. The lease, which commenced on September 1, 1999, and expires on December 31, 2020 provides for annual rental payments of approximately $2.0 million through 2000, $2.4 million through 2005, $2.6 million through 2015, and $2.7 million through the end of the lease.

In addition, through Fiscal 1999, the Company and its subsidiaries used the services of a related importing company. Effective January 31, 2000, the Company acquired this importing operation from Schottenstein Stores Corporation, a related party. As a result, there were no related party merchandise purchases or an accounts payable balance for Fiscal 2000.

The Company has engaged the services of a related party consultant to assist with the liquidation of the Braemar inventory. The agreement is in effect until the Braemar stores are closed and the store locations are turned over to the Company for conversion to American Eagle stores. Compensation is determined by several factors, including proceeds from the sale of inventory and store performance versus plan. During Fiscal 2000, the Company paid $0.1 million to the consultant, excluding reimbursement of direct expenses. The amount included as exit costs at February 3, 2001 was $0.6 million.

Related party amounts follow:

For the years ended	Feb 3, 2001	Jan 29, 2000	Jan 30, 1999
In thousands			
Merchandise purchases through a related party importer	$ –	$ 63,763	$ 46,885
Accounts payable	$ –	$ 682	$ –
Accounts receivable	$ 2,149	$ 2,436	$ 2,829
Rent expense	$ 2,541	$ 1,896	$ 1,548
Merchandise sales	$ 11,540	$ 7,388	$ 3,289

5. Accounts and Note Receivable

Accounts and note receivable is comprised of the following:

	Feb 3, 2001	Jan 29, 2000	Jan 30, 1999
In thousands			
Accounts receivable—construction allowances	$7,346	$3,846	$4,008
Related party accounts receivable	2,149	2,436	2,829
Note receivable	5,904	3,417	–
Accounts receivable—other	14,067	3,772	1,723
Total	$29,466	$13,471	$8,560

AE Annual Report 2000   Consolidated Financial Statements

6. Property and Equipment

Property and equipment consists
of the following:

	Feb 3, 2001	Jan 29, 2000	Jan 30, 1999
In thousands			
Land	$ 1,855	$ –	$ –
Buildings	10,266	–	–
Leasehold improvements	134,930	70,403	46,996
Fixtures and equipment	93,186	52,336	36,307
Subtotal	240,237	122,739	83,303
Less: Accumulated depreciation and amortization	(56,864)	(37,813)	(29,933)
Net property and equipment	$183,373	$84,926	$53,370

Depreciation expense is summarized
as follows:

For the years ended	Feb 3, 2001	Jan 29, 2000	Jan 30, 1999
In thousands			
Depreciation expense	$21,472	$11,782	$8,215

AE Annual Report 2000 Consolidated Financial Statements

7. Note Payable

Unsecured Demand Lending Arrangement

The Company has an unsecured demand lending arrangement (the "facility") with a bank to provide a $125 million line of credit at either the lender's prime lending rate (8.50% at February 3, 2001) or a negotiated rate such as LIBOR. Because there were no borrowings during any of the past three years, there were no amounts paid for interest on this facility. The facility has a limit of $40 million to be used for direct borrowing. At February 3, 2001, letters of credit in the amount of $66.8 million were outstanding, leaving a remaining available balance on the line of $58.2 million.

Non-revolving Term Facility and Revolving Operating Facility

In November 2000, in connection with the Canadian acquisition, the Company entered into a $29.1 million non-revolving term facility (the "term facility") and a $4.9 million revolving operating facility (the "operating facility"). The term facility was used to partially fund the purchase price of the acquisition and the operating facility will be used to support the working capital and capital expenditures of the acquired businesses. The term facility has an outstanding balance, including foreign currency translation adjustments, of $29.2 million as of February 3, 2001. The facility requires annual payments of $4.3 million and matures in December 2007. The term facility bears interest at the one-month Bankers' Acceptance Rate (5.50% at February 3, 2001) plus 140 basis points. Interest paid under the term facility was $0.3 million for the year ended February 3, 2001. The operating facility is due in November 2001 and has six additional one year extensions. There have been no borrowings under the operating facility for the year ended February 3, 2001. The operating facility bears interest at either the lender's prime lending rate (7.50% at February 3, 2001) or the Bankers' Acceptance Rate (5.50% at February 3, 2001) plus 120 basis points.

Both the term facility and the operating facility contain restrictive covenants related to financial ratios. As of February 3, 2001, the Company was in compliance with these covenants.

Interest Rate Swap Agreement

On November 30, 2000, the Company entered into an interest rate swap agreement totaling $29.2 million in connection with the term facility. The swap amount decreases on a monthly basis beginning January 1, 2001 until the termination of the agreement in December 2007. The Company pays a fixed rate of 5.97% and receives a variable rate based on the one month Bankers' Acceptance Rate. This agreement effectively changes the interest rate on the borrowings under the term facility from a variable rate to a fixed rate of 5.97% plus 140 basis points. The Company does not believe there is any significant exposure to credit risk due to the creditworthiness of the bank. In the event of non-performance by the bank, the Company's loss would be limited to any unfavorable interest rate differential.

8. Other Comprehensive Income

The accumulated balances of other comprehensive income included as part of the Consolidated Statements of Stockholders' Equity follow:

In thousands

	Before Tax Amount	Tax Benefit (Expense)	Other Comprehensive Income (Loss), Net
Balance at January 30, 1999	$ –	$ –	$ –
Unrealized loss on investments	(3,766)	1,480	(2,286)
Balance at January 29, 2000	(3,766)	1,480	(2,286)
Unrealized gain on investments and reclassification adjustment	3,766	(1,480)	2,286
Foreign currency translation adjustment	770	(416)	354
Balance at February 3, 2001	$ 770	($416)	$ 354

AE Annual Report 2000   Consolidated Financial Statements

9. Leases

All store operations are conducted from leased premises. These leases generally provide for base rentals and the payment of a percentage of sales as additional rent when sales exceed specified levels. Minimum rentals relating to these leases are recorded on a straight-line basis. In addition, the Company is typically responsible under its leases for common area maintenance charges, real estate taxes and certain other expenses. These leases are classified as operating leases.

Rent expense charged to operations, including amounts paid under short-term cancelable leases, was as follows:

For the years ended	Feb 3, 2001	Jan 29, 2000	Jan 30, 1999
In thousands			
Minimum rentals	$90,467	$66,437	$53,482
Contingent rentals	13,113	10,736	6,177
Total	$103,580	$77,173	$59,659

The table below summarizes future minimum lease obligations under operating leases in effect at February 3, 2001:

Fiscal Years	
In thousands	
2001	$84,586
2002	82,315
2003	78,597
2004	74,708
2005	67,000
Thereafter	286,323
Total	$673,529

The Company may be contingently liable for the remaining rental payments that could total as much as $6.2 million for the outlet stores which were sold in October 1995. In January 2000, the company which owns the outlet stores sought protection under Chapter 11 of the Bankruptcy Act. Currently, there is insufficient information available to determine the amount of loss the Company may incur, if any, related to this potential contingent liability.

AE Annual Report 2000   Consolidated Financial Statements

10. Income Taxes

The significant components of the
Company's deferred tax assets (there are
no deferred tax liabilities) were as follows:

	Feb 3, 2001	Jan 29, 2000	Jan 30, 1999
In thousands			
Current			
Inventories	$4,940	$4,048	$2,826
Accrued rent	5,434	4,055	3,375
Salaries and compensation	8,624	3,565	1,274
Marketable equity securities and capital loss	1,749	1,530	–
Purchase accounting basis differences	3,869	–	–
Other	278	386	724
	24,894	13,584	8,199
Long Term			
Purchase accounting basis differences	6,969	–	–
Basis differences in fixed assets	2,771	2,410	2,200
Other comprehensive loss	–	1,472	–
Other	389	147	–
	10,129	4,029	2,200
Total	$35,023	$17,613	$10,399

AE Annual Report 2000   Consolidated Financial Statements

Significant components of the provision
for income taxes are as follows:

For the years ended	Feb 3, 2001	Jan 29, 2000	Jan 30, 1999
In thousands			
Current			
Federal	$57,675	$55,033	$31,819
State	7,939	10,875	6,305
Total current	65,614	65,908	38,124
Deferred			
Federal	(5,776)	(6,024)	(2,298)
State	(796)	(1,190)	(455)
Total deferred	(6,572)	(7,214)	(2,753)
Provision for income taxes	$59,042	$58,694	$35,371

A tax benefit has been recognized as contributed capital, in the amount of $12.0 million for the year ended February 3, 2001, $16.4 million for the year ended January 29, 2000, and $2.3 million for the year ended January 30, 1999, resulting from additional tax deductions related to vested restricted stock grants and stock options exercised.

A reconciliation between the statutory federal income tax and the effective tax rate follows:

For the years ended	Feb 3, 2001	Jan 29, 2000	Jan 30, 1999
Federal income tax rate	35%	35%	35%
State income taxes, net of federal income tax effect	4	4	4
Other items, net	–	–	1
	39%	39%	40%

11. Profit Sharing Plan and Employee Stock Purchase Plan

The Company maintains a 401(k) retirement plan and contributory profit sharing plan. Full-time employees and part-time employees are automatically enrolled to contribute 1% of their salary if they have attained twenty and one-half years of age, have completed sixty days of service, and work at least 1,000 hours each year. Individuals can decline enrollment or can contribute up to 20% of their salary to the 401(k) plan on a pretax basis, subject to IRS limitations. After one year of service, the Company will fully match up to 3% of participants' eligible compensation. In January 2001, the plan was amended to change the 1,000 hour requirement to an average work week of twenty hours and to increase the automatic enrollment contribution from 1% to 3%. In addition, after one year of service, the Company will fully match up to 3% of participants' eligible compensation and partially match the next 3% of eligible compensation, with a total match of 4.5%.

Contributions to the profit sharing plan, as determined by the Board of Directors, are discretionary. The Company recognized $1.0 million, $2.0 million, and $2.9 million in expense during Fiscal 2000, Fiscal 1999, and Fiscal 1998, respectively, in connection with these plans.

The Employee Stock Purchase Plan is a non-qualified plan that covers employees who are at least 18 years old, have completed sixty days of service, and work on average twenty hours a week. Contributions are determined by the employee, with a maximum of $60 per pay period, with the Company matching 15% of the investment. These contributions are used to purchase shares of Company stock in the open market.

12. Stock Incentive Plan, Stock Option Plan, and Restricted Stock Grants

Stock Incentive Plan

The 1999 Stock Incentive Plan (the "Plan") was approved by the shareholders on June 8, 1999. The Board of Directors authorized 6,000,000 shares for issuance under the Plan in the form of stock options, stock appreciation rights, restricted stock awards, performance units, or performance shares. Additionally, the Plan provides that the maximum number of shares awarded to one individual may not exceed 3,000,000 shares. The Plan allows the Compensation and Stock Option Committee to determine which employees and consultants will receive awards and the terms and conditions of these awards. The Plan provides for a grant of 15,000 stock options annually to each director who is not an officer or employee of the Company. These options are granted in quarterly increments, vest one year from date of grant, and are exercisable for a ten-year period from the date of grant. To date, 5,119,200 non-qualified stock options and 370,906 shares of restricted stock were granted under the Plan to employees and certain non-employees. Approximately half of the options granted vest eight years after the date of grant but can be accelerated to vest over three years if the Company meets annual performance goals. The remaining options granted under the Plan vest primarily over five years. All options expire after ten years. Restricted stock is earned if the Company meets annual performance goals for the year. For Fiscal 2000 and Fiscal 1999, the Company recorded approximately $7.0 and $5.8 million, respectively, in compensation expense related to stock options and restricted stock in connection with the Plan.

During Fiscal 2000, a senior executive assumed a new position within the Company. As a result of this change, the Company accelerated the vesting on grants covering 780,000 shares of stock for this individual. This acceleration does not result in additional compensation expense unless this executive ceases employment with the Company prior to the original vesting dates. If this had occurred at February 3, 2001, the compensation expense would have reduced net income by $12.7 million.

Stock Option Plan

On February 10, 1994, the Company's Board of Directors adopted the American Eagle Outfitters, Inc. 1994 Stock Option Plan (the "Plan"). The Plan provides for the grant of 4,050,000 incentive or non-qualified options to purchase common stock. The Plan was subsequently amended to increase the shares available for grant to 8,100,000 shares. Additionally, the amendment provided that the maximum number of options which may be granted to one individual may not exceed 2,700,000 shares. The options granted under the Plan are approved by the Compensation and Stock Option Committee of the Board of Directors, primarily vest over five years, and are exercisable for a ten-year period from the date of grant.

AE Annual Report 2000   Consolidated Financial Statements

Pro forma information regarding net income and earnings per share is required by SFAS No. 123, which also requires that the information be determined as if the Company has accounted for its employee stock options granted beginning in the fiscal year subsequent to December 31, 1994 under the fair value method of that Statement. The fair value for these options was estimated at the date of grant using a Black-Scholes option pricing model with the following weighted-average assumptions:

For the years ended	Feb 3, 2001	Jan 29, 2000	Jan 30, 1999
Risk-free interest rates	5.8 %	5.5%	5.0%
Dividend yield	None	None	None
Volatility factors of the expected market price of the Company's common stock	.933	.600	.678
Weighted-average expected life	5 years	5 years	6 years
Expected forfeiture rate	9.3%	10.0%	12.0%

The Black-Scholes option valuation model was developed for use in estimating the fair value of traded options which have no vesting restrictions and are fully transferable. In addition, option valuation models require the input of highly subjective assumptions including the expected stock price volatility. Because the Company's employee stock options have characteristics significantly different from those of traded options, and because changes in the subjective input assumptions can materially affect the fair value estimate, in management's opinion, the existing models do not necessarily provide a reliable single measure of the fair value of its employee stock options.

For purposes of pro forma disclosures, the estimated fair value of the options is amortized to expense over the options' vesting period. The Company's pro forma information follows:

For the years ended	Feb 3, 2001	Jan 29, 2000	Jan 30, 1999
In thousands, except earnings per share			
Pro forma net income	$85,028	$83,014	$52,467
Pro forma net income per share			
Basic	$1.22	$1.19	$0.77
Diluted	$1.18	$1.14	$0.73

AE Annual Report 2000   Consolidated Financial Statements

A summary of the Company's stock option
activity under all plans follows:

For the years ended	Feb 3, 2001 (2)		Jan 29, 2000 (2)		Jan 30, 1999 (2)	
	Options	Weighted-Average Exercise Price	Options	Weighted-Average Exercise Price	Options	Weighted-Average Exercise Price
Outstanding—beginning of year	7,281,045	$11.21	5,289,645	$3.47	5,034,357	$1.41
Granted (Exercise price equal to fair value)	2,539,950	$20.49	3,043,350	$22.23	1,854,228	$7.44
Exercised (1)	(1,865,837)	$5.46	(941,580)	$2.84	(1,425,909)	$1.25
Cancelled	(179,820)	$14.80	(110,370)	$15.21	(173,031)	$4.13
Outstanding—end of year (3)	7,775,338	$15.52	7,281,045	$11.21	5,289,645	$3.47
Exercisable—end of year (4)	1,772,151	$13.25	1,515,820	$3.37	829,836	$1.58
Weighted-average fair value of options granted during the year		$16.62		$13.79		$4.61

(1) Options exercised during Fiscal 2000 ranged in price from $0.93- $31.04 with an average of $5.46.
(2) As of February 3, 2001, January 29, 2000, and January 30, 1999, the Company had 845,195 shares, 3,498,558 shares and 431,208 shares available for grant, respectively.
(3) As of February 3, 2001, the exercise price of 2,396,418 options outstanding ranged between $0.93 and $5.94 with weighted-average remaining contractual lives between approximately 5 and 7 years. The exercise price of 1,435,415 options outstanding ranged between $9.35 and $17.98 with weighted-average remaining contractual lives between approximately 7 and 9 years. The exercise price of 2,786,881 options outstanding ranged between $21.67 and $25.50 with weighted-average remaining contractual lives between 8 and 9 years. The exercise price of 1,156,624 options outstanding ranged between $26.29 and $36.56 with weighted-average remaining contractual lives approximating 10 years.
(4) As of February 3, 2001, the exercise price of 774,212 options exercisable ranged between $0.93 and $5.94. The exercise price of 725,285 options ranged between $11.79 and $21.79.

Restricted Stock Grants

The Company maintains a restricted stock plan for compensating certain employees and selected related party consultants. At February 3, 2001, 2,347,317 shares of restricted stock were granted at prices ranging from $0.93 to $28.25, with 1,981,212 shares vested.

For Fiscal 2000, Fiscal 1999, and Fiscal 1998, the Company recorded $6.2 million, $4.8 million, and $1.3 million in compensation expense, respectively, on restricted stock and certain stock options granted during Fiscal 1996 where the exercise price is less than fair value of the underlying stock, and certain options granted to non-employees.

AE Annual Report 2000   Consolidated Financial Statements

13. Quarterly Financial Information—Unaudited

For the quarters ended (2)	Apr 29, 2000	Jul 29, 2000	Oct 28, 2000	Feb 3, 2001
In thousands, except earnings per share				
Net sales	$ 177,999	$ 208,977	$ 282,767	$ 423,734
Gross profit	$ 70,056	$ 63,590	$ 120,079	$ 182,500
Income before income taxes	$ 20,771	$ 4,570	$ 47,912	$ 79,547
Net income	$ 12,608	$ 2,777	$ 29,226	$ 49,147
Basic earnings per common share (1)	$ 0.18	$ 0.04	$ 0.42	$ 0.71
Diluted earnings per common share (1)	$ 0.17	$ 0.04	$ 0.41	$ 0.68

	May 1, 1999	Jul 31, 1999	Oct 30, 1999	Jan 29, 2000
Net sales	$ 145,404	$ 178,582	$ 222,693	$ 285,425
Gross profit	$ 59,027	$ 72,589	$ 95,844	$ 129,048
Income before income taxes	$ 20,169	$ 27,928	$ 40,096	$ 61,161
Net income	$ 12,243	$ 16,949	$ 24,337	$ 37,131
Basic earnings per common share (1)	$ 0.18	$ 0.24	$ 0.35	$ 0.53
Diluted earnings per common share (1)	$ 0.17	$ 0.23	$ 0.33	$ 0.51

(1) Net income per share amounts have been restated to reflect the two-for-one stock split from May 1999 and the three-for-two stock split from February 2001.
(2) Quarters are presented in 13-week periods consistent with the Company's fiscal year discussed in Note 2 of the Consolidated Financial Statements, except for the fourth quarter ended February 3, 2001, which is presented as a 14-week period.

MARKET PRICE INFORMATION

Our stock is traded on The Nasdaq National Market under the symbol "AEOS". The following table sets forth the range of high and low sales prices of the common stock as reported on The Nasdaq National Market during the periods indicated. As of March 20, 2001, there were 186 stockholders of record. However, when including associates who own shares through the Company's 401(k) retirement plan and employee stock purchase plan and others holding shares in broker accounts under street name, the Company estimates the shareholder base at approximately 31,700. The following information reflects the May 1999 and February 2001 stock splits.

Market price For the quarters ended	High	Low
January 2001	$38.58	$22.33
October 2000	$23.92	$9.92
July 2000	$13.83	$7.92
April 2000	$25.29	$11.33
January 2000	$33.09	$23.04
October 1999	$38.42	$21.79
July 1999	$34.46	$25.25
April 1999	$29.25	$20.87

We have never paid cash dividends and presently anticipate that all of our future earnings will be retained for the development of our business and the stock repurchase program (See Note 2 of the Consolidated Financial Statements). We do not anticipate paying cash dividends in the foreseeable future. The payment of any future dividends will be at the discretion of our Board of Directors and will be based on future earnings, financial condition, capital requirements and other relevant factors.

MANAGEMENT AND INDEPENDENT
AUDITORS' REPORTS

**Management Responsibility
for Financial Reporting**

The integrity and objectivity of the financial statements and related financial information in this report are the responsibility of the management of the Company. The financial statements have been prepared in conformity with generally accepted accounting principles and include, when necessary, the best estimates and judgements of management.

We maintain a system of internal accounting controls designed to provide reasonable assurance, at appropriate cost, that assets are safeguarded, transactions are executed in accordance with our authorization, and the accounting records provide a reliable basis for the preparation of the financial statements. The system of internal accounting controls is continually reviewed by management and improved and modified as necessary in response to changing business conditions and recommendations of the Company's independent auditors.

The Audit Committee of the Board of Directors, consisting of independent directors, meets periodically with management and independent auditors to review matters relating to our financial reporting, the adequacy of internal accounting controls and the scope and results of audit work.

Ernst & Young LLP, Certified Public Accountants, are engaged to audit our consolidated financial statements. Their Independent Auditors' Report, which is based on an audit made in accordance with generally accepted auditing standards, expresses an opinion as to the fair presentation of these financial statements.

Report of Independent Auditors

To the Board of Directors and Stockholders of American Eagle Outfitters, Inc.

We have audited the accompanying consolidated balance sheets of American Eagle Outfitters, Inc. as of February 3, 2001, January 29, 2000, and January 30, 1999 and the related consolidated statements of operations, stockholders' equity, and cash flows for the years then ended. The financial statements are the responsibility of the Company's management. Our responsibility is to express an opinion on these financial statements based on our audits.

We conducted our audits in accordance with auditing standards generally accepted in the United States. Those standards require that we plan and perform the audit to obtain reasonable assurance about whether the financial statements are free of material misstatement. An audit includes examining, on a test basis, evidence supporting the amounts and disclosures in the financial statements. An audit also includes assessing the accounting principles used and significant estimates made by management, as well as evaluating the overall financial statement presentation. We believe that our audits provide a reasonable basis for our opinion.

In our opinion, the consolidated financial statements referred to above present fairly, in all material respects, the consolidated financial position of American Eagle Outfitters, Inc. at February 3, 2001, January 29, 2000, and January 30, 1999 and the consolidated results of its operations and its cash flows for the years then ended, in conformity with accounting principles generally accepted in the United States.

Ernst & Young LLP

Pittsburgh, Pennsylvania
March 9, 2001

DIRECTORS AND OFFICERS

Directors

Jay L. Schottenstein
Chairman of the Board and
Chief Executive Officer

Saul Schottenstein
Vice Chairman

George Kolber
Vice Chairman of the Company and CEO
of Value City Department Stores, Inc.

Roger S. Markfield
President and Chief Merchandising Officer

James V. O'Donnell
Chief Operating Officer

Ari Deshe
Chairman and Chief Executive
Officer of Safe Auto Insurance Company

Jon P. Diamond
President and Chief Operating
Officer of Safe Auto Insurance Company

Martin P. Doolan
President of Multitech
Enterprises, Inc.

Gilbert W. Harrison
Chairman of Financo, Inc.

Michael G. Jesselson
President of Jesselson Capital Corporation

Thomas R. Ketteler
Executive Vice President of Finance,
Treasurer, and Chief Operating Officer
of Schottenstein Stores Corporation

John L. Marakas
Retired President of Nationwide
Corporation

David W. Thompson
President of Value City Furniture

Gerald E. Wedren
President of Craig Capital Co.

Executive Officers

Jay L. Schottenstein
Chairman of the Board and
Chief Executive Officer

Roger S. Markfield
President and Chief Merchandising Officer

James V. O'Donnell
Chief Operating Officer

Laura A. Weil
Executive Vice President
and Chief Financial Officer

Joseph E. Kerin
Executive Vice President and
Director of Store Operations

Michael James Leedy
Executive Vice President,
Marketing and E-Commerce

Dale E. Clifton
Vice President, Controller,
and Chief Accounting Officer

Sheila C. Reinken
Vice President of Finance and Treasurer

Corporate Officers

Steven L. Baum
Vice President,
Director of Design

Neil Bulman, Jr.
Vice President,
General Counsel and
Secretary

Andrew M. Calogero
President, Prophecy Company

Joseph C. D'Aversa
Vice President, Men's Design

Michael J. Fostyk
Vice President, Distribution

Robin Gray
Vice President, Planning and Allocation

Frederick W. Grover
Vice President,
General Merchandising Manager

Howard Landon
Vice President, Production and Sourcing

Susan P. Miller
Vice President,
General Merchandising Manager

Jeffrey D. Skoglind
Vice President,
Human Resources

Jeffrey G. Smith
Vice President,
Real Estate

Ken Watts
Vice President,
Information Services

STOCKHOLDER INFORMATION

We will supply to any stockholder, upon written request to Laura A. Weil, at our address, and without charge, a copy of the Report on Form 10-K for the period ended February 3, 2001, which has been filed with the Securities and Exchange Commission.

Independent Auditors

Ernst & Young LLP
One Oxford Centre
Pittsburgh, PA 15219-6403

Common Shares Listed

NASDAQ Symbol

AEOS

Legal Counsel

Porter, Wright, Morris & Arthur
41 South High Street
Columbus, OH 43215-6194

Registrar and Transfer Agent

National City Bank
Stock Transfer Department
P.O. Box 92301
Cleveland, OH 44193-0900
(800) 622-6757

Investor Contact

Laura A. Weil
Executive Vice President and
Chief Financial Officer
(724) 776-4857

Headquarters of the Company

American Eagle Outfitters
150 Thorn Hill Drive
Warrendale, PA 15086-7528
(724) 776-4857

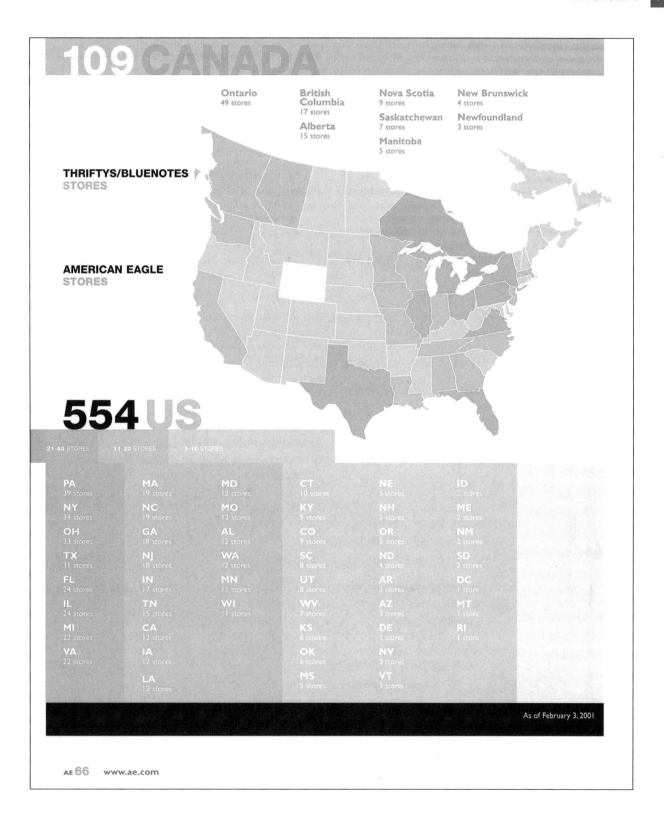

109 CANADA

Ontario	British Columbia	Nova Scotia	New Brunswick
49 stores	17 stores	9 stores	4 stores
	Alberta	Saskatchewan	Newfoundland
	15 stores	7 stores	3 stores
		Manitoba	
		5 stores	

THRIFTYS/BLUENOTES
STORES

AMERICAN EAGLE
STORES

554 US

21-40 STORES	11-20 STORES	1-10 STORES			
PA	MA	MD	CT	NE	ID
39 stores	19 stores	12 stores	10 stores	5 stores	2 stores
NY	NC	MO	KY	NH	ME
34 stores	19 stores	12 stores	9 stores	5 stores	2 stores
OH	GA	AL	CO	OR	NM
33 stores	18 stores	12 stores	9 stores	5 stores	2 stores
TX	NJ	WA	SC	ND	SD
31 stores	18 stores	12 stores	8 stores	4 stores	2 stores
FL	IN	MN	UT	AR	DC
24 stores	17 stores	11 stores	8 stores	3 stores	1 store
IL	TN	WI	WV	AZ	MT
24 stores	15 stores	11 stores	7 stores	3 stores	1 store
MI	CA		KS	DE	RI
22 stores	12 stores		6 stores	3 stores	1 store
VA	IA		OK	NV	
22 stores	12 stores		6 stores	3 stores	
	LA		MS	VT	
	12 stores		5 stores	3 stores	

As of February 3, 2001

AE 66   www.ae.com

ABERCROMBIE & FITCH CO.

Abercrombie & Fitch Co., a Delaware corporation ("A&F"), through its subsidiaries (collectively, A&F and its subsidiaries are referred to as "Abercrombie & Fitch" or the "Company"), is principally engaged in the purchase, distribution and sale of men's, women's and kids' casual apparel. The Company's retail activities are conducted under the Abercrombie & Fitch and abercrombie trade names through retail stores, a catalogue, a magazine/catalogue and a web site, all bearing some form of the Company name. Retail activities are also conducted under the Hollister Co. trade name through retail stores and a lifestyle web site. Merchandise is targeted to appeal to customers in specialty markets who have distinctive consumer characteristics.

At the end of fiscal year 2000, the Company operated 354 stores. The following table shows the changes in the number of retail stores operated by the Company for the past five fiscal years:

Fiscal Year	Beginning of Year	Opened	Closed	End of Year
1996	100	29	(2)	127
1997	127	30	(1)	156
1998	156	41	(1)	196
1999	196	54		250
2000	250	104		354

During fiscal year 2000, the Company purchased merchandise from approximately 100 suppliers and factories located throughout the world.

The Company's policy is to maintain sufficient quantities of inventory on hand in its retail stores and distribution center so that it can offer customers a full selection of current merchandise. The Company emphasizes rapid turnover and takes markdowns where required to keep merchandise fresh and current with fashion trends.

The Company views the retail apparel market as having two principal selling seasons, Spring and Fall. As is generally the case in the apparel industry, the Company experiences its peak sales activity during the Fall season. This seasonal sales pattern results in increased inventory during the back-to-school and Christmas selling periods. During fiscal year 2000, the highest inventory level approximated $147.9 million at the November 2000 month-end and the lowest inventory level approximated $82.1 million at the February 2000 month-end.

Merchandise sales are paid for by cash, personal check, gift certificate and gift card redemption or credit cards issued by third parties, including a private label credit card. The Company offers its customers a liberal return policy stated as "No Sale is Ever Final." The Company believes that certain of its competitors offer similar credit card and service policies.

ABERCROMBIE & FITCH
FINANCIAL SUMMARY

(Thousands except per share and per square foot amounts, ratios and store and associate data)

Fiscal Year	2000*	1999	1998	1997	1996	1995*	1994
SUMMARY OF OPERATIONS							
Net Sales	$1,237,604	$1,030,858	$805,180	$513,109	$329,800	$232,415	$163,156
Gross Income	$ 509,375	$ 450,383	$331,354	$191,890	$118,194	$ 76,550	$ 54,513
Operating Income	$ 253,652	$ 242,064	$166,958	$ 84,125	$ 45,993	$ 23,798	$ 13,751
Operating Income as a Percentage of Sales	20.5%	23.5%	20.7%	16.4%	13.9%	10.2%	8.4%
Net Income	$ 158,133	$ 149,604	$102,062	$ 48,322	$ 24,674	$ 14,298	$ 8,251
Net Income as a Percentage of Sales	12.8%	14.5%	12.7%	9.4%	7.5%	6.2%	5.1%

PER SHARE RESULTS (1)

Net Income Per Basic Share	$1.58	$1.45	$.99	$.47	$.27	$.17	$.10
Net Income Per Diluted Share	$1.55	$1.39	$.96	$.47	$.27	$.17	$.10
Weighted Average Diluted Shares Outstanding	102,156	107,641	106,202	102,956	91,520	86,000	86,000

OTHER FINANCIAL INFORMATION

Total Assets	$587,516	$458,166	$319,161	$183,238	$105,761	$ 87,693	$ 58,018
Return on Average Assets	30%	38%	41%	33%	26%	20%	15%
Capital Expenditures	$153,481	$ 73,377	$ 37,483	$ 29,486	$ 24,323	$ 24,526	$ 12,603
Long-Term Debt	—	—	—	$ 50,000	$ 50,000	—	—
Shareholders' Equity (Deficit)	$422,700	$311,094	$186,105	$ 58,775	$ 11,238	$ (22,622)	$ (37,070)
Comparable Store Sales Increase (Decrease)	(7%)	10%	35%	21%	13%	5%	15%
Retail Sales Per Average Gross Square Foot	$474	$505	$476	$370	$301	$286	$280

STORES AND ASSOCIATES AT END OF YEAR

Total Number of Stores Open	354	250	196	156	127	100	67
Gross Square Feet	2,849,000	2,174,000	1,791,000	1,522,000	1,229,000	962,000	665,000
Number of Associates	13,900	11,300	9,500	6,700	4,900	3,000	2,300

*Fifty-three week fiscal year.

(1) Per share amounts have been restated to reflect the two-for-one stock split on A&F's Class A Common Stock, distributed on June 15, 1999.

MANAGEMENT'S DISCUSSION AND ANALYSIS OF FINANCIAL CONDITION AND RESULTS OF OPERATIONS.

RESULTS OF OPERATIONS

Net sales for the fourth quarter of the 2000 fiscal year were $439.4 million, an increase of 21% from $363.7 million for the fourth quarter a year ago. Operating income was $124.1 million compared to $125.3 million last year. Net income per diluted share was $.76, up 4% from $.73 last year.

Net sales for the 2000 fiscal year increased 20% to $1.24 billion from $1.03 billion last year. Operating income for the year increased 5% to $253.7 million from $242.1 million in 1999. Net income per diluted share was $1.55 compared to $1.39 a year ago, an increase of 12%.

FINANCIAL SUMMARY

The following summarized financial data compares the 2000 fiscal year to the comparable periods for 1999 and 1998:

				% Change	
	2000	1999	1998	2000-1999	1999-1998
Net sales (millions)	$1,237.6	$1,030.9	$805.2	20%	28%
Increase (decrease) in comparable store sales	(7%)	10%	35%		
Retail sales increase attributable to new and remodeled stores, magazine, catalogue and web site	27%	18%	22%		
Retail sales per average gross square foot	$ 474	$ 505	$ 476	(6%)	6%
Retail sales per average store (thousands)	$3,944	$4,487	$4,484	(12%)	—
Average store size at year-end (gross square feet)	8,047	8,695	9,140	(7%)	(5%)
Gross square feet at year-end (thousands)	2,849	2,174	1,791	31%	21%

Number of stores:

Beginning of year	250	196	156
Opened	104	54	41
Closed	—	—	(1)
End of year	354	250	196

NET SALES

Fourth quarter 2000 net sales increased 21% to $439.4 million from $363.7 million in 1999. The increase was due to the addition of new stores offset by a 9% decline in comparable store sales. The decline in comparable store sales, based on a 14 week quarter for both 2000 and 1999, was primarily due to comparable store sales decreases in the men's graphic tees and pants departments. Comparable store sales were positive in the women's business for the quarter based on strong increases in the sweaters, denim and outerwear departments. The Company's catalogue, the *A&F Quarterly* (a catalogue/magazine) and the Company's web sites accounted for 5.0% of net sales in the fourth quarter of 2000 as compared to 3.8% in 1999.

Net sales for the fourth quarter of 1999 increased 21% to $363.7 million from $300.1 million in 1998. The increase was primarily due to the addition of new stores and a comparable store sales increase of 3%. Comparable store increases were driven by men's pants and knits while the women's knit business was very strong. The Company's catalogue, the *A&F Quarterly* and the Company's web site accounted for 3.8% of net sales in the fourth quarter of 1999 as compared to 2.2% in 1998.

Net sales for the 2000 fiscal year increased 20% to $1.24 billion from $1.03 billion in 1999. The sales increase was attributable to the addition of 104 stores offset by a 7% comparable store sales decrease. The decline in comparable store sales, based on a 53 week fiscal year for both 2000 and 1999, was across both the men's and women's businesses. During the year, the assortment in each business was repositioned to be more balanced and less focused on graphics and included items at key opening price points. The Company's catalogue, the *A&F Quarterly* and the Company's web sites represented 3.8% of 2000 net sales compared to 2.9% last year.

Net sales for the 1999 fiscal year increased 28% to $1.03 billion from $805.2 million in 1998. Sales growth resulted from a comparable store sales increase of 10% and the addition of 54 new stores. Comparable store sales increases were driven by both men's and women's knits and pants. Net retail sales per gross square foot for the Company increased 6%, principally from an increase in the number of transactions per store. The Company's catalogue, the *A&F Quarterly* and the Company's web site represented 2.9% of 1999 net sales compared to 2.0% of 1998 net sales.

GROSS INCOME

For the fourth quarter of 2000, gross income, expressed as a percentage of net sales, decreased to 46.2% from 50.9% for the same period in 1999. The decrease was attributable to lower merchandise margins (representing gross income before the deduction of buying and occupancy costs) due to lower initial markups (IMU) and higher markdowns. The IMU was affected by both a change in sales mix and the planned strategy of offering lower opening price points in key product classifications.

Gross income, expressed as a percentage of net sales, increased to 50.9% for the fourth quarter of 1999 from 48.3% for the same period in 1998. The increase was attributable to higher merchandise margins, resulting from higher IMU, and improved control of store inventory shrinkage and merchandise freight costs. The Company also achieved some leverage in buying and occupancy costs, expressed as a percentage of net sales.

For the year, the gross income rate decreased to 41.2% in 2000 from 43.7% in 1999. The decrease was attributable to lower merchandise margins, primarily due to lower IMU caused by both a change in sales mix and the planned strategy of offering lower opening price points in key product classifications.

In 1999, the gross income rate increased to 43.7% from 41.2% in 1998. Merchandise margins, expressed as a percentage of net sales, increased due to slightly higher IMU across most merchandise categories. In addition, buying and occupancy costs, expressed as a percentage of net sales, declined slightly due to leverage achieved from comparable store sales increases. The Company also improved the gross income rate through reduced freight costs and enhanced store inventory control procedures which reduced shrink cost.

GENERAL, ADMINISTRATIVE AND STORE OPERATING EXPENSES

General, administrative and store operating expenses, expressed as a percentage of net sales, were 17.9% in the fourth quarter of 2000 and 16.4% in the comparable period in 1999. The increase in the percentage was primarily due to the inability to leverage fixed expenses as a result of the decrease in comparable store sales. The increase was also due to planned one-time expenses related to the Company's move to a new home office and distribution center. The increases were offset by tightly controlled headcount additions, travel expenses, store payroll hours, outside services and compensation expense related to management bonuses.

General, administrative and store operating expenses, expressed as a percentage of net sales, were 16.4% in the fourth quarter of 1999 as compared to 15.4% for the same period in 1998. The increase in the percentage was primarily due to a change in the accounting for gift certificates and gift cards. This was partially offset by lower compensation expenses related to management bonuses and restricted share grants awarded to key executives of the Company. Additionally, the Company did not incur expenses related to service agreements with The Limited, Inc. that expired prior to the fourth quarter of 1999 and emphasized tighter expense control in travel, relocation and legal expenses.

General, administrative and store operating expenses for the year, expressed as a percentage of net sales, were 20.7%, 20.2% and 20.4% in 2000, 1999 and 1998, respectively. The rate has increased in 2000 primarily due to the inability to leverage fixed expenses as a result of the decrease in comparable store sales. The increase was partially offset by the Company's continued focus on discretionary expense controls. The 1999 improvement was due to the control of expenses and favorable leveraging of expenses due to higher comparable store sales.

OPERATING INCOME

Operating income, expressed as a percentage of net sales, was 28.2% and 20.5% for the fourth quarter and fiscal year of 2000, respectively, compared to 34.5% and 23.5% for the same periods in 1999. The decline in operating income as a percentage of sales in these periods is primarily a result of lower gross income percentages. Higher general, administrative and store operating expenses also added to the decrease in the operating income percentage of net sales.

Operating income, expressed as a percentage of net sales, was 34.5% and 23.5% for the fourth quarter and fiscal year of 1999, respectively, compared to 32.9% and 20.7% for the same periods in 1998. The improvement was the result of higher gross income coupled with lower general, administrative and store operating expenses, expressed as a percentage of net sales. Sales volume and gross income increased at a faster rate than general, administrative and store operating expenses due to the Company's emphasis on cost controls.

INTEREST INCOME/EXPENSE

Net interest income was $2.5 million in the fourth quarter of 2000 and $7.8 million for all of 2000 compared with net interest income of $2.5 million and $7.3 million for the corresponding periods last year. Net interest income in 2000 and 1999 was primarily from short-term investments.

FINANCIAL CONDITION

The Company's continuing growth in net income provides evidence of financial strength and flexibility. A more detailed discussion of liquidity, capital resources and capital requirements follows.

LIQUIDITY AND CAPITAL RESOURCES

Cash provided by operating activities provides the resources to support operations, including seasonal requirements and capital expenditures. A summary of the Company's working capital position and capitalization follows (thousands):

	2000	1999	1998
Working capital	$149,000	$162,351	$ 95,890
Capitalization Shareholders' equity	$422,700	$311,094	$186,105

The Company considers the following to be measures of liquidity and capital resources:

	2000	1999	1998
Current ratio (current assets divided by current liabilities)	1.96	2.18	1.78
Cash flow to capital investment (net cash provided by operating activities divided by capital expenditures)	99%	208%	451%

Net cash provided by operating activities totaled $151.2 million, $152.8 million and $169.0 million for 2000, 1999 and 1998, respectively. Cash was provided primarily by current year net income adjusted for depreciation and amortization, and increased accounts payable and accrued expenses needed to support the growth in inventories. Cash was used primarily to fund inventory purchases required to support the addition of new stores and the investment in new women's categories, including underwear, gymwear and fragrances. The inventory increase is also due to the timing of spring deliveries as a result of the 2000 fiscal year having 53 weeks. Additionally, cash used for income taxes increased due to the timing of income tax payments.

The Company's operations are seasonal in nature and typically peak during the back-to-school and Christmas selling periods. Accordingly, cash requirements for inventory expenditures are highest during these periods.

Cash outflows for investing activities were primarily for capital expenditures related to new and remodeled stores (net of construction allowances) and the construction costs of the new office and distribution center. In 2000 and 1999, investing activities also included maturities and purchases of marketable securities.

Financing activities during 2000 and 1999 consisted primarily of the repurchase of 3,550,000 shares and 1,510,000 shares, respectively, of A&F's Class A Common Stock pursuant to previously authorized stock repurchase programs. A&F is authorized to repurchase up to an additional 2,450,000 shares under the current repurchase program.

In 1998, financing activities consisted primarily of the repayment of $50 million long-term debt to The Limited. This occurred through the issuance of 1.2 million shares of Class A Common Stock to The Limited with the remaining balance paid with cash from operations. Additionally, settlement of the intercompany balance between the Company and The Limited occurred on May 19, 1998. During 1998, A&F also repurchased 490 thousand shares of Class A Common Stock.

CAPITAL EXPENDITURES

Capital expenditures, primarily for new and remodeled stores and the construction of a new office and distribution center, totaled $153.5 million, $73.4 million and $37.5 million for 2000, 1999 and 1998, respectively. Additionally, the noncash accrual for construction in progress totaled $9.5 million, $10.4 million and $4.4 million in 2000, 1999 and 1998, re-

spectively. Expenditures related to the new office and distribution center accounted for $92.3 million of total capital expenditures in 2000, of which $12.9 million was noncash accrual for construction in progress.

The Company anticipates spending $105 to $115 million in 2001 for capital expenditures, of which $85 to $95 million will be for new stores, remodeling and/or expansion of existing stores and related improvements. The balance of capital expenditures will chiefly be related to the construction of the new home office and distribution center. The distribution center was completed in February 2001 and the home office was completed in April 2001. The Company intends to add approximately 825,000 gross square feet in 2001, which will represent a 29% increase over year-end 2000. It is anticipated the increase will result from the addition of approximately 50 new Abercrombie & Fitch stores, 60 abercrombie stores and 20 Hollister Co. stores.

The Company estimates that the average cost for leasehold improvements and furniture and fixtures for Abercrombie & Fitch stores opened in 2001 will approximate $600,000 per store, after giving effect to landlord allowances. In addition, inventory purchases are expected to average approximately $300,000 per store.

The Company estimates that the average cost for leasehold improvements and furniture and fixtures for abercrombie stores opened in 2001 will approximate $500,000 per store, after giving effect to landlord allowances. In addition, inventory purchases are expected to average approximately $150,000 per store.

The Company is in the early stages of developing Hollister Co. As a result, current average costs for leasehold improvements, furniture and fixtures and inventory purchases are not representative of future costs.

The Company expects that substantially all future capital expenditures will be funded with cash from operations. In addition, the Company has available a $150 million credit agreement to support operations.

RELATIONSHIP WITH THE LIMITED

Effective May 19, 1998, The Limited, Inc. ("The Limited") completed a tax-free exchange offer to establish A&F as an independent company. Subsequent to the exchange offer (see Note 1 to the Consolidated Financial Statements), A&F and The Limited entered into various service agreements for terms ranging from one to three years. A&F hired associates with the appropriate expertise or contracted with outside parties to replace those services which expired in May 1999. Service agreements were also entered into for the continued use by the Company of its distribution and home office space and transportation and logistic services. The distribution space agreement terminates in April 2001. The home office space service agreement expires in May 2001. The agreement for transportation and logistic services will also expire in May 2001, although most of these services have already been transitioned to the Company. The cost of these services generally is equal to The Limited's cost in providing the relevant services plus 5% of such costs.

The Company does not anticipate that costs incurred to replace the services provided by The Limited will have a material adverse impact on its financial condition.

RECENTLY ISSUED ACCOUNTING PRONOUNCEMENTS

Statement of Financial Accounting Standards ("SFAS") No. 133, "Accounting for Derivative Instruments and Hedging Activities," subsequently amended and clarified by SFAS No. 138, is effective for the Company's 2001 fiscal year. It requires that derivative instruments be recorded at fair value and that changes in their fair value be recognized in current earnings unless specific hedging criteria are met. The adoption of this standard had no impact on the Company's financial position or results of operations.

IMPACT OF INFLATION

The Company's results of operations and financial condition are presented based upon historical cost. While it is difficult to accurately measure the impact of inflation due to the imprecise nature of the estimates required, the Company believes that the effects of inflation, if any, on its results of operations and financial condition have been minor.

SAFE HARBOR STATEMENT UNDER THE PRIVATE SECURITIES LITIGATION REFORM ACT OF 1995

A&F cautions that any forward-looking statements (as that term is defined in the Private Securities Litigation Reform Act of 1995) contained in this Report or made by management of A&F involve risks and uncertainties and are subject to change based on various important factors. The following factors, among others, in some cases have affected and in the future could affect the Company's financial performance and actual results and could cause actual results for 2001 and beyond to differ materially from those expressed or implied in any of the forward-looking statements included in this Form 10-K or otherwise made by management: changes in consumer spending patterns, consumer preferences and overall economic conditions, the impact of competition and pricing, changes in weather patterns, political stability, currency and exchange risks and changes in existing or potential duties, tariffs or quotas, availability of suitable store locations at appropriate terms, ability to develop new merchandise and ability to hire and train associates.

ABERCROMBIE & FITCH
CONSOLIDATED STATEMENTS OF INCOME

(Thousands except per share amounts)	2000	1999	1998
NET SALES	$1,237,604	$1,030,858	$805,180
Cost of Goods Sold, Occupancy and Buying Costs	728,229	580,475	473,826
GROSS INCOME	509,375	450,383	331,354
General, Administrative and Store Operating Expenses	255,723	208,319	164,396
OPERATING INCOME	253,652	242,064	166,958
Interest Income, Net	(7,801)	(7,270)	(3,144)
INCOME BEFORE INCOME TAXES	261,453	249,334	170,102
Provision for Income Taxes	103,320	99,730	68,040
NET INCOME	$ 158,133	$ 149,604	$102,062
NET INCOME PER SHARE:			
BASIC	$1.58	$1.45	$.99
DILUTED	$1.55	$1.39	$.96

The accompanying Notes are an integral part of these Consolidated Financial Statements.

ABERCROMBIE & FITCH
CONSOLIDATED BALANCE SHEETS

(Thousands)	February 3, 2001	January 29, 2000
ASSETS		
CURRENT ASSETS:		
Cash and Equivalents	$137,581	$147,908
Marketable Securities	—	45,601
Receivables	15,829	11,447
Inventories	120,997	75,262
Store Supplies	17,817	11,674
Other	11,338	8,325
TOTAL CURRENT ASSETS	303,562	300,217
PROPERTY AND EQUIPMENT, NET	278,785	146,403
DEFERRED INCOME TAXES	4,788	11,060
OTHER ASSETS	381	486
TOTAL ASSETS	$587,516	$458,166
LIABILITIES AND SHAREHOLDERS' EQUITY		
CURRENT LIABILITIES:		
Accounts Payable	$ 33,942	$ 18,714
Accrued Expenses	101,302	85,373
Income Taxes Payable	19,318	33,779
TOTAL CURRENT LIABILITIES	154,562	137,866
OTHER LONG-TERM LIABILITIES	10,254	9,206
SHAREHOLDERS' EQUITY:		
Common Stock	1,033	1,033
Paid-In Capital	136,490	147,305
Retained Earnings	350,868	192,735
	488,391	341,073
Less: Treasury Stock, at Average Cost	(65,691)	(29,979)
TOTAL SHAREHOLDERS' EQUITY	422,700	311,094
TOTAL LIABILITIES AND SHAREHOLDERS' EQUITY	$587,516	$458,166

The accompanying Notes are an integral part of these Consolidated Financial Statements.

ABERCROMBIE & FITCH
CONSOLIDATED STATEMENTS OF SHAREHOLDERS' EQUITY

(Thousands)

| | Common Stock | | | | | |
	Shares Outstanding	Par Value	Paid-In Capital	Retained Earnings (Deficit)	Treasury Stock, at Average Cost	Total Shareholders' Equity
Balance, January 31, 1998	102,018	$ 1,022	$117,461	$ (58,931)	$ (777)	$ 58,775
Purchase of Treasury Stock	(490)	—	—	—	(11,240)	(11,240)
Net Income	—	—	—	102,062	—	102,062
Issuance of Common Stock	1,200	11	25,870	—	—	25,881
Tax Benefit from Exercise of Stock Options and Vesting of Restricted Stock	—	—	329	—	—	329
Stock Options, Restricted Stock and Other	86	—	(34)	—	10,332	10,298
Balance, January 30, 1999	102,814	$ 1,033	$143,626	$ 43,131	$ (1,685)	$186,105
Purchase of Treasury Stock	(1,510)	—	—	—	(50,856)	(50,856)
Net Income	—	—	—	149,604	—	149,604
Tax Benefit from Exercise of Stock Options and Vesting of Restricted Stock	—	—	9,389	—	—	9,389
Stock Options, Restricted Stock and Other	700	—	(5,710)	—	22,562	16,852
Balance, January 29, 2000	102,004	$ 1,033	$147,305	$192,735	$ (29,979)	$311,094
Purchase of Treasury Stock	(3,550)	—	—	—	(43,929)	(43,929)
Net Income	—	—	—	158,133	—	158,133
Tax Benefit from Exercise of Stock Options and Vesting of Restricted Stock	—	—	462	—	—	462
Stock Options, Restricted Stock and Other	342	—	(11,277)	—	8,217	(3,060)
Balance, February 3, 2001	98,796	$ 1,033	$136,490	$350,868	$ (65,691)	$422,700

The accompanying Notes are an integral part of these Consolidated Financial Statements.

ABERCROMBIE & FITCH
CONSOLIDATED STATEMENTS OF CASH FLOWS

(Thousands)	2000	1999	1998
OPERATING ACTIVITIES:			
Net income	$158,133	$149,604	$102,062
Impact of Other Operating Activities on Cash Flows:			
Depreciation and Amortization	30,731	27,721	20,946
Noncash Charge for Deferred Compensation	4,340	5,212	11,497
Changes in Assets and Liabilities:			
Inventories	(45,735)	(31,270)	(10,065)
Accounts Payable and Accrued Expenses	21,626	4,999	33,137
Income Taxes	(8,420)	9,258	11,087
Other Assets and Liabilities	(9,486)	(12,773)	355
NET CASH PROVIDED BY OPERATING ACTIVITIES	151,189	152,751	169,019
INVESTING ACTIVITIES:			
Capital Expenditures	(153,481)	(73,377)	(37,483)
Proceeds from Maturities of Marketable Securities	45,601	11,332	—
Purchase of Marketable Securities	—	(56,933)	—
Note Receivable	(3,000)	(1,500)	—
NET CASH USED FOR INVESTING ACTIVITIES	(110,880)	(120,478)	(37,483)
FINANCING ACTIVITIES:			
Settlement of Balance with The Limited	—	—	23,785
Net Proceeds from Issuance of Common Stock	—	—	25,875
Repayment of Long-Term Debt	—	—	(50,000)
Purchase of Treasury Stock	(43,929)	(50,856)	(11,240)
Other Changes in Shareholders' Equity	(6,707)	2,927	941
NET CASH USED FOR FINANCING ACTIVITIES	(50,636)	(47,929)	(10,639)
NET INCREASE/(DECREASE) IN CASH AND EQUIVALENTS	(10,327)	(15,656)	120,897
Cash and Equivalents, Beginning of Year	147,908	163,564	42,667
CASH AND EQUIVALENTS, END OF YEAR	$137,581	$147,908	$163,564
SIGNIFICANT NONCASH INVESTING ACTIVITIES:			
Accrual for Construction in Progress	$ 9,531	$ 10,447	$ 4,393

The accompanying Notes are an integral part of these Consolidated Financial Statements.

ABERCROMBIE & FITCH
NOTES TO CONSOLIDATED FINANCIAL STATEMENTS

1. BASIS OF PRESENTATION

Abercrombie & Fitch Co. ("A&F") was incorporated on June 26, 1996, and on July 15, 1996, acquired the stock of Abercrombie & Fitch Holdings, the parent company of the Abercrombie & Fitch business, and A&F Trademark, Inc., in exchange for 43 million shares of Class B Common Stock issued to The Limited, Inc. ("The Limited"). A&F, through its subsidiaries (collectively, A&F and its subsidiaries are referred to as "Abercrombie & Fitch" or the "Company"), is a specialty retailer of high quality, casual apparel for men, women and kids with an active, youthful lifestyle. The business was established in 1892 and subsequently acquired by The Limited in 1988.

An initial public offering (the "Offering") of 16.1 million shares of A&F's Class A Common Stock, including the sale of 2.1 million shares pursuant to the exercise by the underwriters of their options to purchase additional shares, was consummated on October 1, 1996. The net proceeds received by A&F from the Offering, approximating $118.2 million, and cash from operations were used to repay the borrowings under a $150 million credit agreement. As a result of the Offering, 84.2% of the outstanding common stock of A&F was owned by The Limited, until the completion of a tax-free exchange offer (the "Exchange Offer") on May 19, 1998, to establish A&F as an independent company.

In the Exchange Offer, The Limited accepted 94,150,104 shares of its common stock that were exchanged at a ratio of .86 of a share of A&F stock for each Limited share. On June 1, 1998, The Limited effected a pro rata spin-off to its shareholders of its remaining 6,230,910 A&F shares. Limited shareholders of record at the close of trading on May 29, 1998 received .027346 of a share of A&F stock for each Limited share owned at that time.

The accompanying consolidated financial statements include the historical financial statements of, and transactions applicable to, A&F and its subsidiaries and reflect the assets, liabilities, results of operations and cash flows on a historical cost basis.

2. SUMMARY OF SIGNIFICANT ACCOUNTING POLICIES

PRINCIPLES OF CONSOLIDATION

The consolidated financial statements include the accounts of A&F and all significant subsidiaries that are more than 50% owned and controlled. All significant intercompany balances and transactions have been eliminated in consolidation.

FISCAL YEAR

The Company's fiscal year ends on the Saturday closest to January 31. Fiscal years are designated in the financial statements and notes by the calendar year in which the fiscal year commences. The results for fiscal year 2000 represent the fifty-three week period ended February 3, 2001. The results for fiscal years 1999 and 1998 represent the fifty-two week periods ended January 29, 2000 and January 30, 1999.

CASH AND EQUIVALENTS

Cash and equivalents include amounts on deposit with financial institutions and investments with original maturities of less than 90 days.

MARKETABLE SECURITIES

All investments with original maturities of greater than 90 days are accounted for in accordance with Statement of Financial Accounting Standards ("SFAS") No. 115, "Accounting for Certain Investments in Debt and Equity Securities." The Company determines the appropriate classification at the time of purchase. At January 29, 2000, the Company held investments in marketable securities which were classified as held to maturity based on the Company's positive intent and ability to hold the securities to maturity. All securities held by the Company at January 29, 2000 were corporate debt securities which matured within one year and were stated at amortized cost which approximated market value.

INVENTORIES

Inventories are principally valued at the lower of average cost or market, on a first-in first-out basis, utilizing the retail method.

STORE SUPPLIES

The initial inventory of supplies for new stores including, but not limited to, hangers, signage, security tags and point-of-sale supplies are capitalized at the store opening date. Subsequent shipments are expensed except for new merchandise presentation programs which are capitalized.

PROPERTY AND EQUIPMENT

Depreciation and amortization of property and equipment are computed for financial reporting purposes on a straight-line basis, using service lives ranging principally from 10-15 years for leasehold improvements and 3-10 years for other property and equipment. Beneficial leaseholds represent the present value of the excess of fair market rent over contractual rent of existing stores at the 1988 purchase of the Abercrombie & Fitch business by The Limited and are being amortized over the lives of the related leases. The cost of assets sold or retired and the related accumulated depreciation or amortization are removed from the accounts with any resulting gain or loss included in net income. Maintenance and repairs are charged to expense as incurred. Major renewals and betterments that extend service lives are capitalized. Long-lived assets are reviewed for impairment whenever events or changes in circumstances indicate that full recoverability is questionable. Factors used in the valuation include, but are not limited to, management's plans for future operations, recent operating results and projected cash flows.

INCOME TAXES

Income taxes are calculated in accordance with SFAS No. 109, "Accounting for Income Taxes," which requires the use of the liability method. Deferred tax assets and liabilities are recognized based on the difference between the financial statement carrying amounts of existing assets and liabilities and their respective tax bases.

Deferred tax assets and liabilities are measured using enacted tax rates in effect in the years in which those temporary differences are expected to reverse. Under SFAS No. 109, the effect on deferred taxes of a change in tax rates is recognized in income in the period that includes the enactment date.

Prior to the Exchange Offer, the Company was included in The Limited's consolidated federal and certain state income tax groups for income tax reporting purposes and was responsible for its proportionate share of income taxes calculated upon its federal taxable income at a current estimate of the Company's annual effective tax rate. Subsequent to the Exchange Offer, the Company began filing its tax returns on a separate basis.

SHAREHOLDERS' EQUITY

The Board of Directors declared a two-for-one stock split on A&F's Class A Common Stock, distributed on June 15, 1999 to shareholders of record at the close of business on May 25, 1999. All share and per share amounts in the accompanying consolidated financial statements for all periods have been restated to reflect the stock split.

At February 3, 2001, there were 150 million shares of $.01 par value Class A Common Stock authorized, of which 98.8 million and 102.0 million shares were outstanding at February 3, 2001 and January 29, 2000, respectively, and 106.4 million shares of $.01 par value Class B Common Stock authorized, none of which were outstanding at February 3, 2001 or January 29, 2000. In addition, 15 million shares of $.01 par value Preferred Stock were authorized, none of which have been issued. See Note 13 for information about Preferred Stock Purchase Rights.

Holders of Class A Common Stock generally have identical rights to holders of Class B Common Stock, except that holders of Class A Common Stock are entitled to one vote per share while holders of Class B Common Stock are entitled to three votes per share on all matters submitted to a vote of shareholders.

REVENUE RECOGNITION

The Company recognizes retail sales at the time the customer takes possession of the merchandise and purchases are paid for via cash, credit card or gift certificate and gift card redemption. Catalogue and e-commerce sales are recorded upon shipment of merchandise. Amounts relating to shipping and handling billed to customers in a sale transaction are classified as revenue and the related costs are classified as cost of goods sold. Employee discounts are classified as a reduction of revenue.

CATALOGUE AND ADVERTISING COSTS

Costs related to the *A&F Quarterly,* a catalogue/magazine, primarily consist of catalogue production and mailing costs and are expensed as incurred. Advertising costs consist of in-store photographs and advertising in selected national publications and are expensed when the photographs or publications first appear. Catalogue and advertising costs amounted to $30.4 million in 2000, $30.3 million in 1999 and $24.9 million in 1998.

STORE PREOPENING EXPENSES

Preopening expenses related to new store openings are charged to operations as incurred.

FAIR VALUE OF FINANCIAL INSTRUMENTS

The recorded values of current assets and current liabilities, including receivables, marketable securities and accounts payable, approximate fair value due to the short maturity and because the average interest rate approximates current market origination rates.

EARNINGS PER SHARE

Net income per share is computed in accordance with SFAS No. 128, "Earnings Per Share." Net income per basic share is computed based on the weighted average number of outstanding shares of common stock. Net income per diluted share includes the weighted average effect of dilutive stock options and restricted shares.

Weighted Average Shares Outstanding (thousands):

	2000	1999	1998
Shares of common stock issued	103,300	103,300	103,300
Treasury shares	(3,239)	(429)	(216)
Basic shares	100,061	102,871	103,084
Dilutive effect of options and restricted shares	2,095	4,770	3,118
Diluted shares	102,156	107,641	106,202

Options to purchase 7,875,000 and 5,690,000 shares of Class A Common Stock were outstanding at year-end 2000 and 1999 but were not included in the computation of net income per diluted share because the options' exercise prices were greater than the average market price of the underlying shares. At year-end 1998, no anti-dilutive options were outstanding.

USE OF ESTIMATES IN THE PREPARATION OF FINANCIAL STATEMENTS

The preparation of financial statements in conformity with generally accepted accounting principles requires management to make estimates and assumptions that affect the reported amounts of assets and liabilities as of the date of the financial statements and the reported amounts of revenues and expenses during the reporting period. Since actual results may differ from those estimates, the Company revises its estimates and assumptions as new information becomes available.

RECLASSIFICATIONS

Certain amounts have been reclassified to conform with current year presentation.

3. ADOPTION OF ACCOUNTING STANDARDS

In the fourth quarter 2000, the Company adopted Emerging Issues Task Force ("EITF") No. 00-10 "Accounting for Shipping and Handling Fees and Costs" which changed its classification for shipping revenue. The Company also changed its classification for direct shipping expenses for shipments to customers to cost of goods sold and for employee discounts to a reduction of revenue. All other fulfillment costs are included in General, Administrative and Store Operating Expenses. Previously, shipping revenues, certain shipping expenses and employee discounts were included in General, Administrative and Store Operating Expenses. Prior periods' financial statements presented for comparative purposes have been reclassified to comply with these classification guidelines. These reclassifications did not have an impact on net income.

The Company has adopted Staff Accounting Bulletin ("SAB") No. 101, "Revenue Recognition in Financial Statements." SAB No. 101 provides the Securities and Exchange Commission's views in applying generally accepted accounting principles to selected revenue recognition issues. The adoption of SAB No. 101 did not have a material effect on the Company's results of operations, cash flows or financial position.

4. PROPERTY AND EQUIPMENT

Property and equipment, at cost, consisted of (thousands):

	2000	1999
Land	$ 14,007	$ 14,007
Furniture, fixtures and equipment	212,674	158,753
Beneficial leaseholds	7,349	7,349
Leasehold improvements	31,613	19,572
Construction in progress	118,553	26,100
Total	$384,196	$225,781
Less: accumulated depreciation and amortization	105,411	79,378
Property and equipment, net	$278,785	$146,403

5. LEASED FACILITIES AND COMMITMENTS

Annual store rent is comprised of a fixed minimum amount, plus contingent rent based on a percentage of sales exceeding a stipulated amount. Store lease terms generally require additional payments covering taxes, common area costs and certain other expenses. Rent expense for 1998 included charges from The Limited and its subsidiaries for space under formal agreements that approximated market rates.

A summary of rent expense follows (thousands):

	2000	1999	1998
Store rent:			
Fixed minimum	$65,716	$51,086	$42,774
Contingent	7,079	8,246	6,382
Total store rent	$72,795	$59,332	$49,156
Buildings, equipment and other	2,777	2,574	1,814
Total rent expense	$75,572	$61,906	$50,970

At February 3, 2001, the Company was committed to noncancelable leases with remaining terms of one to thirteen years. These commitments include store leases with initial terms ranging primarily from ten to fifteen years and offices and a distribution center leased from an affiliate of The Limited with a term of three years from the date of the Exchange Offer. A summary of minimum rent commitments under non-cancelable leases follows (thousands):

2001	$ 80,082
2002	83,014
2003	81,672
2004	81,060
2005	78,089
Thereafter	251,391

6. ACCRUED EXPENSES

Accrued expenses consisted of the following (thousands):

	2000	1999
Accrual for construction in progress	$ 24,371	$14,840
Rent and landlord charges	15,634	15,282
Compensation and benefits	11,771	11,588
Deferred revenue	11,636	8,482
Catalogue and advertising costs	7,818	7,005
Taxes, other than income	5,102	4,507
Other	24,970	23,669
Total	$101,302	$85,373

7. INCOME TAXES

The provision for income taxes consisted of (thousands):

	2000	1999	1998
Currently Payable:			
Federal	$ 80,856	$ 84,335	$ 65,778
State	18,403	20,251	14,809
	$ 99,259	$104,586	$ 80,587
Deferred:			
Federal	2,814	(3,885)	(10,038)
State	1,247	(971)	(2,509)
	$ 4,061	$ (4,856)	$(12,547)
Total provision	$103,320	$ 99,730	$ 68,040

A reconciliation between the statutory Federal income tax rate and the effective income tax rate follows:

	2000	1999	1998
Federal income tax rate	35.0%	35.0%	35.0%
State income tax, net of Federal income tax effect	4.1%	4.6%	4.7%
Other items, net	0.4%	0.4%	0.3%
Total	39.5%	40.0%	40.0%

Income taxes payable included net current deferred tax assets of $14.7 million and $14.2 million at February 3, 2001 and January 29, 2000, respectively.

Subsequent to the Exchange Offer, the Company began filing its tax returns on a separate basis and made tax payments directly to taxing authorities. Prior to the Exchange Offer, the Company was included in the consolidated federal and certain state income tax groups of The Limited for income tax purposes. Under this arrangement, the Company was responsible for and paid The Limited its proportionate share of income taxes, calculated upon its separate taxable income at the estimated annual effective tax rate. Amounts paid to The Limited totaled $829 thousand, $9.1 million and $27.4 million in 2000, 1999 and 1998, respectively. Amounts paid directly to taxing authorities were $111.7 million, $81.1 million and $31.7 million in 2000, 1999 and 1998, respectively.

The effect of temporary differences which gives rise to deferred income tax assets (liabilities) was as follows (thousands):

	2000	1999
Deferred tax assets:		
Deferred compensation	$ 8,311	$ 9,333
Property and equipment	—	1,478
Rent	2,414	2,565
Accrued expenses	8,144	10,230
Inventory	2,767	1,650
Total deferred tax assets	21,636	25,256
Deferred tax liabilities:		
Property and equipment	(2,146)	—
Net deferred income tax assets	$19,490	$25,256

No valuation allowance has been provided for deferred tax assets because management believes that it is more likely than not that the full amount of the net deferred tax assets will be realized in the future.

8. LONG-TERM DEBT

The Company entered into a $150 million syndicated unsecured credit agreement (the "Agreement"), on April 30, 1998 (the "Effective Date"). Borrowings outstanding under the Agreement are due April 30, 2003. The Agreement has several borrowing options, including interest rates that are based on the bank agent's "Alternate Base Rate," a LIBO Rate or a rate submitted under a bidding process. Facility fees payable under the Agreement are based on the Company's ratio (the "leverage ratio") of the sum of total debt plus 800% of forward minimum rent commitments to trailing four-quarters EBITDAR and currently accrues at .225% of the committed amount per annum. The Agreement contains limitations on debt, liens, restricted payments (including dividends), mergers and acquisitions, sale-leaseback transactions, investments, acquisitions, hedging transactions and transactions with affiliates. It also contains financial covenants requiring a minimum ratio of EBITDAR to interest expense and minimum rent and a maximum leverage ratio. No amounts were outstanding under the Agreement at February 3, 2001 and January 29, 2000.

9. RELATED PARTY TRANSACTIONS

Prior to the Exchange Offer, transactions between the Company and The Limited and its subsidiaries and affiliates principally consisted of the following:

Merchandise purchases
Real estate management and leasing
Capital expenditures
Inbound and outbound transportation
Corporate services

Subsequent to the Exchange Offer, A&F negotiated arms-length terms with the merchandise and service suppliers that are Limited subsidiaries. A&F and The Limited also entered into various service agreements for terms ranging from one to three years. A&F hired associates with the appropriate expertise or contracted with outside parties to replace those services which expired in May 1999. Service agreements were also entered into for the continued use by the Company of its distribution and home office space and transportation and logistic services. The agreement for use of distribution space terminates in April 2001. The agreement for use of home office space expires in May 2001. The agreement for transportation and logistics services will also expire in May 2001, although most services have already been transitioned to the Company. The cost of these services generally is equal to The Limited's cost in providing the relevant services plus 5% of such costs.

For the periods prior to the Exchange Offer, A&F and The Limited entered into intercompany agreements that established the provision of certain services. The prices charged to the Company for services provided under these agreements may have been higher or lower than prices that would have been charged by third parties. It is not practicable, therefore, to estimate what these costs would have been if The Limited had not provided these services and the Company was required to purchase these services from outsiders or develop internal expertise. Management believes the charges and allocations described above are fair and reasonable.

The following table summarizes the related party transactions between the Company and The Limited and its subsidiaries, for fiscal year 1998. The amounts below reflect activity through the completion of the Exchange Offer.

(Thousands)	1998
Mast and Gryphon purchases	$20,176
Capital expenditures	3,199
Inbound and outbound transportation	2,280
Corporate charges	2,671
Store leases and other occupancy, net	561
Distribution center, IT and home office expenses	2,217
Centrally managed benefits	1,524
Interest charges, net	4
	$32,632

The Company does not anticipate that costs incurred to replace the services currently provided by The Limited will have a material adverse impact on its financial condition.

Shahid & Company, Inc. has provided advertising and design services for the Company since 1995. Sam N. Shahid Jr., who serves on A&F's Board of Directors, has been President and Creative Director of Shahid & Company, Inc. since 1993. Fees paid to Shahid & Company, Inc. for services provided during fiscal years 2000, 1999 and 1998 were approximately $1.7 million, $1.4 million and $1.2 million, respectively.

On August 28, 2000, A&F loaned $4.5 million to its Chairman of the Board, a major shareholder of A&F, pursuant to the terms of a replacement promissory note, which provides that such amount is due and payable on May 18, 2001 together with interest at the rate of 6.5% per annum. This note constitutes a replacement of, and substitute for, the promissory notes dated March 1, 2000 and May 19, 2000 in the amounts of $1.5 million and $3.0 million, respectively, which were cancelled.

10. STOCK OPTIONS AND RESTRICTED SHARES

Under A&F's stock plans, associates and non-associate directors may be granted up to a total of 16.3 million restricted shares and options to purchase A&F's common stock at the market price on the date of grant. In 2000, associates of the Company were granted approximately 1.4 million options, with vesting periods from four to five years. A total of 30,000 options were granted to non-associate directors in

2000, all of which vest over four years. All options have a maximum term of ten years.

The Company adopted the disclosure requirements of SFAS No. 123, "Accounting for Stock-Based Compensation," in 1996, but elected to continue to measure compensation expense in accordance with APB Opinion No. 25, "Accounting for Stock Issued to Employees." Accordingly, no compensation expense for stock options has been recognized. If compensation expense had been determined based on the estimated fair value of options granted in 2000, 1999 and 1998, consistent with the methodology in SFAS No. 123, the pro forma effect on net income and net income per diluted share would have been a reduction of approximately $20.0 million or $.20 per share in 2000, $18.5 million or $.17 per share in 1999 and $6.1 million or $.06 per share in 1998. The weighted-

average fair value of all options granted during fiscal 2000, 1999 and 1998 was $8.90, $23.34 and $9.89, respectively. The fair value of each option was estimated using the Black-Scholes option-pricing model with the following weighted-average assumptions for 2000, 1999 and 1998: no expected dividends; price volatility of 50% in 2000, 45% in 1999 and 40% in 1998; risk-free interest rates of 6.2%, 6.0% and 5.5% in 2000, 1999 and 1998, respectively; assumed forfeiture rates of 10%; and expected lives of 5 years in 2000, 6.5 years in 1999 and 5 years in 1998.

The pro forma effect on net income for 2000, 1999 and 1998 is not representative of the pro forma effect on net income in future years because it takes into consideration pro forma compensation expense related only to those grants made subsequent to the Offering.

Options Outstanding at February 3, 2001

	Options Outstanding			Options Exercisable	
Range of Exercise Prices	Number Outstanding	Weighted Average Remaining Contractual Life	Weighted Average Exercise Price	Number Exercisable	Weighted Average Exercisable Price
$ 8 – $23	5,004,000	7.2	$13.17	1,496,000	$10.82
$23 – $38	2,821,000	7.8	$25.85	590,000	$26.36
$38 – $52	5,169,000	8.4	$43.55	78,000	$40.70
$ 8 – $52	12,994,000	7.8	$28.01	2,164,000	$16.13

A summary of option activity for 2000, 1999 and 1998 follows:

	2000		1999		1998	
	Shares	Weighted Average Option Price	Shares	Weighted Average Option Price	Shares	Weighted Average Option Price
Outstanding at beginning of year	12,809,000	$28.03	7,568,000	$15.87	3,768,000	$ 8.91
Granted	1,414,000	17.25	5,794,000	42.90	3,970,000	22.47
Exercised	(193,000)	14.57	(337,000)	9.39	(60,000)	8.99
Canceled	(1,036,000)	16.06	(216,000)	25.25	(110,000)	19.40
Outstanding at end of year	12,994,000	$28.01	12,809,000	$28.03	7,568,000	$15.87
Options exercisable at year-end	2,164,000	$16.13	556,000	$ 9.85	388,000	$ 8.99

A total of 102,000 restricted shares were granted in 2000, with a total market value at grant date of $2.3 million. A total of 140,000 restricted shares were granted in both 1999 and 1998, with a total market

value at grant date of $5.4 million and $2.7 million, respectively. The restricted share grants generally vest either on a graduated scale over four years or 100% at the end of a fixed vesting period, principally five years. The market value of restricted shares is being amortized as compensation expense over the vesting period, generally four to five years. Compensation expenses related to restricted share awards amounted to $4.3 million, $5.2 million and $11.5 million in 2000, 1999 and 1998, respectively. Long-term liabilities at fiscal year-end 1998 included $8.7 million of compensation expense relating to restricted shares.

11. RETIREMENT BENEFITS

The Company participates in a qualified defined contribution retirement plan and a nonqualified supplemental retirement plan. Participation in the qualified plan is available to all associates who have completed 1,000 or more hours of service with the Company during certain 12-month periods and attained the age of 21. Participation in the nonqualified plan is subject to service and compensation requirements. The Company's contributions to these plans are based on a percentage of associates' eligible annual compensation. The cost of these plans was $3.0 million in 2000, $2.6 million in 1999 and $2.0 million in 1998.

12. CONTINGENCIES

The Company is involved in a number of legal proceedings. Although it is not possible to predict with any certainty the eventual outcome of any legal proceedings, it is the opinion of management that the ultimate resolution of these matters will not have a material impact on the Company's results of operations, cash flows or financial position.

13. PREFERRED STOCK PURCHASE RIGHTS

On July 16, 1998, A&F's Board of Directors declared a dividend of .50 of a Series A Participating Cumulative Preferred Stock Purchase Right (Right) for each outstanding share of Class A Common Stock, par value $.01 per share (Common Stock), of A&F. The dividend was paid to shareholders of record on July 28, 1998. Shares of Common Stock issued after July 28, 1998 and prior to the Distribution Date described below will be issued with .50 Right attached. Under certain conditions, each whole Right may be exercised to purchase one one-thousandth of a share of Series A Participating Cumulative Preferred Stock at an initial price of $250. The Rights initially will be attached to the shares of Common Stock. The Rights will separate from the Common Stock and a Distribution Date will occur upon the earlier of 10 business days after a public announcement that a person or group has acquired beneficial ownership of 20% or more of A&F's

outstanding shares of Common Stock and become an "Acquiring Person" (Share Acquisition Date) or 10 business days (or such later date as the Board shall determine before any person has become an Acquiring Person) after commencement of a tender or exchange offer which would result in a person or group beneficially owning 20% or more of A&F's outstanding Common Stock. The Rights are not exercisable until the Distribution Date.

In the event that any person becomes an Acquiring Person, each holder of a Right (other than the Acquiring Person and certain affiliated persons) will be entitled to purchase, upon exercise of the Right, shares of Common Stock having a market value two times the exercise price of the Right. At any time after any person becomes an Acquiring Person (but before any person becomes the beneficial owner of 50% or more of the outstanding shares), A&F's Board of Directors may exchange all or part of the Rights (other than Rights beneficially owned by an Acquiring Person and certain affiliated persons) for shares of Common Stock at an exchange ratio of one share of Common Stock per Right. In the event that, at any time following the Share Acquisition Date, A&F is acquired in a merger or other business combination transaction in which A&F is not the surviving corporation, the Common Stock is exchanged for other securities or assets or 50% or more of A&F's assets or earning power is sold or transferred, the holder of a Right will be entitled to buy, for the exercise price of the Rights, the number of shares of Common Stock of the acquiring company which at the time of such transaction will have a market value of two times the exercise price of the Right.

The Rights, which do not have any voting rights, expire on July 16, 2008, and may be redeemed by A&F at a price of $.01 per whole Right at any time before a person becomes an Acquiring Person.

Rights holders have no rights as a shareholder of A&F, including the right to vote and to receive dividends.

14. QUARTERLY FINANCIAL DATA (UNAUDITED)

Summarized quarterly financial results for 2000 and 1999 follow (thousands except per share amounts):

2000 Quarter	First (1)	Second (1)	Third (1)	Fourth
Net sales	$205,006	$229,031	$364,122	$439,445
Gross income	75,403	87,765	143,283	202,924
Net income	16,163	21,163	43,592	77,215

(continued)

Net income per basic share	$.16	$.21	$.44	$.78
Net income per diluted share	$.16	$.21	$.43	$.76

1999 Quarter	First (1)	Second (1)	Third (1)	Fourth (1)
Net sales	$186,427	$196,227	$284,510	$363,694
Gross income	69,368	77,346	118,600	185,069
Net income	14,963	18,858	39,059	76,724
Net income per basic share	$.14	$.18	$.38	$.75
Net income per diluted share	$.14	$.17	$.36	$.73

(1) Net sales and gross income for 1999 and the first three quarters of 2000 reflect the reclassification of shipping and handling revenues and costs and employee discounts (see Note 3).

MARKET FOR REGISTRANT'S COMMON EQUITY AND RELATED STOCKHOLDER MATTERS

The following is a summary of A&F's sales prices as reported on the New York Stock Exchange ("ANF") for the 2000 and 1999 fiscal yeas:

	Sales Price	
	High	Low
2000 Fiscal Year		
4th Quarter	$31.31	$14.75
3rd Quarter	$26.56	$15.31
2nd Quarter	$16.69	$ 8.00
1st Quarter	$24.50	$10.06
1999 Fiscal Year		
4th Quarter	$32.56	$19.56
3rd Quarter	$43.25	$21.00
2nd Quarter	$49.69	$36.50
1st Quarter	$50.75	$35.25

Per share amounts have been restated to reflect the two-for-one stock split on A&F's Class A Common Stock, distributed on June 15, 1999 to shareholders of record at the close of business on May 25, 1999.

A&F has not paid dividends on its shares of Class A Common Stock in the past and does not presently plan to pay dividends on the shares. It is presently anticipated that earnings will be retained and reinvested to support the growth of the Company's business. The payment of any future dividends on shares will be determined by the A&F Board of Directors in light of conditions then existing, including earnings, financial condition and capital requirements, restrictions in financing agreements, business conditions and other factors.

On February 3, 2001, there were approximately 7,000 shareholders of record. However, when including active associates who participate in A&F's stock purchase plan, associates who own shares through A&F sponsored retirement plans and others holding shares in broker accounts under street names, A&F estimates the shareholder base at approximately 65,000.

REPORT OF INDEPENDENT ACCOUNTANTS

To the Board of Directors and
Shareholders of Abercrombie & Fitch:

In our opinion, the accompanying consolidated balance sheets and the related consolidated statements of income, shareholders' equity and cash flows present fairly, in all material respects, the financial position of Abercrombie & Fitch and its subsidiaries at February 3, 2001 and January 29, 2000, and the results of their operations and their cash flows for each of the three fiscal years in the period ended February 3, 2001 in conformity with accounting principles generally accepted in the United States. These financial statements are the responsibility of the Company's management; our responsibility is to express an opinion on these financial statements based on our audits. We conducted our audits of these statements in accordance with auditing standards generally accepted in the United States, which require that we plan and perform the audit to obtain reasonable assurance about whether the financial statements are free of material misstatement. An audit includes examining, on a test basis, evidence supporting the amounts and disclosures in the financial statements, assessing the accounting principles used and significant estimates made by management, and evaluating the overall financial statement presentation. We believe that our audits provide a reasonable basis for the opinion expressed above.

PricewaterhouseCoopers LLP
Columbus, Ohio
February 20, 2001

Industry Ratio Report
Family Clothing Stores

Liquidity	
Current Ratio	1.84
Quick Ratio	0.38

Activity	
Inventory Turnover	3.95
Receivables Turnover	132.82
Average Collection Period	2.75 Days
Accounts Payable Turnover	10.36
Fixed Assets Turnover	7.10
Total Asset Turnover	2.30
Days to Sell Inventory	91.04
Operating Cycle	103.86 Days

Profitability	
Gross Profit Margin	36.55%
Operating Profit Margin	5.78%
Net Profit Margin	4.27%
Return on Equity	17.00%
Return on Assets	8.40%
Quality of Income	1.61

Leverage	
Times Interest Earned	14.98
Interest Coverage Ratio	24.34
Total Debt/Total Equity	0.73
Total Assets/Total Equity	1.73

Dividends	
Dividend Payout	3.72%
Dividend Yield	0.31%

Other	
Advertising-to-Sales	3.10%
Sales Growth	9.04%
Capital Acquisitions Ratio	0.65
Price/Earnings	14.12

COMPANIES USED IN INDUSTRY ANALYSIS

Company Name	Ticker Symbol
Abercrombie & Fitch	ANF
American Eagle Outfitters Inc	AEOS
Big Dog Holdings Inc	BDOG
Buckle Inc	BKE
Burlington Coat Factory Warehouse	BCF
Designs Inc	DESI
Factory 2-U Inc	FTUS
Gadzooks Inc	GADZ
Gap Inc	GPS
Goody's Family Clothing Inc	GDYS
Guess Inc	GES
Harold's Stores Inc	HLD
Nordstrom Inc	JWN
Pacific Sunwear California Inc	PSUN
Ross Stores Inc	ROST
Stage Stores Inc	3SGEEQ
Stein Mart Inc	SMRT
Syms Corp	SYM
TJX Companies Inc	TJX
Urban Outfitters Inc	URBN

Industry Return on Equity (ROE) profit driver analysis.

ROE = Net Profit Margin × Asset Turnover × Financial Leverage

17.00 = 4.27 × 2.30 × 1.73

A

Account A standardized format that organizations use to accumulate the dollar effects of transactions on each financial statement item. (4, 56)

Accounting A system that collects and processes (analyzes, measures, and records) financial information about an organization and reports that information to decision makers. (4)

Accounting Cycle The process used by entities to analyze and record transactions, adjust the records at the end of the period, prepare financial statements, and prepare the records for the next cycle. (163)

Accounting Entity The organization for which financial data are to be collected. (7)

Accounting Period The time period covered by the financial statements. (10)

Accounts Receivable (Trade Receivables, Receivables) Open accounts owed to the business by trade customers. (290)

Accrual Basis Accounting Records revenues when earned and expenses when incurred, regardless of the timing of cash receipts or payments. (108)

Accrued Expenses Previously unrecorded expenses that need to be adjusted at the end of the accounting period to reflect the amount incurred and its related payable account. (166)

Accrued Liabilities Expenses that have been incurred but have not been paid at the end of the accounting period. (462)

Accrued Revenues Previously unrecorded revenues that need to be adjusted at the end of the accounting period to reflect the amount earned and its related receivable account. (166)

Accumulated Other Comprehensive Income Net unrealized gains or losses on securities, net minimum pension liability adjustments, and net foreign currency translation adjustment, which are directly credited or debited to the stockholders' equity account. (238)

Acquisition Cost Net cash equivalent amount paid or to be paid for the asset. (399)

Adjusting Entries Entries necessary at the end of the accounting period to measure all revenues and expenses of that period. (165)

Aging of Accounts Receivable Method Estimates uncollectible accounts based on the age of each account receivable. (295)

Allowance for Doubtful Accounts (Allowance for Bad Debts, Allowance for Uncollectible Accounts) Contra-asset account containing the estimated uncollectible accounts receivable. (292)

Allowance Method Bases bad debt expense on an estimate of uncollectible accounts. (291)

Amortization Systematic and rational allocation of the acquisition cost of an intangible asset over its useful life. (419)

Annuity A series of periodic cash receipts or payments that are equal in amount each interest period. (475)

Assets Probable future economic benefits owned by the entity as a result of past transactions. (51)

Assurance Services are independent professional services that improve the quality of information for decision makers. (23)

Audit An examination of the financial reports to ensure that they represent what they claim and conform with generally accepted accounting principles. (23)

Authorized Number of Shares Maximum number of shares of corporation's capital stock that can be issued as specified in the charter. (553)

Average Cost Method uses the weighted average unit cost of the goods available for sale for both cost of goods sold and ending inventory. (347)

B

Bad Debt Expense (Doubtful Accounts Expense, Uncollectible Accounts Expense, Provision for Uncollectible Accounts) Expense associated with estimated uncollectible accounts receivable. (292)

Balance Sheet (Statement of Financial Position) Reports the amount of assets, liabilities, and stockholders' equity of an accounting entity at a point in time. (7)

Bank Reconciliation Process of verifying the accuracy of both the bank statement and the cash accounts of a business. (302)

Bank Statement Monthly report from a bank that shows deposits recorded, checks cleared, other debits and credits, and a running bank balance. (301)

Basic Accounting Equation (Balance Sheet Equation) Assets = Liabilities + Stockholders' Equity. (8)

Bond Certificate The bond document that each bondholder receives. (513)

Bond Discount The difference between selling price and par when a bond is sold for less than par. (515)

Bond Premium The difference between selling price and par when a bond is sold for more than par. (515)

Bond Principal The amount (1) payable at the maturity of the bond and (2) on which the periodic cash interest payments are computed. (512)

C

Callable Bonds Bonds that may be called for early retirement at the option of the issuer. (512)

Capital Expenditures Expenditures that increase the productive life, operating efficiency, or capacity of the asset and are recorded as increases in asset accounts, not as expenses. (403)

Capital Lease meets at least one of the four criteria established by GAAP and results in the recording of an asset and liability. (472)

Capitalized Interest Interest expenditures included in the cost of a self-constructed asset. (401)

Cash Money or any instrument that banks will accept for deposit and immediate credit to the company's account, such as a check, money order, or bank draft. (299)

Cash Basis Accounting Records revenues when cash is received and expenses when cash is paid. (108)

Cash Equivalents Short-term investments with original maturities of three months or less that are readily convertible to cash and whose value is unlikely to change. (299, 647)

Cash Flows from Financing Activities Cash inflows and outflows related to external sources of financing (owners and creditors) for the enterprise. (649)

Cash Flows from Investing Activities Cash inflows and outflows related to the acquisition or sale of productive facilities and investments in the securities of other companies. (649)

Cash Flows from Operating Activities (Cash Flows from Operations) Cash inflows and outflows directly related to earnings from normal operations. (647)

Closing Entries Made at the end of the accounting period to transfer balances in temporary accounts to Retained Earnings and to establish a zero balance in each of the temporary accounts. (179)

Common Stock The basic voting stock issued by a corporation. (555)

Comparable Information Information that can be compared across businesses because similar accounting methods have been applied. (231)

Component Percentage Expresses each item on a particular financial statement as a percentage of a single base amount. (708)

Conservatism Suggests that care should be taken not to overstate assets and revenues or understate liabilities and expenses. (247)

Consistent Information Information that can be compared over time because similar accounting methods have been applied. (231)

Consolidated Financial Statements The financial statements of two or more companies that have been combined into a single set of financial statements as if the companies were one. (614)

Contingent Liability Potential liability that has arisen as the result of a past event; not an effective liability until some future event occurs. (467)

Continuity (Going-Concern) Assumption States that businesses are assumed to continue to operate into the foreseeable future. (50)

Contra-Account An account that is an offset to, or reduction of, the primary account. (164)

Contributed Capital Results from owners providing cash (and sometimes other assets) to business. (53)

Convertible Bonds Bonds that may be converted to other securities of the issuer (usually common stock). (512)

Copyright Exclusive right to publish, use, and sell a literary, musical, or artistic work. (421)

Cost-Benefit Constraint Suggests that the benefits of accounting for and reporting information should outweigh the costs. (231)

Cost of Goods Sold Equation $BI + P - EI = CGS$. (343)

Cost Principle See *historical cost principle.*

Coupon Rate The stated rate of interest on bonds. (514)

Credit The right side of an account. (63)

Credit Card Discount Fee charged by the credit card company for its services. (286)

Cumulative Dividend Preference Preferred stock feature that requires specified current dividends not paid in full to accumulate for every year in which they are not paid. These cumulative preferred dividends must be paid before any common dividends can be paid. (565)

Cumulative Effects of Changes in Accounting Methods Amounts reflected on the income statement for adjustments made to balance sheet accounts when applying different accounting principles. (255)

Current Assets Assets that will be used or turned into cash within one year. Inventory is always considered a current asset regardless of the time needed to produce and sell it. (51)

Current Dividend Preference The feature of preferred stock that grants priority on preferred dividends over common dividends. (565)

Current Liabilities Short-term obligations that will be paid in cash (or other current assets) within the current operating cycle or one year, whichever is longer. (51, 459)

D

Debenture An unsecured bond; no assets are specifically pledged to guarantee repayment. (512)

Debit The left side of an account. (63)

Declaration Date The date on which the board of directors officially approves a dividend. (560)

Declining-Balance Depreciation The method that allocates the cost of an asset over its useful life based on a multiple of (often two times) the straight-line rate. (409)

Deferred Expenses Previously acquired assets that need to be adjusted at the end of the accounting period to reflect the amount of expense incurred in using the asset to generate revenue. (165)

Deferred Revenues Previously recorded liabilities that need to be adjusted at the end of the period to reflect the amount of revenue earned. (165, 466)

Deferred Tax Items Timing differences caused by reporting revenues and expenses according to GAAP on a company's income statement and according to the Internal Revenue Code on the tax return. (481)

Depletion Systematic and rational allocation of the cost of a natural resource over the period of exploitation. (418)

Depreciation Process of allocating the cost of buildings and equipment over their productive lives using a systematic and rational allocation of the cost of property, plant, and equipment (but not land) over their useful lives. (405)

Direct Labor The earnings of employees who work directly on the products being manufactured. (342)

Direct Method The method of presenting the operating activities section of the statement of cash flows reporting components of cash flows from operating activities as gross receipts and gross payments. (647)

Discontinued Operations Financial results from the disposal of a major component of the business and are reported net of income tax effects. (253)

Dividends in Arrears Dividends on cumulative preferred stock that have not been declared in prior years. (565)

E

Earnings Forecasts Predictions of earnings for future accounting periods. (227)

Effective-Interest Method Amortizes a bond discount or premium on the basis of the effective-interest rate; it is the theoretically preferred method. (523)

Effective-Interest Rate Another name for the market rate of interest on a bond. (515)

Efficient Markets Securities markets in which prices fully reflect available information. (723)

Equity Method Used when an investor can exert significant influence over an investee. It permits recording the investor's share of investee's income. (608)

Estimated Useful Life Expected service life of an asset to the present owner. (406)

Expenses Decreases in assets or increases in liabilities from ongoing operations incurred to generate revenues during the period. (106)

Extraordinary Items Gains and losses that are both unusual in nature and infrequent in occurrence; they are reported net of tax on the income statement. (254)

Extraordinary Repairs Infrequent expenditures that increase an asset's economic usefulness in the future. (403)

F

Face Amount Another name for principal or the principal amount of a bond. (512)

Factory Overhead Manufacturing costs that are not raw material or direct labor costs. (342)

Financial Accounting Standards Board (FASB) The private sector body given the primary responsibility to work out the detailed rules that become generally accepted accounting principles. (20)

Finished Goods Inventory Manufactured goods that are completed and ready for sale. (341)

First-In, First-Out (FIFO) Method Assumes that the first goods purchased (the first in) are the first goods sold. (346)

Form 8-K The report used by publicly traded companies to disclose any material event not previously reported that is important to investors. (235)

Form 10-K The annual report that publicly traded companies must file with the SEC. (235)

Form 10-Q The quarterly report that publicly traded companies must file with the SEC. (235)

Franchise A contractual right to sell certain products or services, use certain trademarks, or perform activities in a geographical region. (422)

Free Cash Flow Cash Flows from Operating Activities − Dividends − Capital Expenditures. (667)

Future Value The sum to which an amount will increase as the result of compound interest. (473)

G

Gains Increases in assets or decreases in liabilities from peripheral transactions. (107)

Generally Accepted Accounting Principles (GAAP) The measurement rules used to develop the information in financial statements. (20)

Goods Available for Sale The sum of beginning inventory and purchases (or transfers to finished goods) for the period. (343)

Goodwill (Cost in Excess of Net Assets Acquired) For accounting purposes, the excess of the purchase price of a business over the market value of the business's assets and liabilities. (420, 616)

Gross Profit (Gross Margin) Net sales less cost of goods sold. (240)

H

Held-to-Maturity Investments A long-term investments in bonds that management has the ability and intent to hold until maturity. (598)

Historical Cost Principle Requires assets to be recorded at the historical cash-equivalent cost, which on the date of the transaction is cash paid plus the current dollar value of all noncash considerations also given in the exchange. (55)

I

Income before Income Taxes (Pretax Earnings) Revenues minus all expenses except income tax expense. (241)

Income from Operations (Operating Income) Equals net sales less cost of goods sold and other operating expenses. (241)

Income Statement (Statement of Income, Statement of Earnings, Statement of Operations) Reports the revenues less the expenses of the accounting period. (10)

Indenture A bond contract that specifies the legal provisions of a bond issue. (512)

Indirect Method The method of presenting the operating activities section of the statement of cash flows that adjusts net income to compute cash flows from operating activities. (647)

Institutional Investors Managers of pension, mutual, endowment, and other funds that invest on the behalf of others. (229)

Intangible Assets Assets that have special rights but not physical substance. (397)

Internal Controls Processes by which a company provides reasonable assurance regarding the reliability of the company's financial reporting, the effectiveness and efficiency of its operations, and its compliance with applicable laws and regulations. (300)

Inventory Tangible property held for sale in the normal course of business or used in producing goods or services for sale. (340)

Investments in Associated (or Affiliated) Companies are investments in stock held for the purpose of influencing the operating and financing strategies for the long term. (608)

Issued Shares Total number of shares of stock that have been sold; shares outstanding plus treasury shares held. (553)

J

Journal Entry An accounting method for expressing the effects of a transaction on accounts in a debits-equal-credits format. (63)

L

Last-In, First-Out (LIFO) Method Assumes that the most recently purchased units (the last in) are sold first. (346)

Legal Capital The permanent amount of capital defined by state law that must remain invested in the business; serves as a cushion for creditors. (555)

Lenders (Creditors) Suppliers and financial institutions that lend money to companies. (230)

Liabilities Probable debts or obligations of the entity that result from past transactions, which will be paid with assets or services. (51, 459)

Licenses and **Operating Rights,** obtained through agreements with governmental units or agencies, permit owners to use public property in performing its services. (422)

LIFO Liquidation A sale of a lower-cost inventory item from beginning LIFO inventory. (364)

LIFO Reserve A contra-asset for the excess of FIFO over LIFO inventory. (352)

Liquidity is the ability to pay current obligations. (459)

Long-Lived Assets Tangible and intangible resources owned by a business and used in its operations over several years. (397)

Long-Term Liabilities All of the entity's obligations that are not classified as current liabilities. (470)

Losses Decreases in assets or increases in liabilities from peripheral transactions. (107)

Lower of Cost or Market (LCM) Valuation method departing from the cost principle; it serves to recognize a loss when replacement cost or net realizable value drops below cost. (354)

M

Market Interest Rate Current rate of interest on a debt when incurred; also called *yield* or *effective-interest rate.* (515)

Market Tests Ratios that tend to measure the market worth of a share of stock. (719)

Market Value Method Reports securities are at their current market value. (600)

Matching Principle Requires that expenses be recorded when incurred in earning revenue. (112)

Material Amounts Amounts that are large enough to influence a user's decision. (247)

Merchandise Inventory Goods held for resale in the ordinary course of business. (340)

Merger occurs when one company purchases all of the net assets of another and the target company goes out of existence. (615)

N

Natural Resources Assets occurring in nature, such as mineral deposits, timber tracts, oil, and gas. (417)

Net Book Value (Book Value, Carrying Value) of an asset is the acquisition cost of the asset less accumulated depreciation, depletion, or amortization. (164, 405)

Net Realizable Value The expected sales price less selling costs (e.g., repair and disposal costs). (355)

Noncash Investing and Financing Activities Transactions that do not have direct cash flow effects; reported as a supplement to the statement of cash flows in narrative or schedule form. (670)

No-Par Value Stock Capital stock that has no par value specified in the corporate charter. (555)

Notes (Footnotes) Provide supplemental information about the financial condition of a company, without which the financial statements cannot be fully understood. (16)

Notes Receivable Written promises that require another party to pay the business under specified conditions (amount, time, interest). (291)

O

Operating Cycle (Cash-to-Cash Cycle) The time it takes for a company to pay cash to suppliers, sell those goods and services to customers, and collect cash from customers. (103)

Operating Lease does not meet any of the four criteria established by GAAP and does not cause the recording of an asset and liability. (472)

Ordinary Repairs and Maintenance Expenditures for the normal operating upkeep of long-lived assets. (403)

Outstanding Shares Total number of shares of stock that are owned by stockholders on any particular date. (553)

P

Paid-In Capital (Additional Paid-in Capital, Contributed Capital in Excess of Par) is the amount of contributed capital less the par value of the stock. (238)

Par Value (1) A legal amount per share established by the board of directors; it establishes the minimum amount a stockholder must contribute and has no relationship to the market price of the stock. (2) Also, another name for bond principal or the maturity amount of a bond. (238, 512, 555)

Parent Company The entity that gains a controlling influence over another company (the subsidiary). (614)

Patent Granted by the federal government for an invention; gives the owner the exclusive right to use, manufacture, and sell the subject of the patent. (421)

Payment Date The date on which a cash dividend is paid to the stockholders of record. (560)

Percentage of Credit Sales Method Bases bad debt expense on the historical percentage of credit sales that result in bad debts. (294)

Periodic Inventory System Ending inventory and cost of goods sold determined at the end of the accounting period based on a physical inventory count. (361)

Permanent (Real) Accounts The balance sheet accounts that carry their ending balances into the next accounting period. (179)

Perpetual Inventory System A detailed inventory record maintained recording each purchase and sale during the accounting period. (361)

Post-Closing Trial Balance Should be prepared as the last step in the accounting cycle to check that debits equal credits and all temporary accounts have been closed. (180)

Preferred Stock Stock that has specified rights over common stock. (564)

Present Value The current value of an amount to be received in the future; a future amount discounted for compound interest. (473)

Press Release A written public news announcement normally distributed to major news services. (232)

Primary Objective of External Financial Reporting Provides useful economic information about a business to help external parties make sound financial decisions. (49)

Private Investors Individuals who purchase shares in companies. (230)

Purchase Discount Cash discount received for prompt payment of an account. (367)

Purchase Method records assets and liabilities acquired in a merger or acquisition at their fair market value. (616)

Purchase Returns and Allowances A reduction in the cost of purchases associated with unsatisfactory goods. (367)

R

Ratio (Percentage) Analysis An analytical tool that measures the proportional relationship between two financial statement amounts. (707)

Raw Materials Inventory Items acquired for the purpose of processing into finished goods. (341)

Record Date The date on which the corporation prepares the list of current stockholders as shown on its records; dividends can be paid only to the stockholders who own stock on that date. (560)

Relevant Information Information that can influence a decision; it is timely and has predictive and/or feedback value. (231)

Reliable Information Information that is accurate, unbiased, and verifiable. (231)

Replacement Cost The current purchase price for identical goods. (354)

Report of Independent Accountants (Audit Report) Describes the auditors' opinion of the fairness of the financial statement presentations and the evidence gathered to support that opinion. (22)

Residual (or Salvage) Value Estimated amount to be recovered, less disposal costs, at the end of the company's estimated useful life of an asset. (406)

Retained Earnings Cumulative earnings of a company that are not distributed to the owners and are reinvested in the business. (53)

Revenue Expenditures Expenditures that maintain the productive capacity of an asset during the current accounting period only and are recorded as expenses. (403)

Revenue Principle Revenues are recognized when goods or services are delivered, there is evidence of an arrangement for customer payment, the price is fixed or determinable and collection is reasonably assured. (109)

Revenues Increases in assets or settlements of liabilities from ongoing operations. (104)

S

Sales (or Cash) Discount Cash discount offered to encourage prompt payment of an account receivable. (286)

Sales Returns and Allowances Reduction of sales revenues for return of or allowances for unsatisfactory goods. (288)

Securities and Exchange Commission (SEC) The U.S. government agency that determines the financial statements that public companies must provide to stockholders and the measurement rules that they must use in producing those statements. (20)

Securities Available for Sale All passive investments other than trading securities (classified as either short-term or long-term). (601)

Separate-Entity Assumption States that business transactions are separate from the transactions of the owners. (50)

Specific Identification Method Identifies the cost of the specific item that was sold. (345)

Stated Rate The rate of cash interest per period specified in the bond contract. (512)

Statement of Cash Flows Reports inflows and outflows of cash during the accounting period in the categories of operating, investing, and financing. (14)

Statement of Retained Earnings Reports the way that net income and the distribution of dividends affected the financial position of the company during the accounting period. (13)

Stock Dividend Distribution of additional shares of a corporation's own stock. (562)

Stock Split An increase in the total number of authorized shares by a specified ratio; does not decrease retained earnings. (563)

Stockholders' Equity (Owners' Equity or Shareholders' Equity) The financing provided by the owners and the operations of the business. (52)

Straight-Line Amortization Simplified method of amortizing a bond discount or premium that allocates an equal dollar amount to each interest period. (520)

Straight-Line Depreciation Method that allocates the cost of an asset in equal periodic amounts over its useful life. (407)

Subsidiary Company The entity that is acquired by the parent company. (614)

T

T-account A tool for summarizing transaction effects for each account, determining balances, and drawing inferences about a company's activities. (65)

Tangible Assets (or fixed assets) Assets that have physical substance. (397)

Technology includes costs for computer software and Web development. (421)

Temporary (Nominal) Accounts Income statement (and sometimes dividends declared) accounts that are closed to Retained Earnings at the end of the accounting period. (179)

Temporary Differences Timing differences that cause deferred income taxes and will reverse, or turn around, in the future. (481)

Tests of Liquidity Ratios that measure a company's ability to meet its currently maturing obligations. (714)

Tests of Profitability compare income with one or more primary activities. (709)

Tests of Solvency Ratios that measure a company's ability to meet its long-term obligations. (718)

Time Period Assumption The long life of a company can be reported in shorter time periods. (104)

Time Value of Money Interest that is associated with the use of money over time. (464)

Trademark An exclusive legal right to use a special name, image, or slogan. (421)

Trading Securities All investments in stocks or bonds that are held primarily for the purpose of active trading (buying and selling) in the near future (classified as short-term). (601)

Transaction (1) An exchange between a business and one or more external parties to a business or (2) a measurable internal event such as the use of assets in operations. (56)

Transaction Analysis The process of studying a transaction to determine its economic effect on the business in terms of the accounting equation. (58)

Treasury Stock A corporation's own stock that has been issued but was subsequently reacquired and is still being held by that corporation. (558)

Trial Balance A list of all accounts with their balances to provide a check on the equality of the debits and credits. (163)

Trustee An independent party appointed to represent the bondholders. (513)

U

Unit-of-Measure Assumption States that accounting information should be measured and reported in the national monetary unit. (50)

Units-of-Production Depreciation Method that allocates the cost of an asset over its useful life based on its periodic output related to its total estimated output. (408)

Unqualified (Clean) Audit Opinion Auditors' statement that the financial statements are fair presentations in all material respects in conformity with GAAP. (226)

Unrealized Holding Gains and Losses Amounts associated with price changes of securities that are currently held. (600)

W

Work in Process Inventory Goods in the process of being manufactured. (341)

Working Capital The dollar difference between total current assets and total current liabilities. (468)

Y

Yield (Effective Interest Rate) is the current rate of interest on a debt when incurred. (515)

CREDITS